AF677974

HANDBOOK OF MENTAL HEALTH ECONOMICS
AND HEALTH POLICY
VOLUME I

SCHIZOPHRENIA

HANDBOOK OF MENTAL HEALTH ECONOMICS AND HEALTH POLICY
VOLUME I

SCHIZOPHRENIA

Edited by

M. MOSCARELLI
Association for Research into Costs and Assessment in Psychiatry (A.R.C.A.P.), Milan, Italy

A. RUPP
National Institute of Mental Health, Rockville, USA

N. SARTORIUS
University of Geneva, Switzerland

JOHN WILEY & SONS
Chichester · New York · Brisbane · Toronto · Singapore

Copyright © 1996 by John Wiley & Sons Ltd,
Baffins Lane, Chichester,
West Sussex PO19 1UD, England

National 01243 779777
International (+44) 1243 779777

All rights reserved.

No part of this book may be reproduced by any means, or transmitted, or translated into a machine language without the written permission of the publisher.

Other Wiley Editorial Offices

John Wiley & Sons, Inc., 605 Third Avenue,
New York, NY 10158-0012, USA

Jacaranda Wiley Ltd, 3 Park Road, Milton,
Queensland 4064, Australia

John Wiley & Sons (Canada) Ltd, 22 Worcester Road,
Rexdale, Ontario M9W 1L1, Canada

John Wiley & Sons (Asia) Pte Ltd, 2 Clementi Loop #02-01,
Jin Xing Distripark, Singapore 0512

Library of Congress Catalogue-in-Publication Data

Schizophrenia/edited by M. Moscarelli, A. Rupp, and N. Sartorius.
p. cm.—(Handbook of mental health economics and health policies; 1)
Includes bibliographical references and index.
ISBN 0 471 96108 6
1. Schizophrenia—Economic aspects. 2. Schizophrenia—Treatment—Economic aspects. 3. Schizophrenia—Treatment—Government policy. I. Moscarelli, M. (Massimo) II. Rupp, Agnes. III. Sartorius, N. IV. Series.
[DNLM: 1. Schizophrenia—economics. 2. Schizophrenia—therapy. 3. Schizophrenia—diagnosis. 4. Mental Health Services—organization & administration. 5. Health Policy—economics. WM 203 S337206 1996]
RC514.S33414 1996
616.89'82–dc20
DNLM/DLC
for Library of Congress 95-24232
CIP

British Library Cataloguing in Publication Data

A catalogue record for this book is available from the British Library

ISBN 0 471 96108 6

Typeset in 10/12pt Times by Vision Typesetting
Printed and bound in Great Britain by Bookcraft (Bath) Ltd, Midsomer Norton, Avon
This book is printed on acid-free paper responsibly manufactured from sustainable forestation, for which at least two trees are planted for each one used for paper production.

Contents

Contributors

WOLFRAM AN DER HEIDEN	Central Institute of Mental Health, J5-P.O. Box 122120, D-6800 Mannheim, Germany
ANDRÉ J.H.A. AMENT	University of Limburg, Department of Health Economics, PO Box 616, 6200 MD Maastricht, The Netherlands
NANCY C. ANDREASEN	The University of Iowa, Hospitals and Clinics Mental Health Clinical Research Center, Iowa City, Iowa 52242, USA
GAVIN ANDREWS	Clinical Research Unit for Anxiety Disorders, University of NSW, St Vincents Hospital, Sydney, Australia
JOHN J. BARTKO	5712 Roosevelt Street, Bethesda, Maryland 20817-6742, USA
PAUL BEBBINGTON	Medical Research Council, Social Psychiatry Section, Institute of Psychiatry, De Crespigny Park, London, SE5 8AF, UK
ALLAN BEIGEL	Harvard university, Cambridge, MA, USA
RICHARD P. BENTALL	Department of Clinical Psychology, University of Liverpool, Liverpool, UK
GARY R. BOND	Clinical Rehabilitation, Psychology Program, Purdue University, Department of Psychology LD 3124, 402 N. Blackford Street, Indianapolis, Indiana 46202-3275, USA
PAUL J. CARLING	Center for Community Change Through Housing and Support, Institute for Program Development, Trinity College of Vermont, 208 Colchester Avenue, Burlington, Vermont 05401, USA
ROBIN E. CLARK	Dartmouth Medical School, Department of Community and Family Medicine, Strasenbourgh 7250, Hanover, New Hampshire 03755-3862, USA
JORGE-ALBERTO COSTA E SILVA	Division of Mental Health, World Health Organisation, Geneva, Switzerland
JOHN H. COVERDALE	School of Medicine, Department of Psychiatry and Behavioural Sciences, University of Auckland, Private Bag 92019, Auckland, New Zealand

LINDA DAVIES	Centre for Health Economics, University of York, YO1 5DD, UK
JENNIFER DAY	Department of Nursing, University of Manchester, Manchester, UK
A. DE JONG	Department of Social Psychiatry, Academisch Ziekenhuis, Oostersingel 59, PO Box 30 001, Groningen 9700 RB, The Netherlands
MICHAEL DRUMMOND	Centre for Health Economics, University of York, YO1 5DD, UK
SYLVIA M.A.A. EVERS	University of Limburg, Department of Health Economics, PO Box 616, 6200 MD Maastricht, The Netherlands
IAN R.H. FALLOON	Optimal Treatment Project, Via Case Sparse 10, 28040 Lesa NO, Italy
WAYNE S. FENTON	Chestnut Lodge Research Institute, 500 W Montgomery Ave, Rockville, Maryland 20850, USA
ALLEN FRANCES	Department of Psychiatry, Duke University Medical Center, Durham, North Carolina 27710, USA
RICHARD G. FRANK	Harvard Medical School, Department of Health Care Policy, 25 Shattuck Street, Parcel B-1st Floor, Boston, Massachusetts 02115, USA
HUGH FREEMAN	21 Montagu Square, London W1H 1RE, UK
DAVID GOLDBERG	Institute of Psychiatry, De Crespigny Park, Denmark Hill, London SE5 8AE, UK
HOWARD H. GOLDMAN	University of Maryland, Department of Psychiatry, 645 W Redwood St, Baltimore, Maryland 21201-1549, USA
MICHAEL J. GOLDSTEIN	UCLA Psychology Department, 405 Hilgard Avenue, Los Angeles, California 90024-1563, USA
WALTER GULBINAT	Division of Mental Health, WHO, CH-1211, Geneva 27, Switzerland
HEINZ HÄFNER	Central Institute of Mental Health, J5- PO BOX 122120, D-6800 Mannheim, Germany
WILLIAM A. HARGREAVES	Department of Psychiatry, San Francisco General Hospital, 1001 Potrero Ave, Room 7M36, SF, California 94110, USA
DAVID HEALY	Academic Sub-Department of Psychological Medicine in North Wales, North Wales Hospital, Denbigh, Clwyd, LL16 5SS, UK
JOLINE HENTER	NIMH, Neurosciences Research Center at St Elizabeths, 2700 Martin Luther King Jr Ave, S E Washington DC 20032, USA
MARVIN I. HERZ	Department of Psychiatry, University of Rochester, Strong Ties, 1650 Elmwood Avenue, Rochester, New York 14620, USA
MICHAEL F. HOGAN	Department of Mental Health, 30 East Broad St, Suite 1180, Columbus, Ohio 43215, USA
GARY HOGMAN	NSF National Office, 28 Castle Street, Kingston upon Thames, Surrey, KT1 1SS, UK

TEH-WEI HU	School of Public Health, University of California, Berkeley, California 94720, USA
GAYLE JACKSON	Sector Base, 42 St Mary's Gate, Chesterfield, Derbyshire, S41 7TH, UK
JI JIANLIN	Shanghai Medical University, Department of Psychiatry, 600 Wan Ping Nan Road, Shanghai, 200030 P R China
RACHEL JENKINS	The Elderly and Disability Health Care, Department of Health, Wellington House 133–155 Waterloo Road, London, SE1 8UG, UK
CYNTHIA JONES	Duke University Medical Center, Department of Psychiatry, Durham, North Carolina 27710, USA
JOHN M. KANE	Psychiatry, Hillside Hospital, 754-59 263rd Street, Glen Oaks, New York 11004, USA
ROBERT R. KYDD	School of Medicine, Department of Psychiatry and Behavioural Sciences, University of Auckland, Private Bag 92019, Auckland, New Zealand
DAVID G. KINGDON	Department of Psychiatry, Bassetlaw District General Hospital, Kiltan, Worksop, Nottinghamshire, S81 0BD, UK
MARTIN KNAPP	PSSRU, University of Kent at Canterbury, Canterbury, Kent CT2 7NF, UK
TANNIS M. LAIDLAW	School of Medicine, Department of Psychiatry and Behavioural Sciences, University of Auckland, Private Bag 92019, Auckland, New Zealand
STEVEN S. LAMBERTI	University of Rochester, School of Medicine, Department of Psychiatry, 1650 Elmwood Avenue, Rochester, New York 14620, USA
JULIAN LEFF	MRC Social and Community Psychiatric Unit, De Crespigny Park, London SE5 8AF, UK
ANTHONY F. LEHMAN	University of Maryland, Department of Psychiatry, 645 W Redwood St, Baltimore, Maryland 21201-1549, USA
DAVID B. MALLOTT	University of Maryland, Department of Psychiatry, 645 W Redwood St, Suite P1G08, Baltimore, Maryland 21201-1549, USA
RONALD W. MANDERSCHEID	Center for Mental Health Services, Substance Abuse and Mental Health Service Administration, Rockville, Maryland, USA
ALAN MAYNARD	University of York, Centre for Health Economics, York, YO1 5DD, UK
PAUL McCRONE	PRISM; Psychiatric Research in Services Management, Institute of Psychiatry, De Crespigny Park, Denmark Hill, London SE5 8AF, UK
DAVID R. McDUFF	University of Maryland, Department of Psychiatry, 645 W Redwood St, Suite P1G08, Baltimore, Maryland 21201-1549, USA
BENTSON H. McFARLAND	Oregon Health Sciences University, Department of Psychiatry, OP-02, Portland, Oregon 97201, USA

MARK McGEE	Duke University Medical Center, Department of Psychiatry, Durham, North Carolina 27710, USA
THOMAS G. McGUIRE	Department of Economics, College of Liberal Arts, 270 Bay State Road, Boston, Massachusetts 02215, USA
NEIL MEISLER	Medical University of South Carolina, Department of Psychiatry, 171 Ashley Avenue, Charleston, South Carolina 29425, USA
JUAN E. MEZZICH	The Mount Sinai Medical Center, Department of Psychiatry, One Gustave L. Levy Place, New York, New York 10029-6574, USA
LEONARD S. MILLER	School of Social Welfare, 120 Haviland Hall, University of California, Berkeley, California 94720, USA
MASSIMO MOSCARELLI	Association for Research into Costs and Assessment in Psychiatry (ARCAP), via Daniele Crespi 7, 20123 Milano, Italy
POVL MUNK-JØRGENSEN	Social Psychiatric Research Unit, Institute of Psychiatric Demography, University of Aarhus, Psychiatric Hospital, Skovagervej 2, DK-8240 Risskov, Denmark
GRAYSON S. NORQUIST	NIMH/Division of Epidemiology and Services Research, Room 10-105, 5600 Fishers Lane, Rockville, Maryland 20857, USA
DARREL A. REGIER	NIMH/Division of Epidemiology and Services Research, 5600 Fishers Lane, Rockville, Maryland 20857, USA
DOROTHY P. RICE	Institute for Health and Aging, School of Nursing, University College of San Francisco Room N-531, Box 0612, San Francisco, California 94143-0612, USA
ANN ROGERS	National Primary Care Research and Developmental Centre, University of Salford, UK
AGNES RUPP	Mental Health Economics Research Program, NIMH, Room 10c-06 5600 Fishers Lane, Rockville, Maryland 20857, USA
LUIS SALVADOR-CARULLA	University of Cadiz, Department of Medical Psychology, Minusvalias, – Edificio Cycas 7C, Urbanizacion "El Bosque", Jerez 11405, Spain
ALBERTO B. SANTOS	Medical University of South Carolina, Department of Psychiatry, 171 Ashley Avenue, Charleston, South Carolina 29425, USA
NORMAN SARTORIUS	Department of Psychiatry, University of Geneva, Blvd de la Cluse 51, CH-1205 Geneva, Switzerland
SUSAN K. SCHULTZ	The Mental Health Clinical Research Center and Department of Psychiatry, University of Iowa Hospitals and Clinics, 200 Hawkins Drive, Iowa City, Iowa 52242, USA
STEVEN S. SHARFSTEIN	Sheppard Pratt, 6501 N Charles Street, PO Box 6815, Baltimore, Maryland 21285-6815 USA
MARTHA SHUMWAY	Department of Psychiatry, San Francisco General Hospital, 1001 Potrero Ave., California 94110, USA

RICHARD C. STEVENSON	Department of Economics, Liverpool University, Liverpool, UK
ANNE M. STOLINE	Sheppard Pratt, 6501 N Charles Street, PO Box 6815, Baltimore, Maryland 21285-6815 USA
CHARLIE SWANSON	Duke University Medical Center, Department of Psychiatry, Durham, North Carolina 27710, USA
JOHN A. TALBOTT	University of Maryland, Department of Psychiatry, 645 West Redwood Street, Suite P1G08, Baltimore, Maryland 21201-1549, USA
NICHOLAS TARRIER	University of Manchester, Department of Psychiatry, Withington Hospital, Manchester M20 8LR, UK
MAREE TEESSON	Clinical Research Unit for Anxiety Disorders, University of NSW, St Vincent's Hospital, 299 Forbes St, Durlinghust, NSW, 2010, Australia
JAMES W. THOMPSON	University of Maryland, Department of Psychiatry, 645 West Redwood Street, Suite P1G08, Baltimore, Maryland, 21201-1549, USA
GRAHAM THORNICROFT	PRISM: Psychiatric Research in Service Management, Institute of Psychiatry, De Crespigny Park, Denmark Hill, London SE5 8AF, UK
GARY L. TISCHLER	University of California, Department of Psychiatry, 760 West Wood Plaza, Los Angeles, California 90024-1759, USA
JÜRGEN UNÜTZER	University of California, Department of Psychiatry 760 West Wood Plaza, Los Angeles, California 90024-1759, USA
P.M. VAN DER LUBBE	Department of Social Psychiatry, Academisch Ziekenhuis, Oostersingel 59, P O Box 30 001, 9700 RB Groningen, The Netherlands
REYES VELAZQUEZ	Unidad de Psicologia Medica, Universitad de Cadiz, Centro de Investigation sobre, Minusvalias, Edificio Cycas 7C, Urbanizacion "El Bosque", Jerez 11405, Spain
DURK WIERSMA	Department of Social Psychiatry, Academisch Ziekenhuis, Oostersingel 59, PO Box 30 001, 9700 RB Groningen, The Netherlands
SUSANNE WULFF-SVENDSEN	Social Psychiatry Research Unit, Institute of Psychiatric Demography, University of Aarhus, Psychiatric Hospital, Skovagervej 2, DK-8240 Risskov, Denmark
RICHARD J. WYATT	NIMH Neuroscience Research Center at St Elisabeth's, 2700 Martin Luther King Jr Ave SE, Washington DC 20032, USA

Preface

MASSIMO MOSCARELLI
Association for Research into Costs and Assessment in Psychiatry, Milan, Italy

AGNES RUPP
Mental Health Economics Research Program, National Institute of Mental Health, Rockville, USA

NORMAN SARTORIUS
Institute of Psychiatry, University of Geneva, Switzerland

In a number of countries, the increase in the proportion of health care expenditure in the gross national product has led to the development of policies for controlling costs and evaluating the health and economic return from expenditure for health research, for the prevention of illness and for the care and rehabilitation for those who are ill. The implementation of these policies requires reliable, comprehensive health and economic information that will enable decision makers to obtain the greatest benefits per additional resource unit spent.

Comprehensive information seems particularly important when low-mortality, chronic, disabling illnesses are considered: the World Bank Development Report (1993) showed that disability due to these diseases is a heavy burden on societies. The health status in populations has traditionally been assessed on the basis of mortality data. This has probably obscured the burden which it creates particularly in the case of severe mental illnesses where the lack of social awareness has been reinforced by the stigma historically attached to these illnesses.

The information on the repercussions of illnesses on patients, families, workplaces, society and on the results obtained by financial, clinical and social interventions on health, quality of life and economic status need to take into account the different values given both to health/disability states and to the effects of interventions. Preferences and utilities of the different participants in the health care system (e.g. patients; also taking into account the variation in their individual preferences, relatives, advocate groups, clinicians, administrators, employers, insurance companies, health technology producers and society) need to be separately considered and evaluated, in particular for severe illnesses.

The evaluation of the destructive effects of illnesses and of the effects of clinical, social and financial interventions and their values seems to require an interdisciplinary collaboration between different professionals (mental health professionals, health economists, health policy researchers, sociologists, etc.) who through an integration of their disciplines could produce sound information necessary for the complex activity of decision making.

Pioneering activities aimed at the international integration of the research performed by different disciplines that in the past separately evaluated the mental health field from different perspectives has been performed by the ARCAP since 1990 in collaboration with the World Health Organization, the World Psychiatric Association and some national administrations (in particular US National Institute of Mental Health, and the departments of health of the United Kingdom and The Netherlands). These activities included the organization of biennial international worshops (Venice, 1990, 1992, 1994) in which leading experts presented results of the research performed in this field. The workshops enabled participants from about 40 countries (psychiatrists, psychologists, sociologists, health economists, public health researchers, statisticians who came from academies, administrations, hospitals and private firms, etc., both from the public and the private sectors) in an integrated manner to discuss data from health and economic evaluation and seek ways to use this information in health policy decision making. A selection of the articles presented during the workshops was published (*Schizophrenia Bulletin*, Vol 17, No. 3, 1991, *British Journal of Psychiatry* Vol 166, Suppl. 27, 1995 and *Social Psychiatry and Psychiatric Epidemiology* Vol. 30, No. 5, 1995).

The experience of these years suggested the need for an effort to develop a set of materials that will allow a comprehensive examination of the evidence and facilitate national projects examining the relationship of health and economic policies and interventions.

This handbook, of which we are now presenting the first volume, is a result of this. Each volume of the handbook will focus on one or several illnesses in order to make the interdisciplinary approach easier to apply and demonstrate.

This first volume deals with schizophrenia. Approximately 20 million people in the world suffer from this illness, which causes a heavy burden for patients, families and communities. The incidence rates of schizophrenia seem to be similar in all countries in which investigations were done (Sartorius, 1986). Schizophrenia shares many features with frequently chronic, disabling medical illnesses for which we have only symptomatic treatments, and which require long-term complex co-ordination of different clinical, financial and social interventions (Rupp and Keith, 1993). These shared features and characteristics only related to this illness must be taken into account for the development of sound health policies (Moscarelli, 1994).

This volume opens with specific measures used in the diagnostic evaluation of schizophrenia (McGee *et al.*; Mezzich) and in observing its features over time; it examines: symptoms (Andreasen *et al.*), social disabilities (de Jong *et al.*), work disabilities (Salvador-Carulla *et al.*), quality of life (Lehman), the use of these measures for course and outcome evaluation (Fenton) and the social influences on their severity and course (Bebbington). In order to define the diseases clearly in operational terms, the next set of chapters considers issues of the populations' health status data that are relevent for the attribution of economic values to the illnesses; it principally refers to the evaluation of the economic burden of the illness according to incidence or prevalence and to the evaluation of the changes in prevalence of illnesses over time (Norquist; Munk-Jørgensen *et al.*). The issues of the reliability of measures, when multisite evaluations are performed in separately considered (Bartko).

The interventions currently used, discussed in the chapters which follow, describe the care of schizophrenia, taking into account the variables of importance for economic evaluation: drug treatment (Kane) and its side-effects (Bentall *et al.*); psychological treatment (Tarrier) and the management of relapse (Herz *et al.*); first episode (Falloon *et al.*); case management (Meisler *et al.*; McCrone *et al.*); vocational programs (Clark *et al.*); housing (Carling *et al.*); involuntary treatment (McFarland); and family programs (Leff; Goldstein).

Strategic co-ordination in the care of people with schizophrenia (Talbott; Kingdon *et al.*) is examined next, in preparation for chapters on the issues related to the evaluation of the health services (an der Heiden *et al.*; Jackson *et al.*; Hargreaves *et al.*), to the evaluation of their costing (Hu *et al.*; Knapp *et al.*) to the basic methods of economic evalution (Rice *et al.*) and to the economic evaluation of drug treatment (Drummond *et al.*).

The chapters on financing of health care (Frank *et al.*; Maynard) and research (Wyatt *et al.*) consider the need to evaluate the impact of interventions including financing in terms of health and economic repercussions for the population concerned.

The chapters by Andrews *et al.* (Australia); Evers *et al.* (The Netherlands); Salvador-Carulla (Spain); and Ji Jianlin (China) provide examples of health services and outcome research in several countries.

The last section considers the economic aspects of

introducing policies in the mental health sector and deals with deinstitutionalization (Knapp), financial options (Stoline *et al.*), managed care (Unutzler *et al.*) as well as the use of economic data by policies of intergovernmental (Gulbinat *et al.*), national (Jenkins), state (Hogan) or no-profit organizations (Hogman), and the national health policies of financing mental health economics research (Rupp).

The contents of this volume are intended to provide information on issues relevant to the economic analysis of schizophrenia. We hope that this and subsequent volumes will prove valuable for those engaged in the evaluation of mental health care programs, and that they will encourage further research and the use of this multidisciplinary evaluation by policy makers and all others involved in the process of providing mental health care.

The opinions expressed here by Dr. Rupp are his own and do not necessarily reflect the official position of the NIMH.

REFERENCES

Moscarelli, M. (1994) Health and economic evaluation in schizophrenia: implications for health policies. *Acta Psychiatrica Scandinavica*, **89**, Suppl.382, 84–88.

Rupp, A., and Keith, S.J. (1993) *The Cost of Schizophrenia*, Psychiatric Clinics of North America, **16**, No. 2, June, 413–423.

Sartorius, N., Jablensky, A., Korten, A., Ernberg, G., Anker, M., Cooper, J., and Day, R. (1986) Early manifestations and first-contact incidence of schizophrenia in different cultures. *Psychological Medicine*, **16**, 909–928.

World Bank (1993) *World Development Report 1993—Investing in Health*. New York: Oxford University Press.

ACKNOWLEDGEMENTS

We would like to gratefully acknowledge the support given by Prof. Jorge Alberto Costa e Silva and Mr. Walter Gulbinat (World Health Organization), Prof. Felice Lieh Mak and Prof. Juan Lopez Ibor (World Psychiatric Association), Embassy Counsellor Eugenio Campo and Prof. Immacolata Pannone (Ministry of Foreign Affairs, Italy), Mrs. Irma Balloring (Department of Health, The Netherlands), Dr. Rachel Jenkins (Department of Health, United Kingdom), Dr. Grayson Norquist and Dr. Darrel Regier (National Institute of Mental Health, United States of America), by Prof. Paul Bebbington, Prof. Hugh Freeman, Prof. Samuel Keith and Prof. Greg Wilkinson (Editors of *Social Psychiatry and Psychiatric Epidemiology, British Journal of Psychiatry* and *Schizophrenia Bulletin*) to the activities which led to the development of this *Handbook*. Our thanks go in particular to Dr. Michael Davis, Wiley, for his advice, guidance, patience and understanding and to his collaborators, Ms. Mandy Collison, Ms. Elaine Hutton and Mrs. Hilary Rowe for their precious support.

Issues and Context

Linking Health Economics Research and Health Policy Formulation: The Need for Provision and Use of Scientific Research Information

MASSIMO MOSCARELLI
Association for Research into Costs and Assessment in Psychiatry, Milan, Italy

What sort of difference creates enmity and anger?
If you and I differ about a number . . . don't we go at once to arithmetic, and put an end to them by a sum? . . . if we differ about magnitudes, do we not quickly end the difference by measuring? . . . (do we not) end a controversy about heavy and light by resorting to a weighting machine? . . .
These enmities arise when the matters of difference are the just and unjust, good and evil, honourable and disonourable

Plato, Euthyphro

PROVISION OF SCIENTIFIC INFORMATION

The interaction between the information provided by health and economic research and the development of health policies is an issue currently debated throughout medicine from different perspectives and points of view. The potential consequences of health policy interventions, both related to management or financing, that could produce effects on the health, quality of life and economic status of tens or hundreds of millions of people are rarely strictly evaluated on the basis of experimental studies before implementation (e.g. new financing procedures, economic constraints for drugs reimbursement, providers and third party payers' competition, GPs–specialty physicians' proportion, etc.). The repercussions of these interventions could be particularly negative for more vulnerable populations, e.g. those with chronic and disabling illnesses or sick impoverished people.

Health care reform, which is developing in a number of different countries, has rarely funded and relied on structured research strategies for evaluating implementation of new management and financing programs. Now it seems to have taken on a major awareness by the different participants in the health care system and in different countries, in recognizing the complexity of the health and economic repercussions at different levels of each intervention, and the importance of scientific rigor and comprehensive information about them. From the individual patient to advocacy groups, relatives, clinicians, providers of services, purchasers, insurance companies, health technology producers, etc., the need for information can range from the results of the theoretical efficacy of randomized clinical trials, to information on the practical effectiveness of the application in everyday settings (whether practitioners deviate in a major way in the process of care—inappropriateness and variation phenomenona—and whether the personal style and ability of each physician has significant influence on health outcome results, particularly when the complexity of illness, repercussions, interventions and co-ordination of interventions, could shift the balance from the 'evidence based medicine' to the importance of personal skills in treating and co-ordinating the interventions in individual patients), to information on real health and economic outcomes through monitoring systems on a sample or general basis, in particular for the severe, potentially chronic, disabling illnesses.

BARRIERS TO THE PROVISION OF SCIENTIFIC INFORMATION

There are many interests in the evaluation of the health and economic consequences of illnesses on society and individuals, and of the expected benefits and costs of interventions. These interests refer to local and national administrations, specialty physicians, academics, research organizations, health service providers, employers, employees, patients, families, advocacy groups of individual illnesses, insurance companies, health technology producers, etc. Each of these participants (or their agents) in the health care sector are expected to have their own preferences on *what* is important to evaluate, *how* to evaluate it, *who* should perform the evaluation, *who* should manage the selection and spread of scientific information between different participants according to their interests and points of view and, lastly, *who* should pay for evaluations, spread of information and development of the capacity of the participants (or their agents) to use the data for their decisions and choices properly.

The lack of knowledge among physicians on the application of economic evaluation to the health sector, and the difficulty by clinicians to check the research on cost-effectiveness properly has opened up a discussion on the possible biases which could arise based on whether whoever produces information and/or selects it for distribution has a financial interest in influencing decision-makers' choices.

Two aspects of scientific information derived from cost-effectiveness analysis have recently been of particular interest and in the mean time underline the ethical aspects of possible biases due to conflicting interests: the cost-effectiveness of drugs and the cost/effectiveness of the performances of the medical care system.

A conflict of interests was underlined by Kassirer and Angell (1994), who explained the *New England Journal of Medicine* publication policy of excluding from publication a cost-effective analysis for papers where financial arrangements may exist between the authors and the for-profit companies that fund them.

A number of countries (e.g. Australia) require information on economic data in support of applications by pharmaceutical companies for new drugs. Economic drug trials can be used for pricing a new medicine, repricing an already marketed one, developing promotional material for advertising or other marketing approaches, convincing a formulary committee to place the medicine on their approved list, helping to convince one or more regulatory authorities to approve a medicine, addressing concerns of patients and patients groups, developing clinical strageties, etc. (Spilker, 1993, p. 302).

Information on the performance of the health care system, from the individual physician to the large service provision systems, is another issue. This information is related to 'process' or intermediate measures (e.g. quantity of interventions and their quality, satisfaction with the process of care) and 'product' or outcome measures (e.g. health and economic effects, satisfaction with the outcomes).

The current development and use of practice profiles in the United States based on process and outcome evaluation in decisions about paying physicians has received severe criticism. In particular it was claimed that to monitor and to evaluate practice according to process and outcome must be clinically meaningful and highly reliable, the adjustment for severity of illness and case-mix should be quite precise or physicians might shy away from seeing the sickest patient: companies in the business of producing profiles should also be monitored (Kassirer, 1994). Other aspects, such as financial incentives for physicians and case managers to reduce spending (Rodwin, 1995), difference in preferences given by purchasers (e.g. employers) and patients (e.g. employees), could shift the physician's (or health care provision system's) measure of success from health care results to a reduction in spending.

It seems that research generated information on the financial and human resources lost due to illnesses, information on the resources for research, care and rehabilitation, and information on the health and economic gains due to interventions are now considered a relevant need by the different participants in the health care system. Each of them should have an equal opportunity of production, access and use of relevant information according to their interests and points of view.

Scientific research on cost-effectiveness of a new drug should seriously consider issues such as what is important to evaluate, how to evaluate it, who should perform the evaluation, who should manage the information, and who should pay. Kassirer and Angell (1994) proposed to establish, in case neither the insurance industry nor government were willing or able to fund such efforts, an independent entity funded by a consortium of companies in the drug-and-device industry expressly to support economic analyses. A possible alternative, in the case, for example, of severe, chronic illnesses, could be that an independent evaluation system (from drug companies, insurance companies, clinicians, advocacy groups, administrations, etc.) could be funded proportionately by the different participants for assessing the health and economic effects of new drugs, on the basis of a consensus on the methods and the relevant items to be collected, according to the different interests and preferences of participants.

If the different interests seem to be considered in the production and use of scientific information related to drug development and spread, the multilevel information on the performances of health care over time seems to need equal if not superior attention by participants in the health care system. While information on mortality for illnesses due to its routine collection, is sometimes available to the users of information, the possibility that policy makers and the press adopt outcome measures in addition to mortality to judge the performances of the medical care system seems to be related to the supply of reliable and inexpensive measures of outcome (Newhouse, 1994); or, at least, the expenditures related to the activities of outcome evaluation should be in balance with the gains that information could produce on the health and economic improvement of each different illness. Monitoring outcomes of severe disabling illnesses on a general basis could represent a valuable basis for decision-making information if this activity will not be considered subject to influences of particular interests (e.g. clinicians that evaluate their own health care services provision, companies that evaluate performance profiles on behalf of employers, etc.).

If this activity of monitoring outcomes in particularly severe illnesses should take place, and if these evaluations should be the basis of competition between providers (from whole health care provision systems to individual physicians), it seems that beyond the variables including case-mix, severity, etc. and the availability of large data bases, which need to be considered when comparing performances, the issue of the different interests and possible biases in the development of this information should be given proper attention. It seems again that the program of an independent agency for the evaluation of outcomes, that is able to evaluate comprehensively the performances of the health care systems according to a consensus between the different participants and that is proportionally financed by the different participants in health care, should be considered.

USE OF SCIENTIFIC INFORMATION

Governmental health policies are considered successful if they lead to increased welfare through better outcomes, greater equity, more consumer satisfaction or lower total costs than would occur in the absence of public action. The World Health Organization (WHO) and the World Bank are developing programs for improving awareness in different countries of the importance of supporting health economics and health policy research strategies in developed and developing countries. The WHO division of mental health is in the process of developing multinational initiatives on mental health policy and care that will take into account the use of economic information (Gulbinat *et al.*, 1996). Coordinated financial policies are expected by international organizations, such as the World Bank or the International Monetary Fund, aimed at encouraging governments to invest in research and education programs in this field in the different countries (e.g.

by negotiating a better interest rate on debts for countries that will develop these programs). These organizations are in the position of acting in the general interest of these countries, and are expected to establish research projects aimed at evaluating the balance between the preferences given in each national global priority setting for annual expenditures, where health is in competition with other sources of expenditures, e.g. education or defense. These international policies seem particularly important in low-income developing countries.

Different specialties inside medicine (including psychiatry) are expected to develop over time an informed policy, each of them based on the specific characteristics of the illnesses they consider and the values and utilities of available interventions. It will enable each specialty to support its requests in comparison with other specialties in medicine and to influence on the basis of available data the global health policy development and the health priority setting for health research and care (Barchas & Mazurch, 1994). These policies require the use of specialty related clinical and economic evaluation. The integration of these different aspects will also become more and more common in the everyday decisions of physicians: the cost/effectiveness of individual drugs, their reimbursability, the liberty of judgment in the treatment, the ethics problems related to cost containment, etc. are entering now in the decisions of physicians in the different countries, in relation to particular illnesses, settings and treatments.

The advocacy groups of patients affected by severe illnesses and of their relatives are expected to play a major part in the development of research (e.g. considering the items of major interest to be collected in research on outcomes). They, or their agents, are also expected to develop a major, more sophisticated competence in using multidisciplinary research information according to points of view, interests and preferences of patients (also taking into account individual variations in preferences and the patients' different ability of expressing them in a variety of ways). The doctor–patient relationship is expected to change fundamentally (Morrison & Smith, 1994), and the benefits of these changes should also be evaluated.

The development and reliable use of information by the different participants in the health sector is expected to improve through the development in different countries of governmental strategies for health services, health economics, outcomes evaluation, health policy research and the establishment of a percentage on the annual health budget for funding research grants to academies, research institutes, etc. In the United States the federal standard of a 1% program cost was set aside by legislation for health care program evaluation (health services, economic, outcomes research) and similar percentages on global health care budget can be adopted in other countries.

The activity of financing programs of education aimed at the wise use (and/or support) of research studies according to the points of view and interests of different participants in the health care system (administrations, clinicians, insurance companies, advocacy groups, etc.) seems to be important for developing an informed interaction between providers and health policy makers, a major problem in most of the countries.

The World Bank claiming that 'governments may not have the capacity to administer or implement policies well . . . may suffer from corruption and from sheer incompetence' (World Bank, 1993) underlined the need of developing in the administrations a better capability to fund sound research strategies and to use their results in the activity of decision making of the developing and developed countries.

Some preliminary steps seem to require the establishment of a sufficient number of training programs of health economics, public health and health services and outcomes research, involved in collaboration programs of research and education, in order to train researchers in this interdisciplinary field, and to give to scholars in medicine and economics the fundamentals of this field.

Improving scientific research capacity in different countries will educate researchers in state of the art methods and measures shared by international groups, but it seems also of great importance to invite the researchers to take into account the peculiarities of their own country when they evaluate illnesses, and available new interventions.

This handbook is a first structured effort in considering specialty-related health economics research and health policies and we hope it will be a useful point of reference for the development of similar enterprises in other specialties of medicine.

REFERENCES

Barchas, J.D., and Mazurch, J.D. (1994) Some issues for the new director of NIMH. *Arch Gen Psych*, 998–1000.

Gulbinat, W., Manderscheid, R., Beigel, A., and Costa e Silva, J.-A. (1996) *A Multinational Strategy on Mental Health Policy and Care.* A WHO Collaborative Initiative and Consultative Program. In: M. Moscarelli, A. Rupp and N. Sartorius, eds, *Handbook of Mental Health Economics and Health Policies – Vol. 1, Schizophrenia,* pp. 528–533. Chichester: John Wiley & Sons Ltd.

Kassirer, J. (1994) The use and abuse of practice profiles. *The New England Journal of Medicine,* **330**, No. 9, 633–636.

Kassirer, J.P., and Angell, M. (1994) The journal's policy on cost-effectiveness analysis, *The New England Journal of Medicine,* **331**, No. 10, 669–670.

Morrison, I., and Smith, R. (1994) The future of medicine, *British Medical Journal,* **309**, 1099–1100.

Newhouse, J.P. (1994) Health services research in a post-reform world: presidential address to the Association for Health Services Research, June 1994. *Health Services Research,* **29**, 5 (Dec.), 515–521.

Rodwin, M.A. (1995) Conflicts in managed care. *The New England Journal of Medicine,* **332**, 604–607.

Spilker, B. (1993) Guide to Clinical Trials. Raven Press: New York.

World Bank (1993) *World Development Report 1993—Investing in Health.* New York: Oxford University Press.

Part I

PSYCHIATRIC EVALUATION

1

Diagnosis: The DSM-IV Approach to Schizophrenia

MARK McGEE, CHARLIE SWANSON, CYNTHIA JONES AND ALLEN FRANCES
Department of Psychiatry, Duke University Medical Center, Durham, North Carolina, USA

INTRODUCTION

Any discussion of schizophrenia and its related economic issues must include a consideration of how schizophrenia is defined. Our conceptualization of the illness has changed dramatically over time and only in recent years has there been anything approaching international agreement regarding definitions. DSM-IV is the fourth edition of the American Psychiatric Association's *Diagnostic and Statistical Manual of Mental Disorders*, and is the product of an extensive, empirically documented process aimed at refining and clarifying the nomenclature of mental disorders, including schizophrenia. In this chapter, we review that process and the specific DSM-IV changes for schizophrenia. We have also included a brief review of pertinent theoretical and historical perspectives. ICD-10 and DSM-IV similarities and differences are discussed and we have speculated on the possible economic impact of changing definitions.

The opinions expressed in this chapter are not necessarily those of the American Psychiatric Association and its Task Force on DSM-IV. Because the Task Force was dedicated to keeping the field informed of the development of the manual, there have been a large number of DSM-IV-related papers and presentations, and some of the material presented here represents abbreviated material from earlier work. By arrangement with the American Psychiatric Association, material from the DSM-IV has been borrowed freely.

HISTORICAL CONCEPTS OF DIAGNOSIS

Schizophrenia is a clinical syndrome of unknown etiology and pathophysiology. There are no pathognomonic symptoms and no clinically useful laboratory or imaging markers. The characteristic features of schizophrenia are heterogeneous and the boundaries with other disorders can be difficult to delineate. Clinical diagnosis is curently based on characteristic signs, symptoms, and course of illness. Current nosologies address these issues but cannot be understood without an awareness of their historical precedents and the theoretical concepts that shaped them.

What we now call schizophrenia has been recognized and described throughout much of recorded history. Although there were many earlier literary and medical descriptions, Emil Kraepelin (1856–1926) is typically credited with developing the first comprehensive definition of schizophrenia (Kraepelin, 1919). His term "dementia praecox" gained wide acceptance and emphasized early onset and a chronic, deteriorating course as the defining features of the

Handbook of Mental Health Economics and Health Policy, Volume I, Schizophrenia. Edited by M. Moscarelli, A. Rupp and N. Sartorius.
© 1996 John Wiley & Sons Ltd.

illness. The differentiation of early "dementia" from late-onset dementia and manic-depressive illness had important prognostic utility and remains today as a fundamental distinction in psychiatry. Kraepelin's emphasis on loss of cognitive function and deteriorating course defined a narrow group of severely ill patients with chronic, persistent symptoms, and a poor prognosis.

Complementing Kraepelin's work, Eugen Bleuler (1857–1939) suggested the term "schizophrenia" in an effort to emphasize the fragmentation of thought or "splitting of the mind" that he believed to be fundamental to the illness (Blueler, 1911). Blueler described a group of symptoms including affective blunting, autism (peculiar and distorted thinking), avolition (loss of motivational interest), impaired attention, and ambivalence as "fundamental" to the disorder. He de-emphasized the importance of the course of illness and considered delusions and hallucinations "accessory" symptoms because they occurred in other illnesses. Bleuler's ideas were widely accepted and his "4A's" (associations, affect, autism, and ambivalence) guided diagnostic practice for several decades of European and American psychiatrists. His description of schizophrenia emphasized deficit symptoms and defined a much broader and more heterogeneous group of patients, many of whom were less ill and more functional than those described by Kraepelin.

A third important perspective on the development of the concept of schizophrenia was provided by the German psychiatrist Kurt Schneider (1887–1967). Partly in response to diagnostic uncertainties inherent in Bleuler's broadly defined concepts, he emphasized diagnostically discriminatory symptoms he hoped would be reliably assessed and relatively specific to schizophrenia. He identified a group of delusions and hallucinations and considered them of "first rank" significance in the disorder (Schneider, 1959, 1974). These included thought insertion, thought withdrawal, thought broadcasting, voices communicating with or about the person, and delusions of being externally controlled. Schneider's description of schizophrenia emphasized psychotic symptoms and a cross-sectional view of the illness. His concepts defined an acutely ill group of patients significantly different from either Kraepelin's or Bleuler's. Although later research suggested that Schneiderian symptoms were not specific to schizophrenia, his ideas gained prominence in the 1970s and were incorporated in the diagnostic criteria for schizophrenia in DSM-III.

DIAGNOSTIC SYSTEMS

The classification of mental disorders has, in the broadest sense, been under revision throughout the history of medicine. The many nomenclatures developed in the past differed in their relative emphasis on phenomenology, etiology, and course as defining features. In addition, diagnostic systems have varied with respect to their intended use in statistical, clinical, or research settings. As noted previously, only in recent decades has there been reasonable international agreement on definitions. In this review, we will briefly focus on historical aspects pertinent to the more recent development of DSM-IV and ICD-10.

In the United States, the initial impetus for developing a classification of mental disorders was the need to collect statistical information. A category for the recording of the frequency of "idiocy/insanity" was included in the 1840 census. Categories were gradually expanded and by the 1880 census seven groups were distinguished (mania, melancholia, monomania, paresis, dementia, dipsomania, and epilepsy). In 1917, the American Psychiatric Association's (APA's) Committee on Statistics formulated plans adopted by the Bureau of the Census for the gathering of statistics in mental hospitals. Although some attention was given to clinical utility, this system was still primarily a statistical classification. In the late 1920s, the APA collaborated with the New York Academy of Medicine to develop a nationally acceptable psychiatric nomenclature. This nomenclature was designed primarily for diagnosing hospitalized patients with severe psychiatric and neurological disorders and was incorporated in the first edition of the American Medical Association's Standard Classified Nomenclature of Disease.

Near the end of the Second World War, a much broader nomenclature was developed by the US Army to incorporate the outpatient presentations of servicemen and veterans. With some modifications, this system was adopted by the Veterans Administration (VA) in 1946. At the same time, the World

Health Organization (WHO) published the sixth edition of the *International Classification of Diseases* (ICD-6), which for the first time included a section for mental disorders. ICD-6 was heavily influenced by the VA nomenclature and included 10 categories for psychosis, nine for psychoneurosis, and seven for disorders of character, behaviour, and intelligence.

The APA Committee on Nomenclature and Statistics developed a version of the ICD-6 that was published in 1952 as the first edition of the *Diagnostic and Statistical Manual of Mental Disorders* (DSM-I). DSM-I was the first official manual of mental disorders to focus on clinical utility and was designed for use across a variety of inpatient and outpatient settings. DSM-I (APA, 1952) contained a glossary of descriptions of the diagnostic categories and included nine subtypes of schizophrenic "reactions" (simple, hebephrenic, catatonic, paranoid, acute, undifferentiated, chronic undifferentiated, schizoaffective, and residual). The term "reaction" used throughout DSM-I reflected the influence of Adolf Meyer's psychobiologic view that mental disorders represented reactions of the personality to psychological, social, and biological factors.

DSM-II, developed in coordinations with ICD-8 was published in 1968. DSM-II was similar to DSM-I but eliminated the use of the term "reaction." DSM-II (APA 1968) contained eleven subtypes of schizophrenia (simple, hebephrenic, catatonic, paranoid, acute latent, residual, schizoaffective, childhood, chronic undifferentiated and unspecified).

DSM-III was coordinated with the development of ICD-9 and was published in 1980. DSM-III introduced a number of important methodological innovations, including explicit diagnostic criteria, a multiaxial system, and a descriptive approach that attempted to be neutral with respect to theories of etiology. This approach was a fundamental departure from previous nomenclatures and was due in part to a growing recognition of the importance of diagnosis for both clinical practice and research. DSM-III included expanded descriptions of disorders and many additional categories.

The DSM-III definition of schizophrenia differed significantly from its predecessors. Several forces shaped the development of the DSM-III concept of schizophrenia. Studies done in the early 1970s (Kendell *et al.*, 1971; Cooper *et al.*, 1972; WHO, 1973) suggested that American psychiatrists used a broader definition of schiophrenia than their counterparts in Great Britain and Europe. Specifically, patients with similar presentations were diagnosed as having schizophrenia by American psychiatrists and mood disorder by those in Europe. With the development of specific antimanic therapies (lithium), the discrepancies in diagnosis had specific and potentially deleterious clinical consequences. DSM-III responded to this discrepancy by emphasizing an exclusion for mood disorder in the diagnostic criteria for schizophrenia. This markedly narrowed the DSM-III description of schizophrenia and had a dramatic impact on the diagnostic methods of psychiatrists in the United States.

Other studies (Kreitman *et al.*, 1961; Beck *et al.*, 1962; Sandifer *et al.*, 1964, 1968; Spitzer & Fleiss, 1974) were critical of the reliability of diagnosis. This criticism led in part to an increased emphasis on objective criteria and a shift toward increased reliance on Schneiderian first rank symptoms of delusions and hallucinations to define the disorder.

An additional influence on the DSM-III concept of schizophrenia was a renewed interest in the Kraepelinian emphasis on course of illness. The Washington University criteria, often called the Feighner criteria, required a 6 month duration of symptoms for diagnosis (Feighner *et al.*, 1972). Several studies have shown these criteria to have predictive validity: first episode patients diagnosed with the 6 month criterion were more likely to continue to have the diagnosis of schizophrenia than those patients without the 6 month criterion (Bland & Orn, 1979; Tsuang *et al.*, 1979; Helzer *et al.*, 1981, 1983; Guze et al., 1983; Lloyd & Tsuang 1985; Moller *et al.*, 1989). DSM-III responded to these findings by requiring a 6 month duration of symptoms for diagnosis.

To summarize, the DSM-III definition of schizophrenia (Table 1) emphasized the role of delusions and hallucinations (A criteria) and required continuous signs of the illness for 6 months (C criteria). Manic or depressive syndromes, if present, were to occur only after any psychotic symptoms and were to be brief in duration relative to the duration of the psychotic symptoms (D criteria). DSM-III also required a deterioration from a previous level of functioning (B criteria). The DSM-II concepts of

Table 1. DSM III criteria for schizophrenic disorder

A. At least one of the following during the phase of the illness:
(1) bizarre delusions (content is patently absurd and has *no* possible basis in fact), such as delusions of being controlled, thought broadcasting, thought insertion or thought withdrawal
(2) somatic, grandiose, religious, nihilistic, or other delusions without persecutory or jealous content
(3) delusions with persecutory or jealous content if accompanied by hallucinations of any type
(4) auditory hallucinations in which either a voice keeps up a commentary on the individual's behavior or thoughts, or two or more voices converse with each other
(5) auditory hallucinations on several occasions with content of more than one or two words, having no apparent relation to depression or elation
(6) incoherence, marked loosening of associations, markedly illogical thinking, or marked poverty of content or speech if associated with at least one of the following:
(a) blunted, flat, or inappropriate affect
(b) delusions or hallucinations
(c) catatonic or other grossly disorganized behavior

B. Deterioration from a previous level of functioning in such areas as work, social relations, and self-care.

C. Duration: Continuous signs of illness for at least 6 months at some time during the person's life, with some signs of the illness at present. The 6-month period must include an active phase during which there were symptoms from (A), with or without a prodromal or residual phase, as defined below.

Prodromal phase: A clear deterioration in functioning before the active phase of the illness not due to disturbance of mood or to substance use disorder and involving at least two of the symptoms noted below.

Residual phase: Persistence, following the active phase of the illness, of at least two of the symptoms noted below, not due to a disturbance in mood or to a substance use disorder.

Prodromal or residual symptoms
(1) social isolation or withdrawal
(2) marked impairment in role functioning as wage-earner, student, or homemaker
(3) markedly peculiar behavior (e.g., collecting garbage, talking to self in public, or hoarding (food)
(4) marked impairment in personal hygiene and grooming
(5) blunted, flat, or inappropriate affect
(6) digressive, vague, overelaborate, circumstantial, or metaphorical speech
(7) odd or bizarre ideation, or magical thinking, e.g., superstitiousness clairvoyance, telepathy, "sixth sense," "others can feel my feelings," overvalued ideas, ideas of reference
(8) unusual perceptual experiences, e.g., recurrent illusions, sensing the presence of a force or person not actually present

Examples: 6 months of prodromal symptoms with 1 week of symptoms from (A); no prodromal symptoms with 6 months of symptoms from (A); no prodromal symptoms with 2 weeks of symptoms from (A) and 6 months of residual symptoms; 6 months of symptoms from (A), apparently followed by several years of complete remission, with 1 week of symptoms in (A) in current episode.

D. The full depressive or manic syndrome (criteria A and B of major depressive or manic episode), if present, developed after any psychotic symptoms, or was brief in duration relative to the duration of the psychotic symptoms in (A).

E. Onset of the prodromal or active phase of the illness before age 45.

F. Not due to any organic mental disorder or mental retardation.

acute and latent schizophrenia were essentially eliminated. Acute schizophrenia was partially subsumed under schizophreniform disorder which was introduced to describe presentations that were identical to schizophrenia except for the 6 months duration. Schizophreniform disorder was listed under "Psychotic Disorders Not Elsewhere Classified" to enhance its differentiation from schizophrenia. Also listed in this section were brief reactive psychosis, schizoaffective disorder, and atypical psychosis. The DSM-II concept of latent schizophrenia was largely subsumed under the description of schizotypal personality disorder.

With its emphasis on delusions, hallucinations, course of illness, and mood disorder exclusion, the concept of schizophrenia was significantly narrowed by the DSM-III definition. The change from glossary defined disorders to rigorously defined criteria sets had a significant impact on diagnostic practices. Diagnosis became more discriminating. Clinical presentations previously subsumed under broad pre-DSM-III notions of schizophrenia were more rigorously defined by DSM-III as bipolar illness, schizoaffective, paranoid, schizotypal personality, and schizophreniform disorders. Although the DSM-III concept of schizophrenia was criticized for its simplicity and its relative emphasis on psychotic symptoms, the utility of the approach for clinical and research purposes has been well documented (Andreasen & Flaum, 1991).

DSM-III-R was published in 1987. Relatively minor changes were made in the diagnostic criteria for schizophrenia. Criteria were simplified and the relative weighting of flat and inappropriate affect was increased. Bizarre delusions were redefined and diagnostic boundaries with delusional disorder were clarified. A 1 week duration criterion was added to the psychotic symptoms appearing in the A criteria, and the B criteria, specifying loss of function, was redefined and broadened. A comparison study of DSM-III and DSM-III-R suggested that by excluding patients with non-bizarre delusions (somatic, grandiose, or religious), DSM-III-R reduced the number of patients diagnosed with schizophrenia by 10%, essentially by labelling these individuals as having delusional disorder instead (Fenton *et al.*, 1988).

DSM-IV

DSM-IV, published in 1994, is the result of an extensive process of empirical review and documentation. Previous versions of DSM were primarily reflections of expert consensus on the definition of mental disorders and there was no systematic review of the rationale and empirical support for these decisions. DSM-IV is the first well-documented psychiatric nosology. A three-stage process of comprehensive literature reviews, reanalyses of data sets, and field trials has provided the empirical support for the changes that were made in the text and criteria sets of DSM-IV. This process was carried out by 13 work groups, each of which had responsibility for a specific section of the manual.

The first stage involved a review of the existing literature. The reviewers for each work group were initially instructed to provide a summary of the issues confronting their diagnostic group, stating their significance to the DSM process. An objective and descriptive summary of the existing literature on the subject was then completed. The results of the review led to various recommendations for solutions, with advantages and disadvantages for each option cited. In order to insure a comprehensive and balanced coverage of the literature, the reviews were critiqued by DSM-IV work group members and advisors.

Data reanalysis addressed issues that could not be resolved through the literature reviews. Previously unpublished data sets collected as part of epidemiological, treatment, or other studies were reanalyzed to answer questions from the reviews and generate possible data-based criteria sets for DSM-IV. These reanalyses were funded by a grant to the APA from the John D. and Catherine T. MacArthur Foundation and are referred to as the MacArthur data reanalyses. The data reanalysis studied the preponderant characteristics of a number of possible criteria and compared the DSM-III-R and the ICD-10 approach.

The third stage, field trials, examined questions not entirely resolved by the literature reviews and data reanalyses. The focus of the field trials was to compare options for DSM-III, DSM-III-R, ICD-10, and proposed DSM-IV criteria sets, and to estimate the effect of proposed changes. To represent the array of disease in the diverse fields of usage, field trials examining the criteria sets for psychotic symptoms were conducted across nine sites (including two international sites) with 361 subjects (100 in the international sites).

DEVELOPMENT OF THE SCHIZOPHRENIA SECTION

The DSM-IV criteria for schizophrenia are shown in Table 2. The changes from DSM-III-R are as follows: the A criteria are simplified with bizarre delusions and prominent hallucinations moved to a footnote; two additional negative symptoms are included (i.e. alogia, avolition); the duration of the active characteristic symptoms is increased to 1 month; and the specific list of prodromal and residual symptoms is eliminated. The schizoaffective and mood disorder exclusion is kept intact from DSM-III-R, with minor wording changes. The exclusion due to an organic factor is reworded to reflect the increased influence in DSM-IV given to

Table 2. DSM-IV Diagnostic criteria for schizophrenia

A. Characteristic symptoms: at least two of the following, each present for a significant portion of time during a 1 month period (or less if successfully treated):
(1) delusions
(2) hallucinations
(3) disorganized speech (e.g., frequent derailment or incoherence)
(4) grossly disorganized or catatonic behavior
(5) negative symptoms, i.e., affective flattening, alogia, or avolition
(*Note*: only one A symptom is required if delusions are bizarre or hallucinations consist of a voice keeping up a running commentary on the person's behavior or thoughts, or two or more voices conversing with each other.)
B. Social/occupational dysfunction: for a significant portion of the time since the onset of the disturbance, one or more major areas of functioning such as work, interpersonal relations or self-care are markedly below the level achieved prior to the onset (or when the onset is in childhood or adolescence, failure to achieve expected level of interpersonal, academic, or occupational achievement).
C. Duration: continuous signs of the disturbance persist for at least 6 months. This 6-month period must include at least 1 month of symptoms (or less if successfully treated) that meet criterion (A) (i.e., active phase symptoms), and may include periods of prodromal or residual symptoms. During these prodromal or residual periods, the signs of the disturbance may be manifested by only negative symptoms or two or more symptoms listed in criterion A present in an attenuated form (e.g., odd beliefs, unusual perceptual experiences).
D. Schizoaffective and mood disorder exclusion: schizoaffective disorder and mood disorder with psychotic features have been ruled out because either: (1) no major depressive, manic, or mixed episodes have occurred concurrently with the phase active symptoms; or (2) if mood episodes have occurred during active phase symptoms, their total duration has been brief relative to the duration of the active and residual periods.
E. Substance/general medical condition exclusion: the disturbance is not due to the direct physiological effects of a substance (e.g., a drug of abuse, a medication) or a general medical condition.
F. If there is a history of autistic disorder or another pervasive developmental disorder, the additional diagnosis of schizophrenia is made only if prominent delusions or hallucinations are also present for at least a month (or less if successfully treated).

substance-induced disorders and disorders due to a general medical condition.

Several general principles guided the development of the schizophrenia and other psychotic disorders section. One consensus goal of the work group was not to alter the base rate of schizophrenia. Members believed that any change would be detrimental to research and would confuse clinicians (Andreasen & Flaum, 1991). There was a high threshold for change: in instances where alterations to previous criteria were considered, an overriding conservative approach to change was maintained. Changes had to be supported by clear rationale and a preponderance of data and, as much as possible, be consistent with ICD-10.

First rank symptoms have historical importance in schizophrenia, as described earlier. However, literature reviews demonstrated difficulties with these symptoms (Andreasen & Flaum, 1991; Flaum & Andreasen, 1991). They have been shown to be neither internally consistent nor stable over time. Limitations regarding their reliability, base rate, and specificity suggest they should not be given undue prominence (Carpenter & Strauss, 1974; Koehler *et al.*, 1977; Taylor & Abrams, 1973 & 1975). Also, the MacArthur data reanalysis did not support emphasizing Schneiderian first rank symptoms in the diagnosis of schizophrenia. A literature review as well as MacArthur data reanalysis showed low base rates for incoherence, loosening of associations, and thought broadcasting (Andreasen & Flaum, 1991). Therefore, the A criterion for incoherence or marked loosening of associations in DSM-III-R is replaced with a criterion for disorganized speech (e.g. frequent derailment or incoherence) in DSM-IV. The term "thought broadcasting" is dropped, and the concept is incorporated under bizarre delusions.

In DSM-III-R, bizarre delusions were given added significance. A subsequent study, however, showed low interrater reliability to distinguish bizarre from non-bizarre delusions (Flaum *et al.*, 1991). In addition, Goldman *et al.* (1992) demonstrated that patients with bizarre delusions did not comprise a clinical subgroup except for having more positive symptoms. For these reasons, in DSM-IV, bizarre delusions and prominent hallucinations (such as a commentary voice or two voices conversing) are de-emphasized and moved to a footnote of the A criteria.

Negative symptoms have been given added emphasis in DSM-IV. Two negative symptoms, alogia and avolition, are added to affective flattening in the A criteria. Literature reviews have shown negative symptoms to be reliable, internally consistent, and highly correlated (Crow, 1980; Barnes & Liddle, 1990; Andreasen & Flaum, 1991). They are associated with internal validators such as cognitive impairment, differential treatment response, poor outcome, and motor abnormalities (Andreasen & Flaum, 1991). Negative symptoms are stable over time (Johnstone *et al.*, 1987) and they may be correlated with external validators such as magnetic resonance imaging findings (although there is some controversy over this) (Marks & Luchins, 1990).

In DSM-III-R, the duration criteria specifies continuous signs of the disturbance for 6 months and lists nine prodromal or residual symptoms that can be present in addition to the characteristic psychotic symptoms. A reliability study of the Comprehensive Assessment of Symptoms and History (CASH) (Andreasen, 1985) showed low levels of agreement in prodromal symptoms on the basis of independent interviews (Andreasen & Flaum, 1991). There were doubts as to the ability to assess reliably the duration and onset of these symptoms retrospectively (Andreasen & Flaum, 1991; Keith & Mathews, 1991). Also, there were concerns that this list mixed pre-psychotic symptoms with negative and negative-like symptoms, with their different clinical implications (Keith & Mathews, 1991). In addition, ICD-10 does not list prodromal or residual symptoms. Therefore, in the C criteria, the list of prodromal and residual symptoms is dropped in favor of a more general approach (negative symptoms only or attenuated A criteria symptoms can be used with the characteristic symptoms to meet the criteria for duration).

Field trials assessed 361 patients with a variety of psychotic disorders in seven US sites including: the University of Iowa; New York State Psychiatric Institute; the Medical College of Virginia; Yale Psychiatric Institute; the Long-Island Jewish-Hillside Hospital; the University of Arkansas; and McLean Hospital. In addition, 100 patients were evaluated at two international sites (Autonomous University of Nuevo Leon, Mexico, and Royal Park Hospital, Monash University, Victoria, Australia). Subjects were measured by two raters with a semistructured interview designed especially for the study by Dr. Michael Flaum of the University of Iowa. A variety of criteria sets (including DSM-III-R, ICD 10, and various options for DSM-IV) were included in the field trials. These trials were used to assess the reliability, classification rates, user friendliness, and external validity of the proposed criteria (Flaum & Andreasen, 1991). The field trials confirmed that simplification of the A criteria and the inclusion of additional negative symptoms did not affect the classification rate or reduce reliability (Kline *et al.*, 1993). These trials also suggested that extending the duration of active symptoms to 1 month would reduce false positives in first episode patients (Kline *et al.*, 1993). Extending the duration of active symptoms also increased compatibility with ICD-10.

Substance-related disorders have increased prominence throughout DSM-IV. Each section contains a number of substance-induced disorders. The criteria for substance-induced psychotic disorders include prominent hallucinations or delusions, symptoms developed within 1 month of substance intoxication or withdrawal, and that the disturbance is not better accounted for by a non-substance-induced psychotic disorder. The following classes of substances are associated with psychosis during intoxication: alcohol, amphetamine and related substances, cannabis, cocaine, hallucinogens, inhalants, opioids (meperidine), phencyclidine and related substances, sedatives, hypnotics, and anxiolytics. Classes of substances associated with psychosis during withdrawal are alcohol, sedatives, hypnotics, and anxiolytics.

Another important change in DSM-IV is in the illnesses previously described as organic mental disorders. In DSM-IV, they are referred to as disorders due to a general medical condition, and like substance-induced disorders are found in every section of DSM-IV. The criteria for psychotic disorders due to a general medical condition are prominent hallucinations or delusions with direct history, physical examination, or laboratory evidence that the psychosis is due to the specific medical

Table 3. ICD-*10 schizophrenia criteria*

G1 Either at least one of the syndromes, symptoms, and signs listed under (1) below, *or* at least two of the symptoms and signs listed under (2) should be present for most of the time during the episode of psychotic illness lasting for at least 1 month (or at some time during most of the days).

- (1) At least one of the following must be present:
  - (a) thought echo, thought insertion or withdrawal, or thought broadcasting;
  - (b) delusions of control, influence, or passivity, clearly referred to body or limb movements or specific thoughts, actions, or sensations; delusional perception;
  - (c) hallucinatory voices giving a running commentary on the patient's behavior, or discussing the patient among themselves, or other types of hallucinatory voices coming from some part of the body;
  - (d) persistent delusions of other kinds that are culturally inappropriate and completely impossible (e.g. being able to control the weather, or being in communication with aliens from another world).
- (2) *Or* at least two of the following:
  - (a) persistent hallucinations in any modality, when occurring every day for at least 1 month, when accompanied by delusions (which may be fleeting or half-formed) without clear affective content, or when accompanied by persistent over-valued ideas;
  - (b) neologisms, breaks, or interpolations in the train of thought, resulting in incoherence or irrelevant speech;
  - (c) catatonic behavior, such as excitement, posturing or waxy flexibility, negativism, mutism, and stupor;
  - (d) "negative" symptoms, such as marked apathy, paucity of speech, and blunting or incongruity of emotional responses (it must be clear that those are not due to depression or to neuroleptic medication).

G2 *Most commonly used exclusion clauses*

- (1) If the patient also meets criteria for manic episode (F30.-) or depressive episode (F32.-), the criteria listed under G1(1) and G1(2) above must have been met *before* the disturbance of mood developed.
- (2) The disorder is not attributable to organic brain disease (in the sense of F00–F09), or to alcohol- or drug-related intoxication (F1*x*.0), dependence (F1*x*.2), or withdrawal (F1*x*.3 and F1*x*.4).

Reproduced by permission of WHO, from: *The ICD-10 Classification of Mental and Behavioural Disorders: Diagnostic criteria for research*. Geneva, World Health Organization, 1993.

condition described. There must not be another mental disorder that better describes the psychosis. Also, the diagnosis is excluded if the psychosis only occurs during delirium or is associated with an Alzheimer's or vascular dementia.

Even though one of the aims for the development of DSM-IV was concordance with ICD-10, there remain some important distinctions (WHO, 1989; Andreasen & Flaum, 1991; Flaum & Andreasen, 1991). ICD-10 continues to place more emphasis on cross-sectional Schneiderian first rank symptoms (especially in diagnosing schizoaffective disorder), while DSM-IV adds more emphasis to a Kraepelinian deteriorative course. The duration for active symptoms in both systems is 1 month. In ICD-10, bizarre delusions continue to have added significance and examples of these delusions and prominent hallucinations are specifically delineated. ICD-10 has no corresponding concept to the DSM-IV B criteria for social/occupational dysfunction. Finally, DSM-IV requires a 6 month overall duration while ICD-10 only requires 1 month of active symptoms. Neither system lists specific prodromal or residual symptoms and both opt for a more descriptive approach.

SPECULATIONS ON THE IMPACT OF DSM-IV

The DSM-IV description of schizophrenia compared to past definitions remains relatively narrow. As noted previously, the prevalence of schizophrenia is not expected to undergo any marked change. However, the increase in the duration of active symptoms to 1 month should decrease the number of "false positives" and enhance the recognition of substance-induced psychotic disorder, psychotic disorder due to a general medical condition, and brief psychotic disorder. The exclusion criterion for schizoaffective disorder and mood disorder with psychotic features remains and the criteria for delusional disorder have been slightly refined to enhance diagnostic discrimination.

The relative elevation of negative symptoms in the A criteria may have a subtle impact on research and treatment strategies. The emphasis on Schneiderian first rank symptoms of delusions and hallucinations has had a significant impact on the development of antipsychotic pharmaceuticals. An increased recognition of negative symptoms may encourage the development of more effective therapeutic agents aimed at relieving these symptoms. The enhanced recognition of deficit symptoms could also bolster the prominence of psychosocial therapies now recognized to be central to the effective long-term management of patients.

The substance and general medical conditions exclusion clarifies diagnostic boundaries and should direct clinicians to appropriate therapies. The recognition of substance-related psychotic disorder and psychotic disorder due to a general medical condition may be enhanced and unnecessary exposure to antipsychotic medications may be reduced.

The simplification of the diagnostic criteria may enhance communication among clinicians, researchers, teachers, and administrators. Clinicians will hopefully find the criteria set more user friendly and easier to apply than previous nomenclatures. Research efforts may be enhanced, improving the reliability of findings and encouraging the development of new treatments. The criteria should be easier for all mental health professionals and students to teach, remember, and use. Policy-makers, advocates, and administrators should benefit from the simplification of criteria enhancing the development and administration of systems and programs for patients with schizophrenia.

CONCLUSIONS

The DSM-IV reflects our current understanding of schizophrenia based on the empirical literature and data available at the time of publication. Schizophrenia remains a syndrome of unknown etiology and pathophysiology. DSM-IV is part of a worldwide process directed toward a better, more fundamental understanding of the illness. Future revisions of the nomenclature will benefit from new research findings and developments encouraged in part by the DSM-IV contribution.

Schizophrenia is the most economically burdensome of all psychiatric disorders. Direct treatment costs of patients with schizophrenia were approximately 2.5% of all health expenditures in the United States in 1990. Total costs, including indirect costs such as lost productivity, may have been as high as 33 billion dollars in that year (Rice & Miller, 1992).

Cost estimates are a major determinant of priorities in health care policy and research. In a study of cost, the definition of patient groups to be assessed is by nosology as well as practice standards. As noted previously, the DSM-IV description of schizophrenia is narrow relative to past descriptions. Although there were relatively minor changes in diagnostic criteria, the refinement of diagnostic groups will have an impact on future economic studies.

The diagnosis of schizophrenia in DSM-IV is the narrowest to date. Great care has been taken to exclude conditions that have other etiologies, which may mimic the symptoms of schizophrenia. By increasing emphasis on exclusion criteria for substance use disorders and general medical conditions, DSM-IV describes a more homogeneous condition. This subtle decrease in heterogeneity will shift costs for the excluded conditions to other categories.

In addition to a narrow definition, DSM-IV defines a more ill group of patients. Increasing duration criteria for active symptoms and elevating the significance of negative symptoms defines a group of patients with poorer prognosis. With poorer prognosis come greater costs: both direct (more treatment, more rehabilitative services, more hospitalizations) and indirect (decreased productivity and function, increased family burden).

International economic studies will need to recognize differences between ICD-10 and DSM-IV. ICD-10 defines a more heterogeneous group of patients relative to DSM-IV. Schizophrenia in ICD-10 contains no requirement for 6 months overall duration. Only 1 month of active symptoms is required and thus patients should have a slightly better prognosis than in DSM-IV. In essence, schizophrenia in ICD-10 contains both DSM-IV schizophrenia and schizophreniform disorder, with its better prognosis. Also, DSM-IV places an emphasis on primary mood disorders (even with mood incongruent psychotic features) and therefore schizoaffective disorder by DSM-IV criteria is a narrower, less heterogeneous condition than that described by ICD-10.

The refinement of the diagnostic criteria for schizophrenia does not in any way diminish the magnitude of other psychotic disorders. Any reduction in patient populations defined as having schizophrenia is countered by an equivalent increase in populations with other psychotic disorders (e.g., schizophreniform, substance related, due to a general medical condition, etc.). These populations may require similar treatment considerations, many of which will overlap with programs and protocols developed for patients with schizophrenia. Cost shifting considerations will subsequently play a part in planning.

Although the economic impact of change is hard to predict, the evolution of our understanding of schizophrenia will continue to affect the way we plan and pay for the treatment of patients with this illness. Further refinement of subtypes may help us make more specific economic predictions. Future advances in our understanding of pathology and etiology will lead to more specific treatments and improve our ability to predict course of illness. These advances will enhance the quality of economic projections.

REFERENCES

American Psychiatric Association (1994). *DSM-IV: Diagnostic and Statistical Manual of Mental Disorders*, 4th edn. Washington, DC: APA in press.

American Psychiatric Association (1987). *DSM-III-R: Diagnostic and Statistical Manual of Mental Disorders*, 3rd edn., revised. Washington, DC: APA.

American Psychiatric Association (1980). *DSM-III: Diagnostic and Statistical Manual of Mental Disorders*, 3rd edn. Washington DC: APA.

American Psychiatric Association (1968). *DSM-II: Diagnostic and Statistical Manual of Mental Disorders*, 2nd edn. Washington DC: APA.

American Psychiatric Association (1952). *DSM: Diagnostic and Statistical Manual of Mental Disorders.* Washington, DC: APA.

Andreasen, NC (1985). *The Comprehensive Assessment of Symptoms and History* (*CASH*). Iowa City, IA: The University of Iowa.

Andreasen, N.C., and Flaum, M. (1991). Schizophrenia: the characteristic symptoms. *Schizophrenia Bulletin*, **17**, 27–49.

Barnes, T.R.E., and Liddle, P. (1990). Evidence for the validity of negative symptoms. In N.C. Andreasen, ed., *Modern Problems of Pharmacopsychiatry: Positive and Negative Symptoms and Syndromes*, Vol. 24, pp. 43–72. Basel, Switzerland: S. Karger.

Beck, A.T., Ward, C.H., and Mendelson, M. (1962). Reliability of psychiatric diagnosis: II. A study of consistency of clinical judgements and ratings. *American Journal of Psychiatry*, **119**, 351–357.

Bland, R.C., and Orn, H. (1979). Schizophrenia: Diagnostic criteria and outcome, *British Journal of Psychiatry*, **134**, 34–38.

Bleuler, E. (1911). *Dementia Praecox and the Group of Schizophrenias.* Translated by J. Zinkin (1950). New York, NY: International Universities Press.

Carpenter, W.T., and Strauss, J.S. (1974). Cross-cultural evaluation of Schneider's first rank symptoms of schizophrenia: A report from the International Pilot Study of Schizophrenia. *American Journal of Psychiatry*, **131**, 682–687.

Cooper, J.E., Kendell, R.E., Gurland, B.J., *et al.* (1972). *Psychiatric Diagnosis in New York and London.* Institute of Psychiatry, Maudsley Monograph Series No. 20. London: Oxford University Press.

Crow, T.J. (1980). Molecular pathology of schizophrenia: More than one disease process? *British Medical Journal*, **280**, 66–68.

Feighner, J.P., Robins, E., Guze, S.B., *et al.* (1972). Diagnostic criteria for use in psychiatric research. *Archives of General Psychiatry*, **26**, 57–63.

Fenton, W.S., McGlashan, T.H., and Heinssen, R.K. (1988). A comparison of DSM-III, and DSM-III-R schizophrenia. *American Journal of Psychiatry*. **145**, 1446–1449.

Flaum, M., Arndt, S., and Andreasen, N.C. (1991). The reliability of "bizarre" delusions. *Comprehensive Psychiatry*, **32**, 59–65.

Flaum, M., and Andreasen, N.C. (1991). Diagnostic criteria for schizophrenia and related disorders: Options for DSM-IV. *Schizophrenia Bulletin*, **17**, 133–142.

Goldman, D., Hiew, D.A., Haas, G.L., *et al.*, (1992). Bizarre delusions and DSM-III schizophrenia. *American Journal of Psychiatry*, **149**, 494–499.

Guze, S.B., Cloninger, R., Martin, R.L. *et al.* (1983). A follow-up family study of schizophrenia. *Archives of General Psychiatry*, **40**, 1273–1276.

Helzer, J.E., Kendell, R.E., and Brockington, I.F. (1983). Contribution of the six-month criterion to the predictive validity of the DSM-III definition of schizophrenia. *Archives of General Psychiatry*, **40**, 1277–120.

Helzer, J.E., Brockington, I.F., and Kendell, R.E. (1981). Predictive validity of DSM-II and Feighner definitions of schizophrenia. *Archives of General Psychiatry*, **38**, 791–797.

Johnstone, E.C., Owens, D.G., Frith, C.D., *et al.* (1987). Relative stability of positive and negative features in chronic schizophrenia. *British Journal of Psychiatry*, **150**, 60–64.

Keith, S.J., and Matthews, S.M. (1991). The diagnosis of schizophrenia: A review of onset and duration issues.

Schizophrenia Bulletin, **17**, 51–65.

Kendall, R.E., Copper, J.E., and Gourlay, A.C. (1971). Diagnostic criteria of American and British psychiatrists. *Archives of General Psychiatry*, 25, 123–130.

Kline, M., Sydson–Greenberg, N., Davis, W.W., *et al.* (1993). Using field trials to evaluate proposed changes in DSM diagnostic criteria. *Hospital and Community Psychiatry*, **44**, 621–623.

Koehler, K., Guth, W., and Grimm, G. (1977). First rank symptoms of schizophrenia in Schneider-oriented German centers. *Archives of General Psychiatry*, **34**, 810–813.

Kraepelin, E. (1971). *Dementia Praecox and Paraphrenia* (1919). Translated and edited by R.M. Barclay and G.M. Robertson, Edinburgh, Scotland: E. & S. Livingstone.

Kreitman, N., Sainsbury, P., and Morrissey, J. (1961). The reliability of psychiatric assessment: an analysis. *Journal of Mental Science*, **107**, 887–908.

Lloyd, D.W., and Tsuang, M.T. (1985). Duration criteria and long-term outcome in affective disorder and schizophrenia. *Journal of Affective Disorders*, **9**, 35–39.

Marks, R.C., and Luchins, D.J. (1990). Relationship between brain imaging findings in schizophrenia and psychopathology: A review of the literature pertaining to positive and negative symptoms. In N.C. Andreasen, ed., *Modern Problems of Pharmacopsychiatry: Positive and Negative Symptoms and Syndromes*, Vol. 24, pp. 89–123. Basel, Switzerland: S. Karger.

Moller, H.J., Hohschramm, M., Cording-Tommel, C., *et al.* (1989). The classification of functional psychosis and its implication for prognosis. *British Journal of Psychiatry*, **154**, 467–472.

Rice, D.P., and Miller, L.S. (1992). The economic burden of schizophrenia. Paper presented at the Sixth Biennial Research Conference on the Economics of Mental Health, Bethesda, MD, September 21–22, pp. 1–17.

Sandifer M.G., Horndern, A., Timbury G.C., *et al.* (1968). Psychiatric diagnosis: A comparative study in North Carolina, London, and Glasgow. *British Journal of Psychiatry*, **114**, 1–9.

Sandifer, M.G., Petus, G., and Quad, E.D. (1964). A study of psychiatric diagnosis. *Journal of Nervous and Mental Disease*, **139**, 350–356.

Schneider, K. (1974). Primary and secondary symptoms in schizophrenia. In S.R. Hirsch and M.M. Shepherd, eds, *Themes and Variations in European Psychiatry*, pp. 40–46. Bristol: John Wright.

Schneider, K. (1959). *Clinical Psychopathology*. Translated by M.W. Hamilton. New York, NY: Grune & Stratton, Inc.

Spitzer, R.L., and Fleiss, J.L. (1974). A reanalysis of the reliability of psychiatric diagnosis. *British Journal of Psychiatry*, **125**, 341–347.

Taylor, M.A., and Abrams, R. (1973). The phenomenology of mania: A new look at some old patients. *Archives of General Psychiatry*, **29**, 520–522.

Taylor, M.A., and Abrams, R. (1975). Acute mania: Clinical and genetic study of responders and non-responders to treatments. *Archives of General Psychiatry*, **32**, 863–865.

Tsuang, M.T., Woolson, R.F., and Fleming, J.A. (1979). Long-term outcome of major psychosis: I. Schizophrenia and affective disorders compared with psychiatrically symptom-free surgical conditions. *Archives of General Psychiatry*, **36**, 1295–1301.

World Health Organization. (1989). *Mental Disorders: Glossary and Guide to Their Classification in Accordance with the Tenth Revision of the International Classification of Disease*. Draft of Chapter 5: Mental, Behavioral and Developmental Disorders. Geneva: WHO.

World Health Organization. (1973). *The International Pilot Study of Schizophrenia*, Vol. 1. Geneva: WHO.

2

Assessing the Symptoms of Schizophrenia

NANCY C. ANDREASEN*† and SUSAN K. SCHULTZ*

*The Mental Health Clinical Research Center and †Department of Psychiatry, The University of Iowa Hospitals and Clinics, College of Medicine, Iowa City, Iowa, USA

The reorganization of health care delivery systems throughout the world during the past decade has created new pressures on clinicians and economists to design ways to measure the effectiveness of treatments, clinical services, and the overall outcome of illnesses such as schizophrenia. The assessment of schizophrenia presents particular challenges, as this illness has an impact on so many different aspects of the patient's life. In addition to the symptoms of the illness itself, the disorder affects the patient's ability to work, interpersonal relationships, personal satisfaction, and the welfare and happiness of family members who may be called on to assist in his or her care. While issues pertaining to quality of life and treatment are covered in other chapters in this volume, this chapter focuses specifically on the assessment of the clinical presentation of the illness.

ASSESSING CLINICAL SEVERITY: TYPES OF INFORMATION NEEDED

The types of information that constitute an adequate clinical database are summarized in Table 1. They include diagnostic information, severity and type of symptoms, course of symptoms, a global index of psychopathology, and a global index of cognitive function. In an ideal database, these various types of information will be recorded in a way that can interface with information about psychosocial function, quality of life, hospitalization or community care, pharmacological treatment interventions, and psychosocial treatment interventions.

DIAGNOSTIC INFORMATION

The standardization of diagnostic systems throughout the world by the International Classification of Disease (ICD-10) (WHO, 1992) and the *Diagnostic and Statistical Manual* (DSM-IV) (APA, 1994) of the American Psychiatric Association has created the impression that "diagnosis is easy." Nevertheless, there is still wide variation in both the conceptualization of the boundaries of schizophrenia and in the best methods for establishing a diagnosis (Andreasen & Carpenter, 1993).

Studies of diagnostic reliability and of the comparative classification rates of different diagnostic systems have indicated that the boundaries of the concept of schizophrenia have expanded and contracted over both time and space (Flaum &

This research was supported in part by NIMH Grants MH31593, MH40856 and MHCRC 43271, The Nellie Ball Trust Fund, Iowa State Bank and Trust Company, Trustee; and a Research Scientist Award, MH00625.

Handbook of Mental Health Economics and Health Policy, Volume I, Schizophrenia. Edited by M. Moscarelli, A. Rupp and N. Sartorius.
© 1996 John Wiley & Sons Ltd.

Table 1. Types of information that constitute an adequate clinical database

Diagnostic information
Severity and type of symptoms
Course of symptoms
Global index of psychopathology
Global index of cognitive function

Table 2. Schizophrenia spectrum conditions

ICD-10	DSM-IV
Schizophrenia	Schizophrenia
Schizotypal disorder	Schizophreniform disorder
Persistent delusional disorder	Brief psychotic disorder
Acute and transient psychotic disorders	Schizoaffective disorder
Induced delusional disorder	Delusional disorder
Schizoaffective disorder	Shared psychotic disorder
Other nonorganic psychotic disorders	Psychotic disorder not otherwise specified

Andreasen, 1991). While the American definition of schizophrenia formerly was relatively broad, as was demonstrated by the International Pilot Study of Schizophrenia and the US/UK study, recent efforts to narrow the conceptualization have been successful (Kendell *et al.* 1971; Wing & Nixon, 1975). The American definition of schizophrenia may now be the narrowest in the world. Only DSM-IV requires both one month of active symptoms and six months of the overall syndrome to make a diagnosis of schizophrenia. The 10th edition of the *International Classification of Disease* requires only one month of symptoms. While it is clear that DSM-III and DSM-III-R substantially narrowed the diagnosis of schizophrenia, it seems possible that DSM-IV will narrow the concept even further because of the one and six month duration criteria. Clinical use is likely to lag months to years behind these changes but the net effect is likely to be an increased narrowing in the conceptualization.

Because of this increasing narrowness of conceptualization of schizophrenia, and because related disorders such as schizoaffective disorder produce comparable or related challenges for assessment it is probably more useful to talk about "schizophrenia spectrum conditions" in discussions of schizophrenia.

A listing of schizophrenia spectrum conditions, as they appear in DSM-IV and ICD-10, appears in Table 2. Most of the guidelines concerning the assessment of schizophrenia presented in this chapter apply to this broad range of schizophrenia spectrum conditions, which have a great deal in common with one another. For example, schizophreniform disorder is defined as an illness characterized by the same symptoms that are used to define schizophrenia, but with a shorter duration criterion. Research has shown that the majority of people who present with this group of symptoms continue to have them for more than six months and are eventually classified as having schizophrenia (Helzer *et al.*, 1983; Coryell & Tsuang, 1986; Gupta *et al.*, 1994).

Boundaries exist not only with respect to duration, but also with respect to overlap with mood disorders. Schizoaffective disorder is a "boundary" or spectrum disorder as well. Clinically, both schizoaffective disorder and schizophrenia are characterized by severe psychotic symptoms, which require similar treatment (i.e., neuroleptic medication) and suggest a worse prognosis (McGlashan, 1984).

Paradoxically, although the boundaries of schizophrenia are uncertain and are probably best conceptualized broadly from the perspective of assessing costs, an additional level of complexity is introduced by the fact that this group of spectrum conditions is probably also heterogeneous. Even the narrow construct of schizophrenia is considered by most clinicians and investigators to represent a group of disorders that probably differ in pathophysiology and etiology and potentially in course and treatment (Andreasen & Carpenter, 1993). This heterogeneity was recognized by Eugen Bleuler, who gave the disorder its name and titled his book on this topic *Dementia Praecox or the Group of Schizophrenias* (Bleuler, 1911). The heterogeneity of this spectrum of disorders suggests that it will be very difficult to establish precise cost-assessment guidelines that will apply to all patients classified within this spectrum of disorders. In fact, even the very narrow construct of schizophrenia created by DSM-III or DSM-IV is clearly heterogeneous and does not lend itself to "one size fits all" guidelines about treatment management. This may result in considerable frustration among health care planners who would like to assume that a given specific diagnosis can be used to prescribe treatment or anticipate expected outcome of that treatment.

The assessment of diagnosis is typically done on purely clinical grounds in most studies of the economic aspects of schizophrenia. Although this approach is very far from "state-of-the-art," it does represent the norm. In general, most studies have relied on chart diagnoses. Chart diagnoses are less than ideal and far from reliable, even in our current modern settings in which diagnostic criteria are applied. Ideally, as more sophisticated approaches are utilized in assessing the cost of mental health care, standardized methods will be developed for making diagnoses of conditions within the schizophrenia spectrum. These should rely on symptom checklists and a standardized application of criteria. Because of the complexities in assessing the symptoms described below, the application of symptom checklists should probably be done by individuals with medical training and clinical experience in working with schizophrenic patients.

SEVERITY AND TYPE OF SYMPTOMS

The symptoms of schizophrenia and its related spectrum disorders are heterogeneous. Conventional classification systems currently divide them into two broad categories, positive and negative. At the clinical level, the positive symptoms are those that are florid, command social and medical attention, and represent a disruption or an aberration of functions that are normally present. Negative symptoms, on the other hand, are likely to pass without notice, as they represent a loss or diminution of functions (Andreasen & Olsen, 1982). Nevertheless, although they are less florid, the negative symptoms exact a serious clinical toll. These symptoms tend to prevent patients with schizophrenia from leading normal lives, returning to work, attending school, or having normal interpersonal or family relationships. The positive and negative symptoms of schizophrenia are summarized in Table 3.

Table 3. Positive and negative symptoms of schizophrenia

Symptom	Function lost
Negative symptoms: loss of normal function	
Alogia	Fluency of speech
Affective blunting	Fluency of emotional expression
Avolition–asociality	Volition and drive
Anhedonia	Hedonic capacity
Attentional impairment	Attention
Positive symptoms:	*Distortion or excess of normal function*
Hallucinations	Perception
Delusions	Inferential thinking
Positive formal thought disorder	Language
Disorganized behavior	Behavioral organization and control
Inappropriate affect	Affective regulation

Several standard instruments are available for the assessment of schizophrenia. Perhaps the most widely used are the Scale for the Assessment of Positive Symptoms (SAPS) and the Scale for the Assessment of Negative Symptoms (SANS) (Andreasen, 1983; Andreasen, 1984). Typically, these two groups of symptoms are summed up separately, to produce an index of the severity of positive and negative symptoms. The SANS and SAPS are extensive scales, which include a variety of sub-items. These individual items can be summed, but more commonly the global ratings for the four positive symptoms are added to produce a positive symptom index, while the global ratings for the four negative symptoms are used to produce a negative symptom index.

Recent work using factor analysis has indicated that the positive symptoms should probably be further subdivided into two dimensions: psychoticism and disorganization. Research indicates that these two different dimensions of positive symptoms have different outcomes, psychological correlates, and structural brain abnormalities (Andreasen *et al.*, 1995; Arndt *et al.*, 1995).

Negative symptoms, although they are less colorful and florid, are associated with a poorer prognosis. Negative symptoms can be present at the onset of the illness, and when present, suggest a poorer outcome (Kane, 1988). Many studies have shown that negative symptoms are associated with poor premorbid adjustment, structural abnormalities, poorer response to treatment, and various indicators of neurodevelopmental abnormalities (Flaum & Andreasen, 1991; Andreasen & Carpenter, 1993).

Because the pattern of symptoms may provide

information about possible outcome and appropriate treatment, studies examining economic aspects of schizophrenia should provide adequate documentation of both categories of symptoms. Historically, studies of the efficacy of treatment have focused primarily on treatment responsiveness of positive symptoms (Andreasen *et al.*, 1994). Patients have sometimes been considered "in remission" when their psychotic or disorganized symptoms have remitted, even though negative symptoms are still prominent and persistent. Yet the negative symptoms prevent patients suffering from schizophrenia spectrum conditions from performing such normal role functions as returning to school or holding a job. Consequently, these negative symptoms are perhaps even more important targets for treatment than are the positive symptoms. They are particularly appropriate for the various rehabilitative and cognitive therapies that have been developed for schizophrenia. Studies assessing the effectiveness of various treatment modalities on outcome must be considered severely deficient if they do not include assessment of negative symptoms within their outcome measures.

COURSE OF SYMPTOMS

Schizophrenia and its related spectrum conditions are typically lifelong disorders. In this sense, they differ significantly from many other psychiatric illnesses, which tend to wax and wane. Consequently, the assessment of the clinical presentation of schizophrenia must include not only a cross-sectional measurement of the severity and type of symptoms at a given moment in time, but it must also include a definition of the longitudinal course of the illness. Specifically, it must include descriptors of exacerbation, relapse, and remission.

At present, there are no standard and universally accepted definitions of any of these concepts. Perhaps the most widely accepted is the definition of remission as involving a 20% decrease in symptoms measured during the acute phase of the illness. The most widely used instrument in quantifying symptoms to assess for remission is the Brief Psychiatric Rating Scale (BPRS) (Overall & Gorham, 1962). For example, this instrument and definition were used in the classic study of the efficacy of clozapine in treatment refractory schizophrenia (Kane, 1988). As the BPRS is heavily weighted toward positive symptoms and as it also includes a number of measures that are not core symptoms of schizophrenia spectrum conditions (e.g., anxiety, depression, hostility), it is probably not the best scale to be used to define remission.

Definitions of relapse are even more problematic. The basic problem in assessing the longitudinal course of symptoms is related to the concept of "baseline functioning." If baseline functioning is considered to be normality, which is defined by having a job, absence of any symptoms and healthy interpersonal relationships, then any dysfunction below this level should be considered an exacerbation. The concept of exacerbation has been clouded, however, by the failure to include both positive and negative symptoms in its definition. Prominent negative symptoms have been treated as "normal," as they define the "residual state" (i.e., the persistence of a schizophrenia spectrum disorder without prominent positive symptoms). This perspective has changed, however, with the inclusion of negative symptoms in the definition of schizophrenia in both ICD-10 and DSM-IV, where they appear as core features of the disorder.

Although current definitions of relapse are typically tied to a 20% worsening of symptoms from a poorly defined baseline, while remission is typically defined as a 20% improvement from yet another poorly defined baseline, this inconclusive situation will probably be remedied by future studies that attempt to develop more precise clinical assessment techniques.

GLOBAL INDICES OF PSYCHOPATHOLOGY

Assessments of economic aspects of schizophrenia will often be tied to a global index, in addition to measuring specific types of symptoms, their severity, and their course. The BPRS is often used as a global additive measure of the severity of psychopathology. In addition, other simpler measures are also available. Two of the most widely used scales include the Clinical Global Impression (CGI) and the Global Assessment Scale (GAS) or Global Assessment of Functioning (GAF) (Endicott *et al.*, 1976; APA, 1994)]. These latter two scales are best considered as indices of convenience, as they can be rapidly administered and now enjoy wide familiarity. The GAF has been incorporated into the DSM.

GLOBAL INDICES OF COGNITIVE FUNCTION

Cognitive dysfunction may be the most fundamental component of the schizophrenia spectrum conditions (Weschler, 1944). A global cognitive dysfunction probably underlies the wide range of specific symptoms that are considered to be indicative of this illness, such as hallucinations, delusions, disorganization, or negative symptoms. Although cognitive dysfunction can be measured using relatively sophisticated tools, such as a variety of neuropsychological tests (e.g., Weschler Adult Intelligence Scale, Weschler Memory Scale) (Weschler, 1945; Bilder *et al.*, 1992), use of these tests usually requires experience and training, making them inappropriate for routine clinical assessment. In this regard, perhaps the most useful is the Mini Mental Status Examination (Folstein *et al.*, 1975). This test can be administered in 5 or 10 minutes and provides a rough index of cognitive impairment. The total correct score is 30, and normal individuals usually score in the 28–30 range. Patients with schizophrenia typically score at a lower level, because of problems with inattention, memory, or general cognitive disorganization.

SOURCES OF INFORMATION

If a health economist is attempting to obtain measures that will indicate whether a new type of health care delivery (e.g., single payor versus managed care) has a differential impact on outcome, various questions arise immediately: What source will be used to collect the types of information outlined above? A corollary question includes: What kinds of outcomes will be measured? Clearly, in addition to severity and type of symptoms, course of symptoms, and global indices of psychopathology and cognitive functions, other measures will include patient satisfaction, family satisfaction, a broad range of psychosocial measures (e.g., employment, school attendance, interpersonal relationships, living circumstances), types of treatment administered, their costs, and their adverse side-effects. How can all this information be gathered?

CLINICIAN REPORTS

The types of information summarized in the previous section are best collected by trained clinicians. Training and experience are especially crucial in the assessment of schizophrenia, because of the skill that is required to elicit a full history from a psychotic, suspicious, and defensive individual. If the person has had unfortunate experiences with health care systems, he or she is likely to be quite guarded. Ideally, the information should be collected by a person with extensive training in psychiatry, who also has a specialized interest in caring for schizophrenia spectrum conditions. This type of background is useful not only in establishing rapport with patients, but also to ensure basic familiarity with the definitions of the specific types of symptoms (e.g., particular types of hallucinations such as voices commenting, various forms of disorganized speech, or negative symptoms such as alogia). High-quality information can also be obtained by psychiatric nurses or clinical psychologists with special interest in psychosis. The key element is probably not the type of degree, but rather the level of knowledge and experience. A person with only a few years of training beyond medical school or nursing school is not likely to have sufficient experience to assess the symptoms of schizophrenia spectrum conditions. The method used by many health care delivery systems in order to determine a need for surgery or hospitalization (e.g., assessment of crude indicators of severity of pain or presence of weakness, usually obtained over the telephone by a nurse) is not likely to provide an appropriate model for an illness such as schizophrenia.

SELF-REPORT

Self-report indicators are widely used to assess problems with anxiety or depression (Zung, 1965). These disorders are characterized by intense personal suffering in an individual who has conscious awareness about the suffering and a high level of insight. Almost by definition, however, patients suffering from schizophrenia spectrum conditions lack insight. Studies have repeatedly indicated that people with these disorders are not likely to be aware of their symptoms or able to report them accurately (Amador *et al.*, 1993). Consequently, self-report measures are probably not appropriate assessment techniques in studies of the economics of schizophrenia. The problem with self-report instruments is further enhanced by the fact that patients are likely to be guarded or defensive in addition to lacking insight. Self-report measures will almost certainly lead to a significant level of underreporting.

FAMILY REPORT

If patients lack insight or are too guarded to serve as accurate informants, can family members be used in their place? For some measures, family report is a useful source. For example, family members may be the best informants about the severity of negative symptoms. Fathers and mothers have usually had the opportunity to observe directly their child's inability to get out of bed, have adequate grooming or hygiene, or become involved in relationships with friends or peers.

The positive symptoms of schizophrenia, however, are subjective symptoms experienced only by the patient. Some family members may become knowledgeable about positive symptoms and elicit them from the patient with specific questions; however, most family members become aware of symptoms only if the patient chooses to describe them. Consequently, these symptoms probably cannot be assessed adequately through report measures obtained from family members.

The other indicators that are relevant to the assessment of schizophrenia, such as indices of cognitive function, also do not lend themselves either to family report or patient self-report. These indicators must be evaluated by an experienced clinician.

A final problem with the use of family informants is their unavailability. While family members typically care a great deal about their child or sibling, the illnesss tends to take a severe toll on family relationships. The patient may have frank delusions about family members (e.g., husbands, wives, parents, or siblings) and avoid contact with them altogether. The patient may become violent toward certain family members and may have to live outside the home to insure their safety. In this situation, the family members are not likely to be able to have detailed and accurate information about symptoms or other clinical indicators.

Information from family members is best regarded as an important adjunct to careful assessment by an experienced clinician. Ideally, the assessment will involve all three facets mentioned in this section: evaluation by a clinician, patient self-report, and family report. This combination of sources will give the best information about severity of symptoms, level of functioning, course of illness, and response to treatment.

SUITABLE RATING INSTRUMENTS

In the 1990s standardized instruments have become state-of-the-art. Most methods for assessing the economics of schizophrenia are likely to rely on standardized assessment techniques. These include instruments such as the BPRS, GAS, Mini Mental Status, or SANS and SAPS. Most of these instruments have been widely used in research studies of outcome, familial aggregation, neurobiological substrates, and treatment efficacy. Most have documented reliability and at least some evidence of validity. During the era of the 1990s, when new instruments are likely to be developed, what characteristics should define instruments appropriate for assessing the economics of schizophrenia? A list of desirable characteristics appears in Table 4.

COMPREHENSIVE COVERAGE

As described above, the schizophrenia spectrum conditions are defined by a very wide range of symptoms. These symptoms cut across almost all dimensions of human cognition, emotion, and behavior. They include abnormalities in emotional experience and expression, fluency and organization of language, perception, inferential thinking, volition, attention, hedonic capacity, and insight. A given patient suffering from a schizophrenia spectrum disorder will have abnormalities in some of these domains, but probably not in all. Rating instruments selected to assess symptoms, either cross-sectionally or longitudinally, must be comprehensive in covering a broad range of symptoms. Although the symptoms listed as "characteristic" in DSM-IV or ICD-10

Table 4. Desirable characteristics of rating instruments

Comprehensive	Includes global indices of psychopathology and cognitive function
User friendly	Provides well-designed forms readily adaptable to computerized input
Accurate	Has interrater and test–retest reliability, internal consistency, and validity
Sensitive to change	Can exclude the null hypothesis

should surely be included, this symptom list is not all inclusive or totally sufficient. Further, a rating instrument used to assess symptoms must be supplemented with global indices of psychopathology and cognitive function, and these should be comprehensive as well.

USER FRIENDLINESS

Another desirable characteristic in a rating instrument is "user friendliness." Any instruments used to study the economics of schizophrenia will be filled out by busy clinicians who are operating under a variety of time constraints. Forms should, therefore, be well-designed and easy to use. In the era of "the information highway," they should be readily adaptable to computerized input. The mode of input is likely to vary, with the most likely source being the clinician entering information from a laptop or desktop computer. Alternative and less satisfactory forms of input would include the patient or family member completing pencil and paper instruments or computerized entry systems. Whatever the method for input, the most important feature will be the ease with which the information can be adapted to use by a variety of individuals, including epidemiologists, scientific investigators, or economists.

ACCURACY

Standard instruments such as the BPRS or GAS have been extensively evaluated for reliability and validity (Overall *et al.*, 1988). Consequently, although their accuracy may not be perfect, it is likely to be acceptable for most studies of health economics.

As other chapters will indicate, however, there is a clear need for high-quality instruments to evaluate other aspects of schizophrenia, such as psychosocial functioning, quality of life, cognition, treatment, and patient and family satisfaction. As these instruments are developed, they should be subjected to the same psychometric evaluation as has been applied to early instruments design to assess symptoms. That is, they must be evaluated for interrater and test–retest reliability, internal consistency, and validity.

SENSITIVITY TO CHANGE

The schizophrenia spectrum conditions do not necessarily change over time. Some patients remain chronically ill. Nevertheless, if the value of new forms of treatment or health care are going to be assessed, they must be assessed with instruments that can detect a change in outcome. Otherwise, the null hypothesis will be confirmed, but that confirmation will be completely devoid of meaning. Further, the individuals accepting the null hypothesis are likely to be less aware than the average statistician that confirming the null hypothesis may be totally meaningless (i.e., negative findings in a research study do not necessarily mean that there is no difference between two comparisons, only that no difference has been detected). A variety of factors, such as small sample sizes, experimental noise, or weak rating instruments may prevent investigators from disconfirming the null hypothesis). Ideally, any instruments used to assess the efficacy of treatments or changes in economic management should have established ability to be sensitive to change in some type of relevant group. For example, a rating instrument should be shown to have differentiated the efficacy of clozapine from haloperidol in treatment of refractory patients, or the utility of psychosocial rehabilitation treatments in institutionalized patients, or some other relevant clinical comparisons. This caveat is especially important in an era when health care providers are eager to administer self-report instruments to schizophrenic patients lacking in insight, and cheerfully conclude that a new managed care system is as good as the older one, as the instrument does not detect any difference between the two forms of health care management.

SUMMARY AND CONCLUSIONS

Assessment of the clinical aspects of schizophrenia spectrum conditions will be a major challenge during the coming decade. It is imperative that investigators, clinicians, and economists apply their assessments with rigor, intelligence, and fairness. If the course of schizophrenia and the quality of life of schizophrenic patients are to be accurately and fairly evaluated, the most rigorous possible approach must be used.

REFERENCES

Amador, X.F., Strauss, D.H., Yale, S.A., Flaum, M., Endicott, J., and Gorman J.M. (1993). Assessment of insight in psychosis. *American Journal of Psychiatry*, **150**, 873–979.

American Psychiatric Association (1993). *Diagnostic and Statistical Manual of Mental Disorders*, 4th edn (DSM-IV). Washington, DC: American Psychiatric Press.

Andreasen, N.C. (1983). The Scale for the Assessment of Negative Symptoms (SANS), Iowa City, Iowa, The University of Iowa.

Andreasen, N.C. (1984). The Scale for the Assessment of Positive Symptoms (SAPS), Iowa City, The University of Iowa.

Andreasen, N.C., Arndt, S., Alliger, R., Miller, D., and Flaum, M. (1995). Symptoms of schizophrenia: methods, meanings, and mechanisms. *Archives of General Psychiatry*, **52**, 341–351.

Andreasen, N.C., and Olson, S. (1982). Negative versus positive schizophrenia: Definition and validation. *Archives of General Psychiatry*, **39**, 789–794.

Andreasen, N.O., and Carpenter, W.T. (1993). Diagnosis and classification of schizophrenia. *Schizophrenia Bulletin*, **19**, 199–214.

Arndt, S., Andreasen, N.C., Flaum, M., Miller, D., and Nopoulos, P. (1995). A longitudinal study of symptom dimensions in schizophrenia: Prediction and patterns of change. *Archives of General Psychiatry*, **52**, 352–360.

APA (1994). Global Assessment of Functioning Scale. (*DSM-IV*) Washington: American Psychiatric Association.

Bilder, R.M., Lipschutz-Broch, L., Reiter, G., Geisler, S.H., Mayerhoff, D.I., and Lieberman, J.A. (1992). Intellectual deficits in first episode schizophrenia: Evidence for progressive deterioration. *Schizophrenia Bulletin*, **3**, 18–22.

Bleuler, E. (1911). Translated by J. Zinkin (1950). *Dementia Praecox of the Group of Schizophrenias*. New York: International Universities Press.

Coryell, W., and Tsuang, M.T. (1986). Outcome after 40 years in DSM-III schizophreniform disorder. *Archives of General Psychiatry*, **43**, 324–328.

Endicott, J., Spitzer, R.L., Fleiss, J.L., and Cohen, J. (1976). The Global Assessment Scale: A procedure for measuring overall severity of psychiatric disturbance. *Archives of General Psychiatry*, **33**, 766–771.

Flaum, M., and Andreasen, N.C. (1991). Diagnostic criteria for schizophrenia and related disorders: Options for DSM-IV. *Schizophrenia Bulletin*, **17**, 133–142.

Folstein, M.F., Folstein, S.E., and McHugh, P. (1975). "Mini Mental State": A practical method for grading the cognitive state of patients for the clinician. *Journal of Psychiatric Research*, **12**, 189–198.

Gupta, S., Hubbard, W.C., Arndt, S., Flaum, M.A., and Andreasen, N.C. (1994). The Iowa prospective longitudinal study of recent onset psychoses: One year follow-up of first episode subjects. *Schizophrenia Research*, **11**, 176.

Helzer, J.E., Kendell, R.E., and Brockington, I.F. (1983). Contributions of the six-month criterion to the predictive validity of the DSM-III definition of schizophrenia. *Archives of General Psychiatry*, **40**, 1277–1280.

Kane, J., Honigfeld, G., Singer, J., and Meltzer, H. (1988). Clozapine for the treatment-resistant schizophrenic. A double-blind comparison with chlorpromazine. *Archives of General Psychiatry*, **45**, 789–796.

Kendell, R.E., Cooper, J.E., and Gourlay, A.G. (1971). Diagnostic criteria of American and British psychiatrists. *Archives of General Psychiatry*, **25**, 123–130.

McGlashan, T.H. (1984). The chestnut lodge follow-up study: II. Long-term outcome of schizophrenia and the affective disorders. *Archives of General Psychiatry*, **41**, 586–601.

Overall, J., and Gorham, D. (1962). Brief Psychiatric Rating Scale. *Psychological Reports*, **10**, 799–812.

Overall, J.E., and Gorham, D.R. (1988). Introduction—the Brief Psychiatric Rating Scale (BPRS): Recent developments in ascertainment and scaling. *Psychopharmacology Bulletin*, **24**, 97–99.

Weschler, D. (1944). *The Measurement of Adult Intelligence*. Baltimore: Williams and Wilkins.

Weschler, D. (1945). A standardized memory scale for clinical use. *Journal of Psychology*, **19**, 87–95.

Wing, J., and Nixon, J. (1975). Discriminating symptoms in schizophrenia: A report from the international pilot study of schizophrenia. *Archives of General Psychiatry*, **32**, 853–859.

World Health Organization (1992). Chapter V, Mental and Behavioral Disorders (including disorders of psychological development): Diagnosis Criteria for Research. *International Classification of Diseases*, 10th edn (ICD-10). Geneva: WHO.

Zung, W.W.K. (1965). A self rating depression scale. *Archives of General Psychiatry*, **12**, 63–70.

3

Multiaxial Evaluation and Documentation of Care

JUAN E. MEZZICH
Department of Psychiatry, Mount Sinai School of Medicine of the City University of New York, New York, USA

Multiaxial evaluation represents a comprehensive approach at describing the clinical domain, which involves identifying key informational areas and assessing these systematically. Methodologically, multiaxial evaluation can be quite flexible, as both nominal or categorical and dimensional or quantitative scales can be employed. Initially, and most extensively to date, the multiaxial approach has been identified with comprehensive diagnosis, embodying a biopsychosocial perspective at portraying the patient's clinical condition. However, multiaxial approaches to other important tasks, such as the systematic description of treatment and care, are also emerging.

The articulation of key aspects of clinical problems and treatment, and their methodic, standardized appraisal under the umbrella of multiaxial evaluation, represents a major contribution not only to clinical care but also to the enhancement of their documentation. Clinical records and information systems have always been important in the exercise of patient care as well as for professional training, clinical research, and administration. Recently, the need to justify clinical services through the explicit documentation of the process of care and the measurement of their outcome is making even more compelling the development of effective information systems. The arrangements must be, furthermore, efficient, as clinical care is increasingly taking place under constraints of time and resources.

Accordingly, less and less we can afford to regard clinical information banks as oceans of amorphous data, and more and more we need to focus attention on key parameters, highly informative of the patient's condition and highly relevant to treatment decisions. These challenges explicate the pertinence of multiaxial approaches to the documentation of care.

EARLY MULTIAXIAL APPROACHES

The first multiaxial proposals were aimed at describing key components of psychiatric illness. They were offered by Essen-Möller and Wohlfahrt (1947) in Sweden, Lecomte *et al.* (1947) in France, Bilikiewicz (1951) in Poland, and Leme Lopes (1954) in Brazil. The first two proposals separated syndrome from etiology, while the second pair additionally considered personality patterns.

General medicine also received multiaxial proposals. Best known in this area is the Standard Nomenclature of Pathology (SNOP) (College of

Handbook of Mental Health Economics and Health Policy, Volume I, Schizophrenia. Edited by M. Moscarelli, A. Rupp and N. Sartorius.
© 1996 John Wiley & Sons Ltd.

American Pathologists, 1965), which included axes on topography, morphology, etiology, and symptoms. More recently, the International Classification of Diseases for Oncology (Percy *et al.*, 1990) has proposed two axes: topography (the localization of the tumor) and morphology (its histologic type, behavior, and differentiation).

The first use of the term multiaxial goes back to the schema for child psychiatry developed by Rutter *et al.* (1975) encompassing psychiatric syndromes, mental retardation, specific developmental delays, physical disorders, and abnormal psychosocial situations.

Particularly for schizophrenia, Helmchen (1975) offered a multiaxial schema involving symptomatology; disposition, precipitation and fixation as etiologic concerns; onset age and speed, duration and course; and intensity and certainty of the diagnostic judgments. For the description of the clinical condition of individuals experiencing schizophrenia (also applicable to other forms of psychopathology) Strauss (1975) designed one of the crisper multiaxial systems, composed of axes for symptoms, duration and course, substance abuse, physical illness, environmental stresses, personal relations, and work functioning.

ICD-10 AND DSM-IV MULTIAXIAL SCHEMAS

The two best known current diagnostic systems are the Tenth Revision of the *International Classification of Diseases and Related Health Problems* (ICD-10) (World Health Organization, 1992) and the *Diagnostic and Statistical Manual of Mental Disorders*, 4th edition (DSM-IV) (American Psychiatric Association, 1994). In addition to incorporating a multiaxial schema, these diagnostic systems are characterized by a phenomenological emphasis in the classification of mental disorders and the employment of explicit diagnostic criteria.

The ICD-10 multiaxial schema (Mezzich, 1994) includes three axes: (I) clinical diagnoses (mental and non-mental disorders, (II) disablements, measured in four areas—personal care, occupational functioning, functioning with family, and broader social behaviors; and (III) contextual factors. The relative simplicity of this schema may facilitate its useability not only in psychiatry but also in general medicine.

The DSM-IV multiaxial schema follows the structure of DSM-III (American Psychiatric Association, 1980). Its five axes follow: (I) mental disorders and other conditions of clinical interest; (II) personality disorders and mental retardation; (III) general medical conditions; (IV) psychosocial and environmental problems; and (V) global assessment of functioning. Its major changes from the DSM-III-R (American Psychiatric Association, 1987) involve the move from Axis II to Axis I of pervasive and specific developmental disorders, and the reformulation of Axis IV in terms of specific psychosocial problems instead of a quantification of overall stressor severity.

Table 1 displays comparatively the multiaxial schemas prepared by Helmchen (1975), Strauss (1975), and those included in ICD-10 and DSM-IV. Noticeable is the considerable overlap in terms of domains covered among the Strauss (1975), ICD-10, and DSM-IV schemas.

INTERNATIONAL CLASSIFICATION OF MENTAL HEALTH CARE

This schema developed by the European Regional Office of the World Health Organization, contains eight axes. These follow: (I) psychotherapeutic interventions; (II) biological psychiatric interventions; (III) general medical care; (IV) personal care assistance; (V) rehabilitative interventions (educational, vocational); (VI) crisis management; (VII) social support interventions; and (VIII) housing assistance.

The first three are particularly relevant as treatment interventions to ICD-10 Axis I problems, the fourth and fifth are pertinent to deal with ICD-10 Axis II disablements, and the last three are worth considering to manage ICD-10 Axis III contextual problems.

INSTRUMENTAL STRUCTURES FOR THE DOCUMENTATION OF CARE

Clinical charts, whether in paper or electronic forms, can adopt various degrees of structuration (Mezzich, 1986). At one extreme, one can consider a fully

Table 1. Comparative synopsis of recent multiaxial schemas.

Types of axes	Helmchen (1975)	Strauss (1975)	ICD-10 (1994)	DSM-IV (1994)
Psychopathology	Symptomatology	Symptoms, substance abuse	Clinical diagnoses (mental disorders)	Mental disorders Personality and developmental disorders
Physical disorders		Physical illness	Clinical diagnoses (non-mental)	General medical disorders
Environmental factors		Environmental stresses	Contextual factors	Psychosocial and environmental problems
Functioning or disabilities		Personal relations Work functioning	Disabilities	Global Assessment of Functioning Scale
Etiology	Disposition Precipitation Fixation			
Time frame	Onset age and speed Duration Course	Duration Course		
Other	Intensity and certainty			

informal chart with notes written according to whatever strikes the clinician as interesting. This option offers full descriptive flexibility but few opportunities for systematic exchange of experience among clinicians across the world or across town. At the other end, fully structured charts can be seen as voluminous arrays of checklists, which facilitate comparability of judgments but are limited in informational depth and richness.

A more desirable option involves an intermediate position, which contains both structured components (e.g. areas to be covered, symptoms to be rated) and narrative components. The latter can be employed for the longitudinal description of the patient's illnesses and for complementing the structured coverage of historical markers and symptom severity ratings.

SUMMARY AND CONCLUSIONS

A review has been offered of the concept and role of multiaxial evaluation for diagnostic formulation and the description of clinical service profiles. The identification of key informational domains and their systematic assessment have the potential to enhance the documentation of clinical care. Various structuration options are considered for clinical charts and information systems, with an advantage recognized for semi-structured (partially standardized, partially narrative) arrangements.

REFERENCES

American Psychiatric Association (1980). *Diagnostic and Statistical Manual of Mental Disorders*, 3rd edn (DSM-III). Washington, DC: APA.

American Psychiatric Association. (1987). *Diagnostic and Statistical Manual of Mental Disorders*, 3rd edn, revised (DSM-III-R). Washington, DC: APA.

American Psychiatric Association (1994). *Diagnostic and Statistical Manual of Mental Disorders*, 4th edn (DSM-IV). Washington, DC: APA.

Bilikiewicz, T. (1951). Próba ukladu nozograficznego etioepigenetycznego w psychiatrii. *Neurologia i Neurochirurgia Polska*, **1**, 68–78.

College of American Pathologists (1965). *Standard Nomenclature of Pathology* (*SNOP*). Chicago: College of American Pathologists.

Essen-Möller, E., and Wohlfahrt, S. (1947). Suggestions for the amendment of the official Swedish classification of mental disorders. *Acta Psychiatrica Scandinavica Supplement*, **47**, 551–555.

Helmchen, H. (1975). Schizophrenia: diagnostic concepts in the ICD-8. *British Journal of Psychiatry*, (Special Publication 10), 10–18.

Lecomte, M., Damey, A., Delage, E., and Marty, P. (1947). Essai d'une statistique synoptique de médicine psychiatrique. *Techniques Hospitaliers,* **18**, 5–8.

Leme, Lopes J. (1954). *As Dimensões do Diagnóstico Psiquiátrico.* Rio de Janeiro: Agir.

Mezzich, J.E. (1986). *Clinical Care and Information Systems in Psychiatry.* Washington, DC: American Psychiatric Press.

Mezzich, J.E. (1994). Multiaxial diagnosis: Challenges and proposals. In J.E. Mezzich, Y. Honda, M.C. Kastrup, eds, *Psychiatric Diagnosis: A World Perspective.* New York: Springer-Verlag, pp. 167–174.

Percy, C., van Holten, V., and Muir, C. (1990). *International Classification of Diseases for Oncology.* Geneva: World Health Organization.

Rutter, M., Shaffer, D., and Shepherd, M. (1975). *A Multiaxial Classification of Child Psychiatric Disorders.* Geneva: World Health Organization.

Strauss, J.S. (1975). A comprehensive approach to psychiatric diagnosis. *American Journal of Psychiatry,* **132**, 1193–1197.

World Health Organization. (1992). *Tenth revision of the International Classification of Diseases and Related Health Problems (ICD-10).* Geneva: WHO.

4

Social Dysfunctioning in Rehabilitation: Classification and Assessment

A. DE JONG, P.M. VAN DER LUBBE and D. WIERSMA
Department of Social Psychiatry, University of Groningen, Groningen, The Netherlands

INTRODUCTION

Economic costs associated with mental illness in general and schizophrenia in particular have been discussed for different levels of social organization. It has been argued by Gunderson and Mosher (1975), for example, that for a society at large the total costs of the loss of production resulting from mental illness far exceeds the total costs of treatment. According to McGuire (1991a,b) more than half of the total costs of mental illness in the USA (including costs of treatment but also costs of social welfare organizations, crimes, accidents, and so on) is due to this loss of production. On a different level, Frank (1987) looked into the extra costs for families of psychiatric patients. She concluded that on average $3539 is spent annually. In addition, many hours are spent to support and care for the sick relative, potentially raising the calculated average even further.

No matter for which level these parameters are investigated, their use is questionable. Although it may be quite possible to calculate the costs of production in this way, the interpretation of the resulting amounts is far from clear. To give an example, even if the mental health care system was to succeed in "curing" great numbers of patients, it is far from certain that these patients would then be able to take up full-time jobs as is implicitly taken for granted in this approach of calculating the costs of mental illness.

A much more straightforward and promising approach has been advocated by Beecham and Knapp (1994). These authors propose to study the costs of mental health care by evaluating the effectiveness of the mental health system, using their model for Production of Welfare. The costs of providing mental health care will be the input for this model. The benefits for the individual patients are the outcome of this production process, and can be either positive or negative. With respect to these benefits the question whether and to what extent a patient will be able to live a reasonably normal life in society is perhaps the most important one to be answered (see also Jenkins, 1990). To be able to do so assessments of social dysfunctioning are necessary.

With the possible exception of the personality disorders schizophrenia is the mental illness that is most strongly associated with social dysfunctioning, perhaps even stronger than with its characteristic symptomatology. However, contrary to what is the case in the first mentioned diagnostic group, that can be characterized by inflexible and maladaptive

Handbook of Mental Health Economics and Health Policy, Volume I, Schizophrenia. Edited by M. Moscarelli, A. Rupp and N. Sartorius.
© 1996 John Wiley & Sons Ltd.

behaviors only, social dysfunctions in schizophrenia are very much a part of the disease process.

As to the precise causes of social dysfunctioning of schizophrenic patients much remains to be resolved. According to Bellack *et al.* (1990) two major hypotheses currently exist. The first and most prominent one holds that social dysfunctions result from negative symptoms of the disorder such as emotional apathy, underactivity, slowness of thought and movement, lack of drive, and so on. The second hypothesis arises from the behavioral model of social skills. According to this model schizophrenic patients either lost the ability to use or failed to learn the appropriate social skills, that lie at the basis of effective social performance. Both hypotheses refer (more or less implicitly) to impairments on more basic levels. From the existence of negative symptoms a psychobiological vulnerability can be inferred, making it difficult for the individual to cope successfully with the demands of normal, everyday life (Mueser *et al.*, 1990). The lack of social skills is often thought to be associated with deficits in cognitive–psychological functioning (Morrison & Bellack, 1987).

Unfortunately, until now evidence on which to decide the validity of these hypotheses is lacking. The causal relationships between negative symptoms and social dysfunctions is less clear-cut than initially expected (Bellack *et al.*, 1990; Appelo *et al.*, 1992). And while it has been demonstrated that training of social skills can lead to some improvement in social competence (Liberman *et al.*, 1987; Corrigan *et al.*, 1990), the present models are insufficiently sophisticated to explain the mechanisms underlying this process.

This lack of theoretical clarity may partly explain why for a long time social dysfunctioning was considered to be only an epiphenomenon of psychiatric disorders. Because its manifestation is highly correlated with that of symptoms more characteristic to the disorder it was felt that studying it separately would be of little practical value. This argument has been used by researchers as well as by clinicians.

There is, however, an increasing amount of empirical evidence that the courses of symptomatology and social dysfunctioning may vary relatively independently. This has been found in studies among patients with minor psychiatric disorders (Hurry and Sturt, 1981; Dohrenwend *et al.*, 1983; Casey, Tyrer and Platt, 1985; Wohlfarth *et al.*, 1993), and in patients with schizophrenia (Serban and Gidynski, 1979; Pai and Kapur, 1982; De Jong *et al.*, 1986). From these studies it can be concluded that psychopathology and social dysfunctioning should be considered as independent domains. Separate measurement and classification is therefore not only justified, but should be recommended (Katschnig, 1983; Bellack *et al.*, 1990; De Jong, 1991; Shepherd, 1991; Wohlfarth *et al.*, 1993). This not only applies to research on evaluation and outcome, but also to the planning of treatment. Since the independency between the two domains seems to increase with the severity of the disorder, it will particularly be relevant to the field of rehabilitation, where the distinction between symptoms and dysfunctions 'constitutes a fundamental part of the rehabilitation philosophy' (Shepherd 1991; see also Anthony *et al.*, 1986).

CLASSIFICATION; EXISTING SYSTEMS AND SOME CONCEPTUAL CONSIDERATIONS

The notion that in the treatment and the evaluation of outcome of psychiatric disorders other aspects than the psychiatric syndrome should be considered has given rise to several attempts to develop multi-axial diagnostic classification systems (Mezzich, 1988). Essen-Möller and Wohlfarth (1947) were the first authors to publish such a system, comprising two axes. This initial proposal was followed by several others (Essen-Möller, 1961, 1971; Rutter *et al.*, 1969, 1975; Ottoson & Perris, 1973; Strauss, 1975; Helmchen, 1980; De Jong & Van den Brink, 1986). The number of axes in these proposals ranged from two to five. In each system, of course, there is an axis meant to be used to classify the psychiatric syndrome. Other often mentioned aspects of illness are the personality condition and a etiopathological formulation. Somewhat surprisingly, however, only two of the proposals mentioned above contain an axis for the classification of social adaptation (Strauss, 1975; De Jong & Van den Brink, 1986). This underlines the earlier remark, that until recently social dysfunctioning was considered to be an epiphenomenon of psychiatric illnesses, admittedly often with strong negative consequences for the individual patient, but of too little theoretical and practical value to deserve separate attention. In the last couple of decades, however, this situation started to change.

With the exception of the system used in child psychiatry (Rutter *et al.*, 1969, 1975) the third edition of the *Diagnostic and Statistical Manual of Mental Disorders* (DSM-III; American Psychiatric Association, 1980) was the first widely used multi-axial diagnostic classification in the field of mental health care. To "ensure that certain information that may be of value in planning treatment and predicting outcome for each individual is recorded" DSM-III comprises five axes, the first three of which constitute an official diagnostic evaluation. The two remaining axes pertain to the severity of psychosocial stressors (Axis IV) and the level of adaptive functioning (Axis V). Both were added to the system to be used in special clinical and research settings.

Axis V of DSM-III can be used to record the highest level of adaptive functioning (for at least a few months) in the past year. This information was considered to be of prognostic relevance, because usually an individual returns to his or her previous level of functioning after an episode of illness. While making assessments users of Axis V had to consider functioning in three major areas: social relations, occupational functioning, and use of leisure time. The overall level of adaptive functioning should next be recorded, using a single rating scale, ranging from 1 (superior) to 7 (grossly impaired).

After its introduction the axis has met with considerable criticism. Fernando *et al.* (1986) and Rey *et al.* (1987) both found levels of inter-rater reliability that were lower than the levels found in the official field trials of DSM-III. These disappointing results will no doubt be connected with the following theoretical objections. Kendell (1983), Roth (1983), Fernando *et al.* (1986) and Rey *et al.* (1987) mention the lack of unambiguous criteria for assessment and the deficient operationalization of the axis. This last point is particularly related to the use of a unidimensional rating scale. It is very well conceivable that an individual is for example functioning satisfactorily in two of the major areas to be considered, but is dysfunctioning in the remaining third area. While this information may be of great importance in planning interventions, it is impossible to let this situation be reflected in a single score on the rating scale. For this reason several authors have argued in favor of splitting up the single axis into two or more separate ones (Feder, 1983; Williams, 1985; Fernando *et al.*, 1986; Mellsop *et al.*, 1987; Skodol *et al.*, 1988b). Further objections were raised against the requirement to record the highest level of functioning in the past year. Even if it would be possible to record retrospectively this level in a reliable way it is far from certain that this would be a premorbid level as the accompanying notes in the manual suggest (Kendall, 1983; Skodol *et al.*, 1988a).

This criticism was only partly met in the revised third edition of the classification (DSM-III-R; American Psychiatric Association, 1987). The original rating scale was replaced by a new scale, labelled "Global Assessment of Functioning Scale" (GAFS). It is based on the Global Assessment Scale (Endicott *et al.*, 1976) and the Children's Global Assessment Scale (Shaffer *et al.*, 1983). The GAFS ranges from 1 to 90. In addition to the possibility of recording the highest level of functioning in the past year it is now also suggested to record the present level. The recommendations to use two or more separate axes were not followed.

An important and very regrettable decision was to change the overall instructions for assessment. In addition to the individual's social and occupational functioning the assessor should now also consider his or her psychological functioning. Axis V in DSM-III was already highly correlated with Axis I diagnoses (Schrader *et al.*, 1986; Skodol *et al.* 1988a). It can be expected that this association will only get stronger as a consequence of this new instruction (Beiser *et al.*, 1988; Skodol *et al.*, 1988b).

Based on the above it must be concluded that Axis V in its present form is not suitable for making independent assessments of psychopathology and social functioning as advocated in this chapter. Whether this situation will change with the forthcoming publication of DSM-IV remains to be seen. According to a short report on the progress of the development of the fourth edition (Williams *et al.*, 1990) modifications have been proposed to deal with this particular point. But even after all criticism has been met the question can still be raised whether the overall approach inherent to Axis V is sufficiently refined to make it suitable for clinical purposes (Mellsop *et al.*, 1987). More specifically, it can be argued that there is too little detail in the information recorded with the help of Axis V to make its use relevant to mental health care. This will particularly apply to the field of rehabilitation, where comprehensive knowledge of someone's problems in social functioning is fundamental to treatment (Anthony *et al.*, 1986).

Perhaps the main problem with Axis V (and with the social axis in the upcoming ICD-10 multi-axial scheme, for that matter) is that it is part of a tool, that is first of all meant to be used as a classification of diseases. Understandably (from a historical as well as from a theoretical point of view), the main concern in such a classification is with medical phenomena and not with social ones. And perhaps this is as it should be. For as Lewis already argued in 1955 "the concept of disease (...) has physiological and psychological components, but no essential social ones" (Lewis, 1955). Or, to further pursue this line of thought, social dysfunctioning should not be considered as part of the illness, but as part of the *consequences* thereof.

It is this idea, that lies at the root of the development of the International Classification of Impairments, Disabilities and Handicaps (ICIDH). The ICIDH (the trial version of which was published by the World Health Organization in 1980; see also Badley, 1993) is primarily meant to be used in the process of health care evaluations. The central question to be answered in such evaluations is to what extent the outcome goals have been reached by the end of treatment. This holds true for any evaluation study, irrespective of whether the treatment was provided by an individual clinician, by a health care service, or by a number of collaborating services within a geographical area.

The ICIDH is a classification of the consequences of disease, each of which is a potential target of treatment and therefore an outcome goal. The following three types of consequences are distinguished:

1 *Impairments.* Described as concerned with abnormalities of body structure and appearance and with organ or system function, resulting from any cause; in principle, impairments represent disturbances at the organ level.

2 *Disabilities.* The consequences of impairments in terms of functional performance and activity by the individual; disabilities thus represent disturbances at the level of the person.

3 *Handicaps.* Concerned with the disadvantages experienced by the individual as a result of impairments and disabilities; handicaps thus reflect interaction with and adaptation to the individual's surroundings.

As already evident from these descriptions the ICIDH is based on a (very simple) model, in which it is assumed that impairments may cause the manifestation of disabilities, which in their turn (in a social context) may give rise to handicaps. In this sequence impairments may sometimes lead directly to handicaps without the intermediate step of disabilities. The ICIDH contains three chapters, each devoted to one of the three types of consequences, making it in effect a collection of three distinct and independent classifications.

The ICIDH is a tool meant for general use in all fields of health care. From the text and the way the classification is set up it is evident that its roots are in somatic medicine, making its application to the field of mental health care somewhat problematic. Wiersma (1986; see also De Jong, 1991) mentioned a number of conceptual difficulties which are particularly related to the subject of this chapter. The authors of the trial version of ICIDH seem to have had some trouble in deciding whether social dysfunctions are to be considered as handicaps or as disabilities. Social integration, for example, is part of the handicap section, while functioning in the family and occupational role both fall under the heading of disabilities. This conceptual confusion, the inadequate operationalization of all three key concepts (at least as far as the field of mental health care is concerned) and the all too simple causal pathway from impairment to handicap that serves as the underlying theoretical model led Wiersma (1986) to the conclusion that several aspects of the ICIDH should be reconsidered. An improved conceptualization and operationalization of social dysfunction resulting from psychiatric disorders should definitely be part of the process of improvement. The history of measuring deviant social behavior should of course be taken into account in the course of this process.

MEASURING DEVIANT SOCIAL BEHAVIOUR. THE SOCIAL ROLE CONCEPT

From the early fifties onwards there has been an ever increasing tendency to treat psychiatric patients away from the hospitals in the community. With it came the need to evaluate the effectiveness of this new approach to mental health care (Willer & Biggin, 1976; Katschnig, 1983). Questionnaires were developed to measure what went under different names but was mostly labelled as social adjustment (see for early examples Barrabee *et al.*, 1955; Katz & Lyerly, 1963; Roen *et al.*, 1966). Initially, these assessments were almost exclusively made as part of research projects. With the passing of time, however, information about a patient's level of social dysfunctioning was increasingly collected as part of anamnestic procedures (John & Weissman 1987). This particularly applied to the treatment of the chronically mentally ill, in the rehabilitation of whom the rate of success of their tenure in the community is an important outcome criterium (Wallace, 1986). Since the first questionnaire of Barrabee *et al.* an overwhelming number of instruments have been developed. Even after applying strict criteria of quality Weissman (1975) was still left with 15 instruments to discuss in her review. Only 6 years later another 12 could be added (Weissman *et al.*, 1981). All of these instruments have in common that they are based on social role theories, in all of which it is assumed that someone's position in society can be described on the basis of a limited number of social roles.

There is a widespread confusion and ambiguity as to the question what exactly constitutes a social role (Platt, 1981). A discussion of this topic, however, is beyond the scope of this chapter. The following description composed of common elements found in most of the definitions should suffice. A social role is a complex of expectations which people have as to the behavior of a person who takes up a certain position in society.

Perhaps the most important element in this description is that, referring to "expectations which people have." This means that assessments of someone's behavior in social roles will have to be carried out against the background of how other people expect the individual to behave. By implication it also means that these assessments eventually are about the individual's capacity for interpersonal functioning. This remark may seem to be self-evident and therefore superfluous. As with the concept of social role, however, there is confusion about what is meant by the term "social functioning." Sturt and Wykes (1987) and Wing (1989) are of the opinion that activities like preparing meals, keeping house, using amenities, managing money, etc. fall under this heading. This, however, is not correct. There is no question that the ability to perform these activities is vital to a person's capacity to live independently in the community. As such the assessment of this ability is very relevant, especially in cases of chronic mental illness. But since as a rule these activities do not necessarily presuppose the presence of others (see Cooper, 1993) they are not about social functioning. Instead, labels like "activities of daily living" or (even better) "everyday skills" should be used.

The argument of relevance to treatment is even stronger when applicable to the ability to function adequately in interpersonal situations. Cognitive skills like the ability to accurately predict the expectations and reactions of other people and the consequences of one's own actions are involved, next to the ability to cope with the emotional side of social interactions (Shepherd, 1983). Together, these skills (preferably labelled as "social behavior") form the basis for every kind of social role functioning. Their assessment and the problems that go with it merits a full discussion. This, however, would go beyond the scope of this chapter. The remainder of this text will therefore be devoted to the assessment and classification of social role dysfunctioning.

As already mentioned, many of the instruments developed to assess social functioning of psychiatric patients are based on social role theories. Over the years it was increasingly realized that there are three conceptual problems in these theories that were not always taken into account.

1 First, it is difficult to decide how many and which roles should be assessed to be able to make valid judgements about an individual's level of functioning. The number and content of roles in existing schedules vary. There seem to be agreement about four roles: the occupational role, the marital role, the parental role, and the overall social role in the community are represented in nearly every schedule. There is less agreement about a person's functioning in the nuclear and extended families, in sexual relationships other than marital ones, and in spare-time activities. Dependent upon the schedule that has been chosen functioning in these areas will or will not be part of the assessments. This situation exists because none of the present social role theories has been sufficiently elaborated to provide a conclusive answer (Cooper, 1980; Platt, 1981; Avison & Speechley, 1987). As long as theoretical sophistication is lacking, decisions about the number and content of roles must partly be based on pragmatic considerations.

2 Secondly, the traditional Western family has served as a starting-point in the development of many of the existing schedules. It goes without saying that this is a potential source of problems, especially in research in a transcultural context.

3 Thirdly and most importantly, there is the problem of norms and values against the background of which assessments will have to be made. There is no such thing as a generally accepted standard. Norms and values will vary with the subcultural setting, while the answer to the question whether particular behaviors are acceptable will to a certain extent be the result of negotiations between all those involved (Platt, 1981).

In some conceptualizations and schedules a solution to the third and major problem was sought by comparing observed behavior to an *ideal* norm (not actual behavior, nor what is expected, but what should be done). The danger of an idealogical bias is, however, inherent in this solution. In other schedules the *statistical* or *population* norm is used. But this too is not a good choice, because it does not do justice to the differences between social environments.

In a number of fairly recently published instruments a much better solution has been found (Clare & Cairns, 1978; Remington & Tyrer, 1979; Platt *et al.*, 1980; Hill *et al.*, 1989; Wiersma *et al.*, 1990; Kraaijkamp, 1992). Assessments in the context of these instruments are based on the norms and values that are in force in the specific situation in which the individual to be assessed is living. In other words, assessments are based on behavior as this is expected by relevant others (reference groups; Platt, 1981; Wiersma *et al.*, 1990), given the local conditions and the subcultural setting, and while taking the sociodemographic background of the individual into account. According to Platt (1981) this approach comes closest to what Barrabee *et al.* called the most important characteristic in the definition of a social role; the actual expectations of the public, relevant to the performance of a particular role.

MEASURING DEVIANT SOCIAL BEHAVIOR. SCHEDULES AND QUESTIONNAIRES

As mentioned earlier an overwhelming number of schedules and questionnaires is available for measuring social functioning of psychiatric patients. General reviews have been published by Weissman (1975); Weissman *et al.* (1981) and Katschnig (1983). Other reviews are particularly aimed at the assessment of ward behavior (Hall, 1980), assessments in conjunction with classification on Axis V of DSM-III (Goldman *et al.*, 1992), assessment of social functioning as a result of personality disorders (Tyrer, 1990), assessment of social functioning in the context of rehabilitation programs (Affleck & McGuire, 1984; Wallace, 1986), and assessment of social functioning of patients suffering from schizophrenia (Wallace, 1984; Rosen *et al.*, 1989).

To review all these instruments is an almost impossible task. Not only because of the abundance of instruments available, but also because the criteria by which the instruments would have to be judged are dependent upon the goals of assessment. A short discussion of a number of topics in measurement that may play a part in the choice of instrument should therefore suffice.

SOURCES OF INFORMATION

There are three main sources of information on which assessments of social functioning can be based: the patient him- or herself, an informant or an expert. Each has its disadvantages. Often, a choice for the patient as the main source is not recommendable. The symptoms from which he is suffering may negatively influence his capability to realistically judge his own behavior (Remington & Tyrer, 1979; Platt, 1981; John & Weissman, 1987). Although an informant's judgement may also be influenced by the patient's symptomatology, it will be less so. Their information may be less valid because of their great emotional involvement (Katschnig, 1983). In general, however, because he or she will be better capable of standing aloof an informant will be preferable to the patient as a source of information (Platt, 1981). As far as experts are concerned, mental health professionals involved in the treatment of the individual to be assessed seem to be an obvious choice. Katz and Lyerly (1963), however, mention three reasons why the choice for their consultation may not be a wise one; the differences in their level of education and experience is too great, they have too little opportunity to observe the individual, and there will be too great a variance in their conceptualizations of deviant social behavior. Each of these reasons may have adverse consequences for the validity of their judgements.

Obviously, the use of none of the three sources mentioned can in themselves fully guarantee a valid assessment. The best strategy, therefore, is to use assessors, who are instructed to base their judgement on information from all sources available to them. To enhance the reliability and validity of their judgements the assessors should be well introduced in the theoretical aspects of social assessment and to be trained in administering the instrument chosen (Hill *et al.*, 1989; Wiersma *et al.*, 1990). If this instrument is an interview schedule there are the additional possibilities of making observations on the spot and inquiring after ambiguities (Remington & Tyrer, 1979).

INTERVIEW SCHEDULES VERSUS SELF-REPORT QUESTIONNAIRES

What was written in the previous paragraph about the best strategy for collecting information pertains to interview schedules in particular. Although their use has considerable advantages, there are also a number of disadvantages. As a rule using interview schedules is very time-consuming. Doing an interview may take between 1 and 2 hours and sometimes even more, dependent upon the extent of the problems that are encountered and the ability of the interviewee to disclose the information wanted. In addition, interviewers will often have to be trained in using the instrument. Typically, manuals of interview schedules will contain statements, holding that between 10 and 20 trial interviews are necessary before the interviewer is considered experienced enough to apply the instrument in a clinical or research setting.

In contrast with interview schedules self-report questionnaires can be administered quickly and (if necessary) in groups of patients, while training in their use is not required. But there are also several disadvantages. John and Weissman (1987) mentioned the following: (i) because self-report questionnaires will have to be read and filled out they cannot be used with illiterate respondents; (ii) problems may be underreported as a result of symptomatology; (iii) very disturbed patients may be unable to complete or understand the intent of the task; and (iv) some respondents may falsify their responses.

Other objections are that in self-report questionnaires here is no possibility to correct for the specific characteristics of the respondent's circumstances. In addition, there is a much greater chance on missing data. And last but certainly not least, by definition only those problems that are known to the respondent can be reported. Problems that are unknown to him for whatever reason, but can be observed by others and may have considerable consequences, will be missed.

Whether an interview schedule or a self-report questionnaire should be preferred to assess social dysfunctioning is difficult to say. The choice will largely depend on the purpose for which the instrument will be used. Questionnaires can be used easily and quickly. When there is a need for detailed or more objective information, however, an interview schedule should be applied. There is also the possibility to use both methods in combination. Questionnaires can be used as screening instruments (Weissman & Bothwell, 1976; Corney *et al.*, 1982; De Jong & Van der Lubbe, 1994; Van der Lubbe, 1994). On the basis of the information collected in this way it may be decided to interview those respondents, whose circumstances require a more complete description.

CAUSES OF DEVIANT BEHAVIOR NOT UNDER THE CONTROL OF THE INDIVIDUAL TO BE ASSESSED

Sometimes an individual cannot be held (fully) responsible for the fact, that he/she is not conforming to the expectations others may have with respect to his/her behavior. His "deviant behavior" may have been caused by factors that are not under his/her control. A lack of jobs in the case of unemployment may serve as an example. Severe arguments in the family that were obviously caused by the quarrelsome behavior of other family members is another one. To do justice to the individual to be assessed the instrument used to make assessments should allow for corrections in these situations. This possibility exists in a number of interview schedules (Hill *et al.*, 1989; Wiersma *et al.*, 1990). It is practically impossible to have this opportunity in self-report questionnaires without running the risk of developing a very unwieldy and complicated instrument.

INDEPENDENT ASSESSMENTS OF SYMPTOMS AND SOCIAL DYSFUNCTIONING

Earlier in this chapter it was argued that there are reasons to assess independently psychopathology and social dysfunctioning. This particularly applies to the field of rehabilitation and to treatment and study of patients with schizophrenia and other disabling psychiatric disorders living in the community. In some of the existing schedules and questionnaires, however, items belonging to both domains can be found. Therefore, if the topic of independent measurement will be addressed in the course of the clinical or research application, it will be necessary to choose an instrument in which this hybridization of theoretical domains is not present or is at least avoided as best as possible.

CONCLUSIONS: CLASSIFICATION AND ASSESSMENT REVISITED

A lot of work has been done since the first publications on the social consequences of psychiatric disorders appeared shortly after the Second World War. Although initially the professional world of mental health care did not seem to be very keen on accepting the idea, the pleas for separate classification and assessment of social dysfunctioning eventually has found favor as witnessed by the existence of Axis V in DSM-III.

Axis V, however, can also be used to illustrate that there is definite risk of heading up a dead-end street in pursuing its further development as the instrument for classifying social dysfunctions. Although its methodology will again be changed in the forthcoming fourth edition of DSM, it must be doubted whether the axis will ever bring the idea of separate classification of social dysfunctioning to fruition. Its very limited use up till now in research, but particularly in clinical practice is significant in this respect. The central problem seems to lie in the ambivalence in the reasons for its use. On the one hand it is stated in the manual that the axis is meant for use in special clinical and research settings, implying that it is not developed for use in everyday mental health care. On the other hand the axis is far too less elaborated to be useful in special fields like rehabilitation in general and the treatment of schizophrenic patients in particular. So far the strategy of the developers of DSM seems to be to keep the axis simple. But, as Goldman *et al.* (1992) rightfully commented, the price to pay for this intention may be its validity and reliability.

The solution may lie in a different approach. Outcome of psychiatric disorders is an important topic, that deserves a classification on its own, standing apart from the existing classifications of disease. Preferably this should be a classification of consequences of disease, as advocated in the ICIDH. As mentioned before, however, the present edition of the ICIDH suffers from quite a number of conceptual problems. Where a sound theory of social behavior is still lacking it would be wise to use the experience gained in studies similar to those mentioned in the previous paragraph to solve these problems.

A good starting-point can be found in the commendable series of papers written by Cooper (1993). In it the author addresses several topics, that in this chapter have been identified as problematic in measuring social dysfunctioning. He goes, for example, to some lengths to stress the importance of being very clear about the context of judgements and the social and cultural influences thereof on the process of making assessments. Elsewhere he discusses what he calls imposed and intrinsic reductions in social performance, referring to the distinction between causes of dysfunctioning that are or are not under the control of the individual. Must noteworthy, however, is Cooper's attempt to clarify the conceptual problems. Departing from the original key concepts in the ICIDH Cooper proposes the use of the double terms *personal* disabilities and *role* handicaps to emphasize the difference between reductions in "an activity of the whole person in relation to the immediate physical environment" and "performance of a social role, expressed as interaction with others."

These (re)definitions and the one for impairment ("a reduction in the normal performance of a function, when judged as an isolated task") may not only serve to improve the ICIDH and in that way facilitate the classification of consequences of illness. Their use in the context of a (hopefully) widely accepted instrument may also bring about better demarcations between terms like social dysfunctions, social skills, activities of daily living, negative symptoms, and others. In the long run this may in its turn lead to developments, eventually resulting in more elaborated theories on which to base the development of improved schedules and questionnaires, and (more importantly) decisions pertaining to treatment and rehabilitation.

For the time being a pragmatic approach to the assessment of social dysfunctioning will have to be used. For research purposes the characteristics of the present and intended living environments of the population under study will have to be decisive in choosing an instrument. In addition, criteria of quality like the ones used by Weissman (1975) or Rosen *et al.* (1989) can be applied.

For clinical purposes the use of schedules and questionnaires as standardized methods for assessing an individual's capacities can lead to an increase in the quality of care and should therefore be propagated. Shepherd (1990) recommended a "criterion-oriented" approach to rehabilitation; working backwards from an individual's problems in everyday life the skills needed to survive in his or her particular living environment can be identified. Because it leaves ample room for getting additional information on a more detailed level a semi-structured interview schedule based on social role theories seems to be the obvious choice for this purpose. As all of the existing schedules were first of all developed for use in a research setting, however, some adaptation to their use in clinical settings will probably be necessary.

REFERENCES

Affleck, J.W., and McGuire, R.J. (1984). The measurement of psychiatric rehabilitation status. A review of the needs and a new scale. *British Journal of Psychiatry*, **145**, 517–525.

American Psychiatric Association (1980). *Diagnostic and Statistical Manual of Mental Disorders*, 3rd edn (*DSM-III*). Washington: APA.

American Psychiatric Association (1987). *Diagnostic and Statistical Manual of Mental Disorders*, 3rd revised edn (*DSM-III-R*). Washington: APA.

Anthony, W.A., Kennard, W.A., O'Brien, W.F., and Forbess, R. (1986). Psychiatric rehabilitation: past myths and current realities. *Community Mental Health Journal*, **22**, 249–264.

Appelo, M.T., Woonings, F.M.J., van Nieuwenhuizen, C.J., Emmelkamp, P.M.G., Slooff, C.J., and Louwerens, J.W. (1992). Specific skills and social competence in schizophrenia. *Acta Psychiatrica Scandinavica*, **85**, 419–422.

Avison, W.R., and Speechley, K.N. (1987). The discharged psychiatric patient: a review of social, social–psychological, and psychiatric correlates of outcome. *American Journal of Psychiatry*, **144**, 10–18.

Badley, E.M. (1993). An introduction to the concepts and classifications of the international classification of impairments, disabilities and handicaps. *Disability and Rehabilitation*, **15**, 161–178.

Barrabee, P., Barrabee, E.L., and Finesinger, J. (1955). A normative social adjustment scale. *American Journal of Psychiatry*, **112**, 252–259.

Beecham, J., and Knapp, M. (1994). Cost-effectiveness analysis and schizophrenia. Paper presented during the conference "Una valutazione integrata dei costi e benefici del tratamento della schizofrenia," Turin, 8 July.

Beiser, M., Fleming, J.A., Iacono, W.G., and Lin, T.Y. (1988). Refining the diagnosis of schizophreniform disorder. *American Journal of Psychiatry*, **145**, 695–700.

Bellack, A.A., Morrison, R.L., Wixted, J.T., and Mueser, K.T. (1990). An analysis of social competence in schizophrenia. *British Journal of Psychiatry*, **156**, 809–818.

Casey, P.R., Tyrer, P.J., and Platt, S. (1985). The relationship between social functioning and psychiatric symptomatology in primary care. *Social Psychiatry*, **20**, 5–9.

Clare, A.W., and Cairns, V.E. (1978). Design, development and use of a standardised interview to assess social maladjustment and dysfunction in community studies. *Psychological Medicine*, **21**, 589–604.

Cooper, J.E. (1980). The description and classification of social disability by means of a taxonomic hierarchy. *Acta Psychiatrica Scandinavica*, **27**, 140–146.

Cooper, J.E. (1993). *Draft papers of IDH-93*. Unpublished manuscript, WHO, Geneva.

Corney, R.H., Clare, A.W. and Fry, J. (1982). The development of a self-report questionnaire to identify social problems. A pilot study. *Psychological Medicine*, **12**, 903–909.

Corrigan, P.W., Schade, M.L., and Liberman, R.P. (1990). Social skills training. In R.P. Liberman, ed, *Handbook of Psychiatric Rehabilitation*, pp 95–126, Macmillan: New York.

Dohrenwend, B.S., Dohrenwend, B.P., Link, B.G. and Levav, I. (1983). Social functioning of psychiatric patients in contrast with community cases in the general population. *Archives of General Psychiatry*, **40**, 1174–1182.

Endicott, J., Spitzer, R.L., Fleiss, J.L. and Cohen, J. (1976). The Global Assessment Scale: a procedure for measuring overall severity of psychiatric disturbance. *Archives of General Psychiatry*, **33**, 766–771.

Essen-Möller, E. (1961). On classification of mental disorders. *Acta Psychiatrica Scandinavica*, **37**, 119–126.

Essen-Möller, E. (1971). Suggestions for further improvement on the international classification of mental disorders. *Psychological Medicine*, **1**, 308–311.

Essen-Möller, E. and Wohlfahrt, S. (1947). Suggestions for the amendment of the official Swedish classification of mental disorders. *Acta Psychiatrica Scandinavica*, **47**, 551–555.

Feder, R. (1983). Letter to the editor. *American Journal of Psychiatry*, **140**, 1384–385.

Fernando, T., Mellsop, G., Nelson, K., Peace, K., and Wilson, J. (1986). The reliability of axis V of DSM-III. *American Journal of Psychiatry*, **143**, 752–755.

Frank, D.D. (1987) *The High Cost of Caring. Economic Contribution of Families to the Care of the Mentally Ill.* Unpublished thesis, Brandeis University.

Goldman, H.H., Skodol, A.E., and Lave, T.R. (1992). Revising axis V for DSM-IV: a review of measures of social functioning. *American Journal of Psychiatry*, **149**, 1148–1156.

Gunderson, J.G., and Mosher, L.R. (1975). The cost of schizophrenia. *American Journal of Psychiatry*, **132**, 901–906.

Hall, J.N. (1980). Ward rating scales for long stay patients. A review. *Psychological Medicine*, **10**, 277–288.

Helmchen, H. (1980). Multiaxial systems of classification. Types of axes. *Acta Psychiatrica Scandinavica*, **61**, 43–55.

Hill, J., Harrington, R., Fudge, H., Rutter, M., and Pickles, A. (1989). Adult Personality Functioning Assessment (APFA). An investigator-based standardized interview. *British Journal of Psychiatry*. **155**, 24–35.

Hurry, J., and Sturt, E. (1981). Social performance in a population sample: relation to psychiatric symptoms. In J.K. Wing, P. Bebbington, and L.N. Robins, eds, *What is a Case?* pp. 202–213. London: Grant McIntyre.

Jenkins, R. (1990). Toward a system of outcome indicators for mental health care. *British Journal of Psychiatry*, **155**, 24–35.

John, K., and Weissman, M.M. (1987). The familial and psychosocial measurement of depression. In A.J. Marsella, R.M.A. Hirschfeld, and M.M. Katz, eds, *The Measurement of Depression*, pp. 344–376. Chichester: Wiley.

Jong, A. de (1991). Afwijkend sociaal gedrag van psychiatrische patiënten. Theoretische achtergronden, instrumenten en classificatie (Deviant social behaviour in psychiatric patients. Theoretical backgrounds, instruments and classification). *Tijdschrift voor Psychiatrie*, **33**, 299–316.

Jong, A. de, and van den Brink, W. (1986). Ontwikkelingen in de psychiatrische classificatie. Voorstel voor een polythetische kernclassificatie (Developments in psychiatric classification. Proposal for a polythetic core classification). *Tijdschrift voor Psychiatrie*, **28**, 426–442.

Jong, A. de, Giel, R., Slooff, C.J., and Wiersma, D. (1986). Relationship between symptomatology and social disability. *Social Psychiatry*, **21**, 200–205.

Jong, A. de, and van der Lubbe, P.M. (1994). *Handleiding van de Groningse Vragenlijst over Sociaal Gedrag (Manual of the Groningen Questionnaire about Social Behaviour).* University of Groningen, Department of Social Psychiatry, Groningen.

Katschnig, H. (1983). Methods for measuring social adjustment. In T. Helgason, ed., *Methodology in Evaluation of Psychiatric Treatment*, pp. 205–218. Cambridge University Press.

Katz, M., and Lyerly, S.B. (1963). Methods of measuring adjustment and social behaviour in the community. I. Rationale, description, discriminative validity and scale development. *Psychological Reports*, **13**, 503–535.

Kendell, R.E. (1983). DSM-III: a major advance in psychiatric nosology. In R.L. Spitzer, J.B.W. Williams, and A.E. Skodol, eds., *International Perspectives on DSM-III*, Washington: American Psychiatric Press.

Kraaijkamp, H.J.M. (1992). *Moeilijke rollen. Psychometrisch onderzoek naar de betrouwbaarheid en validiteit van de Groningse Sociale Beperkingenschaal bij psychiatrische patiënten* (Difficult roles. A study into the reliability and validity of the Groningen Social Disabilities Schedule in psychiatric patients). Thesis, University of Groningen.

Lewis, A. (1955). Health as a social concept. *British Journal of Sociology*, **4**, 109–124.

Liberman, R.P., Jacobs, H.E., Boone, S.E. *et al.* (1987). Skills training for the community adaptation of schizophrenics. In J.S. Strauss, W. Böker, and H.D. Brenner, eds, *Psychosocial Treatment of Schizophrenia*, pp. 94–110. Toronto: Hans Huber Verlag.

Lubbe, P.M. van der (1994). *Over de ontwikkeling van de Groningse Vragenlijst over Social Gedrag: GVSG* (On the development of the Groningen Questionnaire about Social Behaviour; GQSB) Thesis, University of Groningen, in press.

McGuire, T.G. (1991a). Measuring the economic costs of schizophrenia. *Schizophrenia Bulletin*, **17**, 375–388.

McGuire, T.G. (1991b). The costs of schizophenia revisited. *Schizophrenia Bulletin*, **17**, 389–400.

Mellsop, G., Peace, K., and Fernando, T. (1987). Preadmission adaptive functioning as a measure of prognosis in psychiatric inpatients. *Australian and New Zealand Journal of Psychiatry*, **21**, 539–544.

Mezzich, J.E. (1988). On developing a psychiatric multiaxial schema for ICD-10. *British Journal of Psychiatry*, **152**, 38–43.

Morrison, R.L. and Bellack, A.S. (1987). Social functioning of schizophrenic patients: clinical and research issues. *Schizophrenia Bulletin*, **13**, 715–725.

Mueser, K.T., Liberman, R.P. and Glynn, S.M. (1990). Psychosocial interventions in schizophrenia. In A. Kales, C.N. Stefanis, and J.A. Tallbott, eds., *Recent advances in schizophrenia*, pp. 213–235. Springer Verlag, New York.

Ottoson, J.O., and Perris, C. (1973). Multidimensional classification of mental disorders. *Psychological Medicine*, **1**, 238–243.

Pai, S., and Kapur, R.L. (1982). Impact of treatment intervention on the relationship between dimensions of clinical psychopatholgy, social dysfunction and burden on the family of psychiatric patients. *Psychological Medicine*, **12**, 651–658.

Platt, S. (1981). Social adjustment as a criterion of treatment success: just what are we measuring? *Psychiatry*, **44**, 95–112.

Platt, A., Weyman, A., Hirsch, S.R., and Hewett, S. (1980). The Social Behaviour Assessment Schedule (SBAS): rationale, contents, scoring and reliability of a new interview schedule. *Social Psychiatry*, **5**, 43–55.

Remington, M., and Tyrer, P.J. (1979). The Social Functioning Schedule. A brief semi-structured interview. *Social Psychiatry*, **14**, 151–157.

Rey, J.M., Plapp, J.M., Stewart, G., Richards, I.N., and Bashir, M.R. (1987). Reliability of the psychosocial axes of DSM-III in an adolescent population. *British Journal of Psychiatry*, **150**, 228–234.

Roen, S.R., Ottenstein, D., Cooper, S., and Burnes, A.J. (1966). Community adaptation as an evaluative concept in community mental health. *Archives of General Psychiatry*, **15**, 36–44.

Rosen, A., Hadži-Pavlović, D., and Parker, G. (1989). The Life-skills Profile: a measure assessing function and disability in schizophrenia. *Schizophrenia Bulletin*, **15**, 325–337.

Roth, M. (1983). The achievements and limitations of DSM-III. In R.L. Spitzer, J.B.W. Williams, and A.E. Skodol, eds, *International Perspectives on DSM-III*. Washington: American Psychiatric Press.

Rutter, M., Lebovici, S. Eisenberg, L., Sneznevskij, A.V., Sadoun, R., Brooke, E., and Lin, T. (1969). A tri-axial classification of mental disorders in childhood. *Journal of Child Psychology and Psychiatry*, **10**, 41–61.

Rutter, M., Schaffer, D. and Shepherd, M. (1975). *A multi-axial classification of child psychiatric disorders*. Geneva: World Health Organisation.

Schrader, G., Gordon, M., and Harcourt, R. (1986). The usefulness of DSM-III axis IV and axis V assessments. *American Journal of Psychiatry*, **143**, 904–907.

Serban, G., and Gidynski, C.B. (1979). Relationship between cognitive defect, affect response and community adjustment in chronic schizophrenics. *British Journal of Psychiatry*, **134**, 602–608.

Shaffer, D., Gould, M.S., Brasic, J. *et al.* (1983). Children's Global Assessment Scale. *Archives of General Psychiatry*, **40**, 1228–1231.

Shepherd, G. (1983). Interpersonal Relationships. In F.N. Watts, and D.H. Bennett, eds, *Theory and Practice of Psychiatric Rehabilitation*, pp. 267–288. Chichester: Wiley.

Shepherd, G. (1990). A criterion-oriented approach to skills training. *Psychosocial Rehabilitation Journal*, **13**, 11–13.

Shepherd, G. (1991). Psychiatric rehabilitation in the 1990s. In F.N. Watts, and D.H. Bennett, eds, *Theory and Practice of Psychiatric Rehabilitation*, pp. xiii–xlviii. Chichester: Wiley.

Skodol, A.E., Link, B.G., Shrout, P.E., and Horwath, E. (1988a). The revision of axis V in DSM-III-R: should symptoms have been included? *American Journal of Psychiatry*, **145**, 825–829.

Skodol, A.E., Link, B.G., Shrout, P.E., and Horwath, E. (1988b). Towards construct validity for DSM-III axis V. *Psychiatry Research*, **24**, 13–23.

Strauss, J.S. (1975). A comprehensive approach to psychiatric diagnosis. *American Journal of Psychiatry*, **132**, 1193–1197.

Sturt, E., and Wykes, T. (1987). Assessment schedules for chronic psychiatric patients. *Psychological Medicine*, **17**, 485–493.

Tyrer, P.J. (1990). Personality disorder and social functioning. In D.F. Peck and C.M. Shapiro, eds, *Measuring Human Problems, A Practial Guide*, pp. 119–142. Chichester: Wiley.

Wallace, C.J. (1984). Community and interpersonal functioning in the course of schizophrenic disorders. *Schizophrenia Bulletin*, **10**, 233–257.

Wallace, C.J. (1986). Functional assessment in rehabilitation. *Schizophrenia Bulletin*, **12**, 604–630.

Weissman, M.M. (1975). The assessment of social adjustment. A review of techniques. *Archives of General Psychiatry*, **32**, 357–365.

Weissman, M.M., and Bothwell, S. (1976). The assessment of social adjustment by patient self-report. *Archives of General Psychiatry*, **33**, 1111–1115.

Weissman, M.M., Sholomskas, D., and John, K. (1981). The assessment of social adjustment. An update. *Archives of General Psychiatry*, **38**, 1250–1258.

Wiersma, D. (1986). Psychological impairments and social disabilities: on the applicability of the ICIDH to psychiatry. *International Rehabilitation Medicine*, **8**, 3–7.

Wiersma, D., de Jong, A., Kraaijkamp, H.J.M., and Ormel, J. (1990). *GSDS-II. The Groningen Social Disabilities Schedule, second version. Manual, Questionnaire and Rating Form.* University of Groningen, Department of Social Psychiatry, Groningen.

Willer, B., and Biggin, P. (1976). Comparison of rehospitalized and non-hospitalized psychiatric patients on community adjustment: Self-Assessment Guide. *Psychiatry*, **39**, 239–244.

Williams, J.B.W. (1985). The multiaxial system of DSM-III: where did it come from and where should it go? I. Its origins and critique. *Archives of General Psychiatry*, **42**, 175–180.

Williams, J.B.W., Goldman, H.H., Gruenberg, A., Mezzich, J.E., and Skodol, A.E. (1990). DSM-IV in progress. The multiaxial system. *Hospital and Community Psychiatry*, **41**, 1181–1182.

Wing, J.K. (1989). The measurement of "social disablement." The MRC social behaviour and social role performance schedules. *Social Psychiatry and Psychiatric Epidemiology*, **24**, 173–178.

Wohlfarth, T.D., van den Brink, W., Ormel, J., Koeter, M.W.J., and Oldehinkel, A.J. (1993). The relationship between social dysfunctioning and psychopathology among primary care attenders. *British Journal of Psychiatry*, **163**, 37–44.

World Health Organization (1980). *International Classification of Impairments, Disabilities and Handicaps*. Geneva: WHO.

5

Quality of Life Issues and Assessment Among Persons with Schizophrenia

ANTHONY F. LEHMAN
Department of Psychiatry, University of Maryland, Center for Mental Health Services Research, Baltimore, Maryland, USA

INTRODUCTION

Schizophrenic disorders afflict approximately 1% of the population during their lifetime. These disorders impose severe hardships on patients and their families and challenge society in the development of public policies that both preserve the public welfare and afford patients a decent quality of life. Among the various conceptual challenges inherent in evaluating services for persons with schizophrenia has been the development of appropriate outcome measures reflecting the broad range of problems faced by these patients (Schulberg & Bromet, 1981; Lehman *et al.*, 1982). Relevant outcome domains include psychiatric symptoms, functional status, access to resources and opportunities, subjective well-being, family burden, and community safety. Because of this broad array of relevant outcomes and because of a prevailing concern that outcome assessments should include the patient's perspective, there has been increased attention paid over the past decade to the development of measures of patient "quality of life" (Baker & Intagliata, 1982; Lehman, 1983a), and the new National Institute of Mental Health (NIMH) research plan on severe and persistent mental illnesses, *Caring for Persons with Severe Mental Illness*, identifies quality of life as one of the major outcome areas to be assessed in new research efforts (Attkisson *et al.*, 1992).

This chapter summarizes those measures of quality of life that have been developed specifically for persons with schizophrenia and other severe and persistent mental illnesses.

The measures reviewed emphasize the patient's "quality of life," that is, measures covering patient's perspectives on what they have, how they are doing, and how they feel about their life circumstances. At a minimum "quality of life" covers persons' *sense of well-being* (*subjective quality of life*); often it also includes how they are doing (*functional status*) and what they have (*access to resources and opportunities*). The latter two dimensions constitute what is commonly referred to as *objective quality of life*. The measures selected for this review were identified from the literature on quality of life through October 1992. In order to be selected a measure had to at least assess the domain of subjective well-being; as will be seen most of these measures also cover the broad areas of functioning and resources.

Handbook of Mental Health Economics and Health Policy, Volume I, Schizophrenia. Edited by M. Moscarelli, A. Rupp and N. Sartorius.
© 1996 John Wiley & Sons Ltd.

DESCRIPTION OF AVAILABLE MEASURES

The measures are presented in order of their chronological development. For each measure, the content and psychometric characteristics of the instrument are described. Also a listing of key references is provided and the seminal reference with regard to the instrument's development is marked with an asterisk (*).

COMMUNITY ADJUSTMENT FORM (CAF)

See (*) Stein and Test (1980) and Hoult and Reynolds (1984).

This semi-structured self-report interview was developed to assess life satisfaction and other quality of life outcomes in a randomized study of an experimental system of community-based care for the severely mentally ill versus standard care in Dane County, Wisconsin. It consists of 140 items and requires approximately 45 minutes to complete.

The areas assessed include: Leisure activities; Quality of living situation; Employment history and status; Income sources and amounts; Free lodging and/or meals; Contact with friends; Family contact; Legal problems; Life satisfaction (21 items); Self-esteem (Rosenberg Scale); Medical Care; and Agency Utilization. No psychometric properties are reported.

The original patient sample studied included 130 patients seeking admission to a state hospital. Over half were men (55%) and their mean age was 31 years. Half carried a diagnosis of schizophrenia. They were treated both in the state hospital and in a community-based Assertive Community Treatment Program. The results of the original Wisconsin study were replicated in Australia using the same measures (Hoult and Reynolds, 1984).

QUALITY OF LIFE CHECKLIST (QLC)

See (*) Malm, May and Dencker (1981).

This checklist was developed to provide information about which aspects of quality of life are particularly important to patients and clinician raters to assist in therapeutic planning. This 93-item rating scale is completed by a trained interviewer after conducting a 1-hour semi-structured interview. Scoring for all areas assessed is dichotomized as "satisfactory" or "unsatisfactory." The areas assessed include: Leisure activities, Work, Vocational rehabilitation, Economic dependency, Social relationships, Knowledge and education, Psychological dependency, Inner experience, Housing standard, Medical care (Psychiatric and General), and Religion.

No psychometric properties are reported. Data analyses report simple frequencies of "*satisfactory*" versus "*unsatisfactory*" by items.

The patients studied included 40 persons with chronic schizophrenia in a Swedish outpatient clinic. They ranged in age from 18 to 50 years and included 68% men.

SATISFACTION WITH LIFE DOMAINS SCALE (SDLS)

See (*) Baker and Intagliata (1982) and Johnson (1991).

This instrument was developed to evaluate the impact of the Community Support Program (CSP) in New York State on the quality of life of chronically mentally ill patients. It is a self-report scale administered by a trained interviewer, consists of 15 items, and requires approximately 10 minutes to complete. Its individual items cover: Satisfaction with housing, neighborhood, food to eat, clothing, health, people lived with, friends, family, relations with other people, work/day programming, spare time, fun, services and facilities in area, economic situation, and place lived in now compared with state hospital. These can be summed into a total life satisfaction score.

The total life satisfaction score correlates at $r = 0.64$ with the Bradburn Affect Balance Scale at $r = 0.29$ with the Global Assessment Scale. No other psychometric data are provided. The frequencies and means on these items can be compared with item scores in a national quality of life survey of the general population (Andrews & Withey, 1976).

The patients studied included 118 chronically mentally ill outpatients, age 18–86, in two community support programs. They had a mean age of 53.3 years, 61% were women, and 84% lived in supervised residential settings. Diagnoses included 56% schizophrenia, 14% affective disorders, 5% substance use disorders, and 3% organic mental syndromes.

OREGON QUALITY OF LIFE QUESTIONNAIRE (OQLQ) (1982, 1990)

See Bigelow *et al.* (1982), Bigelow, Gareau and Young (1990), (*) Bigelow, McFarland and Olson (1991), Bigelow *et al.* (1991).

The OQLQ was originally developed based upon the Denver Community Mental Health Scale and has undergone a series of developments since 1981. The original purpose of the OQLQ was to assess quality of life outcomes among clients served by community mental health programs, especially those developed under the NIMH CSP initiative. Originally published in 1982, the OQLQ has recently been updated by its developer with more recent psychometric data, alternative versions, and further program applications.

The OQLQ exists in two versions: a structured self-report interview (263 items) and a semi-structured interviewer-rated interview (146 items). Both are administered by a trained (not necessarily clinical) interviewer. The theory underlying the OQLQ states that QOL derives from the social contract between an individual and society. Individuals' *needs* are met to the extent that persons fulfill the *demands* placed upon them by society. Most of the items use fixed, ordinal response categories, and the interview requires approximately 45 minutes to administer.

The OQLQ yields 14 scale scores: Psychological distress, Psychological well-being, Tolerance of stress, Total basic need satisfaction, Independence, Interpersonal Interactions, Spouse role, Social support, Work at home, Employability, Work on the job, Meaningful use of time, Negative consequences of alcohol use, and Negative consequences of drug use.

The psychometric properties of the OQLQ have been evaluated extensively. Cronbach's alpha for the 14 scales on the self-report interview versions range from 0.05 to 0.98 with a median of 0.84. Eight of the scales have excellent reliability (alpha >0.8), 2 have intermediate reliability (alpha between 0.8 and 0.4) and 4 have poor reliability (<0.4). Test–retest reliabilities (interval not specified) ranged from 0.37 to 0.64 with a median of 0.50. The inter-rater reliability for the interviewer-rated version has been assessed in a small sample study ($n=6$) and produced inter-rater agreement levels between 58 and 100% on the interviewer judgments. More than half of the items showed greater than 90% agreement, and Cronbach alpha ranged from 0.32 to over 0.80 (more than half over 0.80).

The predictive validity of the OQLQ has been evaluated by comparing: (i) clients in different types of community mental health programs (CSP, drug, alcohol, and general psychiatric clinics); (ii) general community respondents from economically distressed and non-distressed communities; and (iii) changes in community mental health clients over time. Results of these analyses support the overall predictive validity of the OQLQ.

The OQLQ has been applied to outpatients of mental health programs as well as to samples of the general population. The outpatient samples included patients at intake to community mental health programs in Oregon (includes chronically mentally ill, drug abusers, alcoholics, and general psychiatric patients). Their mean age was 33.8 years (range 18–85) and included 60% men and 96% "non-Hispanics." The community sample had 43% men, a mean age of 36.8, and was 92% non-Hispanic.

LEHMAN QUALITY OF LIFE INTERVIEW (QOLI)

See Lehman, Ward and Linn (1982), Lehman (1983a), Lehman (1983b), Lehman, Possidente and Hawker (1986), Franklin *et al.* (1987), (*) Lehman (1988), Simpson, Hyde and Faragher (1989), Levitt, Hogan and Bucosky (1990), Lehman, Slaughter and Myers (1991), Slaughter and Lehman (1991), Lehman, Slaughter and Myers (1992), Sullivan, Wells and Leake (1992), Huxley and Warner (1992), Rosenfield and Neese-Todd (1993) and Rosenfield (1992).

The overall purpose of the QOLI is to assess the life circumstances of persons with severe mental illnesses both in terms of what they actually do and experience ("objective" quality of life) and their feelings about these experiences ("subjective" quality of life). The Interview provides a broad-based assessment of the recent and current life experiences of the respondent in a wide variety of life areas of potential interest, including living situation, family relations, social relations, leisure activities, finances, safety and legal problems, work and school, and health (as well as religion and neighborhood in some versions).

The QOLI is a structured self-report interview administered by trained lay interviewers. It consists of 143 items and requires approximately 45 minutes to administer. It has undergone a variety of revisions over the past 10 years, primarily to improve its psychometric properties and to shorten it. The Core Version contains a global measure of life satisfaction as well as measures of objective and subjective quality of life in eight life domains: living situation, daily activities and functioning, family relations, social relations, finances, work and school, legal and safety issues, and health. The sections *on each life domain* are organized such that information first is obtained about objective quality of life and then about level of life satisfaction in that life area. This pairing of objective and subjective quality of life indicators by domain is essential to the quality of life assessment model (Lehman, 1988).

All of the life satisfaction items in the interview utilize a fixed interval scale, which originally was developed in a national survey of the quality of American life (Andrews & Withey, 1976). The types of objective quality of life indicators utilized vary considerably across the domains. In general they can be viewed as of two types: measures of functioning (e.g., frequency of social contacts or daily activities) and measures of access to resources and opportunities (e.g., income support or housing type). The quality of life indicators include both individual items (e.g., monthly income support) and scales (e.g., frequency of social contacts).

The variables generated by the QOLI include:

1 *Objective quality of life indicators:* Length of Time at Current Residence, Residential Stability, Homelessness, Quality of Living Circumstances, Leisure Activities, Frequency of Family Contacts, Frequency of Social Contacts, Total Monthly Spending Money, Adequacy of Financial Supports, Current Employment Status, Number of Nights in Jail During the Past Year, Victim of Violent Crime During Past Year, Victim of Non-Violent Crime During the Past Year.

2 *Subjective quality of life indicators*: Satisfaction With: Living Situation, Leisure Activities, Family Relations, Social Relations, Finances, Work and School, Legal and Safety, Health (Religion and Neighborhood).

The psychometric properties of the QOLI have been extensively assessed. Internal consistency reliabilities range from 0.79 to 0.88 (median = 0.85) for the life satisfaction scales, and from 0.44 to 0.82 (median = 0.68) for the objective quality of life scales. These reliabilities have been replicated in two separate studies of persons with severe mental illnesses. Test–retest reliabilities (1 week) have also been assessed for the QOLI: life satisfaction scales: 0.41–0.95 (median = 0.72); objective quality of life scales: 0.29–0.98 (median = 0.65). Construct and predictive validity have been assessed as good by confirmatory factor analyses and multivariate predictive models. The QOLI also differentiates between patients living in hospitals and supervised community residential programs in the USA and Britain (Lehman *et al.*, 1986; Simpson *et al.*, 1989). Individual life satisfaction items clearly discriminate between persons with severe mental illness and the general population (Lehman *et al.*, 1982). Further construct validation has been assessed in studies of the predictors of quality of life among day treatment patients in Britain (Levitt *et al.*, 1990) and the relationship between quality of life and feelings of empowerment among persons with severe mental illnesses in the USA (Rosenfeld & Neese-Todd, 1993). A variety of methodologic papers have explored such other issues as the relationship between qualiy of life and clinical symptoms (Lehman, 1983b), gender and age (Lehman *et al.*, 1992), and housing type (Slaughter and Lehman, 1991; Lehman *et al.*, 1991).

The QOLI has been used almost exclusively with persons with severe mental disorders. The samples in published studies have included approximately equal numbers of men and women, about 75% Caucasian, ranging in age from 18 to 65 years. The predominant diagnosis in these studies has been schizophrenia, ranging from 57 to 76% of patients. General population norms for individual life satisfaction items are available (Andrews & Withey, 1976).

QUALITY OF LIFE SCALE (QLS)

See (*) Heinrichs, Hanlon and Carpenter (1984) and Meltzer *et al.* (1990).

The QLS was developed to assess the deficit syndrome in patients with schizophrenia. It is a semi-structured interview rated by trained clinicians.

Its 21 items are rated on fixed interval scales based upon the interviewer's judgment of the patient's functioning in each of the 21 areas. The interview requires approximately 45 minutes.

The 21 items of the QLS cover: Commonplace activities, Occupational role, Work functioning, Work level, Possession of commonplace objects, Interpersonal relations (household, friends, acquaintances, social activity, social network, social initiative, social withdrawal, sociosexual functioning), Sense of purpose, Motivation, Curiosity, Anhedonia, Aimless inactivity, Empathy, Emotional interaction, and Work satisfaction. These items reduce to four scales: Intrapsychic Foundations, Interpersonal Relations, Instrumental Role, and Total Score.

The interrater reliabilities on conjointly conducted interviews range from 0.84 to 0.97 on summary scales. Individual item intraclass correlations range from 0.5 to 0.9. Confirmatory factor analysis has been conducted.

This scale is widely used in the evaluation of psychopharmacologic treatments for schizophrenia, predominantly outpatients (e.g., see Meltzer *et al.*, 1990).

CLIENT QUALITY OF LIFE INTERVIEW (CQLI)

See Goldstrom and Manderscheid (1986) and (*) Mulkern *et al.* (1986).

The CQLI was developed as part of a battery of instruments to assess outcomes among persons with severe mental disorders who were served by the NIMH CSP. These instruments include the Uniform Client Data Instrument (UCDI), the UCDI-Short Form, the CSP Participant Follow-up Form, and the CQLI. The content of these instruments overlap to a considerable degree. All but the CQLI are completed by case managers or other professionals serving the clients and generally focus on functioning, services, and clinical outcomes. Only the CQLI asks clients directly about the quality of their lives and therefore only it is reviewed here. The conceptual model underlying the CQLI assumes that certain life essentials are necessary precursors to a quality life. One major purpose of the Community Support Program was to provide these essentials and thus to enhance quality of life.

The CQLI is a structured self-report interview administered by a trained lay interviewer. It consists of 46 items rated by the respondent as well as 19 interviewer ratings. Ratings are done on fixed, ordinal scales. The content areas covered include: Essentials of Life (food, clothing, shelter, health and hygiene, money, and safety), Job Training and Education, Daily Activities and Recreation, Privacy, Social Supports, Social Time, Self-Reliance, and Peace of Mind. In each area questions generally cover both the quantity of resources or activity as well as the respondents' subjective feelings about these resources and activities. Many of the item sets lend themselves readily to composite scales, although the development or scoring of these scales is not available for the CQLI. Some of the scales parallel the UCDI for which scale computation guidelines as well as psychometric properties are available.

No formal psychometric analyses of the CQLI are available. Correlations of CQLI items rated by the clients with comparable items from the UCDI rated by the case manager were quite low. The CQLI ratings remained stable over a 14 month follow-up period.

The subsample in the CSP study who completed the CQLI were 109 severely mentally ill clients from six exemplary CSP programs. They included 51% men; 82% Caucasian, 11% Black, 6% Hispanic, and 1% other; and had a mean age of 41.5. No diagnoses are indicated, but all were severely mentally ill.

CALIFORNIA WELL-BEING PROJECT CLIENT INTERVIEW (CWBPCI)

See (*) Campbell *et al.* (1989).

The California Well-Being Project was a 3 year initiative funded by the California Department of Mental Health to develop a better understanding of the health and well-being concerns of persons who have been treated for mental illness, the so-called "psychiatrically labeled." The most unique aspect of this initiative is that it was designed and conducted entirely by mental health care consumers. The Project consisted of three components: (i) research and analysis of well-being factors for individuals assessed through a structured survey of consumers, family members, and professionals; (ii) production of educational materials based upon his survey; and (iii) dissemination of these educational materials to consumers, family members, and mental health providers.

Three versions of the survey questionnaire on well-being were developed for consumers (151 items), family members (76 items), and mental health professionals (77 items). Time required for administration is not indicated. The questionnaires consist predominantly of Likert scale questions, but with some open-ended questions interspersed. The questionnaires are designed to be administered either in face-to-face interviews (conducted by trained consumers), self-administered by mail, or group self-administration with an interviewer available to answer questions. The instrument is thus designed for flexibility in administration to provide the multiple perspectives of consumers, family members, and professionals.

In the California survey the CWBPCI was administered to 331 persons who were "psychiatrically labeled" and living in various settings, including psychiatric hospitals (non-state), skilled nursing facilities, board-and-care homes, satellite houses, single occupancy hotels, community residential treatment centers, drop-in centers, client self-help groups, organizations serving people identified as "homeless mentally ill," and on the streets. The final sample consisted of 61 randomly selected members of the California Network of Mental Health Consumers (surveyed by mail), 249 volunteer respondents from various facilities in California (face-to-face interviews, not randomly selected), and 21 randomly selected Project Return clients. The sample was 52% men, 67.5% Caucasian, 14.7% Black, and 4.6% Hispanic. They were predominantly young with 41% below the age of 35 and 75% below age 45, and the authors describe them as predominantly chronically mentally ill, but no further clinical details are given.

No information is provided on the instrument's psychometric properties, and for the most part data from individual items are reported as frequencies (or percentages) in a narrative section that discusses the many concerns of the respondents. Topics covered in this narrative include: Adequate Resources, Age, Alternatives to Psychiatric Hospitalization, Aspirations, Benefit Agencies, Board and Care Residents, Boredom, Causes of Psychological and Emotional Problems, Children, Client/Consumer, Conservatorship, Control of Emotional Problems, Creativity, Stereotype of Dangerousness, Discrimination, Electroconvulsive Therapy, Empowerment, Ethnic/Cultural Group, Family Relationships, Freedom, Friends, Gender, General population, Hallucinations and/or Voices, Happiness, Health, Homelessness, Hospitalization, Income, Informed Consent, Internalized Stigma, Involuntary Treatment/Hospitalization, Labeling, Loneliness/Isolation, Mass Media, Meaningful Work and Achievement/Activity, Medications, Misdiagnosis, Neighborhood Resistance, "Normal" People, Patients' Rights, Personhood, Poverty, Privacy, Pro-choice, Professional/Client Relationship, Public Policy, Quality of Life, Seclusion and Restraint, Self-esteem, Self-help, Sexual Life, Side-effects, Social Life, Spiritual Life, Stigma, Stress, Tolerance, Stereotype of Unpredictability, Validation, Vocational Rehabilitation, Warmth and Intimacy, Well-being, and Young Adult Chronic Mentally Ill.

A key measure derived from the interview is the Well-being Quotient. This measure is derived from two questions providing information about the relative importance assigned to various factors that may affect well-being and whether the respondent currently lacks these factors. The questions read:

1 "Below is a list of things that some people have said are essential for their well-being. Please mark all of those things that you believe are *essential* for your well-being."

2 "Of the things that people have mentioned that are essential for well-being, which of the following, if any, do you lack in your everyday life?"

The response factors include happiness, health, adequate income, meaningful work or achievement, comfort, satisfying social life, satisfying spiritual life, adequate resources, good food and a decent place to live, satisfying sexual life, creativity, basic human freedoms, warmth and intimacy, safety, and other. Besides simply rank ordering these factors according to the percentages of respondents who identify each factor in each of the question, four well-being profiles are computed: (i) for each factor, the proportion of respondents who indicate that they lack a well-being factor that they consider essential; (ii) the proportion of respondents who do not lack a factor they consider essential; (iii) proportion of clients who consider a factor essential regardless of whether they have it; and (iv) the proportion of respondents who lack a given factor regardless of its essentialness.

The most noteworthy aspect of this instrument is that it was entirely consumer-generated. The fact that it is consumer-generated enhances its face validity even though no formal psychometric analyses were conducted. The researchers consider this instrument in a developmental stage.

LANCASTER QUALITY OF LIFE PROFILE (LQOLP)

See (*) Oliver (1991–92) and Oliver and Mohamad (1992).

The LQOLP was developed in the UK during the late 1980s by Oliver and colleagues in response to a mandate by the British government that all community care programs serving persons with severe mental disorders assess the impact of their services on patients' quality of life. The LQOLP is based upon the Lehman QOLI, but modified to reflect cultural variations and the broader survey intent of the government mandate for service-based evaluation of quality of life. The theory underlying the LQOLP is essentially the same as that described under the Lehman QOLI above.

The LQOLP is a structured self-report patient interview designed for administration by clinical staff in community settings. It consists of 100 items and requires approximately 1 hour to administer. It assesses objective quality of life and life satisfaction in nine life domains: Work/Education, Leisure/Participation, Religion, Finances, Living Situation, Legal and Safety, Family Relations, Social Relations, and Health. In addition it includes a measure of General Well-being and Self-concept. Objective quality of life information is collected by means of categorical or continuous measures depending upon the content area. Life satisfaction ratings are on a seven-point Likert scale.

Psychometric properties of the life satisfaction have been evaluated in a series of pilot studies (Oliver, 1991–92). Test–retest reliabilities for life satisfaction scores range from 0.49 to 0.78, depending upon the patient sample. Internal consistency reliabilities (Cronbach's alpha) of these scales range from 0.84 to 0.86. Content, construct, and criterion validities were also assessed using a variety of techniques and judged to be adequate.

The LQOLP has been used with chronically mentally ill patients in a variety of community care settings in the UK and in Colorado. Details of sample characteristics are not available. A briefer version of the LQOLP is currently being piloted in 12 European countries and is being considered by the World Health Organization in conjunction with their broader studies of quality of life.

DISCUSSION

SELECTING A QUALITY OF LIFE MEASURE

The choice of a measure must rest with the investigator's particular purpose and needs. The most comprehensive and best characterized scales from a psychometric standpoint are the Oregon Quality of Life Questionnaire, the Lehman Quality of Life Interview, the Lancaster Quality of Life Profile, and the Heinrichs–Carpenter Quality of Life Scale. The first three cover similar domains of objective and subjective quality of life, are based upon comprehensive quality of life models, and have acceptable psychometric properties. They have been used with typical samples of severely mentally ill patients in the USA, which included high percentages of patients with schizophrenia. The Heinrichs–Carpenter Quality of Life Scale is also a comprehensive and well characterized instrument. However, it was developed for the more focal purpose of assessing the deficit functional symptoms of schizophrenia and requires administration by a trained clinician. As such it does not fit readily into the mainstream of quality of life assessment measures and must be viewed as more disease-specific than the others. All of these instruments require approximately 45 minutes to administer.

The remaining instruments have had much more limited usage and/are less comprehensive. The Satisfaction with Life Domains Scale is a reasonably well characterized and brief measure of life satisfaction that has been used with severely mentally ill populations. As it only measures life satisfaction, measures of quality of life functioning and resources would have to be added to provide a comprehensive quality of life assessment. The QLC was developed specifically for use in a clinic setting and seems particularly adapted to help clinicians assess the various areas of quality of life functioning. However, it has no known psychometric properties and apparently has only been used in one small study. The Community Adjustment Form has demonstrated sensitivity to changes over time among patients assigned to alternative community treatment programs, but lacks adequate psychometric analysis. The WBPCI has not undergone any psychometric evaluation and has been used in only one study, but it has the important distinction of being the only instrument developed primarily by service consumers. Finally, the CQLI has been used as a companion to the UCDI in the major evaluation of the NIMH CSP. Its major shortcoming also is that it has not been characterized adequately from a psychometric perspective.

For some of the measures described above, there are published norms for different samples of patients, thus allowing some comparisons of new patient samples with these samples. For the life satisfaction measures in the QOLI and SLDS, there are also national normative data because these measures were based heavily upon prior work assessing general quality of life in the USA (Andrews & Withey, 1976).

Beyond these instrument-specific comments, some general comments and caveats are warranted for the investigator or program evaluator seeking a quality of life measure for persons with schizophrenia, whether one of those described above or some other. First, a major concern with using normative quality of life measures in this population is that floor effects are frequently encountered, especially in role functioning domains (e.g., spouse, parent, employment roles). Therefore special attention must be paid to instrument sensitivity. Such floor effects are typically not a problem in the domains of life satisfaction and resources. Second, significant numbers of these patients have problems with task perseverance and comprehension; therefore, pencil-and-paper questionnaires are ill-advised. Note that nearly all of the instruments discussed here are interviews.

INTERPRETING QUALITY OF LIFE INFORMATION

Because of the newness of this field in psychiatric research, it is not possible to make specific recommendations about the interpretation of quality of life data. Conceptually, quality of life is generally seen as related to, but distinct from such clinical syndromes as depression and anxiety. Perhaps the most important point about interpretation that can be made at present is the need to distinguish psychological quality of life, for example, life satisfaction or morale, from clinical symptomatology, particularly depression. We know that measures of subjective quality of life are clearly affected by clinical symptomatology (Lehman, 1983). However, at least conceptually, subjective quality of life equivalents are viewed as distinct from clinical syndromes. This distinction has particular relevance with regard to implications for interventions. That is, one might attempt to effect various changes in a patient's environment to improve housing, financial, or work dissatisfaction, whereas one might prescribe a clinical intervention, such as an antidepressant, to alleviate symptoms of depression. Certainly we can foresee the development of an interactive model between quality of life and clinical symptomatology, but at the very least we can say that to interpret adequately quality of life data from psychiatrically impaired populations one needs to assess both quality of life and clinical symptoms.

A common dilemma encountered in the assessment of quality of life among persons with schizophrenia is that at times their perceived quality of life differs from what social norms would predict. Such counterintuitive quality of life results frequently raise concerns about the reliability or validity of their quality of life assessments. While such basic psychometric concerns may be reasonable, the fact is that the psychometric properties of the better quality of life measures for persons with schizophrenia are comparable with those in the general population. Rather than reflecting measurement limitations, such intuitively inconsistent quality of life findings may offer valuable information for clinical interventions and service planning.

Counterintuitive quality of life results may reflect idiosyncratic views and values of persons experiencing schizophrenia and should affect the clinician's approach to service planning. Patients are unlikely to be motivated to change circumstances with which they are content even if the clinician and family feel otherwise. Conversely, failure to address an area of life with which a patient is dissatisfied, even though the clinician and family view the patient's circumstances as satisfactory, can adversely affect the treatment alliance with the patient. Such disagreements about quality of life may signal the need for a period of negotiation regarding treatment and service goals.

Counterintuitive quality of life findings also may represent patients' accommodation to adverse circumstances. Patients who have lived with adversity for extended periods of time may report relative positive life satisfaction. Their satisfaction reflects an accommodation to their circumstances and does not necessarily mean that they would not seek changes in their lives if offered the hope and opportunity for such changes. Conversely, interventions that promote positive change, for example, vocational rehabilitation or a novel antipsychotic medication (e.g. clozapine), may produce transient decreases in life satisfaction in response to change and the renewed awareness that their lives could be better. Such possibilities form the basis for caution and more thoughtful consideration about how we expect interventions to affect quality of life.

RESEARCH NEEDS

In order to advance quality of life assessment for persons with schizophrenia to the point that more scientifically and clinically meaningful applications can be achieved, there are several areas of needed work. First, we need a clearer definition of what quality of life is and what it is not. The existing literature is characterized by conceptually clear but disparate models of quality of life as well as overly broad and vague definitions of the phrase "quality of life." Definitions include life satisfaction, illness-related "deficit states," very comprehensive multi-dimensional models of well-being, and ill-defined, although appealing humanistic notions. Second, with the adoption of a common definition, there needs to be some agreement about how to measure quality of life. This will allow us to begin to accumulate comparable data across studies and populations.

Third, we need to compare quality of life data from psychiatrically impaired populations with those from other non-psychiatric groups, particularly the physically disabled, the general population, and other economically disadvantaged groups to establish some normative perspective. Fourth, we need a better understanding about how quality of life varies naturally over time in psychiatric populations, the predictive validity of quality of life measures for subsequent illness course and outcome, and the sensitivity of quality of life measures for detecting treatment effects among these patients, who may at best experience very modest improvements.

Finally, there is a need for better and more specific conceptual models for integrating quality of life data into the evaluation of interventions for persons with schizophrenia. No matter how well measured, "quality of life" remains a complex, multidimensional outcome that can be unwieldy unless careful consideration is given to the hypotheses that underlie any particular application. Different types of interventions are likely to affect different dimensions of quality of life and to do so over different times frames for different persons. A time-limited efficacy trial for a new antipsychotic medication is likely to need a different type of quality of life impact assessment than a multi-year follow-up assessment of an assertive case management program. For the successful use of quality of life assessment, future research must be driven by more precise theories about how interventions may impact on quality of life.

IMPORTANCE OF QUALITY OF LIFE ASSESSMENT IN ECONOMIC EVALUATIONS

A well known truism asserts, "You can't buy happiness." Nonetheless, it is also true that achievement of well-being can cost money, and it is therefore relevant to consider the relationship between quality of life outcomes and costs. The linkage of quality of life outcomes to costs is relatively virgin territory in mental health services research. Therefore, it is possible to offer only a theoretical rather than an empirical discussion of this topic. It seems useful to consider the issue from two perspectives, cost-effectiveness and cost–benefit.

The cost-effectiveness view is the more straightforward. All of the quality of life measures reviewed in this chapter generate a variety of quality of life indicators that could be used as effectiveness indicators in a cost-effectiveness evaluation. The major methodologic issues are which indicators of effectiveness to choose for a particular study and how to prioritize them. The choice of appropriate quality of life effectiveness indicators, as already discussed, must be governed by the nature of the intervention and the areas of expected or desired impact. More difficult are establishng the priorities among these indicators. For example, appropriate quality of life outcome indicators for a program for homeless persons with severe mental illness may include number of days housed, housing satisfaction, victimization, satisfaction with personal safety, days in jail, amount of income supports, satisfaction with finances, contact with family, and satisfaction with family relations. For each of these quality of life outcomes, a cost-effectiveness ratio could be computed: e.g., the cost of achieving x number of days in stable housing or y units increase in housing satisfaction. It becomes a judgment call, however, to decide which among the various relevant quality of life outcomes are the most important. This is especially critical when a study does not yield consistent effectiveness across multiple indicators. For example, a program for the homeless may reduce days homeless and housing satisfaction, but not improve family relations. In such instances, short of some empirically derived valuation schema, cost-effectiveness ratios for the various outcomes can be reported and their relative significance interpreted within the overall context and goals of the intervention.

The issue of the value of quality of life outcomes brings us to the more difficult cost–benefit perspective. Efforts can be made to estimate the actual monetary value of quality of life outcomes. This seems more feasible for some objective quality of life indicators, such as housing, victimization, arrests, and employment. However, it is quite problematic for other objective quality of life indicators, such as the frequency of contacts with friends and family, and for subjective quality of life indicators. What is the value of life satisfaction or the sense of well-being? It is, of course, possible to imagine procedures for estimating the utilities of alternative levels of these outcomes and relative trade-offs for other outcomes. Hence it may be possible to estimate the value of these for a cost–benefit analysis. These empirical approaches still beg the question, "At what price happiness?"

Given the current emphasis on the costs of outcomes, it is important to develop useful strategies that relate quality of life impacts to costs. The most fruitful avenue would seem to be through the cost-effectiveness perspective with an eye toward the relative priorities for various domains of quality of life outcomes. These priorities must take into consideration both the nature of the intervention and the values of the relevant stakeholders, including providers, payers, patients, families, and communities.

REFERENCES

Andrews, F.M., and Withey, S.B. (1976). *Social Indicators of Well-Being*. New York: Plenum Press.

Attkisson, C., Cook, J., Karno, M., *et al.* (1991). Clinical services research. *Schizophrenia Bulletin*, **18**, 561–626.

Baker, F., and Intagliata, J. (1982). Quality of life in the evaluation of community support systems. *Evaluation and Program Planning*, **5**, 69–79.

Bigelow, D.A., Brodsky, G., Steward, L., and Olson, M. (1982a). The concept and measurement of quality of life as a dependent variable in evaluation of mental health services. In: G. Stahler and W. Tash, eds, *Innovative Approaches to Mental Health Evaluation*, pp. 345–366. New York: Academic Press.

Bigelow, D.A., Gareau, M.J., and Young, D.J. (1990). A quality of life interview. *Psychosocial Rehabilitation J*, **14**, 94–98.

Bigelow, D.A., McFarland, B.H., Olson, M.M. (1991). Quality of life of community mental health program clients: validating a measure. *Community Mental Health Journal*, **27**, 43–55.

Bigelow, D.A., McFarland, B.H., Gareuu, M.J., Young, D.J. (1991). Implementation and effectiveness of a bed reduction project. *Community Mental Health Journal*, **27**, 125–133.

Campbell, J., Schraiber, R., Temkin, T., and ten Tusscher, T. (1989). The Well-Being Project: Mental Health Clients Speak for Themselves. Reports to the California Department of Mental Health.

Heinrichs, D.W., Hanlon, T.E., and Carpenter, W.T. (1984). The quality of life scale: An instrument for rating the schizophrenic deficit syndrome. *Schizophrenia Bulletin*, **10**, 388–398.

Hoult, J., and Reynolds, J. (1984). Schizophrenia: A comparative trial of community oriented and hospital oriented psychiatric care. *Acta Psychiatrica Scandinavica*, **69**, 359–372.

Lehman, A.F. (1988). A quality of life interview for the chronically mentally ill. *Evaluation and Program Planning*, **11**, 51–62.

Lehman, A.F. (1983a). The well-being of chronic mental patients: Assessing their quality of life. *Archives of General Psychiatry*, **40**, 369–373.

Lehman, A.F. (1983b). The effects of psychiatric symptoms

on quality of life assessments among the chronic mentally ill. *Evaluation and Program Planning*, **6**, 143–151.

Lehman, A., Ward, N., and Linn, L. (1982). Chronic mental patients: The quality of life issue. *American Journal of Psychiatry*, **10**, 1271–1276.

Lehman, A.F., Possidente, S., and Hawker, F. (1986). The quality of life of chronic mental patients in a state hospital and community residences. *Hospital and Community Psychiatry*, **37**, 901–907.

Lehman, A.F., Slaughter, J.C., and Myers, C.P. (1991). The quality of life of chronically mentally ill persons in alternative residential settings. *Psychiatry Quarterly*, **62**, 35–49.

Lehman, A.F., Slaughter, J.C., and Myers, C.P. (1992). Quality of life of the chronically mentally ill: Gender and decade of life effects. *Evaluation and Program Planning*, **15**, 7–12.

Levitt, A.J., Hogan, T.P., and Bucosky, C.M. (1990). Quality of life in chronically mentally ill patients in day treatment. *Psychological Medicine*, **20**, 703–710.

Malm, U., May P.R.A., and Dencker, S.J. (1981). Evaluation of the quality of life of the schizophrenic outpatient: a checklist. *Schizophrenia Bulletin*, **7**, 477–487.

Meltzer, H.Y., Burnett, S., Bastani, B., and Ramirez, L.F. (1990). Effects of six months of clozapine treatment on the quality of life of chronic schizophrenic patients. *Hospital and Community Psychiatry*, **41**, 892–897.

Mulkern, V., Agosta, J.M., Ashbaugh, J.W., *et al.* (1986). Community Support Program Client Follow-up Study. Report to NIMH.

Oliver, J.P.J. (1991–92). The social care directive: development of a quality of life profile for use in community services for the mentally ill. *Social Work and Social Sciences Review*, **3**, 5–45.

Rosenfield, S. (1992). Factors contributing to the subjective quality of life of the chronically mentally ill. *Journal of Health and Social Behavior*, **33**, 299–315.

Rosenfield, S., and Neese-Todd, S. (1993). Elements of a psychosocial clubhouse program associated with a satisfying quality of life. *Hospital and Community Psychiatry*, **44**, 76–78.

Schulberg, H., and Bromet, E. (1981). Strategies for evaluating the outcome of community services for the chronically mentally ill. *American Journal of Psychiatry*, **138**, 930–935.

Simpson, C.J., Hyde, C.E., Faragher, E.B. (1989). The chronically mentally ill in community facilities: a study of quality of life. *British Journal of Psychiatry*, **154**, 77–82.

Slaughter, J.C., and Lehman, A.F. (1991). Quality of life of severely mentally ill adults in residential care facilities. *Adult Residential Care Journal*, **5**, 97–111.

Stein, L.I., and Test, M.A. (1980). Alternative to mental hospital treatment: I. Conceptual model, treatment program and clinical evaluation. *Archives of General Psychiatry*, **37**, 392–397.

6

Vocational Assessment in Schizophrenia

LUIS SALVADOR-CARULLA and REYES VELAZQUEZ
Grupo de Investigación en Medicina Psicosocial Universidad de Cádiz, Spain

INTRODUCTION

Work provides means for achieving economic independence, establishing one's identity, and improving social relationships. Thus, employment plays a central part in social integration in the Western cultures, where to be outside work is largely to be outside society (Bluestone, 1989).

Dysfunction in work role is perceived as a major cause of handicap among the mentally ill. This is particularly relevant to schizophrenic patients. The WHO Collaborative Study on the Assessment and Reduction of Psychiatric Disability (WHO, 1988), found work performance as the most impaired role in schizophrenic patients at initial evaluation, well above other survival roles such as self-care or family relationships. In contrast, schizophrenics rated closer to the control population in "interest in getting a job" than in other social role performances. The ability to obtain and maintain employment is considered a major determinant in assessing outcome (Johnstone & Lang, 1994). Impairment in work functioning is also considered a diagnostic feature of schizophrenia, and this deficit may persist without improvement for years (Lysaker *et al.*, 1993).

In spite of all this, the psychosocial aspects of employment are generally overlooked in this population. A person with psychiatric disability is more apt to be stigmatized, blamed, and feared in a work setting than any other disabled person. Furthermore, in contrast to the physically and the developmentally disabled, failure to integrate in work may be seen as the psychiatrically disabled person's fault (Anthony & Blanch, 1987).

The occupational role is not adequately explored in many epidemiological studies. There is considerable controversy about the validity of the optimistic job data provided by the Epidemiology Catchment Area project (43% of persons with schizophrenia curently employed; Angell *et al.*, 1992). Other studies find an employment rate from 10 to 26% among adults with severe mental illness in the USA, most subjects being in unskilled occupations (Anthony & Blanch, 1987; Attkisson *et al.*, 1992). The rates of schizophrenics seeking employment is as low as 6%.

The employment rate for seriously mentally ill people is higher in community support programs, and it ranges from 11 to 60% in those schizophrenic patients receiving some type of vocational rehabilitation (Attkisson *et al.*, 1992). Intensive vocational training may succeed in promoting 25–45% of cases to competitive work. On the other hand, dropout rates are of up to 40% within the first 6 months of such programs, they have a modest impact in placing patients into jobs, and, on many occasions, they fail to prepare patients for future competitive

Handbook of Mental Health Economics and Health Policy, Volume I, Schizophrenia. Edited by M. Moscarelli, A. Rupp and N. Sartorius.
© 1996 John Wiley & Sons Ltd.

employment out from the program (Dauwalder & Hoffmann, 1992).

Vocational integration is an extremely complex, multidisciplinary field, which has not received enough attention until recent years. The history of vocational rehabilitation for chronic mental illness in the USA and Europe has been reviewed by several authors (Anthony & Blanch, 1987; Wesoleck & McFarlane, 1991; Seyfried, 1991; Green, 1991). The rehabilitation programs for chronic mental illness started later than for the developmentally disabled, although they shared many aspects in common. For many years, the issue was centered in changing in the traditional "train-then-place" model for others such as the "place-then-train" or the "choose get-keep" rehabilitation model. Another goal was replacing the "screening-out" favored by the traditional psychological assessment by the "zero-exclusion" that advocates for job promotion for all the handicapped regardless of disability or functional limitation (Wehman & Moon, 1988). The sheltered employment was outrunned by a whole arrangement of supported and transitional employment programs. After being developed in the USA, most of these programs were implemented in Europe without taking into account basic aspects of the European labor markets or the employers' needs and demands. Furthermore, the cooperation between academic institutions, non-governmental organizations, private entrepreneurs, and vocational consulting agencies has been nearly absent. This generates important problems of communication between mental health care providers, vocational rehabilitation workers, and clients (Boevink, 1993).

Thus, regulations are far from real practices, the theoretical background is rarely applied and there is a general lack of high-quality research on outcomes and costs related to different programs. Now, more attention is given to practical experiences, trying to integrate different approaches in flexible programs.

As Attkisson points out (1992), the comparison of studies in this area is extremely difficult due to several factors: conceptual discrepancies, varying definitions, heterogeneity of assessment instruments and techniques, different methodology and lack of adequate epidemiological data. International comparison is hindered by varying factors related to the labor force, such as the rate of women at work, school attendance, age of retirement, sociodemographic trends, and the rate of unemployment. According to Morgan & Cheadle (1975), unemployment rates above 2% may seriously hamper access to competitive work, while unemployment rates above 6% may render competitive jobs almost inaccessible for the mentally ill. The unemployment rates differ greatly from the USA to the European countries, where it is frequently above 10%. Regulations on disability insurance and protection for the handicapped vary greatly as well.

Rehabilitation and treatment may be considered as fairly stable processes if they are compared with the job market. Employment cannot be easily conceptualized as a "treatment technique," and many ongoing employment programs do not fit in any of the supported employment alternatives (e.g. social firms). A tight definition of job alternatives for the handicapped in governmental regulations may impede their adaptation to the changes of the job market.

It is also important to note that vocational programs do not have to be implemented for all the people with severe mental illness such as schizophrenia. First, it is necessary to differentiate between severe mental illness and psychiatric handicap, as not all the chronic patients become handicapped due to their disease. Second, some patients may not want to work, particularly in societies that are not so much work-oriented as in Western cultures. Third, some disabled people obtain work without in-depth vocational assessment because their education, circumstances, or previous work experiences provides them with the potential to be integrated into the work force without too much difficulty. Fourth, some other patients can transition directly from transitional employment into competitive employment without job support. Unfortunately, the current epidemiological and outcome studies do not provide data about these issues.

The growing need for vocational rehabilitation of the psychiatrically disabled is confronted with all these problems. Some of them have been addressed in new regulations such as the "Americans with Disability Act" of July 1990. In Europe many countries tried to establish a "Quota Scheme", fixing the minimal number of handicapped to be employed in medium and large companies. This regulatory strategy failed as a means of encouraging employers to hire mentally ill workers (Floyd, 1991). The increasing provision of vocational programs raises the issue of choosing between alternatives, quality assurance, and adequate assessment of outcome.

CONCEPTUAL AND CLASSIFICATION ISSUES

The lack of an international agreement on the terminology used for vocational assessment is a major burden for an adequate development of this field. The conceptual framework of key concepts such as "normalization," "handicap," and "occupational role," may be determinant in the development of the vocational programs and in their assessment. On the other hand, we lack an operational classification of vocational alternatives.

VOCATIONAL COMPETENCE

According to O'Brien (1986), *vocational competence* (ability to perform functional and meaningful activities with whatever assistance is needed), is part of the accomplishments related to normalization. O'Brien's concept of *competence* differs from the WHO definition (WHO, 1988), at excluding assisted aid. This may contribute to a better understanding of the major differences in vocational rehabilitation of physical and mental handicaps.

IMPAIRMENT, DISABILITY, HANDICAP, AND OCCUPATIONAL ROLE

The Classification of Impairments, Disabilities and Handicaps (ICIDH, WHO, 1980) provides a coding system for describing the personal and social consequences of disease. These three concepts do not have a one-to-one interaction between each other. A person may be impaired and disabled, but not handicapped (Susser, 1990). *Impairment* is defined as a loss or abnormality of psychological, physiological, or anatomical structure or function. A *disability* is any restriction or lack (resulting from an impairment) of the ability to perform an activity in the manner or within the range considered normal for a human being. The *occupational role disability* includes any disturbance of the ability to organize and participate in routine activities connected with the occupation of time, such as motivation, cooperation, or work routine. *Handicap* is defined, in the context of a health experience, "as a disadvantage for a given individual, resulting from an impairment or a disability, that limits or prevents the fulfilment of a role that is normal for that individual. Handicap occurs when there is interference with the ability to sustain what are defined as survival roles" (WHO, 1980; e.g., patient suffering schizophrenia unable to get and keep a job due to his/her impairments and disabilities). For example, schizophrenic symptoms such as lack of drive, social withdrawal, and distractibility are impairments. A schizophrenic individual suffering from these impairments will have subsequent disabilities, such as lack of motivation, lack of cooperation, and problems in keeping a work routine. Eventually, these impairments and disabilities will incapacitate him or her to get and keep a job (occupation handicap). Thus, "psychiatric handicap" may be preferred to "psychiatric disability" for naming this subpopulation of the seriously mentally ill.

"Occupational role" has been defined by the WHO as "a generic designation for a great variety of social roles having work as their common core. Occupational roles are usually defined in terms of specified tasks and duties, requisite skills and knowledge, and standards of performance and output" (WHO, 1988). The reviewed version of the ICIDH for ICD-10, uses the term "Role handicap," and includes more social roles, giving prominence to role handicap that is imposed upon patients by other persons or agencies (Cooper, 1993).

The ICIDH approach to handicap is dimensional and not suitable for categorical classification. It is possible to define the dysfunction level of the patient in several survival roles, but it is not possible to discriminate between the patient who is handicapped from the one who is not. A clear contradiction arises as there is a social demand for detecting, not only the altered roles, but also the handicapped population in order to establish planning strategies at several levels. There is a need for both cut/off points and operational criteria for identifying the "handicapped" population within a group of disorders or within a single disease (e.g. "impairment of 5 or more in at least three survival roles"). Vocational programs may benefit from these operational criteria, as some serious mentally ill are handicapped and others are not. Concepts such as physical, mental, and intellectual handicap are also at odds.

According to its dimensional approach, the ICIDH explicitly advises against the use of the descriptive adjectives "mental" and "physical" in relation to handicaps (WHO, 1980). It is stated that these terms are better applied to impairments, but the role dysfunctions observed in mentally ill patients may be qualitatively different from the roles altered in patients with physical impairments. O'Brien's concept of competence sets a clear-cut difference between, for example, the role dysfunctions of profound visual impairments and schizophrenia. A blind person may reach normal levels of competence in many survival roles, whenever a suitable aid is provided. On the other hand, technical aids are of little relevance for a schizophrenic patient.

Seyfried (1991) has reviewed the major differences between the physically and the mentally handicapped (this term may include the developmental and the psychiatric patients). The vocational rehabilitation of the first group is aimed at enabling the handicapped person to encounter the demand of their physical environment in a new way. The rehabilitation of the mentally ill is, in contrast, aimed at providing the subject with the ability to cope in their social environment. The vocational assessment is also different. Seyfried concludes that "the creation of vocational identity is incomparably harder for the psychiatrically disabled than for the physically handicapped." Thus, concepts such as "mental handicap" and "physical handicap" may be extremely relevant for vocational assessment and rehabilitation. All the same, "mentally handicapped" may be preferred to "serious mentally ill" for naming the group of patients who may benefit from vocational programs, as it is the handicap and not the severity of the condition which determines the need for vocational support. There is also a complex relationship between vocational programs for mental handicap related to serious mental illness and mental handicap related to mental retardation (Anthony & Blanch, 1987).

CLASSIFICATION OF VOCATIONAL PROGRAMS

Vocational programs may be classified into two main groups. First, those programs which promote the patient to the work force. They may include vocational counseling, training, and job clubs. Second, those programs which provide employment for the mentally handicapped. They include a whole range of competitive and supported employment (Wehman & Moon, 1988; Verdugo & Jenaro, 1993). Other programs are halfway from both, being closer to promotion or to provision depending on local or individual factors. This is the case of prevocational work, sheltered workshops, and transitional employment. Nevertheless, the traditional distinction between sheltered versus competitive, supported versus independent, full versus part-time, or permanent versus transitional employment, does not provide an adequate framework for classifying the whole array of employment options which are now available. Furthermore, the meaning of the same term may vary significantly from USA to Europe, from one European country to another, or even among different settings in a single country. The affirmative industries for profit, which are a common alternative in Spain, are difficult to describe in the traditional classification. The same happens with social firms, a vocational model that combines low-paid work with motivation incentives, in a mixed subsidized/for profit organization. Its flexibility allows adaptation to different social policies, fiscal regulations and economic standards, which is extremely relevant for implementing programs in Europe (Le Minotaure, 1993).

VOCATIONAL ASSESSMENT

Vocational assessment can be broadly defined as the process of obtaining information about workers, skills and performance in order to make appropriate training decisions. *Performance* should be applied within the context in which it is expected. The vocational *process* may include the job search and development, the training of a job coach that will help patients in their future work, the job assessment (work place and candidates), the job match between the candidate and the task, the on-the-job training and, at last, the follow-up assessment of ongoing support.

Two types of approaches to vocational assessment have been described: the traditional psychological testing and the ecological approach. The psychological testing promoted selected candidates for specific job tasks according to their performance in several tests. The "screening out" of the mentally handicapped according to this approach and the inconsistency of results in relation to real job performance, led to a general discredit of this procedure. The following are several concerns regarding the use of traditional evaluation for persons with severe disabilities (Wesoleck & McFarlane, 1991): (i) instructions and items often require comprehension levels that exceed the examinee's abilities; (ii) norms are frequently inappropriate for persons with severe disabilities; (iii) skills and abilities (e.g. abstract language facility) required are irrelevant to the construct being predicted (e.g. work performance); and (iv) inadequate consistency, validity, and reliability of the tests for this population.

The ecological model and the so-called "Community referenced assessment procedures," favored the evaluation on the job setting, taking into account a broad number of job dimensions or components and giving less relevance to test performance (Dauwalder & Hoffmann, 1992). At first, any technique related to psychological testing was banned from the ecological evaluation. Thus, cut-off points, centiles, and norm-reference criteria were not considered (Menchetti & Flynn, 1989). After a 20 year hiatus, a renewed interest on employment testing has been favored by the improvement in the research methods and their predictive power (Russell, 1989). At present, the new vocational testing is gaining consideration as a part of the ecolocial assessment.

AREAS OF VOCATIONAL ASSESSMENT

There have been several attempts to classify the different areas of the ecological evaluation (Moos & Lemke, 1983; Chadley-Rusch & Rusch, 1988; Shalock, 1989; Menchetti & Flynn, 1989; Wesoleck & McFarlane, 1991). The final goal of a vocational program is integration. This can be assessed in several areas: physical integration, social integration, relationships, and social networks (Mank & Buckley, 1989).

It is important to establish the minimum number of factors to assess the evaluation in order to obtain reliable and valid information on two main areas: work site or job-and-task analysis, and individual factors related to job competence that can be displayed in a vocational profile. A third area is the environment/individual fit. Every one of these areas can be divided into several components. A general consensus on these components is needed in order to attain international standards of vocational assessment.

Environment/demands

An accurate description of work environments allows a better definition of the demands related to worksite (Table 1).

General environment components

It is important to consider those general factors which are relevant to work site analysis, such as distance from work, transportation, family support, or social climate.

Job environment components

They may be divided into physical and social factors (Table 1). Physical factors include the geographical setting, the building structure, and mainly the physical design of the work site and the workstation. They are related to the physical demands for the job.

The social component includes a broader and more complex number of factors, such as the behavioral setting (particular behaviors related to work function, e.g., hospital, office, church), the organizational structure, and the psychosocial climate (Table 1). Schalock (1989) considers three "dimensions" in the latter: relationship, personal development, and system maintenance/change. Moos and Lemke (1983) described other dimensions: relationships (involvement, cohesion with co-workers, support from supervisor), goal-oriented dimensions (autonomy, task-oriented, work pressure), system maintenance, and change (clarity, control, innovation, comfort), concerning co-workers, supervisors, and employers.

The employer is the individual who is going to hire, so it is important to know what he/she is looking for; what are their expectations, awareness, and knowledge about mental handicap; what are the factors contributing to hiring, their retention criteria, and the incentives they have for hiring (tax credits and support services; Kiernan & Rowland, 1989; Wesoleck & McFarlane, 1991).

Table 1. Environment components of the vocational assessment (adapted from Moos & Lemke, 1983; Judy, 1989; Menchetti & Flynn, 1989)

	Physical	Social
General environment	Housing Distance from work Transportation Community facilities Community services Aids and incentives	Family support Social support Social climate Social network
Job environment	Geographical setting Building structure Physical design of work-site	Behavioral setting Organizational structure Psychosocial job climate with co-workers, supervisors and employers*: *Relationships* *Goal-oriented dimensions* *System maintenance and change*

* See text for explanation

Job restructuring feasibility

Employers should provide "reasonable" job accommodation to qualify handicapped individuals, including "job restructuring," such as task reassignment, task elimination, tasks to provide additional employees or job sharing, reassignment to a vacant position, and "work activities modification." For example: time flexibility, compressed work weeks, alteration of the break/rest periods, or part-time helpers (Judy, 1989). The assessment of these particular issues is enhanced in the Americans with Disabilities Act (ADA; Ravid & Menon, 1993). The functional reinforcement analysis deals with the environmental conditions that influence support and maintain particular behaviors. The *environment adaptability quotient* provides a measure of the capability of change of the environment in order to satisfy the needs of the person (Menchetti & Flynn, 1989).

Individual factors related to vocational competence

There are many different approaches to this issue (Schalock, 1989; Bacon & Crimmins, 1989; Calkins & Walker, 1989; Menchetti & Flynn, 1989; Russell, 1989; Rialland, 1991; Anthony, 1994), and they seldom agree. From a general point of view, vocational competence may be considered as a product of three interacting factors: job responsibility (e.g. punctuality, absenteeism, working continuously at job tasks); task-production competence (e.g. completion of work tasks that meet accuracy and efficiency according to work setting standards); and social–vocational competence (e.g. interaction with co-workers and supervisors, compliance of formal and informal rules at workplace) (Calkins & Walker, 1989). Kiernan and Rowland (1989), differentiate between those factors related to hiring (e.g. personality traits, experience, qualification for job, work history, education), factors related to promotion, and factors leading to termination. There are many other approaches to work competence analysis. A tentative description of these factors is provided below.

Temperaments of jobs

The term "temperaments of jobs" in vocational literature refers to the type of adjustments workers must make in job situations. There have been defined 11 temperaments (Russell, 1989; Schalock, 1989):

1. Directing, controlling, planning
2. Performing repetitive work
3. Influencing people
4. Performing a variety of duties
5. Creative expression
6. Working alone
7. Performing effectively under stress
8. Attaining precise measures
9. Working under specific instruction
10. Dealing with people
11. Making judgments and decisions

Temperaments # 2 and 9 are more relevant to vocational adaptation in people with mental retardation. Different temperaments of jobs may be expected in some schizophrenic patients (e.g. temperaments # 4, 5, and 6). On the other hand, some studies point out a greater impairment of certain temperaments in schizophrenic subjects in comparison with other handicapped people (e.g. temperaments # 7 and 10). Schalock (1989) differentiates between those factors involved in short-term and long-term job tenure (Table 1).

Social skills (social competence)

The relationship between people's social activity or basic social skills and work competence is conflicting. There is a more positive correlation between measures of work adjustment skills and future vocational outcome (Anthony, 1994). According to the "social competence model," three major forms of social competence are required for successful adjustment to competitive employment: (i) *compliance skills* (control disruptive behavior, conforming to interpersonal rules and conventions); (ii) *basic interactions skills* (positive interaction with co-workers, supervisors and others); and (iii) *relationship-building* skills (developing friendship and social support networks) (Calkins & Walker, 1989). A fourth form may be *cooperation* (ability to cooperate and to solicit help or feedback when needed). Subjects with schizophrenia show a poorer performance in this area than in other areas of vocational competence, such as task orientation, work motivation, and work conformance, when they are compared with other disabled groups (Lysaker *et al.*, 1993).

Cognitive functions and work competence

Bowen *et al.* (1994), found significant relationship between schizophrenic individual's cognitive functioning, interpersonal skills, and performance in elemental skills training tasks. They studied several cognitive functions indicators of vulnerability or functions in which schizophrenic individuals remain deficient even when their symptoms have remitted. The cognitive functions assessed were: (i) deficits in signal detection over sustained periods of visual monitoring with minimal short-term memory load measured through two different versions of the Continuous Performance Test (CPT); (ii) short-term auditory recall and auditory distractibility (DSDT); and (iii) efficiency of early iconic memory and readout stages of visual information processing relatively independent of active, short-term memory (Forced-choice Span of Apprehension Test). The vigilance level, as measured by the two versions of the CPT, was the cognitive function most related to performance in roleplays of interpersonal skills. Immediate recall memory was also significantly related to performance in elemental skills independently of vigilance. Their results suggest that enduring cognitive dysfunctions are not only associated with poorer social functioning, but may decrease the training capabilities of these subjects. It is important to consider in the assessment other cognitive deficits relevant to work activity such as planning, categorical sequencing, convergent and divergent thinking, and creativity (Miran & Miran, 1993).

Clinical status and work competence

The role of clinical factors such as medical and psychiatric diagnosis, symptoms, time of onset, and length of the last hospital stay is questioned by some authors (Seyfried, 1991). This finding may be related to methodological problems. Anthony (1994) underline the importance of psychiatric diagnosis and symptomatology as predictors of vocational outcome. Lysaker and Bell (1994) found a significant association of negative symptoms in schizophrenia with deteriorated work function. Patients with prominent negative symptoms had greater difficulties in: (i) task orientation (understanding of work assignments and persistence in tasks without extra supervision); (ii) social skills; and (iii) personal presentation (a measure of behaviors, such as alertness, hygiene, and grooming at work). This study shows the importance of using clinical scales (Positive and Negative Syndrome Scale, PANSS) in the assessment of vocational rehabilitation.

The challenging or disruptive behaviors in regard to the work environment, have been reviewed for short-term and long-term assessment (Table 2) (Schalock, 1989), and in relation to co-workers and supervisors (Calkins & Walker, 1989). The Vocational Assessment Rating Scale (VARS) assesses disruptive behaviors in regard to the work environment (Table 3).

Table 2. Short-term and long-term factors involved in vocational assessment (adapted from Schalock, 1989)

Short-term (social competency)		Long-term (vocational adaptation)	
Enhances	*Impairs*	*Enhances*	*Impairs*
1. Ask questions	1. Steals	1. Leader/co-worker support	1. Seasonal work
2. Follows directions	2. Physically aggressive	2. Job satisfaction	2. Appearance inappropriate to setting
3. Accepts criticism	3. Argues/refuses	3. Task variety	3. Family resistance
4. Follows rules	4. Late/absent	4. Job coach availability	4. Long-term tolerance
5. Neatly groomed	5. Lacks social awareness	5. Quantity of work	5. Economic disincentives
6. Adapts to change	6. Whines/complains	6. Quality of work	6. Transportation
7. Interacts appropriately	7. Easily distracted	7. Ability to learn job	7. Job burnout
8. Courteous to co-workers	8. Bizarre behavior	8. Family support	
		9. Long-term job satisfaction	

Another important clinical variable is the effect of antipsychotic drugs on vocational achievement. Although this variable has been seldom researched, there is a striking consistency of findings that suggest that they may impair work capacity (Anthony, 1994).

Personality factors related to work competence

Some personality traits are extremely relevant for finding and keeping employment: vulnerability to stress and adaptation to changes, frustration threshold, reaction to criticism, and self-esteem. Anthony (1994) stresses the importance of "readiness factors" such as personal preference, satisfaction with current situation, commitment to change, self-efficacy, environmental awareness, and self-awareness. Other related dimensions, frequently overlooked, are goals or aspirations, motivation, and expectations (Waismann, 1988; Vilkkumaa, 1991).

Other individual factors relevant to job tenure

The influence of *sociodemographic factors* such as age and sex on predicting job tenure in the psychiatrically handicapped is stressed by some authors (Kiernan & Rowland, 1989), and questioned by others (Seyfried, 1991). In a selected sample of patients with vocational goals, living in the community, criminal justice involvement, marital status, and symptomatology were the only predictors of vocational outcome (Anthony, 1994). The individual's work history has been considered one of the better predictors of vocational outcome, although a recent research questions the importance of this factor in patients with a clear vocational goal (Anthony, 1994).

Person–environment Wt

Persons and environments can be described in common terms (i.e. environments can be assessed according to which behavioral capabilities they require). Then characteristics of persons and environments can be compared and discrepancies identified and corrected (Schalock, 1989). Once the behavioral capabilities and the environment-specific requirements have been assessed, these data can be used for providing a "goodness-of-fit index" (GOFI), that identifies mismatches and can be displayed as a decision matrix on a set of critical/unacceptable and desirable/undesirable factors that facilitates selecting areas in which functional capabilities have to be enhanced. This index facilitates job-match, planning with individuals and their advocates, and systematic instruction (Schalock, 1989; Mank & Buckley, 1989).

METHODS AND MEASURES OF VOCATIONAL ASSESSMENT

The techniques of vocational assessment have been revised by several authors (Agram, 1986; Mank & Buckley, 1989; Russell, 1989; Menchetti & Flynn, 1989; Wesoleck & McFarlane, 1991). The tools and techniques vary greatly from computer run tests and work samples to community employment settings with very little structure. There are many problems concerning the methods of vocational assessment besides the lack of operational definitions. There is not an agreement about the length of the assessment period. Theorists say that vocational evaluation has to be long enough to provide a comprehensive appraisal of the individual's assets and needs. In practice, vocational assessment may vary from the 1 week or less of the individualized client-centered assessment to the several months or more of the community-based assessment.

An adequate training and standardization of raters is rarely carried forward. Many of the assessment instruments lack the quality criteria currently requested for assessment instruments in psychiatry, such as consistency, reliability, and predictive validity. Questionnaires with global ratings devoid adequate consistency analysis (e.g., Cronbach's alpha, LISREL's factorial analysis, Rasch analysis). There are few studies exploring test–retest and interrater reliability according to kappa coefficient (Agram, 1986). The validation studies are limited to norm-reference, criterion-reference and concurrent validity, or the so-called "social/ecological validity," which refers to the subjective evaluation of the outcomes of an intervention by those persons most affected by the individual behavior (Bason & Crimins, 1989). Meta-analysis has been applied to employment testing in recent years (Russell, 1989). The number of instruments adapted for schizophrenic patients is scarce. Two instruments for assessing work performance, the Occupational Functioning Assessment Scale (OFAS; Bleiser *et al.*, 1994), and the Work Personality Profile (WPP; Lysaker *et al.*, 1993), have been specifically adapted for the schizophrenic population (Table 3).

Integration is assessed in three ways: capacity measures, progress measures, and life-style measures. *Capacity measures* assess the extent to which specific environments allow integration. *Progress measures* assess the quality of service in terms of increasing an individual skills adaptive behavior or community adjustment. Several indicators have been proposed for quality assurance and can be combined with progress measures. *Life-style measures* which examine the lives of the individuals in the environment in which they function (Mank & Buckley, 1989). The Quality of Work Life (QOWL) can be assessed through three types of indicators: objective social indicators (e.g. decreased training and supervision, marketable skills learned, accessibility to promotions), social–psychological and satisfaction indicators (e.g. job satisfaction, pride in workplace, satisfaction with relationships at work), and person–environment fit (e.g. increased GOFI for vocational environment, participatory role in decisions) (Goode, 1989).

Instruments for vocational assessment in schizophrenia

The majority of instruments for vocational assessment in mental handicap have been used in subjects with mental retardation or in heterogeneous groups of handicapped. It is possible to differentiate several types of instruments (Table 3). The *vocational checklists* facilitate the analysis of client vocational data such as interests, temperaments, educational achievements, specific working traits, and physical capabilities (Wesoleck & McFarlane, 1991). The work samples are standardized tests for work simulation, that may be computerized (e.g. ERGOS work simulator). The aptitude-matchng tests allow matching between personal abilities and particular job requirements. Work performance can be assessed either through global scales (e.g. OFAS), or by dimensional scales like the WPP. There are specific tests for assessing disruptive behavior in vocational settings, work-related disease and injury, or decision making. Some systems are comprehensive, including complex batteries for assessing the whole vocational process (environment, individual, fit, and follow-up).

FUTURE TRENDS IN VOCATIONAL ASSESSMENT

There is an urgent need of international consensus in the key concepts and dimensions related to vocational rehabilitation. It is also necessary to adapt the vocational instruments for schizophrenic patients. There is a growing focus on self-directed assessment, systematic reevaluation, better quality measures centered in outcome, and the integration of more complex data in the assessment such as hereditary traits, biorhythms, and temperaments. Computers are playing a growing part in the

Table 3. Instruments for vocational assessment

Name	Reference	Characteristics	Comments
1. Checklists			
VACG *Vocational Assessment and Curriculum Guide*	Rusch (1982)[4]	Checklist for community referenced assessment	Reliability and validity assessed in mental retardation (Menchetti & Rusch, 1988)[4]
SIPB *Prevocational Information Battery*	Halpern (1975)[4]	Checklist	Social validation. Developed for mental retardation
PACG *Prevocational Assessment and Curriculum Guide*	Mithaug (1978)[4]	Checklist for community referenced assessment	Social validation. Developed for mental retardation
2. Work samples			
VCWS *Valpar Component Work Sample Series*	Valpar Corp. (1981)[4] (USA)	Trait-oriented work samples. 18 tools for assessing physical/functional work aptitudes	Used mainly in mental retardation
VIEWS *Vocational Information and Evaluation Work Samples*	Vocational Research Institute, (1977)[4] (USA)	Work-oriented work samples. Work simulation for assessing individual's dexterity in 16 tasks	Work grouped into categories according to task requirements. Use mainly in mental retardation.
SVEV *Singer Vocational Evaluation System*	Singer (1986)[4] (USA)	Work-oriented work samples	
ERGOS Work Simulator	Shervey (1990)[3] (USA)	Computer assessment system. Physical/functional components	Assists the practitioner to establish goals and objectives of individual's work-recovery program
3. Aptitude matching			
AMAS *Activity Matching Ability System*	Rialland (1991) (UK)	Aptitude-matching instrument * Activities required on job	Developed by Remploy and Institute of Consumer Ergonomics. Computer admnistered format.
		* Individual abilities assessed by the factory doctor * Job-match in 103 items grouped in four headings: Work environment Work equipment Physical work demands Other work demands	Competence recorded in the National Record of Vocational Achievement (NRVA) Criterion-referenced.
APTICOM	Vocational Research Institute (1985)[4] (USA)	Aptitude-matching instrument. Dexterity, perceptual and psychomotor components. Match with 10 aptitudinal areas (US Dept. of Labor): general intelligence, verbal, mathematical, spatial, clerical, motor coordination, digital dexterity, manual dexterity, visual-motor coordination	Other similar systems used in US include: OASYS, Valpar System 2000, Choices, Life core, PPS[3] Computer assisted
EEO-*EEO-Match scale* MS	Boles *et al.* (1987)[2] (USA)	Aptitude-matching instrument to assess social competency and behavioral capability in reference to demands of a particular job 11 behavioral enhancing characteristics 8 imparing behaviors	Related to short-term tenure factors. Provides Goodness-of-fit index (GOFI) between 11 behavioral characteristics which enhance job performance and 8 disruptive behaviors

Table 3 (*cont.*)

Name	Reference	Characteristics	Comments
EST *Employment Screening Test*	Schalock *et al.* (1985)[2] (USA)	Aptitude-matching instrument to assess physical and social competencies of persons in reference to the performance demands of a particular job or work environment: 26 physical demands 11 temperant requirements	Related to short-term tenure factors. Provides Goodness-of-fit index (GOFI) between physical/social skills and job's performance demands
GATB *General Aptitude Test Battery*	Hunter (1983)[1] (USA)	Aptitude-matching across a wide range of jobs. Cognitive, perceptual, psychomotor components Predictor of five job families (USES study): Prepare/adjust machines Originate/interpret Manage/problem/solve Examine/ collect/calculate Copy/compare Feed/remove materials from machines	USES study: analysis of 515 validity studies of the GATB for jobs coded in the DOT (Dictionary of Occupational Titles)
FIS *Function Information System*	Tappel (1991) (The Netherlands)	Aptitude-matching instrument. 38 factors matched according to demands and capabilities.	Instrument developed by the Dutch Joint Medical Service
NATB *Non-reading Aptitude Test Battery*	Russell (1989)[1] (USA)	Aptitude-matching instrument for non-reading population. Six tests identic to GATB plus two adapted for this group.	Use mainly for Mental Retardation Cultural-free
PCC *Program Capacity Checklist*	Boles *et al.* (1987)[2] (USA)	Socio-ecological factors reflecting three psychosocial climate dimensions: (i) relationships; (ii) personal development; (iii) system maintenance. 9 factors enhance job tenure 7 factors impair job tenure	Related to long-term job tenure factors.
TAP *Talent Assessment Program*	Nighswonger, (1980)[4] (USA)	Similar to APTICOM with lower requirements	
4. Work performance			
OFAS *Occupational Functioning Assessment Scale*	Beiser *et al.* (1994) (USA)	Global scale for assessing work performance (quantitative and qualitative aspects). 95-point scale: "1": works $<50\%$ of time, "81": full-time job. Adjusted for job complexity (± 10) and job quality (± 4).	Complexity assessed through the Blixen index (Canadian normed scale of occupational prestige) Interrater reliability studied in schizophrenia (ICC: 0.95) (Beiser, 1994)
WPP *Work Personality Profile*	Bolton & Roessler (1986)[5] (USA)	Dimensional scale for assessing work performance five dimensions: Task orientation Social skills Work motivation Work conformance (e.g. to norms at work) Personal presentation	Used in several studies of work performance and occupational aspects of schizophrenia. Internal consistency (alpha coef.), factor analysis, and interrater reliability (intraclass correlation coef.) reported in schizophrenic patients (Lysaker, 1993).

Table 3 (*cont.*)

Name	Reference	Characteristics	Comments
5. Other vocational instruments			
BHI *Battery for Health Improvement*	*Disorbio & Brans* (1988)[3] (USA)	Measures interaction between psychological factors, physical symptoms and work-related illness or injury	Computer administered format
MoRiNi Test	Joint Medical Service (The Netherlands) Tappel (1991)	Psychological screening instrument, to establish motivation, direction, and level of possible future occupation	
VARS *Vocational Adaptation Rating Scale*	Malgady *et al.* (1980)[4] (USA)	Assesses six areas of maladaptative behavior that may interfere with vocational success	
VDMI *Vocational Decision Making Interview*	Czerlinsky (1986)[3] (USA)	63-item verbal questionnaire aimed at providing empirical information regarding the vocational decision-making capabilities in several dimensions	Identifies problem areas and suggests training strategies. Norm-referenced.
6. Comprehensive systems			
EEO *Enhancing Employment Outcomes Guide*	Calkins & Walker (1989) (USA)	Comprehensive system for vocational assessment, two levels: *Person–environment fit* (*level* 1): *EEO match scale (see EEO-MS); *EEO intervention strategies profile; *Program–environment fit:* *Program-capacity check-list	It includes a User's Guide and Resource Manual to Habilitation Planning for Enhanced Employment-Related Outcomes, in order to attain effective adjustment to competitive employment settings. It may be used for quality assurance.
Remploy	Rialland (1991) (UK)	Comprehensive system for vocational assessment, five dimensions: Achievements tests (accreditation prior to learning) Aptitude tests (areas such as clerical or computer functions) Diagnostic tests	
7. Audit and program assessment			
DSS *Decision Support System*	Boles *et al.* (1989) (USA)	Comprehensive model for automated assessment of vocational programs according to three parameters: Self-sufficiency: program economic feasibility Cost-effectivenes: public investment efficiency Consumer benefit: exploitation measure. Wages paid to workers divided by the commercial revenue	Organization of hardware, software, and operating procedures that provide relevant information to groups of decision-makers.

[1] Quoted in Russell (1989); [2] quoted in Schalock, (1989); [3] quoted in Wesoleck & McFarlane (1991); [4] quoted in Menchetti & Flynn (1989); [5] quoted in Lysaker *et al.* (1993).

development of this field. Virtual reality systems are able to simulate thousands of workstations and many more work tasks requiring cognitive and motor functions similar to real jobs (Wesoleck & McFarlane, 1991). Furthermore, computer-assisted work may induce major changes in the integration of schizophrenic patients to the labor force. Home-based computer-oriented employment is a feasible alternative for disabled persons. On the other hand, these jobs may increase the social isolation of the subject and employers may be reluctant to hire people without previous supervision.

Leisure is becoming an important area for rehabilitation. Leisure programs, assessment, and the costs related to these activities may develop a growing number of studies in the coming years.

ACKNOWLEDGMENTS

This work was supported by Grant Biomed/Fondo de Investigationes Sanitarias (FIS) Grant 94/112.

REFERENCES

Agram, M. (1986). Observational reporting of work behavior. In F.R. Rusch, ed., *Competitive Employment Issues and Strategies*, pp. 141–152. London: Paul H. Brookes.

Angell, R.H., Cheng, K., Duncan, E. *et al.* (1992). Guidelines for the mental health and chemical dependency treatments under the Oregon Health Plan. 6th Draft, American Psychiatric Association, 8-24-1992.

Anthony, W.A. (1994). Characteristics of people with psychiatric disabilities that are predictive of entry into the rehabilitation process and successful employment. *Psychosocial Rehabilitation Journal*, **17**, 3–13.

Anthony, W.A., and Blanch, A. (1987). Supported employment for persons who are psychiatrically disabled: An historical and conceptual perspective. *Psychosocial Rehabilitation Journal*, **11**, 5–21.

Attkisson, C., Cook, J., Karno, M., *et al.* (1992). Clinical services research. *Schizophrenia Bulletin*, **18**, 561–626.

Bacon, A. & Crimmins, D.B. (1989). Enhancing functional social capabilities. In W.E. Kiernan and R.L. Schalock, eds, *Economics, Industry and Disability*, pp. 17–26. Baltimore, MD: Paul H. Brookes.

Beiser, M., Bean, G., Erickson, D., Zhang, J., Iacono, W.G, and Rector, N.A. (1994). Biological and psychosocial predictors of job performance following a first episode of psychosis. *American Journal of Psychiatry*, **151**, 857–863.

Bluestone, B. (1989). Employment prospects for persons with disabilities. In W.E. Kiernan and R.L. Schalock, eds, *Economics, Industry and Disability*, pp. 17–26. Baltimore, MD: Paul H. Brookes.

Boevink, W.A. (1993). Working apart together: Vocational rehabilitation and mental health care. Presentation at the 4th Congress of the World Association for Psychosocial Rehabilitation, Dublin, Ireland, 26–29 September.

Boles, S.M., Wald, B.A., and Xiajoan, Y. (1989). Designing decision support systems. In W.E. Kiernan and R.L. Schalock, eds, *Economics, Industry and Disability*, pp. 265–274. Baltimore, MD: Paul H. Brookes.

Bowen, L., Wallace, C.J., Glynn, S.M., Neuchterlein, K.H., Lutzker, J.R., and Kuehnel, T.G. (1994): Schizophrenic individual's cognitive functioning and performance in interpersonal interactions and skills training procedures. *Journal of Psychiatric Research*, **3**, 289–301.

Calkins, F. & Walker, H.M. (1989). Enhancing employment outcomes through habilitation planning for social competence. In W.E. Kiernan and R.L. Schalock, eds, *Economics, Industry and Disability*, pp. 153–166. Baltimore, MD: Paul H. Brookes.

Chadsey-Rusch, J. & Rusch, F.R. (1988). Ecology and the workplace. In R. Gaylord-Ross, ed., *Vocational Education for Persons with Special Needs*, pp. 234–256. Mountain-View, CA: Mayfield Publishing.

Cooper, J.E. (1993). Revision and re-development of the ICIDH of the World Health Organization. Working document. Geneva: WHO.

Dauwalder, J.P., and Hoffmann, H. (1992). Ecological vocational rehabilitation. In R.P. Liberman, ed., *Effective Psychiatric Rehabilitation. New Directions for Mental Health Services*, 53. San Francisco: Jossey-Bass.

Floyd, M. (1991). Disability management and assessment. In *Vocational Assessment and Evaluation.* Report of the Seminar of the Vocational Commission, pp. 10–17. Hoensbroeck (The Netherlands): Rehabilitation International.

Goode, D.A. (1989). Quality of life and quality of work life. In W.E. Kiernan and R.L. Schalock (Eds.): *Economics, Industry and Disability*, pp. 333–349. Baltimore, MD: Paul H. Brookes.

Green, M. (1991). UK Government policies concerning vocational assessment and evaluation. In *Vocational Assessment and Evaluation.* Report of the Seminar of the Vocational Commission. Hoensbroeck (The Netherlands): Rehabilitation International.

Johnstone, E.C., and Lang, F.H. (1994). Onset, course and outcome of schizophrenia. *Current Opinion in Psychiatry*, **7**, 56–60.

Judy, B.T. (1989). Job accommodation in the workplace. In W.E. Kiernan and R.L. Schalock, eds, *Economics, Industry and Disability*, pp. 117–140. Baltimore, MD: Paul H. Brookes.

Kiernan, W.E., and Rowland, S. (1989). Factors contributing

to success and failure in the work environment. In W.E. Kiernan and R.L. Schalock, eds, *Economics, Industry and Disability*, pp. 333–349. Baltimore, MD: Paul H. Brookes.

Le Minotaure (1993). The psychosocial and economic impact of social firms: A European perspective. Presentation at the 4th Congress of the World Association for Psychosocial Rehabilitation, Dublin, Ireland, 26–29 September.

Lysaker, P., and Bell, M. (1994). Negative symptoms and vocational impairment in schizophrenia: Repeated measurements of work performance over six months. Presentation at the annual meeting of the American Psychiatric Association, Philadelphia, May 16–20.

Lysaker, P., Bell, M., Milstein, R., Bryson, G., Shestopal, A., and Goulet, J.B. (1993). Work capacity in schizophrenia. *Hospital and Community Psychiatry*. **44** 278–280.

Mank, D.M., and Buckley, J. (1989). Strategies for integrated employment. In W.E. Kiernan and R.L. Schalock, eds, *Economics, Industry and Disability*, pp. 319–335. Baltimore, MD: Paul H. Brookes.

Menchetti, B.M., and Flynn, C.C. (1989). Supported employment: New directions for vocational evaluation. In F.R. Rusch, ed, *Supported Employment*. Champaign, Il: Sycamore Publishing Company.

Miran, M., and Miran, E. (1993). Systematic rebuilding thinking systems in the brain: An innovative treatment for individuals with schizophrenia. Presentation at the 4th Congress of the World Association for Psychosocial Rehabilitation, Dublin, Ireland, 26–29 September.

Morgan, R., and Cheadle, A.J. (1975). Unemployment impedes resettlement. *Social Psychiatry*, **10**, 63–67.

Moos, R.H., and Lemke, S. (1983). Assessing and improving social-ecological settings. In E. Seidman, ed., *Handbook of Social Intervention*, pp. 143–162. London: Sage Publications.

O'Brien, J. (1986). *A Guide to Personal Futures Planning*. Atlanta, GA: Responsive Systems Associates.

Ravid, R., and Menon, S. (1993). Guidelines for disclosure of patient information under the Americans with Disabilities Act. *Hospital and Community Psychiatry*, **44**, 280–281.

Rialland, A. (1991). Job matching within the framework of sheltered employment in the UK. In *Vocational Assessment and Evaluation*. Report of the Seminar of the Vocational Commission. Hoensbroeck (The Netherlands): Rehabilitation International.

Russell, J.S. (1989). Identifying opportunities through the creative use of aptitude tests. In W.E. Kiernan and R.L. Schalock, eds, *Economics, Industry and Disability*, pp. 77–90. Baltimore, MD: Paul H. Brookes.

Seyfried, E. (1991). Vocational assessment and evaluation for persons with psychiatric disabilities. In *Vocational Assessment and Evaluation*. Report of the Seminar of the Vocational Commission, pp. 34–46. Hoensbroeck (The Netherlands): Rehabilitation International.

Schalock, R.L. (1989). Person–environment analysis. In W.E. Kiernan and R.L. Schalock, eds, *Economics, Industry and Disability*, pp. 105–115. Baltimore, MD: Paul H. Brookes.

Susser, M. (1990). Editorial: Disease, illness, sickness; impairment, disability and handicap. *Psychological Medicine*, **20**, 471–473.

Verdugo, M.A., and Jenaro, C. (1993). El empleo con apoyo. Una nueva posibilidad para personas con discapacidad. *Siglo Cero*, **147**, 5–12.

Tappel, B. (1991). Vocational assessment and evaluation in the Netherlands. In *Vocational Assessment and Evaluation*. Report of the Seminar of the Vocational Commission. Hoensbroeck (The Netherlands): Rehabilitation International.

Vilkkumaa, F. (1991). Present situation and new trends concerning vocational assessment and evaluation in Finland. In *Vocational Assessment and Evaluation. Report of the Seminar of the Vocational Commission*, pp. 62–66. Hoensbroeck (The Netherlands): Rehabilitation International.

Waismann, L.C. (1988). Needs and motivational processes in long-term psychiatric patients in an era of community care, PhD thesis, Institute of Psychiatry, University of London.

Wehman, P., and Moon, M.S. (eds) (1988). *Vocational Rehabilitation and Supported Employment*. Baltimore, MD: Paul H. Brookes.

Wesoleck, J.S., and Mcfarlane, F.R. (1991). Current developments in vocational assessment and evaluation in the USA. In: *Vocational Assessment and Evaluation*. Report of the Seminar of the Vocational Commission, pp. 18–32. Hoensbroeck (The Netherlands): Rehabilitation International.

World Health Organization (1980). *International Classification of Impairments, Disabilities and Handicaps*. Geneva: WHO.

World Health Organization (1988). *WHO Psychiatric Disability Assessment Schedule* (*WHO-DAS*). Geneva: WHO.

7

The Economic Significance of Social Factors Influencing the Outcome of Schizophrenia

PAUL BEBBINGTON
Social Psychiatry Section, Institute of Psychiatry, De Crespigny Park, London, UK

INTRODUCTION

While some patients who develop schizophrenia experience a single episode from which they recover completely, they are in a minority—perhaps a quarter of cases in Western industrialized societies (Wing, 1982; Sartorius *et al.*, 1986; Shepherd *et al.*, 1989). Such patients make relatively few demands on service systems. This means that most of the direct and indirect costs associated with schizophrenia are due to the generally long-term nature of the disorder. The direct costs in the UK, for example, with its population of 57 million and its relatively cheap health care system, has been estimated at about £400 million (Davis & Drummond, 1990). This puts it on a par with depressive illness as one of the great consumers of mental health resources (cf. West, 1992; Kind & Sørensen, 1993; Jönsson & Bebbington, 1994).

The course can vary considerably, depending on the interplay of positive and negative symptoms (Wing, 1982; Shepherd *et al.*, 1989). Positive symptoms comprise odd experiences and beliefs: hallucinations of various types, distorted experiences of thought processes; and delusions. When these dominate the clinical picture they may be associated with behavior that is difficult to contain and often leads to admission to hospital. Indeed, the reemergence of positive symptoms defines the very idea of the acute episode. When patients with schizophrenia are described as vulnerable, this usually implies that they experience a frequent recrudescence of positive symptoms.

Such symptoms usually get better quickly, and typically respond well to neuroleptic medication. However, in perhaps 7% of cases, positive symptoms persist, resulting in a continuing disability even when the sufferer's behavior does not require the supportive environment of a psychiatric hospital. Disability from persistent positive symptoms arises essentially from their capacity to interfere with effective everyday activity. Thus, some patients experience continuing distress at levels that make it difficult for them to carry out sequential tasks in a constructive way, while others, less distressed, are equally distracted by the intrusiveness of their experiences.

Although it is relatively rare for people with schizophrenia to have persistent positive symptoms, this group contributes appreciably to overall disability and suffering, and consequently to overall costs. They usually receive large amounts of medication and may require high-cost interventions, such as

Handbook of Mental Health Economics and Health Policy, Volume I, Schizophrenia. Edited by M. Moscarelli, A. Rupp and N. Sartorius.
© 1996 John Wiley & Sons Ltd.

admission to hospital. Whether positive symptoms are persistent or intermittent, they represent one clear-cut indicator of overall prognosis and thus of potential costs.

Negative symptoms tend to be behavioral deficits. They include lack of energy, drive and initiative, loss of interest, poor concentration and attention, social withdrawal and emotional unresponsiveness, and impaired social and daily living skills. Claims that such symptoms can be ameliorated by medication are relatively unconvincing. While most authorities regard them as the result of the schizophrenic process, there is argument about the degree to which they are reversible (Crow, 1989; Wing, 1989). What is not in doubt is their contribution to the overall disability experienced by sufferers. They are responsible for a huge shortfall in self-fulfillment, and in some cases lead to sufferers being completely unable to look after themselves. Approaching 10%, or even 15%, of cases may end up totally disabled in this way, requiring heavily supported accommodation and constant monitoring.

While the propensity to develop positive symptoms effectively defines vulnerability and the persistence of negative symptoms is largely responsible for disability, the course and outcome of schizophrenia in the individual case is often the result of both.

Moreover, the level of symptomatology is rarely constant for long. While at a clinical level, it is sometimes difficult to account for fluctuations in mental state and performance, I shall argue in this chapter that an appreciable amount of this fluctuation derives from variations in the social environment, which therefore have implications for the cost of care and are potentially open to effective social management.

The costs of care have a particular resonance in Britain at present because of new policies towards the organization and objectives of the National Health Service. The "White Paper," *Working for Patients* (HMSO, 1989), required District Health Authorities to buy care according to need, to buy quality care, and to get value for money. This implies a trade-off between quality and cost; in particular that standards of care must be stipulated, and its effects evaluated. Although clinicians sometimes cavil at this approach, it embodies the central ethical principle of economic evaluation: that resources ought not to be consumed in a given activity if they would generate greater benefit elsewhere. In order to pursue this utilitarian objective, we do need to consider both benefits and costs, and the key concept is *opportunity cost*. It is only because economic evaluation considers both costs and benefits, that it can appraise opportunity costs: more cost here equals less benefit there (McGuire & Drummond, 1993).

Setting standards of care is the responsibility of a *purchasing authority*. However, the *Community Care Act* (1990) stipulated that patients, including those with schizophrenia, should have individual treatment plans. This is in line with what I have said about the extremely variable needs of people with schizophrenia. It also emphasizes that purchasing authorities will have considerable difficulty in setting general standards of care, and in deciding what a good service should look like.

Matheson and her colleagues (1993) have recently argued that in the short-term it is impossible to establish what constitutes quality care, and that purchasers should limit themselves to setting standards of service delivery. This has the advantage of feasibility. However, while it is certainly true that care cannot be good when delivery is poor, good delivery does not guarantee good care unless appropriate levels of clinical expertise are available.

THE SOCIAL REACTIVITY OF SCHIZOPHRENIA

These days it is so well accepted that the course of schizophrenia is influenced by social circumstances that it is hard to reconstruct the genuinely felt scepticism of psychiatrists in the 1950s and 1960s. This scepticism was gradually eroded by a series of writings and investigations dating from that time. First came descriptive reconceptualizations of the behavior of people with schizophrenia accommodated in the large mental institutions of the time, notably Barton's (1959) *Institutional Neurosis* and Goffman's (1960) *Asylums*. These made explicit the view that the social milieu had a major effect on the presence of the negative symptoms of schizophrenia. They were followed by important empirical studies, particularly the series of investigations carried out by

John Wing and his colleagues during the 1960s, in which the poverty of the institutional environment was measured and correlated with the limited range of behavior shown by residents with schizophrenia (Wing & Brown, 1970).

About the same time, or a little later, researchers turned their attention to the relationship between the social environment and the positive symptoms of schizophrenia. The two major areas of interest were the influence of the family environment and the impact of psychosocial stress in the form of life events. The first of these is covered in this volume by Julian Leff (Chapter 21). Life event research in schizophrenia is now long on history, if short on detail and firm conclusions. A further area, examined extensively with reference to depressive disorders, is that of social networks, but in schizophrenia this is fraught with difficulties for the researcher because of the problem of interpreting the direction of causation (Cohen & Sokolovsky, 1978; Henderson, 1980; Cresswell *et al.*, 1992).

In this chapter, I shall review the impact of the social environment on negative symptoms and of life events on positive symptoms, and attempt to set out the cost implications of the variations in course brought about by these factors.

MEASUREMENT AND THE SOCIAL ENVIRONMENT

To the first researchers, the difficulties of measuring something as nebulous as environment must have seemed awesome. As in all such cases, progress came about by simplifying and subdividing the problem. Thus, the degree to which activity was encouraged was assessed by establishing a time budget for each patient. The Ward Restrictiveness Scale was used to measure both the encouragement of activity and the complementary aspect of restraint on activity by rules and regulations (Wing & Brown, 1970). It assessed things like whether bathing was restricted and supervised, whether patients were kept waiting at the end of meals, whether they could visit hospital entertainments at will, whether they had access to all their own clothing, and whether there was an overuse of locked internal and external doors. The scale has very high face validity: a reading of the items in this scale makes clear its potential for tapping the atmosphere of the ward environment.

MEASURING LIFE EVENTS

One way of studying the influence of life events on the development of disorder like schizophrenia is to identify, within a population at moderate risk, a subgroup who experience a single change in their circumstances. This strategy was cleverly exploited by Steinberg and Durrell (1968). They took as their key event recruitment into the army, and then plotted the frequency of schizophrenic breakdown. This was significantly greater in the few months immediately after recruitment than later in the career of their military sample.

However, this strategy is ultimately rather limited, as individuals experience a whole range of events, and these must be taken into account if the general relation between events and disorder is to be established. This means that, for the purpose of analysis, there must be a method of equating the potential effects of events of superficially different character and implication. While the word *event* appears to denote a change in *external* circumstances, the concept is much more complicated because impact is determined by the interaction of circumstances with the individual's prior experiences, aspirations, and value systems. Individual responses are unique. While we cannot be party to all the information we would need to predict a given response exactly, this does not mean that prediction is useless. The more we know, the more often we will be right about the actual subjectively reported reaction.

It might seem most appropriate to rate the impact of events by eliciting a description of the subject's response from them. However, in seeking to assess the relationship between events and disorders, we must allow for the fact that one of the contributors to the subjective response may, to an unknowable degree, be the changes in event-signification brought about by the disorder itself. Clearly, this would run the risk of incorrectly identifying the causal direction. Further problems with the face value of subjective reports of responses to events arise from the fact that lay people are quite likely to share the researcher's hypothesis that events may have been important in provoking their disorder. They may consequently overvalue the events they have experienced in an attempt to give their illness meaning.

There have been two major approaches to overcoming the difficulties associated with self-evaluations of events. The first involved the a priori definition of events by listing them in an *inventory* (Holmes & Rahe, 1967). Subjects are presented, verbally or visually, with a list of possible events and asked to endorse those they have experienced in a given period. This provides an event history simply and cheaply. However, the method is inevitably limited in the amount of detail in which potential events can be described—they are usually covered by a short phrase. In consequence, the descriptions are vague and can be applied to a range of different occurrences. Moreover, the decision about what should count as one of the events is usually left to the respondent, leading to intra-category variability (Dohrenwend *et al.*, 1993).

The events in the list are of different types and likely to differ in impact. The authors of this approach deal with differential impact by using a *rating sample* to ascribe impact scores to each category. These are then averaged to give a definitive rating for the event. The effect is to divorce the event score from any detailed consideration of individual circumstances, which means that the score predicts actual responses rather poorly.

Event inventories have been used in research in schizophrenia. However, many studies rely on an alternative technique, which in my view offers considerable advantages. This is based around a semistructured interview, the Life Events and Difficulties Schedule (LEDS; Brown, 1974; Brown & Harris, 1978), although some authors have adapted it to their own purposes (e.g. Ambelas, 1979, 1987; Kennedy *et al.*, 1983; Al Khani *et al.*, 1986). In the course of the interview, potential life events are identified. The interviewer then presents these in the form of a vignette to a panel of raters, who ascribe an overall severity rating. As the interviewer provides a considerable amount of context, the individual circumstance of the event can be taken into account, in a way that is infeasible using the inventory method. The subject's actual response is not relayed to the raters, so that they must predict the likely response from the relatively objective contextual information they have been given. Recently, Dohrenwend and colleagues (1993) have developed a similar approach in their SEPRATE procedure, in which interviewers collect event descriptions from subjects, but only after they have been endorsed on an inventory provided to the responders. The context of the event is deduced from sociodemographic data.

Once it has been decided to distinguish between events by rating them, appropriate dimensions for the rating must be identified. The original procedure of Holmes and Rahe (1967) involved ratings based on the amount of socioenvironmental *change* implicit in the event. Later researchers came to favor *stress* (Mueller *et al.*, 1977; Tennant & Andrews, 1978), but this was based on its predictive capacity in affective disturbance. It has become traditional to assess events in terms of their threat, and this has been true of most studies of psychosis. However, it is possible that in non-affective conditions the degree of change may be equally relevant; Orrell and Bebbington (1995) have recently shown that, in comparison to threat ratings, change scores are more predictive of deterioration and admission in elderly people with dementia. It is not possible to resolve this issue in the case of schizophrenia as the necessary comparisons have never been made.

Another type of rating relates to the problem of causal direction. The first requirement for inferring cause, that the putative cause preceded the effect, is difficult to meet with certainty in the case of disorders like schizophrenia whose onset may be hard to define. A number of attempts have been made to circumvent this problem: Brown and colleagues, for instance, have developed a rating of *independence*, reflecting the extent to which events are independent of illness-related behavior on the part of the subject (Brown & Harris, 1978). The rating has become increasingly complicated over the years since it was introduced. However, virtually all the schizophrenia research that has used the LEDS has depended on a threefold division of events into *independent, possibly independent,* and *dependent*.

Independent events are essentially those that are logically extremely unlikely to have been brought about by impending breakdown, for instance a traffic accident involving a relative in a distant town. In the possibly independent category, it is not possible to *rule out* that events were the result of changed behavior, but there are no grounds at all for thinking so. Most researchers present data in terms either of the independent category or of the independent and possibly independent categories.

Three main research designs have been used to study the relationship between life events and onset or relapse of schizophrenia. The first two of these are often combined. The retrospective within-patient design involves the comparison of life events in the period immediately before the onset of illness with a more distant period. This is often combined with the classic retrospective case–control design, in which the life event experiences of the cases prior to onset is compared with equivalent period in a normal controls, almost invariably the period immediately preceding interviews. There are appreciable methodological difficulties with each of these designs, and these have been discussed at length elsewhere (Day, 1981, 1989; Brown & Harris, 1989; Creed, 1990; Hirsch *et al.*, 1993; Bebbington *et al.*, 1995). They almost certainly contribute to the inconsistencies in the research findings. Other problems with the case–control design include the difficulty in deciding what the appropriate control group should be, and the possibility that, in any case, people with schizophrenia may be more sensitive to the effect of events of even trivial importance.

The life event hypotheses can also be investigated using a prospective design, that is, prospective in the sense that the life event history is established before the episode of recurrence. Patients are interviewed at regular intervals, at which time the current symptom status and the life events occurring during the interval are evaluated. The researcher thus establishes a continuous series of periods in which life events or exacerbations or both may have occurred. The experience of life events in the period immediately preceding that in which an exacerbation occurred can be compared with periods unrelated to an exacerbation, either in the same subject or in others. In order to follow this design effectively, it is necessary to assess patients quite frequently. Moreover, the intervals between assessments should be constant rather than determined (as it has been in some investigations) by the rhythm of clinic visiting. The disadvantage of the prospective design is that it requires that patients have already suffered a first episode of disorder. Thus, it informs only on the potential causes of *relapse*, rather than of onset.

SOCIAL FACTORS AND THE OUTCOME OF SCHIZOPHRENIA

Evidence for a significant environmental influence on the negative symptoms of schizophrenia has long been established. This is of particular significance, as it is accepted that such symptoms are relatively resistant to modification by psychopharmacological means (Crow, 1989). Belknap (1956), Barton (1959), Dunham and Weinberg (1960), and, perhaps most famously, Goffman (1961) argued strongly that large and environmentally impoverished mental institutions had a damaging effect on long-term inmates. To them, the association between the environment and the impaired social behavior of the residents was quite obvious.

These authors did not consider that individuals handicapped by the chronic effects of severe psychiatric illness could be contributing to their own environment. However, the work of Wing and Freudenberg (1961) made this clear. They arranged for nurses to provide extra social stimulation for patients with long-standing schizophrenia. The patients slowly improved, but when the stimulation was withdrawn they deteriorated again. This strongly suggests that improvement in these patients was dependent on the continuous provision of stimulation from an external source. This is an example of a general rehabilitation principle, the passive exercise of function.

The results of this experiment led Wing and his colleagues to mount a further study (Wing & Brown, 1970). Three area mental hospitals were selected on the basis that they appeared to provide different environments for the patients they housed. A sample of female residents with long-standing schizophrenia was studied in each hospital. Measures of the social environment provided by the hospitals indicated that they did in fact differ in terms of the range of patients' personal possessions, the attitudes of the nurses towards them, the amount of contact with the community outside, the restrictiveness of ward regimes, and the amount of time the patients spent doing nothing. The results confirmed that these

Table 1. Studies of independent life events in schizophrenic illness

Study	Country	Period/method	Patient sample	n	Significant results for time period: 3–5 weeks	Significant results for time period: >3/12
Retrospective						
Brown and Birley (1968)	UK	12/52	Broad group: 30% 1st onset	50	Yes, for 3 weeks	Not addressed
Jacobs and Myers (1976)	UK	1 year: not LEDS	Narrow definition: all 1st onset	62	Not addressed	NS
Malzacher *et al.* (1981)	Germany	6/12	1st onset	90	Not addressed	NS
Canton and Fraccon (1985)	Italy	6/12: not LEDS	24 1st onset	54	Not addressed	Possible support
Chung *et al.* (1986)	USA	6/12	Narrow definition: some 1st onset	15	NS	NS
Al Khani *et al.* (1986)	Saudi Arabia	1 year	Narrow definition: recent onset	48	Small subgroups only	NS
Day *et al.* (1987) WHO	10 centers worldwide	12/52	Broad definition: some 1st onset	13–67	Yes for 5 of 6 analyzed fully	Not addressed
Dohrenwend *et al.* (1987)	USA	6/12: not LEDS	21 1st onset	66	NS	Yes, for "non-fateful" events
Gureje and Adewumni (1988)	Nigeria	6/12: not LEDS	All 1st onset: RDC definition	42	NS	NS
Bebbington *et al.* (1993)	UK	6/12	Narrow definition	52	Not addressed	Yes, for up to 6 months
Prospective						
Leff *et al.* (1973)	UK	Clinical trial	9 on medication relapsed	116	For medicated only (5 weeks)	NS
Hardesty *et al.* (1985)	USA	1 year	2–3 years in remission	36	NS (morbidity 3/52 post LE)	Not addressed
Ventura *et al.* (1989)	USA	1 year on medication (see 1992*)	Recent onset: 11/30 relapsers		Yes for 4 weeks	NS
Malla *et al.* (1990)	Canada	1 year	7 relapsed	22	Not addressed	NS unless trivial events included
Ventura *et al.* (1992)	USA	1 year of medication status (see 1989*)	Recent onset: off medication	13	NS for those off medication	NS
Hirsch *et al.* (1995)	UK	1 year on/off medication status	Narrow. Relapses: off medication 21/35; on medication 5/36	71	NS for both on and off medication groups	Yes, for up to 1 year

Recent onset: illness history <2 years.
Adapted from Bebbington *et al.*, 1994.

characteristics were associated with equivalent clinical differences between the patient samples; in particular, an impoverished and restricted ward environment was associated with prominent negative symptoms.

This cross-sectional association does not guarantee causal direction, but the three groups were followed up over an 8 year period. Intervening improvements in the social environment were associated with impovements in the patients, and this was independent of medication policies. Although negative symptoms rarely disappeared entirely, the degree of improvement was clinically significant. These effects of the social environment have now been confirmed by other studies located outside large institutions (Tidmarsh & Wood, 1972; Hewitt *et al.*, 1975). As a result there is little doubt that, while social disablement in schizophrenia to some extent represents an intrinsic part of the disease process, it should respond considerably to enlightened clinical intervention.

Although the Three Hospitals Study is a classic of careful investigation and had a major impact on the management of long-term mental illness, no attempt to replicate it was made until very recently (Curson *et al.*, 1992). These authors examined the relationship between social and clinical poverty in long-stay patients with schizophrenia at a fourth British hospital. The patients were less than 60 years of age and had been resident for over 2 years. All had a DSM-III diagnosis of schizophrenia. Assessments were made with the same instruments as in the Wing and Brown (1970) study. Levels of disability seemed comparable in the two studies.

In the earlier study, the time the patients spent doing nothing was a particularly important predictor of negative symptoms. Despite the fact that the nurse–patient ratio was two and a half times greater, the patients spent almost 2 hours *more* doing nothing in the later study than in the least stimulating of the three hospitals in the original investigation. Overall, there was a relationship between environmental understimulation and negative symptoms, but the relationship was much weaker than that obtained by Wing and Brown (1970). However, this may reflect a constriction in the variability of the environment rather than unsatisfactory replication: the patients in this study were very much a residual group. Interestingly, the authors also found that there was a relationship between an impoverished social environment and *florid* symptoms.

We must now turn to more direct evidence for an influence of the social environment on the positive symptoms of this disorder. There have been about 16 studies specifically examining the effect of life events on the onset or course of schizophrenia. The first of these is still something of a landmark (Brown & Birley, 1968). The authors used careful methods in a retrospective case–control and within-patient design, and found a significantly raised rate of life events restricted to the 3 week period before onset/relapse. It was felt that this involved triggering an episode that would have happened soon anyway (Brown *et al.*, 1973).

The subsequent studies, listed in Table 1, offer at best inconsistent support for these initial results. Not all found an effect of life events; those that did tended to identify the month or so before admission as the key period.

One of the largest studies was the WHO multicentre collaboration, which used a retrospective within-patient comparison (Day *et al.*, 1987). This gave a pattern of results similar to that of Brown and Birley in five of six centers. Ventura and his colleagues (1989) similarly found support for the triggering hypothesis. Other studies, based on widely varying methods, have found significant increases in independent events over longer periods, up to 6 months or even a year preceding relapse or illness onset (Dohrenwend *et al.*, 1987; Bebbington *et al.*, 1993; Hirsch *et al.*, submitted 1995). Yet others failed to detect a significant excess of independent life events in pre-relapse periods of varying lengths (e.g. Jacobs & Myers, 1976; Malzacher *et al.*, 1981; Chung *et al.*, Gureje & Adewumni, 1988; Malla *et al.*, 1990). A study from Saudi Arabia (Al Khani *et al.*, 1986) obtained no overall effect, but did find a significant difference for a married female subgroup. Other studies have found elevation of life event rates preceding illness onset, but methodological problems limits the weight that can be placed on them.

Prospective life event studies of schizophrenia are increasing in number and avoid some of the methodological problems affecting retrospective studies. However, so far, they too have offered inconsistent support for the triggering hypohesis. Michaux and colleagues (1967) published an early and unsophisticated study in which they gave a life events scale monthly to schizophrenic patients, and were able to show an increase in stress in the month preceding that in which hospitalization occurred. In contrast, Hardesty and colleagues (1985) followed up patients who had been well for 2 or 3 years in the community, but found no increase in morbidity in the 3 weeks following major independent events. However, the study was limited by the small numbers of cases and of major independent events. Two subsequent prospective studies have found no increase in independent major events in the 4 weeks preceding relapse (Hirsch *et al.*, 1993; Malla *et al.*, 1990), and another found a significant excess of events preceding illness, but only in patients on regular neuroleptic medication (Ventura *et al.*, 1989, 1992).

The study of Malla and his colleagues (1990) involved the follow-up of 21 patients over 1 year in an aftercare programme. The PERI life event schedule (Dohrenwend *et al.*, 1978) was administered. In addition, daily hassles were recorded ("minor events"). At weekly or fortnightly intervals, events were rated by a blind rater for whether they arose independently of the patient's symptoms. Relapse was essentially defined as the reemergence of positive psychotic symptoms. There tended to be more events, both major and minor, in the 3 month period before relapse compared with any *other* 3 month periods in relapsing patients, or with *any* 3 month periods in those who did not relapse. However, only in the latter comparison was the trend significant, and then only when events and hassles were taken together. This study is greatly hampered by small numbers, but is at least consistent with the possibility that events tend to peak before onset.

Three recent studies have used different designs to test the relationship between life events and schizophrenic relapse, and are worth describing at somewhat greater length.

The authors of the Camberwell Collaborative Psychosis Study collected a range of biological and social data on a large sample of people suffering from psychosis (Bebbington *et al.*, 1993). Fifty-one subjects with schizophrenia had experienced a datable relapse during the previous year. Life event histories for the 6 month antecedent period were obtained using the LEDS (Brown & Harris, 1978). Community controls provided equivalent histories.

Figure 1 displays results from this study relating to these patients. While the significant excess of events was most notable in the 3 months immediately before relapse, the rate was elevated throughout the period of assessment. The most likely reason for the excess is that events were causally related to relapse, particularly as the findings stood even when based solely on independent events. However, the cases could have experienced more events for other reasons, for instance, because of life-style differences. It is of interest that the elevated rates were not restricted to the more severe events, suggesting that even minor events may have an unsettling effect on people with schizophrenia.

The second recent study is also British (Hirsch *et al.*, 1995?). It follows a prospective design, and so far only it, and the investigation of Ventura *et al.* (1992), have incorporated this design with an examination of the effects of medication. Of 71 patients fulfilling DSM-IIIR criteria for schizophrenia, half were receiving regular neuroleptic medication. A subsample of the cohort were randomized to medication and placebo groups on a double-blind basis. Morbidity and life event evaluations were made every 2 months, and the sample was followed for a year in total. Life events were elicited and rated using the LEDS.

Twenty-one of the patients without medication relapsed, compared with only five of the medicated group. The experience of life events in those who relapsed was not significantly different from their experience in earlier 4 week periods. However, proportional hazards regression analysis suggested a significant association between relapse and the cumulative experience of events over the whole period of assessment. The authors calculated that the reduction of the event rate from mean levels to zero would only reduce the relapse rate by 8%.

Dohrenwend *et al.* (1993) have recently provided results from the New York Risk Factor Study. Part of this involved a comparison of 65 people with recent onsets or relapses of non-affective psychosis with over 400 general population controls, using the SEPRATE procedure for establishing a life event history. The results do suggest that relapse is related to antecedent events, but the relationship was neither large nor significant at conventional levels. It was greatest for non-fateful, negative events (odds ratio 3.4, $p < 0.1$).

If the life event findings described above are taken

on their own, the lack of consistency in the findings would justify the conclusion that social factors are relatively unimportant in relapse in schizophrenia. However, they must be considered in the context of the large and robust effect implied by predictive studies using the Expressed Emotion measure (Leff, Chapter 21, this volume; Bebbington & Kuipers, 1994a). If adverse family relationships have such a marked effect, why is the impact of life events so unconvincing? One possibility is that it is the *persistence* of stress that accounts for the powerful effect of family difficulties. Another, perhaps more likely, is that the threshold for recognizing life events salient for schizophrenia is too high. This may stem from the fact that most of our ideas about levels of stress associated with disorder were derived from the large amount of research on depressive disorder. It is also possible that events even with minor degrees of threat have an influence in schizophrenia because some other dimension is more relevant. There is initial evidence that in dementia changes in routine and environment have more impact than the degree of threat (Orrell & Bebbington, 1995), and this might also be the case in schizophrenia. The potential of events associated with only minor degrees of threat to unsettle people with schizophrenia certainly ties in with clinical experience.

There is a suggestion that psychotic disorders preceded by life events have a more benign course. This is implicit in the Scandinavian concept of *reactive psychosis* (Strömgren, 1985; Cooper, 1986). Earlier prospective studies linking the experience of events before onset with better outcome have had serious methodological defects, particularly in the assessment of events (Vaillant, 1964; Strauss & Carpenter, 1974; Prudo & Blum, 1987).

The Camberwell Collaborative Psychosis Study described above included follow-up after 4 years (van Os *et al.*, 1994). Outcome measures included cross-sectional assessments with, among others, the Global Assessment of Functioning-Symptomatology, the Global Assessment of Functioning-Disability (WHO, 1992), and the Iager Negative Symptom Rating Scale (Iager, 1985). For longitudinal evaluation we used a modification of the *life chart* instrument from the Multi-centre Study on the Course and Outcome of Schizophrenia (WHO, 1992). Multiple sources of information were used. Altogether 59 patients with psychosis and available life event data were followed up successfully. Twenty-nine of these had experienced severe life events before the initial episode. This group was very similar to those without antecedent life events in terms of premorbid adjustment, age of first contact and current age, and the number of prior admissions.

The event-positive subjects generally had better outcome in terms of positive symptoms, spent less time on neuroleptics and more time on antidepressants. However, there was a marked effect of diagnosis. While in the non-schizophrenic groups event-related disorders clearly had better outcome on a number of measures, the differences between the schizophrenic groups were relatively few. Individuals whose index episode of schizophrenia was event-related had received less antipsychotic medication during the follow-up interval but had experienced more compulsory admissions. It is possible that this reflects a tendency towards a more dramatically episodic course in the event-positive group. This in turn probably indicates the social reactivity of these disorders rather than a pathoplastic effect of life events.

THE EFFECTIVENESS, COST-EFFECTIVENESS, AND COST–BENEFIT OF SOCIAL TREATMENTS

There are considerable problems in applying these concepts, both to the treatment of schizophrenia in general and to treatments involving the manipulation of social circumstances. The problems are both conceptual and empirical. The difficulty with the idea of effectiveness is that it is patently a value judgement. In many cases, patients, informal carers, and clinicians will agree on the value of the outcome. Thus, in the case of physical disorders, most people would agree that the relief of distressing pain is worthwhile. Likewise, most would agree that the relief of psychic pain occasioned by unpleasant hallucinations or frightening beliefs is of uncontestable value.

These examples make clear that the concept of effectiveness has very close parallels with that of *need* (Brewin & Wing, 1993). Effectiveness can be defined as the meeting of need. The conceptual problems are correspondingly related. Thus, in some instances, the views of people with schizophrenia about the added value from treatment may differ from those of people caring for them or treating them. For example, a young man with high levels of social anxiety and a tendency towards withdrawal may feel that he would be happiest staying in his room, with only his physical needs being met by relatives. Both his family and the clinical staff involved in his care are likely to feel that this arrangement would not be ideal. The sufferer is regarded as not knowing what is "best" for him. Whose view should be used to define effectiveness?

However, the situation is helped by the fact that, like others, people with schizophrenia change their opinions. In particular, as a result of first-hand experience they change their views about the effects of therapeutic management. Before mental health services are relocated in community facilities, a majority of service users oppose the move, but once the change has occurred, relatively few would consider returning to their old accommodation and facilities.

In general, it is easier to identify as effective changes that involve improvements in social behavior rather than reductions in distress. Another type of good outcome more easily acknowledged than substantiated is the *maintenance* of function, that is the prevention or delay of the deterioration sometimes associated with schizophrenia.

It is probably reasonable to conclude that effectiveness, like need, is best left as an *expert-defined* measure, although in the late twentieth century, it is appropriate to allow the definitions to be colored by the views of service users. This is particularly so because benefits like the relief of distress shade into concepts like satisfaction.

Cost-effectiveness is a type of economic analysis which relates a monetary cost to an outcome identified and measured in non-monetary terms. It requires comparison between the costs of two different methods of achieving an outcome. This looks seductively simple for drug treatments, although less so than at first appears (Jönsson & Bebbington, 1994). It becomes very difficult where treatments are social: the style of service delivery inevitably becomes intertwined with specific expertise in a way that is difficult to tease out.

When outcomes are measured in monetary terms, the evaluation is referred to as cost–benefit analysis. There have been very few of these in psychiatry because of the sheer difficulty of attributing monetary value to many aspects of outcome. The difficulties are compounded by the fact that attributes which in some contexts would be regarded as costs, for instance inpatient treatment, may sometimes be invoked as outcomes, for example, the reduced need for admission.

The social management of schizophrenia comprises a body of knowledge that has been built up both formally and informally. Most of the empirical research on what can broadly be called social interactions has concerned models of service delivery, rather than the evaluation of specific techniques of intervention (e.g. Stein & Test, 1980; Test & Stein, 1980; Muijen *et al.*, 1992), and indeed it is sometimes difficult to work out exactly what the clinicians do within such services. The interventions involving families are a notable exception (Leff, Chapter 21), and techniques of social skills training have also been the subject of appreciable research (Shepherd, 1986; Liberman *et al.*, 1987). Most of the knowledge we have about managing long-standing schizophrenia comes, however, from the efforts of diligent, open-minded clinicians trying out a range of interventions and evaluating the results in individual patients. This has been facilitated by the central principles of long-term management, namely the identification and negotiation of specific goals for treatment, the selection of actions to bring these about, and the regular assessment of results, leading to the recognition of further goals. The consequence is a medley of techniques that all sound sensible but in most cases have not been subject to general empirical evaluation (Bebbington & Kuipers, 1994b; Kuipers & Bebbington, 1994). Indeed this would be difficult in routine clinical practice, as the application of the techniques implies tailor-made treatments.

The social techniques of particular interest to us in this chapter concern the management of negative symptoms and the prevention of the adverse effects of life events. There are a number of ways of creating environments in which negative symptoms are minimized, all devised with the empirical work on the clinical poverty syndrome in mind. They include dealing with social withdrawal by using the key worker relationship to engage patients in activities that foster social contact; encouraging adequate self-care by training specific skills and motivating patients to use them; engineering situations to counteract lack of motivation and self-esteem; encouraging the use of community facilities; and the provision of structure to bring order to lives that have become empty or chaotic (Bebbington & Kuipers, 1994b). These techniques seek to specify an intervention for each separate type of negative symptom. It can be seen from this that while cost-effectiveness and cost–utility analysis (McGuire & Drummond, 1993) might be feasible, cost–benefit analysis would be very difficult and very costly.

As might be expected from the unsatisfactory nature of the research on life events in schizophrenia, no one has so far evaluated the effectiveness of techniques for minimizing the effects of events, or of stress in general. Again there are a number of possibilities that have found their way into imaginative clinical practice. These include the provision of emotional and practical support in the face of stressful situations; planning responses in anticipation of likely stresses; assisting with a problem-solving approach to dealing with the consequences of stress; and modification of medication regimens during periods of stress. In particular, clinicians can protect clients from unnecessary changes by providing genuine continuity of care; this requires a high-morale multidisciplinary team so that staff turnover is quite slow (Bebbington & Kuipers, 1994b).

Because the failure to protect patients from stress is likely to increase the frequency of acute relapse, it might be easier to identify at least some of the cost – benefits of intervention. Thus, Hirsch and his colleagues (1993) have implied that perfect protection from life event stress might reduce the relapse rate by 8%. This result is based on a study that, in the light of the literature overall, may underestimate the effects of events, and good social management of the type described above might reduce relapse by 20%. As nearly three-quarters of all treatment costs for schizophrenia are hospital costs, the potential cost–benefit is considerable. It depends on the additional work of providing the monitoring, practical assistance, and counseling needed to reduce the event-related relapse rate. This in turn depends on the extent to which adequate community-based continuing care is in place. Where such services are already well-developed, the cost of minimizing the impact of events is marginal. Where services are institution-based, the deployment of the necessary techniques is much more difficult. However, the requirement for community-based services is grounded on much wider arguments (Matheson *et al.*, 1993).

CONCLUSIONS

In this chapter, I have summarized evidence that the social environment has a considerable impact on the course of schizophrenia and the quality of life of sufferers. Many current techniques of management are concerned with controlling these social factors. These etiological and management issues must necessarily figure in a competent evaluation of costs and benefits. No work has been done in this area, indeed many of the techniques are the result of wise clinical insights rather than empirical evaluations. This inevitably causes problems for the development of a rational and equitable mental health service. Until empirical evaluations become available, these must still be based on the best clinical opinion, bolstered, it is to be hoped, by rational argument rather than special pleading.

REFERENCES

Al Khani, M.A.F., Bebbington, P.E., Watson, J., and House, F. (1986). Life events and schizophrenia: A Saudi Arabian study. *British Journal of Psychiatry*, **148**, 12–22.

Ambelas, A. (1979). Psychologically stressful events in the precipitation of manic episodes. *British Journal of Psychiatry*, **135**, 15–21.

Ambelas, A. (1987). Life events and mania: A special relationship? *British Journal of Psychatry*, **150**, 235–240.

Barton, R. (1959) *Institutional Neurosis*. Bristol. Wright.

Bebbington, P.E., Wilkins, S., Jones, P., *et al.* (1993). Life events and psychosis: Initial results from the Camberwell Collaborative Psychosis study. *British Journal of Psychiatry*, **162**, 72–79.

Bebbington, P.E., Bowen, J., and Ramana, R. (1995). Life events and psychotic disorders. In T.W. Miller, ed., *Stressful Life Events*, pp. 89–118. Madison, Ct: International University Press Inc.

Bebbington, P.E., and Knipers, L. (1994a). The predictive utility of expressed emotion in schizophrenia: an aggregrate analysis. *Psychological Medicine*, **24**, 707–718.

Bebbington, P.E., and Kuipers, L. (1994b). The social management of long-standing schizophrenia: I The deployment of clinical techniques *Clinician*, **12**, 17–29.

Belknap, I. (1956). *Human Problems of a State Mental Hospital*, New York: McGraw-Hill.

Brewin, C.R., and Wing, J.K. (1993). The needs for care assessment: progress and controversies. *Psychological Medicine*, **23**, 837–841.

Brown, G.W. (1974). Meaning, measurement and stress of life events. In B.S. Dohrenwend and B.P. Dohrenwend, eds, *Stressful Life Events: Their Nature and Effects*, pp. 217–243. New York: John Wiley.

Brown, G.W., and Birley, J.L.T. (1968). Crises and life changes and the onset of schizophrenia. *Journal of Health and Social Behaviour*, **9**, 203–214.

Brown, G.W., and Harris, T.O. (1978). *Social Origins of Depression: A Study of Psychiatric Disorder in Women.* London: Tavistock.

Brown, G.W., and Harris, T. (1989). *Life Events and Illness.* London: Unwin Hyman.

Brown, G.W., Harris, T.O., and Peto, J. (1973). Life events and psychiatric disorders. Part 2: Nature of causal link. *Psychological Medicine*, **3**, 159–176.

Canton, G., and Fraccon, I.G. (1985). Life events and schizophrenia: a replication. *Acta psychiatrica Scandinavica*, **71**, 211–216.

Chung, R.K., Langeluddecke, P., and Tennant, C. (1986). Threatening life events in the onset of schizophrenia, schizophreniform psychosis and hypomania. *British Journal of Psychiatry*, **148**, 680–686.

Cohen, C., and Sokolovsky, J. (1978). Schizophrenia and social networks. *Schizophrenia Bulletin*, **4**, 546–560.

Cooper, B. (1986). Mental disorder as a reaction: the history of a psychiatric concept. In H. Katchnig, ed., *Life Events and Psychiatric Disorder*, pp. 1–32. Cambridge: Cambridge University Press.

Creed, F. (1990). Life events and disorder. *Current Opinion in Psychiatry*, **3**, 259–263.

Cresswell, C.M., Kuipers, L., and Power, M.J. (1992). Social networks and support in long-term psychiatric patients. *Psychological Medicine*, **22**, 1019–1026.

Crow, T.J. (1989). A current view of the Type II syndrome: age of onset, intellectual impairment and the meaning of structural changes in the brain. *British Journal of Psychiatry*, **155** (Suppl. 7), 10–14.

Curson, D.A., Pantelis, C., Ward, J., and Barnes, T.R.E. (1992). Institutionalism and schizophrenia 30 years on. Clinical poverty and the social environment in three British mental hospitals in 1960 compared with a fourth in 1990. *British Journal of Psychiatry*, **160**, 230–241.

Davies, L.M., and Drummond, M.F. (1990). The economic burden of schizophrenia. *Psychiatric Bulletin*, **14**, 522–525.

Day, R. (1981). Life events and schizophrenia: the triggering hypothesis. *Acta Psychiatrica Scandinavica*, **64**, 97–122.

Day, R. (1989). Schizophrenia. In G.W. Brown, and T.O. Harris, eds, *Life Events and Illness.* London: Unwin Hyman.

Day, R., Neilsen, J.A., Korten, A., *et al.* (1987). Stressful life events preceding the acute onset of schizophrenia: a cross-national study from the World Health Organization. *Culture, Medicine and Psychiatry*, **11**, 123–206.

Dohrenwend, B.S., Krasnoff, L., Askenasy, A.R., and Dohrenwend, B.P. (1978). Exemplification of a method for scaling life events: the PERI life events scale. *Journal of Health and Social Behaviour*, **19**, 205–229.

Dohrenwend, B.P., Levav, I., Shrout, P.E. *et al.* (1987) Life stress and psychopathology: progress and research begun with Barbara Snell Dohrenwend. *American Journal of Community Psychology*, **15**, 677–713.

Dohrenwend, B.P., Stueve, A., Skodol, A.E., and Link, B. (1993). Life events vulnerability and schizophrenia episodes: A case–control study. Paper presented at WPA Section of Epidemiology and Community Psychiatry Symposium, Groningen, Netherlands. Sept 1–3.

Dunham, H.W., and Weinberg, S.K. (1960). *Culture of the State Mental Hospital.* Detroit: Wayne State University Press.

Goffman, E. (1961). *Asylums.* New York: Anchor Books.

Gureje, O., and Adewumni, A. (1988). Life events in schizophrenia in Nigerians. A controlled investigation. *British Journal of Psychiatry*, **153**, 367–375.

Hardesty, J., Falloon, I.R.H., and Shirin, K. (1985). The impact of life events, stress and coping on the morbidity of schizophrenia. In I.R. Falloon, ed., *Family Management of Schizophrenia: A Study of Clinical, Family and Economic Benefits.* Baltimore: Johns Hopkins University Press.

Henderson, S. (1980). Personal networks and the schizophrenias. Australian and New Zealand *Journal of Psychiatry*, **14**, 255–259.

Her Majesty's Stationery Office. (1989). *Working for Patients.* London: HMSO.

Hewitt, S., Ryan, P., and Wing, J.K. (1975). Living without the mental hospitals. *Journal of Social Policy*, **4**, 391–404.

Hirsch, S.R.H., Bowen, J., Emami, J., *et al.* (1995). A one year prospective study of the effect of life events and medication in the aetiology of schizophrenia relapse (submitted 1995).

Holmes, T.H., and Rahe, R.H. (1967). The Social Readjustment Rating Scale. *Journal of Psychosomatic Research*, **11**, 213–218.

Iager, A.C., Kirch, D.G., and Wyatt, R.J. (1985). A negative symptom rating scale. *Psychiatry Research*, **16**, 27–36.

Jacobs, S., and Myers, J. (1976). Recent life events and acute schizophrenic psychosis: A controlled study. *Journal of Nervous and Mental Disease*, **162**, 75–87.

Jönsson, B., and Bebbington, P.E. (1994). What price depression? The cost of depression and the cost-effectiveness of pharmacological treatment. *British Journal of Psychiatry*, **164**, 665–673.

Kennedy, S., Thompson, R., Stancer, H.C., Roy, A., and

Persad, E. (1983). Life events precipitating mania. *British Journal of Psychiatry*, **142**, 398–403.

Kind, P., and Sørensen, J. (1993). The costs of depression. *International Clinical Psychopharmacology*, **7**, 191–195.

Kuipers, L., and Bebbington, P.E. (1994). The social management of long-standing schizophrenia: III: social–psychological techniques for helping patients and carers. *Clinician*, **12**, 30–38.

Leff, J.P., Hirsh, S., Gaind, R., Rohde, P., and Stevens, B, (1973). Life events and maintenance therapy in schizophrenic relapse. *British Journal of Psychiatry*, **123**, 659–660.

Liberman, R.P., Jacobs, H.E., Boone, S.E., *et al.* (1987). Skills training for the community adaptation of schizophrenics. In: J.S. Strauss, W. Boeker, and H.D. Brenner, eds, *Psychosocial Treatment of Schizophrenia*. Toronto: Huber.

Malla, A.K., Cortese, L., Shaw, T.S., and Ginsberg, B. (1990). Life events and relapse in schizophrenia: a one year prospective study. *Social Psychiatry and Psychiatric Epidemiology*, **25**, 221–224.

Malzacher, M., Merz, J., and Ebnother, D. (1981). Einschneidende Lebensereignisse im Vorfeld akuter schizophrener Episoden: Erstmals erkrankte Patienten im Vergleich mit einer Normalstichprobe. *Archiv für Psychiatrie und Nervenkrankheiten*, **230**, 227–242.

Matheson, L.A., Cook, H.M., Mckenna, P.J., and Bosanquet, N. (1993). *Purchasing Care for Patients with Schizophrenia. Health Policy Unit Review Paper No. 5*. Cambridge: Daniels.

McGuire, A., and Drummond, M. (1993). Economic evaluation in health care: an introduction for psychiatrists. *Social Psychiatry and Psychiatric Epidemiology*, **28**, 211–217.

Michaux, W., Gansereit, K., McCabe, O., and Kurland, A. (1967). The psychopathology and measurement of environmental stress. *Community Mental Health Journal*, **3**, 358–371.

Mueller, D.P., Edwards, D.W., and Yarvis, R.M. (1977). Stressful life events and psychiatric symptomatology: change or undesirability. *Journal of Health and Social Behaviour*, **18**, 307–317.

Muijen, M., Marks, I.M., Connolly, J., Audini, B., and McNamee, G. (1992). The Daily Living Programme. Preliminary comparison of community versus hospital-based treatment for the seriously mentally ill facing emergency admission. *British Journal of Psychiatry*, **160**, 379–384.

Orrell, M., and Bebbington, P.E. (1995). Life events and senile dementia 1. Admission, deterioration and social environment change. *Psychological Medicine*, **25**, 373–385.

Prudo, R., and Blum, H.M. (1987). Five-year outcome and prognosis in schizophrenia: a report from the London field research centre of the International Pilot Study of Schizophrenia. *British Journal of Psychiatry*, **150**, 345–354.

Sartorius, N., Jablensky, A., Korten, A., *et al.* (1986). Early manifestations and first contact incidence of schizophrenia in different cultures. *Psychological Medicine*, **16**, 909–928.

Shepherd, G. (1986). Social skills training and schizophrenia. In C. Holin and P. Trower, eds, *Handbook of Social Skills Training*, Vol. 2. Oxford: Pergamon Press.

Shepherd, M., Watt, D., Falloon, I.R.H., and Smeeton, N. (1989). The natural history of schizophrenia: A five-year follow-up study of outcome and prediction in a representative sample of schizophrenics. *Psychological Medicine. 19 Monograph supplement*, **15**, 1–16.

Stein, L., and Test, M. (1980). Alternatives to mental hospitals. I. conceptual model, treatment program and clinical evaluation. *Archives of General Psychiatry*, **37**, 392–397.

Steinberg, H., and Durrell, J. (1968). A stressful situation as a precipitant of schizophrenic symptoms: An epidemiological study. *British Journal of Psychiatry*, **114**, 1097–1105.

Strauss, J., and Carpenter, W.T. (1974). The prediction of outcome in schizophrenia. II Relationships between predictor and outcome variables. *Archives of General Psychiatry*, **31**, 37–42.

Strömgren, E. (1985). World-wide issues in psychiatric diagnosis and classification and the Scandinavian point of view. In *Mental Disorders, Alcohol and Drug Related Problems*. Amsterdam: Excerpta Medica.

Tennant, C., and Andrews, G. (1978). The pathogenic quality of life event stress in neurotic impairment. *Archives of General Psychiatry*, **35**, 859–863.

Test, M., and Stein, L. (1980). Alternatives to mental hospitals III. social cost. *Archives of General Psychiatry*, **37**, 409–412.

Tidmarsh, D., and Wood, S. (1972). Psychiatric aspects of destitution. In J.K. Wing and A.M. Hailey, eds, *Evaluating a Community Psychiatric Service*. London: Oxford University Press.

Vaillant, G.E. (1964). Prospective prediction of schizophrenic remission. *Archives of General Psychiatry*, **11**, 509–518.

van Os, J., Fahy, T.A., Bebbington, P.E., *et al.* (1994). The influence of life events on the subsequent course of psychotic illness. *Psychological Medicine*, **24**, 503–513.

Ventura, J., Nuechterlein, K.H., Lukoff, D., and Hardesty, J.P. (1989). A prospective study of stressful life events and schizophrenic relapse. *Journal of Abnormal Psychology*, **98**, 407–440.

Ventura, J., Neuchterlein, K.H., Hardesty, J.P., and Gitlin, M. (1992). Life events and schizophrenic relapse after medication withdrawal: a prospective study. *British Journal of Psychiatry*, **161**, 615–620.

West, R. (1992). *Depression*. London: Office of Health Economics.

Wing, J.K. (1982). Prognosis and outcome of schizophrenia. In J.K. Wing and L. Wing, eds, *Handbook of Psychiatry III: Treatment and Management*. London: Cambridge

University Press.

Wing, J.K. (1989). The concept of negative symptoms. *British Journal of Psychiatry*, **155** (Suppl. 7), 10–14.

Wing, J.K., and Brown, G.W. (1970). *Institutionalism and Schizophrenia. A Comparative Study of Three Mental Hospitals* 1960–68. Cambridge: Cambridge University Press.

Wing, J.K., and Freudenberg, R.K. (1961). The response of severely ill chronic schizophrenic patients to social stimulation. *American Journal of Psychiatry*, **118**, 311–322.

World Health Organization (1992). *International Classification of Disease. Chapter V. Mental and Behavioural Disorders*. Geneva: WHO.

8

Longitudinal Course and Outcome of Schizophrenia

WAYNE S. FENTON
Chestnut Lodge Research Institute and Psychiatry and Behavioral Sciences, George Washington University School of Medicine, Rockville, Maryland, USA

In the absence of knowledge concerning etiology, longitudinal illness course and outcome are frequently used to define and validate psychiatric disorders (Robins & Guze, 1970). As originally described by Emil Kraepelin, dementia praecox was a disorder characterized by a rapidly deteriorating course leading to lifelong disability (Kraepelin, 1919). Beginning with Kraepelin's conception, the longitudinal course of schizophrenia has been extensively studied, and course and outcome have been used over time to modify diagnostic concepts in the direction of more sharply delineating schizophrenia as an illness with a distinct natural history. Despite these efforts, available data indicate that, however defined, schizophrenia is a disorder showing considerable variability in age and type of onset, signs and symptoms, course of illness, long-term disability, and outcome (Fenton *et al.*, 1981; McGlashan, 1988).

It is not unlikely that the variability in clinical presentation and long-term outcome in schizophrenia reflects the possibility that the disorder is a clinical syndrome with multiple underlying etiologies (Tsuang *et al.*, 1990; Carpenter *et al.*, 1993). At the level of the individual patient, the cost of schizophrenia can be expected to vary widely based on the nature and severity of the individual patient's illness course. The costs of schizophrenia accrue in the context of the natural history of what is often a lifelong disorder that evolves, perhaps along predictable trajectories, over time.

This chapter provides a selective overview of schizophrenia as a clinical entity with a focus on the assessment of outcome and prediction of longitudinal course. Findings from the Chestnut Lodge Follow-up Study and Schizophrenia Subtype Study bearing on the prediction of course in schizophrenia will be particularly emphasized.

ORGANIZING ASSUMPTIONS

Three widely held assumptions about schizophrenia are of value in organizing data concerning the clinical course and outcome of the disorder. These include: (i) the vulnerability–stress model; (ii) the phasic nature and progression of schizophrenia; and (iii) the heterogeneity of schizophrenia and individuals who suffer from it.

Handbook of Mental Health Economics and Health Policy, Volume I, Schizophrenia. Edited by M. Moscarelli, A. Rupp and N. Sartorius.
© 1996 John Wiley & Sons Ltd.

VULNERABILITY–STRESS MODEL

Although the cause of schizophrenia is unknown, a number of facts concerning the illness's prevalence, risk factors, treatment response, and course have been established with varying degrees of certainty (Wyatt *et al.*, 1988). The vulnerability–stress model likely represents the best integration of available data concerning the developmental precursors, clinical onset, and longitudinal evolution of the disorder. This model views clinical schizophrenia as occurring in individuals with enduring biologically based vulnerabilities, and views the onset and recurrence of symptomatic periods as a product of the interaction between these vulnerabilities and environmental stressors (Meehl, 1962, 1990; Zubin & Steinhaur, 1981).

The vulnerability to schizophrenia is thought of as a set of stable traits that are likely present prior to illness onset and persist during both acute episodes and remissions. Hypothesized biomedical determinants of vulnerability include genetic predisposition, intrauterine, birth or postnatal neurologic trauma, and viral infections of the central nervous system (Falloon, 1992). At a psychophysiological level, deficits in information processing, attention, and sensor inhibition have been studied as potential vulnerability indicators (Nuechterlain *et al.*, 1992; Braff, 1993). At a psychologic and behavioral level vulnerability may be reflected by impairments in social competence, a tendency towards cognitive disorganization or perceptual distortion, a diminished capacity to experience pleasure or reinforcement, and other general coping deficiencies (Meehl, 1962, 1990). Such traits, particularly when severe, may be responsible for impaired social, academic, and vocational functioning among some vulnerable individuals prior to the onset of symptoms that lead to the diagnosis of schizophrenia. These premorbid disabilities will often impose a functional ceiling on outcome once the illness is established.

The "stress" side of the vulnerability–stress model views a variety of environmental stressors as capable of triggering the emergence or recurrence of symptoms in vulnerable indivduals. Research supports an association between stressful life events, cultural milieu (egocentric versus sociocentric), social class, social network size and density, and the emotional quality of the living environment with the onset and course of schizophrenia (McGlashan, 1986a, Wyatt *et al*, 1988; Lin & Kleinman, 1988; Norman & Malla, 1993a,b). Clinical experience indicates that the specific stressors associated with illness exacerbation are often highly individualized, rendering generalizations, and hence research in this area, difficult. Stressors may be biochemical (as in substance abuse), developmental (e.g., leaving home for college), social (dating, family or work tensions), or environmental (loss of housing, unemployment, poverty).

Within the vulnerability–stress paradigm, learned patient coping strategies, a supportive social network, psychosocial treatment interventions, and antipsychotic medications may act as protective factors mitigating the impact of stress on symptom formation or exacerbation (Nuechterlein *et al.*, 1992).

PHASIC NATURAL HISTORY OF ILLNESS

From a longitudinal perspective, the natural history of schizophrenia can be thought of as consisting of sequential phases. These include: (i) the premorbid period, during which the influence of risk factors and vulnerability indicators on development may be detectable; (ii) a prodromal period of varying lengths in which subclinical signs and symptoms that precede manifest illness and signal impending decompensation are evident; (iii) an early illness onset epoch that includes the onset of positive symptoms, deficit symptoms, and functional disabilities that lead to the diagnosis of schizophrenia; (iv) a middle illness epoch in which symptomatic periods may be episodic so that exacerbations and remissions can be identified, or continuous without identifiable remissions, and during which functional deficits may accrue in severity; (v) a late course epoch, in which illness pattern may be established, disability levels stabilized, or late improvements manifest. Available data suggest that this epoch, in which relatively enduring levels of outcome can be discerned, is established for many patients between 5 and 10 years after illness onset (McGlashan, 1988; Carpenter & Kirkpatrick, 1988; Carpenter & Strauss, 1991).

Although the division of schizophrenia into illness phases provides a useful framework for assessing course and outcome, it should be evident that this delineation is more a researcher's construction than a clinician's reality. Sharp distinctions across phases are rarely possible in individual cases where, for example, premorbid vulnerabilities may blend imperceptibly into illness onset, or the plateauing of disabilities during the late course epoch may only be discernible in the light of hindsight years later.

HETEROGENEITY

Because both schizophrenia and the individuals afflicted with it are heterogeneous, a "typical" illness course and outcome cannot be defined.

Heterogeneity extends across all phases and epochs of schizophrenia. While many vulnerabilities underlying schizophrenia have been hypothesized, none have been shown to be present in all instances. Similarly, although patients with schizophrenia as a group often demonstrate poorer premorbid social, academic, or work functioning than control groups with other psychiatric disorders, substantial interindividual differences are the rule. Many clinical series include highly accomplished individuals with schizophrenia whose histories reveal adequate or superior premorbid adjustment.

The peak age of illness onset for schizophrenia in men is between the ages 18 and 25, with a later (26–45) and broader peak for women (Wyatt *et al.*, 1988; DeLisi, 1992). Childhood or early adolescent onset, and late-life onset schizophrenia, however, are not uncommon (Krausz & Muller-Thomsen, 1993; Castle & Murray, 1993). Onset may be acute, over a period of days or weeks, or insidious, over a period of years.

Substantial interindividual variability in both prodromal and active symptoms is evident. Emerging evidence suggests that the clinical symptoms of schizophrenia cluster into three major groups: (i) delusions and hallucinations; (ii) thought disorder and bizarre behavior; and (iii) deficit or negative symptoms including blunted affect, poverty of speech, anhedonia, asociality, loss of motivation, and loss of a sense of purpose (Liddle, 1987; Arndt *et al.*, 1991; Peralta *et al.*, 1992). Individual patients may demonstrate symptoms from some or all of these clusters, and within individuals the admixture of symptoms may evolve over time.

Heterogeneity in onset, course, and outcome of schizophrenia over a period of decades has been described by Bleuler (1978), Ciompi (1980), Harding (1988), and others. Based on dichotomizing onset as acute or chronic, the middle illness epoch as simple or undulating, and the late illness epoch or end state as mild or severe, Ciompi describes eight prototypic course types. Studies documenting course and outcome over two to four decades have identified patients whose illnesses appeared to correspond to each of these longitudinal trajectories (Harding, 1988).

OUTCOME ASSESSMENT IN SCHIZOPHRENIA

THE FOLLOW-UP STUDY

Given the wide variability in the course and outcome of schizophrenia, it is not surprising that efforts to clarify prognosis and define and predict outcome have been a central theme in research on the disorder. The follow-up study has been the major tool employed in such efforts. In its most rudimentary form, this method involves the identification of a cohort of patients with a given disorder, the characterization of the cohort in terms of potential outcome predictors at the time of identification, and the reexamination of the cohort at a later date to assess outcome and evaluate the strength of predictors. Short-term outcome studies often focus on the efficacy of a particular treatment, while long-term follow-ups reflect illness natural history and aim to clarify diagnosis and prognosis.

Outcome and follow-up studies of schizophrenia likely number in the thousands. Zubin reviewed over 800 performed before 1961 (Zubin *et al.*, 1961) and Stephens reviewed those he considered most important in 1978 (Stephens, 1978). While this vast literature cannot be exhaustively reviewed here, several broad trends can be identified: (i) between studies, wide variation in the outcome of schizophrenia was reported; (ii) overall, the outcome of schizophrenia seemed to conform to a rule of thirds, with one-third of patients achieving significant and lasting improvement, one-third some improvement with intermittent relapses, and one-third permanent incapacity; (iii) the diagnosis of schizophrenia varied widely in different settings, and this had a large impact on observed outcome. Patient samples assembled with broad diagnostic concepts based on cross-sectional signs and symptoms are most heterogeneous in outcome; narrow diagnostic concepts that require evidence of established chronicity as a part of the diagnosis define groups that are less heterogenous in outcome; (iv) generally more and less severe forms of schizophrenia could be identified. The former were often termed chronic, process, nuclear, unremitting schizophrenia, while terms describing the latter included acute, reactive, atypical, schizophreniform, schizoaffective, cycloid psychosis, and others (Stephens, 1978); (v) benign forms of schizophrenia were generally characterized by clinical features that included acute onset, precipitating stress, confusion or depression during the acute episode, a family history of depression, and an extroverted rather than schizoid premorbid personality (Kant, 1941; Chase & Silverman, 1941; Valliant, 1964a,b); (vi) in keeping with Kraepelin's original conceptions, recovery was often taken as evidence of initial misdiagnosis, and many investigators defined good outcome cases as a separate entity leading over time to a narrowing of the definition of schizophrenia (Fenton *et al.*, 1981; Angst, 1988).

A CONCEPTUAL ADVANCE IN UNDERSTANDING OUTCOME

Early follow-up studies used differing and often unspecified definitions of schizophrenia, and global and poorly defined outcome categories (e.g. recovered, unchanged). As a result, cross-study comparisons and the integration of data concerning the outcome of schizophrenia were severely hampered. The introduction of operational diagnostic criteria in the 1970s improved the likelihood that investigators in different settings were studying comparable patients. During this same period, an important follow-up study conducted by Strauss and Carpenter incorporated methodologic elements that allowed a significant conceptual advance in the understanding and prediction of outcome in schizophrenia.

Strauss and Carpenter described the outcome of 85 schizophrenic patients from the Washington, DC Center of the International Pilot Study of Schizophrenia (Strauss & Carpenter, 1972, 1974, 1977). A 14-item prognostic scale including items from earlier studies that could be rated reliably was administered to patients at an index admission. In addition, an outcome scale rating patient functioning in four discrete areas: hospitalization, social functioning, work functioning, and symptom severity was developed. Reproduced here (Table 1), this scale provided concrete anchors that allowed reliable and reproducible rating of outcome. The largely acute or subacute patient cohort was followed up 2 and 5 years after an index admission and the nature and predictors of outcome studied.

Results of this study indicated that major outcome functions or domains were partially independent of each other—for example, some patients remained symptomatic, but were capable of work and maintained social relations. Furthermore, results indicated that for employment and social outcome, pre-illness functioning in each domain was the best predictor in the respective post-illness outcome domain. Thus, poor premorbid social functioning was the best predictor of poor social functioning at outcome, while pre-illness unemployment was the best predictor of work disability at follow-up. In this context, the findings supported the view that simple global outcome ratings such as good or poor inadequately represented the complexity of outcome. Instead, the data suggested that outcome could best be conceptualized as a set of semi-independent domains or open-linked systems that have continuity over time. At both 2 and 5 years, simply summing scores of pre-admission functioning in the domains of hospitalization, work, and social functioning was the most effective means of predicting overall clinical outcome (Strauss & Carpenter, 1974, 1977).

Strauss and Carpenter's follow-up studies led to the recognition that outcome in schizophrenia consists of multiple domains, and that rating scales to reliably measure functioning in these and other domains could be developed. Along with the application of reliable diagnostic criteria, the use of multidimensional and reliable outcome measures has become a minimum methodologic requirement for follow-up and outcome studies in schizophrenia (McGlashan *et al.*, 1988).

ADDITIONAL DOMAINS OF OUTCOME IN SCHIZOPHRENIA

Although symptom severity, social functioning, work functioning, and hospitalization are the four core

Table 1. Outcome dimensions and anchors used by Strauss and Carpenter

1 *Hospitalization*
Duration of nonhospitalization for psychiatric disorder
0. Hospitalized more than 9 months in past year
1. Hospitalized over 6 months, up to 9 months in past year
2. Hospitalized 3–6 months in past year
3. Hospitalized less than 3 months in past year
4. None in hospital in past year (exclude hospitalization at time of first interview if less than 1 month in duration during following interview

2 *Social functioning*
Include all acquaintances
0. Does not meet with friends at all under any conditions
1. Does not meet with friends except "over the back fence" at work, or at school
Social contacts (do not include meetings with friends at work or "over the back fence.")
2. Meets with friends about once a month
3. Meets with friends two to three times a month
4. Meets with friends on average at least once a week

3 *Employment*
Usefully employed (include work as housewife, student. Exclude time in hospital)
0. No useful work
1. "Employed" less than half of the time in the past year
2. "Employed" part-time or full-time about half of the time in the past year
3. "Employed" more than half year but less than continuously
4. "Employed" continuously

4 *Symptoms*
Absence of symptoms (in past month)
0. Continuous and severe signs and symptoms
1. Severe signs and symptoms some of the time, or moderate signs and symptoms continuously
2. Moderate signs and symptoms some of the time
3. Slight signs and symptoms most of the time, or moderate signs and symptoms on rare occasions
4. No signs or symptoms

From: Strauss & Carpenter: The prediction of outcome in schizophrenia, 1: Characteristics of outcome. *Archives of General Psychiatry* (1972), **27**, 740.

domains of clinical outcome in schizophrenia, a comprehensive assessment of outcome can include variables from a number of additional domains. Among these are: (i) cognitive, attentional, and memory functioning (Goldberg *et al.*, 1993); (ii) quality of life and/or satisfaction (Heinrichs *et al.*, 1984; Lehman, 1988; Becker, *et al.*, 1993); (iii) housing and/or independent living status (Daniels, 1992); (vi) psychopathology in areas outside of schizophrenia *per se*, such as depression (Hamilton, 1960; Beck *et al.*, 1961; Addington *et al.*, 1993) or addictive behavior (McLellan *et al.*, 1980); (v) general physical health status and well-being (Hayes *et al.*, 1993); (vi) the acute (akathisia, parkinsonism) and long-term (tardive dyskinesia) neurologic side-effects of antipsychotic medication (Simpson & Angus, 1970; Guy, 1976; Barnes, 1989); and (vii) excess mortality including that referable to suicide. The selection of outcome domains and measures in any particular investigation should be guided by the specific hypotheses under consideration and assessment time frame.

OUTCOME AND OUTCOME PREDICTION IN CHRONIC SCHIZOPHRENIA: CHESTNUT LODGE FOLLOW-UP STUDY

The patients studied by Strauss and Carpenter were acute or subacute in that those who had been ill for more than 2 years or hospitalized more than 3 years were excluded from the sample. Data from the Chestnut Lodge Follow-up Study allowed an assessment of outcome and potential outcome predictors among a cohort of patients with already established chronic forms of schizophrenia (McGlashan, 1984a,b).

The follow-up sample included all patients discharged from Chestnut Lodge between 1950 and 1975 and a smaller cohort of non-discharged inpatients from a comparable time period. Patients without organic brain syndrome who were between 16 and 55 years of age at admission and who were treated at least 90 days were selected for inclusion. In the original follow-up study, two sources of data were collected: (i) medical records for each patient were summarized into 25 page chart abstracts and from these, a range of demographic, premorbid, sign, symptom, and diagnostic data were rated; and (ii) long-term follow-up data including outcome in multiple domains were independently collected by interviews with subjects an average of 19 years after index admissions. The reliability of all measures used for these assessments, including retrospective diagnosis using modern criteria, have been reported (McGlashan, 1984a).

At index admission, the sample of schizophrenics ($n=187$) included 98 males and 89 females. As a group, they were chronically and severely ill: the average duration of illness for these patients was 7 years and they averaged 3.1 past hospitalizations for a mean of 28 months of prior inpatient treatment. The average patient was born in 1931, first became ill in 1951 at age 20 (range 2–44 years), was first hospitalized in 1954 at age 23 (range 11–50), and experienced an index hospitalization at Chestnut Lodge in 1959 at age 28 (range 16–55). The mean age of patients at follow-up in the early 1980s was 47 (range 24–76).

The results of the follow-up study indicated that on average, the long-term outcome of schizophrenia was poorer across all domains than the outcome observed in other major psychiatric disorders (McGlashan, 1984a). The schizophrenic cohort as a whole were described as symptomatic 80% of the follow-up period, spent 45% of the entire follow-up period hospitalized, worked only 30% of the follow-up period. In addition, they were more likely than other patients to have minimal or no social contacts. At the time of follow-up interview, nearly 50% of schizophrenic patients were living in a hospital, other sheltered setting or with their family of origin. The majority of the remainder (28%) lived alone. Outcome was not, however, uniformly poor, and clearly formed a continuum with patients represented at all levels. Nearly 20% of patients, for example, could be described as fully recovered with no further hospitalizations and minimal or no disability over the follow-up period (Fenton & McGlashan, 1987a). Thirty percent of patients were able to pursue further education, 25% had children, and 18% were living with families they had established at the time of follow-up. For most patients, a varying degree of impairment in one or more domains persisted across decades. While these disablities were chronic in the sense of being enduring, overall outcome did not differ as a function of follow-up duration suggesting that for most patients disability level "plateaued" after the first several years of illness. Forty percent of patients reported suicidal thoughts over the follow-up period, 24% attempted suicide, and 8% died by suicide over the follow-up period.

Schizophrenia appeared to be less severe and less frequently resulted in permanent disability among women compared with men (McGlashan & Bardenstein, 1990). In addition, comorbidity with other disorders was not uncommon, and impacted outcome: comorbid borderline or schizotypal personality disorder was associated with a more favorable outcome (McGlashan, 1983, 1986b), while obsessive–compulsive symptomatology was associated with poorer outcome (Fenton & McGlashan, 1986).

Despite the chronicity of the Chestnut Lodge patient sample at index admission, sufficient variability in outcome was observed to generate significant predictor–outcome relationships (McGlashan, 1986c). Although a linkage between premorbid functioning and outcome in specific domains was still discernible, the strength of these associations was attenuated and the specificity of "like predicting like" was diminished. The best predictive model appeared to be one that viewed outcome as the product of the highest level of premorbid work and social functioning achieved prior to illness onset, and the "virulence" of the schizophrenic disorder as manifest by genetic loading (family history of schizophrenia), loss of the capacity for affect (absence of depressed mood), and loss of reality testing (psychotic assaultiveness) (Fenton & McGlashan, 1987b). In general, patients with poor premorbid functioning (which may have represented the developmental impact of the lifelong vulnerability to schizophrenia) were very unlikely to achieve levels of functioning at follow-up that exceeded their level of pre-illness disability. For other patients, a particularly virulent form of schizophrenia appeared to irreversibly erode good premorbid skills. Others with good premorbid functioning and less virulent forms of illness were fully able to maintain their skills and competence after or between acute symptomatic episodes.

SCHIZOPHRENIA SUBTYPES AS PREDICTORS OF COURSE AND OUTCOME

To explore the value of schizophrenia subtypes in defining patient groups with distinctive course and outcome trajectories, index admission subtype diagnoses were obtained for all patients in the follow-up study with a research diagnosis of schizophrenia. As chart abstracts were not sufficiently detailed to allow meaningful subtype ratings, extensive original medical records were used to rate subtype diagnoses and other variables which were assessed blind to both chart abstract and follow-up data collected during the earlier phase of the study (Fenton & McGlashan, 1991a). In addition to rating subtypes at the time of index admission to Chestnut Lodge, sufficiently detailed records from previous hospitalizations were available in the charts of 125 (67%) patients to allow subtype assignment at the time of an earlier (usually first) hospitalization. This admission occurred an average of 4.5 years before index admission.

Using independently collected data from three sources, 26 clinical variables were selected as significant elements of schizophrenia illness natural history. As shown in Table 2, these variables were grouped into eight natural history domains: genetic predisposition, developmental predisposition, premorbid functioning, illness onset features, early illness course, subtype stability, long-term functional outcome, and suicide risk. Patients with differing schizophrenia subtype diagnoses could then be compared across variables in each natural history domain. Both classical (paranoid, hebephrenic, undifferentiated) and newer subtypes based on deficit or negative symptoms were evaluated (Fenton & McGlashan, 1991a,b).

Table 2. Illness natural history domains and variables from Chestnut Lodge Schizophrenia Subtype Study

Domain	Item
1 Predisposition, genetic	Family history of schizophrenia
	Family history of affective disorder
	Family history of hospitalization (any mental disorder)
2 Predisposition, early development	Neonatal trauma
	Childhood behavioral problems
	Asociality in childhood
3 Premorbid functioning	Quantity of social relations
	Marital status
	Quantity of work
	Acquisition of skills and interests
	IQ
4 Illness onset	Age at onset
	Age at first hospitalization
	Age at index admission
	Type of onset
	Distinctiveness of illness
5 Early course	Intermittent versus continuous
	Reactivity to life events
6 Subtype stability	
7 Long-term outcome	Social functioning
	Work functioning
	Symptom severity
	Hospitalization
	Sum global outcome
	Clinical global outcome
	Current living situation
8 Suicide risk	Suicide mortality

CLASSICAL SUBTYPES

Like DSM-III-R, the research diagnoses we employed for classifical schizophrenia subtypes were hierarchical. Hebephrenia was defined as a subtype characterized by disorganized thought, bizarre behavior, and flat or inappropriate affect. Paranoid schizophrenia was characterized by delusions or hallucinations and the absence of symptoms sufficient to meet criteria for hebephrenia. Patients with undifferentiated schizophrenia failed to meet criteria for either specific subtype. Thus, patients with hebephrenia could meet criteria for paranoid schizophrenia, but the converse was not true. Defined in this manner, significant differences in the longitudinal profile of the classical schizophrenia subtypes were discernible. Overall, 78 (42%) were diagnosed with paranoid, 26 (14%) with hebephrenia, and 83 (44%) of patients with undifferentiated schizophrenia.

Paranoid schizophrenia had an older age of onset and often developed rapidly in patients with good premorbid functioning. Early illness course was most often intermittent over the first 5 years, exacerbations and remissions appeared responsive to stresses and life events, and the likelihood of eventual fair to good outcome was nearly 50% despite a relatively high (10%) risk of suicide. Hebephrenia, in contrast, often developed early and insidiously and was associated with poor premorbid functioning and a higher frequency of family history of mental illness. Early illness course was often continuous and remissions, when present, were rarely complete. The illness appeared unreactive to life events and in nearly 90% of cases resulted in permanent disability across all outcome domains. The clinical course of undifferentiated schizophrenia was similar to hebephrenia in terms of early and insidious illness onset and premorbid functioning. Unlike hebephrenia, many patients with undifferentiated schizophrenia had histories of behavioral difficulties in childhood, and in most cases the schizophrenic illness appeared to be a gradual extension of marginal, odd or eccentric premorbid personality functioning. The illness was often continuous with limited remissions, but outcome was variable. Complete recovery was less common than in paranoid schizophrenia, and deterioration and permanent disability was less common than in hebephrenia. Symptomatology was often "quiet" rather than flagrant with a stable degree of disability maintained.

DEFICIT AND NON-DEFICIT SCHIZOPHRENIA SUBTYPES

With the hope of more closely linking the heterogeneity of schizophrenic symptoms with underlying pathophysiologic mechanisms, a variety of methods for subtyping schizophrenia based on positive and negative symptoms have been proposed (Krawiecka *et al.*, 1977; Crow, 1980; Andreasen & Olsen, 1982; Lewine *et al.*, 1983; Kay *et al.*, 1992). A comparison of alternate methods of diagnosing positive and negative subtypes among patients in the Chestnut Lodge sample demonstrated a wide variation in subtype diagnoses depending on what criteria were employed (Fenton & McGlashan, 1992). Among the subtype methods studied, Carpenter's criteria for the deficit syndrome (Carpenter *et al.*, 1988) were unique in their focus on primary enduring negative symptoms. The subtype diagnosis of deficit syndrome requires the enduring presence of two or more negative symptoms (restricted affect, anhedonia, poverty of speech, diminished sense of purpose, and diminished social drive). These symptoms must be judged as primary; that is, not fully accounted for by depression, anxiety, neuroleptic drug effect, or environmental deprivation.

Patients from the Chestnut Lodge cohort were retrospectively rediagnosed as having deficit ($n = 46$) and non-deficit ($n = 141$) forms of schizophrenia and these subtypes were compared across the illness natural history parameters outlined in Table 3. The data revealed that prior to illness onset deficit patients were less likely to be married, but few other differences emerged. Illness onset was often insidious for deficit patients, and once established, the illness was nearly always continuous with few remissions and little reactivity to life events. Negative symptoms were often present at illness onset among deficit patients and increased in severity over the first 5 years of illness. Once established, the deficit syndrome was highly stable, and nearly always associated with poor outcome and permanent disability. The data supported the validity of the deficit concept as a subtype of schizophrenia with a relatively distinct natural history, and perhaps as the subtype most associated with progressive functional impairment (Fenton & McGlashan, 1994).

SUBTYPE OVERLAP AND SUBTYPE PROGRESSION

An analysis of the overlap among the classical and deficit subtype approaches demonstrates partial, but not complete overlap. Among deficit patients,

Table 3. Course type and schizophrenia subtypes in Chestnut Lodge follow-up cohort

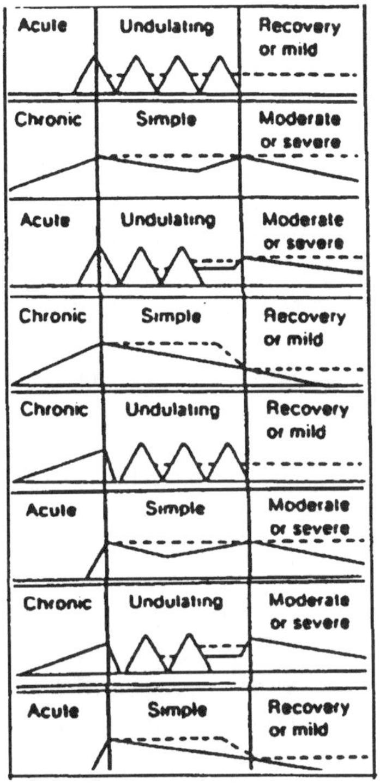

	Onset	Course type	End state	Total sample $n=162$	Classical subtypes: Paranoid ($n=64$)	Hebephrenic ($n=23$)	Undifferentiated ($n=75$)	Deficit subtype: Deficit ($n=41$)	Non-deficit ($n=121$)
1	Acute	Undulating	Recovery or mild	25 (15%)	16 (25%)	—	9 (12%)	1 (2%)	24 (20%)
2	Chronic	Simple	Moderate or severe	41 (25%)	9 (14%)	7 (30%)	25 (33%)	21 (51%)	20 (16%)
3	Acute	Undulating	Moderate or severe	18 (11%)	10 (16%)	3 (13%)	5 (7%)	3 (7%)	15 (12%)
4	Chronic	Simple	Recovery or mild	10 (6%)	5 (8%)	—	5 (7%)	3 (7%)	7 (6%)
5	Chronic	Undulating	Recovery or mild	17 (11%)	6 (9%)	1 (4%)	10 (13%)	2 (5%)	15 (12%)
6	Acute	Simple	Moderate or severe	11 (7%)	6 (9%)	2 (9%)	3 (4%)	4 (10%)	7 (6%)
7	Chronic	Undulating	Moderate or severe	35 (22%)	10 (16%)	9 (39%)	16 (21%)	5 (12%)	30 (25%)
8	Acute	Simple	Recovery or mild	5 (3%)	2 (3%)	1 (4%)	2 (3%)	2 (5%)	3 (3%)

few (9%) are paranoid, many (39%) are hebephrenic and most (52%) are undifferentiated. Conversely, the majority (70%) of hebephrenic, but very few (5%) of paranoid patients meet deficit syndrome criteria.

The availability of subtype diagnoses at both first and index admission separated by approximately 5 years allowed an assessment of subtype progression over the early course of schizophrenia. The classical subtypes were moderately stable between first and index admission: about two-thirds of all patients retained their original subtype diagnosis. When changes occurred, they were in the direction of hebephrenia or undifferentiated subtypes. The deficit syndrome was relatively rare at first admission (10%), but not uncommon (25%) at index admission. Most (10 of 12; 83%) patients with the deficit syndrome at first admission retained this subtype. Thus, when change occurred it was usually in the direction of non-deficit to deficit. Together, the data suggest that for some schizophrenic patients, subtypes evolve over time in the direction of less to more severe (McGlashan & Fenton, 1993). Using Ciompi's graphic representation of longitudinal illness trajectories, the figure in Table 3 visually summarizes the association of schizophrenia subtypes with illness onset, middle course, and outcome.

COMPARISON WITH OTHER STUDIES

Recent North American and European follow-up studies meeting rigorous methodologic standards have been comprehensively reviewed by Angst (1988) and McGlashan (1988), respectively. Although specific rates of recovery and disability differ across studies, much of this variability can be traced by differences in sample characteristics. Significant among these are the diagnostic criteria for schizophrenia employed, patients' degree of chronicity, length of mental illness and institutionalization, exposure and response to neuroleptic medications and/or rehabilitative treatments, and socioeconomic status. Patients in the Vermont Longitudinal Study, for example, were selected on the basis of a positive initial response to medication when neuroleptics were first introduced and 30 hours per week participation in an in-hospital work program (McGlashan, 1988). The Chestnut Lodge sample, in contrast, either did not receive or did not respond to neuroleptic medications, and were selected based on referral to a tertiary care facility. It is not unlikely that these differences in sample characteristics are in part responsible for the greater proportion of patients improving over the long-term in the Vermont sample.

It has been argued that clinicians and follow-up researchers may seriously overestimate the proportion of schizophrenic patients whose illnesses are associated with prolonged disability by falling subject to a "Clinician's Illusion" (Cohen & Cohen, 1984; Harding, 1987)—the statistical process by which patients with the longest duration of illness become substantially overrepresented in a caseload. Because to date, a population-based epidemiologic sample of schizophrenic patients have not been identified and systematically followed over time, specific and widely generalizable outcome rates are not available. Follow-up data from specific hospitals and clinics obviously must be interpreted in light of the specific types of patients referred and treated.

Some data from geographically based case registers may be of value in partially addressing the generalizability of follow-up results. Using case register data from Victoria, Australia; Maryland, USA; Denmark; and Salford, UK, Eaton *et al.* (1992a) estimated that between 50 and 80% of patients were eventually rehospitalized after an initial discharge with a diagnosis of schizophrenia. At the same time, episodes of hospitalization tend to cluster earlier, rather than later suggesting progressive amelioration, rather than deterioration for many patients (Eaton *et al.*, 1992b). A review of follow-up studies of patients treated for a first episode of schizophrenia suggested an overall relapse rate of 60% within the first 2 years of illness onset (Ram *et al.*, 1992). Prospective first episode schizophrenia studies currently underway can be expected to provide further data concerning course progression and disability (Kirch *et al.*, 1992).

ECONOMIC IMPLICATIONS

The enormous economic impact of schizophrenia derives in large measure from the lifelong nature of the disorder and myriad disabilities that may be associated with it. A review of data concerning the longitudinal course and outcome of schizophrenia suggest the following conclusions pertinent to cost assessment:

1 Schizophrenia is heterogeneous in onset, course, outcome, and disability, so that from both a clinical and economic standpoint efforts to define a "typical case" may be futile.

2 Substantial variability in illness cost across individual patients should be anticipated. Data from longitudinal studies suggest that variation in illness severity and/or subtype may be the major source of variance in long-term disabilities and associated costs. Over the long-term, cost variance associated with differences in illness severity may exceed variance attributable to any specific therapeutic intervention or service delivery configuration.

3 The phasic nature of schizophrenia suggests some costs of schizophrenia may be illness stage specific and that the nature of costs may shift over different illness stages. It appears likely, for example, that significant family burden costs accrue during the illness's prodromal phase, that the majority of inpatient hospitalization related costs accrue over the first 5 to 10 years of manifest illness, and that for many patients treatment needs and costs plateau at different levels during the middle to late illness epochs. Economic studies with a longer-term focus may be useful in clarifying these and other relationships between illness course evolution and cost.

4 Despite substantial heterogeneity in course and outcome, robust short- and long-term predictors of outcome have been identified. Over short time periods (6 months to 5 years) premorbid functioning in specific domains are the most powerful predictors of outcome. Thus, for example, the best method for prospectively estimating hospital utilization over a 2 year period would be examination of hospitalization history over the preceding 2 years. Illness severity and subtype may be better predictors of course over a period of decades. The identification of predictors should allow the development of prospective cost models based on severity case mix data.

5 Despite the use of identical operational diagnostic criteria, schizophrenic samples treated in different settings may differ markedly in severity and subtype. To allow for cross-study comparisons and generalization, sample characterization in both clinical and economic outcome investigations should include core predictor and prognostic variables including when possible gender, marital status, premorbid work and social functioning, length of prior hospitalization, medication exposure and response, and schizophrenia subtype. Likewise, patients assigned to differing interventions or service delivery models in studies that focus on clinical effectiveness and cost should be compared across major prognostic variables to assess the possibility of assignment bias.

REFERENCES

Addington, D., Addington, J., and Maticka-Tyndale, E. (1993). Assessing depression in schizophrenia: The Calgary depression scale. *British Journal of Psychiatry*, **163** (Suppl. 23), 39–44.

Andreasen, N.C., and Olsen, S. (1982). Negative vs. positive schizophrenia: definition and validation. *Archives of General Psychiatry*, **39**, 789–794.

Angst, Jules (1988). European followup studies of schizophrenia. *Schizophrenia Bulletin*, **14**, 501–513.

Arndt S., Alliger, R.J., and Andreasen, N.C. (1991). The distinction of positive and negative symptoms: the failure of a two-dimensional model. *British Journal of Psychiatry*, **158**, 317–322.

Barnes, T.R.E. (1989). A rating scale for drug-induced akathisia. *British Journal of Psychiatry*, **154**, 672–676.

Beck, A.T., Ward, C.I., Mendelson, M., *et al.* (1961). An inventory for measuring depression. *Archives of General Psychiatry*, **4**, 561–571.

Becker, M., Diamond, R., and Sainfort, F. (1993). A new patient focused index for measuring quality of life in persons with severe and persistent mental illness. *Quality of Life Research*, **2**, 239–251.

Bleuler, M. (1978). *The Schizophrenic Disorders; The Long Term Patient and Family Studies.* Translated by S.M. Clemens. New Haven: Yale University Press.

Braff, D.L. (1993). Information processing and attention dysfunctions in schizophrenia. *Schizophrenia Bulletin*, **19**, 233–259.

Carpenter, W.T., and Kirkpatrick, B. (1988). The heterogeneity of the long-term course of schizophrenia. *Schizophrenia Bulletin*, **14**, 645–652.

Carpenter, W.T., and Strauss, J.S. (1991). The prediction of outcome in schizophrenia IV: Eleven-year follow-up of the Washington IPSS cohort. *The Journal of Nervous and Mental Disease*, **179**, 517–525.

Carpenter, W.T., Heinrichs, D.W., and Wagman, A.M.I. (1988). Deficit and non-deficit forms of schizophrenia: The concept. *American Journal of Psychiatry*, **145**, 578–583.

Carpenter, W.T., Buchanan, R.W., Kirkpatrick, B., Tamminga, C., and Wood, F. (1993). Strong inference, theory testing, and the neuroanatomy of schizophrenia. *Archives of General Psychiatry*, **50**, 825–831.

Castle, D.J., and Murray, R.M. (1993). The epidemiology of late-onset schizophrenia. *Schizophrenia Bulletin*, **19**, 691–700.

Chase, L.S., and Silberman, S. (1941). Prognostic criteria in schizophrenia: A critical survey of the literature. *American Journal of Psychiatry*, **98**, 360–368.

Ciompi, L. (1980). Catamnestic long-term study on the course of life and aging of schizophrenics. *Schizophrenia Bulletin*, **6**, 606–618.

Cohen, P., and Cohen, J. (1984). The clinician's illusion. *Archives of General Psychiatry*, **41**, 1178–1183.

Crow, T.J. (1980). Molecular pathology of schizophrenia: more than one disease process? *British Medical Journal*, **280**, 66–68.

Daniels, L.V. (1992). *Inventory of CSP Instruments.* National Institute of Mental Health's Community Support Program.

DeLisi, L.E. (1992). The significance of age of onset for schizophrenia. *Schizophrenia Bulletin*, **18**, 209–215.

Eaton, W.W. Mortensen, P.B., Herrman, H., *et al.* (1992a). Long-term course of hospitalization for schizophrenia: Part I. Risk for rehospitalization. *Schizophrenia Bulletin*, **18**, 217–228.

Eaton, W.W., Mortensen, P.B., Hermann, H., *et al.* (1992b). Long-term course of hospitalization for schizophrenia: Part II. Change with passage of time. *Schizophrenia Bulletin*, **18**, 229–242.

Falloon, I.R.H. (1992). Psychotherapy of schizophrenia. *British Journal of Hospital Medicine*, **48**, 165–170.

Fenton, W.S., and McGlashan, T.H. (1986). The prognostic significance of obsessive-compulsive symptoms in schizophrenia. *American Journal of Psychiatry*, **143**, 437–441.

Fenton, W.S., and McGlashan, T.H. (1987a). Sustained remission in drug free schizophrenics. *American Journal of Psychiatry*, **144**, 1306–1309.

Fenton, W.S., and McGlashan, T.H. (1987b). Prognostic

scale for chronic schizophrenia. *Schizophrenia Bulletin*, **13**, 277–286.

Fenton, W.S., and McGlashan, T.H. (1991a). Natural history of schizophrenia. I. Longitudinal study of paranoid, hebephrenic, and undifferentiated schizophrenia. *Archives of General Psychiatry*, **48**, 969–977.

Fenton, W.S., and McGlashan, T.H. (1991b). Natural history of schizophrenia. II. Positive and negative symptoms and long-term course. *Archives of General Psychiatry*, **48**, 978–986.

Fenton, W.S., and McGlashan, T.H. (1992). Testing systems for assessment of negative symptoms in schizophrenia. *Archives of General Psychiatry*, **49**, 179–184.

Fenton, W.S., and McGlashan, T.H. (1994). Deficit syndrome in schizophrenia: Antecedents, symptom progression, and long-term outcome. *American Journal of Psychiatry*, **151**(3), 351–356.

Fenton, W.S., Mosher, L.R., and Matthews, S. (1981). Diagnosis of schizophrenia: A critical review of current diagnostic systems. *Schizophrenia Bulletin*, **7**, 452–476.

Goldberg, T.E., Hyde, T.M., Kleinman, J.E., and Weinberger, D.R. (1993). Course of schizophrenia: Neuropsychological evidence of a static encephalopathy. *Schizophrenia Bulletin*, **19**, 798–804.

Guy, W. (ed.) (1976). *ECDEU Assessment Manual for Psychopharmacology*, revised. DHEW Publication No. (ADM) 76–338. Rockville, MD: National Institute of Mental Health.

Hamilton, M. (1960). A rating scale for depression. *Journal of Neurology, Neurosurgery and Psychiatry*, **23**, 56–62.

Harding, C.M. (1988). Course types in schizophrenia: An analysis of European and American studies. *Schizophrenia Bulletin*, **14**, 633–643.

Harding, C.M., Zubin, J., and Strauss, J.S. (1987). 'Chronicity in schizophrenia: Fact, partial fact, or artifact? *Hospital and Community Psychiatry*, **38**, 477–485.

Hays, R.D., Sherbourne, C.D., and Mazel, R.M. (1993). The RAND 36-Item Health Survey 1.0. *Health Economics*, **2**, 217–227.

Heinrichs, D.W., Hanlon, T.E., and Carpenter, W.T. (1984). The quality of life scale: An instrument for rating the schizophrenic deficit syndrome. *Schizophrenia Bulletin*, **10**, 388–398.

Kant, O. (1941). A comparative study of recovered and deteriorated schizophrenic patients. *Journal of Nervous and Mental Disease*, **94**, 616–624.

Kay, S.R., Opler, L.A., and Fishbein, A. (1992). *Positive and Negative Syndrome Scale (PANSS) Rating Manual*. Toronto: Multihealth Systems, Inc.

Kirch, D.G., Lieberman, J.A., and Matthews, S.M. (1992). First-Episode psychosis: Part I. Editors' Introduction. *Schizophrenia Bulletin*, **18**, 177–178.

Kraepelin, E. (1896). *Dementia Praecox and Paraphrenia*. Translated by R.M. Barclay, 1919. Chicago: Chicago Medical Books.

Krausz, M., and Muller-Thomsen, T. (1993). Schizophrenia with onset in adolescence: An 11-year followup. *Schizophrenia Bulletin*, **19**, 831–841.

Krawiecka, M., Goldberg, D., and Vaughan, M. (1977). A standardized psychiatric assessment scale for rating chronic psychotic patients. *Acta Psychiatrica Scandinavica*, **55**, 299–308.

Lehman, A.F. (1988). A quality of life interview for the chronically mentally ill. *Evaluation and Program Planning*, **11**, 51–62.

Lewine, R., Fogg, L., and Meltzer, H. (1983). The development of scales for the assessment of positive and negative symptoms in schizophrenia. *Schizophrenia Bulletin*, **10**, 371–376.

Liddle, P.F. (1987). The symptoms of chronic schizophrenia: a re-examination of the positive-negative dichotomy. *British Journal of Psychiatry*, **151**, 145–151.

Lin, K-M., and Kleinman, A.M. (1988). Psychopathology and clinical course of schizophrenia: A cross-cultural perspective. *Schizophrenia Bulletin*, **14**, 555–567.

McGlashan, T.H. (1983). The borderline syndrome: II. Is borderline a variant of schizophrenia or affective disorder? *Archives of General Psychiatry*, **40**, 1319–1323.

McGlashan, T.H. (1984a). The Chestnut Lodge Follow-up Study: I. Follow-up methodology and study sample. *Archives of General Psychiatry*, **41**, 573–585.

McGlashan, T.H. (1984b). The Chestnut Lodge Follow-up Study: II. Long-term outcome of schizophrenia and the affective disorders. *Archives of General Pychiatry*, **41**, 586–601.

McGlashan, T.H. (1986a). Psychosocial treatments and the role of psychosocial factors in its etiology and pathogenesis. In A. Frances and R. Hales, eds, *Annual Review of Psychiatry*, Vol. 5, Washington: American Psychiatric Press.

McGlashan, T.H. (1986b). Schizotypal personality disorder: Chestnut Lodge follow-up study: VI. Long-term follow-up perspectives. *Archives of General Psychiatry*, **43**, 329–334.

McGlashan, T.H. (1986c). The prediction of outcome in chronic schizophrenia: IV. The Chestnut Lodge follow-up study. *Archives of General Psychiatry*, **43**, 167–176.

McGlashan, T.H. (1988). A selective review of recent North American long-term followup studies of schizophrenia. *Schizophrenia Bulletin*, **14**, 515–542.

McGlashan, T.H., Carpenter, W.Y., and Bartko, J.J. (1988). Issues of design and methodology in long-term follow-up studies. *Schizophrenia Bulletin*, **14**, 569–587.

McGlashan, T.H., and Bardenstein, K.K. (1990). Gender differences in affective, schizoaffective, and schizophrenic disorders. *Schizophrenia Bulletin*, **16**, 319–329.

McGlashan, T.H., and Fenton, W.S. (1993). Subtype progression and pathophysiologic deterioration in early schizophrenia. *Schizophrenia Bulletin*, **19**, 71–84.

McLellan, K., Luborsky, L., Woody, G.E., and O'Brien, C.P. (1980). An improved evaluation instrument for substance abuse patients: The Addiction Severity Index. *Journal of Nervous and Mental Disorders*, **168**, 26–33.

Meehl, P.E. (1962). Schizotaxia, schizotypy, schizophrenia.

American Psychologist, **17**, 827–838.

Meehl, P.E. (1990). Toward an integrated theory of schizotaxia, schizotypy, and schizophrenia. *Journal of Personality Disorders*, **4**, 1–99.

Neuchterlein, K.H., Dawson, M.E., Gitlin, M. *et al.* (1992). Developmental processes in schizophrenic disorders: Longitudinal studies of vulnerability and stress. *Schizophrenia Bulletin*, **18**, 387–425.

Norman, R.M.G., and Malla, A.K. (1993a). Stressful life events and schizophrenia I: A review of the research. *British Journal of Psychiatry*, **162**, 161–166.

Norman, R.M.G., and Malla, A.K. (1993b). Stressful life events and schizophrenia II: Conceptual and methodological issues. *British Journal of Psychiatry*, 166–172.

Peralta, B., deLeon, J., and Cuesta, M.J. (1992). Are there more than two syndromes in schizophrenia? A critique of the positive–negative dichotomy. *British Journal of Psychiatry*, **161**, 335–343.

Ram, R., Bromet, E.J., Eaton, W.W., Pato, C., and Schwartz, J.E. (1992). The natural course of schizophrenia: A review of first-admission studies. *Schizophrenia Bulletin*, **18**, 185–207.

Robins, E., and Guze, S.B. (1970). Establishment of diagnostic validity in psychiatric illness: Its application to schizophrenia. *American Journal of Psychiatry*, **126**, 983–987.

Simpson, G.M., and Angus, J.W.D. (1970). A rating scale for extrapyramidal side effects. *Acta Psychiatrica Scandinavica (Suppl.)*, **212**, 11–19.

Stephens, J.H. (1978). Long-term prognosis and followup in schizophrenia. *Schizophrenia Bulletin*, **4**, 25–47.

Strauss, J.S., and Carpenter, W.T. (1972). The prediction of outcome in schizophrenia. I. Characteristics of outcome. *Archives of General Psychiatry*, **27**, 730–746.

Strauss, J.S., and Carpenter, W.T. (1974). The prediction of outcome in schizophrenia. II. Relationships between predictor and outcome variables. *Archives of General Psychiatry*, **31**, 37–42.

Strauss, J.S., and Carpenter, W.T. (1977). Prediction of outcome in schizophrenia. III. Five-year outcome and its predictors. *Archives of General Psychiatry*, **34**, 159–163.

Tsuang, M.T., Lyons, M.J., and Faraone, S.V. (1990). Heterogeneity of schizophrenia. Conceptual models and analytic strategies. *British Journal of Psychiatry*, **156**, 17–26.

Vaillant, G.E. (1964a). An historical review of the remitting schizophrenias. *Journal of Nervous and Mental Disease*, **138**, 48–55.

Vaillant, G.E. (1964b). Prospective prediction of schizophrenic remission. *Archives of General Psychiatry*, **11**, 509–518.

Wyatt, R.J., Alexander, R.C., Egan, M.F., and Kirch, D.G. (1988). Schizophrenia: just the facts. What do we know, how well do we know it? *Schizophrenia Research*, **1**, 3–18.

Zubin, J., and Steinhauer, S. (1981). How to break the logjam in schizophrenia. A look beyond genetics. *Journal of Nervous and Mental Disease*, **169**, 477–492.

Zubin, J., Salzinger, S., Burdock, E.I., *et al.* (1961). A biometric approach to prognosis in schizophrenia. In P. Hoch, and J. Zubin, eds, *Comparative Epidemiology of the Mental Disorders*, pp. 143–203. New York: Grune & Stratton.

Part II

EPIDEMIOLOGY

9

Estimates of the Cost of Treating People with Schizophrenia: Contributions of Data from Epidemiologic Surveys

GRAYSON S. NORQUIST, DARREL A. REGIER and AGNES RUPP
Division of Epidemiology and Services Research, National Institute of Mental Health, Rockville, Maryland, USA

Epidemiology is the study of the quantitative distribution of disorders across population groups. In addition, it examines the contribution of certain risk factors to the development of disorders. The focus of epidemiology is population groups rather than individuals. Data from epidemiologic studies of population groups in conjunction with services research data can inform policy, such as determining the treatment needs of large populations and the cost for such treatment.

In this chapter we first provide an overview of epidemiologic definitions and methodologies. We then present prevalence and service utilization data from large epidemiologic data bases. Next, we show current cost data and demonstrate the derivation of a cost estimate for treatment. Although the cost for treating all mental disorders is important, in keeping with the topic of this book we limit our discussion to schizophrenic disorder (DSM-III-R, 1987).

INCIDENCE/PREVALANCE

Incidence refers to the number of people who developed a new case of a disorder during a specific time period. Most studies report annual incidence (i.e., the number of people who develop the disorder during a 1 year period). Prevalence refers to the number of people with a disorder during a defined period of time (period prevalence) or at a specific point in time (point prevalence). Most studies report period prevalence with time periods of 1 month to lifetime. Because budgets are calculated over a 1 year period, 1 year prevalence data are the most useful for estimates of the cost for treating disorders.

DIAGNOSIS

Many people have described the history of epidemiologic research in the mental health field (Dohrenwend, 1983; Regier *et al.*, 1985). Prior to the last decade, studies used symptom scales to determine the existence of mental disorders in populations (Murphy, 1980). Yet, in the early 1980s standardized instruments such as the Diagnostic Interview Schedule (DIS) were developed to determine specific disorders (Robins *et al.*, 1981). If one wants to estimate the total cost of treating all people with schizophrenic disorder, then community surveys

Handbook of Mental Health Economics and Health Policy, Volume I, Schizophrenia. Edited by M. Moscarelli, A. Rupp and N. Sartorius.
© 1996 John Wiley & Sons Ltd.

must adequately detect all people with the disorder. Thus, the advent of standardized instruments that derive valid estimates of the number of people with schizophrenic disorder has been a major advance in the utility of epidemiologic data for policy studies.

CASE FINDINGS

There are several ways to collect data on populations. The four principal methods are: case registers, key informants, facility reports and community surveys (Karno & Norquist, 1989).

CASE REGISTERS

With case registers, all cases of people with a particular disorder in a specific geographical area, and their contacts with the service system, are recorded in community registers. The problem with such registers is that many people with schizophrenic disorder may not come into contact with a given delivery system and thus they may provide low estimates of prevalence and service use. Yet, if one is not concerned with potential use but wants to know only about current use of a particular service system then such data may be adequate.

KEY INFORMANTS

Certain people are identified in the community who have special knowledge of the community and wide social contacts. These people are known as key informants and they have been most helpful in studies in nonliterate societies. Data from key informants are not useful for large-scale studies but they may supplement some community data. For example, when trying to find cases of homeless people with schizophrenia a key informant in the homeless community may be needed to contact these people.

FACILITY REPORTS

Many public agencies use data provided by facilities to estimate the number of people with mental disorders and their use of services in a given area. The problem with such data is that they may represent an undercount of the true number of people in the community with such disorders. Also, unless one has data from every provider in the area, specific types of cases and people with certain sociodemographic characteristics may be missed. Yet, if one is only interested in the costs of providing services at a given facility then such data may be satisfactory.

COMMUNITY SURVEYS

In such studies, one conducts face-to-face interviews with every person possible in the community. If such a community is small, it may be possible to collect data on every person in the community. Yet, most community surveys of heavily populated areas must collect data on selected samples of people in those areas. Mental disorders with low prevalence such as schizophrenic disorder require the sampling of large numbers of people to obtain enough cases for meaningful analysis. Community surveys provide the best estimates of the number of people with mental disorders and they can identify the underserved population (i.e., those with disorder who do not use services).

The best example of a community survey is the National Institute of Mental Health Epidemiologic Catchment Area Survey (NIMH-ECA) (Robins & Regier, 1991). The ECA was the largest epidemiologic community study ever conducted in the United States. Close to 20 000 adults (18 and older) in five geographic areas around the United States were surveyed with face-to-face interviews from 1980 to 1985 with a response rate of about 75%. The study used a highly structured instrument (DIS) for the interviews. Answers to questions on this instrument made it possible to determine DSM-III diagnoses. Because the instrument determined the duration of symptoms, it was possible to diagnose either schizophrenic disorder or schizophreniform disorder (symptoms less than 6 months). The ECA surveyed both community respondents and an institutional sample from prisons, hospitals, and nursing homes. Although the five geographic sites studied are not representative of the rest of the United States, respondents were adjusted by age, sex, and ethnicity groups to the 1980 US census distribution to provide the best estimates of the community prevalence of schizophrenic disorder for adults in the United States.

Another recent study, the National Comorbidity Survey, was designed to provide nationally representative data. Approximately 8000 persons, aged 15–54, were surveyed in face-to-face interviews from across the United States with a response rate of about 83% during 1992. Initial data from this study were recently reported (Kessler *et al.*, 1994). The study reports a summary category of "nonaffective psychosis' and does not separate data for those with schizophrenic disorder.

No national studies have been conducted to determine the prevalence of mental disorders in children and adolescents in the United States. In preparation for such a national study the National Institute of Mental Health (NIMH) recently launched a program known as the Cooperative Agreement for Methodologic Research for Multi-site Epidemiologic Surveys of Mental Disorders in Child and Adolescent Populations (MECA). As part of the initial work of this program, four sites in the United States conducted field trials of parent and child (aged 9–17) interviews with a response rate of about 85% in 1992. Structured interviews (e.g., DIS for Children) were used as well as measures of impairment, functioning, and services utilization. Although data from this study are very preliminary and do not represent the entire United States, initial analyses of these data provide some estimates for the prevalence of schizophrenic disorder in children and adolescents.

PREVALENCE DATA FOR SCHIZOPHRENIA

Studies have reported a range of prevalence for schizophrenic disorder (Karno & Norquist, 1989). Estimates for 6 month prevalence have ranged from 0.4 to 0.7%, 1 year prevalence from 0.2 to 1.0%, and lifetime prevalence from 0.1 to 1.1%. The wide range is primarily due to methodological differences in the studies such as differences in diagnostic criteria, case finding, and limited sample sizes.

The best community prevalence data for adults with schizophrenic disorder now come from the ECA study. Using data from interviews at the start of the survey and 1 year later this study found that 1.1% of adults met criteria for schizophrenic disorder during a 1 year period (Table 1; Regier *et al.*, 1993). Because this study reinterviewed people after 1 year, it was possible to determine the annual incidence of schizophrenic disorder (0.3%). Although one could use these prevalence data to determine the number of people with a potential need for treatment, they would not include those people who no longer meet active criteria for schizophrenic disorder because they are responding to treatment. Therefore, we also determined a 1 year prevalence figure for those adults who met criteria for schizophrenic disorder plus those with a lifetime diagnosis of schizophrenia (but not meeting current criteria) who have received treatment in the past year. This 1 year prevalence figure was 1.5% (National Advisory Council, 1993).

No national data exist for children and adolescents in the United States. Studies in restricted geographic areas have reported that 3–5% of children have a severe emotional or behavioral problem that interferes with daily functioning (Brandenburg *et al.*, 1990; Costello *et al.*, 1993). The MECA study provides preliminary data on schizophrenic disorder. Table 1 shows the 6 month prevalence for children and adolescents (aged 9–17) with schizophrenic disorder and some degree of impairment (1.2%) (National Advisory Council, 1993).

SERVICE UTILIZATION DATA FOR SCHIZOPHRENIA

Although not part of traditional epidemiologic studies, data on service utilization have been incorporated into large surveys, such as the NIMH-ECA to derive estimates of use with specific disorders. In the United States people with schizophrenic disorder may receive treatment services in a variety of public and private settings. Most of these settings can be combined into two major sectors: specialty mental health sector and general medical sector. The former represents those settings where services are delivered by mental health specialists (e.g., psychiatric hospitals, specialists in private practice, crisis centers, etc.). The general medical sector represents those settings where services are delivered by nonspecialty providers (e.g., general hospital emergency departments and general medical physicians). The ECA study collected data on service use (Table 2). Of those people with a diagnosis of schizophrenic disorder, 46% used the

Table 1. Prevalence of schizophrenic disorder

	6 months	1 year
Adults (active)		1.1%
Adults (active/treated)*		1.5%
Children/adolescents	1.2%	

* Adults who either meet current criteria for schizophrenic disorder or have a lifetime diagnosis and are under current treatment (see text).

Table 2. Percentage of adults with schizophrenic disorder using services during 1 year

Specialty outpatient	46%
General medical outpatient	34%
Either outpatient sector	65%
Specialty inpatient	17%

specialty outpatient mental health sector during a 1 year period, 34% used the general medical outpatient sector, and 65% used at least one of these sectors (National Advisory Council, 1993). About 17% of those with schizophrenic disorder had at least one inpatient episode during a 1 year period (Narrow *et al.*, 1993).

Similar national data are not available in the United States for children and adolescents. Previous surveys in restricted geographic areas have found that 6–16% of children with mental disorders received some mental health service during a 1 year period (Bird *et al.*, 1988; Costello *et al.*, 1988, 1993). If one restricts the population to those with some functional impairment, the percentage using mental health services rises to 25%. The MECA study provides some preliminary data for those with the more severe mental disorders (schizophrenic disorder, bipolar disorder, major depressive disorder, obsessive–compulsive disorder, and panic disorder). Table 3 shows that approximately 29% of children and adolescents with these disorders used either the specialty or general medical outpatients sectors for mental health care during a 1 year period (National Advisory Council, 1993). Approximately 10% used inpatient services (National Advisory Council, 1993). If one restricts this group of children and adolescents to those with more significant disability the percentage using either the specialty or general medical sector for mental health care may increase. Although data from the MECA study are the most extensive current data available on this age group, one should use caution in interpreting the results as they are preliminary and not generalizable to the entire US population.

Table 3. Percentage of children/adolescents with severe disorders using services during 1 year*

Specialty outpatient	24%
General medical outpatient	16%
Either outpatient sector	29%
Specialty inpatient	10%

* Severe mental disorders are: schizophrenic disorder, schizoaffective disorder, bipolar disorder and severe forms of major depressive disorder, panic disorder, and obsessive–compulsive disorder.
(Preliminary results from MECA study—see text.)

COST DATA

Early studies of the cost of schizophrenic disorder have provided a range of estimates. The diverse estimates are the result of differing classification systems for schizophrenic disorder, varied demographics and dissimilar estimation techniques (Rupp & Keith, 1993). A study in 1975 estimated the total cost of schizophrenic disorder as $2–4 billion direct and $9–11 billion indirect (Gunderson & Mosher, 1975). A study that followed a small group of patients estimated that the total cost per patient (direct and indirect) was about $13 700 (Muller & Caton, 1983).

The most recent estimate (1985) of the total cost for schizophrenic disorder (direct and indirect costs) in the United States was $22.7 billion (Rice & Miller, 1992). Of this amount $10.3 billion was allocated to direct treatment costs and $12.4 billion was allotted to indirect costs. If one inflates these costs to 1990 dollars then the total cost for schizophrenic disorder was $33 billion in that year (Rice & Miller, 1992). The cost for direct treatment of schizophrenic disorder was approximately $15.9 billion.

ESTIMATE OF COST FOR TREATMENT OF SCHIZOPHRENIA

There is an effort in the United States to reform the health care system. One consideration of that reform is the provision of mental health benefits. Under the current health care system, coverage for mental health care under private health insurance is limited and many people have no insurance (Norquist & Wells, 1991). People with schizophrenic disorder are often eligible for care under a public system (federal, state, or local government programs) as they do not have private insurance or have used services past the limit of their private insurance policies. An accurate estimate of the cost of providing care for those with mental disorders can help to inform policy-makers. Although benefits will not be limited to one disorder, an estimation of the cost of treating those with schizophrenic disorder can serve as an example of how epidemiologic data are used to determine treatment cost.

The first thing to be determined is how many people will be potential users of services. Thus, if one wants to cover all people with schizophrenic disorder one must know how many people have such a disorder. Using our estimates of the prevalence presented above we know that 1.5% of the adult US population has either active symptoms of schizophrenic disorder or are without acute symptoms but in current treatment during a 1 year period. Based on the 1990 US census this represents approximately 2.74 million adults (age 18 and over). The comparable figure for children and adolescents (age 17 and under) would be 770 000 (64.2 million × 1.2%). Thus, in 1990 there were 3.51 million children and adults with schizophrenic disorder in the United States.

From service utilization data we know that about 65% of adults with schizophrenic disorder used services during 1 year. The estimate for children and adolescents varies from 16 to 29%. Both estimates for children and adults are for the current system. If one designs a benefit that allows all people full coverage then one would expect more people to use. The exact figure of this increased demand is unknown. Data from the RAND Health Insurance Experiment show that one could expect an approximately 20% increase in use under a plan that increased coverage from a lower to a more comprehensive level (Wells *et al.*, 1982). Thus, we might expect the proportion of adults who use services to go up to about 85% and for children and adolescents to be about 49% (if we use the high estimate). The figure for children and adolescents is probably low and thus we shall assume a similar utilization to that seen in adults. If one multiplies 85% times the number of children and adults with schizophrenic disorder then 2.98 million people with this disorder would be expected to use services within 1 year.

To derive a cost estimate for the treatment of people with schizophrenic disorder over a 1 year period, one must next attach an estimate of the cost per user to the number of people expected to use services (2.98 million people). Given that financing of mental health services is based on a combination of private insurance and public funds, one must try to subdivide people with schizophrenic disorder into meaningful fiscal groups. Then subtotals for each group can be determined for an accurate summary cost. In a recent report on the cost for covering all severe mental disorders (schizophrenic disorder, schizoaffective disorder, bipolar disorder and severe forms of major depressive disorder, panic disorder, and obsessive–compulsive disorder) we attempted to define more specific subgroups and attach cost figures to each (National Advisory Council, 1993). Using the approach taken in that report we will present a total cost esimate for treating only schizophrenic disorder.

We first separate those with schizophrenic disorder into those with private insurance and those who are covered by the public system. We know that approximately 64% of all people with severe mental disorders have private insurance and the remaining 36% are covered by federal, state, or local funds (National Advisory Council, 1993). If we apply this figure to our total number of potential users (2.98 million) then 1.91 million would have some form of private insurance and 1.07 million would be covered by the public system.

Cost per user data under private insurance are not available for those with schizophrenic disorder. In our recent report, we estimated the annual expenditure per user with a generous benefit plan under private insurance for those with the most severe mental disorders at $7462 (1990 dollars) (National Advisory Council, 1993). Thus, the cost for the 1.91 million with private insurance would be $14.25 billion if one used this figure as an approximation for people with schizophrenic disorder and private insurance. Our estimate per user under private insurance may be high as it is the result of a simulation model that included people with the most severe disorders and who were more likely to use expensive services such as hospital treatment.

Similarly, there are no adequate estimates of the cost per user under the public system for those with schizophrenic disorder. Recent cost estimates that include both state and federal expenditures show that the cost per user for all people in the public system is about $4290 (1990 dollars) (unpublished data from the National Association of State Mental Health Program Directors Research Institute, 1994). Thus, the cost for the 1.07 million with potential coverage by the public sector would be $4.59 billion if one used this figure to represent the cost for people with schizophrenic disorder. This may represent a low estimate as the cost is based on all users and not only those with severe mental disorders.

After summing the cost estimates above, the total 1 year treatment cost for people with schizophrenic disorder in the United States who are likely to use services would be about $18.85 billion in 1990 dollars; representing roughly an increase of $3 billion more than 1990 direct treatment expenditures. This increase is attributable to two components: (i) the number of users will increase due to improved access to coverage, and (ii) the cost per user in the private sector will be higher under a more generous benefit than the current typical benefit coverage.

FUTURE RESEARCH NEEDS

We have shown in this chapter how one can use epidemiologic data with services research data to calculate the cost of treating a particular disorder such as schizophrenic disorder. Yet, one can only consider these calculations an approximation as many uncertainties may exist with the data on which it is based. We assumed the diagnoses of schizophrenic disorder in the population studied were correct. Although structured instruments such as the DIS have improved greatly the ability to assess diagnoses in the community, further work is needed to ensure their validity.

The NIMH-ECA study was conducted in five different geographic sites across the United States and although standardized to the US population it is drawn from predominantly urban areas and does not fully represent the entire US population. The National Comorbidity Study attempts to obtain a representative sample but did not cover all age groups and has not reported specific data on schizophrenic disorder (Kessler *et al.*, 1994). Future studies that need to address national prevalence may choose to obtain a national sample instead of using various community sites.

Data on service utilization may be biased by respondent ability to recall information. In subsequent studies it may be advantageous to employ more frequent assessments of service use and to validate such information with a subsample of actual service use records (Taube *et al.*, 1986). In addition, better definitions are needed of what constitutes a "service."

Another need for further research is improvement in the ability to estimate cost per user. To calculate these estimates we had to use approximate values that may include diverse subgroups of people with schizophrenic disorder. For example, a small percentage of people with schizophrenic disorder may benefit from treatment programs such as Programs of Assertive Community Treatment (Stein & Test, 1980). It would be important to determine the number benefiting from such a program and to derive a cost per user to provide such a program. Total cost estimates are more realistic when one can formulate separate costs for meaningful treatment groups such as this.

Surveys such as those described in this chapter collected data over, at most, a 1 year period. Although this provides a better perspective than data collected at a single point in time, it is still limited. Future studies should consider following people over longer periods of time. This would allow one to understand the variations in cost over time for disorders such as schizophrenia that are chronic but may have fluctuating courses.

Eventually, studies will need to examine community data in the context of data from service systems. Such studies can provide an accounting of the varied costs of schizophrenic disorder under varying service systems. These costs vary depending on the nature of the service system and the appropriateness and adequacy of treatment. In addition, these studies would make it possible to derive more accurate estimates of the indirect costs for those who remain untreated and the potential costs for bringing them into service systems for treatment.

REFERENCES

Bird, H., Canino, G., and Rubio-Stipec, M. (1988). Estimates of the prevalence of childhood maladjustment in a community survey in Puerto Rico. *Arch. Gen. Psychiatry*, **45**, 1120–1126.

Brandenburg, N.A., Friedman, R.M., and Silver, S.E. (1990). The epidemiology of childhood psychiatric disorders. *J. Am. Acad. Child. Adol. Psych.*, **29**, 76–83.

Costello, E.J., Costello, A.J., and Edelbrock, C. (1988). Psychiatric disorders in pediatric primary care. *Arch. Gen. Psychiatry*, **45**, 1107–1116.

Costello, J., Burns, B.J., Angold, A., and Leaf, P.J. (1993). How can epidemiology improve mental health services for children and adolescents? *J. Am. Acad. Child. Adol. Psych.*, **32**, 1106–1114.

Diagnostic and Statistical Manual of Mental Disorders, 3rd edn (1987). Washington, DC: American Psychiatric Association.

Dohrenwend, B.P. (1983). The epidemiology of mental disorder. In D. Mechanic, ed., *Handbook of Health, Health Care and the Health Professions.*New York: Free Press.

Gunderson, J.G. and Mosher, L.R. (1975). The cost of schizophrenia. *Am. J. Psychiatry*, **132**, 901–906.

Karno, M. and Norquist, G.S. (1989). Schizophrenia: epidemiology. In H.I. Kaplan and B.J. Sadock, eds, *Comprehensive Textbook of Psychiatry/V*, pp. 699–705. Baltimore, MD: Williams & Wilkins.

Kessler, R.C., McGonagle, K.A., Zhaos, S., *et al.* (1994). Lifetime and 12-month prevalence of DSM-III-R psychiatric disorders in the United States: results from the national comorbidity survey. *Arch. Gen. Psychiatry*, **51**, 8–19.

Muller, C.F. and Caton, C.L.M. (1983). Economic costs of schizophrenia: A postdischarge survey. *Med. Care*, **21**, 92–104.

Murphy, J. (1980). *Psychiatric Instrument Development for Primary Care Research: Patient Self-report Questionnaire.* Rockville, MD: National Institute of Mental Health.

Narrow, W.E., Regier, D.A., Rae, D.S., Manderscheid, R.W., and Locke, B.Z. (1993). Use of services by persons with mental and addictive disorders. *Arch. Gen. Psychiatry*, **50**, 95–107.

National Advisory Mental Health Council (1993). Health care reform for Americans with severe mental illnesses: Report of the National Advisory Mental Health Council. *Am. J. Psychiatry*, **150**, 1447–1465.

Norquist, G. and Wells, K. (1991). Mental health needs of the uninsured. *Arch. Gen. Psychiatry*, **48**, 475–478.

Regier, D.A., Myers, J.K., Kramer, M., *et al.* (1985). Historical context, major objectives, and study design. In W.W. Eaton and K.G. Kessler, eds, *Epidemiologic Field Methods in Psychiatry: The NIMH Epidemiologic Catchment Area Program.* New York: Academic Press.

Regier, D.A., Narrow, W.E., Rae, D.S., Manderscheid, R.W., Locke, B.Z., and Goodwin, F.K. (1993). The de facto US mental and addictive disorders service system', *Arch. Gen. Psychiatry*, **50**, 85–94.

Rice, D.P. and Miller, L.S. (1992). The economic burden of schizophrenia. Paper presented at the Sixth Biennial Research Conference on the Economics of Mental Health, Bethesda, MD.

Robins, L.N. and Regier, D.A. (1991). *Psychiatric Disorders in America: The Epidemiologic Catchment Area Study.* New York: Free Press.

Robins, L.N., Helzer, J.E., Croughan, J., and Ratcliff, K.S. (1981). The NIMH diagnostic interview schedule: its history, characteristics, and validity. *Arch. Gen. Psychiatry*, **38**, 381–389.

Rupp, A. and Keith, S.J. (1993). The costs of schizophrenia: Assessing the burden. *Psychiatr. Clin. North Am.*, **16**, 413–423.

Stein, L.I. and Test, M.A. (1980). Alternative to mental hospital treatment: I. Conceptual model, treatment program and clinical evaluation. *Arch. Gen. Psychiatry*, **37**, 392–397.

Taube, C.A., Schlenger, W.E., Rupp, A., and Whitmore, R.W. (1986). Validity of medicaid household respondent reporting of ambulatory visits for mental disorders. *J. Econ. Soc. Meas.*, **14**, 243–256.

Wells, K.B., Manning, W.G., Duan, N., Ware, J.E., and Newhouse, J.P. (1982). *Cost Sharing and the Demand for Ambulatory Mental Health Services.* Santa Monica, CA: RAND Corporation.

10

Epidemiology: A Tool in Health Economics

POVL MUNK-JØRGENSEN and SUSANNE WULFF SVENDSEN
Institute for Basic Psychiatric Research, Department of Psychiatric Demography, University Hospital of Aarhus, Risskov, Denmark

Almost 20 million people all over the world are suffering from schizophrenia (Sartorius & de Girolamo, 1991). This indicates that the cost of schizophrenia is huge, both the direct cost and the indirect cost.

The direct cost is the less complicated to calculate, as practically all the necessary data are available, provided that the appropriate monitoring systems have been established. Regarding indirect cost, the picture is far more complicated. For schizophrenic patients, the concept "loss of earnings" is fictive. In societies with severe unemployment problems, a concept such as revenue lost from a schizophrenic person's potential income becomes essentially illusive.

In addition to the calculation of the direct and the indirect costs, it is the duty of any civilized society also to construct an ethical account. Deinstitutionalization in the Western world discharges thousands of schizophrenic patients from the mental hospitals. This is to the advantage of many and appears positively in an ethical account. However, the past two decades have also shown the negative sides of this process. The burden on relatives has increased, thus the direct as well as the indirect cost to schizophrenic patients and their relatives together with the privation and burden which society causes these persons appear negatively in an ethical account. The phenomenon of an increased tendency to schizophrenic patients' residing in institutions for the homeless (Isaac & Armat, 1990), together with the fact that the suicide rate among schizophrenics in Denmark has doubled over the past 15 years (Mortensen & Juel, 1993) must be considered. Schizophrenic patients' utilization of homeless institutions, together with increased suicide rates, clearly lower the direct cost to society, but at the same time, lower the balance of an ethical account. The entry on the indirect account is more complicated.

Although the picture is complicated, we must not abstain from intensifying research in the field. Epidemiological methods and monitoring systems are suitable tools in the calculation of costs connected with schizophrenia.

Epidemiology must be considered as supportative or basic science for health economy.

At the level of overview simplicity is required. Of the common epidemiological measures: prevalence, incidence, duration of illness, utilization of beds, and mortality, prevalence together with utilization of beds, and duration of illness are most significant for health economy. Incidence is of major importance to etiological research and is relevant to the science of health economics in the long-term.

Handbook of Mental Health Economics and Health Policy, Volume I, Schizophrenia. Edited by M. Moscarelli, A. Rupp and N. Sartorius.
© 1996 John Wiley & Sons Ltd.

PREVALENCE

In the present connection, prevalence is certainly the most important concept. Prevalence shows the number of persons with a particular characteristic—*in casu* schizophrenia—present on a given day, in a defined environment or setting. In Denmark, there are approximately 16 000 schizophrenics, corresponding with a prevalence of 0.31% of the total population. The calculation is based on the assumption that schizophrenia is a lifelong disease. In Denmark, such an assumption is probably correct as the Danish concept of schizophrenia is narrow. The figure is calculated on the basis of the Danish Psychiatric Central Register (Munk-Jørgensen *et al.*, 1993), which contains information regarding all admissions to psychiatric hospitals and wards in Denmark since 1969.

The schizophrenics—0.31% of the total population—are those who have been admitted to a psychiatric hospital or ward as in- or day-patient with a main diagnosis of schizophrenia (ICD-8: 295), at least once since April 1, 1969. This group represents not only the treated prevalence, which is a necessary measure in calculation of direct cost of schizophrenia, but also a part of the untreated prevalence, which is important in the calculation of indirect cost. International research shows large differences in prevalence between cultures (Warner & Girolamo, 1995). As most prevalence studies are made on the basis of data from treatment settings, the results are also largely dependent on the structure of the services in the area studied. Consequently, one is forced to use data from the area studied in cost calculations and not to rely upon the findings of others from different cultures.

INCIDENCE

While prevalence figures are directly usable in cost analyses, incidence values play a lesser part in health economic considerations. Incidence, which is a measure of new cases, must however, form a part of the complete picture when discussing long-term or lifetime conditions such as schizophrenia as the occurrence of new cases has a great influence on the prevalence figures of the future. The incidence approach to estimating cost of disease can provide predictions about the economic impact of changes in the occurrence and course of illness (Andrews, 1991). Therefore, the decrease in first-admission rates of schizophrenia in the Western world within the last two to three decades (Munk-Jørgensen & Mortensen, 1992) is interesting from a long-term health economic point of view. However, investigations show that this decrease is largely due to artifacts supervened *pari passu* with the wave of deinstitutionalization (Munk-Jørgensen & Mortensen, 1992; Kendell *et al.*, 1993). Many of the "missing" first-admission schizophrenics are found in shelters, prisons, and are probably also camouflaged by increasing suicide figures (Mortensen & Juel, 1993). In the long-term, the result of deinstitutionalization will be a direct decrease in hospital costs concurrent with a direct increase in social costs. It is most probable that indirect cost will increase. The changes will contribute positively to the ethical account in patients for whom the quality of life increases; but schizophrenic patients who are relegated to shelters, those who are in prison, and those who commit suicide will balance the ethical account negatively.

UTILIZATION OF BEDS

In recent years, the assumption that community psychiatric treatment is less expensive than inpatient treatment has been a major issue in the planning of the psychiatric hospital system. However, both cost and consequences of the alternatives must be examined (Drummond, 1990). If a demand for quality is not met by the community service, which is to replace, or more correctly, to supplement an inpatient service, possible economic profit would be modest (Goldberg, 1991). From a political point of view there are obvious financial incentives to reduce inpatient facilities, intensity of services, and length of stay. The percentage of the direct costs due to hospital treatment fluctuates between 50 and 90–95%, depending on whether treatment is based on outpatient care or hospitalization (Moscarelli *et al.*, 1991). To document a decrease in direct hospital costs is a rather simple task, when the number of bed days is reduced. Presentation, degree of severity,

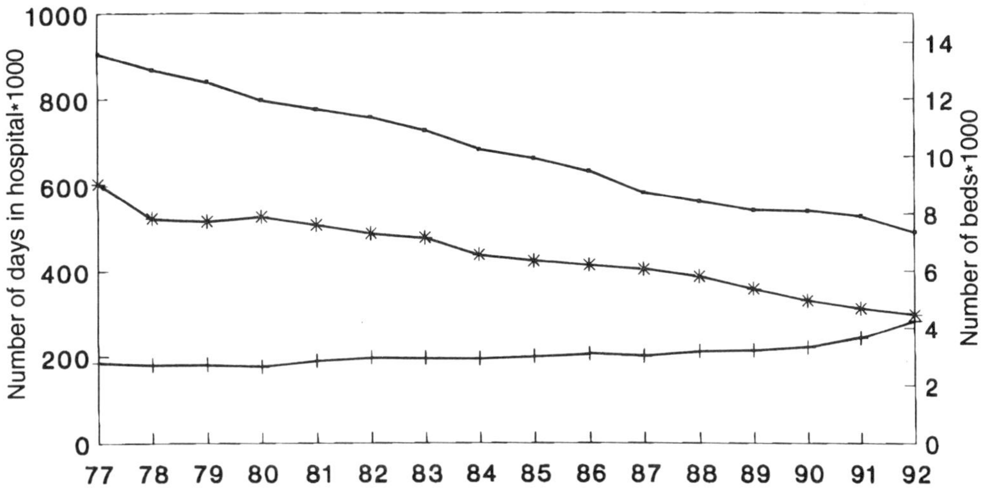

Figure 1. —■—, no. of days; —|—, no. of days excluding patients hospitalized 1 or more; —✳—, beds in psychiatric hospitals

and course of schizophrenia are heterogeneous, as is a schizophrenic patient's utilization of hospital resources. From a health economic angle the determination of average costs is of minor interest, whereas an indication of marginal costs would be more valuable (Holland, 1983). However, it is more difficult to determine the cost of community psychiatric service mainly because registration of community psychiatric care is seldom established. The indirect cost is only measurable in specific research projects, and the concept of an ethical account has hardly been introduced in this area.

Figure 1 shows the decrease in schizophrenia bed days exemplified by data from the Danish psychiatric hospital system from 1977 to 1992, inclusive, performed by means of the Danish Psychiatric Central Register.

A considerable decrease appears, concurrently with a financial gain. In the figure a curve showing the number of beds is added. A comparison of these two curves shows that the number of available beds decreases with approximately the same percentage. The bed days decrease from 900 000 to 500 000 (44%) and the beds from approximately 9000 to 4200, a decrease of 53%. If the bed days utilized by patients hospitalized for 1 year or more are excluded from the statistics, the curve becomes stable during most of the period, increasing over the last years. It can therefore be concluded that the observed decrease in schizophrenia bed days are mainly due to reduction in the actual number of bed days of long-stay patients. Next questions could be: "Where are those patients treated?" "What are the direct, the indirect, and the ethical costs?" The schizophrenic patients who are in long-term inpatient care are often those who have a dominating need of social care, and a lesser need of specialized treatment. It might therefore be an advantage to transfer these patients from expensive wards to less expensive psychiatric nursing homes. A rather simple epidemiological study would provide a survey of the actual size of this group of patients.

All schizophrenic patients hospitalized to psychiatric hospitals and wards in Denmark as at December 31, 1992, were identified from the Psychiatric Central Register.

The 1314 patients in Figure 2 are distributed according to duration of hospitalization. In the calculations we accepted gaps of up to 2 days between hospitalizations in order to correct for, for example, administrative referrals from one hospital to another, minor weekend leaves, etc. 433 patients (32.9%) of the cohort had been hospitalized for 1 year or more, 258 (19.6%) for 3 years or more. In total, the small proportion of patients hospitalized for long periods represents a disproportionate larger part of direct hospital costs due to utilization of beds. It is most probable that a large part of this patient group would profit from the less expensive treatment of social–psychiatric nursing homes.

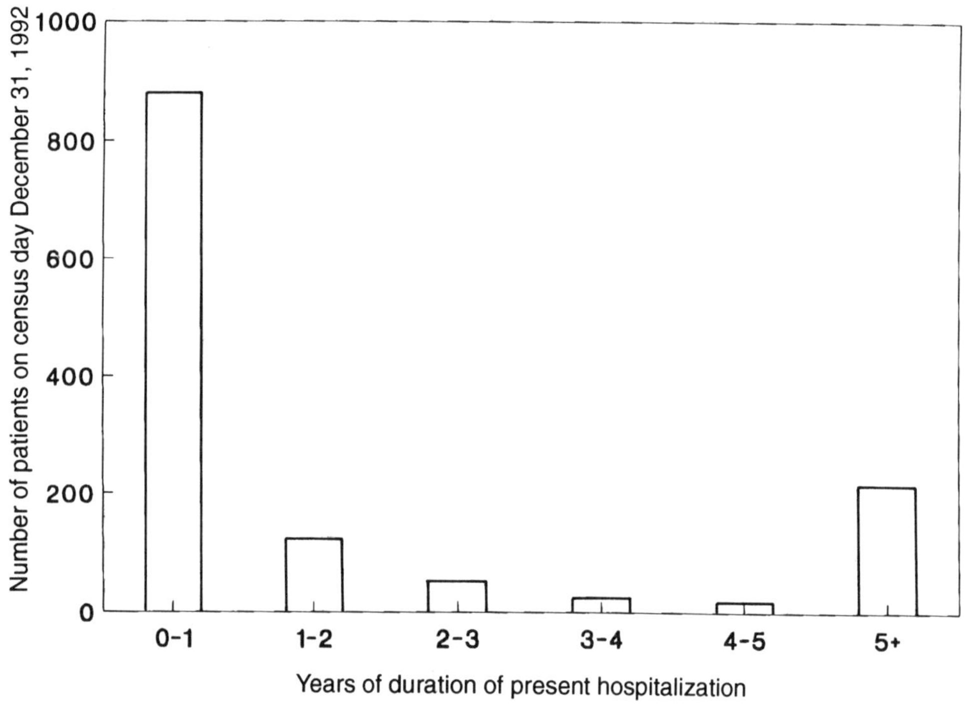

Figure 2. Number of patients on census day December 31, 1992.

On the other hand, from a psychiatric point of view, some schizophrenic patients are inappropriately treated in general psychiatric inpatient facilities. This is the case with revolving-door patients. Figure 3 shows all Danish patients first admitted in 1987, who were diagnosed schizophrenic at least once within a 5-year follow-up period, from the first day of admission. The Figure 3 shows the patients ($n=329$) distributed according to number of readmissions in the period.

A small group of patients ($n=21$, 6.4%), who had been readmitted 15 times or more during the follow-up period, forms 24.1% of the cohort's readmissions. Calculation of this cohort's utilization of beds shows that the revolving-door group which as mentioned, constitutes 6.4% of the cohort, uses 13.1% of the cohort's inpatient days. From a psychiatric point of view, specialized and intensive treatment of long duration would probably be advantageous for the revolving-door group. Such treatment could be initiated by transferring resources used by the group in several geographically spread general psychiatric departments, into few centralized and specialized departments.

DURATION OF ILLNESS

The incidence of schizophrenia influences the prevalence, as it indicates the number of new cases. The higher the incidence the higher the prevalence. Correspondingly, the duration of illness influences the prevalence. The longer the duration, the higher the prevalence. Duration of illness is not directly available from the most common source of data, i.e. registers. However, the registers can provide indirect measures of the duration of illness, i.e. duration of a patient's contact with the hospital system. An example of this is taken from the Danish Psychiatric Central Register. Three cohorts, including all Danish patients diagnosed schizophrenic for the first time in 1971–73, 1975–77, and 1980–82, all had a stable inpatient proportion of 0.1 during the follow-up period of 5–15 years. Inclusion of day-patient contacts increases

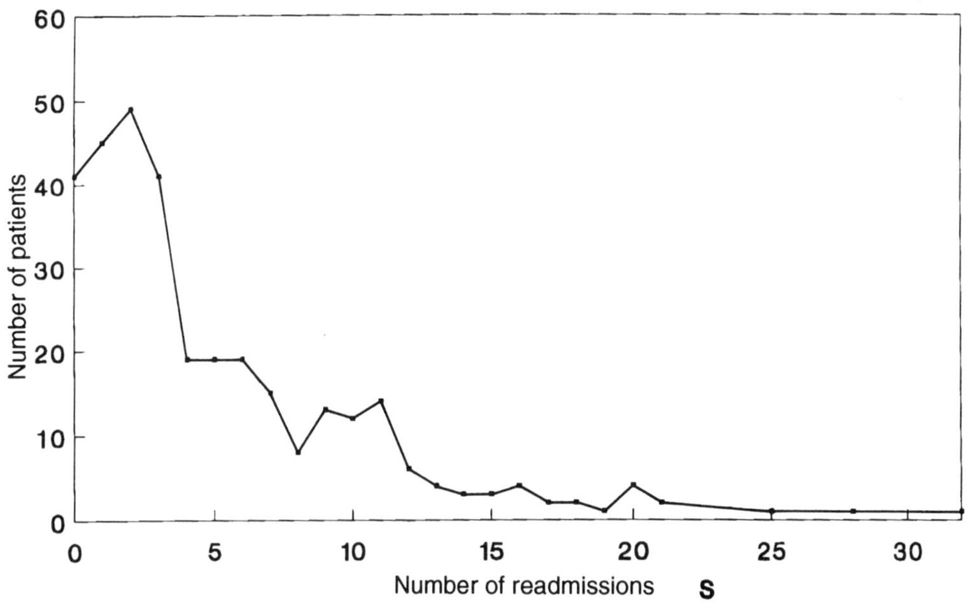

Figure 3. First admitted patients in Denmark, 1987, distributed as to number of admissions in a 5 year follow-up period.

this proportion to 0.2 (Munk-Jørgensen & Mortensen, 1992). Such calculations show the entire cohort's connection with the hospital system and not the connection of each individual patient. In a health economic perspective this is sufficient. In the study mentioned above, each cohort's stable utilization of hospital beds is not the most surprising finding, although the fact that temporally different cohorts had the same use, was somewhat unexpected. It seems that the new organization of Danish psychiatry functions as effective gate-keeping, as first admission rates of schizophrenia are decreasing. However, schizophrenic patients, who are entering the treatment system, have an unchanged utilization of bed days and day-patient contacts in the system.

MORTALITY

As incidence and duration of illness influence the prevalence, mortality among schizophrenics also determines the prevalence. The higher the mortality the lower the prevalence. Mortality among schizophrenic patients has increased in Denmark during the last 20 years. The standard mortality rate (SMR) has approximately doubled in this period (Munk-Jørgensen & Mortensen, 1992). An analysis shows that suicides in particular have been a cause of this increase. Suicides are mostly committed by young schizophrenics, among whom males mainly contribute to the increased suicide mortality (Mortensen & Juel, 1993). This tendency is also seen among patients with other functional psychoses.

MONITORING SYSTEMS

Some common epidemiological measures usable in health economic calculations have been discussed. The premise of data procurement is comprehensive monitoring systems (Häfner & an der Heiden, 1991), if possible on a national level. The core of such well-functioning monitoring systems is person identifiable registers. The Danish Psychiatric Central Register is such a register. The electronic element which registers all in- and day-patient admissions in Denmark was established in April 1969 by the visionary researchers, Professor Erik Strömgren, and Annalise Dupont, previous Director of the Register (Dupont, 1983). The Psychiatric Central Register is conducted by the epidemiological and social psychiatric research unit, Department of

Psychiatric Demography, and was most recently described in international publications by Munk-Jørgensen and colleagues (Munk-Jørgensen, 1991; Munk-Jørgensen *et al.*, 1993). One of these publications (Munk-Jørgensen, 1991) systematically describes the demands which must be made in such a register: (i) it should be based on *person identifiable* information; (ii) it should be *cumulative*; (iii) the data must be *specific as to time and place*, and *specific* regarding the patient's residence; (iv) the data must be of *high validity and reliability* and the registration must be *complete*, e.g. all institutions and services in a catchment area or in a country should be covered by the register; (v) the registration must be *computerized*; (vi) the register must have a *high level of security* and *confidentiality*; (vii) the utilization of data must be of a *high ethical level*; (viii) the responsible persons and authorities for the register should be willing to give information about the *principles and utilization of the register*—not, however, regarding specific person identifiable data in the register; and (ix) it is of the utmost importance that *regular data feedbacks* are provided to the institutions and services reporting to the register as well as being available to researchers and research institutions at a minimum fee.

The data, in the present chapter shown in Figures 1–3, are solely from the Psychiatric Central Register, and were processed within a few hours, for use in this chapter only. The costs can be as low as US$300 at maximum.

LIMITATIONS

In Denmark, the Psychiatric Central Register has blazed a new trail for well-functioning registers, delivering data for planning, evaluation, and research. Gradually, several well-functioning illness and social registers have been established in Denmark. Registers containing information on general practice treatments, pensions, etc. have also been established. In the area of psychiatric outpatient service, however, there is still an omission.

Registration is most valuable when it follows the patient through the entire treatment and care system, often via register linkage. In Denmark this is still difficult. Many registers (e.g. the social welfare registers) are operated by different administrations in the counties and in the municipalities in Denmark, which makes it difficult to follow a person geographically, or for any length of time, even though the registers are person identifiable. Furthermore, the public administration law precludes the task by drawing limits between counties and municipalities and between the many municipalities. In this way the law makes it difficult to evaluate utilization of hospital resources as well as the social system.

The large Danish registers are also in need of further details. In extensive data collection, it is expedient to choose few and simple data, if high validity and reliability is required. In the Danish Psychiatric Central Register it has until now, been impossible to solve the registration problem as to severity of mental illness. This would demand the registration of the psychiatrists' subjective assessment, resulting in low reliability—and, of course, validity. Therefore, epidemiological register-based research projects, including health economic research, should be supplemented with case-study based projects.

SUMMARY AND CONCLUSIONS

As shown in the present chapter, simple epidemiological measures can provide valuable information to health economics. These measures can be calculated from data drawn from well-functioning monitoring systems based upon registers. We recommend the establishment of nationwide person identifiable registers, which should: (i) cover all service units; (ii) maintain high-level data security; (iii) provide routine data collection; (iv) allow researchers controlled access to data; and (v) ensure low cost in data utilization.

The challenge in this area of health economic research is to find a reasonable balance which meets these demands. Collaboration between psychiatrists, health economics, and psychiatric epidemiologists is required (Moscarelli & Capri, 1991).

REFERENCES

Andrews, G. (1991). The cost of schizophrenia revisited. *Schizophrenia Bulletin*, **17**, 389–394.

Drummond, M.F. (1990). Allocating resources. *International*

Journal of Technology Assessment in Health Care, **6**, 77–92.

Dupont, A. (1983). A national psychiatric case register as a tool for mental health planning, research and administration. The Danish model. In E.M. Laska, W.H. Gulbinat, and D.A. Regier, eds, *Information Support to Mental Health Programs. An International Perspective*, pp. 257–274. New York: Human Sciences Press.

Goldberg, D. (1991). Cost-effectiveness studies in the treatment of schizophrenia: a review. *Social Psychiatry and Psychiatric Epidemiology*, **26**, 139–142.

Häfner, H. and an der Heiden, W. (1991). Evaluating effectiveness and cost of community care for schizophrenic patients. *Schizophrenia Bulletin*, **17**, 441–451.

Holland, W.W. (1983). *Evaluation of Health Care*. Oxford University Press.

Isaac, J.I. and Armat, V.C. (1990). *Madness in the Streets. How Psychiatry and the Law Abandoned the Mentally Ill*. New York: The Free Press.

Kendell, R.E., Malcom, D.E., and Adams, W. (1993). The problem of detecting changes in the incidence of schizophrenia. *British Journal of Psychiatry*, **162**, 212–218.

Mortensen, P.B. and Juel, K. (1993). Mortality and causes of death in first admitted schizophrenic patients. *British Journal of Psychiatry*, **163**, 183–189.

Moscarelli, M. and Capri, S. (1991). The cost of schizophrenia: Editors Introduction. *Schizophrenia Bulletin*, **17**, 367–369.

Moscarelli, M., Capri, S., and Neri, L. (1991). Cost evaluation of chronic schizophrenic patients during the first 3 years after the first contact. *Schizophrenic Bulletin*, **17**, 421–426.

Munk-Jørgensen, P. (1991). Fundamental principles of psychiatric registers and examples of their advantages. In T. Sørensen, P. Abrahamsen, and S. Torgersen, eds, *Psychiatric Disorders in the Social Domain. Contributions to a Scientific Basis for Understanding and Action*, pp. 192–199. Oslo: Norwegian University Press.

Munk-Jørgensen, P. and Mortensen, P.B. (1992). Incidence and other aspects of the epidemiology of schizophrenia in Denmark, 1971–1987. *British Journal of Psychiatry*, **161**, 489–495.

Munk-Jørgensen, P., Kastrup, M., and Mortensen, P.B. (1993). The Danish psychiatric register as a tool in epidemiology. *Acta Psychiatrica Scandinavica*, **Suppl. 370**, 27–32.

Sartorius, N. and de Girolamo, G. (1991). Preface. *Schizophrenia Bulletin*, **17**, 371–373.

Warner, R. and de Girolamo, G. (1995). *Epidemiology of Schizophrenia*. Geneva: World Health Organization.

Part III

STATISTICS

11

Some Issues for Consideration in Multi-site and International Reliability Studies

JOHN J. BARTKO
National Institute of Mental Health, National Institutes of Health, Bethesda, Maryland, USA

ABSTRACT

Multi-site and cross-cultural psychiatric reliability studies present issues specific to themselves as well as encompassing common ones. A few points regarding their planning and conduct are outlined. Reliability is defined as the agreement, consistency, reproducibility, or repeatability of ratings for a group of subjects. Validity on the other hand is the degree of conformity with an acceptable arbitrary standard and relates to the correctness of an assessment. There are several statistical measures of reliability, but some purported measures are unacceptable. Many of the statistical procedures for assessing reliability appear in the literature, but a few of the less well known, such as the kappa for multiple and varied diagnoses per patient, are presented here in detail. As much of this material has appeared elsewhere, no originality is claimed.

INTRODUCTION

Any method for evaluating patients in multi-site or cross-cultural settings must apply within each of the sites. It must be capable of generating comparable information necessary to compare benchmarks within sites and results between sites (WHO-IPSS, 1973).

Sound statistical measures of reliability are the intraclass correlation coefficient (ICC) for quantitative data and kappa for categorical data. Reliability is defined as the agreement, consistency, reproducibility, or repeatability of ratings for a group of subjects, and is in concept and computation a ratio of variance components (Bartko, 1966, 1991; Bartko & Carpenter, 1976; Shrout & Fleiss, 1979; Shrout *et al.*, 1987).

One of these variance components is the error variance or within-subjects variance, which is zero if the raters agree for every subject. Reliability indices usually range from zero to unity, although negative values are possible and do occur with real data. Unity represents perfect agreement and occurs when the within subjects variance is zero. The computation of reliability requires differences (variance) between subjects (see Table 1). For kappa and two raters, unity reliability is represented by the occurrence of entries along the main diagonal of the category by category matrix or equivalently by no entries in the off diagonal cells. A zero kappa reflects agreement equal to chance.

Handbook of Mental Health Economics and Health Policy, Volume I, Schizophrenia. Edited by M. Moscarelli, A. Rupp and N. Sartorius.
© 1996 John Wiley & Sons Ltd.

Table 1. Intraclass correlation (ICC) data format
(a) Ratings on a 15-point depression scale

	Raters		
Patients	1	2	3
1	10	11	12
2	5	6	
3	0	0	0
4	15	15	15
5		13	13

(b) ANOVA for ICC

Source	SS	DF	MS	F	ICC
Between subjects	419.2	4	104.8	335	0.99(+)
Within subjects	2.5	8	0.3125		
Total	421.7	12			

(+) ICC=(MSB−MSW)/[MSB+(R_o−1)MSW]; where R_o is defined in Bartko and Carpenter (p. 316, 1976) formula (E5). ICC=(104.8−0.3125)/[104.8+(2.58−1)0.3125]=0.9923.

Thus, a good reliability test setting occurs when: (i) raters are presented with a large and varied number of subjects to rate generating large between subjects variance; and (ii) when most of the raters agree among themselves for each subject rated effecting low within subject or error variance.

By their nature, heterogeneous psychiatric study groups provide many opportunities, for example many diagnostic opportunities, to explore the full range of a rating instrument. Typically this results in large between subjects variance. However, in homogeneous environments such as community surveys where the prevalence or base rate for a disorder may be low, the measurement of reliability is exacting as most often the between subjects variance is low. A low base rate places natural limits on the range and use of the research instrument. This places a greater burden on the raters to minimize within subject mistakes, that is the within subjects error variance. Statistically, low prevalence places restrictions on the adequacy of the estimates of the two variance components necessary for computing reliability measures (Bartko, 1991). In particular, negative values of the ICC occur if the between subjects variance is less than the within subjects variance (see Table 1). Negative values of kappa also can occur, especially if one of the main diagonal agreement cells is a zero for a small contingency table.

RELIABILITY AND SOURCES OF VARIANCE

Some of the issues that must be considered in a reliability study are outlined below (Bartko, 1991).

CRITERIA

Which research, diagnostic, or structured interview instrument should be used? Are some more valid than others? Which have established training environments and thus provide for better rater competence? Is it easier to sort out rater disagreements with some instruments rather than others?

Translation is an issue if the participating sites do not have a common language. For example in the IPSS (WHO-IPSS, 1973), the Present State Examination (PSE) whose original language is English was translated into seven non-English languages.

Werner and Campbell (1971) have listed some rules to be kept in mind with preparing an instrument to be translated for international use. Keep the sentences simple and in active voice, subjunctives should be avoided, metaphors and colloquialisms should not be used, nouns should be repeated rather than replaced by pronouns, and hypothetical phrasing should be avoided.

In the IPSS, back-translation was used to assess the quality of translation. The instrument was first translated into the target language by one person; the translation was then given to another person who translated it back to English. The original and the back-translation were then compared. See chapter 6 of the WHO-IPSS (1973) report for greater detail and procedures.

OCCASION

How and when will the data be collected? What is the time between responses? Test–retest settings have added variance sources in that differences in ratings may be due to the raters or attributed to the changing condition of the patient.

Within sites, structured interviews may be simultaneous using live patients, or the raters may view video tapes of subjects. Data may be from structured prepared case summaries or unstructured case records.

Between sites, logistic, budgetary, and travel restrictions often preclude an assembly of the investigators at one location for joint reliability exercises. The mechanism of a prepared set of video tapes circulated among the sites as well as structured written case summaries has been used by the WHO (WHO-IPSS, 1973) and Prendergast *et al.* (1988).

SIGNAL

Are the data retrospective from case records or from current structured interviews? What is the memory or condition of the subject being rated?

TRAINING

Automobiles and electronic devices have intrinsic reliability; in psychiatry, however, reliability is inherent in the raters, not the research instrument. Raters must have training and demonstrated competence in the use of instruments and their reliability experience should be reported. While perhaps obvious, one can regrettably find in the literature unacceptable statements such as, "... we used instrument XYZ which has demonstrated reliability." These statements are likely to appear without any evidence that raters were trained in the use of the instrument or that reliability exercises were conducted. Training and reliability exercises should begin before undertaking a major research study, not during or after it. Reliability should be reassessed as new raters join the study.

SETTING

Where a large group of heterogeneous patients are evaluated, the resulting reliability measures are usually larger than those where there are few (homogeneous conditions) diagnostic opportunities. An example of the latter is the task of determining prevalence of disorders in epidemiological community surveys where base rates may be low and thus any missed case weighs heavily. The between and within subjects variance components, measure and express the effect of settings on the measure of reliability (Bartko, 1966; Shrout & Fleiss, 1979).

RELIABILITY: QUANTITATIVE DATA

The appropriate measure of reliability for quantitative data is the ICC. Its data format is that for which the analysis of variance arithmetic (ANOVA) is suitable, i.e., quantitative data. The number of raters does not need to be the same per subject rated. For an example of the data format see Table 1. The ANOVA is the natural statistical tool for assembling the variance expressions required to compute the ICC (Bartko, 1966; Bartko & Carpenter 1976 Shrout & Fleiss, 1979).

Inappropriate or unacceptable reliability measures are the Pearson and Spearman correlation coefficient or any correlation as they measure *association*, not agreement. See Bartko & Carpenter (1976) and Shrout *et al.* (1987) for further discussion.

Because unacceptable measures of reliability appear in the literature it is not adequate to report simply that, reliability was 0.7, for example. The name of the reliability measure is essential. If it is an inappropriate measure, the reader will be able to make a judgement regarding the quality of the report.

INTERRELATIONSHIPS AMONG OTHER STATISTICS

Assuming quantitative measurements such that the ICC is appropriate, Bartko (1994) describes a situation in which several agreement statistics may be formulated using one statistical approach. The data format is one in which each randomly selected subject is rated by the same two raters.

With such data, various agreement questions can be posed. How much bias and variance is there between the two ratings? Can the measuring raters be used interchangeably? What is the overall level of agreement? How does one define and measure agreement?

It is axiomatic that statistics should be purposeful and that there is no universal statistic. The ICC is a measure of reliability agreement, but there are other definitions of agreement. The paired *t*-test (Snedecor & Cochran, 1976), can be used to evaluate the overall ratings or bias of two raters. Their variances can be assessed with Pitman's test (Pitman, 1939). A simultaneous test of the two means and variances can be performed using the Bradley and Blackwood test (1989).

Graphic procedures, in particular an ellipse confidence plot of sums and difference of the ratings provides important variance information. For the ellipse, the x-axis reflects the difference between subjects and the y-axis reflects the differences between ratings. It provides visual guidelines for the scatterplot and for focus on outlier responses. It is a convenient way to appreciate the within and between subjects variances. In typical reliability studies it is desirable to have low differences between readings for a given subject and large differences between subjects. Large between subject differences usually reflect the condition where the raters are given a thorough opportunity to test their skills with the full range of a measurement scale. Using only normal subjects or subjects with predefined severity is an example of a narrow range study. Consequently, rater reliability may only be a test of the agreement on the absence of disease or on a subsection of the disease scale, respectively, not a test of the full instrument.

It should not be interpreted that these procedures for exploring agreement are required or even suitable in all instances. Research decisions should be based upon the nature of the study and the purposes of the various agreement measures.

RELIABILITY: CATEGORICAL DATA

Kappa is a chance corrected measure of reliability for categorical data. In the classic setting of two raters and a set of diagnoses the data format is that of a contingency table. With three diagnostic categories and two raters, for example, the table size is three rows by three columns. For an illustration of a data format see Table 2. Computational expressions for kappa can be found, for example, in Fleiss (1981).

Inappropriate measures for categorical data include percent agreement, chi square, and Yule's Y (Yule, 1912). Percent agreement does not make allowances for chance agreement, while kappa does. The chi square measures association not agreement (Bartko

Table 2. Data format for a contingency (3×3) table kappa

(a) Step 1

Patients	Raters 1	Raters 2
1	*Y*	*Y*
2	*N*	*N*
3	?	?
4	*Y*	?
5	*Y*	*N*
6	?	*Y*
7	?	*N*
8	*N*	*Y*
9	*N*	?
etc.	etc.	

(b) Step 2

		Rater 2 *		
		Y	?	*N*
	Y	1	1	1
Rater 1	?	1	1	1
	N	1	1	1

* The cell data entries are for illustrative purposes of the data format steps. These cell sizes are not adequate for a reliability report.

& Carpenter, 1976; Bartko, 1991) as does Yule's Y (Shrout *et al.*, 1987).

Since it was first introduced by Cohen (1960) kappa has been modified and adapted to several data configurations. There are kappas for:

1 *Two raters and two or more diagnostic categories.* The data format is in the usual contingency table format. Weighted kappa is available. Weights for a cell (row i, column j) are often defined by: $w(i,j)=1-(i-j)^2/(k-1)^2$. The weights give full credit for the main diagonal agreements, partial agreement for cells adjacent to the main diagonal, and no weight for the cell in the first row, last column. For an example of the data format see Table 3. See Fleiss (1981) for details on computations.

2 *Three or more raters and two or more diagnostic categories.* The data format for this generalized kappa is of the spreadsheet format where rows are subjects and the columns are diagnostic classes. The data cell entries are the number of times a particular diagnosis is assigned to a subject by the R raters. For a given subject the total of the cell entries is R, the number of raters. For an example of the data format see Table 4. Details of computations can be found in Bartko & Carpenter (1976) and Fleiss (1981).

3 *Two or more categories and variable number of raters per subject.* The data are in spreadsheet format similar to that of Table 4. Fleiss (1981, p. 230).

4 *Bench marks.* Landis & Koch (1977) have given benchmarks for reporting of kappa. For

Table 3. Data format for a contingency (3×3) table kappa. Example of weights

		Rater 2 (Column j)		
		$Y(1)$	?(2)	$N(3)$
	$Y(1)$	(1,1)	(1,2)	(1,3)
Rater 1	?(2)	(2,1)	(2,2)	(2,3)
(row i)	$N(3)$	(3,1)	(3,2)	(3,3)

The (i,j) notation denotes city block coordinates of the cell at row i and column j where $(i,j=1,2,3 \ldots k)$.
Weights defined by: $w(i,j)=1-(i-j)^2/(k-1)^2$, where k is the size of the $k \times k$ table.

Weights for a 3 × 3 table are:

		Rater 2		
		$Y(1)$	?(2)	$N(3)$
	$Y(1)$	1	3/4	0
Rater 1	?(2)	3/4	1	3/4
	$N(3)$	0	3/4	1

Where for example,
$w(1,1)=1-(1-1)^2/(3-1)^2.=1$
$w(1,2)=1-(1-2)^2/(3-1)^2.=3/4$
$w(1,3)=1-(1-3)^2/(3-1)^2.=0$
similarly for the other weights.

Table 4. Kappa data format for three categories and six raters

	Categories		
Subjects	S	MD	NC
1	6	0	0
2	0	6	0
3	0	0	6
4	2	2	2
5	1	2	3

example, values below 0.40 are regarded as poor agreement beyond chance, while values greater than 0.75 are regarded as "substantial" agreement beyond chance. In particular Landis & Koch state:

kappa 0.00–0.20	Poor/slight
kappa 0.21–0.40	Fair
kappa 0.42–0.60	Moderate
kappa 0.61–0.80	Substantial
kappa 0.81–1.00	Almost perfect.

KAPPA: MULTIPLE DIAGNOSES PER SUBJECT

Kappa assumes a broader role that bears emphasizing. It is defined as a function of an index "I" where I assumes the value unity when there is complete agreement among raters. I_o is the observed value of this index and I_c the value that can be expected by chance agreement. Kappa is then expressed as the excess beyond chance, and is written as: $(I_o-I_c)/(1-I_c)$. The denominator is the largest excess possible from chance and serves as a normalizing factor. Kappa is unity indicating perfect agreement if I_o is unity. This occurs if there are no entries in the off diagonals of an agreement matrix. It is zero if observed agreement does not differ from chance agreement.

In the examples mentioned above it is assumed that a rater assigns one and only one diagnosis per subject. Mezzich *et al.* (1981) formulated a kappa for the situation where multiple and varying diagnoses can be assigned to a subject by any number of raters. In this setting, kappa assesses the reliability of a diagnostic system and uses the notion of kappa expressed in the immediate paragraph above. An example of its use can be found in Prendergast *et al.* (1988). A detailed data example of this procedure follows.

Data Example: Multiple Diagnoses

For this diagnostic system kappa it is useful to consider a simple example consisting of two patients, three raters, and a system of four possible diagnoses, coded 1, 2, 3, and 4. The cell entries (1 or 0) correspond to whether a rater assigns the particular diagnosis or not.

Data as it might be recorded:

	Rater 1	Rater 2	Rater 3
Patient 1	1,3,4	1,3,4	1,4
Patient 2	1,3	1,3	1,3

Data reformulated per a given patient in an ANOVA format. Note: that as this is an ICC format that the number of raters does not have to be equal.

Diagnosis	Raters 1	2	3
Patient 1 (ICC=0.7)			
1	1	1	1
2	0	0	0
3	1	1	0
4	1	1	1
Patient 2 (ICC=1.0)			
1	1	1	1
2	0	0	0
3	1	1	1
4	0	0	0

The average (ordinary arithmetic mean) value of the ICCs for these two patients is $(0.7+1.0)/2=0.85=I_o$.

The measure of chance agreement is given by pooling each patient's data and computing another ICC to obtain I_c.

Diagnosis	Patient 1			Patient 2		
1	1	1	1	1	1	1
2	0	0	0	0	0	0
3	1	1	0	1	1	1
4	1	1	1	0	0	0

The arithmetic details of the ANOVA and computation of the ICC follow: ANOVA for ICC:

Source	SS	DF	MS	F	ICC
Between diagnoses	3.50	3	1.1667	10.0	0.60
Within diagnoses	2.33	20	0.1167		
Total	5.83	23			

ICC=(MSB−MSW)/(MSB+5*MSW)=1.05/1.75=0.6=I_c. Kappa as a function of the above indices is:

$$(I_o-I_c)/(1-I_c)=(0.85-0.60)/(1-0.60)=0.625.$$

In summary, an ICC is obtained for each subject. The average value of these ICCs is obtained and this is noted as I_o. The data are pooled and the total experience per diagnostic category is displayed. The ICC from this data format is denoted as the chance ICC, that is I_c. Finally, kappa is given as a function of these indices with a normalizing factor, unity in the denominator.

SAMPLE SIZE AND RELIABILITY

SAMPLE SIZE FOR RELIABILITY EXERCISES

The number of subjects necessary for a reliability exercise, for a quantitative variable should be about 20. Some authors (Fleiss, p. 8, 1986) suggest 15–20. The situation is different for a categorical variable where a larger number of study subjects is required. One way to think about this is to consider two raters and a binary response. The resulting contingency table consists of four cells. With only 20 subjects, for example, and a pure equal chance model (which may not be realistic) the expected number per cell would only be five subjects. Raters will do better than an equal chance model and thus some cells will have very low expected values. General rules for the number of subjects to use in a reliability study of categorical variable are not easy to formulate, but the thinking outlined above can be used as a guideline. With a three by three table, and nine cells a small number of study subjects may lead to very small observed and expected numbers in some of the cells. These suggestions for reliability sample sizes may require serious modification in situations where low frequency of occurrences of responses or diagnoses occur. For a contingency table this may dictate that some marginal totals will be small, which can affect the computation of any reliability measure. Such situations require added training in the use of the reliability instrument. (Bartko, 1991).

THE ROLE OF RELIABILITY IN THE DESIGN OF A STUDY'S SAMPLE SIZE

It may not be appreciated that reliability plays a part in designing the sample size and power of an experimental or treatment study. The lower the demonstrated reliability, the greater the sample size required. This fact emphasizes the importance of the statement made above, that reliability exercises should be conducted *before* launching a research study.

A simple two group study design illustrates the part that reliability plays in sample size and power determinations. Assume a two group *t*-test applies. The sample size formula *N*, for such a test with specified type I error alpha, type II error beta, and delta can be found in numerous statistical sources, Fleiss (chapter 2, 1986) is one source. Delta is an expression of the difference between the two means the investigator wishes to detect.

The *t*-test sample size formula for *N*, where *N* is the sample size for one group is:

$$N = 2s^2(z_{\alpha/2} + z_\beta)^2/(\bar{X}_1 - \bar{X}_2)^2$$

The total sample size for the two groups is 2N. N is adjusted upward by reliability, *R* by $N_R = N/R$. Note, $N_R > N$, except for $R = 1.0$.

To illustrate the computations, suppose that a change in Hamilton Depression Scores of 5 (five) units is important to detect with a two-tail significance level of 0.05 and power of 80%. Assume the pooled standard deviation is 6 Hamilton units.

Then,

$$z_{\alpha/2} = z_{0.025} = 1.96,$$
$$z_\beta = z_{(1-0.80)} = 0.842,$$
$$s = 6,$$

and $$N = 2(36)(1.96 + 0.842)^2/(25) = 23.$$

If the reliability for Hamilton Ratings for this group of investigators is 0.5, $N_R = 23/0.5 = 46$ subjects per group will be required for a total study size of 92 rather than 2*23 = 46. The larger the reliability the smaller the difference between N_R and *N*. This is one illustration of the added costs that additional subjects bring to a study because of unreliable measurements.

CONFIDENCE INTERVALS

While the focus has been on point estimates of reliability coefficients, most of the procedures mentioned above have established confidence intervals of which investigators should be aware. Confidence intervals for kappa can be found in Fleiss (1981), for the ICC, Shrout *et al.* (1979) is a good resource.

JACKKNIFING AND RESAMPLING

JACKKNIFING

There are some cases where reliability variances and confidence intervals of some non-null inferences have not appeared in the literature. The jackknife, a multipurpose tool, introduced by Quenouille (1956) and named by Tukey (1958), can provide an approach to determining variances in such situations. The jackknife may be used to reduce the bias in an estimator of a population parameter and to estimate the standard error of this estimator. Fleiss (1982) illustrates the jackknife to obtain an expression for a version of the kappa variance appropriate for confidence intervals. Schouten (1986) also gives a clear illustration of the use of the jackknife in estimating kappa variance.

PERMUTATION ALGORITHMS

Fisher (1935) introduced the notion of randomization. Randomization is a process to formulate a non-parametric test in which the particular experimental outcome is assessed against all possible outcomes with the given data set.

Within the context of a *N* matched pairs, the particular study result is assessed against all possible occurrences of the matched pair signed differences. This requires enumerating the permutation of all possible arrangements of the *signs* of the observed differences, that is 2^N enumerations. For example, for $N = 10$, $2^{10} = 1024$ enumerations are required. A frequency distribution of these 2^N possible occurrences is made and the resulting two-tail *P* value consists of those numbers of outcomes that are equal to or greater than the observed computed difference. The extremes will be in the positive as well as the negative direction.

For a two group test with sample sizes N_1 and N_2, the number of sample enumerations is $(N_1 + N_2)!/N_1!*N_2!$, where *N*! is read as *N* factorial and is defined to be $N*(N-1)*(N-2)* \ldots 3*2*1$. For $N_1 = 6$ and $N_2 = 9$ a total of 5005 enumerations is required to form the distribution of differences between the two groups. An illustration of these procedures can be found, for example, in Siegel (1956).

Randomization schemes are clearly attractive.

They require no gaussian assumptions and no statistical tables are intuitively understood. R.A. Fisher (1935) was ahead of his time, but it wasn't until the advent of rapid and inexpensive computer power that randomization could be routinely employed, as the numerations for even moderate sample sizes are labor intensive. Mehta *et al.* (1988), have developed efficient permutation algorithms so these and other proposed exact procedures can be implemented.

RESAMPLING ALGORITHMS

Permutation algorithms are complicated and time consuming, but provide for exact statistical inference. Simon and Bruce (1991) have described a resampling procedure to accomplish the task of assessing a particular output against the distribution of outcomes possible with the particular data set. The resampling procedure uses the entire set of data or it uses a data generating mechanism such as a coin toss, that is a model of the process one wishes to understand, to produce new samples of simulated data and to examine the results of those samples. Resampling generates as many samples as the user specifies and does not require permutation algorithms only sampling ones.

SUGGESTIONS

For the simple assessment of variances and bias in categorical measures, such as kappa, where closed form expressions of variance may not be developed, the use of the jackknife as a first approach is recommended. For continuous data and the ICC, at resampling procedures may be the method of choice. These are not hard and fast rules, but suggestions for beginnings.

DISCUSSION

This has been a brief introduction to issues involved with the assessment of reliability in research. Basic tools for appropriate measures of reliability for quantitative data (the ICC) and for categorical data (kappa) have been presented for the reader with reference to more detailed sources in the literature. Sound statistical thinking requires one to reject ersatz measures of reliability such as chi square, correlations, and Yule's *Y*, which measure association not within subject agreement. There are costs associated with improper measurements, unreliable diagnostic systems and inappropriate statistics and measures of reliability. These costs are felt when misleading information leads one on to non-productive avenues of research.

There are many and broader issues required for the consideration in the conduct of mental health research. Kraemer *et al.* (1987) and Bartko *et al.* (1988) discuss some of these. These papers may serve as a companion to this brief discourse on reliability.

REFERENCES

Bartko, J.J. (1966). The intraclass correlation coefficient as a measure of reliability. *Psychological Reports*, **19**, 3–11.

Bartko, J.J. (1991). Measurement and reliability: statistical thinking considerations. *Schizophrenia Bulletin*, **17**, 483–489.

Bartko, J.J. (1994). Measures of agreement: a single procedure. *Statistics in Medicine*, **13**, 737–745.

Bartko, J.J. and Carpenter, W.T. (1976). On the methods and theory of reliability. *Journal of Nervous and Mental Disease*, **163**, 307–317.

Bartko, J.J., Carpenter, W.T. Jr., and McGlashen, T.H. (1988). Statistical issues in long-term follow up studies. *Schizophrenia Bulletin*, **14**, 575–587.

Bradley, E.L. and Blackwood, L.G. (1989). Comparing paired data: A simultaneous test of means and variances. *American Statistician*, **43**, 234–235.

Cohen, J. (1960). A coefficient of agreement for nominal data. *Educational Psychological Measurement*, **20**, 37–46.

Fisher, R.A. (1935). *The Design of Experiments*. Edinburgh: Oliver & Boyd.

Fleiss, J.L. (1981). *Statistical Methods for Rates and Proportions*, 2nd edn. New York: Wiley & Sons Inc.

Fleiss, J.L. (1982). Jackknifing functions of multinomial frequencies, with an application to a measure of concordance. *American Journal of Epidemiology*, **115**, 841–845.

Fleiss, J.L. (1986). *The Design and Analysis of Clinical Experiments*. New York: Wiley & Sons Inc.

Kraemer, H.C., and Pruyn, J.P., Gibbons, R. D., *et al.* (1987). Methodology in psychiatric research. Report on the 1986 MacArthur Foundation Network I Methodology Institute. *Archives of General Psychiatry*, **44**, 1100–1106.

Landis, J.R. and Koch, G.G. (1977). The measurement of observer agreement for categorical data. *Biometrics*, **33**, 159–174.

Mehta, C.R., Patel, N.R., and Wei, L.J. (1988). Computing exact permutational distributions with restricted randomization designs. *Biometrika,* **75**, 295–302.

Mezzich, J.E., Kraemer, H.C., Worthington, D.R.L., and Coffman, G.A. (1981). Assessment of agreement among several raters formulating multiple diagnoses. *Journal of Psychiatric Research,* **16**, 29–39.

Pitman, E.J.G. (1939). A note on the normal correlation. *Biometrika,* **31**, 9–12.

Quenouille, M.H. (1956). Notes on bias in estimation. *Biometrika,* **43**, 353–360.

Prendergast, M., Taylor, E., Rapoport, J.L., *et al.* (1988). The diagnosis of childhood hyperactivity: A US–UK cross-national study of DSMIII and ICD-9. *Journal of Child Psychology and Psychiatry,* **29**, 289–300.

Schouten, H.J.A. (1986). Nominal scale agreement among observers. *Psychometrika,* **51**, 453–466.

Siegel, S. (1956). *Nonparametric Statistics for the Behavioral Sciences.* New York: McGraw-Hill Book Company.

Shrout, P.E. and Fleiss, J.L. (1979). Intraclass correlations: Uses in assessing rater reliability. *Psychological Bulletin,* **86**, 420–428.

Shrout, P.E., Spitzer, R.L., and Fleiss, J.L. (1987). Quantification of agreement in psychiatric diagnosis revisited. *Archives of General Psychiatry,* **44**, 172–195.

Simon, J.J. and Bruce, P. (1991). Resampling: A tool for everyday statistical work. *Chance,* **4**, 22–32.

Snedecor, G.W. and Cochran, W.G. (1976). *Statistical Methods,* 6th edn, p. 197. Ames, Iowa: Iowa State University Press.

Tukey, J.W. (1958). Bias and confidence in not-quite large samples. *Annuals of Mathematical Statistics,* **29**, 614.

Werner, O. and Campbell, D.T. (1971). Translating, working through interpreters and the problem of decentering. In Naroll, R., and Cohen, R., eds. *A Handbook of Cultural Anthropology.* New York: American Museum of Natural History.

Yule, G.U. (1912). On the methods of measuring association between two attributes. *Journal of the Royal Statistical Society,* **75**, 581–642.

WHO-IPSS (1973). *Report of the International Pilot Study of Schizophrenia,* Vol. I. Geneva: World Health Organization.

PART IV

THERAPEUTIC AND MANAGEMENT OPTIONS

12

Drug Treatments

JOHN M. KANE
Department of Psychiatry, Hillside Hospital, Division of Long Island Jewish Medical Center, New York and Albert Einstein College of Medicine, New York, USA

The drug treatment of schizophrenia has provided the greatest single impact in reducing the economic costs associated with this illness. The value of medication in decreasing acute signs and symptoms as well as helping to prevent psychotic relapse and rehospitalization has had a profound effect on the number of hospital days attributable to schizophrenia. In addition, many patients with the help of drug treatment are able to achieve reasonable levels of psychosocial and vocational adjustment, including at times, gainful employment.

This chapter will review the pharmacologic treatment of schizophrenia with an emphasis on resource allocation and cost–benefit assessments.

INDICATIONS FOR PHARMACOLOGIC TREATMENT

Any patient experiencing an acute episode or exacerbation of schizophrenia should receive a trial of antipsychotic medication (unless there is an absolute medical contraindication, which would be very rare).

There are several factors which would influence the cost of such treatment, primarily whether or not hospitalization is indicated. The judgment as to the need for admission will be influenced by the severity and nature of the psychopathlogy (e.g. is the patient a danger to themselves or others), the potential for treatment complications (e.g. adverse effects) which might require careful monitoring, and the alternative treatment settings which are available (e.g. crisis clinic, partial hospital, day hospital, home care, etc.). The extent to which the patient has insight into his or her condition and is willing to accept treatment and take medication on a voluntary basis will also influence the locus of treatment.

HOSPITAL TREATMENT

If hospitalization is indicated, the cost of pharmacologic treatment will involve the medical evaluation of the patient (physical, neurologic, laboratory tests, possibly electrocardiogram depending upon age, screen for drugs of abuse, etc.). In addition, a complete psychiatric history and mental status is necessary to establish diagnosis as well as previous treatment history and response (both therapeutic and adverse effects). The clinician should contact previous physicians and attempt to obtain prior medical records. A parallel history from the perspective of a family member or significant other is also potentially very useful.

Handbook of Mental Health Economics and Health Policy, Volume I, Schizophrenia. Edited by M. Moscarelli, A. Rupp and N. Sartorius.
© 1996 John Wiley & Sons Ltd.

CHOICE OF DRUG

Numerous different classes of antipsychotic drugs have been introduced over the past 35 years. There are no convincing data, with the exception of clozapine (Kane *et al.*, 1988), that any one drug or drug class is consistently more effective than another. A primary consideration in the choice of drug would be the patient's previous history of drug response. Evidence that a patient has responded well to a particular drug would argue strongly for a trial of that specific agent. By the same token, a history of serious adverse effects would argue against a particular drug (with the awareness that patients may misrepresent or overstate a specific drug reaction). An especially costly error in psychopharmacology is the lack of an adequate history. In many instances, treatments which have failed in the past are instituted again because of the lack of an accurate past history. Such an ill-informed clinical decision can easily prolong an acute episode with all of its consequent costs. The same also applies to reoccurence of serious adverse effects, which result in more intensive medical monitoring, evaluation, laboratory tests, and potential change and delay in treatment completion.

Given general equivalency between medications, the cost of drug may become an increasingly important determinant of drug choice. As new compounds are introduced, it will become necessary to have convincing data on added value in terms of clinical outcome (e.g. greater efficacy, reduced adverse effects, higher rates of compliance, etc.) to justify substantially higher costs.

At present the only drug for which some such data are available is clozapine, a drug with a substantially higher cost than other antipsychotic drugs, both in terms of direct cost and the expense of increased surveillance and laboratory tests because of the risk of agranulocytosis (Alvir *et al.*, 1993). At present, clozapine is generally reserved for patients who have failed to respond adequately to, or are intolerant of more typical antipsychotic compounds.

Another consideration in the choice of drug should relate to the long-term treatment plan. If the most recent relapse was precipitated by noncompliance, an especially important consideration would be the use of long-acting injectable medication. Using the oral form of such a drug initially could facilitate the transition to a depot preparation (though this is not essential). In my view, depot drugs are grossly underutilized given their potential to reduce the enormous costs associated with relapse and rehospitalization. Although their use is clearly indicated in those patients who have demonstrated noncompliance, the fact that noncompliance develops in a substantial proportion of patients (Kane, 1985) and is not easily predicted would argue for more widespread use of these agents before noncompliance leads to a relapse and not only afterwards.

DRUG DOSAGE

Although antipsychotic drugs have been in use for over 35 years, there continues to be debate as to what optimal doses are for acute treatment. It became clear shortly after the introduction of chlorpromazine that doses below 400–600 mg/day were much less likely to prove superior to placebo than doses above that range (Klein & Davis, 1969). With the introduction of so-called high-potency drugs, there was increasing interest in exploring the upper ranges of tolerated doses to determine if such dose would produce added benefits either in terms of rapidity of onset of therapeutic effect or the ultimate degree of improvement. In a series of studies comparing high dose (defined as above 2000 mg chlorpromazine equivalents) to standard dose treatment, there has been no statistically significant advantage for the high-dose treatment (see Kane, 1987, for review). Despite lack of clear evidence supporting the value of high doses, there was an increasing trend in the 1970s and 1980s (at least in the USA) to employ high doses of high potency drugs (Reardon *et al.*, 1989). This practice may have been influenced by the desire to bring about a more rapid response given increasing pressure to reduce length of hospital stay coupled with the assumption that such high doses are generally well-tolerated.

The issue of dosage takes on importance from an economic standpoint in the following respects. First, utilizing too low a dose might lead to slower or poorer response overall, including the need for a more intensive level of care, greater number of behavioral accidents, use of PRN medication, etc. On the other hand, use of a higher than necessary dose could result in an increase in adverse effects requiring physician or nurse time, the addition of adjunctive medication or the need to alter the treatment. In addition, the experience of unpleasant adverse effects may have a deleterious effect on the patient's compliance in medication-taking either over the short-term or the long-term. This could ultimately have a major economic impact in leading to subsequent psychotic relapse and rehospitalization.

The fact that the maintenance medication dose is also highly influenced by acute dose leads to additional concerns regarding optimal dose. Even though acute adverse effects may be more obvious or severe during the early phase of treatment, they can continue to be a problem during the maintenance phase of treatment. Side-effects such as akinesia or akathisia can be easily missed or misdiagnosed. At the same time, however, they can produce subjective distress or result in a clinical picture not unlike negative symptoms or what is now being referred to as a neuroleptic-induced deficit state. When viewed in this context, such adverse effects cannot only increase the risk of noncompliance, but they may also interfere with achieving optimal levels of psychosocial and vocational adjustment, thereby having further economic implications.

The use of prophylactic antiparkinsonian drugs should also be mentioned as one strategy to reduce the potential risk of extrapyramidal side-effects. This approach (though involving the cost of additional medication) may be cost-effective in permitting vigorous neuroleptic treatment with a reduced risk of complicating neurologic adverse effects. Though these drugs have their own array of side-effects, the relative impact of these adverse effects is generally far less than acute dystonic reactions or akathisia.

In recent years several studies have attempted to clarify optimal dose, particularly involving the drug haloperidol (Levinson *et al.*, 1990; Van Putten *et al.*, 1990; Rifkin *et al.*, 1991; McEvoy *et al.*, 1991). My conclusion from reviewing these studies is that the optimal dose of haloperidol for an acute trial is between 15 and 20 mg/day. This dosage is likely to produce the maximum therapeutic benefit in the largest proportion of patients. At the same time, however, some studies suggest that the incidence of adverse effect will be significantly higher than that seen with 5–10 mg/day. These adverse effects can be prevented or readily controlled with the addition of antiparkinsonian medication and this combination in my view is the most cost-effective in terms of assuring the highest likelihood of therapeutic response within the shortest time frame while controlling to a large extent the risk of adverse effects. It may be, as suggested by Van Putten *et al.* (1990), that after the first week or two the dosage of haloperidol could be reduced from 20 mg to 15 or 10 mg with the same outcome; however, this hypothesis has not been the subject of appropriate controlled trials. Doses of 15–20 mg may be particularly important in patients who are agitated or hostile. The intensity of supervision, potential injury to staff, the patient, and other patients are issues with considerable management and cost implications.

MANAGING PARTIAL OR NONRESPONDING PATIENTS

It is clear that a substantial proportion of patients with schizophrenia derive little if any benefit from a typical 4–6 week treatment trial with neuroleptic drugs regardless of the type of drug or dosage employed (Davis and Casper, 1977). The treatment of such patients continues to be a major challenge with considerable cost implications in terms of prolonged hospitalization and increased levels of long-term disability.

Despite the magnitude of this problem, there are remarkably few data contrasting (under controlled conditions) commonly used alternatives for managing patients who have failed to respond to an initial trial of an antipsychotic. Kinon *et al.* (1993) have reported initial results from a trial designed to address this issue. The most frequently employed alternatives in this context are to: (i) raise the dose substantially; (ii) switch to a different class of neuroleptic; and (iii) allow more time on the original treatment. Although the third alternative may be the most infrequently utilized, it is essential to have such a group as a control for the passage of additional time. Kinon *et al.* treated schizophrenic, schizoaffective, and schizophreniform patients openly with fluphenazine, 20 mg/

day, for 4 weeks. After this treatment, those patients who failed to meet a priori response criteria were randomly assigned, double-blind, to: (i) fluphenazine 80 mg/day; (ii) haloperidol 20 mg/day; or (iii) to continue on fluphenazine 20 mg/day. The double-blind phase lasted an additional 4 weeks. Only 9% of those who had not met response criteria at 4 weeks responded after 8 weeks and there were no significant differences between the three alternatives. It is possible that some refractory patients would benefit from substantial increases in medication dosage, but such patients appear to be in the minority and better methods would be needed to identify them before exposing the average nonresponding patient to high-dose treatment.

Christison *et al.* (1991) have thoroughly reviewed alternative somatic treatments for nonresponding patients including clozapine, benzodiazepines, electroconvulsive therapy, reserpine, carbamazepine, propranolol, and L-dopa. They concluded that for patients experiencing significant positive symptoms or both positive and negative symptoms, that clozapine, adjunctive lithium, and adjunctive benzodiazepines have the best documented benefit, but that clozapine is the treatment that appears capable of producing the most dramatic benefit in such patients.

CLOZAPINE

The marketing of clozapine in the USA in 1990 represented the first time since the development of antipsychotic drugs that any specific compound was approved by the US Food and Drug Administration based on evidence of superiority over other drugs for the indication of treatment refractoriness or treatment intolerance. Although clozapine is associated with a variety of adverse effects (Safferman *et al.*, 1991) and has an incidence of associated agranulocytosis of 0.8% after 1 year of treatment (Alvir *et al.*, 1993), it has consistently shown substantial benefit in treatment refractory patients (Kane *et al.*, 1988; Safferman *et al.*, 1991). In addition, recent reports suggest that clozapine, despite its expense and the costs associated with required hematologic monitoring, can reduce overall costs associated with the treatment of a subgroup of refractory patients (Revicki *et al.*, 1990; Reid *et al.*, 1993; Meltzer *et al.*, 1993). However, not all such analyses find significant cost savings (Davies & Drummond, 1993).

In treating refractory patients, it is essential that a well-thought out treatment plan be implemented. It is essential that target symptoms be identified and assessed as a baseline against which further improvement can be measured. It is all too common to see a variety of treatments being administered to refractory patients over long periods of time without any clear indication of the degree to which the patient has benefited.

COMORBID SYNDROMES

Given the fact that schizophrenia is a complex disease with a variety of behavioral, affective, and cognitive manifestations, it is not surprising perhaps that comorbid syndromes have frequently been overlooked. Relatively common examples are depression, obsessive–compulsive disorder, panic disorder, and substance abuse. In recent years there has been increasing recognition that these comorbid problems affect many patients and can be difficult to treat. The best studied of these conditions is probably depression. The suffering and disability produced by depressive symptoms can be considerable, and frequently these symptoms can be mistaken for (or overlap with) negative symptoms. When depression is associated with the onset or prodrome of a psychotic episode, antipsychotic medications are usually the most beneficial treatment. When depression occurs in the context of a relatively stabilized schizophrenic illness, then antidepressants can be very helpful (Siris *et al.*, 1987). It is also essential to recognize that akinesia, a neuroleptic side-effect which can be manifested by psychomotor retardation, blunted affect, and diminished spontaneity, can also be confused with depressive symptoms and/or negative symptoms. This differential diagnosis is critical because akinesia can be alleviated by reducing the dosage of the neuroleptic drug or using antiparkinsonian medication.

The management of other syndromes that commonly occur in patients with schizophrenia, such as anxiety disorders, obsessive–compulsive disorder, and alcohol or cocaine abuse have not received adequate attention. Clearly, these syndromes can contribute to increased disability and economic impact.

MAINTENANCE TREATMENT

The benefits of antipsychotic medication in the long-term maintenance treatment of schizophrenia has been established in numerous clinical trials over the past three decades (Davis, 1975; Kane & Lieberman, 1987). More recent maintenance treatment studies have focused on improving the benefit-to-risk ratio of long-term treatment and examining alternative maintenance strategies. In addition, some studies have also focused on the interaction of environmental and psychosocial factors with drug treatment.

Many of the same issues with regard to dosage, benefit-to-risk ratio, and impact on cost that were discussed previously apply in the maintenance phase of treatment; however, in this context the impact is even greater. Too low a dose can result in psychotic relapse with all of the consequent personal suffering and economic cost, whereas too high a dose may lead to adverse effects, reduced compliance, and ultimate relapse. In addition, with long-term treatment we have the added risk of tardive dyskinesia (Kane *et al.*, 1992).

A critical factor in the cost-effectiveness of maintenance treatment is compliance in medication-taking. It is clear that even among patients who are initially compliant enough to participate in controlled trials that approximately one in three develop some degree of noncompliance within 1 year (Kane, 1985). Among patients in general, rates of noncompliance are likely to be substantially higher. Despite the availability of so-called guaranteed medication in the form of long-acting injectable neuroleptics, these agents are used far less frequently than would seem warranted from a cost–benefit standpoint. The use of depot neuroleptics can reduce rate of relapse (Davis *et al.*, 1977) and it is likely that those controlled trials which have been conducted comparing oral and depot routes of administration have underestimated the potential advantages for depot drugs. The reason for this conclusion is that patients who entered such trials were, to a large extent, selected on the basis of initial compliance (in that they would agree to a double-blind clinical trial); and given the time that it might take for them to develop noncompliance and the time-frame of the subsequent relapse (which may not occur for several months), almost all of the studies were too short in duration to adequately identify potential advantages for depot drugs (Kane & Borenstein, 1985).

There are a variety of reasons why clinicians may be reluctant to use depot drugs. First, there is the fear that if adverse effects occur they may be more difficult to treat or more serious in their consequences. There is no evidence that this is true and even in the case of neuroleptic malignant syndrome, where discontinuing the neuroleptic is indicated, there is no evidence that depot drugs are associated with a higher mortality rate assuming the condition is dignosed in a timely fashion and appropriate treatment initiated. Secondly, many clinicians do not consider using depot drugs until noncompliance has been demonstated. As noncompliance is frequent and is not easily predicted, while the potential costs (both personal and economic) are so high, it would seem that more general use of depot drugs would be indicated. Glazer and Kane (1992) have reviewed these issues in more detail.

There have been several studies in recent years examining the benefit-to-risk ratio of different dosages of maintenance neuroleptics. Interestingly, all of these studies have utilized long-acting depot drugs. Clearly, when examining dose–response relationships, it is essential to be certain that the patient is actually taking the intended dose. It would seem that this would also be important in general clinical practice.

In this context the studies which have been conducted suggest that fluphenazine decanoate dosages in the range of 25–50 mg given every other week are associated with 1 year relape rates of 10–20% (average 16%). On the other hand, dosages in the range of 2.5–10 mg are associated with relapse rates of 20–30% (mean 25%).

There are some advantages of the lower doses in terms of fewer adverse effects (Kane *et al.*, 1983; Marder *et al.*, 1984) and possibly lower risk of tardive dyskinesia (Kane *et al.*, 1983), although the latter has not been consistently demonstrated. Clinical judgement is necessary to determine which dosage or dosage range is most appropiate for a given individual.

From a cost management standpoint, the higher the risk of relapse the more carefully (e.g. frequently) the patient should be monitored. The determination of frequency of visits will also be influenced by the availability of other individuals who might be in a position to detect early signs of relapse.

THE ROLE OF PSYCHOSOCIAL AND ENVIRONMENTAL FACTORS

As indicated, the cost of care in the maintenance phase may be influenced by the availability of significant others or a support system to help detect early signs of relapse or a change in clinical status. Psychoeducational approaches have been developed in recent years to help families detect prodromal signs of relapse as well as helping to reduce stressful phenomena in the environment or in family interactions. These strategies can be cost-effective if families, spouses, etc. are available and cooperative.

Environmental stress can increase the risk of relapse, but this may interact with dosage (Kreisman *et al.*, 1988). Among patients receiving very low doses of medication, the impact of stress may be greater than among patients receiving higher doses of medication. Therefore, these kinds of assessments are important to the clinician in establishing the most appropriate treatment plan in terms of medication dosage as well as the need for other forms of therapy. Appropriate psychosocial treatment (e.g. family therapy, social skills training) have been shown in some, but not all studies to reduce rates of relapse as well. Clearly, additional cost–benefit analyses of different approaches or treatment combinations will be necessary to make ultimate decisions when cost becomes an increasing concern.

THE ALLOCATION OF RESOURCES FOR PHARMACOLOGIC TREATMENT

During the acute phase of treatment, extensive physician involvement is desirable in the diagnostic evaluation, medical work-up, treatment plan and initiation, assessment of therapeutic response and adverse effects. At the same time guidelines have not been developed based on empirical data as to what frequency and intensity of, for example, follow-up visits during the first several weeks of treatment, are necessary. Should the patient be seen daily by a physician while in the hospital, less frequently, or determined by need on an individual basis? Does a judgement that the patient need not be seen by a physician every day diminish the justification for inpatient hospitalization? How often should nurses monitor the patient and what should be the targets of such monitoring? These are examples of questions which have not been adequately addressed, but which have considerable potential impact on the cost of care. In the maintenance phase of treatment, patients can be seen by nonphysicians who, if adequately trained, can identify signs of relapse (or prodromal signs of relapse), adverse effects, or other changes in the patient's status that might require physician intervention. To a large extent the success of nonphysician clinicians in this context depends on the adequacy of their training and ongoing supervision.

As increasing emphasis is placed on cost-efficacy analyses, it will become incumbent in the field to determine guidelines for the appropriate allocation of personnel resources, which in the case of psychiatric treatment are likely to represent a significant aspect of cost. Though it is relatively easy to compare different pharmacologic agents in a cost–benefit analysis, even this has yet to be done on a large-scale basis.

REFERENCES

Alvir, J., Lieberman, J., Safferman, A., Schwimmer, J.L., and Scaaf, J.A. (1993). Clozapine-induced agranulocytosis: US incidence and risk factors. *New England Journal of Medicine*, **329**, 162–167.

Kane, J.M. and Borenstein, M. (1985). Compliance in the long-term treatment of schizophrenia. *Psychopharmacolgical Bulletin*, **21**, 23–27.

Christison, G.W., Kirch, D.G., and Wyatt, R.J. (1991). When symptoms persist: Choosing among alternative somatic treatments for schizophrenia. *Schizophrenia Bulletin*, **17**, 217–246.

Davies, L.M. and Drummond, M.F. (1993). Assessment of costs and benefits of drug therapy for treatment-resistant schizophrenia in the United Kingdom. *British Journal of Psychiatry*, **162**, 38–42.

Davis, J.M. (1975). Overview: Maintenance therapy in psychiatry. I. Schizophrenia. *American Journal of Psychiatry*, **132**, 1237–1245.

Davis, J.M. and Casper, R. (1977). Antipsychotic drugs: Clinical pharmacology and therapeutic use. *Drugs*, **14**, 260–282.

Glazer, W.M., and Kane, J.M. (1992). Depot neuroleptic therapy: an underutilized treatment option. *Journal of Clinical Psychiatry*, **53**, 426–433.

Kane, J.M. (1985). Compliance issues in outpatient treatment. *Journal of Clinical Psychopharmacology*, **5**, 22–27S.

Kane, J.M. (1987). Treatment of schizophrenia. *Schizophrenia Bull*, **13**, 133–156.

Kane, J.M. and Lieberman, J. (1987). Maintenance pharmacotherapy in schizophrenia. In H.Y. Meltzer, ed., *Psychopharmacology, The Third Generation of Progress: The Emergence of Molecular Biology and Biological Psychiatry*, pp. 1103–1109. New York: Raven Press.

Kane, J.M., Rifkin, A., Woerner, M., *et al.* (1983). Low-dose neuroleptic treatment of outpatient schizophrenics. *Archives of General Psychiatry*, **40**, 893–896.

Kane, J.M., Honigfeld, G., Singer, J., and Meltzer, H. (1988). Clozapine for the treatment-resistant schizophrenic: A double-blind comparison with chlorpromazine. *Archives of General Psychiatry*, **45**, 789–796.

Kane, J.M., Jeste, D.V., Barnes, T.R.E. *et al.* (1992). *American Psychiatry Association Task Force Report on Tardive Dyskinesia.* Washington, DC: American Psychiatric Press.

Kimon, B.J., Kane, J.M., Johns, C., *et al.* (1993). Treatment of neuroleptic resistant schizophrenic relapse. *Psychopharmacological Bulletin*, **29**, 309–314.

Klein, D.F. and Davis, J.M. (1969). *Diagnosis and Drug Treatment of Psychiatric Disorders.* Baltimore, MD: William & Wilkins.

Kreisman, D., Blumenthal, R., Borenstein, M., *et al.* (1988). Family attitudes and patient social adjustment in a longitudinal study of outpatient schizophrenics receiving low-dose neuroleptics: The family's view. *Psychiatry*, **51**, 3–13.

Levinson, D.F., Simpson, G.M., Singh, H., *et al.* (1990). Fluphenazine dose: Clinical response and extrapyramidal symptoms during acute treatment. *Archives of General Psychiatry*, **47**, 761–768.

Marder, S.R., Van Putten, T., Mintz, J., *et al.* (1984). Costs and benefits of two doses of fluphenazine. *Arch Gen Psychiatry*, **41**, 1025–1029.

McEvoy, J.P., Hogarty, G., and Steingard, S. (1991). Optimal dose of neuroleptic in acute schizophrenia: A controlled study of the neuroleptic threshold and higher haloperidol dose. *Archives of General Psychiatry*, **48**, 739–745.

Meltzer, H.Y., Cola, P., Way, L., *et al.* (1993). Cost effectiveness of clozapine in neuroleptic-resistant schizophrenia. *American Journal of Psychiatry*, **150**, 1630–1638.

Reardon, G.T., Rifkin, A., Schwartz, A., Myerson, A., and Siris, S.H. (1989). Changing pattern of neuroleptic dosage over a decade. *American Journal of Psychiatry*, **146**, 726–729.

Reid, W.H., Pham, V.A., and Rago, W. (1993). Clozapine use by state programs: Public mental health systems respond to a new medication. *Hospital and Community Psychiatry*, **44**, 739–743.

Revicki, D.A., Luce, B.R., Weschler, J.M., *et al.* (1990). Cost effectiveness of clozapine for treatment-resistant schizophrenic patients. *Hospital and Community Psychiatry*, **1**, 850–854.

Rifkin, A., Doddi, S., Karagi, B., Borenstein, M., and Wachspress, M. (1991). Dosage of haloperidol for schizophrenia. *Archives of General Psychiatry*, **48**, 166–170.

Safferman, A., Lieberman, J.A., Kane, J.M., Szymanski, S., and Kinon, B. (1991). Update on the clinical efficacy and side effects of clozapine. *Schizophrenia Bulletin*, **17**, 247–262.

Siris, S.G., Morgan, V., Faugerstrom, R., Rifkin, A., and Cooper, T.B. (1987). Adjunctive imipramine in the treatment of post-psychotic depression: A controlled trial. *Archives of General Psychiatry*, **44**, 533–539.

Van Putten, T., Marder, S.R., and Mintz, J. (1990). A controlled dose comparison of haloperidol in newly admitted schizophrenic patients. *Archives of General Psychiatry*, **47**, 754–758.

13

Side-effects of Neuroleptic Medication: Assessment and Impact on Outcome of Psychotic Disorders

RICHARD P. BENTALL
Department of Clinical Psychology, University of Liverpool, Liverpool, UK

JENNIFER DAY
Department of Nursing, University of Manchester, Manchester, UK

ANNE ROGERS
National Primary Care Research and Development Centre, University of Salford, Salford, UK

DAVID HEALY
Academic Sub-Department of Psychological Medicine in North Wales, North Wales Hospital, Denbigh, UK

RICHARD C. STEVENSON
Department of Economics, Liverpool University, Liverpool, UK

INTRODUCTION: THE CLINICAL EFFICACY OF NEUROLEPTICS

In this chapter we review evidence on psychotic patients' subjective experiences of the benefits and costs of neuroleptic medication, focusing in particular on the impact of adverse reactions on the lives of patients and on their willingness to comply with treatment, and also on the broader costs associated with these reactions. We review various published instruments that have been developed to measure side-effects, which may prove useful both for the purposes of clinical trials and for the routine monitoring of patients receiving neuroleptic therapy.

The development of neuroleptic medications is sometimes portrayed as an unequivocal, perhaps revolutionary advance in the treatment of the severe psychiatric disorders (Iverson & Iverson, 1981; Croyden-Smith, 1982). In the four decades since Delay *et al.* (1952) first demonstrated the antipsychotic properties of chlorpromazine, these drugs have become widely regarded as the treatment of choice for schizophrenic disorders (Lieberman, 1993). Controlled trials have consistently demonstrated that most patients who receive neuroleptics experience less positive symptomatology and are hospitalized less often than patients receiving placebos or other kinds of medication (Leff & Wing, 1971; Green,

Handbook of Mental Health Economics and Health Policy, Volume I, Schizophrenia. Edited by M. Moscarelli, A. Rupp and N. Sartorius.
© 1996 John Wiley & Sons Ltd.

1988). Unfortunately, a proportion of psychotic patients consistently fail to respond to conventional neuroleptics (Brown & Herz, 1989). Although some of these patients may benefit from atypical neuroleptic drugs such as clozapine (Kane *et al.*, 1988), some patients fail to respond even to these newer compounds.

The exact biochemical mechanisms responsible for the therapeutic efficacy of neuroleptics are not fully understood. However, an association between dopamine receptor blockade and the antipsychotic action of neuroleptics was first demonstrated by Carlsson and Lindqvist (1963) and, since that time, substantial research has supported the hypothesis that the clinical effectiveness of neuroleptics is related to their impact on the dopamine system and in particular their ability to occupy D-2 receptors (Van Kammen, 1991; Leonard, 1992; Sunahara *et al.*, 1993).

Continuous medication seems to be the most effective method of neuroleptic treatment; although some investigators have advocated intermittent regimens in which patients receive little or no medication unless they experience life stresses or prodromal symptoms (Carpenter *et al.*, 1987), studies indicate that patients receiving such treatment fair less well in terms of symptoms and vulnerability to relapse (Jolley *et al.*, 1990). Moreover, it is not clear that intermittent medication regimens confer an advantage in terms of reduced side-effects (Herz *et al.*, 1991).

It is only in recent years that the proper dose ranges for neuroleptics have been carefully studied, following a review by Baldessarini *et al.* (1988), which suggested that doses of more than 600 mg of chlorpromazine per day or 30 mg of haloperidol per day might be counter-therapeutic. This review highlighted the fact that no trials had been carried out to establish optimal dosages for neuroleptic maintenance therapy, provoking a series of such studies (Van Putten *et al.* 1990; McEvoy *et al.*, 1991; Rifkind *et al.*, 1991). The basic design of these investigations involved comparing several dosages of haloperidol with each other. The general finding was that 5 mg haloperidol per day was as effective as any other dose and indeed there was some evidence that lower doses might be as effective or even more effective (Rifkind *et al.*, 1991). (See Bollini *et al.*, 1994, for a recent meta-analysis of the relationship between dosage and clinical response, which confirmed that high-dose neuroleptic regimens are associated with severe side-effects but not with increased therapeutic response when compared with low-dose regimens.) This finding coincided with PET scan data from studies employing radiolabelled neuroleptics, which found that doses of the order of 5 mg of haloperidol per day occupy D-2 receptor sites to the level which has been thought sufficient for therapeutic efficacy (Farde *et al.*,1988). Such studies have also revealed that patients who fail to respond to treatment tend to have as high or even higher D-2 occupancy than those who respond to neuroleptic therapy.

Taken together, these observations have been widely taken to imply that low-dose prophylactic medication is the treatment of choice for the majority of psychotic patients. However, this conclusion about the effectiveness of neuroleptic therapy is based mostly on outcome data from clinical trials in the form of clinicians' observations of the behavior of patients or records of patients' statements about their symptoms. Patients' subjective experiences of being medicated are rarely acknowledged and are rarely the target of detailed assessment.

WHAT DO PATIENTS THINK ABOUT NEUROLEPTIC TREATMENT?

Studies show that patients vary widely in their subjective appraisal of the benefits and costs of neuroleptic therapy. For example, in a large survey of psychiatric patients in Great Britain, Rogers *et al.* (1993) observed that 56.8% of patients who had received neuroleptics felt that they were helpful whereas 27.7% rated neuroleptics as "harmful" or "very harmful." Davidhizar (1987) similarly found that patients' beliefs and attitudes towards neuroleptic medication varied widely, and also that some patients held strongly negative and also strongly positive attitudes towards neuroleptics at the same time. This latter observation indicates that patients' views about neuroleptics may be complex and multidimensional, and may not be easily captured along a simple "for versus against" dimension.

Something of this complexity has been revealed in a number of recent studies. Rogers and Pilgrim

(1993), for example, in a qualitative analysis of interview data collected from psychiatric patients, found evidence that satisfaction with treatment may reflect, in part, not only the nature of the treatment but also where it is experienced. In particular, patients seemed to associate neuroleptic therapy with coercion and compulsory admission. In contrast, antidepressants, which are mainly prescribed in primary care settings, were viewed more positively by patients.

Finn *et al.* (1990) argued that, if the costs and benefits of neuroleptic therapy are to be fully appreciated, they must be assessed from at least two different points of view: that of the patient ("individual utility") and also that of all those likely to be affected by the treatment ("institutional utility"), for example the patient's family and local community. Forty-eight patients receiving neuroleptics were interviewed to obtain individual profiles of positive symptoms and side-effects, and then rated the extent to which they were bothered by those symptoms and side-effects which they experienced. A group of 34 experienced psychiatrists performed a similar task using a standard list of symptoms and side-effects, first rating the bothersomeness of these symptoms from the point of view of an average patient and then from the point of view of an average patient's family and society as a whole. Both patients and psychiatrists rated psychotic symptoms as no more bothersome than side-effects. This finding indicates that, from the patient's point of view, the balance between the costs and benefits may be equivocal, and also that this perception is often understood by those who prescribe neuroleptic therapy. However, the psychiatrists who took part in the study rated the side-effects of medication as significantly less bothersome than symptoms when they considered the costs and benefits to society as a whole. Indeed, virtually no relationship was observed between individual and institutional utilities in this study.

In our own work (Day *et al.*, in press), we have attempted to obtain a more detailed picture of patients' attitudes towards neuroleptic therapy, using a social constructionist approach. This approach assumes that individuals actively construct an understanding of events and experiences which are important to them (Gergen, 1985; Stainton Rogers, 1991), and that the understandings achieved by different individuals may vary in structure as well as degree. To take a simple example, two patients may have negative attitudes towards neuroleptics for completely different reasons: one because she or he feels that the requirement to take medication compromises his or her autonomy and the other because of the experience of unpleasant side-effects. The particular technique we used in our study was Q-methodology (Stephenson, 1935; McKeown & Thomas, 1988), which requires participants to sort statements in a particular domain according to agreement or disagreement (thus producing a "Q sort" for each participant). Following further analysis, "prototypical sorts" or viewpoints are identified which represent the dialogues commonly employed by individuals when talking about the particular subject area (in this case, neuroleptic therapy).

Fifty patients who were receiving neuroleptic medication generated Q-sorts, using statements about medication extracted from interviews with patients and professionals. Three main viewpoints were identified. Some patients endorsed statements which suggested that they were "unreflectively compliant," agreeing strongly with such statements as "I can't do without my medication" and disagreeing with such statements as "neuroleptics are just chemical strait-jackets." These patients expressed great trust in the judgement of medical professionals and considerable fear about the consequences of discontinuing medication. A second group of patients was sceptical about the value of medication (agreeing with items such as "neuroleptics aren't good for everyone" and "medication doesn't cure the illness it just controls the symptoms") and expressed the need for personal autonomy in making decisions about medication (agreeing that, "if I started getting any serious side-effects I would stop taking my medication" and disagreeing with the statement "I don't think I should get involved in decisions about my treatment"). For this group, side-effects were not an important issue and did not seem to contribute to their relatively negative view of medication. The third group expressed opinions consistent with having formed a balanced appraisal of the pros and cons of medication. These patients were aware of the benefits of medication, agreeing with statements such as, "If I did not take my medication I'd end up back in hospital," but were also concerned about the impact of side-effects as reflected in their strong disagreement with the statement, "I don't have any side-effects from my medication."

Taken together, the results of these studies indicate that individual patients often reach radically different understandings of the benefits and costs of neuroleptic therapy. For some patients, the benefits clearly outweigh the costs whereas, for others, this is not the case. Of particular importance to patients may be the extent to which they experience adverse rather than positive consequences of therapy. Any understanding of the economic and clinical impact of neuroleptics should therefore take into account patients' experiences of these adverse effects.

SIDE-EFFECTS OF NEUROLEPTIC THERAPY

The range of adverse reactions which may be experienced by patients taking neuroleptics is considerable. Adverse neurological reactions, in the form of extrapyramidal side-effects, are usually particularly noticeable and are of four main types. *Parkinsonian side-effects* include changes in gait, tremor, rigidity, hypersalivation, akinesia (slowing of movements), dysphagia (difficulty swallowing), and a characteristic dazed or expressionless appearance, which is often wrongly attributed to the underlying psychosis. These effects are usually evident after 5–80 days of treatment, and are reversible with the administration of anticholinergic drugs such as procyclidine. Estimates of their prevalence in neuroleptic-treated patients range between 15 and 25% of patients (Ayd, 1961; Kennedy *et al.*, 1971). *Acute dystonic* reactions, characterized by dramatic muscular spasms or sustained tonic contractions of muscles or muscle groups, usually affecting the head and neck, typically occur within the first 5 days of treatment and are quickly reversed by the administration of intramuscular or intravenous anticholinergics. Approximately 10% of patients experience this kind of reaction (Swett, 1975). *Akathisia*, characterized by an inner subjective restlessness often but not always accompanied by motor restlessness, is another commonly observed adverse neurological reaction and can be extremely distressing to patients. In some cases, patients will constantly stand up and sit down, shift from foot to foot or run from side to side in order to relieve inner discomfort. Estimates of the proportion of treated patients affected by this side-effect vary between 20% (Ayd, 1961; Braude *et al.*, 1983) and 75% (Van Putten *et al.*, 1984). Finally, among the neurological side-effects is the best known, *tardive dyskinesia*, a late developing movement disorder, which is often irreversible (Jeste & Wyatt, 1979) and is characterized by involuntary orobuccal movements such as tongue protrusion, fly catching tongue, lip-smacking movements, and lateral jaw movements. Estimates of the number of neuroleptic-treated patients who eventually suffer from this reaction range from as few as 0.5% to as many as 65% (Simpson *et al.*, 1982). The absence of a proven treatment for tardive dyskinesia means that it is a cause of considerable concern to health professionals, although not all patients feel a high level of distress as a result of this side-effect (Rosen *et al.*, 1982).

Although these four side-effects are perhaps the most widely known, neuroleptics can produce a range of additional adverse reactions. They may lower the convulsive threshold and thereby precipitate seizures, both in patients with a history of seizures and in those previously seizure-free (Toone & Fenton, 1977). *Anticholinergic side-effects* are also quite common, including dry mouth, constipation, blurred vision and urinary retention, and may particularly affect patients with preexisting physical disorders such as glaucoma or prostatic hypertrophy. Some drugs such as thioridazine and clozapine are more likely to cause anticholinergic effects due to their intrinsic selectivity for muscarinic receptors. Overall, the prevalence of these kinds of effects has been estimated at about 40% among treated patients (Lingjaerde *et al.*, 1987).

Postural hypotension is the most common drug-induced *cardiovascular* effect of neuroleptics but other cardiac effects include nonspecific ECG abnormalities, cardiac conduction defects, and arrhythmias. There is an increased risk of death due to cardiac arrest in patients taking neuroleptics (Thorogood *et al.*, 1992). Neuroleptics also induce *hormonal and metabolic effects*, with adverse consequences for sexual functioning and body weight. Patients of both sexes may experience orgastic dysfunction and reduced libido. Erectile dysfunction, ejaculatory dysfunction and priapism (prolonged painful erection) may be experienced by males

(Segraves, 1988; Sullivan & Lukoff, 1990).

Neuroleptics elevate prolactin levels, sometimes resulting in amenorrhea (absence of menstruation in females), gynecomastia (breast growth, which may occur in both males and females), and galactorrhea (milk production, also in both sexes). Weight gain is also a common side-effect of neuroleptic medication, particularly of low potency medications, such as chlorpromazine and thioridazine, which may induce an increase in weight of as much as 22 kg (Gordon & Grotte, 1964). The mechanism responsible for this effect is not understood, although it is thought that neuroleptics stimulate carbohydrate craving (Robinson *et al*., 1975).

Neuroleptics also have a number of *hematological consequences*, the most dangerous of which is agranulocytosis (reduction in the white blood cell count), which has a 30% mortality rate (Edwards, 1986). This reaction is reversible on discontinuation of the drug but is often not recognized until it is well advanced. Agranulocytosis usually but not always occurs within the first 3 months of treatment but is quite rare, estimates of the proportion of treated patients affected ranging between 1 in 3000 and 1 in 250 000 (Dukes, 1992). This rises to one to two in 100 for the atypical neuroleptic clozapine (Shopshin & Feiner, 1983) necessitating strict monitoring of blood in patients prescribed this drug.

As neuroleptics are predominantly metabolized in the liver, it is not surprising that *hepatic effects* have been reported. Jaundice, which is particularly associated with the phenothiazines, usually occurs within the first month of treatment. Other minor hepatic abnormalities as revealed by liver function tests have also been reported (Dickes *et al*., 1957).

Additional physical reactions which are often a source of distress to neuroleptic-treated patients include allergic reactions, including skin reactions and photosensitivity (which may necessitate patients using a sun-screen to avoid sunburn, even in mild weather), accumulation of pigmentation in the eyes which sometimes leads to visual impairment, a hypersensitivity syndrome which includes bronchospasm (contraction of the airways), gastrointestinal symptoms, urticaria and cholestatic jaundice, polyuria (excessive urination), and polydipsia (excessive drinking) (Lawson *et al*., 1985; Edwards, 1986). Approximately 0.5–1% of patients may experience *neuroleptic malignant syndrome* characterized by muscular rigidity, fever, fluctuating consciousness, hyperthermia, dyskinesia, and autonomic dysfunction, which may be mistaken for serious bacterial infection leading to inappropriate treatment with antibiotics. In approximately 20% of affected patients this reaction is fatal (Caroff, 1980). This condition may persist for 5–10 days after discontinuation of neuroleptics or considerably longer if a depot preparation has been administered.

Finally, the adverse psychological effects of neuroleptic medication should not be underestimated. In the short-term these may be manifest as feelings of listlessness or panic (Van Putten, 1974; Singh, 1976; Van Putten *et al*., 1976, 1981; Van Putten & May, 1978), which will be discussed in more detail below (see section following on adverse effects and response to treatment). In the longer term, patients may experience a persistent state of lethargy, emotional bluntness, and indifference to the environment.

That neuroleptics have a sedative action has been recognized since their introduction. Indeed, sedation has often been regarded as a useful attribute of neuroleptics, particularly where psychotic symptoms are associated with psychomotor excitation. However, the clinical need for sedation is usually short-term, and the state of lethargy, bluntness, and indifference which is a common adverse consequence of maintenance treatment—sometimes described as the *neuroleptic-induced deficit syndrome* (NIDS)—is usually experienced as unpleasant by patients and undesirable by prescribers. Lewander (1994) has commented on the lack of research carried out into the NIDS. Part of the problem seems to be the lack of agreed terminology for describing this type of response to neuroleptics, which has also been referred to by such terms as *neuroleptic dysphoria* (Emerich & Sanberg, 1991) and *akinetic depression* (Van Putten & May, 1978).

The NIDS can be detrimental to well-being, work output, and general quality of life (Lewander, 1994). For example, in a large clinical trial in which neuroleptics were compared with placebos, Crow *et al*. (1986) found that treated patients, despite being less vulnerable to relapse, made significantly fewer life achievements than patients receiving placebo medication. It has been argued that this kind of effect may impede the efficacy of other kinds of treatments such as psychotherapy (Karon, 1984), although systematic studies of the interaction between neuroleptics and psychosocial therapies have yet to be carried out (Falloon & Liberman, 1983; Bentall & Day, 1994). The NIDS has also been implicated as a major cause of noncompliance with neuroleptics (Van Putten & May, 1978; Weiden *et al.*, 1986).

Several commentators have noted that it is often difficult to differentiate between the negative symptoms of schizophrenia and the NIDS (Lewander, 1994; Schooler, 1994). One possible way of achieving this is to vary neuroleptic dosage. If the effect observed is drug-induced, a dose reduction should result in improved volition and decreased dysphoria whereas, if the effect is a symptom of an underlying psychotic illness, a dose reduction should result in a worsening of these symptoms. A complication is that negative symptoms are often regarded as unresponsive to neuroleptic medication (Crow, 1980), although some authors contend that this is not always the case (Goldberg, 1985; Meltzer *et al.*, 1986; Kane, 1989). In order to clarify the relationship between negative symptoms and both the positive and adverse consequences of neuroleptics, therefore, further studies are required, employing validated tools to assess negative symptoms as well as side-effects prior to and after the administration of neuroleptics to previously neuroleptic naive individuals.

Evidence that the apparent adverse psychological effects of neuroleptics cannot be dismissed as symptoms of an underlying illness is available from animal studies, which have shown that neuroleptics can be used to establish conditioned taste aversions (Bignami, 1991). If the reader should remain in any doubt about the reality of the adverse psychological consequences of neuroleptic drugs for humans it is worth considering the experiences of normal (non-psychotic) people who have cause to take them. Belmaker and Wald (1977), two psychiatrists, have described being administered an intravenous injection of 5 mg of haloperidol as part of a study of the possible role of dopaminergic mechanisms in affective disorders:

> The effect was marked and very similar in both of us: within ten minutes a marked slowing of thinking and movement developed, along with profound inner restlessness. Neither subject could continue work, and each left work for over 36 hours. Each subject complained of a paralysis of volition, a lack of physical and psychic energy. The subjects felt unable to read, telephone or perform household tasks of their own will, but could perform these tasks if demanded to do so. There was no sleepiness or sedation; on the contrary, both subjects complained of severe anxiety.

CLINICAL CONSEQUENCES OF THE ADVERSE EFFECTS OF MEDICATION

Not surprisingly, a number of studies have demonstrated a relationship between patients' experiences of the costs and benefits of neuroleptic therapy and their willingness to undergo treatment. For example, this relationship is reflected in the responses that patients give when asked to explain why they are taking or not taking neuroleptics. Hoge *et al.* (1990), in a large-scale study carried out in the USA, found that refusal to take neuroleptics was associated with negative attitudes towards hospitalization and treatment and with frequent seclusion and restraint. The most common reasons given by patients for noncompliance were side-effects (35% of refusers), denial of mental illness (21%), the avowed ineffectiveness of medication (12%) and "other responses that overtly reflect psychotic or idiosyncratic thought processes" (30%). Psychiatrists interviewed in the course of his study attributed noncompliance to side-effects in only 7% of cases, and blamed psychotic factors in 49% of cases.

Prospective studies have provided clearer evidence of an association between patients' subjective experiences of neuroleptics and compliance with treatment. Hogan *et al.* (1983), developed a 30-item questionnaire (the Drug Attitude Inventory) designed to measure attitudes towards neuroleptic medication, using the recorded statements of patients to generate potential items. Items were included in the scale if they discriminated between patients rated by their therapists to be compliant with medication and those judged to be noncompliant. When the questionnaire was administered to a further 150 patients, the full scale and each of the selected items were found to discriminate between the 46% of the patients who were judged to be compliant and the remaining 54% who were judged to be noncompliant. When the items of the scale were subjected to a factor analysis, seven factors were identified. The first factor, accounting for 59.8% of the variance in the data, contained items expressing positive subjective feelings about neuroleptics (e.g. "I feel more normal," "I feel happier") whereas the second factor, accounting for 11.7% of the variance, contained items expressing subjective negative or dysphoric feelings about neuroleptics ("I feel like a zombie," "Things are more difficult to do"). Thus, maximum variability in responding to the questionnaire reflected how patients felt on medication, rather than specific knowledge or beliefs about neuroleptics.

Similar evidence of a relationship between patients' feelings when on neuroleptics and their subsequent response to therapy has been obtained from studies which have observed patients' early responses to treatment. Singh and Smith (1973) first observed that patients who had an unfavorable response to haloperidol showed a marked dysphoric reaction, characterized by feelings of listlessness or panic, shortly after the commencement of treatment. Subsequent prospective studies by Van Putten and colleagues (Van Putten & May, 1978; May *et al.*, 1981; Van Putten *et al.*, 1981) confirmed this association. For example, Van Putten *et al.*, (1981) studied the response of 63 newly admitted patients to thiothixene. Dysphoria was measured 4 and 24 hours after treatment using a simple rating scale (described in more detail below). Initial dysphoric response was found to be a powerful predictor of drug refusal, and dysphoric patients reported significantly more extrapyramidal side-effects than nondysphoric patients.

Hogan and Awad (1992) compared a 10-item version of the Drug Attitude Inventory with Van Putten's dysphoria scale in 55 recently admitted patients receiving neuroleptic therapy. Scores on the two measures, administered 24 and 48 hours after the commencement of treatment, were found to be highly correlated. Neuroleptic dysphoria was associated with poor clinical response to treatment as measured by symptom scores after 3 weeks. By the third week of treatment, patients classified as dysphoric were also showing more severe extrapyramidal side-effects in comparison with nondysphoric patients.

THE ECONOMIC IMPACT OF SIDE-EFFECTS

In this context it will be helpful to consider some of the economic implications of neuroleptic side-effects. The costs to society of schizophrenia are measured in three main categories: direct treatment costs; indirect costs of loss of production by patients; and indirect costs to families, which may be pecuniary (loss of earnings by carers and the cost of visits to hospitals and clinics) and non-pecuniary (anxiety or the loss of leisure time). One study estimated that the direct cost of treatment for a person with schizophrenia in the UK was £2138 per year in 1991–92 prices (Davies & Drummond, 1994). Although the majority of patients diagnosed as schizophrenic are prescribed neuroleptic medication, drug costs amounted to only 5% of the direct costs. Davies and Drummond estimated the annual direct costs of schizophrenia for medical and social services at £397 million, which amounted to 1.6% of the total health care budget. The loss of patients' earnings was estimated conservatively at £1.7 billion. No account was taken of the cost of the premature mortality of patients, or of costs to families, although two small studies have shown these to be substantial (Johnstone *et al.*, 1986; McGuire, 1991).

Taking the prevalence of schizophrenia in the UK as 136 000 patients, Kavanagh (1994) analyzed the costs of care according to patients' accommodation, including hospital inpatients, those living in private households (receiving general practitioner and specialist care), those in specialist accommodation, those in prison, and the homeless. The largest category of patients was those treated in private households (60 000). Estimates of direct costs differ between studies according to the range of agencies considered, but are consistent in showing the high proportion of costs incurred by relatively few patients. Davies and Drummond (1994) concluded that 97% of direct costs were incurred by less than half the patients, and Kavanagh (1994) drew attention to the very high cost of inpatient care for people with a diagnosis of schizophrenia.

Disease costings are useful as a broad measure of the economic impact of an illness but fall short of an economic evaluation which would relate costs to benefits for alternative treatment regimens and would allow health care purchasers to seek cost-effectiveness in the use of mental health resources. Economic evaluations of this sort are scarce in the treatment of schizophrenia, but a number of studies have attempted to show that clozapine is cost-effective for treatment-resistant patients. Despite the cost of monitoring for agranulocytosis, it is claimed that clozapine performs well in comparison with other medications by reducing hospital admissions for a particularly expensive group of patients, and by enhancing both social functioning and quality of life (Fitton & Benfield, 1993).

So far as we are aware, no studies have addressed specifically the contribution that side-effects of treatment make to the cost of schizophrenia. However, direct costs are undoubtedly incurred in monitoring and treating iatrogenic illness. Side-effects, particularly the NIDS, contribute to the patient's inability to remain in employment and are a major factor in the reluctance of some patients to comply with treatment. Side-effects also add to the pecuniary and psychological costs borne by families.

To separate the cost of iatrogenic illness from the whole cost of schizophrenia would be a difficult and perhaps unprofitable exercise. Of greater practical use would be the economic appraisal of programs designed to reduce side-effects, which might include low-dose maintenance therapy, or perhaps even the complete avoidance of medication for some patients. A patient-centered approach to the economic evaluation of such programs would recognize explicitly the negative as well as the positive utilities of treatment, and would accord well with traditional economic modelling, which assumes the consumer or patient to be the best judge of his or her own interests (although economists readily concede that this sort of rationality is not necessarily characteristic of children or the mentally ill). From an economic perspective noncompliance is of special interest. Noncompliant patients, being prone to periods of inpatient care, are likely to be particularly expensive to treat. There would therefore seem to be potential gains from programs which might increase compliance by reducing the cost to the patient in terms of the disutility generated by side-effects.

The evaluation of changes in treatment designed to reduce side-effects requires the costs of these changes to be compared with benefits. The principles of costing are well understood, although sometimes difficult to apply in practice. However, measuring the costs and benefits of treatment may produce misleading results unless undertaken using well-validated instruments.

MEASURING SIDE-EFFECTS OF NEUROLEPTIC THERAPY

Given the potential damaging impact of neuroleptic side-effects on the quality of life of psychiatric patients, and their potential economic impact, it might be assumed that the careful monitoring of adverse reactions is an essential element of the long-term care of the severely mentally ill. Unfortunately, side-effects are usually monitored unsystematically by prescribing clinicians, and many patients are ill-informed about their nature. Rogers *et al.* (1993), for example, in their survey of a large sample of British people who had received psychiatric treatment, found that few of those who had been taking neuroleptics had been informed about side-effects by the medical and nursing staff who were responsible for their treatment.

There are several explanations for clinicians' reluctance to monitor side-effects and discuss them with patients. One explanation is historical: in the years immediately following the introduction of neuroleptics, and in particular following the introduction of haloperidol, it was widely believed that side-effects were not only inevitable but were required in order to produce an antipsychotic effect. This position, advocated by Delay and Janssen, was resisted by Hippus, who was involved in the early introduction of clozapine, a compound which appeared to have antipsychotic properties but which had few neurological side-effects (see Healy, in press, for interviews with those conducting research into neuroleptics during this period). Unfortunately, clozapine was withdrawn from use because of the risk of agranulocytosis, and has only recently been reintroduced as a treatment for patients who fail to respond to typical neuroleptic compounds. Its reintroduction, together with the discovery that low-dose neuroleptic regimens are as effective as high-dose regimens but produce fewer side-effects, makes it clear that Hippus was right, rather than Delay and Janssen.

A second likely explanation for clinicians' reluctance to discuss possible adverse reactions with patients is the fear that knowledge of side-effects will be associated with poor compliance, a fear which may seem all too reasonable given that many patients cite side-effects as a reason for refusing mediction (Hoge *et al.*, 1990). Paradoxically, this fear is not well-founded. Seltzer *et al.* (1980), although observing an association between fear of side-effects and noncompliance, found that educating patients about the side-effects of neuroleptics reduced fear without compromising compliance. More recently, Kleinman *et al.* (1989) also found that informing patients about the risk of side-effects had no impact on compliance rates.

Third, clinicians may be genuinely unaware of the distress caused to patients by side-effects. It will be recalled that Finn *et al.* (1990) found that psychiatrists and patients gave quite different estimates of which side-effects caused most distress. Further evidence that clinicians often misunderstand the distress caused by side-effects has emerged in a recent study conducted in Liverpool (Day & Bentall, in preparation) in which it was observed that clinicians' decisions about whether to inform patients about potential side-effects were a function of the perceived prevalence of particular side-effects and the perceived distress associated with them. In this study a near to zero correlation was found between psychiatrists' estimates of the distress caused by particular side-effects and the distress reported by patients who were actually experiencing the side-effects.

A final impediment to the practice of monitoring side-effects is no doubt the apparent lack of suitable instruments for this purpose. Ideally, such instruments should be easy and economical to use, and should meet minimum standards or reliability and validity. *Reliability* refers to the degree to which an instrument gives consistent results. For example, an instrument should give similar results when administered by two independent clinicians (inter-rater reliability) and, if measuring a stable trait, should give similar results on two different occasions (test–retest reliability). A further indication of the reliability of an instrument is its internal consistency, for example as measured by Cronbach's alpha coefficient which reflects the extent to which the different items correlate with each other. *Validity* is a more complex criterion, and concerns the extent to which an instrument is useful for the purposes for which it was designed. In the case of an instrument designed to measure neuroleptic side-effects, scores on the instrument should reflect the degree to which patients actually experience side-effects. This might be determined by seeing how scores on the instrument correlate with scores on an established measure of side-effects (concurrent validity), or with other theoretically interesting indices such as dose of medication. Depending on the avowed purpose of the instrument it may be useful to see how well scores on it predict theoretically interesting and useful outcomes (predictive validity) such as compliance with medication.

Despite the relative lack of research devoted to the measurement of neuroleptic side-effects some useful instruments have been reported in the literature. Most have focused on particular groups of symptoms, and been designed for administration by trained raters, e.g. medical practitioners, who make their ratings on the basis of the observed behavior of patients. An example of such an instrument is Simpson and Angus' (1970) scale (developed from an earlier scale by Simpson *et al.*, 1964), which consists of 10 items designed to measure extrapyramidal side-effects. Each item is rated on a five-point scale varying from 0 ("complete absence of the condition") to 4 ("condition in extreme form"). Detailed scoring criteria are given for each of the items, some of which require physical manipulation and examination of the patient. For example, gait is assessed by observing the patient as he or she walks into the examining room. A score of 0 is given for a normal gait; 1 for "diminution in swing while the patient is walking"; 2 for "marked diminution of swing with obvious rigidity in the arm"; 3 for "stiff gait with arms held rigidly before the abdomen"; and 4 for "stooped shuffling gait with propulsion and retropulsion." "Leg pendulousness" is assessed by sitting the patient on a table with legs hanging down and swinging free. The examiner then grasps the patient's ankle and raises the leg until the knee is partially extended, which is then allowed to fall. The resistance to falling and the lack of swinging form the basis for scoring this item.

The reliability and validity of the scale were assessed in a 10 week double-blind trail of haloperidol

(6 mg/day versus 30 mg/day versus placebo). The inter-rater reliability of individual items rated by two psychatrists, as measured by Pearson's correlation coefficient, varied between 0.52 and 0.87. The inter-rater reliability for the total score on the scale was 0.87. Although a factor analysis was reported, yielding a four-factor solution accounting for 69% of the variance, the small number of patients contributing to the study (14) means that this finding must be interpreted with extreme caution. However, the validity of the scale was evident by comparing the scores of patients receiving different dosages. Those receiving 6 mg/day scored significantly higher than those receiving placebo, although the difference between those receving 30 mg/day and those receiving 6 mg/day just failed to reach significance.

Mindham (1976) has described a similar, five-item instrument designed to assess drug-induced extrapyramidal reactions. Ratings for each item are given on a 0–3 scale. Although formal reliability and validity data were not reported by Mindham, changes in scores on this assessment were reported following the start of neuroleptic treatment, peaking approximately 3 weeks after treatment had begun. Mindham also advocated the use of simple psychomotor tests such as the "grooved peg board test" (which requires subjects to place grooved pegs into grooved holes while being timed) noting that patterns of changes in performance on such tests over time are often similar to those observed on his scale.

The American Psychiatric Association (APA) has developed the Abnormal Involuntary Movements Scale (AIMS) as a means of assessing dyskinesias (APA, 1980; Munetz & Benjamine, 1988). The patient is observed unobtrusively prior to a formal examination in which she or he is asked a number of questions (e.g. whether he or she has noticed any abnormal movements in the mouth, face, hands, or feet, and whether he or she is bothered by them) and is asked to perform a number of simple tasks (e.g. sitting with hands hanging unsupported; protruding the tongue). Twelve separate ratings are then made, using scoring procedure provided. The AIMS can be administered by nonmedical staff (McCreadie & Ohaeri, 1994) and has been used in a wide range of studies, including studies with non-English speaking patients (e.g. Koshino *et al.*, 1992; McCreadie & Ohaeri, 1994). Its inter-rater reliability has been demonstrated even with elderly patients (Sweet *et al.*, 1993) and a factor analytic study carried out with a large number of patients has revealed that scores on the AIMS can be accounted for by three factors involving abnormal movements primarily of the jaw and tongue; the face and lips; and the trunk and extremities (Glazer *et al.*, 1988). Evidence of the validity of the AIMS can be inferred from those studies which have shown that AIMS scores correlate with theoretically interesting biological variables such as the density of striatal D-2 receptors (Blin *et al.*, 1989).

The three scales described so far all focus on involuntary movements. Barnes (1989) has described a rating scale for assessing drug-induced akathisia, which yields three main measures: objective akathisia, subjective akathisia, and global clinical assessment of akathisia. Patients are observed while seated, standing, and while engaged in conversation for a period of 2 minutes. Subsequently, patients are asked directly about subjective feelings of restlessness. Both objective and subjective akathisia are then rated on four-point scales, and a separate distress score is recorded for subjective akathisia. The global assessment consists of a six-point scale, which varies between 0 ("absent") and 5 ("severe akathisia"). Inter-rater reliability for the individual items, as assessed by Cohen's kappa, is reported to vary between 0.74 and 0.95. No validity data were reported for the scale. However, Barnes observed that eight of 42 patients receiving neuroleptics were classified by the scales as suffering from akathisia, and that a further nine were assessed as suffering from "pseudoakathisia" in which an inner sense of restlessness was said to be absent. The Barnes Akathisia Scale has been used in a wide range of studies and has been shown to be reliable even when used to assess elderly patients (Sweet *et al.*, 1993).

Van Putten's scale for rating neuroleptic dysphoria (Van Putten & May, 1978; Van Putten *et al.*, 1981) must be included in any list of instruments designed to measure particular neuroleptic side-effects. Patients' subjective responses to neuroleptics are measured by asking four questions: "How does the medication agree with you?" "Did it make you calmer?" "Did it affect your thinking?"; and "Do you think this would be the right medicine for you?" Patients rate themselves on each of these questions using a scale ranging from −11 to +11, yielding an overall score ranging from −44 (maximal dysphoric response) to +44 (maximal syntonic response). The scale is designed for administration soon after the patient is first treated with neuroleptic drugs (several hours to several days).

No reliability data have been reported by Van Putten *et al.* However, Van Putten *et al.* (1981) report strong correlations between an observer's ratings for the first three questions on the scale (that is, whether the observer thought that the medication was agreeing with the patient, making the patient calmer or affecting the patient's thinking). Better evidence of the validity of the scale was obtained by determining its ability to predict both the short-term and long-term outcome of drug treatment. Van Putten and May (1978) found that scores on the scale predicted reduction of psychotic symptoms following treatment with chlorpromazine over an average of 33 days. Van Putten *et al.* (1981) subsequently observed that responses on the scale were good predictors of refusal to take medication, both in the short-term and in the long-term. With some qualification, these findings have been substantially replicated by others, for example by Hogan and his colleagues (Hogan *et al.*, 1985; Hogan & Awad, 1992).

The most comprehensive instrument for measuring psychotropic drug side-effects available today is the UKU rating scale (Lingjaerde *et al.*, 1987), developed by the Scandinavian Society of Psychopharmacology's Committee on Clinical Investigations (Udvalg for kliniske undersøgelser, hence UKU). The scale was carefully constructed over a number of years and consists of an interview schedule with scoring criteria for 48 side-effects. Although no attempt was made to design the scale so that items were intercorrelated, the side-effects measured are categorized into four main groups on a priori grounds: psychic side-effects, neurological side-effects, autonomic side-effects, and others. Because the scale was developed with a view to assessing side-effects as subjectively experienced by the patient the interview questions are constructed so as to avoid leading the patient. Each item is scored on a 0–3 scale.

Lingjaerde *et al.* (1987) reported interrater reliability data from pilot trials carried out in Denmark, Sweden, and Norway. The data from the Norway trial, conducted with a final version of the scale, are the most impressive, with reliabilities for the different groups of symptoms ranging from 0.83 to 0.96 and a reliability for the total score of 0.92. Although validity issues were not addressed in detail, relevant data were reported from a subsequent large study carried out with a total of 2391 patients from Denmark, Finland, Iceland, Norway, and Sweden. For example, the severity of side-effects as measured by the scale was found to increase with duration of treatment. More side-effects of greater severity were observed in those patients who were judged to be most severely ill. Disappointingly, only nonsignificant relationships were observed between side-effects and the type of medication received, and between side-effects and the method of administration (oral versus depot).

A common disadvantage of the instruments so far reviewed, with the exception of Van Putten and May's (1978) neuroleptic dysphoria scale, is the requirement that they be completed by a suitably qualified examiner, usually a psychiatrist (although it seems likely that intelligent research assistants could learn to master the instruments with appropriate training). In the case of the UKU, administration of the instruments may take between 30 and 60 minutes and its inclusion in any research study or audit is therefore likely to contribute substantially to the costs of the project. The other instruments we have reviewed, although less costly, do not cover a wide enough range of side-effects to be useful for most purposes. A comprehensive, self-administered side-effect questionnaire would therefore have a number of practical advantages over these instruments. Such a scale could be employed in routine clinical practice, and would be highly cost-effective if employed in clinical trials or other kinds of research investigations.

Against such a questionnaire, it might be argued that severely ill psychiatric patients will not be able to complete self-report items reliably. Platt (1986), for example, has argued that psychotic patients are likely to be too disturbed to understand questionnaire items, or to report accurately on their own behavior and experiences. However, such pessimism about the abilities of the severely mentally ill may not be justified (and may have contributed to the dearth of research into patients' subjective experience of psychiatric treatment). Self-report instruments for use by psychotic patients have been successfully developed for some purposes. For example, Birchwood *et al.* (1989) have described a reliable method of training patients to monitor their own prodromal symptoms in order to avoid or alleviate relapse. Moreover, some cognitive–behavior therapists have described methods by which patients may effectively rate even florid psychotic symptomatology (Brett-Jones *et al.*, 1987; Chadwick & Lowe, 1990; Bentall *et al.*, 1994). These studies suggest that the majority of psychotic patients should be able to make good use of a neuroleptic side-effects questionnaire.

The Liverpool University Neuroleptic Side Effects Rating Scale (LUNSERS; Day *et al.*, 1995) comprises a 51-item questionnaire. Each item describes a symptom which respondents rate for severity over the last month on a five-point scale ranging from "not at all" to "very much." Forty-one of the items, covering psychological, neurological, autonomic, hormonal, and other miscellaneous side-effects, were constructed by rewording the appropriate UKU items so that they could be easily self-rated. Those UKU items involving sexual dysfunction were collapsed into one LUNSERS item ("difficulty achieving orgasm/climax") in order to simplify the scale. In addition to the UKU-derived items, 10 "red herring" items were also included which referred to symptoms which are not known neuroleptic side-effects (e.g. chilblains, hair loss) in order to check whether patients would report symptoms in response to suggestions. Fifty patients with a DSM-III-R diagnosis of schizophrenia took part in the validation study, together with 50 normal subjects who were not taking neuroleptic medication.

The test–retest reliability of the LUNSERS was assertained by having the patients repeat the questionnaire 1 week after first testing. All known side-effect items were significantly correlated between the two testings and the test–retest correlation between total side-effects score (the sum of the 41 known side-effect items) was highly significant (Pearson $r = 0.811$). The internal consistency of the scale, as measured by Cronbach's alpha coefficient, was satisfactory at both testings.

The validity of the questionnaire was demonstrated in a number of ways. First, it was shown that the medicated patients scored significantly higher than the nonmedicated controls on the known side-effect items but not on the red herring items, as reflected in both mean scores and ROC analysis (Swets & Pickett, 1982), a form of analysis which looks at the way in which different cut-off scores correctly or incorrectly assign subjects to the medicated and the nonmedicated groups. Second, in the medicated subjects a modest correlation was observed between dosage, as measured in chlorpromazine equivalents, and total side-effect scores, which would only be expected if the patients were accurately reporting their side-effects. Finally, all the medicated subjects were assessed on the UKU by either a psychiatrist or a psychiatric pharmacist; the total UKU score correlated very well with the total side-effects score on the LUNSERS ($r = 0.828$, mean r for individual items $= 0.605$). Overall, these findings indicate that the LUNSERS is a reliable and valid instrument and should be considered as a low-cost and effective alternative to the UKU. Subsequent experience with the questionnaire has indicated that even quite severely disturbed patients are usually able to complete it within 20 minutes.

Obviously, the choice of instrument in any attempt to assess neuroleptic side-effects must depend on the purpose of the assessment. If a detailed rating of a particular class of side-effects is required then one of the relevant rating scales will be most appropriate. If the purpose is to predict compliance or response to treatment, Van Putten and May's (1978) neuroleptic dysphoria scale, or Hogan and Awad's (1992) Drug Attitude Inventory are likely to be most useful. For a global assessment of side-effects, the UKU might be used if the relevant staff resources are available, or the LUNSERS might be used if they are not.

CONCLUSIONS

In this chapter we have suggested that many studies of the drug treatment of severely ill psychotic patients have not sufficiently emphasized one important perspective—that of the patient who receives the treatment. Although clinicians and family members may be impressed by the apparent benefits of neuroleptic therapy, from the point of view of the patient, costs and benefits may be finely balanced. This observation has a number of important implications.

First, studies of the outcome of treatments for psychotic patients should take into account all aspects of outcome—not only objectively scored symptoms but also patients' experiences of medication broadly defined. This implication applies as much to studies of the economic impact of neuroleptics as to conventional outcome studies.

Second, patients' subjective experiences of neuroleptic therapy are likely to have important implications for the treatment of individual patients. Given that adverse experiences of neuroleptics are associated with poor compliance (Van Putten & May, 1978; Hogen *et al.*, 1983; Hoge *et al.*, 1990), and that poor compliance is associated with repeated hospitalization (Green, 1988), it seems likely that clinicians will most effectively help their patients by listening carefully to their accounts of the personal impact of medication, and by tailoring the treatment accordingly.

Finally, it is important to consider the policy implications of patients' experiences. The adverse effects of neuroleptics pose a dilemma for those responsible for the development and implementation of mental health policy in the 1990s. On the one hand, people with a diagnosis of schizophrenia are often portrayed in the media and in the public imagination as potentially violent (Monahan, 1992; Philo & Secker, 1994). Reflecting this concern, recent official reports emphasize strategies which ensure that patients receive neuroleptic therapy as the primary means of preventing violence in psychiatric patients (HMSO, 1994). On the other hand, emerging concerns about the iatrogenic effects of neuroleptics (Brown & Funk, 1986), together with the evolution of consumer-oriented approaches to health care which promise to give due regard to patients' views of services and treatment, make the risks associated with neuroleptic therapy less acceptable. A policy which places the autonomy of patients as a central tenet in the management of psychiatric disorders but which at the same time allows patients to experience the benefits of neuroleptic therapy is needed if an equilibrium is to be achieved between these two conflicting sources of concern.

REFERENCES

American Psychiatric Association (1980). Task Force Report—Effects of anti-psychotic drugs: tardive dyskinesia. *American Journal of Psychiatry*, **37**, 1163–1171.

Ayd, F.J. (1961). A survey of drug-induced extrapyramidal reactions. *Journal of the American Medical Association*, **175**, 1054–1060.

Baldessarini, R.J., Cohen, B.M., and Teicher, M.H. (1988). Significance of neuroleptic doses and plasma levels in the pharmacological management of the psychoses. *Archives of General Psychiatry*, **45**, 79–91,

Barnes, T.R.E. (1989). A rating scale for drug induced akathisia. *British Journal of Psychiatry*, **154**, 672–676.

Belmaker, R.H. and Wald, D. (1977). Haloperidol in normals. *British Journal of Psychiatry*, **131**, 222–223.

Bentall, R.P. and Day, J.C. (1994). Psychological factors and neuroleptic therapy: Some neglected issues. *International Review of Psychiatry*, **6**, 217–225.

Bentall, R.P., Haddock, G., and Slade, P.D. (1994). Cognitive behavior therapy for persistent auditory hallucinations: From theory to therapy. *Behavior Therapy*, **25**, 51–66.

Bignami, G. (1991). Neuroleptic dysphoria in animals. *Biological Psychiatry*, **30**, 844–845.

Birchwood, M., Smith, J., and Macmillan, F. (1989). Predicting relapse in schizophrenia. The development and implementation of an early signs monitoring system using patients and families as observers. *Psychological Medicine*, **19**, 649–656.

Blin, J., Baron, J.C., Cambon, H., Bonnet, A.M., Dubois, B., Loc'h, C., Maziere, B., and Agid, Y. (1989). Striatal dopamine D2 receptors in tardive dyskinesia: PET study. *Journal of Neurology, Neurosurgery and Psychiatry*, **52**, 1248–1252.

Bollini, P., Pampallona, S., Orza, M.J., Adams, M.E., and Chalmers, T.C. (1994). Antipsychotic drugs: Is more worse? A meta analysis of the published randomized controlled trials. *Psychological Medicine*, **24**, 307–316.

Braude, W.M., Barnes, T.R.E., and Gore, S.M. (1983). Clinical characteristics of akathisia: A systematic investigation of acute psychiatric inpatient admissions. *British Journal of Psychiatry*, **143**, 139–150.

Brett-Jones, J., Garety, P., and Hemsley, D.R. (1987). Measuring delusional experiences: A method and its application. *British Journal of Clinical Psychology*, **26**, 257–265.

Brown, P. and Funk, S. (1986). Tardive dyskinesia: Barriers to the professional recognition of iatrogenic disease. *Journal of Health and Social Behaviour*, **27**, 116–132.

Brown, W.A. and Herz, L.R. (1989). Response to neuroleptic drugs as a device for classifying schizophrenia. *Schizophrenia Bulletin*, **15**, 123–128.

Carlsson, A. and Lindqvist, M. (1963). Effect of chlorpromazine or haloperidol on formation of 3-methoxytyramine and normetanephrine in mouse brain. *Acta Pharmacologica et Toxicologica*, **20**, 140–144.

Caroff, S.N. (1980). The neuroleptic malignant syndrome. *Journal of Clinical Psychiatry*, **41**, 79–83.

Carpenter, W.T., Heinrichs, D.W., and Hanlon, T.E. (1987). A comparative trial of pharmacologic strategies in schizophrenia. *American Journal of Psychiatry*, **144**, 1466–1470.

Chadwick, P. and Lowe, C.F. (1990). The measurement and modification of delusional beliefs. *Journal of Consulting and Clinical Psychology*, **58**, 225–232.

Crow, J.J. (1980). Molecular pathology of schizophrenia: More than one disease process? *British Medical Journal*, **280**, 66–68.

Crow, T.J., MacMillan, J.F., Johnson, A.L., and Johnstone, E.C. (1986). The Northwick Park study of first episodes of schizophrenia II: A controlled of prophylactic neuroleptic treatment. *British Journal of Psychiatry*, **148**, 120–127.

Croyden-Smith, A. (1982). *Schizophrenia and Madness*. Herts: George Allen & Unwin.

Davidhizar, R.E. (1987). Beliefs, feelings and insight of patients with schizophrenia about taking medication. *Journal of Advanced Nursing*, **12**, 177–182.

Davies, L.M. and Drummond, M.F. (1994). Economics and schizophrenia: The real cost. *British Journal of Psychiatry*, **165** (Suppl. 25), 18–21.

Day, J.C., Bentall, R.P., and Warner, S. (in press). Schizophrenic patients' experiences of neuroleptic medication: A Q-methodological investigation. *Acta Psychiatrica Scandinavica.*

Day, J.C., Kinderman, P., and Bentall, R.P. (in preparation). Side effects of neuroleptic medication: Who knows best?

Day, J.C., Wood, G., Dewey, M., and Bentall, R.P. (1995). A self-rating scale for measuring neuroleptic side effects: Validation in a group of schizophrenic patients. *British Journal of Psychiatry*, **166**.

Delay, J., Deniker, P., and Harl, J.M. (1952). Utilisation en thérapeutique psychiatrique d'une phenothiazine d'action centrale élective. *Annals Medical Psychology*, **2**, 112–117.

Dickes, R., Schenker, V., and Deutsch, L. (1957). Serial liver function and blood studies in patients receiving chlorpromazine. *New England Journal of Medicine*, **256**, 1–7.

Dukes, M.N.G. (ed.). (1992). *Meyler's Side Effects of Drugs*. Amsterdam: Elsevier.

Edwards, J.G. (1986). The untoward effects of anti-psychotic drugs: pathogenesis and management. In P.B. Bradley and S.R. Hirsch, eds, *The Psychopharmacology and Management of Schizophrenia*. Oxford: Oxford University Press.

Emerich, D.F. and Sanberg, P.R. (1991). Neurolpetic dysphoria. *Biological Psychiatry*, **29**, 201–203.

Falloon, I.R.H. and Liberman, R.P. (1983). Interactions between drug and psychosocial therapy in schizophrenia. *Schizophrenia Bulletin*, **9**, 543–554.

Farde, L., Wiesel, F.A., Halldin, C., and Sedvall, G. (1988). Central D-2 dopamine receptor occupancy in schizophrenic patients treated with antipsychotic drugs. *Archives of General Psychiatry*, **45**, 71–76.

Finn, S.E., Bailey, J.M., Scultz, R.T., and Faber, R. (1990). Subjective utility ratings of neuroleptics in treating schizophrenia. *Psychological Medicine*, **35**, 843–848.

Fitton, A. and Benfield, P. (1993). Clozapine: An appraisal of its pharmacoeconomic benefits in the treatment of schizophrenia. *Pharmacoeconomics*, **4**, 131–156.

Gergen, K.J. (1985). The social constructionist movement in modern psychology. *American Psychologist*, **40**, 266–275.

Glazer, W.M., Morgenstern, H., Niedzwiecki, D., and Hughes, J. (1988). Heterogeneity of tardive dyskinesia: A multivariate analysis. *British Journal of Psychiatry*, **152**, 253–259.

Goldberg, S.C. (1985). Negative and deficit symptoms do respond to neuroleptics. *Schizophrenia Bulletin*, **11**, 453–456.

Gordon, H.L. and Grotte, C. (1964). Weight changes during and after hospital treatment. *Archives of General Psychiatry*, **10**, 187–191.

Green, J.H. (1988). Frequent rehospitalisation and non-compliance with treatment. *Hospital and Community Psychiatry*, **39**, 963–966.

Healy, D. (in press). *The Psychopharmacologists*. Chichester: Wiley.

Herz, M.I., Glazer, W.M., Mostert, M.A., *et al.* (1991). Intermittent vs maintenance medication in schizophrenia. *Archives of General Psychiatry*, **48**, 333–339.

HMSO (1994). *The Report of the Inquiry into the Care and Treatment of Christopher Clunis*. London: HMSO.

Hogan, T.P. and Awad, A.G. (1992). Subjective response to neuroleptics and outcome in schizophrenia: a re-examination using two measures. *Psychological Medicine*, **22**, 347–352.

Hogan, T.P., Awad, A.G., and Eastwood, R. (1983). A self-report scale predictive of drug compliance in schizophrenics: Reliability and discriminative validity. *Psychological Medicine*, **13**, 177–183.

Hogan, T.P., Awad, A.G., and Eastwood, M.R. (1985). Early subjective response and prediction of outcome to neuroleptic drug therapy in schizophrenia. *Canadian Journal of Psychiatry*, **30**, 246–248.

Hoge, S.K., Appelbaum, P.S., Lawlor, T., Beck, J.C., Litman, R., Greer, A., Gutheil, T.G., and Kaplan, E. (1990). A prospective, multicenter study of patients' refusal of antipsychotic medication. *Archives of General Psychiatry*, **47**, 949–956.

Iverson, S. and Iverson, L. (1981). *Behavioral Pharmacology*, pp. 248–277. Oxford: Oxford University Press.

Jeste, D.V. and Wyatt, R.J. (1979). In search of treatment of tardive dyskinesia: review of the literature. *Schizophrenia Bulletin*, **5**, 251–293.

Johnstone, E.C., Crow, T.J., Johnson, A.L. *et al.* (1986). The Northwick Park study of first episodes of schizophrenia: I Presentation of the illness and problems relating to admission. *British Journal of Psychiatry*, **148**, 115–120.

Jolley, A.G., Hirsch, S.R., Morrison, E., McRink, A., and Wilson, L. (1990). Trial of brief intermittent neuroleptic prophylaxis for selected schizophrenic outpatients: clinical and social outcome at two years. *British Medical Journal*, **301**, 837–842.

Kane, J.M. (1989). The current status of neuroleptic therapy. *Journal of Clinical Psychiatry*, **50**, 322–328.

Kane, J.M., Honigfeld, G., Singer, J., and Meltzer, H. (1988). Clozapine for the treatment-resistant schizophrenic. *Archives of General Psychiatry*, **45**, 789–796.

Karon, B.P. (1984). The fear of reducing medication, and where have all the patients gone? *Schizophrenia Bulletin*, **10**, 613–617.

Kavanagh, S. (1994). The costs of schizophrenia. *Mental Health Research Review*, **1**, 25–26.

Kennedy, P.F., Hershon, H.I., and McGuire, R.J. (1971). Extrapyramidal disorders after prolonged phenothiazine therapy. *British Journal of Psychiatry*, **118**, 509–518.

Kleinman, I., Schacter, D., and Koritar, E. (1989). Informed consent and tardive dyskinesia. *American Journal of Psychiatry*, **146**, 902–904.

Koshino, Y., Madokoro, S., Ito, T., Horie, T., Mukai, M., and Isaki, K. (1992). A survey of tardive dyskinesia in psychiatric inpatients in Japan. *Clinical Neuropharmocology*, **15**, 34–43.

Lawson, W.B., Karson, C.N., and Bigelow, L.B. (1985). Increased urine volume in chronic schizophrenic patients. *Psychiatry Research*, **14**, 323.

Leff, J.P. and Wing, J.K. (1971). Trial of maintenance therapy in schizophrenia. *British Medical Journal*, **3**, 599–604.

Leonard, B.E. (1992). *Fundamentals of Psychopharmacology*. Chichester: John Wiley.

Lewander, T. (1994). Neuroleptics and the neuroleptic-induced deficit syndrome. *Acta Psychiatrica Scandinavica*, **89**, 8–13.

Lieberman, J.A. (1993). Understanding the mechanism of action of atypical antipsychotic drugs. A review of compounds in use and development. *British Journal of Psychiatry*, **163**, 7–18.

Lingjaerde, O., Ahlfors, V.G., Dech, P., Dencker, S.J., and Elgen, K. (1987). The UKU side effect rating scale for psychotropic drugs and a cross sectional study of side effects in neuroleptic treated patients. *Acta Psychiatrica Scandinavica Supplementum*, **334**, 76.

May, P.R.A., Van Putten, T., Jenden, D.J., Yale, C., and Dixon, W.J. (1981). Chlorpromazine levels and the outcome of treatment in schizophrenic patients. *Archives of General Psychiatry*, **38**, 202–207.

McCreadie, R.G. and Ohaeri, J.U. (1994). Movement disorders in never and minimally treated Nigerian schizophrenic patients. *British Journal of Psychiatry*, **164**, 184–189.

McEvoy, J.P., Hogarty, G.E., and Steingard, S. (1991). Optimal dose of neuroleptic in acute schizophrenia: A controlled study of the neuroleptic threshold and higher haloperidol dose. *Archives of General Psychiatry*, **48**, 739–745.

McGuire, T.G. (1991). Measuring the economic costs of schizophrenia. *Schizophrenia Bulletin*, **17**, 375–388.

McKeown, B. and Thomas, D. (1988). *Q Methodology*. Beverly Hills: Sage.

Meltzer, H.Y., Sommers, A.A., and Luchins, D.J. (1986). The effect of neuroleptics and other psychotropic drugs on negative symptoms in schizophrenia. *Journal of Clinical Psychopharmacology*, **6**, 329–338.

Mindham, R.H.S. (1976). Assessment of drug-induced extrapyramidal reactions and of drugs given for their control. *British Journal of Clinical Pharmacology, Supplement*, **3**, 395–400.

Monahan, J. (1992). Mental disorder and violent behavior: Perceptions and evidence. *American Psychologist*, **47**, 511–521.

Munetz, M.R. and Benjamine, S. (1988). How to examine patients using the Abnormal Involuntary Movement Scale. *Hospital and Community Psychiatry*, **39**, 1172–1177.

Philo. G. and Secker, J. (1994). What the papers say. *Community Care*, **24**, 15.

Platt, S. (1986). Evaluating social functioning: A critical review of scales and their underlying concepts. In P.B. Bradley and S.R. Hirsch, eds, *The Psychopharmocology and Management of Schizophrenia*, pp. 263–285. Oxford: Oxford University Press.

Rifkind, A., Doddi, S., Karagigi, B., Borenstein, M., and Wachspress, M. (1991). Dosage of haloperidol for schizophrenia. *Archives of General Psychiatry*, **48**, 166–170.

Robinson, R., McHugh, P., and Follstein, M. (1975). Measurement of appetite disturbance in psychiatric disorders. *Journal of Psychiatric Research*, **12**, 59–68.

Rogers, A. and Pilgrim, D. (1993). Service user's views of psychiatric treatments. *Sociology of Health and Illness*, **15**, 613–631.

Rogers, A., Pilgrim, D., and Lacey, R. (1993). *Experiencing Psychiatry: Users' Views of Services*. London: Macmillan in association with MIND Publications.

Rosen, A.M., Mukherjee, S., and Olarte, S. (1982). Perception of tardive dyskinesia in outpatients receiving maintenance neuroleptics. *American Journal of Psychiatry*, **139**, 372.

Schooler, N.R. (1994). Deficit symptoms in schizophrenia: negative symptoms versus neuroleptic-induced deficits. *Acta Psychiatrica Scandinavica*, **89**, 21–26.

Segraves, R.T. (1988). Sexual side effects of psychiatric drugs. *International Journal of Psychiatry in Medicine*, **18**, 243–251.

Seltzer, A., Roncari, I., and Garfinkel, P. (1980). Effect of patient education on medication compliance. *Canadian Journal of Psychiatry*, **25**, 638–645.

Shopshin, B. and Feiner, N.F. (1983). Letter to the editor. *Psychopharmacology Bulletin*, **19**, 563–564.

Simpson, G.M. and Angus, J.W.S. (1970). A rating scale for extrapyramidal side effects. *Acta Psychiatrica Scan-*

dinavica, Supplementum, **212**, 11–19.

Simpson, G.M., Amuso, D., Blair, J.H., and Farkas, T. (1964). Aspects of phenothiazine-produced extrapyramidal symptoms. *Archives of General Psychiatry*, **10**, 199–208.

Simpson, G.M., Pi, E.H., and Stramek, J.J. (1982). Management of tardive dyskinesia: current update. *Drugs*, **23**, 382.

Singh, M.M. (1976). Dysphoric response to neuroleptic treatment in schizophrenia and its prognostic significance. *Diseases of the Nervous System*, **4**, 191–195.

Singh, M.M. and Smith, J.M. (1973). Kinetics and dynamics of response to haloperidol in acute schizophrenia in a longitudinal study of the therapeutic process. *Comprehensive Psychiatry*, **14**, 393–414.

Stainton Rogers, W. (1991). *Explaining Health and Illness: An Exploration of Diversity*. London: Harvester Wheatsheaf.

Stephenson, W. (1935). Technique of factor analysis. *Nature*, **136**, 297.

Sullivan, G. and Lukoff, D. (1990). Sexual side effects of antipsychotic medication: evaluation and interventions. *Hospital and Community Psychiatry*, **41**, 1238–1241.

Sunahara, R.K., Seeman, P., Van Tol, H.H.M., and Niznik, H.B. (1993). Dopamine receptors and antipsychotic drug response. *British Journal of Psychiatry*, **163** (Suppl.), 31–38.

Sweet, R.A., DeSensi, E.G., and Zubenko, G.S. (1993). Reliability and applicability of movement disorder rating scales in the elderly. *Journal of Neuropsychiatry and Clinical Neuroscience*, **5**, 56–60.

Swets, J.A. and Pickett, R.M. (1982). *Evaluation of Diagnostic Systems: Methods from Signal Detection Theory*. New York: Academic Press.

Swett, C. (1975). Drug induced dystonia. *American Journal of Psychiatry*, **132**, 532–534.

Thorogood, N., Cowen, P., Mann, J., Murphy, M., and Vessey, M. (1992). Fatal myocardial infarction and use of psychotropic drugs in young women. *Lancet*, **340**, 1067–1068.

Toone, B.K. and Fenton, G.W. (1977). Epileptic seizures induced by psychotropic drugs. *Psychological Medicine*, **7**, 265–270.

Van Kammen, D.P. (1991). The biochemical basis of relapse and drug response in schizophrenia: review and hypothesis. *Psychological Medicine*, **21**, 881–895.

Van Putten, T. (1974). Why do schizophrenic patients refuse to take their drugs? *Archives of General Psychiatry*, **31**, 67–72.

Van Putten, T. and May, P.R. (1978). Subjective response as a predictor of outcome in pharmacotherapy. *Archives of General Psychiatry*, **35**, 477–480.

Van Putten, T., Crumpton, E., and Yale, C. (1976). Drug refusal in schizophrenia and the wish to be crazy. *Archives of General Psychiatry*, **33**, 1443–1446.

Van Putten, T., May, P.R., Marder, S.R., and Wittman, L.A. (1981). Subjective response to antipsychotic drugs. *Archives of General Psychiatry*, **38**, 187–190.

Van Putten, T., May, P.R.A., and Marder, S.R. (1984). Akathisia with haloperidol and thiothixene. *Archives of General Psychiatry*, **41**, 1036–1039.

Van Putten, T., Marder, S.R., and Mintz, J. (1990). A controlled dose comparison of haloperidol in newly admitted schizophrenic patients. *Archives of General Psychiatry*, **47**, 754–758.

Weiden, P.J., Shaw, E., and Mann, J.J. (1986). Causes of neuroleptic non-compliance. *Psychiatric Annals*, **16**, 571–575.

14

Psychotherapy, Relapse Prevention, and Management of Relapse in Schizophrenia

MARVIN I. HERZ and J. STEVEN LAMBERTI
Department of Psychiatry, University of Rochester Medical Center, New York, USA

Schizophrenia is usually a chronic disorder which is characterized by symptomatic exacerbations followed by full or partial remissions. A major goal in the treatment of schizophrenia is to develop clinically effective and cost-effective methods of enhancing functional abilities, and of preventing and managing relapse. An understanding of the course of schizophrenia is essential in planning relapse prevention and management strategies. Although the course of illness is highly variable, it can be broadly divided into three phases: acute or relapse, stabilization, and stable. The acute or relapse phase of illness is characterized by the presence of severe psychotic symptoms including hallucinations, delusions and/or speech disorganization, as well as severely impaired role functioning. The acute phase of schizophrenia is usually preceded by early warning signs called prodromal symptoms (Herz & Melville, 1980). The stabilization or recovery phase follows the acute phase and may last up to approximately 6 months. During this phase patients will experience a gradual improvement of psychotic symptoms and role functioning. The stable or maintenance phase of illness usually marks the return of patients to their symptomatic and functional baselines, although it may involve a plateauing of symptoms at a new level. The most common outcome after recovery from an acute psychotic episode is a nonpsychotic deficit state characterized by apathy, anergia, social withdrawal, and increased vulnerability to stress (Huber *et al.*, 1980). Patients may also exhibit continuing mild psychotic symptoms, nonpsychotic symptoms such as tension, anxiety, and insomnia or be completely asymptomatic.

There is no widely accepted definition of relapse. For the purposes of this discussion, relapse or acute psychosis will be defined operationally as the development of severe psychotic symptoms, a Global Assesment Scale score of 30 or less, and a duration of more than 2 days. A variety of personal and economic costs are associated with the relapse process. It is demoralizing and stigmatizing for many patients, and may be perceived as a recurring personal failure. Also, relapse usually interrupts participation in rehabilitation programs and can pose a burden for family members. Given the high personal and economic costs associated with relapse and hospitalization, relapse prevention is a primary goal in the treatment of schizophrenia. Antipsychotic medications are generally viewed as the principal mode of treatment for preventing relapse and hospitalization. Despite treatment with antipsychotic

Handbook of Mental Health Economics and Health Policy, Volume I, Schizophrenia. Edited by M. Moscarelli, A. Rupp and N. Sartorius.
© 1996 John Wiley & Sons Ltd.

medications, however, up to 40% of schizophrenic patients will experience a relapse within 1 year of hospitalization (Hogarty *et al.*, 1979). Relapse and rehospitalization rates can be reduced when antipsychotic medications are utilized in conjunction with community psychosocial treatment programs. Although treatment has other important aims, this chapter will focus on the roles of individual and group psychotherapy, and of an early intervention strategy in the prevention of relapse. In addition, we will review the roles of hospitalization and alternatives to hospitalization including day hospitalization for the management of relapse. Family, behavioral, and rehabilitative approaches are presented elsewhere in this text.

INDIVIDUAL PSYCHOTHERAPY

A variety of individual psychotherapy approaches have been used in the treatment of schizophrenia. These approaches differ along many dimensions, including the degree to which prevention of relapse is emphasized as a primary goal of treatment. Early studies of individual psychotherapy in schizophrenia utilized psychoanalytically oriented approaches, and for the most part failed to demonstrate significant benefit in patients when compared with supportive therapy (May & Tuma, 1964, 1965; Bookhammer *et al.*, 1966; Grinspoon *et al.*, 1967, 1968, 1972; May, 1968; Karon and O'Grady, 1969; Karon & Vanden-Bos, 1970, 1972). Questions about the design and methodology of early studies led to the most rigorously designed study of individual psychotherapy in schizophrenia to date, the Boston Psychotherapy Study (Gunderson *et al.*, 1984; Stanton *et al.*, 1984). This study was designed to compare the efficacy of exploratory insight-oriented (EIO) psychotherapy with that of reality-adaptive supportive (RAS) psychotherapy. In general, EIO psychotherapy focused upon fostering self-knowledge and understanding, while RAS psychotherapy addressed practical issues of daily living. The study randomly assigned 164 hospitalized schizophrenic patients to receive either EIO or RAS psychotherapy over a 2 year period, and both treatments were conducted by highly experienced and motivated therapists. Patients having either an excellent or very poor prognosis were excluded from the study. Only one-third of the patients in each group remained in the study for the entire 2 year period. All patients received psychotropic medications during the study. Principal findings of this study were that the RAS psychotherapy group spent significantly less time in the hospital and had better occupational functioning compared with the EIO group. While a subsequent analysis of the data suggested a relationship between psychodynamic exploration and improvement in negative symptoms, the findings were limited by a small sample size and other methodological problems (Glass *et al.*, 1989).

A well designed study conducted by Hogarty and co-workers (Hogarty & Goldberg, 1973; Hogarty *et al.*, 1974a,b) examined the effects of individual therapy of a supportive type upon relapse and hospitalization in schizophrenia. This study evaluated the effects of "major role therapy" (MRT), which included social casework and vocational counseling. A group of 374 newly discharged schizophrenic patients were randomized to receive MRT with either chlorpromazine or placebo, or to receive chlorpromazine or placebo alone over a 2 year evaluation period. MRT was associated with a statistically significant reduction in relapse and rehospitalization independently of chlorpromazine during the seventh to 24th month of the study. It was postulated that MRT had a delayed effect. Among those patients who did not relapse, the combination of MRT and medications was associated with significant improvement in interpersonal relations and overall functioning at 2 years. A subsequent report from this study indicated that MRT was actually associated with increased relapse among those patients who were initially highly symptomatic, regardless of medication status (Goldberg *et al.*, 1977).

Review of the experimental literature shows that intensive insight-oriented psychotherapy is not appropriate for most schizophrenic patients (Gomes-Schwarz, 1984; Mueser & Berenbaum, 1990). In examining the nature of the RAS and MRT interventions noted above, these therapies are consistent with the concepts of "psychotherapeutic management" described by May (1968), or supportive psychotherapy. The term "supportive psychotherapy" will be used for the purposes of this discussion. While the type of psychotherapy should always be determined by the characteristics and needs of the patient, supportive psychotherapy should be regarded as the individual psychotherapeutic approach of choice for most schizophrenic patients. In conducting supportive psychotherapy it is desirable for the therapist to have a comprehensive understanding of the patient. Such understanding may include knowledge of the patient's intrapsychic conflicts and defenses, coping skills and strengths, as well as interpersonal, social, cultural, and biological factors affecting the patient's life.

Relapse prevention is an important goal of supportive psychotherapy, and may be accomplished by working with the patient to monitor for prodromal symptoms (Herz, 1984). As noted by Novalis and colleagues, "To varying degrees, each session of supportive psychotherapy requires the psychiatrist to think through with the patient what are the present signs of illness and what are the signs of pending exacerbation that need to be addressed" (Novalis *et al.*, 1993). As schizophrenic patients are vulnerable to stress (Zubin & Spring, 1977; Nuechterlein, 1987), relapse prevention may also be accomplished by assisting the patient in managing current life stresses through enhancement of coping skills, improvement of social and vocational functioning, and development of a sense of competence and increased self-esteem. The extent to which patients may benefit from gaining better insight into their reactions to current life situations should be established individually. In general, interpretations should highlight the connections between stressful life events and the development of prodromal and psychotic symptoms rather than the content of psychotic symptoms (Katz & Gunderson, 1990).

The foundation of supportive psychotherapy, as with other types of psychotherapy, is the therapeutic relationship. Continuity of care with one therapist who engages in a collaborative nonauthoritarian relationship is most beneficial in establishing a therapeutic alliance. Empathy, warmth, and genuineness on the part of the therapist will also enhance development of the relationship. The formation of a good therapeutic relationship has been associated with improved outcome among schizophrenic patients (Frank & Gunderson, 1990). As noted by Stone (1993), concrete survival issues must be addressed in order for therapy to be effective. At the beginning of psychotherapy, and then concurrently, attention should be paid to housing needs, income maintenance, and general medical care. In addition to attending to basic needs, the therapist should provide education about schizophrenia, promote medication compliance, reality test, help solve problems, and provide positive reinforcement for adaptive behaviors. The therapist should be prepared to give practical advice and guidance when needed, to set limits on regressive behaviors when necessary, and to collaborate with family members and other individuals in the patient's support system. For patients in the stable phase of illness, the therapist may also begin the process of assessing and developing readiness for psychiatric rehabilitation. Flexibility is necessary when conducting psychotherapy with schizophrenic patients. Treatment sessions should not be limited to office visits when there are indications for home visits and other forms of active outreach.

Despite the widespread use of psychotherapy in schizophrenia, there is a paucity of studies examining the cost-effectiveness of this treatment. Several factors have likely contributed to this situation, including the difficulty of translating psychotherapy-related improvement into economic terms, and lack of economic expertise and interest among psychotherapy researchers (Krupncik & Pincus, 1992). Considering the high cost of hospitalization and the high indirect cost of lost productivity associated with schizophrenia (Andrews, 1991), however, the findings of the Boston Psychotherapy Study are significant from the standpoint of cost-effectiveness. It is important to note that patients in the RAS group received psychotherapy only weekly to biweekly compared with the EIO group which received psychotherapy twice to three times weekly. Assuming equivalent session durations and hourly costs per session for the two treatments, the cost of EIO psychotherapy was more than twice that of RAS psychotherapy. Furthermore, the superior occupational role functioning achieved by the RAS group could potentially result in less need for governmental income support. Although a cost analysis was not performed in this study, it appears that RAS psychotherapy is both more clinically effective and cost-effective than EIO psychotherapy. No conclusions can be drawn about the cost-effectiveness of psychotherapy versus no psychotherapy from the Boston Psychotherapy Study as there was no nonpsychotherapy control group.

Several unanswered questions remain about the cost-effectiveness of psychotherapy in schizophrenia including questions about optimal conceptual approaches, optimal session frequency, and optimal duration of treatment for particular types of patients. In addition, studies are needed to assess the training and qualifications necessary for conducting particular types of psychotherapy with schizophrenic patients. Reviewing the literature on cost-effectiveness of psychotherapy, Krupnick and Pincus (1992) call for further development of instruments to measure psychotherapy-related change, for development of cost-effectiveness outcome instruments, and for expanded research funding and training opportunities for studying the cost-effectiveness of psychotherapy.

GROUP PSYCHOTHERAPY

A number of articles have examined the efficacy of group psychotherapy for schizophrenia (O'Brien, 1975; Luborsky *et al.*, 1976; Parloff & Dies, 1977; May & Simpson, 1980; Keith & Matthews, 1982; Kanas, 1993). Although differences between studies and weak study designs make it difficult to draw firm conclusions, review of the literature suggests that group psychotherapy is as effective or more effective than individual psychotherapy for many chronic schizophrenic patients (O'Brien, 1983; Kanas, 1993). Advantages of group psychotherapy which have been reported in comparison with individual psychotherapy include reduced rates of rehospitalization, improved compliance, enhanced social effectiveness, and improved staff morale and efficiency.

In general, group approaches are well suited for teaching schizophrenic patients interpersonal and coping skills, and for providing a supportive social network for patients who tend to be socially isolated. Group therapy on a weekly basis is also a cost-effective way of monitoring patients for prodromal symptoms of relapse (Herz *et al.*, 1991). In addressing the social and interpersonal deficits of schizophrenia, group therapy should focus on problem solving, goal planning, social interactions, and on medications and side-effect management (May & Simpson, 1980). The goals of group therapy may vary according to the level of chronicity and interpersonal capacities of the group members (Goldhamer & Leszcz, 1990). As with individual psychotherapy, research suggests that a supportive group approach is more beneficial than an intensive insight-oriented group approach (Kanas, 1986). In contrast to the rules governing psychoanalytically oriented groups, flexibility is required in conducting psychotherapy groups with schizophrenic patients. Examples of such flexibility include allowance for contact between group members outside of the session, less use of confrontation and individualization of attendance contracts (GAP, 1992). Stone (1993) has suggested use of a "flexible-boundaried group contract," which allows patients to determine the frequency of group attendance, enabling them to feel more empowered in deciding about their therapy. Group psychotherapy for schizophrenic patients generally requires a high degree of activity and structure by the therapist. Additional roles of the therapist include fostering group cohesion, managing affect, and creating a safe environment. When group psychotherapy is used as the primary treatment mode, individual sessions may be used adjunctively as needed. Group members may be seen individually either by the group therapist or by a separate therapist, athough it is desirable for all group members to have the same arrangement.

While no clear consensus exists as to the format of outpatient group psychotherapy for schizophrenic patients, some useful guidelines have recently been proposed (Goldhamer & Leszcz, 1990; Malm, 1990; Kanas, 1993; Stone, 1993). The goals, methods, and expectations of the group should be discussed with all prospective members prior to entry into the group. Patients with difficulty identifying treatment goals may require additional preparation in order to engage in group therapy. Outpatients in the stable phase of illness are generally the best candidates for group psychotherapy. Ordinarily, patients whose psychotic symptoms interfere with their ability to attend to the group interactions, including patients who actively respond to frequent auditory hallucinations, are grossly paranoid or severely thought disordered should not be included. Withdrawn patients with prominent negative symptoms may also benefit from group participation. Groups may have one leader or two co-leaders. The presence of co-leadership may offer advantages in providing different role models for the group, in providing continuity during the absence of one therapist, and in providing mutual support for the therapists. However, having two co-therapists is less cost-effective than having one therapist, and it has not been proven to be more clinically effective. The group should consist of approximately eight patients, should include members of each sex, and should be diagnostically homogeneous. In order to ensure adequate attendance at each session, a roster of up to 15 patients may be required. New patients may be allowed to enter the group during its progress, and patients may reenter the group following relapse. All participants should be encouraged to notify the group in advance if unable to attend a session, and the group should always be told why someone is absent. Patients should be seated in a circle in a room without a table in the middle and, if possible, the same room should be used for each session. Groups typically meet for 60 minute sessions on a weekly basis, and a portion of each session may be used to address medication-related concerns.

In a well controlled 2 year study, Malm (1982) demonstrated significantly more improvements in symptomatology and social functioning in patients receiving a combination of communication-oriented group therapy, depot neuroleptics, and living skills instruction compared with patients receiving depot neuroleptics and living skills instruction alone. In addition to illustrating the advantages of a multi-faceted treatment approach, this study demonstrated the efficacy of long-term group psychotherapy with schizophrenic patients. As a primary purpose of group psychotherapy in schizophrenia is to address social and interpersonal deficits, ongoing non-time-limited treatment may be most beneficial. The frequency of group sessions can be decreased to biweekly or monthly in the later stages of treatment. Although some benefits have been reported with short-term group therapy in schizophrenia (Kanas, 1991), further controlled studies with larger patient samples are needed to establish usefulness. As with individual psychotherapy, group therapy should be integrated into an overall treatment approach involving a comprehensive system of care if it is available.

For many schizophrenic patients, group therapy is at least as clinically effective as individual treatment and it is more cost-effective. The cost-effectiveness of group therapy is obvious as the therapist can serve eight patients rather than one or two patients in an hour. It is important, however, to assign patients to group therapy on the basis of clinical rather than economic criteria in order to maintain the efficacy of the intervention. Studies are needed to delineate more clearly the particular types of patients who profit most from group therapy. An important factor determining the cost-effectiveness of group psychotherapy is the level of necessary staff expertise. While several studies have demonstrated the efficacy of group therapy with schizophrenic patients using therapists with limited training (O'Brien *et al.*, 1972; Alden, 1979; Malm, 1982), further studies are needed to establish what staff qualifications are necessary for conducting such treatment.

EARLY INTERVENTION TO PREVENT RELAPSE IN SCHIZOPHRENIA

Despite our understanding of the damaging personal and economic consequences of relapse in schizophrenia, until recently there had been no large-scale systematic studies of the relapse process. Docherty *et al.* (1978) synthesized existing data about the relapse process derived mainly from individual case reports and described the occurrence of nonpsychotic symptoms early in the process of decompensation. Herz and Melville (1980) carried out the first large-scale systematic study of the prodromal phase, including its duration and characteristic symptoms utilizing a structured rating scale, the Early Signs Questionnaire (ESQ). A total of 145 schizophrenic patients including 99 outpatients, 46 recently hospitalized patients, and 80 family members were studied. In response to the question, "Could you tell that there were any changes in your thoughts, feelings, or behaviors that might have led you to believe you were becoming sick and might have to go to the hospital?," approximately 70% of patients and 92.6% of families noticed changes. In 66% of the cases, the patient and the family member agreed on the particular early signs of decompensation. Fifty percent of all patients indicated that the pattern of development of symptoms was similar for each episode of relapse. When asked "What did you do about these changes when you realized that they might become serious?," almost a third of patients reported that they did nothing, and only 4% of patients and family members said that the patients took more medication in response to symptoms. The most common symptoms that appeared or worsened before hospitalization according to all patients and family informants were tension and nervousness, eating less, having trouble sleeping, having trouble concentrating, depression, and seeing friends less. Less frequently reported were mild psychotic symptoms and referential ideas such as feelings of being laughed at. Despite sociodemographic differences (including residence in two different cities, Buffalo, New York and Atlanta, Georgia) between the recently hospitalized patients and stable outpatients, the rank-order correlation of early symptoms reported by these groups was 0.85 ($P \leq 0.001$). The finding that 93% of family members were able to observe early warning signs prior to decompensation suggests that family members can be valuable partners in monitoring for signs of relapse. When the time interval between the onset of noticeable symptoms and hospitalization was examined, most of the patients and family members reported that the interval was more than a week. This interval may be viewed as a window of opportunity for active psychiatric intervention to prevent full relapse.

A number of retrospective and prospective studies have subsequently confirmed the presence of early symptoms of relapse (Heinrichs & Carpenter, 1985; McCandless-Glimcher *et al.*, 1986; Birchwood *et al.*, 1989). Initial efforts to utilize the presence of early signs in order to prevent relapse occurred in a series of intermittent medication studies (Pietzcker *et al.*, 1986, Carpenter *et al.*, 1990; Jolley *et al.*, 1990; Herz *et al.*, 1991). The goal of the intermittent medication strategy was to minimize exposure to antipsychotic medications by administering them only when early signs of relapse appeared. In the Herz *et al.* study the relapse rate for intermittent females was not statistically different than the relapse rate for maintenance males and females (Herz, 1994), and in the study by Pietzcker *et al.* early intervention when prodromal signs appeared proved superior to intervention at relapse in preventing hospitalization. Although the intermittent medication approach was generally found not to be beneficial for most patients, some of these studies demonstrated the efficacy of early intervention and fostered further development of early symptom monitoring strategies.

Herz and co-workers are presently conducting a randomized controlled study of relapse prevention in a group of 88 outpatients with SCID (Structured Clinical Interview for DSM-III-R) confirmed diagnoses of schizophrenia or schizoaffective disorder. All patients receive maintenance antipsychotic drug therapy. Patients were randomly assigned to receive either standard treatment consisting of biweekly individual supportive therapy visits, or early intervention treatment consisting of a combination of the following elements: (i) weekly group therapy emphasizing development of coping skills; (ii) multifamily group psychoeducation; and (iii) active monitoring for prodromal symptoms with psychiatric intervention as soon as prodromal symptoms are observed. A preliminary analysis of data at 6 months showed a trend towards less use of emergency room visits and hospitalization in the experimental group compared with the standard treatment group (Herz *et al.*, 1993). Also, the data showed decreased total treatment costs for the early intervention group.

ALTERNATIVES TO HOSPITALIZATION FOR MANAGEMENT OF RELAPSE

The United States spends approximately 1% of the gross national product on treatment of mental illness each year, totalling \$39.3 billion in 1985 (Rice *et al.*, 1990). Approximately \$10.3 billion of this total was spent on treatment of schizophrenia (Rice & Miller, 1992). Despite deinstitutionalization and ongoing efforts to reduce inpatient lengths of stay, the majority of all dollars spent on treatment of schizophrenia are currently spent on hospital treatment both for acute and long-term care. A recent study of the costs for treatment of a cohort of 3422 seriously and persistently mentally ill patients in Monroe County, NY showed that the average cost for each patient was \$15 503 in 1990; 56% of this amount was spent on inpatient services (Reed & Brown, 1993). Another recent evaluation of the direct costs of treatment for chronic schizophrenic patients was conducted in Italy, and showed that the average yearly cost for each patient was \$9612 (1989 US dollars), 50.5% of which was hospitalization costs (Moscarelli *et al.*, 1991). In a study which examined the relationship between diagnosis and cost of hospitalization based upon data from 1 455 766 hospitalizations at 167 general hospitals, psychotic disorders ranked among the leading causes of high-cost hospitalizations (Fleming *et al.*, 1985). Concern about potential deleterious effects of hospitalization itself has led to the development of alternatives to hospitalization for relapsing patients. Studies have shown that alternatives to hospitalization for many acutely psychotic patients may be more clinically effective as well as more cost-effective than full-time hospitalization. The major controlled studies of day hospital and community-based alternatives to hospitalization will be reviewed in the following section.

A number of randomized (Herz *et al.*, 1971) and non-randomized (Michaux *et al.*, 1973; Fink *et al.*, 1978; Penk *et al.*, 1978) studies have examined the efficacy of day hospitalization as an alternative to inpatient hospitalization for acutely ill patients. While the feasibility of day hospitalization for acutely ill patients was established by Zwerling and Wilder (1964), efficacy was initially established by Herz *et al.* (1971), in a prospective study which randomized newly admitted patients who lived with families to either full-time hospitalization or day hospitalization on the same inpatient ward. Programming for both groups included individual, group, family, milieu, and somatic therapies as well as prevocational evaluation and experiences. Seeking to randomize only those patients for whom both treatments were judged clinically feasible, 90 patients with families entered the study out of a total of 424 admissions. Patients were excluded from participation if they were suicidal, homicidal, or extremely disorganized, or if they were no longer in need of either inpatient or day hospitalization. Approximately half of all patients in the study received the diagnosis of schizophrenia. Upon comparing the groups, patients receiving day hospitalization had greater improvements in symptoms, shorter lengths of stay, and lower rates of rehospitalization with better role functioning over a 2 year period.

Pasamanick and co-workers (Pasamanick *et al.*, 1967) conducted a controlled study comparing the effectiveness of home care versus hospital treatment for 152 acutely symptomatic schizophrenic patients. Patients who were suicidal, homicidal, or who did not have a family willing to care for them at home were excluded from study participation. Over a 3 year period, home care patients received visits from public health nurses, which were weekly for 3 months, and then tapered to monthly. At 3 years the home care group had spent more time in the community and experienced lower rates of rehospitalization than the hospital group. No outcome differences were noted at a 5 year follow-up evaluation during which all patients received routine outpatient care (Davis *et al.*, 1974).

Another study of home care as an alternative to hospital care was conducted by Fenton *et al.* (1979, 1982). Patients with substance abuse, chronic physical illness, and threat of suicide or homicide were excluded. Patients who did not have a significant other, who lived far away, who had lived in the community less than 6 months or who did not speak English were also excluded. Fifty-five percent of those screened were accepted and randomized to home care ($n=78$) or to hospital care ($n=84$). Schizophrenic patients composed 44% of the home care group and 39% of the hospital care group. Follow-up was available on 50% of patients up to 1 year. No differences were observed in clinical symptoms, role functioning, or family burden, although families of home care patients had to assume more responsibility in the first month. Home care patients were hospitalized for an average of 14.5 days compared with an average of 41.7 days for hospital patients, and 24% of both groups required readmission during the 1 year period.

Langsley (1971) reported the results of a study randomizing 350 acutely ill patients to an experimental group receiving outpatient family crisis therapy, or to a control group receiving inpatient treatment. After a 6 month follow-up period, experimental patients had fewer hospitalizations and a trend toward better role performance compared with control patients. However, important information about psychiatric diagnoses, severity of illness, demographic variables, or medications was not provided. Polak and Kirby (1976), randomized 85 patients considered in need of hospitalization to receive either hospitalization or community treatment. Thirty-one percent of all subjects were schizophrenic patients. Community treatment consisted of either boarding with "healthy" host families with 24-hour nursing coverage and a psychiatrist on call, an "intensive observation apartment" staffed by mental health personnel and volunteers, or home day care in the home of a family sponsor. Follow-up at 4 months revealed that home care patients were more satisfied with their treatment outcome, and that they were rated higher on goal attainment and self-disclosure to significant others compared with controls. A number of methodological issues limit the strength of these findings. Methods of choosing between these home care options were not discussed, home care results were combined, and the control hospital treatment was not described in detail. In addition, 10 patients randomized to home care could not be treated there due to behavioral problems and were removed from the analysis.

Mosher (Mosher *et al.*, 1975; Mosher & Menn, 1978) examined use of a supervised residence (Soteria House) as an alternative to hospitalization for acutely ill schizophrenic patients. All patients were diagnosed as schizophrenic by DSM-II criteria, and had no more than one previous hospitalization. Control patients were admitted to an inpatient service which was oriented to short-term care, consistent use of medications, and linkage to aftercare. Experimental patients were given no medications during the initial 6 weeks of the study. Readmission rates did not differ significantly between the two groups during the 2 year follow-up period. Experimental patients achieved a significantly higher occupational level and were more likely to live independently during the follow-up period than controls. The authors acknowledged that their study was limited by a number of factors including that follow-up care was not controlled, and that raters were not blind to treatment assignments. Although they concluded that withholding medication from this selected group of patients did no harm, data were not presented about the length of the acute episode for either group. It was noted, however, that the average length of initial stay was 28 days in the hospital for the controls and 166 days in Soteria House for experimental patients.

A major study of community care was conducted by Stein *et al.* (Stein and Test, 1978, 1980; Test & Stein, 1980; Weisbrod *et al.*, 1980). The study involved patients seeking admission to a state hospital, and the only diagnoses excluded were organic mental disorder and primary alcoholism. The experimental group received Training in Community Living (TCL), using ward staff who were transplanted to the community. Staff were available 24 hours a day, and patient programs were individually tailored with a focus on patient strengths rather than on pathology. Active outreach was provided for patients who missed appointments. Sixty-five subjects were randomized to the experimental condition and 65 subjects were randomized to the control condition, which consisted of inpatient care along with day hospital and outpatient treatment as needed. Results showed that experimental patients spent more time than controls in independent living and had fewer subsequent admissions during the study period (6% versus 58% for controls). Experimental subjects were more satisfied, rated higher on measures of self-esteem, more compliant with medications and showed less symptomatology. Despite spending more time at risk living independently in the community, experimental patients spent less time in psychiatric, penal, and medical institutions than controls. Control subjects also made greater use of emergency room services. Overall, the burden to families was similar for both groups during the study period. It should be noted that the advantages shown by the experimental patients were not sustained during an extended follow-up period where all patients were assigned to standard treatment. The authors concluded that treatment programs for the chronically mentally ill should be ongoing rather than time-limited. Hoult and colleagues in Australia conducted a similar study of community care as an alternative to hospitalization (Hoult *et al.*, 1981, 1983; Hoult & Reynolds, 1984; Hoult, 1986). During the 1 year study period, community patients were less likely to be hospitalized and had better symptom resolution than controls. Both patients and families found the experimental community treatment to be more helpful.

HOSPITALIZATION FOR MANAGEMENT OF RELAPSE

In the United States, a number of investigators have carried out controlled studies examining the relative efficacy of short and long hospital stays. Caffey *et al.* (1968, 1971) reported on a Veterans Administration

(VA) collaborative study of 201 predominantly middle class male schizophrenic patients. Exclusion criteria included lack of a home to return to, hospitalization within the last year, and dangerousness to self or others. Subjects were randomized to one of three groups: group A had usual hospital and outpatient care; group B had a brief hospitalization with special outpatient follow-up; group C had usual hospital care and special outpatient follow-up. Follow-up care of groups B and C was delivered by hospital staff, lasted for 1 year and usually included maintenance on antipsychotic drugs. Families of short-stay patients were visited in their homes during the admission by a social worker for education and preparation for discharge after a brief stay. Average lengths of stay were 75 days for group A, 29 days for group B, and 83 days for group C. Readmission rates and community adjustment of the three groups during the year after discharge were not signficantly different. Patients in groups B and C did show less pathologic disturbance than patients in group A, suggesting that intensive aftercare was associated with better outcome regardless of length of initial hospitalization.

In a series of articles, Glick and Hargreaves (Glick *et al.*, 1975, 1976; Hargreaves *et al.*, 1977) compared the outcome of 141 schizophrenic patients randomly assigned to short-term (average 25 days) or long-term (average 94 days) hospitalization. Outpatient treatment following discharge was not controlled. Both groups were markedly improved at 4 weeks, with the short-term group having a slight advantage. At 1 year, global outcome ratings favored the long-term group. When subjects were separated according to pre-hospital functioning, patients with poor functioning did about equally well in either group while patients with good functioning did better in the long-term group. This study has limited generalizability because of significant baseline differences between the study groups, and because patients in the long-term group received more frequent outpatient visits as well as more antipsychotic medication. Also, studies have suggested that a smooth transition to outpatient care is essential in facilitating the continued recovery of individuals treated only briefly in the hospital. In this study, hospitalization was not provided as part of a comprehensive health service delivery system.

In another series of articles, Mattes *et al.* (Rosen *et al.*, 1976; Mattes *et al.*, 1977a, b, 1979) compared outcome for 126 patients assigned to "short" (average 86 days) or "long" (average 179 days) stays on an analytically oriented inpatient ward with a strong milieu philosophy and primary emphasis on psychotherapy. Assignment to the groups was not random, and was based on administrative requirements. Twenty-one percent of the long-term and 25% of the short-term group had a diagnosis of schizophrenia. There was no difference in outcome for the schizophrenic patients when short and long-term groups were compared. Long-stay patients in general were more likely to have private individual therapy following discharge, were more frequently rehospitalized, and spent more time in the hospital.

DAY HOSPITAL AS A TRANSITION FROM BRIEF HOSPITALIZATION FOR RECOVERING PATIENTS

For patients recovering from the acute phase of illness, studies have examined the efficacy of day hospital as a transition from inpatient treatment, usually brief hospitalization. Herz and colleagues (Herz *et al.*, 1975, 1976, 1979; Endicott *et al.*, 1979) randomized 175 newly admitted patients who lived with their families to one of three treatment groups: (i) standard inpatient treatment (S), where the patient stayed as long as the therapist deemed necessary; (ii) brief-day treatment (B-D), where transitional day treatment was available after the inpatient stay which was to last about 1 week; or (iii) brief-out treatment (B-O), where the patient was to stay in the hospital for 1 week with no transitional day care. All patients received follow-up outpatient treatment. The day treatment patients and inpatients were treated on the same inpatient service by the same clinical staff, with the primary difference being that the day treatment patients returned home on evenings and weekends. Sixty-three percent of the patients received the diagnosis of schizophrenia. In addition to requiring that patients live with a family member, exclusions included serious medical illnesses, substance abuse, and antisocial behavior. Patients requiring readmission during the 2 year follow-up period received the same treatment as initially assigned. The average length of initial inpatient stay was 11 days for both brief groups and 60 days for the S group. At the 2 year follow-up, standard patients spent significantly more days in the hospital (mean 115.5) than had B-D (26.8) or B-O (46.8). However, there was no statistically significant difference in readmission rates between the groups. Approximately half of the B-D patients used day treatment, averaging 43 days during the study period. Differences between the groups regarding psychopathology and role functioning were most striking at 1 year. Ratings of the Global Assessment Scale were most favourable for B-D patients, and least favorable for S patients. Psychopathology, as measured by Psychiatric Status Schedule, was greatest in the S group. The B-O group showed more behavioral disorganization, belligerence, negativism, and speech disorganization than did the brief-day group. In addition, at 1 year the S group families were judged to have a higher level of burden than the B-D families. At 24 months, the proportions failing to perform any occupational role were 40% for S patients, 31% for B-O patients, and 20% for B-D patients. During the second year of the study, families of S patients were least likely to have a favorable attitude toward the treatment staff and were more likely to think that their relative should be back in the hospital.

Hirsch *et al.* (1979) conducted a study comparing brief and standard hospitalization where day treatment was also used as a transition from inpatient treatment. Two hundred and twenty-four patients, about half of whom were schizophrenic, were randomized to brief or standard care. Patients younger than 16 or suffering from "a diagnosable severe brain or physical disorder" were excluded. The median stay was 9 days for the brief group and 17 days for the standard group. Mean lengths of stay were not statistically significantly different. Although day treatment was not built into this study, it was available. No differences in clinical outcome between brief and standard groups were found at 2 weeks or at 3 months as measured by the Present State Examination. Fewer brief-stay patients were rehospitalized in the year following study entry, although it should be noted that many brief-stay patients used the day hospital instead of inpatient care. Forty-seven percent of brief patients versus 34% of standard patients used day hospitalization during the first year. This study replicates the findings of Herz and colleagues, particularly supporting the use of transitional day hospitalization after a brief hospitalization.

Weldon *et al.* (1979) randomized 30 newly discharged schizophrenic patients to either day hospital or outpatient treatment. Outpatient treatment consisted of combinations of medication clinic, group therapy, and individual therapy. Although no differences in symptoms were noted, at 3 month follow-up all of the day hospital patients were working or in job training, compared with only 20% of the outpatients. However, interpretation of the results is difficult due to a small sample size and brief follow-up period. Washburn *et al.* (1976) randomly assigned 29 female patients to day hospital and 30 female patients to inpatient treatment following 2–6 weeks of initial evaluation on an inpatient unit. Suicidal and "destructive" patients were excluded, and 50% of the study patients were schizophrenic. The day hospital patients showed superior improvement up to 18 months versus the hospitalized patients on measures of subjective distress and community adjustment, and their families were more satisfied with treatment. The inpatients were noted to spend more days in the hospital compared with the day hospital patients during the second 6 months of follow-up. Differences in outcome between the two groups disappeared between 18 and 24 months. Results for the schizophrenic patients were not analyzed separately.

CONCLUSIONS ABOUT CLINICAL EFFICACY OF HOSPITALIZATION AND ALTERNATIVES TO HOSPITALIZATION FOR RELAPSED PATIENTS

Review of studies of hospitalization and its alternatives reveals that they had several methodological limitations (Green & De La Cruz, 1981; Cournos, 1987). Many studies lacked modern diagnostic criteria and, although all studies had at least a majority of schizophrenic patients, many examined mixed patient populations. Despite these limitations, the existing literature taken together does support a number of general conclusions. Studies of alternatives to hospitalization suggest that several existing models of alternative treatment can provide better outcomes at lower costs for many schizophrenic patients. Studies on length of stay suggest that short stays are best, particularly for chronic patients, who are prone to develop institutional behaviors during long hospital stays. In addition, the literature suggests that hospitalization in mental institutions tends to be self-perpetuating (Kiesler, 1982). Wing and Brown (1970) showed that the longer a patient had been in the hospital, the more likely it was for that patient to be reluctant to leave. Role functioning is best preserved when the patient is returned to the community as soon as possible. As the studies by Herz and Caffey showed, ensuring availability and utilization of aftercare is probably more important than length of stay in determining outcome. Review of the major length of hospitalization studies also indicates that brief hospitalization is not appropriate for all patients. Reibel and Herz (1976) described nine of 112 patients in the large study by Herz and colleagues who could not be treated briefly. Particular patient characteristics which made it difficult to maintain study failures outside the hospital included persistent poor judgement and impulsive behavior, antisocial behavior, and continued psychotic disorganization. Gudeman and Shore (1984) calculated that approximately 15 long-term beds are required for a catchment area of 100 000, and that 7.5 of these beds would be occupied by patients with schizophrenia.

COST OF ALTERNATIVES TO HOSPITALIZATION, BRIEF HOSPITALIZATION, AND TRANSITIONAL DAY HOSPITALIZATION

It is evident that alternatives to hospitalization can provide comparable or superior clinical outcomes usually at a lower cost for many acutely ill schizophrenic patients. This conclusion is particularly applicable regarding the role of day hospital as an alternative to hospitalization (Luber, 1984; Mostert & Herz, 1990). However, while most studies have found that day hospital is more cost-effective than inpatient treatment, the extent of the savings is difficult to establish as the methods used to assess costs vary substantially. Reporting on costs for the study by Herz *et al.* (1979) which compared standard length hospitalization with brief hospitalization, Endicott *et al.* (1978) found that brief hospitalization with available day hospital care was much less expensive over time than standard length hospitalization. However, while it was more effective in clinical outcomes, it was more expensive than brief hospitalization followed by outpatient care. Three uncontrolled studies have also reported economic advantages for day hospital compared with inpatient hospitalization. A study funded by the Aetna Insurance Company found the cost of treating 31 patients in a day hospital for a total of 1654 days to be $155 611 (Guillette *et al.*, 1978). The authors noted that day hospital was clearly cost-effective as the cost of hospitalizing the same patients during that time would be $411 150 based on a rate of $150 per day. Although this study demonstrated that the per diem cost of day hospital was less than for inpatient treatment, it did not account for the tendency of some patients to have longer day hospital lengths of stay compared with inpatient stays. A study of day hospital by Penk *et al.* (1978) found superior outcomes for day hospital patients compared with patients hospitalized at a VA facility. The average daily direct cost was noted to be $33.26 for the day hospital treatment and $43.16 for inpatient treatment. The difference between indirect costs was even greater, at an average of $39.03 versus $73.49. Another uncontrolled study by Fink *et al.* (1978) which found equivalent clinical outcomes compared with hospitalization, showed lower 12 month treatment costs for the day patients, averaging $2334 versus $4159 for inpatients. In their controlled study of day hospital as an alternative treatment for patients in the recovery phase of illness, Washburn *et al.* (1976) also noted day hospital to be less costly than inpatient hospital treatment.

Despite the evidence that day hospitalization can be a cost-effective alternative to inpatient hospitalization, the day hospital is underutilized (Fink *et al.*, 1978; Luber, 1984; Mostert & Herz, 1990). An American Hospital Association survey of 6304 hospitals in 1985 revealed that only 14.3% had a day hospital program (American Hospital Association, 1986). A recent survey of day hospitalization in New York State revealed that there were no acute facilities substituting day hospital for inpatient care. There are many reasons for the underutilization of day hospital in the United States. Hospitals are under financial pressure to keep inpatient beds full, and thus may divert potential day hospital candidates to inpatient services. Many health insurance programs do not pay for day hospital treatment. In addition, patient characteristics predictive of response to day programs have not been well defined. Also, many psychiatrists and families assume that day care imposes a greater burden on families than inpatient care, although the opposite findings were noted in one study which examined this issue (Herz *et al.*, 1976). Leibenluft and Leibenluft (1988) cite lack of awareness about day hospital on the part of employer groups negotiating benefits, resulting in low consumer demand. They conducted an extensive survey of reimbursement for day hospital, and found that 42% of private insurers reimbursed for this treatment, while 30% did not specify and 28% clearly did not cover it. The authors also noted that private insurers, Medicaid and Medicare tended to favor the use of hospitalization for treatment of acutely ill patients, while the use of day hospital was greater among health maintenance organizations, as it is demonstrably more economical for a capitated system.

Community-based treatment programs can also provide at least comparable clinical outcomes for many acutely ill schizophrenic patients compared with inpatient treatment, often at a lower cost. Weisbrod and colleagues performed a detailed benefit–cost analysis of the Training in Community Living treatment, and found net benefits of $400 per patient per year compared with hospital-based treatment. Examining the costs of their community care program, Hoult and colleagues found that standard treatment was 26% more expensive than experimental treatment ($5669 versus $4489). Eighty-one percent of costs for experimental patients were incurred in the community, while 79% of costs for control patients were due to hospitalization. Two recent studies using matched-group designs have considered the cost-effectiveness of alternatives to hospitalization for acute patients. Bedell and Ward (1989) compared 102 patients admitted to an intensive residential treatment program with 42 patients treated at a state hospital. Pilot data indicate that the majority of patients had a diagnosis of schizophrenia. The authors reported that the residential program achieved comparable results in a shorter time, and cost an average of $9152.50 less per patient compared with the state hospital treatment for the index admission period. In a study comparing two crisis housing alternatives for patients with serious mental illness, Bond *et al.* (1989) compared the efficacy of an eight bed crisis house with lodging purchased in hotels and boarding houses. The authors found that these housing alternatives were associated with comparable rehospitalization rates and costs. The results of these studies should be interpreted with caution due to absence of random subject assignment.

A number of detailed reviews have concluded that day hospital (Greene & De La Cruz, 1981; Luber, 1984; Mostert & Herz, 1990) and various community-based programs (Kiesler, 1982; Herz & Mostert, 1990) are clinically superior and more cost-effective as compared with inpatient hospital treatment for relapsed patients. Further studies are needed to decide the differential indications and benefits of these programs. Despite the advantages of many programs which function as alternatives to hospitalization, however, it is clear that some acutely ill schizophrenic patients require hospitalization. In general, patients who are dangerous to themselves or others, or are so impaired that they require constant supervision, support, and a safe environment should be hospitalized.

DAY TREATMENT TO PREVENT RELAPSE IN STABLE PATIENTS

Day treatment or continuing treatment programs are generally used to provide ongoing supportive care to marginally adjusted schizophrenic patients in the stable phase of illness. While day hospitalization programs are staffed similarly to inpatient hospital programs, day treatment programs generally have lower staff-to-patient ratios, fewer medical and nursing staff, and greater emphasis on recreational and prevocational activities. Early controlled studies comparing day treatment programs with outpatient treatment found day treatment to achieve superior outcomes for chronic schizophrenic patients (Meltzhoff & Blumenthal, 1966), and for schizophrenic patients with schizoaffective features (Guy *et al.*, 1969). Linn *et al.* (1979) conducted a prospective, randomized study comparing day treatment and outpatient drug management in 10 VA hospitals. Subjects were 162 newly discharged chronic schizophrenic patients who had been referred to the VA day treatment program. Eighty were assigned to day treatment and 83 to outpatient treatment, and all were followed with a variety of measures over 2 years. The study showed that day treatment patients had better social functioning and fewer symptoms than outpatients after 2 years. The overall cost of treatment during the 2 year period was higher on average for day treatment patients. However, six of the 10 day centers were noted to achieve significant reductions in both relapse and symptomatology. Successful outcome centers were associated with less use of individual and group therapy, less rapid patient turnover, more occupational therapy and a sustained nonthreatening environment compared with poor-outcome centers. Linn concluded that programs with a high turnover and intensive psychotherapies may have been associated with higher relapse rates, but these two factors could not be sorted out in the analysis. Patients at greatest risk for relapse in these programs appeared to be those with motor retardation, emotional withdrawal and anxiety.

While a consensus exists that there are many cost-effective alternatives to inpatient treatment for acute patients, there are fewer studies examining the costs of continuing day treatment versus outpatient treatment for stable schizophremic patients. Linn's VA study of day treatment showed that total cost for psychiatric care over the 2 year study period was $5895 for day treatment versus $4437 for medication alone (Linn *et al.*, 1979). The study also demonstrated that day treatment programs which had better results tended to be less expensive, perhaps because they provided less intensive treatments which were tolerated better by chronic patients. Another study of VA patients, though retrospective, showed that over a 3 year period, the reduction of inpatient care due to day treatment resulted in a net savings of almost $1.4 million for a group of 64 patients (Guidry *et al.*, 1979). In a randomized study of long-term state hospital inpatients, an experimental on-site residential program was compared with ongoing inpatient treatment for 22 chronic schizophrenic patients (Dickey *et al.*1986). Costs for patients assigned to the residential program were found to average $14 500 less (in 1981 dollars) than for the inpatient control group over a 2 year period.

CONCLUSIONS

Major goals of psychiatric treatment are to improve coping skills and competence, and to prevent and manage relapse. Review of the psychotherapy literature suggests that individual supportive psychotherapy is clinically effective. However, group psychotherapy is at least as clinically effective and more cost-effective for many schizophrenic patients, and is therefore recommended when indicated. The extent to which appropriate use of individual and group psychotherapy can decrease patients' vulnerability to stress through increasing their coping skills, thus decreasing relapse and rehospitalization rates remains to be determined. There is currently a general need to establish the clinical efficacy of particular forms of individual and group psychotherapy. As noted by Strupp and Bergin (1969) we must begin to ask "What specific therapeutic interventions produce specific changes in specific patients under specific conditions?" We support the recommendation of Krupnick and Pincus (1992) for routine inclusion of cost data in all psychotherapy outcome studies in order to begin to define the relative cost-effectiveness of different therapeutic approaches. When prodromal symptoms occur during the course of treatment, early intervention with crisis management and increased antipsychotic medications can often help prevent relapse and hospitalization. For many schizophrenic patients who experience a relapse, alternatives to hospitalization are feasible when there are adequate resources available in the community. Although such alternatives are generally more cost-effective than hospitalization, they have not been adequately supported by third-party payers. Considering the wide diversity of community-based alternatives to hospitalization which currently exist, there is a need for studies to establish both the relative clinical efficacy and cost-effectiveness of these programs. The day hospital can be clinically effective and cost-effective as an immediate alternative to hospitalization and to shorten the inpatient stay for relapsed patients, but remains underutilized in the United States. With the use of day treatment and other community programs for patients in the stable or maintenance phase, only a small minority cannot be managed effectively outside the hospital.

REFERENCES

Alden, A.R., Weddington, W.W., Jacobson, C., and Gianturco, D.T. (1979). Group aftercare for chronic schizophrenia. *Journal of Clinical Psychiatry*, **40**, 249–252.

American Hospital Association: Hospital Statistics (1986). AHA, Chicago, ILL.

Andrews, G. (1991). The cost of schizophrenia revisited. *Schizophrenia Bulletin*, **17**, 389–394.

Bedell, J. and Ward J.C. (1989). An intensive community-based treatment alternative to state hospitalization. *Hospital and Community Psychiatry*. **40**, 533–538.

Birchwood, R., Smith, J., Macmillan, F., Hogg, B., Prasad, R., Harvey, C., and Bering, S. (1989). Predicting relapse in schizophrenia: the development and implementation of an early signs monitoring system using patients and families as observers. *Psychological Medicine*, **19**, 649–656.

Bond, G.R., Witheridge, T.F., Wasmer, D., Dincin, J., McRae, S.A., Mayers, J., and Ward, R.S. (1989). A comparison of two crisis housing alternatives to psychiatric hospitalization. *Hospital and Community Psychiatry*, **40**, 177–183.

Bookhamer, R.S., Meyers, R.W., Schober, C.C., and Piotrowski, Z.A. (1966). A five year follow-up study of schizophrenics treated by Rosen's "direct analysis" compared with controls. *American Journal of Psychiatry*, **123**, 602–604.

Caffey, E.M., Jones, R.D., Diamond, L.S., Burton, E., and Bowen, W.T. (1986). Brief hospital treatment of schizophrenia—early results of a multiple-hospital study. *Hospital and Community Psychiatry*, **19**, 282–287.

Caffey, E.M., Galbrecht, C.R., and Klett, C.J. (1971). Brief hospitalization and aftercare in the treatment of schizophrenia, *Archives of General Psychiatry*, **24**, 81–86.

Carpenter, W.I., Hanlon, T.E., Heinrichs, D.W., *et al.* 1990. Continuous versus targeted medication in schizophrenic outpatients: outcome results. *American Journal of Psychiatry*, **147**, 1138–1148.

Cournos, F. (1987). Hospitalization outcome studies. Implications for the treatment of the very ill patient. *Psychiatric Clinics of North America*, **10**, 165–176.

Davis, A.E., Dinitz, S., and Pasamanick, B. (1974). *Schizophrenics in the New Custodial Community: Five Years After the Experiment* Columbus. OH: Ohio State University Press.

Dickey, B., Cannon, N.L., McGuire, T.G., and Gudeman, K.E. (1986). The quarterway house: a two-year cost study of an experimental residential program. *Hospital and Community Psychiatry*, **37**, 1136–1143.

Docherty, J.P., Van Kammen, D.P., Siris, S.G., and Marder, S.R., (1978). Stages of onset of schizophrenic psychosis. *American Journal of Psychiatry*, **135**, 420–426.

Endicott, J., Herz, M.I., and Gibbon, M. (1978). Brief versus standard hospitalization: the differential cost. *American Journal of Psychiatry*, **136**, 707–712.

Endicott, J., Cohen, J., Nee, J., Fleiss, J.L., and Herz, M.I. (1979). Brief vs standard hospitalization. For whom? *Archives of General Psychiatry*, **36**, 706–712.

Fenton, F.R., Tessier, L., and Struening, E.L. (1979). A comparative trial of home and hospital psychiatric care: one-year follow-up. *Archives of General Psychiatry*, **36**, 1073–1079.

Fenton, F.R., Tessier, L., Struening, E.I., Smith, F.A., and Benoit, C. (1982). *Home and Hospital Psychiatric Treatment*. Pittsburgh, PA: University of Pittsburgh Press.

Fink, E.B., Longbaugh, R., and Stout, R. (1978). The paradoxical underutilization of partial hospitalization. *American Journal of Psychiatry*, **135**, 713–716.

Fleming, S.T., Kobrinski, E.J., and Long, M.J. (1985). A multidimensional analysis of the impact of high-cost hospitalization. *Inquiry*, **22**, 178–187.

Frank, A.F. and Gunderson, J.G. (1990). The role of the therapeutic alliance in the treatment of schizophrenia: relationship to course and outcome. *Archives of General Psychiatry*, **47**, 228–236.

Glass, L.L., Katz, H.M., Schnitzer, R.D., Knapp, P.H., Frank, A.F., and Gunderson, J.G. (1989). Psychotherapy of schizophrenia: an empirical investigation of the relationship of process to outcome. *American Journal of Psychiatry*, **146**, 603–608.

Glick, I.D., Hargreaves, W.A., and Goldfield, M.D. (1974). Short vs. long hospitalization: a prospective controlled study, I. The preliminary results of a one-year follow-up of schizophrenics. *Archives of General Psychiatry*, **30**, 363–369.

Glick, I.D., Hargraves, W.A., Raskin, M., and Kutner, S.J., (1975). Short vs. long hospitalization: a prospective controlled study, II. Results for schizophrenic inpatients. *American Journal of Psychiatry*, **132**, 385–390.

Glick, I.D., Hargreaves, W.S., Drues, J., Showstack, J.A. (1976). Short vs. long hospitalization: a prospective controlled study, IV. One-year follow-up of schizophrenic patients. *American Journal of Psychiatry*, **133**, 509–514.

Goldberg, S.C., Schooler, N.R., Hogarty, G.E., and Roper, M. (1977). Prediction of relapse in schizophrenic outpatients treated by drug and sociotherapy. *Archives of General Psychiatry*, **34**, 171–184.

Goldhamer, P. and Leszcz, M. (1990). Group therapy. In M.V. Seeman and S.E. Greben, eds, *Office Treatment of Schizophrenia*, pp. 101–121. Washington, DC: American Psychiatric Press.

Gomes-Schwartz, B. (1984). Individual psychotherapy of schizophrenia. In A.S. Bellack, ed., *Schizophrenia: Treatment, Management, and Rehabilitation*, pp. 307–335. New York: Grune and Stratton

Greene, L.R. and De La Cruz, A. (1981). Psychiatric day treatment as alternative to and transition from full-time hospitalization. *Community Mental Health Journal*, **17**,

191–202.

Grinspoon, L., Ewalt, J.R., and Shader, R. (1967). Long term treatment of chronic schizophrenia. *International Journal of Psychiatry*, **4**, 116–128.

Grinspoon, L., Ewalt, J.R., and Shader, R. (1968). Psychotherapy and pharmacotherapy in chronic schizophrenia. *American Journal of Psychiatry*, **124**, 1645–1652.

Grinspoon, L., Ewalt, J.R., and Shader, R. (1972). *Schizophrenia: Pharmacotherapy and Psychotherapy*. Baltimore, MD: Williams and Wilkins.

Group for the Advancement of Psychiatry (GAP) (1992). Implications for psychosocial interventions in patients with schizophrenia. In *Beyond Symptom Suppression* (Report No. 134), pp. 59–78. Washington, DC: American Psychiatric Press.

Gudeman, J.E. and Shore, M.F. (1984). Beyond deinstitutionalization: a new class of facilities for the mentally ill. *New England Journal of Medicine*, **311**, 832–836.

Guidry, L.S., Winstead, D.K., Levine, M., and Eicke, F.J. (1979). Evaluation of day treatment center effectiveness. *Journal of Clinical Psychiatry*, **40**, 221–224.

Guillette, W., Crowley, B., Savitz, S.A., and Goldberg, F.D. (1978). Day hospitalization as a cost-effective alternative to inpatient care: a pilot study. *Hospital and Community Psychiatry*, **29**, 525–527.

Gunderson, J.G., Frank, A.F., Katz, H.M., Vannicelli, M.L., Frosch, J.P., and Knapp, P.H. (1984). Effects of psychotherapy in schizophrenia, II: comparative outcome of two forms of treatment. *Schizophrenia Bulletin*, **10**, 564–598.

Guy, W., Gross, M., Hogarty, G.E., and Dennis, H. (1969). A controlled evaluation of day hospital effectiveness, *Archives of General Psychiatry*, **20**, 329–338.

Hargreaves, W.A., Glick, I.D., Drues, J., Showstack, J.A., and Feigenbaum, E. (1977). Short vs. long hospitalization: a prospective controlled study, VI. Two-year follow-up results for schizophrenics. *Archives of General Psychiatry*, **34**, 305–311.

Heinrichs, D.W. and Carpenter, W.T. (1985). Prospective study of prodromal symptoms in schizophrenic relapse. *American Journal of Psychiatry*, **142**, 371–373.

Herz, M.I. (1984). Recognizing and preventing relapse in patients with schizophrenia. *Hospital and Community Psychiatry*, **35**, 344–349.

Herz, M.I. (1994). Intermittent medication in schizophrenia: predictors of outcome. In A. Beigel, E. Costa, J.A. Silva, J.J. Lopez Ibor, eds, *Past, Present and Future of Psychiatry: Proceedings of the World Psychiatric Association IX World Congress of Psychiatry*, pp 502–504. Singapore: World Scientific Publishing.

Herz, M.I. and Melville, C. (1980). Relapse in schizophrenia. *American Journal of Psychiatry*, **137**, 801–805.

Herz, M.I. and Mostert, M.A. (1990). The role of hospitalization. In M.I. Herz, S.J. Keith and J.P. Docherty, eds, *Handbook of Schizophrenia, Volume 4: Psychosocial Treatment of Schizophrenia*, pp. 269–295. New York: Elsevier Science Publishers.

Herz, M.I., Endicott, J., Spitzer, R.L., and Mesnikoff, A. (1971). Day versus inpatient hospitalization: A controlled study. *American Journal of Psychiatry*, **127**, 1371–1382.

Herz, M.I., Endicott, J., and Spitzer, R.L. (1975). Brief hospitalization of patients with families: initial results. *American Journal of Psychiatry*, **132**, 413–418.

Herz, M.I., Endicott, J., and Spitzer, R.L. (1976). Brief versus standard hospitalization: the families. *American Journal of Psychiatry*, 133, 795–801.

Herz, M.I., Endlicott, J., and Gibbon, M. (1979). Brief hospitalization: two-year follow-up. *Archives of General Psychiatry*, **36**, 701–705.

Herz, M.I., Glazer, W.M., Mostert, M.A., Sheard, M.A., Szymanski, H.V., Hafez, H., Mirza, M., and Vana, J. (1991). Intermittent vs maintenance medication in schizophrenia. *Archives of General Psychiatry*, **48**, 333–339.

Herz, M.I., Lamberti, J.S., and Brown, S.W. (1993). Early Intervention to Prevent Relapse in Schizophrenia. Presented at the Sixth Annual New York State Office of Mental Health Conference, Albany, N.Y., December 7, 1993.

Hirsch, S.R., Platt, S., Knight, A., and Weyman, A. (1979). Shortening hospital stay for psychiatric care: effect on patients and their families. *British Medical Journal*, **1**, 442–446.

Hogarty, G.E. and Goldberg, S.C. (1973). Drug and sociotherapy in the aftercare of schizophrenic patients. *Archives of General Psychiatry*, **28**, 54–64.

Hogarty, G.E., Goldberg, S.C., Schooler, N.R., Ulrich, R.F., and the Collaborative Study Group (1974a). Drug and sociotherapy in the aftercare of schizophenic patients. II. Two-year relapse rates. *Archives of General Psychiatry*, **31**, 603–608.

Hogarty, G.E., Goldberg, S.C., and Schooler, N.R., (1974b). Drug and sociotherapy in the aftercare of schizophrenic patients. III. Adjustment of nonrelapsed patients. *Archives of General Psychiatry*, **31**, 609–618.

Hogarty, G.E., Schooler, N.R., Ulrich, R., Mussare, F., Ferro, P., and Herron, E. (1979). Fluphenazine and social therapy in the aftercare of schizophrenic patients. *Archives of General Psychiatry*, **36**, 1283–1294.

Hoult, J. (1986). Community care of the acutely mentally ill. *British Journal of Psychiatry*, **149**, 137–144.

Hoult, J. and Reynolds, I. (1984). Schizophrenia: a comparative trial of a community orientated and hospital orientated psychiatric care. *Acta Psychiatrica Scandinavica*, **69**, 359–372.

Hoult, J., Reynolds, I., Charbonneau-Powis, M., Coles, P., and Briggs, J. (1981). A controlled study of psychiatric hospital versus community treatment: the effect on relatives. *Australia and New Zealand Journal of Psychiatry*, **15**, 323–328.

Hoult, J., Reynolds, I., Charbonneau-Powis, M., Weekes, P., and Briggs, J. (1983). Psychiatric hospital versus community treatment: the results of a randomized trial. *Australia and New Zealand Journal of Psychiatry*, **17**, 160–167.

Huber, G., Gross, G., Schuttler, R., and Linz, M. (1980). Longitudinal studies of schizophrenic patients. *Schizophrenia Bulletin,* **6**, 592–605.

Jolley, A.G., Hirsch, S.R., Morrison, G., McRink, A., and Wilson, L. (1990). Trial of brief intermittent neuroleptic prophylaxis for selected schizophrenia outpatients: clinical and social outcome at two years. *British Medical Journal,* **301**, 847–852.

Kanas, N. (1986). Group therapy with schizophrenics: a review of controlled studies. *International Journal of Psychotherapy,* **36**, 339–351.

Kanas, N. (1991). Group therapy with schizophrenic patients: a short-term, homogeneous approach. *International Journal of Psychotherapy,* **41**, 33–48.

Kanas, N. (1993). Group psychotherapy with schizophrenia. In H.I. Kaplan and B.J. Saddock, eds, *Comprehensive Group Psychotherapy,* pp. 407–418. Baltimore, MD: Williams and Wilkins.

Karon, B. and O'Grady, B. (1969). Intellectual test changes in schizophrenic patients in the first six months of treatment. *Psychotherapy: Theory, Research & Practice,* **6**, 88–96.

Karon, B. and VandenBos, G.R. (1970). Experience, medication, and the effectivness of psychotherapy with schizophrenics: a note on Drs. May and Tuma's conclusions. *British Journal of Psychiatry,* **116**, 427–428.

Karon, B. and VandenBos, G.R. (1972). The consequences of psychotherapy for schizophrenic patients. *Psychotherapy: Research & Practice,* **9**, 111–119.

Katz, H.M. and Gunderson, J.G. (1990). Individual psychodynamically oriented psychotherapy for schizophrenic patients. In M.I. Herz, S.J. Keith, and J.P. Docherty, eds, *Handbook of Schizophrenia, Volume 4: Psychosocial Treatment of Schizophrenia,* pp. 69–90. New York: Elsevier Science Publishers.

Keith, S.J. and Matthews, S.M. (1982). Group, family, and milieu therapies and psychosocial rehabilitation in the treatment of schizophrenic disorders. In L. Grinspoon, ed., *Psychiatry 1982: The American Psychiatric Association Annual Review,* pp. 166–177. Washington, DC: American Psychiatric Press.

Kiesler, C.A. (1982). Mental hospitals and alternative care. Noninstitutionalization as potential public policy for mental patients. *American Psychologist,* **37**, 349–360.

Krupnick, J.L. and Pincus, H.A. (1992). The cost-effectiveness of psychotherapy: a plan for research. *American Journal of Psychiatry,* **149**, 1295–1305.

Langsley, D.G., Machotka, P., and Flomenhaft, K. (1971). Avoiding mental hospital admission: a follow-up study. *American Journal of Psychiatry,* **127**, 1391–1394.

Leibeluft, E. and Leibenluft, R.F., J.D. (1988). Reimbursement for partial hospitalization: a survey and policy implications. *American Journal of Psychiatry,* **145**, 1514–1520.

Linn, M.W., Caffey, E.M., Klett, C.J., Hogarty, G.E., and Lamb, H.R. (1979). Day treatment and psychotropic drugs in the aftercare of schizophrenic patient. *Archives of General Psychiatry,* **36**, 1055–1066.

Luber, R.F. (1984). Partial hospitalization. In A.S Bellack, ed, *Schizophrenia: Treatment, Management and Rehabilitation,* pp. 219–246. New York: Grune and Stratton.

Luborsky, L., Singer, B., and Luborsky, L. (1976). Comparative studies of psychotherapies: is it true that "everybody has won and all must have prizes"? *Proceedings of the American Psychopathological Association,* **64**, 3–22.

Malm, U. (1982). The influence of group therapy on schizophrenia. *Acta Psychiatrica Scandinavica, Supplement* 297.

Malm, U. (1990). Group therapy. In M.I. Herz, S.J. Keith and J.P. Docherty, eds, *Handbook of Schizophrenia, Volume 4: Psychosocial Treatment of Schizophrenia,* pp. 191–211. New York: Elsevier Science Publishers.

Mattes, J.A., Klein, D.F., Millan, D., and Rosen, B. (1979). Comparison of the clinical effectiveness of "short" versus "long" stay psychiatric hospitalization, IV. Predictors of differential benefit. *Journal of Nervous and Mental Disorders,* **167**, 175–181.

Mattes, J.A., Rosen, B., and Klein, D.F. (1977a). Comparison of the clinical effectiveness of "short" versus "long" stay psychiatric hospitalization, II. Results of a 3-year post-hospital follow-up. *Journal of Nervous and Mental Disorders,* **165**, 387–394.

Mattes, J.A., Rosen, B., Klein, D.F., and Millan, D. (1977b). Comparison of the clinical effectiveness of "short" versus "long" stay psychiatric hospitalization, III. Further results of a 3-year post-hospital follow-up. *Journal of Nervous and Mental Disorders,* **165**, 395–402.

May, P.R. (1968). *Treatment of Schizophrenia: A Comparative Study of Five Treatment Methods.* New York: Science House.

May, P.R., and Simpson, G. (1980). Schizophrenia: evaluation of treatment methods. In H.I. Kaplan, A.M. Freedman, and B.J. Sadock, eds, *Comprehensive Textbook of Psychiatry,* 3rd edn, Vol. 2, pp. 1240–1275. Baltimore, MD: Williams and Wilkins.

May, P.R. and Tuma, A.H. (1964). The effect of psychotherapy and stelazine on length of hospital stay, release rate and supplemental treatment of schizophrenic patients. *Journal of Nervous and Mental Disorders,* **139**, 362–369.

May, P.R. and Tuma, A.H. (1965). Treatment of schizophrenia. *British Journal of Psychiatry,* **3**, 505–510.

McCandless-Glimcher, L., McKnight, S., Hamera, E., Smith, B.L., Peterson, K.A., and Plumblee, A.A. (1986). Use of symptoms by schizophrenics to monitor and regulate their illness. *Hospital and Community Psychiatry,* **37**, 929–933.

Meltzoff, J. and Blumenthal, R. (1966). *The Day Treatment Center: Principles, Application and Evaluation.* Springfield, IL: Charles C. Thomas.

Michaux, M.H., Chelst, M.R., Foster, S.A., Pruim, R.J., and Dasinger, E.M. (1973). Post-release adjustment of day and full-time psychiatric patients. *Archives of General Psychiatry,* **29**, 647–651.

Moscarelli, M., Capri, S., and Neri, L. (1991). Cost evaluation of chronic schizophrenic patients during the first 3 years after the first contact. *Schizophrenia Bulletin*, **17**, 421–426.

Mosher, L.R. and Menn, A.Z. (1978). Community residential treatment for schizophrenia: two-year follow-up. *Hospital and Community Psychiatry*, **29**, 715–723.

Mosher, L.R., Menn, A.Z., and Matthews, S.M. (1975). Soteria: evaluation of a home-based treatment for schizophrenia. *American Journal of Orthopsychiatry*, **45**, 455–467.

Mostert, M.A. and Herz, M.I. (1990). The role of partial hospitalization. In M.I. Herz, S.J. Keith and J.P. Docherty, eds, *Handbook of Schizophrenia, Volume 4: Psychosocial Treatment of Schizophrenia*, pp. 297–316. New York: Elsevier Science Publishers.

Mueser, K.T. and Berenbaum, H. (1990). Psychodynamic treatment of schizophrenia: is there a future? *Psychological Medicine*, **20**, 253–262.

Novalis, P.N., Rojcewicz, S.J., and Peele, R. (1993). *Clinical Manual of Supportive Psychotherapy*. Washington, DC: American Psychiatric Press.

Nuechterlein, K.H. (1987). Vulnerability models for schizophrenia: state of the art. In H. Hafner, W.F. Gattaz, and W. Janzarik, eds, *Search for the Causes of Schizophrenia*, pp. 297–316. Berlin: Springer-Verlag.

O'Brien, C.P. (1975). Group psychotherapy for schizophrenia: A practical approach. *Schizophrenia Bulletin*, **13**, 119–130.

O'Brien, C.P. (1983). Group psychotherapy with schizophrenia and affective disorders. In H.I. Kaplan, and B.J. Sadock, eds, *Comprehensive Group Psychotherapy*, 2nd edn, pp. 242–249. Baltimore, MD: Williams and Wilkins.

O'Brien, C.P., Hamm, K.B., Ray, B.A., Pierce, J.F., Luborsky, L., and Mintz, J. (1972). Group vs individual psychotherapy with schizophrenics. *Archives of General Psychiatry*, **27**, 474–478.

Parloff, M.B. and Dies, R. (1977). Group psychotherapy outcome research. *International Journal of Group Psychiatry*, **27**, 281–319.

Pasamanick, B., Scarpitti, F.R., and Dinitz, S. (1967). *Schizophrenics in the Community*. New York: Appleton-Century-Crofts.

Penk, W.E., Charles, H.L., and Van Hoose, T.A. (1978). Comparative effectiveness of day hospital and inpatient psychiatric treatment. *Journal of Consulting and Clinical Psychology*, **46**, 94–101.

Pietzcker, A., Gaebel, W., Kopcke, M., Linden, M., Muller, P., Muller-Spohn, F., Schussler, G., and Tegeler, J. (1986). A German multicenter study of the neuroleptic long term therapy of schizophrenic patients; preliminary report. *Pharmacopsychiatry*, **19**, 161–166.

Polak, P.R. and Kirby, M.W. (1976). A model to replace psychiatric hospitals. *Journal of Nervous and Mental Disorders*, **162**, 13–22.

Reed, S.K. and Brown, S.W. (1993). Populations, Services and Financing in Mental Health: Where Does Your Mental Health Dollar Go? Presented at the Sixth Annual New York State Office of Mental Health Conference, Albany, NY, December 7, 1993.

Reibel, S. and Herz, M.I. (1976). Limitations of brief hospital treatment. *American Journal of Psychiatry*, **133**, 518–521.

Rice, D.P. and Miller, L.S. (1992). The economic burden of schizophrenia. Presented at the Sixth Biennial Research Conference on the Economics of Mental Health, Bethesda, MD, September 21–22, 1992.

Rice, D.P., Kelman, S., Miller, L.S., and Dunmeyer, S. (1990). *The Economic Costs of Alcohol and Drug Abuse and Mental Illness: 1985*. Rockville, MD: National Institute of Mental Health DHHS Pub. No. (ADM) 90-1694.

Rosen, B., Katzoff, A., Carillo, C., and Klein, D.F. (1976). Comparison of the clinical effectiveness of "short" versus "long" stay psychiatric hospitalization, I. Inpatient results. *Archives of General Psychiatry*, **33**, 1316–1322.

Stanton, A.H., Gunderson, J.G., Knapp, P.H., Frank, A.F., Vannicelli, M.L., Schnitzer, R., and Rosenthal, R. (1984). Effects of psychotherapy in schizophrenia, I: design and implementation of a controlled study. *Schizophrenia Bulletin*, **10**, 520–562.

Stein, L.I. and Test, M.A. (eds) (1978). *Alternatives to Mental Hospital Treatment*. New York: Plenum Press.

Stein, L.I. and Test, M.A. (1980). Alternative to mental hospital treatment I. Conceptual model, treatment program, and clinical evaluation. *Archives of General Psychiatry*, **37**, 392–397.

Stone, W.N. (1993). Group psychotherapy for chronically mentally ill patients. In A. Alonso and H.I. Swiller, eds, *Group Therapy in Clinical Practice*, pp. 71–91. Washington, DC: American Psychiatric Press.

Strupp, H.H. and Bergin, A.E. (1969). Some empirical and conceptual bases for coordinated research in psychotherapy: a critical review of issues, trends, and evidence. *International Journal of Psychotherapy*, **7**, 18–90.

Test, M.A. and Stein, L.I. (1980). Alternative to mental hospital treatment III. Social cost. *Archives of General Psychiatry*, **37**, 409–412.

Washburn, S., Vannicelli, M., Longabaugh, R., and Scheff, B.J. (1976). A controlled comparison of psychiatric day treatment and inpatient hospitalization. *Journal of Consulting and Clinical Psychlogy*, **44**, 665–676.

Weisbrod, B.A., Test, M.A., and Stein, L.I. (1980). Alternative to Mental Hospital Treatment II. Economic benefit–cost analysis. *Archives of General Psychiatry*, **37**, 400–405.

Weldon, E., Clarkin, J.E., Hennessy, J.J., and Francis, A. (1979). Day hospital versus outpatient treatment: a controlled study. *Psychiatry Quarterly*, **51**, 144–150.

Wing, J.K. and Brown, G.W. (1970). *Institutionalism and Schizophrenia*. Cambridge University Press.

Zubin, J. and Spring, B. (1977). Vulnerability—a new view of schizophrenia. *Journal of Abnormal Psychology*, **86**, 103–126.

Zwerling, I. and Wilder, J.F. (1964). An evaluation of the applicability of the day hospital in treatment of acutely disturbed patients. *Israel Annals of Psychiatry and Related Disorders*, **2**, 164–185.

15

Early Detection and Intervention for Initial Episodes of Schizophrenia

IAN R.H. FALLOON, ROBERT R. KYDD, JOHN H. COVERDALE and TANNIS M. LAIDLAW
School of Medicine, Department of Psychiatry and Behavioral Sciences, University of Auckland, New Zealand

SUMMARY

Comprehensive programs of drug and psychosocial interventions with adults who show early signs and symptoms of schizophrenic disorders may contribute to a lower incidence and prevalence of florid episodes of schizophrenia. These programs combine early detection of prodromal states by family practitioners, with close liaison with mental health professionals, who are well-trained in psychiatric assessment and rapid deployment of integrated drug and psychosocial strategies that have proven effective in reducing the prevalence of established cases of schizophrenia in controlled studies. Long-term monitoring of signs of recurrence of these prodromal episodes, with further intervention appears essential to maintain these benefits. Preliminary results suggest that the recent advances in clinical management of schizophrenic disorders can be replicated in clinical practice, providing staff are trained to the same standards as those working in the research projects from which the strategies were derived.

INTRODUCTION

Advances in the long-term clinical management of schizophrenia have shown that the skilled application of current therapeutic strategies may provide substantial benefits. While full clinical recovery is rare, at least in the developed nations, there are signs that social recovery is possible for most cases (Shepherd *et al.*, 1989). Florid episodes and exacerbations have been controlled effectively so that the locus of care for most sufferers of this disorder has changed from the mental asylum to residential settings in the community. Low-dosage neuroleptic drugs have halved the rate of florid exacerbations, with an additional reduction of similar proportions achieved where psychosocial stress management strategies have been combined with optimal drug prophylaxis (Figure 1).

Although these benefits appear to be most marked during the first year after a florid episode (Hogarty *et al.*, 1987), the gains may be sustained over longer periods when the programs are continued indefinitely, with careful monitoring by patients, carers and professional services so that intensive periods of

Handbook of Mental Health Economics and Health Policy, Volume I, Schizophrenia. Edited by M. Moscarelli, A. Rupp and N. Sartorius.
© 1996 John Wiley & Sons Ltd.

integrated drug and psychosocial interventions can be targeted to those periods when the risk of exacerbation is high (Falloon, 1985).

These advances have been derived from a series of studies that have associated stress factors with florid episodes of schizophrenia in people who are biologically vulnerable to develop this disorder. Two major sources of stress have been delineated. First, the ambient stress of daily living. This includes a wide range of stressors, such as housing, finances, nutrition, social support network (family, friends, workmates, etc.), work and leisure pursuits, child rearing, as well as the everyday hassles and disappointments that confront every person resident in a community. It is difficult to measure such disparate conditions, but the index of Expressed Emotion is one well-standardized measure that has encompassed several major aspects of ambient stress (Leff & Vaughn, 1985).

The second major stress factor that has been associated with a higher risk of florid episodes is the occurrence of stressful life events. These are discrete stresses, such as the loss of a job, death of a close associate or breakup of an intimate relationship. Only those life events that contribute to long-term increases in ambient stress have been associated with the onset of major schizophrenic episodes (Brown & Birley, 1968, Brown & Harris, 1978).

The *coping behavior* of an individual will modify the level of stress experienced as a result of any stressor. This includes all their efforts to resolve the problems associated with the stressor, and encompasses the problem solving capacity of the individual's intimate social network, particularly the family unit (Pearlin & Schooler, 1978). Where a person is able to communicate readily with other people in his or her social habitat, and together they are able to assist in developing efficient strategies for handling the key problems, the risk of a detrimental outcome is likely to be minimized (Falloon & McGill, 1985).

The precise mechanisms that trigger the pathophysiology of schizophrenia have not yet been elucidated. High levels of physiological arousal associated with neurotransmitter changes have been implicated. However, attempts to specify the physiological changes that are specific to schizophrenic episodes have proved unrewarding, and it is apparent that each individual shows a pattern that is a specific marker of his stress response, rather than a pattern specific to a schizophrenic episode (Dawson & Nuechterlein, 1984).

Thus, the present state of understanding allows us to predict the onset of major episodes of schizophrenia from the presence of high levels of stress in the social and interpersonal environment that are not readily resolved by the individual's coping strategies, the detection of high physiological arousal, and the presence of prodromal clinical features. At the current state of our understanding, the presence of prodromal features of a schizophrenic episode is perhaps the most specific indicator of an impending episode.

The ability to target treatment resources to periods when a person's vulnerability to florid schizophrenia is high has been facilitated by methods that have enhanced the detection of the prodromal phases of florid episodes of schizophrenia (Docherty *et al.*, 1978; Herz & Melville, 1980; Birchwood *et al.*, 1989; Tarrier *et al.*, 1991; Falloon, 1992). It is evident that the phenomenology of prodromes of schizophrenia is as diverse as that reported in early studies of the disorder (Kraepelin, 1913). Attempts to develop checklists of the most commonly reported features have provided a focus for clinical discussions with individual cases, but greater specificity is more readily obtained by defining the idiosyncratic prodromal signs of each individual.

However, early detection of an impending major episode is only of value when intervention strategies are available that are effective in preventing or moderating its development. Over recent years several drug and psychosocial strategies have been devised that offer promise in modifying the severity of schizophrenic episodes.

The first of these has been the development of low dose and targeted pharmacotherapy (Kane *et al.*, 1979; Carpenter *et al.*, 1987; Marder *et al.*, 1987, Jolley *et al.*, 1989). While these approaches have shown a high rate of exacerbations, most of these have been recognized at an early stage and immediate increases of medication have usually prevented major episodes (Herz *et al.*, 1982). Moreover, the low-dose strategies do not appear to impede the early recognition of psychological and physiological responses to stress, which may be blocked by the tranquillizing effects of neuroleptic drugs used in higher doses. Of course the greater sensitivity to stressors that may be associated with low-dosage drug strategies may contribute to a higher number of false alarms, when normal stress responses may be mistaken for possible prodromes. However, all stress responses necessitate problem solving behavior by the patient and his social support network and may provide vital prompts for efforts to learn to cope more effectively with day-to-day life in the community, i.e. rehabilitation.

At the same time that efforts have been made to reduce the levels of drugs used in the prophylaxis of schizophrenic exacerbations, psychosocial strategies for educating patients and their informal carers in the community about the complex nature of schizophrenia, and its management with combined drug and psychosocial treatment, has facilitated sustained involvement in a long-term prophylaxis against florid episodes (Lam, 1992). In addition to providing patients and their informal carers with a self-help framework comprehensive psychosocial strategies have been devised that facilitate long-term stress management. The combination of minimally effective drug therapy with strategies that enable patients to cope more efficiently with the whole range of ambient stressors and life events has minimized long-term clinical, social, and carer morbidity in established cases (Falloon, 1985). As well as enhancing the coping capacities of patients and their immediate social support system comprehensive programs have provided continued social case management to ensure that major social stressors relating to changing needs for housing, finances, and constructive activity have also been resolved in the most efficient manner (Stein & Test, 1980).

The integration of all these factors into a coherent clinical management approach has been facilitated through the formulation of a stress/vulnerability model of mental disorders (Zubin & Spring, 1977). It is postulated that at any point in time the interaction between biological and psychosocial factors determines an individual's risk to succumb to a mental disorder. When pathogenic factors exceed a specific threshold there is a high risk that physiological changes will be triggered that may result in an episode. This threshold may be raised by combinations of prophylactic drugs and psychosocial stress management thereby making episodes less likely. As the biological (e.g. genetic, biochemical, physiological) and psychological (e.g. perceived stress and tension, cognitive and behavioral responses, prodromal phenomena) signs that are associated with achieving this threshold are more readily recognized individuals can learn self-help strategies that ensure that these risk periods are minimized, thereby facilitating recovery from their disorders and preventing chronic disability. Such an approach has been achieved in many medical conditions, such as coronary heart disease, diabetes, and peptic ulceration. While its application in psychiatry is in its infancy the prospects appear quite promising (Falloon & Shanahan, 1990).

In this chapter we will describe preliminary efforts to employ the advances in the comprehensive clinical management of schizophrenia to the early detection and intervention of initial presentations of schizophrenic disorders.

METHODS

EARLY DETECTION OF MAJOR MENTAL DISORDERS

Because the criteria for defining schizophrenic disorders emphasize cognitive–behavioral abnormalities, that cannot yet be supported by specific pathophysiological characteristics (e.g. blood tests, X-rays, etc.), professionals conducting assessments must be highly skilled in the application of these criteria, thereby missing few cases and including few non-cases.

Primary prevention of schizophrenic disorders has not yet been achieved. However, in common with most health problems, treatment of mental disorders appears to be most effective when applied early in their course, and delayed intervention may contribute to higher levels of persisting clinical, social and carer morbidity (Crow *et al.*, 1986; Munk-Jørgensen, 1986; Wyatt, 1992; Loebel *et al.*, 1992). Delays also appear to contribute to difficulty engaging people into treatment, and the need for coercive procedures to ensure treatment for people who are severely disturbed.

Several factors may contribute to delays in achieving effective early intervention. These include peoples' fear about the consequences of having a mental disorder leading to avoidance of consultation with medical services, poor screening by family practitioners, inexact diagnostic assessment by mental health professionals, and inefficient treatment of detected cases. In this chapter the methods we have devised to overcome these problems and to foster early detection and effective treatment of episodes of major mental disorders will be outlined.

SCREENING BY FAMILY PRACTITIONERS

In most health services family practitioners provide the major gatekeeping role. Referrals to specialist services are usually made at the request of the family practitioner, with the exception of major accidental trauma, and long-term case management is monitored by the family practitioner service with whom the great majority of patients are registered. Consultations with the family practitioner are readily accessed and may be requested on a 24-hour basis, every day of the week. As a result, a family practitioner service is likely to consult with almost every patient on an annual basis, particularly if there is any evidence of impaired function. Goldberg and Huxley (1980) suggested that over 90% of all people suffering from mental disorders in the UK consulted their doctors during the course of a year. Similar levels of consultations with primary care services have been noted in other countries (Brodaty & Andrews, 1983; Dilling & Weyrerer, 1984). Despite the often very brief nature of these consultations, and the fact that they are often made expressly for treatment of physical disorders, family practitioners are able to detect about 60% of all mental disorders. In other words, most family practitioners provide reasonably good screening for mental disorders, even in the absence of any formal screening procedures. A recent study by Prince and Phelan (1994) suggests that relatively few first episodes of schizophrenia are missed by family practitioners.

While sorting out the primary diagnosis of people who present with mixtures of clear-cut physical and emotional symptoms is a complex issue, a more common dilemma facing the family practitioner is deciding when a response to a clear life stress is considered a symptom of a mental disorder. Sleep disturbance, appetite loss, muscular tension, agitation, poor concentration, anxious or unhappy mood, and thoughts of suicide are all common responses to serious life stress. They are also all key features of major mental disorders, all of which are precipitated by environmental stress. The ability to predict accurately those cases where the stress response is a prodromal phase of a major mental disorder would enable effective treatment to be initiated early and possibly lead to a more benign presentation of a potentially disabling disorder.

Because of the central role of the family practitioner in the initial screening process and subsequent referral on for specialist consultation, a key feature of the integrated approach is very close liaison with family practitioners and an emphasis on training them to identify accurately mental disorders and their prodromal features.

TRAINING FAMILY PRACTICE AND MENTAL HEALTH STAFF TO CONDUCT RELIABLE ASSESSMENT OF MENTAL DISORDERS

Early detection of potential episodes of schizophrenia is based upon the recognition of changes in a person's mental state that are considered prodromal for the disorder. A two-stage approach has been developed, that entails: (i) training family practitioners to recognize prodromal symptoms and, without delay, to refer such persons for (ii) immediate specialized mental health assessment.

Standardized interview procedures for the assessment of mental disorders are not generally taught in current training programs for family practice or mental health professions. The past two decades have witnessed the development of several standardized methods for assessment of mental disorders. These methods, while preserving rapport with distressed or disturbed people, seek to clarify the psychopathology that underlies these states (Wing *et al.*, 1974; Spitzer *et al.*, 1990). Although these interviews were developed to facilitate diagnosis in research studies, they have been employed by non-psychiatric interviewers after brief training, with reliability similar to that obtained from psychiatric experts (Wing *et al.*, 1977; Robins *et al.*, 1979).

Family practitioners are trained to recognize eight features that might indicate the early stage of an episode of schizophrenia. These symptoms are listed in Table 1. They are derived from the prodromal

Table 1. Prodromal signs checklist

Onset of one of the following without explanation
Marked peculiar behavior
Inappropriate, or loss of, expression of feelings
Speech that is difficult to follow
Marked lack of speech and thoughts
Marked preoccupation with odd ideas
Ideas of reference—things have special meanings
Persistent feelings of unreality
Changes in the way things appear, sound, or smell

Source: From DSM-III (1980).

Table 2. Assessment of risk factors

I: *Vulnerability*
A. Genetic: family history
B. Neurological: birth injury, head trauma, epilepsy, cognitive impairment
C. Endocrinological: hormonal imbalance, post-natal, premenstrual
D. Toxic: stimulant drugs, alcohol, drug withdrawal, injections, vitamin deficiency

II: *Stress*
A. Major life events
B. Persistent high ambient stress: household, social network, occupation, leisure
C. Limited coping abilities: social skills, problem solving

signs outlined in DSM III (1980). A checklist that included brief elaboration of these features is provided for the family practitioners to refer to whenever they suspect a possible case. Training is conducted in a flexible manner, individually for about half the family practitioners and in group seminars for the remainder. Videotaped examples of prodromal symptoms are supplemented with role playing. Most family practitioners report readily recognizing these features when they occurr, but usually hesitate to go to the trouble to refer such cases to a mental health clinic unless they become much worse. Close collaboration with the mental health service facilitates informal consultation, and the family practitioners are assured that any person with any unusual features would receive specialized assessment without delay.

A similar individually tailored approach is applied to training non-psychiatric nurses, such as health visitors and district nurses. Here a major impediment to learning simple diagnostic screening methods has been previous training in counselling methods. Most community nurses had been advised that under no circumstances should they ask their patients any direct questions about their mental states. Instead they were told that patients would self-disclose details such as their plans for suicide, compulsive thoughts and behaviors, or experiences of hallucinations, providing they maintained empathic rapport throughout their contact. Furthermore they have been imbued with a concern for confidentiality, that makes it impossible for them to consider interviewing a spouse or parent of a patient, for fear of damaging their confiding relationship with the index patient. Such attitudes proved very rigid and were only shaken when these community nurses participated in joint assessment interviews with mental health therapists.

Assessment of prodromal states by mental health professionals

The availability of 24-hour assessment by a multidisciplinary team of mental health professionals, including a senior psychiatrist, ensures that assessment can be made within an hour of referral, usually within a few minutes of the request. The mental health assessment includes:

1 Patient and key caregiver (usually a relative or household member) completes the modified version of the Early Signs Questionnaire (ESQ; Herz & Melville, 1980). This lists features found in the prodromes of florid schizophrenic episodes, and is used to prompt patients and their caregivers to identify prodromal symptoms, particularly those of a subtle nature, such as mild interpersonal withdrawal.

2 If features reported by the family practitioner or noted on the ESQ suggest a prodromal state, a trained mental health professional completes a comprehensive psychiatric assessment.

3 A psychiatric, medical, drug, and family history is obtained using the systematic schedule developed for the project (Table 2). The aim of this history taking exercise is to detect people who may have a higher risk of a schizophrenic disorder than others in the community, who may present with non-specific stress responses, and who might merit further monitoring even when the initial presentation does not appear characteristic of a prodrome of schizophrenia.

People with first-degree relatives who have suffered schizophrenia; those with a history of obstetric complications; those who have had prodromal episodes in the past; and those who have made unexplained suicide attempts are all considered to have a higher risk of schizophrenia than the average person living in the community. Substance abuse and organic medical conditions, including convulsive disorders, that may have contributed to the current state are assessed with further specialized consultation when indicated.

4 The differential psychiatric diagnosis is considered in consultation with a psychiatrist. This includes consideration that the prodromal features could be the early stage of a manic episode, atypical depression or acute anxiety disorder. A history of previous episodes of mental disorders and family history provide additional information to assist in defining the probability that the current state represents the initial phase of a first episode of a schizophrenic psychosis. In all such cases a project psychiatrist conducts an independent assessment to validate key aspects of the mental health assessment, usually on the day the patient presents at the family practice.

5 Patients are invited to discuss any stresses that have occurred in their social environment that may have preceded the onset of prodromal features, or may have occurred as a result of the changes. All changes in the social network that might have necessitated adjustment by the patient are considered, whether they are positive or negative, or whether they involved the patient directly or indirectly.

6 The assessment always includes an interview with key people in the patient's social environment, usually family members or friends. The aims of this interview are: (i) to obtain validation for important aspects of the assessment and initial formulation and to provide further information when necessary; (ii) to assess the strengths and weaknesses of home-based support in assisting with clinical management (this includes potential caregivers' understanding of mental and psychological disorders, so that any education may be tailored to their levels of comprehension); and (iii) to assess the mental health of other household members, and their own vulnerability to develop disorders as a result of the stress associated with caring for the disturbed person.

EARLY INTERVENTION STRATEGIES

Once it has been established that a person is suspected of experiencing a prodrome of schizophrenia an integrated program of crisis management is initiated without delay. This includes education, stress management, and neuroleptic medication. Each component is targeted according to individual needs within a structured clinical management protocol.

Increasing understanding of the nature of schizophrenia

Within 24 hours of detection the patient and his key caregivers are provided with an informal educational seminar that provides a rationale for the early intervention program. They are told that the features displayed by the patient are possible early signs of an impending episode of schizophrenia, and that the application of treatment strategies that have proven highly effective in prevention of major exacerbations in persons with established schizophrenic disorders, may ameliorate the current condition. The characteristic symptoms of schizophrenia, theories of etiology, prognosis, and effective integrated drug and psychosocial treatment methods are outlined in an informal discussion in the home. The high rates of remission and recovery from long-term application of effective treatment methods are emphasized, as well as the benefits that could be derived from continued support from family/friends backed up around the clock by a well-trained, committed domiciliary mental health service. Questions and concerns were discussed in a frank and open manner that endeavour to foster an optimal therapeutic alliance.

The aim of this education is primarily to enhance the collaboration between people experiencing prodromal features, and their informal and professional carers. We hypothesize that through enhancing understanding of mental disorders in a specific manner, people become informed of these disorders in a highly personalized way that may assist in their own mental health care. The link between the levels of *early insight* (i.e. shared understanding between patient and professional) appears a major predictor for the successful application of monitoring prodromes in established cases (Heinrichs *et al.*, 1985). It has been argued that such education may have detrimental effects and lead to escape and avoidance responses by patients and their carers. We have not yet encountered such responses. On the contrary, education provided in this interactive, personalized, and home-based manner appears highly reassuring to all those involved.

At the completion of this education informed consent to pursue the early intervention program is sought from patient and key carers. In every case this has been granted with alacrity.

Home-based stress management

At the conclusion of the initial educational meeting the rationale for a stress management approach that includes key carers is provided. A formulation of the vulnerability and stress factors that may have triggered the patient's current condition is made. Where a major life event or persistent ambient stressor is identified as a clear precipitant of the prodromal features, immediate efforts are made to assist patient and carers to cope and begin to seek ways to resolve this.

Further assessment of stresses associated with life events and persisting ambient stress, as well as the coping capacity of the patient and carers is conducted as soon as convenient. Daily sessions, usually including key carers, are conducted to plan efficient management of significant stresses. Intensive domiciliary nursing care is available where necessary, supported by a team of psychological, social work, and occupational therapists. This crisis management is conducted according to the Training in Community Living model of Stein and Test (1980).

At all times the level of support is targeted according to the expressed needs of the patient and carers. Efforts are made to train efficient problem solving within the household unit according to the behavioral family therapy model of Falloon *et al.* (1984). For cases where coping skills are excellent and stress levels not excessive, stress management training is brief, usually no more than one or two 1-hour sessions. However, in some cases where persisting social or interpersonal stresses are implicated, such as unemployment, housing, marital conflicts, or interpersonal inadequacy, stress management may be prolonged.

Targeted neuroleptic medication

Where features of perceptual or cognitive impairment, agitation or sleep disturbance are prominent, the family practitioner is advised to prescribe a small dose of a low potency neuroleptic drug (usually thioridazine or chlorpromazine 25–100 mg daily). This drug therapy is carefully targeted to a clearly specified impairment (e.g. "sleeping 4 hours per night," "unable to concentrate on television for more than two minutes"). The minimal effective dose is given (McEvoy *et al.*, 1991). The effectiveness of this intervention strategy is monitored daily by nurses and psychiatrists, who alert the family practitioner to the onset of any unwanted effects. This drug therapy is time-limited, seldom lasting more than 1 week. Where no specific symptoms that are likely to respond to neuroleptic medication are evident, no neuroleptic drug is prescribed.

CONTINUED CARE PROCEDURES

Stress management and drug therapy

The combined crisis-oriented stress management and drug strategies are continued until the prodromal features have remitted. Continued monitoring of stress in the environment enables the therapist to define the specific coping capacities of the patient and the household unit, both the strengths and weaknesses in efficiently resolving the stresses that they encounter daily. This ongoing analysis provides the basis for further training in problem solving skills for all members of the household unit. This training is continued until the unit displays proficiency in coping with all major stresses that currently exist, as well as those considered likely to occur in the near future. A regular weekly household meeting, convened at home, that specifically addresses problem issues for the patient, as well as other household members, attended regularly by key household members, is considered the optimal format to ensure sustained stress management. This recommendation is based upon empirical observations obtained in the earlier

EARLY WARNING SIGNS

Name ______________________

I have a risk of developing episodes of a ____________ disorder.

My early warning signs are:

1. ______________________

2. ______________________

3. ______________________

Whenever I experience *any* of these signs I will respond by:

a) ______________________

b) ______________________

c) ______________________

My Doctor is: ______________________ Phone: __________

My Home Contact is: ______________________ Phone: __________

If I have any concerns about my disorder I will contact __________ immediately.

Figure 1. Early warnings signs.

studies of family-based stress management for schizophrenia (Falloon, 1985).

Monitoring recurrence of prodromal features

Patients and their carers are trained to recognize the specific signs displayed by the patient during the prodromal phase. A wallet-sized card is provided for each patient that lists the one to three signs that are most likely to discriminate a future prodromal episode (see Figure 1). Detailed procedures for immediate contact of family practitioner and mental health therapist are included on the card. Additional prompt sheets detailing identical information are provided for display on personal and household noticeboards, so that future episodes can be detected at the earliest possible phase.

Mental health monitoring

The mental health therapist conducts assessments of clinical, social, and carer status at 3, 6, 12, and 24 months after complete resolution of the prodromal state. Early warning signs are reviewed with patients and carers. Stress levels and coping functions are assessed and booster sessions provided where the efficiency of household problem solving functions has not been well maintained. In cases where disability persists further psychosocial rehabilitation strategies are provided, such as social skills, parenting, vocational or leisure skills training. After 24 months free of psychiatric impairment and associated disability, patients are transferred back to routine family practitioner monitoring.

EVIDENCE FOR EFFECTIVENESS: A PILOT STUDY

A mental health service that was fully integrated with 18 family practitioners provided care for a population of 30 000–35 000 in a semi-rural area of England (Falloon & Fadden, 1993). All general practitioners and mental health professionals were trained to apply the early detection and intervention strategies. A previous study had revealed an annual

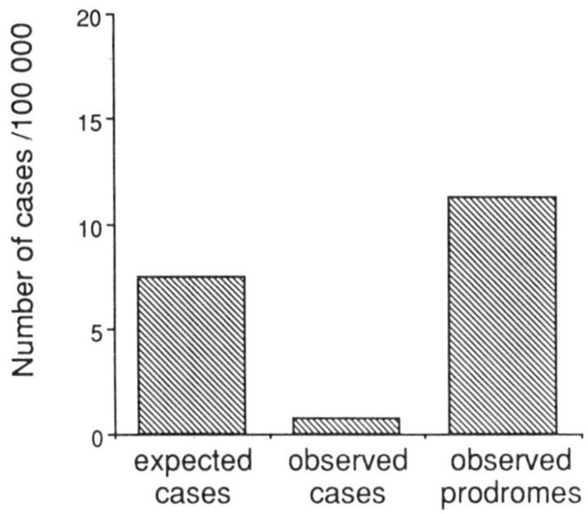

Figure 2. Annual incidence of schizophrenia: 1984–88.

incidence of 7.4 new cases of schizophrenia per 100 000 population as defined by PSE (Present State Examination)/CATEGO classes S and P in Buckinghamshire during the years 1974–75 (Shepherd *et al.*, 1989). This study was considered to have included a highly representative sample of persons who experienced the onset of schizophrenia in this region, although cases who did not present with serious behavioral disturbance sufficient to warrant hospital admission would not have been included. Thus, it represents a more conservative estimate than that expected using the methodology of the current study, and is similar to the average hospitalized incidence found across the UK (Der *et al.*, 1990).

Observed incidence of new cases of schizophrenic disorders

During the 4 years, 1984–88, one person was defined as having an initial episode of schizophrenia according to Present State Examination (PSE)/CATEGO criteria for classes S and P (Figure 3). This represented an annual incidence rate of 0.75 per 100 000. This person was not admitted to hospital and experienced a full remission after 4 weeks of low-dose neuroleptic and stress management intervention. She presented to her family practitioner complaining of sleep disturbance. Rather than immediately prescribing a brief course of sedative medication, as had been her previous management choice for such a presentation, her family practitioner asked her what was contributing to the sleep problem and was told that when she went to bed she heard voices talking about her. The family practitioner immediately contacted the mental health therapist in her practice, a PSE was completed, a diagnosis of schizophrenia confirmed, and after consultation with the psychiatrist integrated psychosocial and drug management was started.

Observed incidence of "prodromal" symptoms

During the 4-year period 15 further cases were observed with symptom patterns suggestive of prodromal states, who had not experienced previous episodes of functional psychoses. All but two of these cases experienced full and rapid recovery after brief integrated intervention. One developed a bipolar disorder, with recurrent depressive and hypomanic episodes that were readily treated in their early stages, using a similar integrated drug and stress management approach, with monitoring of early warning signs. Another 21-year-old man experienced three episodes of prodromal symptoms and has remained under continuous mental health supervision throughout the 4 years. After several years of intermittent medication targeted to prodromal periods he was prescribed continuous low-dosage oral neuroleptics. A combination of family-based stress management, social and vocational skills training, enabled him to progress slowly, but steadily towards his life goals without major setbacks.

Detection of "hidden" cases

The low incidence of new cases of schizophrenia prompted a specific effort to uncover any cases that may not have been detected in this project. A review was conducted of all persons in the area who were prescribed psychoactive drugs on a continual basis. Social services and general community nursing services were asked to review any cases that might be suffering from a major mental disorder. Six additional cases of schizophrenia were detected. All had experienced the onset of the disorder prior to the study period; in three the onset was more than 10 years earlier. Appropriate clinical management was instigated with beneficial results. Four other cases with diagnoses of schizophrenia were reviewed and considered to have alternative conditions. Their clinical management was altered accordingly.

DISCUSSION

This chapter presents a methodology for the early detection and intervention of initial episodes of schizophrenic disorders that may enable persons to receive effective clinical management during the prodromal phase of the disorder. A small pilot study suggested a reduction in the observed incidence of florid episodes of schizophrenic disorders. While such an observation appears dramatic, extreme caution should be applied to its interpretation. The following points must be considered in assessing the validity of this finding: (i) What evidence is there to support the efficiency of the case finding used in this study, particularly those cases where the onset is insidious? (ii) What evidence is there to suggest that the prodromes detected are specific to schizophrenic disorders? (iii) Could this finding be an artifact of a narrowing of diagnostic criteria? (iv) Could this finding be a function of drift of persons most vulnerable to schizophrenic disorders out of the area studied? (v) What are the costs and benefits of this approach when applied in clinical practice?

The methodology of early detection of major health problems always invites controversy, despite its inherent appeal to clinicians and consumers. Clearly, considerable work is required before the approach that we have outlined should be applied more widely. However, several research groups are already developing similar projects. They include, Patrick McGorry and Jane Edwards in Melbourne, Thomas McGlashan in New Haven, Tor K. Larsen and Jan Olaf Johanssen in Stavanger, Nicholas Tarrier in Manchester, Max Birchwood in Birmingham, and Robert Kydd and John Coverdale in Auckland. This ground swell of interest seems likely to ensure that many of the research problems will be resolved and the clinical benefits of this approach substantiated.

Schizophrenia remains one of the major public health problems in industrialized countries, with substantial economic costs compounding human suffering. Any strategies that appear to reduce the morbidity associated with this disorder must be considered seriously, particularly if this reduction appears to be sustained. The key element of the approach we have developed is close collaboration between comprehensively trained mental health and family practice professionals. Such a service may be the most difficult component to replicate. This may be especially true if the service is restricted to providing early intervention solely for schizophrenic disorders. In the absence of well-defined prodromal syndromes, projects that focus exclusively on preventing schizophrenic episodes would appear to make inefficient use of resources. However, a generic program that integrates stress management with targeted drug therapy can be applied to all functional psychoses, with the selection of the specific drug determined by the predominant pattern of symptoms. Staff in the Buckingham Project divided their time equally between early detection, crisis management, and long-term rehabilitation of all major mental disorders.

Although evidence for drug-related disability is a major concern for prescribers of neuroleptic drugs, brief use of low doses tend to minimize the risk of serious side-effects. Close monitoring of the effects on specific symptoms ensures that ineffective strategies are readily adjusted and the benefit/cost ratio remains positive.

Educating people about schizophrenia and other major mental disorders appears to have considerable benefits, with very rare deleterious effects. Inevitably, some people who would not develop any significant disorder will receive stress management and drugs that they do not need. They may also worry needlessly about the possibility of developing schizophrenia in the future. Promising research on information processsing suggests that we may soon be able to differentiate those persons most vulnerable to this disorder, and thereby alleviate the concern of those we have considered vulnerable solely on phenomenological grounds (Nuechterlein, 1990). This future research must estimate the relative costs and benefits of this approach and consider whether it is an advance over waiting till persons developed florid episodes, receive accurate diagnosis and effective treatment (cf. Crow *et al.*, 1986).

It is concluded that a comprehensive mental health service that is integrated within the ambit of an effective primary care program may be able to provide specific interventions for persons who present with features consistent with prodromes of schizophrenia. This very limited preliminary survey suggests that this may prove feasible, and may even contribute to a lower incidence of florid episodes of schizophrenia, or at least to a more benign presentation of the disorder. Although a random-controlled outcome study of such an approach presents a major undertaking, this is an essential step in validating the approach outlined in this report.

REFERENCES

Birchwood, M. (1992). Early intervention in schizophrenia; Theoretical background and clinical strategies. *British Journal of Clinical Psychology*, **31**, 257–278.

Birchwood, M., Smith, J., Macmillan, J., *et al.* (1989). Predicting relapse in schizophrenia: The development and implementation of an early signs monitoring system using patients and families as observers, a preliminary investigation. *Psychological Medicine*, **19**, 649–656.

Brodaty, H. and Andrews, G. (1983). Brief psychotherapy in family practice: a controlled prospective intervention trial. *British Journal of Psychiatry*, **143**, 11–19.

Brown, G.W. and Birley, J.L.T. (1968). Crises and life changes and the onset of schizophrenia. *Journal of Health & Social Behaviour*, **9**, 203–214.

Brown, G.W. and Harris, T. (1978). *Social Origins of Depression: A Study of Psychiatric Disorder in Women.* London: Tavistock.

Carpenter, W.T., Heinrichs, D.W., and Hanlon, T.E. (1987). A comparative trial of pharmacologic strategies in schizophrenia. *American Journal of Psychiatry*, **144**, 1466–1470.

Crow, T.J., MacMillan, J.F., Johnson, A.L., and Johnstone, E.C. (1986). A randomised controlled trial of prophylactic neuroleptic treatment. *British Journal of Psychiatry*, **148**, 120–127.

Dawson, M.E. and Nuechterlein, K.H. (1984). Psychophysiological dysfunctions in the developmental course of schizophrenic disorders. *Schizophrenia Bulletin*, **10**, 204–232.

Der, G., Gupta, G., and Murray, R.M. (1990). Is schizophrenia disappearing? *Lancet*, **335**, 513–516.

Dilling, H. and Weyrerer, S. (1984). Prevalence of mental disorders in the small town rural region of Traunstein (Upper Bavaria). *Acta Psychiatrica Scandinavica*, **69**, 60–79.

Docherty, J.P., van Kammen, D.P., and Siris, S.G. (1978). Stages of schizophrenic psychosis. *American Journal of Psychiatry*, **135**, 420–426.

Falloon, I.R.H. (1985). *Family Management of Schizophrenia.* Baltimore: Johns Hopkins University Press.

Falloon, I.R.H. (1992). Early intervention for first episodes of schizophrenia: a preliminary exploration. *Psychiatry*, **55**, 4–15.

Falloon, I.R.H. and Fadden, G. (1993). *Integrated Mental Health Care.* Cambridge: Cambridge University Press.

Falloon, I.R.H., Boyd, J.L., and McGill, C.W. (1984). *Family Care of Schizophrenia: A Problem-Solving, Approach to the Treatment of Mental Illness.* New York: Guilford Press.

Falloon, I.R.H. and McGill, C.W. (1985). Family stress and the course of schizophrenia: a review. In I.R.H. Falloon, ed., *Family Management of Schizophrenia.* Baltimore: Johns Hopkins University Press.

Falloon, I.R.H. and Shanahan, W.J. (1990). Community management of schizophrenia. *British Journal of Hospital Medicine*, **43**, 62–66.

Goldberg, D.P. and Huxley, P. (1980). *Mental Illness in the Community: The Pathway to Psychiatric Care.* London: Tavistock.

Herz, M.I. and Melville, C. (1980). Relapse in schizophrenia. *American Journal of Psychiatry*, **137**, 801–805.

Herz, M.I., Szymanski, H.V., and Simon, J.C. (1982). Intermittent medication for stable schizophrenic outpatients: an alternative to maintenance medication. *American Journal of Psychiatry*, **139**, 918–922.

Hogarty, G.E., Anderson, C.M., and Reiss, D.J. (1987). Family psychoeducation, social skills training, and medication in schizophrenia: the long and short of it. *Psychopharmacology Bulletin*, **23**, 12–15.

Jolley, A.G., Hirsch, S.R., McRink, A., and Manchanda, R. (1989). Trial of a brief intermittent neuroleptic prophylaxis for selected schizophrenic outpatients: clinical outcome at one year follow-up. *British Medical Journal*, **298**, 985–990.

Kane, J.M., Rifkin, A., Quitkin, F., *et al.* (1979). Low dose fluphenazine decanoate in maintenance treatment of schizophrenia. *Psychiatry Research*, **1**, 341–348.

Kraepelin, E. (1913). *Clinical Psychiatry.* New York: William Wood.

Lam, D.H. (1991). Psychosocial family intervention in schizophrenia: a review of empirical studies. *Psychological Medicine*, **21**, 423–441.

Leff, J.P. and Vaughn, C.E. (1985). *Expressed Emotion in Families.* New York: Guilford Press.

Loebel, A.D., Lieberman, J.A., Alvir, J.M.J., Mayerhoff, D.I., Geisler, S.H., and Szymanski, S.R. (1992). Duration of psychosis and outcome in first-episode schizophrenia. *American Journal of Psychiatry*, **149**, 1183–1188.

Marder, S.R., Van Putten, T., Mintz, J., *et al.* (1987). Low- and conventional-dose maintenance therapy with fluphenazine decanoate. *Archives of General Psychiatry*, **44**, 518–521.

McEvoy, J.P., Hogarty, G.E., and Steingard, S. (1991). Optimal dose of neuroleptics in acute schizophrenia. A controlled study of neuroleptic threshold and higher haloperidol dose. *Archives of General Psychiatry*, **48**, 739–745.

Munk-Jørgensen, P. (1986). Decreasing first admission rates of schizophrenia among makes in Denmark from 1970 to 1984: changing diagnostic patterns? *Acta Psychiatrica Scandinavica*, **73**, 645–650.

Nuechterlein, K.H. (1990). Methodological considerations in the search for indicators of vulnerability to severe psychopathology. In J.W. Rorbaugh, R. Johnson, and R. Parasuraman, eds, *Event-related Potentials of the Brain.* New York: Oxford University Press.

Pearlin, L. and Schooler, C. (1978). The structure of coping. *Journal of Health & Social Behavior,* **19**, 2–21.

Prince, M. and Phelan, M. (1994). Invisible schizophrenia: A postal survey of the incidence and management of new cases of schizophrenia in primary care. *Journal of Mental Health,* **3**, 91–98.

Robins, L., Helzer, J., Croughan, J., Williams, J.B.W., and Spitzer, R.L. (1979). *The NIMH Diagnostic Interview Schedule (DIS), Version II.* Washington, DC: National Institute of Mental Health.

Shepherd, M., Watt, D., Falloon, I., and Smeeton, N. (1989). *The Natural History of Schizophrenia. Psychological Medicine Monograph, No. 16.* Cambridge: Cambridge University Press.

Spitzer, R.L., Williams, J.B.W., Gibbon, M., and First, M. (1990). *Structured Clinical Interview for DSM-III-R, (SCID-R).* Washington, DC: American Psychiatric Press.

Stein, L.I. and Test, M.A. (1980). An alternative to mental hospital treatment: I. Conceptual model, treatment program, and clinical evaluation. *Archives of General Psychiatry,* **37**, 392–399.

Tarrier, N., Barrowclough, C., and Bamrah, J.S. (1991). Prodromal signs of relapse in schizophrenia. *Social Psychiatry and Psychiatric Epidemiology,* **26**, 157–161.

Wing, J.K., Cooper, J.E. and Sartorius, N. (1974). *Measurement and Classification of Psychiatric Symptoms.* Cambridge: Cambridge University Press.

Wing, J.K., Nixon, J.M., Mann, S.A., and Leff, J.P. (1977). Reliability of the PSE used in a population survey. *Psychological Medicine,* **7**, 505–516.

Wyatt, R.J. (1991). Neuroleptics and the natural course of schizophrenia. *Schizophrenia Bulletin,* **17**, 325–351.

Zubin, J. and Spring, B. (1977). Vulnerability: a new view of schizophrenia. *Journal of Abnormal Psychology,* **96**, 103–126.

16

Case Management of Persons with Schizophrenia and Other Severe Mental Illnesses in the USA

NEIL MEISLER and ALBERTO B. SANTOS
Department of Psychiatry, Medical University of South Carolina, Charleston, South Carolina, USA

In 1969, Ernest M. Gruenberg, predicted the failure of new US policy for community based treatment of mental illness:

> Many hope that the new mental health centers in the U.S.A. will assign comprehensive responsibility to one treatment team for each patient. The outcome is by no means certain since most plans emphasize the availability of comprehensive services (no matter how nominal their coordination might be); they do not concentrate on ensuring continuity of attention through the provision of a single team which cares for each patient throughout his illness.

INTRODUCTION

Most persons with schizophrenia experience disability in a wide range of instrumental and social functioning, which limits their self-sufficiency. Fifty percent of the approximately 90 000 patients residing in state and county psychiatric hospitals in the United States have schizophrenia (Center for Mental Health Services, 1993). A majority of the mentally ill among the homeless population have schizophrenia and are apt not to receive treatment between episodes of hospitalization (Freeman *et al.*, 1979; Arce *et al.*, 1983; Bassuk *et al.*, 1984). Many others with schizophrenia are confined to nursing and shelter care homes (Goldman, 1983; Goldman *et al.*, 1981, 1984; US Department of Health and Human Services, 1982; Strahan & Burns, 1991). Although recent advances in psychopharmacology hold promise for improved treatment of schizophrenia, improved systems of psychosocial interventions are also needed to make community living more than a euphemism for material and social impoverishment. For the past decade, case management has been widely promoted as a means to prevent such conditions.

This chapter reviews the evolution of public policy in the United States regarding the treatment of schizophrenia and other severe mental illnesses, tracing the development of the present emphasis on case management as a means to diminish fragmentation and increase continuity in service delivery. One approach, Assertive Community Treatment (ACT), which integrates case management, treatment, rehabilitative and supportive services within a

Handbook of Mental Health Economics and Health Policy, Volume I, Schizophrenia. Edited by M. Moscarelli, A. Rupp and N. Sartorius.
© 1996 John Wiley & Sons Ltd.

self-contained system of care, is described in detail. The research literature on ACT approaches is reviewed and issues of program dissemination and financing are discussed.

ORIGINS OF CASE MANAGEMENT

"Outreach," "assertive community treatment," and "case management" are relatively new terms in the vernacular of the mental health professions. Historically, psychiatric theory and state policy in regard to the treatment of mental illness has revolved around one type of facility or another as the locus of care (Goldman & Morrisey, 1985). When the federal government entered the arena of reform of the public mental health service system with the passage of the Community Mental Health Centers Act in 1963, it also did so from this perspective. The Community Mental Health Centers Act provided construction and time-limited operating grants to government and private non-profit organizations to start up community mental health centers (CMHCs). The Community Mental Health Centers Act grew out of a presidential task force, The Joint Commission on Mental Illness and Health, appointed by Congress during the Eisenhower Administration to recommend reforms to improve the care of persons with mental illness (Joint Commission on Mental Illness and Health, 1961).

Based on the Joint Commission's recommendations, President Kennedy introduced the Community Mental Health Centers Act as a 'bold new direction" to reduce the population of state hospitals by half by 1980. CMHCs were intended to replace state hospitals as the primary locus of care for persons with severe mental illness and be funded in the long-run by the states and insurance mechanisms. In the Congressional legislative process, however, the mandate of CMHCs because much broader than the care of persons with severe mental illness. Unfortunately, there were no requirements in the Community Mental Health Centers Act or in regulations to make it likely that persons with schizophrenia and other severe mental illness would be cared for by CMHCs. CMHCs were directed and staffed by professionals with little experience or interest in treating severe mental illness. Consequently, during the formative years of the federal CMHC program, when, coincidently, state hospital admissions were shifting from long- to short-term care, persons with schizophrenia were underserved by CMHCs. This critical shortcoming only began to be addressed in the late 1970s as described below. For most CMHCs, the care of persons with severe mental illness was a secondary concern and the services they offered did not address their limitations in actively seeking treatment or their needs for assistance in daily living. CMHCs left the social welfare and rehabilitative needs of persons with severe mental illness to other systems, accepting responsibility for mental health treatment only; and this narrow responsibility was limited by a passive and office-based orientation to treatment. In most localities, CMHCs had no impact on reducing the use of hospitals.

President Kennedy's vision of reduction in the census of overcrowded state hospitals was realized, but occurred primarily as a consequence of other federal programs; notably Supplemental Security Income for the Aged, Blind, and Disabled (SSI) and Medicaid. SSI, which provides a monthly subsistence income for persons with mental illness outside of state hospitals, spawned the development of a cottage industry of shelter care homes. Although Medicaid did not cover state hospital patients between the ages of 21 and 64, it did cover patients of all ages in nursing homes. The reduction in state hospital census between 1965 and 1980 was largely a spread of custodial care to shelter care and nursing homes as well. While state hospital census decreased to 140 000 by 1980, approximately 750 000 persons with severe mental illness were by then residing in shelter care and nursing homes (Allen, 1974; Bassuk & Gerson, 1978; Goldman *et al.*, 1981). The reduction in long-term hospitalization was also accompanied by an increase of recurrent episodic hospital admissions, with little or no intervening community treatment (Goldman & Morrisey, 1985; Committee on Government Operations, 1988).

By the mid-1970s, enthusiasm for the CMHCs program waned as reports appeared in both the popular media and professional literature of the abandonment of persons with severe mental illness in the process of deinstitutionalization. The Carter Administration and Congress took several steps to address the issue. A report by the Congressional

General Accounting Office, *Returning the Mentally Disabled to the Community: Government Needs to do More* (1977), prompted Congress to fund the Community Support Program (CSP), an initiative conceived by staff of the National Institute of Mental Health in collaboration with mental health professionals and advocates outside of government. The CSP was launched by the National Institute of Mental Health in 1977 without a specific appropriation. It diverted a small amount of funds authorized for state hospital improvement to enter into contracts with state mental health agencies for "community support systems strategy development" and local "demonstration/replication" projects. In 1978, the CSPs first appropriation was $3.5 million, compared with approximately $300 million for the CMHC program that year.

The CSP sought to assist the states to integrate a broad array of mental health, social, and rehabilitative services within local systems of care in order to effectively address the needs of persons with severe mental illness in the community (Turner & TenHoor, 1978). Agencies providing the components of this service array within a service area needed to be linked, with one of the agencies assuming a "lead agency" role. The CSP also addressed the problems of fragmentation and discontinuity of care by introducing the concept of the case manager, defined as a single person or team at the client level responsible for remaining in touch with the client on a continuing basis, regardless of how many agencies get involved [sic]. Its strategy was to influence state mental health agencies, and federal agencies operating programs to which persons with mental illness are entitled, to adopt policies and approaches that would ensure that these persons had access to local systems of support for community living. The CSP used some of its funds to link states to sources of technical assistance, to develop monographs on successful approaches, and to bring state mental health agency and federal staff together with advocates at local, regional, and national conferences.

In 1977, President Carter appointed the President's Commission on Mental Health to undertake a 1 year study and report recommendations to overhaul federal policy concerning the care of persons with severe mental illness. The Commission's recommendations were embodied in the National Mental Health Systems Act submitted to Congress during the spring of 1979 to replace the Community Mental Health Centers Act which was due to expire in September 1980. The thrust of the Mental Health Systems Act was to increase federal funding for services for adults and youths with severe mental illness, redirecting it along with the existing CMHC funding to the state mental health agencies for them to coordinate the provision of hospital and community services. The Mental Health Systems Act also focused on developing increased cordination between the Department of Health and Human Services and other federal agencies to improve the flow of federal financing to meet the needs of persons with severe mental illness. It continued funding for those among the nearly 700 federally funded CMHCs that had not reached the end of their 8 year grants, but gave states broad latitude in directing the use of those funds. The CSP was embodied in the Mental Health Systems Act. Accompanying the Mental Health Systems Act, the Department of Health and Human Services drafted a National Plan for the Chronically Mentally Ill with specific service and financing recommendations for an improved system of care. The Plan was consonant with the CSP, but went beyond it in specifying the needs of clinical subpopulations and committed the Department of Health and Human Services to work toward improved coordination of federal programs.

The National Mental Health Systems Act was enacted in October 1980 and the National Plan was released in December 1980. However, the change of administrations in January 1981 brought the momentum of federal policy reform for the mentally ill to a sudden halt. President Reagan successfully sought the repeal of the Systems Act prior to its September 1981 implementation and shifted the funding of the Community Mental Health Centers Program to a block grant to the states, with a 25% reduction in funding. Block grants were made with literally no requirements other than that states had to continue providing funding to agencies that had been recipients of CMHC grants when the CMHC Act expired and could not spend block grant funds on construction or hospital care. With the repeal of the Mental Health Systems Act, the CSP became the only remaining expression of federal policy regarding the care of persons with severe mental illness.

With control of the CMHC funds, many states began to place conditions on the use of both state and block grant funds to promote community treatment of persons with severe mental illness. With the CSP framework for organizing service delivery systems as a guide, many states also placed emphasis on a more systemic approach to serving these persons. Case management became a core element in the service array.

During the mid-1980s, two other Congressional initiatives reinforced a federal policy emphasizing case management for persons with severe mental illness. In 1985, Congress amended Title XIX of the Social Security Act to include "targeted case management services" as an optional Medicaid covered service. The legislation defined targeted case management as services which will assist individuals eligible under the medical assistance plan in gaining access to needed medical, social, educational, and other services [*sic*]. Subsequently, the Health Care Financing Administration promulgated regulations further defining case management as an activity under which responsibility for locating, coordinating and monitoring necessary and appropriate services for an individual rests with a specific person or organization [*sic*]. States are permitted to provide case management to all Medicaid eligible persons or to target them to subgroups of the Medicaid eligible populations such as persons with severe mental illness. In 1988, only 13 states were providing Medicaid financed case management services to persons with mental illness. By 1992, the number of states had grown to at least 35 (National Assocation of State Mental Health Program Directors, 1992).

In 1986, Congress enacted legislation requiring states to obtain annual approval from the Department of Health and Human Services of a Comprehensive Mental Health Service Plan as a condition of receipt of block grant funds. The Plan must address the provision of case management services to all persons with prolonged mental illness who use substantial amounts of public funds or services. States are required to estimate number of persons who require case management services, set objectives to extend case management services to them, and report progress toward meeting these objectives.

The CSP, the Planning Act, and the Medicaid provision for targeted case management have collectively influenced the states to place emphasis on case management services. Most often, case management has been layered on to existing facility-based services and has been limited as to: (i) the degree of outreach case managers undertake to assist clients; (ii) the kinds of assistance they provide; (iii) the days and hours of the week that they are available to provide assistance; and (iv) the degree of integration with other interventions over the course of a person's illness. Despite the positive impact of the CSP, some states still have not implemented a statewide service system design that successfully engages mentally disabled persons in continuous treatment and meets their social and rehabilitative needs.

CASE MANAGEMENT IN THE CONTEXT OF OVERALL CARE

In a narrow sense, as defined by Medicaid policy, case management is assistance in assessing clients' human service needs, linking clients to needed human services, and monitoring the provision of services to ensure that identified needs are met. However, while these functions are important, they are not a sufficient response to the needs of persons with schizophrenia (Marx *et al.*, 1973). Without ongoing encouragement and assistance, about half the persons with schizophrenia tend not to take prescribed medications, both because of their denial of mental illness and uncomfortable medication side-effects (Babiker, 1986; Hogarty & Anderson, 1986). Even those who comply with psychiatric treatment often experience chaos in their daily lives because of their susceptibility to ordinary stress, tendency to distort and misinterpret communication, feelings of hopelessness, and extreme poverty. Substance use also contributes to instability among a substantial minority of persons with schizophrenia (Drake & Wallach, 1989).

These factors combine to make it very difficult for most persons with schizophrenia to live independently or to interact with complex human service systems. Many persons with schizophrenia need a broad range of direct assistance including: (i) ongoing encouragement to participate in prescribed psychiatric treatment, whether it be the taking of medicine or attendance at appointments; (ii) guidance in obtaining and managing entitlements; (iii) support in home making; (iv) encouragement and prompting to be involved in social activities; (v) help in avoiding or resolving conflict with family, friends, landlords, and others; and (vi) support in getting and keeping a job (Marx *et al.*, 1973).

Case management for persons with schizophrenia and other severe mental illness, therefore, involves assistance that transcends the definition of targeted case management. It seems logical that such assistance would best be provided in the context of supportive, psychotherapeutic relationships in which all mental health professionals involved with a client are working cooperatively to coordinate and integrate their efforts. Because most persons with schizophrenia need case management of modulating intensity over long periods of time, it also seems logical that having a team of staff sharing these roles in a relationship with a client would promote continuity of care more so than assigning this responsibility to a single case manager. Given that the acceptance by a client of the case management relationship is based on trust, it would seem that a risk of loss of the client's confidence and willingness to accept help would accompany each change of case manager assignment. These assumptions suggest that case management should be a shared responsibility, woven within a system of care.

CASE MANAGEMENT APPROACHES IN PRACTICE

The term "case management" does not connote a standard intervention. Although it developed as a social casework function intended to mitigate the difficulty persons with mental illness experienced in obtaining needed services and entitlements (Intagliata, 1982), it has evolved into many different types of intervention in place across and within the states that share the same label. Case management programs can be differentiated by *organization* (e.g., free-standing case management specialist programs, case managers within treatment programs, or case management as a function of each member of a treatment team), *orientation* (e.g., service broker, strengths facilitator, rehabilitation agent, network facilitator, clinician, or full support), *intensity* (e.g., client to staff ratios varying from 1:40 to 1:10), and *availability* (varying from weekdays to around the clock and from office bound to home- and community-based provision of assistance).

Several recent reports summarizing the descriptive and research literature on case management approaches with persons with severe mental illness group contemporary case management approaches into six models: (i) broker or generalist; (ii) personal strengths; (iii) rehabilitation; (iv) social network; (v) clinical; and (vi) full support (Chamberlain & Rapp, 1991; Solomon, 1992; Harris & Bergman, 1993). These models differ in terms of the role of the case manager in the life of the client, based on values about the helping relationship, theories about the needs of persons with severe mental illness, and beliefs about the functioning of complex delivery systems.

The broker or generalist model is closest to the initial conception of case management dating back to the 1960s (Intagliata, 1982); an integrative function that helps the client make optimal use of human services. It is a social casework intervention that is viewed as ancillary to mental health treatment. The case manager is not a treatment or rehabilitation agent and typically has bachelors level or less education in human services. Rather, the case manager is an advocate for the client who identifies unmet needs, develops a case management plan in collaboration with the client, assists the client directly and indirectly to obtain services, and attempts to increase communication with and among the various services in which the client is involved.

Through experience, providers of broker case management services have learned that many clients need assertive outreach to continue with a given service or treatment intervention and direct, concrete assistance in daily living to preserver. Case management caseloads have tended to decrease in order to allow the case manager to provide this type of support in addition to brokering services. "Expanded broker" or "intensive case management" (Solomon, 1992) are terms used to denote this more comprehensive role of the generalist case manager. The generalist approach is the most prevalent type of case management among the states. It fits the prevailing organization of community mental health services: outpatient clinics, day activity programs, psychosocial clubhouses and supervised residential settings which operate with a high degree of autonomy from one another, and with clients frequently involved in two or more programs concurrently. Generalist case managers have been added to these settings to provide outreach, linkage, monitoring, and advocacy functions. They work, more or less, as a manager of a loose "treatment team," with other professionals attending to clinical management, counseling, and/or rehabilitation of the client.

The personal strengths model (Freddolino & Moxley, 1992; Rapp, 1993) is based on a theoretical rationale that views the client with severe mental illness as having difficulty in access to needed services and supports primarily caused by the stigma of being a "mental patient." Hence, case management according to the strengths model focuses on capitalizing on the client's personal strengths to help themselves with as little imposition of the case manager's wants or judgement as possible. The case manager is an assistant to the client, whose focus is to help the client accomplish those objectives which the client identifies as important. The goal of case management in the personal strengths model is to empower clients, primarily by enabling their success at accomplishing *their* objectives rather than by directing or imposing the expedient or professionally valued alternative. Personal strengths case managers take their lead from their client and adapt an advocacy relationship that is a true partnership with the client. Personal strengths case management is intended to be intensive (at least weekly contact) with the case manager reaching out assertively to establish and maintain a helping relationship. It is intended to be adjunctive to, and independent of, the provision of mental health services. Primarily, the difference between the intensive broker and personal strengths models is the specific foundation of values from which the personal strengths case manager proceeds.

The rehabilitation model (Anthony *et al.*, 1993) is also an adaptation of the intensive case management broker model that provides a specific theoretical framework and set of skills to the case manager designed to empower the client to progress toward self-sufficiency. The case manager does this through a rehabilitation approach which is the learning of skills and development of environmental supports that compensate for the disabling effects of the person's illness. Achievement of skills and supports that enable the client to live independently and to work are primary goals of rehabilitation case management. Rehabilitation case management shares the core values of personal strengths case management regarding the case management process proceeding from the client's needs and wants as expressed by the client in a collaborative assessment and service planning process.

Social network (or contextual) case management focuses on the potential for improving and expanding the client's social network as a means to meet the client's needs for material, emotional, and social support (Bebout, 1993). Rather than primarily focusing on the client's adaptation to community living with a disability, it seeks to strengthen the willingness and ability of others to cope with, compensate for, and support the client. The approach is based on experimental evidence that the variety and interconnectedness of persons involved with the client makes a difference in the client's ability to achieve stable community living. Like personal strengths and rehabilitation case management, social network case management proceeds from a specific theoretical basis, grounded in social psychology. The social network approach differs from the others primarily in the dimension of emphasis on adapting the social environment to compensate for the client's disability, but not to the exclusion of helping the client gain mastery. It builds on an intensive case management approach of assertive outreach and frequency of contact.

Clinical case management (Roach, 1993) incorporates the intensive case management broker role within the scope of responsibilities of a mental health clinician who approaches the client from the perspective of developmental and psychodynamic theory. Thus outreach, assistance with obtaining needed services, assistance with daily living and social relations are integrated within a psychotherapeutic relationship aimed at the client gaining increased recognition, understanding, and control of their illnesses. The clinical case manager maintains the primary clinical as well as supportive relationship with the client and mediates the client's involvement with the psychiatrist and providers of other mental health services (residential, day treatment, etc.). As with other psychotherapy relationships, the clinical case manager exercises considerably more power in relationship to the client than in the other models described above.

In all of the above models, the case manager works on a solo basis with a specific caseload of clients. Caseloads tend to range from 1:10 to 1:20 in the more intensive approaches. By contrast, the case management broker model may range up to a ratio of 1:40 with minimum if any direct assistance in daily living provided. In all of these models, case managers either work as a specialist within a loose treatment team or as a discrete homogeneous unit within a comprehensive mental health agency or as a free-standing agency, not affiliated with the mental health service program(s) in which the client is enrolled. Case managers work with clients on a solo basis to facilitate their access to, and appropriate use of, services across the mental health, health, and social welfare systems.

The full support case management model differs from the others in several key organizational contexts, yet integrates the theoretical underpinnings of several of them. The full support model is a self-contained interdisciplinary treatment team program in which intensive case management functions are imbedded within the roles of each member of the team. Responsibility for case management for each client is shared by multiple team members, although each client has a specific team member as a primary therapist/case manager. The multidisciplinary treatment team model contains psychiatry, nursing, social work, and rehabilitation disciplines and is therefore able to provide a comprehensive array of psychotherapeutic, rehabilitative, and supportive services, minimizing the use of other mental health programs. The treatment team shares responsibility for clients in an intensive client to staff ratio of 15:1 or lower. It delivers treatment by becoming very involved in clients' lives and social networks with the goals of improving clients' control over symptoms, achieving independent living and positive social relations, and attaining a vocation. The prototype for this approach, the Training in Community Living (TCL) model, was developed in the early 1970s by the Program of Assertive Community Tretment (PACT), a unit of the Mendota Mental Health Institute in Madison, Wisconsin. A group of Mendota Mental Institute staff conceptualized a service delivery system in which the same clinician provided persons at high risk for frequent or long-term hospitalization with flexible, long-term, and intensive outpatient intervention. The work site of a hospital treatment team was transposed from the inpatient setting to the community and the team delivered nearly all interventions in natural settings, assisting clients to establish independent residence while supporting them (as well as the members of their social network) in a variety of material as well as therapeutic ways (Marx *et al.*, 1973; Stein *et al.*, 1975; Stein & Test, 1976a). Several descriptive and research reports of the dissemination of the TCL model have applied various labels including "Continuous Treatment Teams" (Torrey, 1986) and "Assertive Community Treatment" (Taube *et al.*, 1990). We use the term Assertive Community Treatment (ACT) to refer to community treatment team programs based on the TCL model. Controlled studies of ACT conducted at PACT and elsewhere (described below) have consistently shown it to produce greater benefit to clients than outpatient psychiatry, counseling, and related facility-based treatments.

The ACT model addresses two frequent shortcomings of the community mental health system: service fragmentation and gaps in continuity of care. Community mental health systems are multi-agency systems; and, while a lead agency may promote multi-agency cooperation, it is extremely difficult to achieve coordination at the client level when clinical responsibility is divided among separate programs. Inconsistent and confusing guidance to clients is likely when multiple staff in separate programs seldom if ever meet together with and about shared clients. Even with the advent of a case manager, who addresses issues impeding a cooperative effort on behalf of a client among programs and agencies, communication is disrupted with each change of case manager. Considering the difficulties in communication and social relations that persons with schizophrenia experience, the multidisciplinary team approach appears to be a more logical means to achieve clients' clinical stability and functional rehabilitation than the case-managed, multiprogram approach (Test, 1979). Figure 1 illustrates the opportunities for communication failure, service fragmentation, and gaps in continuity of care when

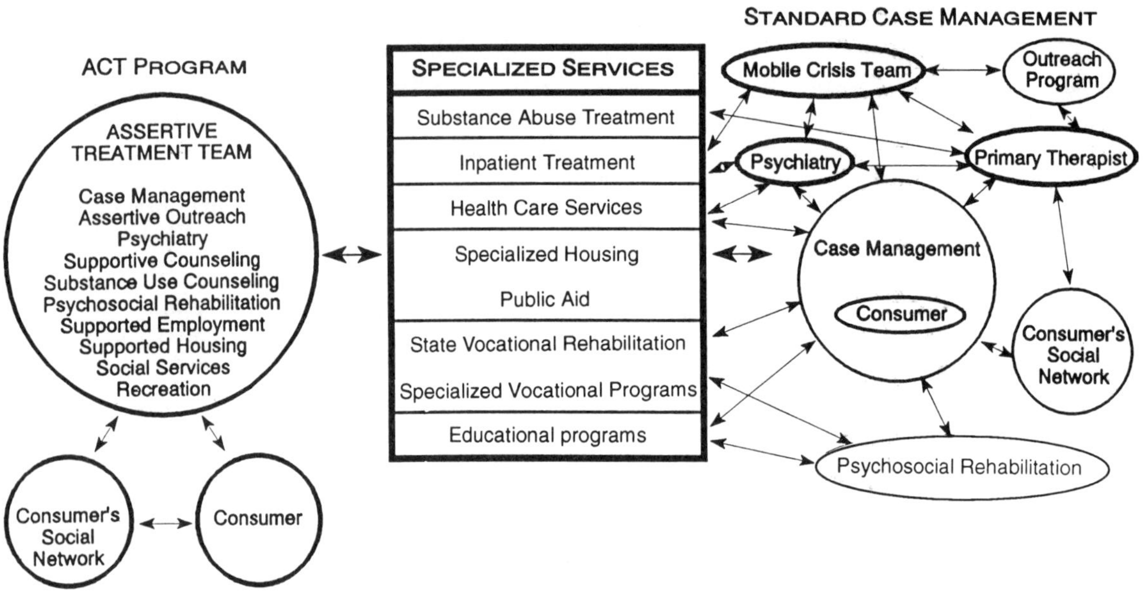

Figure 1. ACT approach versus standard case management. Adapted from Essock, S.M. and Kantos, N.I. Cost-effectiveness of assertive community treatment, Connecticut Department of Mental Health.

case management is layered on to a community support system and the coherence of the TCL model.

ACT APPROACH

ACT represents an integration of biological, psychological, and social interventions with innovations over traditional community mental health services in the organization and delivery of services (Table 1). ACT allows for the application of pharmacologic and psychosocial treatments within an intensive field-based support system enabling most clients to live independently in their communities.

The ACT approach directly address the multiple and complex needs of persons with severe mental illness in a pragmatic, flexible, and comprehensive manner. The core of ACT is a treatment team which assumes global responsibility for a group of clients. The treatment team is characterized by multidisplinary composition, shared responsibility for clients, and an intensive staff to client ratio. The ACT team's approach toward clients is *assertive*, emphasizing outreach and out-of-office interventions 24 hours a day, 7 days per week. To engage and retain persons in treatment, the team assumes a *can-do attitude*, using a comprehensive array of treatment, rehabilitative, and supportive interventions, as well as environmental modifications, to promote independent and productive functioning. ACT operates as a *self-contained* program, incorporating core psychiatric, supportive, and rehabilitative services within the team which serves as a fixed point of responsibility, accountable for clients' psychiatric and social welfare. The desired client outcomes are reduced symptomatology and subjective distress, increased community tenure, enhanced satisfaction with life, and improved psychosocial functioning (Test, 1991). Specific tasks include: (i) close psychiatric monitoring including the taking of medications; (ii) facilitating the acquisition of basic resources (housing, entitlements, and general health care); (iii) support in dealing with life's daily problems which can easily overwhelm clients; (iv) teaching and reinforcing essential skills in the natural environment (e.g. homemaking, financial management, communication, and employment); (v) modifying pathologic dependency relationships; and (vi) developing a supportive

Table 1. Differences between traditional mental health care systems and Assertive Community Treatment (ACT)

Service element	Traditional systems	ACT
Primary locus of care	Hospital, residential programs, day programs, offices	In the field (community, home, neighborhood, work site)
Provider	Individual clinician for individual outpatients, multidisciplinary teams for inpatients. Treatment time highly variable. Outpatient caseloads high; inpatient caseloads low. Fragmented continuity of care across loci of care	Generalist teams share a fixed caseload. Ratio of staff to clients, 1:10–15. Treatment time unlimited. Direct services continuously available.
Treatment approach	Specific individual and/or group psychosocial therapies, and biological treatments provided mostly in a health care facility. Providers not held directly accountable for outcomes.	Medication monitoring and social support (help with housing, health, basic needs) in natural community environment. Providers held accountable for outcomes.

network among family and significant others decreasing their stress and frustration in relating to the client (Stein & Test, 1980).

The TCL model includes a mix of disciplines (psychiatrist, nurses, social workers, rehabilitation therapists) who care for a shared caseload of up to 120 clients. There is considerable variation among ACT programs in team size and composition, but all integrate psychiatry with one or more other professional mental health disciplines. Detailed psychosocial assessments and specific treatment plans are the core around which all interventions are organized in a weekly schedule for each client. The nature and frequency of client contact is determined by these, and by close monitoring of the individual's changing needs. Daily staffing sessions (clinical rounds) are held during which staff schedules are adjusted according to each client's present status. When a client is hospitalized or jailed, team members consult with the institution's staff and remain directly engaged with the client to facilitate resolution of the problems which contributed to the crisis episode.

The ACT approach is consistent with the federal CSP systems model (Turner & TenHoor, 1977; Stroul, 1989). It incorporates all 10 of the services identified as essential within a community support system. It also incorporates the attributes of a community support system for service coordination at both system and client levels (see Table 2).

RESEARCH ON ACT

Since the seminal controlled studies of the implementation of the TCL model (Marx *et al.*, 1973; Stein *et al.*, 1975; Stein & Test, 1980), controlled studies have accompanied ACT program development in Australia and Great Britain as well as in several sites in the United States. None of these studies has included as comprehensive a set of measurement domains (hospitalization, independent living, symptoms, self-esteem, quality of life, criminal justice involvement, employment, economic cost–benefit, and social costs) as the TCL study by Stein & Test. (1980); nor has demonstrated as clear benefit of ACT over facility-based outpatient services across multiple domains. In these trials, the experimental (ACT) treatment condition has ranged from close fidelity (Mulder, 1985; Hoult *et al.*, 1983; Muijen *et al.*, 1992) to loose fidelity (Bond *et al.*, 1988, 1990; Jerrell & Hu, 1989) to the TCL model. The following review, therefore, groups the studies into these two categories.

The TCL study (Weisbrod *et al.*, 1980) and two randomized trials of ACT closely based on the TCL model (Mulder, 1985; Hoult *et al.*, 1983), in which treatment costs were measured, demonstrated its cost-effectiveness. In each of these studies, as well as another which did not measure treatment costs (Muijen *et al.*, 1992), the ACT approach demonstrated improvements in community tenure. The two studies

Table 2. Elements of community support systems for SMI adults and their compatibility with Assertive Community Treatment (ACT)

Community support systems*	ACT†
I. Philosophical principles	I. Organization and delivery of services
A. Services should:	A. Core services team (continuous treatment team)
1. be consumer centered	1. Fixed point of responsibility (all needs)
2. empower clients	2. Primary provider of services
3. be racially and culturally appropriate	3. Continuity of care and caregivers across functional areas and across time
4. be flexible	B. Assertive outreach and *in vivo* treatment
5. focus on strengths	C. Individualized treatment
6. be normalized/ incorporate natural supports	1. Between clients
7. meet special needs	2. Within clients across time
8. be coordinated	D. Ongoing treatment and support
B. Service systems should be accountable	
II. Service components	II. ACT: Treatments and services provided
A. Client identification and outreach	A. Direct assistance with symptom management
B. Mental health treatments	1. Medications
C. Crisis response services	2. 24-hour crisis availability
D. Health and dental care	3. Brief hospitalization
E. Housing	4. Long term 1:1 clinical relationship
F. Income support and entitlements	B. Facilitation of an optimally supportive environment
G. Peer support	1. Assistance with meeting basic needs (housing, etc.)
H. Family and community support	2. Assistance with a supportive social environment
I. Rehabilitation services	3. Assistance with a supportive family environment (psychoeducation)
J. Protection and advocacy	C. Direct assistance with instrumental functioning (work, social relations, activities of daily living)
K. Case management	1. *In-vivo* skill teaching
	2. *In-vivo* support
	3. Environmental modifications

* Adapted from Stroul (1989).
† Adapted from Test (1991).

that compared the living arrangements of the two groups found that the ACT clients were more likely to be living independently (Stein & Test, 1980; Mulder, 1985). All of these studies included a majority of patients with schizophrenia-related disorders. The one study that reported specifically about clients with schizophrenia in detail (Hoult & Reynolds, 1984) found significant differences in hospital use, satisfaction with treatment, and psychotic symptoms between ACT and control clients, with ACT having the advantage.

Regarding controlled studies of ACT programs more loosely based on the TCL model, two found ACT to be more effective than office-based interventions in reducing hospital use (Bond *et al*., 1988, 1990), and one (Jerrell & Hu, 1989) that found comparable improvements in reduction of hospital use and comparable costs.

In all of the ACT studies, with the exception of the one by Jerrell and Hu (1989), the control conditions were fairly standard, consisting of office visits for medication maintenance and counseling. In the study reported by Jerrell and Hu (1989), although control group clients were assigned to outpatient clinics, which provided only medication maintenance and counseling in a staff to client ratio varying from 1:40 to 1:70, clients also had access to a generalist case manager program that provided community-based assistance with social, vocational, and housing needs and to a variety of social support and vocational rehabilitation programs operating parallel to the clinics.

The study by Jerrell and Hu (1989) had more mixed results than the others. Experimental group clients received more clinical and case management contacts than control group clients but the groups had comparably positive outcomes in regard to decreased inpatient service use. The reduction in inpatient use was less dramatic than in the case of other ACT studies that employed the TCL model. During the first three measurement intervals, the experimental group experienced improvements in psychosocial measures while the control group did not; however, these differences were not evident at the end of the 2 year follow-up period. Total direct care costs for the experimental group increased over the course of the study while costs for the control group decreased by a comparable amount; however, there was no significant difference in total costs between the groups. This study would suggest comparability of benefit between ACT programs and comprehensive, but less coordinated, community mental health services. However, because the experimental condition varied from multiple core elements of the TCL model the meaning of its findings is less clear.

Taube and colleagues (1990) recommended eight steps that would improve the comparison of findings among future research on ACT: (i) the control condition should include case management, emergency treatment, and psychosocial services reflective of services now delivered in most local mental health systems; (ii) costs should be fully assessed; (iii) studies should have follow-up periods of 18 months or more; (iv) mature programs should be evaluated in operation; (v) client subgroups should be evaluated; (vi) study design should test the differential effects of specific approaches within a program (close monitoring of medication taking, efforts to strengthen social networks, direct assistance in daily living); (vii) outcome indicators should be standardized; (viii) cost shifting should be measured. To these we would add the recommendations that: (i) additional close replications of the TCL model be undertaken to further test its effectiveness compared with client involvement in large, less coordinated comprehensive systems of care; and (ii) that ACT variations on the TCL model limit the number of varying conditions so that the effects can be compared.

There are several studies in progress in which the experimental conditions are the TCL model and the control conditions are CMHCs that provide comprehensive, but less coordinated, services including all 10 core elements of the federal CSP systems model (Test *et al.*, 1985; Test, 1992; Drake *et al.*, 1993; Santos *et al.*, 1993a, b; Essock & Kontos, 1993). These studies may shed light on the effects of incorporating key principles of TCL (e.g., fixed point of accountability for care, assertive outreach, practical assistance, community-based contacts, support to social networks) within larger systems of care that incorporate a variety of programs and case management approaches. Preliminary results reported for two of these studies indicate advantage for TCL.

A 12 year prospective study is comparing 5–10 year outcomes of clients with schizophrenic disorders randomly admitted as young adults early in the course of their illnesses to PACT or the Dane County mental health system, which evolved into a comprehensive system early in the course of the study (Test *et al.*, 1985; Test, 1992). Findings after 2 full years of treatment indicate that clients receiving TCL through PACT experienced significantly fewer hospitalizations and hospital stays and significantly more time living in independent arrangements than clients in the comparison group. The groups did not differ in the amount of time spent incarcerated or in homeless shelters which was small in both cases.

An 18-month study in three Connecticut cities is comparing effects and costs of ACT programs, closely adhering to the TCL model, and case management by individual case management practitioners combined with access to comprehensive CMHC services (Essock & Kontos, 1993). In both conditions, case management functions include assertive outreach and provision of direct assistance in the community. Preliminary results for a 6 month period early in the study indicated that ACT clients spent less time than control group clients in inpatient settings or shelters. The above cited randomized trials are summarized in Table 3.

If the TCL model is superior to the prevailing structure of community support systems, the public policy implications for restructuring existing systems would be daunting. However, it may be that the approach and intensity of the TCL intervention has more to do with client outcome than its structural

Table 3. Outcomes of randomized trials of Assertive Community Treatment (ACT) for seriously mentally ill (SMI) subjects

Investigations	Site	Clinical and psychosocial outcomes
Marx, Test, Stein	Madison, Wi. * (1970–72)	ACT more effective (5 months trial) in reducing use of hospitals and ER's, in improving residential status, and in preserving occupational status
Stein, Test, Weisbrod	Madison, Wi. * (1974–78)	ACT more effective (12 months trial) in reducing use of hospitals, nursing homes, and law enforcement services; in improving residential status, and improving socialization, instrumental functioning, and symptom profiles
Hoult and Reynolds	Sidney, Aust. * (1979–81)	ACT more effective (12 months trial) in reducing use of hospitals and ER's; in improving instrumental functioning, symptom profile, residential status, and occupational activity
Muldar, Mowbray	Grand Rapids, Mi. † (1982–85)	ACT more effective (30 months trial) in reducing use of hospitals and law enforcement services; and in improving instrumental functioning and residential status
Bond, Miller, Krumwied, Ward	3 MHC's Indiana † (1986–88)	ACT more effective (6 months trial) in reducing use of hospitals in two of three sites
Jerrell and Hu	Santa Clara, CA † (1985–88)	ACT more effective in reducing use of hospitals and ER's. Positive changes in functioning and quality of life at 12 months not present at 24 months
Bond, Witheridge, Dincin, Wesmer, Webb, DeGraaf-Kaser	Chicago, Ill. † (1984–87)	ACT more effective (12 months trial) in reducing use of hospitals, and in improving instrumental functioning, satisfaction with life, and residential status
Muijen, Marks, Connolly, Audini	London, Eng † (1985–90)	ACT more effective (36 months trial) in reducing use of hospitals
Test	Madison, Wisc † (1978–90)	ACT more effective (2 year follow-up) in reducing use of hospitals; in improving residential and mental health status

* Acute phase SMI.
† Stable phase SMI.

characteristics. For example, positive findings similar to those reported above (Stein & Test, 1980; Mulder, 1985; Hoult & Reynolds, 1984; Muijen, 1992) have occurred in controlled clinical trials of family preservation using multisystemic therapy (FP/MST), and assertive case management approach to a variety of adolescent clinical problems (Henggeler *et al.*, 1986, 1990, 1991; Brunk *et al.*, 1987; Borduin *et al.*, 1990, 1993). While team size and composition of ACT and FP/MST differ, they have similar staff to client ratios and program approaches to which their mutual success may be attributed. First, they assume a social ecological model of behavior. That is, they proceed from the assumption that the client's capacity to function in the community is linked both to his/her psychological and social characteristics and key elements in the environment, such as family, work/school, and neighborhood. Moreover, the client's psychosocial characteristics and social environment are inexorably linked. Second, their treatment approaches are pragmatic, with an emphasis on action-oriented and well-specified interventions. Third, interventions are delivered in the client's natural environment. Such delivery of services reduces the frequency of missed appointments, enables the acquisition of assessment data that have greater ecological validity, and facilitates a practical approach to the acquisition of skills and changing behavior. Fourth, therapeutic goals are specific and intervention strategies are flexible. Essentially, staff are encouraged to do "whatever it takes" to attain specified treatment goals. Fifth, treatment team members are held accountable for therapeutic outcomes. Outcomes are continuously monitored to allow rapid feedback regarding the viability of interventions and the possible need to alter or refine treatment plans.

Thus, rather than being passive in the face of lack of progress by clients, staff are openly challenged in team meetings and supervisory sessions to seek creative solutions to intervene successfully with clients. These approaches, which could be incorporated within a variety of program structures, should be more widely tested.

Another focus of future research should be the use of ACT to promote clients' community adjustment and self-sufficiency through employment. The initial TCL study at PACT (Weisbrod *et al.*, 1980) and the TCL study at Harbinger (Mulder, 1985) found that TCL clients earned more through paid employment than did control group clients. PACT has maintained clinical and programmatic emphasis on employment outcome since its inception and much higher rates of employment than typical for persons with severe mental illness (Knoedler, 1979; Frey & Godfrey, 1991; Russert & Frey, 1991). Analysis of the experience of programs that have attempted to replicate the TCL model but which have poor employment outcomes, compared with the specific approaches and activities used by PACT to obtain employment outcome, is needed. Additional controlled studies of TCL strategies that are believed to promote employment outcome are also needed.

Finally, there are several states (including Michigan, Wisconsin, Rhode Island, and Delaware) where large numbers of clients are enrolled in ACT programs that have been developed in conformance with state standards. A meta-analysis of relationships between variables such as team size, team composition, staff to client ratio, proportion of client contacts occurring in the community, and easily measured outcomes such as hospital utilization and living arrangements could provide very useful information for state mental health agencies.

ACT COSTS AND FINANCING

Notwithstanding its limitations, the available research evidence on the effectiveness of the ACT approach is already sufficient to justify more widespread dissemination and use of the ACT models. However, despite its demonstrated effectiveness, the approach has not proliferated as rapidly as might have been expected. A primary reason for this is the inertia of the existing systems of community and hospital care. Financing streams, which have both shaped and been shaped by the historical emphasis on hospital- and office-based care, have not been altered to promote the provision of ACT-based care. No third parties provide specific coverage for ACT. Only under Medicaid, can the cost of ACT be recouped through the insurance mechanism. Even for Medicaid-covered populations, the considerable start-up costs of launching an ACT program combined with the state share of Medicaid expenditures represent barriers to state mental health agencies interested in its development.

Cost analyses in controlled studies of ACT have demonstrated ACT to be less costly, or at least no more costly, than alternative outpatient care, only when expenditures for hospital treatment are factored in the analyses. Among states that have undertaken statewide or large-scale development of ACT programs, average annual per client expenditures range from \$5000 to \$18 000 (Meisler, 1994), varying primarily in accordance with the intensity of the ratio of clients to staff. Expenditures based on the TCL model (1:10 staff to client ratio and multidisciplinary professional staff) range from \$8000 to \$10 000. A survey of CMHCs (Emery & Goplerud, 1988) identified that 45% of CMHC expenditures were for clients with severe mental illness who make up 45% of CMHC caseloads. That is, expenditure levels for persons with severe mental illness and those with less serious problems were similar. The average expenditure per client was \$2300. Adjusting for the 5 year gap between the collection of these CMHC data and those for ACT, it appears that ACT represents at least a doubling of the average CMHC expenditure per client. Financing for large-scale development of ACT programs could potentially be offset by reductions in expenditures for hospital care. Without radical, systematic reform, however, "savings" from reduced use of inpatient services do not necessarily result in an actual shift of resources to expand a preferred mode of care. Financing the start-up costs of such a strategy also poses a challenge. The recent momentum at the federal and state levels to stem the growth of health care expenditures may lead to increased attention to the cost containment potential of ACT.

CONCLUSIONS

Although there is no broad agreement about its definition or a preferred organizational approach, case management has emerged as a core element in most state mental health systems. This emergence has been a response to problems of fragmentation and discontinuity which have characterized the community mental health service system. Research comparing clients who are offered case management (including, at a minimum, outreach and direct assistance to persevere with daily life and psychiatric treatment) has repeatedly demonstrated it to be more beneficial than the offer of office-based psychiatric and counseling services alone in reducing hospital use.

As both state mental health agencies and third parties confront the pressure to contain increases in annual expenditures, the momentum to identify and develop alternatives to traditional care is likely to increase. Using an ecological model of intervention with pragmatic therapeutic aims, an intensive staff to client ratio, and an emphasis on therapist accountability, seem to be factors in the success of case management.

REFERENCES

Allen, P.A. (1974). A consumer's view of California's mental health care system. *Psychiatric Quarterly*, **48**, 1–13.

Anthony, W.A., Forbess, R., and Cohen, M.R. (1993). Rehabilitation-oriented case management. In M. Harris and H.C. Bergman eds, *Case Management for Mentally Ill Patients: Theory and Practice*, USA: Harwood Academic Publishers.

Arce, A.A., Tadlock, M., Vergare, J.J., and Shapiro, S.H. (1983). A psychiatric profile of street people admitted to an emergency shelter. *Hospital and Community Psychiatry*, **34**, 812–817.

Babiker, I.E. (1980). Non-compliance and schizophrenia. *Psychiatric Developments*, **4**, 329–337.

Bassuk, E.L. and Gerson, S. (1978). Deinstitutionalization and mental health services. *Scientific American*, **238**, 46–53.

Bassuk, E.L., Rubin, L., and Lauriat, A. (1984). Is homelessness a mental health problem? *American Journal of Psychiatry*, **141**, 1546–1550.

Bebout, R. (1993). Contextual case management: restructuring the social support networks of seriously mentally ill adults. In M. Harris and H.C. Bergman, eds, *Case Management for Mentally Ill Patients: Theory and Practice*. USA: Harwood Academic Publishers.

Bond, G.R., Miller, L.D., Krumwied, R.D., and Ward, R.S. (1988). Assertive case management in three MHCs: a controlled study. *Hospital and Community Psychiatry*, **39**, 411–418.

Bond, G.R., Witheridge, T.F., Dincin, J., Wasmer, D., Webb, J., and DeGraaf-Kaser, R. (1990). Assertive community treatment for frequent users of psychiatric hospitals in a large city: a controlled study. *American Journal of Community Psychology*, **18**, 865–872.

Borduin, C.M., Henggeler, S.W., Blaske, D.M., and Stein, R. (1990). Multisystemic treatment of adolescent sexual offenders. *International Journal of Offender Therapy and Comparative Criminology*, **34**, 105–113.

Borduin, C.M., Mann, B.J., Cone, L.T., *et al.* (1993). Multisystemic treatment of serious juvenile offenders: Long-term prevention of violent offending. *Journal of Consulting & Clinical Psychology* (in press).

Brunk, M., Henggeler, S.W., and Whelan, J.P. (1987). A comparison of multisystemic therapy and parent training in the brief treatment of child abuse and neglect. *Journal of Consulting and Clinical Psychology*, **55**, 311–318.

Center for Mental Health Services (1993). *Additions and Resident Patients at End of Year, State and Community Mental Hospitals, by Age and Diagnosis, by State, United States*, 1991. Rockvile, MD: Author.

Chamberlain, R. and Rapp, C.A. (1991). A decade of case management: a methodological review of outcome research. *Community Mental Health Journal*, **27**, 171–188.

Committee on Government Operations Forty-First Report (1988). *From Back Wards to Back Streets: The Failure of the Federal Government in Providing Services for the Mentally Ill*. Washington, DC: US Government Printing Office.

Drake, R.E. and Wallach, M.S. (1989). Substance abuse among the chronically mentally ill. *Hospital and Community Psychiatry*, **13**, 103–113.

Drake, R.E., McHugo, G.J., and Noordsy, D.L. (1993). Treatment of alcoholism among schizophrenic outpatients: 4-year outcomes. *American Journal of Psychiatry*, **150**, 328–329.

Emory, B.D. and Goplerud, E.N. (1988). *Services for the Seriously Mentally Ill: A Study of Community Mental Health Agencies*. Washington, DC: National Council of Mental Health Centers.

Essock, S.M. and Kontos, N.J. (1993). Cost effectiveness of assertive community treatment. *Proceedings of the 1992 NASHPD Research Institute Conference*. Baltimore, MD: NASHPD.

Freeman, S.J.J., Formo, A., Alampur, A.G., and Sommers, A.F. (1979). Psychiatric disorder in a skid-row mission population. *Comprehensive Psychiatry*, **20**, 454–462.

Freddolino, P.P. and Moxley, D.P. (1992). Refining an advocacy model for homeless people coping with psychiatric disabilities. *Community Mental Health Journal*, **28**, 337–352.

Frey, J.L. and Godfrey, M. (1991). A comprehensive clinical vocational assessment: the PACT approach. **22**, 25–28.

General Accounting Office (1977). *Returning the Mentally Disabled to the Community: Government Needs to do More*. Washington, DC: General Accounting Office.

Goldman, H.H. (1983). The demography of deinstitutionalization. *New Directions for Mental Health Services*, **17**, 15–29.

Goldman, H.H. and Morrissey, J.P. (1985). The alchemy of mental health policy: homelessness and the fourth cycle of reform. *American Journal of Public Health*, **75**, 727–731.

Goldman, H.H., Gattozzi, A.A., and Taube, C.A. (1981). Defining and counting the chronically mentally ill. *Hospital and Community Psychiatry*, **32**, 21–25.

Goldman, H.H., Adams, N.H., and Taube, C. A. (1984). Deinstitutionalization: the data demythologized. *Hospital and Community Psychiatry*, **34**, 129–134.

Gruenberg, E.M. (1969). From practice to theory community mental health services and the nature of psychoses. *Lancet*, **1**, 721–724.

Harris, M. and Bergman, H.C. (1993). *Case Management for Mentally Ill Patients: Theory and Practice*. Harwood Academic.

Henggeler, S.W. and Borduin, C.M. (1990). *Family Therapy and Beyond: A Multisystemic Approach to Treating the Behavior Problems of Children and Adolescents*. Pacific Grove, CA: Brooks/Cole.

Henggeler, S.W., Rodick, J.D., Borduin, C.M., Hanson, C.L., Watson, S.M., and Urey, J.R. (1986). Multisystemic treatment of juvenile offenders: Effects on adolescent behavior and family interactions. *Developmental Psychology*. **22**, 132–141.

Henggeler, S.W., Borduin, C.M., Melton, G.B., *et al.* (1991). Effects of multisystemic therapy on drug use and abuse in serious juvenile offenders: A progress report from two outcome studies. *Family Dynamics of Addiction Quarterly*, **1**, 40–51.

Hogarty, G.E. and Anderson, C.M. (1986). Medication, family, psychoeducation, and social skills training: first year relapse results of a controlled study. *Psychopharmacology Bulletin*, **22**, 860–862.

Hoult, J. and Reynolds, I. (1984). Schizophrenia. A comparative trial of community oriented and hospital oriented psychiatric care. *Acta Psychiatrica Scandinavica*, **69**, 359–372.

Hoult, J., Reynolds, I., Charbonneau-Powis, M., *et al.* (1983). *Psychiatric Hospital Versus Community Treatment: A Controlled Study*. NSW, Australia: Department of Health.

Intagliata, J. (1982). Improving the quality of community care for the chronically mentally disabled: the role of case management. *Schizophrenia Bulletin*, **8**, 655–674.

Jerrell, J.M. and Hu, T. (1989). Cost-effectiveness of intensive clinical and case management compared with an existing system of care. *Inquiry*, **26**, 224–234.

Joint Commission on Mental Illness and Health: Final Report (1961). New York: Basic Books, Inc.

Knoedler, W.H. (1979). How the training in community living program helps patients work. *New Directions for Mental Health Services*, **2**, 57–66.

Marx, A.J., Test, M.A., and Stein, L.I. (1973). Extrohospital management of severe mental illness: feasibility and effects of social functioning. *Archives of General Psychiatry*, **29**, 505.

Meisler, N. (1994). Statewide dissemination of the training in community living program: the making of public policy. *Administration and Policy in Mental Health*, **23**, 71–76.

Muijen, M., Marks, I., Conolly, J., and Audini, B. (1992). Home based care and standard hospital care for patients with severe mental illness: a randomized controlled trial. *British Medical Journal*, **304**, 749–754.

Mulder, R. (1985). Evaluation of the Harbinger Program, 1982–1985. Lansing, MI: Department of Mental Health.

National Association of State Mental Health Program Directors (1992). Funding Sources and Expenditures of State Mental Health Agencies: Revenue/Expenditure Study Results, Fiscal Year 1990. Alexandria, VA.

Office of the Inspector General (1982). *A Study of Federal and State Actions to Safeguard the Health and Safety of Board and Care Home Residents*. Washington DC: US Department of Health and Human Services.

Randolf, F.L. (1992). NIMH funded research demonstration of (PACT) models. *Outlook*, **2**, 9–11.

Rapp, C. (1993). Theory, principles and methods of the strengths model of case management. In M. Harris and H.C. Bergman, eds, *Case Management for Mentally Ill Patients: Theory and Practice*. Langhorne, PA: Harwood Academic Publishers.

Roach, J. (1993). Clinical case management with severely mentally ill adults. In M. Harris and H.C. Bergman (eds), *Case Management for Mentally Ill Patients: Theory and Practice*. Langhorne, PA: Harwood Academic Publishers.

Russert, M.G. and Frey, J.L. (1991). The PACT vocational model: a step into the future. *Psychosocial Rehabilitation Journal*, **14**, 11–17.

Santos, A.B., Hawkins, G.D., Julius, B., Deci, P.A., Hiers, T.H., and Burns, B.J. (1993a). A pilot study of assertive community treatments for patients with chronic psychotic disorders. *American Journal of Psychiatry*, **150**, 501–504.

Santos, A.B., Deci, P.A., Lachance, K.R., *et al.* (1993b). Providing assertive community treatment for severely mentally ill patients in a rural area. *Hospital and Community Psychiatry*, **44**, 34–39.

Solomon, P. (1992). The efficacy of case management services for severely mentally disabled clients, *Community Mental Health Journal*, **28**, 163–180.

Stein, L.I. and Test, M.A. (1976a). Training in community

living-one year evaluation. *American Journal of Psychiatry,* **133**, 917–918.

Stein, L.I. and Test, M.A. (1976b). Retraining hospital staff for work in a community program in Wisconsin. *Hospital and Community Psychiatry,* **27**, 266–268.

Stein, L.I. and Test, M.A. (1980). Alternatives to mental health hospital treatment, I. Conceptual model, treatment program and clinical evaluation. *Archives of General Psychiatry,* **37**, 392–397.

Stein, L.I., Test, M.A., and Marx, A. (1975). Alternative to the hospital: a controlled study. *American Journal of Psychiatry,* **132**, 517–522.

Strahan, G. and Burns, B.J. (1991). Mental illness in nursing homes. *Vital and Health Statistics.* Hyattsville, MD: DHSS Publication No. (PHS) 91-1766.

Stroul, B.A. (1989). Community support systems for persons with long-term mental illness: a conceptual network. *Psychosocial Rehabilitation Journal,* **12**, 9–26.

Taube, C.A., Morlock, L., Burns, B.J. and Santos, A.B. (1990). New directions in research on community treatment. *Hospital and Community Psychiatry,* **41**, 642–647.

Test, M.A. (1979). Continuity of care in community treatment. *New Directions for Mental Health Services,* **1**, 15–23.

Test, M.A. (1991). The training in community living model: delivering treatment and rehabilitation services through a continuous treatment team. In R.P. Liberman, ed., *Handbook of Psychiatric Rehabilitation.* New York: Pergamon Press.

Test, M.A. (1992). Training in community living. In R.P. Liberman, ed., *Handbook of Psychiatric Rehabilitation.* New York: Macmillan.

Test, M.A., Knoedler, W.H., and Allness, D.J. (1985). The long-term treatment of young schizophrenics in a community support program. In L.I. Stein and M.A. Test, eds, *The Training in Community Living Model: A Decade of Experience. New Directions for Mental Health Services,* No. 26. San Francisco: Jossey-Bass.

Test, M.A. and Stein, L.I. (1980). Alternative to mental hospital treaatment III. Social costs. *Archives of General Psychiatry,* **37**, 409–412.

Thompson, K.S., Griffith, E.H., and Leaf, P.J. (1990). A historical review of the Madison model of community care. *Hospital and Community Psychiatry,* **41**, 625–634.

Torrey, E.F. (1986). Continuous treatment teams in the care of the chronic mentally ill. *Hospital and Community Psychiatry,* **37**, 1243–1247.

Turner, J.C. and TenHoor, W.J. (1978). The NIMH community support program: pilot approach to a needed social reform. *Schizophrenia Bulletin,* **4**, 319–349.

U.S. Department of Health and Human Services (1982). *Board & Care Homes: A Study of Federal and State Actions to Safeguard the Health and Safety of Board & Care Home Residents.* Washington, DC: US Government Printing Office.

Weisbrod, B.A., Test, M.A., Stein, L.I. (1980). Alternative to mental hospital treatment II. Economic benefit-cost analysis. *Archives of General Pychiatry,* **37**, 400–405.

17

The Economic Evaluation of Case Management

PAUL McCRONE and GRAHAM THORNICROFT
PRiSM (Psychiatric Research in Service Measurement), Institute of Psychiatry, London, UK

INTRODUCTION

In recent years the UK has seen emphasis placed on the provision of community mental health services as opposed to institutional care. This has resulted in a range of departures from traditional mental health services. Much of the recent focus has been on community mental health services as opposed to hospital care (Griffiths, 1988; Thornicroft & Bebbington, 1989). Enormous scope exists for innovative and radical initiatives to implement community care. Clearly though this move to the community requires effective, coordinated, and efficient service provision, otherwise benefits may be lost (Marks, 1992). Does this occur? Kingdon (1989) discovered that only 60% of all district health authorities in England and Wales had a mental health plan. Strathdee and Thornicroft (1992) note that there are a variety of planning strategies that may be pursued. The needs of users of mental health care services are extensive and varied. Some individuals will be going through a process of rehabilitation after discharge from long-stay institutions (Leff, 1991). Other people will have always been living in the community other than for occasional stays in psychiatric hospitals or units, but who now attend small community mental health centers (Sayce *et al.*, 1991) for contacts with the psychiatric services, rather than attending the large institutions. In addition there will inevitably be people living in the community who may never have had contact with the psychiatric services before but who do now come into contact with them. Therefore, there should be endeavors to provide a wide range of services in a way in which these needs may be met. Case management is one proposed method to facilitate the coordination, planning, and implementation of community care services.

One of the many changes introduced and encouraged by the 1990 National Health Service and Community Care Act was a policy preference for community over institutional care, and the employment of care programs and case management to coordinate the support which service users needed. Case management has been allocated a major role by the UK government in the provision of community care for people with long-term mental health problems, people with learning difficulties, and the elderly (Secretaries of State, 1989). It has been suggested that "case management is a process or method for ensuring that consumers are provided with whatever services they need in a coordinated, effective, and efficient manner" (Intagliata, 1982). Case management

Handbook of Mental Health Economics and Health Policy, Volume I, Schizophrenia. Edited by M. Moscarelli, A. Rupp and N. Sartorius.
© 1996 John Wiley & Sons Ltd.

aims to prevent fragmentation of services and to enable ongoing support that changes if necessary (Holloway *et al.*, 1991). However, there exists no clear consensus as to how the "ideal" case management system should operate. This is appropriate. The varied needs of different client groups requires varied services and methods of operation. Perhaps the main factor that influences case management (and any other health care initiative) is finance. In the present era of parsimony a crucial issue that needs to be addressed concerns the cost of community care provision.

Mental health care is resource hungry. In the UK mental health problems account for 10% of all health care expenditure, 23% of all National Health Service inpatient costs, and 25% of pharmaceutical charges (Department of Health, 1991). The move from institutional care to community care has major financial implications. Rather than one body (the health authority) bearing the burden of cost, a multiplicity of agencies will be called upon to provide services. The transfer of these financing responsibilities is potentially problematic. The necessary transfer of resources *within* agencies can also cause difficulties. This is particularly so with regard to health authorities. Eighty-five percent of the mental health budget has been located in the large institutions which serve only 10% of patients (Mental Health Foundation, 1987). The 1991 Act came into effect in April 1993 and gives local authorities a far greater role than they had previously. Purchasing of residential care is now the responsibility of these authorities.

The cost implications of any program of mental health care are important. Resources in an economy are invariably scarce and therefore it is imperative that they are allocated in an efficient and effective manner so as to maximize the benefit given to clients. This does not mean choosing the least costly service—usually the least costly option is to do nothing—but to link costs with clinical and social outcomes to achieve the best possible use of the given resources. To gauge fully the effectiveness of case management programs it is important to ascertain their associated economic costs.

Case management effectively originated in the United States and a number of models, such as the Training in Community Living Program (Stein & Test, 1980), the COSTAR home-based treatment (Thornicroft & Breakey, 1991), and the NIMH Model Plan (NIMH, 1987), have been widely acclaimed and replication has been sought after. Mention should also be made of the community mental health care system in Sydney (Hoult *et al.*, 1984). Elsewhere in this volume Gary Bond discusses the economics of case management in the United States (see Chapter 19). In this chapter we will be focusing primarily on case management in the UK.

CASE MANAGEMENT: DEFINITION, AIMS, PRACTICE

WHAT IS CASE MANAGEMENT?

Broadly, we can define case management as a method for the distribution and coordination of services, both clinical and social, for and in liaison with the client. This calls for great skill and expertise. Care needs to be provided to the individual within an environment of limited resources and competing alternatives (hence the needs for economic evaluation). Two broad forms of case management exist, although the number of possible models is numerous. "Brokerage" case management involves case managers arranging care for the user. The case manager does not have a tangible therapeutic part to play, but coordinates other professionals who are unlikely to work within a single team. It would be quite feasible for the case manager to purchase care and then to allocate it according to his/her caseload. This is similar to the system of capitation that exists in the United States (Lehman, 1987; Lurie *et al.*, 1992). Brokerage models tend to be popular among policy-makers and planners (Holloway *et al.*, 1991). However, the systems that appear to have more popularity among clinicians and other carers takes the form of "direct care," where case managers do perform a therapeutic role. They are often part of a multidisciplinary team and may undertake tasks not normally performed by their profession (Thornicroft, 1991). An important issue is whether the case management programs should be centered around the project or the individual. The former is perhaps easier, with the individual adapting to the services on offer. However, it is felt that a more flexible situation should prevail whereby it is the services which are tailor-made to the client. In practice it is inevitable that there will be some short-term rigidity.

WHAT ARE THE AIMS OF CASE MANAGEMENT?

Case management aims to provide a coordinated, continuous, flexible, and efficient approach to mental health care provision (Intagliata, 1982). It is an attempt to avoid fragmentation of services and to allow long-term care if necessary (Holloway *et al.*, 1991). Another aim is that case management should meet needs and be efficient, without costs becoming too great (Renshaw, 1987).

WHAT ARE THE COMPONENTS OF CASE MANAGEMENT?

The concept of case management allows for a rich variety of community mental health schemes—a richness which is desirable given the diverse needs of people with mental health problems. Case managers must attempt to address all relevant needs of the client without duplicating services. The belief of the UK government is that case management should contain certain essential components in order to be effective. These core tasks are: case identification, assessment of need, planning and delivering care, monitoring the quality of care, and the review of clients' needs (Secretaries of State, 1989). Other proponents of case management have agreed with, and added to, this list of core tasks (Renshaw, 1987; RDP, 1991; Thornicroft, 1991; Onyett, 1992). Additional functions, therefore, may include evaluating service effectiveness, repeating the cycle of care, collaboration with the client and the client's relatives, control over resources, and advocacy. Particular areas of work should be diverse. In Greenwich, Community Psychiatric Nurse (CPN) case managers were involved in housing issues and liaised with families (McCrone *et al.*, 1993; Muijen *et al.*, 1994). Welfare benefits are also an area where clinicians and therefore case managers could be involved (Stewart, 1988; Steadman, 1992).

WHO SHOULD THE CASE MANAGER BE?

The term "case manager" is often used interchangeably with "key worker." An individual, who is part of a multidisciplinary team, will be responsible for operationalizing the care that a client receives. This will usually involve liaison with the other professionals in the team, the client's family, and most importantly the client themself. The flexible approach to case management allows for staff from different professions to perform the role. Therefore case managers may be nurses (McLoughin, 1990; Tyrer *et al.*, 1990; McCrone *et al.*, 1994; Muijen *et al.*, 1994), social workers (Wooff & Goldberg, 1988), the user's family (Intagliata *et al.*, 1986; Falloon *et al.*, 1985), the multidisciplinary team (Onyett *et al.*, 1990; Jackson *et al.*, 1993), or the psychiatrist. With the proliferation of fundholding, general practitioners (GPs) may become brokerage case managers purchasing services on behalf of their clients. Who the case manager is could define the shape of the community mental health service, and therefore have an impact on cost.

A useful framework to bring together the various aspects of case management has been developed (Thornicroft, 1993). This framework is based around 12 axes which are detailed in Table 1. The range of combinations given these 12 axes justify the belief that there are as many ways to implement the principles of case management as there are case management programs.

METHODOLOGICAL GUIDELINES

Little is known about the costs of community mental health service provision for people with mental health problems (Peck & Cockburn, 1993). Performing an economic evaluation of a case management project entails following a well-defined methodology. The cost implications of a project are vital to ascertain, yet they are often ignored or wrongly assessed. This importance is caused by the scarcity of resources, which leads to limited budgets. Consequently parsimony is "encouraged." However, even if resources are plentiful it is important to ensure that they are allocated in an efficient and effective manner so as to provide maximum benefits to the users of services.

Knapp and Beecham (1990) have developed a costing framework based upon the following four principles which should be followed in a cost evaluation. This framework has been widely used in

Table 1. The 12 axes to define case management

1	Individual/team case management
2	Direct care/brokerage
3	Intensity of interventions
4	Degree of budgetary control
5	Health/social service function
6	Status of case manager
7	Specialization of case manager
8	Staff/patient ratio
9	Patient participation
10	Point of contact
11	Level of intervention
12	Target population

the field of mental health care research (Renshaw *et al.*, 1988; Beecham *et al.*, 1991; Melzer *et al.*, 1991; McCrone *et al.*, 1994) and other social research programs, particularly sentencing options for young offenders (Robertson *et al.*, 1986; Knapp *et al.*, 1993). First, costs should be comprehensively measured to range over all relevant service components of the care packages under consideration. This is crucial in the evaluation of case management projects where a large number of services will be used from a range of providing agencies. Second, cost variations between users need to be examined. Information on the causes of such variations can be far more valuable than looking at a simple average cost figure. Also, as will be seen, an understanding of the causes of cost variations is advantageous to a wide range of individuals (planners, clinicians, carers, financiers, users, families, etc.). Third, we need to ensure in an economic evaluation of different systems that we are making relevant comparisons. Systems evaluated must be substitutes for one another. If the experimental project was not implemented then we should assume that people would use the control service. Finally, costs must be integrated with outcomes. This cannot be over-emphasized. Focusing on only the cost side of the equation reveals little about economic efficiency (which is concerned with maximizing output from given resources) and causes suspicion to arise of economics. Economists need to be wise as to how policy-makers will use their findings. Equally, of course, neglecting costs when making policy decisions, or when undertaking the evaluations which inform them, should also prompt questions about validity and relevance.

THE COSTING PROCESS

With the departure from the hospital-based mental health care system it is likely that more agencies will be offering services to the client. Local authorities will inevitably be playing a greater part in the provision of services than before. This multiplicity of service provision calls for a careful examination of costs and where the cost burden lies. Other agencies that are likely to be involved in an extensive community service are the voluntary sector, the private sector, and the family/friend network of the client.

The costing process involves identifying the costs that are likely to be significant and, especially for policy-making, to be clear about where they fall. We would obviously strive to be as accurate as possible in calculating costs. It is perhaps ironic, though, that research in this area is also influenced by the limitation of resources. Therefore, some pragmatism is required in determining how far the costing process should go (Challis *et al.*, 1993). Three areas of cost in particular need to be identified. *Direct costs* refer to the costs that accrue due to contact with services operated by the psychiatric agency. These include psychiatric hospital inpatient episodes, outpatient appointments, day-patient attendances, psychiatrist/psychologist/CPN contacts, etc. *Indirect costs* are generally borne by other agencies who would normally provide services to a range of individuals. Services here include day centers, GP visits, dental appointments, etc. Accommodation costs are also included. *Hidden costs* are not often measured. Three main types exist: informal care, time travelling and waiting, and the cost of lost employment. Table 2 details many of the costs that occur when services are used. Each client will perhaps only have contact with a handful of these services and some services will be used by very few people. Having said this, the list is not exhaustive. Experience shows that any study which attempts to comprehensively cost a package of care will come across services not used by clients in other studies.

Costs are calculated according to the amount of time that a client is in contact with them. For example, we can ask the client how many times they visited their GP during the previous 6 months and for how long on average. This total contact time can then be multiplied by the unit cost of a GP to arrive at the cost of this service. For a fuller explanation of this procedure the reader is referred to Allen and Beecham (1993).

Table 2. The range of service costs

Direct costs	
Psychiatric hospital:	*Community:*
inpatient	community psychiatric nurse
outpatient	psychiatrist home visit
day patient	community mental health center
depot clinic	crisis house
emergency clinic	respite house
psychologist	drop-in
occupational therapy	day center
Indirect costs	
Accommodation:	*Law and order:*
supported residential care	police
private accommodation	probation service
Family health sevices:	court
GP	solicitor
GP home visit	legal aid
optician	prison
chiropodist	*Social services:*
gynecologist	field social worker
family planning clinic	field social worker home visit
nurse	home help
domiciliary nurse	meals on wheels
dentist	*Employment:*
General hospital:	job center
inpatient	job club
outpatient	disablement rehabilitation officer
day patient	careers advice
accident and emergency	*Others:*
physiotherapy	counsellor
dental services	security officer
	education course
Hidden costs	
Informal care:	
lost employment of friends and relatives	
lost leisure time of friends and relatives	
User time:	
travelling	
waiting	
Lost employment:	
time off work due to mental health problem	
foregone potential employment	
Lost production to economy	
Benefits:	
opportunity cost of welfare payments	

CASE STUDIES

Case management, and evaluations of case management, have primarily come from the United States (Weisbrod *et al.*, 1980; Franklin *et al.*, 1987; Meuller & Hopp, 1983). Possible replication of successful systems should clearly be explored. It may be the situation that particular idiosyncrasies of one mental health care system do not exist elsewhere entailing the need for "home-grown" projects. Case management systems in the UK have been developed and implemented, but have seldom undergone a full (clinical, social, and economic) evaluation. Case management may have superior outcomes to standard care but be economically inferior. This undermines their relevance. Other studies do include a costing process but this is not performed correctly. However, some projects and their associated evaluations are worthy of discussion.

THE MAUDSLEY DAILY LIVING PROGRAMME

The Daily Living Programme (DLP) in South London consisted of a multidisciplinary team offering intensive home-based support to users who would otherwise have been admitted to hospital. An evaluation of the project was undertaken and work continues (Marks *et al.*, 1988; Marks, 1992; Muijen *et al.*, 1992; Knapp *et al.*, 1994). The DLP operated about seven guiding principles: continuity of care, coordination of care by key-worker, crisis intervention, rehabilitation including skills training, support for families and others associated with clients, 24-hour care, and user advocacy.

The DLP was evaluated by randomizing a sample of clients requiring immediate inpatient care to either community care (the DLP) or to standard hospital care. The majority of users had a diagnosis of schizophrenia. The DLP team cared for users who went in to hospital and arranged for their discharge. Eighty-three percent of DLP users and 100% of the control required inpatient care at some stage during the following 18 months. However, the people on the DLP used only 20% of the bed days than the control. The service provided by the DLP team was deliberately intensive and involved employers, social workers, families, and the users themselves. The DLP and hospital care did not differ significantly on clinical or social outcomes. But DLP users and their relatives did prefer care in the community. Over the 18 months the DLP direct costs were 4% less than standard hospital care. The latter 5 months (i.e. after the start-up costs) saw a DLP saving of 25% over traditional therapy on these costs.

THE GREENWICH COMMUNITY SUPPORT TEAM

The Greenwich Community Support Team (CST) comprised 4 CPNs who provided an intensive support service for people with severe mental health problems who had been referred to the specialist psychiatric services. In addition, there were four mental health workers who supported clients in their daily living activities. Each member of the CST had case management responsibilities for a number of users. This departure from standard psychiatric care—routine outpatient consultations and time-limited involvement of CPNs—required a wider job specification for the CPNs and mental health workers. Duties and roles were performed which previously would have been carried out by other, albeit related, professionals, such as social workers, GPs, psychiatrists, home helps, or resettlement officers. The initial emphasis of the CST was to respond to the service needs of clients by providing a more intensive service where the CPN was acting as case manager and user advocate. Each CPN had a small caseload of about 10 clients. Tasks were often performed which were not traditionally CPN duties. The CST needed new skills, such as knowledge of bureaucracy, of social security benefits, and housing issues. Undertaking such a wide range of tasks was also seen as a way of building relationships with clients and their relatives. Nobody was discharged from the CST caseload. However, after 1 year, if they refused nursing input they were put on an "inactive" list but were offered services again at a later date if they were needed.

The support team was a departure from traditional models of CPN care and an evaluation was seen as important. As with the DLP there were found to be no significant differences in clinical and social outcomes (number of admissions, length of stay, psychopathology, social functioning, and client and family satisfaction) between people using the CST service and a control group receiving generic CPN care (Muijen *et al.*, 1994). The direct CPN costs for the control group were 25% of the CST cost during the first 6 months of the study period, 18% during the second 6 months, and 13% during the final 6 months (McCrone *et al.*, 1994). All of these differences were significant. Thus far it would appear that this form of case management costs more than traditional care and is no more effective. However, when comprehensive costs (both direct and indirect) are taken into account we see that over the 18 month study period the users of the generic service on average cost £110 more per week than did the users of the CST. However, the cost difference was only significant during the initial 6 months. In the short run this unidisciplinary case management system was more cost-effective than traditional care.

DAY TREATMENT IN THE NETHERLANDS

In the Netherlands, day treatment for people with schizophrenia, who would normally require admission, was compared with standard psychiatric hospital inpatient care (Wiersma *et al.*, 1991). The day treatment incorporated case management integrated with joint consultation between staff, and aftercare. Users of this new system did not experience gains in symptomatology, social role disabilities, or number of readmissions in the first follow-up year. The economic costs were also not found to be significantly different. However, only direct costs are reported.

OTHER PROJECTS AND EVALUATIONS

A hostel ward catering for new long-stay patients in the UK was evaluated with standard hospital care as a control (Hyde *et al.*, 1987). This project was not specifically case management dominated but some of the features were from the same genre. The management of clients was structured according to a rehabilitation program, which aimed to help clients to improve/maintain self-care and other social functions. If inpatient stays were required the clients were still considered to be in the "index" group. The residents on the hostel ward developed better domestic skills and used more community facilities. Costs were less for this form of care than for standard hospital care. The costs were measured relatively comprehensively. Another study examined multidisciplinary care delivered from a day hospital, with nurse therapists in effect taking the case management role (McLoughin, 1990). Only direct costs were mentioned. This was described "without doubt" as cost-effective. More analysis and evidence is required to make this claim.

A number of other case management projects have been developed, and evaluated. However, the process of evaluation, like mental health care itself, does absorb valuable resources. Consequently, many studies are not able to provide full economic, social, and clinical evaluations. The concept of economic efficiency is vital to grasp and many studies clearly recognize this even though we should not place great emphasis on all the findings presented in all such papers, Unfortunately, some evaluations could incorporate an economic component but choose not to, or do so in an inappropriate manner.

THE USE OF COST DATA

When economic costs are discussed in the arena of health care controversies often arise. This is sometimes understandable as costs can be quoted out of context and used by influential parties primarily for political reasons. However, we have seen that costs can be an effective way of indicating the amount of service input that an individual requires. It can be argued that it is as appropriate to report that a user used £300 of a day center's resources as to report that the user attended the day center for 2 weeks. The two figures are essentially giving the same information in different ways.

Once a package of services has undergone a comprehensive costing process it is vital to interpret and use the costs with wisdom. Merely looking at an average cost figure for the "average" user is not particularly fruitful. It is far more interesting and beneficial to examine cost variations. What factors cause the cost of the services used by one individual to deviate from the average cost? Using multivariate regression analyses we can develop cost functions which include cost as the dependent variable and an array of background characteristics, clinical features, and social factors as independent variables (Knapp, 1993). With careful construction it is possible to predict what the total service costs and also the component service (e.g. GP time) costs are for a given client. If a robust equation can be created from a representative sample of users we would have a very powerful planning tool. Clearly, the usefulness of such an approach is dependent upon the predictive power of the original equation (Goldberg, 1991).

CLIENT IDENTIFICATION, NEEDS ASSESSMENT, AND ECONOMIC EVALUATION

It is imperative that case managers know what population they are working with so that services can be developed accordingly. The need for information is paramount (Stevens & Raftery, 1992). Consequently, client identification is a major task of the case management system. Many users who previously received hospital-based care will now receive care from a new case management team. It is likely that most of the clients will be known to the team especially if they too were based in the hospital. However, it is felt that there are many individuals living in the community who have mental health problems and have not been in contact with the psychiatric services. Therefore, links should be forged between case managers and other professionals, such as GPs and social workers. Also liaison is important with the police, churches, and voluntary organizations. Case identification should be a coordinated, ongoing procedure. Once case identification has been completed it would be advantageous to group patients according to their needs so that resources may be directed towards them (Anthony, 1993; McCrone, 1994). However, to date this process has been limited to inpatient care in the form of diagnosis-related groups. These have not been able to predict the amount of resource utilization an inpatient has required (English *et al.*, 1986; Oydebode, 1990).

A mental health care system should aim to address the needs of the relevant user population, that has been identified in the community, rather than to be service led (Strathdee & Thornicroft, 1992). Since April 1993 local authorities in the UK have had the task of assessing the needs of their local population. One of the core tasks of case management is the assessment of needs; however, there is no clear consensus as to what the relevant needs of a user are or how they can be measured. Distinctions may be drawn between basic human needs and those that specifically relate to mental health problems (Holloway, 1991). There must be a pragmatic trade-off between totality and time if needs are to be assessed frequently. Those areas of need which are likely to have a major impact on the client's life should be assessed (such as accommodation, food, welfare benefits, social networks, etc.). It should be an essential part of the case manager's clinical work to have a knowledge of the client's needs so that services can be allocated accordingly.

Needs can be linked to service utilization and costs. Using the cost function approach it would be possible to have a range of "needs indicators" as independent variables in a regression equation with cost (whether total or component) as an independent variable. A more refined model would be to incorporate *changes* in such needs indicators into the equation and thus costs, needs, and outcomes would be combined to assess the efficiency of the service.

CONCLUSIONS

Case management is an innovative way of ensuring coordinated and continuing community care and can benefit service users (Holloway *et al.*, 1995). However, it requires much thought (and imagination) and certainly resources. The continued move towards effective community provision does require the redeployment of resources (Mahoney, 1992). Case management should not become an "empty phrase" (Holloway, 1991) but should be instrumental in formulating and implementing care programs that are flexible enough to address the needs of the clients. One often cited criticism of case management is that it has no clear definition. Should this not be considered to be an asset? Clients of mental health services are no less diverse than the general population and therefore heterogeneity is to be applauded as long as the diverse nature of services is as a result of needs.

It is important to ascertain the economic implications of any new case management project. The fact that resources are scarce has already been discussed. However, possible cost savings should not be the sole driving force behind the further development of case management. Costs need to linked with outcomes. In any case it is not clear that case management is a cheap option. The evaluation of the Greenwich CST discovered no long-term significant cost saving. In other areas of community care evaluation it has been discovered that improvements in outcome are associated with higher costs (Beecham *et al.*, 1991). Often only direct costs are examined. This may result in distorted findings. However, if joint plans are not formulated or desired then one agency may regard the costs to another agency with indifference. This attitude may unfortunately often be the reality, but it is doubtful that it benefits clients. With case management a variety of services are likely to be utilized and costs will be apportioned between different agencies.

With the emergence of the NHS internal market, self-governing trusts, and GP budget holders the emphasis on economic issues is likely to remain. However, even if parsimony was not being enforced by the government, economic efficiency and maximizing care from given resources should be pursued. Case management offers the opportunity for this to occur. However, if costs are to be calculated, and they should be, it is vital that they are calculated well and analyzed in their correct context.

If case management is to be an effective model of community care then certain things need to be achieved. Liaison between different professionals both within multidisciplinary teams and between teams and others needs to be enhanced (Brook, 1987; Stansfield, 1991). Members of teams need adequate training in skills which they would not necessarily use in their more traditional roles. Neither the Greenwich or DLP teams, for example, received such vital extra training.

This chapter has emphasized the desirability of economic evaluation in the area of case management. The future of case management can be guided by the results of careful economic evaluation, to ensure that its further development is both effective and cost-effective.

REFERENCES

Allen, C. and Beecham, J. (1993). Costing services: ideals and reality. In A. Netten and J. Beecham, eds, *Costing Community Care: Theory and Practice*, pp. 25–42. Aldershot: Ashgate.

Anthony, P., Elphick, M., and Lelliott, P. (1993). Casemix in psychiatry. *Psychiatric Bulletin*, **17**, 8–9.

Beecham, J., Knapp, M., and Fenyo, A. (1991). Costs, needs and outcomes. *Schizophrenia Bulletin*, **17**, 427–439.

Brook, S. (1987). Nursing and the social services: collaboration or conflict? *Social Work Today*, **May 18**, 12–13.

Challis, D., Chesterman, J., and Traske, K. (1993). Case management: costing the experiments. In A. Netten and J. Beecham, eds, *Costing Community Care: Theory and Practice*, pp. 143–161, Aldershot: Ashgate.

Department of Health (1991). *The Health of the Nation*. London: HMSO.

English, J.T., Sharfstein, S.S., Scherl, D.J., Astrachan, B., and Muszynski, I.L. (1986). Diagnosis-related groups and general hospital psychiatry: the APA study. *American Journal of Psychiatry*, **143**, 131–139.

Falloon, I.R.H. (1985). *Family Management of Schizophrenia: A Study of Clinical, Social, Family, and Economic Benefits*. Baltimore: Johns Hopkins University Press.

Franklin, J.L., Solovitz, B., Mason, M., Clemons, J.R., and Miller, G.E. (1987). An evaluation of case management. *American Journal of Public Health*, **77**, 674–678.

Goldberg, D. (1991). Cost-effectiveness studies in the treatment of schizophrenia: a review. *Social Psychiatry and Psychiatric Epidemiology*, **26**, 139–142.

Griffiths, R. (1988). *Community Care: An Agenda for Action*. London: HMSO.

Holloway, F. (1991). Case management for the mentally ill: looking at the evidence. *The International Journal of Social Psychiatry*, **37**, 2–13.

Holloway, F., McLean, E., and Robertson, J. (1991). Case management. *British Journal of Psychiatry*, **159**, 142–148.

Holloway, F., Oliver, N., Collins, T, Carson, J. (1995). Case management: a critical review of the outcome literature. *European Psychiatry*, **10**, 113–128.

Hoult, J., Rosen, A., and Reynolds, I. (1984). Community orientated treatment compared to psychiatric hospital orientated treatment. *Social Science and Medicine*, **18**, 1005–1010.

Hyde, C., Bridges, K., Goldberg, D., Lowson, K., Sterling, C., and Faragher, B. (1987). The evaluation of a hostel ward: a controlled study using modified cost–benefit analyses. *British Journal of Psychiatry*, **151**, 805–812.

Intagliata, J. (1982). Improving the quality of community care for the chronically mentally disabled: the role of case management. *Schizophrenia Bulletin*, **8**, 655–674.

Intagliata, J., Willer, B., and Egri, G. (1986). Role of the family in case management of the mentally ill. *Schizophrenia Bulletin*, **12**, 699–708.

Jackson, G., Gater, R., Goldberg, D., Tantam, D., Loftus, L., and Taylor, H. (1993). A new community mental health team based in primary care: a description of the service and its effect on service use in the first year. *British Journal of Psychiatry*, **162**, 375–384.

Kingdon, D. (1989). Mental health services: results of a survey of English district plans. *Psychiatric Bulletin*, **13**, 77–78.

Knapp, M. (1993). Principles of applied costs research. In A. Netten and J. Beecham, eds, *Costing Community Care: Theory and Practice*, pp. 61–72, Aldershot: Ashgate.

Knapp, M. and Beecham, J. (1990). Costing mental health services. *Psychological Medicine*, **20**, 893–908.

Knapp, M., Beecham, J., Koutsogeorgopoulou, V., Hallam, A., Fenyo, A., Marks, I.M, Connolly, J., Audini, B., Muijen, M. (1994). Service use and costs of home-based versus hospital-based care to people with serious mental illness. *British Journal of Psychiatry*, **165**, 195–203.

Knapp, M., McCrone, P., Drury, C., and Gould, E. (1993). Intermediate treatment: user characteristics and the prediction of costs. In A. Netten and J. Beecham, eds, *Costing Community Care: Theory and Practice*, pp. 178–195, Aldershot: Ashgate.

Leff, J. (1991). Evaluation of the closure of mental hospitals. In P. Hall and I. Brockington, eds, *The Closure of Mental Hospitals*, pp. 25–32. London: Gaskell.

Lehman, A.F. (1987). Capitation payment and mental health care: a review of the opportunities and risks. *Hospital and Community Psychiatry*, **38**, 31–38.

Lindow, V. (1993). A chance for change. *Nursing Times*, **March 24**, 33–34.

Lurie, N., Moscovice, I.S., Finch, M., Christianson, J.B., and Popkin, M.K. (1992). Does capitation affect the health of the chronically mentally ill? *Journal of the American Medical Association*, **267**, 3300–3304.

Mahoney, J. (1992). Resources available to develop mental health services. *Psychiatric Bulletin*, **16**, 490–492.

Marks, I. (1992). Innovations in mental health care delivery. *British Journal of Psychiatry*, **160**, 589–597.

Marks, I., Connolly, J., and Muijen, M. (1988). The Maudsley Daily Living Programme. *Psychiatric Bulletin*, **12**, 22–24.

McCrone, P. (1994). Allocating resources in psychiatric hospitals according to casemix. *Psychiatric Bulletin*, **18**, 212–213.

McCrone, P., Beecham, J., and Knapp, M. (1993). Community psychiatric nurses in a community support team: a cost evaluation of the Greenwich innovation. *Discussion Paper*, **794/2**. University of Kent at Canterbury: Personal Social Services Research Unit.

McCrone, P., Beecham, J., and Knapp, M. (1994). Community psychiatric nurses in an intensive community support team: cost-effectiveness comparisons with generic

CPN care. *British Journal of Psychiatry*, **165**, 218–221.

McLoughlin, M. (1990). Day care and a hostel—a cost effective approach. *Psychiatric Bulletin*, **14**, 203–205.

Melzer, D., Hale, A., Malik, S., *et al.* (1991). Community care and schizophrenia: one year after hospital discharge. *British Medical Journal*, **393**, 1023–1026.

Mental Health Foundation (1987). *Schizophrenia: A Briefing for all Those Concerned with the Treatment and Care of Schizophrenia.* London: Mental Health Foundation.

Mueller, J. and Hopp, M. (1983). A demonstration of the cost benefits of case management services for discharged mental patients. *Psychiatric Quarterly*, **55**, 17–24.

Muijen, M., Marks, I.M., Connolly, J., Audini, B., and McNamee, G. (1992). The Daily Living Programme: preliminary comparison of community versus hospital-based treatment for the seriously mentally ill facing emergency admission. *British Journal of Psychiatry*, **160**, 379–384.

Muijen, M., Cooney, M., Strathdee, G., Bell, R. and Hudson, A. (1994). A randomised controlled study of an intensive support CPN team versus generic CPN care for long term mentally ill patients in the Greenwich district. *British Journal of Psychiatry*, **165**, 211–217.

National Institute of Mental Health (1987). *Toward a Model Plan for a Comprehensive Community Based Mental Health System.* Washington, DC: NIMH.

Onyett, S. (1992). *Case Management in Mental Health.* London: Chapman and Hall.

Onyett, S., Tyrer, P., Connolly, J., *et al.* (1990). The Early Intervention Service: the first 18 months of an Inner London demonstration service. *Psychiatric Bulletin*, **14**, 267–269.

Oyebode, F., Cumella, S., Garden, G., and Binyon, S. (1990). Diagnosis-related groups: implications for psychiatry. *Psychiatric Bulletin*, **14**, 1–3.

Peck, E. and Cockburn, M. (1993). Comparative costs of adult acute psychiatric services. *Psychiatric Bulletin*, **17**, 79–81.

Renshaw, J. (1987). Care in the community: individual care planning and case management. *British Journal of Social Work*, **18** (Suppl.), 79–105.

Renshaw, J., Hampson, R., Thomason, C., Darton, R., Judge, K., and Knapp, M. (1988). *Care in the Community: The First Steps.* Aldershot: Ashgate.

Research and Development for Psychiatry (1991). *The RDP Case Management Project: Information Update.* London: Research and Development for Psychiatry.

Roberston, E., Knapp, M., Crank, D., and Wood, C. (1986). The comparative costs of intermediate treatment and its alternatives in Thameside. *Discussion Paper*, **374**, University of Kent at Canterbury: Personal Social Services Research Unit.

Sayce, L., Craig, T.K.J., and Boardman, A.P. (1991). The development of Community Mental Health Centres in the UK. *Social Psychiatry and Psychiatric Epidemiology*, **26**, 14–20.

Secretaries of State for Health, Wales, Northern Ireland, and Scotland (1989). *Working for Patients.* London: HMSO.

Stansfield, S. (1991). Attitudes to developments in community psychiatry among general practitioners. *Psychiatric Bulletin*, **15**, 542–543.

Steadman, P. (1992). Disability Living Allowance—how it affects psychiatrists. *Psychiatric Bulletin*, **16**, 349–350.

Stein, L.I. and Test, M.A. (1980). Alternative to mental hospital treatment: I. Conceptual model, treatment program, and clinical evaluation. *Archives of General Psychiatry*, **37**, 392–397.

Stevens, A. and Raftery, J. (1993). The purchasers' information requirements on mental health needs and contracting for mental services. In G. Thornicroft, C. Brewin, and J. Wing, eds, *Measuring Mental Health Needs*, pp. 42–61, London: Gaskell.

Stewart, G. (1988). Maintaining people with mental disabilities in the community. In S. Baldwin, G. Parker, and R. Walker, eds, *Social Security and Community Care*, pp. 93–112. Aldershot: Averbury.

Strathdee, G. and Thornicroft, G. (1992). Community sectors for needs-led mental health services. In G. Thornicroft, C. Brewin, and J. Wing, eds, *Measuring Mental Health Needs*, pp. 140–162, London: Gaskell.

Thornicroft, G. (1991). The concept of case management for long-term mental illness. *International Review of Psychiatry*, **3**, 125–132.

Thornicroft, G. (1993). Case management for the long-term mentally ill. In D. Bhugra and J. Leff, eds, *Principles of Social Psychiatry*, pp. 412–423, Oxford: Blackwell Scientific Publications.

Thornicroft, G. and Bebbington, P. (1989). Deinstitutionalisation—from hospital closure to service development. *British Journal of Psychiatry*, **155**, 739–753.

Thornicroft, G. and Breakey, W.R. (1991). The COSTAR progamme. 1: Improving social networks of the long-term mentally ill. *British Journal of Psychiatry*, **159**, 245–249.

Tyrer, P., Hawksworth, J., Hobbs, R., and Jackson, D. (1990). The role of the community psychiatric nurse. *British Journal of Hospital Medicine*, **43**, 439–443.

Weisbrod, B.A., Test, M.A., and Stein, L.I. (1980). Alternative to mental hospital treatment: II. Economic benefit–cost analysis. *Archives of General Psychiatry*, **37**, 400–405.

Wiesma, D., Kluiter, H., Nienhuis, F.J., Ruphan, M., and Giel, R. (1991). Costs and benefits of day treatment with community care for schizophrenic patients. *Schizophrenia Bulletin*, **17**, 411–419.

Wooff, K. and Goldberg, D.P. (1988). Further observations on the practice of community care in Salford: differences between community psychiatric nurses and mental health social workers. *British Journal of Psychiatry*, **153**, 30–37.

18

Economic Implications of Involuntary Treatment for Schizophrenia

BENTSON H. McFARLAND
Department of Psychiatry, Oregon Health Sciences University, Portland, Oregon, USA

INTRODUCTION

Persons having a diagnosis of schizophrenia are often involved with involuntary treatment. For example, in the United States individuals with a diagnosis of schizophrenia comprised some 43% of patients admitted involuntarily to psychiatric hospitals in 1980 (Rosenstein *et al.*, 1986). In contrast, people with schizophrenia make up only about 1% of the adult US population (Keith *et al.*, 1991; Kessler *et al.*, 1994) and represented only 29% of all patients admitted (voluntarily and involuntarily) to psychiatric hospitals during 1980 (Rosenstein *et al.*, 1986).

Given the substantial differences between the mental health system in the United States and those found in other countries (Segal, 1989; Appelbaum, 1994) the overrepresentation of people with schizophrenia among patients treated involuntarily may or may not be found worldwide. Nonetheless, involuntary treatment represents an important aspect of caring for people with schizophrenia (Torrey, 1994). Much of this chapter will focus on involuntary psychiatric treatment within the United States and its economic implications for people with schizophrenia.

A typology of involuntary treatment will be helpful (see Table 1). It is important to distinguish between civil (i.e., non-criminal) involuntary treatment and obligatory care provided to offenders involved with the criminal justice system. In the civil sector, there can be emergency treatment, inpatient civil commitment, and outpatient civil commitment (Faulkner *et al.*, 1986). Emergency involuntary treatment is typically initiated by police and/or physicians and often takes place in a local, general hospital. Civil commitment (in the United States) involves a judicial decision (i.e., by a judge) to commit a patient for involuntary treatment. Civilly committed patients can receive treatment at local, general hospitals; specialized, private sector psychiatric hospitals; state mental hospitals; or in outpatient programs.

The civil commitment system serves two purposes: to protect society from mentally ill people who are dangerous and to provide treatment for mentally ill people who decline to obtain care. At least in the United States, the relative emphasis on social control versus treatment provision has changed back and forth over the last few decades (Segal, 1989; LaFond & Durham, 1992). Generally speaking, though, civil commitment in the United States is usually reserved for people believed to be dangerous to themselves or

Handbook of Mental Health Economics and Health Policy, Volume I, Schizophrenia. Edited by M. Moscarelli, A. Rupp and N. Sartorius.
© 1996 John Wiley & Sons Ltd.

Table 1. Typology of involuntary treatment

	Treatment duration	Authorized by	Location
Civil (non-criminal)			
Emergency	Short-term	Police and/or physicians	General hospital
Inpatient commitment	Long-term	Judge	Psychiatric hospital
Outpatient commitment	Long-term	Judge	Outpatient
Criminal			
Jail	Short-term	Police	Jail
Prison	Long-term	Judge	Prison
Insanity acquittees/ incompetent for trial	Long-term	Judge	Psychiatic hospital, prison, and/or outpatient
Juvenile	Long-term	Judge	Juvenile facility
Probation/parole	Long-term	Judge	Outpatient

others by virtue of mental illness. In other countries civil commitment appears to be used for people who are in need of but decline to obtain mental health treatment (Segal, 1989). In any event, an important consideration is that treatment of the mentally ill patient is a component of civil commitment. An interesting feature of civil commitment in the United States is the right of involuntary patients to refuse psychotropic drug treatment (Schouten & Gutheil, 1990; Torrey, 1994).

The criminal justice system is also a significant provider of involuntary mental health service in the United States (Torrey *et al.*, 1992). For example, in some US jurisdictions mentally ill people can be detained in local community jails whether or not they are accused of committing crimes (Torrey *et al.*, 1992). In contrast with civil commitment, the overriding purpose of the criminal justice system is protection of society. Treatment, *per se*, of mental illness within the criminal justice system may be a low priority (Torrey *et al.*, 1992).

Persons with severe mental illnesses such as schizophrenia are overrepresented in local jail populations (Teplin, 1990) and in US prisons (Jemelka *et al.*, 1989; Keith *et al.*, 1991). Also, many states have special programs for persons with severe mental illness who have committed crimes and subsequently been adjudicated "not guilty by reason of insanity" (Bloom & Williams, 1994). Persons accused of crimes who are found unfit to stand trial due to mental illness may also be detained in criminal justice facilities—presumably while treatment takes place (Brown, 1992). It is reasonable to suppose that there are youths with schizophrenia involved in juvenile justice systems but little is known about this population (Burns *et al.*, 1992). Again, it is important to recognize that the criminal justice system may or may not provide mental health treatment, *per se*, to offenders with conditions such as schizophrenia (Torrey *et al.*, 1992). Treatment (e.g., medication) for mentally ill offenders can be provided involuntarily in some but not all parts of the United States (Torrey *et al.*, 1992).

The nature of involuntary treatment is also worth describing. Incarceration is the oldest form of obligatory "treatment." Obviously one can wonder what, if any, actual treatment is delivered to mentally ill inmates. Hospitalization is also a frequently used form of involuntary treatment. Presumably, both incarceration and hospitalization provide some protection for society at large and, perhaps, offer some protection to persons who are dangerous to themselves. Other aspects of involuntary treatment include use of psychotropic drugs. As noted, at least in some US jurisdictions involuntary patients have a right to refuse drug treatment. Table 1 provides a typology of involuntary treatment services.

More controversial, at least in the United States, are questions about the quality and effectiveness of involuntary treatment. Recall that involuntary treatment has the dual goals of protecting society and improving patients' health. Presumably these two dimensions are inter-related. For example, Torrey (1994) suggests that much of the violence attributable to persons with severe mental illness (e.g., schizophrenia) can be accounted for by untreated individuals. One might hypothesize that involuntary treatment could lead to reductions in violence. Whether or not this conjecture is true remains to be seen. Observational data from Sweden do suggest a causal relationship between psychiatric treatment of mentally disordered offenders and subsequent reduction in criminal activity (Belfrage, 1991).

A potential adverse effect of involuntary treatment is the development of antipathy between mental health care consumers and those providers who advocate obligatory treatment (McFarland, 1989). On the other hand, some surveys of mental health program clients show that consumers recognize the value of involuntary treatment (McFarland, 1989). Of course, consumers (or survivors) who have abandoned the mental health treatment system are unlikely to be represented in such surveys.

At least in the United States, involuntary treatment of schizophrenia is a large, costly yet poorly understood enterprise. This chapter will discuss the epidemiology of involuntary treatment in the United States and then address financial considerations.

EPIDEMIOLOGY OF INVOLUNTARY TREATMENT AND SCHIZOPHRENIA

In the United States, persons with schizophrenia appear to be greatly over-represented in all types of involuntary treatment programs. For example, in Shore *et al.*'s (1981) early study of acute involuntary patients in Oregon, persons with schizophrenia comprised 37% of the sample. Urrutia *et al.* (1987) found that 33% of their Tennessee sample was diagnosed as schizophrenic whereas for Segal *et al.* (1988a,b) the figure was 32% in California.

Table 2 gives demographic characteristics of acute involuntary non-criminal patients in Multnomah County (greater Portland), Oregon as well as analogous data from California, North Carolina, and Pennsylvania. Notice that the definitions of "involuntary clients" are not the same in all the states. For example, less than half (94 of 251) California emergency psychiatric patients are involuntary. Nonetheless, the California demographic data are so rich that the information is worth presenting. On the other hand, the North Carolina data pertain to civil commitment "candidates" who are held involuntarily prior to a court hearing. The Oregon data, in contrast, include individuals who had been detained involuntarily by police or physicians but were released prior to hearing (in addition to patients who went on to have a hearing). The Oregon data appear to correspond most closely to the Pennsylvania statistics. To summarize Table 2, the acute involuntary non-criminal population consists chiefly of younger, single men with diagnoses of schizophrenia and/or substance abuse.

Table 3 shows estimated point prevalences of schizophrenia in different US involuntary treatment systems. Although the data are incomplete it is clear from Table 3 that people with schizophrenia comprise a substantial fraction of individuals receiving involuntary treatment.

Some comments and caveats about Table 3 will be helpful. First, there is considerable missing data. For example, although outpatient commitment has been recommended strongly for some persons with schizophrenia (Torrey *et al.*, 1992) there is little quantitative information on the extent of its use (Torrey & Kaplan 1995). Similarly, few data are available about involuntary treatment in non-hospital settings such as residential facilities or shelter care (Segal & Kotler, 1989). As noted, at least in the United States little work has been done to date on the epidemiology of schizophrenia within the juvenile justice system. However, the US National Institute of Mental Health is now beginning a large research project on Utilization, Need, and Outcomes of Child and Adolescent Psychiatric Services (UNOCAP), which may address this issue. There is also little or no information available about the prevalence of schizophrenia among offenders on probation or parole.

A second concern about Table 3 is the validity of the data. Some of the citations are over a decade old but represent the most recent information available. In the last decade there have been substantial changes in the numbers of persons admitted to psychiatric facilities annually as well as a continuing decline in patients' lengths of stay. State and county mental hospitals continue to shrink. For example, a recent survey of 145 state mental hospitals located in 46 states (representing at least 70% of state hospital capacity nationwide) examined the facilities' 1992 censuses compared with that of 1991 (Backlar & McFarland, 1993, 1994). The survey showed that

Table 2. Demographics of acute involuntary non-criminal patients in several states

	Oregon(1)	California(2)	North Carolina(3)	Pennsylvania(4)
n (persons)	2092	251	727	39
Sex				
Male	52%	57%	57%	51%
Female	48%	43%	43%	49%
Age				
20–40	58%	60%[a]	56%	41%
Other	42%	40%	44%	59%
Race				
White	84%	68%	46%	44%
Other	16%	32%	54%	56%
Marital status				
Never married	50%	48%	51%	80%[b]
Other	50%	52%	49%	20%
Living arrangements				
Alone	44%	20%	?	?
Other	56%	80%	?	?
Employment				
None	63%	71%[c]	?	?
Other	37%	29%	?	?
Primary diagnoses				
Schizophrenia	30%[d]	32%	?	41%
Alcohol–Drugs	17%[d]	8%[e]	?	5%
Mania	11%[d]	10%	?	5%
Other	42%[d]	50%	?	49%
Reason				
n	1213[f]	94[g]	727	49
Danger to self	34%	60%	23%	44%
Danger to others	24%	49%	48%	28%
Disabled	42%	32%	30%	28%

(1) Multnomah County data taken from State of Oregon Mental Health and Developmental Disability Services Division reports of investigations 7/1/88 through 6/30/89.
(2) From Segal *et al.* (1988a, and b).
(3) From Hiday (1991).
(4) From Rothman and Dubin (1982).
(a) Ages 25–44.
(b) Includes divorced.
(c) Includes unemployed and disabled.
(d) Based on 2770 episodes.
(e) Acute organic or substance use disorder.
(f) Reasons for recommending court hearing.
(g) More than one reason permitted.

67% of the responding facilities had a lower 1992 census with the average reduction being about 4%. On the other hand since 1980 there has been dramatic growth in the numbers of general hospital psychiatric beds and private psychiatric hospital beds.

A current (i.e., 1990) estimate of the average daily census for psychiatric inpatients in the United States is about 232 000 with 90 000 in state mental hospitals; 62 000 in private psychiatric hospitals; 38 000 in general hospitals; and 42 000 in other facilities such as veterans' hospitals (Manderscheid & Sonnenschein, 1992; US Bureau of the Census, 1993). Based on methodology described by McFarland *et al.* (1990) one can estimate that about 56% of state mental hospital patients are involuntary compared with 9% of private psychiatric inpatients and 13% of general hospital psychiatric patients. No data are available for inpatients in other facilities.

Other difficulties with Table 3 include the need to extrapolate data from local studies or to use

Table 3. Schizophrenia prevalence in United States involuntary treatment systems

System	Annual involuntary Admissions	% with Schizophrenia	Average involuntary Census	% with Schizophrenia
Civil commitment				
Hospital				
General[a]	100 333	42%	2363	50%
Private psychiatric[a]	17 643	39%	1190	44%
State mental[a]	188 492	45%	77 897	77%
Outpatient	?	?	?	86%[b]
Criminal justice				
Jails	104 435[c]	5%[d]	426 479[e]	5%[d]
Prisons	316 215[e]	?	789 347[e]	5%[f]
Insanity acquittees/Incompetent for trial	31 611[a]	42%[a]	3494[a]	77%[a]
Juvenile justice	766 504[e]	?	96 148[e]	?
Pobation/parole	?	?	3 201 600[g]	?

(a) 1980 data from Rosentein *et al.* (1986) and Manderscheid and Barrett (1987) with prevalences calculated according to McFarland *et al.* (1990).
(b) 1988 estimate based on data from Hiday and Scheid-Cook (1991).
(c) 1991 data from US Bureau of the Census (1993).
(d) Estimate based on data summarized by Torrey *et al.* (1992).
(e) 1989 through 1991 data from US Bureau of the Census (1993).
(f) From Keith *et al.* (1991).
(g) 1990 data from US Bureau of the Census (1993).

approximate national figures. For example, the prevalence of schizophrenia among jail inmates derives from a number of local studies (see, for example, Teplin, 1990 as well as reviews by Steadman *et al.*, 1989 and by Torrey *et al.*, 1992). Similarly, crude national data suggest that about 77% of persons found not guilty by reason of insanity have diagnoses of schizophrenia (Rosenstein *et al.*, 1986) whereas a detailed study of Oregon's program for this population (the Oregon Psychiatric Security Review Board) found the corresponding figure to be 60% (Bloom & Williams, 1994).

These caveats notwithstanding, Table 3 suggests that in the United States there are substantial numbers of people with schizophrenia who are being treated involuntarily. In terms of civil commitment, adjusting the figures in Table 3 for population growth gives a rough 1993 point prevalence estimate of about 45 000 individuals with schizophrenia receiving involuntary, inpatient treatment. On the criminal justice side, the numbers are comparable with roughly 50 000 offenders having schizophrenia being involved in the corrections system during 1993. Of course, one can certainly wonder whether (and to what extent) people with schizophrenia in the criminal justice system are actually receiving treatment (voluntarily or otherwise).

It is useful to compare these rough point prevalence figures (45 000 civil and 50 000 criminal) to data on schizophrenia prevalence obtained from the Epidemiologic Catchment Area (Keith *et al.*, 1991) and National Comorbidity Study (Kessler *et al.*, 1994) projects. Both these epidemiologic studies estimated that there are about two million people in the United States with schizophrenia. In other words, at any given time about 2% of people in the United States with schizophrenia are receiving involuntary (civil) treatment while slightly more than 2% are under the jurisdiction of the criminal justice system. Looking at the entire adult (over age 18) population of the United States (about 180 million), some 61 000 people or 0.03% are receiving involuntary (civil) mental health treatment at any time while about 1.2 million or some 0.7% are under criminal justice confinement. The relative risk estimates are 67 and 3.6 respectively. In other words, viewed in isolation as a risk factor, schizophrenia elevates one's risk of civil commitment by a factor of about 67 while one's risk of criminal justice system incarceration is elevated by over threefold. This latter relative risk estimate is somewhat higher than earlier calculations pertaining to chronic mental illness and the criminal justice system (McFarland *et al.*, 1989).

Despite the magnitude of involuntary treatment in the United States, there have been surprisingly few longitudinal studies of this population (see, e.g., Gove & Fain, 1977). One of the earliest was by Shore *et al.* (1981). Those investigators followed a group of patients admitted involuntarily to a local general hospital in Portland, Oregon. The follow-up time was approximately one and a half years. As noted, some 37% of the subjects carried diagnoses of schizophrenia. Noteworthy findings were substantial mortality and morbidity in the cohort.

A longitudinal follow-up study of acute involuntary patients in rural Oregon was conducted by McFarland *et al.* (1993). Again, there were substantial numbers of subjects with schizophrenia (24%). Over a 6 year follow-up there was significantly elevated mortality (three times the expected figure).

Hiday (1991) and Hiday and Scheid-Cook (1989) have followed some 1200 subjects in North Carolina who had civil commitment hearings. Follow-up in that study was approximately 6 months after the initial incident. The North Carolina project found that involuntary patients had considerable involvement with the criminal justice system but often for relatively minor crimes.

These follow-up studies suggest that economic analyses of involuntary treatment for persons with schizophrenia will need to include examinations of health, mental health, and criminal justice service utilization. Wolff *et al.* (1991, 1995) provide a model for such a comprehensive cost finding methodology. While not addressing the issue of involuntary treatment *per se*, Wolff *et al.* (1991, 1995) did conduct a remarkably detailed cost analysis of 100 community mental health center clients, 75% of whom were diagnosed as having schizophrenia. These workers found initially that during the year 1988 the 100 clients incurred costs of 578 163 US dollars. Of this amount some 157 067 US dollars (27%) was due to involvement with the legal system. The majority of these legal costs were related to police contacts and/or arrests.

As noted, little is known about the financial aspects of involuntary treatment for schizophrenia. The limited economic work in this area will now be briefly summarized.

ECONOMIC ASPECTS OF INVOLUNTARY TREATMENT FOR SCHIZOPHRENIA

Indeed, given its importance for people with schizophrenia there have been surprisingly few studies on the financial aspects of involuntary treatment in the United States (Rubin, 1991). McFarland *et al.* (1990) performed a crude calculation which suggested that involuntary treatment as a whole in the United States cost some two billion dollars in 1980. Updating this figure to 1993 health care prices (i.e., a 254% increase based on figures from US Bureau of the Census, 1993) and adjusting for the prevalence of schizophrenia in the civil commitment system (calculated at 72% based on Table 3 and current numbers of involuntary inpatients as described above), one can estimate that the direct costs for involuntary (civil) treatment of schizophrenia are currently about 3.7 billion US dollars annually. It may be more useful to say that the direct costs of involuntary, civil treatment for schizophrenia represent about 0.4% of US direct health care expenditures in 1993 (US Bureau of the Census, 1993).

On the criminal justice side, Rice *et al.* (1990, 1992) provide a framework for estimating direct expenses for schizophrenia associated with the corrections system. Based on the prevalence data in Table 3, this figure is estimated to be about 2.2 billion US dollars in 1990 or some 3% of criminal justice expenses (US Bureau of the Census, 1993). Of course, one can wonder whether or not treatment is actually being provided to people with schizophrenia in criminal justice facilities.

Even though there are few detailed economic studies of involuntary treatment systems (Rubin, 1991) several questions arise pertaining to the clinical and financial aspects of involuntary care. Obviously, one can wonder about the extent to which involuntary treatment achieves its dual goals of providing health care to mentally ill persons and protecting society from potentially dangerous individuals (Hiday, 1988). As involuntary treatment is, by definition, an abrogation of civil liberties, one can also wonder if the same clinical ends could be attained by voluntary treatment. There are surprisingly few observational studies (Faulkner *et al.*, 1989) and very few randomized trials (Swartz, personal communication,

1993) in this area. Nonetheless, observational data (Shore *et al.*, 1981) do suggest that involuntary treatment is worthwhile.

Assuming, then, that there is clinical and social value to involuntary treatment (broadly defined), one can reasonably ask questions about the efficiency of various approaches to obligatory mental health care. There has been some work on the relative value of local (i.e., general hospital) involuntary treatment versus involuntary hospitalization in state mental hospitals.

Superficially, the state hospital would appear to be an attractive facility from the financial point of view. The charges at a state mental hospital are typically some 20–30% of those for a general hospital psychiatric unit. For example, in 1988 the charge at Oregon's state mental hospital was 110 US dollars per day, whereas the charges for inpatient psychiatric treatment at a local general hospital were approximately 500 US dollars per day (Governor's Commission, 1988). This difference in charges is not surprising given the different ratios of staff to patients at the two types of facility. For example, looking just at registered nurses national figures show that for state mental hospitals there are approximately 15 patients for every registered nurse, whereas for general hospitals there is roughly one patient for each registered nurse (Taube & Barrett, 1986).

Faulkner *et al.* (1989) and McFarland *et al.* (1990) took advantage of a "natural experiment" to examine the question of state versus local treatment for involuntary subjects some 76% of whom had major mental illnesses such as schizophrenia. These workers compared lengths of stay for involuntary patients treated locally in Oregon's second largest county with those of patients admitted to a state mental hospital. During 1983 a local "Mental Health Emergency Unit" provided the vast majority of involuntary treatment. Due to financial pressures, the local facility was only able to operate for a year. This situation created two cohorts of involuntary patients: (i) those treated at the state hospital before the local unit opened and after it closed plus (ii) locally treated persons who received involuntary care when the unit was open during 1983. All patients (in both cohorts) had been detained involuntarily because they were dangerous to self or others or were gravely disabled. In accordance with Oregon law, all patients in the cohorts were evaluated shortly after their detention by a mental health professional who determined whether or not the person should appear before a judge for a civil commitment hearing. This process is called a "precommitment investigation." Using methodology similar to that of Rappaport *et al.* (1987), Faulkner *et al.* compared the involuntary patients treated locally with those treated at the state hospital.

Faulkner *et al.* (1989) found that comparable subjects treated involuntarily in a local facility had much shorter lengths of stay than did individuals treated in a state mental hospital. Indeed, the difference in length of stay was sufficiently great that the local facility's total charges were actually less than those of the state hospital (McFarland *et al.*, 1990). Follow-up of the study subjects showed that both groups had comparable hospital and criminal justice recidivism (Faulkner *et al.*, manuscript, 1994).

In a detailed examination of the subjects' hospital utilization McFarland *et al.* (1990) found that involuntary patients treated in the local facility had much shorter lengths of stay than those treated at the state hospital even though the case mix was similar at both institutions. The demographic, diagnostic, and clinical characteristics of the two cohorts were virtually identical. However, locally treated patients were quickly returned to the community. In contrast, state hospital patients were detained longer and were more often civilly committed by a judge.

The Oregon data suggested that treatment in the local facility was less costly than involuntary state hospital admission provided the ratio of local to state hospital costs per diem was no greater than 4.6:1. The data implied that local facilities may well be more cost-effective than state hospitals for treating involuntary patients. While it was possible to follow subjects using administrative records, it was not possible to interview the subjects.

Similarly, a retrospective study by Santos *et al.* (1988) in South Carolina examined lengths of stay for involuntary patients in a "decentralized treatment program." The investigators found lower costs associated with use of a local facility versus use of a state hospital. The explanation was that locally treated patients were committed less often than state hospital patients. Moreover, the authors also noted "improvements in quality and continuity of local alternatives for psychiatric hospitalization" (Santos *et al.*, 1988). On the other hand, in the Santos *et al.* study subjects were not interviewed and there was no follow-up. It is unknown whether or not state and local patients in South Carolina were truly comparable.

Outpatient civil commitment has generated considerable interest (Torrey *et al.*, 1992; Torrey & Kaplan, 1995), but there has as yet been rather little economic research in this area. Fernandez and Nygard (1990) studied North Carolina's outpatient civil commitment system by examining state mental hospital usage before and after initiation of the involuntary outpatient treatment program. These workers found substantial decreases in both numbers of admissions and lengths of stay. However, in that observational study it was not possible to determine causality. It should also be noted that Fernandez and Nygard (1990) did not examine the financial aspects of the outpatient civil commitment program. Nor was the possibility that patients were "relocated" from hospitals to jails or prisons addressed in that study. In another North Carolina study, Hiday and Scheid-Cook (1991) suggested that outpatient commitment can improve compliance. Again, financial aspects of the program were not examined.

There has also been considerable attention to the economic implications of involuntary patients' right to refuse drug treatment. For example, Schouten and Gutheil (1990) studied psychiatric inpatients in Massachusetts who refused medications during 1986. These workers found that the state initiated more than five legal actions each working day to obtain judicial decisions about involuntary medication. In fewer than 1% of the cases was the patient's right to refuse medication upheld by the court. Schouten and Gutheil (1990) estimated that the "right to refuse treatment" cost the state at least 800 000 US dollars in 1986.

On the criminal justice side there is growing evidence that involuntary patients' dangerousness can be a nearly overwhelming factor in attempting to devise community-based alternatives to incarceration for mentally disordered offenders. For example, McFarland and Blair (1995) report that an intensive outpatient program aimed at severely mentally ill jail inmates appeared to have increased subjects' use of the state mental hospital. One possible explanation is that the close monitoring associated with intensive outpatient treatment leads to detection and reporting (to the judicial system) of violent acts that may otherwise be overlooked. Indeed, a key issue in the economic analysis of involuntary treatment systems is the need to weigh the greater costs of inpatient treatment against the greater protection for society afforded by institutionalization.

The issue of balance among individual liberty, treatment of mental illness, and protection for society is especially striking for persons found not guilty by reason of insanity. One of the few detailed financial analyses pertinent to this population has examined the Oregon Psychiatric Security Review Board (Bigelow *et al.*, 1990; Bloom & Williams, 1994; McFarland & Bigelow, 1994). The Psychiatric Security Review Board (PSRB) program is considered to be a model approach to dealing with the "criminally insane" population (some 60% of whom carry diagnoses of schizophrenia).

An interesting feature of the Oregon system (which is also found in other states) is the possibility of "conditional release" (Griffin *et al.*, 1991). Under this option, offenders found not guilty by reason of insanity (i.e., "acquittees") may leave the state mental hospital and live in the community provided they participate in closely supervised outpatient care. From the social perspective, inpatient treatment is more secure (i.e., offenders have a much lower rate of re-offending when they are hospitalized) but it is also much more expensive than conditional release (Bigelow *et al.* 1990; McFarland & Bigelow, 1994). Recently data have become available that can be used to begin calculations on the relative cost of "preventing" a felony (or misdemeanor) for hospitalized as opposed to conditionally released offenders.

For illustrative purposes we will limit our definition of costs to the state mental health agency's daily expenditures for the state hospital and for community conditional release "slots." Program (i.e., hospital versus conditional release) "effects" will be measured as the frequency of felonies (per acquittee per year) and the frequency of misdemeanors (per acquittee per year).

We wish to calculate the cost of a given reduction in felonies and misdemeanors for acquitees in hospital

Table 4. Persons, person-time, offenses, and rates for Oregon insanity acquittees

	Before* PSRB Jurisdiction	During PSRB Hosp	During PSRB Cond Rel	After† PSRB Jurisdiction
Events				
Persons	365	335	183	364
Person-years	4914	380	266	1538
Hospital-years	398	n/a	n/a	151
Risk-years	4516	380	266	1387
Misdemeanors—w/o	848	0	21	286
Misdemeanors—with	1010	0	21	286
Felonies—w/o	794	0	17	174
Felonies—with	997	0	17	174
Calculated average number of offenses per year at risk				
Misdemeanors—w/o	0.188	0	0.079	0.206
Misdemeanors—with	0.224	0	0.079	0.206
Felonies—w/o	0.176	0	0.064	0.125
Felonies—with	0.221	0	0.064	0.125

Data are from Bloom and Williams (1994).
PRSB = Oregon Psychiatric Security Review Board.
Hosp = hospitalization (forensic inpatient).
Cond Rel = conditional release (supervised outpatient).
* Adult (over age 18) years prior to PSRB jurisdiction.
† Years between termination of PRSB jurisdiction and end of study.
Risk-years = person-years minus hospital-years.
w/o = excludes PSRB crime.
with = includes PSRB crime.
n/a = not applicable.
Note: It is assumed that no misdemeanors or felonies were committed while in hospital during PSRB jurisdiction. Other qualifications about these data are found in Bloom and Williams (1994).

and for those on conditional release. To do so we will use three "baseline" figures: (i) based on the acquittee's adult (after age 18) years prior to PSRB jurisdiction excluding the crime leading to involvement with PSRB; (ii) based on the acquittee's adult years before PSRB but including the PSRB crime; and (iii) based on the time between the end of PSRB jurisdiction and the end of the study.

To perform these calculations we rely on the data in Table 4 which were derived from Bloom and Williams (1994). Table 4 shows person-time at risk plus the numbers of offenses committed by the acquittees during the several different time periods. Notice that the "before PSRB" time period and the "after PSRB" time period are adjusted for time the individual spends in hospital (and, therefore, is presumably at low risk of offending).

Based on data in the upper portion of Table 4, we then compute the average number of misdemeanors per person-year and the average number of felonies per person-year during the time periods: adult years prior to PSRB jurisdiction, hospital time during PSRB jurisdiction, conditional release time while under PSRB jurisdiction, and time from termination of Board jurisdiction to end of the study. Notice that the computations "before PSRB" are done both excluding and including the "index" crime leading to involvement with the PSRB. Also note that we have assumed no offenses are committed while the acquittee is in hospital under PSRB jurisdiction.

We next calculate the figures in Table 5. These numbers are the years of conditional release and the years of hospitalization, respectively, necessary to "prevent" one misdemeanor and one felony (calculated using the three baseline figures). These calculations are performed as follows. We assume that the number of offenses "prevented" by a year of PSRB jurisdiction is equal to the baseline rate of offending minus the rate of offending while under PSRB. For example, from Table 4 we have that hospitalization under PSRB "prevents" $0.188-0=0.188$ misdemeanors per year (using

Table 5. Numbers of jurisdiction-years and associated expenditures necessary to "prevent" one misdemeanor or felony

Baseline	Hospital	Conditional release
Misdemeanors		
Before—w/o*	5.32 ($180 603)	9.17 ($44 392)
Before—with†	4.46 ($151 408)	6.90 ($33 403)
After‡	4.85 ($164 648)	7.87 ($38 099)
Felonies		
Before—w/o*	5.68 ($192 825)	8.93 ($43 230)
Before—with†	4.52 ($153 445)	6.37 ($30 837)
After‡	8.00 ($271 584)	16.39 ($79 344)

Data from Bloom and Williams (1994) and McFarland and Bigelow (1994).
Expenditures are those assigned to the state mental health agency for the operation of forensic programs and are in 1987 US dollars.
* Adult years prior to PSRB jurisdiction excluding PSRB crime.
† Adult years prior to PSRB including PSRB crime.
‡ Years between termination of PSRB jurisdiction and end of study.
PSRB = Oregon Psychiatric Security Review Board.

Misdemeanor—w/o as the baseline). Similarly, conditional release under PSRB "prevents" 0.188 − 0.079 = 0.109 misdemeanors per year (again using "Misdemeanor—w/o" as the baseline). Now, taking the reciprocal of these figures we can say that 1/0.188 = 5.32 years of hospitalization are necessary to prevent one misdemeanor whereas 1/0.109 = 9.17 years of conditional release are required to prevent one misdemeanor. These figures are given in Table 5.

Finally, we can convert the years of hospitalization or conditional release into (1987) US dollars as shown in Table 5. Here we see that the costs to prevent one misdemeanor are $151 000–181 000 during the hospitalization period but only $33 000–44 000 during the time on conditional release. Regarding felonies, Table 5 shows that the figures are $31 000–79 000 to prevent one felony under conditional release versus $153 000 to $272 000 during hospitalization. The range in the figures is due to choosing different "baseline" estimates of the rate at which offenses are committed when not under PSRB jurisdiction. Table 6 gives the ratio of hospital to conditional release costs for misdemeanors and felonies, respectively.

Calculating the variances for the ratios given in Table 6 is fairly straightforward. The formula for the ratio (y) is

$$y = (\$33\,948/x_1)/\{\$4841/(x_1 - x_2)\} \quad (1)$$

Table 6. Ratio of hospital to conditional release expenditures to "prevent" one offense

Baseline	Misdemeanor	Felony
Before—w/o*	4.07 (2.77, 5.37)	4.46 (3.21, 5.71)
Before—with†	4.53 (3.44, 5.62)	4.98 (3.99, 5.97)
After‡	4.32 (3.11, 5.53)	3.42 (1.60, 5.24)

Data are from Bloom and Williams (1994) and McFarland and Bigelow (1994).
Calculations are based on 1987 state mental health agency forensic program expenditures.
* Adult years prior to PSRB jurisdiction excluding PSRB crime.
† Adult years prior to PSRB including PSRB crime.
‡ Years between termination of PSRB jurisdiction and end of study.
PSRB = Oregon Psychiatric Security Review Board.
Note: Figures in parentheses are the 95% confidence interval.

$$= \{7.01\,(x_1 - x_2)\}/x_1 \quad (2)$$
$$= 7.01\,\{1 - (x_2/x_1)\} \quad (3)$$

where: 7.01 is the ratio of hospital to conditional release yearly costs; x_1 = (offenses in baseline/risk-years of baseline); and x_2 = (offenses during conditional release/risk-years of conditional release). We have made the assumption that no offenses are committed while the subject is in hospital. Therefore,

$$\text{Variance of } y = (7.01^2)\,[\text{Variance of } \{1 - (x_2/x_1)\}] \quad (4)$$
$$= 49.14\,[\text{Variance of } (x_2/x_1)] \quad (5)$$
$$= 49.14\,\{[(\text{risk-years of baseline})/(\text{risk-years of conditional release})]^2\}\,[\text{Variance of } (z_2/z_1)] \quad (6)$$

where: z_1 = offenses in baseline, and z_2 = offenses during conditional release.

It is important to recognize that z_1 and z_2 might be correlated. As it happens, the sample correlation coefficients between the annualized rates of offending (baseline versus the period of time during PSRB jurisdiction) are not statistically significantly different from zero (see Table 7). Therefore, the variance of (z_2/z_1) is calculated according to Armitage and Berry (1987, p. 91). The quantities z_1 and z_2 are considered to be independent Poisson variables. Thus, the estimated variance of y is proportional to:

$$\{z_2/(z_1{}^2)\} + \{(z_2{}^2)/(z_1{}^3)\}$$

These considerations lead to the confidence intervals given in Table 6.

Table 7. Correlations between annualized offending rates (baseline versus during PSRB jurisdiction)

Baseline	n	Misdemeanor	Felony
Before—w/o*	179	0.049	0.069
Before—with†	179	0.040	0.007
After‡	176	−0.056	0.000

Data are from Bloom and Williams (personal communication, 1994).
* Adult years prior to PSRB jurisdiction excluding PSRB crime.
† Adult years prior to PSRB including PSRB crime.
‡ Years between termination of PSRB jurisdiction and end of study.
PSRB = Oregon Psychiatric Security Review Board.
Note: no correlation coefficient is statistically significant.

Obviously, these calculations are quite crude. We have access only to the state mental health agency expenditures for our cost figures. We are assuming that the PSRB program itself is responsible for the reduction in crime whereas other factors (e.g., the passage of time) could also be responsible. Our three baseline measures of crime frequency are helpful in dealing with this "regression to the mean" phenomenon and provide us with a range for the estimated cost-effectiveness of the PSRB program.

Therefore, we can say that, by these measures, conditional release is a cost-effective program when it is compared with hospitalization. Naturally, it must be understood that there is a trade-off here. While conditional release is cost-effective, it does not offer the public the guaranteed safety afforded by hospitalization. Conditional release does lower the rate of offending but does not lower the rate to zero. On the other hand, conditional release is much less expensive than hospitalization. Again, these calculations are presented as an example of approaches that can be taken to examine the economic aspects of involuntary treatment for schizophrenia.

CONCLUSIONS

Studies from the United States reviewed in this chapter show that individuals with schizophrenia are greatly over-represented in civil commitment programs and in criminal justice systems. While precise figures are not available, it does appear that obligatory treatment is a large and costly enterprise. Despite its importance for persons with schizophrenia there has been surprisingly little research on the economic aspects of involuntary treatment. Future work in this area will require at a minimum careful attention to resource utilization in both the mental health and the criminal justice sectors. Important issues to be addressed include the need to balance individual liberty with protection of society in an environment of fiscal restraint.

ACKNOWLEDGMENT

Supported in part by National Institute of Mental Health grants numbers MH R01 45015 and MH P50 43458.

REFERENCES

Appelbaum, P.S. (1994). Mental health law and ethics in transition: a report from Japan. *Hospital and Community Psychiatry*, **45**, 635–644.

Armitage, P. and Berry, G. (1987). *Statistical methods in medical research.* Boston: Blackwell.

Backlar, P. and McFarland, B.H. (1993). A national survey of ethics committees in state mental hospitals. *Healthcare Ethics Committee Forum*, **5**, 272–288.

Backlar, P. and McFarland, B.H. (1994). Ethics committees in state mental hospitals: a national survey. *Hospital and Community Psychiatry*, **45**, 576–580.

Belfrage, H. (1991). The crime preventive effect of psychiatric treatment on mentally disordered offenders in Sweden. *International Journal of Law and Psychiatry*, **14**, 237–243.

Bigelow, D.A., Bloom, J.D., and Williams, M.H. (1990). Costs of managing insanity acquitees under a Psychiatric Security Review Board system. *Hospital and Community Psychiatry*, **41**, 613–621.

Bloom, J.D. and Williams, M.H. (1994). *Management and Treatment of Insanity Acquitees: A Model for the 1990s.* Washington, DC: American Psychiatric Press, Inc.

Brown, D.R. (1992). A didactic group program for persons found unfit to stand trial. *Hospital and Community Psychiatry*, **43**, 732–733.

Burns, B.J., Angold, A., and Costello, E.J. (1992). Measuring child, adolescent, and family service use. In L. Bickman and D.J. Rog, eds, *Evaluating Mental Health Services for Children.* New Directions for Program Evaluation, No. 54, pp. 17–29. San Francisco: Jossey-Bass.

Faulkner, L.R., McFarland, B.H., Bloom, J.D., and Stern, T.O. (1986). A methodology for quantifying and comparing civil commitment processes. *American Journal of Psychiatry*, **143**, 744–750.

Faulkner, L.R., McFarland, B.H., and Bloom, J.D. (1989).

An empirical study of emergency commitment. *American Journal of Psychiatry,* **146**, 182–186.

Fernandez, G.A. and Nygard, S. (1990). Impact of involuntary outpatient commitment on the revolving-door syndrome in North Carolina. *Hospital and Community Psychiatry,* **41**, 1001–1004.

Gove, W.R. and Fain, T. (1977). Comparison of voluntary and committed psychiatric patients. *Archives of General Psychiatry,* **34**, 669–676.

Governor's Commission on Psychiatric Inpatient Services (1988). *Report to Governor Neil Goldschmidt on improving the quality of Oregon's psychiatric inpatient services.* Salem: Oregon Mental Health and Developmental Disability Services Division.

Griffin, P.A., Steadman, H.J., and Heilbrun, K. (1991). Designing conditional release systems for insanity acquitees. *Journal of Mental Health Administration,* **18**, 231–241.

Hiday, V.A. (1988). Civil commitment: a review of empirical research. *Behavioral Sciences & the Law,* **6**, 15–43.

Hiday, V.A. (1991). Arrest and incarceration of civil commitment candidates. *Hospital and Community Psychiatry,* **42**, 729–734.

Hiday, V.A. and Scheid-Cook, T.L. (1989). A follow-up of chronic patients committed to outpatient treatment. *Hospital and Community Psychiatry,* **40**, 52–59.

Hiday, V.A. and Scheid-Cook, T.L. (1991). Outpatient commitment for "revolving door" patients: compliance and treatment. *Journal of Nervous and Mental Disease,* **179**, 83–88.

Jemelka, R., Trupin, E., and Chiles, J.A. (1989). The mentally ill in prisons: a review. *Hospital and Community Psychiatry,* **40**, 481–485.

Keith, S.J., Regier, D.A., and Rae, D.S. (1991). Schizophrenic disorders. In L.N. Robins and D.A. Regier, eds, *Psychiatric Disorders in America: the Epidemiologic Catchment Area Study.* New York: Free Press.

Kessler, R.C., McGonagle, K.A., Zhao, S. Nelson, C.B., *et al.* (1994). Lifetime and 12-month prevalence of DSM-III-R psychiatric disorders in the United States. *Archives of General Psychiatry,* **51**, 8–19.

LaFond, J.Q. and Durham, M.L. (1992). *Back to the Asylum: The Future of Mental Health Law and Policy in the United States.* New York: Oxford University Press.

Manderscheid, R.W., and Barrett, S.A. (1987). *Mental Health United States, 1987.* DHHS Publication Number (ADM) 87–1518. Washington, DC: Superintendent of documents.

Manderscheid, R.W. and Sonnenschein, M.A. (1992). *Mental Health, United States, 1992.* DHHS Publication Number (SMA) 92-1942. Washington, DC: Superintendent of Documents.

McFarland, B.H. (1989). Overview of mental health services research. In J.D. Bloom, ed., *State-University Collabortion: the Oregon Experience.* New Directions for Mental Health Services, No. 44, pp. 55–63. San Francisco: Jossey-Bass.

McFarland, B.H. and Bigelow, D.A. (1994). Financial aspects of the Psychiatric Security Review Board. In J. Bloom and W.H. Williams, eds, *Management and Treatment of Insanity Acquitees: a Model for the 1990s,* pp. 191–202. Washington, DC: American Psychiatric Press.

McFarland, B.H. and Blair, G. (1995). Delivering comprehensive services to homeless mentally ill offenders: challenges for community programs. *Psychiatric Services,* **46**, 179–181.

McFarland, B.H., Faulkner, L.R., Bloom, J.D., Hallaux, R., and Bray, J.D. (1989). Chronic mental illness and the criminal justice system. *Hospital and Community Psychiatry,* **40**, 718–723.

McFarland, B.H., Faulkner, L.R., and Bloom, J.D. (1990). Predicting involuntary patients' length of stay. *Administration and Policy in Mental Health,* **17**, 139–149.

McFarland, B.H., Brunette, M., Steketee, K., Faulkner, L.R., and Bloom, J.D. (1993). Long-term follow-up of rural involuntary clients. *Journal of Mental Health Administration,* **20**, 46–57.

Rappaport, M., Goldman, H., Thornton, P., *et al.* (1987). A method for comparing two systems of acute 24-hour psychiatric care. *Hospital and Community Psychiatry,* **38**, 1091–1095.

Rice, D.P., Kelman, S., Miller, L.S., and Dunmeyer, S. (1990). *The Economic Costs of Alcohol and Drug Abuse and Mental Illness: 1985.* San Francisco, Ca: Institute for Health and Aging, University of California.

Rice, D.P., Kelman, S., Miller, L.S. (1992). The economic burden of mental illness. *Hospital and Community Psychiatry,* **43**, 1227–1232.

Rosenstein, M.J., Steadman, H.J., MacAskill, R.L., and Mandersheid, R.W. (1986). *Legal Status of Admissions to Three Inpatient Psychiatric Settings– US 1980.* Mental Health Statistical Note Number 178. National Institute of Mental Health, Rockville, Maryland.

Rothman, M. and Dubin, W.R. (1982). Patients released after psychiatric commitment evaluation: comparison with the committed. *Journal of Clinical Psychiatry,* **43**, 90–93.

Rubin, J. (1991). Economic aspects of law and psychiatry. *International Journal of Law and Psychiatry,* **14**, 299–304.

Santos, A.B., Thrasher, J.W., and Ballenger, J.C. (1988). Decentralized services for public hospital patients: a cost analysis. *Hospital and Community Psychiatry,* **34**, 827–829.

Schouten, R. and Gutheil, T.G. (1990) Aftermath of the Rogers decision: assessing the costs. *American Journal of Psychiatry,* **147**, 1348–1352.

Segal, S.P., Watson, M.A., Goldfinger, S.M., Averbuck, D.S. (1988a). Civil commitment in the psychiatric emergency room I. The assessment of dangerousness by emergency room clinicians. *Archives of General Psychiatry,* **45**, 748–752.

Segal, S.P., Watson, M.A., Goldfinger, S.M., and Averbuck, D.S. (1988b). Civil commitment in the psychiatric emergency room. II. Mental disorder indicators and three dangerousness criteria. *Archives of General Psychiatry*, **45**, 753–758.

Segal, S.P. (1989). Civil commitment standards and patient mix in England/Wales, Italy, and the United States. *American Journal of Psychiatry*, **146**, 187–193.

Segal, S.P. and Kotler P. (1989). Community residential care. In D.A. Rochefort, ed., *Handbook on Mental Health Policy in the United States*, pp. 237–265. New York: Greenwood Press.

Shore, J.H., Breakey, W., and Arvidson, B. (1981). Morbidity and mortality in the commitment process. *Archives of General Psychiatry*, **31**, 930–934.

Steadman, H.J., McCarty, D.W., Morrissey, J.P. (1989). *The Mentally Ill in Jail: Planning for Essential Services*. New York: Guildford Press.

Taube, C.A. and Barrett, S.A. (1986). *Mental Health, United States, 1985*. DHHS Publication Number (ADM) 86-1378. Rockville, Maryland: National Institute of Mental Health.

Teplin, L.A. (1990). The prevalence of severe mental disorder among male urban jail detainees: comparison with the Epidemiologic Catchment Area program. *American Journal of Public Health*, **80**, 663–669.

Torrey, E.F. (1994). Violent behavior by individuals with serious mental illness. *Hospital and Community Psychiatry*, **45**, 653–662.

Torrey, E.F., and Kaplan, R.J. (1995). A national survey of the use of outpatient commitment. *Psychiatric Services*, **46**, 778–784.

Torrey, E.F., Stieber, J., Ezekiel, J., Wolfe, S.M., Sharfstein, J., Noble, J.H., and Flynn, L.M. (1992). *Criminalizing the Seriously Mentally Ill*. Washington, DC: Public Citizen's Health Research Group and the National Alliance for the Mentally Ill.

Urrutia, G., Morrissey, J.A., and Matthews, J.G. (1987). Commitment patients in a private psychiatric hospital: a pilot program in Tennessee. *The Psychiatric Hospital*, **18**, 115–119.

US Bureau of the Census (1993). *Statistical Abstract of the United States: 1993*. Washington, DC: US Bureau of the Census.

Wolff, N., Helminiak, T., and Diamond, R. (1991). *Sharing Responsibilities for the Mentally Disordered: A Legal System and Mental Health Center Cost Profile*. Madison, Wisconsin: Mental Health Research Center Research Paper Series, 15.

Wolff, N., Helminiak, T., and Diamond, R. (1995). Estimated societal costs of assertive community mental health care. *Psychiatric Services*, **46**, 898–906.

19

Costs and Benefits of Vocational Programs for People with Serious Mental Illness

ROBIN E. CLARK
Department of Community and Family Medicine at Dartmouth Medical School and New Hampshire-Dartmouth Psychiatric Research Center, Hanover, New Hampshire, USA

GARY R. BOND
Department of Psychology, Indiana University–Purdue University at Indianapolis, USA

Exclusion from the workforce has long placed people with serious mental illness (SMI) at the margins of society. In the United States alone, lost productivity attributable to SMI exceeded 47 billion dollars during 1985 (Rice *et al.*, 1990). Increased workforce participation is the next logical step in the journey from the asylum to full citizenship for people with psychiatric disabilities. Unfortunately, our ability to help is limited by our knowledge of how to help and by lingering public skepticism about the effectiveness of vocational programs for people with SMI.

Is competitive employment a realistic goal for people with severe mental illness? Increasing numbers believe it is. Yet vocational programming for persons with SMI remains one of the least understood and most inadequately researched areas of mental health services. Conducting such research is not easy and, unlike other psychiatric rehabilitation domains, it has been difficult to show that vocational programs have an impact on employment (Bond, 1992).

Vocational services have been largely ignored by the mental health system in the United States (Tashjian *et al.*, 1989; Torrey *et al.*, 1990). This has meant that vocational services have not been well integrated into the mainstream of psychiatric services. Moreover, there has been substantial ambiguity about program models. Terminology is defined poorly and there is no accepted typology of programs. Credible research demonstrating the effectiveness of vocational programs has been lacking (Bond, 1992), but recent investigations of supported employment (SE), are promising.

In this chapter, we hope to lay a foundation for future cost-effectiveness studies of vocational programs to make more definitive judgments about their role in the treatment and rehabilitation of persons with SMI. We will first present a typology of vocational programs; then we will review several cost and benefit studies of vocational programs, emphasizing supported employment for people with SMI. Building on the preceding discussions, the third section identifies several problems in determining the cost-effectiveness of various interventions and suggests some possible remedies.

Handbook of Mental Health Economics and Health Policy, Volume I, Schizophrenia. Edited by M. Moscarelli, A. Rupp and N. Sartorius.
© 1996 John Wiley & Sons Ltd.

A TYPOLOGY OF VOCATIONAL APPROACHES

Of the many different vocational approaches for persons with SMI, some focus on specific aspects of the vocational process, whereas others are more comprehensive. No single schema adequately captures all the possible variations. Nor is terminology consistent within the literature. The typology shown in Table 1 offers a framework for discussing various models, their popularity, effectiveness, costs from the standpoint of the agency providing services, and suitability for different types of clients. Since the most recent reviews of the literature on the effectiveness of vocational programs for persons with SMI (Bond & Boyer, 1988; Dion & Anthony, 1987; Bond, 1992), several SE studies have been completed. Several popular models continue to have little evidence for program effectiveness.

Hard estimates of program costs are not feasible at this time, because of the lack of consensus on program models. Because of this, no comments are offered on the staffing patterns for these program models. A bachelor's degree is the typical requirement for most employment specialist positions. Similarly, there is little consensus about the requisite staff–client ratios, as would be needed to make sound budget estimates from an agency perspective.

1 Vocational counseling refers to office-based interactions between clients and professionals. It typically involves identification of client needs, development of a rehabilitation plan, and career selection (Anthony, 1980). Although widely used in the United States (e.g., by rehabilitation counselors in the vocational rehabilitation (VR) system), counseling alone is not associated with increased competitive employment rates (Vandergoot, 1986; Bond, 1992).

2 Skill training involves goal-setting, focused instructions, modeling, behavioral rehearsal, prompting, social reinforcement, corrective feedback, and homework (Mueser & Liberman, 1988). As applied to the vocational arena, skill training may focus on interviewing skills, job-finding skills (as discussed below, under the job club model), interpersonal skills, and job retention. Skill training groups are widely used in hospitals and community mental health centers (CMHCs). Although there are over 60 studies of skill training for persons with SMI (Dilk, 1994), none have developed and evaluated a comprehensive skill training approach for employment. At the very least, this approach is unproved with respect to employment outcomes.

3 Volunteer work experiences include unpaid work experiences and training activities in community settings. Volunteer work experiences are intended to provide a chance for persons to experience realistic job previews (Bond & Dietzen, 1993) and to gain confidence in their work abilities. The literature on this approach is anecdotal.

4 Unpaid prevocational work units involve work necessary for the operation of the agency providing the training (Beard *et al.*, 1982). Examples include kitchen crews, responsible for preparing a lunch meal; and maintenance crews, responsible for cleaning the building. The literature suggests that this approach is ineffective for helping clients obtain jobs (Bond, 1992) and a less desired option than SE (Bond *et al.*, 1995). It also has high dropout rates (Bell *et al.*, 1993). Nonetheless, prevocational work activities remain a popular vocational approach (Connors *et al.*, 1987; Tashjian *et al.*, 1989). One early study reported annual costs of $20 000 (in 1968 Canadian dollars) for a prevocational program serving about 25 clients a year (Symington & Lewis, 1973).

5 Sheltered workshops provide paid employment opportunities (usually paying subminimum wage) in protected settings, either on jobs subcontracted from industry, or manufacturing goods for sale (Carpenter & Black, 1986). Of the more than 5000 sheltered workshops operating in the United States today (Black, 1988), the large majority serve a mixed disability population, only a small proportion of which have psychiatric disabilities. Workshops have proven to be an ineffective means for attaining competitive employment (Black, 1988; Bond, 1992), and some clients with SMI viewed it as demeaning and stigmatizing (Estroff, 1981; Warner & Polak, 1993).

Even though agencies employing persons with disabilities receive federal and state subsidies and/or preferential treatment in bidding for contracts, workshop administrators face the dilemma that financial pressures of running a business sometimes conflict with clients' rehabilitation needs (Salkind, 1971; Black, 1988). From a business perspective, retaining productive workers in workshops is

Table 1. Typology and hypothesized characteristics of vocational approaches

(a) Dissemination and effectiveness

	Dissemination	Effectiveness in helping clients with: Paid work	Getting competitive jobs	Keeping jobs
Vocational counseling	Extensive	Poor	Poor	Poor
Skill training	Extensive	Poor	Poor	Poor
Volunteer work	Moderate	?	?	?
Unpaid prevocational	Extensive	Poor	Poor	Poor
Sheltered workshops	Extensive	Excellent	Poor	Poor
Paid work crews	Moderate	Excellent	?	?
Job club	Moderate	Excellent	Excellent	Unproven
Workplace interventions	New	?	?	?
Transitional employment	Extensive	Excellent	Unproven	Unproven
Supported employment	Growing	Promising	Promising	Promising
Train and place	Minimal	?	?	?
Clubhouse	Extensive	Variable	Variable	?
Psychosocial rehabilitation	Extensive	Variable	Variable	?
Community lodge	Moderate	Variable	Variable	?
Assertive Community Treatment	Extensive	Variable	Variable	Promising

(b) Costs from agency perspective

	Staff	Facilities	Running a business	Interacting with businesses (e.g., job development)
Vocational counseling	Minimal	Minimal	No	No
Skill training	Minimal	Minimal	No	No
Volunteer work	Minimal	Minimal	No	Yes
Unpaid prevocational	Moderate	Moderate	No	No
Sheltered workshops	Moderate	Extensive	Yes	Yes
Paid work crews	Moderate	Variable	Yes	Yes
Job club	Minimal	Minimal	No	No
Workplace interventions	?	Minimal	No	Yes
Transitional employment	Extensive	Minimal	No	Yes
Supported employment	Extensive	Minimal	No	Yes
Train and place	Extensive	Moderate	No	Yes
Clubhouse	Extensive	Extensive	Variable	Variable
Psychosocial rehabilitation	Extensive	Extensive	Variable	Variable
Community lodge	Moderate	Extensive	Variable	Variable
Assertive Community Treatment	Most extensive	Minimal	No	Variable

(c) Types of clients for which approach may be most suitable

Vocational counseling	Highly verbal clients with good work histories
Skill training	Same as above
Volunteer work	Clients with little work history seeking information about different types of work
Unpaid prevocational	Poor option for most clients; disliked by many clients
Sheltered workshops	Poor option for most clients; may be suitable for clients who function poorly in competitive settings
Paid work crews	May be suitable for clients who are fearful of competitive employment
Job club	Suitable for higher functioning clients who have good work histories
Workplace interventions	Not yet determined
Transitional employment	Requires willingness of client to take temporary jobs offered, which are often menial
Supported employment	Requires willingness of client to try competitive employment
Train and place	Must have aptitude in skill area being trained

advantageous, although from a rehabilitation perspective, productive workers are the best candidates for competitive employment.

6 Paid work crews include variety of paid work opportunities which rehabilitation agencies have a direct role in organizing. Paid in-house work crews are similar to unpaid work crew units, except that clients receive wages (e.g., Wilder, 1976). An enclave consists of a group of clients who work together in a factory or other business setting, typically trained and supervised by nonhandicapped workers (e.g., Bond, 1987). Marrone (1993) defines affirmative industries as "a business entity set up for the purpose of employing people with disabilities, usually subsidized heavily by rehabilitation or social services moneys." Typical examples include janitorial services and bakeries. In a national survey, Granger (1990) located 142 affirmative industries for persons with SMI, most operated by mental health agencies. Handyman work crews are organized efforts by agencies to get groups of clients together for day-labor, such as yard work or house repairs (Schultheis & Bond, 1993). None of these approaches have been studied systematically. The single exception is a recent controlled study showing favorable employment outcomes for a program operating several affirmative industries (Meisel *et al.*, 1993).

7 The job club is a behavioral approach developed by Azrin and Besalel (1979) to help unemployed persons systematically develop job leads, make telephone and in-person contacts, and to obtain jobs. Although some job club research has reported promising employment outcomes, it appears to work best with higher functioning clients (Jacobs *et al.*, 1992a). Jacobs *et al.* (1992a) report that the cost per placement in the job club is $400–$600.

8 Workplace interventions encompass two types of activities: Facilitating early return to work for workers who are newly disabled (Gates *et al.*, 1989), and workplace accommodations, which are changes to the work environment to enable persons with disabilities to perform job duties they otherwise could not. The Americans with Disabilities Act (ADA) of 1990 requires most employers to make "reasonable accommodations" for persons with disabilities, provided it does not cause the employer "undue hardship". The ultimate impact of the ADA on employment outcomes or on costs is not yet known. While accommodations could have the impact of increasing job tenure with the resulting benefits to employers of lower turnover (Fabian *et al.*, 1993), possibly even with most accommodations costing $500 or less (Mancuso, 1990), early studies have not calculated typical long-term costs such as increased supervision on an ongoing basis.

9 Transitional employment (TE) owes its origin to the Fountain House in New York. TE consists of work experiences for clients in normal places of business on a temporary basis. Placements are typically entry-level jobs, such as in food service, janitorial services, and messenger services (Beard *et al.*, 1982.

Rutman and Armstrong (1985) located 185 TE programs in the United States. Its proponents cite favorable employment rates, based on samples of clients who are active participants (e.g., Malamud & McCrory, 1988). The experimental evidence for its effectiveness is modest (Bond, 1992).

10 SE was first developed during the late 1970s as a more productive and self-enhancing alternative to sheltered approaches that were the major rehabilitation options available for persons with severe disabilities in the United States (Wehman & Moon, 1988). The Rehabilitation Amendment of 1986 with its 1992 revisions defines SE as including these features: clients are working for pay (preferably the prevailing wage rate), as regular employees (and in regular contact with nonhandicapped workers), and receiving ongoing support (i.e., two contacts per month). For persons with SMI, SE also usually includes: (i) minimal prevocational assessment and training; (ii) client involvement in the selection of jobs; (iii) staff assistance in helping clients find competitive employment; (iv) jobs viewed as permanent, although multiple job tryouts are acceptable. Although federal guidelines define three types of SE (individual placements, enclaves, and mobile work crews), individual placement appears to be the predominant model used with clients with SMI (Kregel *et al.*, 1989).

By 1991, SE programs in 2600 agencies were providing SE services to approximately 90 000 individuals (Revell *et al.*, 1994), a ninefold increase from a 1986 survey (Wehman & Melia, 1990). In various SE surveys, between 10 and 17% of the clients served have had psychiatric disabilities (NARF,

1989; Wehman & Melia, 1990). SE is an increasingly popular vocational approach in mental health case management programs (Toms-Barker *et al.*, 1993).

Of all the vocational approaches reviewed, SE has the most empirical support. Several recent studies (Bond *et al.*, 1995a; Gervey & Bedell, 1994; Meisel *et al.*, 1993; Drake, *et al.*, 1994) and several studies still in progress suggest that SE is a promising approach yielding consistently higher competitive employment rates, and longer retention rates, than approaches that depend heavily on VR services and prevocational preparation.

11 Train-and-place approaches offer systematic training for a specific technical field (e.g., word processing). In the 1980s a number of training programs were developed to prepare mental health consumers to be employed as case manager aides (Sherman & Porter, 1991). Of the 70 graduates of a Denver program, 62% were employed for at least 1 year (Warner & Polak, 1993). An Indiana project has estimated training costs of $8000 per trainee (Bond *et al.*, 1994).

12 Comprehensive approaches.

a The clubhouse model was first developed by Fountain House in 1948 (Beard *et al.*, 1982). Clubhouse activities are organized around a central meeting place. Clients attending clubhouses are referred to as "members". Clubhouses meet basic needs of affiliation and acceptance. Fountain House developed the concept of the "work-ordered day" in which members are expected to be involved in productive activity necessary for the operation of the clubhouse. Since 1976, Fountain House has been active in promulgating the model throughout the world, with a network of over 200 clubhouses (Propst, 1992). A single study, now three decades old, offers the only experimental evidence on the effectiveness of the clubhouse model (Beard *et al.*, 1963). This study suggested that participation in the Fountain House program reduced hospital use, but had no impact on employment.

b Psychosocial rehabilitation (PSR) centers include a substantial number of agencies sharing some, but not all, of the clubhouse assumptions. One such program is Thresholds, located in Chicago. Thresholds differs from Fountain House by including psychiatric services within the agency, and it has expanded its vocational program to include SE and numerous vocational options (Cook & Hoffschmidt, 1993).

Many of the comments regarding the lack of data on program effectiveness for clubhouses also apply to PSR centers. The Dincin and Witheridge (1982) study showing significant impact in the areas of hospitalization and independent living (but not employment) remains the only rigorously controlled study to date comparing PSR to regular mental health services. Black (1988) reported a 1984 cost analysis of an Indiana PSR program estimating a per diem rate of $25, or less than half the cost of visit to an outpatient clinic.

c The community lodge was developed by Fairweather *et al.* (1969) in an early deinstitutionalization effort. It involved the formation of cohesive groups of psychiatric inpatients who were then discharged to group homes. The lodge is intended to be a self-contained and self-governing society in which members live, work, and socialize together. The initial lodges had client-run businesses.

As state hospitals became depopulated, the original lodge process was rendered obsolete. The lodge concept has survived, however, with over 100 lodges nationwide (Fergus & Balzell, 1990). Little research has been done on the lodge model since the original study (Fairweather *et al.*, 1969), which showed a substantial cost advantage to the lodge, as compared with inpatient treatment. The original expectation that lodges would become financially independent through income generated by their businesses has not been realized (Black, 1988).

d Assertive community treatment (ACT) is a comprehensive treatment and rehabilitation approach emphasizing assertive outreach, attention to details of everyday living, and frequent contact, usually in community settings, not agency offices (Test, 1992). First developed in Madison, Wisconsin, in the 1970s (Stein & Test, 1985), ACT has spread throughout the United States, especially in the Midwest, where Michigan has 86 ACT teams serving 3500 clients (Plum & Lawther, 1992). Programs based on the ACT model are found in 26 states ("Health Reform," 1993). States attempting to integrate vocational services with their ACT teams are Wisconsin, Rhode Island (Detrick, 1991), and Delaware (Kirszner *et al.*, 1991). Most ACT programs, however, have departed from the Madison model by having little focus on employment issues. Budget considerations have often driven the decision not to include employment specialists on ACT teams (Bond, 1991).

OTHER VOCATIONAL APPROACHES

Although the above listing is a relatively comprehensive typology of approaches used in the United States, it does not reflect the philosophy in other countries. In most of Europe, federal laws require businesses to hire persons with handicaps (Black, 1988). Black (1988) contrasted the American and European attitudes toward disabilities; the American attitude has been to attend to individual needs and to help the person with a disability adjust to the community, whereas in Europe, employment is seen as a right, with the goal of rehabilitation to help clients find their niche.

STUDIES WITH COST AND BENEFIT ESTIMATES

We searched the literature for studies that met the following criteria: (i) vocational programs, or comprehensive programs with an explicit vocational focus; (ii) programs serving exclusively persons with SMI, or study presented separate statistics for this subgroup; (iii) study conducted since 1975; (iv) costs and benefits reported. Cost–benefit analyses conducted before 1975 were excluded because mental health services have changed to the extent to render these earlier studies obsolete (e.g. Fairweather *et al.*, 1969). We found eight studies meeting our criteria, five of which focused on specific vocational programs (Nichols, 1989; Noble, 1991; Bond *et al.*, 1995b; Meisel *et al.*, 1993; Rogers *et al.*, 1995) and three which evaluated comprehensive programs (Weisbrod *et al.*, 1980; Mulder, 1982; Bond, 1984). As can be seen in Table 2, all of the studies fall short on several criteria for an ideal study.

STUDIES OF VOCATIONAL PROGRAMS

Bond *et al.* (1995b) compared 74 clients randomly assigned to either gradual entry into SE (a minimum of 4 months in prevocational preparation prior to eligibility for SE) to accelerated entry (immediate entry into SE services). Costs included the SE program and mental health treatment (partial hospitalization, social club, clubhouse, psychiatrist, outpatient, substance abuse, education, and medication clinic). Although hospitalization costs were not included in the analysis, the mean number of days hospitalized was similar (5.8 days for accelerated and 5.3 days for gradual). The mean annual per-client cost was $6176 for accelerated clients and $8474 for gradual clients, with decreased costs of mental health treatment offsetting costs of the SE program for the accelerated group. Mean annual per client earnings were $1525 for accelerated clients and $574 for gradual clients.

Meisel *et al.* (1993) have reported preliminary findings for three demonstration projects in California. The intent of these projects is to create new treatment teams, based loosely on the ACT model. Two of the projects have had little impact on employment. Of interest in this review is the remaining site, known as the Village, where program staff developed an extensive array of employment options, using a mixed strategy described as "transitional work sites and employment opportunities (a cafe and catering service, a mini-mart, a bank, a janitorial service, and clerical positions)" (p.v.). During the second year of the project, the program staff shifted to spending more time to finding job placements in the community. Altogether, 40% of all direct service staff time was devoted to client vocational goals.

Table 2. Cost studies of vocational programs for persons with SMI

Study	Program type	New program	Design	Sample size	Follow-up period	Study dates	Economic assumptions/methods: Alternative program costs	Future earnings estimated?	Cost estimation sources	Accounting framework
Vocational program evaluations										
Bond *et al.* (1995b)	SE	Yes	Exp.	E = 38 C = 35	12 months (fixed)	1989–91	Control group	No	Agency Records	Limited
Meisel *et al.* (1993)	Affirm Ind. and SE	Yes	Exp.	E = 102 C = 101	21 months (fixed)	1990–92	Ignored	No records?	Agency	Limited
Nichols (1989)	SE	Yes	Post only	25	21 months (var.)	1985–87	Ignored	No	Agency Records	Limited to vocational program
Noble (1991)	SE	Yes	Post only	250 + 50	26 months (var.)	1988–90	Hypothetical	No	Agency	Vocational program only
	TE	No	Post only	27	26 months (var.)	1988–90	Hypothetical	Yes	Agency Complete	Moderately
Rogers *et al.* (1995)	SE	Yes	Pre-Post	19	12 months (fixed)	1990–?	Pre-study	No	Agency/self-report	Moderately complete
Evaluations of comprehensive programs										
Bond (1984)	PSR (mainly prevoc)	No	Exp.	93	12 months (fixed)	1975–77	Control	No	Retrospective	Limited
Mulder (1982)	ACT	Yes	Exp.	E = 59 C = 62	30 months (var.)	1979–82	Control group	No	Multiple	Comprehensive
Weisbrod *et al.* (1980)	ACT	Yes	Exp.	E = 65 C = 65	12 months (fixed)	1972–74	Control group	No	Multiple	Comprehensive

Exp. = experimental; Post only = only follow up data analyzed; Pre-Post = variables measured before and after the intervention

A total of 203 clients were randomly assigned to the Village or to a control group receiving usual mental health services. During the second study period, 52% of Village clients and 7% of controls were employed. Of the 52 Village clients who were working, 20 were competitively employed, and 44% of wages earned were from competitive employment. The Village had no negative impact on mental health outcomes (e.g., hospital rates, self-esteem, symptomatology, independent living, etc.), as compared with the control group or to the other two demonstration programs.

The cost analysis for this study was done in two parts, a cost comparison limited to the vocational component, and a cost–benefit analysis for the total treatment/rehabilitation program, from a state and county budget perspective. For the second study period (of 9 months), the mean annualized cost for vocational services was $4893 for Village clients and $351 for controls. Revenue generated by the agency-businesses was not factored in. Within this limited comparison and time frame, the Village clearly had an unfavorable benefit–cost ratio.

Nichols (1989) conducted a rudimentary cost analysis in an early SE demonstration project. Unit costs were derived from expenditures for staff (job developer and job coaches), staff training, vocational evaluation, work adjustment, and administrative overhead. These unit costs were then used to calculate per-client cost, based on actual service utilization during the time clients participated in the program. Over an average of 53.4 weeks, mean per-client costs were $575 for vocational evaluation and work adjustment, $1568 for job development and administration, $1036 for job coaching, and $980 for a support group, for a per-client average of $4663 in program costs. During this time, the average per-client earnings were $1979.

This study had several weaknesses. Unfortunately, Nichols did not attempt to estimate the costs of mental health services before or after admission to the program. Because all of the clients had been referred by a CMHC, it is likely that some had a reduction in use of the CMHC's day treatment program. Second, because this was a demonstration project, it is possible that the clients were atypical. Although none were employed at the time of program admission, it is possible that the CMHC referred clients they thought were most likely to succeed. A third weakness was that the program costs were based on the demonstration grant budget, which may not have identified all program costs (e.g., costs for office space were not built into the budget).

Noble (1991) examined costs and benefits for clients served by 45 newly funded SE projects in New York state. His sample consisted of clients with a range of disabilities, including 76 persons with "non-psychotic" mental illness, 250 with "psychotic" mental illness, and 27 clients with mental illness receiving TE from clubhouses. Noble based his analysis on unaudited financial reports. His accounting framework included SE program costs, "alternative program" (AP) placement costs, earnings from employment, and intangible benefits. (For TE participants, the program costs included all clubhouse services including TE.) The AP placement costs were calculated from either the day treatment program in which the client was enrolled before starting SE or, when these data were not available, a program the client otherwise may have entered had SE not been available. Intangible benefits included measures of psychosocial functioning, social integration, and the impact on the family.

The benefit–cost ratios for SE participants were 0.51 for clients with nonpsychotic mental illness and 0.75 for clients with psychotic mental illness. Intangible benefits did not change pre- and postprogram admission. Between 55 and 65% of the monetary benefits for SE was attributable to the avoidance of AP placements. Noble speculated that one reason for the unfavorable benefit–cost ratio may have been the lack of fidelity in implementing the SE program model, suggested by substantial costs for preplacement assessment and training, even though these activities are expressly avoided in the SE model (Wehman, 1986).

Using similar assumptions as for the SE sample, Noble found a benefit–cost ratio of 0.62 for the TE sample. He subsequently recalculated the benefit–cost ratio making assumptions about future earnings. Based on information supplied by the TE program, he estimated that 20% of clients achieve independent employment after completing the TE program. He also optimistically assumed that once permanently employed, these clients would continue in independent employment until retirement age. Under these assumptions, the benefit–cost ratio for TE clients was 6.5.

Rogers, *et al.* (1995) evaluated a university-based SE program. The investigators compared data collected retrospectively for the year prior to enrollment in the SE program to a period of at least 1 year postenrollment. Costs and benefits were calculated from the societal, participant, and taxpayer perspectives. The per-client program cost was \$7128, compared with \$6335 in benefits (\$1846 in earnings and \$4489 in reduced use of alternative programs), yielding a benefit–cost ratio of 0.89.

STUDIES OF COMPREHENSIVE PROGRAMS

In a secondary analysis, Bond (1984) conducted a rudimentary cost study of Dincin and Witheridge's (1982) controlled study comparing clients admitted to Thresholds, a comprehensive PSR center, or to a social club providing no vocational services. At the time of the study, Thresholds offered a continuum of vocational services, including unpaid work units and TE. Considering the costs of inpatient care and the experimental and control group programs, Bond (1984) estimated that the per-client treatment costs for Thresholds clients (\$6512) to be \$2500 less than for control (\$8999). However, each Thresholds client averaged \$154 in wages over this period, compared with \$371 for each control client, a comparison that actually significantly favored controls.

Weisbrod *et al.* (1980) compared costs and benefits for randomly assigned groups of ACT clients and controls receiving existing community services. Using a comprehensive accounting framework, the investigators found that the average per-client costs for ACT clients (\$7296) were slightly higher than for controls (\$8093), but that when mean per-client earnings from employment were also considered (\$2364 for ACT; \$1168 for controls), that the net difference (benefits–costs) slightly favored ACT (−\$5729 versus −\$6128).

Mulder's (1982) controlled study of a Michigan ACT program examined costs from mental health treatment, social services, and criminal justice, comparing them with earnings from competitive and sheltered employment. The annual mean per-client estimates for costs were \$8924 for ACT and \$8120 for controls, while the benefits were \$2762 for ACT and \$2225 for controls. Comparing mental treatment costs for the earlier 18-month analysis to the 30-month analysis, Mulder found a decline in annual per-client costs from \$8924 to \$6470 in ACT. The decline for controls was from \$8129 to \$7600.

All three evaluations of comprehensive programs suffer the same drawback: it is difficult to know how much of the costs to attribute to the treatment program and how much to attribute to the vocational intervention. A related problem is identifying the exact nature of the vocational effort in each of these studies. In the Thresholds study, most of the clients received prevocational training and no other vocational assistance (e.g., TE). In both ACT studies, the vocational strategies were still evolving. None of these studies measured intensity of vocational services.

STUDIES REPORTING COST OFFSETS

A study by Drake *et al.* (1994), offers information on "cost offsets" from vocational programs. They compared 183 clients enrolled in two partial hospitalization programs, one of which converted its services over to SE, and the other which continued to offer day treatment and to use traditional brokered VR services to assist clients seeking employment. In the program converting to SE, the rate of competitive employment increased from 25 to 39% over a year's time. Results were especially favorable for regular attendees, whose rate of employment increased from 33 to 56%. By contrast, in the partial hospitalization program not converting to SE, employment rates did not change for either the total group (13% in the baseline year and 13% during the study year) or its regular attendees (14% during the baseline year and 8% during the study year). No negative outcomes (e.g., increased hospitalization, incarceration, homelessness, dropouts) were detected for the program converting to SE. This report is the only published study describing specific outcomes from converting from day treatment to SE. A cost-effectiveness analysis focusing on the 58 study participants who were frequent users of day treatment before conversion to SE showed a trend toward lower costs at both sites after the change (Clark *et al*, in press). Although the trend was not statistically significant, the study demonstrated that vocational outcomes can be improved significantly without increasing costs.

The issue of cost offset has not been examined extensively, although it is intuitively plausible. Clients who are working during the day typically have less time available to attend day treatment programs. Therefore, programs accelerating the process of linking clients to community jobs will reduce utilization of prevocational programs (e.g., Bond & Dincin, 1986). The costs associated with placement and follow-up in theory may be recouped by reduced staff of prevocational programs.

DETERMINING THE COST-EFFECTIVENESS OF VOCATIONAL PROGRAMS

As we have seen, there are a variety of vocational programs and services that people with SMI may use. Each approach has it own unique features that determine its cost and its effectiveness. In this section, we will discuss some important considerations for assessing the cost-effectiveness of vocational interventions with particular emphasis on SE models.

Although the focus is on SE, the issues we will address are also important for other forms of vocational rehabilitation. Specifically, we will discuss different views of vocational rehabilitation and their implications for measuring effectiveness, the importance of perspective in measuring costs and benefits, and several problems that researchers have encountered in analyzing the costs and benefits of SE for people with serious mental illnesses.

THE OBJECTIVES OF VOCATIONAL REHABILITATION: TREATMENT OR EMPLOYMENT?

To the casual observer, the purpose of vocational rehabiliation is clear: to help clients get jobs. Given this goal, the most obvious performance measures of vocational programs are the number of participants getting jobs, the number of hours they work, and their earnings from employment. Without doubt, such measures are critical outcomes for most vocational programs; but people with mental illness, their families, or their service providers may emphasize other outcomes as well. Clients may value enhanced feelings of self-esteem and increased social interaction; families may cite their relatives' increased independence or lower caregiving demands; and, service providers may focus on the therapeutic aspects of vocational programs. None of these outcomes are clearly reflected in earnings or in hours of competitive employment.

It is theoretically possible for a program to perform poorly at helping clients get jobs, but to succeed in improving participants' self-esteem, social skills and general functioning. Such a program could also reduce use of other, more expensive, treatment services. An evaluation that focused only on the program's ability to help participants get competitive jobs would probably consider it a failure. But an assessment based on other client benefits might consider the program both effective and efficient.

Admittedly, the scenario above is somewhat implausible. Most people believe that gainful employment, rather than vocational service by itself, produces positive benefits for participants. Still, it illustrates the importance of defining expectations clearly. If the goal of an economic analysis is to provide information that helps policy-makers make informed choices, it is important to include all relevant outcomes, including nonmonetary ones.

Different emphases on the outcomes of vocational rehabilitation programs also suggest different forms of economic analysis. Earnings from employment and program savings are easily measured in dollars and lend themselves well to a cost–benefit analysis. Because both costs and benefits are measured in dollars, a cost–benefit analysis has certain apparent advantages over a cost-effectiveness analysis in which benefits may be measured in any of a number of units. A single net benefit (total benefits minus total costs), benefit–cost ratio (benefits divided by costs), or rate of return (percent of costs returned in a given period) can be calculated in a cost–benefit analysis. A cost-effectiveness analysis typically yields more than one ratio of costs to benefits, which can make it difficult to draw clear conclusions for policy purposes. Although cost–utility analytical techniques consolidate multiple effectiveness measures in a single unit (Kamlet, 1992), the resulting policy conclusions still may not be as unambiguous as those produced by a net benefit or average net benefit figure. On the other hand, the difficulty of measuring some benefits in dollars means that they are often left out of cost–benefit comparisons. What is gained in apparent analytical clarity may be lost in a failure to account comprehensively for all relevant benefits. Ultimately, evaluators and policy-makers must decide which type of analysis is most useful for their purposes. In part, this depends on whether they view vocational rehabilitation as a jobs program, an alternative form of treatment, or some combination of the two.

COSTS AND BENEFITS TO WHOM?

Critical for any economic analysis is the point of view from which costs and benefits are measured. Unlike natural phenomena, costs and benefits are identifiable only within the context of a given perspective. Conley and Noble (1990) suggested four perspectives for measuring the costs and benefits of a supported employment program for a heterogeneous group of people with severe disabilities: individuals/families, employers/private sector, government, and society. Other perspectives for consideration might include taxpayers, county or state mental health agencies, and service providers. Each of these perspectives represents a group with an important, but very different, stake in the success of a given vocational program. To illustrate, increased individual earnings benefit individuals directly but have little direct impact on service providers or on state mental health agencies. And from a societal perspective, decreases in income support payments (e.g. Supplemental Security Income, SSI or Social Security Disability Insurance, SSDI, in the United States), that may result from increased earnings are of no consequence, as they do not represent societal costs, but simply are transfers of money from one group to another. Obviously, decreases in such payments *do* affect federal spending and, therefore, are a benefit from the perspectives of the governmental unit issuing such payments and from that of taxpayers. Given these and other differences in how economic events are viewed, it is essential to know whose perspective guides a particular cost analysis.

Deciding whether to count an economic change as a cost, as a benefit, or to leave it out of the analysis altogether is not always an easy decision. For example, the prevailing standard for including or excluding an event from the societal perspective is whether or not it affects a nation's gross national product (GNP). This standard is the reason cash transfers, in which no goods or services are produced or consumed, are not considered costs or benefits; money is simply redistributed within a society. Viewed in this way, private earnings, which represent the value of labor inputs used to produce new goods or services, benefit society. But the societal benefits of money earned by participants in vocational programs have been viewed differently in the literature.

Heal *et al.* (1989) argue that, when there is less than full employment in a society, it is plausible to assume that if a program participant had not gotten a particular job, someone else would have. If this is the case, then individual earnings do not represent new production, but are simply a transfer of earnings from one member of society to another. Put differently, the GNP was not increased or decreased by program participants' earnings. Hill and Wehman (1983) excluded earnings in analyzing the societal costs of a vocational program for people with moderate and severe handicaps. Heal *et al.* (1989) went one step further: arguing that the cost of unemployment benefits paid to (hypothetical) workers displaced by supported employment program participants should be added to the calculation of taxpayer costs.

From a different viewpoint, Conley *et al.* (1989) and Weisbrod (1983) treated *increased* individual earnings as a benefit to society. Weisbrod argued that increases in earnings represent heightened productive potential as a result of an intervention and, as such, are new benefits to society, not simply transfers. Whichever side of the debate an evaluator chooses, this and other controversies emphasize the importance of having a consistent, theoretically based rationale for identifying costs and benefits. Unfortunately, lack of agreement on how to analyze these and other events hampers our ability to compare the cost-effectiveness of interventions from one study to another (Drummond *et al.*, 1993).

In addition to these more generic concerns about how costs and benefits are defined, there are some specific issues that should be considered in evaluating

SE services for people with SMI. For example, the relevant perspectives from which to evaluate vocational programs for people with schizophrenia and other forms of severe mental illness may differ from those appropriate for other employment or treatment programs. Studies of families show that they may spend a great deal of time and money and experience a significant amount of stress and role strain in caring for a relative with mental illness (Noh & Avison, 1988; Lefley, 1989; Franks, 1990; Clark & Drake, 1994). Given these findings, it is likely that families face costs and benefits that are different from those of program participants. Specific governmental units that have statutory responsibility for the care of people with SMI, e.g., a state or county mental health authority, also represent a distinct group whose perspective is different from that of all governmental units together and might, therefore, be considered separately.

To illustrate how conclusions about cost-effectiveness might differ across groups, a study of supported employment for people with developmental disabilities (Tines *et al.*, 1990) reported substantial net benefits for program participants, but a societal return of $0.75 per $1.00 invested, and a taxpayer return of $0.66 for every dollar spent. Another study conducted by Hill *et al.* (1987a) and subsequently reanalyzed by Heal and colleagues (1989) found that net benefits to clients averaged from $4405 to $7293 while taxpayer benefits ranged between $6084 and $8013. Both studies included the cost-savings for alternative services as a societal and taxpayer benefit. These and similar findings from research on supported employment programs (Conley & Noble, 1990) serve as important reminders that cost–benefit/effectiveness analyses are heavily influenced by values, by perspectives, and by interpretations of theory. They emphasize the importance of making such factors explicit in research and evaluation reports. Practices such as sensitivity analyses and reporting a range or confidence interval for summary values (instead of a single net benefit, cost-effectiveness ratio, or rate of return) are standard in good evaluations of health and social programs (Weinstein & Stason, 1977; Udvarhelyi *et al.*, 1992; Drummond *et al.*, 1993).

EVALUATING VOCATIONAL OUTCOMES FOR PEOPLE WITH SMI

Defining outcomes clearly and choosing perspectives that are relevant for people with mental illness are important, although frequently neglected, steps for evaluating vocational interventions, but there are other considerations as well. Among these are: which groups are most appropriate for comparison, the extent to which vocational services are integrated with other treatment services, a program's geographic location, how long it has been in operation, and what, if any, future benefits might accrue from an intervention.

COMPARED WITH WHAT?

Unfortunately, there have been few controlled trials of supported employment and none of a scale sufficient to allow firm conclusions. Many existing evaluations rely on extrapolations based on "business as usual" or before and after comparisons for calculating increased earnings and savings in alternate services. These types of comparisons present several different problems for interpretation.

Lacking random assignment, one of the most troubling difficulties is the inability to establish clearly that the comparison group is equivalent to the group enrolled in the vocational program being evaluated. Even if groups are equivalent, it is impossible to say with confidence how a comparison group might behave without actually observing and measuring the group. Fraker and Maynard (1987) demonstrated the importance of true control groups in their evaluation of an SE program for high-school dropouts and welfare recipients. They used two comparison groups (a true control group and a matched comparison) and found large discrepancies in effect sizes depending on which comparison group was used.

Conley and Noble (1990) point out another problem: estimating the costs of alternative services that a comparison group might consume. By establishing a new program alternative, the pool of applicants available for the comparison program may be changed. If the number of people enrolled in alternative programs changes, costs are also likely to change. Fixed costs such as buildings, equipment, and some administrative expenses, will be spread over more or fewer clients and, if client characteristics change, the resources necessary to serve them are also likely to change. All of these problems diminish the confidence we can have in cost-effectiveness analyses that do not employ a randomly selected control group.

WHAT IS RESPONSIBLE FOR CHANGE?

ACT and many of the case management approaches patterned after it include a vocational specialist as a member of a case management team that provides a comprehensive package of treatment services. Such configurations make sense clinically and organizationally, but they make it difficult to untangle the effects of vocational rehabilitation from those of other services.

Some integrated programs have shown significant gains in employment, hours worked, and earnings; decreased use of alternate services such as partial hospitalization; and clinical and/or functional improvements (Kirszner *et al.*, 1991; McFarlane *et al.*, 1992; Meisel *et al.*, 1993). Although these results are encouraging and suggest that vocational programs can make a difference, it is impossible to determine clearly which parts of these programs were responsible for the favorable outcomes. Ideally, alternate vocational interventions should be compared with all other service factors held constant. For example, an ACT program with a vocational component could be compared with an ACT program that offers a similar approach, but without VR services. Again, this can be done only in the context of a randomized trial in which only the type of vocational intervention employed distinguishes groups.

Another problem that makes it difficult to measure effectiveness is poor program implementation. Fidelity of program implementation is especially problematic when introducing a new approach in several sites simultaneously. Thornton (1992), noting the less favorable results in statewide SE initiatives in Illinois and New York, compared with findings from early demonstration projects, suggested variability in program operations as one explanatory factor.

HOW DOES LOCATION AFFECT OUTCOMES

Although evaluators and researchers have paid little attention to the geographic location of a program, it seems likely that differences in the availability and type of jobs, in population density, and in barriers to employment, e.g. transportation, discrimination, education, will affect vocational outcomes. Although it seems that unemployment rates in an area would affect the success of rehabilitation programs, there is, as yet, little evidence that they are important. Purlee (1993) found a weak correlation (−0.12) between unemployment rates and job placement for people with mild mental illness and no association for people with more severe illness. One explanation for this lack of association is that people with SMI tend to enter low-paying jobs that are available even in an economic downturn.

Marrone (1993) has suggested that TE programs work better in urban and suburban areas, because they have a larger number of entry-level jobs and more diverse employers. Intuitively, individual placement models are more feasible in rural areas, but there has been no research testing this assumption. A large, multisite trial would be required to advance our knowledge significantly in this area. In the interim, researchers could improve the usefulness of their findings by describing carefully the characteristics of the areas in which programs are located.

OVER WHAT PERIOD SHOULD OUTCOMES BE MEASURED?

As most evaluations focus on a fairly short period of time, typically 1 year, findings may not represent accurately the long-term effects of a mature program. Problems with model implementation are fairly typical of new programs (e.g. Meisel *et al.*, 1993; Kaufmann *et al.* 1993), and start-up costs such as capital purchases, training, or down time due to slow enrollment may inflate program costs. Later, economies (or diseconomies) of scale may also affect costs. Finally, some types of interventions, particularly those involving a substantial training or educational component, may take longer than a year to reach their full potential. All of these potential problems argue for longer evaluation periods and for careful measurement of changes in service cost over time. In addition to inefficiencies, new programs may be less or more effective than more mature programs due to staff inexperience or to Hawthorne effects. Evaluating new programs for short periods may not render an accurate assessment of how such models will perform with more seasoned staff or when other start-up problems have been solved.

Hill *et al.* (1987b), in an 8-year study of SE for people with mental retardation, found that from a taxpayer's perspective the benefit–cost ratio improved steadily (i.e., 0.19, 0.79, 1.3, 1.64, 1.83, 2.49, 2.97, 2.93). In addition to cutting program costs in half during this period, factors influencing this change included increased taxes paid and reduced SSI payments. The largest benefit was the avoidance of alternative program costs, which alone was more than twice the SE program's cost during the final year.

A related issue, yet to be addressed in SE research, is: How long should intensive vocational support continue after a client is employed? A recent large-scale study shows that short-term gains in employment rates from rehabilitation dissipate rapidly once vocational support is removed (GAO, 1993). Although supported employment implies ongoing support, it seems likely that clients' needs for intensive support would diminish as their employment tenure increases. The short-time horizon of most evaluations has prevented examination of longitudinal effects such as these.

ARE THERE FUTURE BENEFITS?

A final consideration is whether all costs and benefits of vocational programs for people with mental illness are contemporaneous or whether there are future benefits for current services. Although future benefits are more likely to be an issue with disorders that are associated with less chronicity than schizophrenia or other serious mental illnesses, some programs may claim future benefits. If this is the case, evaluators should include the actual or estimated value of such benefits, discounted at a standard social rate of return (Lipscomb, 1989). As estimates of future costs or benefits are usually highly sensitive to changes in the assumptions on which they are based (e.g. Noble, 1991), it is often advisable to test the effects of different assumptions on conclusions.

Estimation of future benefits may not be relevant for SE models. As they carry an implicit assumption that ongoing support will be needed, it may be reasonable to assume that costs and benefits are concurrent.

WHAT OTHER FACTORS AFFECT VOCATIONAL OUTCOMES?

Program participants' decisions to work and their ability to secure and maintain employment may be strongly affected by circumstances that are independent of the services they use. Although we know very little about how different models of vocational rehabilitation affect costs and benefits, we know even less about how personal characteristics, such as diagnosis, cognitive capacity, functional abilities, gender, race, and age affect these outcomes. And, since a large percentage of people with schizophrenia receive public benefits such as SSI and SSDI (income support programs) or Medicaid and Medicare (public health insurance), understanding the incentives and barriers that these and other alternate sources of income present is critical.

Some correlational data suggest that diagnosis may affect work outcomes, but these findings are not clear. An early study by Walls *et al.* (1977) found that vocational rehabilitation clients with psychotic disorders got jobs more quickly but required more rehabilitative services than clients with less severe diagnoses. Noble (1991) observed similar differences. Other data from Jacobs *et al.* (1992b) suggest that clients with psychotic disorders have more difficulty getting jobs than others with nonpsychotic diagnoses. The discrepancies in findings may be due to differences in diagnostic criteria and processes or in programs, nevertheless, research suggests that clients with SMI respond differently to vocational interventions than do clients in other diagnostic categories.

Mental illness is not the only "disability" with which vocational rehabilitation participants must contend. Data also suggest that, among people with a variety of disabilities, members of racial minority groups and individuals with less education have more difficulty in obtaining employment and in rebounding from downturns in the national economy (Burkhauser *et al.*, 1993). Cook (1992) found poorer vocational outcomes for African Americans than for others, leading her to conclude that minority status operates in much the same way for persons with and without psychiatric disability. Societal prejudice and cultural differences might explain these differences.

Gender differences that affect income and vocational success among the nondisabled population are likely to have a similar impact on people with mental illness. These and other individual characteristics should be taken into account when designing and evaluating supported employment programs. Test *et al.* (1990) found no gender differences in out-of-home employment. Cook and Roussel (1987) found that females took longer to achieve their first paid employment position. They argued that "Women may require a targeted series of services designed specifically to provide behavioral incentives for achievement" (p. 21).

Recently, the work incentives (or disincentives) inherent in various public benefits have captured the interest of policy-makers in the United States. Benefit programs are complex in design and often present conflicting work incentives. Correlational and anecdotal data (Berkowitz, 1981; Walls *et al.*, 1990; Jacobs *et al.*, 1992b; Warner & Polak, 1993) indicate strongly that people with serious mental illnesses are sensitive to the incentives of these programs. Particularly problematic for people with chronic illnesses who live in the United States is that public medical insurance (Medicaid and Medicare) is often tied to earnings. Increased earnings may actually mean a decrease in overall income if a person loses health benefits. Because obtaining Medicaid or Medicare is a difficult, time-consuming process and because they need ongoing treatment, people with SMI, understandably, can be very reluctant to risk losing such benefits due to increased earnings from employment.

CONCLUSIONS

Supported employment has significant potential for reducing costs and for improving client outcomes, but several problems need to be addressed before we know conclusively whether SE is a cost-effective alternative to other interventions. We discussed seven general areas that research on SE and other vocational programs must address more effectively: (i) measuring costs and benefits comprehensively; (ii) defining clearly and consistently the perspective(s) for viewing costs and benefits; (iii) using appropriate comparison groups; (iv) controlling for the effects of other mental health treatment on outcomes; (v) examining the longitudinal effects of SE; (vi) assessing the cost-effectiveness of mature as well as new programs; and, (vii) exploring how location, client characteristics, welfare payments, and other factors affect program outcomes. Diversity in the ways evaluators have addressed these and other problems make it very difficult to compare results from one study with another. In particular, different assumptions about future costs and benefits, about the value of particular resources and even how important outcomes like employment earnings should be treated add to the difficulty of comparing the results of one study with those from another.

Research in vocational rehabilitation for people with SMI will benefit not only from increased rigor but also from greater consensus about what methods and assumptions are most appropriate for comparisons. In the interim, researchers must report their methods explicitly and, where appropriate, test how the chosen methodology affected their conclusions.

We have focused on areas we believe are particularly urgent, but there are a number of other areas that need exploration. Although we used several studies of people with developmental disabilities for illustration, we need to learn more about the similarities and differences between SMI interventions and those for people with other disabilities. The relationship between social welfare benefits and employment decisions is another area in need of exploration. There are many more.

Renewed interest in vocational opportunities is a hopeful sign that policy-makers are beginning to look beyond their preoccupation with decreasing hospital use and toward a more complete integration of people who have serious mental illness with their communities. Good research is essential if we are to make wise choices about how to spend the scarce resources available for treatment. Careful, relevant research can be time-consuming and expensive, but these costs may be much lower than the cost of continued ignorance.

ACKNOWLEDGMENTS

Dr. Bond was supported in part by Research Scientist Development Award K02 MH 00842 from the National Institute of Mental Health.

REFERENCES

Anthony, W.A. (1980). *The Principles of Psychiatric Rehabilitation.* Baltimore: University Park Press.

Azrin, N.H. and Besalel, V.B. (1979). *Job Club Counselor's Manual: A Behavioral Approach to Vocational Counseling.* Baltimore: University Park Press.

Beard, J.H., Pitt, R.B., Fisher, S.H., and Goertzel, V. (1963). Evaluating the effectiveness of a psychiatric rehabilitation program. *American Journal of Orthopsychiatry,* **33**, 701–712.

Beard, J.H., Propst, R.N., and Malamud, T.J. (1982). The Fountain House model of rehabilitation. *Psychosocial Rehabilitation Journal,* **5**(1), 47–53.

Bell, M.D., Milstein, R.M., and Lysaker, P.H. (1993). Pay as an incentive in work participation by patients with severe mental illness. *Hospital and Community Psychiatry,* **44**, 684–686.

Berkowitz, M. (1981). Disincentives and the rehabilitation of disabled persons. *Annual Review of Rehabilitation,* **2**, 40–57.

Black, B.J. (1988). *Work and Mental illness: Transitions to Employment.* Baltimore, MD: Johns Hopkins Press.

Bond, G.R. (1984). An economic analysis of psychosocial rehabilitation. *Hospital and Community Psychiatry,* **35**, 356–362.

Bond, G.R. (1987). Supported work as a modification of the transitional employment model for clients with psychiatric disabilities. *Psychosocial Rehabilitation Journal,* **11**(2), 55–73.

Bond, G.R. (1991). Variations in an assertive outreach model. *New Directions for Mental Health Services,* **52**, 65–80.

Bond, G.R. (1992). Vocational rehabilitation. In R.P. Liberman, ed., *Handbook of Psychiatric Rehabilitation,* pp. 244–275. New York: Macmillan.

Bond, G.R. and Boyer, S.L. (1988). Rehabilitation programs and outcomes. In J.A. Ciardiello and M.D. Bell, eds, *Vocational Rehabilitation of Persons with Prolonged Mental Illness,* pp. 231–263, Baltimore, MD: Johns Hopkins Press.

Bond, G.R. and Dietzen, L. (1993). Predictive validity and vocational assessment: Reframing the question. In R.L. Glueckauf, L.B. Sechrest, G.R. Bond, and E.C. McDonel, eds, *Improving Assessment in Rehabilitation and Health,* pp. 61–86. Newbury Park, CA: Sage.

Bond, G.R. and Dincin, J. (1986). Accelerating entry into transitional employment in a psychosocial rehabilitation agency. *Rehabilitation Psychology,* **31**, 143–155.

Bond, G.R., Dietzen, L.L., McGrew, J.H., and Miller, L.D. (1995a). Accelerating entry into supported employment for persons with severe psychiatric disabilities *Rehabilitation Psychology,* **40**, 91–111.

Bond, G.R., Dietzen, L.L., Vogler, K., Katuin, C., McGrew, J.H., and Miller, L.D. (1995b). Toward a framework for evaluating costs and benefits of psychiatric rehabilitation: Three case examples. *Journal of Vocational Rehabilitation,* **5**, 75–88.

Bond, G.R., Katuin, C.H., and Webb, P. (1994). Indiana's Consumer Human Service Provider Training Project. Study in progress.

Burkhauser, R.V., Haveman, R.H., and Wolfe, B.L. (1993). How people with disabilities fare when public policies change. *Journal of Policy Analysis and Management,* **12**, 251–269.

Carpenter, M.D. and Black, B.J. (1986). Review of research and evaluation. In B.J. Black, ed., *Work as Therapy and Rehabilitation for the Mentally Ill,* pp. 41–83. New York: Altro Health and Rehabilitation Services.

Clark, R.E. and Drake, R.E. (1994). Expenditures of time and money by families of people with severe mental illness and substance use disorders. *Community Mental Health Journal,* **30**, 145–163.

Clark, R.E., Bush, P.W., Becker, D.R., Drake, R.E. (in press). A cost-effectiveness comparison of supported employment and rehabilitative day treatment, *Administration and Policy in Mental Health.*

Conley, R.W. and Noble, J.H. (1990). Benefit–cost analysis of supported employment. In F.R. Rusch, ed., *Supported Employment: Models, Methods, and Issues,* pp. 271–287. Sycamore, IL: Sycamore Publishing.

Conley, R.W., Rusch, F.R., McCaughrin, W.B., and Tines, J. (1989). Benefits and costs of supported employment: an analysis of the Illinois supported employment project. *Journal of Applied Behavior Analyses,* **22**, 441–447.

Connors, K.A., Graham, R.S., and Pulso, R. (1987). Playing the store: Where is the vocational in psychiatric rehabilitation? *Psychosocial Rehabilitation Journal,* **10**(3), 21–33.

Cook, J.A. (1992). Social work implications of vocational rehabilitation for persons with severe mental illness. Presentation at the NIMH Workshop on Building Social Work Knowledge for Effective Mental Health Services, Bethesda, MD.

Cook, J.A. and Hoffschmidt, S.J. (1993). Comprehensive models of psychosocial rehabilitation. In R.L. Flexer and P.L. Solomon, eds., *Psychiatric Rehabilitation in Practice,* pp. 81–97. Boston: Andover.

Cook, J.A. and Roussel, A.E. (1987). Who works and what works: Effects of race, class, age, and gender on employment among the psychiatrically disabled. Presentation at the Annual Meeting of the American Sociological Association, Chicago, IL.

Detrick, A. (1991). Assessing outcomes in Rhode Island's mobile treatment team demonstration program. In

Proceedings from the Second Annual Conference on State Mental Health Agency Services Research, pp. 156–165. Alexandria, VA: NASMHPD Research Institute.

Dilk, M.N. (1994). A meta-analytic evaluation of skills training for persons with severe mental illness. Unpublished dissertation, Department of Psychology, Indiana University–Purdue University at Indianapolis.

Dincin, J. and Witheridge, T.F. (1982). Psychiatric rehabilitation as a deterrent to recidivism. *Hospital and Community Psychiatry*, **33**, 645–650.

Dion, G.L. and Anthony, W.A. (1987). Research in psychiatric rehabilitation: A review of experimental and quasi-experimental studies. *Rehabilitation Counseling Bulletin*, **30**, 177–203.

Drake, R.E., Becker, D.R., Biesanz, J.C., Torrey, W.C., McHugo, G.J., and Wyzik, P.F. (1994). Partial hospitalization vs. supported employment: I. Vocational outcomes. *Community Mental Health Journal*, **30**, 519–532.

Drummond, M., Brandt, A., Luce, B., and Rovira, J. (1993). Standardizing methodologies for economic evaluation in health care. *International Journal of Technology Assessment in Health Care*, **9**, 26–36.

Estroff, S.E. (1981). *Making it Crazy*. Berkeley: University of California Press.

Fabian, E.S., Waterworth, A., and Ripke, B. (1993). Reasonable accommodation for workers with serious mental illness: Type, frequency, and associated outcomes. *Psychosocial Rehabilitation Journal*, **17**(2), 163–172.

Fairweather, G.W., Sanders, D.H., Maynard, H., Cressler, D.L., and Bleck, D.S. (1969). *Community Life for the Mentally Ill*. Chicago, IL: Aldine.

Fergus, E.O. and Balzell, A. (1990). *A National Directory of Fairweather Programs*. East Lansing, MI: Michigan State University Fairweather Lodge Project.

Fraker, T. and Maynard, R. (1987). The adequacy of comparison group designs for evaluations of employment-related programs. *Journal of Human Resources*, **22**, 194–227.

Franks, D.D. (1990). Economic contribution of families caring for persons with severe and persistent mental illness. *Administration and Policy in Mental Health*, **18**, 9–18.

General Accounting Office (GAO) (1993). *Vocational Rehabilitation: Evidence for Federal Program's Effectiveness is Mixed*. PEMD-93-19. Washington, DC: US General Accounting Office.

Gates, L.B., Taler, Y., and Akabas, S.H. (1989). Optimizing return to work among newly disabled workers: A new approach toward cost containment. *Benefits Quarterly*, **5**, 19–27.

Gervey, R. and Bedell, J.R. (1994). Supported employment. In J.R. Bedell, ed., *Psychological Assessments and Treatment of Persons with Severe Mental Disorders*, pp. 139–163. Washington, DC: Taylor & Francis.

Granger, B. (1990). Agency-sponsored entrepreneurial businesses employing individuals with long-term mental illness: Findings from a national survey. Unpublished paper, Matrix Research Institute, Philadelphia, PA.

Heal, L.W., McCaughrin, W.B., and Tines, J.J. (1989). Methodological nuances and pitfalls of benefit–cost analysis: A critique. *Research in Developmental Disabilities*, **10**, 201–212.

Health Reform Must Cover "Hospital Without Walls". (1993). NAMI Advocate, **14**(9), 1, 5.

Hill, M. and Wehman, P. (1983). Cost benefit analysis associated with the competitive employment of moderately and severely handicapped persons. *Journal of Association for Severely Handicapped*, **8**, 30–38.

Hill, M.L., Banks, P.D., Handrich, R.R., Wehman, P.H., Hill, J.W., Shafer, M.S. (1987a). Benefit–cost analysis of supported competitive employment for persons with mental retardation. *Research in Development Disabilities*, **8**, 71–89.

Hill, M.L., Wehman, P.H., Kregel, J., Banks, P.D., and Metzler, H.M. (1987b). Employment outcomes for people with moderate and severe disabilities: Eight-year longitudinal analysis of supported competitive employment. *Journal of the Association for Persons with Severe Handicaps*, **12**, 182–189.

Jacobs, H.E., Collier, R., and Wissusik, D. (1992a). The job finding module: Training skills for seeking community competitive employment. *New Directions for Mental Health Services*, **53**, 105–115.

Jacobs, H.E., Wissusik, D., Collier, R., Stackman, D., and Burkeman, D. (1992b). Correlations between psychiatric disabilities and vocational outcome. *Hospital and Community Psychiatry*, **43**, 365–369.

Kamlet, M. (1992). The Comparative Benefits Modeling Project: A Framework for Cost-Utility Analysis of Government Health Care Programs. Office of Disease Prevention, US Public Health Service, Washington, DC., 1992. (Available from ODPHP, National Health Information Center, PO Box 1133, Washington, DC 200131133).

Kaufmann, C.L., Ward-Colasante, C., and Farmer, J. (1993). Development and evaluation of drop-in centers operated by mental health consumers. *Hospital and Community Psychiatry*, **44**, 675–678.

Kirszner, M.L., McKay, C.D., and Tippett, M.L. (1991). Homeless and mental health replication of the PACT model in Delaware. *Proceedings from the Second Annual Conference on State Mental Health Agency Services Research*, pp. 68–82. Alexandria, VA: NASMHPD Research Institute.

Kregel, J., Wehman, P., and Banks, P.D. (1989). The effects of consumer characteristics and type of employment model on individual outcomes in supported employment. *Journal of Applied Behavior Analysis*, **22**, 407–415.

Lefley, H.P. (1989). Family burden and family stigma in major mental illness. *American Psychologist*, **44**, 556–560.

Lipscomb, J. (1989). Time preference for health in cost-effectiveness analysis. *Medical Care*, **27** (Suppl.),

S233–253.
McFarlane, W.R., Stastny, P., and Deakins, S. (1992). Family aided assertive community treatment: A comprehensive rehabilitation and intensive case management approach for persons with schizophrenic disorders. *New Directions in Mental Health Services,* **53**, 43–54.
Malamud, T.J. and McCrory, D.J. (1988). Transitional employment and psychosocial rehabilitation. In J.A. Ciardiello and M.D. Bell, eds., *Vocational Rehabilitation of Persons with Prolonged Mental Illness,* pp. 150–162. Baltimore, MD: Johns Hopkins Press.
Mancuso, L.L. (1990). Reasonable accommodation for workers with psychiatric disabilities. *Psychosocial Rehabilitation Journal,* **14**(2), 3–19.
Marrone, J. (1993). Creating positive outcomes for people with severe mental illness. *Psychosocial Rehabilitation Journal,* **17**(2), 43–62.
Meisel, J., McGowen, M., Patotzka, D., Madison, K., and Chandler, D. (1993). Evaluation of AB 3777 client and cost outcomes: July 1990 through March 1992. Report prepared by Lewin-VHI, Inc. Available from California Department of Mental Health. 1600 9th St., Sacramento, CA 95814.
Mueser, K.T. and Liberman, R.P. (1988). Skills training in vocational rehabilitation. In J.A. Ciardiello and M.D. Bell, eds., *Vocational Rehabilitation of Persons with Prolonged Mental Illness,* pp. 81–103. Baltimore, MD: Johns Hopkins Press.
Mulder, R. (1982). Final evaluation of the Harbinger program as a demonstration project. Unpublished manuscript. Michigan Department of Mental Health, Lansing, MI.
National Association of Rehabilitation Facilities (NARF) (1989). Supported employment in context: NARF's national scope supported employment survey and policy implications. Washington, DC: NARF.
Nichols, M.E. (1989). Demonstration study of a supported employment program for persons with severe mental illness: Benefits, costs, and outcomes. Unpublished masters thesis, Department of Psychology, Indiana University–Purdue University at Indianapolis.
Noble, J.H. (1991). The benefits and costs of supported employment for people with mental illness and with traumatic brain injury in New York state. Final Report No. C-0023180, Amherst, NY: Research Foundation of the State University of New York.
Noh, S. and Avison, W.R. (1988). Spouses of discharged patients: Factors associated with their experience of burden. *Journal of Marriage and the Family,* **50**, 377–389.
Plum, T.B. and Lawther, S. (1992). How Michigan established a highly effective statewide community-based program for persons with serious and persistent mental illness. *Outlook,* **2**, 2–5.
Propst, R.N. (1992). Introduction. *Psychosocial Rehabilitation Journal,* **16**, 3–4.
Purlee, G.D. (1993). Predictors of employment outcome for persons with serious mental illness. Unpublished dissertation, Bloomington: Indiana University.
Revell, W.G., Wehman, P., Kregel, J., West, M., and Rayfield, R. (1994). Supported employment for persons with severe disabilities: Positive trends in wages, models, and funding. *Education and Training in Mental Retardation and Developmental Disabilities,* **291**, 256–264.
Rice, D.P., Kelman, S., Miller, L.S., and Dunmeyer, S. (1990). *The Economic Costs of Alcohol and Drug Abuse and Mental Illness: 1985.* DHHS Pub. No. (ADM) 90-1694. Rockville, MD: National Institute of Mental Health.
Rogers, E.S., Sciarappa, K., MacDonald-Wilson, K., and Danley, K. (1995). A benefit–cost analysis of a supported employment model for persons with psychiatric disabilities. *Evaluation and Program Planning,* **18**, 105–115.
Rutman, I.D. and Armstrong, K. (1985). A comprehensive, national evaluation of transitional employment programs for the psychiatrically disabled. Unpublished paper, Matrix Research Institute, Philadelphia, PA.
Salkind, I. (1971). Economic problems of workshops. In H.R. Lamb *et al.*, eds., *Rehabilitation in Community Mental Health,* pp. 71–91. San Francisco: Jossey-Bass.
Schultheis, A.M. and Bond, G.R. (1993). Situational assessment ratings of work behaviors: Changes across time and between settings. *Psychosocial Rehabilitation Journal,* **17**(2), 107–119.
Sherman, P.S. and Porter, R. (1991). Mental health consumers as case management aides. *Hospital and Community Psychiatry,* **42**, 494–498.
Stein, L.I. and Test, M.A. (1985). The evolution of the Training in Community Living model. *New Directions for Mental Health Services,* **26**, 7–16.
Symington, D.C. and Lewis, M.P. (1973). Cost–benefit analysis of a hospital and university based prevocational program. *Archives of Physical Medicine and Rehabilitation,* **54**, 341–347.
Tashjian, M.D., Hayward, B.J., Stoddard, S., and Kraus, L. (1989). *Best Practice Study of Vocational Rehabilitation Services to Severely Mentally Ill Persons.* Washington, DC: Policy Study Associates.
Test, M.A. (1992). Training in Community Living. In R.P. Liberman, ed., *Handbook of Psychiatric Rehabilitation,* pp. 153–170. New York: Macmillan.
Test, M.A., Burke, S.S., and Wallisch, L.S. (1990). Gender differences of young adults with schizophrenic disorders in community care. *Schizophrenia Bulletin,* **16**, 331–344.
Tines, J., Rusch, F.R., McCaughrin, W., and Conley, R.W. (1990). Benefit–cost analysis of supported employment in Illinois: A statewide evaluation. *American Journal on Mental Retardation,* **95**, 44–54.
Thornton, C. (1992). Uncertainty in benefit–cost analysis of supported employment. *Journal of Vocational Rehabilitation,* **2**, 62–72.
Toms-Barker, L., Raffe, S., and Leff, S.H. (1993). How case management can improve employment outcomes: Effective programs and practices. Presentation at the

annual conference of the International Association of Psychosocial Rehabilitation Services, New Orleans, LA.

Torrey, E.F., Erdman, K., Wolfe, S.M., and Flynn, L.M. (1990). *Care of the Seriously Mentally Ill: A Rating of State Programs.* Washington, DC: Health Research Group.

Udvarhelyi, I.S., Colditz, G.A., Rai, A., and Epstein, A.M. (1992). Cost-effectiveness and cost–benefit analyses in the medical literature: Are the methods being used correctly? *Annals of Internal Medicine,* **116**, 238–244.

Vandergoot, D. (1986). *Review of Placement Research Literature: Implications for Research and Practice* (Rehabilitation Research Review, NARIC). Washington, DC: DATA Institute.

Walls, R.T., Tseng, M.S., and Ellis, W.D. (1977). Time and money for vocational rehabilitation of clients with psychotic and psychoneurotic disabilities. *Journal of Occupational Psychology,* **50**, 37–44.

Walls, R.T., Dowler, D.L., and Fullmer, S.L. (1990). Incentives and disincentives to supported employment. In F.R. Rusch, ed., *Supported Employment: Models, Methods, and Issues,* pp. 251–269. Sycamore, IL: Sycamore Publishing.

Warner, R. and Polak, P. (1993). *An Economic Development Approach to the Mentally Ill in the Community.* Available from the Community Support Program, Center for Mental Health Services, SAMHSA, Rockville, MD.

Wehman, P. (1986). Supported competitive employment for persons with severe disabilities. *Journal of Applied Rehabilitation Counseling,* **17**, 24–29.

Wehman, P. and Melia, R. (1990) *A National Analysis of Supported Employment Growth and Implementation.* Richmond, VA: Virginia Commonwealth University (NIDRR Grant No. H133B80052).

Wehman, P. and Moon, M.S. (eds) (1988). *Vocational Rehabilitation and Supported Employment.* Baltimore: Paul Brookes.

Weinstein, M.C. and Stason, W.B. (1977). Foundations of cost-effectiveneness analysis for health and medical practices. *New England Journal of Medicine,* **296**, 716–721.

Weisbrod, B.A. (1983). A guide to benefit-cost analysis, as seen through a controlled experiment in treating the mentally ill. *Journal of Health Politics, Policy, and Law,* **7**, 808–845.

Weisbrod, B.A., Test, M.A., and Stein, L.I. (1980). Alternative to mental hospital treatment, II: Economic benefit–cost analysis. *Archives of General Psychiatry,* **37**, 400–405.

Wilder, J.F. (1976). The case for a flexible, long-term sheltered workshop for psychiatric patients. *Hospital and Community Psychiatry,* **27**, 112–116.

20

Emerging Approaches to Housing and Support for People with Psychiatric Disabilities

PAUL J. CARLING
Center for Community Change through Housing and Support, Trinity College of Vermont, Burlington, Vermont, USA

INTRODUCTION

THE ECONOMICS OF HOUSING AND SUPPORT

In the final decade of the twentieth century, the hallmark of mental health systems throughout the world appears to be their ability to reintegrate and successfully support individuals with the most significant psychiatric disabilities, regardless of age, in their local communities, and to reduce or eliminate institutional care. Several major factors have emerged which appear to be critical to the success of these efforts including: the willingness, at all levels of government, to embrace a new set of expectations about rehabilitation, integration, and recovery among this clientele; the political will to shift funding and clinical service models to those which are demonstrably more effective in promoting community tenure and success, rather than models which assume low expectations and high levels of control; the level of competence in finding or developing affordable housing; and the capacity to develop outreach-oriented supports, which are based on the preferences of the individuals themselves and their families, and which combine the best of professional skills, with those of support by families, friends, and other community members, such as neighbors and co-workers.

Mental health systems are undergoing a fundamental change in their vision of what is possible for people with significant psychiatric disabilities, but to date most of this change has taken place at a policy level, rather than in people's lives and in local communities. To be sure, some of the model program approaches described in the literature provide ample evidence that successful community reintegration is possible, but major structural barriers within mental health systems, and in our society as a whole, continue to prevent the great majority of people with these disabilities from fully and successfully participating in community life. These barriers include pervasive poverty, exacerbated by health insurance programs which tend to keep people terminally dependent; a crisis in the availability of affordable housing; a continued commitment of the predonderance of mental health resources to institutional programs and to facility-based services, which serve only a small number of people in need; and a

Handbook of Mental Health Economics and Health Policy, Volume I, Schizophrenia. Edited by M. Moscarelli, A. Rupp and N. Sartorius.
© 1996 John Wiley & Sons Ltd.

continued emphasis within these systems on devoting nearly all available funding to professional treatment services, rather than to concrete benefits such as rent subsidies, employment training programs, and peer support.

During the last decade, the critical need for stable housing linked to effective supports has emerged as a major policy dilemma within the mental health field (Carling & Ridgway, 1987). In the early 1980s, it was found that a majority of the 1.7–2.4 million Americans with "long term mental illness" based on diagnosis, disability, and duration of disorder (Goldman *et al.*, 1981), lived in inadequate housing, lacked needed supports, or were homeless (Department of Health and Human Services, 1983; Public Health Service, 1980), and these problems continue today. The reasons for this situation are complex: the United States, Canada, and other industrial countries have been undergoing an affordable housing crisis, homelessness is becoming more widespread, and the mental health field has been unclear about its responsibility, or the most effective approaches, for addressing these issues within its traditional service system. Each of these problems is discussed in depth below.

POVERTY AND THE AFFORDABLE HOUSING CRISIS

Two factors reduce access to housing for *all* people with limited incomes: a decade-long decline in affordable housing stock, and the rising cost of housing in relation to income. This combination puts home ownership out of the reach of many middle-income citizens, and decent housing out of reach of most of those at or below the poverty level. Many people with psychiatric disabilities in the United States, for example, with reported average annual incomes from \$3000 to \$7000, rely on social insurance or Supplemental Security Income (SSI) as their primary income source and have unemployment rates as high as 85% (Anthony & Dion, 1986), making their access to decent housing tenuous at best. With a cut of nearly 80% in federally assisted housing for low-income and special needs groups since 1981, representing a decline of the national investment in affordable housing from 7% of the federal budget in 1978 to 0.7% in 1988, there has been a dramatic increase in homelessness (Low Income Housing Information Service, 1988).

Because disabilities can be economically catastrophic, people with disabilities are disproportionately represented in that group which is "very poor," or well below the poverty level. A recent study comparing SSI income and affordability of housing in every area of the United States found that *there is not a single county* where people with SSI income alone can afford to rent either an efficiency or a one-bedroom apartment (McCabe *et al.*, 1991), using the federal Department of Housing and Urban Development's standard of affordability, i.e. 35% of one's total income. For the approximately one-third of people with psychiatric disabilities who need housing that can accommodate children (Carling & Ridgway, 1987), the situation is even more dire. Figures 1 and 2 detail these findings. It also is difficult for individuals with psychiatric disabilities to maintain SSI as a stable source of income. Segal and Choi (1991), for example, found that among board and care residents receiving SSI, those with the most severe psychiatric disabilities spent the least amount of time receiving SSI because of revolving-door hospitalizations and inadequate coordination of treatment and benefits.

In addition, housing discrimination based on stigma is a day-to-day reality: landlords refuse to rent to individuals with psychiatric disabilities, cutting off access to available rental housing. A recent study found that over 40% of landlords immediately rejected individuals with a known psychiatric disability (Alisky & Iczkowski, 1990) who were otherwise qualified applicants for the apartments. Of those individuals who find independent housing in the community, many do so in very low income neighborhoods where substandard housing and high crime rates are typical. "Oversaturation" of these neighborhoods by people with disabilities often leads to community backlash, referred to as the NIMBY (not in my back yard) syndrome (Coulton *et al.*, 1984; Ridgway, 1987). In addition, community opposition to mental health residences is widespread (Rizzo *et al.*, 1992; Segal *et al.*, 1980), in spite of the fact that claims that they will have adverse effects on neighborhoods appear to be groundless (Boydal *et al.*, 1989).

These findings, along with results of studies of

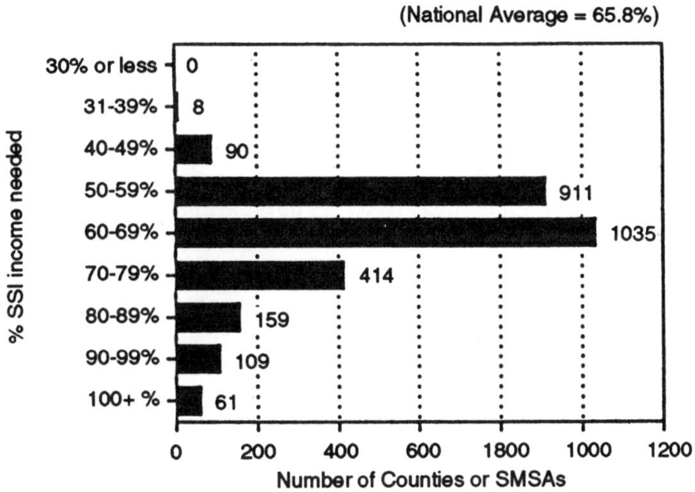

Figure 1. Percentage of SSI income needed to rent an efficiency apartment in US counties. Total $n=2787$. Source: McCabe *et al.* (1993).

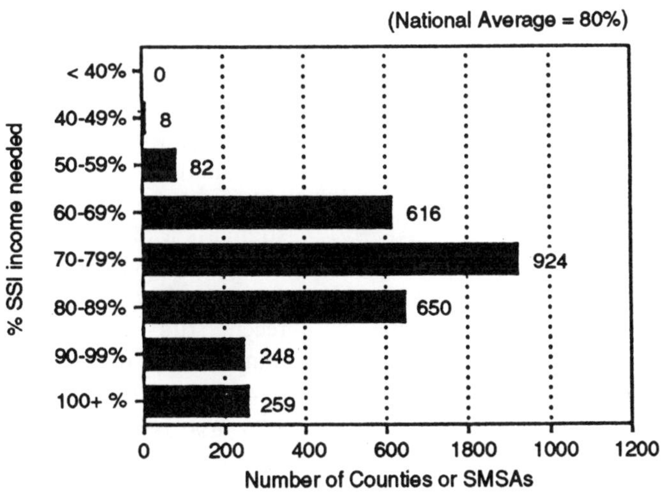

Figure 2. Percentage of SSI income needed to rent a one-bedroom apartment in US counties. Total $n=2787$. Source: McCabe *et al.* (1993).

consumer perceptions of the housing problem (Ridgway, 1988), suggest that income and stigma may be the major barriers to housing, rather than the psychiatric disability itself. These are especially vexing barriers, given the results of consumer preference studies, described below, that indicate that most consumers prefer their own apartment, in housing that is integrated, i.e. not developed specifically for people with a label or disability, and in urban areas, where much of the affordable housing stock (e.g. welfare hotels, boarding homes, and other "marginal" settings) has been lost to "gentrification."

THE CRISIS OF HOMELESSNESS

Because of the decade-long decline in affordable housing, increasing unemployment, and the erosion of resources for community services for people with psychiatric disabilities and with alcohol and substance abuse problems, homelessness has become a widespread phenomenon in the United States, with estimates that 736 000 Americans are homeless on a given night, and 2.3 million over the course of a year (Low Income Housing Information Service, 1988). In addition, 27 million Americans are considered "shelter poor" and at risk of homelessness (National Alliance to End Homelessness, 1988). Within these numbers, estimates of the proportion of homeless individuals who have "serious mental health problems" range from 25 to 90% (Bassuk, 1984; Lamb, 1984; Benda & Datallo, 1988), although major methodological questions have been raised about the definition of homelessness, and about methods for estimating the numbers of these individuals (Morrison, 1989; Breakey & Fischer, 1990). Furthermore, many of these studies fail to make important distinctions between key subpopulations of homeless persons, such as women (Morse & Calsyn, in press; Roth *et al.*, in press), and minority group members (First *et al.*, 1988).

Although the popular press often equates homelessness with deinstitutionalization policies, there is considerable debate about the extent to which homelessness is a consequence of the disabling nature of mental illness (Lamb & Lamb, 1990), or is a precipitant of psychiatric disabilities itself (Cohen & Thompson, 1992). Research studies tend to overestimate the numbers of homeless people with mental illness by describing some behaviors as characteristic of mental illness rather than homelessness itself (Koegel & Burnham, in press). In fact, the literature describes a new process, similar to early accounts of learned helplessness in psychiatric hospitals, called "shelterization" (Grunberg & Eagle, 1990), characterized by a decrease in interpersonal responsiveness, a neglect of personal hygiene, increased passivity, and increased dependence on others.

HOUSING AND SERVICE STRATEGIES TO ADDRESS HOMELESSNESS

A variety of strategies for addressing the housing and support needs of homeless people with psychiatric disabilities has emerged in the literature and from the National Institute of Mental Health's (NIMH) demonstration projects. Several studies (Morse & Calsyn, in press: Mulkern & Bradley, 1986; First *et al.*, 1990) report that the priorities for most homeless persons are social resources and support rather than mental health treatment, and that the key needs related to housing stability are for engagement, case management, and "linkages" with other services. The most effective approach in helping most people to overcome homelessness appears to consist of outreach-oriented health and mental health services, a focus on the perspectives and demands of clients, work options, and supported housing (Schutt *et al.*, 1992; Gelberg & Linn, 1988). Goering and associates (1990a) summarize key service principles for working with people who are homeless: normal community living in long-term or permanent housing is the desired goal for homeless people; permanent housing with flexible supports rather than residential treatment programming is the preferred model; consumer involvement in planning and governing is essential; and a commitment to ongoing review of both the quality of the housing, and the adequacy of the services provided is necessary. In spite of these findings, some continue to call for new forms of "asylum" (Drake *et al.*, 1989), or for a variety of institutional solutions (Belcher, 1988).

MENTAL HEALTH'S RESPONSE TO HOUSING AND SUPPORT NEEDS

TRADITIONAL TREATMENT-ORIENTED RESPONSES

The mental health field's response to people who need both housing and treatment is undergoing significant change. Historically, mental health agencies have viewed housing as a social welfare problem, and defined their role exclusively in terms of "treatment." Public housing agencies, in turn, contended that consumers need "specialized residential programs," and viewed housing needs as a mental health responsibility (Carling & Ridgway, 1987). Thus, housing needs have often been ignored. When mental health systems have responded to housing needs, they have typically combined treatment needs and living needs in a "residential service."

These residential services include a variety of models, such as "quarterway houses" and "halfway houses" (Budson, 1981), family foster care (Carling, 1984), Fairweather Lodges (Fairweather, 1980), apartment programs (Carling, 1978; Goldmeier *et al.*, 1977), boarding homes (Segal & Liese, 1991), and nursing homes (Carling, 1981). "Crisis alternative models" (Mosher & Menn, 1979; Stein & Test, 1985; Stroul, 1988) also may involve group residences, family settings, or apartments reserved for that purpose. Shelters for homeless persons and transitional or permanent "housing for the homeless" have become the latest in a series of quasi-institutional solutions to housing and support needs (Baxter & Hopper, 1984; Kozol, 1988). Practically speaking, this means that consumers have typically been offered therapeutic facilities, not housing.

Despite broad development of residential programs in the last decade, a recent survey of over 2500 community residential programs across the United States serving adults with psychiatric disabilities (Randolph *et al.*, 1991) found that only a small number of agencies actually provide these services in most states. Few agencies offer more than one option, and most programs identified were large congregate settings. The newer supervised apartment and supportive housing approaches used larger number of households, each of which served a small number of people. Intermediate care facilities, nursing homes, and shelters had few formal ties with mental health services. Transitional housing also was not as common as expected; most programs provided long-term housing. Surprisingly, residential services were *not* "intensive": they were staffed by paraprofessionals who have received little mental health training (Spaulding *et al.*, 1987). While some of these programs have explicitly attempted to incorporate a rehabilitation approach (Benoit, 1992; Campanelli *et al.*, 1992; Mills & Hanson, 1991), others are oriented toward "maintenance" (Carling & Ridgway, 1987). Follow-up services were informal and inconsistent. Residents were primarily young adults with major mental disorders, but these programs served *twice* as many persons who were functional as they did those who were gravely disabled. Most of these residential programs had been developed to combine housing and services in a single setting, and have typically been segregated, professionally staffed, and congregate in nature.

RESEARCH ON THE EFFECTIVENESS OF TREATMENT-ORIENTED HOUSING APPROACHES

Empirical knowledge about "what works" in residential programs is hampered by both methodological and conceptual problems. In spite of their proliferation, there is no commonly used nomenclature for these programs, a fact which makes any evaluation of their impact especially difficult. Furthermore, in six major reviews covering several hundred "alternatives to hospitalization," only a handful of studies met basic criteria of experimental design (Braun *et al.*, 1981; Carpenter, 1978; Dellario & Anthony, 1981; Keisler, 1982; Test & Stein, 1978). Taken as a whole, however, these studies indicate that "community-based treatment" is virtually always as effective or more effective than "hospital-based treatment" in helping people with psychiatric disabilities to achieve employment outcomes, to gain re-entry into the community, and to reduce the use of medication and outpatient services. Apparently, any of a wide range of community services can assist in achieving some measure of community integration.

With regard specifically to residential programs, however, a total of 109 studies (Cometa *et al.*, 1979) concluded that evidence of the effectiveness of transitional halfway houses in reducing recidivism, improving economic self-sufficiency, and improving community adjustment was "highly suspect" (p. 25). Transitional residential programs may in fact be preferable to institutional care, but they fall short of helping people to achieve community integration (Segal & Aviram, 1978). In fact, serious questions have been raised about failing to distinguish between residential treatment and housing, or even about the assumption that people need to reside in residential programs prior to "independent living" (Taylor *et al.*, 1987). It has been suggested (Carling & Ridgway, 1987) that the notion of help through a series of time-limited stays in specialized residential settings in order to achieve "independent living," is simplistic. First, it confuses a person's need for stable affordable housing with the person's need for treatment, which in effect, makes receiving housing—which is a basic human need, and a right—contingent on accepting treatment. This is an especially problematic notion in what purports to be a voluntary service setting.

As treatment needs change, individuals may experience chronic dislocation through successive moves, because often improvement in functioning requires a physical move to another setting. In addition, alternative housing is often not available at precisely the time that a person's needs change. A "residential continuum" also focuses on *preparing* people for living in their own housing, even though rehabilitation research strongly suggests that the most effective learning of such skills is in the actual environment in which they will be applied (Anthony & Blanch, 1989).

Furthermore, the idea that people will move from these settings to "independent living" without any mental health supports appears to be contradicted by the need for ongoing, yet flexibly available support among many people with a psychiatric disability. Finally, these facilities appear to be settings that are generally not desired by consumers themselves, but instead represent professional notions of what consumers need (Tanzman *et al.*, in press).

The failure of mental health systems to focus on people's permanent housing needs has had multiple effects. Many individuals remain in psychiatric hospitals because of the lack of housing (Public Health Service, 1980). Others cycle through emergency rooms and general hospitals in costly and often inappropriate stays (Chatetz & Goldfinger, 1984; Geller, 1982). Many others have been moved to "custodial" nursing and boarding homes, many of which lack active rehabilitation or treatment, contribute to declines in functioning, and are often exploitative (Carling, 1981; Segal & Aviram, 1978; Kohen & Paul, 1976). In addition, the lack of permanent housing and support options often results in a substantial burden on families (Hatfield *et al.*, 1982; Wasow, 1982; Housing Committee, California Alliance for the Mentally Ill *et al.*, 1986), who serve as case managers and landlords with little or no support. Residential facilities are typically offered to only 2–5% of people with psychiatric disabilities, yet consume the great majority of system resources allocated to "housing" (Randolph *et al.*, 1991).

The field of mental health has a great deal to learn from other groups who require special supports in their housing: people with low incomes, those who are elderly or homeless, and those with developmental disabilities, including mental retardation. A recent comprehensive review of the research related to housing and community integration for all of these groups (Carling *et al.*, 1987) concluded that: (i) housing needs are similar for each of these groups, although support needs are more varied; (ii) supports appear to be the critical factor in whether people can remain in a housing situation of their own choice; (iii) housing problems are less closely related to disability than they are to economic and social factors such as poverty, affordable housing trends, and discrimination; (iv) strong differences of opinion often exist between professionals and consumers about specific needs for housing and supports, regardless of which disability group is involved: (v) choices and control over one's environment are critical necessities regardless of special need, and consumers wish to be centrally involved in planning their own housing and supports, and to have the opportunity to manage their own services; (vi) because of the lack of in-home supports and services, elders and people with disabilities are plagued by transience, dislocation, and the risk of institutionalization; and (vii) the model of a "residential continuum" is increasingly beset by conceptual and practical problems. This review concluded that the broader disability and low income communities are increasingly emphasizing normal housing and the need to avoid transforming housing into service settings. Thus, community integration approaches avoid congregation and segregation, and instead focus on building relationships between disabled and non-disabled individuals and among those with a variety of incomes.

With specific regard to individuals with psychiatric disabilities, two recent reviews of the outcome research literature on psychiatric disabilities (Anthony & Blanch, 1989; Wilson, in press) have implications for housing and support needs. They concluded that: (i) a psychiatric disability is not necessarily a life-long degenerative process which requires more intensive supports over time; (ii) most people with psychiatric disabilities can maintain homes, jobs, friends, and families; (iii) mental health services must be highly flexible in order to be responsive to individual needs, which vary over time; correspondingly, people with the highest level of disability seem to have the most individual needs; (iv) given choice, most people don't define themselves principally as "chronic mental patients"; instead, they value independence and productivity more than any other treatment outcomes; and (v) people *can* make positive choices about the kind and intensity of supports they receive. In an indication that people will exercise choice regardless of options available, clients seem to use residential facilities, such as boarding homes, as they define their need at a given time, rather than as the program planners intended these settings to be used (Segal & Liese, 1991).

RESEARCH ON WHAT PEOPLE WITH PSYCHIATRIC DISABILITIES AND THEIR FAMILIES WANT IN HOUSING AND SUPPORT

A growing body of information describes what kinds of housing and supports consumers actually want. A recent review of over 43 consumer housing and support preference studies conducted in North America, and summarized by Tanzman (1993), concluded that people with psychiatric disabilities generally want the same kinds of housing as all other citizens want. This review also indicates that most people with psychiatric disabilities, whether homeless, residing in psychiatric hospitals, living in residential programs, with families, or in their own housing, generally place the highest value on privacy and autonomy; prefer not to live with other mental health consumers, in spite of prevailing "placement" policies; want integrated housing; want mental health services, but not on a live-in basis; and see a lack of income as the major barrier to achieving their housing goals.

A national housing policy forum of U.S. consumer leaders who have themselves been homeless and in residential programs, and who also have experienced providing services to people with psychiatric disabilities (Ridgway, 1988) provides concrete suggestions for implementing systems that will achieve these desired outcomes: (i) systems should develop the housing options that most people prefer; (ii) housing should be decent, safe, permanent, and near shopping, services, and transportation; (iii) services should be voluntary and skills oriented; (iv) an increased focus on benefits, flexible funding, and jobs is needed; (v) case management should be expanded, using a personal care attendant model; (vi) staff need training related to housing and choice; (vii) consumers should be hired to provide and manage services; (viii) more self-help and empowerment options are needed; (ix) public education is needed to reduce stigma; (x) more regulation of board and care homes, and more affordable housing legislation is needed; and (xi) developing coalitions to work on housing issues is critical. In short, these consumer leaders favored a shift from a traditional mental health approach to an adaptation of the "independent living" model that has been successfully used with people with severe physical disabilities (Tanzman, 1993; Deegan, 1992).

EMERGING APPROACHES

A NEW CONCEPTUAL MODEL FOR HOUSING, SUPPORTS AND COMMUNITY INTEGRATION: THE FRAMEWORK FOR SUPPORT

The field of mental health is in the midst of a "paradigm shift" with regard to people with the most severe disabilities (Blanch *et al.*, 1988; Carling, 1989; Ridgway & Zipple, 1990), from an era of institutional and facility-based thinking, to a transitional period in which people were seen principally as service recipients needing a comprehensive community support system (Turner & TenHoor, 1979), to a view in which people are seen principally as citizens with a potential for, and a right to, full community participation and integration (Wilson, in press; Racino, 1991). The learnings from the community support and rehabilitation literature in mental health, from other fields, and from consumers themselves suggest that the key ingredients for achieving community integration are a focus on consumer goals and preferences, an individualized and flexible rehabilitation process, and a strong emphasis on normal housing, work, and social networks (Carling *et al.*, 1987; Blanch *et al.*, 1988).

The dramatic change in thinking which is challenging mental health systems today represents a fundamental shift in how we view the person with psychiatric disability, what outcomes we believe are possible in people's lives, and what approach to services makes the most sense in achieving those outcomes. During the twentieth century, the mental health field has changed its answers to these questions in several fundamental "waves" of reform. The first half of the century could be described as the era of institutionalization, a condition which resulted in significant isolation for the individual. The focus of the person's role was on patienthood, and the predominant service approach was delivered through the medical model. Service characteristics included custodial care or treatment and protection (i.e. deprivation) from the community. From the 1950s to the 1980s the focus of the person's role was on clienthood, i.e. on being a commodity labelled "service recipient." The predominant service model shifted during that time from "symptom maintenance" to a developmental/rehabilitation model. Program characteristics focused on the "continuum" of services, on preparation for life in the community, and on individuals fitting into program "slots." By contrast, the emerging integration approach of the 1990s focuses on the role of citizen, has as a primary service approach an emphasis on functional supports, and prioritizes networking, self-determination, choice, and supports that are based in reciprocal, respectful relationships.

The integration paradigm differs dramatically from prior service approaches in several key ways. We perceive the individual as a person, rather than a disabled client. We define the person's needs in terms of capacities, instead of deficits. We see the community as a resource of possibilities, understanding, awareness, acceptance, and inclusion, rather than as an obstacle, or as a source of fear, prejudice, ignorance, or rejection. In a community integration approach, power is located in the person, through self-determination and through "circles of support," rather than in the hierarchical structures of service systems, in which policy-makers regulate the behavior of professionals "in the best interests of" the person with a disability. Our role is that of enabler and supporter, rather than service provider. And finally, our vision of the future is one of a citizen pursuing his/her dreams and using his/her gifts, rather than one of continuing clienthood, a role that is in fact created directly by the service models we have used in the past. In an integration approach, the support role is played by the same diversity of individuals, who support people without a label, principally those connected in freely given relationships. Even formal services are more often provided through community resources and by peers.

Referring to the work of Kuhn, Ridgway and Zipple (1990) present a compelling case that the integration approach represents a paradigm shift for the mental health field in how it approaches housing needs. In this shift, we can expect that national, state, and local policy changes, which have themselves been somewhat slow in coming, will be followed by an increasing intensity of change, as old assumptions upon which traditional services are based, are seen as no longer viable, no longer describing people with disabilities as we have come to see them, and no longer helpful in promoting the kinds of outcomes that people with disabilities have come to value. Just as in the case of the undoing of a major scientific theory or way of explaining reality, once this basic shift occurs, one can expect a period of chaos until a new explanation of reality is accepted. Thus, it is likely that the increasing conflict which we see in the mental health field, conflict which primarily represents the differences in goals and power between professionals and people with disabilities may, in fact, continue and intensify until the integration paradigm is finally broadly accepted.

In many ways, the field of mental health is in a most advantageous position to make major changes, since it has developed, over the last decade, an excellent set of service models. To the extent that these models incorporate the new assumptions about people with disabilities, and transform the power relationships between professionals and individuals with disabilities, they are quite adaptable as one element (albeit not the most crucial one) in an integration approach. Professional services are necessary, but are hardly sufficient for achieving integration. Thus, we need to understand the current "state of the art" thinking about professional services—the "comprehensive community support systems" model—in order to consider an alternative model—a "framework for support"—which views the individual within a vibrant and supportive community. The differences between these two conceptualizations are crucial: the comprehensive community support systems model is essentially a professional one, while the framework for support is, in essence, a self-help model.

THE CURRENT PROFESSIONAL SERVICE MODEL: COMPREHENSIVE COMMUNITY SUPPORT SYSTEMS

As mental health systems began to rely less on hospitals, and began gaining valuable experience in supporting individuals with psychiatric disabilities in communities, the concept of a "comprehensive community support system" (CSS) (Turner & Ten-Hoor, 1979) emerged, primarily through the leadership of the NIMH's Community Support Program. This model, updated by NIMH in 1990 as guidance for all U.S. state mental health plans (NIMH, 1987a) is described below. However, a word of caution is in order. Although the following model represents the "state of the art" from a professional perspective, the reader is advised to be sensitive to the residual focus on incapacity, the emphasis on the need for professionally delivered services over the life span, rather than those offered by peers, family members and others, and the assumptions about medically oriented supports, even as the model attempts to incorporate some of the new thinking about integration.

The core CSS components are:

1 *Client identification and outreach* to locate potential clients, and to offer them assistance, whether in shelters, soup kitchens, drop-in centers or the streets.

2 *Mental health treatment,* including diagnostic evaluation, supportive counseling, medication, and services for those with mental illness and substance abuse.

3 *Crisis response services,* including acute care and quick response crisis stabilization services available on a 24 hour basis, including a 24 hour hotline; walk-in crisis services; mobile outreach; community crisis residential beds; and a small number of inpatient beds.

4 *Health and dental care,* including access to general health care and to dental services.

5 *Housing*: permanent, affordable, acceptable housing in normal community housing arrangements; individuals should exercise choice and control over housing; skills training, supports, and services should be available regardless of where people live.

6 *Income support and entitlements*: assistance to help clients obtain income supports and other entitlements.

7 *Peer support for clients*: consumer self-help groups and consumer-operated services in each locality, which are self-defined and consumer-controlled, including peer-support groups; drop-in centers or social clubs; independent living programs that assist individuals to obtain financial benefits, housing, counseling and referral, independent living skills training, job counseling, and employment; consumer-run housing businesses, respite care or crisis assistance services, and community education.

8 *Family and community support*: assistance to families, including education, consultation and supportive counseling, involvement in treatment planning, respite care, and referrals to family support and advocacy groups; backup support to landlords, employers, friends, and community agencies and others.

9 *Employment and rehabilitation services*: rehabilitation to gain or regain practical skills, including teaching clients how to cope with their disabilities; assistance in developing social skills, interests, and leisure-time activities; and teaching daily living skills; including vocational services and employment opportunities to assist clients to prepare for, obtain, and maintain employment, including vocational assessment and counseling; pre-vocational job readiness; career development; on-the-job-training; job sharing; transitional employment; supported employment; competitive employment; job development with local employers; and innovative approaches to using recovering consumers as mental health workers.

10 *Protection and advocacy*: grievance procedures and mechanisms to protect client rights, both in and outside of mental health and residential facilities, and ways to inform each client and family of their legal rights and resources.

11 *Case management services*: this involves having a single person or a team of persons responsible for maintaining a long-term supportive relationship with the client. Specific functions include: identifying clients who need and desire case management services; working with the client to develop a comprehensive service plan based on the client's needs and goals; providing information to help the client make an informed choice about opportunities and services; assisting the client, as requested, to obtain needed

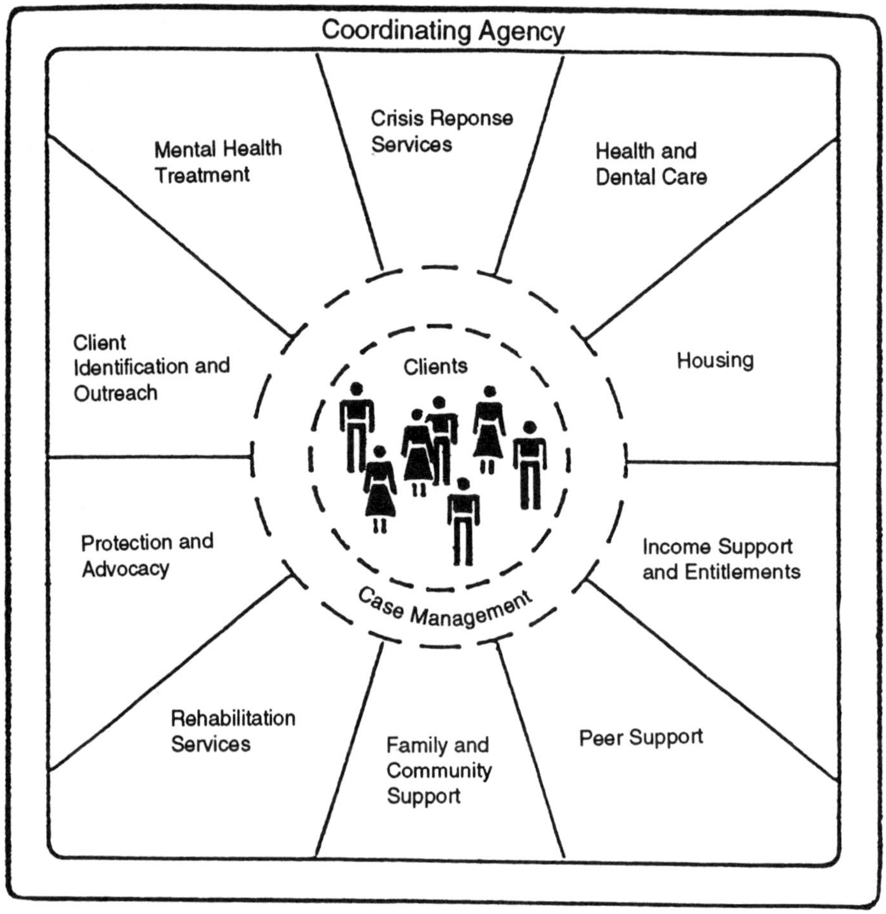

Figure 3. The community support system model. Source: NIMH (1987a).

services, supports, and entitlements; being available and accessible during and after regular working hours; and advocating at the systems level for needed systems improvements. For homeless mentally ill individuals, effective case management must be intensive, ongoing, and take place in shelters or on the streets.

Figure 3, taken from the NIMH Model Plan, graphically describes the community support system.

A SELF-HELP ALTERNATIVE TO THE PROFESSIONAL MODEL: THE FRAMEWORK FOR SUPPORT

It should be noted that, in spite of the widespread acceptance of the "community support systems" perspective in the United States, Canadian mental health systems have adopted a different, and some feel more progressive set of policies that are referred to as a "framework for support" (Trainor & Church, 1984; Pape, 1990). In this conceptualization, the core support which is expected to lead to integration and success is not professional services, but self-help. Secondly, people are expected to draw upon family, friends, and close, freely given relationships for support. Thirdly, people should expect support from generic community organizations and associations, such as churches, social clubs, and community service agencies that are organized for all community members, not just those with "special needs" or labels. Lastly, people should expect services from the formal mental health service system, which is

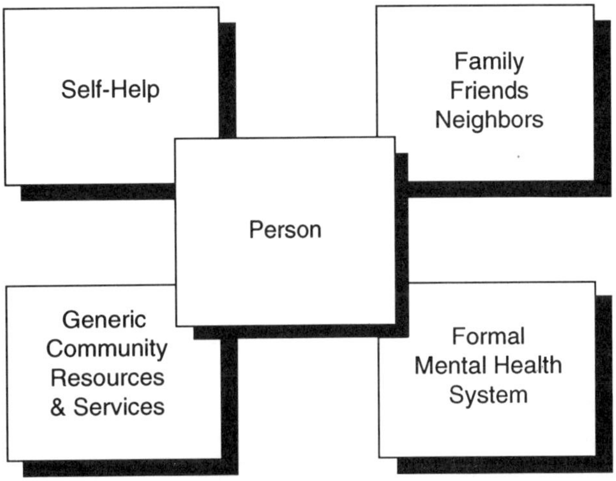

Figure 4. The framework for support. Source: Canadian Mental Health Association (Pape, 1990, p. 2).

organized primarily to "support the supporters," or, in other words, to bolster the efforts of self-help, natural relationships, and community resources. This conceptual approach seems to be a more effective way of thinking about integration, as it more closely approximates the manner in which all citizens, regardless of any special need or circumstance, expect to receive support in their communities. The "framework for support" asserts that change will only come when there are powerful and clear partnerships developed between those who are involved in each part of the framework. Figure 4 graphically displays this model.

The "model" suggested by the "framework of support," is one in which the major supports in a person's life are identified first and foremost as the person (self-help); then friends and family (peer support and family support); then generic community services (housing assistance, employment and training, local recreational opportunities, health care, and so forth); and *only then* the formal mental health system. It is within this framework that we can best examine the capacity of our communities to support people, and then to propose changes in each of these four "sectors" of support. It is important *not* to begin this examination from the narrow perspective of formal mental health services alone (e.g. the community support systems model), as the tendency in communities is always for formal services to take on the responsibility of, or overwhelm, the other three sectors of support, and instead of being the "backup" to those sectors, becoming the *only* support system, with the person becoming increasingly isolated from natural supports, and the formal system, typically underfunded, becoming increasingly burdened.

The goal of the framework for support (Pape, 1990) is to ensure that people with mental disabilities live rich and fulfilling lives in the community. Mental health services, in turn, should be oriented to assisting and buttressing each of these other elements of the support system, in whatever ways are necessary, so as to minimize the ongoing need for professional intervention. The two basic requirements to meet this goal are that individuals with mental health problems be empowered to control their own lives and to make choices about which supports to use; and that the community be mobilized to use all of its capacity to welcome and support people with mental health problems. This approach has major implications for communities and systems, as consumer participation and empowerment are essential to its success. Further, all sectors are equally balanced (instead of being dominated by the formal mental health system); a legislative framework is necessary; and roles in the formal mental health system are redefined (Pape, 1990).

The Framework for Support Project has been tested in three pilot communities in Canada. In a summary of the learnings, Pape (1990) found that achieving a balance of power is both complicated and chaotic; that consumer participation requires groundwork; that the framework cannot work without community reinvestment (i.e. shifting resources from institutional and professional services to community- and consumer-controlled services); that there must be an articulated and explicit set of values, and the leadership to catalyze these values into action.

STRATEGIES FOR SEPARATING HOUSING AND SUPPORTS WHILE INTEGRATING SERVICES

More specifically, with regard to housing, the "paradigm" is shifting toward homes, not residential treatment settings; choices, not placement; normal roles, not client roles; client control, not staff control;

physical and social integration, not segregated/congregate grouping by disability; *in vivo* learning in permanent settings, not preparatory learning in transitional settings; individualized, flexible services and supports, not standardized levels of service; most facilitative, not least restrictive environments; and long-term supports/interdependence, not independence (Ridgway & Ziple, 1990). In the field of mental health, this approach has been termed "supported housing," and is organized around three central principles: (i) consumers choose their own living situations; (ii) consumers live in integrated, stable housing, not in mental health programs; and (iii) consumers have the services and supports required to maximize their opportunities for success over time.

In most instances, successful programmatic implementation of supported housing at the local level has been facilitated by state-level interventions (Livingston & Srebnik, 1991), such as increasing mental health consumers' access to affordable housing, by increasing the number of state staff working on housing issues, by developing housing units, and by increasing consumers' income, such as through rent subsidy approaches. Legislative mandates and financial incentives also have been used to encourage service providers to offer more flexible support services. States have promoted consumer involvement in the mental health system by encouraging their participation in state-level decision-making, and by providing financial support to consumer organizations.

Because of national and state policy support for this approach (Livingston & Srebnik, 1991; NIMH, 1987b; Parrish, 1990; National Association of State Mental Health Program Directors, 1987) supported housing appears to be in the process of broad replication throughout the United States (Livingstone & Srebnik, 1991). Examples are beginning to appear in the literature, including adaptations focused on consumer empowerment and on cultural diversity (Mandiberg & Telles, 1990); for youth in transition (Birmingham *et al*.,, 1990); in combination with an assertive community treatment approach in urban areas (Witheridge, 1990); through the use of non-professional staff and volunteers (Pace & Turkel, 1990); and in Canada as well as the United States (Chipperfield & Aubry, 1990). This approach has been used as a strategy for "decongregating" traditional residential programs (Nagy, 1989), as an alternative to transitional housing for people who are homeless (Goering *et al*., 1990a); and for people with the most severe psychiatric disabilities and the most challenging behaviors (Brown & Wheeler, 1990). This latter study suggests that the following critical skills and supports be included: apartment search assistance; help in moving; money management; structuring time and leisure activities; medication management; crisis support; and limit setting. Staff are recruited who can establish rapport quickly, and who see themselves as client advocates. Key organizational supports include transportation, telephone support, flexible funds, minimal paperwork, low caseloads, and a posture of supporting staff's independent decisions.

In the United States, supported housing has also been the subject of a five-state, 10-site, NIMH national demonstration program, (Livingston & Srebnik, 1991) which found that nearly all clients were living in integrated apartments. Some of the housing was less scattered than others, and most was privately owned, although some units were owned by mental health agencies. The housing quality was generally very decent. All programs provided housing services to access housing units, all had services to help clients keep their housing, and most provided financial assistance with rent. Programs provide a broad range of community support services (case management, crisis services, mental health, rehabilitation, and peer support), and case management caseloads averaged two to 15 clients. Services ranged from 8 to 16 hours per day. All services were available in peoples' homes. Projects were not focused as much on self-determination as the conceptual model might suggest: most picked a roommate for the person, who could then say yes or no. Few programs offered more than one or two housing choices. Some programs held the lease to the housing, while others did not. Most had expectations that clients who received housing would also participate in services. Thus, implementation of supported housing varied widely along nearly every dimension studied.

There also are a variety of special issues of concern to those involved in the practical implementation of supported housing (Livingston & Srebnik, 1991). These include the need for special supports at the time of moving into housing; making arrangements for ongoing support and monitoring of needs, including the development of a crisis plan; the usefulness of successful role models for those just beginning to live in their own housing; the special needs of women (Culhane, 1992; Goering *et al.*, 1990b), people who are homeless (Goering *et al.*, 1990b; Benda, 1991; Lipton *et al.*, 1988), who have children, or who have alcohol and substance use problems (Brown & Wheeler, 1990); as well as critical cultural and racial issues (First *et al.*, 1988). There are also important differences in the implementation of supported housing in rural (Tanzman *et al.*, 1991), and in urban (Richman, 1992) areas. A number of creative approaches to housing finance have surfaced recently (Randolph *et al.*, 1987; Applebaum, 1988). These strategies are used for three purposes: to access existing housing, to preserve existing housing, and to develop new affordable housing. To *access* housing, systems are creating rent subsidy programs at the state level in connection with, or as an alternative to, the federal Section 8 subsidy program, as well as "contingency funds" to help with furnishings, utility hook ups, other start-up costs, and emergency housing payments. To *preserve* existing affordable housing, systems are creating limited pools of capital dollars to be used to purchase and renovate such housing, usually in coalition with other low income advocacy groups. To *develop* housing, systems are using a variety of approaches, from targeting capital funds (formerly used for facilities) to develop integrated housing in partnership with others, to purchasing distressed properties, creating capital funds which can "internally subsidize" the cost of housing so that it remains perpetually affordable, or mixing public and private funds, such as in limited equity ventures, or through the use of tax credits. Many of these innovative financing strategies have been refined through the Robert Wood Johnson Program on Chronic Mental Illness, a nine-city demonstration project to develop housing and supports on a system-wide basis for people with psychiatric disabilities (Cohen & Somers, 1990). One other creative example is the use of "back payments" from an SSI law suit to develop housing (Applebaum, 1988).

Even with these policy developments and creative financing approaches, Hatfield (1993) raises legitimate family concerns about whether people with psychiatric disabilities will be able to compete for housing on the open market, and about whether landlords will be willing to keep housing open while a person is in crisis or hospitalized. In fact, as indicated by Knisley and Fleming (1993), mental health agencies which have broadly implemented supported housing have found that a variety of organizational changes, such as the development of housing development corporations; funding strategies, such as the ongoing payment of rent during hospitalization; as well as service strategies, such as the provision of intensive case management, are needed to assure this ongoing housing access for many consumers. Hatfield is also concerned about the issue of loneliness and social isolation for those who choose to live alone. In fact, a national evaluation of supported housing implementation (Livingston & Srebnik, 1991) found that this was a real problem for many consumers, and that mental health agencies, with the exception of "exemplary" programs (Tanzman *et al.*, 1991; Richman, 1992) are generally not yet effective in meeting this need. This lack is found in residential facilities as well, in which social integration only occurs with specifically focused efforts (Segal & Holschuh, 1991), and even then typically excludes social relationships with people without disabilities (Burchard *et al.*, 1992). Hatfield is also concerned that group homes will not be available for those who want them. This is a major concern in that choice in housing, even in supported housing programs (Livingston & Srebnik, 1991), appears to be given much less emphasis than the underlying philosophy of rehabilitation would suggest. In fact, "placement" still appears to be the dominant approach in mental health. This is confounded by the enormous pressures on mental health systems to reduce the use of costly facilities, by transferring people, often quickly, to other settings, which effectively reduces choice even further. The supported housing philosophy clearly specifies that choice is paramount, and that if an individual wishes to use a residential treatment setting, or to live in a group arrangement, then that choice should be respected. Whether these choices will be honored, however, in increasingly difficult financial times is indeed an open question.

On a related issue, Hatfield (1993) is concerned about whether supported housing will cost more than traditional approaches. Systematic cost data are not yet available to make these comparisons. The cost of implementing a variety of supported housing programs in the NIMH demonstration program (Livingston & Srebnik, 1991; Livingston *et al.*, 1992) averaged $8000–9000 (U.S.) for each person with a severe psychiatric disability. Other cost data on the provision of comprehensive community support services to people with the most severe psychiatric disabilities in Dane County, Wisconsin, (Diamond, 1992) average about $12 000, (U.S.) confirming the early studies of the PACT (Program in Assertive Community Treatment) Program, which suggested that this comprehensive approach was a cost-effective alternative to hospital care (Stein & Test, 1985). A more recent statewide study in Tennessee (Carling *et al.*, 1992) suggests that the state could save nearly 800 million dollars over the next 20 years by converting from a facility-based system to one that used state-of-the-art community support services. There is no systematic evidence about comparative costs for residential programs. The above studies, however, while certainly not conclusive, do not appear to suggest that a home-based housing and supports approach would be any more expensive than traditional residential treatment. In fact, these findings suggest that such comparisons may even be specious, in that the focus of these facility-based programs may properly be one of treatment, not long-term housing.

A small number of studies have documented family preferences for housing for their affected family member (Housing Committee, California Alliance for the Mentally Ill *et al.*, 1986; Edgar, 1989; Pandiani & Glesne, 1992; Rogers *et al.*, 1992; Tanzman, 1990; Akers, 1989). In general, these studies indicate that families see an enormous need for affordable housing and better community services, and that they have roughly equal preferences for residential program models or for supported housing. The conclusion one draws in reading these studies is that the housing need is so desperate that virtually *any* option is acceptable. Interestingly, family and professional assessments about what consumers need appear to vary, at least in part, as a function of what is available in a given area. This is also the case, but to a lesser extent, with consumer preferences. For example, mental health professionals, in a Washington state assessment of needs, believed that consumers primarily needed residential programs, while consumers preferred integrated housing with supports (Daniels & Carling, 1986). By contrast, a more recent study in Vermont, a state in which community support services are more widely available, revealed little difference between consumer and professional perception of need, both of which heavily emphasized a supported housing approach. (Pandiani & Glesne, 1992). In the Vermont study, families continued to see a need for group homes or residential programs, while also concluding that there is a greater need for housing and supports in integrated settings.

As the previous discussion indicates, a crucial policy issue involves the future of residential services programs. While it appears that states are funding fewer of these settings (Randolph *et al.*, 1991), and that the settings themselves are evolving (Nagy, 1989), there is little consensus in the field as to whether they represent a set of institutions whose time has passed, or a resource which, with adaptations, represents a valuable element of the service system of the future. This latter policy perspective has been articulated by Fields (1990), who contends that a full range of residential treatment programs, and the widespread availability of affordable, permanent housing with supports, are both essential elements of a fully delineated system of services for people with psychiatric disabilities. He contends that residential treatment is essential to prevent the use of institutional care for those who would otherwise remain in hospitals, jails, or nursing homes, and thus, is a specific treatment element that represents one of the critical supports in an overall supported housing approach. Although this question continues to fuel debate, evidence suggests that as the mental health field develops more responsive services, even people with the most severe psychiatric disabilities can be successfully served with a supported housing approach (Brown & Wheeler, 1990; O'Rear & O'Rear, 1990).

THE NEED FOR FURTHER RESEARCH

As public policy appears to be shifting away from an expectation that residential facilities will meet any significant proportion of the need for stable housing and community support services, additional research into questions of where and how consumers prefer to live, successful strategies for facilitating meaningful client choices and for developing housing and supports, documentation of the costs and benefits of housing and support initiatives, identification of clinical interventions best suited to normal housing, and an elaboration of the role of peer support in community success, will all be vital.

Research on supported housing, to date, has largely consisted of descriptive studies of current programs (Hall *et al.*, 1987), although several outcome studies specifically focused on supported housing have been reported. A recent study (Brown *et al.*, 1991), for example, which compared clients with a history of involuntary hospitalization, who were assigned to a supported housing program, with clients who had voluntarily selected that program, found that the involuntary clients rated higher on such risk factors as history of suicide attempts, self-neglect, homelessness, and medication non-compliance. The involuntary clients showed a much higher utilization of supported housing services and case management, psychiatric and shelter services during the 9 months after entry into the program, and they had a higher 1 year re-hospitalization rate. However, they used substantially fewer inpatient days in the 6 months after entry to the program than the 6 months before. A similar program (O'Rear & O'Rear, 1990) reports successfully reducing hospitalization rates with "more difficult to serve" clients through the use of multidisciplinary teams, including psychiatrists, available on a mobile basis, 24 hours a day, and through the use of scattered site housing.

In order to demonstrate the effectiveness of this approach, further studies which assist the field in operationalizing the supported housing concept, as well as studies that assess its impact on consumers and their families, are essential. A recent review of the research on community integration of people with psychiatric disabilities (Carling *et al.*, 1987) concluded that further research is *not* needed on hospital versus community alternatives, or on the efficacy of residential treatment settings (e.g., group homes), particularly as these settings are so rarely operationally defined. The key unresearched questions, according to that review, are: "Where do people with mental illness live?" "Where do they want to live?" and "How can we help them succeed there?" (p. 23). Finally, the authors note that answering these questions requires a shift from professionally defined to consumer-defined research. This is consistent with recent calls for research on psychiatric disability to focus more on the commonalities between people with and without disabilities, and to begin defining "success" in terms of quality of life variables such as physical and material well-being; relations with other people; social, community, and civic activities; personal development and fulfillment; and recreation (Wilson, 1992).

The supported housing approach itself suggests a broad research agenda (Carling, 1990). In promoting active consumer choice of their housing and supports, for example, we need to understand better the process of choice and how to assist people with making choices. We need to understand better the power of control and autonomy in promoting success. We need further information on consumers' perspectives about what kinds of housing people prefer, what services and supports are helpful, and how they might best be provided. We need to understand better the capacity of consumers to manage their symptoms and their own lives, and to assist each other, both individually, and through consumer-operated services.

With regard to supports, we need to understand effective ways to organize services which assist people with the most severe disabilities to succeed in housing of their choice, and which support their families as well. Key issues to be explored include strategies for achieving flexibility and individualization of services, and the continuity of relationships involved. In effect, we need to discover the ways in which services can eliminate the perceived need for specialized living arrangements (Test & Stein, 1977; Test, 1981).

Finally, with regard to housing, we need to understand the impact of choice versus "placement" on success, and the contribution to success of particular types of housing strategies. Broad dispersion of housing, for example, versus physical proximity, may have an impact on the capacity of consumers to support each other, and for staff to be available and readily accessible to provide requested assistance. We need to understand the positive value of a shared consumer or ex-patient housing arrangement, at the same time as we assist people to become part of the larger community. In order to understand better how to facilitate integration, it would be helpful to study the impact of different types of living arrangements, including size, number of residents, location and make-up of the housing, and its appearance and stability; and on relevant integration outcomes, such as the number and types of relationships and activities which involve people without disabilities. Through expanded research on consumer choice, housing, and supports, we can begin building the critical knowledge base necessary to achieve community integration for people with psychiatric disabilities.

SUMMARY AND CONCLUSIONS: FUTURE CHALLENGES IN HOUSING AND SUPPORT

In summary, the field of mental health has begun to make significant progress in reconceptualizing its roles and responsibilities for housing and supports. New knowledge about what consumers actually want, and about the needs of families, new policies and funding mechanisms through which agencies and systems can respond to these needs, and new program approaches are all emerging. As the field continues to experience major change, it is both significant and hopeful that this change is resulting in an increased focus on the basic need for a home, and on a deepening commitment to pursue a variety of strategies that will assist people to have their own homes, with the supports they want, in spite of their psychiatric label.

This paradigmatic shift mirrors similar shifts in the broader fields of disability and affordable housing. Because access to affordable housing has become a national crisis, the public's support for increased federal and state spending and taxation for housing is at an all time high (O'Rear & O'Rear, 1990). Thus, even as federal housing programs are being cut, the U.S. Congress has passed new housing legislation. The National Affordable Housing Act and the Fair Housing Amendments Act are intended to further promote housing integration, including for people with a psychiatric disability; and the Americans with Disabilities Act (ADA) is a landmark piece of legislation that specifically promotes the goal of full community integration for people with psychiatric disabilities. These larger trends will continue to shape mental health's response to housing and support needs.

The supported housing approach, while an exciting response to some of the limitations of traditional approaches, brings with it a wealth of difficulties and challenges, largely because it represents a far more ideal way of thinking about people and their needs than is reflected in current attitudinal, programmatic, and funding realities (Racino, 1991). By advocating major change throughout a system, it also flies in the face of many vested interests, both professional and economic. Systems that take on a supported housing approach can easily become overwhelmed with such goals as basing housing on consumers' preferences, especially as they are typically acting in "crisis mode," with little time to ask *anyone* else's views. Listening to consumers, whether in a process of formulating new goals with an individual, or planning a new statewide approach to housing, takes time; more time than implementing current approaches. Furthermore, much of what policy-makers or professionals hear from consumers they may not like, and most of the resources and tools they have to create housing are only useful for facility-based approaches. Similarly, services are rarely organized to support people wherever they wish to live. With regard to housing, systems and local agencies have significant real estate holdings in their facilities. Often they do not have the management or practice-level staff who have skills in housing access, preservation, financing, and development, nor do they have the relationships with housing systems that they need. Systems face resistance from local agencies, from professional groups, and from other advocates in moving too quickly toward a consumer driven approach. Implementing supported housing also takes resources which are currently unavailable in mental health systems, at least in the form they are needed, and therefore need to be created. Rent subsidies, pools of capital that can be accessed quickly to make opportunistic deals, flexible funds for furnishings for consumers, expanded case management and crisis services: all of these represent bureaucratic nightmares in some systems. In these cases, trying to implement supported housing often makes it crystal clear to a mental health system that the major barriers clients face are, in fact, the characteristics of the system itself. In spite of these formidable barriers to change, however, it seems clear that most states are moving in this direction, albeit at very different paces, and with differing strategies.

For all of these reasons though, it is also clear, that while policy change in this area can proceed relatively rapidly, implementing a supported housing approach is essentially a long-term proposition for most mental health systems. Policies, planning practices, financing structures, relationships, and expectations with service providers and with other government agencies, such as housing, management information systems, and staff roles all need to change. It is likely that, in most systems, residential facilities and group living settings will continue to be used, even as other systems begin "decongregating" them. In this way, supported housing is no different from any other change in mental health; implementation is always widely variable.

The difference with supported housing, however, is its "ripple effect" on other aspects of the system. Once a mental health system begins to take consumer choice and voice seriously, for example, it is exceedingly difficult to make decisions based on more traditional methods.

ABSTRACT

This chapter focuses on the housing and community living needs of people with psychiatric disabilities within the context of powerful economic forces which limit their opportunities for successful community integration. It describes how the field's approach to meeting these needs is changing, and how consumers are severely affected by the international affordable housing crisis, by the crisis of homelessness, and by the continued investment of the preponderance of mental health resources into institutions, facility-based settings, and professional treatment, rather than for such basic supports as housing, employment and peer support. A variety of community "program models," and research on their effectiveness is described, along with some critical programmatic and financial problems associated with using residential treatment facilities as housing. Finally, "supported housing," a new approach based on principles of consumer choice, integrated housing, and flexible personal and financial supports, is described. The implications of this approach for mental health systems are discussed.

REFERENCES

Akers, L. (1989). *Residential Programs for Kentuckians with Mental Illness.* Louisville, KY: Kentucky Department for Mental Health and Mental Retardation Services.

Alisky, J.M. and Iczkowski, K.A. (1990). Barriers to housing for deinstitutionalized psychiatric patients. *Hospital and Community Psychiatry,* **41**, 93–95.

Anthony, W.A. and Blanch, A. (1989). Research on community support services: What have we learned? *Psychosocial Rehabilitation Journal,* **123**, 55–81.

Anthony, W.A. and Dion, G. (1986). A review of psychiatric rehabilitation research. Washington, DC: National Rehabilitation Information Center.

Anthony, W.A., Cohen, M., and Farkas, M.A. (1982). A psychiatric rehabilitation treatment program: Can I recognize one if I see one? *Community Mental Health Journal,* **18**, 182–192.

Applebaum, P. (1988). Housing for the mentally ill: An unexpected outcome of a class action suit against the SSA. *Hospital and Community Psychiatry,* **39**, 479–480.

Bassuk, E.L. (1984). The homelessness problem. *Scientific American,* **251**, 40–45.

Baxter, E. and Hopper, K. (1984). Troubled in the streets: The mentally disabled homeless poor. In J.A. Talbott, ed., *The Chronic Mental Patient: Five Years Later.* New York: Grune, & Stratton.

Belcher, J.R. (1988). Defining the service needs of homeless mentally ill persons. *Hospital and Community Psychiatry,* **39**, 1203–1205.

Benda, B.B. (1991). Undomiciled: A study of drifters, other homeless persons, their problems, and service utilization. *Psychosocial Rehabilitation Journal,* **14**, 39–67.

Benda, B.B. and Datallo, P. (1988). Homelessness: consequence of a crisis or a long term process? *Hospital and Community Psychiatry,* **39**, 884–886.

Benoit, B. (1992). Promoting the rehabilitation potential of community residential facilities. *Psychosocial Rehabilitation Journal,* **15**, 109–113.

Birmingham, M., MacLeod, R.J., and Farthing, G.R. (1990). A supported independent living program for youth. *Hospital and Community Psychiatry,* **41**, 924–927.

Blanch, A.K., Carling, P.J., and Ridgway, P. (1988). Normal housing with specialized support: A psychiatric rehabilitation approach to living in the community. *Rehabilitation Psychology,* **432**, 47–55.

Boydall, K.M., Trainor, J.N., Pierri, A.M. (1989). The effect of group homes for the mentally ill on residential property values. *Hospital and Community Psychiatry*, **40**, 957–958.

Braun, P., Kochansky, G., Shapiro, R., *et al.* (1981). Overview: Deinstitutionalization of psychiatric patients—a critical review of outcome studies. *American Journal of Psychiatry*, **138**, 736–749.

Breakey, W.R. and Fischer, P.J. (1990). Homelessness: The extent of the problem. *Journal of Social Issues*, **46**, 31–47.

Brown, M.A. and Wheeler, T. (1990). Supported housing for the most disabled: suggestions for providers. *Psychosocial Rehabilitation Journal*, **13**, 59–68.

Brown, M.A., Ridgway, P., Anthony, W.A., *et al.* (1991). Comparison of outcomes for clients seeking and assigned to supported housing services. *Hospital and Community Psychiatry*, **42**, 1150–1153.

Budson, R.D. (1981). *New Directions for Mental Health Services: Issues in Community Residential Care*. San Francisco, Jossey-Bass.

Burchard, S.N., Rosen, J.W., Gordon, L.R., *et al.* (1992). A comparison of social support and satisfaction in three types of community residential alternatives. In J.W. Jacobson, S.N. Burchard, and P.J. Carling, eds, *Community Living for People with Developmental and Psychiatric Disabilities*, pp. 137–154. Baltimore, MD: Johns Hopkins University Press.

Campanelli, P.C., Sacks, J.Y., Heckart, K., *et al.* (1992). Integrating psychiatric rehabilitation within a community residence framework. *Psychosocial Rehabilitation Journal*, **16**, 135–153.

Carling, P.J. (1978). Residential services in a psychosocial rehabilitation context: The Horizon House model. In *New Directions in Mental Health Care: Cooperative Apartments*, pp. 52–64. Adelphi, MD: National Institute of Mental Health.

Carling, P.J. (1981). Nursing homes and chronic mental patients: A second opinion. *Schizophrenia Bulletin*, **7**, 574–579.

Carling, P.J. (1984). *Developing Family Foster Care Programs in Mental Health: A Resource Guide*. Rockville, MD: National Institute of Mental Health.

Carling, P.J. (1989). Access to housing: cornerstone of the American dream. *Journal of Rehabilitation*, **553**, 6–8.

Carling, P.J. (1990). Supported housing: an evaluation agenda. *Psychosocial Rehabilitation Journal*, **134**, 95–104.

Carling, P.J. (1993). Supports and rehabilitation for housing and community living. In R.W. Flexer, and P. Solomon eds, *Contemporary Practice in Rehabilitation and Mental Health Services*, pp. 99–118. Boston, MA: Andover Medical Publishers.

Carling, P.J. and Ridgway, P. (1987). Overview of a psychiatric rehabilitation approach to housing. In W.A. Anthony and M. Farkas, eds, *Psychiatric Rehabilitation: Turning Theory into Practice*, pp. 28–80. Baltimore, MD: Johns Hopkins University Press.

Carling, P.J., Randolph, F.L., Blanch, A.K., *et al.* (1987). *Rehabilitation Research Review: Housing and Community Integration for People with Psychiatric Disabilities*. Washington, DC: D:ATA Institute, National Rehabilitation Information Center Review.

Carling, P.J., McCabe, S.S., and Besio, S.F. (1992). *The Tennessee Mental Health Master Plan*. Burlington, VT: Center for Community Change through Housing and Suport.

Carpenter, M.D. (1978). Residential placement for the chronic psychiatric patient: A review and evaluation of the literature. *Schizophrenia Bulletin*, **4**, 384–398.

Chatetz, L. and Goldfinger, S.M. (1984). Residential instability in a psychiatric emergency setting. *Psychiatric Quarterly*, **56**, 20–34.

Chipperfield, S. and Aubry, T. (1990). The supportive housing program in Winnipeg. *Psychosocial Rehabilitation Journal*, **13**, 91–94.

Cohen, M.D. and Somers, S. (1990). Supported housing: insights from the Robert Wood Johnson Foundation Program on chronic mental illness. *Psychosocial Rehabilitation Journal*, **13**, 43–50.

Cohen, C.I. and Thompson, K.S. (1992). Homeless mentally ill or mentally ill homeless? *American Journal of Psychiatry*, **6**, 816–822.

Cometa, M.S., Morrison, J.K., and Ziskoven, M. (1979). Halfway to where? A critique of research on psychiatric halfway houses. *Journal of Community Psychology*, **7**, 23–27.

Coulton, C.L., Holland, T.P., and Fitch, V. (1984). Person–environment congruence and psychiatric patient outcome in community care homes. *Administration in Mental Health*, **12**, 71–88.

Culhane, D.P. (1992). Ending homelessness among women with severe mental illness: A model program from Philadelphia. *Psychosocial Rehabilitation Journal*, **16**, 63–76.

Daniels, L.V. and Carling, P.J. (1986). *Community Residential Rehabilitation Services for Psychiatrically Disabled Persons in Kitsap County*. Boston, MA: Boston University Center for Psychiatric Rehabilitation.

Deegan, P.E. (1992). The independent living movement and people with psychiatric disabilities: Taking back control over our own lives. *Psychosocial Rehabilitation Journal*, **15**, 3–19.

Dellario, D. and Anthony, W. (1981). On the relative effectiveness of institutional and alternative placements of the psychiatrically disabled. *Journal of Social Issues*, **37**, 21–33.

Department of Health and Human Services. (1983). *Report to Congress on Shelter and Basic Living Needs of Chronically Mentally Ill Individuals*. Washington, DC: Department of Health and Human Services.

Diamond, R. (1992). Supporting people with mental illness over time in a comprehensive community support system: costs and benefits. Final Report to NIMH. Madison, WI: University of Wisconsin.

Drake, R.E., Wallach, M.A., and Hoffman, J.S. (1989). Housing instability and homelessness among aftercare patients of an urban state hospital. *Hospital and Community Psychiatry*, **40**, 46–51.

Edgar, B. (1989). Family and case manager perspectives on consumers' housing and support needs. *Journal of the California Alliance for the Mentally Ill*, **3**, 10–11.

Estroff, S. (1981). *Making it Crazy: An Ethnography of Psychiatric Clients in an American Community*. Berkeley, CA: University of California Press.

Fairweather, G. (1980). The Fairweather Lodge: A twenty-five year retrospective. In H.R. Lamb, ed., *New Directions for Mental Health Services*, No. 7. San Francisco, Jossey-Bass.

Fields, S. (1990). The relationship between residential treatment and supported housing in a community system of services. *Psychosocial Rehabilitation Journal*, **13**, 105–113.

First, R., Roth, D., and Arewa, B. (1988). Homelessness: understanding the human dimensions of the problem for minorities. *Social Work*, **33**, 120–124.

First, R.J., Rife, J.C., and Kraus, S. (1990). Case management with people who are homeless and mentally ill: Preliminary findings from an NIMH Demonstration Project. *Psychosocial Rehabilitation Journal*, **14**, 87–91.

Gelberg, L. and Linn, L. (1988). Social and physical health of homeless adults previously treated for mental health problems. *Hospital and Community Psychiatry*, **39**, 510–516.

Geller, M.P. (1982). The "revolving door": A trap or a life style? *Hospital and Community Psychiatry*, **33**, 388–389.

Goldman, H.H., Gatozzi, A.A., and Taube, C.A. (1981). Defining and counting the chronically mentally ill. *Hospital and Community Psychiatry*, **32**, 21–27.

Goering, P., Durbin, J., Trainor, J. *et al.* (1990a). Developing housing for the homeless. *Psychosocial Rehabilitation Journal*, **13**, 33–42.

Goering, P., Paduchak, D., and Durbin, J. (1990b). Housing homeless women: a consumer preference study. *Hospital and Community Psychiatry*, **41**, 790–794.

Goldmeier, J., Shore, M.F., and Mannino, F.V. (1977). Cooperative apartments: New programs in community mental health. *Health and Social Work*, **2**, 119–140.

Grunberg, J. and Eagle, P.F. (1990). Shelterization: How the homeless adapt to shelter living. *Hospital and Community Psychiatry*, **41**, 521–525.

Hall, G.B., Nelson, G., and Fowler, H.S. (1987). Housing for the chronically mentally disabled: Part I—conceptual framework and social context. *Canadian Journal of Mental Health*, **26**, 65–78.

Harding, C., Brooks, G., Ashikaga, T., Strauss, J., and Brier, A. (1987). The Vermont longitudinal study of persons with severe mental illness. II: Long-term outcome of subjects who retrospectively met DSM-III criteria for schizophrenia. *American Journal of Psychiatry*, **144**(6), 718–726.

Hatfield, A.B. (1990). *Coping with Mental Illness in the Family: A Family Guide*, 2nd edn. Baltimore, MD: Mental Hygiene Administration.

Hatfield, A.B. (1993). A family perspective on supported housing. *Hospital and Community Psychiatry*, **44**, 496–497.

Hatfield, A.B., Fierstein, R., and Johnson, D. (1982). Meeting the needs of families of the psychiatrically disabled. *Psychosocial Rehabilitation Journal*, **6**, 27–40.

Housing Committee, California Alliance for the Mentally Ill. (1986). B.A. Castaneda and R. Sommer, eds, Patient housing options as viewed by parents of the mentally ill. *Hospital and Community Psychiatry*, **37**, 1238–1242.

Howie the Harp (1990). Independent living with support services: The goal and future for mental health consumers. *Psychosocial Rehabilitation Journal*, **13**, 85–89.

Kiesler, C.A. (1982). Mental hospitals and alternative care: noninstitutionalization as potential public policy for mental patients. *American Psychologist*, **37**, 349–360.

Knisley, M.B. and Fleming, N. (1993). Implementing supported housing in state and local mental health systems. *Hospital and Community Psychiatry*, **44**, 456–461.

Koegel, P. and Burnam, M.A. (in press). Problems in the assessment of homelessness: An empirical approach. In M.J. Robertson and M. Greenblatt, eds, *Homelessness: The National Perspective*. New York: Plenum Press.

Kohen, W. and Paul, G.L. (1976). Current trends and recommended changes in extended care placement of mental patients: The Illinois system as a case in point. *Schizophrenia Bulletin*, **2**, 575–594.

Kozol, J. (1988). *Rachel and Her Children: Homeless Families in America*. New York: Crown Publishers.

Lamb, H.R. (1984). *The Homeless Mentally Ill*. Washington, DC: American Psychological Association.

Lamb, R.H. and Lamb, D.M. (1990). Factors contributing to homelessness among the chronically and severely mentally ill. *Hospital and Community Psychiatry*, **41**, 301–305.

Lipton, F.R., Nutt, S., and Sabatini, A. (1988). Housing the homeless mentally ill: A longitudinal study of a treatment approach. *Hospital and Community Psychiatry*, **39**, 40–45.

Livingston, J. and Srebnik, D. (1991). States' strategies for promoting supported housing for persons with psychiatric disabilities. *Hospital and Community Psychiatry*, **42**, 1116–1119.

Livingston, J.A., Srebnik, D., King, D.A. *et al.* (1992). Approaches to providing housing and flexible supports for people with psychiatric disabilities. *Psychosocial Rehabilitation Journal*, **16**, 27–43.

Low Income Housing Information Service (1988). *Low Income Housing, Bulletin 12*. Washington DC: Low Income Housing Information Service.

Mandiberg, J.M. and Telles, L. (1990). The Santa Clara County Clustered Apartment Project. *Psychosocial Rehabilitation Journal*, **14**, 21–28.

McCabe, S.S., Edgar, E.R., King, D.A., *et al.* (1991). Holes in the Housing Safety Net: Why SSI is Not Enough: A National Comparison Study of Supplemental Security Income and HUD Fair Market Rents. Burlington, VT: University of Vermont, Center for Community Change through Housing and Support.

McCabe, S.S., Edgar, E., Mancuso, L., King, D., Ross, E.C., and Emery, B.D. (1993). Access to affordable housing: a national comparison study of supplemental security income and HUD fair market rents, *Hospital and Community Psychiatry*, **44** (55), 494–495.

McKnight, J. (1977). Professionalized service and disabling help. In *Disabling Professions*. London: Marion Boyers.

Mills, P.D. and Hanson, J.C. (1991). Short term group interventions for mentally ill young adults living in a community residence and their families, *Hospital and Community Psychiatry*, **42**, 1144–1150.

Morrison, J. (1989). Correlations between definitions of the homeless mentally ill population. *Hospital and Community Psychiatry*, **40**, 952–954.

Morse, G. and Calsyn, R.J. (in press). Mental health and other human service needs of homeless people. In M.J. Robertson and M. Greenblatt, eds, *Homelessness: The National Perspective*. New York: Plenum Press.

Mosher, L.R. and Menn, A.Z. (1978). Community residential treatment for schizophrenia: two year follow up. *Hospital and Community Psychiatry*, **29**, 715–723.

Mulkern, V. and Bradley, V. (1986). Service utilization and service preferences of homeless persons. *Psychosocial Rehabilitation Journal*, **10**, 22–30.

Nagy, M. (1989). De-congregating a residential program for people with psychiatric disabilities. *Psychosocial Rehabilitation Journal*, **12**, 70–73.

National Alliance to End Homelessness (1988). *Housing and Homelessness: A Report of the National Alliance to End Homelessness*. Washington DC: National Alliance to End Homelessness.

National Association of State Mental Health Program Directors (1987). *Position Statement on Housing and Support for People with Long-term Mental Illness*. Alexandria, VA: NASMHPD.

National Housing Institute (1988). *A Status Report on: The American Dream*. Princeton, NJ: RL Associates.

National Institute of Mental Health (1987a). *Model Plan for Meeting the Needs of People with Serious Psychiatric Disabilities:* P. L. 99-660 Guidelines. Rockville, MD: NIMH.

National Institute of Mental Health (1987b). *Guidelines for Meeting the Housing Needs of People with Psychiatric Disabilities*. Rockville, MD: NIMH.

O'Rear, G. and O'Rear, T.M. (1990). Way station: A comprehensive approach to residential services for and with people with serious mental illness. *Psychosocial Rehabilitation Journal*, **13**, 77–80.

Pace, S. and Turkel, W. (1990). Participants community volunteers and staff: A collaborative approach to housing and support. *Psychosocial Rehabilitation Journal*, **13**, 81–83.

Pandiani, J. and Glesne, C. (1992). Interpreting divergent results of triangulated research: A review of three studies of housing needs of adults with psychiatric diagnoses. *Sociological Practice Review*, **3**, 87–93.

Pape, B. (1990). Building a framework for support for people with mental disabilities. *CMHA Social Action Series*. Toronto: Canadian Mental Health Association.

Parrish, J. (1990). Supported housing: A critical component of effective community support. *Psychosocial Rehabilitation Journal*, **13**, 9–10.

Public Health Service (1980). Toward a National Plan for the "Chronically Mentally Ill": Report to the Secretary by the DHHS Steering Committee on the Chronically Mentally Ill. Rockville, MD.

Racino, J.A. (1991). Living in the community: independence, support and transition. In F.R. Rusch, L. DeStafano, J. Chadsey-Rusch, L.A. Phelps, and E. Suzaminski, eds, *Transition from School to Work for Youth and Adults with Disabilities*, pp. 31–42. Sycamore II: Sycamore Publishing Company.

Randolph, F.L., Laux, R., and Carling, P.J. (1987). *In Search of Housing: Creative Approaches to Housing for People with Psychiatric Disabilities*. Monograph Series on Housing and Mental Health. Boston, MA: The Center for Psychiatric Rehabilitation.

Randolph, F.L., Ridgway, P., and Carling, P.J. (1991). Residential programs for persons with severe mental illness: A nationwide survey of state-affiliated agencies. *Hospital and Community Psychiatry*, **42**, 1111–1115.

Richman, E. (1992). Supported housing in urban areas. *In Community*, **2**, 24.

Ridgway, P. (1987). *Avoiding Zoning Battles*. Washington DC: Intergovernmental Health Policy Project.

Ridgway, P. (1988). Coming home: ex-patients view options and needs. *Proceedings of a National Consumer Housing Forum*. Burlington VT: University of Vermont, Center for Community Change through Housing and Support.

Ridgway, P. and Zipple, A.M. (1990). The paradigm shift in residential services: From the linear continuum to supported housing approaches. *Psychosocial Rehabilitation Journal*, **134**, 11–31.

Rizzo, A.M., Zipple, A.M., Pisciotta, J., *et al.* (1992). Strategies for responding to community opposition in an existing group home. *Psychosocial Rehabilitation Journal*, **15**, 85–95.

Rogers, S.E., Walsh, D., and Masotta, L., *et al.* (1992). Massachusetts Survey of Family Preferences for Community Support Services: Final Report. Boston, MA: Massachusetts Department of Mental Health.

Roth, D., Toomey, B.G., and First, R.J. (in press). Homeless women: characteristics and service needs. Affilia: *Journal of Women and Social Work*.

Schutt, R.K., Goldfinger, S.M., and Penk, W.E. (1992). The structure and sources of residential preferences among seriously mentally ill homeless adults. *Sociological Practice Review*, **3**, 148–156.

Segal, S.P. and Aviram, U. (1978). *The Mentally Ill in Community-based Sheltered Care: A Study of Community Care and Social Integration*. New York: John Wiley.

Segal, S.P. and Choi, N.G. (1991). Factors affecting SSI support for sheltered care residents with serious mental illness. *Hospital and Community Psychiatry,* **42**, 1132–1137.

Segal, S.P. and Holschuh, J. (1991). Effects of sheltered care environments and resident characteristics on the development of social networks. *Hospital and Community Psychiatry,* **42**, 1125–1131.

Segal, S.P. and Liese, L.H. (1991). A ten year perspective on three models of sheltered care. *Hospital and Community Psychiatry,* **42**, 1120–1124.

Segal, S.P., Baumohl, J., and Moyes, E.W. (1980). Neighborhood types and community reaction to the mentally ill: A paradox of intensity. *Journal of Health and Social Behavior,* **21**, 345–359.

Spaulding, W., Harig, R., and Schwab, L.O. (1987). Preferred clinical skills for transitional living specialists. *Psychosocial Rehabilitation Journal,* **11**, 5–21.

Stein, L.I. and Test, M.A. (1985). The training in community living model: A decade of experience. In H.R. Lamb, ed., *New Directions for Mental Health Services,* No. 26. San Francisco: Jossey-Bass.

Stroul, B. (1988). *Crisis Residential Services in a Community Support System.* Rockville, MD: National Institute of Mental Health.

Tanzman, B.H. (1990). Minnesota Department of Human Services Housing Study. In B.H. Tanzman, ed. *Researching the Preferences of People with Psychiatric Disabilities for Housing and Supports: A Practical Guide.* Monograph Series on Housing and Rehabilitation in Mental Health. Burlington, VT: University of Vermont, Center for Community Change through Housing and Support.

Tanzman, B. (1993). An overview of surveys of mental health consumers' preferences for housing and support services. *Hospital and Community Psychiatry,* **44**, 450–455.

Tanzman, B., McCabe, S.S., and Curtis, L. (1991). When a little is a lot: implementing supported housing in rural areas. *In Community,* **1**, 24.

Tanzman, B., Wilson, S.F., and Yoe, J. (1992). Mental health consumer preferences for housing and supports: The Vermont consumer housing preference study. In J.W. Jacobson, S.N. Burchard, and P.J. Carling, eds, *Community Living for People with Developmental and Psychiatric Disabilities*, pp. 155–166. Baltimore MD: Johns Hopkins University Press.

Taylor, S.J., Racino, J., Knoll, J., *et al.* (1987). *The Nonrestrictive Environment: A Resource Manual on Community Integration for People with the Most Severe Disabilities.* New York: Human Policy Press.

Test, M. (1981). Effective community treatment of the chronically mentally ill: What is necessary? *Journal of Social Issues,* **37**, 71–86.

Test, M.A. (1992). Training in community living. In R.P. Liberman, ed., *Handbook of Psychiatric Rehabilitation.* New York: Macmillan.

Test, M.A. and Stein, L. (1977). Special living arrangements: a model for decision making. *Hospital and Community Psychiatry,* **28**, 608–610.

Test, M. and Stein, L. (1978). Community treatment of the chronic patient: Research overview. *Schizophrenia Bulletin,* **4**, 350–364.

Test, M.A., Senn Burke, S., and Wallish, L. (1990). Gender differences of young adults with schizophrenic disorders in community care. *Schizophrenia Bulletin,* **16**, 331–344.

Test, M.A., Knoedler, W.H., Allness, D.J., *et al.* (1991). Long-term community care through an assertive community treatment team. In C.A. Tamminga and S.C. Schuley, eds, *Advances in Neuropsychiatry and Psychopharmacology,* Vol. 1: *Schizophrenia Research*, pp. 111–128. New York: Raven Press.

Trainor, J. and Church, K. (1984). *A Framework for Support for People with Severe Mental Disabilities.* Toronto: Canadian Mental Health Association.

Turner, J. and TenHoor, W. (1979). The NIMH community support program: pilot approach to a needed social reform. *Schizophrenia Bulletin,* **4**, 319–344.

Wasow, M. (1982). *Coping with Schizophrenia: A Survival Manual for Parents Relatives and Friends.* Palo Alto: Science and Behavior Books.

Wilson, S.F. (1992). Community support and integration: New directions for client outcome research. In S. Rose, ed., *Case Management: An Overview and Assessment*, pp. 113–129. White Plains, NY: Longman, Inc.

Witheridge, T.F. (1990). Assertive community treatment as a supported housing approach. *Psychosocial Rehabilitation Journal,* **13**, 69–75.

United States Senate Special Committee on Aging, Sub-Committee on Long-Term Care (1976). Supporting paper, No. 7: *The Role of Nursing Homes in Caring for Discharged Mental Patients and the Birth of a For-Profit Boarding Home Industry.* Washington DC: US Government Printing Office.

Zinman, S., Harp, H.T., and Budd, S. (1987). *Reaching Across: Mental Health Clients Helping Each Other.* Sacramento, CA: The California Network of Mental Health Clients.

21

Working with Families of Schizophrenic Patients: Effects on Clinical and Social Outcomes

JULIAN LEFF
MRC Social and Community Psychiatry Unit, Institute of Psychiatry, London, UK

THE ECONOMICS OF SCHIZOPHRENIA

As with any disease, the costs to society attributable to schizophrenia can be calculated under three headings: the direct costs of treatment, the indirect costs of lost production, and the human costs of pain and suffering to the patient and family. The course of schizophrenia differs widely between individuals: about 25% of patients in the West will suffer a single episode from which they will recover completely and remain well for years. At the other extreme, about 10% of patients worldwide will never recover from the initial episode and will be severely disabled for the rest of their life. Hence, the calculation of average costs is misleading. Davies and Drummond (1990) have estimated that 40% of people with schizophrenia incur 97% of direct treatment costs and 77% of indirect costs. The estimated lifetime cost of patients with the best outcome is only £1715, while the lifetime cost of patients with the worst outcome is £315 776. The latter is calculated on the basis of 37 years of institutional care. The direct costs are obviously very large, but are dwarfed by the indirect costs. It is estimated that the total annual direct cost of schizophrenia in the UK is £397 million, whereas the total annual indirect cost is £1.6 billion, more than four times as large. Burns and Raftery (1991) calculated the total catchment area health care costs for patients referred to the psychiatric services. They found that the costs for schizophrenic patients were more than twice as great as those for non-schizophrenic patients. Virtually all the cost difference was accounted for by an increased use of inpatient beds. Kavanagh *et al.* (1993) found that the costs of care for the relatively small proportion of schizophrenic patients accommodated in hospital was larger than the total cost of schizophrenia to all other public agencies combined. Any form of treatment that can keep people with schizophrenia out of hospital and can increase their productivity is almost bound to be cost-beneficial.

With the shift in the locus of care for schizophrenia from the hospital to the community, families are inevitably carrying a larger burden of the care. There are emotional strains involved which are not easy to cost, but family members give up time to look after the patient, and this can be costed. Franks

Handbook of Mental Health Economics and Health Policy, Volume I, Schizophrenia. Edited by M. Moscarelli, A. Rupp and N. Sartorius.
© 1996 John Wiley & Sons Ltd.

(1987) surveyed responses from 408 members of the National Alliance for the Mentally Ill in the USA: they reported that they spent an average of 66.5 hours per week caring for the ill family member. However, there was a big variation in the time estimated: some asserted that they provided care for 24 hours a day. Rice *et al.* (1985) calculated that the value of the time contributed by family members to the care of the mentally ill (not just schizophrenia) was $2.5 billion. Hence, programs that succeed in increasing the independence of people with schizophrenia will reduce the time spent by relatives in giving care, with a consequent saving in costs.

THE PREDICTIVE VALUE OF THE EXPRESSED EMOTION MEASURE

At the beginning of the era of deinstitutionalization, a study by Brown *et al.* (1962) showed that long-stay patients with schizophrenia were more likely to be readmitted if they were discharged to the care of relatives than if they went to live alone or with private landlords. This finding focused attention on the interaction between schizophrenic patients and their relatives and its possible influence on the course of the disease. The interest in the area eventually led to the development of a technique of measuring the relative's emotional attitudes towards a family member with a psychiatric illness. The technique can be adapted for non-psychiatric illnesses and has already been used for conditions such as diabetes (Stevenson *et al.*, 1991) and inflammatory bowel disease, but the first studies were conducted on schizophrenia.

The basis of the technique is a semi-structured interview—the Camberwell Family Interview (CFI), which is administered to a relative, initially when the patient is experiencing a first episode or recurrence of their illness. The relative is asked about the patient's symptoms and behavior in the 3 months before the interview. The interview is audiotaped and ratings are made later from the tape. The rater pays as much attention to the way the respondent uses their voice to convey emotion, as to the content of the respondent's remarks (Brown & Rutter, 1966). Ratings are made on four principal scales: critical comments, hostility, overinvolvement, and warmth.

Patients were followed up for 9 months after they returned from hospital to the family home. Outcome was assessed in terms of relapse, that is, a recurrence of psychotic symptoms in patients who were free of them at discharge (type I), or an increase in the level of psychotic symptoms in those who never lost them (type II). In practice, the great majority of relapses (over 80%) are type I in nature. It should be noted that relapse is not identical with rehospitalization, as some patients who relapse are not readmitted but are managed as outpatients, while some patients are rehospitalized for social reasons.

Relapse was significantly more frequent if the relative expressed a high level of critical comments, any degree of hostility, or a high degree of overinvolvement. However, if the relative was rated low on these negative emotions but high on warmth, the relapse rate was significantly lower than when the relative was rated low on warmth (Brown *et al.*, 1972). These findings suggested that relatives might be able to influence the course of schizophrenia in both a positive and a negative way. Ratings on the negative emotional scales were used to create an index of Expressed Emotion (EE). The criteria for high EE are now established as six or more critical comments expressed in the course of the CFI, any rating on hostility, or a score of three or above on the overinvolvement scale (Vaughn & Leff, 1976a). Patients most commonly live with a spouse, or with one or both parents. If one member of the household is rated as high EE, the household is categorized as high EE. In practice most dual parent households are consistently high or low EE.

In the original study, the relapse rates in high and low EE households were 58% and 16% respectively over 9 months (Brown *et al.*, 1972). Vaughn and Leff (1976b) replicated these results almost exactly. Since then, there have been 11 published studies from a variety of cultures involving a number of different languages which have repeated these findings. Three or four studies have failed to find a difference in relapse rates between high and low EE families. Bebbington and Kuipers (in 1994) have recently conducted an aggregate analysis on all the published studies and have found that EE is the principal predictor of relapse when all other factors measured are taken into account.

It should be noted, however, that EE is not only predictive of relapse in schizophrenia. Significant associations with relapse have been found in manic-depressive psychosis (Miklowitz *et al.*, 1988) depressive neurosis (Vaughn & Leff, 1976b; Hooley *et al.*, 1986), obesity (Fischmann-Havstad & Marston, 1984), anorexia nervosa and bulimia (Szmukler *et al.*, 1985; van Furth, 1991), and diabetes (Koenigsberg, personal communication). Consequently, relatives' EE cannot be a specific etiological factor in the origin of schizophrenia.

PROTECTIVE FACTORS IN HIGH EE HOUSEHOLDS

Approximately half the patients' living in high EE households suffer a schizophrenic relapse over a 9-month period. This raises the question of how the other half manages to stay well. The answer lies in two protective factors. One is prophylactic anti-psychotic medication, the effectiveness of which has been demonstrated in a multitude of studies (e.g. Leff & Wing, 1971). The other is the amount of social contact the patient has with the high EE relatives. Patients who are in low social contact have a significantly lower relapse rate than those in high contact. In an analysis of combined data from the study of Brown *et al.* (1972) and their own study, Vaughn and Leff (1976b) showed that the protective effects of drugs and reduced social contact were additive. Patients who employed either protective factor reduced their relapse risk by a half, while if both were present, the relapse rate was only 15%, comparable with that in a low EE home. This finding has recently been confirmed by the aggregate analysis of Bebbington and Kuipers (1994).

These results suggested that it might be possible to substantially reduce the risk of relapse for patients in high EE homes by maintaining them on medication and by lowering relatives' EE and/or social contact between patient and relative.

FAMILY INTERVENTIONS FOR SCHIZOPHENIA

Consequently in 1976 we began to put together a package of interventions which were aimed specifically at reducing relatives' EE and social contact between relatives and patients. The package has been modified as a result of experience in working with families and has now reached a final form (Kuipers *et al.*, 1992). It consists of an education component given in two sessions in the patient's home, and interventions aimed at teaching problem-solving, improving communication, reducing criticism, conflict and overinvolvement, reducing contact, expanding social networks, and lowering relatives' expectations.

These interventions were delivered in two ways: through therapists visiting families at home, including the patient, and through a group run by therapists for relatives, but excluding patients. The family sessions were held once a fortnight for an hour and usually included two therapists. After the first few months their visits were often reduced to once monthly, and eventually might be only once every 3 months before being discontinued. The group was held regularly once a fortnight for an hour and a half. It was run by two therapists and supported up to eight families at a time.

The program of intervention always begins with the education sessions. We decided to give these in the home on the grounds that family members would feel more comfortable on their own territory and hence more able to take in information. This proved to be a sensible decision for another reason, namely it ensured a high success rate in engaging families in the program. Families appreciated the effort professionals made to come to them and were eager to receive information about the illness. Consequently, very few families refused the offer of a visit by the therapists to provide them with an education program. The engagement of families is an important issue when considering the effectiveness of a program.

The rationale for the education program is worth exploring in detail. One of the principal aims of the intervention was to reduce criticism, which is the commonest component of the high EE measure. In order to design an appropriate intervention it is first necessary to determine the major targets of relatives' criticism. This was achieved by analyzing the content of 100 critical comments derived from the CFI recordings. It turned out that only 30% of the critical remarks were concerned with the positive symptoms of schizophrenia such as delusions and hallucinations. The majority of criticisms were focused on the negative symptoms (Leff & Vaughn, 1985). Whereas positive symptoms are *distortions* of normal behavior and experience, negative symptoms are the *absence* of normal behavior and are manifested by apathy, inertia, social withdrawal, paucity of speech, and lack of emotion. It is not surprising that many relatives fail to recognize these symptoms as stemming from an illness, and instead criticize patients for being lazy and selfish. Hence, we thought that if we educated relatives to accept negative symptoms as part of the picture of schizophrenia, they might modify their critical attitude.

POSITIVE AND NEGATIVE SYMPTOMS

The distinction between positive and negative symptoms is of great importance for the economics of schizophrenia. Negative symptoms severely impair the patient's motivation and ability to engage in productive work. Patients find it very difficult to get up in the mornings, have little motivation to do anything, do not interact with colleagues at work, neither fellow employees nor supervisors, and have a short attention span. Work in the competitive environment of open employment is out of the question. Even productive work in a sheltered environment such as a day center may be too much to expect. Many patients with severe negative symptoms can just about manage to attend an unstructured drop-in center, where they will sit in company with others, drinking tea or coffee and smoking, but engaging in negligible social activity.

In an observational study of the patients' club at a large psychiatric hospital, a group of "asocial" individuals was identified (Dunn *et al.*, 1990). These patients had obvious disabilities and difficulties, for example with buying tea, and were generally ignored by other patients, although occasionally they would be offered help. They were noted to sit evenly spaced around the walls, smoking or staring into space in silence. They did not initiate social interactions. Lack of occupation is not confined to the "asocial" group, although they seem to be the most affected by negative symptoms. In surveying the patients in two large psychiatric hospitals, Friern and Claybury, who stayed more than 1 year, 81% were given a diagnosis of schizophrenia (O'Driscoll *et al.*, 1993). Five hundred of these long-stay patients who were discharged as part of a program of reprovision were assessed while they were in hospital and again 1 year after moving to the community. It was found that 37% of them engaged in no structured activity while in the hospital. This proportion rose to 46% when the patients moved to the community as the well-developed industrial therapy in the hospital was not replaced by equivalent community facilities. This degree of inactivity obviously contributes to the massive indirect cost of schizophrenia attributable to lost production (Davies & Drummond, 1990). Any treatment that could ameliorate negative symptoms would make a major impact on the cost of schizophrenia. Unfortunately, the standard antipsychotic drugs in use for many decades are ineffective in treating negative symptoms. A new generation of antipsychotic drugs, such as clozapine and risperidone, has now been introduced and there are claims that they reduce negative symptoms, but these remain to be substantiated.

One of the main targets of the family intervention is negative symptoms, because of the frequency with which they elicit critical comments. A number of the components of the family work are applicable to negative symptoms. One or other of these symptoms is often cited by the family as a priority problem, which can then be tackled with a problem-solving approach. For example, if the problem is the patient's inability to get out of bed in the morning, the first step is to analyze the problem. The common reasons are: (i) that the patient has reversed their day–night rhythm, staying up all night and sleeping during the day (this effectively reduces contact between patient and relative with a consequent protective function); (ii) the patient is on too high a dose of medication, going to bed at a reasonable hour but sleeping through the first half of the next day and feeling drowsy on waking; and (iii) the patient has nothing to get up for. The analysis of the problem cannot be accomplished without a major contribution from the patient. This has the advantage of establishing the patient as an "expert" on the problem, hence raising their status in the family, which is often lowly.

If the problem is excessive medication, a reduction in dosage will have to be negotiated with the patient's doctor. If a day–night reversal has taken place, the patient should be encouraged gradually to shift their sleeping pattern to normal. To start with, they could go to bed and get up half-an-hour earlier. The patient's feeling that there is nothing to get up for epitomizes the negative symptoms of apathy, inertia, and lack of motivation.

In attempting to motivate the patient, it is useful to identify some activity he/she used to enjoy before becoming ill. Then attempts can be made to help the patient engage in the activity again, starting in a small way and with the help of the family. In working on the problem of motivation, the family need to lower their expectations for the patient. Very often family members expect patients to return to full-time work or to their course of study once the acute episode is over. The therapists stress the fact that there is a long convalescent period following an episode of schizophrenia and that it may take 1–2 years before the patient returns to a normal level of activity. It is also stressed that the family should praise patients for small advances, for example bathing twice a week instead of once a week.

REDUCING CONTACT BETWEEN PATIENT AND RELATIVES

During periods of high unemployment, as at the moment in Europe and the USA, it is almost impossible for a person with a history of schizophrenia to obtain a job in open employment, unless they conceal their history. Consequently, most people with schizophrenia spend many hours at home with nothing to do. If they live with parents, it is quite likely that one or both parents will have retired, spending much of the day in their home. As we have seen, high contact between a patient and a high EE relative increases the risk of relapse. Thus, a key objective of the intervention is to reduce this contact by altering the life-styles of both patient and relatives.

This entails focusing on both work and leisure activities. As finding a job is impractical for most patients, effort is directed at helping the patient to obtain a place in a day hospital, day center, or other sheltered work situation. Such facilities have traditionally accepted contract work from businesses and industry, usually involving simple assembly of components or packing. In addition, some workshops have designed their own products which patients make from raw materials, for instance dolls house furniture. An innovatory scheme, known as Fountain House, was introduced by Fairweather in the States (Fairweather *et al.*, 1969). The basis of this was a group of patients and staff who offered services to the public, such as car washing and gardening. The group guaranteed that someone would always turn up to perform the service. Patients would cover for each other if someone felt too unwell to work, and if necessary a member of staff would fill in for an absent worker. This approach to generating paid work for patients has unfortunately not been implemented in more than a few locations.

Most sheltered work facilities operate between 10 a.m. and 4 p.m. for 5 days a week. This leaves patients with many hours during the week and at the weekend with little or nothing to do. Therefore it is important to encourage the patient to take up leisure activities which can be pursued outside of the home, and preferably in the company of other people. Adult education is well developed in the UK and the courses are relatively inexpensive to join. They do not necessarily involve academic demands and are a useful resource for patients. It is often the case in high EE households that patients and relatives spend most of their leisure time together, resulting in high levels of social contact. When arranging for the patient to undertake leisure activities outside the home, the relatives' needs for leisure should also be addressed. They can be encouraged to join different adult education classes from the patients. In addition, attention needs to be given to their social networks. Relatives often withdraw from their natural social networks, made up of family and friends, through shame and embarrassment. They stop visiting people and they stop inviting people to their home. As a consequence their home becomes a fortress against the outside world. It is the therapists' task to persuade the relatives to utilize their social networks again. The process begins with education about schizophrenia, which can help to dispel the mystery surrounding the condition and to reduce the stigma. The relatives' group is an asset in this area, because relatives feel more comfortable in being with people who have experienced similar problems. Much of their shame and embarrassment is removed when they find the issues being openly discussed. We have found that relatives who attend the group make social contact with each other outside of group sessions. Hence the relatives' group acts as a stepping stone to informal socialization.

SEPARATING OVERINVOLVED PATIENTS AND RELATIVES

One of the characteristics of an overinvolved relationship is that it is symmetrical. The patient is often as anxious about and protective of the relative as the relative is of the patient. Consequently, it is necessary to work with both partners' anxieties in order to achieve any degree of separation. The relative's anxieties center on the patient's perceived inability to look after themself and to perform adequately in other social roles. For example, one mother would not allow her daughter of 20, who had recently developed schizophrenia, to cross the road on her own. This parental overprotectiveness undermines the patient's confidence in themself, so that they develop anxieties about being able to manage without the parent doing things for them. As a result of this mutual reinforcement of anxiety, both patient and relative are prevented from realizing their potential productivity.

A good example is provided by a married couple in which the wife had given up her job as a nurse tutor to look after her husband, who had had 10 previous episodes of schizophrenia. She took total responsibility for her husband, did all the housework, and ran the household. He lacked confidence in himself to begin with, and as a response to her overprotectiveness he did virtually nothing for himself. We held a small number of family sessions in which we explored the anxieties the husband felt about taking on responsibilities. We also emphasized to the wife that she had accepted a very heavy burden for herself and that she had earned a rest. The wife attended the relatives' group regularly, where pressure was put on her by other relatives to return to work. She eventually decided to take up her job again, and on returning home after the first day at work, found that her husband had coped very efficiently with the housework and had prepared an evening meal for both of them. This arrangement continued and in addition the husband became an active official in the local church. He remained free of relapse for the next 10 years until his death from a physical illness. The therapeutic interventions had been successful both in improving the course of the illness and in enabling patient and relative to become productive members of society in their own ways. Costing would be easy for the wife's return to work, somewhat more difficult for the patient's domestic chores, and problematic for his voluntary activities for the church, but each represents an increase in productivity resulting from the interventions.

Having outlined the approach to working with families, we can now consider its efficacy as tested in a series of clinical trials.

TRIALS OF FAMILY INTERVENTIONS FOR SCHIZOPHRENIA

A number of trials have been conducted in the UK and the USA. We will start by reviewing our own studies, and then compare them with others.

THE LONDON TRIALS

Our two trials were conducted on patients in high contact with high EE relatives as we were interested to determine whether the intervention was efficacious in reducing contact, EE or both. We knew from the previous research that this type of patient was at high risk of relapse, so that it was unethical to withhold maintenance antipsychotic medication. Thus we aimed to maintain most, if not all, the patients on depot injections.

The first question is whether it was possible to reduce relatives EE by the intervention. In the first trial we conducted, families were randomly assigned to the intervention package or to a control group, which received routine clinical care (Leff *et al.*, 1982, 1985). In effect, the control relatives were offered no help. The experimental families showed a significant reduction in critical comments at the 9-month follow-up, the average falling from over 12 initially to six. There was also some spontaneous reduction in criticism in the control families, but this was not significant. Overinvolvement was moderately reduced in the experimental families, but not to a significant extent, while it remained unchanged in the control families (Leff *et al.*, 1982). Overall, a reduction from high to low EE was achieved in 50% of experimental families compared with 20% of control families.

A reduction in social contact from high (more than 35 hours per week) to low also occurred in 50% of experimental families. However, some families changed both in EE and in contact, so that one or both of these therapeutic aims were achieved in 75% of experimental families.

These alterations in the emotional and social environment were paralleled by a reduction in the relapse rate of schizophrenia. Virtually all the patients remained on maintenance neuroleptics, so that compliance with medication was not a complicating factor. The relapse rate in the experimental patients was only 8% over 9 months compared with 50% in the control patients.

The majority of patients who relapsed were rehospitalized, so that the direct cost for the experimental group would have been considerably less than that for the control group, although no economic analysis was conducted. In terms of the patients' social and occupational activities, there were small gains by most of the experimental subjects. Four patients began attending day hospitals or day classes, two increased their leisure activities considerably, and one unemployed patient obtained a job. The wife of one patient resumed employment after a gap. These changes represent improvements in the quality of life, although no attempt has been made to put a cost value on them.

A 2-year follow-up of this first trial showed that the relapse rate in the control group had risen to 75% compared with 33% in the experimental group (Leff *et al.*, 1985). Unfortunately, two experimental patients committed suicide and when these are added to the relapsed patients, the rate rises to 50%, which is not significantly different from the relapse rate of the control patients.

The next step was to investigate the relative efficiency of the components of the intervention package. We had already evaluated the effect of the education component and found it to be relatively small (Berkowitz *et al.*, 1984). Therefore our main comparison was of education plus a relatives' group with education plus family sessions in the home.

The relatives' group can be run for up to eight families by two therapists meeting once a fortnight, while the family sessions require two therapists to visit each family at the same time interval. Hence, if they are of comparable efficacy, the relatives' group must be the more efficient means of delivering the intervention.

In the second trial, suitable families were randomly assigned to a relatives' group or to family sessions in the home (Leff *et al.*, 1989). Both forms of intervention produced equally large reductions in critical comments by 9 months. Both samples of relatives also showed a significant increase in warmth. This is important as in earlier studies, high warmth was associated with a lower relapse rate for the patients (Brown *et al.*, 1972; Vaughn & Leff, 1976b). As in the previous trial, overinvolvement showed a non-significant reduction at 9 months. However, a 2-year follow-up was conducted of relatives EE, which revealed that overinvolvement had fallen significantly (Leff *et al.*, 1990). These data indicate that for many relatives overinvolvement can be modified if the therapists continue working with them for 1–2 years.

A serious problem with attendance at the relatives' group became apparent in this trial. Nearly half the relatives assigned to the group failed to attend even once. In families of the non-attenders there was very little change in relatives EE or social contact and the patients had a high relapse rate (60%). By contrast, the relapse rate of patients in the family sessions stream was 8% over 9 months, and was 17% for patients whose relatives attended the group. We conclude from these results that a relatives' group on its own is not efficient because a high proportion of needy relatives will not attend. However, family sessions on their own, while effective, are an expensive mode of delivering the intervention. The combination of family sessions and a relatives' group, as used in the first trial, is most efficient, because a high proportion of relatives can be persuaded to attend the group once they have experienced some family sessions, which can then be held relatively infrequently, thus saving therapists' time in making home visits to individual families. However, it needs to be recognized that there will always be some relatives who refuse to attend the group and for whom family sessions will be the only way to deliver the intervention.

A 2-year follow-up was conducted of the patients in the second trial and the findings amalgamated with those of the first trial (Leff *et al.*, 1990). The 2 year relapse rate (including suicide) for the three groups of patients who received an experimental intervention was 40% compared with 75% for the control group in the first trial ($P<0.05$). Hence the efficacy of the intervention was sustained over 2 years.

As in the first trial, patients in the second trial achieved improvements in their social performance. Two patients moved to independent living, two gained a stable sexual partner, and two increased their social activity considerably. Two patients took on full-time employment, one attended day classes, and another started college. Once again the social interventions were followed by social gains for the patients, some of which improved their quality of life, while others increased their productivity.

OTHER TRIALS

Six other trials of family interventions for schizophrenia have been published. Two failed to show any advantage for an experimental group compared with a control group. One utilized psychodynamic groups for relatives and for patients, a different approach from any other center. The second applied the method used by Leff's group from reading a brief account of it and without undergoing any training. These studies will not be considered further. The other four trials were conducted in Los Angeles (Goldstein *et al.*, 1978; Falloon *et al.*, 1982, 1985), Pittsburgh (Hogarty *et al.*, 1986, 1987), and Salford, UK (Tarrier *et al.*, 1988, 1989). They each employed a similar combination of interventions with emphasis on psychoeducation, problem-solving, improving communication, lowering expectations, reducing contact, and expanding social networks. All patients were maintained on antipsychotic medication. Control patients received either routine care or social skills training. The outcome in terms of relapse rates is shown in Table 1, with the London trials included for comparison.

The results are remarkably consistent across the six studies, providing a substantial body of evidence supporting the efficacy of family interventions for schizophrenia. In addition to recording relapse rates, some of the investigators studied the effects of intervention on patients' social functioning and relatives' experience of burden. Falloon *et al.* (1987) calculated the number of months patients spent in employment or rehabilitation programs. This averaged 12.6 months for patients in the experimental group and 7.2 months for control patients. Standardized interviews with the relatives showed that experimental patients made greater improvements in household tasks, work, or study activities, and friendships than control patients. Furthermore the relatives' experience of subjective burden was significantly eased at both 9 months and 2 years.

In the Salford study, Barraclough and Tarrier (1990) found that experimental patients compared with control patients made significant gains in the Withdrawal and Prosocial Activities subscales of the Social Adjustment Scale (Birchwood *et al.*, 1990) and in the total score. Thus, all the measures of patients' social functioning and relatives' experienced burden favor family intervention over routine care. However, family interventions involve an added cost. The judgement as to whether this is worthwhile needs to be based on cost–benefit and cost-effectiveness analyses. Only the study by Falloon *et al.* (1982) employed an economic analysis.

ECONOMIC ANALYSIS

Cardin *et al.* (1985) calculated all treatment-related costs for the patients throughout the 2 years of the study. Costs and benefits associated with family members were not assessed. A cost–benefit analysis was conducted on the treatment costs, community costs, and the benefits that accrued for each patient during the first year of participation in the study. A set formula was used to adjust for staff travel time for home-based sessions.

Earnings from open and sheltered employment were included under benefits and savings stemming from reductions in inpatient stays were also added.

Contrary to the authors' expectations, family management did not differ from individual management in terms of direct costs. While home visits added a significant extra cost to family management, this was largely offset by the cost of nursing visits to individual patients for injectable medication and missed and extra appointments. As anticipated, there was a considerable saving in costs of hospital care for the family management patients. There was no significant difference between the two treatment groups in patients' earnings from open and sheltered employment.

Overall, family management cost 19% less than individual management, the saving being largely attributable to the reduction in inpatient stays.

Cardin *et al.* (1985) went on to conduct a cost-effectiveness analysis, using the data on outcome in the three main areas measured, psychopathology, social functioning, and family functioning. A standard score was devised for each area, and the three scores were combined to provide an index of effectiveness.

Table 1. The outcome of family intervention trials

Trial	Relapse rates: Short-term follow-up (6–12 months) Control	Short-term Experimental	Long-term follow-up (2 years) Control	Long-term Experimental
Goldstein *et al.* (1978)	48%	0%	—	—
Falloon *et al.* (1982)	44%	6%	83%	17%
Leff *et al.* (1982)	50%	8%	78%	50%
Hogarty *et al.* (1986)	46%	16%	66%	33%
Tarrier *et al.* (1987)	53%	12%	59%	33%
Leff *et al.* (1989)		8%*		33%*
		17%†		36%†

* Family sessions.
† Relatives group.

The total cost of each approach was then divided by the total units of therapeutic effectiveness. On the basis of this calculation, it was concluded that "family management was more than twice as cost efficient than the more traditional individual-based management in achieving the goals of community care." The meaningfulness of standardizing and combining scores across such disparate areas as patients' symptoms and family functioning is dubious, eroding confidence in the final figure.

CONCLUSIONS

We began this chapter with a brief review of the costs of schizophrenia to society. These are of such a magnitude that any innovative treatment that promises to reduce them should be examined with great care. The family interventions that have been developed over the past two decades are of proven efficacy in reducing the relapse rate of schizophrenia over a 2-year period. Unfortunately, in only one of the six studies with positive results has any attempt at an economic analysis been mounted, and this left much to be desired. While researchers have studied both the efficacy and efficiency of family interventions, their effectiveness remains to be established. Any attempt to do this should be combined with a sophisticated economic analysis that calculates direct and indirect costs, and also includes the impact on family members in terms both of the time they devote to caring for their sick relative and their subjective sense of burden.

REFERENCES

Barrowclough, C. and Tarrier, N. (1990). Social functioning in schizophrenic patients. I. The effects of expressed emotion and family intervention. *Social Psychiatry and Psychiatric Epidemiology*, **25**, 125–129.

Bebbington, P. and Kuipers, L. (1994). The predictive utility of Expressed Emotion in Schizophrenia: An aggregate analysis. *Psychological Medicine*, **24**, 707–718.

Berkowitz, R., Eberlein-Friess, R., Kuipers, L., and Leff, J. (1984). Educating relatives about schizophrenia. *Schizophrenia Bulletin*, **10**, 418–429.

Birchwood, M., Smith J., Cochrane, R. *et al.* (1990). The social functioning scale: the developenent and validation of a scale of social adjustment for use in family intervention programmes with schizophrenic patients. *British Journal of Psychiatry*, **157**, 853–859.

Brown, G.W. and Rutter, M. (1966). The measurement of family activities and relationships: a methodological study. *Human Relations*, **19**, 241–263.

Brown, G.W., Birley, J.L.T., and Wing, J.K. (1972). Influence of family life on the course of schizophrenic disorders: a replication. *British Journal of Psychiatry*, **121**, 241–258.

Brown, G.W., Monck, E.M., Carstairs, G.M., and Wing, J.K. (1962). Influence of family life on the course of schizophrenic illness. *British Journal of Preventive and Social Medicine*, **16**, 55–68.

Burns, T. and Raftery, J. (1991). Cost of schizophrenia in a randomized trial of home-based treatment. *Schizophrenic Bulletin*, **17**, 407–410.

Cardin, V.A., McGill, C.W., and Falloon, I.R.H., (1985). An economic analysis: Costs, benefits, and effectiveness. In I.R.H. Falloon J.L. Boyd, and C.W. McGill, eds, *Family Management of Schizophrenia*. Baltimore, MD: John Hopkins University Press.

Davies, L. and Drummond, M. (1990). The economic burden of schizophrenia. *Psychiatric Bulletin*, **14**, 522–525.

Dunn, M., O'Driscoll, C., Dayson, D., Wills, W., and Leff, J. (1990). The TAPS Project, 4: An observational study of the social life of long-stay patients. *British Journal of*

Psychiatry, **157**, 842–848.

Fairweather, G.W., Sanders, D.H., and Maynard, J. (1969) *Community Life for the Mentally Ill: An Alternative to Institutional Care.* Chicago: Aldine.

Falloon, I.R.H, Boyd, J.L., McGill, C.W., Razini, J., Moss, H.B., and Gilderman, A.M. (1982). Family management in the prevention of exacerbations of schizophrenia. *New England Journal of Medicine,* **306**, 1437–1440.

Falloon, I.R.H., Williamson, M., Razani, J., Moss, H.B., Gilderman, A.M., and Simpson, G.M. (1985). Family versus individual management in the prevention of morbidity of schizophrenia: I. Clinical outcome of a two-year controlled study. *Archives of General Psychiatry,* **42**, 887–896.

Falloon, I.R.H., McGill, C.W., Boyd, J.L., and Pederson, J. (1987). Family management in the prevention of morbidity of schizophrenia: a social outcome of a two-year longitudinal study. *Psychological Medicine,* **17**, 59–66.

Fischmann-Havstad, L. and Marston, A.R. (1984). Weight loss maintenance as an aspect of family emotion and process. *British Journal of Clinical Psychology,* **23**, 265–271.

Franks, D.D. (1987). The high cost of caring: economic contribution of families to the care of the mentally ill. Unpublished PhD Dissertation, Brandeis University.

Goldstein, M.J., Rodnick, E.H., Evans, J.R., May, P.R.A., and Steinberg, M.R. (1978). Drug and family therapy in the aftercare treatment of acute schizophrenia. *Archives of General Psychiatry,* **35**, 169–177.

Hogarty, G.E., Anderson, C.M., *et al.* (1986). Family psychoeducation, social skills training, and maintenance chemotherapy in the aftercare treatment of schizophrenia: I. One-year effects of a controlled study on relapse and Expressed Emotion. *Archives of General Psychiatry,* **43**, 633–642.

Hogarty, G.E., Anderson, C.M., and Reiss, D.J. (1987). Family psychoeducation, social skills training and medication in schizophrenia: The long and the short of it. *Psychopharmacology Bulletin,* **23**, 12–13.

Hooley, J.M., Orley, J., and Teasdale, J.D. (1986). Levels of Expressed Emotion and relapse in depressed patients. *British Journal of Psychiatry,* **148**, 642–647.

Kavanagh, S., Knapp, M., Beecham, J., and Opit, L. (1993). *The Costs of Schizophrenia Care in England.* University of Kent, Canterbury: Personal Social Services Research Unit DP 920.

Kuipers, L., Leff, J., and Lam, D. (1992). *Family Work for Schizophrenia: A Practical Guide.* London: Gaskell.

Leff, J. and Vaughn, C. (1985). *Expressed Emotion in Families: Its Significance for Mental Illness.* New York: Guilford.

Leff, J.P. and Wing, J.K. (1971). Trial of maintenance therapy in schizophrenia. *British Medical Journal,* **3**, 599–604.

Leff, J., Kuipers, L., Berkowitz, R., Eberlein-Fries, R., and Sturgeon, D. (1982). A controlled trial of social intervention in the families of schizophrenic patients. *British Journal of Psychiatry,* **141**, 121–134.

Leff, J., Kuipers, L., Berkowitz, R., and Sturgeon, D. (1985). A controlled trial of social intervention in the families of schizophrenic patients: two year follow-up. *British Journal of Psychiatry,* **146**, 594–600.

Leff, J., Berkowitz, R., Shavit, N., Strachan, A., Glass, I., and Vaughn, C. (1989). A trial of family therapy v. a relatives group for schizophrenia. *British Journal of Psychiatry,* **154**, 58–66.

Leff, J., Berkowitz, R., Shavit, N., Strachan, A., Glass, I., and Vaughn, C. (1990). A trial of family therapy versus a relatives' group for schizophrenia, two year follow-up. *British Journal of Psychiatry,* **157**, 571–577.

Miklowitz, D.J., Goldstein, M.J., Nuechterlein, K.H., Snyder, K.S., and Mintz, J. (1988). Family factors and the course of bipolar affective disorder. *Archives of General Psychiatry,* **45**, 225–231.

O'Driscoll, C., Wills, W., Leff, J., and Margolius, O. (1993). The TAPS Project. 10: The long-stay populations of Friern and Claybury Hospitals. In J. Leff, ed., Evaluating Community Placement of Long-Stay Psychiatric Patients. *British Journal of Psychiatry,* **162** (Suppl. 19), 18–24.

Rice, D.P., Kelman, S., Miller, L.S., and Dunmeyer, J. (1985). *The Economic Costs of Alcohol and Drug Abuse and Mental Illness.* Rockville, MD: National Institute of Mental Health, DHHS Publ. No. (ADM) 90-1694 (1990).

Stevenson, K., Sensky, T., and Petty, R. (1991). Glycaemic control in adolescents with Type 1 diabetes and parental Expressed Emotion. *Psychotherapy and Psychosomatics,* **55**, 170–175.

Szmuckler, G.I., Eisler, I., Russell, G.F.M., and Dare, C. (1985). Anorexia nervosa, parental "expressed emotion" and dropping out of treatment. *British Journal of Psychiatry,* **147**, 265–271.

Tarrier, N., Barrowclough, C., Vaughn, C., *et al.* (1988). The community management of schizophrenia: a controlled trial of a behavioural intervention with families to reduce relapse. *British Journal of Psychiatry,* **153**, 532–542.

Tarrier, N., Barrowclough, C., Vaughn, C., *et al.* (1989). Community management of schizophrenia: A two-year follow-up of a behavioural intervention with families. *British Journal of Psychiatry,* **154**, 625–628.

van Furth, E.F. (1991). *Parental Expressed Emotion and Eating Disorders.* The Hague: CIP-Gegevens Koninklijke Bibliotheek.

Vaughn, C.E. and Leff, J.P. (1976a). The measurement of expressed emotion in the families of psychiatric patients. *British Journal of Clinical and Social Psychology,* **15**, 157–165.

Vaughn, C.E. and Leff, J.P. (1976b). The influence of family and social factors on the course of psychiatric illness: a comparison of schizophrenic and depressed neurotic patients. *British Journal of Psychiatry,* **129**, 125–137.

22

A Psychological Approach to the Management of Schizophrenia

NICHOLAS TARRIER
Department of Clinical Psychology, School of Psychiatry and Behavioural Science, University of Manchester, Withington Hospital, Manchester, UK

INTRODUCTION

When initially described schizophrenia was thought to follow an inevitably deteriorating course, later clinical observation and longitudinal studies carried out in Europe and the USA (e.g. Ciompi, 1980; Harding *et al.*, 1987) have indicated that there can be considerable variation in the long-term natural history of schizophrenia, and the course over the short- and medium-term is frequently episodic. The development of neuroleptic medication four decades ago heralded a major advance in the management of schizophrenia, both to reduce positive symptoms during acute episodes and prophylactically to prevent relapse. However, certain inadequacies of neuroleptic medication have now become apparent. Many patients fail to comply with their medication, especially when used prophylactically, and of those who do 30–50% will relapse in the short-term (Falloon *et al.*, 1978; Hogarty *et al.*, 1979; Johnson *et al.*, 1987). Furthermore, a considerable number of patients, approximately 50% in some estimates, will continue to experience persistent positive symptoms, such as hallucinations and delusions (Harrow & Silverstein, 1977; Silverstein & Harrow, 1978; Curson *et al.*, 1985, 1988).

Conceptualization of schizophrenia in terms of vulnerability–stress models have been useful in integrating the social, psychological, and biological literature (Zubin & Spring, 1977; Nuechterlein & Dawson, 1984; Nuechterlein, 1987). The principle of this type of formulation is that psychosocial factors such as psychological and social stressors can contribute to the variance in the outcome and course of schizophrenia. This has lent impetus to the development of psychosocial management strategies to modify these factors and hence bring about positive change in the course of the disorder. These innovative psychological and psychosocial management strategies have the potential for enormous impact on the management of serious mental illness in the community (Birchwood & Shepherd, 1992; Birchwood & Tarrier, 1992).

PSYCHOSOCIAL FACTORS AND SCHIZOPHENIA

EXPRESSED EMOTION

In the early 1950s a series of research studies carried out by Brown and his colleagues at the Medical Research Council's Social Psychiatry Unit in London

Handbook of Mental Health Economics and Health Policy, Volume I, Schizophrenia. Edited by M. Moscarelli, A. Rupp and N. Sartorius.
© 1996 John Wiley & Sons Ltd.

investigated the outcome of patients discharged from psychiatric hospitals (Brown, 1985; Leff & Vaughn, 1985). The initial finding that patients diagnosed as suffering from schizophrenia who returned to live with their parents and close family did worse than those who lived alone or in hostel accommodation (Brown *et al*,. 1958) stimulated an attempt to investigate the nature of the home environment (Brown, 1985). This culminated in the development of the measure of expressed emotion (EE). Although, what EE actually represents is still the subject of much debate (see Kavanagh, 1992). It was initially formulated as an index of the emotional climate within the home environment, an attempt to assess the quality of the relationship between patient and relative. The nature of this emotional climate was viewed as potentially important in the development of the course of schizophrenia, if this was true then such a measure as EE could predict outcome. The initial studies of Brown and colleagues (Brown *et al*., 1962, 1972) and the later study of Vaughn and Leff (1976) demonstrated an association between EE and relapse. In these studies patients were recruited during hospitalization for an acute episode of schizophrenia. During this hospitalization their relatives were interviewed using an audiotaped semi-structured interview known as the Camberwell Family Interview (CFI). The CFI covered: household composition and time budget; psychiatric history of the patient; current problems and symptoms; relationships between family members; and general information about activities of household members. From this a number of scales were rated (see chapter 2 of Leff & Vaughn, 1985 for details of the CFI and chapter 3 for details of the EE scales). The established method of categorizing EE is through the rating of the following scales: (i) critical comments—this is a frequency count of the number of criticisms the relative makes about the patient, a critical comment needs to include an expression of dissatisfaction and a critical tone in the voice of the respondent; (ii) hostility—which is an expression of rejection of the patient and is indicated by the presence of a generalized negative comment or a rejecting comment; (iii) marked emotional overinvolvement (EOI)—which includes assessment of: exaggerated emotional responses; self-sacrificing and devoted behavior; extremely overprotective behavior; and examples of dramatization and emotional display during the interview. Each of these scales has a threshold above which the relative is classified as high on EE. If the threshold is not reached on any of these three scales than the relative is classified as low EE.

In the predictive EE studies, once discharged from hospital the clinical condition of patients are monitored over a follow-up period, usually of 9–12 months. Relapse rates are then compared between patients returning to live with high EE relatives compared with those returning to live with low EE relatives. Well over 25 prospective studies have now been published, these have been reviewed by Kavanagh (1992). The median relapse rate over the first year after discharge is 48% in high EE households compared with 21% in low EE households. Kavanagh (1992) concluded that the ability of EE to predict relapse is remarkably robust and this effect does not appear to be due to a confounding with other variables.

The results of EE research have stimulated much interest and some controversy and prompted researchers both to examine correlates of EE and to construct explanatory models. Briefly, research has investigated the following areas:

1 *Behavioral correlates of EE*. Laboratory interaction studies have found that high EE critical relatives make more critical remarks and that relatives rated high on EOI are more intrusive during interactions (Valone *et al*., 1983; Miklowitz *et al*., 1984; Strachan *et al*., 1986; Hahlweg *et al*., 1989). High EE relatives also talk more and listen less effectively (Kuipers *et al*., 1983). Naturalistic studies of the relative–patient interaction have yet to be performed, probably due to the immense methodological and logistic difficulties of such studies. Other studies have also indicated that living with a high EE relative is associated with lower levels of social functioning (Barrowclough & Tarrier, 1990).

2 *The patient's psychophysiological reactions to EE*. These studies have indicated that interaction with a high EE relative is associated with higher levels of physiological arousal in the patient (see Tarrier & Turpin, 1992 for a review). The association of elevated electrodermal activity in the presence of relatives rated as high EE has been advanced as evidence for the mediating role of arousal in schizophrenic relapse. A 9 month follow-up study

demonstrated that changes in relatives' EE from high to low was associated with a decrease in patients' electrodermal reactivity in the presence of their relative (Tarrier, 1991a).

3 *Causal attributions and EE.* An attributional model has been advanced to explain why individual relatives differ in their responses and attitudes to schizophrenic patients (Barrowclough *et al.*, 1994). This study has utilized a modified version of the Leeds Attributional Coding System (Stratton *et al.*, 1986) to assess explanations or spontaneous causal attributions made by the relative about negative events associated with the patient and the illness. The results of the study support the attributional model. High EE relatives made more attributions about the illness than did low EE relatives. Within the high EE group there were differences in the type of beliefs that the relative held. The attributions of relatives with marked EOI were similar to low EE relatives, with problems being attributed to factors more external to and uncontrollable by the patient. Relatives who were high on criticism gave more causes internal to the patient, while the relatives who were high on hostility also tended to perceive the causes to be controllable by, and be personal to the patient. This study also found that attributional variables were better predictors of patient relapse at 9 month follow-up than were EE variables. This last finding has the potential to influence greatly the development of behavioral family management methods towards a more cognitive approach which would target beliefs and cognitions of relatives.

FAMILY MANAGEMENT OF SCHIZOPHRENIA

FAMILY MANAGEMENT AND FAMILY INTERVENTIONS

Perhaps the greatest influence of EE has been in stimulating the development of family interventions. These interventions have aimed to reduce further relapses in schizophrenic patients after an acute episode. In these studies EE has been used as an index of high risk of relapse, as in the studies of Falloon and colleagues and Hogarty and colleagues (Falloon *et al.*, 1982, 1985; Hogarty *et al.*, 1986, 1991) or as important focus of the intervention itself, in which there has been an explicit attempt to change relatives' EE status from high to low in the intervention families, as in the studies of Leff and colleagues and Tarrier and colleagues (Leff *et al.*, 1982, 1985; Tarrier *et al.*, 1988, 1989). To date seven studies have been published that have compared family intervention versus a control intervention with high EE families.

Three trials of family intervention have taken place in the UK, two in London (Leff *et al.*, 1982, 1989) and one in Salford (Tarrier *et al.*, 1988). Two studies have been completed in the USA, one in California (Falloon *et al.*, 1982) and one in Pittsburgh (Hogarty *et al.*, 1986). Single studies have been carried out in Hamburg, Germany (Kottgen *et al.*, 1984) and in Sydney, Australia (Vaughan *et al.*, 1992). The interventions have varied from behavioral (e.g. Falloon *et al.* 1982; Tarrier *et al.*, 1988) and eclectic (e.g.. Leff *et al.*, 1982) to group psychodynamic (Kottgen *et al.*, 1984). All the interventions, except those of Kottgen *et al.* (1984) and Vaughan *et al.* (1992), have focused on the family as a unit. Kottgen *et al.* (1984) utilized group treatments separately for relatives and patients, and Vaughan *et al.* (1992) intervened solely with the relatives. The majority of interventions have been carried out over an extended period of at least 9 months with most workers concluding that to be effective family interventions need to be part of a continuing care program (e.g. Tarrier *et al.*, 1989). The exception being Vaughan *et al.* (1992) who implemented a short intervention with relatives lasting only 3 months.

These studies are all characterized by the recruitment of patients suffering an acute psychotic episode, with relative(s) rated as high EE. The vast majority of patients being hospitalized at the time of recruitment. The intervention commences on their discharge and the patient is followed up over a 9 or 12 month period. Except in the Sydney study the intervention takes place over this follow-up period.

OUTCOMES

These studies have used a range of outcome measures, but the outcome of primary interest has been relapse. A number of investigators have called for the use of a wide range of outcome measures (e.g.

Table 1. Relapse rates in percentages for high EE households from published family intervention studies. Percentages in parentheses represent "treatment takers" only and exclude those who did not complete the intervention program

Study	Relapse rates	
	9 or 12 months	24 months
London study 1 (Leff *et al.*, 1982, 1985)		
Family intervention	8%	20%
Routine treatment	50%	78%
London study 2 (Leff *et al.*, 1989, 1990)		
Family therapy	8%	33%
Relatives groups	17%	36%
California study (Falloon *et al.*, 1982, 1985)		
Family intervention	6%	17%
Individual intervention	44%	83%
Hamburg study (Kottgen *et al.*, 1984)		
Group psychodynamic intervention	33%	
Control group	43%	
Pittsburgh study (Hogarty *et al.*, 1986, 1991)		
Family intervention	23% (19%)	(32%)
Social skills training	30% (20%)	(42%)
Combined FI & SST	9% (0%)	(25%)
Control group	41%	66%
Salford study (Tarrier *et al.*, 1988, 1989)		
Family intervention	12% (5%)	33% (24%)
Education program	43%	57%
Routine treatment	53%	60%
Sydney study (Vaughan *et al.*, 1992)		
Relatives' counselling	41%	
Control group	65%	

Barrowclough & Tarrier, 1984), both because this reflects comprehensive evaluation and because measures other than relapse may better reflect levels of functioning and quality of life. Some investigators have made more strenuous efforts than others to measure a range of outcomes. These outcomes can be classified as follows: relapse; social functioning; family functioning; burden of care; and economic cost.

RELAPSE

The percentage relapse rates for the seven published studies are presented in Table 1. All studies present relapse rates over 9–12 months.

It can be seen from Table 1 that four of six studies (Leff *et al.*, 1982; Falloon *et al.*, 1982; Hogarty *et al.*, 1986; Tarrier *et al.*, 1988) demonstrate significant reductions in relapse rates for families receiving the family intervention at 9–12 months. Neither the Hamburg study (Kottgen *et al.*, 1984) nor the Sydney study (Vaughan *et al.*, 1992) were able to demonstrate significant benefits of their interventions. It should be noted that both these studies used interventions which differed markedly from those implemented by the successful trials. The second study of Leff and colleagues compared two parts of the original intervention package but was not able to show a superiority of one over the other. Tarrier and colleagues were unable to demonstrate a short, two session education program to be significantly better than routine care. Hogarty and colleagues found that at 12 months family intervention and social skills training were approximately equivalent, but in combination the intervention prevented relapses in families who completed treatment. Relapses were fewer in the family intervention group if treatment dropouts were excluded.

Five studies have included a 2 year follow-up, which demonstrated that although relapses increase in the second year a significant benefit is still maintained. Tarrier and colleagues (Tarrier *et al.*, 1994) have followed up their patient cohort from the Salford study through examination of the psychiatric notes and hospital records. Relapse was assessed at both 5 and 8 years after the initial discharge. The groups have been collapsed into three groups: family intervention, high EE control (including patients who received the short education intervention and routine care) and low EE control. The relapse results are presented in Figure 1 in terms of percentage of patients in the group who were well at each follow-up point: 9 months; 2 years; 5 and 8 years.

These results indicate that although there is an accumulating increase in the number of patients who relapse over the extended follow-up period the significant difference between the family intervention group and the high EE control group is maintained

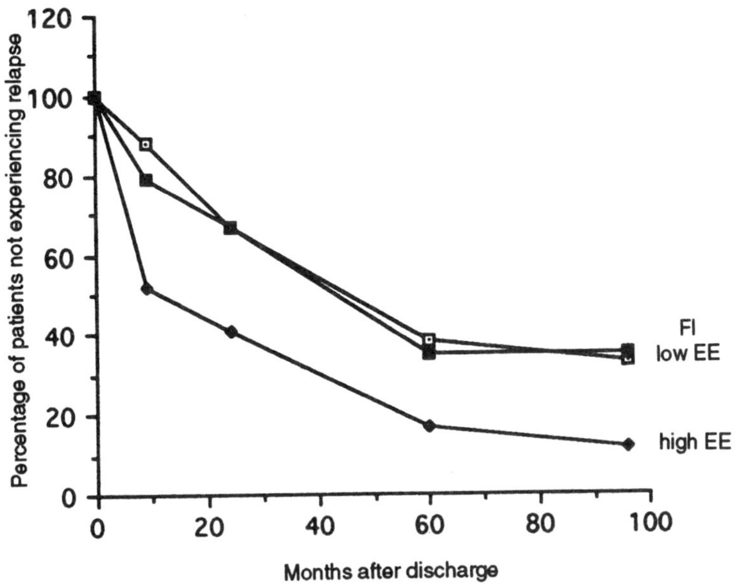

Figure 1. Salford family intervention project: 8 year follow-up.

for up to 8 years. However, over two-thirds of patients who received family intervention with their families do eventually relapse. A further point of note from Figure 1 is the similarity in relapse rates between the low EE group and the high EE family intervention group.

SOCIAL FUNCTIONING

Both the California study (Falloon *et al.*, 1984) and the Salford study (Barrowclough & Tarrier, 1990) systematically measured social functioning in their patients. Both studies found patients in the family intervention group showed significant improvements in social functioning. In the Salford study the patients social functioning was assessed using Birchwood *et al.*'s (1990) Social Functioning Scale (SFS). Changes, although significant, were quite small.

FAMILY FUNCTIONING

Family functioning is difficult to conceptualize and measure. Within the EE research tradition high EE is not necessarily thought of as poor functioning, it is not in itself pejorative. Expressed emotion may reflect different styles of coping or different response strategies to difficult and negative events in the relatives' lives (Vaughn, 1986; Barrowclough *et al.*, 1994). As such, changes in EE from high to low may indirectly reflect improvements in relatives' ability to cope with difficulties and to adjust to living with someone with schizophrenia. Whether this reflects family functioning is, of course, a moot point. A number of studies have demonstrated a significant reduction from high to low EE in relatives receiving the family intervention (Leff *et al.*, 1982, 1989; Hogarty *et al.*, 1986; Tarrier *et al.*, 1988). These reductions in EE were also associated with decreases in relapse (Hogarty *et al.*, 1986; Leff *et al.*, 1989). It should also be noted that there is doubt about the stability of EE in some families. Approximately one-third of relatives rated as high EE when the patient is in hospital will show a change to low EE if reassessed sometime after discharge (Dulz & Hand, 1986; Tarrier *et al.*, 1988).

Falloon and colleagues assessed whether the problem solving abilities of families had improved after they received the family intervention. The intervention consisted of training in problem solving (Falloon & Pederson, 1985). They were able to demonstrate, perhaps not unsurprisingly, significant improvements.

BURDEN OF CARE

There is a considerable body of evidence to show that relatives carry a substantial burden in caring for the mentally ill (Creer & Wing, 1974; Fadden *et al*., 1987). Measurement of burden is methodologically difficult. Subjective burden is often conceptualized in term of distress and assessed by measuring affective and emotional symptomatology. For example, Tantum (1989) has suggested that the General Health Questionnaire (GHQ; Goldberg & Williams, 1988) is a satisfactory measure of subjective burden. In the Salford study the relatives completed the GHQ during the patients' index admission, 2 weeks after discharge, at 4.5 and 9 month follow-up. However, there were no significant changes or group differences over the follow-up periods for the intervention or control groups (Tarrier *et al*., unpublished data). These data suggest that the family intervention had no impact on relatives' subjective burden. Positive results were reported by Falloon (Falloon & Pederson, 1985) who found significant reductions in symptomatology in relatives in the family management group using the Hopkin's Symptom Check List. Brooker *et al*. (1992a) evaluated the effectiveness of community psychiatric nurses (CPNs) trained in the Tarrier and Barrowclough intervention did find a significant reduction in GHQ scores in relatives of families receiving family intervention. This was contrary to the negative results of Tarrier and colleagues reported from the Salford project.

ECONOMIC COST

Falloon and colleagues (Cardin *et al*., 1986) undertook a detailed analysis of all direct and indirect costs to the patients, families, health, welfare, and community agencies associated with their intervention. A cost–benefit analysis of the 12 months data showed the total cost for family management was 19% less than for the individually managed patients. A much less ambitious analysis of the Salford project was undertaken by Tarrier *et al*. (1991) in which only direct costs were analyzed. The treatment of patients who received family intervention showed an overall saving of 36.4% over the high EE control group and a saving of 26.2% on mean costs per patient. These costings included the cost of the psychologists' time who carried out the family intervention. In both the California and Salford studies reducing inpatient stay was a big factor in reducing costs. The potential of family interventions for reducing relapse and hence hospitalizations in the short-term represents a large financial saving, which far outweighs the costs of the extra resources in staff time required to carry out the intervention.

ENGAGEMENT AND MAINTENANCE IN TREATMENT

Another important area is that of engagement of families into treatment. Despite the proven success of family interventions there is considerable evidence that a sizable number of families either refuse family intervention or dropout at a very early stage (Smith & Birchwood, 1990; Tarrier, 1991b). The percentage of families refusing intervention ranges from 7 to 21% (median 13%), and the percentage withdrawing from treatment ranges from 7 to 14% (median 9.5%). Some treatments, such as relatives' groups run by Leff and colleagues have reported refusal rates of 50%. Furthermore, patients who become treatment refusers and treatment dropouts appear to be particularly vulnerable to relapse with 67% of this group relapsing over 9 months in the Salford study (Tarrier, 1991b). The difficulty of engaging and maintaining families in treatment is a crucial issue that needs to be addressed. Explanatory models of adherence and health behavior have emphasized a cost–benefit, decision-making perspective and the adoption of such a conceptualisation to engagement and maintenance in family intervention may well be productive (Tarrier, 1991b).

INPATIENT FAMILY INTERVENTION

One randomized clinical trial of inpatient family intervention which compared standard inpatient treatment with standard inpatient treatment plays psychosocial family education has been reported in the literature (Spencer *et al*., 1988). The results indicate that female schizophrenic patients, with a chronic condition characterized by poor levels of social functioning, benefit from the inpatient family intervention but these benefits do not become apparent until the 18 month follow-up (Glick *et al.*, 1990). This intervention did not include any outpatient family intervention, whereas the results presented earlier in this chapter suggest that recruitment during hospitalization followed by family intervention with the patient and family in the community produces the best results.

PSYCHOLOGICAL MANAGEMENT OF POSITIVE PSYCHOTIC SYMPTOMS

Despite advances in pharmacological treatments many schizophrenic patients continue to experience hallucinations and delusions. Although these symptoms may be less severe than during an acute episode they can be extremely distressing, resulting in anxiety and depression (Breier & Strauss, 1983; Tarrier, 1987), and contribute significantly to general disability and handicap (Falloon, 1986). There is also a high risk of suicide among patients experiencing persistent symptoms (Falloon & Talbot, 1981). A number of psychological approaches to alleviating psychotic symptoms have been reported in the literature, for example: operant methods such as, social reinforcement (Liberman *et al.*, 1973; Bulow *et al.*, 1979), time out (Davis *et al.*, 1976), and punishment (Weingaertner, 1971; Turner *et al.*, 1977; Fonagy & Slade, 1982); assertive training (Nyedegger, 1972); exercise (Belcher, 1988); stimulus control (Slade, 1972; 1973); self-instruction (Meichenbaum & Cameron, 1973); thought stopping (Lamontagne *et al.*, 1983); control of stimulus input (Birchwood, 1986; Morley, 1987); biofeedback (Schneider & Pope, 1982); and self-control (Alford *et al.*, 1982). Most of these reports have been of single case studies or small uncontrolled trials, so the general efficacy of these methods has still to be demonstrated. Furthermore, many of these studies, especially those involving contingency management techniques, have dealt with chronic institutionalized populations and it is unclear whether the symptoms themselves or merely the patient's report of them have been reduced (Tarrier, 1992a).

Considerable effort has been devoted to investigating the putative information processing deficits that underlie the schizophrenic disorder. Despite this, and the frequent calls for attention to be directed into cognitive remediation as a productive clinical advance (Greene, 1993) this advance has yet to take place. The exception to this lack of applied treatment research has been the work of Brenner and colleagues in Bern (Brenner *et al.*, 1985, 1990). Notwithstanding the paucity of clinical application to come out of information processing research there has been considerable interest in possible application of cognitive and cognitive–behavioral therapy to the treatment of schizophrenic symptoms. Although famous for his work on depression, Beck's early work on cognitive therapy was in the treatment of schizophrenic delusions (Beck, 1952). Small studies have been published describing the success of belief modification methods in treating delusional beliefs (Watts *et al.*, 1973; Milton *et al.*, 1978; Hole *et al.*, 1979). Kingdon and Turkington (1991) describe the successful use of cognitive–behavior therapy with 64 consecutively referred schizophrenic patients experiencing hallucinations and delusions. They aimed to provide a "destigmatizing rationale" which proved safe to use and acceptable to patients and their carers. Furthermore, patients were managed with relatively low use of medication and hospitalization.

A further cognitive–behavioral approach has been developed by Slade *et al.* in Liverpool, UK (Haddock *et al.*, 1993; Bentall *et al.*, 1994) for the treatment of hallucinations. They have developed an approach which they term *focusing*. In a previous review of the psychological treatment literature they classified these treatments into three main groups: (i) those that emphasized distraction from the hallucination; (ii) those that emphasized focusing on the hallucination; and (iii) those that involved anxiety reduction (Slade & Bentall, 1988). A controlled trial of focusing versus distraction is currently near completion, some preliminary data have been presented which tentatively supports the efficacy of their focusing treatment (Bentall *et al.*, 1994).

A final approach has been developed by Tarrier *et al.* in Manchester, UK (Tarrier, 1992a, b; Tarrier *et al.*, 1990, 1993a, b). This was based on an earlier observation that the majority of patients who experienced persistent delusions and/or hallucinations would take active efforts to reduce the symptoms or their negative emotional effects (Tarrier, 1987). A treatment approach termed *coping strategy enhancement* (CSE) was developed which utilized the natural coping strategies of the patient together with a detailed behavioral analysis of the determinants and consequences of the symptoms. On the basis of this analysis the patient was systematically trained in methods aimed at increasing their ability to cope with the symptoms either by decreasing their occurrence or by decreasing the negative emotional reactions associated with the symptoms. This approach shared many features with other cognitive–behavioral approaches such as, involving a collaborative approach, including homework exercises, and involving *in vivo* work should symptoms occur during the session. But there were some differences, for example: the treatment of both hallucinations and delusions, the use of a composite treatment consisting of an array of individual techniques, and the utilization of the patient's own coping repertoire as an entry point into teaching coping skills. The CSE approach was evaluated on schizophrenic patients suffering from drug-resistant hallucinations and delusion against another cognitive–behavioral approach, problem solving. It was predicted that problem solving would be a plausible treatment which would have beneficial effects, probably to increase levels of functioning, but would not act directly upon psychotic symptoms themselves. It was predicted that CSE, on the other hand, would have a direct action on hallucinations and delusions, and that social functioning would also improve due to the reduction of impairment caused by the experience of positive symptoms. Hence, it was predicted that CSE would result in both a significant reduction of symptoms and an increase in social functioning while problem solving would result solely in an increase in social functioning. The first thing to note from the results is the large attrition rate in subjects. Of the 49 patients who were considered suitable, 27 continued through treatment and 23 continued to 6 month follow-up. There are parallels here with the difficulties in engaging patients and their families in family interventions and maintaining them in treatment, which were noted earlier.

The results demonstrated that patients who received either cognitive–behavioral treatment show significant improvements in positive psychotic symptoms compared with patients who were in a waiting list group (see Figure 2). Patients on the waiting list did not demonstrate any change in their psychotic

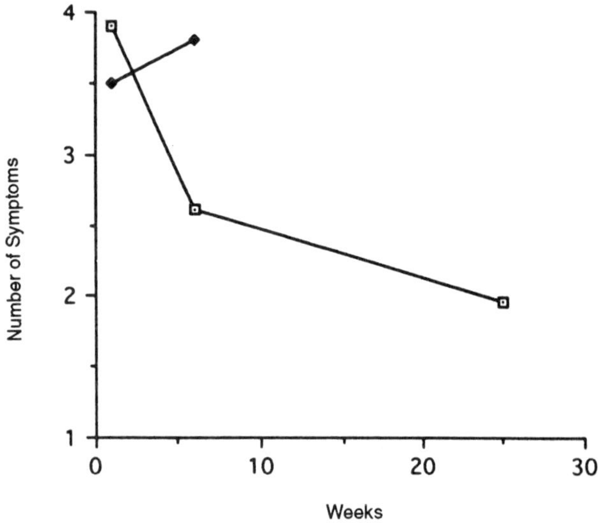

Figure 2. Mean number of symptoms per patient: —⊡—, CBT; —♦—, WP.

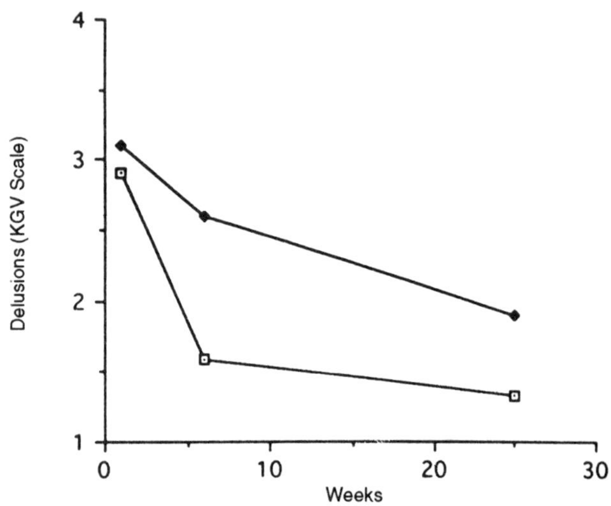

Figure 3. Changes in delusions: —⊡—, CSE; —♦—, PS.

symptoms. Comparison between CSE and problem solving produced less clear-cut results, both groups show significant improvements and there was some evidence that patients who received CSE show greater improvement especially in the reduction of delusional beliefs (see Figure 3). Treatment benefits were shown to be maintained at 6 months follow-up.

Examination of whether improvement was clinically significant as well as statistically significant was carried out by examining the percentage of patients in each treatment group who showed a 50% of greater decrease in their hallucination and/or delusions. Sixty percent of patients who received CSE and 25% of those who received problem solving reached this criterion at post-treatment assessment, the difference between the two groups approached significance. These figures were 42 and 36% respectively at 6 month follow-up. Analysis of negative symptoms and social functioning data failed to show any change for any treatment over any time period.

Hence the predictions were only partially confirmed. Positive symptoms were significantly reduced by CSE as predicted. That similar results were also demonstrated by problem solving was not predicted. The prediction that both treatments would effect an improvement in social functioning failed to be confirmed. Despite this, quite dramatic clinical improvements were demonstrated in some patients all of whom had failed to show any further improvements in response to medication for at least 6 months prior to entry into the study.

Coping and problem solving skills were also assessed (Tarrier *et al.*, 1993b). It was found that patients who received CSE significantly improved their coping skills and that improvements in coping were significantly related to decreases in hallucinations and delusions. Patients who received problem solving did not show an improvement in coping skills. All patients showed an improvement in problem solving skills, whether they received CSE or problem solving. Improvements in problem solving skills, unlike improvements in coping skills, were not related to symptomatic improvement.

It was further hypothesized that a positive response to psychological treatments, such as CSE, may be influenced by the presence and magnitude of negative symptoms experienced by the patient. To examine this question, patients were assessed with the Scale for Assessment of Negative Symptoms (SANS) prior to treatment and these results were correlated with the changes in positive symptoms achieved through treatment. It was found that affective flattening and alogia, but not avolition, anhedonia, or attention were significantly related to symptom change scores, so that high initial scores on these negative symptoms were associated with a poor response to treatment. Affective flattening here is defined as a "characteristic impoverishment of emotional expression, reactivity and feeling." While alogia refers to an "impoverished thinking and cognition." Hence, patients who show negative symptoms characterized by a poverty of emotion and thought appear to respond poorly to cognitive–behavioral approaches. This may be an important finding in that if replicated patients who are likely to respond well to psychological treatment approaches can be identified and prioritized. We intend to investigate this further and in more detail.

These results were considered promising because of the dramatic improvements that some patients showed over a relatively short period of time with a small number of sessions. Each intervention consisted of 10 sessions spread over 5 weeks. We have now embarked on further study, funded by the Wellcome Trust (Tarrier, 1993), which combines both CSE and problem solving with a third intervention component designed to teach the patient to identify early signs of relapse and to use their coping skills to abort the relapse. It is reasoned that a much longer intervention, 30 sessions over 3 months, which combines coping skills, problem solving skills, and relapse prevention skills will have a greater impact on the patient by reducing symptomatology and increasing functioning than did the short intervention of the first trial. It is also anticipated that non-specific factors will be important, especially the building of a strong therapeutic relationship. To control for the effect of non-specific factors alone a supportive counselling control intervention of the same duration is to be included, as is a routine care control group. Factors which predict treatment response will also be examined.

DISSEMINATION AND TRAINING

EVALUATION OF TRAINING

Despite the successful results reported for family interventions the point has often been made that these results were the products of enthusiastic and highly trained specialist research teams and the case for family interventions working in a normal service setting remains unproven. There is some truth in this argument, although the Salford project was performed by National Health Service psychologists attempting to run a District service. If family interventions and other psychosocial and psychological treatments are to become standard practice then appropriate training needs to be available.

Some progress has been achieved in training. The Department of Nursing at Manchester University set up a project in 1988 to train CPNs in family management methods and to evaluate the effectiveness of this training. This project was stimulated by the research results reporting the benefits of family intervention and also by concern in the "drift" in the role and activity of CPNs. CPN services had been established in the mid-1950s for the after-care and follow-up of psychotic patients receiving the newly introduced neuroleptics (Simmonds & Brooker, 1986). Recent evidence suggested that CPNs were spending considerably less time with psychotic patients than non-psychotic affective disordered patients (Wooff *et al.*, 1988) and that schizophrenic patients "constituted a mere 27% of all total CPN caseloads throughout the UK" (White, 1990). The advances in psychosocial interventions with schizophrenic patients appear not to have been reflected in an increased input of relevant material in CPN training and the lack of such psychosocial management skills had resulted in CPNs "drifting away" from contact with patients with psychoses. So a training scheme was devised which aimed to train CPNs in family intervention and provide them with clinical supervision with the hope that the provision of these skills alongside clinical supervision would rekindle interest in working with psychotic patients.

In the initial trial (Brooker *et al.*, 1992a, b), nine CPNs were recruited from three regional Health Authorities through advertisement. Each selected CPN was matched with a "control" colleague from the same health authority on a number of variables such as: length of experience as a CPN; amount of post-qualification training; age and sex. The aim of the study was for each CPN to recruit three schizophrenic patients and their families into their caseload, a total of 54 families. Initially, 87% of the target was achieved; however, 17 of these families dropped out during 1-year follow-up. The 30 families who completed the trial represented 64% of the recruited sample. All CPNs, both experimental and control, were trained in the clinical assessment methods and the nine experimental CPNs attended a training course in family management derived from that used in the Salford project (see Barrowclough & Tarrier, 1992). The course was of 6 months duration and consisted of didactic and workshop teaching, and clinical supervision throughout the 6 months. The continuous clinical supervision was considered an essential constituent of the course and was led by clinical psychologists experienced in the area. Evaluation of the patients and families indicated that there were small but significant improvements in patients' symptomatology. Depression, anxiety, delusions, and physical retardation improved in patients managed by the CPNs who were receiving training, whereas only delusions improved in the control group. There was a trend towards a reduction in neuroleptic medication for patients in the experimental group that was not evident in the control group. Furthermore, there was evidence for significant improvements in personal functioning and social functioning in the experimental group but not the control group. There was also evidence that relatives of patients in the experimental group showed a significant decrease in the presence of minor psychological symptoms as measured by the GHQ while there was no change in the control group. Such differences may indicate a decrease in the perceived or subjective burden of care in relatives who received family intervention compared to those who did not. Interestingly, this result contrasts to that of Tarrier and colleagues who report no change in GHQ scores for relatives who participated in family intervention. An evaluation of knowledge about schizophrenia held by the relatives using the Knowledge About Schizophrenia Interview (KASI) evaluation method (Barrowclough *et al.*, 1987) found that relatives in the experimental group significantly increased their functional knowledge about schizophrenia whereas the control group did not (Brooker *et al.*, 1992a).

In a subsequent study, Brooker *et al.* (1994) carried out a trial of the effectiveness of CPN training using a within-subject design. Ten CPNs recruited six patients and their families, of which three patients and families received family intervention and the other three acted as controls. After 6 months follow-up data were collected, the control families were then offered active family intervention and

65% of this group accepted. Seventy-eight percent of families in the intervention group and 96% of control families remained in the study until follow-up. The family intervention in this study was taught by Falloon and his colleagues (see Falloon *et al.*, 1984 for details of this treatment approach). The patients who received the intervention showed a significant improvement in positive and negative symptoms and a significant increase in social functioning. There was also evidence for a dramatic decline in hospital usage when the mean number of days spent in hospital per patient were compared between the 12 months prior to the intervention and a comparable period post-intervention. The experimental group demonstrated a decline from 18.4 days per annum, before treatment to 1.8 days per annum, after treatment. In the untreated controls this figure increases from a baseline of 23.5 days per annum to 73.5 days.

Both studies carried out by Brooker and his colleagues in Manchester, indicate the positive benefits of training CPNs in family intervention even though two different types of intervention were used and were taught by different groups of workers.

In an Australian study of family intervention training, Kavanagh and his colleagues (1993) trained mental health workers in a cognitive–behavioral approach to family intervention. However, despite the considerable efforts by the training team the training appeared to have little impact upon clinical practice with few of the trainees actually engaging families for any length of time. Trainees received didactic and workshop training of approximately 30–35 hours duration, they were then asked to participate in a controlled evaluation of family intervention by acting as trial therapists. Initially, 160 therapists received training but only 44 of these elected to take part in the treatment trial and 28 of these saw only one family. In fact, 57% of the families in the study were seen by 6 therapists. Therapists reported particular difficulty in integrating the family work with their other duties and interests. In an evaluation of the training program only 4% of the sample reported that their knowledge of cognitive–behavioral approaches was a significant problem, but in a written test most therapists failed to demonstrate even the minimum recall of the material they had been taught (Kavanagh *et al.*, 1993). The authors report that in families receiving intervention 13% of patients receiving family intervention had experienced a marked exacerbation of symptoms compared with 27% in the group who received an individual intervention (Kavanagh *et al.*, 1993). But they conclude "as a demonstration that the structured family intervention could be disseminated into routine community health practice, the project clearly was of limited success."

There are two possible reasons why the training program of Kavanagh and colleagues yielded such poor results compared with the comparative success of Brooker and colleagues. Successful training requires continuity and progressive clinical supervision, time limited didactic and workshop teaching is unlikely to result in skill acquisition in the absence of guided practice. It is probable that without supervision within a structured teaching program trainees will very quickly abandon the new approach. The second important factor is the necessity for management commitment for the training and practice of the new approach. In Kavanagh's program there appears to have been little in the way of management commitment to the reorganization of workloads so that family intervention could be given a high priority. It appears that for most trained therapists in this study family work was just one more activity that had to compete in an already overloaded schedule. It is perhaps not surprising that very few therapists attempted to implement what they have been taught without management prioritizing of their family work, and clinical supervision to shape their practice.

An ongoing project funded by the Jules Thorn Charitable Trust, in Manchester and London, is dedicated to evaluating the training of CPNs in problem-oriented case management. This will include training in three modules: family intervention; psychological management of psychotic symptoms; and case management. The training effectiveness is being extensively evaluated with the assessment of knowledge and skills acquired by the nurses being assessed by academic measures, and evidence of practical skills assessed through clinical casework. Trainees will also assess the clinical effectiveness of their work through the use of standardized clinical assessments and monitoring of problems and goals. An objective clinical assessment will be performed by an independent evaluator on a sample of the patients and their relatives.

ACKNOWLEDGMENTS

The Salford Family Intervention project was funded by a project grant (no. 5062) from the North West Regional Health Authority. The Salford Symptom Project was funded by a project grant (no. 5107) from the North West Regional Health Authority. The Manchester Psychotic Symptom Management Project is funded by The Wellcome Trust project grant (no. 03670/1.5/WRE/JL). All grants were awarded to the author. I am indebted to: Dr. Barrowclough for many of the ideas expressed in this chapter, to Dr. Brooker for information relating to the CPN training studies, to the Thorn Nurse Project for information relating to the Thorn CPN training study.

REFERENCES

Alford, G.S., Fleece, L. and Rothblum, E. (1982). Hallucinatory-delusional verbalisations: modification in a chronic schizophrenic by self-contol. *Behavior Modification,* **6**, 421–435.

Barrowclough, C. and Tarrier, N. (1984). Psychosocial interventions with families and their effects on the course of treatment. *Psychological Medicine,* **14**, 629–642.

Barrowclough, C. and Tarrier, N. (1990). Social functioning in schizophrenic patients. I: the effects of expressed emotion and family intervention. *Social Psychiatry and Psychiatic Epidemiology,* **25**, 125–129.

Barrowclough, C. and Tarrier, N. (1992). *Families of Schizophrenic Patients: Cognitive Behavioural Intervention.* London: Chapman & Hall.

Barrowclough, C., Tarrier, N., Watts, S., Vaughn, C., Bamrah, J.S., and Freeman, H.L. (1987). Assessing the functional knowledge about schizophrenia: a preliminary report. *British Journal of Psychiatry,* **151**, 1–8.

Barrowclough, C., Johnston, M., and Tarrier, N. (1994). Attributions, expressed emotion and patient relapse: an attributional model of relatives' response to schizophrenic illness. *Behavior Therapy,* **25**, 67–88.

Beck, A.T. (1952). Successful out-patient psychotheapy of a chronic schizophrenic with a delusion based on borrowed grief. *Psychiatry,* **15**, 305–312.

Belcher, T.L. (1988). Behavioral reduction of overt hallucinatory behavior in chronic schizophrenics. *Journal of Behavior Therapy & Experimental Psychiatry,* **19**, 69–71.

Bentall, R.P., Haddock, G., and Slade, P. Cognitive–behaviour therapy for persistent hallucinations: from theory to therapy. *Behavior Therapy,* **25**, 51–66.

Birchwood, M. (1986). Control of auditory hallucinations through occlusions of monoaural auditory input. *British Journal of Psychiatry,* **149**, 104–107.

Birchwood, M. and Shepherd, G. (1992). Controversies and growing points in cognitive–behavioural interventions for people with schizophrenia. *Behavioural Psychotherapy,* **20**, 305–342.

Birchwood, M. and Tarrier, N. (1992). *Innovations in the Psychological Management of Schizophrenia: Assessment, Treatment & Services.* Chichester: John Wiley.

Birchwood, M., Smith, J., Cochrane, R., *et al.* (1990). The social functioning scale: the development and validation of a scale of social adjustment for use in family intervention programmes with schizophrenic patients. *British Journal of Psychiatry,* **157**, 853–859.

Breier, A. and Strauss, J.S. (1983). Self-control in psychotic disorders. *Archives of General Psychiatry,* **40**, 1141–1145.

Brenner, H.D., Boker, W., Andres, K., and Stramke, W.G. (1985). Efforts at compensation with regard to basic disorders among schizophrenics. In U. Laaser, R. Senault, and K. Viefhues, eds, *Primary Health Care in the Making*, pp. 136–151. Berlin: Springer-Verlag.

Brenner, H.D., Kraemer, S., Hermantz, H., and Hodel, B. (1990). Cognitive treatment in schizophrenia. In E.R. Straube and K. Hahlweg, eds, *Schizophrenia: Concepts, Vulnerability, and Interventions*, pp. 161–192. New York: Springer.

Brooker, C., Barrowclough, C., and Tarrier, N. (1992a). Evaluating the impact of training community psychiatric nurses to educate relatives about schizophrenia. *Journal of Clinical Nursing,* **1**, 19–25.

Brooker, C., Tarrier, N., Barrowclough, C., Butterworth, A., and Goldberg, D. (1992b). Training community psychiatric nurses for psychosocial intervention: report of a pilot study. *British Journal of Psychiatry,* **160**, 836–844.

Brooker, C., Falloon, I.R.H., Butterworth, A., Goldberg, D., Graham-Hole, V., and Hillier, V. (1994). The outcome of training community psychiatric nurses to deliver psychosocial intervention. *British Journal of Psychiatry,* **165**, 222–230.

Brown, G.W. (1985). The discovery of expressed emotion: induction or deduction. In J.P. Leff and C.E. Vaughn, eds, *Expressed Emotion in Families.* Guilford: New York.

Brown, G.W., Carstairs, G.M., and Topping, G. (1958). Post hospital adjustment of chronic mental patients. *Lancet,* **ii**, 685–689.

Brown, G.W., Monck, E.M., Carstairs, G.M., and Wing, J.K. (1962). Influence of family life on the course of schizophrenia. *British Journal of Preventative and Social Medicine,* **16**, 55–68.

Brown, G.W., Birley, J.T.L., and Wing, J.K. (1972). Influence of family life on the course of schizophrenia: a replication. *British Journal of Psychiatry,* **121**, 241–258.

Bulow, H., Oei, T., and Pinkey, B. (1979). Effects of contingent social reinforcement with delusional chronic schizophrenic men. *Psychological Reports,* **44**, 659–666.

Cardin, V.A., McGill, C.W., and Falloon, I.R.H. (1986).

An economic analysis: costs, benefits and effectiveness. In I.R.H. Falloon, ed., *Family Management of Schizophrenia*. Baltimore, MD: Johns Hopkins University Press.

Ciompi, L. (1980). The natural history of schizophrenia in the long term. *British Journal of Psychiatry*, **136**, 413–420.

Creer, C. and Wing, J.K. (1974). *Schizophrenia at Home*. Surrey: National Schizophrenia Fellowship.

Curson, D.A., Barnes, T.R.E., Bamber, R.W., Platt, S.D., Hirsch, S.R., and Duffy, J.D. (1985). Long term depot maintenance of chronic schizophrenic out-patients. *British Journal of Psychiatry*, **146**, 464–480.

Curson, D.A., Patel, M., Liddle, P.F., and Barnes, T.R.E. (1988). Psychiatric morbidity of a long stay hospital population with chronic schizophrenia and implications for future community care. *British Medical Journal*, **297**, 819–822.

Davis, J.R., Wallace, C.J., Liberman, R.P., and Finch, B.E. (1976). The use of belief isolation to suppress delusional and hallucinatory speech. *Journal of Behavior Therapy & Experimental Psychiatry*, **7**, 269–275.

Dulz, B. and Hand, I. (1986). Short term relapse in young schizophrenics: can it be predicted and affected by family (CFI), patient and treatment variables? An experimental study. In M.J. Goldstein, I. Hand, and K. Hahlweg, eds, *Treatment of Schizophrenia: Family Assessment and Intervention*, pp. 159–75. Berlin: Springer-Verlag.

Fadden, G., Bebbington, P., and Kuipers, L. (1987). Caring and its burden. *British Journal of Psychiatry*, **151**, 660–667.

Falloon, I.R.H. (1986). Cognitive and behavioural interventions in the self-control of schizophrenia. In J. Strauss, W. Boker, and H.D. Brenner, eds, *Psychological Treatment of Schizophrenia*, pp. 180–190. Bern: Hans Huber.

Falloon, I.R.H., and Pederson, J. (1985). Family management in the prevention of morbidity of schizophrenia: the adjustment of the family unit. *British Journal of Psychiatry*, **147**, 156–163.

Falloon, I.R.H. and Talbot, R.E. (1981). Persistent auditory hallucinations: coping mechanisms and implications for management. *Psychological Medicine*, **11**, 329–339.

Falloon, I.R.H., Watt, D.C., and Shepherd, M. (1978). A comparative controlled trial of pimozide and fluphenazine decanoate in the continuation therapy of schizophrenia. *Psychological Medicine*, **7**, 59–70.

Falloon, I.R.H., Boyd, J.L., McGill, C.W., Razani, J., Moss, H.B., and Gilderman, A.M. (1982). Family management in the prevention of exacerbations of schizophrenia. *New England Journal of Medicine*, **306**, 1437–1440.

Falloon, I.R.H., Boyd, J.L., and McGill, C.W. (1984). *Family Care of Schizophrenia*, New York: Guilford Press.

Falloon, I.R.H., Boyd, J.L., McGill, C.W., *et al.* (1985). Family management in the prevention of morbidity of schizophrenia: clinical outcome of a two year longitudinal study. *Archives of General Psychiatry*, **42**, 887–896.

Fonagy, P. and Slade, P. (1982). Punishment vs negative reinforcement in the aversive conditioning of auditory hallucinations. *Behaviour Research & Therapy*, **20**, 483–492.

Glick, L.D., Spencer, J.H., Clarkin, J.F., *et al.* (1990). A randomised clinical trial of in-patient family intervention: IV. followup results for subjects with schizophrenia. *Schizophrenia Research*, **3**, 187–200.

Goldberg, D. and Williams, P. (1988). *A User's Guide to the General Health Questionnaire*. Windsor: NFER Nelson.

Green, M.F. (1993). Cognitive remediation in schizophrenia: is it time yet? *American Journal of Psychiatry*, **150**, 178–187.

Haddock, G., Bentall, R.P., and Slade, P. (1993). Psychological treatment of chronic hallucinations: two case studies. *Behavioural & Cognitive Psychotherapy*, **21**, 335–346.

Hahlweg, K., Goldstein, M.J., Nuechterlein, K.H., *et al.* (1989). Expressed emotion and patient–relative interaction in families of recent onset schizophrenia. *Journal of Consulting and Clinical Psychology*, **57**, 11–18.

Harding, C., Brooks, G.W., Ashikaga, T., Strauss, J.S., and Breier, A. (1987). The Vermont longitudinal study of persons with severe mental illness: II. Long term outcome of subjects who retrospectively met DSM III criteria for schizophrenia. *American Journal of Psychiatry*, **144**, 727–735.

Harrow, M. and Silverstein, M.L. (1977). Psychotic symptoms in schizophrenia after the acute phase. *Schizophrenia Bulletin*, **3**, 608–616.

Hogarty, G.E., Schooler, N.R., Ulrich, R.F., Mussare, F., Ferro, P., and Herron, E. (1979). Fluphenazine and social therapy in the aftercare of schizophrenic patients. *Archives of General Psychiatry*, **36**, 1283–1294.

Hogarty, G.E., Anderson, C.M., Reiss, D.J., *et al.* (1986). Family psychoeducation, social skills training and maintenance chemotherapy in the aftercare treatment of schizophrenia. 1: One year effects of a controlled study on relapse and expressed emotion. *Archives of General Psychiatry*, **43**, 633–642.

Hogarty, G.E., Anderson, C.M., Reiss, D.J., *et al.* (1991). Family psychoeducation, social skills training, and maintenance chemotherapy in the aftercare treatment of schizophrenia. II. Two year effects of a controlled study on relapse and adjustment. *Archives of General Psychiatry*, **48**, 340–347.

Hole, R.W., Rush, A.J., and Beck, A.T. (1979). A cognitive investigation of schizophrenic delusions. *Psychiatry*, **42**, 312–319.

Johnson, D.A.W., Ludlow, J., Street, K., and Taylor, R. (1987). Double blind comparison of half-dose and standard dose flupenthixol decanoate in the maintenance treatment of stabilised out-patient schizophrenics. *British Journal of Psychiatry*, **151**, 634–638.

Kavanagh, D. (1992). Recent developments in expressed emotion and schizophrenia. *British Journal of Psychiatry*,

160, 601–620.

Kavanagh, D., Clark, D., Piatkowska, O., *et al.* (1993). Application of cognitive-behavioural family intervention for schizophrenia in multidisciplinary teams: what can the matter be? *Australian Psychologist*, **28**, 1–8.

Kingdon, D.G., and Turkington, D. (1991). Preliminary report: the use of cognitive behaviour therapy and a normalising rationale in schizophrenia. *Journal of Nervous and Mental Disease*, **179**, 207–211.

Kottgen, C., Soinnichsen, I., Mollenhauer, K., and Jurth, R. (1984). Results of the Hamburg Camberwell family Interview study, I-III. *International Journal of Family Psychiatry*, **5**, 61–94.

Kuipers, L., Sturgeon, D., Berkowitz, R., and Leff, J.P. (1983). Characteristics of expressed emotion: its relationship to speech and looking in schizophrenic patients and their relatives. *British Journal of Clinical Psychology*, **22**, 257–264.

Lamontagne, Y., Audet, N., and Elie, R. (1983). Thought stopping for delusions and hallucinations: a pilot study. *Behavioural Psychotherapy*, **11**, 177–184.

Leff, J.P. and Vaughn, C.E. (1985). *Expressed Emotion in Families*. New York: Guilford Press.

Leff, J.P., Kuipers, L., Berkowitz, R., Eberlein-Fries, R., and Sturgeon, D. (1982). A controlled trial of intervention with families of schizophrenic patients. *British Journal of Psychiatry*, **141**, 121–134.

Leff, J.P., Kuipers, L., Berkowitz, R., and Sturgeon, D. (1985). A controlled trial of social intervention in the families of schizophrenic patients. *British Journal of Psychiatry*, **146**, 594–600.

Leff, J.P., Berkowitz, R., Shavit, A., Strachan, A., Glass, I., and Vaughn, C.E. (1989). A trial of family therapy v. relatives' groups for schizophrenia. *British Journal of Psychiatry*, **154**, 58–66.

Leff, J.P., Berkowitz, R., Shavit, A., Strachan, A., Glass, I., and Vaughn, C.E. (1990). A trial of family therapy v. relatives' groups for schizophrenia: two year follow up. *British Journal of Psychiatry*, **157**, 571–577.

Liberman, R.P., Teigan, J., Patterson, R., and Baker, V. (1973). Reducing delusional speech in chronic paranoid schizophrenics. *Journal of Applied Behavior Analysis*, **6**, 57–64.

Meichenbaum, D. and Cameron, R. (1973). Training schizophrenics to talk to themselves: a means of developing attentional control. *Behavior Therapy*, **4**, 515–534.

Miklowitz, D.J., Goldstein, M.J., Falloon, I.R.H., *et al.* (1984). Interactional correlates of expressed emotion in families of schizophrenics. *British Journal of Psychiatry*, **144**, 482–487.

Milton, F., Patwa, V.K., and Hafner, J. (1978). Confrontation vs belief modification in persistently deluded patients. *British Journal of Medical Psychology*, **51**, 127–130.

Morley, S. (1987). Modification of auditory hallucinations: experimental studies of headphones and earplugs. *Behavioural Psychotherapy*, **15**, 240–251.

Nydegger, R.V. (1972). The elimination of hallucinatory and delusional behaviours by verbal conditioning and assertive training: a case study. *Journal of Behavior Therapy & Experimental Psychiatry*, **3**, 225–227.

Nuechterlein, K.H. (1987). Vulnerability models: state of the art. In H. Hafner, W. Gattaz, and W. Jangerik, eds, *Searches for the Cause of Schizophrenia*. Berlin: Springer-Verlag.

Nuechterlein, K.H. and Dawson, M.E. (1984). A heuristic vulnerability-stress model of schizophrenic episodes. *Schizophrenia Bulletin*, **10**, 300–312.

Schneider, S.J. and Pope, A.T. (1982). Neuroleptic-like electroencephalographic changes in schizophrenics through biofeedback. *Biofeedback & Self-Regulation*, **7**, 479–490.

Silverstein, M.L. and Harrow, M. (1978). First rank symptoms in the post acute schizophrenic: a follow-up study. *American Journal of Psychiatry*, **135**, 1481–1486.

Simmons, S. and Brooker, C. (1986). *Community Psychiatric Nursing: A Social Perspective*. London: Heinemann.

Slade, P.D. (1972). The effects of systematic desensitisation on auditory hallucinations. *Behaviour Research & Therapy*, **10**, 85–91.

Slade, P.D. (1973). The psychological investigation and treatment of auditory hallucinations: a second case report. *British Journal of Medical Psychology*, **46**, 293–296.

Slade, P.D. and Bentall, R.P. (1988). *Sensory Deception: A Scientific Analysis of Hallucination*. Baltimore, MD: Johns Hopkins University Press.

Smith, J. and Birchwood, M. (1990). Relatives and patients as partners in the management of schizophrenia: the development of a service model. *British Journal of Psychiatry*, **150**, 645–652.

Spender, J.H., Glick, I.D., Haas, G.L., *et al.* (1988). A randomised clinical trial of inpatient family intervention, III: effects at 6 months and 18-month follow-ups. *American Journal of Psychiatry*, **145**, 1115–1121.

Strachan, A.M., Leff, J.P., Goldstein, M.J., *et al.* (1986). Emotional attitudes and direct communication in the families of schizophrenics: a cross national replication. *British Journal of Psychiatry*, **149**, 279–287.

Stratton, P., Heard, D., Hanks, H.G.I., Munton, A.G., Brewin, C.R., and Davidson, C. (1986). Coding causal beliefs in natural discourse. *British Journal of Social Psychology*, **25**, 299–313.

Tantam, D. (1989). Family factors in psychiatric disorders. *Current Opinion in Psychiatry*, **2**, 296–302.

Tarrier, N. (1987). An investigation of residual psychotic symptoms in discharged schizophrenic patients. *British Journal of Clinical Psychology*, **26**, 141–143.

Tarrier, N. (1991a). Changes in the electrodermal activity of schizophrenic patients associated with changes in the expressed emotion status of their relatives. *Psychopathology*, **24**, 203–208.

Tarrier, N. (1991b). Some aspects of family interventions in schizophrenia. I; adherence to intervention programmes. *British Journal of Psychiatry*, **159**, 475–480.

Tarrier, N. (1992a). Psychological treatment of schizophrenic symptoms. In D. Kavangh, ed., *Schizophrenia: An Overview and Practical Handbook*. London: Chapman & Hall.

Tarrier, N. (1992b). Management and modification of residual positive psychotic symptoms. In M. Birchwood and N. Tarrier, eds, *Innovations in the Psychological Management of Schizophrenia: Assessment, Treatment & Services*. Chichester: John Wiley & Sons.

Tarrier, N. and Turpin, G. (1992). Psychosocial factors, arousal and schizophrenic relapse: the psychophysiological data. *British Journal of Psychiatry*, **161**, 3–11.

Tarrier, N., Barrowclough, C., Vaughn, C.E., *et al.* (1988). The community management of schizophrenia: a controlled trial of a behavioural intervention with families to reduce relapse. *British Journal of Psychiatry*, **153**, 532–542.

Tarrier, N., Barrowclough, C., Vaughn, C.E., *et al.* (1989). The community management of schizophrenia: a controlled trial of a behavioural intervention with families to reduce relapse: a two year follow up. *British Journal of Psychiatry*, **154**, 625–628.

Tarrier, N., Harwood, S., Yusupoff, L., Beckett, R., and Baker. A. (1990). Coping strategy enhancement (CSE): a method of treating residual schizophrenic symptoms. *Behavioural Psychotherapy*, **18**, 283–293.

Tarrier, N., Lowson, K., and Barrowclough, C. (1991). Some aspects of family interventions in schizophrenia. II: Financial considerations. *British Journal of Psychiatry*, **159**, 481–484.

Tarrier, N., Beckett, R., Harwood, S., Baker, A., Yusupoff, L., and Ugarteburu, I. (1993a). A trial of two cognitive–behavioural methods of treating drug-resistant psychotic symptoms in schizophrenia: I, outcome. *British Journal of Psychiatry*, **162**, 524–532.

Tarrier, N., Sharpe, L., Beckett, R., Harwood, S., Baker, A., and Yusupoff, L. (1993b). A trial of two cognitive–behavioural methods of treating drug-resistant psychotic symptoms in schizophrenia: II, treatment specific changes in coping and problem-solving. *Social Psychiatry & Psychiatric Epidemiology*, **28**, 5–10.

Tarrier, N., Barrowclough, C., Porceddu, K., and Fitzpatrick, E. (1994). The Salford Family Intervention Project for schizophrenic relapse prevention: five and eight year accumulating relapses. *British Journal of Psychiatry*, **165**, 829–832.

Turner, S., Herson, M., and Bellack, A. (1977). Effects of social disruption, stimulus interference and aversive conditioning on auditory hallucinations. *Behavior Modification*, **1**, 249–258.

Valone, K., Norton, J.P., Goldstein, M.J., *et al.* (1983). Parental expressed emotion and affective style in an adolescent sample at risk for schizophrenia spectrum disorders. *Journal of Abnormal Psychology*, **92**, 399–407.

Vaughan, K., Doyle, M., McConaghy, N., Blaszczynski, A., Fox, A., and Tarrier, N. (1992). The Sydney intervention trial: a controlled trial of relatives' counselling to reduce schizophrenic relapse. *Social Psychiatry & Psychiatric Epidemiology*, **27**, 16–21.

Vaughn, C.E. (1986). Patterns of emotional response in the families of schizophrenic patients. In M.J. Goldstein, I. Hand, and K. Hahlweg, eds, *Treatment of Schizophrenia: Family Assessment and Intervention*, pp. 76–78. Berlin: Springer-Verlag.

Vaughn, C.E. and Leff, J.P. (1976). The influence of family and social factors on the course of psychiatric illnesss: a comparison of schizophrenic and depressed neurotic patients. *British Journal of Psychiatry*, **129**, 125–137.

Watts, F.N., Powell, G.E., and Austin, S.V. (1973). The modification of abnormal beliefs. *British Journal of Medical Psychology*, **46**, 359–363.

Weingaertner, A.H. (1971). Self-administered aversive stimulation with hallucinating hospitalised schizophrenics. *Journal of Consulting & Clinical Psychology*, **36**, 422–429.

White, E. (1990). *The Third National Quinquennial Survey of Community Psychiatry Services*. Leeds: CPNA Publications.

Wooff, K., Goldberg, D., and Fryers, T. (1988). The practice of community psychiatric nursing and mental health social work in Salford. *British Journal of Psychiatry*, **152**, 783–792.

Zubin, J. and Spring, B. (1977). Vulnerability: a new view of schizophrenia. *Journal of Abnormal Psychology*, **86**, 103–126.

23

Psychoeducational Family Programs in the United States

MICHAEL J. GOLDSTEIN
Department of Psychology, University of California, Los Angeles, USA

INTRODUCTION

The development of any program of psychosocial treatment of schizophrenia is best understood within the cultural context of the health delivery system of the country in question. Unlike other western European countries, the USA does not have a national health system in which mental health treatment is guaranteed to all. Instead, multiple treatment systems exist in different communities, some supported by private insurance mechanisms, and others by public funding, with limited coordination of these different systems. Further, the linkages between systems designed to provide inpatient care for severely ill psychiatric patients and those designed to provide post-hospitalization community aftercare are tenuous and sometimes lacking entirely. Thus, any statement concerning the status of psychoeducational family programs in the USA must recognize the enormous diversity of mental health delivery systems and the unique infrastructure in which the programs have evolved. There is no one set of standardized programs in the USA, but rather a number of different approaches which arose from the unique characteristics of the particular service delivery system and the availability of funding for implementing family-oriented programs.

In general, there is wide support in the USA for psychoeducational family programs developed for psychotic patients (schizophrenic and bipolar, in particular), from both mental health professionals and advocacy groups, such as the National Alliance for the Mentally Ill (NAMI), a group which has played a very significant part in emphasizing the importance of relatives' involvement in the care of psychotic patients. The major problems in implementing these psychoeducational family programs on a much broader scale have been: (i) the lack of opportunities for persons to be trained in the delivery of these programs, and therefore a lack of trained personnel to implement them; and (ii) the difficulty in convincing public and private funders of mental health care that these programs serve important therapeutic functions which can reduce or delay recurrence of psychiatric disorders, with consequent cost-savings. Unless these two issues can be addressed, psychoeducational family programs in the USA will be present in only a minority of mental health delivery systems, and may be implemented in watered-down versions in many others.

Handbook of Mental Health Economics and Health Policy, Volume I, Schizophrenia. Edited by M. Moscarelli, A. Rupp and N. Sartorius.
© 1996 John Wiley & Sons Ltd.

THE ORIGINS OF PSYCHOEDUCATIONAL FAMILY PROGRAMS

DEINSTITUTIONALIZATION AND ITS CONSEQUENCES

The rapid trend in the USA toward deinstitutionalization of chronic schizophrenic patients and the great reductions in periods of inpatient care have led to an increasing reliance on community care as the major phase in the treatment of these patients. As indicated in a previous paper by the author (Goldstein, 1992), these changes in philosophy had led to a three-phase model of treatment for schizophrenia: *resolution* of the acute phase of the disorder in a relatively brief period of inpatient stay; *stabilization* for some period, usually measured in months, after discharge from the hospital; and *maintenance* of the stabilized state for as long as possible thereafter. This model of treatment has had important implications for the formulation of psychoeducational family programs in the USA. For example, a brief hospitalization of 1–3 weeks, which is the norm in the USA does not permit extensive therapeutic work with the patient or the family members. As articulated by Anderson *et al.* (1980), the major goal of this period is for the family psychoeducational therapist to "connect" with the patient and significant relatives. The goal of the connection is to provide support during this crisis period, to provide information about the patient's treatment while in the hospital, and to set the stage for continuing contact after the patient is discharged. While these goals may seem minimal, most professionals have found this sort of alliance-building essential, in order to insure that the patient and relatives will participate in an outpatient program of combined pharmacological and family treatment.

Most persons now recognize that a psychoeducational family program should last from 9 months to 1 year after the schizophrenic person is discharged from the hospital, and is most likely to play a major part in the *stabilization* phase of treatment. Here, we refer to the importance of these programs in assisting patients and relatives in dealing with residual symptoms and social deficits, which wax and wane, during the immediate post-discharge period, to set realistic expectations for the patient and to provide a support system for the patient and relatives during a period of relative clinical instability.

Of course, these programs can also play a part during the maintenance phase of treatment, to promote further improvement in general family functioning and to assist patients and families to set realistic goals for the patient's social and occupational functioning.

THE IMPACT OF COMMUNITY CARE ON RELATIVES

An important consequence of the model of treatment for schizophrenia outlined above is that patients are likely to be discharged into the community in states of *partial* remission and clinically unstable. Unless extensive resources exist to provide transitional, therapeutically oriented living environments for recently discharged patients, many, if not the majority of younger, schizophrenic patients end up living with relatives or remaining in very frequent contact with them. This has frequently required that relatives play some sort of caretaker role with their schizophrenic family member. This role has indirectly been foisted on relatives without clear guidelines as to how to deal with the inevitable problems posed by a less than fully recovered family member, and without a support system to assist with crises that are almost inevitable during the stabilization period. Thus, the re-design of the mental health delivery system in the USA in the last 20 years has had the unintended effect of increasing the burden on relatives. The sense of frustration about these burdens, including the difficulties in locating inpatient facilities or outpatient programs when needed, has led relatives, either through formal advocacy groups such as NAMI, or as individuals, to demand attention to their needs. The increasing proliferation of psychoeducational family programs in the USA has been, in part, a response to these cries for help from relatives, and to mental health professionals' awareness of the need for such programs.

THE EXPRESSED EMOTION LITERATURE

It is one thing to recognize the need for a community-based program for schizophrenic patients and their families, and quite another to have a clear rationale for the design of a potentially effective one. Here, the literature on what has been termed expressed emotion (EE; Vaughn & Leff, 1976) has been very significant. This literature, originally carried out in Great Britain, but also replicated in many other countries, including the USA (see Kavanagh, 1992 for a review of these studies), identified certain attitudes, particularly criticism and emotional overinvolvement, that were predictive of relapses in recently discharged schizophrenic patients. These attitudes have been found to correlate with intricate patterns of transactions, observable in direct interactions between patients and relatives (Goldstein *et al.*, 1994). These findings have provided clues to the ultimate goals of psychoeducational family programs, namely to reduce the probability of reciprocal criticism by patients and relatives, to limit excessive involvement by relatives in the patient's day-to-day activities, and to increase positive and clear communication among all family members. While the EE literature identified certain ultimate goals for these interventions, it did not define the strategies or tactics for realizing those objectives.

MODELS OF PSYCHOEDUCATIONAL FAMILY TREATMENT

Almost all family intervention programs that have been tested in controlled clinical trials (Goldstein *et al.*, 1978; Leff *et al.*, 1982; Falloon *et al.*, 1982; Hogarty *et al.*, 1986; Tarrier *et al.*, 1988) have had certain common features. While not all aspects of these programs were designed specifically to modify the transactional processes indexed by high EE attitudes, there is considerable evidence that they operate to achieve this objective. The common ingredients in effective family psychoeducational programs are summarized in Table 1. In addition to these common features, all but the original Leff *et al.* (1982) approach involved individual family units, and the patient was an active participant in the sessions.

As this author has had much experience implementing programs with these features, he has come to recognize certain critical issues that must be approached if the patient and family are to achieve maximum benefit from the program. These are summarized in Table 2. We will briefly review these issues.

Table 1. Common ingredients in effective family intervention programs

Engagement of the family early in the treatment process in a "no fault" atmosphere
Education about schizophrenia concerning:
The vulnerability–stress model
Etiologic theories
Variations in prognosis
Rationale for various treatments
Recommendations for coping with the disorder
Communication training directed at:
Improving communication clarity in general
Improving ways of providing positive and negative feedback within the family
Problem-solving training directed at improving:
Management of day-to-day problems and hassles
Management of discrete stressful life events
Generalized problem-solving skills
Crisis intervention:
In times of extreme stress involving one or more members of the family
When incipient signs of recurrence are evident

INTEGRATION OF THE PSYCHOTIC EXPERIENCE

An episode or multiple episodes of schizophrenia are very disruptive to the patient and to his or her close relatives. Akin to a major natural disaster, the experience is shattering to all, and leaves much residue. Thus, it is necessary to review the experience of psychosis in detail, and to permit the patient and relatives to share their experiences with it. This may involve a review of the syndrome and the common symptoms, as well as residual symptoms in the post-acute state. By integration, we refer to a process in which patients and relatives understand that the symptoms are characteristic of a known psychiatric disorder, and can comprehend its causes, both biological and psychological.

ACCEPTANCE OF VULNERABILITY TO FUTURE EPISODES

As the evidence is very strong that persons with schizophrenia rarely have a single episode in their lifetime, most psychoeducational programs are built around what has been termed the "vulnerability–

Table 2. Critical issues in the psychoeducational treatment of psychotic patients and their relatives

Integration of the psychotic experience
Acceptance of vulnerability to future episodes
Dependence on psychotropic medication for symptom control
The significance of stressful life events as triggers for the recurrence of the disorder
Distinguishing personality from disorder

stress" hypothesis (Zubin & Spring, 1977). A key element of the model is that the vulnerability to schizophrenia is an enduring one, and that effective management of one's life can reduce the probability of recurrence. Effective management of life refers to the use of coping techniques which reduce the impact of stressful life events, and continued adherence to maintenance medication, where indicated. Thus, to realize these objectives, both patients and relatives need to accept the often painful notion that, while an episode of schizophrenia has been resolved successfully, vulnerability can endure.

DEPENDENCE ON PSYCHOTROPIC MEDICATION FOR SYMPTOM CONTROL

As indicated above, effective management of one's life may involve continued adherence to a program of maintenance antipsychotic medication. Knowledge about the evidence for the effectiveness of medication is helpful, but rarely sufficient to insure compliance. Continued reliance on medication involves numerous complex issues for the patient and his/her relatives, such as tolerating some of the noxious side-effects of antipsychotic medications, the idea of dependence on an outside agent (a drug) to control one's behavior, and the stigmatizing impact of having others know that he/she requires a psychotic medication. These issues require careful and sensitive handling in psychoeducational family therapy for their resolution.

THE SIGNIFICANCE OF STRESSFUL LIFE EVENTS AS TRIGGERS FOR THE RECURRENCE OF THE DISORDER

While the notion that stress plays a part in the recurrence of schizophrenia is readily comprehensible, patients and relatives frequently have difficulty recognizing specific stressors associated with prior onsets of the patient's disorder. Also, because the vulnerability–stress model emphasizes biological and psychological factors as relevant to schizophrenia, participants in psychoeducational family therapy frequently struggle with the relative significance of each factor in their, or their relatives', particular case. Thus, it is frequently necessary to focus in detail on the types of life events that preceded the most recent episode, as well as any earlier ones, to help patients and relatives identify those events to which the patient was most sensitive. Once these connections are established, plans for dealing effectively with future stressors, anticipated or unanticipated, can be more readily designed. This type of review of stressors also permits relatives and patients to become more aware of interactions within the family which can increase stress for all members.

DISTINGUISHING PERSONALITY FROM DISORDER

An important objective of psychoeducation family therapy is to have the family members appreciate that their patient-relative has experienced an episode of a major psychiatric disorder—schizophrenia. However, there is a great danger in this process that both the patient and his/her relatives may conclude that the patient *is* his/her disorder, such that all aspects of his/her personality are signs of the disorder. Thus, an important objective of psychoeducational family therapy is to help family members recognize that many personality traits of the patient are quite independent of his/her disorder, and can be valued qualities. In other terms, the goal is to help all participants to see that the patient is a person first and a person with a disorder second.

THE COSTS OF THE TYPICAL PSYCHOEDUCATIONAL PROGRAM IN THE USA

The typical psychoeducational family program directed at in individual family has tended to follow the model outlined originally by Falloon *et al.* (1982). This is a program which begins very soon after discharge and lasts for a minimum of 9 months, sometimes extending longer based on the needs of the family and the patient. Generally, the program consists of 21 sessions, more intense initially (once per week for 3 months; biweekly for the next 3 months) and at longer monthly intervals in the latter phases of the program. While not essential, most programs have used a co-therapist model, as this has been found useful in dealing with the many crises experienced by the families of psychotic patients, and providing a support system for therapists. Thus, a 9-month program of 21 sessions involves a minimum of 42 direct contact hours (based on two therapists per session) with a family. When we factor in missed or rescheduled appointments, and the inevitable crisis calls between sessions, 50 person-hours per 9-month program seems appropriate.

Translating these hourly costs into monetary amounts is difficult because the rates for professional services are dependent on the training experience and professional discipline of the therapists. If we assume that high-level professionals are the psychoeducational family therapists (psychiatrists, psychologists, social workers) and set an average hourly rate of \$100 per hour (not an unusual figure in the USA), then a series for one family will cost \$5000 for two therapists, and \$2500 if one therapist runs the family sessions. The latter is certainly a possibility in general practice.

THE ECONOMIC BENEFITS OF A PSYCHOEDUCATIONAL PROGRAM FOR SCHIZOPHRENIC PATIENTS

The best estimates regarding the economic benefits come from two major controlled clinical trials conducted in the USA, those of Falloon *et al.* (1982) and Hogarty *et al.* (1986). The former was a 9-month trial and the latter a 12-month trial. Although the models used varied somewhat, both programs showed many of the common features as outlined earlier in Table 1. These two trials compared a psychoeducational family program and maintenance drug treatment with the effects of maintenance drug treatment alone in reducing the rate of relapse following discharge from the hospital after an index episode of the disorder. The rates of relapse at 9 months post-discharge in both studies were substantially reduced in the groups who received the psychoeducational family programs, when compared with those who received medication alone. While the figures vary between the two studies, if we use the more conservative figures from the Hogarty *et al.* (1986) study which found less dramatic group differences, the relapse rate was reduced to one-third of that seen in the medication-only condition. Note that the medication-only condition is frequently the most common aftercare program in the USA.

If we assume that many of these relapses result in the re-hospitalization of patients, which, in the USA will involve a minimum cost of \$800 per day for an average of 14 days, then the cost of the average relapse will be approximately \$11 200. This is more than twice the cost of a two-therapist psychoeducational family program, and over four times the cost of a single-therapist program.

Thus, each averted relapse represents a cost savings of approximately US\$6200. The reduction of the relapse rate by one-third, as has been found in the controlled clinical trials conducted in both the USA and Great Britain (see Figure 1), suggests that routine psychoeducational family programs could be highly cost-effective. This conclusion does not even address the impact of those programs on symptomatic and social functioning.

ALTERNATIVE MODELS FOR PSYCHOEDUCATIONAL PROGRAMS

The above review and economic calculations are based on one model of family psychoeducation in which individual family units meet with one or two therapists. Other models have been suggested which promise even greater cost-effectiveness. At one extreme are what are termed "relatives' groups," in which the relatives of schizophrenic patients meet with a trained leader who implements a program of education, and encourages group support. Patients are generally not included in these sessions, and this model seems more appropriate to relatives of chronic schizophrenic patients who have lived with the patient's disorder for some time, than for relatives of recent onset patients. This approach, while very popular in the USA, has not received

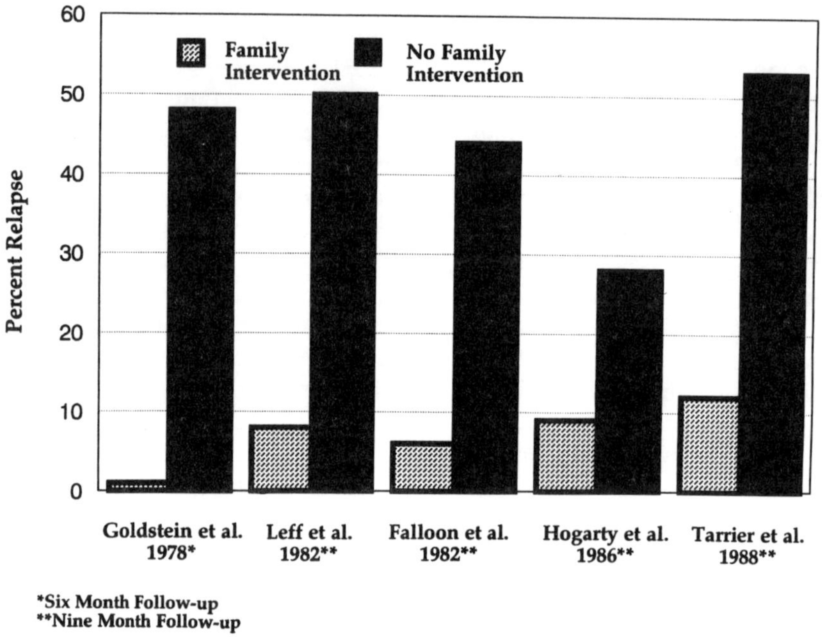

Figure 1 Relapse rates from five studies – Goldstein *et al.* (1978), Leff *et al.* (1982), Falloon *et al.* (1982), Hogarty *et al.* (1986) and Tarrier *et al.* (1988) contrasting a family intervention program with the absence of such program (schizophrenic patients on continuous medication).

careful evaluation in controlled clinical trials.

The one study (Leff *et al.*, 1989) which tested relatives' groups against psychoeducational family therapy for individual family units yielded confusing results. The rate of attrition in the relatives' groups was so high (50%) that a careful comparison of the two conditions was not possible. Perhaps the main conclusion of that study was that you are more certain to deliver the treatment when the individual family is the focus than when relatives are invited to join an ongoing group. A secondary conclusion was that those relatives who did participate in the group had schizophrenic family members whose relapse rates were reasonably low, and comparable with the rate found for the larger sample who received the individual family treatment.

The issue of the pros and cons of leaving the schizophrenic person out of the psychoeducational treatment process has never been clearly addressed in the writings on this subject. In a sense, relatives' groups, carried out in the patient's absence, can imply a disability model in which the primary goal of the program is to help the relatives adapt as best they can to a chronically disabled person. The introduction of the patient into the process carries a different message, namely that the patient has a part in his/her recovery, and in contributing to improvements in his/her life inside and outside of the family. These two views represent very different philosophical positions about the nature of schizophrenia and the degree of personal responsibility a person with this disorder has for his/her own recovery and rehabilitation. Possibly, with very chronic, poor-functioning patients, a disability model is appropriate, while for younger, recent onset patients, exclusive reliance on relatives to modify their behaviors, as implied by a disability model, could be highly counterproductive.

An intermediate position on this issue is represented by the work of McFarlane (1990), who advocate the application of the psychoeducational model within multiple family groups, in which patients and relatives both participate. Clearly, multiple family groups are a more economical method for delivering this type of problem. Recent data from a multicenter trial presented by McFarlane (1994) indicate that psychoeducational multiple family groups were as, if not more effective, than a comparable program targeted at individual family units.

CONCLUSIONS

Research has consistently supported the value of a psychoeducational family program as a significant component in the community care of schizophrenic patients. Despite the broad acceptance of this approach, major barriers exist in the USA to the general implementation of these programs. These include the lack of an infrastructure for training personnel in the delivery of these programs, the absence of a clear funding mechanism for incorporating these programs into the mental health delivery systems in the USA, and a lack of general agreement concerning the most cost-effective model for the psychoeducational program (relatives only or patients with relatives; single or multiple family groups). Despite these problems which demand further data on efficacy, there is little question that some variant of a psychoeductional program is cost-effective and likely to meet important needs of schizophrenic persons and their relatives.

REFERENCES

Anderson, C.M., Hogarty, G., and Reiss, D.J. (1980). Family treatment of adult schizophrenic patients: A psychoeducational approach. *Schizophrenia Bulletin*, **6**, 490–505.

Falloon, I.R.H., Boyd, J.L., and McGill, C.W. (1982). Family management in the prevention of exacerbations of schizophrenia: A controlled study. *New England Journal of Medicine*, **306**, 1437–1440.

Goldstein, M.J. (1992). Psychosocial strategies for maximizing the effects of psychotropic medications for schizophrenia and mood disorder. *Psychopharmacology Bulletin*, **28**, 237–240.

Goldstein, M.J., Rodnick, E.H., Evans, J.R., May, P.R.A., and Steinberg, M.R. (1978). Drug and family therapy in the aftercare of acute schizophrenics. *Archives of General Psychiatry*, **35**, 1169–1177.

Goldstein, M.J., Rosenfarb, I., Woo, S.M., and Nuechterlein, K.H. (1994). Intrafamilial relationships and the course of relationships and the course of schizophrenia. *Acta Psychiatrica Scandinavica Supplement*, **90**, 60–66.

Hogarty, G.E., Anderson, C.M., Reiss, D.J., *et al.* (1986). Family education, social skills, training, and maintenance chemotherapy in the aftercare of schizophrenia. *Archives of General Psychiatry*, **43**, 633–642.

Kavanagh, D.J. (1992). Recent developments in expressed emotion and schizophrenia. *British Journal of Psychiatry*, **160**, 601–620.

Leff, J., Kuipers, L., Berkowitz, R., Eberlein-Fries, R., and Sturgeon, D. (1982). A controlled trial of social intervention in the families of schizophrenia patients. *British Journal of Psychiatry*, **141**, 121–134.

Leff, J., Berkowitz, R., Shavit, N., Strachan, A., Glass, I., and Vaughn, C. (1989). A trial of family therapy versus a relatives group for schizophrenia. *British Journal of Psychiatry*, **154**, 58–66.

McFarlane, W.R. (1990). Multiple family groups and the treatment of schizophrenia. In: M.I., Herz, S.J., Keith, and J.P., Docherty, eds, *Psychosocial Treatment of Schizophrenia*. New York: Elsevier.

McFarlane, W.F. (1994). Multiple family group, psychoeducation and maintenance medication in the treatment of schizophrenia. Unpublished paper presented at the XIth International Symposium for the Psychotherapy of Schizophrenia.

Tarrier, N., Barrowclough, C., and Porceddu, K. (1988). The community management of schizophrenia: a controlled trial of a behavioural intervention with families to reduce relapse. *British Journal of Psychiatry*, **153**, 532–542.

Vaughn, C. and Leff, J. (1976). The influence of family and social factors on the course of psychiatric illness: A comparison of schizophrenic and depressed neurotic patients. *British Journal of Psychiatry*, **129**, 125–137.

Zubin, T. and Spring, B. (1977). Vulnerability—A new view of schizophrenia. *Journal of Abnormal Psychology*, **86**, 103–126.

Part V

PERSONNEL COORDINATION

24

Personnel Options in the Treatment of Schizophrenia in the USA

JOHN A. TALBOTT, ANTHONY F. LEHMAN, DAVID R. McDUFF, DAVID B. MALLOTT and JAMES W. THOMPSON
Department of Psychiatry, University of Maryland School of Medicine, Baltimore, Maryland, USA

INTRODUCTION

Services in the United States for persons suffering from schizophrenia are varied and complex. There are no widely adopted staffing standards or service requirements. Indeed, many services have sprung up because of the failure of "traditional" inpatient and ambulatory programs to serve the severely mentally ill (e.g., community care teams, psychosocial rehabilitation centers, etc.).

In this chapter, therefore, we will use national and local data and examples to discuss personnel options, but caution the reader not to assume that these represent universal standards. We will begin with a description of the various types of professionals and paraprofessionals serving persons suffering from schizophrenia, then describe the settings in which they work, define several current issues involving personnel options, and conclude with a summary, including the necessity for future studies.

PERSONNEL CATEGORIES

In the following section, we will provide some basic information about the types of professionals and paraprofessionals in the United States who work with persons suffering from schizophrenia. This includes data on their history and numbers, training, settings, and roles. We are indebted to several sources of information for these descriptions (Barton & Barton, 1983a, b; Manderscheid & Sonnenschein, 1990).

Psychiatrists comprise the oldest medical specialty in American (Mora, 1967). The father of American psychiatry was Benjamin Rush (1745–1813) who signed the Declaration of Independence. In 1844, 13 asylum superintendents founded the American Psychiatric Association (APA) that currently is comprised of approximately 40 000 members, representing 90% of currently practicing psychiatrists and psychiatrists in training.

Psychiatrists must complete 4 years of university education (where they graduate with a Bachelors of Arts or Sciences), 4 years of Medicine School and 4 years of post-graduate training in general medicine, neurology, and psychiatry. Now, many also take 1–2 year fellowships (or more lengthy experiences in the case of psychoanalysis) in addiction psychiatry, administrative psychiatry, child and adolescent psychiatry, consultation-liaison psychiatry, forensic

Handbook of Mental Health Economics and Health Policy, Volume I, Schizophrenia. Edited by M. Moscarelli, A. Rupp and N. Sartorius.
© 1996 John Wiley & Sons Ltd.

psychiatry, geriatric psychiatry, psychoanalysis, psychopharmacology, or research.

Psychiatrists work in many settings where they treat persons suffering from schizophrenia. A recent (1988–89) membership survey conducted by the American Psychiatric Association (Dorwart *et al.*, 1992) showed that psychiatrists' primary work settings are: 45% private practice, 33% hospitals, 10% outpatient clinics, 6% university medical schools, and 1% governmental administrative agencies. In addition, 25% reported secondary work settings in private practice, 23% in hospitals, 6.5% in outpatient clinics, 7.7% in university medical schools, and 1% in governmental administrative agencies. The percentage in salaried employment has remained steady between 1988 and 1991 at over 30%, but there were shifts elsewhere. While those in self-employed solo private practice have gone from almost 60% to under 50%, the percent in group settings or working on contract has increased from 10 to 20%. We continue to experience a major problem in the national distribution of psychiatrists, with an estimated 4 per 100 000 in Idaho versus 77 per 100 000 in Washington, DC.

Psychiatrists have many roles in regards their dealings with persons suffering from schizophrenia. These roles include evaluation, diagnosis, and triage; direct treatment with drugs, psychotherapy, group therapy, and family therapy; supervision of other professionals, paraprofessionals, or trainees; administration of programs, services, or systems of care; and policy-making, governmental administration, and legislative liaison.

Psychiatric nurses represent the second oldest group of mental health specialists. The training of psychiatric nurses began as an apprenticeship experience, but evolved into specialized training programs in 1882, beginning with McLean Hospital near Boston, MA. There were approximately 40 000 nurses practicing in psychiatric areas in 1976 and by 1988 10 000 were Masters-degree prepared, 4000 of whom are certified as clinical specialists in adult or child/adolescent psychiatric nursing.

There are several routes to psychiatric nursing practice. Generalist nurses can: (i) attend a 4-year liberal arts college from which they graduate with a nursing degree (receiving a Bachelors of Science); or (ii) attend a 3-year "diploma" school, usually connected to a general hospital; or (iii) attend a 2-year "community college" (receiving an associate degree). Specialists in psychiatric nursing attend university for an additional 2 years (receiving a Masters degree) after completion of their first 4 years. Forty percent of these go on to receive a 2-year experience that prepares them for certification as a clinical specialist. In addition, a small percentage go on to earn doctoral (PhD) degrees.

The settings nurses work in are much more likely to be hospital- and inpatient-oriented than psychiatists; in 1988, 45% worked in hospitals, 17% in clinics, 13% in academic settings, 8.5% in individual or group practice and 0.3% in nursing homes. There are no data on secondary settings. As with psychiatrists, there are large geographical differences in the distribution of psychiatric nurses, especially of Masters-prepared specialists; e.g., from 7 per 100 000 in New England to 1 per 100 000 in the Midwest and West.

The roles psychiatric nurses assume can also vary from those of being a staff nurse delivering psychiatric nursing care, medication, group therapy or home visiting to serving as a program director or in policy-making or in administrative positions. However, the vast majority of psychiatric nurses work in direct patient care settings involving the seriously mentally ill, such as those suffering from schizophrenia. Whereas 20 years ago nurses were almost exclusively working in acute inpatient hospital settings, more and more now work in ambulatory settings (outpatient departments, day hospitals, etc.) and on outreach teams (assertive community teams, mobile treatment teams, etc.), which involve more varied roles and responsibilities than inpatient work. One function traditionally assumed primarily by generalist nurses was education of the patient about medication, etc. Now, with the emphasis on family psycho-education, this function too has been assumed by some psychiatric nurses.

Psychiatric social workers date their birth to about 1900, following the introduction of "aftercare" of seriously-ill patients when they were discharged from state mental hospitals. The first formal training program in the United States was established at Smith College in 1918. By 1979, there were 80 000 social workers who were members of the National Association of Social Workers; this includes psychiatric social workers.

Like nursing, there are multiple levels of education and paths to practice psychiatric social work. There are 2-year Associate degree (AA) programs in community colleges, 4-year Bachelors degree (BA, BS) programs in colleges and universities, some of which also offer additional Master's degree (MS, MSW or Doctoral degree (DSW, or PhD) programs. Special interests are taught and organized in areas such as community organization, policy development and case work, rather than in what psychiatrists think of as subspecialties (alcohol and drug abuse, child and adolescent psychiatry, geriatrics, etc.)

Psychiatric social workers, in contrast to psychiatric nurses, are found much more in outpatient than in inpatient settings. In 1989, 27% of Masters level social workers worked primarily in community social service agencies, 19% in private practice and 17% in clinics versus 21% in hospitals (5% were in academic settings). Secondary sites involved private practice (49%), social service agencies (24%), clinics (12%), hospitals (7%), and academic settings (9%). Geographically, their distribution varies from 8 per 100 000 in a very poor state, i.e., Mississippi, to 85 per 100 000 in Massachusetts, which before the current recession was a moderately affluent state.

While the roles of psychiatric social workers involve many of the therapeutic activities mentioned before (individual, group, and family therapy), in addition, child guidance, individual case work, and family therapy have been bedrock activities of the profession. In the 1960s and 1970s, with the growth of community mental health centers (CMHCs) and services, social workers became the dominant members of the workforce. In addition, many assumed the role of program directors in community psychiatric programs serving the severely mentally ill and some became involved with policy-making. Most recently, after deinstitutionalization, the traditional role of discharge planning from inpatient settings has served as a jumping-off point to assuming the roles of community treatment coordination, community support, and case management.

Psychologists have been trained for many years in academic settings, but the role of *clinical* psychologist is a relatively new one. Much of the impetus for the growth of clinical psychology is attributed to the introduction of such practitioners into the Veterans' Administration hospitals established or expanded following the Second World War. There are currently about 56 000 members of the American Psychological Association who practice clinical psychology.

As mentioned above, psychologists, clinical and otherwise (e.g., experimental, counselling, school, etc.) come to the profession through academic channels—4 years of college or university (BA/BS), 2 years in Master's degree training (MS) and/or 2–4 years in PhD or PsyD training. Those wishing to be clinical psychologists do an additional 1–2-year internship.

Forty-three percent of psychologists work primarily in private practice, 21% in academia, 13% in hospitals, and 11% in clinics. In addition, practice data reveal that they treat fewer persons with psychoses and other serious mental disorders than do psychiatrists. Regarding secondary settings, there are 44% in practice, 20% in academia, and only 11% in clinics and 9% in hospitals. As with other professional groups, there are large geographic distributional differences, with a high of 78 per 100 000 in Washington, DC versus a low of 6 per 100 000 in Mississippi.

While clinical psychologists assume many of the same roles as others in the fields enumerated above—e.g., therapist, program directors, etc.—their academic research and psychometric training make these activities more likely. In addition, the interest of psychologists in behavioral and cognitive therapies has enabled them to specialize in these areas.

Mental health workers represent a group of different types of paraprofessional mental health workers; such as mental hygiene therapy aides on wards, outpatient case aides, psychological technicians, case managers, etc. The earliest such workers in the United States were ward attendants in psychiatric hospitals during the 1800s, but their numbers and job descriptions have increased as alternative services were developed. We do not know how many such individuals there are, but Barton and Barton, in 1983(b), estimated that there were "perhaps 150 000."

Training for hospital and community mental health aides has always tended to take place at the work site—e.g., "in-service education"—although some workers receive training in 2-year community colleges (leading to an AA degree). Most states have extensive in-service educational programs coordinated by the State Director of Human Resources Development (HRD).

The programs in which mental health workers are employed vary from inpatient to ambulatory settings. With the new emphasis on day hospitals, community care teams, and case management, new opportunities for such employment are now available.

The roles assumed by mental health workers tend to be concentrated in activities of daily living, supportive psychotherapy, monitoring, and escort services. Helping patients to receive various services and coordinating between agencies is also important.

Rehabilitation workers represent another group where persons of different backgrounds do varying jobs in a variety of programs. Their numbers can only be inferred from data on rehabilitation services, but with the increase in psychosocial rehabilitation and drug and alcohol rehabilitation programs, there is an increasing number of such workers.

Barton and Barton report that in 1983(b), there were 100 training programs for these personnel, from weeks to months in length, 25 of which prepared persons at the doctoral level (e.g., PhD). They note that of the 9000 members of the National Rehabilitatiion Counseling Association, 8000 have received certification as of 1983.

The settings rehabilitation workers can be found in vary, but prime examples include: psychosocial rehabilitation centers, sheltered workshops, drug rehabilitation programs, and partial hospitals.

The roles assumed by such workers can vary from counselling to helping patients master generic and specific jobs; from monitoring medication compliance to assessing and teaching social skills; from direct instruction on skills of everyday living to negotiating with allied agencies (e.g., State Divisions of Rehabilitation.)

Activity Therapists include those who are involved with occupational therapy, recreational therapy, and creative therapies, e.g., art, music, and dance. Occupational therapy dates back to the turn of the twentieth century and, along with the other modalities, was until recently centered in hospital settings. Barton and Barton (1983b) state that there were 20 000 occupational therapists in the United States in 1983.

Training for occupational therapists involves a 4-year college program leading to a Bachelor's degree (BA/BS) with the option of an additional 2-year period leading to a Master's degree (MA/MS). To be certified as an OTR (Registered Occupational Therapist), 6–9 months of field work must be completed, followed by a national exam.

Training of recreational and creative therapists tends to occur in their basic area, e.g., art therapists often come from art programs or art schools rather than medical or psychiatric routes.

As mentioned previously, activity therapists have tended to work in inpatient settings until relatively recently. Now more and more, they work in outpatient clinics, psychosocial rehabilitation centers, day hospitals, etc.

Their roles combine education and some of the given activity itself, whether this involves working, painting, singing, etc. Over time, such therapists have moved from being seen as teaching patients irrelevant activites such as basket-weaving to assessing and preparing patients for mainstream work or productive activity.

PRACTICE SETTINGS

In this section, we will describe each setting's typical leadership; the personnel used in each; and its staffing and patient load. The figures provided are not meant to represent optimal or baseline figures, but are real examples in private and public settings at the University of Maryland in Baltimore.

Inpatient units in the United States are found in psychiatric hospitals (both public and private), general hospitals and community mental health centers. Because of the medical nature of hospitals, as well as the fact that physicians are responsible and liable for patient treatment and care, psychiatrists are in charge of psychiatric units in hospitals in the United States.

The personnel used include psychiatrists, nurses, social workers, psychologists, activity therapists, rehabilitation workers, and mental health workers. On specialized units, such as research, geropsychiatric, medical–psychiatric, dual diagnosis (mental illness and substance abuse), etc., there may also be primary care physicians and others.

Below are typical staffing patterns (all staffing is given as full-time equivalents) at two psychiatric

Table 1

UMMC Adult Inpatient Unit	WPCC Adult Inpatient Unit
15 Beds; 275 Admissions/year	18 Beds; 250 Admissions/year
1.0 Psychiatrist Unit Chief	1.0 Psychiatrist
2.0 Psychiatry Residents (PGY-2)	1.0 Psychiatry Resident (PGY-1)
7.0 Nurses (per 24 hours)	5.0 Nurses
3.0 Technicians (per 24 hours)	5.0 Technicians
1.5 Social Workers	1.5 Social Workers
1.0 Occupational Therapist	0.5 Occupational Therapist
	0.5 Activity Therapist
	1.0 Psychologist
1.0 Unit Secretary	

Table 2

UMMC Emergency Room		WPCC Screening and Evaluation Clinic	
(2300 Visits a year)		(1800 Visits a year)	
0.15	Psychiatrist Director	1.0	Psychiatrist Director
3.70	Psychiatric Residents (PGY-2)	2.0	Psychiatric Residents (PGY-2)
0.10	Chief Resident (PGY-2)	1.0	Social Worker
1.55	Psychiatric Social Workers	3.0	Psychiatric Nurses
2.0	Substance Abuse Technician		
0.20	Secretary		

inpatient units administered by the Department of Psychiatry at the University of Maryland; the first, a general hospital unit, the Institute of Psychiatry and Human Behavior (IPHB) a part of the University of Maryland Medical Center (UMMC) and the second, the Walter P. Carter (Community Mental Health) Center (WPCC) (Table 1).

Emergency rooms are found predominately in general hospitals, although some governmental (e.g., Veterans' Administration) and private hospitals may have them. They are typically run by emergency medical, surgical, or internal medical physicians, with psychiatrists and other mental health professionals serving as consultants.

The personnel used include psychiatrists, social workers, nurses, and mental health workers. Where there are expanded duties, e.g., crisis intervention, holding beds, screening, evaluation, etc., such as in the example that follows, staffing may vary.

Typical staffing patterns are as follows, at two emergency settings connected with the Department of Psychiatry at the University of Maryland Medical Center (UMMC): (i) a general hospital emergency unit in the University of Maryland Hospital (UMMS), and (ii) a Screening and Evaluation Clinic (S&E) at the Walter P. Carter (Community Mental Health) Center (WPCC) (Table 2):

Outpatient clinics are found under a variety of auspices; in psychiatric hospitals, general hospitals and community mental health centers, as well as free-standing clinics. While in hospitals, leadership tends to be psychiatric, in community settings, others, including social workers and psychologists, are often in charge.

The personnel used include psychiatrists, psychologists, nurses, social workers, activity therapists, rehabilitation workers, and mental health workers. In specialized clinics, there may also be persons with an educational background, e.g., for tutoring programs, primary care physicians, etc.

Typical staffing patterns are as follows at two psychiatric outpatient clinics administered by the Department of Psychiatry at the University of Maryland; the first part of the general hospital, the University of Maryland Medical Center (UMMC) and the second, in one central and one satellite location of what was formerly the Walter P. Carter (Community Mental Health) Center (WPCC) (Table 3):

Table 3

UMMC Adult Outpatient Clinic		WPCC Adult Outpatient Clinic	
5000	Visits a year	28 000	Visits a year
(300	Patients a year)	(1300	Patients a year)
1.0	Psychiatrist Director	0.6	Medical Director
		1.0	RN/MSW Program Director
		2.0	MSW Satellite Clinic Coordinators
		0.6	Medical (psychiatrist) Dir.
0.6	Psychiatrists	4.5	Psychiatrists
0.7	Chief Resident (PGY-4)		
4.4	Psych. Residents (PGY-2,3,4)	2.0	Psych. Residents (PGY-3)
2.0	Psychiatric Nurses	4.5	Psychiatric Nurses
1.0	NSW Social Worker	18.6	MSW Psych. Social Workers
0.05	MA Psychologist	1.5	PhD Psychologists
		3.65	Other trainees

Table 4

UMMC Adult Day Hospital		WPCC Adult Day Program	
18	Patients/day (24 enrolled)	20	Patients/day (45 enrolled)
0.5	Psychiatrist Director	0.8	Psychiatrist
2.0	Psychiatric Nurses	3.0	Nurses
1.0	Social Worker	1.0	Social Workers
1.75	Occupational Therapists	0.5	Occupational Therapist
1.0	Secretary	1.0	Psychologist

Day hospitals are usually connected with or in the actual building(s) run by psychiatric hospitals, general hospitals, or community mental health centers, but some are free-standing. Leadership may or may not be medical, but there is usually a state requirement for at least a 1/2 time psychiatric commitment.

The personnel used includes psychiatrists, psychologists, nurses, social workers, activity therapists, rehabilitation workers, and mental health workers. Depending on whether the setting is a high-intensity, time-limited (e.g., 30–60 days) day hospital program or a low-intensity, longer-term day program, or even longer-term drop-in center, there are increasing percentages of non-professional staff members.

Typical staffing patterns are as follows at two psychiatric day programs administered by the Department of Psychiatry at the University of Maryland; the first, a part of the Outpatient Clinic in the University of Maryland Medical Center (UMMC) and the second, in the hospital building portion of the Walter P. Carter (Community Mental Health) Center (WPCC) (Table 4).

Community care teams can be either closely connected with hospitals or clinics or can be located in the community. Leadership is usually non-medical, with psychiatric input, although there are teams with psychiatrist leaders.

The personnel used includes social workers, nurses, psychiatrists, psychologists, and mental health workers (including patient advocates). Teams that concentrate on special populations, e.g., dual diagnosis, the homeless mentally ill, geriatrics, may have other specialized personnel (e.g., housing experts, addictionists, primary care physicians, etc.).

Typical staffing patterns are as follows in three community care teams administered by the Department of Psychiatry at the University of Maryland; the first, a mobile treatment unit (MTU) that is housed in a part of the hospital building portion of Walter P. Carter (Community Mental Health) Center (WPCC); the second, a continuous care team (CCT) located adjacent to the outpatient

Table 5

Assertive Community Treatment	Mobile Treatment Unit	Continuous Care Team
68 Patients enrolled	45 Patients enrolled 3501 Visits/year	43 Patients enrolled 5000 visits/yr
1.0 MSW Prog Dir		.1 MSW/RN Prog Dir
0.5 Medical Director	1.0 RN/MSW Prog Dir.	
0.5 Psychiatrist	0.64 Psychiatrist	0.6 Psychiatrist
2.0 Psychiatric Nurses		
2.0 Psych Soc Workers	2.0 Psych Soc Workers	1.0 MSW Social Worker
2.0 Counsellors		
2.0 Consumer Advocates		
	1.0 Secretary	
	0.2 Business Manager	

clinic in the hospital building portion of Walter P. Carter (Community Mental Health) Center (WPCC); and the third, an assertive community treatment (ACT) team in the tradition of the Madison, Wisconsin, PACT Program, located in the community in the building also occupied by a psychosocial rehabilitation program, Harbor City Unlimited (HCU) (Table 5).

Rehabilitation centers are usually located apart from hospitals and medical centers, although there are exceptions. Leadership is usually non-medical, with minimal psychiatric input.

The personnel used include rehabilitation specialists, social workers, nurses, psychiatrists, psychologists, and mental health workers. Programs that focus on vocational rehabilitation usually have heavier concentrations of vocational counsellors, occupational therapists, and employment experts than those that focus on social rehabilitation, which have more social workers, educators, and psychologists.

A typical staffing pattern at a psychosocial rehabilitation center, HCU, administered by the Department of Psychiatry at the University of Maryland, is as given in Table 6.

Case management programs may be located apart from hospitals and medical centers or work from them as a base. Leadership is usually non-medical, with psychiatrists serving as consultants. There is disagreement about whether clinicians should become case managers as an extension of their role (e.g., therapist–case managers) (Lamb, 1980) or whether case managers should be generically trained. (In the United States, the term "case manager" is also used by managed care companies to denote persons who attempt to cut or control costs in patients' care.)

Table 24.6

Harbor City Unlimited
Administration
1 MSW Program Director
1 Financial Operations Manager
2 Account Clerks
1 Billing Clerk
1 Secretary
Community Rehabilitation Program (includes vocational rehab)
185 Members enrolled in a typical week
0.1 Psychiatrist consultant
23.0 Rehabilitation workers
1.0 MSW intake
2.0 MA Rehabilitation Coordinators
20.0 Rehabilitation Workers (BA, AA, LS)
Residential Rehabilitation
102 Persons enrolled in a typical week
53 Persons in Residential Rehabilitation
36 Persons Receiving 24-hour Coverage
7 Persons in Supported Housing
6 Persons in Crisis Beds
1.0 Nurse Director
0.1 Psychiatrist Consultant for Young Adult Program
0.1 Psychiatrist Consultant for Crisis Beds
38.0 Rehabilitation Workers
3.0 BA Rehabilitation Coordinators
35.0 Rehabilitation Workers (BA, AA, LS)

The personnel used include social workers and mental health workers.

A typical staffing pattern exists at the Community Support Program (CSP) administered by the Department of Psychiatry at the University of Maryland: 45 patients enrolled in a typical week; 1 MSW Social Worker Director; and 2 counsellors.

WHO DOES WHAT?

From the sections above, it is clear that a large number of differently trained and oriented clinicians are involved currently in the evaluation, treatment, and rehabilitation of persons suffering from schizophrenia. One may wonder: Who should be the leader and how is this decided? Who should be the therapist and how is this decided? Who should perform the triage of individual patients? Who should choose the components necessary to treat this population and how? Who should decide what personnel should work in each program and how? Who should secure the financing and how?

The answers to these questions are not simple. They depend on history and tradition; laws, litigation, and regulation; politics; and funding and philosophy.

Historically, the first psychiatric services in this country were psychiatric hospitals, administered by psychiatrists and staffed by psychiatrists, nurses, and ward attendants. Tradition, therefore, has placed administration of such facilities in the hands of psychiatrists. As alternatives to hospitals were established in America starting in 1855 (Galt, 1885) and new specialties were established (e.g., social work, rehabilitation) to meet new tasks, psychiatrists were less likely to have the same administrative responsibility or burden. With free-standing outpatient clinics, rehabilitation centers, and day hospitals, their role as administrators becomes even more remote a possibility. Now, with the newer emphasis on housing, case management, and community care teams, many others direct programs.

In American psychiatry, because of the long tradition of asylum care and administrative responsibility, most policy and leadership positions have been occupied by physicians, including state commissioners, state superintendents, psychiatric hospital directors, etc. Power, e.g., the ability to do, has been in psychiatric hands: power to make decisions about services needed, both individually and collectively, personnel to be selected, treatment to be followed and how funding would be secured.

The psychiatrist has also usually been the leader at the inpatient and outpatient unit level, at least in hospital and university settings, but as alternatives to hospitals and community mental health services proliferated, this too has become less common.

Laws, litigation, and regulations are also powerful determinants of leadership choices. By law, until recently, most states were required to have psychiatrist commissioners or psychiatric hospital directors. By regulation, only physicians were allowed to admit or discharge patients. And by litigation precedent, physicians are held liable for malpractice committed to patients under their or their staff's care.

Now, many states have changed their laws about commissioners, but the responsibility for admissions, discharges, diagnoses, and treatment adequacy still rests with the psychiatrist. In hospitals and hospital systems, psychiatrists (as part of the medical board and medical staff) set standards of care, monitor that care and credential clinicians. They do not, however, by law or regulation, necessarily become involved with state or regional or hospital planning, although many regulations establishing planning efforts and advisory boards do specify some physician participation. Accreditation processes continue to place central importance on physician/psychiatrist management and responsibility for clinical issues.

Politics have entered the arena of who, how, and where decisions about personnel and service provision are made. As psychiatrists, we cannot have an unbiased opinion on this issue. But it seems clear that, in the last few decades, there has been an enormous push by other clinicians to assume increased power in decision-making in regards to both programs and patients, combined with the pressure of generic administrators, business officers, and accountants to assume more control of administrative and fiscal decisions.

Some of this has dangerous clinical consequences. For instance, at the height of the community mental health movement, there was great pressure for equality and power-sharing and clinical teams were "voting" on diagnoses and discharges. At the height of the push for non-psychiatrist leadership in state offices of mental health, only one commissioner was a psychiatrist. And, at the current height of the managed care effort, decisions on triage and treatment choice as well as treatment length are being made by non-psychiatrists. Currently in the United States, several psychologists are enrolled in a federal university-sponsored training program designed to teach them psychopharmacology—what will happen when they actually write prescriptions that result in malpractice suits will probably determine the fate of this effort.

Funding and philosophy are also important contributors to who makes which decisions. There are currently several models for clinical care, prominent among them: the biologic medical model, the education–rehabilitation model, and the biopsychosocial medical model.

With the *biologic medical or physician model,* schizophrenia is seen as a brain disease that requires medical diagnosis, treatment, and rehabilitation. Administrative and clinical leadership, therefore, rests in medical hands. Staffing is hierarchical, with nurses and nurse's aides being prominent.

With the *education–rehabilitation model,* while the etiology may be felt to be biological, the disabilities concomitant with schizophrenia are felt to be most amenable to educational efforts (e.g., psychoeducation), social rehabilitation training, and vocational rehabilitation. Administrative and clinical leadership, here is more likely to reside in persons with a social or rehabilitative background.

Finally, however, with a balanced *biopsychosocial model,* the disease and disability are seen as intertwined and interventions guided by causation (e.g., the bio (logical) via somatic treatment by physicians and nurses, the psycho (logical) by psychotherapy from a number of clinicians and the social through social intervention, environmental change, and family involvement by social workers, mental health workers, etc.) Most psychiatrists, however, firmly believe that consolidation of biological and psychological treatment approaches in one individual, e.g., the psychiatrist, is necessary to ensure effective and efficient treatment of persons suffering from schizophrenia. Splitting the treatment often leads to duplication, misunderstanding, and tension, especially in persons with severe cognitive disabilities.

Even in this preferred model, however, imbalance can lead to movement to a totally biological or social orientation and the tug of war over the psychological element may, as it has in the recent past, occupy much of our professional organizations' energies.

Staffing and funding stem from these models; e.g., medical wards depend on medical fees for treatment of disease, community housing efforts depend on disability or social welfare payments. As we have turned away from the egalitarian, power-sharing headiness of the 1960s to tighter controls on medical reimbursement and tighter money for social programs, however, more and more programs, despite their philosophy, staffing, and orientation, have attempted to secure medical reimbursement.

The psychiatrist's role, therefore, depends on the setting of the program or service serving persons suffering from schizophrenia, its history, connection with university or hospital settings versus communities, the laws, regulations, and judicial actions governing it and its philosophy and funding. Thus, on a medical center's inpatient ward, where they are present daily to admit, evaluate, treat, and discharge patients, the psychiatrists' power, ability to make decisions, and scope are vastly different from their role in a psychosocial rehabilitation program, where they may visit for only 1–2 hours a week to check on patients who cannot or will not go to their regular clinic or physician.

Most psychiatrists think that because of their training (e.g., ability to prescribe medication, do psychotherapy, and evaluate complex medical–psychiatric problems) they should be the leader of treatment planning efforts, on either an inpatient or ambulatory service, but when these efforts are conducted in free-standing community programs, their role may consist of primarily being consulted about decisions, or not involved at all.

In the 1960s, in the passion of several social movements, many community and other mental health services argued for "role-blurring." At best, this was compared with a combat military team, the Green Berets being the fashionable parallel at the time, where every invididual had "cross-training" to perform the job of at least one other, in case of death or disability. At its most neutral, it was a naive belief that all training was equivalent, all intellect equal, and all mentally ill persons as amenable to all interventions. At its worst, however, it represented a raw grab for power on the part of untrained or differently trained individuals. "Power to the people" in many instances really meant "Take it from them and give it to us."

One of the concerns that motivated the American Psychiatric Association (Talbott, 1984) to study the problem of patients with chronic mental illness in the 1970s was the complaint by some psychiatrists in public systems that they were hired and expected simply to write prescriptions and *not* either to deliver the psychotherapy or participate in treatment planning.

Ironically, with the increase in managed care in the private sector in the United States, we are now hearing the same complaint from psychiatrists in private practice or in what are euphemistically called health maintenance organizations (HMOs). Likewise, some managed care operations prefer to use psychiatrists to conduct the evaluation of patients and their preferred treatment face to face while others use social workers to do this over the telephone for periods as short as 10 minutes. Both claim their system is more cost-effective; those advocating psychiatrists because despite a larger "front-end" cost, the diagnosis and decisions are more likely to be accurate; those advocating social workers on the phone because of lower front-end costs, despite the possibility of increased cost due to having the patient go through more than one trial or modality of treatment.

There has also been a trend in recent years in the United States to find the least-expensive professional or paraprofessional to perform services. As we do not have good studies demonstrating, say, the superiority in outcome of psychiatrists over psychologists, or social workers over nurses, in performing certain tasks, public and private payers will often seek to "substitute" one professional or paraprofessional for another. The paucity of good comparative treatment studies coupled with a poor understanding of the etiology of schizophrenia allows this political rather than clinical choice.

Service array decisions are made on the basis of several determinants. First, there may be laws or regulations that determine their array. For instance, community mental health centers were originally legislated to have 10 components (inpatient, outpatient, partial hospital, 24-hour emergency and consultation, and education services as well as diagnostic, precare, aftercare, rehabilitation services, and research and evaluation).

Second, needs assessments in local areas will or should dictate the array. For instance, an absence of services for the hearing-impaired mentally ill, homeless mentally ill, addicted mentally ill, mentally ill offenders, etc.

Third, however, and regrettably, often the primary determinant is dictated by neither policy nor assessment, but by convenience and funding. For instance, some psychiatrists trained in the pre-psychopharmacological era are still reluctant and uncomfortable with some if not all medications. In addition, if a program receives $800 a day if a patient is on an inpatient unit but only $50 a day in an outpatient clinic, there is no question which service will be used more.

Coordination is a vexing problem too, as all have seen who have worked in the field in recent years, as we have moved from a predominately hospital-based system to a more balanced hospital–community system. Even with a full array of services, coordination at governmental, programmatic, and patient levels must be established.

In the United States (Talbott, 1984) each level of government has separate requirements for funding separate services in separate departments for the *same individual target recipients*. For example, the federal Departments of Health and Human Services, Housing and Urban Development and Social Security all have different requirements and funding streams for the same mentally ill patients. Some increased coordination has occurred since 1978, but more has occurred at local and state levels than the federal one.

Second, programs in a city or catchment area must be coordinated. The Robert Wood Johnson Foundation recently funded a 5-year study in nine of America's large cities, to see if providing money for such coordination and housing could influence positively the outcome of its recipients (Goldman, 1994).

Finally, in the post-deinstitutionalization era, patients need help in knowing what services exist, how to apply for them, and in actually getting to them. In most areas of the country now, CSPs are available that provide some or all of the following (Turner & TenHoor, 1978): (i) identification of the population; (ii) assistance in applying for entitlements; (iii) crisis stabilization; (iv) psychosocial rehabilitation; (v) supportive living and working; (vi) medical and mental health care; (vii) backup support to families; (viii) community involvement in planning, housing, and work; (ix) protection of rights; and (x) case management.

Case management (Harris & Bergman, 1993), the last of the elements listed above, is the most common current method used to coordinate services for persons suffering from schizophrenia. Linking persons to services has become *one* if not *the* key task in our current system, for even if all the services required by patients were available, which they are not in most American communities, without access to those programs, they could just as well not exist.

Choosing the personnel is also a process with multiple determinants. Again, there may be regulations or quasi-regulations, that dictate that certain personnel perform certain tasks. For instance, regulations for state Medicaid (which is actually federal money matched with state taxes, intended for persons below a certain income level) or "voluntary" national accreditation guidelines (established by the Joint Commission on the Accreditation of Health Organizations—JCAHO) may state how much time a psychiatrist must spend in a program or that certain functions that require specially trained persons must be performed (e.g., social services, nursing, medical records, credentialling, laboratory services, etc.)

In addition, because of fluctuations in both the national pool and local geographic distribution of professionals, personnel may be hired because of these realities. For instance, for a decade we had a severe nursing shortage but a glut of social workers. Advertisements for nursing jobs would generate many times more applications, albeit inappropriate, from social workers than nurses for a variety of positions.

As mentioned in a prior section, some personnel decisions are based on history coupled with function. For instance, nurses on some inpatient units performed what others would consider tasks usually performed by activity therapists. Likewise, mental health workers on inpatient units tend to be "nursing" aides, while in outpatient services they are "social work" aides, although their work may be quite similar.

Philosophy and treatment approach may also play a part. In a medical–psychiatric unit, more physicians may be used; in an educationally oriented rehabilitation unit, more rehabilitation-oriented individuals may be used. In the area of case management, for instance, a team may define its role as both therapeutic and linking, which leads to hiring clinical case managers, versus one that sees its role as brokering, in which case, non-clinicians are hired (Harris & Bergman, 1993). In addition, we are aware of emergency rooms that believe that nurses should play a leading part because of the importance of medication and the medical contributions to patients' conditions, etc; whereas others predominately use social workers, believing that most emergencies are prompted by social conditions (e.g., family rejection, lack of housing, etc.) and solved by addressing these conditions.

Finally, finances may again play a key part. For instance, the decision on whom to hire to assist in emergency room decisions and dispositions may become predominately a financial one. Again, as stated above, many organizations, under pressure from public and private cost-cutting forces, may make decisions for entirely economic reasons. Also again, however, without adequate data showing superiority of one professional or paraprofessional performing a task over another, countering such decisions becomes impossible.

Staffing level decisions are another area of complexity. For a period of time, the APA published staffing levels. This was in the days when money and litigation were not major problems. The APA stopped this practice because they feared government or regulatory bodies would take these guidelines as minimum standards and reduce personnel to a minimum regardless of need, acuity, and severity or local circumstances.

There have been intrusions by the courts into staffing levels as well, with the most famous or infamous being Judge Johnson (1980), who decreed that the state of Alabama must provide certain minimal staffing for one of its state mental hospitals. This court order was complicated by the fact that such resources could be raised and allocated only by the state's legislature which did not share Judge Johnson's preference for funding personnel to work in psychiatric hospitals rather than for roads and prisons.

Several organizations have looked at staffing levels but no requirements have stemmed from these efforts. The American Hospital Association (Trends in Hospital Personnel 1982–1984, 1986) periodically samples its 5000 member hospitals and reports staffing, but suggests no optimal levels.

In addition, the Institute of Medicine, a part of the National Academy of Science, which receives funding from the Congress of the United States to perform certain research, recently studied staffing in psychiatric departments in Veterans' Administration Hospitals, but no correction of current imbalances vis-à-vis medical or surgical departments has yet resulted (Lipscomb & Alexander, 1992).

SUMMARY AND FUTURE NEEDS

As the reader is now aware, most chapters in this book contain more economic and research data than does this one. While we do know something about current personnel options and staffing, we do not have definitive answers to the critical question: "What persons should conduct which treatments for which sub-groups of patients suffering from schizophrenia in what settings?"

In the United States, the field of differential therapeutics (research to answer the question "what treatment for which sub-groups") has begun (Frances *et al.*, 1984). At the University of Maryland, the first federally funded PORT grant to study treatment effectiveness in schizophrenia, was recently received. In addition, we are beginning to be able to determine whether some "alternative" settings (e.g., day hospitals) are able to serve severely ill persons as well as more traditional ones (e.g., 24-hour hospitals). However, much remains to be done regarding the question of personnel and we will probably have to live with the current blurred boundaries and political decisions until scientific research provides us more definitive answers into the nature of schizophrenia itself.

Future research will, therefore, have to concentrate on both efficiency (cost–benefit) and efficacy (cost–impact). Until we have these data, we will continue to endure initiatives aimed primarily at cutting costs rather than ensuring appropriate patient outcomes.

REFERENCES

Barton, W.W. and Barton, G.M. (1983a). The psychiatrist: role and pattern of practice. In W.E. Barton and G.M. Barton, eds, *Mental Health Administration Principles and Practice*, pp. 667–694. New York: Human Sciences Press, Inc.

Barton, W.E. and Barton, G.M. (1983b). The mental health team. In W.E. Barton and G.M. Barton, eds, *Mental Health Administration: Principles and Practice*, pp. 695–744. New York: Human Sciences Press, Inc.

Dorwart, R.A., Chartock, L.R., Thomas, D., *et al.* (1992). A National Study of Psychiatrists' Professional Activities. *American Journal Psychiatry*, **149**, 1499–1505.

Frances, A., Clarkin, J., and Perry, S. (1984). *Differential Therapeutics in Psychiatry: The Art and Science of Treatment Selection*. New York: Brunner/Mazel.

Galt, J.M. (1885). The Farm of St. Anne. *American Journal of Insanity*, **11**, 352–357.

Goldman, H., Morrissey, J., and Ridgely, M.S. (1994) Evaluating the Program on Chronic Mental Illness (RWJ PCMI). *Milbank Quarterly*, **72**, 37–47.

Harris M. and Bergman, H.C. (eds) (1993). Case management for mentally ill patients: theory and practice. In *Chronic Mental Illness*, Vol. I (Series Editor J.A. Talbott). New York: Harwood Academic.

Judge Johnson Takes Steps to Secure Compliance with Landmark Wyatt Order (1980). *Hospital and Community Psychiatry*, **31**, 144–145.

Lamb, H.R. (1980). Therapist–case managers: more than brokers of services. *Hospital and Community Psychiatry*, **31**, 762–764.

Lipscomb, J. and Alexander, B. (1992). Physician staffing for the VA, *Institute of Medicine*. Washington, DC: National Academy Press.

Manderscheid, R.W., and Sonnenschein, M.A. (eds) (1990). Mental Health, United States 1990. Rockville, MD: National Institute of Mental Health. U.S. Department of Health and Human Services.

Mora, G. (1967). History of psychiatry. In A.M. Freedman and H.I. Kaplan, eds, *Comprehensive Textbook of Psychiatry*, pp. 2–34. New York: Williams & Wilkins.

Talbott, J.A. (1984). *The Chronic Mental Patient: Five Years Later*, New York: Grune & Stratton.

Trends in Hospital Personnel 1982–1984: From the American Hospital Association Annual Surveys (ODAM Report No. 9-86) (1986).

Springfield, VA, US Department of Commerce, National Technical Information Service.

Turner, J.C. and TenHoor, W.J. (1978). The NIMH Community Support Program: pilot approach to a needed social reform. *Schizophrenia Bulletin*, **4**, 319–348.

25

Personnel Options in the Treatment of Schizophrenia in the UK

DAVID G. KINGDON
21 Montagu Square, London, UK

HUGH FREEMAN
Department of Psychiatry, Bassetlaw District General Hospital, Kilton, Worksop, Nottinghamshire, UK

ORGANIZATION OF HEALTH CARE

The UK National Health Service (NHS), funded by central taxation, provides almost all health care to residents of the UK, which consists of four parts—England, Scotland, Wales, and Northern Ireland. This is particularly the situation for schizophrenia. There is a small private sector funded by individual fee-for-service or private insurance, but this accounts for only 4% of total health funding; this provides some acute psychiatric care and psychotherapy, but very little longer-term or community psychiatric services, and so has little relevance in this context. This chapter will therefore concentrate on health services provided by the NHS and on social services provided by the Local Authorities (counties and metropolitan boroughs) in the UK.

The NHS has undergone a series of reorganizations over the past decade. Centrally, the Department of Health in England (and similar departments in Scotland, Wales, and Northern Ireland) have been responsible for developing policy and central management of services through the NHS Management Executive, which has eight English Regional Offices. Each office is responsible for 11–12 District Health Authorities, who are developing the means to assess need for health care in the geographical area they serve and then purchase services to meet that need. Primary care services are purchased from general practioners, while specialist services are mainly purchased by contract from quasi-independent NHS Trusts, consisting of hospitals and community services.

Local Authorities, of which there are about 125 in the UK, are also undergoing reorganization so that their Social Service Departments become purchasers of social care and social work services from, for example, private and voluntary nursing and residential homes. For the foreseeable future, however, they will also be providers of such services.

Mental health services, parts of which are provided by both the NHS and local Social Services, have also been much affected by the long-term policy of developing services that are local and accessible to peoples' own communities. These are intended to replace activities based in large and often remote

Handbook of Mental Health Economics and Health Policy, Volume I, Schizophrenia. Edited by M. Moscarelli, A. Rupp and N. Sartorius.
© 1996 John Wiley & Sons Ltd.

Table 1. Range of service provision

Location	Acute/emergency care	Rehabilitation/continuing care
Home-based	Intensive home support Emergency duty teams ("out-of-hours") Sector mental health teams	Domiciliary services Key workers Care management
Day care	Day hospitals	Drop-in centres Support groups Employment schemes Day care
Residential support	Crisis accommodation Acute units Local secure units	Ordinary housing Unstaffed group homes Residential care homes Specialist mental nursing homes 24 hour NHS accommodation Local secure units Medium secure units High security units (Special hospitals)

mental hospitals; by the end of 1993, 89 of 130 such hospitals had been closed and replaced by a range of community-based services. These include psychiatric units attached to District General Hospitals and community health teams responsible for a geographical sector of the area covered by a District Health Authority; a sector usually contains a population of 50–100 000. The range (see Table 1) and comprehensiveness of such services varies considerably, and there has been much concern about the fragmentation of services, as a result of recent changes.

Government policy has emphasized the importance of prioritizing the distribution of mental health services on the basis of assessed need. As patients with schizophrenia, particularly when it is severe and enduring, are among the patients who are most severely mentally ill, services are increasingly being targeted on them. Guidance from central government described as "The Care Programme Approach" (1990), has specified that: (i) patients accepted by specialist services should have their health and social needs assessed, a key worker allocated to each, and a care plan developed and regularly reviewed; (ii) they should not be discharged from hospital if their minimal care needs cannot be met outside; and (iii) assertive outreach of services and renegotiation of care plans should occur where the patient is in danger of falling out of contact. This has been substantially reinforced in England by the selection of mental illness as one of five key areas for particular attention under the government's health strategy *The Health of the Nation* (DOH, 1992), and in subsequent guidance (DOH, 1994) which includes reference to the small number of cost-effectiveness studies available.

The major changes occurring in service delivery over the past 40 years have affected the ways of working of individual professions and collaboration between them. The focus of care has moved away from the highly centralized, traditional mental hospital into dispersed, smaller locally based settings. This has meant that major changes have been necessary in the practices of the various professionals involved. Principles of normalization have been widely introduced, with attempts to make such facilities domestic rather than clinical in atmosphere, and to reduce artificial divisions between staff and patients, exemplified by the wearing of uniforms. The more widespread use of psychosocial methods of treatment, for example, family, cognitive, and behavioral therapies, as well as the expectation that they will be employed, involve more collaborative styles of working than those which were used in the past.

The total amount of specialist accommodation for mentally ill people in England (population 48 million) is estimated to have remained just above 80 000 during the 1980s. However, the number of locations has increased from about 1000 to 2500, with an increase in community provision matched by a decrease in the number of hospital inpatient beds. At March 31, 1992, the number of current inpatients with mental illness was 45 100 (93 places/100 000). Of these, 21 500 had been in hospital under 6 months, 15 400 between 6 months and 5 years, and 8200 over 5 years. Only 300 were aged under 14, 23 100 were 15–64, and 21 800 aged 65 and over.

PRIMARY CARE

In the UK, most psychiatric morbidity is managed by the primary health care team, which includes general practitioners (GPs; of whom there are approximately 35 000 in the UK—1 to 1600 residents), health visitors, and practice nurses. Health visitors are nurses who have had post-registration training in maternal and child care; they work mainly on a domiciliary basis. GPs have, not unsurprisingly, been ambivalent towards the changes occurring in mental health services; while some have regarded their role as that of "coordinator" (Shepherd, 1991), others see it as predominantly providing physical care, at least towards the severely mentally ill (Kendrick *et al.*, 1991).

A substantial amount of psychiatric disorder is undetected in primary care, leading to inappropriate treatment or referral. This has been estimated to be about 50% (Goldberg & Huxley, 1980), and 40% of people who commit suicide have consulted their GP in the previous week. Training and further education are being developed for all staff who work in primary health care—GPs, practice nurses, health visitors, district nurses, and midwives—in the recognition and effective treatment of depression (as part of a "Defeat Depression" campaign) and in the assessment and management of suicide risk. A senior fellow at the Royal College of General Practitioners has been appointed to take a national lead in continuing GP education in mental illness, with the task of expediting the education of the primary health care team in this area and cascading this information through Regional Advisors in General Practice.

SECONDARY CARE

MULTIDISCIPLINARY TEAM WORKING

The integrated delivery of services to meet the social and health needs of users of mental health services require a high degree of collaboration between staff. Each member of a multidisciplinary team brings specific skills, although there will be some overlap between them, particularly in relation to psychological management. A multidisciplinary team will, wherever possible, consist of nurse, psychiatrist, social worker, occupational therapist, and psychologist members. These will cover a specified geographical area and be responsible for the provision of mental health services within it.

Emergency duty teams and crisis intervention teams are expected to include a psychiatrist who is qualified to arrange compulsory admission under the Mental Health Act, a specially trained social worker and, in crisis intervention teams a community psychiatric nurse (CPN). They are intended to be available on a 24-hour basis for the assessment and management of patients, and will respond to requests from GPs, police doctors, hospitals, etc.

PSYCHIATRISTS

Psychiatrists complete a 5- or 6-year course leading to a medical degree (Bachelor of Medicine) awarded by a University, and then have to complete work satisfactorily for 1 year as a House Physician and House Surgeon on general medical and surgical wards, before being registered by the General Medical Council. They are then eligible to commence general training in psychiatry and, typically, will apply to work as a Senior House Officer on a rotational training scheme. Over the next 1–2 years, they will receive basic training before taking the first part of the examination leading to Membership of the Royal College of Psychiatrists (MRCPsych). Once passed, the next 2–3 years are spent as a Registrar with clinical work and training in both general and specialist areas of psychiatry (e.g. general adult, old age, substance abuse, learning disability, and child and adolescent psychiatry). The final part of the Membership examination is then taken and, once this is passed, progression to the Senior Registrar level is possible. Further specialist training then occurs over 3 years, after which stage the trainee can apply for the specialist grade (consultant) post. (Alternatively, a small number may be appointed to lecturer posts in Universities—equivalent to registrar and senior registrar—and, at specialist levels, to senior lecturer posts and professorial chairs.) Virtually all specialists have either full- or part-time salaried appointments in the NHS.

At present, there are 999 senior house officers, 798 registrars, 655 senior registrars and 2168 consultants (i.e. 4.34/100 000) in England (see Table 1), although long-standing vacancies (possibly about 20%) exist in particular districts outside university areas as well as in particular subspecialties, especially learning disability and old-age psychiatry. These difficulties in recruitment are progressively but slowly being remedied as part of national planning for medical staff, with increased numbers of training posts at the senior registrar level over the past few years; a relative lack of posts at this level has distorted the whole training program for psychiatrists.

The development of District General Hospital psychiatric units since the 1960s, has generally led to closer contact between psychiatrists and psychiatric nurses with colleagues in other specialities and the increasing development of "liaison" psychiatry. It has been shown to be a cost-effective way of delivering services (Jones *et al.*, 1980).

Within psychiatry, the acceptance of multidisciplinary working by the profession has gradually emerged (Bennett & Freeman, 1991). Presidential statements from the Royal College of Psychiatrists have changed in emphasis from "the multidisciplinary team approach is fashionable in psychiatric practice" (1982—quoted in Rodhe, 1984) to it is "a necessity, not a fad" (Royal College of Psychiatrists, 1987).

NURSING STAFF

Nurses, midwives, and health visitors are considered to have an important contribution to the management of psychiatric disorder, but require appropriate education and training to enable them to make that contribution. The training of all nurses has been radically changed in recent times under the national "Project 2000." This involves an 18-month Common Foundation Program, covering both mental and physical aspects of nursing, which is expected to give students a better understanding of psychological needs and problems. A further 18 months is then completed in specialist areas before registration by the UK Central Council (UKCC).

The Registered Mental Health Nurse (RMN) is a specialist nurse who is educated and trained to provide care and treatment for people with mental illness and to contribute to prevention and health promotion. Mental health nursing has undergone radical changes over recent years and a review has been instituted by the government to report on how best, in the interest of patient care, to equip and deploy valuable nursing resources. Qualified mental health nurses work in both inpatient and community settings, e.g. in acute care, care of elderly people with mental illness, rehabilitation settings, substance misuse, and forensic psychiatry. The total number of RMNs is 52 033, of whom 3600 work as CPNs.

Areas in which CPNs are becoming increasingly involved include behavior therapy, family therapy, as well as psychodynamics and other psychosocial treatments. The CPN has been described as expected to be "a model of versatility who should be able to assess psychiatric status, set up treatment programmes in behaviour and family therapy, have a good working knowledge of psychotherapy and dynamic principles, understand the principles of care management and be aware of developments in rehabilitation" (Tyrer & Gelder, 1990). However, preparation and training for such changes have repeatedly been reported to be insufficient (e.g. Brooker & Beard, 1985).

CLINICAL PSYCHOLOGISTS

Clinical psychologists initially take a 3-year degree course in psychology (Bachelor of Science [BSc]) and then a 3-year clinical training course. There are 2070 clinical psychologists in the NHS, but shortages remain in many areas which have a high demand for the expansion of mental health services. Greater involvement of local services in the personnel planning is intended to remove such disparities in the supply of professional staff to the NHS, but has yet to be demonstrated to be effective in so doing. A consultancy model of working has been advocated by the Department of Health Manpower Planning Advisory Group which examined these issues in 1990.

SOCIAL WORKERS

Social workers train for a minimum of 2 years, on courses leading to registration with the Central Council for Education and Training in Social Work (CCETSW). Approval to take action under the Mental Health Act (1983) on behalf of Social Services Departments requires further specific training in the diagnosis and management of mental illness and in the use of the Act.

Unlike other members of mental health teams, social workers are employed by Local Authorities (Metropolitan and County Councils). Since the reorganization of social work in 1971, major changes have occurred in practice: previously, apart from the statutory duties of compulsory admissions, the "mental welfare officer" was primarily concerned with monitoring patients' clinical state and with practical matters of finance and home circumstances. After the Seebohm Report (Report of Committee, 1968), both area and hospital social workers emerged with a wider remit to provide family support and therapy which had previously been undertaken by Psychiatric Social Workers, although these were relatively few in number. Social work became more generic, although this does not appear to have been wholly the intention of the Committee, which did not focus on mental health as a major issue. Specialist workers became fewer, until this trend was reversed in the past decade, at least in part, because of the introduction of the necessity for social workers to be approved under the Mental Health Act in order to exercise compulsory powers. Other mental health workers, particularly those across the "Local Authority/Health Authority divide" have found this reduction in specialization frustrating (Challis & Ferlie, 1986), while the benefits of closer integration with other Local Authority colleagues in Social Service and Housing Departments, even where realized, have been uncertain.

A minimum of 50% of all people on social workers, caseloads have a psychiatric disorder, irrespective of whether individuals are accepted as clients by the mental health services, other specialist (e.g. elderly, child) teams, or generic teams. Reviewing the involvement of social workers in mental health health teams, Huxley (1988) found that when they work as part of such teams, in contrast to being in generic teams, there is increased contact with clients, together with improved social outcome and satisfaction for the clients. It therefore appears that attaching social workers to mental health rather than generic, area-based teams leads to the provision of better mental health care, though this is not universal. The total number of social workers of all kinds is 24 456; the number working specifically in mental health or who are approved as ASWs (Approved Social Workers) is not known, but has been estimated at 3600.

OCCUPATIONAL AND OTHER THERAPISTS

The main therapists working in the treatment of psychiatric disorder are occupational therapists, who assist patients in developing the skills of independent living while art, music, and drama therapists work in specific forms of therapy. Physiotherapists influence psychological health through physical approaches such as the use of relaxation, exercise, and the management of disabilities. Both speech therapists, who develop speech and communication skills, and dietitians, who provide dietary advice for anorexia, dietary neglect, and before discharge from hospital, are available to participate in management of psychiatric patients, but do not usually work full-time in mental health services. As with other professions, staff trained in the provision of these services are generally in short supply.

UNQUALIFIED STAFF

More than 50% of staff working in psychiatric units and residential settings do not have specific qualifications, although the development of a National Vocational Qualification may improve a situation where individuals with considerable experience were not credited with it. The expansion of community services has not been matched with developing an appropriate skill-mix to match changing circumstances, and few unqualified staff are employed by the NHS in domiciliary care—limited the support made available. However, with the development of case (renamed "care") management teams, it is hoped that this situation will be improved.

Professionalization has also led to some duties being relinquished by community mental health teams, for example, welfare rights advice. Where this has led to specialist welfare rights workers being employed, it may have resulted in improvement, but often this area has simply been neglected. Clients' expressions of need have tended to be for practical assistance rather than "counselling," but the latter is generally more popular with providers, so that the former may be neglected. Concern (WHO, 1987) has been expressed that an appropriate balance between professional and other staff should be struck, such that they are used to best effect.

AN EXAMPLE OF THE STAFFING OF A MENTAL HEALTH SERVICE

Mental health services in England vary greatly, particularly between urban and rural settings and relative to the deprivation levels of the population. However, a brief description of the service provided in Bassetlaw District may illustrate staffing configurations and numbers in a district in the English Midlands which has a population of 103 000, focused on two towns and a variety of villages. It is demographically average on most population indicators, but has unemployment above average and the proportion of those from black and ethnic minorities below. Prior to 1984, psychiatric services were based in Saxondale Hospital, a mental hospital located 30 miles away, outside Nottingham. A psychiatrist and social worker visited the district to do outpatient clinics and visit patients in their own homes. A local authority day centre opened in 1976. In 1984, a district service was established in active collaboration with local authority and voluntary agencies. It consisted of a District General Hospital unit, hospital hostels which provided 24-hour nursing care for those who required it after the mental hospital closed, and a range of other residential provision (Kingdon *et al.*, 1991). Facilities in the community were developed including a small residential unit for crisis intervention (Turkington *et al.*, 1991), social support groups (Pym, 1989), and a befriending scheme (Kingdon *et al.*, 1989). Medical and other students from Sheffield University (outside the catchment area) are trained within the service. An overall appraisal of the service was published in the *British Medical Journal* (Groves, 1990). Health and Local Authority staffing of the child and adolescent, adult, and old age psychiatric services is given in Table 2. Only four psychiatric patients from the district are known to be currently resident outside in mental or secure hospitals. Occasional referrals (approximately four to six per year) are made to psychiatric units elsewhere for in-patient psychotherapy and specialist opinion.

INTERPROFESSIONAL COLLABORATION

The importance of interprofessional collaboration in the provision of mental health services has been reiterated by the World Health Organization (1987), and has also been UK government policy for many years (e.g. DHSS, 1975). However, both in the UK and in the USA (Borus, 1978), there is evidence that in the development of many community mental health teams, a diversion of care has occurred away from those who are most chronically disabled (Patmore & Weaver, 1991), and that institutional practices have been transferred inappropriately into community settings. On the other hand, there are controlled studies showing the successful use of teams providing support and crisis intervention to patients and their relatives in their own homes (Stein & Test, 1980; Dean *et al.*, 1993). However, where teams work in areas that are very deprived socially or where there are very high levels of chronic severe morbidity, the problem of "staff burn-out" has proved to be significant, although not well documented.

Collaboration can occur through the establishment or emergence of teams and also of networks; both seem essential in providing a balance package of care to most individuals. A team has been described (Muir, 1984) as referring to "continuing interaction between a small, clearly bounded group of the same people who share a common task, similar values and who hold distinctive knowledge and skills"; a network, on the other hand, is composed of "a range of people with different knowledge and skills, who may meet infrequently with a changing constituency, yet who work on a common task when the occasion demands."

The efficient provision of services which is directed to actual needs and avoids duplication of effort requires the existence of both teams and networks,

Table 2. Staffing in a mental health service

Component of services	Psychiatrists		Psychiatric nurses		Social workers		Occupational therapists		Psychologists	
	Consultants	Others	Qualified	Unqualified	Qual.	Unqual.	Qual.	Instructor	Clinical	Asst.
Psychiatric ward			13	8						
Hospital hostels		3	9.2	10.5			0.5			
Day hospital	2		4	2	5		2.5	2	1	
Community team			6							1
Day centre					2	3	1	1		
Psychogeriat-tric assessment ward		1	9	10.5				0.5		
	1				1					
Community team for elderly			3							
Child & Family therapy team	1		1		1				2	

Additionally: 1 Art Therapist & 1 Physiotherapist work across the service as a whole.

Table 3. Medical staff in England and Wales: number of staff in post at September 30, 1991

	Consultants		Senior Registrar		Registrars		Senior house Officers	
Specialties	Total	% female	Total	% female	Total	% female	Total	% female
All medical hospital specialties	17612	15.1	3875	29.1	6565	24.1	12040	37.1
Psychiatric specialties	2168	25.7	655	44.2	798	41.5	999	45.2
Mental illness	1286	22.4	406	37.2	696	41.5	920	46.8
Child and adolescent	384	36.4	129	60.1	31	48.1	28	29.6
Forensic	80	18.2	28	34.7	22	25.0	2	0.0
Mental handicap	182	29.2	52	48.0	32	42.9	13	15.3
Old age psychiatry	118	22.8	8	42.9	8	42.9	30	58.6
Psychotherapy	118	29.2	32	66.8	9	50.0	6	50.0

but this has proved difficult to arrange where agencies with widely differing philosophies and funding mechanisms have apparently overlapping responsibilities. Key members of mental health teams include employees of both NHS units and Social Service Departments, as well as GPs who have responsibilities for providing primary medical care and assessing the need for social care. However, many others may also participate in a network of care for individuals; these include personnel from education, probation, housing, social benefits agencies, police, prisons, legal services, and both voluntary and private sectors. In such circumstances, coordination and advocacy—assisting a patient to negotiate a pathway through complex bureaucracies—are essential, but not easy.

In developing mental health services, the focus of attention has been on teams: their advantages "include the opportunity to pool skills and share work by using the specialist knowledge of team members, gaining wider professional awareness of problems of the client group, exploring a variety of potential solutions to problems, understanding the role of other professionals, thus breaking down stereotypes, and the giving and receiving of support" (Muir, 1984). Their disadvantages, however, have also to be considered, and can be glossed over too easily: they include "having to work closely with people you may dislike and not agree with, spending time in lengthy meetings where efforts may be directed towards group maintenance rather than towards the task, individual initiatives may be hindered by pressure towards group conformity, and less contact with clients because of team demands" (Muir, 1984).

Consultants and nurses have often found such changes threatening, and may have resisted them. While there have been increases in overall staff numbers, smaller psychiatric units have meant that contact with colleagues of the same discipline is reduced. The support network available is restricted particularly in professions whose numbers are relatively small, e.g. psychiatrists and psychologists. The changes involved in moving into urban environments from the quieter pace of mental hospitals located in more rural settings also constitutes a major alteration in life circumstances.

Philosophical and practical differences have also bedevilled interprofessional cooperation. Differential models of care have been stereotyped—the "medical model" of psychiatrists and "antipsychiatry" of social workers. The former has been taken to mean a narrow, exclusively biological conception of mental illness; the latter a sociopolitical model, which blames families and society for its behavior towards those who it labels as mentally ill. However, it has been demonstrated that only a small minority of professionals occupy such extreme positions (Fisher *et al.*, 1984).

Evaluation of different treatment methods has been criticized as either insufficiently rigorous, even anecdotal, or narrowly analytical and insufficiently holistic (Ramon, 1985). Diagnostic and assessment systems have differed markedly; psychiatric systems have become progressively more reliable, although their validity continues to raise concerns (Crow, 1988). Nursing systems are more problem-oriented, while social work particularly emphasize holistic approaches. Consideration of issues of individual rights, e.g. user involvement, sexism, and racism, have been given differing priorities within and between professional groups. Differences in status, and remuneration between groups have also been, usually unspoken, factors impeding collaboration.

With role changes, the blurring of both role and professional boundaries has increased, and misperceptions may arise. This has particularly occurred between social workers and CPNs, whereas psychologists, in establishing their identity as an independent profession, have tended to stress the distinctive contribution that they have to make. Interprofessional difficulties between psychologists and psychiatrists (as well as other doctors) have been not infrequent. A common medical view is that psychologists are highly selective in their choice of cases, for example, rarely working with psychotic patients, yet not accepting continuing responsibility for them. In Salford, Wooff and Goldberg (1988) found some differences between CPNs and social workers: CPNs applied a mainly biomedical model of care to patients with schizophrenia, and simple psychotherapeutic support to others, whereas social workers were more concerned with the social adjustment of clients and used counselling techniques extensively. Working patterns differed in this setting: the mental health social workers worked more closely than the CPNs with the multidisciplinary team and received more supportive supervision. While seeing fewer clients, the social workers' caseloads remained stable; those of the CPNs rose substantially over the period of the study.

The issue of leadership is a vexed one and remains controversial: conceptions of leadership of multidisciplinary teams have varied dramatically. One team, as an example, has described itself as aiming to develop a "...more egalitarian relationship both among professionals and between professionals and clients. The team has no formal leader, this function being asumed by whoever is most appropriate at the time and in the circumstances. Decisions are reached by consensus. The medical model of treatment is seen as a valid approach for some clients, but not the dominant one. The team psychiatrist is responsible for the proper application or the medical model, but other team members are autonomous when they apply social, psychological or non-medical interventions" (Peet, 1986). This contrasts with views, such as that of Cockburn (1989), that "the leadership role (*sic*) of the consultant in the clinical team implies some accountability of members of other disciplines to be consultant—(who)—must be able to delegate work to... clinical team members of other disciplines." Watts and Bennett (1983) have identified six different functions of leadership in an interdisciplinary setting: (i) structuring of tasks; (ii) demonstrating effective involvement with patients; (iii) communicating high expectations of other staff and showing confidence that they can be met; (iv) articulating a grasp of the goals of the team; (v) providing a broad view of the nature and significance of care; and (vi) taking responsibility for relationships to external organizations. They go on to suggest that "these are best assumed by those who have the appropriate skills rather than investing them in one individual" and that "increasing members contributions to leadership tasks improves the team's integration."

However, hierarchical management arrangements exist for all professions—with the general exception of consultant psychiatrists (Harrison, 1989). Such arrangements "provide clear lines of accountability, give authority to those in the top tiers and are comprehensive to most individuals" (Soni *et al.*, 1989); used appropriately—as good management practice dictates—they can improve interprofessional collaboration and seem particularly important in allocation of workload (Patmore & Weaver, 1991).

Training methods for similar tasks varies radically between professional groups. There are distinct areas which need to be more clearly outlined. However, marked similarities can be found between much of the work of mental health professionals and the skills required; these include the following: (i) establishing a rapport with client/patients conducting an assessment; different professionals cover very similar territory, e.g. demographic detail, social circumstances including housing, finances, current relationships, significant life events (current and past), present symptoms, past service contact; (ii) collaboratively developing a care plan with the client/patient, and, when appropriate, with carers; (iii) developing the relationship with the client/patient to encourage specific action to be taken, e.g. acceptance of medication, a program of treatment, or access to family members; (iv) using techniques of counselling and psychotherapy; (v) coordinating care between a number of professional groups; and (vi) monitoring and responding to developments.

It is clear that "the running down and eventual closure of the large psychiatric institutions is a far more complicated process than originally anticipated" (Cooper, 1990); the complexities of developing effective interprofessional collaboration to provide improved replacement services must be a major reason for this. Nevertheless, it does appear that such collaboration is emerging at both national and local levels (e.g. Hall & Brockington, 1991; Groves, 1990).

ECONOMIC CONSIDERATIONS

Definition of the specific skills of individual professional groups is still not fully agreed and is, any case, evolving. For example, medical tasks such as prescription of medication can be undertaken by both GPs and psychiatrists, while psychotherapeutic skills are claimed by virtually all professional groups in greater or lesser degree. Overlaps and inefficiencies in the deployment of mental health personnel are rife, and it is likely that these will be commented upon by an investigation into them that is currently being undertaken by the national Audit Commission. Some appraisal of the effectiveness of individual groups has already occurred, though: social workers have been shown to be effective in treating women with minor depression (Corney & Clare, 1983) as have CPNs and nurses trained in behavior therapy, with neurotic disorders (Marks, 1985). However, this is initial work which requires further development, including the incorporation of cost-effectiveness measures; it clearly cannot be read across to schizophrenia. Government-funded studies into, for example, care management, treatment compliance in schizophrenia, and the implementation of the care program approach are now routinely involving health economists, and a wider understanding should result of the effectiveness of these measures.

REFERENCES

Bennett, D.H. and Freeman, H.L. (1991). *Community Psychiatry*. London: Churchill Livingstone.

Borus, J.F. (1978). Issues critical to survival of mental

health. *American Journal of Psychiatry*, **135**, 1029–1035.

Brooker, C. and Beard, P. (1985). Psychiatric nursing—Quo Vadis? *Bulletin of Royal College of Psychiatrists*, **9**, 70–72.

Challis, D. and Ferlie, E. (1986). Changing patterns of fieldwork organisation. *British Journal of Social Work*, **16**, 181–202.

Cockburn, J.J. (1989). Clinical decisions about patients: Management within multidisciplinary clinical teams. *Psychiatric Bulletin*, **13**, 130–134.

Cooper, J. (1990). Professional obstacles to implementation and diffusion of innovative approaches to mental health care. In I. Marks and R. Scott, eds, *Mental Health Delivery*. Cambridge: Cambridge University Press.

Corney, R. and Clare, A. (1983). The effectiveness of attached social workers in the management of depressed women in General Practice. *British Journal of Social Work*, **13**, 57–74.

Dean, C., Phillips, J., Gadd, E.M. *et al.* (1993). Comparison of community based service with hospital based service for people with acute severe psychiatric illness. *British Medical Journal*, **307**, 473–476.

Department of Health. (1990). *Joint health/social services circular: health and social services development: 'Caring for People'. The care programme approach for people with a mental illness referred to the special psychiatric service.* Heywood, Lancs: Department of Health. (Joint circular: HC(90)23, LASSL(90)11).

Department of Health (1992). *The Health of the Nation.* London: HMSO.

Department of Health (1994). *The Health of the Nation. Key Area Handbook: Mental Illness*, 2nd edn. London: HMSO.

Department of Health Manpower Planning Advisory Group (1990). *Clinical Psychology Project: Full report.* London: Department of Health.

Department of Health & Social Security (1975). *Better Services for the Mentally Ill.* Cmnd 6233. London: HMSO.

Fisher, M. *et al.* (1984). Mental health social work observed, National Institute Social Services Library No. 45.

Groves, T. (1990). After the asylums: the local picture. *British Medical Journal*, **300**, 1128–1130.

Hall, P. and Brockington, I. (1991). *The Closure of Mental Hospitals.* London: Gaskell.

Harrison, T. (1989). The role of the consultant psychiatrist in the clinical team. *Psychiatric Bulletin of the Royal College of Psychiatrists*, **13**, 347–350.

Huxley, P. (1988). *Social Work Practice in Mental Health: Teamwork*, pp. 24–28. Aldershot: Gower.

Jones, R., Goldberg, D., and Hughes, D. (1980). A comparison of two different services treating schizophrenia: a cost benefit approach. *Psychological Medicine*, **10**, 493–505.

Kendrick, T., *et al.* (1991). Role of general practitioners in care of long term mentally ill patients. *British Medical Journal*, **302**, 508–510.

Kingdon, D.G., Turkington, D., Collis, J., *et al.* (1989). Befriending: cost-effective community care. *Psychiatric Bulletin*, **13**, 350–351.

Kingdon, D.G., Turkington, D., Malcolm, K., *et al.* (1991). Replacing the mental hospital: community provision for a district's chronically psychiatrically disabled in domestic environments. *British Journal of Psychiatry*, **158**, 113–116.

Marks, I.M. (1985). Controlled trial of psychiatric nurse therapists in primary care. *British Medical Journal*, **290**, 1181–1184.

Muir, L. (1984). Teamwork, in M.R. Olsen, ed., *Social Work and Mental Health*, pp. 168–176. London: Tavistock.

Patmore, C. and Weaver, T. (1991). Unnatural selection. *Health Service Journal*, **10th October**, 20–22.

Peet, M. (1986). Network Community Mental Health Care in North-West Derbyshire. *Psychiatric Bulletin*, **10**, 262–265.

Pym, B. (1989). Run it your own way. *Community Care*, **6th April**, 17–19.

Ramon, S. (1985). *Psychiatry in Britain: Meaning and Policy*, pp. 60–96. London: Croom Helm.

Report of Committee on Local Authority and Allied Personal Social Services (1968). *The Seebolm Report.* Cmnd 3703. London: HMSO.

Rodhe, P. (1984). An open letter to the President: the future of the consultant in psychiatry—a continuing debate. *Bulletin of Royal College of Psychiatrists*, **8**, 65–66.

Royal College of Psychiatrists (1987). The new president. *Psychiatric Bulletin*, **11**, 210.

Shepherd, S. (1991). Expert opinion. Community ward rounds. *Psychiatric Bulletin*, **15**, 363–364.

Soni, S.D. *et al.* (1989). Multi-disciplinary teams and line management. *Psychiatric Bulletin*, **13**, 657–661.

Stein, L., and Test, M. (1980). Alternatives to mental hospitals. I. Conceptual model, treatment program and clinical evaluation. *Archives of General Psychiatry*, **37**, 392–397.

Turkington, D., Kingdon, D.G., and Malcolm, K. (1991). The use of an unstaffed flat for crisis intervention and rehabilitation. *Psychiatric Bulletin*, **15**, 13–14.

Tyrer, P. and Gelder, M. (1990). Research report: The future of community psychiatric nursing: some research findings. *Psychiatric Bulletin*, **14**, 550–551.

Watts, F.N. and Bennett, D.H. (eds) (1983). Management of the staff team. In *The Theory and Practice of Psychiatric Rehabilitation.* Chichester: Wiley.

World Health Organization Regional Office for Europe Copenhagen (1987). *Mental Health Services in Pilot Study Areas.* WHO: Copenhagen.

Wooff, K. and Goldberg, D. (1988). Further observations on the practice of community care in Salford: differences between community psychiatric nurses and mental health social workers. *British Journal of Psychiatry*, **153**, 30–37.

Part VI

SERVICES USE EVALUATION AND ECONOMIC EVALUATION METHODS

26

The Economic Burden of Schizophrenia: Conceptual and Methodological Issues, and Cost Estimates

DOROTHY P. RICE
Institute for Health & Aging, University of California, San Francisco

LEONARD S. MILLER
School of Social Welfare, University of California, Berkeley, California, USA

ABSTRACT

Schizophrenia is costly to the nation in medical resources used for care, treatment, and rehabilitation; reduced or lost productivity; and pain and suffering of patients, their families, and friends. This paper discusses the conceptual and methodological issues related to cost of illness studies and summarizes the methods and sources of data used in estimating the direct and indirect costs of schizophrenia and presents the results.

Schizophrenia imposed a \$22.8 billion burden on the United States economy in 1985 and \$32.5 billion in 1990. Schizophrenia costs comprise 22% of the costs of all mental illness. Direct treatment and support costs comprised 53% of the total in 1990; morbidity costs, the value of reduced or lost productivity, 33%; mortality costs, 4%, based on a 6% discount rate of the value of productivity forgone in future years as a result of premature mortality in 1985; and other related costs, including the cost of caregivers' services, 10%. Private sources account for 36% of the total direct expenditures for treatment of persons with schizophrenia. The remaining 64% is borne by public sources, 40% from state and local funds, and 24% from federal funds.

In light of the high burden of schizophrenia on societal resources, more attention should be directed at comprehensive, research-based strategies to reduce the prevalence of this disorder in the United States.

INTRODUCTION

Schizophrenia is a chronic mental disorder characterized by social withdrawal, disordered thinking, hallucinations, and bizarre delusions. Its onset may begin early in life and cause considerable morbidity and reduced productivity. The costs to patients and their families are high in terms of pain, suffering,

Handbook of Mental Health Economics and Health Policy, Volume I, Schizophrenia. Edited by M. Moscarelli, A. Rupp and N. Sartorius.
© 1996 John Wiley & Sons Ltd.

financial, and social costs. Schizophrenia also is costly to the nation in medical resources used for care, treatment, and rehabilitation, and in reduced or lost productivity. Results from recent surveys document the prevalence of schizophrenia in the general population: 0.7% of the population 18 years and over report schizophrenia during a 1-month period, 0.9% during a 6-month period, and 1.5% during their lifetime (Regier *et al.*, 1988). About 2.5 million persons aged 18–64 suffer from this disorder.

This chapter presents estimates of the economic burden of schizophrenia in 1985 and 1990. The methodology is based on a larger study, *The Economic Costs of Alcohol and Drug Abuse and Mental Illness: 1985* (Rice *et al.*, 1990) conducted for the Alcohol, Drug Abuse, and Mental Health Administration (ADAMHA). The first part of this chapter discusses the conceptual and methodological issues related to cost of illness studies, focusing on those that relate to cost of schizophrenia; the second part summarizes the methods and sources of data used in estimating the direct and indirect costs of schizophrenia: the third part presents the results; and the final part presents the conclusions.

CONCEPTUAL AND METHODOLOGICAL ISSUES

PREVALENCE VERSUS INCIDENCE-BASED COST ESTIMATES

Prevalence-based costs estimate the direct and indirect economic burden incurred in a period of time (the base period) as a result of the prevalence of the disease, a period most often a year. Included are the costs of the base year or any time prior to the base year. Prevalence-based costs measure the value of resources used or lost during a specified period of time, regardless of the time of disease onset. Incidence-based costs represent the lifetime costs resulting from a disease or illness. In the aggregate, incidence-based costs refer to the total lifetime costs of all cases with onset of disease in a given base year.

The approach used depends on the purpose of the analysis. If the results are to be used for cost control, then prevalence-based costing is appropriate; it identifies the major components of current expenditures and forgone resources and identifies possible targets for economy. If the analysis is aimed at making decisions about which treatment or research strategy to implement, then the incidence-based approach is more appropriate because it provides the basis for predictions about the likely savings from programs that reduce incidence or improve outcomes. In general, prevalence-based estimates are larger than incidence estimates (Andrews *et al.*, 1985). Because the aim of this chapter is to estimate the burden and magnitude of schizophrenia on the economy, the prevalence-based approach is employed.

HUMAN CAPITAL VERSUS WILLINGNESS-TO-PAY APPROACHES

Economists generally employ two approaches to valuing human life. One is the human capital approach, refined by Rice (1966) and her colleagues (Rice *et al.*, 1985); the second is the willingness-to-pay approach, first proposed by Schelling (1968) and Mishan (1971). In addition, there have been attempts to further refine these methods and link them together (Landefeld & Seskin, 1982). In the human capital approach, a person is seen as producing a stream of output that is valued at market earnings and the value of life is the discounted future earnings stream. Morbidity and mortality destroys labor, a valuable economic resource, by causing persons to lose time and effectiveness from work and other productive activities, forcing them out of the labor force completely, or bringing about premature death. Disease thus creates an undeniable loss to individuals and society, and it is this loss that the human capital approach attempts to measure (Hodgson & Meiners, 1982). This method has some disadvantages. Because it values life using market earnings, it yields very low values for children and the retired elderly. It also undervalues life if labor market imperfections exist and wages do not reflect true abilities. In addition, psychosocial costs, such as pain and suffering, are components of the burden of illness omitted from the human capital computation of indirect costs.

The willingness-to-pay approach values life according to what individuals are willing to pay for a change that reduces the probability of illness or death. This method could be helpful in indicating how individuals value health and life, in deriving social preferences regarding public policy, and in assessing the burden of pain and suffering, which have an intangible quality not amenable to evaluation in terms of the monetary value of resources used or forgone. A review by Robinson (1986) makes a strong case that the willingness-to-pay method is a fundamentally "incorrect" method of valuing life for cost-effective public policy. Robinson concludes that it is subjective and suffers from circularity because the values placed by individuals on government health programs are clearly influenced by those policies.

The human capital approach is still most often used in cost–benefit and cost-effectiveness analyses that seek to evaluate alternative demands for scarce health resources and promote economic rationality in health services policy, planning, and management. This approach is used in the current study of the cost of schizophrenia in the United States.

VALUING HOUSEHOLD SERVICES

Marketplace earnings underestimate losses resulting from illnesses that affect women and men who are not in the labor force and who keep house. Time and motion studies of housekeepers' activities are measured and the hours are valued on the basis of relevant market wages. For example, the time spent cooking may be valued using the prevailing wage rate for a cook. For this study, estimates are developed of hours spent on household labor, employing regression analysis to control for socioeconomic and demographic factors (Douglass *et al.*, 1990).

EARNINGS

Estimates of output losses are generally based on annual mean earnings by age and sex, adjusted by wage supplements such as employer contributions for social insurance, private pensions and welfare funds. Cross-sectional profiles of mean earnings by age and gender are used to estimate lifetime earnings. In applying these data, it is assumed that the future pattern of earnings for an average individual within a gender group will follow the pattern reported by the Bureau of the Census during the base year. This model recognizes that the average individual may expect earnings to rise with age and experience in accordance with the cross-sectional data for that year. Future changes in productivity of wage earners also need to be taken into account. Based on average changes in hourly earnings between 1980 and 1986, a 1% annual increase in productivity is assumed (US Bureau of the Census, 1987a).

CONSUMPTION

Questions have been raised in the past as to whether the cost of morbidity and mortality due to illness should be estimated based on an individual's output or an individual's output minus consumption (Weisbrod, 1961). The concern of this study is with the cost of illness to society. The individual, not just the output he or she contributes in excess of consumption, is valued by society. Economists today generally agree that consumption should not be deducted. In accordance with current accepted methodology, consumption is not deducted from the individual's output in the present study.

COSTS VERSUS CHARGES

In measuring direct costs, charge data are more frequently used than cost data, despite the fact that charges do not necessarily reflect resource use. Most researchers use charge data in cost studies because of accessibility and the lack of alternatives. The present study uses charges or expenditure data for the direct cost components.

TRANSFER PAYMENTS

Welfare, disability, and other benefit payments under public and private programs constitute a reallocation of resources and the net cost to society is zero. Inclusion of transfer payments would result in double counting and are not included in the cost estimates.

NONMARKET USE OF RESOURCES

A large share of the burden of caring for sick patients falls on relatives, friends, and community networks of volunteers. If individuals are unable to provide these services informally, they might have to be purchased in the marketplace. The value of caregiver services is included in this study.

NONHEALTH-RELATED COSTS

These costs encompass direct and indirect costs. Direct costs include expenditures for transportation to providers, criminal justice, property losses, etc. Indirect costs include the opportunity costs of time for individuals who are incarcerated as a result of conviction for an affective disorder related crime as well as the imputed value of caregiver services. The present study includes estimates of other related direct and the indirect costs of schizophrenia.

COMORBIDITY

Comorbidity of schizophrenia in relation to other diagnoses, especially for hospitalized persons, is a major problem that requires quantification in estimating hospital costs. For the larger study, *The Economic Costs of Alcohol and Drug Abuse and Mental Illness: 1985*, we measured comorbidity in short-stay hospitals by estimating the annual days of care associated with a primary diagnosis of alcohol, drug abuse, and mental illness (ADM) as well as the additional days of care reported for hospitalizations with secondary or comorbid ADM disorders. A similar procedure was used in this study of the cost of schizophrenia.

METHODS AND DATA SOURCES

Cost of illness studies are typically divided into two major categories: core costs are those resulting directly from the illness and other related costs are the costs of the nonhealth costs of the illness. Within each category, there are direct and indirect costs. Direct costs are those for which payments are made, and indirect costs are those for which resources are lost. Indirect costs consist of: morbidity costs, the value of lost productivity by persons unable to perform their usual activities or to perform them at a level of full effectiveness due to the illness; and mortality costs, the value of lost productivity due to premature death resulting from the illness, calculated as the present discounted value of future market earnings plus an imputed value for housekeeping services.

For estimation of the direct and mortality costs, schizophrenia includes those persons with a diagnosis of schizophrenia (code 295) and paranoid states (code 297), based on the *International Classification of Diseases Ninth Revision, Clinical Modification* (ICD-9-CM) (WHO, 1978). For morbidity costs, the *Diagnostic and Statistical Manual of Mental Disorders* (DSM-III) (APA, 1980) was used; included are schizophrenia and schizophreniform.

A prevalence-based approach is used in this study. This method estimates the direct and indirect cost incurred during 1985 as a result of the prevalence of this illness during that year, including cases of onset in that year or at any prior time period. Estimates of the cost of schizophrenia are also presented for 1990.

DIRECT COSTS

In general, direct costs (medical expenditures) are estimated as the product of two components: number of services and unit prices or charges. For example, short-stay hospital days of care were obtained from the 1985 National Hospital Discharge Surveys (NCHS, 1987). Included are the annual days of care for hospitalizations with a primary diagnosis of schizophrenia as well as the additional days of care associated with a secondary diagnosis of schizophrenia (Rice & Kelman, 1989). Expenses per patient day (AHA, 1988) were applied to the total days of care to obtain total short-stay hospital costs.

Nursing home costs are estimated by multiplying the number of residents with a primary or secondary diagnosis of schizophrenia at admission by the annual charge for all residents in the 1985 National Nursing Home Survey (NHCS, 1989). Costs of outpatient care by office-based physicians are based on visit data from the 1985 National Ambulatory Care Survey (NCHS, 1988) and charges of psychiatrists and other physicians obtained from the American Medical Association (1987). Costs of other office-based professional services are limited to psychologists and social workers and are based on the proportion that schizophrenia ambulatory costs represent of total mental illness ambulatory costs. Expenditures for care in mental specialty institutions are based on data from the National Institute of Mental Health (1988). Expenditures for prescription drugs include amounts spent for antipsychotics (phenothiazine, nonphenothiazine, and lithium) and are based on national estimates of outpatient prescription sales from the National Prescription Survey conducted by Pharmaceutical Data Services (1985).

Support costs related to the treatment of schizophrenia include federal expenditures for medical and health services research, training costs for physicians and nurses, program administration, and the net cost of private health insurance and are based on national health expenditure data from the Health Care Financing Administration (1987). Other related direct costs of schizophrenia include the following components: public and private criminal justice system and social welfare administration and are estimated as the proportion that these components represent of other related mental illness costs reported for these components in the larger study, *The Economic Costs of Alcohol and Drug Abuse and Mental Illness: 1985*.

MORBIDITY COSTS

Morbidity costs for the noninstitutionalized population, the value of reduced or lost productivity due to schizophrenia, are estimated as the product of: (i) population size; (ii) schizophrenia prevalence rates; (iii) impairment rates per person with schizophrenia or percentage income loss; and (iv) average income the individual would have earned had he or she not been affected by this disorder. Calculating this four-term product by age and sex and then summing them provides an estimate of the aggregate loss of income due to schizophrenia among the entire noninstitutionalized population aged 18–64.

The identity is given below:

$$\$LOSS = \Sigma\Sigma\Sigma\ (POP_{as} * PREV_{asd})\ (b_{asd} * Y_{as})$$

Where:

$\$LOSS$ is the aggregate loss in income due to the disorder (d);

POP_{as} is the size of the population of age (a) and sex (s);

$PREV_{asd}$ is the prevalence rate of a, s, and d;

b_{as} is the percentage income loss per individual with the disorder, by a, s, and d; and

Y_{as} is the average income by a and s for individuals without d.

A timing model employing regression analysis was developed to estimate the percentage income loss per disordered individual (impairment rate). This model measures the lifetime effect on current income of individuals with schizophrenia, taking into account the timing of onset and the duration of this disorder. Calculations were based on measures of time of onset and of last symptom relative to the time of interview reported in the Epidemiologic Catchment Area Surveys (NIMH, 1980–85).

Three different models of behavioral translation of schizophrenic disorders into impairment were hypothesized, specified, and estimated. In the first model, a short period of disorder is assumed to immediately reduce productivity, causing a small immediate percentage loss in income. In the second model, a short period of disorder is again assumed to immediately reduce productivity, causing a small immediate percentage loss in income as it did in the first model. But the effects of a particular short period of disorder continue to reduce productivity into the future, resulting in future income losses which are occurring at exponentially declining rates. The third model is exactly like the second, except for the feature describing what happens in remission, in which new disorder effects are no longer added, but the effects from past disorders are still experienced at their exponentially declining rates. The timing measure expressions are approximated by:

Model 1: Minimum $[A - tb,\ te - tb]$.
Model 2: Minimum $[(A - tb)^2,\ (te - tb)^2]$.
Model 3: $(A - tb)^2 - (A - te)^2$, for $A > tb$ and $A > te$.

Where:

A is the age at interview;
tb is the age at onset; and
te is the age at last symptom.

In the analysis, equations were estimated using each of the three timing models for each of the disorders studied. A final equation was run, using the model with the highest significance level for its parameter estimate. More complete descriptions and explanations appear in appendices B and C of the full report, *The Economic Costs of Alcohol and Drug Abuse and Mental Illness: 1985* and in Miller and Kelman (1992).

Morbidity costs for the institutionalized population

are based on the number of residents in state and county mental hospitals and in nursing homes with schizophrenia. The number of institutionalized persons is adjusted by labor force participation rates and then multiplied by the estimated mean earnings adjusted for wage supplements or fringe benefits for each age and sex group.

MORTALITY COSTS

If an individual had not died prematurely from schizophrenia, he or she would have continued to be productive for a number of years. The estimated mortality costs are the product of the number of deaths from schizophrenia, including 10% of suicides (Goodwin, 1990), and the expected value of an individual's future earnings with sex and age taken into account. This method of derivation considers life expectancy for different age and sex groups, changing pattern of earnings at successive ages, varying labor force participation rates, an imputed value for housekeeping services, and the appropriate discount rate to convert a stream of earnings into its present worth. Cross-sectional profiles of mean earnings by age and sex as reported by the US Bureau of the Census (1987b) are employed based on the assumption that future earnings of an average individual will rise with age and experience in accordance with the cross-sectional data for that year.

Marketplace earnings underestimate losses resulting from illnesses that affect women and men who are not in the labor force and who keep house. The value of household work must be added to the earnings loss for people who died. For this study, estimates are developed of hours spent on household labor, employing regression analysis to control for socioeconomic and demographic factors (Douglass *et al.*, 1990). The hours are then valued on the basis of 1985 wage rates.

The formula for calculating the present value of lifetime earnings is presented below:

$$V=\sum_{n=a}^{85+}\frac{(X_nW_nP_a^n+H_nK_nP_a^n)}{(1+i)^{n-a}}$$

Where:

- a is the midyear age for the given cohort of persons;
- X_n is the annual mean earnings for all persons with earnings in an age group where the midpoint is age n;
- i is the discount rate;
- H_n is the annual mean imputed value of housekeeping services for all persons in an age group where the midpoint is age n;
- K_n is the average keeping house participation rate in the age group with midpoint n;
- P_a^n is the approximate probability that an individual age a survives to n;
- W_n is the average labor force participation rate in the age group with midyear age n, resulting from the single year labor force participation rate W.

Given these definitions,

$W_nP_a^n$ estimates the number of labor force years per person in an age group and determined as follows:

$$W_nP_a^n=\frac{\sum_{j=t}^{t+r-1}L_jW_j}{L_a}$$

Where:

- j is the specific single year of age under consideration;
- t is the beginning year of the age group;
- r is the number of years in this age group; in any age group j can go from t to $t+r-1$;
- L_j is the number of individuals surviving to j out of a cohort of 100 000 live births, based on 1985 Life Tables;
- W_j is the single year labor force participation rate;
- L_a is the number of persons living at the midyear age a for a given single subgroup out of a cohort of 100 000 live births.

OTHER RELATED COSTS

Other related direct costs include public and private expenditures for crime (police protection, legal and judicial services, and correctional institutions) and social welfare program administrative costs associated with schizophrenia. Costs are based on data from the Department of Justice Uniform Crime report (US DOJ, 1985) and social welfare expenditures (Bixby, 1988).

Table 1. Economic costs of schizophrenia and total mental illness by type of cost, 1985 and 1990 (in millions)

Type of cost	Schizophrenia (1985)	1990* Schizophrenia	1990* Total mental illness	1990* Percent of mental illness
Total	$22 798	$32 538	$147 847	22.0
Core costs	20 257	29 292	141 887	28.2
Direct	11 130	17 296	67 000	25.8
Mental health organizations	4 288	6 520	19 516	33.4
Short-stay hospitals	1 706	2 595	13 392	19.4
Office-based physicians	239	406	3 655	11.1
Other professional services	373	710	6 599	10.8
Nursing homes	3 414	5 316	16 478	32.3
Drugs	263	397	2 191	18.1
Support costs	847	1 352	5 169	26.2
Indirect costs	9 127	11 996	74 887	16.0
Morbidity	8 105	10 694	63 083	17.0
Noninstitutionalized Popn	6 605	8 837	58 988	15.0
Institutionalized Popn	1 500	1 857	4 095	45.3
Mortality†	1 022	1 302	11 804	11.0
Other related costs	2 541	3 246	5 960	54.5
Direct	439	599	2 292	26.1
Crime	340	464	1 777	26.1
Social Welfare Admin.	99	135	515	26.2
Indirect	2 102	2 647	3 668	72.2
Incarceration	85	150	573	26.2
Family caregiving	2017	2 497	3 095	80.7

* 1990 costs are based on socioeconomic indices applied to the 1985 costs.
† Discounted at 6%.

Two types of other related indirect costs are estimated: (i) productivity losses for individuals incarcerated in prisons as a result of a conviction for a schizophrenia-related crime; and (ii) the value of time spent to care for family members. The first costs are based on the number of persons incarcerated (US DOJ, 1988) multiplied by the 1985 average, year-round full-time mean earnings adjusted for supplements and fringe benefits. The value of time spent by caregivers for care provided to family members of schizophrenic patients is estimated by Franks in a study conducted for the National Institute of Mental Health in 1987. Included is time spent in the following activities: caregiving; work loss; time with lawyers, clergy, professionals; recreation; and other activities based on a survey of the membership of the Massachusetts Alliance for the Mentally Ill, a family support and advocacy group (Franks, 1990).

RESULTS

The prevalence of schizophrenia is high, resulting in considerable use of medical care services and substantial costs to society in productivity losses as summarized below.

TOTAL ECONOMIC IMPACT

Schizophrenia imposed a $22.8 billion burden on the United States economy in 1985 (Table 1). Direct treatment and support costs comprised 48.8% of the total; morbidity costs, the value of reduced or lost productivity, 35.6%; mortality costs, 4.5%, based on a 6% discount rate of the value of productivity forgone in future years as a result of premature mortality in 1985; and other related costs, including the cost of caregivers' services, 11.1%.

The costs of schizophrenia were updated to 1990 employing economic data and indices with known relationships to mental illness cost estimates. To obtain the 1990 values, both inflationary and real changes were taken into account. Direct costs were adjusted using the percentage change in the components of total personal health care expenditures between 1985 and 1990 (Levit *et al.*, 1991). These data incorporate inflation in the medical care market as well as the effect of changing demographics and patterns of medical care utilization.

For indirect costs, inflation and real change were estimated separately. The change in hourly compensation in the business sector was used to reflect real change for morbidity. The change in the total number of deaths due to suicides and schizophrenia was used to reflect real change for mortality. Similarly, for other related crime expenditures, the Gross National Product implicit price deflator for government purchases of goods and services was used to reflect inflation, and the change in the number of arrests was used for real change.

The costs of schizophrenia in 1990 are estimated at $32.5 billion, a 43% rise during the 5-year period, 1985–90. Schizophrenia costs comprise 22% of the costs of all mental illnesses. The proportion varies by type of cost. Direct costs of schizophrenia comprise 26% of total mental illness costs; indirect costs comprise 16% of the total. Other related costs, however, comprise a much larger share of the total—55%, with family caregiving representing four-fifths of total caregiving costs for all mental illnesses. It is clear that schizophrenia patients place a great burden on families in the form of caregiving services.

DIRECT COSTS

Direct costs for persons suffering from schizophrenia totaled $11.1 billion in 1985 or 3% of total personal health care spending for all illnesses in that year. Almost two-fifths of the direct costs, $4.3 billion, are expenditures for care in specialty institutions (federal, state, county, and private psychiatric hospitals, residential treatment centers for emotionally disturbed children, freestanding mental health centers, and correctional facilities). About 15% of the direct costs, $1.7 billion, was spent for short-stay hospital care. Other treatment costs included $239 million for office-based physicians and $373 million for other professional services, including psychologists and social workers. Nursing home expenditures for persons with schizophrenia amounted to $3.4 billion, 31% of direct costs. Prescription drugs were estimated at $263 million, 2.4% of the direct costs. Support costs, including expenditures for research training costs of physicians and nurses, program administration, and the net cost of private health insurance, amounted to $847 million, comprising 8% of direct costs.

INDIRECT COSTS—MORBIDITY

Schizophrenia morbidity costs, the value of reduced or lost productivity, amounted to $8.1 billion, almost nine-tenths of the total indirect costs of schizophrenia. Morbidity costs for the noninstitutionalized population, $6.6 billion, were based on an estimated prevalence of 2.5 million persons with schizophrenic disorders, 900 000 men and 1.6 million women (Table 2). Schizophrenia prevalence rates for women are higher than for men at all ages. For women, the rates rise from 2.5% for persons aged 18–24 to 2.9% for persons aged 25–34 and then decline to 2.0% for women aged 35–54 and less than 1% for women aged 55–64. A similar trend is shown for men, but the rates are lower: 18–24 years, 1.8%; 25–34 years, 1.4%; 35–54 years, 1.3%; and 55–64 years, 0.4%.

Impairment rates or percent of income loss for men, however, are significantly higher than for women, rising from 7.1% for men aged 18–24 to 77.4% for men aged 55–64 compared with 3.0% loss for women aged 18–24 rising to 15.3% for those aged 55–64.

As noted earlier, a timing model employing regression analysis was developed to estimate these impairment rates. This model measures lifetime effect of current income of the individual, taking into account timing of onset and the duration of schizophrenia. The impairment rates are the adjusted cross-sectional regression coefficients obtained when the natural logarithm of personal income is regressed on lifetime measures of individual schizophrenia prevalence and other control variables.

Table 3 presents the results of the regression analysis for the demographic control variables for

Table 2. Prevalence and morbidity loss of noninstitutionalized persons with schizophrenic disorders by age and sex 1985

Age	Male	Female	Total
Prevalence rates (%)			
18–24	1.77%	2.46%	—
25–34	1.43	2.86	—
35–54	1.33	2.04	—
55–64	0.04	0.08	—
Prevalence (thousands)			
Total	906	1604	2510
18–24	237	346	583
25–34	287	597	884
35–54	344	562	906
55–64	38	99	137
Impairment rates (percent)			
18–24	7.14%	2.95%	—
25–34	7.49	6.13	—
35–54	29.40	9.05	—
55–64	77.40	15.30	—
Average loss per person			
18–24	$649	$264	—
24–34	1994	1079	—
35–54	10477	1624	—
55–64	19064	1559	—
Morbidity losses (millions)			
Total	$4802	$1803	$6605
18–24	153	91	244
25–34	571	644	1215
35–54	3608	914	4522
55–64	470	154	624

Source: based on Epidemiology Catchment Area Surveys.

income loss associated with schizophrenia. The age variable demonstrates the expected signs, with the first-order variables positive and the second-order variables negative, suggesting that after some age, income begins to decline controlling for everything else. Marital status, as expected, is strongly positive for males and equally strongly negative for females. The number of children appears to bear no relationship to the incomes of men, but has a strong negative effect on that of women.

Race generally has the expected effects. For Hispanic and black men, incomes are 51 and 45%, respectively, below those of white men. For Hispanic women this pattern persists, but there is no statistically discernible difference between incomes of black and white women. For women of "other" races, there is a marginally significant difference of approximately 12.5%.

Being "sick all one's life" has a very substantial effect on income, lowering that of men and women by about 62 and 45%, respectively. The time and location of survey variables also have the expected signs and values. The signs are negative for two reasons: first, incomes generally rise over time; and second, the west Los Angeles locale surveyed in 1983, the excluded category, is a relatively wealthy district. Income differences by year and location of survey range from 17% for men in Los Angeles (1983) to 57% loss in Durham (1982), controlling for all other effects. For women, income differences range from 13% in Los Angeles (1983) to 84% loss in Baltimore (1981).

As indicated above, three timing models were employed. Table 4 shows the specific timing model used for males and females, the average values of the timing measures for the eight age–sex groups, and the regression coefficients by sex. The impairment rate for any age–sex group is the product of the timing measure for the group and the sex specific regression coefficient.

In addition to morbidity costs for the noninstitutionalized population, losses for the institutionalized populations were also estimated. Persons institutionalized because of schizophrenia include those in mental hospitals and in nursing homes, and their morbidity costs amounted to $1.5 billion, 16% of total indirect costs in 1985.

INDIRECT COSTS—MORTALITY

A total of 3154 deaths due to schizophrenia occurred in 1985. Included are 2945 suicide deaths, 10% of the total deaths due to suicide. The 3154 schizophrenia deaths represent more than 100000 person years lost, or 32 years per death and a loss of $1.0 billion to the economy at a 6% discount rate, or $324033 per death (Table 5). Males account for 76% of the deaths, 76% of the person years lost, and 83% of the productivity losses. The higher costs for men reflect their higher death rates due to schizophrenia, higher labor force participation rates, and higher earnings than for women.

Table 3. Regression coefficients for demographic and location variables in the timing model by sex

	Male			Female		
Variable	Coefficient	Standard Error	*t*-value	Coefficient	Standard Error	*t*-value
Intercept	3.773	0.334	11.289	3.278	0.390	8.415
Age	0.246	0.157	15.662	0.263	0.018	14.314
Age 25–34†	4.679	0.430	10.873	6.127	0.502	12.205
Age 35–54	6.718	0.377	17.845	6.979	0.434	16.070
Age 55–64	8.340	0.809	10.313	7.448	5.284	8.839
Age* Age 25–34‡	−0.200	0.018	−10.937	−0.251	0.021	−11.854
Age* Age 35–54	−0.257	0.016	−15.882	−0.275	0.019	−14.571
Age* Age 55–64	−0.265	0.020	−14.235	−0.282	0.022	−12.599
Married	0.380	0.033	11.570	−0.460	0.038	−12.199
No. of children§	0.009	0.010	0.922	−0.104	0.009	−11.592
Hispanic	−0.509	0.052	−9.782	−0.620	0.060	−10.424
Black	−0.452	0.039	−11.696	0.025	0.046	0.548
Other race	−0.478	0.066	−7.242	−0.125	0.085	−1.467
Sick¶	−0.619	0.087	−7.149	−0.451	0.084	−5.378
New Haven (1980)	−0.508	0.057	−8.922	−0.817	0.076	−10.793
New Haven (1981)	−0.520	0.073	−7.146	−0.700	0.093	−7.550
Baltimore (1981)	−0.527	0.062	−8.553	−0.844	0.079	−10.716
Durham (1982)	−0.571	0.060	−9.533	−0.533	0.080	−6.659
Durham (1983)	−0.519	0.086	−6.057	−0.306	0.120	−2.542
Los Angeles (1983)	−0.168	0.058	−2.917	−0.132	0.073	−1.806

†This and the following two variables are an adjustment to intercept for age group.
‡This and the following two variables are an adjustment to slope for age group.
§Maximum of seven children.
¶Sickly for the majority of subjects' life.
Note: The demographic and location variables in this table as well as other mental illness timing measures constitute the full specification of the model. Results are available from the authors.

More than one-third (36%) of the deaths due to schizophrenia occur among persons aged 25–44 years. Owing to the longer life expectancy and higher earnings of this age group, person-years lost amount to 46% of total person-years lost and mortality costs comprise 56% of the total mortality costs. By contrast, 23% of the deaths are among persons aged 65 and over, accounting for 7% of person-years lost and only 1% of total productivity losses.

OTHER RELATED COSTS

Other related direct and indirect costs were estimated at $2.5 billion for 1985. Of this total, direct costs accounted for $439 million (17%) and indirect costs for the remaining $2.1 billion (83%). The value of time spent to care for family members because of schizophrenia comprises the major portion of indirect costs—$2.0 billion.

SOURCE OF PAYMENT

The direct costs of schizophrenia, distributed by source of payment and treatment setting, are shown in Table 6. Private sources account for 36% of the total direct expenditures for treatment of persons with schizophrenia. The remaining 64% is paid by public sources, 40% from state and local funds and 24% from federal sources.

There is considerable variation in source of payment by treatment setting. About 70% of the cost of treatment by mental health organizations, including public and private psychiatric hospitals and other institutions (residential treatment centers for emotionally disturbed children, freestanding

Table 4. Schizophrenia* timing measures and regression coefficients by sex

	Male (model 3)	Female (model 1)
Timing measure†		
18–24	123.2	4.832
25–34	129.6	10.21
35–54	578.2	15.30
55–64	2471.0	26.70
Regression coefficients	−0.601 E-03	−0.620 E-02
Standard error	0.138 E-03	0.758 E-02
t-values	(−4.359)	(0.818)

* Includes schizophrenia and schizophreniform.
† Each entry represents the average value by age, sex, and the power series approximation of the degree of clinical impairment among prevalent individuals, specific to the particular Timing Model used. Timing measures are expressed in units of years or years squared and represent measures of clinical impairment, not duration of time.

facilities, multi-services mental health organizations, and correctional facilities) is supported by state and local funds, 17% comes from federal funds, and 13% from private sources. In contrast, for short-stay hospital care of patients with schizophrenia, 41% comes from federal sources, 16% from state and local funds, and the remaining 43% from private sources. About three-fifths (58%) of the expenditures for nursing home care comes from public sources, with 28% from federal funds, and 31% in state and local payments; the remaining two-fifths come from private sources.

For office-based physicians, other professional services, and drugs, private funds cover the bulk of the expenditures—about 90% of the total.

DISCUSSION AND CONCLUSIONS

The cost estimates presented in this study are based on the most current and reliable data available and new methodology developed specifically for this study. Nonetheless, several qualifications are in order:

Several known costs, such as pain and suffering, are excluded because data are unavailable. No estimates are made for schizophrenia income loss among the homeless and military populations, resulting in underestimation of costs. Some of the costs estimates are likely to be low due to data limitations. For example, hospital discharge and ambulatory data records may not list schizophrenia diagnoses because of the stigma associated with this disorder.

Capital costs of construction of facilities are not included in these cost estimates because there was no basis for making such estimates (McGuire, 1991).

Estimates of income loss among the civilian resident noninstitutionalized population are calculated only for the population aged 18–64. To the degree that those under age 18 and over 64 suffering earnings losses due to schizophrenia, the costs are understated. Productivity losses are based on personal income rather than earnings. Personal income, which includes receipt of transfer payments, may be less sensitive to the effects of schizophrenia than earnings, resulting in possible understatement of costs.

A 6% discount rate is employed to estimate the present value of future earnings lost to be consistent with the discount rates employed in earlier studies. Use of a 4% discount rate would yield higher mortality costs than the costs based on a 6% discount rate.

For these reasons, the cost estimates presented in this study can be interpreted as a lower limit of the true cost of schizophrenia. As better data become available, the approach can be refined and improved.

A variety of cost-effectiveness studies in the treatment of schizophrenia have been conducted in the past (Goldburg, 1991). Most of these studies focus on treatment costs in hospital settings and at home. These studies limit their analyses to direct costs. However, there have been relatively few studies of the societal costs of schizophrenia that include indirect costs. Andrews and his colleagues have estimated the costs of schizophrenia in New South Wales, Australia (Andrews *et al.*, 1985; Andrews, 1991). They employ an incidence approach for their cost estimates, in which the lifetime direct and indirect costs are estimated for new cases of the disorder. They note that the approach to costing depends on the purpose. The prevalence-based costing will suffice if cost control is the aim of the study because it identifies the major contributors to current expenditure and identifies possible targets for economy. If the aim of the study is to make decisions about which treatment or research strategy to implement, then the incidence-based approach is the more appropriate because it provides predictions

Table 5. Schizophrenia mortality*: number of deaths, person-years lost, and discounted productivity losses by age and gender (1985)

Age and gender	Number of deaths	Person-years lost		Productive losses†	
		Number	Per death	Amount (thousands)	Per death
Total	3154	101 195	32	$1 022 182	$324 033
Under 15	27	1 676	62	9 678	358 444
15–24	518	27 798	54	257 824	497 730
24–44	1122	46 650	42	567 692	505 964
45–64	766	17 842	23	172 482	224 512
65+	721	7 229	10	14 507	20 121
Males	2406	76 437	32	847 111	352 084
Under 15	20	1206	60	7 496	374 800
15–24	431	22 638	53	222 200	515 545
25–44	875	35 393	40	473 920	541 623
45–64	561	12 305	22	134 381	239 538
65+	519	4 895	9	9114	17 561
Females	748	24 758	33	175 071	234 051
Under 15	7	470	67	2182	311 714
15–24	87	5 160	59	35 625	409 483
25–44	247	11 257	46	93 771	379 640
45–64	205	5 537	27	38 101	185 859
65+	202	2 334	12	5392	26 693

* Includes 10% of all suicides that are attributed to schizophrenia.
† 6% discount rate.
Note: numbers may not add up to totals due to rounding.

Table 6. Direct costs of schizophrenia by treatment and source of payment (1985)

Treatment setting	Total	Federal	State and local	Private*
		Amount (millions)		
Total	$11 130	$2707	$4394	$4029
Mental health organizations	4288	733	2988	567
Short-stay hospitals	1706	693	277	736
Office-based physicians	239	17	6	216
Other professional services	373	26	9	338
Nursing homes	3414	946	1041	1427
Drugs	263	23	8	232
Support costs	847	269	65	513
		Percent distribution		
Total	100.0	24.3	39.5	36.2
Mental health organizations	100.0	17.1	69.7	13.2
Short-stay hospitals	100.0	40.6	16.2	43.2
Office-based physicians	100.0	7.1	2.5	90.4
Other professional services	100.0	7.0	2.4	90.6
Nursing homes	100.0	27.7	30.5	41.8
Drugs	100.0	8.7	3.1	88.2
Support costs	100.0	31.8	7.7	60.5

* Includes private health insurance, direct payments by patients, and philanthropy.

about the likely savings from programs that reduce incidence or improve outcome. According to Andrews *et al.* (1985) prevalence estimates are generally larger than incidence estimates. Our study presents current prevalence-based estimates of the societal costs of schizophrenia in the United States. Incidence-based estimates of schizophrenia also would be useful for policy purposes.

These cost estimates indicate that substantial potential savings to society could be gained by timely and appropriate treatment interventions to patients suffering from schizophrenia. In light of the high burden of schizophrenia on societal resources, more attention should be directed at comprehensive, research-based strategies to reduce the prevalence of this disorder in the United States.

REFERENCES

American Hospital Association (AHA) (1988). *Hospital Statistics, 1987 Edition.* Chicago, IL: American Hospital Association.

American Medical Assocation (AMA) (1987). *Socioeconomic Characteristics of Medical Practice.* Chicago, IL: American Medical Association.

American Psychiatric Association (APA). (1980). Committee on Nomenclature and Statistics. *Diagnostic and Statistical Manual,* 3rd edn (DSM-III). Washington, DC: American Psychiatric Association.

Andrews, G. (1991). The cost of schizophrenia revisited. *Schizophrenia Bulletin,* **17**, 389–394.

Andrews, G., Hall, W., Goldstein, G., Lapsley, H., Bartels, R., and Silove, D. (1985). The economic costs of schizophrenia. *Archives of General Psychiatry,* **42**, 537–544.

Bixby, A.K. (1988). Public social welfare expenditures, fiscal year 1985. *Social Security Bulletin,* **51**, 21–31.

Douglass, J.B., Kenney, G.M., and Miller, T.R. (1990). Which estimates of household production are best? *Journal of Forensic Economics,* **4**, 25–45.

Franks, D.D. (1990). Economic contribution of families caring for persons with severe and persistent mental illness. *Administration and Policy in Mental Health,* **18**, 9–18.

Goldburg, D. (1991). Cost effectiveness studies in the treatment of schizophrenia: a review. *Schizophrenia Bulletin,* **17**, 453–459.

Goodwin, F.K. (1990). *Manic Depressive Illness.* New York: Oxford University Press.

Health Care Financing Administration (1987). National health expenditures, 1986–2000. *Health Care Financing Review,* **8**, 1–36.

Hodgson, T.A. and Meiners, M. (1982). Cost-of-illness methodology: a guide to current practices and procedures. *Milbank Memorial Fund Quarterly,* **60**, 429–462.

Landefeld, J.G. and Seskin, E.P. (1982). The economic value of life: linking theory to practice. *American Journal of Public Health,* **72**(6), 555–566.

Levit, K.R., Lazenby, H.C., Cowan, C.A., and Letsch, S.W. (1991). National health expenditures, 1990. *Health Care Financing Review,* **13**, 29–54.

Mcguire, T.G. (1991). Measuring the economic costs of schizophrenia: a review. *Schizophrenia Bulletin,* **17**, 367–370.

Miller, L.S. and Kelman, S. (1992). Estimates of the loss of individual productivity from alcohol and drug abuse and from mental illness. In R.G. Frank and W.B. Manning, eds, *Economics and Mental Health,* pp. 91–129. Baltimore, MD: Johns Hopkins University Press.

Mishan, E.J. (1971). Evaluation of life and limb: a theoretical approach. *Journal of Political Economy,* **79**, 687–705.

National Center for Health Statistics (NCHS) (1987). Detailed diagnoses and procedures for patients discharged from short-stay hospitals, United States, 1985. *Vital and Health Statistics,* Series 13, No. 90. DHHS Pub. No. (PHS) 87-1751. Washington, DC: US Government Printing Office.

National Center for Health Statistics (NCHS) (1988). Office visits to psychiatrists, United States, 1985. *Vital and Health Statistics.* Series 13, No. 94. DHHS Pub. No. (PHS) 88-1755. Washington, DC: US Government Printing Office.

National Center for Health Statistics (NCHS) (1989). The national nursing home survey: 1985 summary for the United States. *Vital and Health Statistics,* Series 13, No. 97. DHHS Pub. No. (DHS) 89-1758. Washington, DC: US Government Printing Office.

National Institute of Mental Health (NIMH) (1980–85). *Epidemiologic Catchment Area (ECA) Program Community Surveys in Five Sites: St. Louis, MO; Baltimore, MD; New Haven, CT; Durham, NC; and Los Angeles, CA.* Public use data tapes. Rockville, MD: National Institute of Mental Health.

National Institute of Mental Health (NIMH) (1988). Specialty mental health organizations: United States, 1985. *Mental Health Statistical Note No. 189.* Rockville, MD: Department of Health and Human Services.

Pharmaceutical Data Services (1985). *National Prescription Survey.* Scotsdale, AZ: Pharmaceutical Data Services.

Regier, D.A., Boyd, J.H., Burke, J.D., *et al.* (1988). One-month prevalence of mental disorders in the United States. *Archives of General Psychiatry,* **45**, 977–986.

Rice, D.P. (1966). Estimating the cost of illness. *Health Economics Series,* No. 6. DHEW Pub. No. (PHS) 947-6. Rockville, MD: US Department of Health, Education and Welfare.

Rice, D.P., Hodgson, T.A., and Kopstein, A.N. (1985). The economic costs of illness: a replication and update. *Health Care Financing Review,* **7**, 61–80.

Rice, D.P., Kelman, S., Miller, L.S., and Dunmeyer, S. (1990). *The Economic Costs of Alcohol and Drug Abuse and Mental Illness: 1985*. Publication No. (ADM) 90-1694. Rockville, MD: US Alcohol, Drug Abuse, and Mental Health Administration.

Rice, D.P. and Kelman, S. (1989). Measuring comorbidity and overlap in the cost of hospitalization for alcohol and drug abuse and mental illness. *Inquiry*, **26**, 249–260.

Robinson, J.C. (1986). Philosophical origins of the economic value of life. *Milbank Memorial Fund Quarterly*, **64**, 133–135.

Schelling, T.C. (1968). The Life You Save May Be Your Own. In S.B. Chase, ed., *Problems in Public Expenditure Analysis*, pp. 127–176. Washington, DC: The Brookings Institution.

US Bureau of the Census (1987a). *Statistical Abstract of the United States: 1988*, 108th edn. Washington, DC: US Department of Commerce.

US Bureau of the Census (1987b). Money income of households, families, and persons in the United States, 1985. *Current Population Reports*, Series P-60, No. 156. US Government Printing Office, Washington, DC.

US Department of Justice (DOJ) (1985). *Crime in the United States, 1985: Uniform Crime Reports*. Federal Bureau of Investigation, Washington, DC

US Department of Justice (DOJ) (1988). *Profile of State Prison Inmates*, 1986. NCJ 109926. Bureau of Justice Statistics, Washington, DC.

Weisbrod, B.A. (1961). *Economics of Mental Health*. University of Pennsylvania Press, Philadelphia, PA.

World Health Organization (WHO) (1978). *International Classification of Diseases, Ninth Revision, Clinical Modification*.

27

Evaluating the Effectiveness of Services by Means of Mental Health Care Information Systems

WOLFRAM AN DER HEIDEN and HEINZ HÄFNER
Central Institute of Mental Health, Mannheim, Germany

INTRODUCTION

Empirical results derived from studies on institutionalism and schizophrenia such as those conducted by Wing and Brown (1970) were not the only factors inolved in initiating a fundamental reform in mental health care. The deplorable conditions in the traditional large psychiatric hospitals were just too obvious, the lack of alternative treatment within the community too apparent for there to be even a need to justify a change with empirical findings. When the reform began, it seemed like any measure which would prevent admission to a psychiatric hospital was appropriate, even if this went so far as to make inpatient treatment illegal.

However, it was impossible to prevent disillusionment. In the course of the last two decades, critics have even spoken of failure when taking a look at the chronically ill neglected within the community (Caton, 1981; Goldman *et al.*, 1983; Torrey, 1988). Instead of being grounded in scientific research and experience, decisions regarding mental health care have too often been dependent on the good will of those in charge or determined by a limited budget. Furthermore, pressure to make decisions based on the effectiveness of treatment and rehabilitation measures already taken have aggravated this trend.

EVALUATIVE RESEARCH

Science has long been able to use established methods of basic research when evaluating an isolated aspect of psychiatric treatment, particularly when testing the effectiveness of drug treatment. The experimental design with which it is possible to manipulate and control variables stands out as an example of this process. On the other hand, evaluative research, an area which tries to measure the effectiveness of complex treatment processes, services, or even a section of the care system itself, has long been neglected. The gap between the standards set in a laboratory experiment and the uncontrollable conditions of the social world outside of the laboratory seemed simply too big. However, Cambell and Stanley's work on quasi-experimental research design (1963) found that the differences between basic research and evaluative research are not qualitative

Handbook of Mental Health Economics and Health Policy, Volume I, Schizophrenia. Edited by M. Moscarelli, A. Rupp and N. Sartorius.
© 1996 John Wiley & Sons Ltd.

but quantitative. Thanks to sophisticated statistical methods and ingenious analytical strategies, the necessary causal statements for testing the effectiveness of treatment can also be made on the basis of data from observational studies. (Blalock, 1964, 1968, 1971; Kenny, 1979; Bentler & Woodward, 1979; an der Heiden *et al.*, 1989).

In contrast to the routine assessment that merely labels a patient "improved" or "deteriorated", evaluative research requires a scientific method which can measure the changes. According to Weiss (1972), the basic components of assessment are: measurement, outcome, explicit goals, and judging the program's worth. It is moreover indispensable to ascertain the internal validity of the results of evaluative research. More precisely, one must determine to what extent the changes were brought on by the measures assessed in the study instead of other (uncontrollable) factors.

The term "evaluative research" can be used for different approaches, depending on the process being assessed (Milne, 1987).

1 "Effort evaluation" examines the relationship between the characteristics and activities of a program or service (e.g. physician–patient ratio; utilization of beds) and the money spent on it (e.g. staff, equipment, expenditures, etc.).

2 "Process evaluation", in the traditional sense, is limited to a simple outline of services over time. An example of this would be recording the number of patients or the type and extent of the offered services. Indeed, this type of evaluation is descriptive rather than evaluative, providing none or little information on what brought about the observed changes. A more elaborate form deals with the relationship between the individual components of a program and the individual or collective outcome.

3 "Efficiency evaluation" establishes the relationship between the cost of a service and the goal it aims to achieve. Psychiatric care is efficient when better results are achieved on the same budget or the same results on a lower budget.

4 "Client satisfaction evaluation" examines the patients' acceptance of treatment measures.

5 "Outcome evaluation" is the core of evaluative research; in this case, the result of a measure or series of measures is in the focus of the study. This strategy is chosen if the efficiency of interventions or services is to be examined.

MENTAL HEALTH INFORMATION SYSTEMS

Reliable information and data collection systems are essential prerequisites for evaluative research, as they provide the basis for the description of the organization, operation, and use of mental health services.

Information systems exist at different levels. A system serves different purposes, depending on the level. A primary-level health information system is established when a hospital keeps records or files. It may serve as a monitoring advice when running hospital records as a uniform event reporting system. At this level it may also form the basis for the evaluation of an individual treatment service. Yet, conventional single-service information systems provide no insight into interactions between different professions, facilities, and agencies. The evaluation of a whole network of mental health care facilities therefore requires a linked uniform reporting system. In this way, a change in one section may be noticed in other parts (Eaton, 1993). In its most elaborate form, this system constitutes a comprehensive population-based case register.

A case register is a "patient-centered longitudinal record of contacts with a defined set of psychiatric services, originating from a defined population (... that has been used more than at one occasion)" (ten Horn, 1983; Jennings, 1985). Case registers have the following features (cf. Wing, 1986a; ten Horn, 1986; Häfner & an der Heiden, 1986; Dupont, 1987): a case register is patient-related instead of event-related. Each patient is assigned a singular code, to prevent him/her from being counted twice. When combining the longitudinal and cumulative collection data on services, a single patient, who has made contact with different agencies, can thus be traced. In addition, a case register is population-based, which makes it possible to calculate rates or to include information from other registers covering the same area. The standardized, prospective, cumulative, and population-based collection of patient-centered data, with the possibility of making record linkages covering different services and time periods, provide some of the essential prerequisites for the evaluation of, respectively, psychiatric services and parts of care systems. Even so, there are also a couple of formal differences.

1 Registers covering a defined district/area (Aberdeen, Aarhus, Baltimore, Camberwell, Cardiff, Groningen, Mannheim, Monroe County, Nottingham, Oxford, Salford, Sheffield, Southampton, Samsø, Worcester) or even a whole country or state (Denmark, Hawaii, Israel, Maryland, Scotland).

2 Registers covering certain specific disorders (Norway) or the entire field of mental illness.

3 Registers covering all psychiatric institutions, or only a part of the mental health care delivery system, for example inpatient treatment only. The register in Salford is the only one in which data from social services were routinely collected (Fryers & Wooff, 1989).

Besides the psychiatric case registers as defined in the narrow sense, there are further types of registers. The London Department of Health and Social Security, for instance, collects information on every patient admitted to or discharged from one of the approximately 500 state mental hospitals in England and Wales. This register not only contains data on age, gender, family status, occupation, etc., but also an ICD diagnosis and information on how the patient was referred to psychiatric treatment. The National Inpatient Register in the Netherlands also covers university and addiction clinics and produces annual tabulations for planning purposes. The Irish National Psychiatric Inpatients Reporting System covers both private and public services and publishes annual reports.

However, formal differences in the structure and methods of the different registers are not the only hindrance making direct comparisons difficult. One must also take into account a certain margin of error when using data on the evaluation of psychiatric services. Indeed, an essential characteristic of psychiatric case registers is their service orientation; information is obtained exclusively from affiliated services. Even if one excludes those case registers in which data are overtly limited to inpatient care (e.g. the Danish national register as well as the former register of psychoses in Norway), those who claim to cover a wider range of services still neglect outpatient care and even omit it completely. However, outpatient services are becoming more and more important, due to the shift from inpatient to community-based care. This fact is confirmed by a prospective study of a cohort of schizophrenic patients from Mannheim. Over a period of 18 months, 136 of 145 patients used medical outpatient services after discharge (an der Heiden *et al.*, 1989). Also, Engelhardt *et al.*, 1982) examined 646 chronically ill schizophrenics in New York and found that 20.6% had during 15 years never been in hospital for inpatient treatment.

With respect to the range of affiliated services another limitation results from not covering primary care data in most registers, representing a significant underreporting of milder cases of psychiatric morbidity, that may result in an underestimation of the real need for care. But also for major psychiatric disorders the exclusion of general medical care may lead to incomplete data on the actual extent of contacts with psychiatric services: one-quarter (24.7%) of all outpatient medical contacts in the mentioned Mannheim Schizophrenia Study was with physicians and not psychiatrists. Another limitation is that clinical diagnoses are not standardized. The usefulness of register data heavily relies upon the quality of the diagnoses made by staff members of the participating services (Jones *et al.*, 1986).

Unfortunately, since the 1950s and 1960s many of the case registers in the United States and England were forced to close due to lack of funds (e.g. Camberwell Case Register) and the implementation of data protection laws (Mannheim Case Register, National Icelandic Register). In Great Britain, of eight registers (see Gibbons *et al.*, 1984) only four managed to survive (Fryers & Greatorex, 1992): Aberdeen, Nottingham, Oxford, and Salford.

THE EVALUATION OF MENTAL HEALTH SERVICES

Before mental health care can be meaningfully evaluated, it is necessary to define the goals by which its effectiveness can be measured. It is not realistic to set a goal such as "a patient with treatment recovers faster than a patient without treatment" (WHO, 1991), unless these goals are translated in more specific and measurable objectives (Häfner and an der Heiden, 1995). As a general rule, it is necessary to know the goal of a procedure or service. Assessing a procedure for which no goals have been set is useless.

Besides this, the following characteristics of the treatment of (chronic) psychiatric patients have to be taken into account.

1 Ideally, a treatment measure is adapted to the patient: his/her individual needs and impairments as well as the abilities he or she retains. Consequently, the evaluation must allow for individual goals, as is done within the goal-attainment scaling (Kiresuk & Lund, 1979; Lewis *et al.*, 1987).

2 Therapeutical and rehabilitation measures not only attempt to reduce or even eliminate the effects of an illness. They often aim at developing abilities compensating for such effects as well as at the avoidance of possible primary and secondary disabilities.

3 The majority of therapeutic and rehabilitation efforts are set up to promote a medium- to long-term recovery.

Thus, for one case successful treatment means that symptoms have not deteriorated, and in another case it will mean that symptomatology has been significantly reduced. It is obvious that the operationalization of such goals for the use of health information system is very limited in practicality. The registers must confine themselves to a few "hard facts" for the sake of simplicity. There are on average between 20 and 40 items collected (Häfner & an der Heiden, 1986). They usually encompass sociodemographic characteristics such as age, gender, family status, occupation, etc., as well as administrative data, for instance how the patient was referred, and type and frequency of previous outpatient or inpatient treatments. Medical data are usually limited to the diagnosis. Besides the assignment of the main diagnosis, some registers also allow for the coding of additional diagnoses; in the Danish Case Register three additional diagnoses can be given (Dupont, 1979). However, registers do not usually incorporate data which would give insight on the patient's health status in more detail. Such data would be suitable as outcome measures. Technically, linking psychiatric case registers with registers containing data on the health status of patients would no longer pose a problem at present (cf. Gulbinat & Katz, 1986). However, because there are so few registers that cover long periods, there is not enough information on the feasibility of such a project. In addition, ethical issues and data protection laws have often hindered such linkages.

Despite these limitations, register data still seem to be the most suitable method for evaluating one of the main objectives of community psychiatric care: the prevention or reduction of the need of inpatient treatment.

ANALYSIS OF THE EFFECTIVENESS OF PSYCHIATRIC SERVICES ON THE BASIS OF HEALTH INFORMATION SYSTEMS DATA: EXAMPLES

Wing (1986b)—being aware of the limitations, both formal and with regard to the contents of data from health information systems—differentiated three methodical approaches within evaluative research: (i) monitoring; (ii) descriptive surveys; and (iii) evaluation.

MONITORING (PROCESS EVALUATION)

Monitoring usually involves the use of relatively "hard" structural indices of care—such as bed occupancy or number of physicians, nurses, social workers, etc. per 100 beds—for the description of developments in a given area over time. These indices can be broken down by age groups, length of stay in hospital, or diagnostic groups. This is this way that register data are most often used as a basis for planning purposes.

In many European countries, a change in policy in psychiatric care has been the subject of intensive case register analyses (e.g. Wing & Hailey, 1972; Hailey, 1973, 1974; Wing & Fryers 1976; Häfner & Klug, 1981, 1982; Giel & ten Horn, 1982; Dupont, 1983; Gibbons *et al.*, 1984; Giel, 1986; ten Horn *et al.*, 1986; Munk-Jørgensen, 1986; Fryers & Wooff, 1989; Tansella, 1991). A comparison of results, however, has turned out to be difficult. Besides the mentioned differences in the structure and method of the registers, the structure of psychiatric care also varies greatly between regions. These differences also become apparent when observing the large discrepancies in user rates. In Groningen, the average number of patients using outpatient, inpatient, or complementary services, first registered between 1974 and 1977, was 10.5 per 1000. For Camberwell and Salford, the comparable 1974 rates were 7.3 and

5.0 respectively (Giel & ten Horn, 1982). In Finland the rate of occupied beds in psychiatric hospitals was, even as late as 1980, not much different to that of the highest rate found in England in 1954 (Salokangas *et al.*, 1985).

The greater offer of psychiatric facilities, resulting from the building of community-based care structures, has in part led to a significant rise in the overall treatment prevalence. In Mannheim, for example, the number of outpatient and inpatient treatment episodes doubled between 1974 and 1977 (Häfner & Klug, 1982). The number of episodes of schizophrenic patients increased from 485 in 1974 to 756 in 1977 (Häfner & Klug, 1980)—while long-term hospital stays decreased over the same period. Similar results, at least in terms of a general trend, were achieved by other registers; following the establishment of a community psychiatric service in south Verona, the point prevalence of patients in out- or daypatient care rose by 51% from 239.8 per 100 000 in 1979/80 to 361.9 in 1987/88 (Tansella *et al.*, 1991). In England the situation is not as clear. An analysis of five British case registers (Salford, Southampton, Nottingham, Oxford, Aberdeen) for the period of 1976–81 (Gibbons *et al.*, 1984) showed the following development of yearly overall prevalence of inpatient and daypatient care, as well as contacts with outpatient clinics, domiciliary visits, and ward referrals (rates per 100 000 population): a slight to moderate rise in Nottingham (1441 + 4.7%), Aberdeen (1382 + 9.3%), Salford (1340 + 15%), virtually no change in Southampton (1657 + 1.4%), and Oxford (1320 + 0.4%). An additional analysis of the Salford case register (Fryers & Wooff, 1989) aiming to determine the point prevalence for the period 1976–87, demonstrated that the increase was mostly on the part of patients over 65 years of age.

In other countries, however, the wave of deinstitutionalization led to a massive decline in bed occupancy (Häfner, 1993): the rate per 100 000 population in England decreased between 1965 and 1992 from 276 to 94, in Denmark between 1970 and 1991 from 232 to 110 and in Germany ("old" federal states) between 1973 and 1990 from 170 to 107. It seems obvious that the decline was greater in countries starting out with the highest occupancy levels.

The developmental trends in the need for inpatient treatment is not as clear-cut when doing an analysis of regional and local case registers. These registers usually cover shorter periods of time. A comparison of utilization rates per 100 000 population from eight English case registers for the period 1977–83 (Jennings *et al.*, 1989) revealed rates ranging from slight decrease (Camberwell: 506–9%) to significant increase (Worcester: 420 + 50%), with part of the starting points in 1977 differing considerably (Oxford: 385; Southampton: 671). Five of eight registers showed an increase. In Mannheim the number of hospital admissions increased by 40% for patients of all diagnostic groups from 1974 to 1977, whereas the number of beds occupied by schizophrenic patients dropped from 243 to 209 (Häfner & Klug, 1980).

When a decrease in bed occupancy was accompanied by the establishment of community-based services, these results may suggest that the provision of services outside the hospital will reduce the risk of relapse and thus the probability of rehospitalization. However, the following analysis of a case register in Italy is an example of what kind of difficulties one can encounter when interpreting the data on different levels: The data of the case register in south Verona (Balestieri *et al.*, 1987), which was studied over a period of 6 years (1979–84), showed that parallel to the establishment of a community psychiatric service the rate of long-stay patients in the psychiatric hospital decreased steadily from approximately 55 per 100 000 to 35 per 100 000. Towards the end of the observation period, a dramatic rise in long-term community patients could be observed, i.e. patients who during 1 year were being treated almost incessantly by the community service. While a relationship between the two developments seems plausible, this decrease may be due to still another reason which seems just as likely: the authors themselves state that it may be due to Law no. 180 from 1979, which prohibited admissions to psychiatric hospitals in Italy. The problematic nature of an interpretation becomes obvious when looking at the development of these rates on a yearly basis. The number of "long-term" patients in the community dropped from approximately 80 per 100 000 to approximately 50 per 100 000 and did not rise again until 2 years before the end of the observation period, when it reached the original value once again.

On the whole, the building of community-based mental health care systems in many European countries did not result in the hoped for decrease in the need for inpatient psychiatric treatment, as is evident from case register analysis. Where the decline in bed occupancy is especially marked, e.g. in England on the national level, it is more likely due to the reduction in hospital beds than the reduced need for psychiatric care on account of extramural measures. As Wing (1986b, p. 38) already stated, administrative indices of this kind can be used to monitor trends, but, "... they cannot allocate value to the policies or practices that are responsible for those trends occurring." The direction of causes and effects cannot be specified without further investigations.

DESCRIPTIVE SURVEYS

Descriptive surveys use health information system data as a framework for carrying out studies on special issues. For example, case register data are used to draw a subsample or a random sample of patients, who are then interviewed to investigate factors that seem important for a better understanding of the observed trends. Descriptive surveys thus allow for the collection of data that seem more suitable for the evaluation of services. This is for example patients' data on symptomatology, impairments, disabilities, or even on consumer satisfaction and quality of life.

One of the first studies of this kind has been provided by Wing *et al.* (1972). Using data from the Camberwell Psychiatric Case Register, out of a total of 380 schizophrenic patients recorded in 1968 they identified 75 patients, who had been living at home for at least 1 year without occupation. Twenty-eight of these patients were chosen to evaluate the effectiveness of preparatory training for occupational rehabilitation by a day clinic program within a quasi-experimental design. A follow-up evaluation after 2 years indicated no differences in employment status or social adjustment against the control condition not being involved in the day clinic program—four patients in each group were employed. But the study yielded some other interesting results: it seemed obvious that the intensive methods of social intervention in the quasi-experimental group led to a deterioration and to acute relapses. In addition, five patients were found to have committed suicide. It was concluded that in chronic schizophrenic patients special attention has to be paid to an environment in which handicaps are accepted and excessive social stimulation is avoided. Wykes (1982) also used the Camberwell Psychiatric Case Register to select a sample of long-stay patients in order to evaluate a new hostel-ward as an alternative to long-stay hospital care. The sample consisted of those patients who were not long-stay patients on December 31, 1970 (known as "old" long-stay patients) but had been inpatients for more than 1 year on December 31, 1977 ("new" long-stay patients). Among other things he tried to answer the following questions: (i) Is there any decrease in the severity of disability in the hostel ward residents compared with those staying in hospital? (ii) What is the outcome, over a 3-year-period, of candidates transferred to the hostel ward, compared with the rest? Out of a total of 29 patients who met the inclusion criteria 14 were transferred to the new facility, 15 patients remained in hospital serving as a control group. All but six had a diagnosis of schizophrenia. Apart from data routinely available on the Camberwell register additional data were collected concerning basic social and demographic characteristics, social performance, type of care received, and patients' attitudes. After three and a half years no one from the hostel-ward group had to be transferred back to conventional wards. Not only this, but eight patients could be discharged during the period of observation, two of whom were readmitted and two of whom had died. On average patients improved in social behavior compared with those who stayed in conventional wards.

A more recent study carried out by Ferguson *et al.* (1992) aimed at the evaluation of a new psychiatric service based on general practice psychiatric units in Nottingham. This new service, built up between 1979 and 1981, consists of five general practitioner psychiatric clinics augmented by a day hospital and other community facilities. The community psychiatric service was compared with a conventional hospital-oriented service. Ferguson and his coworkers used the Nottingham Psychiatric Case Register to identify two cohorts of patients (in total 272 patients) who were treated in either service during 1983, matched by age, sex, and type of contact. According to ICD most of the patients had neurotic disorders (41%), affective disorders (19%), or schizophrenia (13%). Follow-up data from 181 patients were obtained between 1986 and 1988 including measures of psychopathology and social functioning. At follow-up 33% of the "community" cohort were still being seen by a member of the psychiatric team, compared with only 6% of the "hospital" cohort. Both patient groups achieved similar outcomes concerning psychopathology and social functioning. Although patients expressed acceptance of both services at an equal level the main differences occurred with respect to more frequent use of day-hospital facilities, wider involvement of all members of the psychiatric team, willingness to maintain contact, and the use of more senior medical staff in the delivery of outpatient care, in favor of the community service.

Mignolli *et al.* (1991) evaluated psychopathological and social outcome in a cohort of patients suffering from schizophrenic psychosis by comparing mental hospital patients and patients treated by community services in south Verona. The South Verona Community Psychiatric Service was established in 1980 and today it comprises a broad range of psychiatric services including a mental health center providing day care and rehabilitation, a domiciliary service supplying both emergency and elective care, an outpatient department, and a 15-bed inpatient unit at the University general hospital (Tansella *et al.*, 1991). In addition there exists a liaison service for other medical and surgical departments and a psychiatric emergency room service at the hospital. All south Verona residents who in 1979 had at least one contact with the services monitored by the South Verona Psychiatric Case Register and received a diagnosis of "schizophrenia or other functional non-affective psychoses" according to ICD-9 were included in the study, comprising a total of 60 patients. Forty-nine patients were living in the community ("community" patients), 11 were living in the hospital (patients). Fifty patients could be traced and 46 could be interviewed in 1986. At the time of follow-up nine were long-stay inpatients—eight had been continuously in hospital since inclusion—and 41 lived outside the hospital. In MH patients there were no changes in the sociodemographic characteristics during the follow-up period. The major changes in the "community" patients group occurred in work status: only three of 14 patients who had a regular job in 1979 were still working, only two patients had found a job meanwhile. In total, the comparison between mental hospital and community patients revealed that the clinical and social conditions and the psychiatric status of the mental hospital patients remained stable at a low level through the years. In contrast, the sociodemographic characteristics in the community patients showed a greater variation: in 1986 more patients lived alone and most of those formerly holding jobs had lost employment. Despite prolonged contacts with community-oriented psychiatric services patients were characterized by disturbances in occupational and heterosexual role behavior and were socially withdrawn.

Since 1985 the Team for the Assessment of Psychiatric Services (TAPS) has been evaluating the closure of two psychiatric hospitals, Friern and Claybury, in north-east London (Leff, 1993). The aim of the project is to examine the consequences of this measure, the three main concerns being (O'Driscoll & Leff, 1993): (i) assessment of the well-being of the patients in the new community services after discharge; (ii) understanding the processes by which significant decisions in planning are made; and (iii) estimating community costs of closing psychiatric hospitals. After the decision to close down the two hospitals had been made, they had a total of just under 2000 beds. Long-stay patients (duration of stay more than 1 year) occupied about one-half of these beds. This group—all of them long-stay patients under the age of 65, including brain-damaged adults and those with presenile dementia—constituted the core group of the evaluation. Also included were patients over 65 years who were not demented. The naturalistic design matched each discharged patient with a "control patient" with similar characteristics (age, gender, diagnosis, duration of stay, etc.) but remaining as an inpatient. After a baseline measure of all relevant variables the "movers" were then to be reinterviewed 12 months after discharge and to be compared with their matched controls so as to assess the effects of the changing service. The following areas were taken into account for the outcome measurement: personal data and psychiatric history, physical health, mental state, social behavior, patient attitude to services, environmental autonomy, and social networks. The discharged patients were cared for in different services, according to their needs. Most were accommodated in various kinds of staffed group homes. An analysis of data of 260 patients of the first 3 yearly cohorts showed that 12 months after discharge the "leavers" had a larger social network and were more autonomous than the matched controls (Anderson *et al.*, 1993). There were no differences in clinical features. The comparison of the two groups was, however, complicated by the fact that the "leavers" differed in essential characteristics from those staying behind: they were younger, their overall duration of stay was shorter, they were less often diagnosed with schizophrenia, and their social network was larger (Jones, 1993).

An evaluative study on the basis of data from all psychiatric services of a London district has been carried out since 1992. The PRiSM (Psychiatric Research in Service Measurement) research team is working on evaluating a community mental health service recently built up in the Nunhead sector. To this end, all persons with serious mental health problems are established on the basis of case notes from all in- and outpatient as well as complementary psychiatric services in the Nunhead area. Then, a random sample of patients from the basic group is drawn to be interviewed on their biography and their illness. A follow-up study after 4 years should provide answers on the patients' course of illness and the effectiveness of the community service (reduction of inpatient treatment, costs, strain on family members, etc.). To evaluate the effectiveness of the service, a parallel data collection will be performed in another London sector (west Norwood), where the population has a similar social structure, but where there is no community mental health service. Even though as yet there are no results available, the method and the control group design of the study seem appropriate for the evaluation of a community service.

In an equally ongoing control group study, Wiersma and colleagues (1989) examine the effects of a new kind of day treatment combined with ambulatory and domiciliary care offered by a social psychiatric service together with the outpatient department of a hospital. The service is being compared with the conventional 24-hour residential care in the mental hospital, including routine outpatient aftercare. An essential characteristic of the study is the random allocation of patients according to the terms of the study. After index admission each patient is reinterviewed three more times over a 2-year period. The information gathered should show the different effects of the new care form on different levels (patient level, family level, care level, institutional level, level of the regional mental health care systems). During the whole follow-up period, the utilization of mental health services will be recorded by means of a psychiatric case register.

A somewhat different approach was chosen in Mannheim (Häfner & an der Heiden, 1989): schizophrenic patients were studied to determine the effects of psychiatric treatment in the community on outcome measures, such as duration and frequency of rehospitalizations and symptomatology, and to find out whether community care can be provided less expensively than hospital care. In this study case register data were used to control for population-related changes in the utilization of mental health services while the cohort data were used to test the effectiveness of outpatient care. Between 1973 and 1984 the number of beds in specialized homes for psychiatric patients in Mannheim increased from 19 to 153, and the number of places in group homes increased from 0 to 60. As a consequence between 1973 and 1980 the number of hospital beds occupied by schizophrenic patients on a given day dropped by some 25% while the number of schizophrenics in psychiatric homes during the same period almost doubled. Thus case register data provided information about the respective proportions of schizophrenic patients in (long-term) hospital care and complementary accommodation home treatment care and the trends over time. In order to gain insight into the outpatient medical sector of care we supplemented the case register data with a prospective cohort study. The cohort consisted of all Mannheim residents with a diagnosis of schizophrenia, who were admitted to inpatient facilities serving the Mannheim area during 1 year (October 1977–September 1978). The cohort patients were reassessed three times at 6-monthly intervals resulting in an observation period of 18 months for each patient. During this time the utilization of all kinds of care was registered by means of a special record system. A total of 145 schizophrenics—of group of 195 patients meeting the inclusion criteria—could be followed up for the whole interval. A model-based analysis, controlling for the patient's psychopathological status, living conditions, and chronicity of illness, revealed a relationship between increased psychiatric outpatient treatment and reduced hospital care, as reflected by the total duration of hospitalization during the last year of the observation period. It also showed a relationship between psychiatric aftercare and a reduction of psychopathological symptoms and disease-related behavior.

The quantified utilization data of our cohort in a next step formed the basis for a case-related calculation of the direct costs of community treatment. While the mean total cost of community care—including readmissions to inpatient treatment because of relapses—was about 43% of total costs of continued hospital care, in eight patients the actual costs indeed were above the threshold of continued inpatient treatment. So, in combination with the findings from the case register analysis, this may be interpreted in a way that, as a larger number of chronic patients are discharged from hospital into community care, a larger proportion have more serious disorders and are in need of more intensive care. So, one can expect that increasing the share of long-term institutionalized schizophrenic patients in the community will consequently result in a rise of the mean costs of community care.

DISCUSSION

Undoubtedly, the main use of psychiatric case registers is monitoring. Provided that it is possible to include all health care services, the analysis of utilization can give valuable hints on medium- and long-term trends on different care levels. They allow routine longitudinal and cross-sectional analyses which cannot be replaced by any other method of data collection. Examples of this are analyses of long-stay patients in hospitals or changed utilization patterns following the establishment of new facilities. As of yet, the emphasis has been on description. The analysis of the effectiveness of types of service, however, requires a procedure that is characterized by the generation and confirmation of hypotheses.

In a preface of the Monograph Supplement 2 of *Psychological Medicine* regarding two surveys from Camberwell, Wing (1982, p. 2) wrote: "Exploratory studies, even those with an epidemiological base, specified samples and a replicable methodology, cannot supply final answers to the questions they are designed to investigate. Indeed, they are of little use unless they lead to further studies, including some with more controlled designs, which will put to test the ideas and hypotheses they have generated." This statement on the one hand considers the boundaries of monitoring, on the other it stresses the hypothesis-generating character of descriptive surveys and calls for further studies. This we are doing at the present time.

Measured by what is required from evaluative research, mental health information systems only in part provide the prerequisites needed for evaluating the effectiveness of a service. To establish essential dependent and independent variables, additional information needs to be collected in further studies. Suchman (1967) once saw "evaluative research" as a bridge between basic and applied research: applying the best methods and theories from basic research in "natural" settings. A critical look at the evaluative approach in studies on mental health care shows that it is still a long way from this function. Changes in utilization are still recorded in a descriptive way (monitoring, or "process evaluation" in the traditional sense). Although these descriptions are indispensable in the framework of evaluative research, as they supply the basic information making possible a testing of effectiveness of single services or parts of care systems, they are unable to take the place of evaluative research.

REFERENCES

Anderson, J.G., Dayson, D., Wills, W., Gooch, C., Margolis, D., O'Driscoll, C., and Leff, J.P. (1993). The TAPS Project. 13: Clinical and social outcome of long-stay psychiatric patients after one year in the community. *British Journal of Psychiatry*, **162** (Suppl. 19), 45–56.

Balestrieri, M., Micciolo, R., and Tansella, M. (1987). Long-stay and long-term psychiatric patients in an area with a community-based system of care. A register follow-up study. *International Journal of Social Psychiatry*, **33**, 251–262.

Bentler, P.M. and Woodward, J.A. (1979). Nonexperimental evaluation research: Contributions of causal modelling. In L-E. Datta and R. Perloff, eds, *Improving Evaluations*, pp. 71–102. Beverly Hills: Sage Publications.

Blalock, H.M. (1964). *Causal Inferences in Nonexperimental Research*. Chapel Hill: University of North Carolina Press.

Blalock, H.M. (1968). Theory building and causal inference. In H.M. Blalock and A.B. Blalock, eds, *Methodology in Social Research*, pp. 155–198. New York: McGraw-Hill.

Blalock, H.M. (1971). *Causal Models in the Social Sciences*. London: Macmillan.

Campbell, D.T. and Stanley, J.C. (1963). Experimental and quasi-experimental designs for research on teaching. In N.L. Gage, ed., *Handbook of Research on Teaching*. Chicago: MacNally.

Caton, C.L.M. (1981). The new chronic patient and the system of community care. *Hospital and Community Psychiatry*, **32**, 475–478.

Dupont, A. (1979). Psychiatric case registers. In H. Häfner, ed., *Estimating Needs for Mental Health Care*, pp. 43–51. Berlin: Springer.

Dupont, A. (1983). A national psychiatric case register as a tool for mental health planning, research and administration. The Danish Model. In E.M. Laska, W.H. Gulbinat, and D.A. Regier, eds, *Information Support to Mental Health Programs*, pp. 257–274. New York: Human Sciences Press.

Eaton, W.W. (1993). *Strategies of measurement*. Paper presented at the 'NATO Advanced Research Workshop' on 'Research Evaluation of Community Psychiatric Services', Il Ciocco/Italy, September 3–7.

Engelhardt, D.M., Rosen, B., Feldman, J., Engelhardt, J.A.Z., and Cohen, P. (1982). A 15-year followup of 646 schizophrenic outpatients. *Schizophrenia Bulletin*, **8**, 493–503.

Ferguson, B., Cooper, S., Brothwell, J., Markantonakis, A., and Tyrer, P. (1992). The clinical evaluation of a new community psychiatric service based on general practice psychiatric clinics. *British Journal of Psychiatry*, **160**, 493–497.

Fryers, T. and Greatorex, I. (1992). Case registers and mental health information systems. In G. Thornicroft, C.R. Brewin, and J.K. Wing, eds, *Measuring Mental Health Needs*, pp. 81–98. London: Gaskell, Royal College of Psychiatrists.

Fryers, T. and Wooff, K. (1989a). A decade of mental health care in an urban community. In J.K. Wing, ed., *Health Services Planning and Research: Contributions from Psychiatric Case Registers*, pp. 31–52. London: Gaskell, Royal College of Psychiatrists.

Fryers, T. and Wooff, K. (1989b). A decade of mental health care in an English urban community: patterns and trends in Salford, 1976–87. In J.K. Wing, ed., *Health Services Planning and Research. Contributions from Psychiatric Case Registers*, pp. 31–52. London: Gaskell, Royal College of Psychiatrists.

Gibbons, J., Jennings, C., and Wing, J.K. (1984). *Psychiatric Care in Eight Register Areas, 1976–1981*. Southampton: University of Southampton, Department of Psychiatry.

Giel, R. (1986). Care of chronic mental patients in the Netherlands. *Social Psychiatry*, **21**, 25–32.

Giel, R. and ten Horn, G.H.M.M. (1982). Patterns of mental health care in a Dutch register. *Social Psychiatry*, **17**, 117–123.

Goldman, H.H., Adams, N.H., and Taube, C.A. (1983). Deinstitutionalization: The data demythologized. *Hospital and Community Psychiatry*, **34**, 129–134.

Gulbinat, W.H. and Katz, A. (1986). Linkage of psychiatric case registers with other data bases: introduction. In G.H.M.M. ten Horn, R. Giel, W.H. Gulbinat, and J.H. Henderson, eds, *Psychiatric Case Registers in Public Health. A Worldwide Inventory 1960–1985*, pp. 200–216. Amsterdam: Elsevier.

Hailey, A.M. (1973). The chronic mental hospital population: a six-year follow-up study. *British Journal of Preventative and Social Medicine*, **27**, 255–260.

Hailey, A.M. (1974). The new chronic psychiatric population. *British Journal of Preventative and Social Medicine*, **28**, 180–186.

Häfner, H. (1993). *Psychiatric rehabilitation – General issues*. Paper presented at the AEP-Symposium, Strasbourg/France, November 19–20

Häfner, H. and an der Heiden, W. (1986). The contribution of European case registers to research on schizophrenia. *Schizophrenia Bulletin*, **12**, 26–51.

Häfner, H. and an der Heiden, W. (1989). Effectiveness and cost of community care for schizophrenic patients. *Hospital and Community Psychiatry*, **40**, 59–63.

Häfner, H. and an der Heiden, W. (1995). Background and goals of evaluative research in community psychiatry. In H.C. Knudsen and G. Thornicroft, eds, *Mental Health Service Evaluation*, Cambridge University Press (in press).

Häfner, H. and Klug, J. (1980). Der Aufbau einer gemeindenahen Versorgung in Mannheim—erste Ergebnisse einer wissenschaftlichen Begleitung. In H. Häfner, W. Picard, and Aktion Psychisch Kranke e.V., eds, *Psychiatrie 5 Jahre nach der Enquete. Tagungsberichte Bd. 5*, pp. 29–42. Köln: Rheinland Verlag.

Häfner, H. and Klug, J. (1982). The impact of an expanding community mental health service on patterns of bed usage: evaluation of a four-year period of implementation. *Psychological Medicine*, **12**, 177–190.

an der Heiden, W., Krumm, B., and Häfner, H. (1989). *Die Wirksamkeit ambulanter psychiatrischer Versorgung. Ein Modell zur Evaluation extramuraler Dienste*. Berlin: Springer-Verlag.

ten Horn, G.H.M.M. (1983). *Psychiatric Case Registers. Report on a Working Group. Mannheim, May 1983*. Copenhagen: World Health Organization.

ten Horn, G.H.M.M. (1986). A classification of different types of psychiatric case registers. In G.H.M.M. ten Horn, R. Giel, W.H. Gulbinat, and J.H. Henderson, eds, *Psychiatric Case Registers in Public Health. A Worldwide Inventory 1960–1985*, pp. 388–401. Amsterdam: Elsevier.

ten Horn, G.H.M.M., Giel, R., Gulbinat, W.H., and Henderson, J.H. (1986). *Psychiatric Case Registers in Public Health.* Amsterdam: Elsevier.

Jennings, C. (1985). *The Use of Psychiatric Case Registers in Public Health. Report on a WHO Working Group. Groningen, September 1985.* Groningen: WHO Collaborating Centre, Department of Social Psychiatry.

Jennings, C., Der G., Robinson, C., Rose, S., de Alarcon, J., Hunter, D. Hollyday, R., and Moss, N. (1989). In-patient statistics from eight psychiatric case registers, 1977–83. In J.K. Wing, ed., *Health Services Planning and Research. Contributions from Psychiatric Case Registers,* pp. 13–20. London: Gaskell, Royal College of Psychiatrists.

Jones, D. (1993). The TAPS Project. 11: The selection of patients for reprovision. *British Journal of Psychiatry,* **162** (Suppl. 19), 36–39.

Jones, S.J., Cooper, J.E., and Davis, N. (1986). Diagnostic validity and comparability of register data. In G.H.M.M. ten Horn, R. Giel, W.H. Gulbinat, and J.H. Henderson, eds, *Psychiatric Case Registers in Public Health: A Worldwide Inventory 1969–1985,* pp. 175–178. Amsterdam: Elsevier.

Kenny, D.A. (1979). *Correlation and Causality.* New York: John Wiley.

Kiresuk, T.J. and Lund, S. (1979). Goal attainment scaling: Research, evaluation, and utilization. In C. Schulberg and F. Baker, eds, *Program Evaluation in the Health Fields,* Vol. 2. New York: Human Sciences.

Leff, J.P. (1993). *The TAPS Project: Evaluating Community Placement of Long-stay Psychiatric Patients. British Journal of Psychiatry (Suppl. 19).* London: The Royal College of Psychiatrists.

Lewis, A.B., Spencer, J.H., Haas, G.L., and DiVittis, A. (1987). Goal attainment scaling. Relevance and replicability in follow-up of inpatients. *Journal of Nervous and Mental Disease,* **175**, 408–418.

Mignolli, G., Faccincani, C., and Platt, S. (1991). Psychopathology and social performance in a cohort of patients with schizophrenic psychosis. A seven-year follow-up. In M. Tansella, ed., *Community-based Psychiatry: Long-term Patterns of Care in South-Verona. Psychological Medicine Monograph (Suppl. 19),* pp. 17–26. Cambridge University Press.

Milne, D. (1987). *Evaluating Mental Health Practice: Methods and Applications.* London: Croom Helm.

Munk-Jørgensen, P. (1986). Schizophrenia in Denmark: incidence and utilization of psychiatric institutions. *Acta Psychiatrica Scandinavica,* **73**, 172–180.

O'Driscoll, C. and Leff, J.P. (1993). The TAPS Project. 8: Design of the research study on the long-stay patients. *British Journal of Psychiatry,* **162** (Suppl. 19), 18–24.

Salokangas, R.K.R., Der, G., and Wing, J.K. (1985). Community services in England and Finland. *Social Psychiatry,* **20**, 23–29.

Suchman, E.A. (1967). *Evaluative Research. Principles and Practice in Public Health Service and Social Action Programs.* New York: Russell Sage Foundation.

Tansella, M. (1991). *Community Based Psychiatry: Long-term Patterns of Care in South Verona. Psychological Medicine Monograph (Suppl. 19).* Cambridge University Press.

Tansella, M., Balestrieri, M., Meneghelli, G., and Micciolo, R. (1991). Trends in the provision of care. In M. Tansella, ed., *Community-based Psychiatry: Long-term Patterns of Care in South-Verona,* pp. 6–16. Cambridge University Press.

Torrey, E.F. (1988). *Nowhere to Go.* New York: Harper & Row.

Weiss, C.H. (1972). *Evaluation Research.* Englewood Cliffs, NJ: Prentice-Hall.

WHO (1991). *Evaluation of Methods for the Treatment of Mental Disorders.* Report of a Scientific Group on the Treatment of Psychiatric Disorders. WHO Technical Report Series 812. Geneva: WHO.

Wiersma, D., Kluiter, H., and Nienhuis, F.J. (1989). *Day-Treatment with Community Care as an Alternative to Standard Hospitalisation: An Experiment in the Netherlands.* Groningen: Department of Social Psychiatry, University of Groningen.

Wing, J.K. (1982). *Long-term Community Care: Experience in a London Borough. Psychological Medicine (Suppl. 2).* Cambridge University Press.

Wing, J.K. (1986a). Epidemiological research using psychiatric case registers. In G.H.M.M. ten Horn, R. Giel, W.H. Gulbinat, and J.H. Henderson, eds, *Psychiatric Case Registers in Public Health. A Worldwide Inventory 1960–1985,* pp. 14–25. Amsterdam: Elsevier.

Wing, J.K. (1986b). The cycle of planning and evaluation. In G. Wilkinson and H. Freeman, eds, *The Provision of Mental Health Services in Britain: The Way Ahead,* pp. 35–48, Oxford: Gaskell, Royal College of Psychiatrists.

Wing, J.K. and Brown, G.W. (1970). *Institutionalism and Schizophrenia.* London: Cambridge University Press.

Wing, J.K. and Fryers, T. (1976). *Psychiatric Services in Camberwell and Salford. Statistics from the Camberwell and Salford Psychiatric Registers,* 1964–1974. London: MRC Social Psychiatry Unit; and Manchester: Department of Community Medicine.

Wing, J.K. and Hailey, A.M. (1972). *Evaluating a Community Psychiatric Service: The Camberwell Register, 1964–1971.* London: Oxford University Press.

Wing, L., Wing, J.K., Stevens, B., and Griffiths, D. (1972). An epidemiological and experimental evaluation of industrial rehabilitation of chronic psychotic patients in the community. In J.K. Wing and A. Hailey, eds, *Evaluating a Community Psychiatric Service,* pp. 283–308. London: Oxford University Press.

Wykes, T. (1982). A hostel-ward for "new" long-stay patients: an evaluation study of a "ward in a house". In J.K. Wing, ed., *Long-term Community Care: Experience in a London Borough. Psychological Medicine Monograph (Suppl. 2),* pp. 57–97. Cambridge University Press.

28

Measuring Services Use and Delivery

WILLIAM A. HARGREAVES and MARTHA SHUMWAY
School of Medicine, University of California, San Francisco, California, USA

TEH-WEI HU
School of Public Health, University of California at Berkeley, California, USA

INTRODUCTION

This chapter discusses methods for measuring the *amount* and *kind* of services provided to persons with schizophrenia. Information on the amount of service consumed is used to compute total cost for each study subject. Information on the kind of service consumed enables the investigator to confirm that the service models being compared were implemented as intended.

Amount of service is counted in "units" of various types. These units are then assigned a monetary value to compute total cost of resources consumed by each study subject. The first part of this chapter is intended to expand on methods for counting units, as described in Chapter 29.

The kind of services consumed by study subjects is partly described by the types of units consumed. However, the central components of services, which define specfic treatment "models," will often need to be studied in more detail, both quantitatively and qualitatively, in order to specify the kinds of service models to which study results can be generalized. Sometimes this is a matter of reminding users of study results about the realities of actual services delivery in routine practice settings outside the research clinic or university hospital. Just as often it is a message to those who administer routine services, suggesting management principles and monitoring controls that may be necessary in order to apply an innovative service model effectively or efficiently. The second part of this chapter, "measuring service implementation," discusses various approaches to measuring the character of services.

MEASURING AMOUNT OF SERVICE USE

IDENTIFYING THE UNITS TO BE COUNTED

To design cost-effectiveness analyses to fit a particular study or site, one must enumerate the types of service patients may receive, and what the countable unit is for each service. One should also enumerate the possible sources of patient income. An example of a service list is provided in chapter 29. It may help to start with such a list, eliminate service types that have no local counterpart, add local services not on the list, adjust the names to match those used locally, and check that the unit listed for each service is the one used locally.

Research activities, such as study recruitment or assessment interviews and special laboratory tests,

Handbook of Mental Health Economics and Health Policy, Volume I, Schizophrenia. Edited by M. Moscarelli, A. Rupp and N. Sartorius.
© 1996 John Wiley & Sons Ltd.

should not be included in treatment costs. While research contacts with patients or their families may have clinical benefits, the authors recommend that one not count them when the primary purpose of these contacts is research data collection.

UNITS THAT REPRESENT PROMINENT COSTS

The second step is to select for special attention the units likely to represent large proportions of the total cost. Such units may usefully be separated into subunits to gain a more detailed picture of costs. Cost estimation methods for such high cost or frequently used service units need to be as accurate as possible, as errors in these estimates could greatly distort findings. One may estimate the cost of minor components more approximately without jeopardizing the overall accuracy of the analysis. In many communities mental health service utilization is easier to track than other types of costs.

In designing a study one will usually disaggregate prominent cost elements. For example, long-stay hospital patients who improve with an innovative treatment but who remain in the hospital may require fewer hours of seclusion, physical restraint, or special observation by nursing staff. Transfer to a unit with a lower staff–patient ratio may reflect this improvement. Thus it may be useful to record days that patients spend on specific inpatient wards and divide wards into groups with different cost levels. It may also be worthwhile to measure seclusion, restraint, and observation costs separately, and not include them in the per diem rate for an inpatient day. A study of patients recruited in the community may require a different emphasis. If hospital days are fewer, one may need to disaggregate outpatient and case management units.

When disaggregating units of service, it is necessary to guard against "double counting" costs. For example, the average hospital day may cost a certain amount, including overhead, food, lodging, and average staff effort. When a patient spends time in seclusion, restraint, or special observation, requiring more staff contact, the resources consumed on that hospital day increase. If one treats separately these added costs, one should subtract the average cost of seclusion, restraint, and special observation from the estimate of the hospital per diem cost.

In drug studies it will usually be important to disaggregate costs of antipsychotic medications and any related clinical laboratory work. One may wish to record the dose level of antipsychotic drugs and the concurrent use of other psychoactive drugs, with more approximate data on subsidiary drugs. One can then model the impact on costs of price changes for antipsychotic medications. One can also assess the relative adequacy of pharmacologic treatment in naturalistic settings from the analysis of detailed information on antipsychotic drug dose, when examining service packages whose aim is to optimize the delivery of pharmacological treatment (Klein, 1993).

DATA SOURCES FOR COUNTING UNITS

The primary potential sources of data on services are: (i) agency records; (ii) interviews of patients and family members; (iii) existing databases; and (iv) various *ad hoc* methods for gathering information that eludes the first three approaches. One cannot rely completely on any one of these sources, and comparsons of multiple sources is necessary for accuracy in the information obtained. The patient's permission to contact providers, releases to obtain medical or billing records, and permission to use databases linked to the patient's social security number or other universal identifier are important tools.

AGENCY RECORDS

This source is an important one, but one that shows the most variation across jurisdictions. Some governmental units have well developed service information systems that gather individual-level data centrally and provide a useful resource for research. Ideally, each unit of service is identified with a different accounting cost center. Other localities have no reporting system or only an aggregate reporting system that may require units-of-service data to be abstracted from paper records at each provider organization. If there are many community providers, this will increase the cost and difficulty of the study. When designing new data collection methods that one hopes will be compatible with mental health reporting systems, one should be aware of existing data standards regarding such systems (e.g., Leginski *et al.*, 1989). In most services studies, however, it is not feasible to install new patient contact reporting systems. One must depend on existing agency records.

PATIENT AND FAMILY INTERVIEW

While patient and family interviews are a standard feature of effectiveness studies, they also have a part to play in measuring services utilization and patient income. It is hard for an interview respondent to remember specific information about the dates and amounts of services consumed. The primary value of interview report is to alert project staff to providers from whose records utilization data should be obtained.

Family interviews in effectiveness studies have been used for two rather different purposes: obtaining the family member's report of cognitive, social, and occupational functioning of the patient; and obtaining cost and "family burden" information. Assessing either kind of information takes considerable interview time, and investigators have usually chosen to focus on one type of information or the other. In cost-effectiveness studies the more common choice is to focus on family burden.

An example of a widely used patient interview as a source of effectiveness measures is the Quality of Life Interview (QOLI), an hour-long interview typically carried out every few months (Lehman, 1988). The QOLI also serves as a source of data on services utilization, although this is not its primary purpose. It is an occasion to identify additional service providers and to obtain releases to contact providers not included in the original consent process. In addition to providing measures of six areas of social and instrumental functioning, the QOLI yields indications of mental health, other health, social, and legal services use, measures of patient time burden, and sources and amounts of income.

The Family Burden Interview Schedule (FBIS) is a 30-minute interview completed periodically in person or by telephone, and is an example of a way to obtain both financial and psychological burden measures (Tessler *et al.*, 1992). While not a primary source of utilization data, providers are noted and this alerts one to seek utilization information. The FBIS estimates two aspects of cost, family time burden and family financial burden related to the care of the patient. An additional focus of the FBIS is family psychological burden, an aspect of effectiveness rather than cost.

Modified interview methods for assessing patient and family costs have been described (e.g., Clark & Drake, 1994). The reader is advised to examine available assessment approaches and choose measures that best fit the aims of the planned study.

Clark *et al.* (1994) suggest several ways to improve the validity of data on resources used. We have already noted the value of interviews in prompting a search of primary data sources. Recall is also a problem when interviewing about frequent events. Infrequent but prominent events like a hospitalization or an arrest will be remembered over several months, but frequent events are best recorded with a time-sampling technique rather than trying to recall the entire interval since the last interview. It is preferable to ask only about the past 2 weeks on such items as family assistance with transportation, and total hours of care. Clark *et al.* (1994) found that asking the "typical" level leads to reports of fewer hours of care.

STUDY-SPECIFIC FORMS

One nearly always needs to design study-specific forms for recording data from agency records or for integrating data from multiple sources. These forms are in some ways as difficult to develop as good interview forms, and require adequate field testing during their development. Because these forms are so specific to the needs of particular studies, there are not very many published forms already developed and tested for their psychometric properties. One also should not underestimate the amount of staff time required to train record abstractors and to obtain data from institutional records. The record-keeping practices of each agency must be learned, access to records must be developed, research assistants must spend time and expense travelling to multiple agencies and reading agency records on site, sampled records must be rescored to estimate data collection reliability, and completed forms must be edited prior to data entry and analysis.

The Medication and Ancillary Treatment (MAT)

form (Hargreaves and Essock, personal communication) is an example of a study-specific form used to record both cost and effectiveness measures for persons with schizophrenia. It is completed for successive 30-day periods from clinical records in facilities managing patients' medication. For studies of inpatients this will initially be an inpatient ward, but the form spans all types of facilities. MAT data contribute to checking implementation and assessing effectiveness as well as counting units of service. Antipsychotic medication is measured in daily total dose of each antipsychotic agent, distinguishing depot from other routes of administration, as cost results may be sensitive to drug dosage levels and route of administration. Ancillary and side-effect medications are measured more globally (days on a particular class of drug). The day-by-day location of the medication management responsibility reveals the number of days the patient is on different specific wards of a hospital (which may differ in daily cost). Items on seclusion, restraint, special observation, clinical laboratory tests, and psychiatric hearings provide the primary source of data on these units of service. Items on other mental health, medical, dental, and social services received and legal system contacts are intended to provide search clues rather than primary data on these units of service.

OTHER DATABASES

In the United States in the early 1990s, Medicaid billings provide a potential sources of data on mental health and other medical care provided in both the public and private sector. This source is valuable for persons with schizophrenia served in the public sector, as most of them are eligible for Medicaid coverage. Medicaid bills from individual providers are processed in each state by a company that serves as the Medicaid fiscal intermediary. The fiscal intermediary is required to convey complete billing tapes to a common federal repository. The state fiscal intermediary can usually provide data more quickly than the federal government. In order to link patients with their Medicaid bills one needs to obtain the patient's social security number during the consent process. In other countries the investigator will need to explore the accessibility and cost of access to centralized health system information systems that may provide similar data. As such databases are very large, the investigator needs to anticipate the need for skilled computer programming assistance in accessing the information.

In the United States, the Department of Veterans Affairs operates a separate national health care system that maintains centralized units-of-service data for individual veterans, linked to an accounting cost-center system that provides a reasonable way to estimate the cost of each unit in each facility. A number of investigators have developed methods for accessing and analyzing these data (Beattie *et al.*, 1992; Rosenheck *et al.*, 1995).

AD HOC PROCEDURES NEEDED TO COMPLETE THE COLLECTION OF UTILIZATION DATA

Large database approaches will not be feasible for obtaining data from many providers. One must obtain data from these agencies in whatever method is most efficient. This may mean hand abstracting of paper records. Patients will also report receiving services from many small or private providers for which large database approaches are unavailable. In one study of persons with severe mental illness, 198 subjects reported services from 151 such providers within a 12 month period (Shern *et al.*, 1990). For these providers one should attempt to obtain bills that report services provided and charges. Shern *et al.* sent letters to providers requesting this information, which yielded a 74% response rate.

INTEGRATING DIVERSE DATA SOURCES

When resource use occurs in episodes, such as involuntary hospitalization or arrest, it is important to learn the typical patterns of resource use in each site. Police involvement, transportation, legal hearings, and other events may be common events during an involuntary hospitalization. Similarly, an arrest may lead to much later court costs and incarceration. One should attribute the cost of these later events (with their value appropriately discounted) to the time of the arrest or the illegal behavior. On the other hand, costs incurred due to illegal behavior before the study period should not be attributed to the intervention being evaluated. One may not be able to know future costs for an individual arrest, but information about the usual resource use associated with each type of offense among a subsample of study subjects will provide an alternate estimate.

As utilization information is collected it will be found that the different sources often do not agree on the occurrence or nature of the services consumed. One needs to develop decision rules for resolving conflicting data and estimating missing data. Records made at the time a service unit occurs are probably the most reliable, and might be accepted even when other sources do not report an event. On the other hand, when a respondent suggests from memory that an event occurred but it cannot be confirmed, then further checking of alternate providers or times is wise when feasible.

After exhausting consistency checking and other analysis approaches, one is left with a residue of missing or conflicting data. Here one needs rules for estimating missing or conflicting data using average values from similar situations, or other decision rules. As Clark *et al.* (1994) remind us, decision rules are needed that strike a balance between failing to identify resource use and wrongly attributing consumption to study participants. Decision rules that set unrealistically high standards for verifying events may under-represent costs, while unquestioningly accepting all reports may exaggerate resource use.

The many judgments needed in designing and implementing a study of cost leaves considerable room for variation in methods. Wolff and Helminiak (1994) have shown that variations in research question formulation, data source choice, service use definition, and value calculation method can lead to widely different estimates of social cost. They propose that investigators reach a consensus on data collection, analysis, and reporting standards to reduce this variation. Drummond *et al.* (1933) have made some specific standardization proposals, while Clark *et al.* (1994) and Udvarhelyi *et al.* (1992) have suggested more general principles to guide the application of cost methods. Clark *et al.* (1994) have cautioned that some data collection, especially for non-treatment resource use, requires careful, inventive work and may be hindered by premature standardization. The reader who is initiating a study of cost-effectiveness might like to review these sources and monitor developing consensus on standards.

SOURCE OF PAYMENTS

The public policy implications of study results are enhanced if service costs can be analyzed by source of payment. For some studies (in the United States) it may be sufficient to distinguish the following sources of payment: (i) state and state-administered federal mental health funds; (ii) federal (block grant, Medicaid, Medicare) mental health funds; (iii) federal Department of Veterans Affairs funds; (iv) county or other local mental health funds; (v) other public funds (e.g., most legal system costs); and (vi) private payers. One should distinguish mental health and general health funds within these categories. It is useful to gather data that identifies more specific sources of payment and information on what agency controls the reimbursement decision. Many types of service, such as police contacts, can be assumed to be paid from a single source. Nevertheless, data collection forms and interviews should include information about source of payment.

MEASURING SERVICE IMPLEMENTATION

The latter part of this chapter will discuss measuring the qualitative aspects of service implementation. Investigators have attended to measuring treatment implementation in efficacy studies, and this experience has guided the development of relevant methods for studies of the cost-effectiveness of services.

In drug efficacy research, where the focus is on the physiological effect of a compound, attention to treatment implementation is usually quite narrow. We often are concerned only with the amount of the medication that each subject consumes, or the plasma levels of drug and active metabolites that are achieved. Complexities do arise when comparing two active compounds, as often the relative therapeutic potency of the two compounds is not known, nor whether there is an optimum therapeutic window for one or the other drug. With antipsychotic drugs there is also a question whether onset of therapeutic effect is hastened by pushing the dose to the level of intolerable side-effects or sticking within a fixed level in the therapeutic range of dosage or plasma level. The psychosocial concomitants of medication administration are rarely examined unless drug and psychosocial interventions are being compared, as in the ground-breaking study by Elkin and co-workers (1985). Here the psychosocial aspects of drug (or placebo) management are crucial to specify and implement consistently if results implying relative efficacy are to be interpretable (Fawcett *et al.*, 1987).

In psychotherapy efficacy research investigators have vigorously developed methods for specifying and monitoring the implementation of different psychotherapy models being compared (Waltz *et al.*, 1993). This trend was greatly stimulated by the example of the National Institute of Mental Health (NIMH) Treatment of Depression Collaborative Research Program (Elkin *et al.*, 1985, 1989; Elkin, 1993). Investigators developed treatment manuals, trained experienced clinicians up to a treatment performance criterion, and monitored recorded patient sessions throughout the study using detailed rating procedures (Waskow, 1984; Hill *et al.*, 1992). The treatment design, training, and monitoring groups were separate from the treatment site investigators, and separate for each of the three modalities being compared, interpersonal psychotherapy (Weissman *et al.*, 1982; Chevron & Rounsaville, 1983; Chevron *et al.*, 1983; Rounsaville *et al.*, 1984, 1986, 1987), cognitive therapy (Shaw, 1984; Dobson *et al.*, 1985; Vallis *et al.*, 1986; Shaw & Dobson, 1988) and antidepressant and placebo medication strategies (Fawcett *et al.*, 1987). This example has set a very high standard for subsequent psychotherapy research, although a standard that is probably necessary if meaningful conclusions are to be drawn.

Cost-effectiveness research on services for persons with schizophrenia has grown out of these psychopharmacology and psychotherapy research traditions, and presents new challenges not encountered in efficacy research. Effectiveness research, by definition carried out under conditions of usual services delivery, cannot itself impose the kinds of treatment management controls used in efficacy research. Such controls would conflict with the aims of the research. However, services investigators often ask whether the service model under study incorporates management practices that efficacy research has indicated may be necessary to deliver established treatments effectively. For example, one might examine the cost-effectiveness of incorporating structured diagnostic procedures as an aid to selecting appropriate treatments (Rush & Basco, 1993). A more general issue for services research is the specification of the operating nature of whole service programs in their contacts with patients. These include not only the specific treatments that are provided, but social services that may need to be integrated with the treatment process such as assistance in obtaining financial entitlements, adequate housing, and employment. The methods used to maintain the continuity and appropriateness of services is also a central issue for persons with severe disabilities.

DISTINGUISHING KEY FEATURES OF A PROGRAM TYPE

In defining or monitoring service program implementation we generally identify a set of "key features" that we believe are important to measure. One might think of these key features as those characteristics we hypothesize to account for a program model's cost-effectiveness. One aim of services research is to confirm such hypotheses. The field thus far has paid much attention to "model programs" that combine a set of features that their proponents believe make them cost-effective (Bachrach, 1980, 1989). Only a few model programs, such as assertive community treatment, have been sufficiently studied in controlled cost-effectiveness trials to establish their potential cost effectiveness and the limits of the generalizabiity of their cost-effective application (Olfson, 1990; McGrew *et al.*, 1994). Even now the critical ingredients of assertive community treatment are a matter of expert judgment rather than being based on evidence from systematic dismantling studies (McGrew & Bond, 1995). Implementation of assertive community treatment probably varies more than these experts imagine, resulting from variation in interpretation and application of the common principles.

Implementation differences can be both quantitative and qualitative. For example, assertive community treatment programs have always aspired to a set of common, mostly qualitative principles (Witheridge, 1991; Test, 1992). These include a problem-solving orientation in which staff attend to specific life issues, no matter how mundane; provision of most services directly, rather than referring patients to another program; a team approach, in which the outreach staff meets together daily and shares responsibility for every patient on the caseload; and a long-term commitment to patients, providing services for as long as their needs persist. While there is good agreement among experts on these principles, in practice their implementation probably varies according to quantitative variables like staffing size and staff/patient ratio. Indeed, McGrew and Bond (1995) found that the opinions of the experts they surveyed suggested the existence of subtypes of implemented assertive community treatment programs related to total staff size.

Caseload characteristics are an important though conceptually distinct aspect of program implementation. Even programs of similar type may vary widely in the type and level of disability of their clientele. As programs will normally adapt to their modal patient, caseload characteristics are often included in program implementation descriptions.

Not all program types can be compared meaningfully, because the characteristics of their physical setting and caseload are very different and they are intended to serve very different purposes. Comparison across gross differences in restrictiveness (locked 24-hour care versus office-based outpatient psychotherapy) is one example. One is not usually comparing such services because they are not substitutable. Program models designed to have similar functions are the ones most often compared in cost-effectiveness trials.

Nevertheless it would be valuable to have implementation measures that were meaningful across a wide array of program models. For example, an array of non-residential mental health programs showing wide variation in practice compete with each other as the primary source of community services for persons with schizophrenia in many contemporary mental health systems. These services range from office-based outpatient services and other facility-based services such as day programs and socialization centers, to case management, visiting nurse, and assertive community treatment models that emphasize out-of-office contact. Clearly stated model specifications and established measures of model implementation meaningful across this spectrum of program types would aid investigators examining the relative cost-effectiveness of models within this spectrum.

FROM PROGRAM TYPE TO SERVICE MODEL SPECIFICATION

We are used to thinking of the variety of services for persons with schizophrenia by the names of major program types (inpatient, outpatient, day treatment, halfway house, etc.), such as those used to identify units of service in cost studies. Clinicians familiar with such programs will require only a moment's reflection to remind themselves that the practice variation within any of those program types can be huge, sometimes seeming greater that the typical differences between program types. Mental health services investigators seem to be in agreement that a program typology at this level is not specific enough for informative cost-effectiveness studies.

The first step in model specification is a written operating manual. Sometimes published descriptions of model programs can serve this purpose, but when one attempts to operationalize measures of model components it becomes clear that greater clarity and specificity is needed. This may not become clear until the model program has been replicated in multiple sites and practice variations become apparent. An example of a program manual is provided by McFarlane and Stastny (1987) for the assertive community treatment model.

The next stage of model specification is often the expert consultant or site visit team that aims to help replication sites implement the model as originally intended. Examples of this are the dissemination of the Fairweather Lodge model (Fairweather, 1980), the dissemination of the assertive community treatment model (Thompson *et al.*, 1990; Test, 1992), site visit activities of the International Center for Clubhouse Development (Propst, 1992) with regard to the Fountain House model, and the Boston University site visits of psychosocial rehabilitation programs (Anthony *et al.*, 1982; Farkas *et al.*, 1988). These consultants and site visitors see practice variations and sharpen their concepts of the key elements of their model.

The cost-effectiveness investigator then needs measures of model implementation. These measures should fully reflect the key features of the model being studied, but also the features of competing models that may or may not be implemented. When an innovative model is being compared with "usual services," adequate measures of the implemented usual services are important. All of these purposes could be accommodated efficiently if we had established, psychometrically sound measures that encompassed the range of key service elements across the entire spectrum of services for persons with schizophrenia. The authors' view is that this methodology needs to attend separately to 24-hour residential/inpatient services versus community maintenance and rehabilitation services. Emergency services may need separate attention as well. At present we have pieces of this methodology. Vigorous pursuit of measurement development in this area will facilitate future studies of cost-effectiveness.

MEASUREMENT APPROACHES

The types and sources of data can be seen to fall into seven different categories (Table 1). Examples of measures will be discussed with regard to the full range of inpatient/residential and community service models.

Table 1. Program implementation measures

Program structure
Caseload characteristics
Units of service
Staff time logs
Staff survey of practices
Patient survey of practices
Participant observation

Program structure characteristics are objective features that can easily be recorded accurately from program records, a key informant, or a participant observer. These include the number and characteristics of staff, the staff/patient ratio, ownership and management structure, and physical characteristics of the facility and its community environment. Within a given model or program type many of these characteristics are taken for granted by program staff and are not thought of as part of the program design, yet they of necessity influence the service process. Are there staff licensed to dispense medication or give injections? Is the program reimbursed fee-for-service or is the program forced to share financial risk? Are all physical spaces in the facility open to patients or are parts reserved for staff only? Is public transportation available and the neighborhood safe? Do patients (or staff) come to a facility at all or is all patient contact in the community? Is a residential facility locked or entirely open? Are necessary health and social services provided by the program, available on site, or available only at a (physical or organizational) distance? Timko (1995) provides an example of the range of program structure (and caseload) characteristics that might be gathered for residential treatment programs.

Caseload characteristics also influence program practice, especially if the target schizophrenic subgroup being studied is only a subset, perhaps a small subset, of the program caseload. Age, gender, ethnicity, and diagnosis mix can often be obtained from annual reports or other program statistical reports. Gross level of functioning distributions may be possible to rate by a key informant, including the proportion who have a legal guardian or conservator, the proportion eligible for income entitlements or various categories of reimbursement for medical and mental health services. Length of stay distributions in the studied program may be important, including whether the distribution differs for the investigator's target group versus other types of patients. History of lengths of stay or lifetime total time in hospital or other intense 24-hour care may also be important caseload characteristics in community programs.

Units of service data will be gathered at the individual patient level for purposes of cost estimation, and can provide excellent information about program operating characteristics. Brekke and Test (1992) illustrate how the pattern of service units over time following patient admission may reveal differences in community program practice even though the overall types of service units are similar from patient to patient. Service units are often recorded with the amount of time involved, whether the contact was face-to-face, by telephone, or with a collateral, and whether the contact was in the office or the community.

Staff time logs are usually necessary to supplement and validate units of service data. Brekke (1988) shows an example of such a log used in studying community mental health programs, while Dennis *et al.* (1992) show a "client encounter checklist" for describing substance abuse counseling. Often the service units that are required to be reported (e.g., "case management") do not give sufficient detail, or different programs are required to show all of their work under somewhat inappropriate service unit categories. For example, some jurisdictions allow one program to bill psychotherapy units but not case management units, while for other programs the reverse is true, in an effort to force work patterns into cost centers for the purpose of cost accounting. When staff do both types of activities, they are all recorded as psychotherapy in one type of program and case management in the other. Staff logs that record more specific details of the content and focus of patient contacts enable the investigator to further define the average meaning of service unit types in each program studied. Staff logs are time consuming for staff and may distort the workload distribution slightly, but usually can be time sampled. For example, staff might be asked to keep logs for 2-week periods two or three times per year. During this time it is advisable to audit the time logs against service units reported and resolve discrepancies immediately while staff can recall their activities. Staff logs are less often used for inpatient and residential programs, as the unit of service is an inpatient/residential day. However, if the investigator plans to disaggregate the cost of a service day, staff logs or other time-and-motion sampling may be needed to determine how to disaggregate costs of different staff activities. While time-and-motion sampling is used to quantify the amount or cost of service received, such data may also help characterize qualitative differences among inpatient wards or residential programs.

Surveys of program practices are a very efficient way to gather qualitative ratings of program practices. Instruments with adequate psychometric development and available norms from various program models can facilitate comparison of findings from different studies. The earliest inventories were developed to reflect program philosophy or social milieu. One of the earliest was the Community Mental Health Ideology Scale (Baker & Schulberg, 1967) that measured the new ideology growing in the field in the 1960s that emphasized: (i) focus on a total population; (ii) primary prevention; (iii) total community involvement; (iv) comprehensive continuity of care; and (v) social treatment goals. That scale focused on the ideology of individual clinicians, not the operating style of programs. The most extensive empirical work has been done by Moos and his colleagues, who initially measured psychiatric ward "atmosphere" (Moos & Schwartz, 1972), then extended this method to community-oriented programs in general (Moos, 1988). They further elaborated this procedure into a comprehensive environmental assessment procedure (Moos & Lemke, 1984) that includes instruments for recording physical features, policies and services, characteristics of residents and staff, and treatment climate. This approach has been adapted to nursing homes (Lemke & Moos, 1986) and alcoholism programs (Finney & Moos, 1984). A revised and extended set of instruments for inpatient substance abuse treatment programs (Peterson *et al.*, in press) has been used to examine the determinants of readmission in a national sample of 101 Veterans Administration programs (Swindle *et al.*, 1994). This group and others have focused on more specific aspects of psychiatric service models in inpatient and residential care (Olfson *et al.*, 1993; Timko, 1995) and in non-residential psychiatric services (Jerrell & Hargreaves, 1990). Jerrell and hargeaves (1990) developed the Community Program Philosophy Scale that aims to characterize the spectrum of community maintenance and rehabilitative programs for clinic-based outpatient models through various types of case management to assertive community treatment. This scale has shown some success in distinguishing service models (Brekke & Test, 1992; Rosenheck *et al.*, 1993) and a normative sample of programs is being gathered. Staff ratings of program operating style also reflect the adaptation of programs to differences in caseload mix, so the two kinds of information should be used in combination (Rosenheck *et al.*, 1993).

Patient survey instruments have been used in a number of studies, but no major instrument has yet been developed that could be widely applied. A brief patient survey focused on client-to-client interaction has been described by Brekke and Aisley (1990), which contains 12 items that factor into scales Affective Attachment, Instrumental Involvement, and Negative Experience of Environment. A more comprehensive scale is under development by Martha Burt (personal communication) at the Urban Institute in Washington, DC. The Burt scale asks respondents for ratings of "what has been helpful" in their program, and attempts to cover content that will be relevant for the full range of non-residential mental health programs.

A *participant observer* may be in a unique position to observe certain characteristics of a program, such as qualities of the interpersonal process between staff and patients, among patients, and among staff. Participant observation has been incorporated into a number of ongoing cost-effectiveness studies of community programs for persons with schizophrenia, usually engaging a qualitatively trained anthropologist or sociologist for extensive participation in one or two programs. This type of qualitative observation and synthesis aims to identify unforseen or unrecognized characteristics of service programs. However, participant observers (and site visitors with more structured, briefer contact with a program) might also be asked to complete a structured rating instrument. Cathaleene Macias (personal communication) is developing such an instrument in collaboration with the site visitors/consultants of the International Center for Clubhouse Development. Its content is such that it may serve well across a variety of program models.

COMMENT

We have reviewed measurement issues for counting units of services consumed and measuring program implementation. We have tried to show how the two tasks can complement each other with regard to some aspects of the measurement effort. In historical perspective, the two tasks come from rather different roots. The measurement of the cost of schizophrenia and its treatment is an application of established cost-effectiveness principles from economics to studying a particular disorder and relevant service interventions. Measuring program implementation comes more directly from the traditions of mental health efficacy research in psychopharmacology and psychotherapy.

To count units of services consumed, the investigator needs to select and construct instruments that will efficiently collect both cost and effectiveness information from each data source. This may require a collaboration of economist and clinical investigator to choose the right balance and complexity of measurement of these two types of data.

To select measures of implementation, the investigator must obtain or write program manuals for each model, draw upon the experience of available experts, and select among the available measurement techniques those that can most appropriately and easily be adapted to the needs of the planned study.

We have reviewed a developing measurement technology that largely grew out of the needs of specific studies. With time, a full catalog of program manuals and measurement tools needs to be developed to facilitate good quality studies of the cost-effectiveness of services for persons with schizophrenia.

REFERENCES

Anthony, W.A., Cohen, M., and Farkas, M. (1982). A psychiatric rehabilitation treatment program: Can I recognize one if I see one? *Community Mental Health Journal*, **18**, 83–96.

Bachrach, L.L. (1980). Overview: model programs for chronic mental patients. *American Journal of Psychiatry*, **137**, 1023–1031.

Bachrach, L.L. (1989). The legacy of model programs. *Hospital and Community Psychiatry*, **40**, 234–235.

Beattie, M.C., Swindle, R.W., and Tomko, L.A. (1992). *Department of Veterans Affairs Databases Resource Guide.* Palo Alto, CA: HSR&D Center for Health Care Evaluation.

Brekke, J.S. (1988). What do we really know about community support programs? Strategies for better monitoring. *Hospital and Community Psychiatry*, **39**, 946–952.

Brekke, J.S. and Aisley R.A. (1990). The Client Interaction Scale: A method for assessing community support programs for persons with chronic mental illness. *Evaluation and the Health Professions*, **13**, 215–226.

Brekke, J.S. and Test, M.A. (1992). A model for measuring the implementation of community support programs: Results from three sites. *Community Mental Health Journal*, **28**, 227–247.

Chevron, E.S. and Rounsaville, B.J. (1983). Evaluating the clinical skills of psychotherapists: A comparison of techniques. *Archives of General Psychiatry*, **40**, 1129–1132.

Chevron, E.S., Rounsaville, B.J., Rothblum, E.D., and Weissman, M.M. (1983). Selecting psychotherapists to participate in psychotherapy outcome studies: Relationship between psychotherapist characteristics and assessment of clinical skills. *Journal of Nervous and Mental Disease*, **171**, 348–353.

Clark, R.E. and Drake, R.E. (1994). Expenditures of time and money by families of people with severe mental illness and substance use disorders. *Community Mental Health Journal*, **30**, 145–163.

Clark, R.E., Teague, G.B., Ricketts, S.K., Bush, P.W., Keller, A.M., and Zubkoff, M. (1994). Measuring resource use in economic evaluations: Determining the social costs of mental illness. *Journal of Mental Health Administration*, **21**, 32–41.

Dennis, M.L., Fairbank, J.A., and Rachal, J.V. (1992). *Measuring Substance Abuse Counselling: The Methadone Enhanced Treatment (MET) Study Approach*. Research Triangle Park, NC: Research Triangle Institute.

Dobson, K.S., Shaw, B.F., and Vallis, T.M. (1985). Reliability of a measure of the quality of cognitive therapy. *British Journal of Clinical Psychology*, **24**, 295–300.

Drummond, M., Brandt, A., Luce, B., and Rovira, J. (1993). Standardizing methodologies for economic evaluation in health care. *International Journal of Technology Assessment in Health Care*, **9**, 26–36.

Elkin, I. (1993). The NIMH Treatment of Depression Collaborative Research Program: where we began and where we are. In A.E. Bergin and S.L. Garfield, eds, *Handbook of Psychotherapy and Behavior Change*, 4th edn, pp. 114–139. New York: Wiley.

Elkin, I., Parloff, M.B., Hadley, S.W., and Autrey, J.H. (1985). NIMH Treatment of Depression Collaborative Research Program: Background and research plan. *Archives of General Psychiatry*, **42**, 305–316.

Elkin, I., Shea, M.T., Watkins, J.T., *et al.* (1989). National Institute of Mental Health Treatment of Depression Collaborative Research Program: general effectiveness of treatments. *Archives of General Psychiatry*, **46**, 871–892.

Fairweather, G.W. (ed) (1980). The Fairweather lodge: A twenty-five year retrospective. *New Directions for Mental Health Services*, Number 7.

Farkas, M.D., Cohen, M.R., and Nemic, P.B. (1988). Psychiatric rehabilitation programs: Putting concepts into practice? *Community Mental Health Journal*, **24**, 7–21.

Fawcett, J., Epstein, P., Fiester, S.J., Elkin I., and Autry, J.H. (1987). Clinical Management—Imipramine/Placebo Administration Manual: NIMH Treatment of Depression Collaborative Research Program. *Psychopharmacology Bulletin*, **23**, 309–324.

Finney, J. and Moos, R. (1984). Environmental assessment and evaluation research: Examples from mental health and substance abuse programs. *Evaluation and Program Planning*, **7**, 151–167.

Hill, C.E., O'Grady, K.E., and Elkin, I. (1992). Applying the Collaboratve Study of Psychotherapy Rating Scale to rate therapist adherence in cognitive–behavior therapy, interpersonal therapy, and clinical management. *Journal of Consulting and Clinical Psychology*, **60**, 73–79.

Klein, D.F. (1993). Clinical psychopharmacologic practice: The need for developing a research base. *Archives of General Psychiatry*, **50**, 491–494.

Leginski, W.A., Croze, C., Driggers, J. *et al.* (1989). *Data Standards for Mental Health Decision Support Systems.* NIMH Series FN No. 10, DHHS Pub. No. (ADM) 89-1589. Washington, DC: Supt. of Docs., US Government Printing Office.

Lehman, A. (1988). A quality of life interview for the chronically mentally ill. *Evaluation and Program Planning*, **11**, 51–62.

Lemke, S. and Moos, R. (1986). Quality of residential settings for elderly adults. *Journal of Gerontology*, **4**, 268–276.

McFarlane, W.R. and Stastny, P. (1987). *Treatment Manual for Training in Community Living*. New York: New York State Psychiatric Institute.

McGrew, J.H. and Bond, G.R. (1995). Critical ingredients of assertive community treatment: Judgments of the experts. *Journal of Mental Health Administration*, **22**, 113–125.

McGrew, J.H., Bond, G.R., Dietzen, L., and Salyers, M. (1994). Measuring the fidelity of implementation of a mental health program model. *Journal of Consulting and Clinical Psychology*, **62**, 670–678.

Moos, R. (1988). *Community Oriented Programs Environment Scale Manual*, 2nd edn. Palo Alto, CA: Consulting Psychologists Press.

Moos, R. and Lemke, S. (1984). *Multiphasic Environmental Assessment Procedure Manual.* Palo Alto Social Ecology Laboratory, Veterans Administration Medical Center, Stanford University.

Olfson, M. (1990). Assertive community treatment: An evaluation of the experimental evidence. *Hospital and Community Psychiatry*, **41**, 634–641.

Olfson, M., Glick, I.D., and Mechanic, D. (1993). Inpatient treatment of schizophrenia in general hospitals. *Hospital and Community Psychiatry*, **44**, 40–44.

Peterson, K., Swindle, R., Phibbs, C.S., Recine, B., and Moos, R.S. (1994). Determinants of readmission following inpatient substance abuse treatment: A national study of VA programs. *Medical Care*, **32**, 535–550.

Propst, R.N. (1992). Standards for clubhouse programs: Why and how they were developed. *Psychosocial Rehabilitation Journal*, **16**, 25–30.

Rosenheck, R., Neale, M., and Gallup, P. (1993). Community-oriented mental health care: Assessing diversity in clinical practice. *Psychosocial Rehabilitation Journal*, **16**, 39–50.

Rosenheck, R.A., Neale, M.S., and Frisman, L.K. (1995). Issues in estimating the cost of innovative mental health programs. *Psychiatric Quarterly*, **66**, 9–31.

Rosenheck, R.A., Neale, M.S., Leaf, P., Milstein, R., and Frisman, L.K. (1995). A multi-site experimental cost study of intensive psychiatric community care. *Schizophrenia Bulletin*, **21**, 129–140.

Rounsaville, B.J., Chevron, E.S., and Weissman, M.M. (1984). Specification of techniques in interpersonal psychotherapy. In J.B.W. Williams and R.L. Spitzer, eds, *Psychotherapy Research: Where Are We and Where Should We Go?*. pp. 160–172, New York: Guilford.

Rounsaville, B.J., Chevron, E.S., Weissman, M.M., Prusoff, B.A., and Frank, E. (1986). Training therapists to perform interpersonal psychotherapy in clinical trials. *Compehensive Psychiatry*, **27**, 364–371.

Rounsaville, B.J., Chevron, E.S., Prusoff, B.A., *et al.* (1987). The relation between specific and general dimensions of the psychotherapy process in interpersonal psychotherapy of depression. *Journal of Consulting and Clinical Psychology*, **55**, 379–384.

Rush, A.J. and Basco, M.R. (1993). *Progress Summary.* Mental Health Clinical Research Center, Department of Psychiatry, University of Texas Southwestern Medical Center, Dallas.

Shaw, B.F. (1984). Specification of the training and evaluation of cognitive therapists for outcome studies. In J.B.W. Williams and R.L. Spitzer, eds, *Psychotherapy Research: Where Are We and Where Should We Go?*. pp. 173–189, New York: Guilford.

Shaw, B.F. and Dobson, K.S. (1988). Competency judgments in training and evaluation of psychotherapists. *Journal of Consulting and Clinical Psychology*, **56**, 666–672.

Shern, D.L., Coen, A.S., Nelson, L., Wilson, N.A., and Vasby, K.O. (1990). *Innovative Service Models and the Cost of Chronic Mental Illness: Final Report.* Denver: State of Colorado Division of Mental Health.

Swindle R., Peterson, K., Paradise, M., and Moos, R. (1995). Measuring substance abuse program treatment orientations: The Drug and Alcohol Program Treatment Inventory. *Journal of Substance Abuse*, **7**, 79–98.

Tessler, R.C., Fisher, G.A., and Gamach, G.M. (1992). *Family Burden Interview Schedule.* Amherst: Social and Demographic Research Institute.

Test, M.A. (1992). Training in community living. In R.P. Liberman, ed, *Handbook of Psychiatric Rehabiliation.* New York: Macmillan.

Thompson, K.S., Griffith, E.E.H., and Leaf, P.J. (1990). A historical review of the Madison model of community care. *Hospital and Community Psychiatry*, **41**, 625–634.

Timko, C. (1995). Policies and services in residential substance abuse programs: Comparisons with psychiatric programs. *Journal of Substance Abuse*, **7**, 43–59.

Udvarhelyi, I.S., Colditz, G.A., Rai, A., and Epstein, A.M. (1992). Cost-effectiveness and cost-benefit analysis in the medical literature: Are the methods being used correctly? *Annals of Internal Medicine*, **116**, 238–244.

Vallis, T.M., Shaw, B.F., and Dobson, K.S. (1986). The Cognitive Therapy Scale: Psychometric properties. *Journal of Consulting and Clinical Psychology*, **54**, 381–385.

Waltz, J., Addis, M.E., Koerner, K., and Jacobson, N.S. (1993). Testing the integrity of a psychotherapy protocol: Assessment of adherence and competence. *Journal of Consulting and Clinical Psychology*, **61**, 620–630.

Waskow, I.E. (1984). Specification of the technique variable in the NIMH Treatment of Depression Collaborative Research Program. In J.B.W. Williams and R.L. Spitzer, eds, *Psychotherapy Research: Where Are We and Where Should We Go?*, pp. 150–159, New York: Guilford.

Weissman, M.M., Rounsaville, B.J., and Chevron, E. (1982). Training psychotherapists to participate in psychotherapy outcome studies. *American Journal of Psychiatry*, **139**, 1442–1446.

Wolff, N. and Helminiak, T.W. (1994). The anatomy of cost estimates: The "other outcome." In T.W. Hu and A. Rupp, eds, *Advances in Health Economics and Health Services Research*, Volume 14, pp. 159–180. Greenwich, CT: JAI Press.

29

Estimating Costs of Schizophrenia and its Treatment

TEH-WEI HU
School of Public Health, University of California at Berkeley, California USA

WILLIAM A. HARGREAVES and MARTHA SHUMWAY
School of Medicine, University of California, SanFrancisco, California, USA

INTRODUCTION

Insight into the relationships between costs and outcomes is essential to the provision of effective treatments for schizophrenia in the face of growing fiscal constraints in both public and private sectors. As alternative strategies for health care reform are considered and debated, it is increasingly important to understand the full range of costs of schizophrenia and appreciate the extent to which the burdens of schizophrenic illness and the benefits of its treatment are shared among all segments of society. Analyzing the costs of schizophrenia and its treatment provides an empirical basis for accounting for expenditure of public and private funds, evaluating the cost-effectiveness of alternative treatment strategies and identifying cost-efficient approaches to treatment delivery. Such cost–outcome analyses facilitate improved allocation of the limited resources available for schizophrenia treatment.

Costs can be examined at the national, or "macro," level or at the individual treatment program, or "micro" level. In this chapter, we focus on the micro level, where the goal is to estimate and evaluate the costs and economic impact associated with a specific treatment program or set of programs. We will first provide a conceptual framework for defining the societal costs of schizophrenia and its treatment along with specific guidelines for estimating these costs. These concepts will then be illustrated with examples from a recent cost–outcome study conducted in the United States.

CONCEPTUAL FRAMEWORK OF COST EVALUATION

Conceptually, the societal cost of schizophrenia is equivalent to the value of resources consumed or lost by ill individuals, treatment providers, government entities, or other segments of society as a result of the illness. Two key words in this definition are "resources" and "value." Resources include time inputs by clinicians and other service providers, medication, supplies, and space. Resources can be used by providers, patients, or others. Resources can

Handbook of Mental Health Economics and Health Policy, Volume I, Schizophrenia. Edited by M. Moscarelli, A. Rupp and N. Sartorius.
© 1996 John Wiley & Sons Ltd.

be purchased in either the public sector or the private sector. The task of cost evaluation is to identify the resources used or lost, enumerate the quantities of these resources, and assign appropriate monetary values to each resource. When this information is assembled, the unit cost for each resource is multiplied by the number of units used and the total cost is calculated as the sum of all resource costs.

It is usually easier to identify resources than it is to assign values to them, as assigning monetary values can be a very subjective task. The market price of a resource is the most desirable monetary value for cost comparison. If there is a competitive market for a resource, then the observed market price is assumed to reflect the best possible compromise between producers' and consumers' valuations of the resource and this market price is taken as a true measure of the value, or cost, of the resource.

It is relatively easy to assign values to resources which are available in the market-place. Markets usually exist for resources such as outpatient and inpatient psychiatric services and medications, therefore, market prices can be obtained and used in cost estimation. However, markets do not exist for other resources, such as patient and caregiver time and voluntary informal care. When no market price exists, it is necessary to impute resource values using available information as the basis for estimation. Methods for imputation are discussed later in the chapter.

In cost estimation, it is generally thought useful (Rice, 1966; Hu & Jerrell, 1991) to divide costs into two categories: direct costs and indirect costs. Direct costs are incurred when resources are used directly to provide treatment, services or other assistance. Inpatient and residential care, outpatient and medication visits, emergency room visits, case management, jail and other correctional services, and travel expenses are direct costs. As most direct costs reflect actual expenditures, it is usually possible to obtain data on units of service used and the value of each unit. However, some direct costs, such as travel time and voluntary informal care, do not reflect actual expenditures and it is necessary to impute their market value. In contrast, indirect costs are defined as resources lost as a result of illness. These costs, such as loss of employment or productivity, are not incurred directly and it is usually necessary to impute their value.

A number of prior studies illustrate the evolution and application of methods for evaluating the costs of treatments for schizophrenia and other serious mental disorders (May, 1971; Cassell *et al.*, 1972; Murphy & Datel, 1976; Sharfstein & Nafziger, 1976; Guillette *et al.*, 1978; Jones *et al.*, 1980; Weisbrod *et al.*, 1980; Hoult *et al.*, 1981, 1983; Hoult & Reynolds, 1984; Fenton *et al.*, 1982, 1984; Bond, 1984; Giel, 1984; Dickey *et al.*, 1986; Bond *et al.*, 1988; Hafner & an der Heiden, 1989; Jerrell & Hu, 1989; Burns & Raftery, 1991; Moscarelli *et al.*, 1991; Wiersma *et al.*, 1991). Central concepts common to these studies are discussed in the following sections.

The first step in cost analysis is to identify all service elements and other resources related to the treatments being evaluated and to determine a standard unit of measurement for each resource. For example, inpatient and residential treatment are usually measured in days, while outpatient and emergency services are often measured in hours. An example of a list of resources and their measurement units is presented in Table 1. Sources of utilization data for each resource are also shown in Table 1. Typically, a resource list such as this one is compiled in an iterative fashion. The investigators first list all the resources that they would like to include in their cost analysis and note the level of desirable measurement detail. They must then search for accessible data sources. Some information is usually available from existing mental system or provider data bases, some information may be extracted from individual clinical records, while other information must be obtained through interviews with clients, providers, or other persons. The resource list must then be revised based on data availability. For example, definitions of service elements and resource units may be revised to match definitions used in an existing agency data base or the measurement of informal care may be modified to match an existing interview protocol. As available data sources are identified, the list of resources and level of measurement detail are reevaluated in light of the relevant importance of each resource and the difficulty of obtaining data. Trade-offs between the specificity of each data element and the associated data collection expense merit careful consideration. Clearly, more effort should be devoted to collecting detailed and

Table 1. Resources, units, and data sources

Resource	Unit	Data source
Direct costs		
Mental health treatment		
Inpatient hospitalization	day	mental health agency
Skilled nursing facility/IMD	day	mental health agency
Residential treatment	day	mental health agency
Psychiatric emergency room visit	visit	mental health agency
Ambulance	trip	hospital billing
Medication management	visit	mental health agency
Outpatient treatment	visit	mental health agency
Case management	hour	mental health agency
Day treatment	day	mental health agency
Partial hospitalization	day	mental health agency
Medication	dose/day	mental health agency
Laboratory tests	procedure	laboratory billing
Medical care		
Inpatient hospitalization	day	insurance claims
Outpatient care	visit	insurance claims
Medical emergency room visit	visit	insurance claims
Laboratory tests	procedure	laboratory billing
Nursing home	day	insurance claims
Criminal justice contacts		
Police contact	contact	police records
Court appearance	hour	judicial records
Jail/prison	day	penal records
Probation supervision	day	probation records
Parole supervision	day	parole records
Conservatorship/ guardianship	day	conservator records
Social services		
Transfer payment administration	month	social welfare agency
Rehabilitation services	hour	social service agency
Supported housing	day	social service agency
Family/informal care activities		
Informal care	hour	interview
Transportation	trip	interview
Maintenance assistance	dollar	interview
Indirect costs		
Loss of patient productivity	hour/day	interview
Loss of family/caregiver productivity	hour/day	interview

complete data on frequently used, high-cost resources than on infrequently used, low-cost resources.

DIRECT COSTS

The direct costs shown in Table 1 are divided into four categories: mental health treatment, medical treatment, criminal justice and social services, and family and informal care. Typical resources in each category and potential sources of utilization data are discussed below.

Mental health treatment

This includes days of inpatient care, skilled nursing care, residential treatment, emergency visits, ambulance trips, medication visits, outpatient visits, case management hours, day services, partial hospitalization days, medication, and laboratory procedures. Data on publicly sponsored programs are generally available in existing data bases maintained at the local or regional level. Such data bases are desirable sources because data are collected routinely and all providers are subject to common data collection and reporting requirements. In some cases, however, existing data bases may not provide the data required for a specific cost analysis. for ecample, if private mental health programs are not included or necessary data on different components of a treatment are not available, it may be necessary to collect additional utilization data from agency records or to directly monitor the provision of treatment.

Medical services

In most cost analyses of schizophrenia treatment it is informative to collect and examine data on medical services in addition to data on mental health services because schizophrenic illness and its treatment may be related to medical care utilization. Some individuals may seek assistance for their mental health problems from medical care providers because appropriate mental health services are unavailable or unappealing. In other cases, mental health treatment may link clients to necessary medical services which they were not able to obtain on their own. Medical treatment includes inpatient, outpatient and emergency visits, laboratory procedures, and nursing care. The wide variety of providers, insurance plans, and payment options makes it more difficult to obtain complete data on medical care utilization than to obtain data on mental health care utilization. Data on public insurance payments can be obtained from public claims data bases, such as Medicaid and Medicare in the United States, and data on private payments can be obtained from private claims data bases. Individual hospital or provider billing records may also be useful in some situations. Given the vast array of medical illnesses and procedures, all of these data sources tend to be difficult to access and complex and costly to work with. The extent and importance of medical care utilization should be considered in the context of each study before extensive data collection is undertaken.

Criminal justice and social services

Persons with schizophrenia are occasionally involved with the criminal justice system and may receive social services. Data on the costs of these resources should be collected as need for these services may be related to schizophrenic illness. Criminal justice resources include police contacts, arrests, court appearances, attorney services, jail, probation and conservator services. Collecting data on these activities is much more difficult than collecting data on mental health or medical care. Most criminal justice agencies do not routinely generate billing or cost reimbursement data. Data are scattered at different locations and tracing relevant records is complex and time consuming. These records are often difficult to access and interpret and special confidentiality rules may apply.

Data on social services, such as mental health conservatorship or guardianship, supported housing and rehabilitation services are often collected from client interviews and/or clinician or public guardian records. Information on transfer payments, such as government disability benefits, can be obtained either from client interview or guardian records. The government's cost of administering the program, which can be calculated as a percentage of the payment, may be included as a cost.

Family and informal care costs

Many persons with schizophrenia require assistance with food, lodging, transportation, clothing, and shopping above and beyond services that treatment programs provide. Family members and friends often provide this type of informal care, which is essential to some severely disabled persons. Interviews with clients or caregivers are usually the only way to collect data on this kind of resource use.

INDIRECT COSTS

Indirect costs reflect the loss of productive resources as a result of illness. These could include time costs incurred by patients and time costs incurred by family or other informal caregivers. Two methods are commonly used to value this lost productivity:

the human capital approach and the willingness-to-pay approach.

The human capital approach is based on the concept of opportunity cost, assuming that the best alternative use of an individual's time is contributing to the economy and receiving wages in return. Thus, the indirect cost due to lost productivity is valued at each individual's wage for competitive employment. The human capital approach is often criticized because wages are influenced by factors such as age, gender, race, location, and occupation and may not accurately reflect indirect costs.

The willingness-to-pay approach is intended to avoid the potential biases of the human capital approach by valuing lost productivity at the amount individuals would pay to avoid illness and its consequences. Despite its conceptual appeal, the willingness-to-pay approach is difficult to implement because subjective assessment is required to obtain individual values. Furthermore, it is also biased by personal perception and subjective endowment (i.e., differences in income, wealth, and status). As both methods are subject to bias, the more straightforward human capital approach is used to estimate indirect costs in most cost of illness studies.

The preceding discussion of resource categories illustrates that collecting utilization data becomes increasingly more difficult as we move from mental health treatment to medical care, to criminal justice and social services, and finally to family and caregiver activities. As data collection expenses increase as data become more difficult to obtain, it is clear that each investigator must carefully evaluate the need for data in each resource category in the context of the time and expense required for data collection and the specific goals of the study. As noted earlier, it is more important to obtain accurate data on resources that are very costly or are used frequently than to obtain accurate data on inexpensive or infrequently used resources.

After resource categories and service units are defined, values must be assigned to each unit so that total cost can be calculated. Determining reliable, accurate values for resources is much more difficult than obtaining data on resource utilization. The next section is devoted to the valuation process.

VALUATION AND COST ASSIGNMENT

The crucial aspect of any cost evaluation is the assignment of appropriate costs, or monetary values, to the resource units. If values are readily available, such as unit costs of public mental health services available in agency data bases, then we should attempt to review agency cost accounting and cost allocation procedures to determine whether the values accurately represent the true cost. If no resource values are available then we need to impute costs. Several common issues in valuation and cost assignment are discssed below.

CHARGES VERSUS COSTS

Most private sector providers and some public sector providers send bills to patients, government agencies, or insurance companies reflecting their charges for specific services. Although they are often easier to obtain than costs, charges are not usually accurate or reliable proxies for the true cost or value of the resources used to provide services. Charges commonly include a share of the cost of uncompensated care for other patients or reflect cost shifting between different departments in a hospital or clinic. Charges may also reflect profits to private sector providers. One provider's charge for the same service may vary from patient to patient if the provider has negotiated special rates with a government program or a private insurance plan.

In some circumstances it is possible to determine costs from charges. In the United States, for example, many institutions prepare for a Medicare Cost Report for the Health Care Fnancing Administration (HCFA) for reimbursement purposes and the charge-to-cost ratios contained in these reports can be used to adjust charges to yield cost estimates. For example, if the charge for an inpatient day in a private hospital is \$900 and the hospital's charge-to-cost ratio for inpatient care is 1.44, the actual cost would be \$625 per day. Likewise, costs of physician fees and medications can be calculated using similar standard reports, such as the Medicare physician fee schedule, or actual payment data from patient claims files. If cost data are not available, payments may provide a superior alternative to charges, as payment is likely to reflect negotiation of an amount closer to actual cost than the original charge.

These important concerns about the distinctions between costs and charges may not be applicable to all of the public sector services which provide the majority of treatment for schizophrenia. Many public health agencies operate services directly or contract for services at cost. Thus, in some cases costs may equal charges. However, even with such publicly provided services, there may be cost sharing and cost shifting among different departments or treatment programs and the cost accounting procedures used to compute costs and charges should be examined before equivalence is assumed.

CAPITAL COSTS

Capital costs refer to the value of land and buildings used to provide treatment. It is essential to consider capital costs because they often constitute a major cost component which dominates the total cost of services (Weisbrod, 1983; Cannon *et al.*, 1985; McGuire 1991). Capital costs are estimated using the basic economic principle of "opportunity cost," which is the cost of the best alternative use of a resource. If a program rents space, capital costs do not need to be independently calculated because the opportunity cost is equal to the rent which is already included in the unit costs for the treatment.

However, when a treatment program owns the building it operates in or is located in a publicly owned building, the cost of the space and, hence, the cost of the treatment, is at least partially subsidized. The opportunity costs of such buildings may vary a great deal, depending on factors such as the age and location of the building. Four types of methods have been used to determine the capital cost of such a building. One could use the historical value of a building, an estimate of the replacement cost, the current assessed value, or the fair market rental price for similar space. The use of historical cost may underestimate the current value of property, while the replacement cost or assessed value may overestimate the value. For simplicity, the literature indicates that a sensible approach would be to use the regional rental price listings, such as the list compiled by the US Office of Economic Development, in combination with estimates provided by community realtors (Rosenheck *et al.*, 1993).

ALLOCATION OF JOINT COSTS

Joint costs are incurred when one program or facility provides two or more distinct services, for example day treatment and outpatient psychotherapy, and the two services share resources such as space or staff. Two general methods are used to allocate joint costs between the services that share them. One is based on the amount of inputs used (i.e., amount of time space is used or time spent by a clinician) and the other is based on the amount of outputs produced (i.e., the number of patients treated).

Using the first, input-based approach, if 5% of emergency room clinician time was devoted to serving schizophrenic patients then the total cost of emergency room clinician time for these patients would be equal to 5% of the cost of all clinician time and the unit cost would be that amount divided among the number of service units provided. Using the second, output-based approach, if 8% of the clients seen in the emergency room were schizophrenic, then the cost of services for these clients would be 8% of the total emergency room cost and the unit cost would be that total divided by the number of service units provided. Similarly, the joint costs associated with a case management program could be calculated by the input-based approach by computing the percent of case managers' time devoted to a specific group of clients. With the output-based approach, the percentage of case-managed clients in that specific group would be calculated.

Some economists (Enthoven, 1965; Alchian & Allen, 1967) have argued that joint costs are not a major concern, as marginal costs—the additional cost of treating one additional client—are more important than average costs. If the marginal cost is constant, regardless of the number of units provided, then the average cost and the marginal cost are equivalent. If the use of a facility by one treatment program does not reduce the ability of another program to use the same facility, then the two treatment programs do not have any joint costs. The more detailed the information on units of inputs and outputs, the easier it is to identify and allocate joint costs.

CRIMINAL JUSTICE COSTS

Persons with schizophrenia may have contact with the criminal justice system and it is possible that these contacts may be related directly or indirectly to their mental illness. Furthermore, the extent and appropriateness of cost shifting between the mental health costs and criminal justice systems is of concern. The major challenge in estimating criminal justice costs is the complexity of the process which can include one or more of the following types of contacts: citation, arrest, hearing, court trial, sentencing, jail, probation, or conservatorship. All of these processes may involve multiple agencies, each with its own information needs and data management systems. In one California county, criminal justice data were obtained through the sheriff's office which functioned as a central source of interagency data. Some localities prepare cost reports and cost analyses, which calculate the unit costs of different types of criminal justice contacts and others have computerized cost accounting systems which facilitate data acquisition.

If local data cost data are not available, national estimates may be used. For example, the US National Institute of Justice has estimated offender processing costs in five locations across the country (Jacoby *et al.*, 1987; Wayson & Funke, 1989). Such estimates, adjusted for inflation and regional cost differences, can be used as estimates of local criminal justice costs.

Empirical evidence indicates that criminal justice costs are usually underestimated because many of the initial stages of the process, such as citation and arrest, are underreported (Clark *et al.*, 1994). Criminal justice records may be difficult for outsiders to interpret and expert advice is necessary if these data are to be meaningfully incorporated into a cost analysis. While only a small percentage of schizophrenic patients are involved in the criminal justice system, several studies suggest that those individuals who are incur substantial costs. Thus, the average cost per patient in a treatment program could be relatively low, but the distribution of these costs is likely to be highly skewed.

FAMILY AND INFORMAL CARE COSTS

There are two approaches to valuing the assistance with daily living activities that family members and other informal caregivers provide to persons with schizophrenia (McGuire, 1991). One approach treats informal caregiver time as an indirect cost reflecting resources lost as a result of the illness. With this approach, if a caregiver forgoes competitive employment to care for an ill friend or relative, this time is valued at the opportunity cost of the informal caregiver's time. This opportunity cost is typically the wage the caregiver earns from his or her competitive employment. Such estimates correctly reflect the indirect costs incurred by the individuals being studied, but there may be great variability in these estimates due to occupational, gender, and age biases in wage rates that is unrelated to the amount or quality of care. The second approach treats informal care as a direct cost related to treatment and values time spent providing informal care at the market value of the type of assistance provided rather than at the wage rate of the person providing the care. Wage rates for home health workers or housekeepers often provide the best estimate of the market value of these resources. This method may permit more objective comparison of treatments, because informal care provided by an appropriate paid provider could be incorporated into a treatment program.

TIME COSTS

There are two categories of time costs. One is the amount of time patients spend in treatment, traveling to treatment or waiting for treatment. The second time cost is the value of productive activity that patients lose because of illness. In evaluating the cost of treatment, the value of the time a patient spends in treatment should be considered a direct cost of treatment and this time should be valued at the opportunity cost of that time. Thus, if the patient must leave competitive employment to participate in treatment then the opportunity cost patient's wage rate at that job. However, if the patient is not in the job market, the opportunity cost of time spent in treatment would be zero.

In contrast to the direct cost of time spent in treatment, time lost due to illness is an indirect cost. Traditionally, in cost of illness studies, wage rates have been used to calculate the value of lost productivity. However, the chronic disability often associated with schizophrenic illness frequently begins in early adulthood before individuals are fully established in the labor market. Thus, it is difficult to assign a meaningful value to their time. Given this high level of inaccuracy and variability, most cost-effectiveness studies of schizophrenia treatments do not treat lost productivity as an indirect cost. Instead they use data on earnings from competitive employment as an outcome variable reflecting one facet of treatment effectiveness.

MAINTENANCE COSTS

The issue of whether maintenance costs, such as food, lodging, clothing, and transportation, should be included in the costs of treatment is debatable. When clients are in jail, in an inpatient facility, or other supervised housing or treatment facility, maintenance costs are usually incorporated in the unit cost of treatment and are included in cost analyses.

There are two different approaches to estimating the value of treatment related maintenance costs. One approach is to treat all maintenance costs as treatment costs (Rice *et al.*, 1992), and the other is to treat only a portion of the total as treatment costs (Dickey *et al.*, 1986). The justification for including all maintenance expenses is that these expenditures are an integral part of the treatment and the amount often reflects the relative share of burden incurred by different parties (i.e., government, social welfare agencies, families). The rationale for using only a proportion of maintenance costs is that some level of food, clothing, and room expense are necessary for every individual whether healthy or ill and only the extra costs of providing these necessities in a special setting are truly part of treatment.

Maintenance costs incurred while living with family members or alone in a house or apartment are not usually considered treatment costs because these maintenance expenditures are part of daily living expenses, even for persons who are not ill. However, there are two types of situations in which maintenance costs may be considered as direct costs. Costs of employing a paid caretaker to assist a patient with basic daily living activities should be included. Similarly, if family members or others make extensive contributions to a patient's basic living expenses, these contributions are clearly a cost of illness and are ideally included as a family cost. However, information on the frequency and value of these contributions must be obtained through lengthy and complex interviews with family members which may not be feasible in all evaluations.

TRANSFER PAYMENTS

Transfer payments are payments from one party to another which are not accompanied by exchange of services or goods of comparable value. Examples of transfer payments are government entitlements such as welfare assistance and disability payments, and charitable contributions. These payments are particularly relevant in studying schizophrenia because the high level of persistent disability associated with the illness leads to high levels of eligibility for entitlement programs. These payments are not treatment costs because they reflect only a shifting of existing resources. However, they are an important focus of any cost evaluation because transfer payments are indicators of the government and taxpayer share of the cost of illness. The amount of transfer payments also serves as a useful outcome indicator demonstrating treatment providers' success in linking clients to entitlement programs which are likely to increase their level of well-being.

Although transfer payments themselves are not direct costs of treatment or illness, the cost of administering the program is a direct cost. This administrative cost can be calculated as a proportion of the amount of payment. For instance, if a client received $4800 per year in supplemental security income while participating in a treatment program, this $4800 would constitute the government's monetary burden. In addition, if local administrative costs were equal to 15% of the actual payment, an additional $720 (15% of $4800) in administrative costs could be considered as a direct cost.

DISCOUNTING

When evaluating a treatment that lasts for more than 1 year, it is necessary to adjust costs in later years to reflect the present value of those costs; this adjustment is called "discounting." The rationale for discounting is that the value of a dollar in the current year is always greater than the value of the

Table 2. Average annual costs per schizophrenic client in a California county (1990 dollars)

Resource type	Average cost ($)	Cost summary ($)
Direct costs		
Mental health treatment		
Public sector		
Inpatient hospitalization	11 000	
Skilled nursing facility	7 500	
Psychiatric emergency care	990	
Medication visit	970	
Outpatient treatment	2 920	
Case management	1 610	
Day treatment	240	
Partial hospitalization	90	
Subtotal		25 920 (74.3%)
Private sector		
Inpatient hospitalization	2 800	
Skilled nursing facility	1 200	
Subtotal		4 000 (11.5%)
Medical treatment		
Public sector		
Inpatient hospitalization	1 470	
Medical emergency care	320	
Outpatient treatment	160	
Subtotal		1 950 (5.5%)
Private sector		
Inpatient hospitalization	50	
Medical emergency care	10	
Subtotal		60 (0.1%)
Criminal justice contacts		
Police contacts	60	
Court appearances	420	
Jail/prison	850	
Conservatorship	190	
Subtotal		1 520 (4.2%)
Social services		
Administrative costs of transfers	960	
Subtotal		960 (2.8%)
Family/informal care		
Informal care	170	
Transportation	60	
Subtotal		1 190 (3.4%)
Total direct costs		34 640 (99.3%)
Indirect costs		
Loss of patient productivity	170	
Loss of caregiver productivity	80	
Total indirect costs		250 (0.7%)
Total societal costs		34 890 (100%)

same dollar in a future year, even if there is no inflation, because the opportunity to use the dollar now is forgone, as is the opportunity to earn additional income through investment. For example, if one could earn a 7% return on the foregone investment, the present value of a \$100 cost 1 year from now would be \$94.46 $(100/(1+0.07))$. It is obvious from the formula that the higher the discount rate, the lower the present value of the cost.

For example, consider a 4 year treatment program with annual costs over the 4 years of $19 000, $13 000, $10 000 and $9000, respectively. Without discounting, the total cost would be $51 000, while with a 7% discount rate, the present value of the total cost would be $47 231. Clearly, discounting can have a major impact on total treatment cost.

The choice of the discount rate is a complex and controversial topic in economics. A common rule of thumb when evaluating a public program is to set the discount rate at the interest rate that the government must pay to borrow money. It can vary from year to year depending on economic conditions, and has ranged from 4 to 12% over the last 20 years in the United States. At present, the discount rate is between 4 and 5%. Given the variability of rates over time, it is important to explicitly state the discount rate used in any analysis.

EMPIRICAL EXAMPLE OF ESTIMATING COSTS FOR TREATING SEVERELY MENTALLY ILL PATIENTS

As illustration of the methods discussed in the preceding sections, we now present an empirical example of a cost evaluation of one specialized treatment program for severely mentally ill patients in one California county (Hu & Jerrell, 1994). The costs presented below reflect average costs per patient for 124 patients treated during a 12 month period in 1990. Table 2 shows the overall program costs.

Direct public mental health treatment costs were obtained from the county mental health bureau. Information on resource use was obtained from the bureau's data system. This system, designed primarily for reimbursement purposes, contains utilization information reflecting service type and provider type for all encounters for each client. Thus, units of service for inpatient days, skilled nursing care, residential treatment, psychiatric emergency services, and all outpatient services could be extracted for the entire year. Unit costs were also obtained from the county mental health bureau. Each provider was required to submit cost calculations in a standardized format to permit cost auditing. Researchers in the study reviewed cost allocation procedures with the county financial officer, especially capital costs and depreciation calculations. In the county's original cost calculations, space in depreciated buildings was considered to be cost-free. Although this method is appropriate from an accounting perspective, it does not accurately reflect the value of the space used to provide treatment. Therefore, for study cost calculations such space was valued at the prevailing rental price of similar space. Once the data were adjusted, the number of service units were multiplied by the unit cost of each service.

The results show that the average annual public cost of treating these schizophrenic patients was $25 920, which included $11 600 in inpatient costs, $7500 in skilled nursing costs, $2950 in outpatient costs, and $1610 in case management costs. Table 2 shows that public inpatient costs accounted for almost three-fourths of the total public mental health treatment costs, while total public mental health costs accounted for three-fourths of the cost to society.

Private sector mental health treatment costs were more difficult to obtain than public sector costs. The source and type of private mental health service units were identified through client interview and mental health bureau records. As most of these clients were eligible for government disability benefits, the county reimbursed private providers for these services. Therefore, utilization and cost data were available from the county's public insurance data base. In this county, private sector inpatient services accounted for 11.5% of treatment costs. It is obvious from this example that inpatient care costs account for the majority of treatment costs.

Data on medical care utilization were obtained in two ways. As noted above, most of these clients were eligible for government disability benefits. Therefore, much of their medical care was provided by the county's public health system and detailed utilization and cost data were available from health system data bases. Data on private sector medical care were more difficult to obtain. Utilization information was obtained through client interview and this data is clearly less accurate and complete than that from health system data bases. Results indicate that medical treatment accounted for only 5.5% of the societal cost, or $1950, with the vast majority of costs incurred in the public sector.

The local criminal justice system's database was used to trace criminal justice contacts of the 124

Table 3. Sources of patient support

Source of support	Amount of financial support (annual average per patient) ($)
Earned income	610
Subtotal	610
Government entitlements	
SSI/SSA	6300
Welfare	15
Unemployment	90
VA disability	90
Subtotal	6495
Other	180
Subtotal	180
Family support	
Housing assistance	10
Maintenance assistance	210
Subtotal	220
Total financial support	7505

patients in the treatment program studied. All types of contacts, including citations, arrests, hearings, sentencing, incarceration, and probation, are recorded in the data system. Study investigators collaborated with criminal justice system staff to estimate the average cost of each type of contact based on the type and amount of resources (personnel, equipment, overhead, etc.) involved in each.

The average criminal justice system cost of $1520 reflects criminal justice system contacts for only eight of the 124 patients studied. Thus, while involvement was limited, these contacts were very costly. Jail costs were most expensive, followed by court appearance costs. In addition, there were social and family services which include the administrative costs of transfer payments, transportation costs, and informal care costs. The administrative costs of transfer payments were estimated as 15% of the payments to program recipients. These costs may be considered as secondary costs to society which are not directly related to illness or treatment and some economists would not include them as social costs. Family and informal care costs were obtained through caregiver and client interviews. On the whole, these costs accounted for only 3.4% of total costs. The average total direct cost per patient was $34 640.

In this sample, most of the schizophrenic patients did not work in the labor force and few family members spent time caring for patients. Thus, the indirect opportunity costs of loss productivity were very minimal, 0.7% of total cost.

Table 3 provides a detailed financial support summary to illustrate the distribution of economic burden, including government contributions in the form of transfer payments and family expenditures on maintenance costs. Note that these items are not included in the total costs of treatment, but are considered as financial support given to these patients. Among the government support, government disability payments ($6300) account for the largest share of financial support. In one sense, this reflects success of local treatment providers in linking clients to entitlement programs. Of course, higher income earned by patients is another positive outcome of the treatment.

SUMMARY AND CONCLUSIONS

Cost analysis is a useful tool for maintaining accountability for spending of public and private funds, examining the efficacy of treatment programs and comparing the cost and effectiveness of alternative treatment strategies. This paper has summarized the methodology of estimating the costs of illness and treatment associated with individual treatment programs for schizophrenia.

Treating schizophrenia is extremely costly and requires an extensive array of services, ranging from mental health and medical care, to social and legal services, to informal family assistance. Therefore, it is essential to identify carefully the many associated societal costs and to develop a cost allocation methodology which accurately reflects the value of resources used. Conducting comprehensive evaluations of the costs of schizophrenia and its treatment requires close collaboration between treatment providers, clients, and health economists.

REFERENCES

Alchian, A.A. and Allen, W.R. (1967). *University Economics.* Belmont, CA: Wadsworth Publishing Company.

Bond, G.R. (1984) An economic analysis of psychosocial

rehabilitation. *Hospital and Community Psychiatry*, **35**, 356–362.

Bond, G.R., *et al.* (1988). Assertive case management in three CMHCs: A controlled study. *Hospital and Community Psychiatry*, **39**, 411–418.

Burns, T. and Raftery, J. (1991). Cost of schizophrenia in a randomized trial of home-based treatment. *Schizophrenia Bulletin*, **17**, 407–410.

Cannon, N.L., McGuire, T.G., and Dickey, B, (1985). Capital costs in economic program evaluation: The case of mental health services. In J. Catterall, ed, *Economic Evaluation of Public Programs. New Directions for Program Evaluation*, Vol. 26, pp. 69–82. San Francisco: Jossey-Bass.

Cassell, W.A., Smith, C.M. Grunberg, F., Boan, J.A., and Thomas, R.F. (1972). Comparing costs of hospital and community care. *Hospital and Community Psychiatry*, **23**, 17–20.

Clark, R.E., Teague, G.B., Ricketts, S.K. *et al.* (1994) Measuring resource use in economic evaluations: Determining the social costs of mental illness. *Journal of Mental Health Administration*, **21**, 32–41.

Dickey, B., Cannon, N.L., McGuire, T.G., and Gudeman, J.E. (1986). The quarterway house: A two-year cost study of an experimental residential program. *Hospital and Community Psychiatry*, **37**, 1136–1143.

Dickey, B., McGuire, T.G., Cannon, N.L., and Gudeman, J.E. (1986). Mental health cost models: Refinements and applications. *Medical Care*, **29**, 857–867.

Enthoven, A. (1965). Appendix: The simple mathematics of maximization. In E. Hitch and R. McKean, eds, *The Economics of Defense in the Nuclear Age*, pp. 239–242. New York: Atheneum Co.

Fenton, F.R., Tessier, L., Straening, E., Smith, F., and Benoit, C. (1982). A comparative trial of home and hospital psychiatric treatment: Financial costs. *Canadian Journal of Psychiatry*, **27**, 177–187.

Fenton, F.R., Tessier, L., Straening, E., Smith, F., and Benoit, C. (1984). A two-year follow-up of a comparative trial of the cost-effectiveness of home and hospital psychiatric treatment. *Canadian Journal of Psychiatry*, **29**, 205–211.

Guillette, W., *et al.* (1978). Day hospitalization as a cost-effective alternative to inpatient care: A pilot study. *Hospital and Community Psychiatry*, **29**, 525–527.

Hafner, H. and an der Heiden, W. (1989). Effectiveness and cost of community care for schizophrenic patients. *Hospital and Community Psychiatry*, **40**, 59–63.

Hoult, J. and Reynolds, I. (1984). Schizophrenia: A comparative trial of community orientated and hospital orientated psychiatric care. *Acta Psychiatrica Scandanavica*, **69**, 359–372.

Hoult, J., Reynolds, I., and Rosen, A. (1981). A controlled study of psychiatric hospital versus community treatment: The effect on relatives. *Australian and New Zealand Journal of Pschiatry*, **15**, 323–328.

Hoult, J. Reynolds, I., Rosen, A. Chanbonneau-Powes, M., and Weeks, P. (1983). Psychiatric hospital versus community treatment: The results of a randomized trial. *Australian and New Zealand Journal of Psychiatry*, **37**, 26–31.

Hu, T-W. and Jerrell, J. (1991). Cost-effectiveness of alternative approaches in treating severely mentally ill in California. *Schizophrenic Bulletin*, **17**, 461–468.

Hu, T-W. and Jerrell, J. (1994). *Estimating the cost impact of three case management programs for treating people with severe mental illness*, a paper presented at the Seventh Biennial Research Conference on Economics of Mental Health, September 1994, Bethesda, Maryland.

Jacoby, J., McEwen, T., and Guynes, R. (1987). *National Baseline Information on Offender Processing Costs: Source Data*. Washington, DC: National Institute of Justice.

Jerrell, J. and Hu. T-W (1989). Cost effectiveness of intensive clinical and case management compared to an existing system of care. *Inquiry*, **26**, 224–234.

Jones, R., *et al.* (1980). A comparison of two different services treating schizophrenia: A cost–benefit approach. *Psychological Medicine*, **10**, 493–505.

May, P.R.A. (1971). Cost efficiency of treatments for the schizophrenic patient. *American Journal of Psychiatry*, **127**, 118–121.

McGuire, T.G. (1991). Measuring the economic costs of schizophrenia. *Schizophrenia Bulletin*, **17**, 375–388.

McGuire, T., Dickey, B., Shively, G.E., and Strumwasser, I. (1987). Differences in resource use and cost among facilities treating alcohol, drug abuse, and mental health disorders: implications for design of a prospective payment system. *American Journal of Psychiatry*, **144**, 616–620.

Moscarelli, M., Capri, S., and Neri, L. (1991). Cost evaluation of chronic schizophrenic patients during the first 3 years after the first contact. *Schizophrenic Bulletin*, **17**, 421–426.

Murphy, J.G. and Datel, W.E. (1976). A cost–benefit analysis of community versus institutional living. *Hospital and Community Psychiatry*, **27**, 165–170.

Rice, D.P. (1966). Estimating the cost of illness. *Health Economics Series*, No. 6 (DHEW Pub. No. (PHA)947-6). Rockville, MD: US Department of Health, Education and Welfare.

Rice, D.P., Kelman, S., and Miller, L.S. (1992). The economic burden of mental illness. *Hospital and Community Psychiatry*, **43**, 1227–1232.

Rosenheck, R., Neale, M., and Frisman, L. (1993). Program cost of intensive case management: estimating costs and identifying sources of inter-site variation. Unpublished manuscript.

Sharfstein, S.S. and Nafziger, J.C. (1976). Community care: Costs and benefits for a chronic patient. *Hospital and Communty Psychiatry*, **27**, 170.

ten Horn, G.H.M.M. and Giel, R. (1984). The feasibility of cost–benefit studies of mental health care. *Acta Psychi-*

atrica Scandanavica, **69**, 80–87.

Wayson, B.L. and Funke, G.S. (1989). *What Price Justice? A Handbook for the Analysis of Criminal Justice Costs.* National Institute of Justice.

Weisbrod, B.A. (1983). A guide to benefit–cost analysis, as seen through a controlled experiment in treating the mentally ill. *Journal of Health Politics, Policy and Law*, **7**, 808–845.

Weisbrod, B.A., Test, M.A., and Stein, L. (1980). Alternatives to mental hospital treatment. II. Economic cost–benefit analysis. *Archives of General Psychiatry*, **37**, 400–405.

Wiersma, D., Kluiter, H., Nienhuis, F.J., *et al.* (1991). Costs and benefits of day treatment with community care for schizophrenic patients. *Schizophrenia Bulletin*, **17**, 411–419.

30

Methodology of Economic Evaluations of Mental Health Services: the Clinician's Perspective

GAYLE JACKSON
Mental Illness Research Unit, University of Manchester

DAVID GOLDBERG
Institute of Psychiatry, London, UK

WHY DO AN ECONOMIC EVALUATION?

In developing and running mental health services, planners and managers must make choices between different ways of spending limited resources and this implies making value judgements about different forms of care. These judgements have often been based on political expediency, personal opinion, or immediate financial pressures and there is a need for objective data to inform them. An economic evaluation concerns itself with measuring value for money, the techniques link costs and benefits and provide objective data as to what is being bought by resources spent in different ways. Many doctors wishing to include an economic dimension to an evaluative study may not be familiar with the necessary techniques, and in this chapter we discuss some of the methodological issues relevant to the clinician designing a study. Table 1 lists the steps necessary in carrying out an economic evaluation of a service. The rest of the chapter follows these steps.

THE IMPORTANCE OF A CLEAR AIM

The evaluation of a service is a complex task and a clear aim and precise hypotheses will focus and structure the data collection.

The hypotheses should relate to the likely effects of the new service and the evaluation should concentrate on measuring them. A new physical treatment for example might be expected to affect florid psychotic symptoms and the main outcome measures might therefore be an assessment of the patient's mental state and of the side-effects of medication. In evaluating the effect of community occupational therapy, however, the investigator would postulate an effect on patients' activity levels and skills. If there is no thought given to the hypotheses, the researchers may attempt to assess a very broad range of possible effects wasting time on areas which are unaffected and possibly performing inadequate assessments in relevant areas.

Handbook of Mental Health Economics and Health Policy, Volume I, Schizophrenia. Edited by M. Moscarelli, A. Rupp and N. Sartorius.
© 1996 John Wiley & Sons Ltd.

Table 1. Steps in an economic appraisal

1 State the aim of the investigation and formulate the hypotheses to be tested
2 Design the study
3 Establish a register of study patients
4 Gather basic information about the services
5 Measure the monetary effects:
   Design and administer the economic questionnaire
   Count the items of service used
   Estimate unit costs
6 Measure the non-monetary costs and benefits
7 Interpret the results

Table 2. Costs of patients with neurotic illness (per capita cost in £ over the 6 months following first contact)

Type of cost	Community service	Hospital service
Per capita cost including all the patients in the analysis		
Costs of services	321	567
Cost to patients	99	151
Lost market output	732	269
(days lost)	(69)	(66)
Total cost	1152	987
Per capita cost excluding the outlier in the index group		
Lost output	315	269
Total cost	735	987

DESIGNING THE STUDY

An economic evaluation must be a comparison either between two novel ways of treating a disorder or between a novel method and a good example of standard clinical practice. It is not possible to evaluate adequately a psychiatric treatment without a matched comparison group as the natural history of psychiatric disorders and the costs associated with them are variable and are affected by factors other than the provision of services.

The best experimental design is that of prospective random assignment of individual patients to the two services to be compared. Weisbrod *et al.* (1980) used this design in their well known controlled study of home versus hospital treatment for patients with acute psychosis, consecutive patients presenting for inpatient care were randomly assigned to the experimental group receiving home care or control group receiving standard hospital treatment. This design is not always feasible and others have been used. Jones and Goldberg (Goldberg & Jones, 1980; Jones *et al.*, 1980) wished to compare the effectiveness of a mental hospital and a District General Hospital psychiatric unit in caring for patients with chronic schizophrenia. They did this by interviewing retrospectively defined cohorts of patients with schizophrenia 4 and 12 years into their illness. They first identified consecutive admissions to each service over the same periods 4 and 12 years prior to the start of the study and then selected patients for whom the index admission was a first admission with a diagnosis of schizophrenia. Hyde and Goldberg comparing hospital and hostel ward care of long-stay patients used another design (Hyde *et al.*, 1985). They defined two groups of long-stay inpatients who were carefully matched for chronicity, severity of symptoms and problem behaviors and randomly assigned the groups to continued hospital care or to care in a hostel ward. On a larger scale, Goldberg *et al.* (1992) defined two populations of 20 000 people matched for sociodemographic characteristics and randomly assigned them to have access to contrasting services.

Whichever design is used, the study groups must be economically comparable as well as matching on conventional measures of clinical and social severity of disorder. If one study group has more employed people, or more people in highly paid jobs, there are likely to be higher monetary costs and benefits in that group because the economic consequences of their illness will be greater. This is illustrated in Table 2. These are data drawn from a study of the treatment of patients with neurotic disorders by a new community-based team compared with a traditional hospital service (Goldberg *et al.*, 1992). Table 2 shows a summary of the costs of the two services. Care by the new team entailed lower costs in services and to the patients, but this advantage was outweighed by higher costs of lost marketed output in the index group. This was not because index patients were off work for longer, as the time lost from work was similar in both groups. One index patient earned a very high salary: four times higher than that of any other study patient and so his time off work resulted in much greater costs. The figures also show that lost marketed output is a major component of the cost of mental illness and it is of interest to note that the monetary value of the atypical patient's time off work alone outweighed all the savings made in hospital costs by the new service.

This patient is an "outlier," as his earnings are unrepresentative of the group. One way to deal with outliers is to exclude them from the analysis, considering them separately. The second part of Table 2 shows the costs if this patient is excluded. It can be seen that the difference in costs between the two services now reverses!

COLLECTING THE DATA

Table 1 shows that the data collection is in two parts: the measurement of the monetary effects of the services and the assessment of the non-monetary effects. In a classical economic analysis, all costs and benefits are quantified and expressed in monetary terms. This poses difficulties in evaluative research in psychiatry where monetary valuation of the non-monetary effects would be controversial and of doubtful validity (see Goldberg, 1983 for a full discussion). A widely accepted method is that of Glass and Goldberg (1977) where in a modified cost–benefit analysis the investigators carry out a conventional analysis of the monetary effects and in a separate exercise measure the non-monetary or "soft" costs and benefits. The results of the economic comparison are then used to interpret the comparison of the soft costs and benefits: if a service which produces more soft benefits is also cheaper it is said to dominate the other, while if the better service is more expensive, the evaluation gives health planners objective data as to how much the added quality will cost.

ESTABLISHING A STUDY REGISTER

Data collection for an economic appraisal is complex. Data are needed from a number of sources and the service use must be recorded longitudinally for the whole of the study period. For all but the simplest of studies, a computerized register of the study patients will make the task much easier and the development of personal computers means that most projects can now afford to establish one. A register normally contains for each patient basic demographic and clinical information, the circumstances of referral to the service, and a longitudinal record of contacts with it (Ten Horn, 1986). If the quality of the information is good, this will allow the data to be analyzed in different ways, comparing for example patterns of care for patients of different diagnoses. Maintaining a good quality register is labor intensive and needs skilled staff (Fryers, 1986).

INFORMATION ABOUT THE SERVICES

Much information can usually be collected without the need for specialized instruments. For example, data on staffing, location of services, and the range of services offered can be routinely collected as factual data. Basic information relevant to the quality of care offered by a service is also factual and can be collected without special instruments: the study patient register is helpful for recording waiting times, patterns of care, admission rates, etc. Large program evaluations have used care indices available from case register data as measures of outcome: admission or readmission rates, length of inpatient treatment, and time spent out of hospital (Hafner & an der Heiden, 1991). These are only proxies for individual outcomes and they are influenced by factors other than the patients' health or social functioning. On the other hand they are unequivocal statistics and as such are hard data which carry important service implications.

ESTIMATING THE MONETARY EFFECTS

The costs of services are measured in three stages. First the patients' utilization of services over the study period must be measured. Then a unit cost is estimated for each type of care. Finally, for each patient the number of items and the cost are multiplied to give overall costs. In addition to the cost of services used, the monetary effects also include the economic consequences of the patients' mental illness to the patient and to their family: their loss of earnings and the need for others to care for them and for their dependants.

It may be helpful for the researchers to start by

Table 3. Services used by the patients showing the sources of information used to collect the data on resource use

Use of hospital services, community health services, general practice resources, and social services day center and residential facilities from services registers, medical notes, and the health authority computerized database
Use of social workers, other rehabilitation facilities, criminal justice system, and voluntary services from an economic questionnaire administered to the patients at interview
Costs to the patient (money and time costs accessing and receiving treatment, employment history, income) from an economic questionnaire administered to the patients at interview
Costs to the family (money and time costs resulting from the patients' illness) from an economic questionnaire administered to the relatives at interview

making a list of all the different types of resources which patients are likely to use. Table 3 shows the list of services drawn up for an evaluation of the care of patients with schizophrenia by a community team in south Manchester with the sources of information used. The list should be comprehensive including health services, other statutory agencies, voluntary organizations, and self-help groups and also the resources of the patients and their families. If the costings are not comprehensive, the evaluation will not detect cost shifting from one agency to another. An illustration of this might be a service development where shorter hospital stays was leading to patients' families having to take more time off work to care for them and to more patients spending time in prison. The consequent shifting of costs from the hospital budget on to families and the criminal justice system would not be detected by a study looking only at health service costs. A pilot study and wide consultation with colleagues and patients will help to ensure that the list is as complete as possible.

THE ECONOMIC QUESTIONNAIRE

The patient or their principal carer is an important source of information about the use they have made of services. Although information on service receipt will be obtained in many instances from the facilities themselves, it is important to ask the patients too. Community care in particular is often delivered in a fragmented system and the patient may be the only person who knows about all the different agencies involved with him/her. Information from the patient is usually obtained on interview using an economic questionnaire.

Areas to be covered will be information on accommodation, on employment history and earnings, and other income such as State benefits. For facilities where it is not possible to obtain records of service use, the patient must be asked to estimate the frequency and length of attendances. The time and costs of travelling to treatment facilities and any other costs of treatment, such as charges made for the service should be asked about. Information is also needed about aids and adaptations made to the patient's accommodation, this may be especially relevant for older patient groups, and about the burden of care falling on informal carers. Some studies may wish to interview informal carers themselves to obtain a more detailed estimate of the time and resources they spend on caring for the patient.

In many cases, investigators have developed their own economic questionnaires but researchers should consider using or adapting one of the instruments which have been developed for this purpose. The Economic Questionnaire used by Weisbrod *et al.* (1980) is a comprehensive instrument which was used in one of the classic economic evaluations of home treatment. In Britain the Personal Social Services Research Unit (PSSRU) has built on this and other instruments to develop the Client Receipt Interview (CSRI) (Beecham & Knapp, 1992). This is a questionnaire, but is best completed by a trained interviewer and takes about 40 minutes to complete. The questions are mostly structured but some require narrative answers. It is comprehensive and has been designed to be adaptable to varied research settings.

COUNTING ITEMS OF SERVICE

For frequently used facilities, the most reliable way to collect service utilization by study patients is to go through the service registers or the patients' medical records for the study period recording all service contacts by study patients. This data collection is tedious and time consuming but it is essential that it should be accurate. The reliability of the sources of information should be checked. In Manchester for example, we found that computerized records of hospital utilization were easy to use but often incomplete and an examination of the written lists and patients' records were needed to collect good quality information. The process is helped by well designed data collection sheets tailored to the lay-out of the sources of data and laid out to facilitate data entry into the computer.

Collecting and costing a large number of services is itself a costly exercise and it may not be possible to collect data from all sources with the same thoroughness. The research team should give priority to collecting accurate data about services which carry high unit costs: these are inpatient care, residential care, day care, and child care. If many study patients are employed, lost marketed output may be another area carrying high costs. Less emphasis may be paid to areas with low unit costs: for example, the costs of drugs prescribed in primary care in a project where the major expenditure is on inpatient care. Knapp and Beecham (1993) have produced a shortened list of services which have accounted for over 80% of expenditure on services for patients with long-term mentally ill people in a number of studies. The authors discuss the circumstances under which using this reduced list of costings alone may give valid cost information.

ESTIMATING UNIT COSTS

The cost per item of care used in an economic evaluation should be its *long run marginal opportunity cost*. The term opportunity cost means that the cost is estimated not as the amount spent but as the value of the resource used in the best alternative way: the value of the opportunities forgone. The marginal cost is that associated with one extra person using the service. The short run marginal costs would be the small cost of extending the service to one extra person by using present resources more intensively. Most evaluation is concerned with long-term planning for which the long run costs are more relevant. Many investigators have used the current average revenue cost plus capital costs and overheads as an estimate of the long run marginal cost (Beecham & Knapp, 1992). The current average revenue cost is the amount spent on staff and equipment divided by a measure of workload. Capital cost is the cost of depreciation of the buildings and overheads, and includes the cost of services shared by all using the facility: heating, lighting, cleaning, etc.

Table 4. Components of the cost of an inpatient day in a Manchester psychiatric unit (in £, 1990/91 price base)

Type of cost	Value
Nursing staff	£28.20
Medical staff	£16.03
Cleaning, heating, etc.	£7.22
Paramedical services	£2.58
Catering	£5.93
Portering	£1.15
Residual overheads	£7.08
Pharmacy	£1.82
Diagnostic facilities	£0.94
Direct administration	£2.43
Secure facilities	£9.95
Capital costs	£2.54
Total cost	£85.87

Unit costs should be built up by estimating the cost of each individual component of the service and Table 4 shows as an example the components of the cost of a hospital inpatient day taken from a recent study carried out in Manchester (Goldberg *et al.*, 1992).

The research team may need to spend time observing the work of the unit to measure the resource used per item of care. This may show that costs are different for different groups of patients: for example, detailed observation of the resource used by inpatients on a general psychiatric ward showed that patients received much more staff time in the first few days of their admission (Hyde *et al.*, 1985). This information may be used to weight overall costs for subgroups of patients.

Sources of information for estimating costs are the accounts of the service for facility specific costs such as the cost of a day in hospital or an attendance at a day center. For costing the time of peripatetic staff details are needed about their pay and working conditions either on a local or national level as is relevant to the study (Beecham & Knapp, 1992).

Building up valid estimates of unit costs is complicated and the help and advice of a health economist is essential. Increasingly, costing work is being carried out in health facilities and access to any previous estimates may be very helpful. PSSRU have published a report with estimates of British unit costs for a range of services involved in community care with enough detail to allow them to be adapted for specific studies (Netten & Smart, 1993).

MEASURING THE NON-MONETARY EFFECTS

Having information about the costs of a service without an assessment of the benefits it brings is like shopping from a list of prices without knowing what the items are which are being bought. Measuring benefits tells planners what they are going to get for their money.

Rating scales are widely used in psychiatric research to convert descriptive data such as clinical interviews into numerical data which can be subjected to statistical analysis. Nowadays, most studies collecting data on individual patients use rating scales for most of their assessments, but where a study is exploring new ground or examining unique local issues it may be useful to record at least some of the data in descriptive form.

Methodological issues in choosing instruments and collecting data for a number of measures are discussed below and selected individual instruments are reviewed. Comprehensive lists of instruments developed for psychiatric research are available, one has been compiled by the British Royal College of Psychiatrists (The Royal College of Psychiatrists, 1992) and there are also good reviews of individual instruments (Thompson, 1989; Dennis *et al.*, 1992).

ASSESSING THE QUALITY OF CARE

There is no blueprint for a perfect psychiatric service. There is, however, a consensus based on research on a number of characteristics and features of a good quality service and there are instruments available for assessing many of these features.

In residential settings, Wing and Brown (1961) were among the first to try to measure the quality of patients' environment and to demonstrate that this affected patients' outcomes. They assessed the restrictiveness of the ward management, the extent to which patients were able to keep personal possessions, the amount of medication prescribed, the amount of contact with the outside world and the amount of time patients spent doing nothing. Wykes *et al.* (1982) built on their work in developing the Hostel Hospital Practices Profile, which measures the restrictiveness versus the permissiveness of the setting. Lavender (1987) developed the Model Standards Questionnaire expanding on Wykes' work to include assessments based on the theory of psychiatric rehabilitation and standards of the physical environment.

Wing (1988) has consistently argued that an important measure of the quality of a service is the extent to which its clients needs are met or remain unmet. The assessment of needs is a two-stage procedure: first, an assssment is made of what problems a patient has and then the extent to which these problems are being addressed by the service is explored. The results of the assessment will show how often patients' needs for care are met or unmet. A research instrument has been developed by Brewin and colleagues using this approach (1987). The Needs for Care Assessment is an instrument which links an individualized assessment of need for each patient using standardized research instruments to a schedule which prescribes apropriate actions to be followed to meet each need. It is a lengthy instrument and more recently the Camberwell Assessment of Need (Phelan *et al.*, 1993) has been designed for an evaluation of new community services in Camberwell. This is a shorter instrument taking about 20 minutes to complete. It relies on staff and patients to make judgements as to the presence of need and to assess whether adequate interventions have been offered.

ASSESSING CONSUMER SATISFACTION

Patients' views of services are an important component of the quality of care. In the Western world, consumer views are increasingly influencing formulation of health care and social policy. Furthermore, dissatisfaction with treatment has been shown to be a correlate of non-compliance (Ley, 1982). Studies comparing hospital- or community-based care have consistently shown that patients prefer community-based treatments (Hoult & Reynolds, 1984; Tyrer, 1984; Onyett *et al.*, 1990; Goldberg *et al.*, 1992), although there is often little difference in the outcomes of patients treated by the two styles of service. El-Gualeby (1993) has reviewed the methodological issues in the measurement of patient satisfaction. Sampling is an important issue, dissatisfied customers often drop out of contact with services and may not be included in research. The timing of the assessment is significant, satisfaction has been shown to change over a course of treatment. Assessing the views of very disabled people with mental handicap, florid psychotic symptoms or thought disorder may be difficult and corroborative data from relatives for this group of patients can be helpful.

McPhee *et al.* (1975) review the measurement of satisfaction in 67 community mental health centers. They found that many used short instruments asking very general questions. They recommend assessment of specific issues such as cost, accessibility, physical surroundings, and staff–patient interactions and mention the importance of the patients' frame of reference, their cultural background, past experience of psychiatric care and expectations.

THE OUTCOME OF CARE

Individual outcome for a patient with schizophrenia has many dimensions: mental state, disturbed behavior, negative symptoms, physical health, the possession of skills needed for independent community living and social relationships, subjective quality of life, and employment. The first step as with the overall assessment of benefits is to be clear about the stated aims of the new treatment so as to concentrate on the dimensions of outcome which are most likely to be affected.

Standardized assessments of mental state fall into three categories. Screening instruments such as the General Health Questionnaire (GHQ) are useful for identifying patients who are likely to have a mental illness. Diagnostic instruments such as the Present State Examination (Wing *et al.*, 1974) are lengthy and detailed standardized interviews, which may be used to establish a research diagnosis at the beginning of the study. They are not suitable for rating a change in severity of symptoms: for this purpose observer-rated scales such as the KGV (Krawiecka *et al.*, 1977) or the CPRS (Asberg *et al.*, 1978) are more appropriate.

The REHAB (Baker & Hall, 1988) scale and the SBS (Wykes *et al.*, 1982) both cover behavior and clinical and social functioning in patients with chronic illness, including measures of negative symptoms. They are both observer-rated instruments which ask care staff or relatives to make the ratings and this limits their usefulness in community settings where many patients may have no regular contact with anyone. They have both been widely used, have been shown to be valid instruments, and are quick and easy to administer.

Increasingly, quality of life is being used as an outcome measure. An advantage is that it is a common measure which can be compared across diagnoses and even across specialities. It has been cited by the Department of Health in Britain as the principal outcome measure to be used to assess social care in community mental health services (Department of Health and Social Security, 1989). It is influenced by the other dimensions of outcome listed above but includes a subjective measure of the patients' perception of overall outcome. Health-related quality of life measures such as the Nottingham Health Profile (McEwan, 1983) or the Rosser Index (Rosser & Watts, 1976) are short and easy to administer. However, they have not been designed for use in patients with long-term mental illness and they emphasize physical symptoms such as pain or physical disability. Lehman (1983) was the first to develop a quality of life measure designed for patients with long-term mental illness. His instrument was a lengthy interview but it has been shortened and developed by Oliver (1992) in Britain to a semistructured interview taking about 20 minutes. It combines factual information and patients' satisfaction with their circumstances and skills in a number of different areas of their lives such as work, social relations, accommodation, and finance. It also includes brief ratings of mental state and a rating by the patients of their overall satisfaction with their lives. It has been used both as an outcome measure in large service evaluations and as a way of charting individual outcome in clinical rehabilitation programs.

Table 5. Comparison of a community team and a hospital service in the care of patients with chronic schizophrenia

	Superior service
Non-monetary effects	
Extent to which patients' needs were met	Community team
Extent to which relatives' needs were met	Community team
Patients' satisfaction with the service	Community team
Family doctors' views of the service	Community team
Monetary effects	
Health service costs	Hospital service
Costs of other services	Hospital service
Cost of families	Hospital service
Patients' earned income	Community service

INTERPRETING THE RESULTS

Classically, the results of economic appraisals have been presented as the overall costs and benefits summed for each study group. More recently there has been increasing interest in disaggregating the data to examine the differences between patients.

The overall results are generally presented in a table showing the costs and benefits of each type of service. Table 5 shows an example drawn from the study comparing the care of patients with chronic schizophrenia living at home by a community-based team and a hospital-based outpatient service (Goldberg *et al.*, 1992). In this case, the new community team led to improvements in the quality of care: more of the patients' needs were met and patients were more satisfied. Costs of care in the group with access to the new service were higher by the cost of the new service. The study has therefore shown that the new style of service has led to better quality care and has given an estimate of what this improvement has cost.

These results are unusual, a more common finding is that services with more intensive treatments leading to higher unit costs may lead to better outcomes and to lower overall cost to the community (Goldberg, 1991). Jones and Goldberg found this in their study comparing a mental hospital and a District General Hospital unit in the treatment of patients with chronic schizophrenia (Goldberg & Jones, 1980; Jones *et al.*, 1980). The District General Hospital (DGH) was the more expensive unit: it was better staffed and had higher unit costs. However, at follow up, the DGH patients not only had better outcomes but their overall costs to society were less. The lower costs of the 4 year cohort were largely because they were more likely to be in employment, and of the 12 year cohort because they had spent less time in hospital. The clinical outcomes of DGH patients in both cohorts were better in that they were less likely to have developed chronic symptoms and a defect state, they were also less socially impaired. Weisbrod's study of home versus hospital treatment of acute phsychosis showed a similar pattern (Weisbrod *et al.*, 1980). Home treatment carried higher treatment costs but patients had better outcomes and when the wider social costs were taken into consideration, home treatment was found to be cheaper overall. This result is an important finding of economic evaluation: it shows that it may in the long run be cheaper to provide better quality services even if they lead to higher initial health care costs.

Only a few of the classical economic evaluations have published the statistical significances of the reported overall differences in cost. Commonly, apparently large differences in per capita cost fail to reach statistical significance because of the high variability of the data. These are intensive studies needing extensive data collection and the cost of including sufficient patients for the reported differences to reach statistical significance would often be prohibitive. This has been an important limitation of many of the studies in the literature.

Most costing studies have found wide varations in costs incurred by individual patients and Beecham *et al.* (1991) emphasize that analysis of these variations will give important information. They disaggregated the costs of a large group of long-term inpatients resettled in the community and found that over a third of the variation in the cost of care in the community could be explained by patients' symptoms, behavior, and personal characteristics at least 1 year earlier (Knapp *et al.*, 1993). Much of the remaining variation could be linked to their outcomes in their first year in the community, higher expenditure leading to improved outcomes.

Disaggregation by diagnosis of the data in Weisbrod's study referred to above (Weisbrod *et al.*, 1980), shows very different patterns for patients of different diagnoses: patients with schizophrenia cost less in community and benefited more, while for patients with personality disorders community treatment was much more expensive (Goldberg, 1991). This information might indicate the need for targeting intensive community services at groups for whom it was shown to be cost-effective.

In the study comparing community- and hospital-based services in the treatment of patients with schizophrenia referred to above (Goldberg *et al.*, 1992), disaggregation of the data showed that among patients seen by the community team, resources were targeted at the most needy patients whereas in the hospital-based service, there was no relationship between patients' need and the amount of resource they received. This additional analysis therefore indicates that the community service was more efficient at allocating resources and targeting the patients most in need and suggests that even without the input of new resource, this model of service would improve the efficiency of mental health care delivery.

Another factor to take into account in interpreting results is the time frame of the study: a short study may not capture clinical improvements in patients with long-standing disorders. Carrier (1988), has compared the provision of rehabilitation services to the long-term mentally ill to an investment and emphasizes the need to follow patients over a long period. The Manchester study comparing DGH and mental hospital care of schizophrenia illustrates this point: the differences in outcome and costs were all more marked after 12 years than after 4 (Goldberg, 1983), so that it may take time for the benefits of better quality care to become clear. The expected timing of costs and benefits should be made clear in reporting the studies, with future costs and benefits discounted using a standard discount rate.

For some resources, the estimate of unit costs involves making value judgements: for example the valuation of the unpaid time spent caring by relatives. It is important to make explicit what estimates were used. If this cost is critical in influencing the outcome of the study, a sensitivity analysis should be carried out. This involves carrying out several analyses of the data with differing values for these estimates to show how this affects the results.

Common preconceptions are that economic evaluation is concerned with cost cutting or is equivalent to accountancy. Health economics attempts to provide a framework in which expenditure can be assessed and its effects valued. There are several examples where economic appraisals have supported investment in high-quality psychiatric services on the grounds that they ultimately prove to be cheaper to society than less-effective alternatives. Information from the analysis of individual variations in data may help to predict future expenditure or target services at groups for which they are most effective. In the current widespread climate of limited resources, it may be argued that evaluative research which neglects the measurement of costs is incomplete and clinicians wishing to carry out such research will need to familiarize themselves with the relevant techniques.

REFERENCES

Asberg, M., Perris, C., Schalling, D., and Sedvall, G. (1978). The CPRS—development and applications of a psychiatric rating scale. *Acta Psychiatrica Scandinavica,* **271** (Suppl. 5).

Baker, R. and Hall, J. (1988). REHAB: a new assessment instrument for chronic psychiatric patients. *Schizophrenia Bulletin,* **14**, 97–111.

Beecham, J. and Knapp, M. (1992). Costing psychiatric interventions. In G. Thornicroft, C. R. Brewin and J, Wing, eds, *Measuring Health Needs,* pp. 163–183. London: Gaskell.

Beecham, J., Knapp, M. and Fenyo, A. (1991). Costs, needs, and outcomes. *Schizophrenia Bulletin,* **17**, 427–439.

Brewin, C.R., Wing, J.K., Mangen, S.P., Brugha, T.S. and MacCarthy, B. (1987). Principles and practice of measuring needs in the long-term mentally ill: the MRC Needs for Care Assessment. *Psychological Medicine,* **17**, 971–981.

Carrier, J. (1988). Discussion of "Economic dimensions of mental health evaluation." In I. M. Marks, J. Connolly, and M. Muijen, eds, *New Directions in Mental Health Care Evaluation,* pp. 30–33. London: Institute of Psychiatry.

Dennis, M., Ferguson, B., and Tyrer, P. (1992). Rating instruments. In C. Freeman and P. Tyrer, eds, *Research Methods in Psychiatry,* pp. 98–134. London: Gaskell.

Department of Health and Social Security (1989). *Caring for People, Community Care in the Next Decade and Beyond.* HMSO: London.

El-Guabely, N., Toews, J., Leckie, A., and Harper, D. (1983). On evaluating patient satisfaction: methodological issues. *Canadian Journal of Psychiatry*, **28**, 24–29.

Fryers, T. (1986). Practical issues in the establishment, maintenance and exploitation of registers. In G.H.M.M. Ten Horn, R. Giel, W.H. Gulbinat and J.H. Henderson, eds, *Psychiatric Case Registers in Public Health*, pp. 262–268. Amsterdam: Elsevier Science.

Glass, N. and Goldberg, D.P. (1977). Cost–benefit analysis and the evauation of psychiatric services. *Psychological Medicine*, **7**, 701–707.

Goldberg, D. (1983). Measurement of the benefits in psychiatry. In G. Teeling Smith, ed., *Measuring the Social Benefits of Medicine*, pp. 68–74. London: Office of Health Economics.

Goldberg, D. (1991). Cost-effectiveness studies in the treatment of schizophrenia: a review. *Schizophrenia Bulletin*, **17**, 453–459.

Goldberg, D.P. and Jones, R. (1980). The costs and benefits of psychiatric care. In L. Robins, P. Clayton and J. Wing, eds, *The Social Consequences of Psychiatric Illness*, pp. 55–70. New York: Brunner/Mazel, Inc.

Goldberg, D., Tantam, D., Gater, R., Jackson, G., Jennett, N. and Lowson, K. (1992). *The Interface Between Primary Care and Specialist Mental Health Services in the Community*. Mental Illness Research Unit, University of Manchester, Occasional paper, No. 2.: Manchester, Report to the Department of Health.

Hafner, H. and an den Heiden, W. (1991). Methodology of evaluative studies in the mental health field. In H. Freeman and J. Henderson, eds, *Evaluation of Comprehensive Care of the Mentally Ill*, pp. 1–17. London: Gaskell.

Hoult, J. and Reynolds, I. (1984). Schizophrenia, a comparative trial of commmunity orientated and hospital orientated psychiatric care. *Acta Psychiatrica Scandinavica*, **69**, 359–372.

Hyde, C., Bridges, K., Goldberg, D., Lowson, K., Sterling, C., and Farragher, B. (1985). The evaluation of a hostel ward: A controlled study using modified cost–benefit analysis. *British Journal of Psychiatry*, **151**, 805–812.

Jones, R., Goldberg, D., and Hughes, B. (1980). A comparison of two different services treating schizophrenia: a cost–benefit approach. *Psychological Medicine*, **10**, 493–505.

Knapp, M. and Beecham, J. (1993). *Reduced List Costings: Examination of an Informed Short Cut in Mental Health Research*. Personal Social Services Research Unit, University of Kent at Canterbury: Canterbury, Discussion Paper 939.

Knapp, M., Beecham, J., Fenyo, A., and Hallam, A. (1993). *Predicting Costs From Needs and Diagnoses: Community Mental Health Care for Former Hospital In-patients*. Personal Social Services Research Unit, University of Kent at Canterbury: Canterbury, Discussion Paper 935.

Krawiecka, M., Goldberg, D., and Vaughan, M. (1977). A Standardized Psychiatric Assessment Scale for Rating Chronic Patients. *Acta Psychiatrica Scandinavica*, **55**, 299–308.

Lavender, A. (1987). The measurement of the quality of care in psychiatric rehabilitation settings: development of the Model Standards Questionnaires. *Behavioural Psychotherapy*, **15**, 201–214.

Lehman, A.F. (1983). The well being of chronic mental patients, assessing their quality of life. *Archives of General Psychiatry*, **40**, 369–373.

Ley, P. (1982). Satisfaction, compliance and communication. *British Journal of Clinical Psychology*, **21**, 241–254.

McEwan, J. (1983). The Nottingham health profile: a measure of perceived health. In G. Teeling Smith, ed., *Measuring the Social Benefits of Medicine*, pp. 75–83. London: Office of Health Economics.

McPhee, C.B., Zusman, J. and Joss, R.H. (1975). Measurement of patient satisfaction: a survey of practices in community mental health centers. *Comprehensive Psychiatry*, **16**, 399–404.

Netten, A. and Smart, S. (1993). *Unit Costs of Community Care*. Canterbury: Personal Social Services Research Unit, University of Kent.

Oliver, J.P.J. (1992). The social care directive: development of a quality of life profile for use in community services for the mentally ill. *Social Work & Social Sciences Review*, **3**, 5–45.

Onyett, S., Tyrer, P., Connolly, J., *et al.* (1990). The Early Intervention Service: The first 18 months of an Inner London Demonstration Project. *Psychiatric Bulletin*, **14**, 267–269.

Phelan, M., Slade, M., Dunn, G., *et al.* (1993). *The Camberwell Assessment of Need*. London: PRiSM, Institute of Psychiatry.

Rosser, R.M. and Watts, V.C. (1976). The measurement of illness. *Journal of the Operational Research Society*, **29**, 529–540.

Ten Horn, G.H.M.M. (1986). Definitions and classifications: introduction. In G.H.M.M. Ten Horn, R. Giel, W.H. Gulbinat and J.H. Henderson, eds, *Psychiatric Case Registers in Public Health*, pp. 170–174. Amsterdam: Elsevier Science.

The Royal College of Psychiatrists (1992). *Psychiatric Instruments and Rating Scales, A Select Bibliography*. Occasional Paper OP16. London: Royal College of Psychiatrists.

Thompson, C. (ed.) (1989). *The Instruments of Psychiatric Research*. Chichester: John Wiley and Sons.

Tyrer, P. (1984). Psychiatric clinics in general practice: an extension of community care. *British Journal of Psychiatry*, **145**, 9–14.

Weisbrod, B.A., Test, M.A. and Stein, L.I. (1980). Alternative to mental hospital treatment. (2) Economic benefit–cost analysis. *Archives of General Psychiatry*, **37**, 400–405.

Wing, J. (1988). Evaluative research: an underpopulated science. In I.M. Marks, J. Connolly and M. Muijen, eds, *New Directions in Mental Health Care Evaluation*, pp. 8–14. London: Institute of Psychiatry.

Wing, J.K. and Brown, G.W. (1961). Social treatment of chronic schizophrenia, a comparative survey of three hospitals. *Journal of Mental Science,* **107**, 847–860.

Wing, J., Cooper, J.E., and Sartorius, N. (1974). *The Measurement and Classification of Psychiatric Symptoms.* London: Cambridge University Press.

Wykes, T. (1982). A Hostel Ward for "new" long-stay patients: an evaluative study of a "ward in a house." In J.K. Wing, ed., *Psychological Medicine Monograph,* Supplement 2: *Long-term Community Care: Experience in a London Borough.* Cambridge: Cambridge University Press.

Wykes, T., Creer, C., and Sturt, E. (1982). The measurement of social behaviour in psychiatric patients: an assessment of the reliability and validity of the SBS scedule. *British Journal of Psychiatry,* **148**, 1–11.

31

The Health Economics of Schizophrenia Treatment

MARTIN KNAPP
Centre for the Economics of Mental Health, Institute of Psychiatry, University of London, UK and Personal Social Services Research Unit, University of Kent at Canterbury, Canterbury, UK

> Look to your health; and if you have it, praise God, and value it next to a good conscience; for health is the second blessing that we mortals are capable of; a blessing that money cannot buy (*The Compleat Angler,* 1653).

Three centuries after Izaak Walton wrote these words there are fewer doubts about whether spending more money produces better health. But there are certainly many doubts as to how much should be spent, on whom, in what setting, and under what circumstances. The treatment and support of people with schizophrenia demonstrate these uncertainties well: there are still relatively few clear indicators to guide national and local policy-makers or clinical practitioners as to the most efficacious and efficient treatment options and their targeting.

Health economics has an important part to play in assisting these policy and practice decisions, but has made only a modest contribution to date. However, findings from health economics studies of the treatment of schizophrenia are beginning to accumulate, and are beginning to be influential.

HEALTH ECONOMICS

The growing demand for, and impact of, health economics is particularly noticeable in the UK, although it is in fact a worldwide phenomenon. Were it not for the shortage of people with health economics skills, the contribution of the subdiscipline would be even larger.

Before describing what health economics can do, it is important to clear up a common misunderstanding. It is not the aim of health economics to cut health spending or to pare down costs, but to improve both the efficiency with which health care resources are employed and the targeting of those resources on needs and demands (the equity objective). It might prove to be the case that the pursuit of efficiency and equity requires cost or expenditure reductions in particular areas of clinical practice or community care, but this would be because careful analysis had revealed that resources could be better used elsewhere. Although the need for efficiency examinations might appear to be greater at a time of macroeconomic difficulty, the relevance of health economics does not, in fact, stem solely from the challenges of a recession-bound economy or government expenditure cuts. Economics has relevance because there is, and always will be, scarcity of resources relative to needs. Scarcity means that difficult choices will be necessary. A central aim of economics is to offer information and analysis which can inform such choices.

This paper is a slightly revised version of a paper published in *The Clinician.* 1994, **12**, pp. 39–52.

Handbook of Mental Health Economics and Health Policy, Volume I, Schizophrenia. Edited by M. Moscarelli, A. Rupp and N. Sartorius.
© 1996 John Wiley & Sons Ltd.

Responding to scarcity does not just mean conducting cost-effectiveness analyses (CEA) of alternative treatments, but requires, for example, examination of the patterns of employment, the forces of demand and supply, the roles of markets in resource and treatment allocation, and the incentives and disincentives to better practice. Good health economics textbooks illustrate this diversity of activities and interests (McGuire *et al.*, 1988; Donaldson & Gerard, 1993).

THE DEMAND FOR HEALTH ECONOMICS

Public expenditure constraints in a country which pays for almost all of its health care from general taxation will obviously leave their mark. Even though the National Health Service (NHS) has arguably suffered fewer expenditure cuts than most other areas of the UK public sector in recent years, there is still a scarcity of resources relative to needs which has generated a demand for the kinds of resource allocation analyses which health economists can perform. But there are other sources of demand. The reforms introduced by the 1990 NHS and Community Care Act put great emphasis on bottom-up, needs-led decision-making. Patients and users are more involved, and there have been concomitant increases in the power of community and primary care agencies, particularly social services care managers and general practitioner fundholders. Increasingly, competitive markets are encouraged in the expectation, first, that service responsiveness and systems efficiency will improve, and second, that financial incentives will encourage innovation and extend choice. Policy-makers and local strategists clearly need better information on costs, outcomes, and needs.

There are also longer-standing demands for a health economics perspective. The full evaluation of the implications of different policies, practices and products requires data on both resources and outcomes, and the links between them. In Australia, Quebec and Ontario, pharmaceutical companies must provide cost-effectiveness data before the licensing of new products (Drummond, 1992), and the UK pharmaceutical industry has been encouraged to undertake economic evaluations. Costs data are needed for "burden of illness" calculations, the pricing of services for sale and the performance reviews required for public probity, now often built around "value for money audits" and "efficiency scrutinies." Responses to some of these demands are illustrated below.

THE CHALLENGE OF SCARCITY

What causes scarcity of resources relative to needs? Government expenditure decisions are clearly important, but to lay all the blame at that door would be mistaken. Many other factors are at work. In particular, society's demands for health care will always outstrip available supplies. New drugs, other therapies and service arrangements help health care professionals to meet mental health and other needs, and so reduce the need for further or more expensive treatment, but they can also raise expectations. Scarcity, and the economic and ethical issues which it poses, can be seen in relation to the treatment of schizophrenia.

There are between 500 and 1250 people with schizophrenia in a typical District Health Authority population of 250 000 people (including 35 000 people aged over 65), although only between 33 and 50% will be in contact with mental health services (Department of Health, 1993). Each year, the same typical district could expect to have approximately 30 new cases referred to specialist psychiatric services (Kavanagh *et al.*, 1995). The aging of the UK population, more elderly people and fewer young people of working age may lead to a decrease in the number of people with schizophrenia needing treatment and support, assuming that incidence rates and standardized mortality ratios remain broadly similar. However, there will also be fewer people paying taxes to support them.

A more pressing influence on relative scarcity is raised expectations of sufferers and families as new treatment modes are developed and become known. This is particularly important in relation to new drugs. Pharmaceutical companies' claims of big breakthroughs (both *real* breakthroughs as well as occasionally inflated claims) will obviously raise expectations. Why, sufferers and families might ask, should they be denied clozapine or risperidone or other new drug treatments which appear to be effective (Pelonero & Elliott, 1990; Eichelman & Hartwig, 1990)?

The refocusing of government policy and the reconfiguration of health care aims have also contributed to, or at least highlighted, the scarcity of resources. Central to the UK health service reforms of 1990 was the creation of an internal market, separating purchasers (health authorities and budget-holding general practitioners) from providers (NHS Trusts, directly managed units, and non-NHS facilities). Costs are now more transparent: they are being calculated for most health care procedures, and *real* money is changing hands. The need to use money wisely has always been there, of course, but the internal market and other changes greatly encourage the pursuit of value for money and effective targeting.

Society's expectations have also changed. When Ben Silcock, a schizophrenia sufferer, climbed into the lions' enclosure at London Zoo on New Year's Day 1993 he had his own motivations and his own private suffering. He was not to know that his action would receive enormous media attention or prompt the Secretary of State for Health to raise again the question of compulsory supervision orders. A small number of attacks and murders by people with schizophrenia have also attracted attention generally disproportionate to the albeit tragic events, although they lead public opinion to a broader consideration of community care and its successes and failings. The specific demands of the media and society at large might sometimes appear misjudged, but they reflect growing realization of the need to provide effective support and treatment for schizophrenia. The murder in 1993 of Jonathon Zito by a schizophrenia sufferer living in the community and the subsequent inquiry (reporting in 1994) could bring quite marked policy changes, especially with respect to compulsory treatment and the provision of adequate numbers of acute inpatient beds.

People with schizophrenia are more likely to attempt suicide than other people with mental health problems or the population generally, and the mortality rate (all causes) for people with schizophrenia is twice that of the general population. One of the core targets of the health strategy announced in *The Health of the Nation* White Paper is "to reduce the overall suicide rate by at least 15 per cent by the year 2000" (Secretary of State, 1991). This specific improvement in health care has probable resource implications, adding to the challenge of scarcity.

PEOPLE WITH SCHIZOPHRENIA—PLACE OF RESIDENCE

In an examination of some of the economic effects of altering the balance of care, Kavanagh *et al.* (1995) tentatively estimated that there were 109 250 people with schizophrenia in contact with psychiatric services in England in 1993. The direct service and accommodation costs of their care and treatment, plus their living costs when not in hospital, amounted to £1.9 billion (at 1992/93 prices). These people were accommodated and supported in a variety of settings. The estimated balance of care and associated costs are given in Table 1.

An earlier estimate of the economic burden of schizophrenia in the UK was provided by Davies and Drummond (1990). Their overall cost figure now looks low, but their estimates of their indirect annual and lifetime costs of lost production and premature mortality point to the enormous social implications above and beyond the direct NHS and other intervention costs. "The economic implications of the disease extend beyond the use of health and personal social services to its morbidity and mortality implications as well as its impact on the quality of life of patients and their families" (Davies & Drummond, 1990, p. 522).

Rupp and Keith (1993) provide the most recent US estimates of the costs of schizophrenia, again pointing to the many and long-term implications. Andrews *et al.* (1985) offer similar evidence for Australia. Cost estimates of this kind need to be employed carefully. None of these authors makes the mistake of equating the costs of a disease or condition with the benefits of intervention. The correct interpretation is that resources which would otherwise have been expended can be utilized elsewhere to realize additional health gain. Although cost projections of a disease can be used to evaluate changes in the balance of care or treatment, in order to make allocative decisions, policy-makers require

Table 1. Schizophrenia—the balance of care, 1993

Accommodation/care setting	Estimated no. of people	Estimated weekly costs per person†
Private household—GP support only	10 150	159
Private household—using specialist services‡	50 350	206
Specialist supported accommodation	17 700	526
Short stay hospital inpatients	5 500	821
"New long stay" hospital inpatients	4 700	780
"Old long stay" hospital inpatients	3 900	780
Special hospitals (forensic)	850	708
Homeless—board and lodgings	3 500	272
Homeless—hostels	10 500	170
Homeless—sleeping rough	800	39
Prisoners—sentenced	550	462
Prisoners—remand	750	495
	109 250	—

Source: Kavanagh *et al.* (1995).
† Includes all NHS, local authority, education, criminal justice, voluntary sector services, housing and living expenses. Excludes costs of lost employment and informal (family) care. Costs at 1992/93 price levels.
‡ Including outpatient and day patient services.

information about the interventions that realise the greatest health gain and at what *marginal* resource implications.

ALLOCATION CRITERIA—EFFICIENCY AND EQUITY

Faced with this level of need in a context of scarcity and some tough resource allocation decisions, is it possible to make improvements to the balance of treatment and care? And how do we judge whether improvements have been made?

Improvements are most commonly gauged by reference to the two criteria of efficiency and equity.

Efficiency refers to a situation in which the allocation of a given level of resources maximizes the outcomes of a system of care, or minimizes the resource requirements to achieve specified standards or effects. Absolute efficiency is hard to conceptualize for activities with such varied objectives as most mental health care interventions, making it difficult to identify the *most* efficient utilization of resources. Nevertheless, it ought to be possible to identify policy or practice changes, which represent the *more* efficient utilization of resources. Relative efficiency is an accessible concept both in principle and practice. The term "cost-effectiveness" is often used as a synonym.

Equity, which alternatively can be described as fairness or justice, is also concerned with the distribution of resources. Now, however, the primary concern is not the transformation of inputs into outputs, or resources into outcomes, but their fair distribution. A desired allocation would be consistent with an individual's or society's value judgements as to the equal or unequal treatment of equivalent wants or needs, and the different responses to different levels of need or eligibility.

In broad terms, the concepts of efficiency and equity are straightforward, although there are many alternative definitions and concepts for practical applications. Common parlance might use the word efficiency as a euphemism for cheap, but it should really be reserved for a criterion which looks at both achievements and resources, outcomes and costs, ends and means. Another common mistake is to equate equity with equality, when what is generally sought is a fair and acceptable *unequal* distribution.

OUTCOMES

Most evaluations of health care procedures and medications define outcomes as changes over time in the health and welfare of patients or users and their families. Outcome dimensions in the case of schizophrenia commonly include clinical measures (such as positive and negative symptoms), behavioral characteristics, social networks, quality of life, and self-care abilities. There are, of course, well developed instruments for measuring well-being along each of these and other dimensions. A number of UK health economics evaluations include outcome measures of this kind (Mangen *et al.*, 1983; Beecham *et al.*, 1991; Knapp, 1995a; and see the review by O'Donnell, 1991).

Some health economists have taken a different tack, attempting to measure outcomes using "utility" indices which combine individual preferences on quality of life and data on enhanced life duration to produce measures such as quality-adjusted life-years (QALYs). Some people see the QALY as a useful generic measure of health status that can be used to compare interventions across therapeutic categories, and can be combined with cost data to produce, for example, a marginal cost per QALY (Maynard, 1993). The logical corollary would be that allocating resources to interventions which deliver QALYs at lowest marginal cost will improve health service efficiency. On the other hand, the QALY might be seen as too simplistic and reductionist—wasting relevant information on health and welfare. Ethical objections have also been raised, for example because the QALY might discriminate against groups such as the elderly (Rosser, 1990). In mental health applications, the QALY may be too blunt an instrument adequately to reflect variations in the severity of mental disorder, as the scaling for disability primarily reflects physical as opposed to social functioning (Wilkinson *et al.*, 1990, 1992; O'Donnell *et al.*, 1992). Obviously, the limitations of specific, especially simple QALY measures do not mean that quality of life considerations must be excluded from mental health evaluations, or that quality of life measures of one form or another cannot be employed. Selai and Rosser (1993) review the main QALY measures and their relevance for mental health evaluations. They conclude that: "[quality of life] measures are invaluable in psychiatry for identifying need, evaluating therapies, monitoring change, and assisting in decisions about the allocation of scarce resources" (p. 70), but that there is as yet no simple or appropriate measure for mental health service uses.

COSTS

It is possible to distinguish different types of cost. The *direct costs* are the health services provided to people with schizophrenia, the largest cost item often being in-patient hospital care, with others including community nursing and medications. *Indirect costs* are the necessary complements to direct expenditure from local authorities and other agencies. The *hidden costs*, as their label suggests, are not immediately identifiable but are nevertheless measurable. Examples are family and volunteer support and other informal care. Finally, there are probably some *immeasurable costs*, necessary elements of a package of care which are difficult or perhaps impossible to express in monetary terms, such as premature mortality, family anxiety or burden. In fact, some economists have attached costs to some of these elements, but the methods and figures remain contentious (McGuire *et al.*, 1988; Netten, 1993).

Where possible, costs should be measured as long-run marginal opportunity costs. These ensure that a long-term perspective on resource implications is employed, that only those effects on resources attributable to the program or service user are counted, and that costs are reckoned as opportunities forgone, not just money expended. Long run marginal opportunity cost is the usual measure employed in economic evaluations (O'Donnell *et al.*, 1992; Knapp, 1993, 1995b).

MODES OF ECONOMIC EVALUATION

The most common economic evaluations are cost-effectiveness, cost–benefit, and cost–utility analyses (CEA, CBA, and CUA, respectively). There are also simple cost evaluations. They each set out to measure costs comprehensively in accordance with the principles just outlined. The differences between them relate to outcome measurement. Simple cost evaluations do not measure outcomes at all, and are therefore of limited usefulness. CEAs compare the costs of different policies in achieving an identical outcome, such as a uniform reduction in hospital readmission rates or different degrees of success, such as cost per readmission avoided. A multivariate CEA admits more than one outcome, and then seeks to examine the different cost–outcome links *statistically* (see below). Virtually every economic evaluation in the mental health care area is a cost or cost-effectiveness analysis.

A CBA values all outcomes in monetary terms. This is useful in that it allows the policy-maker to compare treatment costs with benefits using the same measure of value, but has the disadvantage of sometimes squeezing multifarious, complex effects into a monetary straitjacket. The simple comparison of costs incurred with costs saved is *not* a CBA. It may be a worthwhile exercise, but it neglects to look at the impacts of services or treatments on patients—it is a simple cost comparison. A CUA compares cost with a global measure of outcome such as the QALY, allowing treatments to be compared in terms of cost per QALY.

Thus a CUA can be useful for comparing the costs of securing more QALYs across different clinical interventions, a CBA can indicate whether the outcomes of an intervention exceed the resources expended, and a (simple) CEA compares the costs of achieving a single consistent outcome. More complex CEAS—using what economists would identify as cost–function analyses using multivariate statistical methods—offer the opportunity to analyze more than a single outcome and to adjust for extraneous influences. They can also explore the sources of cost and outcome differences (see below).

EVALUATION DESIDERATA

The well conducted economic evaluation will therefore measure costs and outcomes comprehensively, or will employ partial measures advisedly. Davies and Drummond's (1993) CEA evaluation of clozapine for treatment-resistant schizophrenia needed to include the costs of the regular blood tests, accommodation, outpatient attendances, GP consultations, and so on. This evaluation examined a narrower set of outcomes than is usual, as the researchers recognized. This aspect of their study was probably forced on them by the unusual design (the retrospective UK interpretation of US trial data plus judgements from a small Delphi panel of psychiatrists). An economic evaluation of psychiatric reprovision in the community in North London for long-stay psychiatric hospital residents computed comprehensive service and support costs alongside a many dimensional assessment of the effects of rehabilitation on individuals (Knapp *et al.*, 1993, 1995). More than three-quarters of the people in the study sample had a diagnosis of schizophrenia. On both outcome and cost criteria, community care compared favorably with hospital.

Economic evaluations should also aim to make comparisons between treatments or policies on a careful like-with-like basis. Economic evaluations are therefore often designed around or linked to randomized controlled trials (RCTs), or they employ matching or statistical analyses in an attempt to control for extraneous factors. For example, a recently commenced economic evaluation of a cognitive versus a psychoeducational approach to improving compliance with a depot neuroleptic regimen (being conducted by the Centre for the Economics of Mental Health (CEMH), Institute of Psychiatry, integrated with the outcomes study of Professor Barnes and colleagues at Charing Cross and Westminster Medical School) is built upon a controlled trial. A second example of an RCT-based economic evaluation is the study of a new acute psychiatric service in south London, comparing a prompt, home-based assessment with standard procedures (Burns *et al.*, 1993). Although there were no clinical or other outcome differences between the control and experimental groups, the new service was significantly less costly. A third of the people initially recruited to the study were psychotic.

Less commonly undertaken, but almost always revealing, are examinations of outcome and the cost variations between patients, facilities, or areas of the country. These variations should be examined for their policy and practice insights. Could there, as Bosanquet and Zajdler (1993, p. 30) ask, "be less distance between the average standard of treatment and the best available?" Is it possible within a broad organizational arrangement (such as community care) or a standard medication response (such as prescription of neuroleptics or risperidone) to identify and "explain" different service utilization patterns or individual patient outcomes?

An example of this more searching interrogation of data is the evaluation of psychiatric reprovision referred to earlier. Costs ranged from £69 to £1429 per week (1989/90 price levels) among the people with schizophrenia who moved in the first 5 years of the hospital closure program, and closer examination found a number of needs-related and other individual characteristics (as assessed in hospital) to be associated with community costs (Knapp *et al.*, 1995). Indeed more than a third of the intra-sample difference in community care costs could be explained by: gender, marital status, age, time spent in psychiatric hospitals prior to discharge, psychiatric symptoms (non-specific neurotic syndrome, negative symptoms, delusions, and hallucinations), social behavior, daily nursing care needs, and social networks. Within the overall finding that community care was much less costly on average than hospital for the people leaving hospital in the early years of a closure program, the analyses of cost variations therefore pointed to those individual characteristics which push or pull costs away from the average.

KEY TREATMENT QUESTIONS

Health economics evaluations can provide valuable information needed for a variety of treatment decisions. There are perhaps five main types of evaluation question (Williams, 1974):

1 *What care service or treatment mode is more or most appropriate in given circumstances?* Recent attention has particularly focused on two new pharmaceutical products—clozapine and risperidone—for which there is some evidence of comparative cost-effectiveness over conventional neuroleptic therapy (Davies & Drummond, 1993; Addington *et al.*, 1993). But neither study conforms to the standard principles of an economic evaluation. Davies and Drummond's UK study was retrospective, based on US data not obtained from randomization, and used Delphi judgements rather than actual placements and outcomes. After sensitivity analysis (allowing key assumptions to vary) they concluded that clozapine was cost-saving or cost-neutral under the conditions of psychiatric practice in the UK (p. 41). For people with severe, chronic schizophrenia clozapine appeared to be cost-effective. Healy (1993) and McKenna and Bailey (1993) debate some other aspects of the US clozapine trials.

The Canadian study by Addington *et al.* was also retrospective, using a before–after design with a small sample. The authors themselves enter a number of methodological and empirical caveats about their study. Costs were not calculated, but instead a comparison was made of the number of inpatient hospital days during a year of open therapy with risperidone compared with the number in the preceding year of antipsychotic medication for the same sample. During the risperidone period, the amount of time spent in hospital was 20% lower ($P = 0.003$). This result is encouraging though incomplete. Hospital inpatient stays certainly account for a high proportion of direct and indirect costs for people whose symptoms of schizophrenia require specialist psychiatric attention (almost two-thirds of total cost over a 20-month period for the control group in the Daily Living Program (DLP) evaluation described below). The hidden costs (of lost employment and informal care) may or may not swamp these service and associated costs—the jury is still out—but a reduction in inpatient stays is important to the health service, to the patient, and to society at large.

Full prospective, controlled studies, embodying economic evaluations are needed for both clozapine and risperidone in the UK. The same is true for other forms of treatment. There is evidence of significant benefits from a variety of psychological therapies, including cognitive–behavioral therapy, in tackling residual psychotic symptoms (Tarrier *et al.*, 1993; Kingdon & Turkington, 1993). The randomized trial of Tarrier and colleagues was based on a comparatively small sample but found significant improvements associated with two cognitive–behavioral therapies. Current work at the Centre for the Economics of Mental Health is examining this dimension alongside two other randomized trials of cognitive therapies.

2 *When should care or treatment be provided?* A number of health economics studies have examined the efficiency of preventative measures, but not in

relation to psychiatric problems. For example, Backhouse *et al.* (1992) list more than 300 English language health economics studies of prevention, but only one (of case registers, published in 1980) in psychiatry. Burns *et al.* (1993) examined prompt or early intervention services, but the timing of treatment has generally not been the focus of much evaluative attention.

3 *Where should care or treatment be provided?* The most common "placement question" to be addressed is the balance between inpatient and community care. UK evidence should encourage the continued shift in the locus of care away from hospital, particularly long-stay residence. The north London study described earlier found evidence of lower community care costs for most former long-stay inpatients, except those with more challenging symptoms and behavioral problems (Knapp *et al.*, 1993; Hallam *et al.*, 1994). Outcomes after 1 year of community residence were at least as good as, and in some respects better than, the outcomes for matched stayers in hospital (Anderson *et al.*, 1993). Equivalent findings have emerged from smaller scale studies in England (Knapp *et al.*, 1992) and Northern Ireland (Donnelly *et al.*, 1994).

These are *discharge* studies. There is also evidence that *diversion* away from inpatient admission can be cost-effective. The DLP at the Maudsley Hospital offered problem-oriented, home-based care for people with severe mental illness facing emergency admission. The DLP was modelled on earlier experiments with intensive community support teams, particularly the Madison approach (Stein & Test, 1980). A randomized, controlled evaluation of the DLP compared with standard hospital-based care found that the new service improved symptoms and social adjustment slightly more, and enhanced patients' and relatives' satisfaction over a period of 20 months after admission (Marks *et al.*, 1994). Half of the 189 people included in the study had a diagnosis of schizophrenia. For the full sample (all diagnoses), the DLP was also significantly less costly than standard treatment over the 20-month evaluation period (Knapp *et al.*, 1994b). The costs of treatment for people with schizophrenia—ranging over all health, social services, housing, education, and criminal justice services, and including accommodation and living expenses—are illustrated in Figure 1.

The cost differences between the control and DLP samples are significant in every period except 0–4 months after admission. Over the full 20-month treatment period, the DLP was considerably less expensive than standard hospital-based care (£207–£328 per patient per week at 1989/90 prices; $P=0.000$). There were no differences between the groups in the estimated costs of lost employment or informal care.

4 *To whom should care or treatment be provided?* It is rare for an evaluation in psychiatry to pose this question, although some of the controversy over the efficacy of clozapine relates to its targeting during the US trial on particular groups of schizophrenics (Healy, 1993). The results for inpatient hospital stays for risperidone relate only to patients who completed a year of treatment and who thus tolerated the drug well (Addington *et al.*, 1993). However, the factors which limit the generalizability of trial results might simultaneously assist in the targeting of comparatively expensive treatments.

What is also needed is the disaggregation of trial and other data to tease out the *individual* characteristics of patients associated with better or worse outcomes and higher or lower costs. The disaggregation of costs in the north London psychiatric reprovision study described earlier has predictive power—it shows how community care costs respond to patient's predischarge symptoms and needs—and can therefore guide health care purchasers. Disaggregated cost analyses within the DLP study similarly have predictive power: they indicate the association between the downstream costs of both DLP and standard services and the characteristics of patients at admission (Knapp, 1995a). Of course, neither of these studies directs purchasers or providers to concentrate available treatment on particular groups of patients; rather they demonstrate the cost consequences of doing so. Under conditions of resource scarcity, such interpersonal comparisons are inevitable. Those who must decide on the allocations of treatment resources need health economics and much other evidence to assist their decisions.

5 *How should care or treatment be provided?* This fifth evaluative question is closely tied to others, for the organization of treatment cannot easily be separated from its location or targeting. A distinguishing feature, however, is the recent emphasis

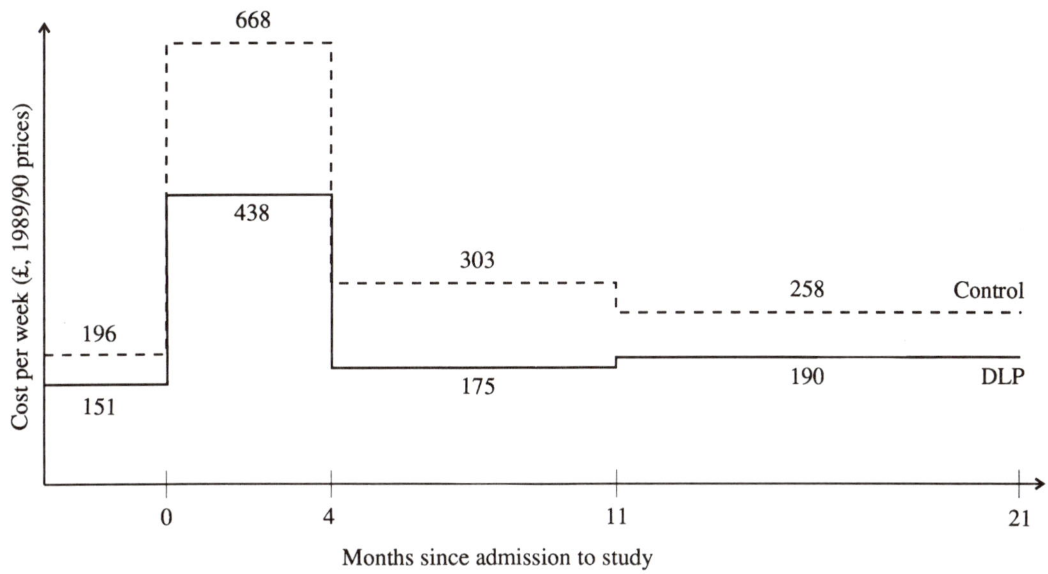

Figure 1. Daily Living Program and costs over time for people with schizophrenia.

on better *coordination* of support and treatment, whether through care programs (North & Richie, 1993; Schneider, 1994) or care management (Huxley, 1992). These case-level coordinating activities seek to achieve better and multi-agency assessments, clearer lines of professional responsibility, closer links between assessed needs and service responses, and monitoring of the results. Full evaluation of these coordinating procedures is awaited in the UK (but see Clark & Fox, 1993, for a helpful discussion of cost-effectiveness evidence in the USA). The consequences of not having such arrangements could be dire (Melzer *et al.*, 1991). Earlier arrangements—such as the community support team of psychiatric nurses in Greenwich—bear many similarities and suggest relative cost-effectiveness (Muijen *et al.*, 1994; McCrone *et al.*, 1994).

CONCLUSIONS

Schizophrenia affects only a small proportion of the population but can be extremely burdensome. "It begins early in life, produces maximal morbidity with minimal mortality, and lacks a comprehensive efficacious treatment. The personal cost to patients and their families is great ..." (Andreasen, 1991, p. 475). The cost, of course, is not only private: "In the form of tax dollars, the entire society pays for the treatment and maintenance of people disabled by schizophrenia for a lifetime and also pays for the costs of the non-negligible externalities of the disease. Solution can only come from more effective treatment developed by research" (Rupp & Keith, 1993, p. 421).

There is still relatively little health economics evidence on schizophrenia in the UK, whether from research or elsewhere, to help society move towards a solution, which is not only effective but also cost-effective. We are beginning to learn more about *what* treatments work *where* and with *whom*, and organizational experience is accumulating on *how* to coordinate them. Returning to the quote at the beginning of this chapter, were Izaak Walton to reflect upon late twentieth century health care rather than the practices of the mid-seventeenth century he might have more cause for optimism. Money *can* buy health, but there is still a great deal to be learnt about how best to use it.

ACKNOWLEDGMENTS

I wish to thank colleagues, especially Shane Kavanagh (PSSRU), for the use of previous joint work in this chapter.

REFERENCES

Addington, D.E., Jones, B., Bloom, D., Chouinard, G., Remington, G., and Albright, P. (1993). Reduction of hospital days in chronic schizophrenia patients treated with risperidone: a retrospective study. *Clinical Therapeutics*, **15**, 917–926.

Anderson, J., Dayson, D., Willis, W., *et al.* (1993). The TAPS Project. 13: Clinical and social outcomes of long-stay psychiatric patients after one year in the community. *British Journal of Psychiatry*, **162** (Suppl. 19), 45–56.

Andreasen, N.C. (1991). Assessment issues and the cost of schizophrenia. *Schizophrenia Bulletin*, **17**, 475–481.

Andrews, G., Hall, W., Goldstein, G., *et al.* (1985). The economic costs of schizophrenia: implications for public policy. *Archives of General Psychiatry*, **42**, 537–543.

Backhouse, M.E., Backhouse, R.J., and Edey, S.A. (1992). Economic evaluation bibliography. *Health Economics*, **1** (Suppl.), 1–236.

Beecham, J.K., Knapp, M.R.J., and Fenyo, A.J. (1991). Costs, needs and outcomes. *Schizophrenia Bulletin*, **17**, 427–439.

Bosanquet, N. and Zajdler, A. (1993). Psychopharmacology and the ethics of resource allocation. *British Journal of Psychiatry*, **162**, 29–32.

Burns, T., Raftery, J., Bearsmoore, A., McGuigan, S., and Dickson, M. (1993). A controlled trail of home-based acute psychiatric services. II: treatments patterns and costs. *British Journal of Psychiatry*, **163**, 55–61.

Clark, R.E. and Fox, T.S. (1993). A framework for evaluating the economic impact of case management. *Hospital and Community Psychiatry*, **44**, 469–473.

Davies, L.M. and Drummond, M.F. (1990). The economic burden of schizophrenia. *Psychiatric Bulletin*, **14**, 522–525.

Davies, L.M. and Drummond, M.F. (1993). Assessment of costs and benefits of drug therapy for treatment-resistant schizophrenia in the United Kingdom. *British Journal of Psychiatry*, **162**, 38–42.

Department of Health (1993). *Mental Illness Handbook* (*of The Health of the Nation*). London: HMSO.

Donaldson, C. and Gerard, K. (1993). *Economics of Health Care Financing*. London: Macmillan Press.

Donnelly, M., McGilloway, S., Mays, N. *et al.* (1994) *Opening New Doors: An Evaluation of Community Care for People Discharged from Psychiatric and Mental Handicap Hospitals*, London: HMSO.

Drummond, M.F. (1992). Cost-effectiveness guidelines for reimbursement of pharmaceuticals: is economic evaluation ready for its enhanced status? *Health Economics*, **1**, 85–92.

Eichelman, B. and Hartwig, A. (1990). Ethical issues in selecting patients for treatment with clozapine: a commentary. *Hospital and Community Psychiatry*, **41**, 880–882.

Hallam, A., Beecham, J.K., Knapp, M.R.J., and Fenyo, A. (1994). The costs of accommodation and care: community provision for former long-stay psychiatric hospital patients. *European Archives of Psychiatry and Clinical Neuroscience*, **243**, 301–310.

Healy, D. (1993). Psychopharmacology and the ethics of resource allocation. *British Journal of Psychiatry*, **162**, 23–29.

Huxley, P. (1992). Social services assessment and care management: getting it right. *Journal of Mental Health*, **1**, 285–294.

Kingdon, D.F. and Turkington, D. (1993). *Cognitive Therapy in Schizophrenia*. New York: Guilford Press (forthcoming).

Knapp, M.R.J. (1993). Background theory. In A. Netten and J. Beecham, eds, *Costing Community Care*. Aldershot: Ashgate.

Knapp, M.R.J. (1995a). Costing mental health services: towards an understanding of cost-effectiveness. In F. Creed and P. Tyrer, eds, *Evaluation of Community Psychiatric Services*. Cambridge University Press: Cambridge.

Knapp, M.R.J. (ed.) (1995b). *The Economic Evaluation of Mental Health Care*. Aldershot: Ashgate.

Knapp, M.R.J., Beecham, J.K., Hallam, A., and Fenyo, A.J. (1993). The costs of community care for former long-stay psychiatric hospital residents. *Health and Social Care in the Community*, **1**, 193–201.

Knapp, M.R.J., Beecham, J.K., Fenyo, A., and Hallam, A. (1995). Community mental health care for former hospital in-patients: Predicting costs from needs and diagnosis. *British Journal of Psychiatry*, **166** (suppl. 27) 10–18.

Knapp, M.R.J., Beecham, J.K., Koutsogeorgopoulou, V., *et al.* (1994). Service use and costs of home-based versus hospital-based care for people with serious mental illness, *British Journal of Psychiatry*, **165** 195–203.

Knapp, M.R.J., Cambridge, P., Thomason, C., Beecham, J.K., Allen, C., and Darton, R. (1992). *Care in the Community: Challenge and Demonstration*. Aldershot: Ashgate.

McCrone, P., Beecham, J.K., and Knapp, M.R.J. (1994). Community psychiatric nurses teams: cost-effectiveness of intensive support versus generic care. *British Journal of Psychiatry*, **165**, 218–221.

McKenna, P.J. and Bailey, P. (1993). The strange story of clozapine. *British Journal of Psychiatry*, **162**, 32–37.

McGuire, A., Henderson, J., and Mooney, G. (1988). *The Economics of Health Care*. London: Routledge.

Marks, I.M., Connolly, J., Muijen, M. *et al.* (1994). Home-based versus hospital-based care for people with serious mental illness, *British Journal of Psychiatry*, **165**, 179–194.

Maynard, A. (1993). Cost management: the economist's viewpoint. *British Journal of Psychiatry*, **163** (Suppl. 20), 7–13.

Melzer, D., Hale, A.S., Malik, S.J., Hogman, G.A., and Woods, S. (1991). Community care for patients with schizophrenia one year after hospital discharge. *British Medical Journal*, **303**, 1023–1026.

Muijen, M., Cooney, M. Strathdee, G., *et al.* (1994). Community psychiatric nurse teams: intensive support versus generic care, *British Journal of Psychiatry*, **165**, 211–217.

Netten, A. (1993). Costing informal care. In A. Netten and J. Beecham, eds, *Costing Community Care*. Aldershot: Ashgate.

North, C. and Ritchie, J. (1993). *Factors Influencing the Implementation of the Care Programme Approach*. London: HMSO.

O'Donnell, O. (1991). Cost effectiveness of community care for the chronic mentally ill. In H. Freeman and J. Henderson, eds, *Evaluation of Comprehensive Care for the Chronic Mentally Ill*. London: Gaskell.

O'Donnell, O., Maynard, A., and Wright, K.G. (1992). Evaluating mental health care: the role of economics. *Journal of Mental Health*, **1**, 39–51.

Pelonero, A.L. and Elliott, R.L. (1990). Ethical and clinical considerations in selecting patients who will receive clozapine. *Hospital and Community Psychiatry*, **41**, 878–880.

Rosser, R. (1990). From health indicators to Quality Adjusted Life Years: technical and ethical issues. In A. Hopkins and D. Costain, eds, *Measuring the Outcomes of Medical Care*. London: RCP Press.

Rupp, A. and Keith, S.J. (1993). The costs of schizophrenia. *Psychiatric Clinics of North America*, **16**, 413–423.

Schneider, J. (1994). Costing the care programme approach. In M.R.J. Knapp, ed., *Economic Evaluation of Mental Health Care*. Aldershot: Ashgate.

Secretary of State for Health (1991). *The Health of the Nation*. Cmd 1523. London: HMSO.

Selai, C. and Rosser, R. (1993). The role of quality of life measurement in psychiatry. *Current Medical Literature–Psychiatry*, **4**, 67–71.

Stein, L.I. and Test, M.A. (1980). Alternative to mental hospital treatment: conceptual model, treatment program and clinical evaluation. *Archives of General Psychiatry*, **37**, 392–397.

Tarrier, N., Beckett, R., Harwood, S., Baker, A., Yusupoff, L., and Ugarteburn, I. (1993). A trial of two cognitive–behavioural methods of treating drug-resistant residual psychotic symptoms in schizophrenic patients: I. Outcome. *British Journal of Psychiatry*, **162**, 524–532.

Wilkinson, G., Croft-Jeffreys, C., Krekorian, H., McLees, S., and Falloon, I. (1990). QALYs in psychiatric care? *Psychiatric Bulletin*, **14**, 582–585.

Wilkinson, G., Williams, B., Krekorian, H., McLees, S., and Falloon, I. (1992). QALYs in mental health: a case study. *Psychological Medicine*, **22**, 725–731.

Williams, A. (1974). The cost benefit approach. *British Medical Bulletin*, **30**, 252–256.

Part VII

ECONOMICS OF DRUG TREATMENT

32

Economic Evaluation of Drug Therapy for Schizophrenia

MICHAEL DRUMMOND and LINDA DAVIES
Centre for Health Economics, University of York, York, UK

ABSTRACT

There is an increasing worldwide interest in assessing the value for money from health care interventions. For drug therapy some jurisdictions have proposed or adopted formal guidelines for the provision of cost-effectiveness data prior to reimbursement (public subsidy) of new pharmaceutical products.

This chapter reviews the current evidence of the cost-effectiveness of drug therapy for schizophrenia. It considers the alternative therapies assessed and the key methodological features of published studies.

It is concluded that a number of improvements could be made in the methodology of studies in: (i) selecting appropriate alternative treatments for comparison; (ii) basing the economic study on good clinical evidence, (iii) considering a broad range of costs and consequences; and (iv) modelling long-term consequences.

INTRODUCTION

THE GROWING INTEREST IN VALUE FOR MONEY

There is an increasing worldwide interest in assessing the value for money from health care interventions. Although drug therapy only accounts for 6–15% of overall health care expenditure in most developed countries, pharmaceuticals have been a target for efficiency measures. In particular, new pharmaceutical products are often perceived to be expensive because of their high acquisition costs compared with existing drug therapies.

Some measures have a direct impact on the use of drugs, such as the establishment of national or local drug formularies. Also, in some jurisdictions measures have been introduced to influence directly prescribing patterns by changing the incentives to prescribers or patients. These include allowing practitioners to redeploy savings they make on their drugs budget, or establishing a "reference price" system, where the government or health insurance scheme reimburses only a minimum amount for a given class of medicine. If a more expensive medicine is prescribed then the patient must pay the difference.

The effects of other efficiency measures are more indirect, although no less important. For example, a change in the method of reimbursing hospitals, from a global budget to a system based on individual diagnostic categories of cases treated, will lead those hospitals to search for more cost-effective methods of treatment. A more cost-effective treatment method

Handbook of Mental Health Economics and Health Policy, Volume I, Schizophrenia. Edited by M. Moscarelli, A. Rupp and N. Sartorius.
© 1996 John Wiley & Sons Ltd.

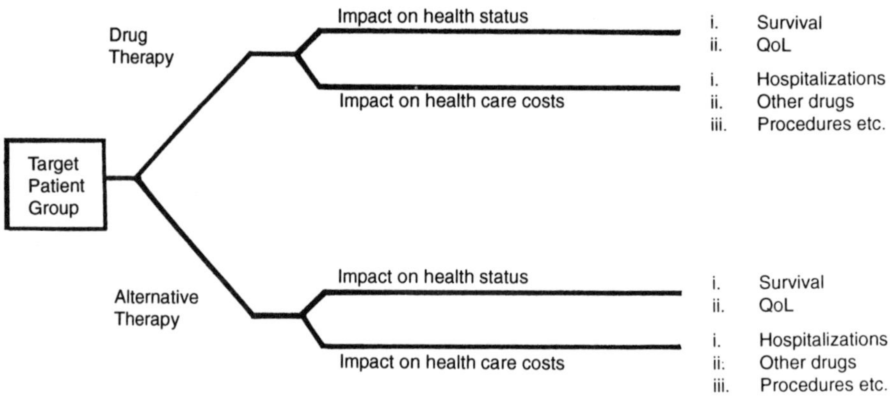

Figure 1. Nature of economic assessments

would either allow a better service to be offered within the amount reimbursed for each category of case, or enable the hospital to make a bigger surplus. This may not necessarily lead to cuts in expenditure on pharmaceuticals. Indeed, it provides the opportunity to argue that the use of a more expensive but more effective medicine is justified because other resources are saved as a result.

A more recent development is the requirement in some jurisdictions to provide economic data in support of applications (by pharmaceutical companies) for reimbursement (public subsidy) of medicines (Drummond, 1994). This was first proposed in Australia, where the provision of cost-effectiveness data became mandatory in January 1993. A similar approach has been proposed in the Province of Ontario (Canada) (Detsky, 1993) and is also being debated in a number of European countries (Drummond *et al.*, 1993).

The significance is that economic evidence is elevated to a status similar to that of efficacy and safety, which is required prior to licensing or market approval of new pharmaceutical products. As the majority of economic data need to be gathered prior to launch of a given product, this changed regulatory requirement has a profound impact on the clinical trials programs of pharmaceutical companies. Some resource use or cost data may have to be gathered alongside particular trials. More fundamentally, the design of trials may need to be modified to include different comparator drugs or different outcome measures.

METHODS AND APPLICATION OF ECONOMIC EVALUATION

It is currently unclear whether the provision of economic data will be a *mandatory* requirement in many jurisdictions. However, given the growing interest of health care decision-makers at all levels, it is likely to become an *essential* requirement of drug development. These data are gathered by economic evaluation.

Economic evaluation involves a comparison of the costs and consequences of alternative health care treatments or interventions for a given target patient group. (The alternative could be another drug, a non-pharmacological intervention such as counselling, or "doing nothing" if no other effective intervention exists.)

The evaluation considers not only the relative costs of the interventions themselves, but the broader impacts on health status and other health care resource use. The impacts on health status could be measured in survival or quality of life, both of which would be relevant outcomes in the field of schizophrenia. These are affected both by the efficacy of a given drug and its side-effects. The impacts on health care resource use could include hospitalizations, the use of medical procedures, the use of community care resources, and costs imposed on the family.

Some economic evaluations also consider the impacts on production in the economy, as successful therapy may enable the patient, or someone caring for them, to return to work. Inclusion of these items, however, is more controversial and is not universally done. Economic evaluation has now been widely applied to all forms of care, including mental illness treatments. The methods of economic evaluation, the different forms of analysis and examples of application to non-pharmacological interventions are discussed in Drummond (1987) and in other chapters of this book.

Given the growing need for evidence on the cost-effectiveness of drug therapy for schizophrenia, this chapter reviews the studies published to date and indicates how the quality of economic evaluations can be improved in the future.

EXISTING EVIDENCE ON THE COST-EFFECTIVENESS OF DRUG THERAPY

DRUG THERAPY IN GENERAL

Despite the important role of drug therapy in the treatment of schizophrenia, there are no published studies assessing the general value for money of drug therapy compared with other forms of treatment. Davies and Drummond (1990) point out that drug costs only accounted for about 3% of the overall economic burden of schizophrenia in the UK in 1987. On the other hand Healy (1993) points to the high price of a number of the newer drugs and questions the size of pharmaceutical company profits. However, as pointed out above, the way to assess whether a given treatment justifies its cost is to undertake a comparative evaluation, of costs and consequences, with a relevant alternative.

EVIDENCE ON PARTICULAR DRUGS

The only published studies adopting this approach all relate to clozapine, a drug that has been marketed for the treatment of individuals who are resistant to neuroleptic therapy. This claim is based primarily on a trial by Kane *et al.* (1988), where patients who were initially refractory and who were subsequently resistant to a 6-week course of haloperidol (60 mg/day) were then randomized to treatment with clozapine or a combination of chlorpromazine plus benzotropine. Of those on clozapine, 30% responded, whereas of those on chlorpromazine, only 4% responded to therapy.

Table 1. Average mental health services costs for patients treated with clozapine and conventional neuroleptics during pre- and post-treatment years

Treatment period	Clozapine[1]	Conventional neuroleptics[2]
One year before index date[3]		
Hospital costs	$73 403	$72 121
Total costs[4,5]	$80 440	$73 067
First year after index date[3]		
Hospital costs	$58 941	$67 934
Total costs[4,5]	$80 454	$70 414
Second year after index date[3]		
Hospital costs	$28 367	$61 518
Total costs[4,5]	$55 867	$64 878

[1] n patients = 87 1 year before and first year index date; 46 in second year.
[2] n patients = 51.
[3] For the clozapine group, index date is the date clozapine treatment was started; for the conventional-neuroleptic group, index date is the date patients were screened for entry into the humanitarian study ($n = 24$) or the study of tardive dyskinesia ($n = 27$).
[4] Includes cost of the drug, the monitoring system, and hospital and non-hospital services.
[5] Annual cost per patient for clozapine and the monitoring system estimated at $8500; for neuroleptic treatment, $500 per year.

Clozapine attracted economic attention for two reasons. First, being heralded as the first pharmacological breakthrough in the treatment of schizophrenia for 20 years, it was likely to attract a considerable amount of clinical interest, and hence usage. (However, diffusion of clozapine throughout treatment practice has been partly tempered by the risk of agranulocytosis, a point which will be returned to later.) Secondly, clozapine had a price much higher than that of other commonly used neuroleptic drugs. Therefore, the obvious question was whether the additional benefits of clozapine therapy justified the costs.

The first economic evaluation of clozapine was carried out in the USA by Revicki *et al.* (1990). They compared the costs and clinical outcomes of care over a 2-year period for 133 patients started on clozapine with 51 patients treated with conventional neuroleptics. The economic study was not based on a prospective randomized trial. Rather, attempts were made to match the two groups of patients.

Their results are shown in Table 1. It can be seen that in the year before the study began, the costs of care for the group subsequently given clozapine were higher than those of the group that continued on neuroleptic therapy. This difference was maintained in the first year of the study but, by the end of the second year, the average mental health services costs for the clozapine group (excluding the cost of clozapine) had fallen below those of the group continuing on neuroleptic therapy. This was primarily a result of a reduction in hospital costs, through patients being discharged as a consequence of improvement in their condition. The authors concluded that, after 2 years, the net saving to the mental health system may be \$12 000 to \$15 000 per patient.

A number of limitations and qualifications to this study have been noted both by the authors and other commentators. The main problem relates to the historical cohort design. The clozapine patient group was itself highly selected and despite attempts to find a matching group of patients receiving conventional neuroleptic care, the two groups differed in several demographic characteristics and Brief Psychiatric Rating Scale (BPRS) scores. Also, different methods of measurement were used for the two groups of patients. The clozapine patients were participating in an ongoing clinical study in which data on use of aftercare services were easily available, resulting in a more accurate enumeration of these services for clozapine patients than for patients treated with conventional neuroleptics.

Not all of the limitations would necessarily bias the study in favor of clozapine. Indeed some may operate in the opposite direction. However, one concern is that the study excluded consideration of the costs and outcomes for those patients (about 35%) who dropped out of clozapine therapy, although the reasons for discontinuation were given.

In a second study performed in the UK, Davis and Drummond (1993) adopted a modelling approach, using data from the earlier US study (Revicki *et al.*, 1990), supplemented by data from other sources. Their problem was that, given differences in clinical practice and organization of psychiatric services between the USA and the UK, the results of the earlier US study were not simply transferable to the USA. (For example, rates of hospitalization for schizophrenia were known to differ between the two settings.) Ideally, one would like to undertake a new prospective study, but this opportunity was not available.

The method adopted was to construct a clinical decision tree, shown in Figure 2. The decision tree shows the probabilities of patients achieving the different outcomes depending on whether they continued with standard neuroleptic therapy or changed to clozapine. The square box in the tree represents the decision to change therapy and the circles "chance nodes", show the probability of patients having certain outcomes. Patients changing to clozapine therapy will either continue with the drug if the outcome is satisfactory, or will discontinue therapy if the drug is ineffective or there are clinically significant side-effects (chance node B) or if there is a problem with compliance.

Data for some of the probabilities in the tree were taken from the US study (e.g. the probability of clozapine being discontinued, or the probability of clozapine patients attaining a particular BPRS score). However, other data, relating to the effectiveness of neuroleptic therapy or the type of community-based care received by patients discharged in either group, were used to supplement those from the US study.

In particular a Delphi (consensus) panel of five UK psychiatrists was used to assess the level of resource use in the UK setting for patients of different clinical status. From total BPRS scores observed in the US study, six patient profiles were constructed and considered by the panel. To avoid bias, the members of the Delphi panel were *not* given information about the actual location of care or drug therapy for the six patients. They were asked to make their own assessment prior to the meeting of how they would manage a patient corresponding to each profile and, through discussion at the meeting, consensus was reached on how each of the patients would have been managed in the UK. This formed the basis for costing care.

The authors concluded that clozapine would lead to a net gain of 5.87 years of life with no disability or only mild disability (defined as a BPRS score <35 or Clinical Global Impression Scale Score <3). Also, the direct costs of using clozapine (including the costs of the drug) would be £91 less per annum or £1333 per lifetime less than that for standard neuroleptic therapy. Because the study involved a number of key assumptions, the authors also under-

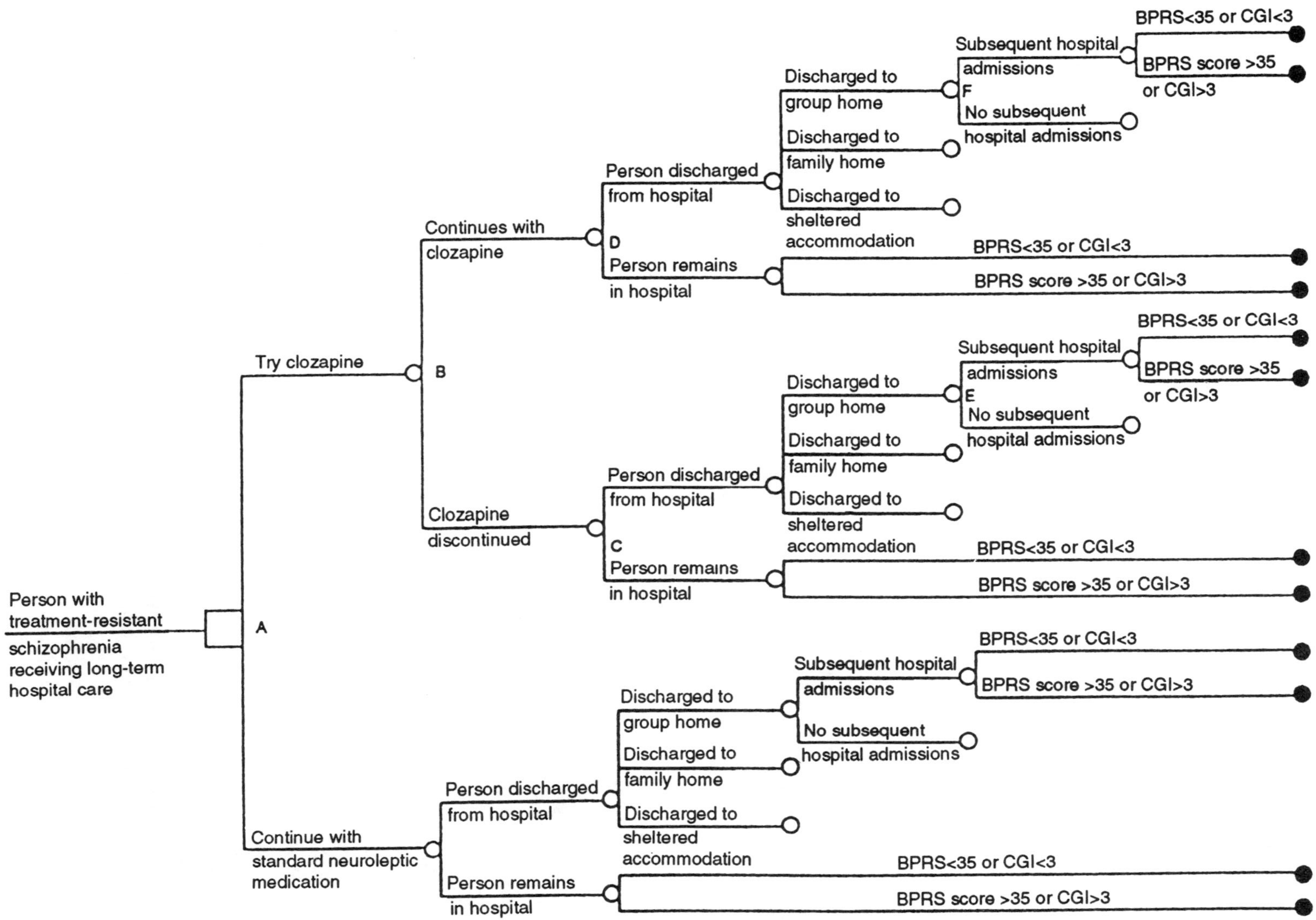

Figure 2. Decision tree used by panel to decide on care likely to be received by chronic, treatment-resistant schizophrenic patients.

took an extensive analysis of the sensitivity of the results to the main estimates. They concluded that use of clozapine would be cost saving or cost neutral under many assumptions but that a prospective health economic study with clozapine in the management of schizophrenia would be desirable to confirm these results.

One of the criticisms of this study was in the costing of clozapine therapy itself. Because of the potentially serious side-effects, clozapine was only able to be licensed in the UK along with an accompanying blood monitoring service, which was provided by the pharmaceutical company. The approach adopted by Davies and Drummond (1993) was to assume that the costs of this service, which was provided free by the company, were reflected in the price of clozapine. Certain other costs falling on the health care system, such as the taking of blood samples, were not included in the analysis but are unlikely to be substantial.

A more important issue is whether the overall charge for the drug was unnecessarily inflated by the addition of the blood monitoring system, as this could possibly have been provided by the health care system itself, or other commercial laboratories, at a lower cost (Salzman, 1990). This is hard to establish given the information available. However, if the overall cost of clozapine therapy could indeed be reduced by separating, or "unbundling", the cost of the drug and the blood monitoring system, the conclusions of the Davies and Drummond study would be further reinforced.

The third and most recent economic evaluation of clozapine is the study by Meltzer *et al.* (1993), undertaken in the USA. Data were collected on 96 treatment-resistant patients with schizophrenia for 2 years before they entered a clozapine treatment study and for at least 2 years after. Information was collected on the cost of inpatient and outpatient treatment, housing costs, and family burden through direct interview or questionnaire. (This was available for 47 of the 96 patients.) Data on lost income and Social Security disability insurance were also obtained. Outcome measures included psychopathology, quality of life (measured by an instrument for rating the schizophrenic deficit syndrome), global functioning, work function, and rehospitalization.

It was found that the cost of treatment was significantly decreased in the patients who continued clozapine treatment for at least 2 years. This was primarily due to a dramatic decrease in the frequency and cost of hospitalization. Costs were not significantly lower in patients who dropped out of treatment. Taking into account all patients there was a saving of \$8700 per patient per year over the 2 years. There was a decrease in total costs of \$22 936 per year for the 37 patients who continued clozapine and for whom cost data were available.

Clozapine also produced a marked improvement in BPRS total scores as well as positive negative symptom scores, Global Assessment Scale scores, Quality of Life Scale scores, work functioning, capacity for independent living, and rehospitalization rates. Having a stronger design than the two earlier studies, the Meltzer *et al.* study provides the best evidence on the likely costs and consequences of switching neuroleptic-resistant patients to clozapine therapy.

ASSESSING COST-EFFECTIVENESS OF DRUG THERAPY IN THE FUTURE

GROWING IMPORTANCE OF THE PROBLEM

It can be seen from the discussion above that none of the existing published studies employed an ideal methodology. Some interesting data have been generated on clozapine in relation to treatment-resistant patients. However, a number of new schizophrenia drugs have been recently launched or are in development. These may be shown to have similar advantages to clozapine, in relation to the absence or lower incidence of extrapyramidal side-effects, without the serious side-effects such as agranulocytosis. Therefore they may not necessarily be reserved for the treatment-resistant patients in the long-term. However, the acquisition costs of these new drugs are high compared with older neuroleptics, such as haloperidol. For example, the average cost per day of clozapine is approximately £6, and that of risperidone £4, compared with less than £1 for haloperidol (Davies & Drummond, 1993; *Drug and Therapeutics Bulletin*, 1993).

While the development of new, more effective or more easily tolerated, medicines will bring undoubted benefits to patients, there will be consequent increases in the total drugs bill for schizophrenia. This may, or may not, increase the total expenditure on health care for schizophrenia, depending on the costs of the new medicines and the extent of savings in the use of other resources, most notably hospitalization. Nevertheless, it is likely to focus attention on the cost-effectiveness of therapy for schizophrenia and increase the need for economic evaluation of drugs. What should be the essential methodological features of such an evaluation strategy?

LINK TO PROSPECTIVE CLINICAL TRIALS

None of the existing economic evaluations of drug therapy for schizophrenia was linked to a prospective randomized controlled trial. The randomized controlled trial is universally accepted as the preferred form of medical evidence about the efficacy of drug therapy. There is therefore a growing trend towards undertaking economic analysis alongside clinical trials and several successful studies have been carried out in other clinical fields.

The conduct of economic studies alongside trials is not without its methodological difficulties (Drummond and Davies, 1991). In the main these relate to the fact that many clinical trials are undertaken under conditions that would not pertain in regular clinical practice. However, with careful selection of the trial alongside which to undertake economic analysis and with adjustments to the data (e.g. exclusion of protocol-driven costs) many of the difficulties can be overcome. Nevertheless, several logistical and methodological challenges remain, in relation to the statistical analysis of economic data gathered alongside trials and the additional time and expense of data collection.

SELECTION OF RELEVANT COMPARATORS

In economic evaluation the objective is to explore the implications, in costs and consequences, of employing alternative clinical strategies in practice. However, many clinical trials of pharmaceuticals compare the new drug with a placebo or baseline therapy. In an economic evaluation the ideal comparator would be the therapy that the new drug was most likely to replace, with the exception of breakthrough drugs, where the realistic alternative may be "doing nothing." Therefore, there should be an increased emphasis on comparing new drugs with realistic comparators, especially after the needs of licensing agencies like the Food and Drug Administration have been satisfied.

Also the comparator therapy should itself be delivered in the most effective way. Some of the commentators on the clinical and economic studies of clozapine have argued that the comparisons made with neuroleptic drugs were unfair, either because the dosages used were inappropriate, or because they were given to a population that might have been known in advance to be likely to benefit (Healy, 1993). Whether or not these particular claims can be substantiated, it is clear that when assessments of new drugs are made, these should be compared with an alternative therapy that is itself being delivered appropriately.

ADEQUATE FOLLOW-UP

Because of the economic incentives and pressures facing pharmaceutical companies, there is a tendency for the clinical development program to be undertaken as quickly as possible. In turn this means that clinical trials may be small or be of short-term duration. However, the length of follow-up should be commensurate with the need to demonstrate the efficacy, side-effect profile and economic consequences of therapy over an adequate period. In the case of the economic studies of clozapine, the 2-year results were often different from the 1-year results, as it sometimes takes time for improvements in the patient's clinical status to be reflected in measures such as hospital discharge or impact on the family. This suggests that exploration of some of the economic consequences may require longer studies. Certainly, given the nature of schizophrenia it is necessary to follow the patient beyond the first discharge from hospital as readmissions are common.

Also, where possible, economic evaluations should be undertaken on an intent-to-treat basis. This is particularly important in situations where treatment failures could be costly. Sometimes this poses practical difficulties, but should be easier to handle in prospective studies. The problems in following dropouts in some of the clozapine evaluations arose from the fact that the studies were retrospective.

ACCURATE COST MEASUREMENTS

This has two components: measurement of the appropriate *range* of costs and accurate estimation of those costs that are considered. In the field of schizophrenia a particular challenge is that many of the important costs are incurred outside the hospital, in the use of community health care services, social welfare, and voluntary services, or in increased economic burden on the family. These items are harder to track than hospital-based costs.

The accurate estimation of costs involves *quantification* of the physical quantities of the resources used (e.g. number of hospital days, number of community psychiatric nurse visits) and reliable *valuation* of the unit costs of those items. Now that more economic evaluations are being carried out alongside clinical trials the quantification of resource use is more frequently being made through the trial case report forms, rather than by expert assessment as in the Davies and Drummond (1993) study of clozapine. Where the clinical trial is being conducted in a setting typical of regular clinical practice these assessments are likely to be more reliable.

The main issue relating to valuation of resource items is whether the financial amounts observed reflect true costs. One instance of this, relating to the "bundling" of the clozapine drug cost with that of the patient monitoring system, was discussed earlier. However, there is a much broader debate in economic evaluation over the use of health care charges, as in the study by Meltzer *et al.* (1993) for some resource items. Often the level of charges, for physicians' services or hospitalization, reflect local market conditions rather than real resource costs (Finkler, 1982). If the evaluation is being performed from the perspective of the health insurer or third party payer, the use of charges (or rather payments) may be defensible. However, it should be recognized that these financial estimates may not be accurate reflections of the sacrifices borne by society, in terms of resources denied other uses. The financial estimation of other resource items, such as lost worktime and family time spent in informal care of sick relatives, is even more controversial.

RELEVANT RANGE OF QUALITY OF LIFE MEASURES

Most clinical and economic evaluations of drug therapy for schizophrenia have used measures of clinical status of the patient as guides to the overall impact of therapy on quality of life. As measures like the BPRS are useful for clinical practitioners wishing to assess whether therapy is working they should continue to be used. However, economic evaluations usually require the inclusion of other, broader, measures of the impact of therapy on quality of life.

For example, in Figure 3 the BPRS may be viewed either as a traditional clinical measure, or a disease-specific measure of quality of life. These measures have the advantage that, being targeted on the disease in question, they have the maximum responsiveness to change. However, quality of life could also be measured by using a general health profile, such as the Short Form 36 or Nottingham Health Profile. This would enable comparisons to be made between the quality of life of people with schizophrenia, and the possible benefits of therapy, with those experienced by people suffering from other diseases. Finally, in order to influence public policy and resource allocation decisions, it may be necessary to measure changes in quality of life on a utility scale. This would enable the estimation of benefits of therapy in terms of quality-adjusted life-years (QALYs). The problems related to its use in schizophrenia are discussed in this book (Chapter 31). This is important as one way of approaching priority setting in health care is to compare the relative cost per QALY gained from alternative health care interventions. If developments in drug therapy lead to increased expenditure on schizophrenia it may be important to have evidence on the costs and QALYs gained in order to justify extra resources.

CONCLUSIONS

In summary, there is a growing need for economic evaluation of drug therapies for schizophrenia. The data from these evaluations are likely to be required either for reimbursement decisions, or to justify the

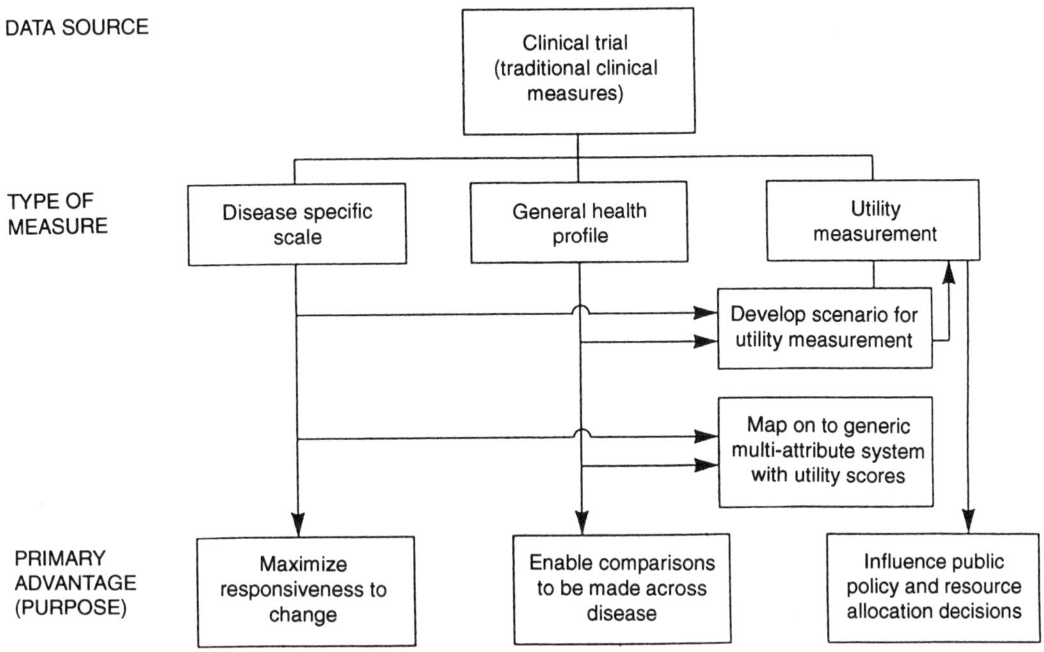

Figure 3. Inter-relationships between health-related quality of life measures.

additional expense of new drugs to health care decision-makers at all levels. In particular, the acquisition costs of new drugs will be substantially higher than currently available therapies. However, as the economic studies of clozapine indicate, these new medicines may result in savings in the use of other health care resources and improve the quality of life of patients. Therefore, it is important that these broader costs and benefits are assessed.

Furthermore, economic evidence will be required either prior to, or at, product launch. This means that economic data will need to be collected as part of the drug development process. The criticisms of the economic studies of clozapine indicate that the requirement to collect economic data may have a profound impact on the design of clinical trials. Clinical trials would need to include relevant comparator drugs, at appropriate doses. The period of follow-up may need to be substantially longer, as changes in health care resource use may only occur after 1–2 years of use. Finally, a wider range of outcome measures may need to be included. This would enable assessment of the impact of new therapies on broader aspects of patients' quality of life.

REFERENCES

Davies, L.M. and Drummond, M.F. (1990). The economic burden of schizophrenia. *Psychiatric Bulletin*, **14**, 522–525.

Davies, L.M. and Drummond, M.F. (1993). Assessment of costs and benefits of drug therapy for treatment resistant schizophrenia in the United Kingdom. *British Journal of Psychiatry*, **162**, 38–42.

Detsky, A.S. (1993). Guidelines for economic analysis of pharmaceutical products. A draft document for Ontario and Canada. *Pharmacoeconomics*, **3**, 354–361.

Drug and Therapeutics Bulletin (1993). Risperidone and Remoxipride for schizophrenia. *Drug and Therapeutics Bulletin*, **31**, 101–102.

Drummond, M.F. (1994). The emerging government requirement for economic evaluation of pharmaceuticals. *Pharmacoeconomics*, **6** (Suppl. 1), 42–50.

Drummond, M.F. and Davies, L.M. (1991). Economic analysis alongside clinical trials: revisiting the methodological issues. *International Journal of Technology Assessment in Health Care*, **7**, 561–573.

Drummong, M.F., Stoddart, G.L., and Torrance, G.W. (1987). *Methods for the Economic Evaluation of Health Care Programmes*. Oxford: Oxford University Press.

Drummond, M.F., Rutten, F.F.H., Brenna, A., Gouveia Pinto, C., and Horisberger, B. (1993). Economic evaluation of pharmaceuticals: a European perspective. *Psychiatric Bulletin*, **14**, 522–525.

Finkler, S.A. (1982). On the distinction between costs and charges. *Annals of Internal Medicine*, **96**, 102–109.

Healy, D. (1993). Psychopharmacology and the ethics of resource allocation. *British Journal of Psychiatry*, **162**, 23–29.

Kane, J., Honigfeld, G., Singer, J., and Meltzer, H. (1988). Clozapine for the treatment-resistant schizophrenic: a double-blind comparison with chlorpromazine. *Archive of General Psychiatry*, **45**, 789–796.

Meltzer, H.Y., Cola, P., Way, L., *et al.* (1993). Cost-effectiveness of clozapine in neuroleptic-resistant schizophrenia. *American Journal of Psychiatry*, **150**, 1630–1630.

Revicki, D.A., Luce, B.R., Weschler, J.M., Brown, R.E., and Adler, M.A. (1990). Cost-effectiveness of clozapine of treatment-resistant schizophrenia patients. *Hospital and Community Psychiatry*, **41**, 850–854.

Salzman, C. (1990). Mandatory monitoring for side effects: the "bundling" of clozapine. *New England Journal of Medicine*, **323**, 827–829.

Part VIII

FINANCING

33

Insuring Severe Mental Disorders: a Comparison of Approaches

RICHARD G. FRANK
Harvard University, Boston, Massachusetts, USA

HOWARD H. GOLDMAN
Department of Psychiatry, University of Maryland, Baltimore, Maryland, USA

THOMAS G. McGUIRE
Department of Economics, College of Liberal Arts, Boston, Massachusetts, USA

INTRODUCTION

As the United States debates health care reform, the mental health community has focused attention on the design of the benefit. What will be the nature of health care coverage for individuals with mental illness? Who will be insured; what conditions will be covered; with what limits?

Recent policy has shifted the priority for the expenditure of public mental health resources toward services for individuals with *severe* mental disorders. Naturally, advocates and policy-makers have focused a great deal of attention on offering better health care insurance protection against the financial consequences of severe mental illness (National Advisory Mental Health Council, 1993; Lamb, 1993). Interest in this issue has expanded as the federal government and individual states have developed specific legislative proposals to reform the health system (see for example, US Senate, Equitable Health Insurance Coverage of Severe Mental Disorders, 1992 and Texas Insurance Code 3.50-2, 1993).

Three general approaches to health insurance benefit design have been proposed to assure that the care needs of individuals with severe mental disorders will be met through appropriate coverage. Legislative proposals and the health care literature refer to *service-based, diagnosis-based,* and *disability-based* approaches. The objective of each approach is to offer adequate protection by suporting the treatment of individuals with severe mental disorder as the first priority for insurance coverage, recognizing the need to allocate scarce resources carefully (and sometimes differentially).

As a standard we can consider three goals for public policy which are commonly advanced in discussions of insurance coverage and severe mental illnesses. The first goal, stemming from the traditional literature on insurance (Arrow, 1963), is to protect patients and families against the catastrophic financial consequences of severe mental disorders. The most valuable form of insurance from this perspective is

Handbook of Mental Health Economics and Health Policy, Volume I, Schizophrenia. Edited by M. Moscarelli, A. Rupp and N. Sartorius.
© 1996 John Wiley & Sons Ltd.

that which offers protection against large losses. In the case of mental illnesses a small percentage of all individuals account for a very large portion of total mental health care expenditures. For example, a privately insured individual hospitalized for treatment of schizophrenia will have expenditures made on their behalf of approximately $23 800 in 1993. In contrast the average level of expenditure made on behalf of all users of mental health services is about $1200.

The second major goal for insurance policy is to promote use of cost-effective care. That is, the insurance plan can be viewed as defining the dimensions of a contingent contract which specifies the treatments that will be paid for given various states of mental health. The choice of treatments is typically influenced by the patient, the treating clinician, and increasingly, a managed care organization representing the payer. Policy towards insurance design seeks to encourage matches between patients and treatments that lead to effective care.

A third common goal of policy towards health insurance is to control the costs of mental health care. Mental health care costs, like all health care costs, have been rising at rates well above the general rate of inflation (Frank *et al.*, 1991). Thus decisions concerning benefit design and payment methods have increasingly focused on the control of utilization and costs.

The remainder of this chapter is aimed at assessing how effectively and efficiently each of the three approaches towards offering coverage for severe mental disorders addresses these three policy goals. Our assessment will proceed by discussing each approach to insurance policy in terms of four key questions. Those questions are as follows: (i) How well does each approach to insuring against severe mental illness protect patients against the financial risks of illness? (ii) How well does the structure of the "contingent contract" implicit in each approach correspond to what is known about effectiveness of treatments and the needs of individuals with severe mental disorders? (iii) What are the administrative costs associated with each approach? and (iv) How much does each approach cost overall?

Questions (i) and (iv) are commonly raised in discussions of insurance policy. Question (ii) is newer and is increasingly being incorporated into the debate regarding the use of managed care techniques and practice guidelines in the context of health insurance and payment policy. Question (iii) is critical to the problem at hand because each approach differs significantly in its administrative requirements for defining eligibility for coverage.

The paper consists of four main sections. In the second section we describe each approach. The third section offers a detailed discussion of each approach in terms of incentives and costs. The third section presents an overview of how well each approach accomplishes the policy goals and a discussion of the trade-offs decision-makers face in choosing between the three approaches to insurance policy.

THE APPROACHES

Ideal insurance would cover effective services for persons who would benefit from them and who need protection against financial risk. Insurance for mental health care has historically limited coverage for inpatient and office-based care below that which was available for treatments of other illnesses. Doubts about the cost-effectiveness of psychotherapy and hospitalization have been reasons behind some of the restrictions. The high demand response characterizing mental health services exacerbates the concern about cost-effectiveness. Services only purchased when insurance is present are particularly suspect on cost-effectiveness grounds.

In light of the past difficulties associated with restrictions on coverage for mental health services, it seems worthwhile to consider basing coverage on other criteria. In this paper, we compare the traditional means of defining eligibility for insurance based on services used (with a broad notion of qualified diagnoses) to a definition based on a characteristic of the person, such as diagnosis or a level of disability. If the person is determined to be eligible in terms of their clinical state, then a broad range of services would be covered in a favorable way.

As can be pointed out immediately, however, ultimately, insurance pays for service use. Questions of cost-effectiveness and demand response are not avoided when the clinical state of the person is used to determine eligibility. The same questions merely reappear in another form.

The *diagnosis-based* approach to providing insurance coverage for severe mental illnesses has recently been discussed in a report prepared on behalf of the National Advisory Mental Health Council (NAMHC, 1993). The operational definition of severe mental disorders consists of two major components. There are those disorders that are *per se* indicators of severe mental illness and those that are *qualified* indicators of severe mental illness. The *per se* indicators are diagnoses of schizophrenia, schizoaffective disorder, manic depression (or bipolar mood disorder), and autism. The qualified indicators are the severe forms of major depression, panic disorder and obsessive–compulsive disorder (NAMHC, 1993, appendix B, p. 37). Severity criteria were defined in terms of symptoms, functional status, and receipt of treatment. Specifically, the criteria included inpatient use, psychotic symptoms, use of antipsychotic medication, or a Global Assessment of Functioning scale (GAF) score of 50 or less.

Given this definition of severe mental illness, the diagnosis-based approach would offer qualifying individuals insurance coverage for the treatment of their mental illnesses that would be "commensurate with other illnesses" (NAMHC, 1993, p. 20). The implications of this condition are several. First, there would be no special limits placed on inpatient coverage of mental disorders, in contrast with most existing insurance plans (BLS, 1991). Second, psychotherapy would not be subject to any visit limits and cost sharing would be at the 20% levels rather than the typical 50% level (BLS, 1991). Brief office visits to physicians would also be covered without limits and at 20% cost sharing. Third, lifetime and annual limits on mental health care would be eliminated. Finally, the benefit would include case management services (as is meant in the mental health system), residential treatment, rehabilitation services or day hospital programs—all services most existing insurance plans do not cover.

The *services-based* approach does not set any specific criteria concerning eligibility for insurance coverage other than those typically used by insurers: a diagnosed mental disorder according to DSMIII-R criteria. Thus, everyone in the risk pool (population) has the same coverage. The services approach relies on the structure of the "contingent contract" to meet policy goals. The insurance plan defines services to be covered and the terms of coverage with respect to cost sharing and payment methods, in order to provide catastrophic coverage and a menu of services that have (in combination) been shown to be effective in treating severe mental disorders. The services-based approach, as exemplified by Frank *et al.* (1992), provides the greatest coverage for services associated with (i) large financial losses (facility-based care) and (ii) services where utilization has a relatively modest response to cost sharing arrangements (less price elasticity of demand).

The *disability-based* approach to insurance coverage of severe mental disorders is similar to the diagnosis-based approach in concept. The disability-based approach seeks to identify those individuals experiencing levels of impairment due to mental illness that are in some sense catastrophic. The idea is to identify individuals whose illnesses are particularly severe and whose treatment needs are presumably great in order to provide them with special coverage. As in the case of the diagnosis-based approach, meeting disability criteria would entitle one to enriched coverage for treatment of mental disorders. As no specific proposals have appeared using this approach, the nature of the coverage is assumed to be similar to that discussed in conjunction with the diagnosis-based approach. (We make this assumption because all discussion of the disability approach occurs in the context of making mental health coverage for the disabled commensurate with that of other disorders.)

In sum, in the services-based approach *all* people (subject to a broad diagnostic requirement that they have some mental disorder), are covered for *some* services. In the diagnostic- and disability-based approaches, *some* people are covered for *all* services.

DISCUSSION OF THE APPROACHES

In this section we discuss issues related to: (i) the structure of the contingent contract; (ii) the incentives; and (iii) costs associated with each of the three approaches.

THE CONTINGENT CONTRACT

The descriptions in the previous section indicate several features that distinguish between the services-based approach on the one hand and the diagnosis- and disability-based approaches on the other. Under the services-based approach the extent of financial protection against illness depends on the pattern of services used for treating a particular diagnosed condition. All individuals in the population are eligible for the same level of coverage. The structure of the insurance benefit defines the out of pocket cost of care to the patient. Higher cost sharing provisions for specific services will discourage their use. Limits and service definitions define the types and quantity of services that can be paid for by insurance. Cost sharing arrangements can be used to encourage use of certain services (e.g. those shown to be effective or those viewed as more appropriate) and to limit services that are used very liberally when insurance coverage is provided (McGuire, 1989).

Additional clinical considerations can be incorporated via appropriate application of utilization management techniques such as pre-admission certification, concurrent review, high-cost case management and establishment of provider networks. The "Model Benefit" proposed by Frank *et al.* (1992) offers a specific formulation of the contingent contract within a services-based approach.

The services-based approach can be very effective in protecting the severely ill from financial risk. In the Model Benefit, extensive hospital- and other facility-related costs were fully covered after a small deductible. Even the patients with the highest costs face very little cost sharing in aggregate. By targeting cost sharing to the services used by the "low utilizers," primarily psychotherapy and the initial costs of facility-based care, the Model Benefit uses a services approach to fully cover the costs of services used by the seriously ill at a relatively low total plan cost.

Outpatient medical management, which is commonly used by the severely mentally ill for the purposes of monitoring medications, brief counseling, and assistance in management of a complicated treatment regimen, carries cost sharing comparable with that for other medical conditions (20% copayment) with no limits on the volume of services used. Outpatient psychotherapy in contrast carries substantially higher cost sharing (50% copayment). This formulation (currently in force in Medicare Part B) was proposed because: (i) psychotherapy services have been shown to be more responsive to cost sharing arrangements than are other types of treatment (Keeler *et al.*, 1986), and (ii) the expected financial losses to those with severe mental illnesses and most others are low. In sum, the benefit design offers a set of covered services that provide protection against financial outlays for the types of treatment that are currently used to treat severe mental disorders. The benefit design offers the same coverage to individuals in need of other forms of care. No attempt is made to determine which types of individuals may make use of coverage. This approach assures that severely mentally ill individuals get the services they need with catastrophic coverage and reasonable cost controls.

The diagnosis-based and disability-based approaches represent a very different approach to structuring a contingent contract relative to the services-based approach. Because the two approaches are quite similar in the way they handle benefit design, we discuss them together. Both the diagnosis and disability approach define a more complex contingent contract than does the service-based approach. The benefit design that is relevant to any given person depends on whether or not they meet criteria for classification as severely mentally ill (by either diagnostic or disability criteria). What is envisioned in the NAMHC report is that individuals not classified as severely ill would face coverage for mental health care that resembles the median health plan in 1992. Such a plan would generally cover 30 days per year of inpatient psychiatric care, 20 psychotherapy visits at a 50% copayment rate and possibly some partial hospital care that might count against the inpatient benefit (BLS, 1991; Hay Huggins, 1993).

The insurance coverage offered to individuals who meet criteria for severe mental illness would remove all special limits (on visits, inpatient days, and access to partial hospital care) and make copayments for psychotherapy and other ambulatory mental health care equal to those for other ambulatory care procedures (20%). Thus, severe mental illness qualifies an individual for more of everything. As in the case of the service-based benefit further clinical considerations can be introduced into utilization control by making use of managed care techniques (Hodgkin, 1992). One important question that arises is the extent that this formulation of the contingent contract corresponds well to either what is known about treatment effectiveness or cost control.

The principal problem with providing more of everything is that it does not distinguish between effective and ineffective nor between appropriate and inappropriate services for the individual with severe mental illness. The consequence may be a greatly increased cost for the care of this already expensive population. Such a policy may expose beneficiaries to unnecessary (or unnecessarily long) hospital stays—or to ineffective psychotherapy—simply because coverage with little cost sharing was available ("moral hazard") and/or because it was recommended by a provider ("supply-induced demand"). On the other side of the contract, for those who are not determined to be categorically "severe" but who have similar needs, the benefit provides inadequate coverage.

INCENTIVES

Central to the incentives under each of the three approaches to offering insurance coverage for severe mental disorders is identifying the relevant units of payment. In our analysis of the unit of payment we will discuss the diagnostic and disability approaches together as the units of payment are essentially the same. The services-based approach will be considered separately.

Traditionally, insurance coverage of health services means that the out of pocket price of a covered service is well below the so-called supply price paid to the provider. This divergence between the social and private costs of care results in a tendency to "overuse" care. By overuse we refer to a situation where the incremental benefits of the service (in terms of offering well-being to a consumer) are less than the incremental social costs of providing the service. This is the well known moral hazard problem that has been discussed extensively in the literature on economics and mental health (McGuire, 1989). A variety of policies have been proposed for limiting moral hazard (McGuire, 1989). Those proposals include: higher level of cost sharing for some mental health services, provider incentives, and coverage limits. This type of moral hazard is common to all three approaches to coverage of severe mental disorders. The services-based approach addresses the moral hazard problem in a very different manner than do the diagnostic- and disability-based approaches.

The services-based approach deals with moral hazard or cost control by applying three types of utilization control techniques directly to the services of concern according to the technical feasibility of implementing the utilization controls. The three techniques consist of: (i) financial incentives to providers of mental health care; (ii) managed care mechanisms; (iii) consumer cost sharing provisions. Where feasible the services-based approach as articulated in the plan of Frank *et al.* (1992) depends first on financial incentives to providers. Financial gains and penalties associated with different levels of utilization are placed on the provider of care via reimbursement methods. Per case utilization are placed on the provider of care via reimbursement methods. Per case prospective payment is an example of such a method which is used to control the duration of facility-based care. Pre-admission screening is proposed as a control on the initiation of facility-based care given the mounting evidence of its effectiveness (Hodgkin, 1992; Brookmeyer & Frank, 1993). Finally, when neither provider side payment nor utilization management offers a practical solution to utilization control, consumer cost sharing provisions are proposed to control use of services. This usually entails higher levels of copayments for specific services (e.g. 50% for psychotherapy). The terms of the utilization controls apply to all enrollees in an insurance plan equally. Different services carry different sets of arrangements.

What is unique to the diagnostic- and disability-based approaches to coverage is that payment is jointly determined by clinical status and the design of the mental health benefit within a health plan. Hence, there may therefore be major financial consequences associated with the determination of an individual's clinical status. The diagnosis- and disability-based approaches thereby creates a two-stage payment process.

In the first stage an individual's "clinical" status is determined. Depending on the results of the clinical determination the benefit package is then assigned to the individual. The second stage then involves paying for *covered services* on behalf of the mentally ill individual. For a substantial array of circumstances the payments that can be made for specific treatment services depend on the results of the first-stage determination process. For example, whether a readmission to a psychiatric hospital following a previous stay of 30 days during the benefit period will be paid for by an individual's health plan is determined by whether or not an individual is classified as severely mentally ill.

By offering essentially unlimited coverage of mental health services without specifying either specific cost sharing provisions or payment methods the diagnosis and disability approaches rely on limiting the size of the eligible population to control utilization and costs. Thus, control of the population that qualifies as severely mentally ill is central to determining the cost of coverage. The diagnosis and disability approaches create strong financial incentives for individuals in need of relatively extensive treatment to seek ways to become eligible for the enriched coverage offered to those designated as severely mentally ill. This implies that there will be incentives for clinicians serving as advocates for their patients to "upcode" cases in order to make them eligible for richer coverage.

In the definition of severe mental illness used by the NAMHC one severity criterion relates to use of inpatient care. Tying access to the enriched benefit to utilization of inpatient psychiatric care, during an era when public policy has been aimed at reducing such service use, creates undesirable incentives for individuals in any category but especially for those in the depression, panic disorder, and obsessive–compulsive disorder categories to overuse inpatient care.

Limiting access to the enriched coverage may control costs in the aggregate, but it does not fully solve the moral hazard problem. The same forces that produce a tendency to make excessive use of services in the general population of mental health care users will produce a similar phenomenon. While it is broadly agreed upon that individuals with severe mental disorders have more complicated treatment needs (NIMH, 1991) and are more prone to require care that carries catastrophic financial consequences, this does not mean that all services are equally beneficial to this population and that overuse cannot occur. For this reason there remains the incentive for excessive use of care even within the diagnosis and disability approaches.

COSTS

The costs of each approach can be viewed as consisting of several components. The components of cost are: (i) the costs of services used under each approach; (ii) the costs of administering the benefit including utilization review, monitoring of copayments, limits and deductibles, and the like; (iii) the costs of determining and policing eligibility standards; (iv) the costs of incorrectly limiting insurance coverage to those who are truly "severely mentally ill" but are incorrectly classified or do not use needed services because of the financial disincentives in the benefit; and (v) the costs of inappropriate treatment arising from distortions in benefit design.

Various estimates of the costs of mental health services used have been made for the service-based and diagnosis-based plans. They are not entirely comparable as they were conceived to apply to different populations. The service-based plan proposed by Frank *et al.* (1992) was designed for use in the context of private insurance and would have to be altered in important ways to be used for individuals currently enrolled in Medicaid or those who are poor and uninsured. Thus the existing cost estimates for a services-based plan only project costs for implementing the services-based approach for insured populations.

Frank *et al.* (1992) estimate that applying their specific formulation of the services-based approach would cost $135.50 per covered person in 1989. This is comparable in cost with plans with more restrictive benefit designs that rely on limits to control costs. It is also less costly than the most generous existing corporate plans in the USA.

The NAMHC (1993) report contains cost estimates for a diagnosis-based approach assuming that it applies to the entire non-elderly population of the USA. Thus no direct comparison is made.

The services-based plan relies on managed care techniques to control utilization to a larger extent than do either the diagnosis- or disability-based approaches. Unfortunately, we have not been able to locate any clear estimates of the cost of using various managed care techniques to control utilization. Moreover, it is not clear how managed care techniques would be used under the diagnosis- or disability-based approaches. The literature does report savings net of the costs of management but one cannot glean the costs of management from those studies (Hodgkin, 1992). The three approaches all make use of cost sharing and deductibles while the diagnosis- and disability-based approaches make relatively heavier use of limits on services than does the services-based approach. We do not expect that the administrative costs of each approach would differ substantially with respect to those benefit design provisions.

The diagnosis and disability approaches both require that determinations be made regarding eligibility for the expanded set of insurance benefits. Under the diagnosis-based approach one could rely simply on the diagnoses assigned by a clinician. One potentially important strength of the diagnosis-based approach is that it relies on a relatively easily observed (and administered) indication of illness. Diagnoses are commonly reported on insurance claims, hospital discharge abstracts, and patient charts. If one were to rely on this source of information, one must consider two types of consequences that stem from such a policy. The first is the costs stemming from upcoding. The second is the costs of excluding individuals who meet clinical criteria for severe mental illness but are not captured by simple diagnostic criteria.

There is evidence of diagnostic upcoding in the health sector generally and in the mental health area specifically. The RAND Corporation has performed a series of studies on the coding responses under Medicare's Prospective Payment System (PPS). Carter *et al.* (1991) show that between 1987 and 1988 Medicare's Diagnosis Related Group (DRG) based Case Mix Index (CMI) increased 3.3%. This change was decomposed into increases due to changes in patient resource needs and increases due to altered coding and administrative practices. The results of the analysis show that 1.7 of the 3.3% increase in the CMI was attributable to upcoding. A study by Sharfstein *et al.* (1980) raises a similar point for mental health services specifically. They show wide discrepancy in diagnostic coding under the US Federal Employees Benefit Program. They offer two explanations for the results. The first relates to a practice of assigning patients "socially benign" diagnoses in order to protect confidentiality. The other suggests that individuals who did not meet diagnostic criteria but who "needed" therapy were assigned a diagnosis for reimbursement purposes. No direct evidence on the importance of each hypothesis in explaining the results was reported. The available evidence suggests that when diagnoses are part of a unit of payment increases in costs will be generated by upcoding.

The operational definition given by the NAMHC adds additional criteria for determining which cases are severe within the major depression, panic disorder, and obsessive–compulsive disorder diagnostic groups. Thus, relying on simple diagnoses as reported on claims forms will result in a majority of the cases of severe mental illness being misclassified (Regier *et al.*, 1993). This raises the issue of how additional criteria will be assessed and monitored. If the criteria relate to utilization of inpatient care one might expect substantial increases in admissions to inpatient care. Research on capitation programs, selective contracting (Schmitz, 1992), and prospectively set budgets (Frank & Jackson, 1989) show that when one ceases paying for units of inpatient care (either admissions or days) admissions are significantly reduced.

An alternative strategy to determining eligibility to the enriched insurance coverage would focus on the symptomatology and GAF criteria exclusively for individuals with diagnoses of depression, panic disorder, and obsessive–compulsive disorder. In this case one has to choose between relying on clinician reports as the basis for eligibility or establishing an external eligibility determination process. If clinician judgements are to be relied upon the issue of costly upcoding arises once again. Putting into place an eligibility determination process may also be quite costly. We discuss this in more detail in connection to the disability-based approach.

Basing insurance coverage on an assessment of disability is more complex than one based on diagnosis. Defining disability is difficult. Our society uses many definitions of disability for different purposes. One of the most important uses of the term disability is one that entitles one to social insurance benefits under the Supplemental Security Income (SSI) program and Social Security Disability

Insurance (SSDI). In those instances the term disability refers to "the inability to engage in any substantial gainful activity by reason of any ... mental impairment which can be expected to result in death or has lasted or can be expected to last for a continuous period of not less than 12 months" (Social Security Act, Section 223). The Social Security standard is very strict. Others use the term disability to refer to impairment in social functioning that falls short of the inability to engage in any gainful activity (Goldman *et al.*, 1981). In practical terms psychosocial rehabilitation programs, partial hospitalization programs, and other supports for the severely mentally ill are utilized regularly by many individuals who do not meet the SSI/SSDI criteria. Nevertheless, eligibility for an enriched insurance policy based on disability status requires: (i) defining disability and (ii) developing a system to determine eligibility. Allowing clinicians to make that determination has the same costs and benefits as were discussed in the context of the diagnosis-based approach above.

Creating an eligibility process will be costly. The SSI/SSDI eligibility process offers one estimate of those costs. The cost of that program offer some insight into what it might cost to create an eligibility system for a national plan. The processing of initial disability claims submitted to the Social Security Administration cost the government between \$410 and \$500 per claim in 1992 (unpublished SSA Administrative Data). Of the initial claims submitted, 13.6% were appealed in 1992. The appealed cases cost the government between \$200 and \$450 depending on the specific type of claim being made. Roughly 49% of the appealed cases resulted in a hearing at a cost of between \$800 and \$2500 to the SSA. Finally, about 18% of cases are reviewed by the SSA Council at a cost of between \$360 and \$595. Given these costs and probabilities of appeal, the expected processing cost of a new claim is about \$575. An estimate of the incidence of severe mental disorders in any one year can be made at 1.5% based on Regier *et al.* (1993). Based on this incidence estimate the cost of processing mental health disability claims might be at least \$2 billion per year or roughly 3% of what we currently spend on mental health services.

The costs of misclassification may be significant for both the diagnostic- and disability-based approaches to insuring severe mental illnesses. To day most attempts to define and codify severe mental illness have appealed to three dimensions of the illnesses: diagnosis, disability, and duration (Goldman *et al.*, 1981). In this case diagnosis *per se* does not correspond closely to either clinically or financial characterizations of severe mental illness. This leaves open the costs of exposing individuals and their families to financial risks over which they have little control. A similar point can be made with respect to disability. That is, attempting to set boundary conditions for complicated phenomena such as mental illness is certain to result in misclassification. These misclassifications can be costly both in terms of the lost benefits of risk spreading and due to the treatment distortions that might occur.

For example, certain patients might be discouraged from obtaining ongoing low-intensity treatment for a condition prior to its reaching a stage where severity criteria were met. A second episode of unipolar depression might call for maintenance therapy. However, if severity criteria were not met, such individuals might have exhausted their ambulatory mental health benefit prior to obtaining the full course of treatment. Such a patient might then require a costly hospitalization—either in the public sector or privately when ultimately reclassified as disabled.

It is important to note that similar distortions can occur within a services-based approach. Relative out-of-pocket prices defined by the benefit package may encourage say, medical management (possibly using drug treatments) over psychotherapy. This may result in non-optimal treatment from a clinical standpoint especially in the cases of mild depressions and childhood mental disorders.

ASSESSMENT

AN ANALYTICAL PERSPECTIVE

In attempting to sum up the discussion we offer a simple analytical structure for organizing the discussion of the issues presented above. The aim of the framework is to offer a basis for an empirical assessment of many of the key issues raised above. A central issue in making a comparison between the three coverage approaches is the trade-off between the gains of targeting coverage and the costs of misclassification.

Let S_1 be the optimal benefit for individuals who do not meet criteria for severe mental illness, S_2 is the optimal benefit for individuals who qualify as severely mentally ill and S^* is the optimal benefit if all individuals are pooled into a single risk group. We define P_1 as the portion of non-severely ill people in the population (type 1). The portion of severely mentally ill individuals is therefore $(1-P_1)$ (or type 2). The goal of the exercise here is to compare the value of the services approach with the value of two approaches to classifying people as severely mentally ill. The value of the service approach is

$$S^*=(P_1+(1-P_1))S \tag{1}$$

This is compared with the value of the diagnostic or disability approach.

$$V=[(1-\delta)P_1+\lambda(1-P_1)]S_1 + [\delta P_1+(1-\lambda)(1-P_1)]S_2 \tag{2}$$

where δ is the portion of type 1 people misclassified and λ is the portion of type 2 people misclassified.

Assume that when correct matches between people and coverage are made the following conditions hold:

$U_1(S_1)>U_1(S^*)>U_1(S_2)$ for type 1 people and for type 2 people
$U_2(S_1)<U_2(S^*)<U_2(S_2)$

Hence for type 1 people a more limited benefit is more valuable in a social sense than either the services-based benefit or the enriched benefit targeted at severely mentally ill people. The reverse is true for type 2 individuals.

We can now define gains and losses that rise from going to a diagnostic/disability approach from a services-based approach. Define the utility or benefits of coverage as $U(S)$. Then

$$U_1(S_1)-U_1(S^*)=g>0 \tag{3a}$$
$$U_1(S_2)-U_1(S^*)=l_1<0 \tag{3b}$$
$$U_2(S_2)-U_2(S^*)=g_2>0 \tag{3c}$$
$$U_2(S_1)-U_2(S^*)=l_2<0 \tag{3d}$$

Equations (3a) and (3c) represent the gains from making the "right matches" between individuals and coverage compared with the services-based coverage. Equations (3b) and (3d) define the losses stemming from mismatches relative to the benefits of the services-based approach. Using Equations (1), (2), and (3) we form the expression for the gain from moving from a services-based approach to a diagnostic/disability approach.

$$G=(1-\delta)P_1g_1+\lambda(1-P_1)l_2 + \delta P_2l_1+(1-\lambda)(1-P_1)g_1 \tag{4}$$

Equation (4) makes clear that the values for δ and λ are critical for defining the gains from various alternative approaches. The magnitude of the g's and l's are also important.

MISCLASSIFICATION COSTS

Each of the three approaches offers different coverage to potentially quite different populations. The services-based approach offers the same coverage to all covered individuals, yet the expectation is for different types of people to use different services. The structure of the insurance coverage, as proposed in Frank *et al.* (1992) offers relatively complete coverage for the types of services that put severely mentally ill individuals at serious financial risk. This implies what might be termed an economic view of severe mental illness. One might define cases in terms of the financial risks imposed on families. Thus, a severe mental disorder might be defined as one where appropriate and effective treatment results in large financial outlays. Given this definition, provision of broad insurance coverage may be efficient. If one subscribes to such a view, the services-based approach offers all who are at risk, coverage for severe mental illness. The weakness here is that many low-cost services may be available to those who may not benefit from receiving them (medical management for minor conditions). These in part, create the gains captured in g_1 and g_2.

Clinical definitions of severe mental illness focus on three dimensions of illness and its consequences: diagnosis, disability, and duration. Focusing on one dimension is by definition limiting. It is particularly limiting as a mechanism for establishing eligibility to insurance designed to protect against catasrophic illness. This is because research related to classification systems has shown that diagnoses (DRGs) are a poor predictor of variation in duration of hospital stays and costs (Frank & Lave, 1985; Horgan & Jencks, 1987). Little research has been done on classification systems and their ability to predict all mental health care utilization. It is, however, likely that the explanatory power of a diagnostic-based system for all mental health utilization would be even weaker than that found for DRGs and inpatient care. This suggests that the magnitudes of δ and λ may be substantial in the diagnostic-based approach.

It is also troublesome to note that a significant portion of individuals who meet the strict mental disability standards set by the Social Security Administration (SSA) have primary diagnoses of somatoform and personality disorders (unpublished data) and would therefore not meet diagnostic criteria set out by the NAMHC (1993). This indicates some important conflicts between any classification scheme that relies primarily on a single dimension to classify people with an illness that has complex effects on those suffering from the condition.

The disability-based approach is as yet not well defined. We believe that there is considerable potential to classify people along the multiple dimensions that correspond to most definitions of disability in such a way as to offer catastrophic coverage to those who are truly severely ill. There is, however, much work to be done in specification of definitions of disability. Although the SSA definition identifies some individuals who do not meet the NMHAC definition of severe mental illness, in other instances it is too strict and misses substantial segments of the population suffering from severe mental illness (NAMHC, 1993). Private disability insurance which covers about 40% of all workers in the USA uses a variety of definitions. It would be important to align clinical definitions with appropriate treatment patterns that expose beneficiaries to large financial losses.

Setting up strict boundaries with relatively restrictive definitions of severe mental illness suggests great weight is being placed on Type I errors. That is, it is important not to pay for extended care for people who are not severely mentally ill. It is also important to explicitly consider Type II errors. Individuals who are severely impaired by a mental illness and who incur large financial losses but are denied protection against those losses. Those costs are captured by the I_1 and I_2 terms in Equation (4).

COSTS OF MATCHING

Under the services-based approach the insurance plan does not attempt to distinguish which types of people are most appropriate to receive one form of coverage over another. Thus there are no direct costs of matching. There are of course the costs associated with the failure to control moral hazard and those associated with distortions in the treatment choices stemming from the benefit design.

In its simplest form the diagnosis-based approach has few direct costs of matching, if it relies solely on clinician-reported diagnoses or other clinical information. The consequence of making such a design decision would be the likelihood of upcoding on the costs stemming from such behavior. If a formal determination process is put into place which would establish (or verify) diagnoses and assess other criteria necessary for classification of individuals as suffering from severe mental illness, the costs are unknown. One reasonable approximation is the expected per claim cost under the SSI/SSDI programs. These were estimated to be $575 per claimant. The disability-based approach would almost certainly require a determination process to be established. The SSI/SSDI costs are probably the best estimate of what such a mechanism would cost per claimant. The expected volume of claims is difficult to anticipate.

DEFINING COVERAGE

The services-based approach represents a balance of concerns with providing catastrophic coverage, controls on use of services that are responsive to insurance coverage and coverage of services shown to be effective. In some instances this may make for a good match, as in the case of medical management. In other cases the link between benefit design and treatment is less clear such as for borderline personality disorders or childhood disorders. This is why $U_1(S^*) < U_1(S_1)$ and $U_2(S^*) < U_2(S_2)$. In addition, the services-based approach proposed by Frank *et al.* (1992) is not well suited for covering the medically indigent, the poor, and the unemployed. Substantial changes in that approach would have to be made to make it relevant to most disadvantaged population. The main reason for that is the reliance of that formulation of the services-based approach on cost sharing.

Both the diagnosis- and disability-based approach link the coverage of the enriched benefit package to benefit design for all medical conditions. While this is sensible as an avenue for eliminating special limits imposed on mental disorders, it fails to recognize some of the unique treatment needs of individuals with severe mental disorders that are not typically covered under traditional insurance plans. These include: day hospital services, residential treatment, psychosocial rehabilitation, and case management. Such omissions could be remedied by simply specifying the sets of services that constitute mental health treatment and the terms of coverage thereby making $U_1(S_1)$ and $U_2(S_2)$ larger. This issue, however, is important because it suggests that for both the diagnosis-based and the disability-based approaches, it is important to move beyond simply making mental health benefits commensurate to those in general health care. It is unlikely that specifying a rule such as: if one qualifies as severely mentally ill one is entitled to more of everything, creates a cost-effective public policy towards insurance coverage.

SUMMARY

One rationale for targeting coverage for persons meeting diagnostic or disability criteria is that services may be more effective for these persons. While this is quite possible, evidence on such differential effectiveness does not exist, or at least not in sufficient force to justify such a strong distinction. The other possible rationale is that these persons need financial protection because they use more services. This goal can readily be met by a services-based approach emphasizing coverage for services used by persons most severely ill, such as the model plan.

Against these "advantages" would be weighed the administrative complexity and cost, fairness costs, and extra services costs generated by a system administered with error. Comparison of these approaches ultimately is an empirical issue concerning the parameters of Equation (4) above.

ACKNOWLEDGMENTS

Financial support for the project came from NIMH Grant MH43703.

REFERENCES

Arrow, K. (1963). Uncertainty and the welfare economics of medical care. *American Economic Review*, **December**, 941–973.

Brookmeyer, R. and Frank R.G. (1993). *Cost Sharing, Managed Care and Inpatient Psychiatric Utilization in Private Insurance*. Baltimore, MD: Johns Hopkins University Press.

Bureau of Labor Statistics (1991). *Employer Benefits Survey*. Washington, DC: US Department of Labor.

Carter, G.M., Newhouse, J.P., and Relles, D.A. (1990). How Much Change in the Case Mix Index if DRG Creep. Rand Report R-3826-HCFA.

Carter, G.M., Newhouse, J.P., and Relles, D.A. (1991). Has DRG Creep Crept Up? Rand Report R-4098-HCFA/PROPAC.

Frank, R.G. and Jackson, C.A. (1989). The impact of prospective set hospital budgets on psychiatric admissions. *Social Science and Medicine*, **28**, 861–867.

Frank, R.G. and Lave, J.R. (1985). The psychiatric DRGs: are they different? *Medical Care*, **23**, 1148–1155.

Frank, R.G., Salkever, D.S., and Sharfstein, S.S. (1991). A new look at rising mental health insurance costs. *Health Affairs*, **10**, 116–123.

Frank, R.G., Goldman, H.H., and McGuire, T.G. (1992). A model mental health benefit in private health insurance. *Health Affairs*, **11**, 98–117.

Goldman, H.H., Gatozzi, A., and Taube, C.A. (1981). Defining and counting the chronically mentally ill. *Hospital and Community Psychiatry*.

Hay Huggins, Inc. (1993). *Benefits Report*. Washington, DC: Hay Huggins, Inc.

Hodgkin, D. (1992). Utilization management and psychiatric care: a review of the literature. *Journal of Mental Health Administration*, **19**, 143–157.

Horgan, C. and Jencks, S.F. (1987). Research on psychiatric classification systems. *Medical Care*, **26** (Suppl.) S37–41.

Keeler, E., *et al.* (1986). *The Demand for Episodes of Mental Health Services*. RAND Report R-3432-NIMH Santa Monica, CA: RAND Corporation.

Lamb, H.R., *et al.* (1993). Ensuring services for persons with chronic mental illness under national health care reform. *Hospital and Community Psychiatry*, **44**, 542–545.

McGuire, T.G. (1989). Financing and demand for mental health services. In C. Taube, D. Mechanic and Holman, A. eds, *The Future of Mental Health Services*. Washington: DHHS-(ADM)89-160.

National Advisory Mental Health Council (1993). *Health*

Care Reform for Americans with Severe Mental Illnesses. Washington, DC: NAMHC.

National Institute of Mental Health (1991). *Caring for Persons with Severe Mental Disorders: A National Plan for Research to Improve Services.* Washington: USGPO.

Regier, D.A., *et al.* (1993). The DeFacto US Mental and Addictive Disorders Service Systems: Epidemiological Catchment Area Prospective 1 year prevalence rates of disorders and services. *Archive of General Psychiatry,* **50**, 85–94.

Schmitz, R.J. (1992). The shortrun effects of a contracted provider arrangement for mental health care. In R. Frank and W. Manning, eds, *Economics and Mental Health.* Baltimore, MD: Johns Hopkins University Press.

Sharfstein, S.S., Towery, O.B., and Milowe, I. (1980). Accuracy of diagnostic information submitted to an insurance company. *American Journal of Psychiatry,* **137**, 70–73.

34

Financing and Paying for Care in Schizophrenia

ALAN MAYNARD
Centre for Health Economics, University of York, York, UK

INTRODUCTION

The design of systems of finance and payment in health care in general, and in schizophrenia in particular, depends on the objectives of policy-makers and their societies. In Europe over the centuries the aristocracy developed a sense of "noblesse oblige," recognizing their responsibility for the health of their workers and the need to provide care for them. In more recent times the Bismarckian reforms, and their parallels in Britain, again reflected public concern about the health of the disadvantaged and how this impaired not only industrial productivity but also the health of soldiers needed to fight wars in Africa, Europe, and elsewhere. Thus out of self-interested and altruistic concerns, the ruling elites of European states created extensive bureaucratic apparatuses to provide health care.

The logic and extent of these activities tended to be masked by the complexities of humanitarian intent, fiscal rectitude, and a residual Puritanism, which questioned the need to succour the "undeserving," advocating sometimes explicitly "survival of the fittest." The resulting ambiguities in the setting of policy targets is explored in the first section where it is argued that the purpose of health policy is to allocate access to health care services on the basis of the patients' ability to benefit. In the second section, the inconsistency in policy formulation and debate is elaborated by a description of the stereotypes used by the political "left" and "right" to criticize the *actual* performance of the system they oppose and compare it with the *ideal* performance of the system for which they have ideological sympathy. The implications of this policy debate for financing and paying for the care of patients with schizophrenia is explored in a third section.

DETERMINING ACCESS TO CARE

In the Yom Kippur (Day of Atonement) prayer book the central question about resource allocation in health care was set out clearly: "Who shall live and who shall die, who shall fulfil his days and shall die before his time?"

In ancient and quite recent times the question of "who shall live" and mortality has been central to decisions about whether and how to treat. In recent decades, with increased longevity and the dominance of chronic complex diseases, treatment choices are not only about increasing the duration of survival

Handbook of Mental Health Economics and Health Policy, Volume I, Schizophrenia. Edited by M. Moscarelli, A. Rupp and N. Sartorius.
© 1996 John Wiley & Sons Ltd.

but also about enhancing the quality of survival (or the quality of life) of patients and their "nearest and dearest" (e.g. carers).

European societies have been reluctant to define explicitly the objectives of their health care policies. This can be illustrated by the rhetoric used by British policy-makers at the inception of the National Health Service (NHS) in the 1940s. The Churchill government's policy promised: "the Government... want to ensure that in the future every man and woman and child can rely on getting ... the best medical and other facilities available; that their getting them shall not depend on whether they can pay for them or on any other factor irrelevant to real need." The Labor government subsequently stated that the NHS: "imposes no limits on availability e.g. limitations based on financial means, age, sex, employment or vocation, area of residence of insurance qualification."

What did these policy-makers mean? They listed the factors which would *not* determine access to health care but their discussion of the determinants of *access* (i.e. need) was noticeable by its absence. Was "need" a demand or a supply side concept? Was it to be defined by patients or by their "guardians" in the health care system, the physician?

Confusion about the answers to such questions was worsened by politicians who defined arbitrary limits to care and used the rhetoric of their ideological opponents to rationalize their decisions. Thus Aneurin Bevan, the socialist architect of the UK NHS, argued in relation to the financing of assistants who provide domestic services to support community care (i.e. home helps) as follows:

> I really must resist this amendment. Does the Hon Member suggest that everything shall be free? ... It is a perfectly reasonable proposition that, where domestic help of this sort is needed and the persons concerned are able to provide it for themselves, they should do so, and, where they are able to make a contribution, they should make it ... it seems to me to be wholly unjustified that we should provide a service of this sort without any payment whatever.
>
> Our objection to the means' test was that it was devised for the purpose of withholding money from people. This means' test is for the purpose of giving services to people who are in need of these services ... and where people can make a contribution towards the cost, they should make it (House of Commons Debates, 1946).

Such inconsistency between ideology and policy choice by politicians can be seen in all European countries: policy reflects the feasibility of convincing evolving and dissolving coalitions of patients, providers and financiers to support often ill conceived policies, to mitigate the effects of poorly defined problems! Thus Margaret Thatcher in 1982, confronted by public and provider opposition to the privatization of health care finance and provision in Britain, argued in a clearly socialist fashion: "the principle that adequate health care should be provided for all, regardless of their ability to pay, must be the foundation of any arrangements for financing health care" (Margaret Thatcher, 1982).

Politics, as ever, is "the art of the possible" and this, rather than a "science" base determines the course of health care policy and the way in which services are financed and provided.

Access to health care can be determined in two ways: (i) allocation of care on the basis of willingness and ability to pay; (ii) allocation of care on the basis of need, where need is defined as the patient's ability to benefit from care per unit of expenditure.

In Europe the latter approach, some form of benefit approach derived from the solidarity or collectivist principle, underlies the design of the health care system and the system of financing and providing care for schizophrenics.

INCONSISTENCY IN THE POLICY DEBATE

A number of conflicts and inconsistencies permeate the debate about health care policy: the Puritan or Protestant ethic has influenced the survival of the liberal market paradigm in health care. The social-collectivist paradigm reflects the development of corporate "noblesse oblige" in most west European societies.

The essentials of these paradigms are outlined in Table 1. From this it can be seen that liberals (viewpoint A) seek the decentralization of power into competing local markets, as a defense against the power, and the abuse of power, by the State. For advocates of this ideology, freedom is the desired end of policy and competing markets are seen as a means to this end. The fear of the State inherent in

Table 1. Attitudes typically associated with viewpoints A and B

	Viewpoint A	Viewpoint B
Personal responsibility	Personal responsibility for achievement is very important, and this is weakened if people are offered unearned rewards. Moreover, such unearned rewards weaken the motive force that assures economic well-being, and in so doing they also undermine moral well-being, because of the intimate connection between moral well-being and the personal effort to achieve.	Personal incentives to achieve are desirable, but economic failure is not equated with moral depravity or social worthlessness.
Social concern	Social Darwinism dictates a seemingly cruel indifference to the fate of those who cannot make the grade. A less extreme position is that charity, expressed and effected preferably under private auspices, is the proper vehicle, but it needs to be exercised under carefully prescribed conditions, for example, such that the potential recipient must first mobilize all his own resources and, when helped, must not be in as favorable a position as those who are self-supporting (the principle of "lesser eligibility".	Private charitable action is not rejected but is seen as potentially dangerous morally (because it is often demeaning to the recipient and corrupting to the donor) and usually inequitable. It seems preferable to establish social mechanisms that create and sustain self-sufficiency and that are accessible according to precise rules concerning entitlement that are applied equitably and explicitly sanctioned by society at large.
Freedom	Freedom is to be sought as a supreme good in itself. Compulsion attenuates both personal responsibility and individualistic and voluntary expressions of social concern. Centralized health planning and a large governmental role in health care financing are seen as an unwarranted abridgement of the freedom of clients as well as of health professionals, and private medicine is thereby viewed as a bulwark against totalitarianism	Freedom is seen as the presence of real opportunities of choice; although economic constraints are less openly coercive than political constraints, they are nonetheless real, and often the effective limits on choice. Freedom is not individisible but may be sacrificed in one respect in order to obtain greater freedom in some other. Government is not an external threat to individuals in the society but is the means by which individuals achieve greater scope for action (that is, greater real freedom).
Equality	Equality before the law is the key concept, with clear precedence being given to freedom over equality wherever the two conflict.	As the only moral justification for using personal achievement as the basis for distributing rewards is that everyone has equal opportunities for such achievement, then the main emphasis is on equality of opportunity; where this cannot be assured, the moral worth of achievement is thereby undermined. Equality is seen as an extension to the many of the freedom actually enjoyed by only the few.

Source: Maynard and Williams (1984).

this ideology was a determining factor in the migration of groups such as the Pilgrim Fathers to America 300 years ago. The power of adherents to this ideology in creating subsequently the US constitution, with its emphasis on rights rather than responsibilities and entitlements, and the survival of the individualistic ethic, has influenced the development of US health care policy to the present day and provides a rationale for its inequalities and cost inflation.

Indeed these qualities, rejected in Europe but still

beloved of some European ideologies, maintain freedom for those with the ability and willingness to pay for health care. Those without the cash to buy care deserve, in the extreme version of this ideology, their fate. Indeed their fate is functional as it creates incentives for people to work and invest in the market.

Collectivists (viewpoint B) reject the market and the principle of allocating resources on the basis of willingness and ability to pay. Their primary objective is equality. This objective, often poorly defined and failing to distinguish between equality in access to health care and equality in health, has emerged from a cumulative recognition by ruling elites of their collective self-interest. This process was accentuated by the nineteenth and twentieth centuries by the fear of Marxism and the power by labour by ruling economic groups, and resulted in increased intervention in health care markets by government.

Choices in health care policy reflect the transient or more permanent dominance of one of these ideologies. In Europe the collectivist perspective of solidarity has dominated policy during the last 50 years. However, this policy perspective is continually assaulted by ideologies of the right. Nowhere is this more acute now than in the countries of the former Soviet Empire where states such as the Czech republic have developed liberal market-oriented policies throughout the economy including the health care sector.

The characteristic of the policy debate between adherents of the competing ideologies is that advocates of one viewpoint present their "ideal" and criticize the *actual* workings of the perspective they reject. In terms of supply, demand, adjustment processes and success criteria the actual and ideal of each model are set out in Tables 2 and 3.

The advocates of the market describe their ideal health care system in totally unrealistic terms. The advocates of the opposing paradigm behave in a similar fashion. This ensures repetitive policy debates conducted at the level of principle and often with too little regard to empirical data. This debate is at once wasteful but the essence of the political process in democracies.

FINANCING AND PAYING FOR THE CARE OF SCHIZOPHRENICS

In all health care systems the funding of health care comes from households who, directly and indirectly, own all assets and acquire income in the form of wages, interest, profit, and rent. The households can purchase or contribute to the cost of health care in a variety of ways (Figure 1). Householders can buy health care directly. They can purchase private insurance as well as paying general taxation (e.g. income and sales taxes) or earmarked taxes such as social insurance. Finally, households can contribute to health care costs by paying copayments (or user charges) for the services they consume.

The four sources of finance (or "pipes") generate a stock of resources: health care finance. This stock is used to pay providers in a variety of ways. Physicians and pharmaceutical companies may be paid on an item of service basis: for every medical act or drug used the provider is paid some fixed sum. Alternatively, these providers may be paid on a capitation basis. In this case they acquire a fixed sum of money for the delivery of a service with the sum being determined on a capitation or per capita basis. The final way in which providers may be paid is a salary.

What householders expend through their four "pipes" of funding provides the income of providers: expenditure equals income. In the health care systems of western Europe, governments have chosen to finance the delivery of care largely from taxation, whether general or based on employment (social insurance) contributions.

One significant potential benefit of relying predominately on a single pipe to finance health care is that it is easier to control total expenditure. In health care systems where there are many sources of finance, attempts to control one source leads to pressure on, and expansion of the flows of funds in the other pipes, making control of total expenditure very difficult.

An example of this is the attempt of the German government to control drug expenditure. The German policy was to take the 1993 drug expenditure to 1991 levels and decree that the first 260 million DM of overspend would be financed out of funds available to pay physician fees. The consequent sharp financial incentive to reduce drug expenditure reduced the

Table 2. Idealized health care systems

		Private	NHS
Demand	1	Individuals are the best judges of their own welfare.	When ill, individuals are frequently imperfect judges of their own welfare.
	2	Priorities determined by own willingness and ability to pay.	Priorities determined by social judgements about need.
	3	Erratic and potentially catastrophic nature of demand mediated by private insurance.	Erratic and potentially catastrophic nature of demand made irrelevant by provision of free services.
	4	Matters of equity to be dealt with elsewhere (e.g. in the tax and social security systems).	As the distribution of income and wealth unlikely to be equitable in relation to the need for health care, the NHS must be insulated from its influence.
Supply	1	Profit is the proper and effective way to motivate suppliers to respond to the needs of demanders.	Professional ethics and dedication to public service are the appropriate motivation, focusing on success in curing or caring.
	2	Priorities determined by people's willingness and ability to pay and the costs of meeting their wishes at the margin	Priorities determined by where the greatest improvements in caring or curing can be effected at the margin.
	3	Suppliers have strong incentive to adopt least-cost methods of provision.	Predetermined limit on available resources generates a strong incentive for suppliers to adopt least-cost methods of provision.
Adjustment mechanism	1	Many competing suppliers ensure that offer prices are kept low, and reflect costs.	Central review of activities generates efficiency audit of service provision and management pressures keep the system cost-effective.
	2	Well-informed consumers are able to seek out the most cost-effective form of treatment for themselves.	Well-informed clinicians are able to prescribe the most cost-effective form of treatment for each patient.
	3	If, at the price that clears the market, medical practice is profitable, more people will go into medicine, and hence supply will be demand responsive.	If there is resulting pressure on some facilities or specialties, resources will be directed towards extending them.
	4	If, conversely, medical practice is unremunerative, people will leave it, or stop entering it, until the system returns to equilibrium.	Facilities or specialities on which pressure is slack will be slimmed down to release resources for other uses.
Success criteria	1	Consumers will judge the system by their ability to get someone to do what they demand, when, where and how the want.	Electorate judges the system by the extent to which it improves the health status of the population at large in relation to the resources allocated to it.
	2	Producers will judge the system by how good a living they can make out of it.	Producers judge the system by its ability to enable them to provide the treatments they believe to be cost-effective.

Source: Maynard and Williams (1984).

pharmaceutical bill by 25%. However, physicians, rather than prescribe expensive drugs for the mentally ill, those with Parkinson's disease, and other chronically sick groups, referred them to inpatient and outpatient hospital care. The costs of this were greater (by some 800 million DM) than the savings made on the drug bill! (Schulenberg, 1994).

The lesson to be learnt by policy-makers is

Table 3. Actual health care systems

		Private	NHS
Demand	1	Doctors act as agents, mediating demand on behalf of consumers.	Doctors act as agents, identifying need on behalf of patients.
	2	Priorities determined by the reimbursement rules of insurance funds.	Priorities determined by the doctor's own professional situation, by his assessment of the patient's condition, and the expected trouble-making proclivities of the patient.
	3	Because private insurance coverage is itself a profit seeking activity, some risk-rating is inevitable, hence coverage is incomplete and uneven, distorting personal willingness and ability to pay.	Freedom from direct financial contributions at the point of service, and absence of risk rating, enables patients to seek treatment for trivial or inappropriate conditions.
	4	Attempts to change the distribution of income and wealth independently, are resisted as destroying incentives (one of which is the ability to buy better or more medical care if you are rich).	Attempts to correct inequities in the social and economic system by differential compensatory access to health services leads to recourse to health care in circumstances where it is unlikely to be a cost-effective solution to the problem.
Supply	1	What is most profitable to suppliers may not be what is most in the interests of consumers, and as neither consumers nor suppliers may be very clear about what is in the former's interests, this gives suppliers a range of discretion.	Personal professional dedication and public spirited motivation likely to be corroded and degenerate into cynicism if others, who do not share those feelings, are seen to be doing very well for themselves through blatantly self-seeking behavior.
	2	Priorities determined by the extent to which consumers can be induced to part with their money, and by the costs of satisfying the pattern of "demand."	Priorities determined by what gives the greatest professional satisfaction.
	3	Profit motive generates a strong incentive towards market segmentation and price discrimination, and tie-in agreements with other professionals.	As cost-effectiveness is not accepted as a proper medical responsibility, such pressures merely generate tension between the "professionals" and the "managers."
Adjustment mechanism	1	Professional ethical rules are used to make overt competition difficult.	Because it does not need elaborate cost data for billing purposes, it does not routinely generate much useful information on costs.
	2	Consumers denied information about quality and competence, and, since insured, may collude with doctors (against the insurance carriers) in inflating costs.	Clinicians know little about costs, and have no direct incentive to act on such information as they have, and sometimes even quite perverse incentives (i.e. cutting costs may make life more difficult, or less rewarding for them).
	3	Entry into the profession made difficult and numbers restricted to maintain profitability.	Very little is known about the relative cost-effectiveness of different treatments, and even where it is, doctors are wary of acting on such information until a general professional consensus emerges.

Table 3. (*cont*).

		Private	NHS
	4	If demand for service falls, doctors extend range of activities and push out neighboring disciplines.	The phasing out of facilities which have become redundant is difficult because it often threatens the livelihood of some concentrated specialized group and has identifiable people dependent on it, whereas the beneficiaries are dispersed and can only be identified as "statistics."
Success criteria	1	Consumers will judge the system by their ability to get someone to do what they need done without making them "medically indigent" and/or changing their risk-rating too adversely.	As the easiest aspect of health status to measure is life expectancy, the discussion is dominated by mortality data and mortality risks to the detriment of treatments concerned with non-life-threatening situations.
	2	Producers will judge the system by how good a living they can make out of it.	In the absence of accurate data on cost-effectiveness, producers judge the system by the extent to which it enables them to carry out the treatments which they find the most exciting and satisfying.

Source: Maynard and Williams (1984).

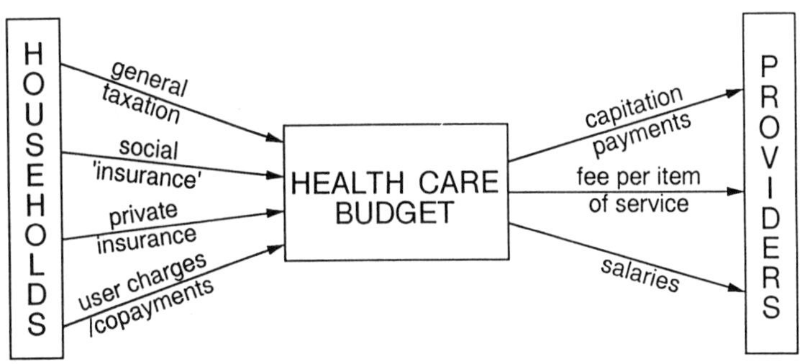

Figure 1 The Expenditure–Income Identity.

obvious but ignored generally: if you squeeze the health care "balloon" in one place (e.g. drugs), expenditure expands elsewhere (in this case hospital care). Another example of this has been provided in a US study of the capping of the Medicaid drug budget with regard to the treatment of schizophrenics.

Soumerai *et al.* (1994) analyzed the effects of a prescription cap on the use of psychotropic drugs and acute mental health care by non-institutionalized patients with schizophrenia. The effects of the cap were to reduce drug utilization of a range of drugs used to control schizophrenia. This was accompanied by increased visits (one to two per month) to Community Mental Health Centres and increases in the use of emergency mental health services and partial hospitalization (1.2–1.4 episodes per patient per month), but no increases in complete hospitalization. The estimated average increase in mental health care costs per patient during the cap ($1530) exceeded the savings in drug costs to Medicaid by a factor of 17, and these financial effects take no account of the reduced quality of life produced by the policy for low income patients with chronic mental illness.

Naive manipulation of service delivery in this way is not uncommon: the basis of health policy reform and clinical practice generally reflects optimism, values, and beliefs and is not knowledge based. Cochrane (1972, p. 82), writing over 25 years ago, noted that: "the allocation of funds and facilities are nearly always based on the opinions of senior consultants." He looked forward to an era when: "requests for additional facilities will be based on detailed argument with 'hard evidence' as to the gain to be expected from the patients' angle and the cost. Few would object to this."

Unfortunately, this optimism about the likely creation of knowledge-based medical practice has been unfulfilled and many clinicians continue to object to being challenged about the bias of their decision-making. Worldwide clinicians continue to object to being challenged about the basis of their decision-making. Worldwide clinicians continue to confuse their clinical experience with knowledge about what is cost-effective in the treatment of patients.

The care of schizophrenics has shifted in recent decades from long-stay institutions to community care provided in residential homes, hostels, the family, and elsewhere outside the hospital: the latter is often "care" or neglect in the street. For instance Bachrach (1992) has estimated that a third to a half of American homeless are schizophrenics. In Europe many homeless people and prisoners have a similar diagnosis.

This is a product of the imperfect organization of care of this vulnerable, and potentially dangerous, group in the community. Integrated and well managed systems of care are not available in many areas. For instance in London care is poorly financed and badly organized with the result that isolated incidents (e.g. one schizophrenic leapt into the lions' enclosure in London Zoo, and was badly mauled, and another stabbed an innocent bystander to death in the London underground) can cause much public concern, which is justifiable.

When care is available it is often provided by different agencies in different geographical locations. Attempts to create new managerial structures are emerging such as, the community care purchaser in England, who is responsible for identifying the patient's needs and purchasing care from public and private providers (Griffiths, 1988). However, with a deficient knowledge base about the cost-effectiveness of community care interventions, and sometimes inadequate financing, the success of these reforms are uneven. The purchaser, as the guardian of the schizophrenic patient, has to be sensitive and efficient to compensate for the patient's lack of drive, insight, and purpose.

Furthermore, purchasers have to act in conjunction with providers whose pecuniary self-interest may inhibit the development of appropriate care structures. Changes in the flow of funds will redistribute expenditure among providers (Figure 1). Thus the shift in care from the hospital to the community affects incomes and jobs for providers who, if not efficiently managed, will resist change in order to maintain their income and employment.

CONCLUSIONS

There is very limited scope to introduce market or privatization principles into the finance of care for patients with schizophrenia. Their needs for care are acute and long-term longitudinal studies (for a review of the area see Carpenter and Buchanan (1994) suggest that many patients recover and only a minority encounter progressive decline in their state and a poor long-term outcome. For many patients, perhaps in part because of poor diagnosis and treatment, schizophrenia has a significant impact on social and economic functioning and patients and their carers have long-lasting and severe impairment in their quality of life.

Such characteristics suggest that public funding, through taxation, is the appropriate method of finance. Patients and their carers will not have the resources to finance long-term chronic care which can stabilize the illness and bring relief. The use of financial controls to influence the provision of care should be exercised with care in order to avoid perverse effects seen in studies in the USA and Germany (Carpenter & Buchanan, 1994; Schulenberg, 1994).

An important input into decision-making about the treatment of schizophrenic (and all other) patients is the production and use of data about the cost-effectiveness of pharmaceutical and other interventions in the hospital and the community (Freemantle and Maynard, 1994). The use of anti-psychotic drugs produces effects for about 80% of patients but most schizophrenics have an incomplete response. The use of clozapine for patients resistant to such treatments is hazardous and expensive, but useful. The market for new drugs, such as risperidone, if they provide enhanced control of positive and negative symptoms may be significant.

At present in European health care systems the organization and provision of care for patients with schizophrenia is uneven with major variations in the funding and provision of support to patients and their carers. The security of appropriate financing of care is a necessary but not sufficient condition for the provision of efficient care: the establishment of treatment protocols on the basis of good scientific knowledge about the costs and effects of alternative treatment packages is also essential (See Drummond and Knapp chapters in this book).

REFERENCES

Bachrach, L.I. (1992). What we know about homelessness among mentally ill persons: an analytical review and commentary. In H.R. Lamb, L.L. Bachrach, and F.I. Kass, eds, *Treating the Homeless Mentally Ill*. Washington, DC: American Psychiatric Press.

Carpenter, W.T. and Buchanan, R.W. (1994). Schizophrenia: medical progress. *New England Journal of Medicine*, **330**, 681–690.

Cochrane, A.L. (1972). *Effectiveness and Efficiency*. London: Nuffield Provincial Hospitals Trust.

Freemantle, N. and Maynard, A. (1994). Something rotten in the state of clinical and economic evaluations? *Health Economics*, **3**, 63–67.

Griffiths, Sir Roy (1988). *Community Care*. London: Agenda for Action, HMSO.

Maynard, A. and Williams, A. (1984). Privatisation and health care. In J. Le Grand and R. Robinson, eds, *Privatisation and the Welfare State*. London: Allen and Unwin.

Schulenberg, M. (1994). The German health care system at the crossroads. *Health Economics*, **3**, 5, 301–304.

Soumerai, S.B., McLaughlan, T.J., Ross-Degnan, D., *et al.* (1994). Effects of limiting Medicaid drug reimbursement benefits on the use of psychotropic agents and acute mental health services by patients with schizophrenia. *New England Journal of Medicine*, **331**, 651–655.

Part IX

THE ECONOMICS OF RESEARCH

35

Research as an Investment

RICHARD WYATT and IOLINE HENTER
NIH-NIMH Neuroscience Center at St. Elizabeths, Neuropsychiatry Branch, Washington, DC, USA

If you think medical research is expensive, try disease.
W.C. Gibson

INTRODUCTION

Five centuries ago, when Christopher Columbus and Queen Isabella, his financial supporter, sought a shorter, more lucrative route to India, they could not have imagined that parallels would be drawn between their success and those of contemporary scientists and their backers. Although the romance associated with science, exploration, and discovery has been the inspiration of many, a substantial return on investment is a more compelling goal for most of society. Nevertheless, as is often the case with targeted research (research aimed at a specific goal), Columbus's discovery produced something far more valuable than was originally sought. Similarly, most major discoveries in biological psychiatry have come at a time when accepting minds, like Columbus's, were able to develop new concepts from unanticipated observations (Jeste *et al.*, 1979).

While the value of targeted research can be found everywhere, the benefits of basic medical research—research not specifically directed at a clinical problem—are equally, if less obviously, important. Development of the Salk polio vaccine, for example, relied on a number of seemingly unrelated findings, including the development of tissue culture. In 1907, Ross Granville Harrison cultured the kidney tissue of monkeys; his pupil, John Enders, then grew the polio virus on that tissue, eventually leading to sufficient viral propagation for the development of the vaccine. During each of the first 6 years following the introduction of the Salk vaccine, 70 times the cost (including field trials) of its development was saved in the United States alone (Gibson, 1980).

Comroe and Dripps, who carefully examined the origins of clinical advances in cardiovascular and pulmonary diseases from the early 1940s through the mid-1970s, came to a similar conclusion regarding basic research (Comroe & Dripps, 1976); over 60% of the research essential for a later clinical advance was not considered clinically oriented at the time it was done.

Change based on adequate research often results in substantial savings. This chapter discusses, from our parochial (American) viewpoint, how effective measures for preventing AIDS (screening of blood donors), treating manic-depressive illness (lithium) and treating schizophrenia (clozapine) have all brought about substantial monetary savings, in addition to decreasing the suffering brought about by these illnesses. On the other hand, change based

Handbook of Mental Health Economics and Health Policy, Volume I, Schizophrenia. Edited by M. Moscarelli, A. Rupp and N. Sartorius.
© 1996 John Wiley & Sons Ltd.

on inadequate data or change purely for the sake of change, as in the case of deinstitutionalization in America, can be extremely expensive. Finally, this chapter will introduce a method of measuring costs based on actual and potential productivity rather than on dollar amounts.

INFECTIOUS DISEASES AND THE FIRST SUCCESSFUL TREATMENTS FOR A NEUROPSYCHIATRIC ILLNESS—SYPHILIS

The cause of dementia paralytica, or general paralysis of the insane, which once accounted for 10–20% of admissions to state hospitals, confounded physicians for centuries until its relationship to syphilis and the syphilitic spirochete was clarified at the beginning of the twentieth century. About the same time, Paul Ehrlich systematically synthesized and screened 606 arsenic-containing organic compounds in his search for the "magic bullet." His 1910 discovery of arsphenamine (Salvarasan) as a treatment for syphilis was the beginning of informed mass drug screening, which has become a standard procedure of many modern pharmaceutical houses (Wyatt, 1988). Salvarasan, however, was difficult to administer, toxic, and rarely successful by itself. More importantly, it often killed patients who had central nervous system syphilis. Other treatments were sought.

After years of trial and error, in 1917, Julius Wagner van Jauregg, who was familiar with the several thousand year old observation that some psychiatric patients recover after having a fever, developed a treatment for dementia paralytica which became the first successful treatment for a major psychiatric illness. Injections of blood from patients with a benign form of malaria produced a cure in approximately 30% of patients with dementia paralytica. In addition, his fever therapy significantly helped another 30% of those affected. Careful screening of patients prevented serious side-effects, but the treatment still required long hospitalizations and uncomfortably high temperatures (Dennie, 1962).

In the 1940s, however, penicillin therapy was so effective that the previously used arsenic compounds and fever induction were quickly supplanted (Freedman & Kaplan, 1967). In the first 2 years that it was widely available (1945–47), the price of penicillin dropped from $20 to 30¢ per 100000 units and, within 10 years, new admissions to psychiatric hospitals for syphilis were halved (Brandt, 1987). Penicillin has been credited with decreasing the number of psychiatric inpatients worldwide by 10% (Gibson, 1980). While few studies measured these monetary benefits in a comprehensive manner, a number of cost studies do exist for another transfusion-transmitted disease which affects the central nervous system: AIDS.

INFECTIOUS DISEASES AND PREVENTION OF NEUROPSYCHIATRIC ILLNESS—AIDS

The neuropsychiatric symptoms which sometimes accompany AIDS are some of the most disabling aspects of this illness. For 1991, projected estimates of the direct costs to the United States of AIDS ranged from $5 to $10 billion (Scitovsky & Rice, 1987; Hellinger, 1990), and indirect cost estimates were over $50 billion (Scitovsky & Rice, 1987). Prevention of HIV infection is the only known method of significantly altering the morbidity of AIDS, and screening of blood donors, implemented by the United States in April of 1985, was the first preventive measure to have a major effect.

Were blood and blood products not screened on a regular basis, the cost of AIDS would be even more staggering than it is. Approximately one-third of all surgery done in the United States requires blood, and an additional one-third of all surgery requires that blood be available (Capra, personal communication, 1993). All alternate approaches to blood transfusion have serious drawbacks (Capra, personal communication, 1993; McCullough, 1993). For instance, while it is widely believed that direct blood donation—blood donated through an individual's friends rather than obtained from blood banks—is safer, most studies have found just the opposite (McCullough, 1993). In addition, neither direct donation nor autologous donation (donating one's own blood for future use) cover the majority of cases where blood is needed: accidents, emergency surgeries, etc. It is likely that without an HIV test, much surgery and most transfusions would have stopped

(Klein, 1990). Also, the use of blood products to treat individuals with hemophilia would be impossible. Transfusions of contaminated blood presently account for approximately 8% of AIDS cases, virtually all of which were contracted before blood screening measures could be implemented (Scitovsky *et al.*, 1986).

The development of a specific assay for detection of HIV antibodies in sera of infected individuals was accomplished at the National Institutes of Health by Dr. Robert Gallo at an investment of $7 million 1988 dollars. Commercialization and standardization, as well as later refinements for large scale screening, raised these costs (National Institutes of Health, 1990). The economic advantages of the test, however, have been sizable. France is said to have delayed introduction of the "American test" in order to market a "French test," and that delay tragically led to a large number of French hemophiliacs developing AIDS with costly financial and human consequences.

Nevertheless, since screening precautions for blood donors were implemented a combination of routine laboratory screening, donor counseling and self-exclusion has been 99.83–99.95% effective in eliminating the risk of HIV infection from blood transfusions (Cumming *et al.*, 1989). In 1986, the total cost of such screening in the United States, including testing, discarding processed blood, marginal donor recruiting, and notifying and evaluating positive donors, totaled approximately $36 million (Eisenstaedt & Getzen, 1988). The same study found that, in 1986, donor screening saved roughly $43 million in direct and indirect costs by preventing approximately 300 new cases of HIV infection. This number is probably low, as the study was conducted when most of the infected individuals were not yet ill and therefore not contributing to the enormous treatment costs. Results from a 1990 study conducted by the National Institutes of Health found that the annual cost of screening the US blood supply for HIV was still about $34 million, while the savings due to reduction of transfusion-associated HIV infection and AIDS, in a 1 year cohort, had increased to approximately $64 million (National Institutes of Health, 1990). Current HIV blood testing procedures generate net economic, not to mention human, benefits.

LITHIUM

Lithium was used f or a variety of medical disorders during the second half of the nineteenth century; indeed, bromide of lithium was still being used as a hypnotic in the early part of the twentieth century. Not until 1949, however, did John Cade suggest that lithium might be useful for treating manic-depressive illness and not until 1954 did Mogens Schou elegantly prove lithium's efficacy (Cade, 1949; Schou, 1954). Prior to lithium's introduction, individuals with manic-depressive illness often required months or years of hospitalization, experienced both a severe disruption in their social lives and a loss of productivity, and frequently killed themselves. While many individuals with manic-depressive disorder remain untreated, those who are treated usually respond well and live remarkably improved lives.

The element lithium is a readily available natural salt, and is consequently inexpensive. Although a handful of American psychiatrists appreciated its value early, it was not until 1964 or 1965 "that anything like general awareness that lithium might be important dawned on the psychiatric profession" (Kline, 1973). Despite controlled trials performed in Europe (Baastrup & Schou, 1967), a number of factors slowed lithium's acceptance by American psychiatrists (Gershon & Shopsin, 1973). First, many psychiatrists, especially in 1949, were not oriented to pharmacological intervention for manic-depressive illness, which was thought to be a purely psychological disorder. Second, lithium's reputation was tainted by the fact that, as late as the 1940s, it was being indiscriminately used as a table salt substitute and had caused several deaths. Third, manic-depressive illness was thought to be an uncommon disorder, and few psychiatrists had much experience treating it. Fourth, because lithium's introduction into psychiatry took place in Australia, physicians in the United States did not learn about it for many years. Finally, because lithium is a cheap, non-patentable medication, and therefore commercially unprofitable, pharmaceutical companies did not heavily investigate or promote its use.

Although affective disorders are expensive (Hertzmann,, 1983; Stoudemire *et al.*, 1986; Greenberg *et al.*, 1993b; Wyatt and Henter, 1995a), few studies have attempted to estimate just what effect treatment can have on costs (Greenberg *et al.*, 1993a, b). In a previous study, we estimated the savings attributable to lithium between 1970 and 1980 (Reifman & Wyatt, 1980; Wyatt, 1984, 1985). Since that report was published, however, more detailed information has become available, primarily from the Epidemiological Catchment Area (ECA) study (Robins & Regier, 1991), which allows for an improved estimate.

We have recently conducted a study (Wyatt *et al.*, submitted) which estimates, in 1991 dollars, the savings to the United States from lithium use between 1970 (the year lithium was approved by the FDA) and 1991. Savings were divided into direct and indirect components. Direct cost savings totaled close to $15 billion, and consisted of a *mélange* of inpatient and outpatient care categories. Indirect cost savings were close to $120 billion (or roughly $155 billion), and included the lost productivity of both wage-earners and homemakers, individuals who were in institutions or who committed suicide, and caregivers who took care of their manic-depressive family members.

Since its introduction in 1970, lithium has saved the United States approximately $8 billion per year, or a total of roughly $170 billion. Some categories showed only modest savings; in other categories, such as inpatient care, or indirect costs, the savings are impressive. In those few instances where costs shifted (for example from state hospitals to nursing homes), the care became more expensive (see Table 1).

Table 1. Total savings from lithium, 1970–91 (in 1991 dollars)

Category	Total savings ($) 1970–91 (in millions)
Direct costs	15 400
Inpatient costs (State and County Hospitals, Private Hospitals, Veterans Administration Hospitals, Veterans Administration Domicillary and Partial Care, Non-Federal General Hospitals, Multiservice Hospitals and Freestanding Partial Care Centers, Indian Health Service, Department of Defense)	24 000
Outpatient costs (Veterans Administration, CHAMPUS, Federally Funded Community Mental Health Centers, Freestanding Outpatient Clinics, Indian Health Service, Department of Defense)	3 400
Nursing homes, shelters and case management	(11 900)
Medications	(750)
Research and training	(300)
Suicide (direct)	1 000
Indirect costs	155 000
Lost compensation	25 700
Lost productivity from caregivers	36 8000
Lost productivity from homemakers	7 300
Lost productivity from those in institutions	15 000
Lost wages from suicide	70 300
Total	170 700

Approximately $1 billion has been spent worldwide on research into manic-depressive illness (Wyatt, unpublished data). The return on this investment has been enormous and continues to grow yearly. Although these numbers are only estimates, they demonstrate how the cost of chronic diseases such as manic-depressive illness can be reduced, and large savings in human and economic terms realized, when effective treatments are found.

CLOZAPINE

Synthesized in 1958, clozapine (Clozaril) was soon found to be effective in chronic schizophrenia. While not marketed in the United States, it was licensed in over 30 countries in the 1960s. In 1975, following the tragic bone marrow failure and death of eight Finnish patients, clozapine was withdrawn from most markets (Terkelsen & Grosser, 1990; Hirsch & Puri, 1993).

Clozapine's reintroduction in 1988, particularly in the United States, followed a large trial by Kane and associates, which showed that clozapine was more effective than standard antipsychotic medications in treatment-resistant patients with chronic schizophrenia (Kane *et al.*, 1988). This suggested that potentially hundreds of thousands of patients could benefit from clozapine. Because of the associated risk of agranulocytosis, however, intensive hematologic monitoring was required, making clozapine very costly. Nevertheless, its cost-effectiveness has now been demonstrated. For patients with a history of repeated hospitalizations, clozapine use is accompanied by a sizable reduction in hospital bed days, the costliest aspect of treating schizophrenia (Revicki *et al.*, 1990; Davies & Drummond, 1993; Grinfield, 1993; Meltzer *et al.*, 1993). One recent study found that the mean number of annual days in the hospital for patients with schizophrenia decreased from 128 days on standard antipsychotic medication to 7.4 days on clozapine. This reduction in bed days was accompanied by a 22.6% reduction in costs, even when the cost of patients who began a trial of clozapine but had adverse reactions (and thus discontinued treatment) were included (Meltzer *et al.*, 1993). Decreases in inpatient costs were accompanied by increases in outpatient costs; such reallocation of costs still yields substantial savings as inpatient and outpatient costs are of a different magnitude.

Between 1990 and 1994, approximately 75 000 individuals in the United States began a trial of clozapine (Hirsch, personal communication, 1994). The 1993 Meltzer *et al.* study followed a group of chronic schizophrenic patients taking clozapine and found that, over a 2 year period, the total savings for each of these patients, including the ones who interrupted or discontinued their treatment, was $8700, or roughly $10 000 per year, per patient, in 1991 dollars (Meltzer *et al.*, 1993). Based on these data, our own calculations suggest that, between 1990 and 1994, clozapine has saved approximately $1.6 billion. Already impressive, this number is likely conservative as it does not take into account those patients who have begun a trial of clozapine since January 1994, nor does it include indirect costs.

Ultimately, the decision to pursue clozapine as a viable treatment for schizophrenia came about because an enthusiastic and visionary group of investigators both demonstrated clozapine's clinical value and, despite its toxicity, found a way of making it available and relatively safe.

CHANGE FOR THE SAKE OF CHANGE—DEINSTITUTIONALIZATION AND THE HOMELESS

Although the benefits of research are highly visible, such benefits often require focused and lengthy efforts. The impatience of politicians, or scientists, with science, as well as insufficient commitment to the future, can divert these efforts, leading to human and financial waste. Certain societal concerns, which seem to demand quick decisions are often "solved" because the time seems right and/or because strong scientific claims are based on weak data. The decision to rapidly empty large state psychiatric hospitals during the last few decades is such a case.

In the United States, deinstitutionalization had been considered for a number of years both inside and outside of Congress and, in 1963, it became public policy with the enactment of the Mental Retardation Facilities and Community Mental Health Centers Act. A number of factors contributed to the push for deinstitutionalization, including the successful introduction of antipsychotic medications. Also, in response to the National Mental Health Act of 1946, more mental health professionals were being trained with a community-based perspective. Finally, the institutions which housed the mentally ill were typically lonely, horrible places. Change was needed and its advocates were eloquent, but the scientific base for direct action was lacking. Only one controlled, small study describing how to provide care to discharged inpatients (Wing, 1960) had been conducted, and that study had taken place in England. Ultimately, the emptying of large state hospitals was a response to a convergence of events and circumstances that had set the momentum for change, rather than a decision based on systematic studies in the American environment in which it was going to take place.

Although the original and admirable objectives of deinstitutionalization were to hasten patient rehabilitation and reintegration into community life, to provide greater continuity of patient care, and to make this care more economical, these goals remain largely unrealized three decades later. Even during and after deinstitutionalization, large-scale controlled trials demonstrating how to care for the deinstititionalized were rarely performed. This absence of knowledge, married with guesses about the long-term outcomes of deinstitutionalized patients, has cost patients, families, and our society dearly.

One study of geriatric patients discharged from a psychiatric hospital that was being abruptly closed broke patients down into three groups matched for age, gender, race, and diagnosis. The first group remained in the original hospital and experienced little change. The second group was transferred to another state hospital and experienced a fourfold increase in their death rate. The third group, which was transferred to a nursing home, had a death rate 900% higher than the first group (Killian, 1970). While these findings are undoubtedly extreme, they demonstrate that good intentions can be devastating when not based on knowledge.

Nor has deinstitutionalization produced the expected financial savings. Originally, it was claimed that costs of community care would be lower than costs for large state-run facilities. At the time this claim was first made, however, there were almost no data to support it (Wyatt, 1985). Currently, a number of studies have been conducted showing that comprehensive community care can be accomplished; a review of these findings suggests, however, that the savings from these programs are minimal (Herz, in press).

At the time institutions were emptied, controlled clinical trials of new pharmacological agents became accepted practice. Now as well as then, new medications could not be introduced without first performing large-scale controlled trials in diverse patient populations, and even after these trials, post-marketing surprises were, and are, common. Although it may be impractical to compare relatively simple drug trials with the study of complex community treatment systems, the point remains that well-designed and replicated controlled experiments are necessary to prevent future difficulties. Unfortunately, the problems associated with deinstitutionalization, at least in the United States, have continued for the last 30 years because as a society, we have either been incapable or unwilling to treat our social problems with the same scientific rigor required of medical science.

While homelessness is a multidimensional socioeconomic and medical problem, not merely a consequence of a misguided psychiatric movement, deinstitutionalization is responsible for the presence of a great majority of the homeless mentally ill on America's streets. Depending on the criteria used, estimates indicate that between half a million and three million people in the United States are homeless (Caton, 1990). Rates of mental illness in this population vary widely, from 15 to 90% depending on the study (Caton, 1990). Homelessness, especially that of the mentally ill, has become a social tragedy, and is an example of how poor communication and inadequate research in psychiatry have been very costly (Wyatt & DeRenzo, 1986).

PRODUCTIVE PERSON-YEARS

Many of the costs described in this chapter amount to billions of dollars—numbers which, though concrete, are too massive to be readily understandable. A clearer method of estimating these costs and savings is needed. The use of lost actual and potential productivity to measure these numbers provides an easily understandable index for both medical disorders and other social issues. Below, a simple aid, which relies on the concept of productivity, is described.

THE CONCEPT OF PRODUCTIVE PERSON-YEARS

While direct national health care costs are so vast that they often lose their meaning, indirect costs are even more difficult to understand. Indirect costs are "what if costs," meaning that if the ill individuals were well, indirect costs would equal the amount that they would be expected to contribute to the gross domestic product (GDP). Indirect cost estimates, however, are not always accurate because they assume that some individuals contribute to the GDP when they do not. Furthermore, some components of "what if" indirect costs, such as the productivity lost from homemakers, are not included directly in the GDP, despite the fact that these individuals are being productive. Finally, the "human capital" method, which is based on the assumption that earnings reflect productivity and has become the traditional way of measuring indirect costs, is inequitable (Fein, 1958; Rice, 1966; Rice *et al.*, 1990). It places a higher value on the lives of the rich than the poor, a higher value on white Caucasians than on black people, and a higher value on males than on females.

The concept of productive person-years (PPY) was developed to describe the costs of medical disorders in a manner that estimates the lost quality of life, values all individuals equally and also includes direct expenditures. Incorporating direct costs and quality of life into the same measure allows for a clearer understanding of a burden of the illness, and for more equitable comparisons across medical disorders. In most cases, the *ability* to produce is an estimate of functionality, which, with some exceptions, should be roughly associated with quality of life. A PPY is therefore defined as actual plus potential productivity and can be expressed as a loss or gain. Actual productivity would, for example, include employed individuals, homemakers who are not paid a wage but are productive, as well as individuals who volunteer their time. In contrast, healthy, unemployed individuals would have the same ability or *potential* to function as employed full-time workers. Such productivity would be measured by potential rather than by actual PPY. All adult individuals have the potential to be productive, although there may be obstacles such as illness preventing them from being fully functional.

In order to convert direct costs into PPY, dollar costs are divided by the average total compensation for a full-time worker. In the United States, total compensation was roughly equal to \$33 000 in 1991. As mentioned above, all individuals, including the unemployed, volunteers, or homemakers, are considered to be potentially productive, and thus all are assigned the \$33 000 value. Direct costs of an illness can then be calculated as follows: assuming that in 1991 the average direct cost per patient for a hypothetical illness was \$100 000, the cost per patient would be approximately three PPY (\$100 000/\$33 000). If there were 500 000 people in the country with that illness, the total direct cost would be \$50 billion or 1.5 million PPY.

Measuring indirect costs using the PPY method largely depends on calculating lost productivity. A number of factors can contribute to the loss of a PPY, including decreases in productivity stemming directly from an illness. This lost productivity can extend to the families of the ill, to others who provide uncompensated help to the family, and to those whose productivity is slowed because they are partially dependent on an ill person. The method used to calculate lost productivity is a mixed economic and quality of life approach. If an individual dies prematurely at the beginning of a year, or is hospitalized for a year because of a specific illness, he or she is assigned a value of one, meaning that one PPY is lost.

The traditional way of estimating future lost productivity due to premature death is to discount years. Discounting estimates the economic value of a life by projecting an individual's future earnings and translating those earnings into current dollars. The PPY system uses a stream of life method and keeps the lost productivity in the year where the loss will actually be felt. For an illness such as schizophrenia, where the number of premature deaths is relatively constant, a steady state can be assumed and the calculations become fairly straightforward.

When individuals occupy an institutional bed for a year, they have also largely lost their economic value. Contrasting lost productivity in PPY to other forms of life-year measurements shows that PPY differ from quality-adjusted life years (QALY) (Carr-Hill, 1989) or disability-adjusted life years (DALY) (Jamison *et al.*, 1993). Both those systems might assume that the quality of life of a hospitalized individual could be relatively high, while in the PPY system, institutionalization is considered both non-productive and non-functional. Using PPY in this manner avoids the more complex issue of how to place a value on such concepts as pain, suffering, feelings of uselessness, or increased social dependence. To an extent, it also avoids the issue of who makes the judgment. An ill person may well see quality of life differently than an observer when more abstract concepts such as pain and suffering are used instead of productivity. The major advantage of PPY over the other systems, however, is that it allows direct and indirect costs to be placed into one number.

Lost productivity for individuals who are not institutionalized for a full year but are nevertheless unproductive for a portion of it are calculated in roughly the same manner. For instance, an individual who was severely ill, but not hospitalized, might lose anywhere from 0.8 to 0.6 PPY depending on the nature of the illness. Moderately ill individuals might lose 0.4 PPY, while family members caring for an ill relative could lose 0.3 PPY. On the other hand, individuals who were well during the year would lose zero PPY. Quality of life between zero and one is subjective, but actual and potential productivity can be measured objectively.

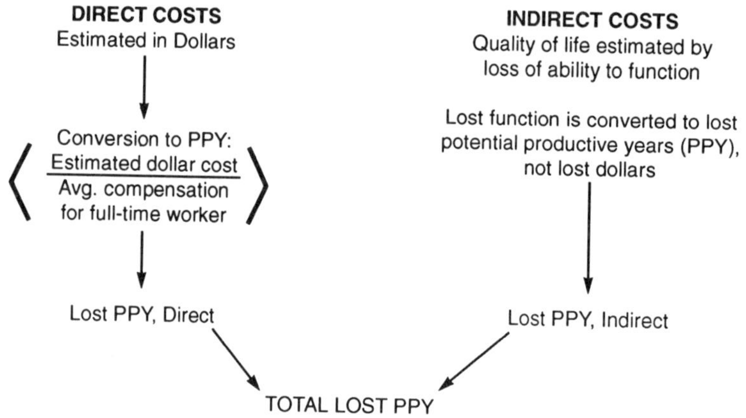

Figure 1. Calculating lost PPY.

THE PPY INDEX

To facilitate comparisons between populations and across time, a relative scale was developed, the PPY Index (Figure 2). The PPY Index measures the lost percent of a population's potential PPY, and can be used as a tool for measuring costs and benefits, or the gained percent of PPY produced by an intervention.

$$\left\langle \frac{\text{Total Lost PPY from illness or intervention}}{\text{Total Productive Person Years in Population, Ages 18-65}} \times 100\% \right\rangle$$

Figure 2. Calculating the PPY Index.

In the United States in 1991, there were approximately 158 million individuals between the ages of 18 and 65, or about 158 million potential PPY[18–65]. While selecting individuals between ages 18 and 65 is somewhat arbitrary, the ages approximate the normal span of paid work in the United States. Broader indexes, such as between age 18 and normal life expectancy (PPY[18–]), could also be chosen—ideally, all individuals have the potential to be productive until the time of their death, and in other cultures the average individual might begin work prior to age 18.

CALCULATING PPY AND THE PPY INDEX FOR SCHIZOPHRENIA AND OTHER DISORDERS

In 1991, the combined direct and indirect costs of schizophrenia were $66 billion (Wyatt *et al.*, 1995). The same year, 3.4 million PPY were lost due to schizophrenia. Use of the PPY Index reveals a loss of 2.2% of the entire US PPY in 1991 from schizophrenia.

On the other hand, the savings brought about by use of clozapine can also be calculated using the PPY method. Table 2 shows that, since 1990, clozapine has saved almost 50 000 PPY in direct costs. This roughly translates into a saving of 0.03% of the total potential productivity of the United States for 1 year.

The PPY system was also used to find the savings from lithium for the treatment of manic-depressive illness. Table 3 shows that, between 1970 and 1991 in the United States, lithium saved almost a million productive person-years in direct and indirect costs. As measured by the PPY Index, lithium saved approximately 0.5% of the potential productivity of the entire United States.

The PPY system has a wide variety of applications. It could be used, for instance, in analyzing the cost-effectiveness of specific medical as well as non-medical interventions. Although medical issues may spring to mind because of their cost and visibility, this index can also be used for resolving complex environmental issues as well as social ones such as crime and education. The concept of PPY

Table 2. Savings (in PPY) from use of clozapine. United States, 1990–94

Number of PPY saved	
Direct	49 388
Amount saved on PPY index	0.03%

Table 3. Savings (in PPY) from use of lithium. United States, 1970–91

	Projected PPY of manic-depressive illness without lithium	Actual PPY of manic depressive illness with lithium	PPY saved
Direct PPY	4 469	3 878	591
Indirect PPY	1 614 648	789 477	825 171
PPY index			
Direct	0.0028%	0.0024%	0.0004%
Indirect	1.02%	0.50%	0.52%
Total	1.02%	0.50%	0.52%

and the PPY Index has considerable utility; it provides a simple and intelligent way of understanding the huge costs of some of society's biggest problems.

CONCLUSIONS

Comparing the costs and benefits of various treatments has been proposed as a method for allocating scarce therapeutic resources and is being used in some places (Jamison *et al.*, 1993). Rarely, however, have similar procedures been implemented in large-scale medical research plans. When pharmaceutical houses consider investing in new research projects, they certainly consider their potential return, but their consideration of profits generally focuses on financial gain rather than on a total return for society. Still, their view of investment into research is a sound one, and, if implemented on a much broader scale, could be used as a model for allocating resources targeted at specific research interventions for society as a whole.

The theme of this chapter has been simple: investing in our own health through medical research is not only part of the common good, it is a good investment. In medicine, nothing is more precious than knowledge, and nothing helps to build that knowledge as well as research.

REFERENCES

Baastrup, P.C. and Schou, M. (1967). Lithium as a prophylactic agent: its effect against recurrent depressions and manic-depressive psychosis. *Archives of General Psychiatry*, **16**, 162–172.

Brandt, A.M. (1987). *No Magic Bullet*. New York: Oxford University Press.

Cade, J. (1949). Lithium salts in the treatment of psychotic excitement. *Medical Journal of Australia*, **36**, 349–352.

Carr-Hill, R.A. (1989). Assumptions of the QALY procedure. *Social Science Medicine*, **29**, 469–477.

Caton, C.L.M. (1990). *Homeless in America*. New York: Oxford University Press.

Comroe, J.H. and Dripps, R.D. (1976). Scientific basis for the support of biomedical science. *Science*, **192**, 105–111.

Cummings, P.D., Wallace, E.L., Schorr, J.B., and Dodd, R.Y. (1989). Exposure of patients to human immunodeficiency virus through the transfusion of blood components that test antibody-negative. *New England Journal of Medicine*, **321**, 941–946.

Davies, L.M. and Drummond, M.F. (1993). Assessment of costs and benefits of drug therapy for treatment-resistant schizophrenia in the United Kingdom. *British Journal of Psychiatry*, **162**, 38–42.

Dennie, C.C. (1962). *A History of Syphilis*. Springfield: Charles C. Thomas.

Eisenstaedt, R.S. and Getzen, T.E. (1988). Screening blood donors for human immunodeficiency virus antibody: cost–benefit analysis. *American Journal of Public Health*, **78**, 450–454.

Fein, R. (1958). *Economics of Mental Illness*. New York: Basic Books.

Freedman, A.M. and Kaplan, H.I. (eds) (1967). *The Comprehensive Textbook of Psychiatry*. Baltimore, MD: Williams and Wilkins.

Gershon, S. and Shopsin, B. (eds) (1973). *Lithium: Its Role in Psychiatric Research and Treatment*. New York: Plenum Press.

Gibson, W.C. (1980). The cost of not doing medical research. *Journal of the American Medical Association*, **244**, 1817–1819.

Greenberg, P.E., Stiglin, L.E., Finkelstein, S.N., and Berndt, E.R. (1993a). Depression: a neglected major illness. *Journal of Clinical Psychiatry*, **54**, 419–424.

Greenberg, P.E., Stiglin, L.E., Finkelstein, S.N., and Berndt, E.R. (1993b). The economic burden of depression. *Journal of Clinical Psychiatry*, **54**, 405–418.

Grinfeld, M.J. (1993). Bed-days decline with clozapine usage. *Psychiatric Times*.

Hellinger, F. (1990). Updated forecasts of the costs of medical care for persons with AIDS, 1989–93. *Public Health Report*, **105**, 1–12.

Hertzman, P. (1983). The economic costs of mental illness in Sweden 1975. *Acta Psychiatrica Scandinavica*, **68**, 359–367.

Herz, M.I. (ed.) (in press). *Practice Guidelines for the Treatment of Schizophrenia*. Washington DC: American Psychiatric Association.

Hirsch, S.R. and Puri, B.K. (1993). Clozapine: progress in treating refractory schizophrenia. *British Medical Journal*, **306**, 1427–1428.

Jamison, D.T., Mosley, W.H., Measham, A.R., and Bobadilla, J.L. (eds) (1993). *Disease Control Priorities in Developing Countries*. New York: Oxford University Press.

Jeste, D.V., Gillin, J.C., and Wyatt, R.J. (1979). Serendipity in biological psychology—A myth? *Archives of General Psychiatry*, **36**, 1173–1178.

Kane, J., Honigfeld, G., Singer, J., and Meltzer, H.Y. (1988). Clozapine for the treatment-resistant schizophrenic: a double-blind comparison with chlorpromazine. *Archives of General Psychiatry*, **45**, 789–796.

Killian, E.C. (1970). Effect of geriatric transfers on mortability rates. *Social Work*, **15**, 19–26.

Klein, R.S. (1990). Transmission of human immunodeficiency virus type 1 (HIV-1) by exposure to blood: defining the risk. *Annals of Internal Medicine*, **113**, 729–730.

Kline, N.S. (1973). A narrative account of lithium usage in psychiatry. In S. Gershon and B. Shopsin, eds, *Lithium: Its Role in Psychiatric Research and Treatment*, pp. 5–13. New York: Plenum Press.

McCullough, J. (1993). The nation's changing blood supply system. *Journal of the American Medical Association*, **269**, 2239–2245.

Meltzer, H.Y., Cola, P., Way, L., *et al.* (1993). Cost effectiveness of clozapine in neuroleptic-resistant schizophrenia. *American Journal of Psychiatry*, **150**, 1630–1638.

National Institutes of Health (1990). *Health Care Cost Savings Resulting from HIV Antibody Testing of the Nation's Blood Supply*. Rockville, MD: National Institutes of Health.

Reifman, A. and Wyatt, R.J. (1980). Lithium: A brake in the rising cost of mental illness. *Archives of General Psychiatry*, **37**, 385–388.

Revicki, D.A., Luce, B.R., Weschler, J.M., Brown, R.E., and Adler, M.A. (1990). Cost-effectiveness of clozapine for treatment-resistant schizophrenic patients. *Hospital and Community Psychiatry*, **41**, 850–854.

Rice, D.P. (1966). *Public Health Service Publication 947-6*. Health Economic Series No. 5. Washington, DC: US Department of Health, Education and Welfare.

Rice, D.P., Kelman, S., Miller, L.S., and Dunmeyer, S. (1990). *Report submitted to the Office of Financing and Coverage Policy of the Alcohol, Drug Abuse, and Mental Health Administration*. US Department of Health and Human Services, San Francisco, CA: Institute for Health and Aging, University of California.

Robins, L.N. and Regier, D.A. (1991). *Psychiatric Disorders in America: The Epidemiologic Catchment Area Study*. New York: The Free Press.

Schou, M. and Al, E. (1954). The treatment of manic psychoses by the administration of lithium salts. *Journal of Neurological and Neurosurgical Psychiatry*, **17**, 250–260.

Scitovsky, A.A. and Rice, D.P. (1987). Estimates of the direct and indirect costs of acquired immunodeficiency syndrome in the United States, 1985, 1986, and 1991. *Public Health Report*, **102**, 5–17.

Scitovsky, A.A., Cline, M., and Lee, P.R. (1986). Medical care cost of patients with AIDS in San Francisco. *Journal of the American Medical Association*, **255**, 3101–3106.

Stoudemire, A., Frank, R., and Hedemark, N. (1986). The economic burden of depression. *General Hospital Psychiatry*, **8**, 389–394.

Terkelsen, K.G. and Grosser, R.C. (1990). Estimating clozapine's cost to the nation. *Hospital and Community Psychiatry*, **41**, 863–869.

Wing, J.K. (1960). Pilot experiment in the rehabilitation of long-hospitalized male schizophrenic patients. *British Journal of Preventive and Social Medicine*, **14**, 173–180.

Wyatt, R.J. (1984). Cost-benefits of lithium as a treatment. In Z. Taintor and S.A. Barrett, eds, *Cost Considerations, Modalities and Providers*, pp. 50–51. Rockville, MD: National Institute of Mental Health.

Wyatt, R.J. (1985). Science and psychiatry. In H.I. Kaplan and B.J. Sadock, eds, *Comprehensive Textbook of Psychiatry IV*, pp. 2016–2027. Baltimore, MD: Williams and Wilkins.

Wyatt, R.J. (1988). Earl Usdin as a communicator of science. In J.D. Barchas and W.E.J. Bunney, eds, *Perspectives in Psychopharmacology: A Collection of Papers in Honor of Earl Usdin*, pp. 31–37. New York: Alan R. Liss, Inc.

Wyatt, R.J. and DeRenzo, E.G. (1986). Scienceless to homeless (Editorial). *Science*, **234**, 1309.

Wyatt, R.J. and Henter, I. (1995a). An economic evaluation of manic-depressive illness—1991. *Social Psychiatry and Psychiatric Epidemiology*, **30**, 213–219.

Wyatt, R.J., Henter, I., Leary, M.C., and Taylor, E. (1995b). An economic evaluation of schizophrenia—1991. *Social Psychiatry and Psychiatric Epidemiology*, **30**, 196–205.

Wyatt, R.J., Henter, I., and Jamison, J.C. (submitted). Lithium revisited: savings brought about by the use of lithium between 1970 and 1991.

Part X

APPLICATIONS IN DIFFERENT COUNTRIES

36

Some Get More Than They Pay For: Mental Health Services in Australia

GAVIN ANDREWS and MAREE TEESSON
Clinical Research Unit for Anxiety Disorders and Inner City Mental Health Service, School of Psychiatry, University of New South Wales, Sydney, Australia

Schizophrenia is, or at least used to be, a costly disorder. Ten years ago we (Andrews *et al.*, 1985; Hall *et al.*, 1985) used case register data to calculate, following the incidence-based costing method of Hartounian *et al.* (1981), the stream of direct treatment costs likely to be incurred during their lifetimes by the new cases of schizophrenia identified in 1975 in New South Wales, the largest state in Australia. Schizophrenia, although only one-twelfth as common as myocardial infarction, was estimated to cost nearly as much ($24.6M versus $33.3M, in 1975 US dollars). The direct treatment costs per case for these two disorders were very different, schizophrenia being nine times more expensive than heart disease. In 1975, even though bed numbers had been falling for a decade or more, there were still 150 public sector psychiatric beds per 100 000 population, and because hospital was such a major part of treatment, the direct treatment costs were virtually equivalent to the hospital costs, with the young onset and poor outcome cases generating the greatest stream of costs.

The following 20 years have seen the bed ratio continue to fall so that Australia in 1993 only had 46 psychiatric beds per 100 000 population, and spent an average of $45 per capita on all public inpatient services, $12 on public sector community mental health services, and a further $22 per capita on Federal Government supported private psychiatrists and general practitioners dealing with patients with mental disorders (First National Mental Health Report, 1993). Australia has 17 million inhabitants who live in six states linked by a Federal Government: 12% of the population live on farms; 63% live in cities with more than 100 000 people; and more than 80% of the population are of European, largely British descent. Australia is characterized by the emphasis placed on home ownership and is very much a family-oriented, and rather tolerant and optimistic society. The size of the country is in stark contrast to the urbanization of the small population. For example, New South Wales is the most populous state with nearly 6 million inhabitants. Five of those six million live in one urban conurbation, the remaining million inhabitants being rural or small town dwellers distributed across a state that is bigger than France or Texas, and twice as big as California. Medical services in Austalia are divided into state (i) public sector services (72% of funds), and (ii) federally funded private sector services for

Handbook of Mental Health Economics and Health Policy, Volume I, Schizophrenia. Edited by M. Moscarelli, A. Rupp and N. Sartorius.
© 1996 John Wiley & Sons Ltd.

psychiatist and general practitioner fee-for-service payments (28% of funds).

The problem with mental health services in Australia, as in many other countries, is that direct spending on mental health services remains largely inpatient based and has not fallen commensurately with bed numbers (Raftery, 1992). On average, half the total mental health service expenditure is on stand-alone psychiatric hospitals, a quarter on hospitals integrated with general medicine, and only a quarter on community mental health services. In 1992, the Health Ministers of all Australian States and the Federal Government endorsed a National Mental Health Policy (1992) that would guide the states in terms of mental health policy, planning, service provision, and funding. The isolation of mental health services from other health services and the lack of a national policy or funding focus were given as reasons for the variability in mental health service quality and costs. The Policy identifies three main aims: (i) to promote the mental health of the Australian community and, where possible, prevent the development of mental health problems and mental disorders; (ii) to reduce the impact of mental disorders on individuals, families, and the community; and (iii) to assure the rights of people with mental disorders.

The process of reform is guided by a set of 38 objectives and 49 indicators of mental health services outlined by the National Mental Health Policy. One of the clear objectives is to transfer funds into the community until they comprise half the budget, implying that the current level of funding is sufficient for the development of an adequate mental health service. We have argued elsewhere (Andrews, 1991a) that the level of funding which the hospital-oriented services currently receive should be sufficient to develop appropriate community-oriented services. We have also argued (Andrews, 1991b) that the funds, once dominated by the needs of patients with schizophrenia, are now progressively being freed up and should become available for the treatment of patients with other disorders.

However, funding is not the entire story. An analysis of expenditure for each state and territory across Australia suggests that high per capita spending levels do not imply comprehensive and adequate services. Fuller Torrey and the US National Alliance for the Mentally Ill are well known for their ratings of services for the seriously mentally ill. Hoult and Burchmore (1994), in conjunction with Schizophrenia Australia, have just completed a similar analysis of the Australian public sector services. Information was sought by questionnaire from service providers, administrators, and consumers. Independent site visits were also conducted. For these authors, the definition of seriously mentally ill can be taken to be equivalent to chronic schizophrenia. The report was focused on services for the type of patient who would have once inhabited the back ward of a mental hospital. They rated New South Wales as the state with the best overall services: hospital, community, rehabilitation and housing. The Hoult and Burchmore survey identified the provision of 24-hour community-based services for the seriously mentally ill as the outstanding achievement of the Australian mental health services. For example, every mental health service in Sydney (population 4 million) has an extended hours service which can undertake an emergency home assessment 7 days a week. Extended hours services on such a scale are rare elsewhere in the world. In contrast, the National Mental Health Report (1993) identified New South Wales as the state that spends the least per capita ($46, 1993 Australian dollars) on public sector mental health services, the national average expenditure being $57 per capita (see Table 1).

The disparity between cost and quality across Australia warrants further attention: Is it credible that the state that spends the least has the best services? Do the differences in Hoult and Burchmore's rankings of the services provided by the states represent real differences? Regional scores varied 10-fold, from 34 points which represented an excellent service, to 3 points, which measured what the authors termed a shameful service. Even when aggregated by state, the highest ranking state averaged 21, three times higher than the score of the worst state. The best and the worst states adjoin, and Hoult and Burchmore saw the differences as so major that they advised anyone with a serious mental illness to migrate from Queensland to adjoining New South Wales. The next question is whether the budget differentials are significant. Victoria spends 58% more than the adjoining state of New South Wales, a difference of $158 million per

Table 1. Excellence of service for the seriously mentally ill versus costs and resources for the six Australian states

	NSW	VIC	SA	TAS	WA	Q	Australia
Excellence score	21	18	12	10	8	7	
Public sector							
Total expenditure per capita	$46	$73	$64	$59	$62	$47	$57
(expenditure on community services)	($12)	($20)	($16)	($17)	($13)	($10)	($14)
Community staff per 100 000	10.9	10.2	3.9	7.0	4.5	7.7	7.7
Psychiatric beds per 100 000	43	41	52	50	44	59	46
% beds in general hospitals	25%	16%	12%	34%	30%	30%	24%
Private services							
Expenditure on private psychiatrists per capita	$9	$11	$11	$7	$5	$7	$9
General practitioners per 100 000	118	120	125	124	111	115	118

annum. This addition would effectively treble the community mental health budget of New South Wales.

Accepting, therefore, that there is an issue that should be explained—that New South Wales provides significantly better services on much less money—what are the options? A number of options spring to mind and the data about each are also displayed in Table 1. As beds consume money in quite a disproportionate fashion, could New South Wales simply have developed the service with the fewest beds? At 43 beds per 100 000 it is close to the national average and Victoria, which spends the most money, has the fewest beds. Queensland spends the second least and has the most beds. Perhaps psychiatric beds integrated into general hospital settings are expensive. But no. Again New South Wales is close to the national average and some of the good states have few and some of the poor states have many, even though the National Mental Health Policy asks that all acute psychiatric services be mainstreamed with other health services.

We will argue later that the design of the Community Mental Health Services is important. At this point, it is sufficient to note that the amount of money each state spends on community services has no strong relationship to overall excellence even though the number of community mental health staff is 40% higher in the two states with the best services. Because expenditure is split between state and federal sources, another explanation could be that New South Wales had transferred the most costs to the federal government by attracting the most private psychiatrists and general practitioners per capita to work in that state. Again the answer seems negative, with New South Wales figures for dollars per capita spent on private psychiatrists and numbers of general practitioners per 100 000 being identical to the national averages.

The next explanation, that New South Wales is cheaper to service than the other states simply because most people live in the coastal conurbation, is also difficult to support. Victoria has a greater population density, and South Australia is essentially a city state with very few people in the rural areas. If population density provided economies of scale then they should be among the most economical of states, but they are the two that spend the most. Thus, this geographical explanation does not explain the conundrum. The next possibility, that inhabitants of New South Wales are less mentally ill than the rest of Australia, is attractive but probably not true. Andrews *et al.* (1990a), showed that a quasi-population sample of New South Wales twins who completed the Diagnostic Interview Schedule showed prevalences of mental disorders consistent with age, sex, and site variation of rates in the US Epidemiological Catchment Area Studies and a similar survey of a South Australian rural area has revealed comparable figures. It is difficult to think that the inhabitants of the other Australian states suffer from higher rates of mental illness.

The two remaining explanations as to how New South Wales can offer the best services yet spend the least money are not quite so simple to resolve. They are, first, that by restricting services to patients once hospitalized with schizophrenia, New South Wales is able to treat these patients well at the significant social cost of providing minimal services for patients seriously ill with other disorders. There have been surveys of the workload of the public and private sector psychiatrists in Australia (Andrews, 1989) that show that public sector patients are twice as likely to suffer from a psychotic illness and half as likely to suffer a neurosis as are patients treated in the private sector. There are data for both Victoria and for New South Wales that echo this, that is that only one-third of the private sector workload, but two-thirds of the public sector workload both in hospital and in the community mental health clinics, suffer from a serious mental illness (Andrews & Hickie, 1986; Solomon *et al.*, 1993). Hence there is no evidence that New South Wales has an abnormally restricted service but we do not have data for the other states.

The second alternative is that the organization of services in New South Wales have made it possible to provide excellent services at minimal cost. The area health service boards of management have responsibility for the funding and allocation of monies to mental health service delivery within their areas which vary in population from 60 000 to 600 000. Hoult and Burchmore (1994) highlight differences in the way services have been organized for these different areas. We would argue that part of the success of the New South Wales services is the delivery of comprehensive mental health services for given catchment areas and almost all of the top 10 rated regions in the Hoult and Burchmore report were from New South Wales. This state has a long history of planned deinstitutionalization with successful placement of the chronically ill in sheltered accommodation in the community (Andrews *et al.*, 1990b). We describe two comprehensive area mental health services in New South Wales: one in an intact suburban area and the other serving the inner city area of Sydney. Both have been rated as having adequate resourcing and good organization.

RYDE–HUNTERS HILL

This region is a middle class area with a population of about 90 000. It is a mostly residential area with a few industrial estates. There are two old mental hospitals which are being downsized. Acute admissions go to a 30 bed ward in one of these hospitals. There is no separate acute general hospital unit. The community services are available 24 hours, 7 days a week. An assessment team of 14 staff deal with all new patients including patients prior to admission to the hospital unit. The three psychiatrists do home visits regularly. The service has a team of 17 other staff who supervise several residential facilities, operate a day program and also provide both individual and team case management. Staff of these teams are all tertiary-trained mental health professionals. Seven of the staff operate as an assertive treatment team for a pool of about 40 of the most severely impaired patients. This assertive component operates 7 days a week (Teesson & Hambridge, 1992). The region generates 120 admissions a year and uses only five beds. Research has shown that this low hospital utilization did not result in additional burden on the families (Reynolds *et al.*, 1990).

INNER CITY MENTAL HEALTH SERVICE

Providing a mental health service to an inner city area is very different to providing services in an intact suburban area. The inner city of Sydney has a population of 66 000, there are over 1000 beds in refuges for the homeless, and 25% of residents in these refuges meet criteria for schizophrenia (Teesson & Buhrich, 1990). The area is indistinguishable from many other inner city areas in large cities throughout the world, characterized by cheap rooming houses, squats, the homeless, the skid-row alcoholic, and the sex and drug industry all concentrated in the one small area. The area is served by a 28 bed psychiatric ward in a general hospital which takes 600 admissions a year. As with the Ryde–Hunters Hill service the inner city community service is available 24 hours, 7 days a week and the 40 staff are organized into functional teams. The service has a current case load of about 450 patients who are provided with ongoing clinical case management. Five staff operate as an assertive treatment team for a pool of about 35 of the most severely impaired patients and research has proven the efficacy of this team (Teesson & Hambridge, 1992). Seven staff undertake case management of clients who are more stable. The most innovative component of the inner city service is the provision of outreach services to the refuges for the homeless. This team deals with emergency referrals from the refuges in the area, conducts weekly evening outreach clinics in the refuges, and provides assertive follow up. The clinics are conducted in conjunction with psychiatrists from the inpatient unit. This service has proven to be effective in reducing hospitalization of the homeless with schizophrenia who live in the refuges.

CONCLUSIONS

We don't know what makes a good inexpensive service but it seems that a coherent and optimistic society is a good starting point. From our experience in New South Wales we regard the following features as important: access to 24 hour mobile crisis assessment; clinical case management (Andrews & Teesson, 1994); integrated hospital and community services; and, for the reluctant yet seriously disabled patient, provision of assertive outreach services. While such community services seem essential, a large number of psychiatric beds is not. Good data on patients, their illness, disability, and needs, are essential if one is to deliver effective services efficiently.

REFERENCES

Andrews, G. (1989). Private and public psychiatry: A comparison of two health care systems. *American Journal of Psychiatry,* **146**, 881–886.

Andrews, G. (1991a). *The Tolkien Report: A Description of a Model Mental Health Service.* Sydney, NSW: Clinical Research Unit for Anxiety Disorder.

Andrews, G. (1991b). The cost of schizophrenia revisited. *Schizophrenia Bulletin,* **17**, 388–394.

Andrews, G. and Hickie, C. (1986). The people seen by Sydney psychiatrists. *Australian and New Zealand Journal of Psychiatry,* **20**, 492–495.

Andrews, G. and Teesson, M. (1994). Smart versus Dumb Treatment: Services for mental disorders. *Current Opinion in Psychiatry,* **7**, 182–185.

Andrews, G., Hall, W., Goldstein, G., Lapsley, H., Bartels, R., and Silove, D. (1985). The economic costs of schizophrenia: Implications for public policy. *Archives of General Psychiatry,* **42**, 537–543.

Andrews, G., Stewart, G.W., Morris-Yates, A., Holt, P.E., and Henderson, A.S. (1990a). Evidence for a general neurotic syndrome. *British Journal of Psychiatry,* **157**, 6–12.

Andrews, G., Teesson, M., Stewart, G., and Hoult, J. (1990b). Follow-up of community placement of the chronic mentally ill in New South Wales. *Hospital and Community Psychiatry,* **41**, 184–188.

First National Mental Health Report (1993). Canberra: Australian Government Publishing Service.

Hall, W., Goldstein, G., Andrews, G., Lapsley, H., Bartels, R., and Silove, D. (1985). Estimating the economic costs of schizophrenia. *Schizophrenia Bulletin,* **11**, 598–610.

Hartounian, N.S., Smart, C.N., and Thompson, M.S. (1981). *The Incidence and Economic Costs of Major Health Impairments.* Lexington, MA: Lexington Books.

Hoult, J. and Burchmore, H. (1994). *Care of the Seriously Mentally Ill in Australia: A Rating of State and Regional Programs.* North Fitzroy, Victoria: Schizophrenia Australia Foundation.

National Mental Health Policy (1992). Canberra: Australian Government Publishing Service.

Raftery, J. (1992). Mental health services in transition: the United States and the United Kingdom. *British Journal of Psychiatry,* **161**, 589–593.

Reynolds, I., Jones, J.E., Berry, D.W., and Hoult, J.E. (1990). A crisis team for the mentally ill: the effect on patients, relatives and admissions. *Medical Journal of Australia,* **152**, 646–652.

Solomon, S., Buckingham, B., and Epstein, M. (1993). *Report of Consultancy for the Mental Health Workforce Committee on Medical Workforce Financing Arrangements.* Canberra: Australian Government Publishing Service.

Teesson, M. and Buhrich, N. (1990). Prevalence of schizophrenia in a refuge for homeless men: a five year follow-up. *Psychiatric Bulletin,* **14**, 597–600.

Teesson, M. and Hambridge, J. (1992). Mobile community treatment in inner city and suburban Sydney. *Psychiatric Quarterly,* **63**, 119–128.

37

Economic Impact of Schizophrenia on the Dutch Society

SILVIA M.A.A. EVERS and ANDRÉ J.H.A. AMENT
University of Limburg, Department of Health Economics, Maastricht, the Netherlands

INTRODUCTION

Like other European countries, the Netherlands is currently facing increases in the need and demand for health care services, due to demographic changes (aging population) and changing attitudes to health. Demand is also growing due to advances in medical treatment and the changing preferences of consumers. This means that the costs are rising sharply. In 1990 48 billion guilders was spent on health care, in 1994 this amount is expected to rise to some 58 billion guilders. Cost containment is necessary because macro-economic policies aim to reduce the level of public expenditures (Ministry of Welfare, Health and Cultural Affairs, 1993). Until recently the magnitude of the burden that schizophrenia posed to the Dutch community was unknown. Therefore, in 1992 the Department of Health Economics of the University of Limburg performed a study which tries to identify and estimate the health care costs of schizophrenia in the Netherlands and to determine in a broader sense the total costs of schizophrenia for the Dutch society in terms of productivity loss caused by absence from work and early retirement (Evers *et al.*, 1992) In this study, the medical consumption, and the social consequences of schizophrenia are examined.

In a report by the Government Committee on Choices in Health Care (1992) it is examined whether or not all that is medicotechnically possible and is developed ought to be introduced into the Dutch health care system. To this question, the committee, in principle, answers "no." Economic evaluation of new developments on the basis of costs, benefits, and risk can serve to underpin choices at the macro-level of health care. In a later section some remarks are made regarding economic evaluation in psychiatry. Finally, a conclusion and discussion can be found.

METHOD

The purpose of the study which is performed by the Department of Health Economics is to assess the burden which schizophrenia puts on the Dutch society. The study can be characterized as a prevalence-based cost-of-illness study. In cost-of-illness studies a distinction is made between direct and indirect costs.

Direct costs are defined as the actual expenditures related to an illness or disorder, including money spent on hospital and nursing home care, the

Handbook of Mental Health Economics and Health Policy, Volume I, Schizophrenia. Edited by M. Moscarelli, A. Rupp and N. Sartorius.
© 1996 John Wiley & Sons Ltd.

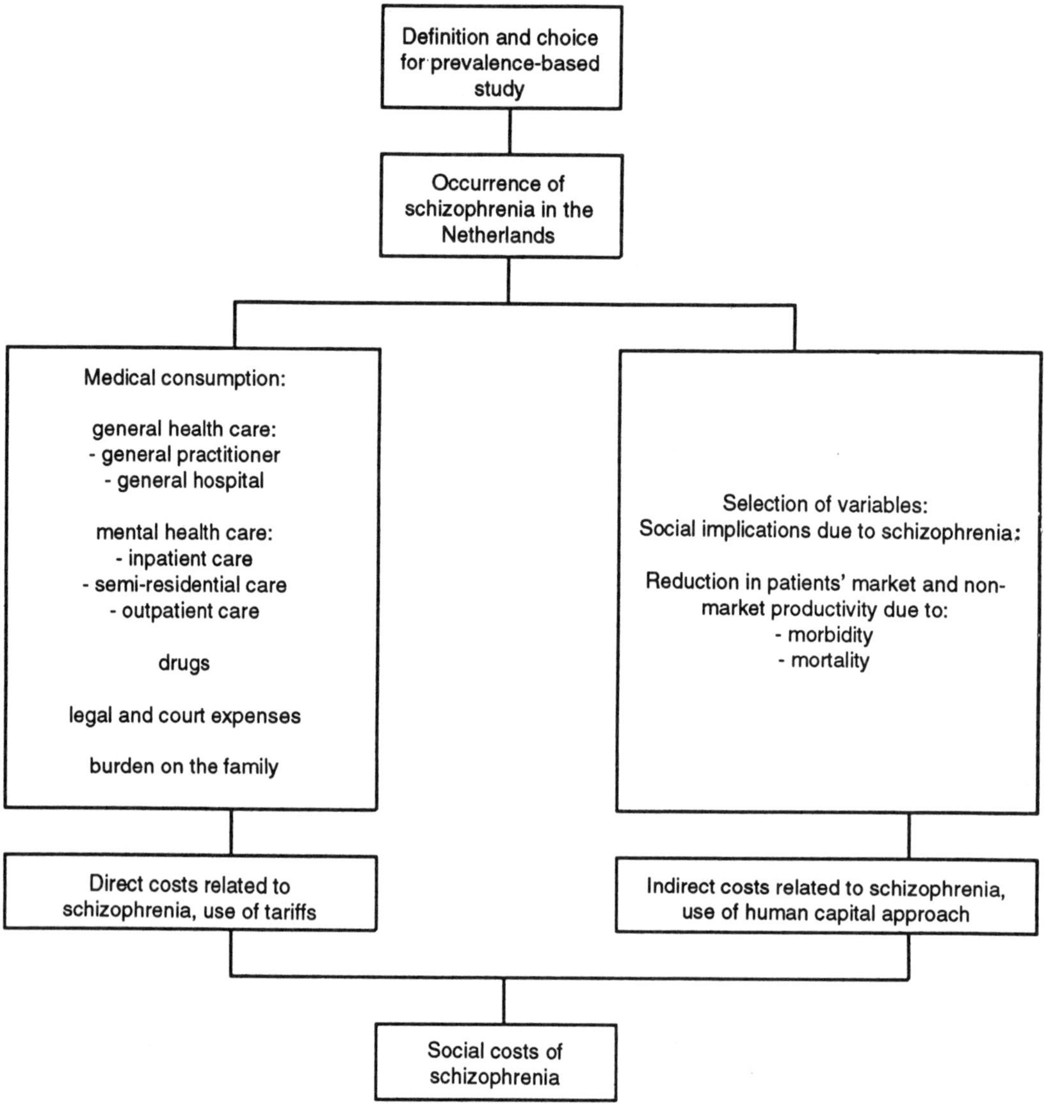

Figure 1. Method.

services of physicians and other medical professionals, drugs and appliances, rehabilitation, etc.

Indirect costs are broadly defined as the value of lost output due to reduced productivity caused by illness, disability, or injury. This includes the value of lost working days, housekeeping days, and diminished productivity.

By using data bases and relevant studies, an estimate was made of the social consequences of schizophrenia in 1989. The epidemiologic figures had to be translated into direct and indirect costs (see Figure 1). The costs of medical consumption, e.g. consultations and treatment days, are based on figures provided by the *Financieel Overzicht Zorg* (FOZ) (Tweede Kamer, 1991–92). The FOZ is a government publication which gives an integrated overview of the financial developments in the Netherlands during recent years. The costs of drugs are calculated by means of the Information Medical Statistics (IMS) on-line sales data at public price level. To quantify the indirect costs the human capital approach is used.

COST-OF-ILLNESS

PREVALENCE OF SCHIZOPHRENIA

Little is known about the incidence and prevalence of schizophrenia in the Netherlands. In an overview by the Scenario Commission for Mental Health Care, an incidence of 0.11 per thousand of the general population using extramural or intramural care facilities for the first time was reported (Giel *et al*., 1980). The Dutch Schizophrenia Society estimates the yearly incidence at 0.23 per thousand. According to the Scenario Commission the prevalence in the Netherlands varies from six per thousand to 6.7 per thousand. In our study a conservative estimate of six per thousand is assumed.

MEDICAL CONSUMPTION

General health care

The Dutch health care system can be divided into general health care, e.g. general practitioners, general hospitals, and more specific mental health care, e.g. psychiatric hospitals, sheltered residences, and community care. People with schizophrenia use both health care subsystems.

General practitioners play an important part in serving people with mental problems. In a national study (van der Velden, 1991) focusing on the prevalence of diseases, complaints, and problems in the practice of the general practitioner, the morbidity of schizophrenia was also examined. Based upon this study it is estimated that the year prevalence for schizophrenia is one per thousand of people visiting a general practitioner (age 0–75+ years).

The total costs of general practitioners' practices in 1989 was 1814 million guilders (Tweede Kamer, 1991–92). Based on the estimate that about one in every thousand visits to the general practitioner are due to schizophrenia the total costs in 1989 would be about 1.8 million guilders.

Schizophrenics are admitted to general hospitals for various reasons. The LMR (Landelijke Medische Registratie, 1990) registers patients who are admitted to general hospitals, academic hospitals or specialized hospitals (e.g., children's hospitals). Our study focuses on people who were admitted to a general hospital because of schizophrenia. In 1989, 1004 schizophrenics were discharged from a general hospital, after a mean length of stay of 45.8 days. Some general hospitals have a special department for the treatment of people with a psychiatric disease. In 1989 694 discharged patients were diagnosed as having schizophrenia. The total number of hospitalization days in the psychiatric departments was 27961 with an average length of stay of 41.5 days. Based on the cost per hospital day of 687.40 guilders for a general department and 423.94 guilders for a psychiatric department the total costs due to schizophrenia in general hospitals would be about 25 million guilders.

Mental health care

In the course of the twentieth century the Netherlands have developed a complex and differentiated system of mental health care for psychiatric patients, which can be divided into three parts: inpatient care, semimural care (i.e., part-time care), and outpatient care.

Little information is available about the use of mental health care facilities by schizophrenics in the Netherlands (Scenariocommissie Geestelijke Volksgezondheid, 1990). It is only from the psychiatric hospitals that data are gathered on a national level by the PIGG (patiëntenregister intramurale geestelijke gezondheidszorg) using the ICD-9 classification. The PIGG registers prevalences on December 31, 1989.

On December 31, 1989, 6563 schizophrenics (30.4% of the population present) were staying in a general psychiatric hospital, 38 (10.0%) in a forensic hospital, and 42 (16.3%) in an academic psychiatric hospital. According to the FOZ (Tweede Kamer, 1991–92), the total costs of psychiatric hospitals in 1989 were 2255 million guilders, of which the general psychiatric hospitals accounted for 2020 million. Based on the figure of 30.4% the costs of schizophrenia would be about 614.1 million guilders.

In 1989, 93 million guilders (Tweede Kamer, 1991–92) were spent in forensic psychiatric hospitals. On December 31, 1989, 10% of those present in these institutions were schizophrenic. Because of

Table 1. Costs due to drug consumption

Main category	Consumption schizophrenia (out-patient)	Sales at public price level in 1989 (in millions)
N4A Anti-parkinson	10.7%	3.42
N5A Neuroleptics	13.9%	3.94
N5B Hypnotics/Sedatives	1.1%	0.61
N5C Tranquillisers	0.5%	0.22
N6A Anti-depressants	0.9%	0.45
Total		8.64

this, the costs that can be attributed to schizophrenia would be about 9.3 million. The FOZ figures do not allow us to trace the costs in academic psychiatric hospitals.

In the Netherlands the semimural and outpatient institutions do not keep a central register of the kinds of disease which their care groups exhibit. Therefore a rough estimation of the medical consumption in this sector due to schizophrenia was made.

The sheltered residences are one important group of institutions in the mental health care sector. In our study two Regional Institutes for Sheltered Residences (in Drenthe and Zeeland) were asked to give us the schizophrenia prevalence rates in a certain year. In 1989, in the Regional Institute for Sheltered Residences in the region of Drenthe, 60 of the 112 patients resident on December 31, 1991 (54%) were classified using the DSM-III-R or the ICD-9 as schizophrenic (Regionale Instelling Beschermende Woonvormen, 1992, personal communication). In the sheltered residences in Zeeland 21% (19 of 92) of the people present were schizophrenic (Beschermende Woonvormen Zeeland, 1992, personal communication). Tholen *et al.* (1988) found in his research that 39% of the persons in sheltered residences had schizophrenic disorders.

On December 31, 1989 there were 3250 people in sheltered homes throughout the Netherlands. Assuming that the overall percentage of people with schizophrenia in sheltered homes is equal to the mean of the three figures for Drenthe (54%), Zeeland (21%), and from the research by Tholen *et al.* (39%), this would imply that 1235 people (38%) were in care in a sheltered home due to schizophrenia. The total costs for sheltered homes in 1989 were 125 million guilders (Tweede Kamer, 1991–92), which means that about 47.5 million can be attributed to schizophrenia.

In general and academic psychiatric hospitals the number of schizophrenic patients admitted to part-time care is recorded. In 1989, of the day care in general psychiatric hospitals and academic psychiatric hospitals, 11.1% can be attributed to schizophrenics. According to the National Hospital Institute (1990a–d) the total expenditure on day care in 1989 was 83 million, of which therefore 9.2 million can be attributed to schizophrenia.

Wiersma *et al.* (1988) found in his research on chronic patients in mental health care that for every one long-stay patient in a general psychiatric hospital there are five chronic patients in outpatient mental health care. In 1989, 6643 clients were present in inpatient psychiatric hospitals. A tentative conclusion on the basis of the available data would be that 33 215 schizophrenic patients were receiving treatment from an outpatient mental health care institution. This would be 9.4% of all outpatients in mental health care (Jacobs & Bijl, 1991). The outpatient settings in the Netherlands consist for the most part of the Regional Institutes for Out-patient Mental Health Care and Out-patient Centers for Addicts. In 1989, the total costs for this type of care were 670 million guilders (Tweede Kamer, 1991–92). If 9.4% of the patients in the outpatient sector were schizophrenic, then the costs which can be attributed to schizophrenia in outpatient care would be about 62.9 million guilders.

The most important treatment for schizophrenia is the administration of medicine. Extensive information about drug administration is registered by the Information Medical Statistics (IMS). Table 1 gives an overview of the costs of drug treatment due to schizophrenia. Based upon the IMS figures for

Table 2. Spells of absence[1] due to schizophrenia and mental disorders in 1989

Diagnosis	Cases of absence	Average sickness duration	Total duration
Not seen by an insurance physician	2995431	10	29134267
Mental disorders	175070	96	16744077
Of whom with schizophrenia	134	219	29317
Total	4146694	24	99545039

[1] Benefits of employees insured under the Sickness Insurance Act with the occupational associations
Source: Central Bureau of Statistics, 1991 Statistical Bulletin, 11

on-line sales per sector at public price level it is estimated that the outpatient drug costs due to schizophrenia were about 8.6 million guilders.

INDIRECT COST

Along with the direct consequences due to medical consumption and the use of drugs schizophrenia also leads to absence from work due to illness. The larger part of the data regarding absenteeism is registered by occupational associations, covering persons who are voluntarily or compulsorily insured under the Sickness Insurance Act and whose employers are members of an occupational association. The classifications used by these associations are based on the International Classification of Diseases, 9th revision.

Table 2 gives an overview of the spells of absence due to mental disorders and schizophrenia which ended in 1989. In 1989 there were 134 cases of absence due to schizophrenia, with a total duration of 29 317 days.

In the Netherlands if a person fulfils certain conditions one can get a benefit due to "work disability" after the 1 year period of absence from work described above. In 1989 921 990 persons were receiving a benefit as being unfit for work, of whom 27% receive the benefit because of psychological disturbances. Of these persons only a small part, 1212 persons (Algemeen Arbeidsongeschiktheidsfonds/Arbeidsongeschiktheidfonds, 1990) or 1.3‰ of all people receiving a disability benefit, are schizophrenic.

Schizophrenia makes people unable to carry on with their work, which leads to losses of productivity for society. The human capital approach calculates the productivity losses by means of earnings. Average earnings, including non-wage labor costs, are generally used to measure this loss. The average daily income in 1989 for people between 16 and 64 years old was about 132.60 guilders. It was estimated that the total absence from work due to schizophrenia in 1989 was 52 352 days. Multiplying this by the average earnings per day yields about 6.9 million guilders. In addition to absence from work, a number of persons (1212 in 1990) are also more or less permanently disabled because of schizophrenia. The production losses due to permanent disability can be calculated in the same way. Multiplying the number of disabled schizophrenics by the average gross yearly income (48 400 guilders) gives total costs of 58 660 800 guilders. The total production loss due to schizophrenia is therefore 65.6 million guilders.

In conclusion, Table 3 shows that in the Netherlands 778 million guilders are spent on the treatment of schizophrenic patients, which is about 2% of the total health care budget. Of the total health care costs devoted to schizophrenic patients, the largest part goes to the inpatient costs of psychiatric hospitals. Only a relatively small percentage is related to outpatient care. Furthermore it can be seen that the total drug costs are relatively low in the treatment of schizophrenia.

ECONOMIC EVALUATION

Cost-of-illness studies are able to measure the total change in resource use for a given year. They fail, however, to identify which intervention is responsible

Table 3. Costs of schizophrenia in The Netherlands

	Effects due to schizophrenia (rate used)	Costs in guilders (in millions)
General practitioners	0.1%	1.8
Hospital (excluding psychiatry)	46 024	24.7
General psychiatric hospitals	30.4%	614.1
Forensic psychiatric institutions	10.0%	9.3
Sheltered residences	37.8%	47.5
Psychiatric day-care	11.1%	9.2
Out-patient care	9.4%	62.9
Total health care		769.5
Drugs out-patient		8.6
Total direct costs		778.1
Absenteeism	29 317 days	6.9
Disability	1 212 cases	58.7
Total indirect costs		65.6
Legal and court costs	More often admitted by means of a committal to custody or by judicial authorization than the total population. Comparatively speaking there are more schizophrenics who have a been detained by means of special eglal sentences	
Mortality	Twice that in general population due to suicide, violent death and natural causes	
Burden on the family	Emotional and economic strain that family members, neighbours and friends experience when a realative is mentally ill	
Total all costs		843.7

for this (potential) change, and they fail to link them with the potential improvement in health status. Economic evaluation is the comparative analysis of alternative courses of action (e.g. interventions) in terms of both their costs and consequences (Drummond, 1987). Economic evaluation can serve to make choices between interventions. In the Netherlands in 1988, approximately 8% of the health care budget is spent within the health care system for mentally ill patients (Tweede Kamer, 1991–92). Despite the amount of money spent on the mental health care economic analysis of this sector is relatively rare. One of the few studies in the Netherlands which compared costs and benefits of day treatment with community care for schizophrenic patients is a study by Wiersma *et al.* (1991). One can think of several reasons (Fried, 1989a, b) why economic evaluation is not so popular in psychiatry. Measurement of effectiveness in mental health care is often complicated because of the known difficulties with the reliability of psychiatric diagnosis, and frequent lack of consensus about etiology and appropriate treatment for many psychiatric illnesses. Additionally, the treatments are sometimes ill-defined and many have not been "proven" effective. Furthermore, the success of treatment for any chronic disease may vary over time. For instance, how long must an alcoholic be alcohol-free in order to label the outcome of the treatment a success? Finally, an important item in economic evaluation are "foregone wages" as the way of measuring productivity loss as a result of being in treatment. The mentally ill are more less likely to be employable. Furthermore, schizophrenics often lose their jobs in the predromal phase, before they are actually diagnosed as being schizophrenic.

DISCUSSION

If one looks at the prevalence rate of schizophrenia in the Netherlands of 0.6%, one can say that the costs figures of schizophrenia 2% of the health care budget are rather high. Schizophrenics often need treatment during the rest of their lives, which are only slightly shorter than average lives. In the Netherlands treatment is not drug-oriented. In our study we estimated the economic burden of schizophrenia of the Dutch society. In order to allow better decisions regarding the use of resources in mental health care one should evaluate the effectiveness and efficiency of the health care intervention. For this reason economic evaluation of interventions in psychiatry remains obligatory.

REFERENCES

Algemeen Arbeidsongeschiktheidsfonds/Arbeidsongeschiktheidfonds (1990). *Jaarverslag 1989*. Zoetermeer: Algemeen Arbeidsongeschiktheidsfonds/Arbeidsongeschiktheidfonds.

Beschermende Woonvormen Zeeland (1992). *Information on the sheltered residences in the region 'Zeeland', regarding the year 1989*. (Personal communication P. Hoondert).

Central Bureau voor de Statistiek (1991). Beëindigde verzuimgevallen en hun gemiddelde duur naar diagnosehoofdgroep, leeftijd en geslacht. *Statistisch Bulletin*, **47**, 3.

Drummond, M.F., Stoddart, G.L., and Torrance, G.W. (1987). *Methods for the Economic Evaluation of Health Care Programmes*. Oxford: Oxford University Press.

Evers, S.M.A.A., Ament, A.J.H.A., van den Boom, G., and Warndorff, D.K. (1992). *Cost of Schizophrenia in The Netherlands*. Maastricht: University of Limburg, Department of Health Economics, R92-01.

Fried, B.J., Worthington, C., and Deber, R.B. (1989a). Economic evaluations in the Canadian mental health, System I: Theory behind economic evaluation. *Canadian Journal of Psychiatry*, **34**, 633–636.

Fried, B.J., Worthington, C., and Deber, R.B. (1989b). Economic evaluations in the Canadian mental health, System II: From theory to practice in mental health care. *Canadian Journal of Psychiatry*, **34**, 637–640.

Giel, R., Sauër, H.C., Slooff, C.J., and Wiersma, D. (1980). Over epidemiologie van functionele psychosen en invaliditeit. *Tijdschrift voor Psychiatrie*, **22**, 709–722.

Government Committee on Choices in Health Care (1992). *Choices in Health Care*. Rijswijk: Ministry of Welfare, Health and Cultural Affairs.

Information Medical Statistics (IMS). *On-line sales data at public price level*.

Jacobs, C. and Bijl, R. (1991). *GGZ in getallen, 1991*; kwantitatief overzicht van de geestelijke gezondheidszorg: instellingen, zorgcircuits, trends 1980–2000. Utrecht: Nederlands Centrum voor de Geestelijke Volksgezondheid.

Landelijke Medische Registratie (LMR) (1990). *Bedrijfs- en medische informatie*. Psychiatrische Afdelingen van Algemene Ziekenhuizen (PAAZ) Diagnoses Utrecht: SIG, 1990.

Ministry of Welfare, Health and Cultural Affairs (1993). *Fact sheet* Health care reform in the Netherlands. Rijswijk: Ministry of Welfare, Health and Cultural Affairs.

National Hospital Institute (1990a). Sectie geestelijke gezondheidszorg & Stichting Informatiecentrum voor de gezondheidszorg (SIG). *Patiëntenregister Intramurale Geestelijke Gezondheidszorg (PIGG), algemene psychiatrische ziekenhuizen*. Utrecht: NZR/SIG.

National Hospital Institute (1990b). Sectie geestelijke gezondheidszorg & Stichting Informatiecentrum voor de gezondheidszorg (SIG). *Patiëntenregister Intramurale Geestelijke Gezondheidszorg (PIGG), psychiatrische universiteitsklinieken*. Utrecht: NZR/SIG.

National Hospital Institute (1990c). Sectie geestelijke gezondheidszorg & Stichting Informatiecentrum voor de gezondheidszorg (SIG). *Patiëntenregister Intramurale Geestelijke Gezondheidszorg (PIGG), justitiële TBS-inrichtingen*. Utrecht: NZR/SIG.

National Hospital Institute (1990d). Sectie geestelijke gezondheidszorg & Stichting Informatiecentrum voor de gezondheidszorg (SIG). *Patiëntenregister Intramurale Geestelijke Gezondheidszorg, klinieken voor verslavingsziekten*. Utrecht: NZR/SIG.

Regionale Instelling Beschermende Woonvormen (1992). *Information on the sheltered residences in the region 'Drenthe', regarding 1991*. (Personal communication A. van der Heiden).

Scenariocommissie Geestelijke Volksgezondheid (1990). *Zorgen voor de geestelijke gezondheid in de toekomst*. Toekomstscenario's geestelijke volksgezondheid en geestelijke gezondheidszorg 1990–2010. Utrecht: Bohn, Scheltema & Holkema.

Tholen, A.J., Giel, R., Hoek, H.W., de Jong, A., and Wiersma, D. (1988). De psychopathologie in voorzieningen voor langdurig verblijf. *Tijdschrift voor Psychiatrie*, **30**, 54–72.

Tweede kamer der Staten-Generaal (1992). *Financieel Overzicht Zorg 1992*. Tweede Kamer, vergaderjaar 1991–1992, 22311, nrs. 1–2, 's-Gravenhage: Sdu.

Velden van der, J. (1991). *Een nationale studie naar ziekten en verrichtingen in de huisartspraktijk*. Utrecht: Nederlands Instituut voor onderzoek van de eerstelijnsgezondheidszorg.

Wiersma, D., Giel, P., Hoek, H.W., de Jong, A., Nienhuis, F., Ruphan, M., Tholen, A.J. (1988). Chronische patiënten in de geestelijke gezondheidszorg, een epidemiologische verkenning van hun behoefte aan zorg. *Tijdschrift voor Psychiatrie*, **30**, 388–400.

Wiersma, D., Kluiter, H., Nienhuis, F.J., Rüpman, M., and Giel, R. (1991). Costs and benefits of day treatment with community care for schizophrenic patients. *Schizophrenia Bulletin*, **17**, 411–419.

38

Mental Health Services in Spain

LUIS SALVADOR-CARULLA
Centro de Investigación en Minusvalías (CIM), Jerez, Spain

GENERAL BACKGROUND

The general background for the provision of services for the mentally ill was set forth by Spain's General Law of Health and the Law for the Social Integration of the Handicapped—known by its Spanish initials: LISMI (Cabrera & Fuertes, 1990). Their goals have been unequally fulfilled in Spain's different autonomous regions. This is mainly due to the following factors.

LACK OF COORDINATION BETWEEN THE SOCIAL SERVICE AND THE HEALTH CARE SYSTEM

The poor coordination between both services has favored the duplication of resources in some areas and the lack of them in some others. There is a general tendency to transfer competencies in critical areas from the health service to the social service (e.g. mental retardation, and social care for dementia and AIDS). This has been done without any general planning, leaving some topics aside. Furthermore, in a period of economic restraint, the health service may decline responsibilities in certain areas, while the social service cannot implement alternatives. This is particularly important in the case of schizophrenia.

TRANSFERENCE OF SERVICES TO THE AUTONOMOUS REGIONS

Since 1977, Spain is gradually changing from a central state to a federal one. During the last 10 years many services have been transferred from the central government to 17 autonomous regions. The transfer of services has been negotiated between every region and the central government. Thus, some regions have transferred either the health service or the social service, while some others have transferred both of them. Local governments may also apply different policies in their own regions. Although this process may eventually improve the situation, at present it constitutes a supplementary handicap for general planning.

LACK OF COORDINATION BETWEEN THE PUBLIC AND THE PRIVATE SECTORS

This problem affects both the health and the social services. As a matter of fact, the studies available up to date refer only to the public settings, those private facilities which have agreements with the public sector or some non-governmental organizations involved in European programs.

Handbook of Mental Health Economics and Health Policy, Volume I, Schizophrenia. Edited by M. Moscarelli, A. Rupp and N. Sartorius.
© 1996 John Wiley & Sons Ltd.

LACK OF A NATIONAL AGENCY FOR MENTAL HEALTH

The lack of such an institution worsens the problems referred to above.

HEALTH SERVICES FOR SCHIZOPHRENIA IN SPAIN

DEINSTITUTIONALIZATION PROGRAMS

Since the late 1970s the mental health service in Spain has been involved in a strong deinstitutionalization program. This shift from an inpatient model to a community-based model is still the major objective in mental health. This reform follows the recommendation of the European Council and is based upon the report of the National Commission for Psychiatric Reform, published in 1985. Among others, the goals set by the commission were: (i) integration of the mental health service in the general health system; (ii) development of a community-oriented model based upon geographical area (sector); (iii) development of intermediate services and rehabilitation programs; (iv) reform and "overcoming" of the mental hospital, with a progressive shift to psychiatric services within general hospitals; and (v) priority to programs in specific areas, such as child psychiatry, psychogeriatrics, drug abuse, and convicted subjects.

This report sets forth the guidelines for the Spanish reform on mental health services and it has been followed by Spain's autonomous regions. Nevertheless, the differences among the various regions are outstanding. From a regulatory point of view, six of 17 autonomous regions do not have a general plan for mental health. Three have developed partial regulations, and eight have a fully developed plan (Defensor del Pueblo, 1992). The degree of implementation is in some way unrelated to this regulatory process. Thus, the three regions with partial regulation (Asturias, Catalonia, and Galicia) have gone a considerable way to their reform, while other regions with a general plan are still at their first phase of deployment (e.g. the Balearic Islands, where the responsibilities on mental health are divided among five different local and central agencies).

Furthermore, a full implementation of the mental health plan does not warrant an efficient functioning. An example of this can be seen in Andalusia. This is the largest autonomous region in Spain with more than 6 million inhabitants. Andalusia has approved a mental health plan, both the health and the social services have been transferred, and the psychiatric reform is nearly complete. In spite of all that, the present situation is far from acceptable, as the closing of psychiatric hospitals has not been accompanied with a full deployment of alternate structures. While regions like Andalusia, Madrid, or Asturias opt for the closing of psychiatric hospitals, other regions like the Basque Country, Navarre, and Catalonia prefer to remodel and include them in the mental health system. In Andalusia the entire closing of the psychiatric hospitals is planned for the end of 1995. On the other hand, the local government of the Basque Country opened a new psychiatric hospital in 1994 (Salvador-Carulla & Martínez-Maroto, 1993).

The problems mentioned above have been recently analyzed in a special report by the Spanish ombudsman (Defensor del Pueblo, 1992). This report discusses the need for a better coordination between the central government and the autonomous regions, the social service and the health service, and the need for more intermediate services both for outpatients and patients in residential settings. The report demands a quick transfer to the social service of those aged or mentally retarded without a psychiatric disorder. It also states that the "overcome" and closing of psychiatric hospitals cannot be accomplished without a full warrant of proper housing and attendance for this population.

PSYCHIATRIC INSTITUTIONS

During the 1970s the total number of institutionalized people in psychiatric hospitals was about 40 000 (41 942 in 1978). In spite of the population increase, the total number of patients in public psychiatric hospitals was 30 084 in 1985, when the national deinstitutionalization program started. During that period the rate of schizophrenic patients in public institutions was 43% (range: 15–60%; Jorda *et al.*, 1986). Six years later, the number of psychiatric hospitals fell to 97, with a total of 23 282 beds −55.5% in comparison with 1978. Chronic patients occupied 11 535 beds (29.58 per 100 000 inhabitants).

The 1991 report on the psychiatric hospitals by the Spanish ombudsman revealed that the overall proportion of schizophrenic patients in those institutions was 50% or about 5700 people (Defensor del Pueblo, 1992).

It is difficult to assess the number of schizophrenic patients living in private settings. For example, one single Catholic institution, *Sisters of the Sacred Heart*, shelters 1500 chronic patients in three psychiatric institutions.

HEALTH COMMUNITY PROGRAMS

Several epidemiological studies provide reliable data about the rate of schizophrenia in some areas of Spain (e.g. Vazquez-Barquero *et al.*, 1992). There are also case registers in several autonomous communities, such as the Basque Country (Ozamiz, 1986).

Mental health care is organized by sectors. Every sector includes a unit for adult outpatients, a unit for child psychiatry, a rehabilitation unit, and an inpatient unit. Protected housing is also provided by the mental health system. Day hospitals, therapeutic communities, and sheltered homes are also functioning in some sectors. The hospitalization system may differ from one region to another (for example, in Catalonia there are three different units of hospitalization—acute, subacute, and chronic—whereas in Andalusia or Asturias hospitalization is provided by a single inpatient unit per sector. The revolving-door effect is quite significant in some of these areas. The level of implementation varies from one sector to another. For instance, in the province of Cadiz (Andalusia), only one sector out of seven is fully developed. It is difficult to make a guess on the future development of this model, as the public health system is submitted to privatization or mixed systems in some areas (Salvador-Carulla & Martínez-Maroto, 1993). Non-governmental organizations also play an important part in providing support, shelter, and employment for these people.

HEALTH ECONOMICS AND SCHIZOPHRENIA RESEARCH

The Spanish Society of Health Economics is a young organization which is pushing forward the research in this field. Quality assurance and economic studies are major goals of the Spain's Ministry of Health through a special agency for assessment and health planning. Unfortunately, the interest in mental health is scarce. There is only one cost-analysis study of schizophrenia published to date (Ozamiz & Cabases, 1988). This situation is changing quickly through international cooperation and ongoing projects in this field.

ACKNOWLEDGMENT

This work has been supported by the Fondo de Investigationes Sanitarias FiS Grant 95–1961

REFERENCES

Cabrera, J. and Fuertes, J.C. (1990). Psiquiatría y Derechos. Madrid: Ed. Arán.

Comisión Ministerial para (1) la Reforma Psiquiátrica (1985). Informe de la Comisión Ministerial para la Reforma Psiquiátrica. Ministerio de Sanidad y Consumo. Madrid: Secretaría General Técnica.

Defensor del Pueblo (1991). La Situacion juridica del enfermo mental en Espana. Oficina del Defensor del Pueblo Report, Madrid.

Oefensa del Pueblo (1992). Situación jurídica y asistencial del enfermo mental en España. Madrid: Defensor del Pueblo.

Jorda, E., Espinosa, J., and Gomez-Beneyto, M. (1986). Estudio de los pacientes de larga estancia internados en ocho hospitales psiquiátricos españloes. In J. Espinosa, ed., *Cronicidad en Psiqiatría*, pp. 121–236. Madrid: Asociación Española de Neuropsiquiatría.

Ozamiz, J.A. (1986). The establishment of a psychiatric case register in the Basque Country. In G.H.M.M. ten Horn, R. Giel, W.H. Gulbinat, and J.H. Henderson, eds, *Psychiatric Case Registers in Public Health*, pp. 146–150. Amsterdam: Elsevier.

Ozamiz, J.A. and Cabases, J.M. (1988). Economic analysis of different patterns of psychiatric treatment and management of chronic psychotic patients in the Basque country. In D. Schwefel, H. Zollner, and P. Potthoff, eds, *Costs and Effects of Managing Chronic Psychotic Patients*, pp. 97–105. Berlin: Springer-Verlag.

Salvador-Carulla, L. and Martínez-Maroto, A. (1993). Description of general services for people with mental handicap in Spain. *Journal of Intellectual Disability Research*, **37** (Suppl. 1), 34–37.

Vazquez-Barquero, J.L., Diez-Manrique, J.F., Peña, C., *et al.* (1992). A community mental health survey in Cantabria: a general description morbidity. *Psychological Medicine*, **17**, 227–241.

39

The Application of Mental Health Economics Methods in the People's Republic of China

JI JIANLIN
Department of Psychiatry, Shanghai Medical University, Shanghai, China

As early as 2000 years ago ancient Chinese medical literature described and reported psychiatric diseases, referring to their possible causes, pathogeneses, and diagnoses as well as prevention and management. Modern psychiatry, however, developed in the twentieth century. In 1899 the first psychiatric hospital which attempted to provide Western modern psychiatric care was opened with 30 beds by Dr John Kerr in Guangzhou (in South China) (Wong, 1950). From then until 1949, only a few mental hospitals and institutions were set up in eight cities. However, since 1949, Chinese psychiatry has developed rapidly under the present government's lead and support, particularly during the last 20 years. Three research and training centers in mental health have been set up in collaboration with the World Health Organization in Beijing, Nanjing, and Shanghai since 1980. This chapter describes the application of mental health economics approaches for the management of schizophrenic patients in China in recent years.

BACKGROUND

China is a very big country, with a population of over 1.3 billion people and 30 provinces, municipalities, and autonomous regions on the mainland. Despite its apparent homogeneity to the outside world, China has a multicultural population, with 93.3% of its population belonging to the Han "nationality" and the remaining 6.7% belonging to 55 different minority "nationalities." About 80% of the population live in rural areas and are thus not very easily accessible to services available in metropolitan areas. In a national survey conducted in 1982, covering 12 districts in different parts of the country with a total population of 38 136 subjects aged 15 and over, involving 6000 urban households and a similar number of households from rural areas, the prevalence of schizophrenia is 5.69 per thousand. Comparing the prevalence of schizophrenia between urban and rural areas, it is higher in urban areas (6.06 per thousand) than in rural areas (3.43

Handbook of Mental Health Economics and Health Policy, Volume I, Schizophrenia. Edited by M. Moscarelli, A. Rupp and N. Sartorius.
© 1996 John Wiley & Sons Ltd.

per thousand) (Chen *et al.*, 1986).

The national budget spent on public health is small; for example, it was 3.25% in 1985 (Tan & Lipton, 1988). There are no figures available on what percentage of this 3.25% was spent on mental health. Compared with industrialized countries, the health service in China is run on a low budget. According to 1984 figures (Tan & Lipton, 1988), there were 325 psychiatric hospitals and a total bed capacity of 63 997 in the whole country. However, psychiatric hospitals constituted only 0.48% of all hospitals and psychiatric beds made up 2.96% of all hospital beds in the country.

The problem of how to provide much needed services to the vast number of people in this immense land with very limited labor and economic resources has been, and will remain, a paramount concern of Chinese mental health professionals. In accordance with the special situation in China, the mental health services must be developed in a simple, economic, practical, and effective way.

THE THREE-LEVEL SCHEME OF ORGANIZATION

Using the theory and experience of community psychiatry in western Europe for reference, a three-level (municipal/province, district/prefecture, and community/county) mental health network was established in China in the late 1970s and has been progressively continued since. Currently, there are three models for mental health care in the different areas, such as a city model (Shanghai), suburban model (Beijing Haidian), and rural model (Yantai). For example, the Shanghai mental health delivery system is representative of the city model (see Figure 1; Ji Jianlin, 1993). The municipal authority acts through the health offices in the districts or county, then street or area levels, then at neighborhood or village levels. The organization at the municipal level, for example, comprises representatives of the Shanghai Health Bureau, Civil Welfare Agency, and Police Department, and its main tasks are to: (i) draw up a coordinated program for mental health care in the whole municipality; (ii) coordinate the methods and strategies of the professional and all social agencies carrying out mental health work; (iii) mobilize and organize medical staff and social agencies to push forward the development of mental health work; and (iv) advise and supervise the district and county facilities to carry out various programs of primary mental health care (Ji Jianlin, 1993).

THE PRIMARY MENTAL HEALTH CARE SERVICE

The mental health service in China, which was much neglected during the political turmoil of the Great Proletarian Cultural Revolution, is currently being rapidly improved and strengthened. The present government of China is conscious of the needs of mental health in the country, especially primary mental health care in rural areas. Various efforts have been made to cater for the needs of the mentally ill and to take preventive measures on mental health issues. In 1980, a meeting on the care of the mentally ill was held in Shanghai by the Ministry of Health with the Police and the Ministry of Civil Affairs. This has resulted in the improvement of the management of patients with mental disorders in this city. Since then other municipalities and provinces have followed suit drawing on the practical experience of Shanghai. In 1985, a Joint Co-ordinating Council for Mental Health at national level was formed by the Central Government with representatives from the Ministries of Public Health, Public Security (Police), Civil Affairs, Education, Labour, Finance, etc., to implement preventive measures on mental health and to coordinate mental health programs. Thus, currently, the primary mental health care services (PMHCSs) in China get support from various levels of administrative organs as well as all social agencies. The main forms of PMHCSs have four aspects.

NETWORK OF PSYCHIATRIC FAMILY CARE UNIT AND FAMILY EDUCATION INTERVENTION

Although inpatient services are available if needed, it is believed that a larger proportion of the mentally ill are looked after by their families at home. Discrimination against the mentally ill is believed to be at a low level, especially in those areas where

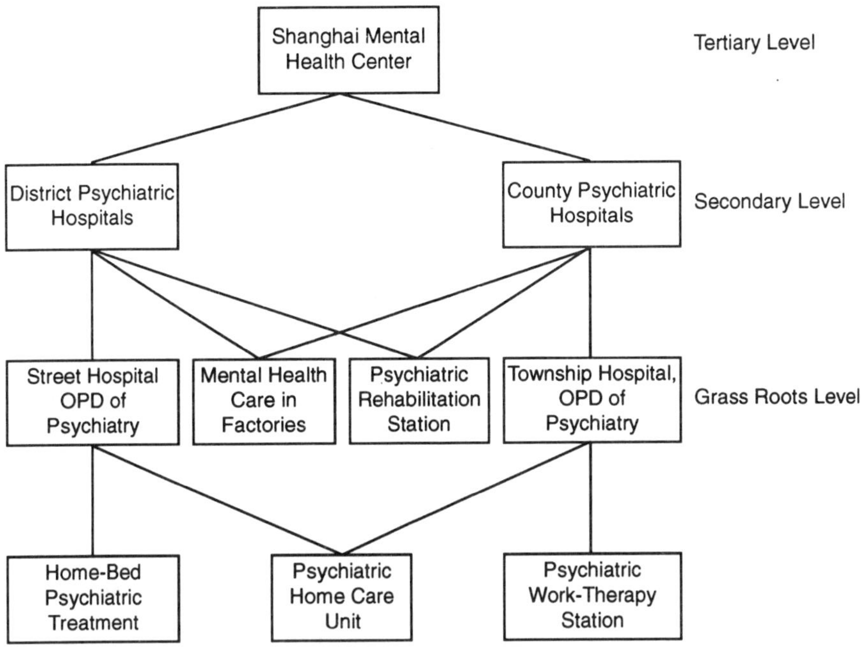

Figure 1. The Shanghai Model: a three-level scheme

community mental health care has been organized (e.g. Shanghai, Beijing, and Shandong).

The psychiatric family care unit and home-bed treatment are one of the PMHCSs in some areas. The former consists of the patient's neighbors, retired workers, and family members to assist in the care of chronic schizophrenics with a couple of people devoting their time to care for each patient. Their duty is to observe the patient's mental condition and report to the health personnel concerned if abnormal behavior occurs. Meanwhile, they help to guide and advise the patients, solve their related social or psychological problems and administer medications as prescribed. The home-bed treatment refers to the community mental health program under which mental patients are cared for at home with adequate treatment and nursing provided by mental health personnel. It aims at making good use of the favorable family and community environment for improving the patient's mental condition and social rehabilitation. A follow-up control study was conducted in 1982 between 100 schizophrenic patients in remission from the psychotic condition through home-bed treatment before 1979 and 100 schizophrenics discharged as remitted from psychiatric hospital in the same period (Yao, 1985). The relapse rates of the two groups were 24 and 67% ($P=0.01$), respectively. The average expense of medical care was 24.94 yuan (US\$1≈3.5 yuan in 1982) for home-bed treatment and 55.93 yuan for hospital treatment. It took an average of 144 days for the home-bed group to recover work capacity from clinical remission while the corresponding hospital group needed an average duration of 265 days. In another study conducted by Shen and her colleagues in Beijing (Shen, 1985), more than 200 schizophrenic patients received this type of home care in combination with psychotropic medication. Good remission and marked improvement were achieved in 64.9% of the patients during 8 years. The recovery of social functioning was even more satisfactory. Before the initiation of the home-care program, only 2.9% could keep up full-time farm work while the percentage rose to 47.1% after 5 years. Meanwhile, the percentage of patients who could neither do household work nor take part in farm work has decreased from 82 to 5.8%. Briefly, the psychiatric family care unit and the home-bed treatment can be considered to be beneficial economically and to be well accepted by patients and their families because they are very convenient.

Currently, a multicenter cooperative study on family-based intervention of schizophrenic patients is conducted in five cities of China (Zhang *et al.*, 1993). The purpose of this research is to explore the feasibility and effectiveness about psychosocial education for the relatives of schizophrenics as one of the community interventions. The results showed that in experimental patients the status of disorder improved significantly, relapse rate per year reduced from 35.01 to 20.40%, the admission rate per year decreased from 22.9 to 11.7%, the social functional disability measured by the Psychiatric Disability Assessment Schedule (DAS) was alleviated, and various kinds of family burden recorded in the Family Burden Interview Schedule (FBIS) were eased.

OCCUPATIONAL THERAPY GROUPS (OR STATIONS)

The occupational therapy (OT) groups conducted in Shanghai area are more or less the same as day hospitals, half-way stations, or sheltered workshops in North America and Europe. However, there are four points which characterize OT groups in China: (i) they are run by the community, neighborhood committees and district; (ii) most of the staff are volunteers and non-professional paramedics with short-term training in clinical psychiatry; (iii) they serve not only as psychiatric treatment and rehabilitation units, but also as units of patients' self-supportive organizations; and (iv) they chiefly lay emphasis on OT combined with psychotropic drugs, behavioral modification, social skills training, reeducation, and recreational treatments.

OT groups admit schizophrenic patients who have partially recovered but are not quite capable of taking up definite jobs and those who were unemployed before their illness. The administration is composed of district officers, paramedics, and retired workers, among which retired workers play a main part in community mental health care service. They often keep in contact with the regional psychiatrists and psychiatric nurses. Recently, there were more than 100 OT stations in Shanghai providing care for about 300 chronic mental patients (most are schizophrenics).

CARE OF MENTAL PATIENTS IN BIG FACTORIES

There are many big factories and companies in the main industrial and commercial cities (e.g. Beijing and Shanghai) in China. For this reason, in factories and other workplaces, especially those with over 2000 employees, the mental health service is integrated into the factory general health care system (parallel to their administrative organization), under the supervision of district mental health staff.

TRAINING OF PRIMARY MENTAL HEALTH WORKERS

Since 1985, in China, a 5 year training program for psychiatrists has been set up. However, the program of shorter training of clinical psychiatry for medical staff working at the grassroots level in neighborhoods, district or county hospitals, and the factory health stations started to be provided in the 1970s. The training course often lasts 6 weeks, 2 weeks of which are devoted to theoretical lectures, which are followed by 4 weeks of clinical practice. The object of such training is to provide the trainee with basic and practical knowledge about psychopathology, diagnostic criteria for common mental disorders, psychopharmacology, and mental care and prevention so that the medical staff can provide effective and direct PMHCSs at their grassroots levels.

COMPREHENSIVE TREATMENT APPROACHES

In China, a lot of traditional Chinese treatment methods, such as herb therapy, acupuncture and moxibustion, qi-gong (a system of deep breathing exercises), and tai-ji-quan (a kind of traditional Chinese shadow boxing), can be chosen to add to the management of schizophrenics because China is a very old country with a continuous history of a 5000 year old culture. For this reason, some Chinese psychiatrists consider these comprehensive treatments to be economic and effective approaches suited to the Chinese condition (Xu, 1989). Of course, the application of comprehensive treatment approaches is a challenge for the Chinese mental health professional that requires sophistication in nosology, competence in psychology, psychiatry, and general medicine, as well as mastery of the art and science of psychosocial and pharmacologic treatment.

COMMENT

Although the achievements made since the network of mental health care was established in part areas of China are quite encouraging, there is plenty of room for improvement, particularly in community psychiatry in rural areas. In the near future, Chinese psychiatrists will strengthen the systematic training of mental health workers (including residents, nurses, social workers, and clinical psychologists, etc.), helping them to pay more attention to psychosocial factors and to master the professional knowledge of psychiatry together with the modern biopsychosocial medical model.

REFERENCES

Chen, C.H., Zhang, W.X., and Shen, Y.C. (1986). Analysis of the data of a survey of mental disorders, drug and alcohol dependence and personality disorders: A collaborative survey of 12 districts. *Chinese Journal of Neuropsychiatry*, **19**, 70–72.

Ji Jianlin (1993). Mental health delivery system in Shanghai, China. *Psychiatric Bulletin*, **17**, 44–46.

Shen, Y.C. (1985). Community mental health services in primary health care in the Beijing countryside: A suburban model. In T.Y. Lin and L. Eisènberg, eds, *Mental Health Planning for One Billion People: A Chinese Perspective*, pp. 119–131.

Tan, E.S. and Lipton, G. (eds) (1988). *Mental Health Service in the Western Pacific Region: A Report on a Ten-Country Survey*, pp. 39–42. Manila: WHO Regional Office for the Western Pacific.

Wong, K.C. (1950). A short history of psychiatry and mental hygiene in China. *Chinese Medical Journal*, **68**, 44.

Xu, T.Y. (1989). Forty years overview: the Chinese psychiatry. *Shanghai Archives of Psychiatry*, **1**, 7–9.

Yao, C.Y. (1985). Mental health in primary health care in Yantai Prefecture: A rural model. In T.Y. Lin and L. Eisenberg, eds, *Mental Health Planning for One Billion People: A Chinese Perspective*, pp. 133–138. Vancouver: University of Columbia Press.

Zhang, M.Y., Yan, H.Q., and Xu, G.Y. *et al.* (1993). A study of education for the relatives of schizophrenic patients in the five cities of China. *Shanghai Archives of Psychiatry*, **5**, 55–58.

Part XI

MENTAL HEALTH POLICIES AND ECONOMICS

40

From Psychiatric Hospital to Community Care: Reflections on the English Experience

MARTIN KNAPP

Centre for Economics of Mental Health, Institute of Psychiatry, University of London, UK and Personal Social Services Research Unit, University of Kent at Canterbury, Canterbury, UK

FROM HOSPITAL TO COMMUNITY

In government policy, community-based provision is the favored locus of care for people with mental health problems in the UK, as in many other countries. The movement away from hospital has been quite fast. The number of people resident as inpatients under the psychiatric specialty in England in March 1993, was approximately a third of the number 30 years earlier. By March 1993, 42 of the 130 large psychiatric hospitals in England in 1960 had closed (Davidge *et al.*, 1993).

The purpose of this chapter is to describe briefly the UK policies on these psychiatric hospital closures and on the development of community care, and in particular to focus on the *economic* issues raised by this policy. The chapter will offer economic evidence on how the implementation of the policy is proceeding within a framework which should assist the continued discussion of this important policy trend.

Some parts of this chapter draw on early work by Knapp (1990) and Knapp *et al.* (1992).

HOSPITAL CLOSURE

Long before the UK central government or local health authorities were formulating the community care policies which were eventually made law by the *1990 National Health Service and Community Care Act*, there were moves to run down hospital provision for people with mental health problems, learning difficulties (mental handicaps), and age-related needs. The hospital rundown policy has been part medical preference, part public opinion, and part "hard political economy" (Korman & Glennester, 1990, p. 11), although it is not always easy to disentangle their respective influences.

Chlorpromazine, the first of the benzodiazepine anxiolytics, and other pharmaceutical developments in the 1950s, allowed the acceleration of the "dehospitalization" trend in the treatment and care of mental illness. One of the most commonly quoted statistics in the English debate is the peaking of the hospital inpatient population at about 150 000 in 1954 or 1955, but the *per capita* population may have peaked 30 years earlier (Goodwin, 1989), and "all the techniques of rehabilitation and resettlement

Handbook of Mental Health Economics and Health Policy, Volume I, Schizophrenia. Edited by M. Moscarelli, A. Rupp and N. Sartorius.
© 1996 John Wiley & Sons Ltd.

now accepted as good psychiatric practice were introduced . . . well before the introduction of reserpine and chlorpromazine" (Wing, 1990, p. 823).

The work of the Royal Commission on Lunacy and Mental Disorder during the 1920s led to the *1930 Mental Health Treatment Act*, which introduced voluntary admission (later informal admission) to mental hospitals. This open-door policy reduced the numbers of certified patients; and custody was gradually replaced by treatment. Although admission rates to mental hospitals continued to grow, so too did discharge rates, with mean length of stay falling. Psychiatric wards appeared in general hospitals, industrial therapy was introduced, and outpatient services started to replace inpatient accommodation. There was growing recognition that people with mental health problems needed to maintain links outside hospitals if they were to progress and to be successfully rehabilitated, and realization that physical and social environments of institutions had undesired, and perhaps iatrogenic effects upon the welfare and health of residents. This realization is most obviously associated with a series of influential post-war publications, but is in fact not a peculiarly post-war perspective (Stanton & Schwartz, 1954; Belknap, 1956; Goffman, 1961; and in Britain, Barton, 1959; Freeman & Farndale, 1963; Morris, 1969; Wing & Brown, 1970). The associated development of therapeutic communities, halfway houses, hospital–hostel wards, community mental health centers, and intensive support programs are the more recent examples of this trend in professional preference, built on assumptions about more effective treatment or support away from the psychiatric hospital.

There were other influential changes. Over at least half a century public attitudes to mental health problems appear to have become gradually more understanding, or perhaps it is just that greater indifference is generating less overt hostility. Whatever the true situation, there is still a long way to go before mental health problems are accepted as readily as physical health problems. Whether or not public opinion has changed over the years (Jones, 1981; Scull, 1984; Goodwin, 1989), policy decisions have sometimes been justified on the assumption that they *have*, helping to support proposals for hospital closure. The view that there is a need to incarcerate people with particular characteristics, in order to protect them from stigma and ridicule, and to protect the public from the disturbing spectacle of "odd" behaviors is less readily propounded today.

It would be a mistake to underestimate the impact of public opinion and the non-medical professions in shaping services. One eminent psychiatrist commented that the move to close hospitals was: "supported by a motley group of civil libertarians, who maintained in the name of various creeds and ideologies that mental hospitals were effectively prisons, depriving their inmates of 'freedom' under an authoritarian medical regime from whose yoke discharge represented a release and a return to normal life" (Shepherd, 1989, p. 667). This is a common theme. Two months later, again in the *British Medical Journal*, an editorial opined: "A generation of sociologists convinced themselves that mental illness was a myth and the disabilities of those so labelled were largely a consequence of their incarceration and mistreatment" (Kendell, 1989, p. 1237).

Misplaced or not, these ideologies or myths, coupled with revelations of scandalous practices and conditions in various hospitals, starting with Ely in 1969 and continuing for some years (Martin, 1984), and in a period in which government ministers were sensitive to threats to civil liberties, ensured that limited action to close the hospitals ensued. The *Mental Health Act 1983* addressed many of these human rights issues.

Although the stark economic realities of maintaining the hospitals were brought home in the 1950s and 1960s, the physical decline of the predominantly Victorian hospital stock had presented problems somewhat earlier. In the early post-war years, with all their economic privations, it would have been perverse to inject substantial capital sums into institutions which were not regarded by all psychiatrists as efficacious in the treatment of mental illness, or by public opinion as appropriate. The initial response was not to develop community care but to lament the shortage of beds, psychiatrists and nurses, and the poor condition of the hospital fabric. Capital allocations to mental hospitals increased over the 1950s, and financial incentives were offered to attract psychiatric nurses, but neither was sufficient to improve standards to an acceptable level. The cost of improving the mental hospitals was simply too great (Ministry of Health, 1962). A similar argument surfaced in the 1970s, propelled into the policy debate by fiscal crises and, subsequently, the "value-for-money imperative." This was the comparative cost argument: hospitals providing long-term care were believed to be more expensive than community services of comparable quality. Moreover, in this recent revival of the political–economic argument, there was the additional attraction that many hospitals were sitting on prime building land. This certainly helped to accelerate the closure program in the late 1980s.

In a characteristically colorful 1961 speech about the "isolated, majestic, imperious [hospitals], brooded over by the gigantic water tower and chimney combined, rising unmistakably and daunting out of the countryside," Enoch Powell, Minister of Health, announced the intention to halve the acute population of psychiatric hospitals in 15 years, and to work towards the eventual disappearance of the long-term (chronic) inpatient population. The former aim was virtually realized in the time-scale envisaged, although the latter is taking longer to achieve. The 1975 White Paper, *Better Services for the Mentally Ill*, emphasized early recognition and prevention, and recommended the integration of support from families and community services (Cmnd 6233, 1975). A few years later a central government White Paper, *Care in Action*, carried the clear message that closure plans should be introduced for some hospitals, phased over a 10-year period, and the *Care in the Community* consultative document of the same year set out proposals to encourage joint working and joint finance (Department of Health and Social Security, 1981a, b).

Numerous academic and media commentaries on the hospital rundown program have criticized the government either for its failure to implement policy quickly enough, or for doing so too fast. Relatives of people in hospital or with long-term needs for care or support have argued vociferously that beds have closed precipitately. The slump in property prices and land values at the end of the 1980s halted some reprovision programs, frustrating the plans of many health authorities, yet ministers are still urging them to speed up closures.

COMMUNITY CARE POLICY

For many years community care was seen simply as getting people out of hospital. Quite what was to happen thereafter was not tackled thoroughly in official publications in the UK until the reports of the Audit Commission (1986) and Sir Roy Griffiths (1988). Given that most community care is provided informally by relatives and neighbors, and most community care clients have never spent long periods in hospital, there is a case for arguing that a community care policy *per se*—that is a policy in which community care was the primary and not the residual aim, and in which service plans were not confined to formal nursing home, residential care home, and day care provision—did not arrive until the late 1980s, despite its permanent place in policy rhetoric.

Government's role in making community care policy has, until recently, looked more reactive than proactive. The introduction of community care by the Ministry of Health in the 1950s "was not so much generating a new and progressive policy as responding to changing circumstances" (Goodwin, 1989, p. 45). Indeed, the reforms contained within the *Mental Health Act 1959*, like earlier government statements, sought to foster or establish, not community care for people with mental health problems, but "treatment in the community." These reforms were necessary to overcome problems already arising as a result of changes in professional practice and political–economic realities. Attempts to initiate a concerted, coherent, and internally consistent community care policy were a long way off. "Rather than simply constituting a reformist measure resulting from enlightened thinking, the community care policy in fact represented a response to a crisis of institutional care" (Goodwin, 1989, p. 41). The absence of a rounded, comprehensive community care policy left its mark on the information baseline from which local practice could move forward, including (usually) woefully inadequate costs perspectives.

Partly for this reason there was no clear definition of what community care is or what it can achieve. Bulmer (1987, ch. 1) identified four different usages of the term. In its original usage it was "care outside of large institutions," meaning anything other than the remote and massive asylums. A second meaning was the delivery of various professional services outside all hospitals, as in "community nursing." Third, it can connote care *by* the community (Bayley, 1973), principally via the involvement of families and voluntary agencies. Finally, community care has been used to describe provision which is as close to normality or ordinary living as possible. The last three definitions are still in use in policy discussions in the UK, generating obvious difficulties of interpretation.

Community care was encouraged as a desirable policy goal, but not supported by financial incentives until the arrival of arrangements for "joint finance" by health authorities (part of the National Health Service) and social services departments (parts of elected local authorities) in the 1970s, and then was fettered by so many disincentives and limitations as to lead the House of Commons Social Services Committee (1985, para. 21) to complain of "under-financed and under-staffed" community provision. Not surprisingly, the history of community care has been described as "painfully slow progress towards timid goals" (Walker, 1982, p. 16).

The development of community care as an explicit, internally consistent, comprehensive goal of public policy has until recently followed rather than shaped professional opinion and preferences. Like the hospital rundown policies of the past 50 years, it has been spurred on by economic forces. The 1975 government White Paper posited that community care would be cheaper than hospital, although the government's 1981 consultative document was more circumspect. These views from central government were based on fairly comprehensive cost concepts, ranging over many but not all relevant services and agencies. A more partial or fragmented view of costs—such as a health authority calculating only its own expenditure implications of closing a hospital—would be likely to encourage overenthusiastic internal support for such a closure policy, especially because until the *1990 National Health Service and Community Care Act*, public sector health and social services authorities could transfer much of the cost of community care on to the social security budget by encouraging people to use private and voluntary sector nursing homes and residential care homes. This expensive loophole has now been closed, with the associated intention to provide care for people in more appropriate domiciliary-based settings. This chapter will return to the comparative cost and fragmented expenditure questions later, for these have been among the more contentious issues in the UK community care debate.

Other criticisms of community care practice (and lack of policy) prior to the 1990 Act centered on the uncompensated, inequitable burdens placed on relatives and neighbors (and women in particular), the speed of hospital rundown compared with the slow development of community facilities, and the neglect of disabled and defenseless people without adequate assistance or personal resources. There was also, it was argued, insufficient recognition of a continuing need for asylum, not necessarily in "large or isolated institutions ... [but] in a physical and psychological sense [perhaps] in the middle of a normal residential community" (House of Commons Social Services Committee, 1985, para. 26). Some of these criticisms of government policy started out as hypotheses constructed from observations of the mistakes that were made in parts of the USA and Italy when hospitals were emptied over-hastily (see, for example Kirk & Therrein, 1975; Scull, 1984; Jones & Poletti, 1985, 1986; Torrey, 1988), although they are not unique to modern times (for example, see Titmuss, 1963; Brown *et al.*, 1966; Jones, 1972). What many of the accounts of community care failure themselves fail to do is to distinguish between the discharge of long-stay hospital residents into the community and the diversion (or early discharge) of people who would previously have become inpatients (or stayed longer). This was an unfortunate and slightly distracting oversight in the 1985 House of Commons Social Services Committee Report, for example, and continues to arise.

> It is perhaps surprising—although possibly revealing of the current climate of opinion in the UK—that such an ill-researched and poorly reasoned polemic [as Weller (1989)] can find its way into the prestigious columns of *Nature*. None can doubt Dr Weller's sincere desire to protect the long-term mentally ill from precipitate discharge from hospital and inadequate services in the community, but the way in which he plays "fast and loose" with the figures is really very difficult to defend.... Weller raises some important points, but his failure to distinguish between the needs of the people who can no longer get *in* to the psychiatric system, as opposed to the

> needs of the people who may have just been thrown out, seriously undermines his arguments (Shepherd, 1990, p. 279).

These logical errors notwithstanding, the fundamentally correct point was that "community care [had] become a slogan, with all the weakness that implies" (House of Commons Social Services Committee, 1985, para. 8). It was not a rounded policy. The inadequacy of much previous research, particularly the neglect of the costs dimension, is a direct corollary of the inadequacy of policy—both were preoccupied for too long with the rundown of hospitals, making a few concerted attempts to tackle the problem of developing good community care.

Community care policy in the UK in the 1990s—covering community health care and social care—seeks to move away from treatment, support, and placement decisions which are dominated by available patterns of supply, towards a system which is strongly influenced by the needs and preferences of patients and users. The policy also puts great emphasis on community-based alternatives to institutional care, shifting the balance away from hospitals, nursing homes, and residential care facilities towards smaller, more domestic accommodation arrangements *where this is possible.* A third key feature of community health and social care policy is the emphasis on developing a mixed economy, introducing an "internal market" within the health service and encouraging private and voluntary suppliers of social services and some mental health services. Although not currently on the political agenda, there will doubtless soon be moves to shift more of the financial responsibility for purchasing health and social care on to patients and users and away from taxpayers. At present, the formal care systems are heavily dominated by public expenditure. (For more details and discussions of these reforms see, for example, Wistow *et al.*, 1994.)

THE COST-EFFECTIVENESS QUESTION

One of the most comprehensive evaluations of psychiatric hospital closure and community "re-provision" is being conducted in North London. The Team for the Assessment of Psychiatric Services (TAPS), under the direction of Professor Julian Leff, and the Personal Social Services Research Unit (PSSRU), University of Kent at Canterbury, are evaluating the community care arrangements set in place to allow the closure of Friern and Claybury Hospitals. Full details of this wide-ranging evaluation are given elsewhere (Leff, 1993; Hallam *et al.*, 1994), but a number of findings by these research teams help to illustrate both the pitfalls of inadequate cost analyses and the benefits that can flow from a more complete picture. This chapter focuses mainly on former Friern and Claybury long-stay inpatients who, if aged over 65, do not have a current diagnosis of dementia. Data are also being gathered on acute patients and elderly people with dementia, but the associated analyses are as yet incomplete.

One of the important early findings to emerge from this study is that "psychiatric reprovision" in the community is less costly and more cost-effective than hospital residence for the first six annual cohorts of leavers. It is certainly the case that less dependent people left hospital in the first few years of the hospital closure programs (see below), and that their costs in the community were often comparatively low. But for the whole long-stay population in each hospital, the extrapolated costs of community care are probably not much greater than hospital costs (Knapp *et al.*, 1990, 1995). Outcomes thus far are at least as good and probably marginally better in the community (Anderson *et al.*, 1993).

These findings are for *groups* of people, but individual experiences and costs can be markedly different. It must be recognized that good community care is not necessarily or always cheaper than hospital provision, although it may prove more cost-effective. But on its own this is still an inadequate basis for moving forward, for we need to know for *whom* and under *what circumstances* is community care more cost-effective than hospital. By moving away from the grand generalization and the reliance on broad averages, attention is properly focused on individuals, their needs and the consequences for their carers and the associated individual costs and outcomes. This in turn encourages attention to be focused on the appropriate *balance* between community and hospital care, rather than viewing the two settings as stark opposites.

Individual level data are, however, costly to collect in terms of both research time and conceptualization. For example, comparatively few evaluations of psychiatric service innovations have analyzed or presented their findings below the aggregate or group level. Conclusions to the effect that community psychiatric nurses (CPNs) are "more cost-effective" than routine psychiatric follow-ups as found by Magnen *et al.* (1983), are certainly interesting and, as demonstrated by this well-designed study, undoubtedly valid. But this and other evaluative studies would be additionally useful if—data permitting—further analyses were conducted at the level of the individual patient or user. Are there, for example, people for whom CPNs are *not* the most cost-effective option? And if so, are there (simple) procedures available to psychiatric service managers to identify these people?

The need for sensitivity to differences in individual circumstances, community placement options, areas of the country, collaborative links between care agencies, and so on is particularly important in relation to hospital closure. Community-based provision will be more cost-effective than hospital for some people, and for some it will be less. Häfner (1987) illustrated this problem by noting that the total costs of "complementary care" in psychiatric homes and group homes in Mannheim amounted to an average of only 43% of the costs of continuous inpatient hospital care for a cohort of 145 people with schizophrenia admitted to inpatient treatment, and followed in a prospective study. But for eight of these 145 people, the complementary care was *more* costly than continuous hospital treatment: "certain patients require such intensive care that it is more economical to treat them in in-patient than extra-mural services" (Häfner, 1987, p. 123). In the North London hospital closure study, a third of the people who left hospital in the first 5 years of the reprovision program had costs after 1 year in the community which were greater than the average hospital cost at the start of the program (and for 2% of people, community care was more than 40% more costly than hospital). In other studies with which I have been associated, there have been sizeable numbers of people in the lowest cost *group* whose *individual* costs have nevertheless been much higher than the average for the highest cost group (Knapp *et al.*, 1994; McCrone *et al.*, 1994).

Ideally, the evaluative evidence offered about alternative treatment modes or locations will be more than just descriptive, and will offer *predictive* advice: treatment option A is less costly (more cost-effective or whatever) than option B for persons with characteristic X and under familial or social circumstances Y. For example, Knapp *et al.* (1996) describe how costs four years after admission either to inpatient treatment or to an intensive community-based support service (the Maudsley Daily Living Program) could be partially predicted by the characteristics of patients at admission. The *cost prediction equations* were estimated by multiple regression analysis and used as the basis for standardized cost comparisons between the inpatient and community groups. These revealed the probable differential costs of the two treatment options for people with different combinations of symptoms and characteristics.

The psychiatric reprovision study in North London could not examine this exact same question because available data on inpatient costs were not disaggregated to a sufficiently low level to permit the estimation of a hospital cost prediction equation, but other disaggregated cost and cost-effectiveness analyses have been undertaken and are described below. Disaggregated enquiries are to be encouraged to suggest caution, for grand, dramatic policy shifts might be justified on the basis of broad research generalizations, but they also need focused, individual-level understandings to offer a better information base for matching resources to needs.

FRAGMENTATION OF FUNDING: COST-EFFECTIVENESS FOR WHOM?

Problems can often arise with incomplete information. Most of the cost data routinely available to policy-makers are incomplete. Inpatient treatment costs fall mainly to hospitals and the health authorities which manage them. For long-stay psychiatric hospital patients in England, treatment costs to agencies other than the National Health Service amount to no more than about 4% of the total (Knapp *et al.*, 1987). The community care cost distribution is very different. For the recent leavers from long-stay inpatient care in Friern and Claybury hospitals only 50% of the aggregate costs fall to the health service (Hallam *et al.*, 1995). The other costs of community support are picked up by local authority social services, housing and education departments, voluntary organizations, social security budgets, and users (often subsidized out of pensions or social security benefits) and their informal carers. The aggregate costs of community-based psychiatric services may exceed the costs of the hospitals they are intended to replace—they certainly do for some individuals, as we have just seen—and community-based services may also be no more effective than hospital for some people. Under these circumstances and for these people, a policy based only on health service costs would be inappropriately encouraging the emptying of the hospitals. Without sight of the "hidden costs" of all care options we cannot expect policies to be taking us in the direction of a more sensible allocation of available resources. And even if some of the hidden costs are not readily expressed in monetary magnitudes, there is no reason why they should not be included in an evaluative study and taken into account in the policy process (Glass & Goldberg, 1977; Jones *et al.*, 1980).

One reason why there are often sizeable hidden costs is the fragmentation of funding of services for persons with a mental illness and the multiple lines of managerial responsibility. No single public agency in the UK can shift the balance of provision unilaterally and guarantee an adequate quality of service. Even when all services are offered by public sector agencies, flows of funds across agencies, together with flows of users and responsibilities, must often be painfully negotiated to effect any satisfactory shift.

This is again well illustrated by the difficulty of setting up community care services for people leaving hospital. Local authorities, facing central government grant penalties ("capping") and bombarded with demands upon their limited budgets, may be reluctant to set up services for former health service patients without a subsidy. They may also receive little encouragement to participate: transferred payments from health authorities are often made net of any social security benefits, sometimes leaving little scope for capital development or peripatetic support. Resettled hospital patients can stretch an already heavily demanded local authority service like day care or peripatetic social work support.

There may be other difficulties, especially if financial transfers from hospital to community budgets are based on the present average costs of running hospitals. It is usually the least dependent inpatients who move out first to the community, and the cost of providing for them in hospital is below the hospital average. On top of this, many overhead costs are not saved until wards or perhaps whole hospitals close down. If money is transferred from hospital based on an overall average cost, the result will be a faster rate of financial transfer than warranted by the cost savings, and hospitals will be left with insufficient resources for their most dependent inpatients.

The alternative, of course, is that hospitals try to hang on to the money (and maybe, therefore, also the patients) to the detriment of community-oriented programs of care. Many proposed developments in acute services—psychiatric or otherwise—can only be funded from the run-down of inpatient hospital care for chronic patients. There is a strong economic incentive to move the patient without the money, and that surely was much too common in Britain in previous decades and in other countries—notably parts of the United States and Italy—more recently. The loss of money may not be the only disincentive, of course, for hospital staff—especially nursing staff—may be reluctant to participate in rehabilitation programs which appear to threaten their livelihoods or—and this now seems more common in the UK—it is the younger and more mobile staff who move from hospital to community employment first, leaving some hospitals with difficulties.

VALID COMPARISONS

It must not be forgotten that the people discharged from hospitals over the past two decades in the UK are quite different from those who are yet to move to be supported in the community. Most hospitals have released their least dependent residents first, leaving behind a group of people who on average need greater help and support. In these circumstances, it would be easy for projections of the future

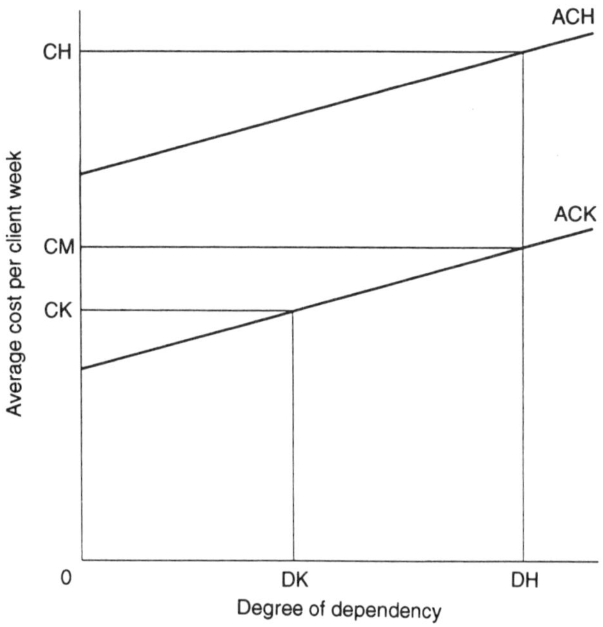

Figure 1. Costs and dependency for hospital and community care.

responsibilities of community care to underestimate the real cost to health and social service agencies and to society as a whole. The situation is complicated by many extant financial transfer arrangements. As just argued, using the average cost of hospital care as the baseline for financial transfers will leave hospitals depleted of resources. As each successive person leaves hospital, the average hospital cost must rise, first because the overhead costs are spread between fewer individuals and, second, because the average dependency of the hospital population will rise as the most able people tend to leave first. This can be illustrated with the help of Figure 1.

The two lines of the graph represent the average cost of care in hospital (ACH) and in the community (ACK). Each is drawn to represent average cost as an increasing function of dependency (with the latter defined as an amalgam of symptoms, self-care skills, behavioral problems and so on). We can assume that hospital is always more expensive than community care, although it is easy to demonstrate that relaxing this assumption by allowing hospital costs to be *lower* than community costs for people of higher levels of dependency will strengthen the argument below. The "average inpatient" is rather more dependent (DH) than the average community-based client (DK). This reflects the finding that hospital is not only more costly than community care on a like-with-like basis, but that the average hospital patient is also the more dependent. A health authority which seeks to resettle the "average" hospital patient will have to find, not funding amounting to CK, but the larger sum CM. Thus the savings of dehospitalization will be exaggerated by today's observed average costs. The outcome could well be underfunding of the new community placements for the former hospital residents.

Of course, the typical dehospitalization policy not only resettles the "easiest" or less dependent people first, but tends to move people into the community who are more dependent than the community average. (On the diagram, this would be illustrated by the movement of someone of dependency between DK and DH from hospital to community.) The result is that *both* average dependency and average cost go up in *both* settings. Policy-makers will observe inflated costs in hospital and in the community, causing them some anxiety if they originally supported a dehospitalization policy on the grounds of economy. (For example, cost per inpatient week in English non-teaching psychiatric hospitals was almost three times higher in real terms in 1984–85 than it was 20 years earlier, with the real cost inflation as high as 32% in the last 5 years of that period. Not all of this inflation can be laid at the door of changes in patient "dependency"—and part of the dependency change is due not to the discharge policy but to the general aging of the hospital population—but this has undoubtedly had a marked effect.) The policy of altering the balance of provision away from inpatient care is, in fact, economical because *total* expenditure is falling.

CAPITAL FUNDING

The selective resettlement of the more independent hospital residents has some advantages, including reducing the risks sometimes associated with community reprovision and also reducing the initial bridging costs of new community services. But problems could arise later when subsequent cohorts of leavers present more behavioral problems or are more dependent on staff or informal carers for their activities of daily living, and when existing community facilities no longer have the spare capacity to accommodate them. This applies to living accommodation, day care, industrial and other "therapeutic" workshops, family practitioner services, and so on. The marginal cost of community-based services could well be very small for the early movers from the hospital, but the acute shortage of housing, the other demands on scarce day center places and employment schemes, and the apparently higher demands of ex-hospital patients on general practitioners (Hallam *et al.*, 1994) will combine to push up marginal costs for subsequent leavers. Part of this rising marginal cost is obviously the capital element—the need for newly-built or converted facilities.

It is clear from the earlier evaluation of the English Care in the Community demonstration program that pump-priming was absolutely essential for community care development, yet ordinarily health and social care agencies do not have sufficient resources "up front" to permit such an initial investment (Knapp *et al.*, 1992). The Friern and Claybury reprovision program would probably not have achieved the successes revealed by the outcomes research had there not been a well-planned capital funding program. In this paper it is not possible to address capital funding issues associated with community reprovision. What is clear, however, is that capital needs should be articulated and addressed *before* hospital closure programs commence.

COSTS, NEEDS, AND OUTCOMES

The links between expenditure and the effects of community and hospital care on patients or users and their carers should obviously be central to most policy and practice debates. We need a better understanding of the effects of patient characteristics on services (the needs question), the effects of service interventions on patient health and welfare (the outcome question), and the associated resource implications (the cost question). What little evidence has accumulated in the UK is broadly encouraging.

In the North London study, Anderson *et al.* (1993) report that the outcomes for former inpatients after 1 year in the community were at least as good as their "matched" counterparts who had remained in hospital. Moreover, their mental state and social disabilities were stable, the leavers had more diverse social networks, lived under less restrictive conditions, and preferred life in the community. There was also a clear link between costs and outcomes.

Employing data for people in the first three annual cohorts of leavers, variations in the cost of community care 1 year after discharge were examined alongside individual characteristics (many of them interpretable as needs) and changes in well-being (Beecham *et al.*, 1991). Outcomes were thus measured by the differences in scores on the instruments used to assess people in hospital and 1 year after discharge. Other factors examined in relation to the cost variations included certain characteristics of the care settings. Together, these factors could explain (statistically) almost two-thirds of the cost variation. Among other findings, there was an encouragingly strong link between costs and outcomes. Higher community care costs (higher levels of spending) were associated with greater improvements in the health and welfare of former hospital inpatients. In particular, improvements in negative symptoms, delusions and hallucinations, social networks (broadening), and the general need for care (from an index of physical health) were all associated with higher costs.

The earlier evaluation of the Care in the Community demonstration program found that former long-stay hospital residents were quite well integrated into a number of community-based activities a year after discharge, were more likely to express positive attitudes about their activities in the community than they did about their activites in hospital, had more opportunities to make choices, and experienced no changes in skills, behavioral problems, or symptoms (Knapp *et al.*, 1992). There was again a link between costs and outcomes, although with a smaller sample and a less comprehensive set of outcome measures.

CONCLUSIONS

The UK policy of emptying the long-stay hospitals has gathered a momentum which is unlikely to stop. There remain numerous challenges, although—as illustrated by some of the evidence summarized in this chapter—there is an accumulation of material and experience which should help the policy and practice communities to rise to the challenge. The experience and evidence suggest at least four "resource keys" to the successful reprovision of support for people with mental health problems in community settings.

RESOURCE ADEQUACY

The development of alternatives to long-term in-patient care requires inputs from a range of services, in turn demanding the adequate funding of service-providing agencies. In the North London dehospitalization program, the transfer of funds from the hospital budgets has generally been adequate to finance good quality community care. Capital funding has been made available. On average across the research sample, these service inputs have produced a quality of community care and brought changes in individual health and welfare that are no worse than long-stay hospital residence, and in some respects significantly better. Resource adequacy is clearly fundamental to successful community care.

RESOURCE TIMELINESS

Community care services need these funds early, and often *before* hospitals can release them. Timely funding is necessary in order to finance capital investment, to recruit and train staff, and to build services up to their full or most economical operating levels. This will often require bridging funds or some form of "double funding" of hospitals as they run down towards closure (see Renshaw *et al.*, 1988, ch. 10; Knapp, 1990). There is also the need for the financial capacity to respond flexibly to changing individual needs. Generally, service planning and capital investment need to precede, not follow changes to the locus of care.

RESOURCE DISTRIBUTION

The funding balance needs to change, not only to move resources from hospitals to the community, but also from health service budgets to other agencies. The financial responsibilities of community reprovision are not distributed in the same way as hospital-related costs. This also implies a need for coordination between the different purchasers and providers to ensure that appropriate, equitable, and efficient care is offered.

RESOURCE COORDINATION

This feeds directly into the fourth "resource key." Service coordination is needed at both the micro- and the macro-levels—for area planning as well as case planning. Care management offers a route to the better coordination of services for individual service users (and can simultaneously extend the influence of user choice over service arrangements), while long-term strategic planning involving all relevant public, voluntary, and private agencies—as well as user and carer representatives—would help to set the broader context within which service and quality of life improvements can be made.

Hospital closures offer long-stay residents the opportunity to establish new life-styles in the community. The costs of failure will be reckoned in terms of neglect, destitution, homelessness, perhaps criminality, and certainly high rates of inpatient readmission. Turning the right "resource keys" will help to prevent these failures and will help to ensure that people with mental health problems making the momentous moves from hospital residence to the community enjoy a good quality of life.

ACKNOWLEDGMENTS

My thanks to CEMH and PSSRU colleagues, especially Jeni Beecham, Andrew Healey and Sandra Semple, for comments on earlier versions of some of the arguments in this paper.

REFERENCES

Anderson, J., Dayson, D., Wills, W., *et al.* (1993). Clinical and social outcomes of long-stay psychiatric patients after one year in the community. *British Journal of Psychiatry*, **162** (Suppl.), 45–56.

Audit Commission (1986) *Making a Reality of Community Care*. London: HMSO.

Barton, R. (1959). *Institutional Neurosis*. Bristol: Wright.

Bayley, M. (1973). *Mental Handicap and Community Care*. London: Routledge & Kegan Paul.

Beecham, J., Knapp, M., and Fenyo, A. (1991). Costs, needs and outcomes: community care for people with long-term mental health problems. *Schizophrenia Bulletin*, **17**, 427–439.

Belnap, I. (1956). *Human Problems of a State Mental Hospital*. New York: McGraw-Hill.

Brown, G.W. *et al.* (1966). *Schizophrenia and Social Care*. Oxford University Press.

Bulmer, M. (1987.) *Social Basis of Community Care*. London: Allen & Unwin.

Cm 849 (1980). *Caring for People: Community Care in the Next Decade and Beyond*. London: HMSO.

Cmnd 6233 (1975). *Better Services for the Mentally Ill*. London: HMSO.

Davidge, M., Elias, S., Jayes, B., Wood, K., and Yates, J. (1993). *Survey of English Mental Illness Hospitals, March 1993*. Paper prepared for The Mental Health Task Force, Department of Health.

Department of Health and Social Security (1981a). *Care in the Community: A Consultative Document on Moving Resources for Care in England*. London: Department of Health and Social Security.

Department of Health and Social Security (1981b). *Care in Action*. London: HMSO.

Department of Health and Social Security (1987). *Public Support for Residential Care: Report of a Joint Central and Local Government Working Party* (Firth Report). London: HMSO.

Freeman, H. and Farndale, J. (eds) (1963). Wanderers in a promised land: the chronically mentally ill and deinstitutionalization. *Medical Care*, **22** (Suppl.), 12.

Glass, N.J. and Goldberg, D. (1977). Cost–benefit analysis and the evaluation of psychiatric services. *Psychological Medicine*, **7**, 701–707.

Goffman, I. (1961). *Asylums: Essays on the Social Situation of Mental Patients and other Inmates*. Harmondsworth: Penguin.

Goodwin, S. (1989). Community care for the mentally ill in England and Wales: myths, assumptions and reality. *Journal of Social Policy*, **18**, 27–52.

Griffiths, R. (1988). *Community Care: Agenda for Action*. London: HMSO.

Häfner, H. (1987). Do we still need beds for psychiatric patients? *Acta Psychiatrica Scandinavica*, **75**, 113–126.

Hallam, A., Knapp, M.R.J., Beecham, J., and Fenyo, A. (1995). Eight years of psychiatric reprovision: an economic evaluation. In M.R.J. Knapp, ed., *The Economic Evaluation of Mental Health Care*. Aldershot: Ashgate.

House of Commons Social Services Committee (1985). *Community Care*. HCP 13-1, Session 1984–85. London: HMSO.

Jones, K. (1972). *A History of Mental Health Services*. London: Routledge & Kegan Paul.

Jones, K. (1981). Re-inventing the wheel. In *Mind, Future of the Mental Hospitals: A Report of Mind's 1980 Annual Conference*. Brighton: Marshallarts Print Services.

Jones, K. and Poletti, A. (1985). Understanding the Italian experience. *British Journal of Psychiatry*, **146**, 341–347.

Jones, K. and Poletti, A. (1986). Italian experience reconsidered. *British Journal of Psychiatry*, **148**, 144–150.

Jones, R. *et al.* (1980). A comparison of two different services treating schizophrenia: a cost–benefit approach. *Psychological Medicine*, **10**, 493–505.

Kendell, R.E. (1989). The future of Britain's mental hospitals. *British Medical Journal*, **299**, 1237–1238.

Kirk, S. and Therrein, M. (1975). Community mental health myths and the fate of former hospitalized patients. *Psychiatry*, **38**, 209–217.

Knapp, M. (1990). Economic barriers to innovation in mental health care. In *Mental Health Care Delivery: Innovations, Impediments and Implementation*. Cambridge University Press.

Knapp, M., Renshaw, J., and Beecham, J. (1987). The cost-effectiveness of psychiatric reprovision services. Discussion Paper 533, Personal Social Services Research Unit, University of Kent at Canterbury.

Knapp, M., Beecham, J., Anderson, J., *et al.* (1990). Predicting the community costs of closing a psychiatric hospital, *British Journal of Psychiatry*, **157**, 661–670.

Knapp, M., Cambridge, P., Darton, P., *et al.* (1992). *Care in the Community: Challenge and Demonstration*. Aldershot: Ashgate.

Knapp, M., Beecham, J., Fenyo, A., and Hallam, A. (1995). Community mental health care for former hospital patients: predicting costs from needs and diagnosis. *British Journal of Psychiatry*, **160** (Suppl. 27), 10–18.

Knapp, M., Beecham, J., Koutsogeorgopoulou, V., *et al.* (1994). Service use and costs of home-based versus hospital-based care for people with serious mental illness. *British Journal of Psychiatry*, **165**, 195–203.

Knapp, M.R.J., Wolstenholme, J., Marks, I., *et al.* (1996). Cost-effectiveness over four years of home-based versus hospital-based care for people with serious mental illness. *Archives of General Psychiatry*, forthcoming.

Korman, N. and Glennester, H. (1990). *Hospital Closure*. Milton Keynes: Open University Press.

Leff, J. (ed.) (1993). The TAPS project: Evaluating community placement of long-stay psychiatric patients. *British Journal of Psychiatry*, **162** (Suppl.).

McCrone, P., Beecham, J., and Knapp, M.R.J. (1994). Community psychiatric nurse teams: cost-effectiveness of intensive support versus generic care. *British Journal of Psychiatry*, **165**, 218–221.

Mangen, S.P., Paykel, E.S., Griffiths, J.H., Burchell, A., and Mancini, P. (1983). Cost-effectiveness of community psychiatric nurse or out-patient psychiatrist care of neurotic patients. *Psychological Medicine*, **13**, 407–416.

Martin, F.M. (1984). *Between the Acts: Community Mental Health Services, 1959–1983*. London: Nuffield Provincial Hospitals Trust.

Ministry of Health (1962). *A Hospital Plan for England and Wales.* Cmnd 1604. London: HMSO.

Morris, P. (1969). *Put Away: A Sociological Study of Institutions for the Mentally Retarded.* London: Routledge & Kegan Paul.

Renshaw, J., Hampson, R., Thomason, C., Datron, R., Judge, J., and Knapp, M. (1989). *Care in the Community: The First Steps.* Aldershot: Gower.

Scull, A. (1984). *Decarceration: Community Treatment and the Deviant: A Radical View,* 2nd edn. Cambridge: Polity Press.

Shepherd, G. (1990). Rehabilitation and the long-term mentally ill. *Current Opinion in Psychiatry,* **3**, 278–283.

Shepherd, M. (1989). Primary care of patients with mental disorder in the community. *British Medical Journal,* **299**, 666–669.

Stanton, A.H. and Schwartz, M.S. (1954). *The Mental Hospital: A Study of Institutional Participation in Psychiatric Illness and Treatment.* New York: Basic Books.

Titmuss, R. (1963). Community care: fact or fiction? In H. Freeman, ed., *Trends in the Mental Health Services.* London: Pergamon Press.

Torrey, E.F. (1988). *Nowhere To Go.* New York: Harper & Row.

Walker, A. (1982). *Community Care: The Family: the State and Social Policy.* Oxford: Blackwell.

Weller, M.P.I. (1989). Mental Illness: who cares? *Nature,* **339**, 249–252.

Wing, J.K. (1990). The functions of asylum. *British Journal of Psychiatry,* **157**, 822–827.

Wing, J.K. and Brown, G.W. (1970). *Institutionalism and Schizophrenia.* Cambridge University Press.

Wistow, G., Knapp, M., Hardy, B., and Allen, C. (1994). *Social Care in a Mixed Economy.* Buckingham: Open University Press.

41

Funding the Continuum of Care: a Rational Social Policy for the Care and Support of Persons with Schizophrenia

ANNE M. STOLINE and STEVEN S. SHARFSTEIN
Sheppard Pratt Health System, University of Maryland, Baltimore, Maryland, USA

The lack of comprehensive private insurance coverage and the need for restraint or control of those with behavior dangerous or outside societal norms create a need for publicly funded services to care for those suffering from mental illnesses. The policies creating and funding these services have influenced the types of mental health services and the development of the public health sector. In fact, it is difficult to underestimate the effects of public policies and private insurance coverage on clinical care and the development of health care delivery systems. As a result of these factors, the evolution of mental health service systems, treatment, and scientific progress all reflect their close relationship to financing.

This chapter will explore the relationship between funding and mental health services. It will describe the problems in the current non-system of care, as well as make proposals for more rational financing and service systems, with a particular emphasis on funding a continuum of care for patients with schizophrenia.

HISTORIC BACKGROUND

Mental health care in the USA in the nineteenth century was generally purchased directly by patients or their families. States also had a role in care provision through contracts bid by individual homeowners. Some of the mentally ill were kept in local prisons. Specialized institutional care was a new form of housing and treatment for those with mental illness. Over time, asylums became the most common treatment facility, initially intended to provide individualized care and an attitude hopeful for recovery. As the number of chronically ill individuals increased, these idealistic attitudes declined, transforming institutions in the latter half of the nineteenth century into large public warehouses for those with mental illnesses.

Between the late nineteenth century and the Second World War, many states shifted financial and service delivery responsibilities from the local or county level to the state level. Although the intention of these policies was to improve the quality

Handbook of Mental Health Economics and Health Policy, Volume I, Schizophrenia. Edited by M. Moscarelli, A. Rupp and N. Sartorius.
© 1996 John Wiley & Sons Ltd.

of care and treatment of the mentally ill, the state institutions which evolved during this time were convenient facilities for housing elderly and cognitively impaired citizens without financial resources. As turnover rates decreased, the state facilities developed a chronic patient profile, with a much higher proportion of long-term residents. The state assumed responsibility for custodial care for these patients, many of whom manifested behavioral or psychiatric symptoms for which no treatments were available. As state governments assumed the financial burden of caring for the chronically ill, clinical approaches changed in state asylums from active treatment to chronic custodial care; many patients were housed for years. Locally funded asylums disappeared, while state hospital populations and regulations grew.

Health insurance, both private and public, provided the impetus for change in the twentieth century. The first health insurance policies, created in the 1930s, generally excluded mental health services. These policy decisions reflected: ambiguous descriptions and classifications of mental disorders; misunderstanding of the types of care provided for mental disorders; perception that liberalization of benefits would unduly increase demand for services; the existence of public sector funding of these services; and the stigma attached to mental illness, substance abuse, and their treatments.

Reflecting the exclusion of mental health services from private insurance coverage, as well as the lack of reliable medical treatments for psychotic and affective symptoms, much of the treatment for those with severe mental illnesses such as schizophrenia remained in public institutions for the next 100 years.

These practice patterns were relatively stable until the mid-1950s. The number of persons hospitalized in state and county mental hospitals reached its peak of 558 900 at that time. Since then, remarkable changes have occurred in the role of public insitutions in the mental health sector, reflecting the process of deinstitutionalizing those with mental illness.

DEINSTITUTIONALIZATION—A PROCESS, NOT A POLICY

In the past 40 years, the balance has reversed between institutional and community care, inpatient and outpatient services, and individual and group practice. Deinstitutionalization, or the departure of thousands of individuals from the large state hospital system, has occurred over the last three decades and has had a significant impact on the mental health care delivery system. This process for patients began in 1955, a change reflecting both clinical and political developments.

CLINICAL FACTORS IN THE DEINSTITUTIONALIZATION PROCESS

The first major clinical factor in the deinstitutionalization process occurred in the mid-1950s with discovery of the major tranquilizers, thioridazine and chlorpromazine. These breakthroughs provided psychiatrists, for the first time, with pharmacologic tools effective in treating primary symptoms through reduction of hallucinations, delusions, and thought disorder, with secondary benefits of sedation and decreased aggressiveness. Reserpine's effectiveness in treating psychiatric symptoms was discovered at about the same time.

By allowing many patients to behave more rationally, these medicines facilitated patient discharge, or enabled them to avoid hospitalization entirely. As a result, many patients receiving treatment in an inpatient setting on the basis of aggressive or unmanageable behavior could be safely treated in an outpatient setting. Thus, clinical progress resulted from the introduction of major tranquilizers, and brought promise for the restoration of many patients, housed custodially for years in large public asylums, to community-based settings. As the philosophy of care shifted from an institutional to a community-based approach, the number of units in general hospitals increased, providing a source for short-term, hospital-based care. Effective drug treatment also stimulated the introduction of milieu therapy, halfway houses, and aftercare.

THE ROLE OF PRIVATE INSURERS IN THE DEINSTITUTIONALIZATION PROCESS

As the clinical care and management of psychiatric patients on an outpatient basis became possible, private insurance policies began including mental health services in the benefits package. For example, Blue Cross/Blue Shield in the early 1950s included coverage of inpatient services in general hospitals for psychiatric care on the same basis as all medical conditions.

Despite the inclusion of mental health services in benefit packages, however, private insurance companies do not cover mental health services at parity with other medical conditions.

> The vast majority of private insurance policies have *inside limits* in which psychiatric care is treated differently from other medical conditions. Inside limits include higher cost sharing and caps on outpatient visits and hospital days. These limits generally result in non-coverage of catastrophic expenses while providing a partial subsidy for expenditures up to an arbitrary limit. Patients then pay out-of-pocket, forego care, or when severely impaired, may seek care in the public sector (Sharfstein *et al.*, 1933).

As a result of inside limits, private insurance plans provide some financial protection for those with mental illness, although they generally fail to protect those with mental illness and their families against catastrophic financial losses. In addition, most private plans have lacked any coverage for the continuum of care, especially day treatment, psychosocial rehabilitation, and group homes. Outpatient care was most severely discriminated against.

As mental health coverage became more commonplace, public policy-makers were able to justify moving some patients out of state psychiatric facilities. Public facilities were still necessary, particularly for those with severe and persistent illness.

THE ROLE OF PUBLIC POLICIES IN THE DEINSTITUTIONALIZATION PROCESS

Public policy developments also encouraged the trend toward deinstitutionalizing the long-term residents of public psychiatric facilities. The Joint Commission on Mental Illness and Health was established by Congress in 1955 to examine the nation's mental health care. The commission's report, *Action for Mental Health*, was released in 1961. This group concluded that half the patients in the state mental hospitals were not receiving active treatment. They recommended establishing a national network of multidisciplinary community mental health clinics. The commission also recommended a bed limit of 1000 in psychiatric hospitals. Their encouragement of the use of community-based, short-term inpatient care, and outpatient care whenever possible, set the stage for the emphasis on community mental health care that marked the 1960s.

> Many of the commission's recommendations were incorporated in a 1963 Message to Congress by President Kennedy, the first presidential message Congress had ever received on behalf of the mentally ill and the mentally retarded. Congress responded with the Mental Retardation Facilities and Community Mental Health Centers Construction Act, which, in part, created federal support for community-based mental health services delivered by community mental health centers (Sharfstein *et al.*, 1995).

Passed during the era of rapid deinstitutionalization, the Community Mental Health Center (CMHC) Act was intended to address the needs of those without the resources to afford private outpatient care. These public subsidies were intended to support the belief that coordinated community-based services were the appropriate way to deliver mental health care as well as to provide a focus for the prevention of mental illness. The CMHC Act provided federal funds for the development of a network of outpatient day treatment and inpatient services, further shifting the cost of care of those with mental illness from the state government to the federal government. Reflecting the effects of this legislation, the number of CMHCs and public clinics increased substantially in the 1960s and 1970s.

To complement these subsidies for psychiatric care, federal welfare support and food stamps for those with established psychiatric disability provided a minimal level of economic support for those who were discharged from state facilities. Most of the long-term residents were ill-equipped to function independently in the community. Unfortunately, the necessary networks of community medical, mental health, and human service agencies which could have facilitated a successful transition of this population were inadequately organized and underfunded. There was no continuum of care.

From the outset the CHMC Program was very

long on promises and short on funding. It proclaimed public health goals to manage all the mental health as well as mental illness needs of a "catchment area," that is, a defined population and yet, provided limited Federal and matching State funding hoping that the shortfall in finances would be made up by private insurance. Limits on coverage in private insurance made this task problematic. The Vietnam War and health care cost inflation allowed less than one-half of the country's catchment areas to be funded with Federal grants. Conflicting priorities within local jurisdictions allowed for the diversion of these limited funds away from patients with schizophrenia, toward problems of adolescent children and families, the elderly, and those with substance abuse, leading to a relative neglect of the seriously and persistently ill patients with schizophrenia. As Federal funds declined, however, and State funds came into play, more programs emphasizing psychosocial rehab and day treatment were funded. It should be noted that the CMHC Program did bring these services into areas which previous to this Federal initiative, had virtually no expertise in the diagnosis and treatment for patients with schizophrenia. Yet on the whole, the Federal CMHC Program has been seen as contributing more to the problem of the deinstitutionalized schizophrenic patient than to the solution (Foley and Sharfstein, 1983, Torrey, 1988).

The 1965 legislation creating the Medicare and Medicaid programs represented a compromise to supporters of national health insurance reform. Medicare is the federal health insurance program for all people age 65 and over who are eligible for Social Security and for those under age 65 who have been receiving Social Security disability payments for at least 2 years. Medicaid is the program funded by federal and state governments to subsidize medical care for means-tested indigent persons in the USA. Medicare and Medicaid benefits have been structured to ensure that these programs would not pay for long-term custodial support of the mentally ill, either in public or in private hospitals. Neither program pays for extended care in free-standing psychiatric hospitals, with Medicare imposing a lifetime limit of 190 days in these facilities, and Medicaid excluding coverage for such services for beneficiaries aged 22–64. As a result of the policy decision to cover only the costs of acute services, many rehabilitative services for those with chronic and persistent mental illness remain uninsured by the public sector. Medicare and Medicaid also encouraged the shift of many patients with chronic illness from state facilities to alternative housing as well as nursing homes, in an effort to reduce state financial burdens. Despite their limitations, since 1966 the Medicare and Medicaid programs have shifted many of the costs of caring for the mentally ill to the federal treasury.

SUBSEQUENT PUBLIC AND PRIVATE POLICY TRENDS

From the liberal increases in public spending which characterized the 1960s, concerns about cost began in the 1970s and continued to the present time. The 1970s saw a decline in federal support for mental health research and training and slow growth in funding for CMHCs. Fiscal retrenchment continued in the 1980s, with increasing numbers of Americans on the poverty rolls, cutbacks in programs for the poor, and an increase in the number of homeless.

The desire for minimal government prevailed throughout the 1980s and early 1990s. President Clinton's election in 1992 reflected another shift in national mood, as many Americans became dissatisfied enough with the health care system to support major reform. (Reform proposals put forth by the Clinton Administration will be described later.)

The private insurance sector has generally followed trends set by the Medicare and Medicaid programs. Private insurance policies have not covered long-term treatment costs, and have also implemented serious cost control efforts in the last decade.

As a result, responsibility has fallen to state and local agencies to provide services and subsidies for those with severe and persistent illness. As public budgets have plateaued or dwindled in this era of fiscal constraint, programs providing these services have had reduced ability to provide services adequate in quality and quantity.

COST SHIFTING AND ITS EFFECTS

Many cost control policies reflect *cost shifting*, which occurs when one group's policies or financial services leave unmet needs which are then assumed by another group, either directly or indirectly, through price increases. Cost shifting is ubiquitous in the current non-system of care, both between private and public insurance and treatment programs, and within these systems, such as shifts between federal, state, and local systems.

Cost-shifting highlights the piecemeal nature of the US health care system. Cost control efforts in the public and private sectors affect only one part of the system at a time—like squeezing a balloon, reduction in one area causes expansion in another. As a result, the elusive goal of overall improvement in the economic health of the system has not been achieved.

Similar to cost shifting, reduction of the inpatient state hospital census led to increases in outpatient and community treatment populations. The ability of these systems to adapt to this shift is explored in the next section.

EFFECTS OF THE DEINSTITUTIONALIZATION PROCESS

Several factors in today's mental health sector have resulted in the movement of patients and money in an unplanned manner, including emptying state hospitals, cost shifting, and budget constraints. Without adequate community and private financial protection or active treatment, reinstitutionalization of those with severe and persistent mental illness is perhaps an inevitable consequence of these non-policies.

Although admissions to state mental hospitals and the number of psychiatric beds in general hospitals increased dramatically during the deinstitutionalization era, most admissions were actually readmissions. This has been termed the "revolving door" syndrome, with patients admitted for multiple brief stays. Nursing homes have also become a substitute for state mental hospitals, assuming a long-term-care function. Currently, nearly one million Americans with chronic mental illness reside in nursing homes.

> Decline in the use of state hospitals has had negative effects. Many patients—perhaps a million—have been discharged into communities that are ill-prepared to provide the therapeutic and rehabilitative services they need, such as halfway houses, aftercare programs, sheltered workshops, and psychosocial rehabilitation. Many patients now reside in unlicensed and uninspected board-and-care homes that do not offer or arrange active treatment. Some have become homeless wanderers, shifted from the back wards to living on the streets.
>
> As a result of failed public and private health policy decisions, a major public mental health problem in this country became the sight of the homeless with mental illness wandering the streets, often hallucinating, rummaging through garbage and sleeping on grates. This issue more than others has received attention through legislative hearings, the media, and public outcry. It is symptomatic of the release of thousands of patients from state facilities and the imperfect psychiatric technology that can help patients in the acute phase of a psychosis but does not provide a long-term cure. Patients have found themselves in underfunded community mental health programs, and when they discontinue treatment, they are readmitted to hospitals for short-term stays (Sharfstein *et al.*, 1995).

INCENTIVES: HOW TO MOVE THE MAJORITY OF PATIENTS TO THE LEAST COSTLY AND MOST EFFECTIVE SETTING FOR TREATMENT OF SCHIZOPHRENIA: FUNDING THE CONTINUUM OF CARE

The USA now has almost a 15-year history of private and public sector efforts toward cost containment, but these efforts have been without major success. Some analysts feel that this failure is attributable to the piecemeal nature of reform.

Global budgeting sets a total spending cap within which resource effectiveness is maximized. By eliminating cost shifting, this approach theoretically permits payers and providers to assess the effects of their behavior and prohibits overruns and expansions in other systems from creating false appearances of cost control. It is conceivable that real success will be possible only with a national health reform effort, such as all other industrialized nations (with the exception of South Africa) have implemented. Whether such reforms will be implemented in the USA depends on conducive sociopolitical factors.

Because of the close connection between reimbursement method and provider incentives, the method of financing health services strongly impacts the types of services provided and the demand for those services. In creating programs and financing existing services for the treatment of schizophrenia, policy-makers are challenged to optimize resources through reimbursement methods which maximize benefits from their investments (whether public or private).

REIMBURSEMENT TO ORGANIZED SYSTEMS OF CARE

Fee-for-service reimbursement has been the mainstay financing method in the US health care system. While this method has advantages in clinician flexibility, its potential disadvantages include an inflationary more-is-better incentive. Policy-makers in the cost control era have searched for methods offering incentives for care providers to use resources in a cost-conscious manner. Capitation is one such method.

> [Under capitation,] the self-insured corporation or the insurer pays a provider organization in advance on a per head or "capitated" basis for the care of a group of employees. In return for this payment, the provider organization agrees to provide all necessary care to the group for a predetermined period of time; thus, total payment is independent of the amount of services eventually given.
>
> Such an arrangement usually occurs only within ... non-traditional delivery settings such as HMOs ... Capitation plans rarely require cost sharing except for small co-payments for some services. Services are usually comprehensive in scope, although with limited depth. HMOs usually offer a broader benefit package than conventional private insurance policies, including preventive care, immunizations, and annual checkups. The enrollee has no financial disincentive to use the HMO, as there is no significant additional cost once the capitation payment is made. Therefore, financial survival of the HMO requires that services be limited. Nonfinancial barriers may include time delays between appointment and visit, telephone triage using gatekeepers, and visit limits. Since all psychotherapy depends on development of a therapeutic alliance, mental health patients may be put off by bureaucratic procedures, in many cases opting to forego treatment.
>
> Federal standards have been developed for HMOs. Minimal mental health care benefits include short-term (up to twenty visits) outpatient evaluation and crisis intervention mental health services, medical treatment, and referral services for alcohol and drug abuse or addiction. Of note, it is thus possible to meet federal standards without offering inpatient psychiatric coverage. Furthermore, the federally legislated benefits do not entitle the enrollee to care; while gatekeepers and other bureaucratic procedures concurrently used to minimize resource use to not technically prohibit the use of services, in reality that is often the result.
>
> The financial incentives facing the HMO organization may be different from the incentives facing the providers it employs. However, these incentives may be tightly linked through contractual arrangements that pass along financial risk to the provider. Alternatively, the link may be quite loose, with the organization absorbing the financial risk. It is therefore difficult to generalize about the effects of financing on care received within an HMO. However, it is clear that because the HMO receives lump payment in advance for the care of all patients, the incentive is to provide as few services as possible, so as to maximize revenue. The provider organization and its practitioners (depending on the contractual financial arrangement) bear the financial risk instead of the third-party payer or enrollee. Because the capitation payment depends only on the number of people cared for, rather than on the quantity of services, there is no incentive to maximize the volume of services provided. In fact, there is some incentive to enroll more members and provide fewer services for each.
>
> As a result of this potential for compromise, much has been written about HMOs concerning their financial incentives and the resulting quality of care that patients receive compared to other health care delivery systems. Opinions about quality of care differ, although anecdotal evidence would suggest that at least some enrollees receive suboptimal care. However, the main conclusion is that HMOs save money over FFS systems because of the low rate of patient hospitalization (for medical and surgical conditions)—about 40 percent lower than within FFS systems. The lower rate of hospitalization within HMOs does not represent a higher quality of medical care. Apart from the financial incentive not to hospitalize, healthier enrollees self-select into HMOs. Given that HMOs are not mandated to provide inpatient psychiatric care, their rate of hospitalization for these conditions is likely even less than 40 percent of the rate within FFS systems (Stoline & Sharfstein, 1993).

PROSPECTIVE PAYMENT FOR THE SEVERELY MENTALLY ILL

Policy-makers considering reform opportunities for financing mental health services have access to a growing body of experience with previous efforts to use mental health resources in a cost-effective manner. Public policies have several advantages, including capitalizing on economies of scale, the ability to legislate and regulate when free market economic forces fail to control costs, and utilization of public budgets as prototypes for planned system of care. Efforts to reform financing and service delivery in private sector health care systems such as health maintenance organizations (HMOs) are evolving as well, as increasing numbers of HMOs are moving from acute to intermediate and long-term care models.

PROSPECTIVE PAYMENT

In a prior publication, one of the co-authors (SSS) proposed a prospective cost allocation methodology as a specific model to finance the continuum of care for patients with schizophrenia. This methodology provided for incentives for continuous interdisciplinary teams to assume total responsibility for a defined group of patients. This responsibility included case management of such services as: income maintenance, structured and supervised housing, psychosocial rehabilitation, and psychoeducation of families. What was critical to the model was the ability to provide access to an array of needed medical, psychiatric, and rehabilitative services. Flexibility was the key so that funding would be able to respond to the intermittent and changing needs of individuals with schizophrenia. This system of "prospective capitation" would set rates based on health, status, or risk for patients with schizophrenia. The methodology of "risk-adjusted capitation" is based on the patients' past use of services, current health status, and level of disability. The model proposed has been put into place in Rochester, New York. This funding system is designed to encourage the use of cost effective treatment in least restrictive settings with a special focus on outpatient, medication management, day treatment with an emphasis in psychosocial rehab, and less-restrictive residential facilities (Sharfstein, 1991).

RECENT EFFORTS TOWARD NATIONAL HEALTH REFORM

President Clinton's Health Care Task Force considered options for national health care reform. The group was asked to develop a proposal based on the principles of security, choice, quality, cost control, comprehensiveness, and simplicity. Prospective, capitated payment was the designated financing arrangement, as this approach was considered to have the best potential to provide high-quality, cost-effective services to those enrolled in a national health care plan.

The President's Task Force included a working group on mental health care, the only working group devoted to a specific diagnosis. This group was included in order to consider the aspects of mental health care unique from other health services, such as the existence of a large public mental health sector.

One option strongly considered by the Task Force's working group on mental health care was a mental health benefit covering a full continuum of care, with incentives to use alternatives to hospitalization and other outpatient services when clinically possible. The working group also considered the clinical, social, and financial ramifications of combining funding and services of the public and private mental health sectors. The Clinton proposal minimized a major risk of prospective payment—the tendency to minimize resource use for enrollees—by making health plan accountability an integral aspect of the proposal.

The working group's eventual proposal included a full continuum of care, accessed through benefit trade-offs. This strategy is intended to maximize flexibility of service provision and to permit treatment in the least restrictive (and least costly) setting. Merging of the public and private sectors in the year 2001 was endorsed, with states required to submit plans for these mergers in the late 1990. As a result, while the President's plan for national health reform is ambitious but does not offer immediate parity for mental health services, necessitating continuation of the public mental health sector.

Unfortunately, the President's proposal died during the Congressional debate in 1994. This creates problems for offering flexible benefits in a full range of treatment settings, and maintaining hope for full parity of benefits.

HOUSING, VOCATIONAL TRAINING AND ADVOCACY—OTHER ELEMENTS IN THE PROSPECTIVE PAYMENT APPROACH

Development of mental health policy should include the essential non-medical services needed by the severely mentally ill, most of which are inadequately reimbursed in the current system. In a 1976 paper, Boris Astrachan and coauthors elaborated the four major tasks included in comprehensive psychiatric care. *Medical tasks* under psychiatric care include inpatient and outpatient evaluation and treatment. These tasks are required to care for acute psychiatric conditions, as well as for exacerbations of chronic illness. *Humanistic tasks* foster personal growth and development, primarily through psychotherapeutic interventions. Psychiatric tasks with goals of *social control* overlap with legal enforcement and are required for persons with socially deviant behavior. *Reparative tasks* are intended to help in the rehabilitation of patients with psychiatric impairments and disability.

> Reparative needs begin while patients are acutely ill and continue into the recovery period. They are a particularly important component of the treatment plan for patients who remain severely and persistently ill. Reparative tasks include day care, assistance with household management skills, other types of community outreach, "Meals on Wheels" transportation, special education, vocational counseling and training, shopping assistance, protective services, and recreational activities.
>
> Reparative services are cost-effective and help to reduce hospital readmission rates. They also optimize a patient's potential for return to productive activity after the onset of severe psychiatric illness. Although some insurance policies cover outpatient, day hospital, and psychosocial rehabilitation programs, many Americans are without any coverage for such reparative services. Some patients and their families can pay for these services out of pocket, but most are unable to afford them, particularly after paying for the costs of acute care. Lack of financing for long-term support and rehabilitation of the chronically mentally ill is a public health disaster (Sharfstein Stoline, 1992).

Any effort toward comprehensive reform of the mental health sector should include coverage for these reparative tasks, as they are intimately related to the ultimate success or failure in rehabilitating many persons with psychiatric illness. Several demonstration projects in the USA have successfully included these services under capitated or flexible financing arrangements.

CONCLUSIONS

For patients with schizophrenia, flexibility in service delivery and financing is essential if patients are able to access the continuum of care. This continuum includes the most restrictive, staff intensive, and expansive inpatient alternative and also the full range of day treatment, residential, home and outpatient care alternatives. Opportunities for treatment and rehabilitation are essential for the care of the patient with schizophrenia. In the USA, ongoing efforts to implement national health reform emphasizing prospective rate setting and capitation as the means to finance this continuum is the latest chapter in a long history of mental health economics.

REFERENCES

Astrachan, B.M., Levinson, D.J., and Adler, D.A. (1976). The impact of national health insurance on the tasks and practice of psychiatry. *Archives of General Psychiatry*, July, 785–794.

Foley, H.A., and Sharfstein, S.S. (1983). *Madness and Government: Who Cares for the Mentally Ill?* Washington DC: American Psychiatric Press.

Sharfstein, S.S. (1991). Prospective cost allocations for the chronic schizophrenia patient. *Schizophrenia Bulletin*, **17**, 395–400.

Sharfstein, S.S. and Stoline, A.M. (1992). Reform issues for insuring mental health care. *Health Affairs*, **11**, 84–97.

Sharfstein, S.S., Stoline, A.M., and Goldman, H.H. (1993). Psychiatric care and health insurance reform. *American Journal of Psychiatry*, **150**, 7–18.

Sharfstein, S.S., Stoline, A.M., and Koran, L. (1995). Mental health services. In A.R. Kovner, ed., *Health Care Delivery in the United States*, pp. 232–266, 5th edn. New York: Springer.

Stoline, A.M. and Sharfstein, S.S. (1993). Mental health care: providers, delivery systems, and cost containment. In J.P. Kahn, ed., *Mental Health in the Workplace: A Practical Psychiatric Guide*, pp. 26–52. New York: Van Nostrand Reinhold.

Torrey, E.F. (1988). *Nowhere To Go: The Tragic Odyssey of the Homeless Mentally Ill.* New York: Harper and Row.

42

The Many Faces of Managed Care

JÜRGEN UNÜTZER and GARY L. TISCHLER
Department of Psychiatry and Biobehavioral Sciences, University of California, Los Angeles, California, USA

INTRODUCTION

Health care in the United States represents a social enterprise that accounts for 14 of every 100 dollars worth of purchased goods and services. Thirty percent of all health care expenditures are borne by the federal government, while business spends well over $100 billion yearly on health insurance premiums and contributions to the Medicare Hospital Insurance Trust Fund. Confronted by a segment of the economy expanding continuously at rates in excess of inflation, government and business have strong incentives to bring health care expenditures under control.

The same incentives exist within the mental health specialty sector. Over the past quarter century, a predominantly inpatient-oriented, public sector-based mental health system of care has been transformed into a pluralistic one where the majority of services are dispensed on an outpatient basis by private sector providers. Concurrently, there has been an increase in the capacity of the mental health system, a surge in the demand for mental health care and rising costs—the same triad of events that accompanied the expansion of the general health care system.

To contest these trends and promote greater efficiency in the delivery of care, government and business have resorted to a number of managed care approaches. The approaches are intended to regulate access to care and mediate service utilization in both the general health and mental health sectors. They include: (i) benefit limits, cost sharing, and pricing approaches; (ii) organizational arrangements; and (iii) case management techniques.

These are the major tools of managed care which will be elaborated on in the pages to follow.

BENEFIT DESIGN, PRICING, AND COST SHARING APPROACHES

Attitudes of payers in relation to insurance for mental illness have been shaped by the view that generous coverage promotes adverse selection. Adverse selection refers to the tendency of individuals most likely to use a particular service to opt for a plan providing the most generous benefits in relation to their perceived need. It can result in high utilization with the result that premiums may fail to cover the costs of care. An association between a patient's benefits and inpatient length of stay has been documented (Frank & Lave, 1985; Tsai *et al.*, 1987). Other studies have shown that rates of outpatient utilization are quite sensitive to cost sharing (Horgan, 1986; Taube *et al.*, 1986). For payers, these findings undermine the credibility of providers as arbiters of

Handbook of Mental Health Economics and Health Policy, Volume I, Schizophrenia. Edited by M. Moscarelli, A. Rupp and N. Sartorius.
© 1996 John Wiley & Sons Ltd.

"need" and reinforce the view that the allocation of mental health care is highly discretionary. As a result, mental illness continues to receive less generous coverage in health insurance plans than physical illness.

Managed care organizations use a variety of payment schemes for providers ranging from salaried practice to discounted fee-for-service practice with additional rewards or penalties depending on outcomes and service utilization. A common way to structure such incentives is to establish risk sharing pools which individual providers and insurers divide up at the end of a year presuming that everyone has practiced in an efficient way and money is left in the pool. The implications of such incentives for provider behavior and ultimately quality of care are not well studied (Hillman *et al.*, 1989) and will be discussed in the quality of care section below.

BENEFIT DESIGN AND PRICING

Restrictions on mental health benefits usually take the form of lower benefit limits, increased cost sharing and annual or lifetime limits on inpatient days or total expenditures. Still, innovations in benefit design are occurring. Tenneco, for example, is using a variable benefit approach towards inpatient care that requires a 20% copayment for psychotic and neurotic disorder and 50% for personality and developmental disorders (Tsai *et al.*, 1987). Medicare has modified its outpatient benefit for patients with Alzheimer's disease and related organic mental disorders so that coverage equivalent to that provided for physical illness is provided for office visits for medical management as opposed to psychotherapy of these conditions.

An alternative pricing strategy involves reimbursement at preestablished rates for diagnosis-related groups (DRGs). Although the DRG system introduced by Medicare in 1982 has been successful in reducing costs mainly by shortening hospital stays (Russell & Manning, 1989), the predictive validity of the system for psychiatric disorders has been called into question from the onset (Jencks *et al.*, 1987). In one study, for example, only 5.6% of the variance in patients' lengths of stay were explained by psychiatric DRGs (English *et al.*, 1986). Despite this limitation, prospective payment approaches have been shown to reduce the lengths of hospital stays in psychiatry as well. From the perspective of adequate care for the severely mentally ill, however, these approaches have also been shown to be associated with increased hospital readmission rates and a shift in care from private to an already overburdened and underfunded public sector (Rupp *et al.*, 1984; Frank & Lave, 1985).

The public sector has also turned to supply-side cost sharing in their efforts to deal with rising costs and reduced levels of funding (Sharfstein *et al.*, 1992). *Capitation* experiments have been undertaken in New York, Pennsylvania, Minnesota, and Rhode Island (Christianson & Linehan, 1989; Rothbard *et al.*, 1989; Shinnar *et al.*, 1989; Babigian and Reed, 1992; Christianson *et al.*, 1992; Marshall, 1992). In these projects, providers are paid a set amount per year for delivering comprehensive mental health services to an identified group of patients. Sharfstein (1991) argues that capitation funding for schizophrenic patients provides the necessary incentives to increase system flexibility and encourage early interventions which, in turn, prevent expensive hospitalizations. He makes an important point not always included in capitation approaches by highlighting the importance of a "risk-adjusted" approach that takes into account such factors as past service use, perceived health status, and level of disability. The experience in Rochester lends credibility to the capitation approach. Here, community mental health centers acted as "lead agencies." Working for a fixed cost, they were shown to deliver appropriate community services to patients previously dependent on state hospitals. Reduced overall costs, increased flexibility in treatment planning, and improved patient functioning was documented (Marshall, 1992; Reed *et al.*, 1992).

In order to bid rationally for capitated contracts, however, providers must have access to data on the utilization and costs of services for a given population (Traska, 1988). In a 1-year study of service use of 55 clients in a hospital-based community mental health center, Smith and Loftus-Rueckheim (1993) found that having a physical or developmental disability or a history of frequent hospitalization were the only clinical variables useful in predicting service consumption. This underlines the problems of confronting agencies wishing to develop an accurate system for predicting the cost of providing services on a capitated basis to severely mentally ill patients.

COST SHARING

To limit the cost of mental health services, most benefit plans introduce copayments and deductibles. This represents an effort at using out-of-pocket expense as a way of controlling use. As opposed to capitation or supply-side approches aimed at the provider, the effort to modify utilization behavior is aimed at the consumer. It is a demand-side intervention aimed at shifting a portion of the cost for care from the payor to the consumer.

Although carefully controlled studies of how cost sharing affects accessibility, frequency of use and the outcome of mental health care are extremely limited, the results indicate a sensitivity of outpatient utilization to levels of cost sharing (Horgan, 1986). The substantial price elasticity of outpatient mental health care was most recently demonstrated in a study by Wells *et al.* (1991), in which persons with lower incomes enrolled in a plan with copayments and deductibles were found to use significantly less outpatient services. In another study, however, Wells and coworkers (1992) found that patients in a fee-for-service plan who selected a preferred provider option with lower cost-sharing had reduced outpatient mental health care costs without significant differences in access to care. There is some concern that shifting financial risk to patients and their families is particularly disadvantageous for individuals with severe and chronic mental disorders such as schizophrenia, who are often difficult to engage in treatment, and may prevent them from getting appropriate and needed outpatient mental health services. Confirmation for this position comes from the work of McGuire (1989). He has developed a model which demonstrates the effect of demand versus supply-side cost sharing on the use of inpatient mental health services. The model indicates that cost shifting to providers—capitation or supply-side cost sharing approaches—is less of a barrier to care than demand-side stratagems which place the consumer at financial risk.

Preliminary data suggest that, when compared with indemnity insurers, health maintenance organizations (HMOs) may have more exclusions, a narrower range of service benefits, and provide care which is less intensive and focuses on the short-term only (Dorwart & Epstein, 1992). Many managed care contracts cover only "acute" mental health problems and exclude maintenance and rehabilitative treatments for patients with chronic mental illness. A recent survey of HMO benefits by Shadle and Christianson (1988) showed that 53% of HMOs surveyed excluded treatment of chronic mental illness. Based on such findings, Christianson *et al.* (1992) have suggested that "many HMOs may have limited experience in delivering services to severely mentally ill persons." Sharfstein and coworkers have pointed out that managed care companies often refer patients with serious and chronic mental illness who will require additional services such as intensive case management and rehabilitation to agencies in the public sector (Scharfstein *et al.*, 1992). Treatment options in HMOs are limited in the locus of care (usually a choice between emergency room, inpatient and outpatients services) and in the focus of care.

More recently, however, managed care organizations have been limiting inpatient care (Thompson *et al.*, 1992) and are developing alternative and "less restrictive" treatment settings such as day treatment programs and rehabilitation centers. They have also become more flexible in their allocation of benefits. In a recent survey of member hospitals by the National Association of Psychiatric Health Systems (1993), 16.4% of survey respondents said that reviewers were "often" or "always" willing to negotiate benefits and treatment settings according to patient need, up from 6.8% who said the same in 1992.

ORGANIZATION OF SERVICE DELIVERY

Managed care entities use a variety of service delivery strategies to mediate utilization. They vary from organizational arrangements that shift financial risk from the payor to the provider via capitation (HMOs) or discounting (preferred provider organizations) to policies and procedures which regulate the entry and throughput systems of health care enterprises. Many contend that these practices and procedures are diabolic innovations by the Darth Vaders of managed care. Others argue that they are merely contemporary variants of more traditional approaches for controlling access, with the only significant difference being that the locus of control is shifted from the provider to the third party. The unspoken issue is not whether it is necessary to regulate access and throughput in a health care system, but which of two "disinterested" parties is better suited to decide who receives care and adjudicate what services should be furnished—a health care provider or a third party.

THE ENTRY SYSTEM

Increasingly, primary care physicians are used as *gatekeepers* charged with managing a patient's use of resources. Although the stated goal of gatekeeping is to reduce inappropriate use and duplication of services, there is a strong cost containment component to the activity. For example, financial disincentives may be used to shape gatekeeper behavior. This involves placing the gatekeeper at financial risk for making specialty referrals rather than providing a service themselves. Alternatively, the referral decision may be based strictly on price to the exclusion of professional background, experience or competence (Jellinek & Nurcombe, 1993).

That is not to say that all programs use gatekeepers to regulate entry to mental health specialty care. During a recent redesign of its mental health benefits, for example, the Harvard Community Health Plan allowed patients to bypass the gatekeeper and self-refer for mental health services (Abrams, 1993). Still, it is well documented that administrative procedures and treatment practices such as waiting times, encouragement of self-help, cumbersome triage procedures, and other sources of "inconvenience" are used as barriers to access (Grumet, 1989). Whether gatekeepers or policies/procedures are the mechanism, any activity which restricts access risks denying interventions that could prevent costly hospitalizations, (Stein, 1992, 1993; England, 1993; Lazarus, 1993).

Perhaps the most significant limitation of gatekeeping models, however, is the inadequate preparation of gatekeepers in either case identification or the treatment of mental illness. The literature is replete with examples of the failure of physicians in medical settings to identify mental disorder. The shortcoming is compounded by a tendency to use psychotropic medication in idiosyncratic and undiscriminating ways (Tischler, 1990a,b). Further confounding the situation is the penchant of many primary care patients to refuse or fail to comply with referrals for mental health care. Indeed, Olfson (1991) found that these patients impose a considerable burden on the general health care system. Not only do they account for 37% more medical visits than a comparison population, but many visits were for difficult-to-explain somatic symptoms.

MANAGING THROUGHPUT

The techniques for managing throughput begin with efforts to limit those providing care. This may be done by limiting providers to members of *networks*, also referred to as *provider panels*. At one end of the spectrum is the HMO which directly employs and salaries providers; at the other, a loose network of providers contracted with to render services at a predetermined fee. Both models give managed care organizations some control over their providers and a more predictable pricing structure.

Third parties exert additional influence on practice through *provider credentialing* and *profiling*. This involves monitoring patterns of care including such factors as availability, cooperation with the managed care company, willingness to use lower cost brief treatments, patient outcomes, and patient satisfaction. The inherent pitfalls in attempting to judge performance both in terms of clinical efficiency/effectiveness and compliance with corporate goals have been pointed out (Dorwart, 1990; Tischler, 1990a, b; Lasker *et al.*, 1992), as have the significant methodological problems involved in profiling, such as adequate sample size and failure to introduce case mix adjustments (McNeil *et al.*, 1992).

Substitution is another approach used to mediate throughput. While traditional insurers rely heavily on psychiatrists for mental health services, HMOs tend to use alternate and "cheaper" non-physician providers but not as part of a multidisciplinary team of professionals which is needed to provide cost-effective care for patients with chronic mental illnesses such as schizophrenia (Stein, 1993). Falloon and Shanagan (1990) have described the composition of such multidisciplinary teams which include psychiatrists, psychiatric nurses, social workers, mental health workers, rehabilitation counselors, and occupational therapists in cooperation with general practitioners.

Interventions designed to modulate the frequency and intensity of service are characteristically emphasized by managed care entities. For example, HMOs encourage the use of brief treatment techniques such as group therapies, short-term psychotherapy, and crisis work (Wells *et al.*, 1986; McGovern *et al.*, 1990; Budman, 1992; Budman & Armstrong, 1992; Merwin & Fox, 1992; Nahmias, 1992). As Stein (1992, 1993) and Docherty (1990) point out, these briefer and time-limited interventions may not be sufficient when dealing with severe mental disorders such as schizophrenia. The dilemma is compounded by the failure of many HMOs to incorporate services needed to manage effectively patients with such disorders in their treatment armamentarium. These include case management, rehabilitative services, family interventions, assistance with housing, protective services, and recreational activities (Stein, 1992; Scheffler *et al.*, 1993; Vaccaro *et al.*, 1993).

CASE MANAGEMENT

Preadmission certification, concurrent utilization review, and case management, the essential tools in utilization management, have in common the fact that they are all apply a "clinical means test" in making decisions concerning medical necessity. Preadmission certification primarily involves judgments concerning the necessity for treatment. Concurrent review and case management focus on the appropriateness and adequacy of ongoing or proposed services. In both, the clinician and third party actively explore a patient's needs and the alternatives available for meeting them. They differ primarily in terms of focus and intensity. Case management is usually targeted at instances of care characterized by a lack of timeliness in implementing a treatment plan, significant treatment complications, minimal clinical improvement, questionable patterns of care, or deficient discharge planning. Case managers are more likely than reviewers to adopt an aggressive proactive posture in relation to treatment decisions. Their interventions are generally perceived as more clinically intrusive.

Public and private sector case management differ in their essential foci—resource acquisition versus cost efficiency. These emphases reflect different origins. Public sector case management originated as a valuable treatment adjunct aimed at coordinating the care provided patients with long-term mental disorders. Private sector case management evolved from administrative procedures intended to contain costs and achieve efficiencies in the delivery of care. The different origins have resulted in the term *case manager* taking on many meanings. On one hand, the term applies to an individual playing a coordinative role central to the care of people with serious mental disorder (Test, 1992; Vaccaro *et al.*, 1993); on the other hand, it portrays an administrative capacity which Caplan (1992) notes: "... most clearly differentiates managed care from fee-for service."

PUBLIC & PRIVATE SECTOR CASE MANAGEMENT MODELS

In the public sector, case management commonly includes activities such as outreach, case finding, assessment, treatment planning, triage, linkage, advocacy, facilitation of access to a broad range of services, resource development, continuity of care, follow-up, aftercare, monitoring of care, and direct treatment by the case manager such as crisis intervention, counseling, rehabilitation and skills training, and involvement with the patient's social network (i.e. family therapy or education). Current public sector models fall into two basic types (Bachrach, 1989; Corrigan, 1993). In the broker model, case managers do not provide direct treatment and characteristically carry a large caseload. Functioning as expediters and coordinators, their primary role is to link clients with the appropriate services. This requires frequent communication with patients, support systems, and service providers. In the clinical model, also referred to as intensive case management or assertive community treatment (ACT), caseloads tend to be much lower, rarely exceeding 10 cases (Taube *et al.*, 1990a). The case managers have both a clinical and coordinative role.

In the past, case management in the private sector

has primarily been a term used to describe activities more akin to utilization management techniques such as preadmission certification and continued stay reviews. That is much less true today. Private sector managed care has now come to broadly incorporate elements of the broker models. Case managers are both more assertive in their interactions with clinicians and more directly involved in the management of care (E.E. Anderson, 1993).

At the same time, there is a closer approximation of cost containment and case management activities in the public sector. In Great Britain, a new kind of worker has emerged, the "care manager." The care manager is responsible to "organize and budget for packages of care" and obtain services from a range of providers, while adhering to local community care budgets (Holloway, 1990; Holloway *et al.*, 1991; Thornicroft *et al.*, 1993).

Although similarities between public and private sector case management have increased, there still are salient differences between the private and public sector approaches. They include:

1 Private sector case management rarely incorporates outreach or case identification efforts. These functions, if they exist at all, are more likely to devolve to gatekeepers ranging from employee assistance programs (EAP) to primary care physicians.

2 Patient advocacy plays, if any, a secondary role in private sector case management. The principal focus in the private sector remains cost containment through utilization management.

3 Hands-on involvement of a case manager in the assessment or clinical care/treatment of a patient is unusual in the private sector (D.F. Anderson, 1993). There is a growing tendency, however, for case managers to play a prominent part in formulating treatment plans. Practice guidelines are increasingly being used as the basis for authorizing specific treatment interventions (Panzarino and Wetherbee, 1990).

4 Within the private sector, case managers often become fixated on interventions geared to the acute phase of an illness. They are far less likely than their public sector counterparts to expend effort insuring the availability of the comprehensive and continuous services required for severe and recurrent disorders where relapse prevention is the goal (Vaccaro *et al.*, 1993).

5 Private sector case managers concentrate on monitoring the treatments/benefits covered under a specific insurance plan, rather than the "needs-based" acquisition/coordination of the totality of health, mental health, and social services that may be required particularly when treating the severely disabled, mentally ill. To their credit, managed care firms have begun to work with clinicians to achieve a more flexible use of benefits. This has been described as "appropriate substitution" (Tischler, 1990a, b) and creative benefit allocation (D.F. Anderson, 1993; Kongstved, 1993). While Panzarino and Wetherbee (1990) suggest that this can be an effective approach for containing costs and improving outcomes, they caution that one should not underestimate the considerable clinical skill and knowledge that greater flexibility in benefit allocation demands of a case manager.

The differences between the public and private sector approaches noted here are summarized in Table 1 and are quite real. As both sectors struggle to contain costs while maintaining reasonable standards of quality at a time when health care costs continue to escalate at rates in excess of inflation, the two approaches have become less distinguishable.

IMPACT ON COST AND EFFECTIVENESS

Studies of case management programs have yielded mixed results (Solomon, 1992; Belcher, 1993; Holloway *et al.*, 1991; Corrigan, 1993). The most consistent finding is of a decrease in inpatient days (Stein & Test, 1980; Hoult *et al.*, 1983; Hoult & Reynolds, 1984; Test *et al.*, 1985; Witheridge & Dincin, 1985; Marks *et al.*, 1988; Borland, 1989; Jerrel & Hy, 1989; Taube *et al.*, 1990a; Bush *et al.*, 1990). Effects on patient symptoms and level of functioning are less consistent. Curtis *et al.* (1992), Rossler *et al.* (1992), Hornstra (1993), and Lehman *et al.* (1993) have reported negative results. There is also evidence that cost savings from reduced inpatient services may be offset by increases in the utilization and cost of community care (Wasylenski *et al.*, 1985; Franklin *et al.*, 1987; Borland *et al.*, 1989).

Much less data exist concerning the effectiveness of private sector case management. The data that do exist are predominately anecdotal. They are derived mainly from "internal evaluations" conducted by

Table 1. Public and private sector case management

Role of case manager	Public sector (ACT)	Private sector (managed care)
Direct contact with client	Yes	No
Outreach and case finding	Yes	No
Assessment	Yes	No
Treatment plan	Yes	No
Triage and linkages	Yes	Sometimes
Services limited to range of insurance plan benefits	No	Yes
Patient advocacy	Yes	No
Determine access to services	Sometimes	Yes
Monitor care	Yes	Yes
Follow-up/continuity of care	Yes	No
Treatment (i.e., crisis intervention, counseling, rehabilitation, etc.)	Yes	No
Resource development	Sometimes	No
Financial responsibility/budgetary control	Sometimes	Yes

large employers and managed care companies. The fairly consistent findings suggest that these programs do lead to cost savings (England & Vaccaro, 1991). Panzarino and Wetherbee (1990) go further intimating that case management, when well done, not only saves costs but ensures clinically superior care.

CONCLUSIONS

One should be mindful of the fact that case management alone cannot insure good outcomes. Service availability and accessibility are as critical to the equation as are the appropriateness and adequacy of the care provided. Lehman's (1993) analogy of case managers as bus drivers who take clients to a shopping mall of services highlights this relationship. If stores are empty and needed services are unavailable, even the best case management systems have grave difficulties in assuring an adequate end result.

Belcher (1993) and Baker and Vischi (1989) indicate the potential for conflict between the managed care goals of maximizing patient outcomes and minimizing costs. Despite a general acknowledgment of the dilemma, there are few data concerning the impact of managed care on factors such as clinical status, course of disorder, social function, role performance or postdischarge use of medical mental health, and social services. The research that exists focuses on matters of efficiency rather than quality of care or effectiveness. Efforts to evaluate the latter two factors are complicated by considerations such as lack of operational definitions for managed care activities, heterogeneity of the managed care programs, confidentiality, and problems with access to proprietary data (Wells *et al.*, 1995).

Ginsberg (1990) points out that the cost–quality dichotomy in the United States is further complicated by the commitment of Americans and American medicine to translating advances in medical science and technology into improved diagnostic, therapeutic and rehabilitative procedures. The field of psychiatry is particularly ripe for such an outcome given the explosive growth of knowledge emanating from basic and clinical neuroscience research. As we enter an era where patients will be able to benefit from the application of new technologies, it is highly likely that there will be even greater reliance on the application of managed care approaches to ensure that the innovations are neither used inappropriately nor excessively. As the scope of managed care expands, it will become an even more pivotal mediator of change in practice patterns.

Because of the conservative bias inherent in the cost containment goals of managed care, however, there is the omnipresent danger that advances in practice will be constrained. It is not unusual for there to be a lag between the development of new knowledge and its application. As a result, today's premises concerning acceptable care may not always be based upon the most current knowledge. In the eighteenth century, for example, adequate psychiatric practice involved bleeding and purging patients, spinning patients rapidly in revolving chairs, and alternating hot and cold baths. As knowledge accumulates, it should be accompanied by changes in practice. As practice changes, the standards by which practice is judged must also change.

Today, consumers and purchasers are more knowledgeable about health care, more inclined to question the care provided and more insistent that the services they receive live up to their claims. A clinician is no longer regarded as the sole arbiter of the need for care. Changing economic circumstances and shifts in public attitudes have created an ambiance supportive of initiatives aimed at altering traditional patterns of health care and increasing the cost consciousness of providers and patients. Managed care represents an initiative introduced with these aims in mind. It is a vehicle for monitoring practice and practice patterns. It is not a mechanism for reifying established practices or constraining advances that would lead to improved care.

If one accepts the premise that our clinical sciences are far from static, then it is critical for the professions both to promote and to remain actively involved in the development of practice standards and the oversight of managed care activities. The federal government and private foundations should be encouraged to increase their investment in research on the effectiveness of current treatments for mental illness. Additional support is needed for health services research aimed at evaluating the impact of managed care initiatives on the availability, appropriateness, adequacy, and effectiveness of care. Professional societies and governmental agencies should intensify their efforts to promote the effective and timely translation of advances in knowledge into clinical practice and to ensure that quality of care issues are adjudicated not solely in economic terms, but on the basis of clinical merit.

What the preceding review of managed care alerts us to is the pressing need to replace heat with light. It is insufficient for the merits of the activity to be argued solely in economic or utilization terms. Managed care is an intervention aimed at affecting clinical decision-making in ways that may impact either positively or negatively on health status. If we are to make informed judgments about the worth of the intervention, then we need to move beyond description or anecdotal empiricism and evaluate the health consequences of the intervention.

REFERENCES

Abrams, H.S. (1993). Harvard Community Health Plan's mental health redesign project: a managerial and clinical partnership. *Psychiatric Quarterly*, **64**, 13–31.

Anderson, E.E. (1993). Life Link: closed-panel behavioral health program. In P. Boland, ed., *Making Managed Health Care Work*. Gaithersburg, MD: Aspen Publishers, 238–239.

Anderson, D.F. and Berlant, J.L. (1993). Managed mental health and substance abuse services. In P.R. Kongstvedt, ed., *The Managed Health Care Handbook*, 2nd edition, pp. 130–141. Gaithersburg, MD: Aspen Publishers.

Babigian, H.M. and Reed, S.K. (1992). Capitation and management of mental health in the public sector. In J.L. Feldman and R.J. Fitzpatrick, ed., *Managed Mental Health Care: Administrative and Clinical Issues*, pp. 111–124. Washington, DC: American Psychiatric Press.

Bachrach, L.L. (1989). Case management: towards a shared definition. *Hospital and Community Psychiatry*, **40**, 883–884.

Baker, F.. and Vischi, T. (1989). Continuity of care and the control of costs: can case management assure both? *Journal of Public Health Policy*, **10**, 204–213.

Belcher, J.R. (1993). The trade-offs of developing a case management model for chronically mentally ill people. *Health and Social Work*, **18**, 20–31.

Borland, A., McRae, J., and Lycan, C. (1989). Outcomes of five years of continuous intensive case management. *Hospital and Community Psychiatry*, **40**, 369–376.

Budman, S.H. (1992). Models of brief individual and group psychotherapy. In J.L. Feldman and R.J. Fitzpatrick, eds, *Managed Mental Health Care: Administrative and Clinical Issues*, pp. 231–248. Washington, DC: American Psychiatric Press.

Budman, S.H. and Armstrong, E. (1992). Training for managed care settings: how to make it happen. *Psychotherapy*, **29**, 416–419.

Bush, C.T., Langford, M.W., Rosen, P., *et al.* (1990). Operation Outreach: intensive case management for severely psychiatrically disabled adults. *Hospital and Community Psychiatry*, **41**, 647–649.

Caplan, R. (1992). Treatment of drug abuse in the managed care setting. In J.L. Feldman and R.J. Fitzpatick, eds, *Managed Mental Health Care: Administrative and Clinical Issues*, p. 315. Washington, DC: American Psychiatric Press.

Christianson, J.B. and Linehan, M.S. (1989). Capitated payments for mental health care: the Rhode Island programs. *Community Mental Health Journal*, **25**, 121–131.

Christianson, J.B., Lurie, N. Finch, M., *et al.* (1992). Use of community-based mental health programs by HMOs: evidence from a Medicaid demonstration. *American Journal of Public Health*, **82**, 790–796.

Corrigan, P.W. and Kayton-Weinberg, D. (1993). "Aggressive" and "problem-focused models of case management for the severely mentally ill. *Community Mental Health Journal*, **29**, 449–458.

Curtis, J.L., Millman, E.J., Struening, E., *et al.* (1992). Effect of case management on rehospitalization and use of ambulatory care services. *Hospital and Community Psychiatry*, **43**, 895–899.

Docherty, J.P. (1990). Myths and mystifications of managed care. *Journal of Mental Health Administration*, **17**, 138–144.

Dorwart, R.A. and Epstein, S.S. (1992). Economics and managed mental health care: the HMO as crucible for cost-effective care. In J.L. Feldman, and R. Fitzpatrick, eds, *Managed Mental Health Care: Administrative and Clinical Issues*, pp. 11–27. Washington, DC: American Psychiatric Press.

England, M.J. (1993). Discussion Section. *Journal of Clinical Psychiatry*, **54** (Suppl.), 35–36.

England, M.J. and Vaccaro, V.A. (1991). New systems to manage mental health care. *Health Affairs*, **10**, 129–137.

English, J.T., Sharfstein, S.S., Sherl, D.J., *et al.* (1986). Diagnosis-related groups and general hospital psychiatry: the APA study. *American Journal of Psychiatry*, **143**, 135.

Falloon, I.R. and Shanaghan, W.J. (1990). Community management of schizophrenia. *British Journal of Hospital Medicine*, **43**, 62–66.

Frank, R.G. and Lave, J. (1985). The impact of Medicaid benefit design on length of hospital stay and patient transfers. *Hospital and Community Psychiatry*, **36**, 749–753.

Franklin, J.L., Solovitz, B., Mason M., *et al.* (1987). An evaluation of case management. *American Journal of Public Health*, **77**, 674–678.

Ginsberg, E. (1990). High-tech medicine and rising health care costs. *Journal of the American Medical Association*, **263**, 1820–1822.

Grumet, G.W. (1989). Health care rationing through inconvenience. The third party's secret weapon. *New England Journal of Medicine*, **321**, 607–611.

Hillman, A.L., Pauly, M.V., and Kerstein, J.J. (1989). How do financial incentives affect physicians' clinical decisions and the financial performance of health maintenance organizations? *New England Journal of Medicine*, **321**, 86–92.

Holloway, F. (1990). Caring for people: a critical review of Government policy for the mentally ill. *Psychiatric Bulletin*, **14**, 641–645.

Holloway, F., McLean, E.K., and Robertson, J.A. (1991). Case management. *British Journal of Psychiatry*, **159**, 142–148.

Horgan, C.M. (1986). The demand for ambulatory mental health services from specialty providers. *Health Services Research*, **21**, 291–319.

Hornstra, R.K., Bruce-Wolfe, V., Sagduyu, K., *et al.* (1993). The effect of intensive case management on hospitalization of patients with schizophrenia. *Hospital and Community Psychiatry*, **44**, 844–847.

Hoult, J. and Reynolds, I. (1984). Schizophrenia. A comparative trial of community oriented and hospital oriented care. *Acta Psychiatrica Scandinavica*, **69**, 359–372.

Hoult, J., Reynolds, I., Charbonneau-Pouris, M., *et al.* (1983). Psychiatric hospital versus community treatment: the results of a randomized trial. *Australian and New Zealand Journal of Psychiatry*, **17**, 160–167.

Jellinek, M.S. and Nurcombe, B. (1993). Two wrongs don't make a right. Managed care, mental health, and the market place. Commentary. *Journal of the American Medical Association*, **270**, 1737–1738.

Jencks, S., Horgan, C., Goldman, H., *et al.* (1987). Bringing excluded psychiatric facilities under the Medicare PPS. *Medical Care Supplement*, **25** (9S), S1-51.

Jerrell, J.M. and Hu, T.W. (1989). Cost-effectiveness of intensive case management compared with an existing system of care. *Inquiry*, **26**, 224–234.

Kongstvedt, P.R. (1993). Controlling hospital utilization. In *The Managed Health Care Handbook*, 2nd edn, pp. 102–115. Gaithersburg, MD: Aspen Publishers.

Lasker, R.D., Shapiro, D.W., and Tucker, A.M. (1992). Realizing the potential of practice pattern profiling. *Inquiry*, **29**, 287–297.

Lazarus, A. (1993). Managed competition and access to emergency psychiatric care. *Hospital and Community Psychiatry*, **44**, 1134–1136.

Lehman, A.F. (1993). Case management: theoretic assumptions and implications for practice. A Symposium at the 45th Institute on Hospital and Community Psychiatry, Baltimore, MD, October 1993.

Lehman, A.F., Herron, J.D., Schwartz, R.P., and Myers, C.P. (1993). Rehabilitation for adults with severe mental illness and substance use disorders. A clinical trial. *Journal of Nervous and Mental Disease*, **181**, 86–90.

Marks, I., Connoly, J., and Muijen, M. (1988). The Maudsley Daily Living Programme. *Bulletin of the Royal College of Psychiatrists*, **12**, 22–24.

Marshall, P.E. (1992). The mental health HMO: capitation funding for the chronically mentally ill. Why an HMO? *Community Mental Health Journal*, **28**, 111–120.

McGovern, M.P., Lyons, J.S., and Pomp, H.C. (1990). Capitation payment systems and public mental health care: implications for psychotherapy with the seriously mentally ill. *American Journal of Orthopsychiatry*, **60**, 298–304.

McGuire, T.G. (1989). Combining demand and supply-side cost sharing: the case of inpatient mental health care. *Inquiry*, **26**, 292–303.

McNeil, B.J., Pedersen, S.H., and Gatsonis, C. (1992). Current issues in profiling quality of care. *Inquiry*, **29**, 298–307.

Merwin, E. and Fox, J. (1992). Cost-effective integration of mental health professions. *Issues in Mental Health Nursing*, **13**, 139–148.

Nahmias, V.R. (1992). Training for a managed care setting. *Psychotherapy in Private Practice*, **11**, 15–19.

National Association of Psychiatric Health Systems (1993). 1993 Survey Report on Utilization Management Firms Conducting Psychiatric Review, Washington, DC.

Olfson, M. (1991). Primary care patients who refuse specialized mental health services. *Archives of Internal Medicine*, **151**, 129–132.

Panzarino, P.J. and Wetherbee, D.G. (1990). Advanced

case management in mental health: quality and efficiency combined. *Quality Review Bulletin*, **16**, 386–390.

Reed, S.K., Hennessy, K., Brown, S.W., and Fray, J. (1992). Capitation from a provider's perspective. *Hospital and Community Psychiatry*, **43**, 1173–1175.

Rossler, W., Loffler, W., Fatkenheuer, B., *et al.* (1992). Does case management reduce hospitalization rate? *Acta Psychiatrica Scandinavica*, **86**, 445–449.

Rothbard, A.B., Hadley, T.R., Schinnar, A.P., *et al.* (1989). Philadelphia's capitation plan for mental health services. *Hospital and Community Psychiatry*, **40**, 356–358.

Rupp, A., Steinwachs, D., and Salkever, D. (1984). The effect of hospital payment methods on the pattern and cost of mental health care. *Hospital and Community Psychiatry*, **35**, 456–459.

Russel, L.B. and Manning, C.L. (1989). The effect of prospective payment on Medicare expenditures. *The New England Journal of Medicine*, **320**, 439–444.

Scheffler, R., Grogan, C., Cuffel, B., *et al.* (1993). A specialized mental health plan for persons with severe mental illness under managed competition. *Hospital and Community Psychiatry*, **44**, 937–942.

Schinner, A.P., Rothbard, A.B., and Hadley, T.R. (1989). Opportunities and risks in Philadelphia's capitation financing of public psychiatric services. *Community Mental Health Journal*, **25**, 255–266.

Shadle, M. and Christianson, J. (1988). The organization of mental health care delivery in HMOs. *Administration Mental Health*, **15**, 201–225.

Sharfstein, S.S. (1991). Prospective cost allocations for the chronic schizophrenic patient. *Schizophrenia Bulletin*, **17**, 395–400.

Sharfstein, S.S., Goldman, H.H., and Arana, J. (1992). The market for mental health care: new rules of reimbursement and new delivery services. In J.A. Talbott, R.E. Hales, and S.L. Keill, eds, *Textbook of Administrative Psychiatry*. Washington, DC: American Psychiatric Press Inc.

Smith, M.E. and Loftus-Rueckheim, P. (1993). Service utilization patterns as determinants of capitation rates. *Hospital and Community Psychiatry*, **44**, 49–53.

Solomon, P. (1992). The efficacy of case management services for severely mentally disabled clients. *Community Mental Health Journal*, **28**, 163–180.

Stein, L.I. (1992). On the abolishment of the case manager. *Health Affairs*, **Fall**, 172–177.

Stein, L.I. (1993). A system approach to reducing relapse in schizophrenia. *Journal of Clinical Psychiatry*, **54** (Suppl.), 7–12.

Stein, L.I. and Test, M.A. (1980). Alternative to mental hospital treatment: I: conceptual model, treatment program, and clinical evaluation. *Archives of General Psychiatry*, **37**, 392–397.

Taube, C.A., Kessler, L.G., and Burns, B.J. (1986). Estimating the probability and level of ambulatory mental health services use. *Health Services Research*, **21**, 321–340.

Taube, C.A., Morlock, L., Burns, B., *et al.* (1990a). New directions in research on assertive community treatment. *Hospital and Community Psychiatry*, **41**, 642–647.

Taube, C.A., Goldman, H.H., and Salkever, D. (1990b). Medicaid coverage for mental illness: balancing access and costs. *Health Affairs*, **9**, 5–18.

Test, M. (1992). Training in community living. In R. Liberman, ed., *Handbook of Psychiatric Rehabilitation*, pp. 153–170. New York: Macmillan.

Test, M.A., Knoedler, W.H., and Allness, D.J. (1985). The long term treatment of young schizophrenics in a community support program. *New Directions for Mental Health Services*, **26**, 17–27.

Thompson, J.W., Burns, B.J., Goldman, H.H., *et al.* (1992). Initial level of care and clinical status in a managed care program. *Hospital and Community Psychiatry*, **43**, 599–603.

Thornicroft, G., Ward, P., and James, S. (1993). Care management and mental health. *British Medical Journal*, **306**, 768–771.

Tischler, G.L. (1990a). Utilization management and the quality of care. *Hospital and Community Psychiatry*, **41**, 1099–1102.

Tischler, G.L. (1990b). Utilization management of mental health services by private third parties. *American Journal of Psychiatry*, **147**, 967–973.

Traska, M.R. (1988). Managed care: whoever has the data wins the game. *Hospitals*, **62**, 50–55.

Tsai, S.P., Bernacki, E.J., and Reedy, S.M. (1987). Mental health care utilization and costs in a corporate setting. *Journal of Occupational Medicine*, **29**, 812–816.

Vaccaro, J.V., Young, A.S., and Glynn, S. (1993). Community-based care of individuals with schizophrenia: combining psychosocial and pharmacologic therapies. *Psychiatic Clinics of North America*, **16**, 387–399.

Wasylenski, D.A., Goering, P.N., Lancee, W.J., *et al.* (1985). Impact of a case manager program on psychiatric aftercare. *Journal of Nervous and Mental Disease*, **173**, 303–308.

Wells, K.B., Manning, W.G., and Benjamin, B. (1986). Use of outpatient mental health services in HMO and fee-for-service plans. *Health Serv Res*, **21**, 452–474.

Wells, K.B., Marquis, M.S., and Hosek, S.D. (1991). Mental health and selection of preferred providers. Experience in three employee groups. *Medical Care*, **29**, 911–924.

Wells, K.B., Hosek, S.D., and Marquis, M.S. (1992). The effects of preferred provider options in fee-for-service plans on use of outpatient mental health services by three employer groups. *Medical Care*, **30**, 412–427.

Wells, K.B., Astrachan, B., Tischler, G.L., and Unützer, J. (1995). Issues and approaches in evaluating managed mental health care. *Millbank Quarterly*, **73**, 57–75.

Witheridge, T. and Dincin, J. (1985). The Bridge: an assertive outreach program in an urban setting. *New Directions for Mental Health Services*, **26**, 65–76.

43

Use of Health Economic Data by Health Administrators in National Health Systems

RACHEL JENKINS
Department of Health, London, UK

MARTIN KNAPP
Centre for Economics of Mental Health, Institute of Psychiatry, University of London, UK and PSSRU, University of Kent at Canterbury, Canterbury, Kent, UK

BASIC NEEDS FOR HEALTH ECONOMICS

The challenge of scarce resources is the principal rationale for seeking, constructing, and employing economic data. Where resources are limited—as is the case in every country, whatever its relative wealth—economic data are needed to assist in making decisions about their most rational deployment in order to address society's needs and wants. This applies as much to health needs and health care preferences as to any other aspect of modern day living. However, countries with health care systems dominated by government funding and/or state provision may have different needs for economic data than countries where health care provision or purchasing is dominated by the private market.

Administrators in national health systems need economic data which will assist rational decision-making to achieve objectives specified either at the systems level or for individual programs and services. This chapter briefly examines this need in relation to mental health services. These offer an excellent example of the pressure and complexity of need for economic data by administrators in national health services, not only because mental health services are such a complicated infrastructure of primary, secondary, and tertiary care, but also because they interface with social care, voluntary and private sector services, family support, and other services and activities. Thus inadequacies in some areas of provision or planning may be partially compensated by higher levels of provision in other areas, and particular strengths can guide the complementary interventions of other agencies. Adequate interfacing arrangements between components of the infrastructure are as crucial for successful functioning of mental health care as are adequate inputs into each component, for otherwise the service provided will not be used to maximum effectiveness, nor will it achieve the standards of efficiency or equity demanded of a national system. It is for these reasons that economic evaluation needs to address, at some

This paper is lodged as PSSRU Discussion Paper 1084 and CEMH Working Paper 036.

Handbook of Mental Health Economics and Health Policy, Volume I, Schizophrenia. Edited by M. Moscarelli, A. Rupp and N. Sartorius.
© 1996 John Wiley & Sons Ltd.

stage, the full and rich tapestry of a system as well as its component parts, and that the agencies or individuals responsible for guiding the system, at whatever level, ensure that they adopt economic as well as other perspectives. As we argue later in this chapter, the needs for an economic perspective stem from many sources, particularly needs associated with accountability, policy-making, evaluation of interventions, product development, and research.

UK STRUCTURES—FUNDING AND HEALTH ECONOMICS

THE NATIONAL HEALTH SERVICE

The UK Government decides the level of resources for publicly funded health and social services as part of the annual public expenditure survey (PES), the level being determined by the overall public expenditure plans of government and the priorities accorded different spending departments. Its expenditure plans are published each year in the Departmental Report for the Department of Health and Office of Population Censuses and Surveys.

The National Health Service (NHS) is funded mainly from general taxation allocated in this way, and relatively small amounts of revenue come from fees paid by patients, sales of services to other agencies, or borrowing. In England, the Department of Health (DoH) allocates revenue resources for the hospital and community health services to regional health authorities by a formula which is at least partly determined by assessed need and inter-regional priorities. The formula currently uses forecast resident population figures, which are weighted for age, and relative mortality data (as a proxy for morbidity), and allows for higher costs in the Thames regions. Regions allocate resources to district health authorities and general practitioner (GP) fundholders (who are the purchasers in the new "internal market"). By adapting the formula to take account of the different health needs of the resident population and (partially) of local circumstances, these districts and fundholders decide what provision to purchase in the light of local needs, local priorities, and central guidance.

The purchaser/provider split was introduced by the 1990 National Health Service and Community Care Act, and represents a concerted attempt to inject market forces into a system previously dominated by the familiar structures and incentives of a public administration, with its attendant strengths and weaknesses. Although the NHS is now an "internal market", it clearly remains a national health system. Markets for mental health services generate potential benefits and harbor their own drawbacks (Kavanagh & Knapp, 1995a, b).

In 1992/93, about £1775 million was spent on mental illness inpatient services in England, £155 million on mental illness outpatient services, £195 million on mental illness day patient services and £255 million on community mental illness services. This amounted to some 12% of overall expenditure on hospital and community health services.

SOCIAL CARE

Social care or personal social services, together with other local government services, are funded through a combination of central government revenue support grant and other grants, unified business rates, local council taxes, and contributions from service users. The distribution of general resources to local authorities is based on standard spending assessment formulae which take account of resident populations, socioeconomic factors, and prices. Funds actually come from the Department of Environment, and the formulae are negotiated each year with local authority representatives, although they embody a significant needs element. Local authorities determine the allocation of their total income between departments (principally social services, education, leisure, and housing, although complications can arise because of the different tiers of local government) and between services *within* departments in the light of local needs and priorities, and in accordance with central guidance.

In addition to general resources for social services, there are special and specific grants. The DoH allocates the Community Care Special Transitional Grant (STG), which was part of the community care reforms introduced by the 1990 Act. The STG is the means by which responsibilities for public finance for independent (private and voluntary) residential and nursing home care were transferred from the social security department and budget to local authority social services. The DoH also allocates the Mental Illness Specific Grant (MISG), which was also introduced as part of the community care reforms. Unlike other grants or resources, the MISG is earmarked for services for severe mental illness. In 1991/92, gross social services expenditure on mental illness services included some £50 million on residential care, £50 million on day care and an estimated £55 on fieldwork, and about £35 million on other services. This amounted to about 3% of overall gross expenditure on personal social services, but excludes some of the expenditure on services for elderly mentally infirm people, generic support services (including social workers), and administration.

HEALTH ECONOMISTS

The DoH employs about 20 economists. They are divided between the NHS Executive headquarters in Leeds and the wider Department in London. Economists are also employed by the NHS in Regional Health Authorities/Executive outposts, District Health Authorities, and NHS Trusts (the new semi-independent provider units within the internal market). Economists within the Department provide advice to Ministers and senior officials on a range of issues. These include resources and resource allocation, methods of financing health care, policy appraisal, policy evaluation, investment appraisal, costs of health and social services, the cost-effectiveness of health promotion measures, the cost-effectiveness of health and social care, labor market issues, market regulation, and performance measurement. The DoH and other bodies—particularly the NHS regions, charitable foundations and the Medical Research Council—fund health economics research, either from the centrally commissioned program, or from the NHS. Increasingly, research funders are demanding a health economics dimension to evaluations of clinical practice or policy change (see below). In consequence, few research briefs issued by the DoH fail to include health economics inputs among the necessary research tasks. This is a significant, recent, and welcome development.

The DoH is also concerned that there should be an adequate supply of health economists. The DoH, which has direct responsibilities across England, sponsors a number of studentships (currently 16) for students taking the well-regarded MSc in health economics at the University of York. The other health departments in the UK (in Scotland, Wales, and Northern Ireland) and some health authorities also sponsor studentships at York. Graduates of the York MSc course are employed in academic teaching and research posts, the NHS, economics consultancies, and the DoH. Many of those economics graduates are now employed in research units across the UK working on health and social care programs funded by the DoH. There are no government-funded doctoral programs in health economics, and no specific taught degree programs at all in *mental* health economics. However, focused *short* courses in mental health economic evaluation are now offered by two modestly sized research groups active in this area: the Personal Social Services Research Unit (PSSRU) at both the University of Kent at Canterbury and the London School of Economics and the Centre for the Economics of Mental Health (CEMH) at the Institute of Psychiatry, London. In addition, a growing number of health economists at other universities carry out research on mental health services as part of a wider organizational brief.

The PSSRU mental health economics program is mainly funded by the DoH and examines a number of key aspects of mental health policy and practice. Current research includes: health economics analyses of data collected in the recently completed, DoH-funded Psychiatric Morbidity Survey; the role of employment and meaningful occupation (including evaluation of work schemes); monitoring the developing mixed economy; continued evaluation of psychiatric reprovision in the community for former long-stay inpatients; and some other, smaller-scale evaluations (Knapp, 1994). The CEMH program at the Institute of Psychiatry has a shorter pedigree but is more varied, ranging over just about every subspecialty of psychiatry, usually working in collaboration with clinical researchers. A number of cross-national studies are now underway. The PSSRU and CEMH jointly run short courses and produce the *Mental Health Research Review*, an annual summary of their research in mental health economics.

POLICY AND PRACTICE CONTEXTS

As we have argued, the needs for health economics are pervasive, whatever the health service system or structure. Nonetheless, the reforms introduced in the UK by the 1990 National Health Service and Community Care Act provide a helpful context for understanding the relevance and application of economics in mental health service evaluations, as they have increased the demand for better information on costs and cost-effectiveness, as well as generating a better understanding of the meaning and value of cost-effectiveness data. Moreover, the reforms have encouraged wider debate of allocation criteria such as efficiency and equity, even though such terms may not be part of the everyday currency of public discourse.

Among other things, the 1990 reforms aim to change the balance between institutional and community care, moving the emphasis away from long-term hospital provision in favor of treatment and support in settings which are either at home or are as home-like and convenient as possible. It is, of course, recognized that a small proportion of people in every district need 24-hour nursing care for long periods of time. The balance of provision for elderly people is being moved away from nursing and residential care homes in favor of domiciliary based support. A second important facet of the 1990 reforms is the emphasis on market forces. The new "internal markets" in health separate the purchasers (or commissioners) of services from the providers within the public sector NHS, and make fundholding general practices into purchasers of secondary care as well as providers of primary care, with more control over the deployment of their financial resources. The more "external" markets (or "quasi-markets") in social care also separate purchasers and providers, the latter including a large number of private and voluntary sector organizations.

One rationale behind the reforms is the intention to improve decision-making about the deployment of resources by making it purchaser-dominated rather than provider-dominated, and hence needs-led rather than supply-led. The changes have thus facilitated—indeed, they have actively encouraged—the growth of important developments such as care management and care programs, more comprehensive and sensitive assessment procedures, and greater influence and choice for users and carers (Kavanagh & Knapp, 1995b).

The two pre-legislation White Papers published in 1989 set out the government's underlying policy aims to give patients better health care, greater choice of the services available and greater satisfaction, and also to improve service innovation and quality (Secretaries of State, 1989a, b). Both documents were unequivocal in their emphasis on cost-effectiveness. In 1992, the Government produced *The Health of the Nation* White Paper, (DoH, 1993), which set out a strategic framework for the achievement of health gains in five big areas—including mental illness—and set targets for the improvement of morbidity and mortality. The ensuing *Mental Illness Key Area Handbook* also sets out the need for cost-effectiveness information: "In a situation where 'need is limitless and resources finite', organisation of the available resources is critical to ensure that allocations are used as cost-effectively as possible in order to provide the maximum possible health benefits" (DoH, 1993, p. 13).

An increase in the demand for cost-effectiveness information is thus a predictable consequence of the 1990 Act, particularly with its requirement that health and social care decision-making should become user-sensitive, bottom-up, needs-led, and multiple-agency. As we have seen, financial allocations are now becoming more market-inspired rather than simply being driven in a hierarchical, top-down, provider-led, single-agency manner. This has introduced new financial incentives, but has also emphasized the importance of considering financial implications for the broader health and social care sectors rather than merely in terms of the drain on a single public sector agency's budget. In these new circumstances, policy-makers, planners, purchasers, and providers need more and better cost and outcome information to underpin a more strategic approach to resource utilization and management.

UK GOVERNMENT OBJECTIVES FOR MENTAL HEALTH

The English DoH's objectives for mental health are summarized in Box 1. Similar objectives will be shared by other countries, although those with centrally planned systems will perhaps have a better chance of achieving social efficiency and an equitable or fair allocation of services in meeting identified needs. Also shared across countries and systems will be a large number of social and economic constraints, each of them implying some difficult choices in the allocation of health care resources, between mental health and other health priorities, and within mental health between different client groups at policy level. Health economics studies are a vital ingredient for ensuring that such choices are made on scientific and ethical grounds, and that they pursue equity and efficiency alongside other aims. However, economic constraints apply in other areas, and health economists are themselves relatively scarce, with the consequence that there remain comparatively few completed economics studies in the mental health area.

In order to address the policy objectives outlined in Box 1 for mental health problems, the DoH needs information not only on inputs, processes, and outcomes, but also (and especially) on the links between them. The resources put into the health and social care systems in terms of finance, education and training, personnel, drugs, buildings, and equipment are the "resource inputs"; the activities of personnel—in conjunction with the non-staff resources and the so-called "non-resource inputs" (the care milieu, staff attitudes, user experiences, etc.) form the "process"; and the changes in social functioning, symptomatology, quality of life, and mortality are the outcomes. Fleshing out these concepts and the links between them can be achieved within the so-called "production of welfare" framework. As described in another chapter, this framework offers a sound, flexible, and informative starting point for the conduct of economic evaluations (Knapp, 1995, 1996).

Information needs within national health systems are many and various. For example, there are numerous cost needs. For resource inputs we need to know the direct expenditure levels and the opportunity costs of providing the structures and the teams. For processes we need to know the relative opportunity costs of deploying those structures and staff in different ways; for example, on implementing the care program approach and supervision registers as opposed to deployment in usual clinical practice. For outcomes, we need to know the costs of achieving different levels of user and carer health and welfare, and the resource consequences of inadequate interventions. Overall, we need to pull the information together to give us an informed view of the full mental health delivery system and cost-effectiveness indications of how much intervention at what cost is required to achieve specific health, social, and quality of life gains.

BOX 1. DEPARTMENT OF HEALTH OBJECTIVES FOR MENTAL HEALTH

(a) To reduce the incidence and prevalence of mental disorders.
(b) To reduce the mortality associated with mental disorders.
(c) To reduce the extent and severity of other problems associated with mental disorders including poor physical health, impaired personal and social functioning, poor social circumstances, and the family burden.
(d) To ensure that appropriate services and interventions are provided to address (a), (b) and (c).
(e) To reverse the public's negative perception of mental disorders in order to counter the fear, ignorance and stigma which surround mental disorders, to create a more positive social climate in which it is acceptable to seek help without fear of labelling or feelings of failure, and to improve the quality of life of people with mental health problems, their families and friends.
(f) To research the causes, consequences, and care of specific mental disorders.

England, in common with some other NHS administrations, is starting to focus much more on achieving specific health outcomes (Jenkins, 1990) as the central goal, with improved processes seen not as main goals in themselves, but rather as intermediate steps *en route* to real health gains. The strategy enunciated in *The Health of the Nation* therefore sets targets to reduce morbidity and mortality in mental illness. The way to achieve this is through use of a public health framework for primary, secondary, and tertiary prevention, and reduction of mortality. So, taking schizophrenia as the focus, the DoH wants to use health economics frameworks and findings, in conjunction with clinical and other evidence, to find cost-effective ways of: (i) reducing the incidence of schizophrenia; (ii) reducing relapse rates and readmission rates; (iii) reducing the total disability and deterioration in social functioning; (iv) preventing patients from "falling through the net"; (v) reducing the suicide rate; (vi) reducing the premature mortality from all causes, especially cardiovascular malignancy and respiratory diseases; (vii) reducing unemployment in people with schizophrenia; (viii) providing satisfactory housing for people with schizophrenia; and (ix) continuing research into the causes, consequences, and care of schizophrenia.

In planning the collection, analysis, and interpretation of health economics data to inform these aims in relation to people with schizophrenia, it is necessary to operate at three different levels: at *policy level*, where government decides on the appropriate method to achieve its objectives; at *program level*, where government establishes a set of related actions to enact policy; and at *project level*, where government sets up self-contained activities often in specific locations, generally as part of a wider program.

USE OF HEALTH ECONOMIC DATA

This leads naturally and finally to consideration of the broader demands for health economics in national health systems (and elsewhere). These demands take us beyond the issues and illustrations given earlier; indeed, they also take us beyond the current set of UK government policy emphases. They therefore help to describe the contributions which health economics can make to the continuing development of mental health services. (What follows is adapted from Knapp, 1996.)

ACCOUNTABILITY

Costs and other economic data are needed for the various performance reviews which are bringing new control to public probity. In England these are often built around value-for-money audits and efficiency scrutinies undertaken at local, regional, or national levels. Besides public accountability to the taxpayer for money spent, there have been initiatives in quality assurance and major recent developments in clinical audit promoted by the DoH which have also stimulated demands for health economics data and argument. Of course, we need good theoretical models to provide a coherent framework within which data and arguments from a *variety* of sources can be combined to provide the evidence needed for accountability, just as clear and valid conceptual frameworks are needed for health economics inputs to meet the other demands discussed below.

The DoH has commissioned a series of *Effectiveness Bulletins* on the outcomes of health service procedures and interventions, and their implications for decision makers. The fifth in this ongoing series reviewed the treatment of depression in primary care. It pointed out that the widespread substitution of the selective serotonin reuptake inhibitors for the cheaper antidepressants could result in an increase in the NHS drug budget for antidepressants in Engand of about £100 million a year (School of Public Health, 1993). Clearly, we need careful long-term health economic studies to establish whether such action would be cost-effective in terms of better patient outcome and reduced direct and indirect health and social costs (Jönsson & Bebbington, 1994; Stewart, 1994).

POLICY

The shift from hierarchical, top-down, provider-led services to the post-1990 developments in macro-planning and delegation of case coordination responsibilities has precipitated a greater need for a clear costs perspective in mental health care, including information on how to price services, how to compare costs across alternatives, how to adjudge trade-offs between higher costs and greater effectiveness, how to respond to price or output changes of other providers or to purchasing changes of other buyers, and so on. At the highest policy level, it is important to evaluate all of the macro, micro, and market developments which have been set in train by the 1990 Act reforms and subsequent development.

For example, better cost information can assist policy-makers in at least four different ways: (i) by supporting and justifying overall budgets that are of more appropriate size (for example, supporting the DoH's arguments in the annual PES round with the Treasury, the central government finance ministry); (ii) by promoting more equitable access to treatment according to assessed need because better cost data can assist at all levels in encouraging the equitable allocation of resources; (iii) through the development of more effective policies by the appraisal of the cost-effectiveness of alternative options; and (iv) by creating pressures for greater efficiency in the use of resources to benefit clients. Good cost information can, for example, generate comparisons (yardstick competition) and assist with efficient pricing.

PRACTICE

Care management in social care and the "care program approach" in mental health care promote the integrated and coordinated assessment of need for individual service users and the deployment of personal and relevant interventions to meet those needs. Both practices have obvious cost information needs, particularly if budgetary responsibilities are devolved to fieldwork teams or individual professionals.

Choices *within* and *between* different diagnoses or mental health problem areas also pose challenges for local purchasers, care managers, and systems-level decision-makers. How many mental health care resources should be allocated to the treatment and support of people with dementia and how much to schizophrenia? Should purchasers target more resources on affective disorders? Is there a mismatch between adult and child psychiatric provision? What is the appropriate local balance between primary and secondary care, and which patient groups should be seen in secondary care? How much hospital-based treatment should be relocated in the community? What means can be used to improve compliance with medication prescriptions? These are just a few of the practice questions which can benefit from an economic perspective.

PRODUCT DEVELOPMENT AND DISTRIBUTION

Different GPs have widely different approaches to drug prescribing in the UK. Independently, the UK NHS has strongly encouraged (though not mandated) pharmaceutical companies to undertake valid, robust economic evaluations of new pharmaceutical products to justify their utilization, and urged formularies also to bear the cost-effectiveness dimension in mind as part of the decision-making process about treatment (DoH, Press Release, 19 May 1994). The *Effectiveness Bulletin* on treatment of depression in primary care referred to above is another example of national health administrators' inputs to the product development process.

RESEARCH

As part of the process of demonstrating the cost-effectiveness of new interventions, it is helpful to establish the costs of an illness if it is not treated, the costs when treated in the previous usual way, as well as the costs of the new interventions themselves. There is increasing political concern about the overall cost of mental illness to society, and the overall public health burden, as evidenced by the recent World Bank report (1993). Burden-of-illness calculations are becoming more common and increasingly sophisticated. However, great care is needed in merging individual costs into global aggregated figures, and in using figures from these burden-of-illness calculations. Costs projections of a disease can be used to inform changes in the balance of care or treatment, but, in order to make allocative decisions, policy-makers also require information about the interventions that realize the greatest health gains, and at what marginal resource implications.

In addition to this directly policy-related research, there is always an amount of "intellectual curiosity" health economics research being conducted in universities, research institutes, consultancy companies, and elsewhere, sometimes with only long-term or unspecific objectives and few immediate implications for accountability, policy, practice, or product development. The DoH stimulates and finances health economics research to feed into the other four demand areas of accountability, policy, practice, and product development, whereas the Medical Research Council, the Economic and Social Research Council (ESRC), and Wellcome have tended to fund proportionately more studies of the "intellectual curiosity" (basic science) variety. Both types of research are fundamentally important. The developing close links between good psychiatric practice and mental health services research is ensuring that there is now a great deal of health economics research informed by, and itself forming, both the pressing mental health issues of the day and the patterns of clinical and service intervention.

CONCLUSIONS

The Health of the Nation White Paper has set an agenda for the UK for the next 10 years which firmly shifts the focus of attention to the examination of improved patient outcomes in relation to given inputs and processes, rather than focusing solely on improving processes. This is far-reaching in its implications, both for the formulation of policy and for the collection and analysis of relevant information in the NHS. Health economics has major contributions to make and many potential points of entry to debate, analysis, and decision-making in relation to almost all aspects of mental health care.

REFERENCES

Department of Health (1993). *The Health of the Nation: Mental Illness Key Area Handbook.* London: HMSO.

Jenkins, R. (1990). Towards a system of mental health outcome indicators. *British Journal of Psychiatry*, **157**, 500–514

Jönsson, B. and Bebbington, P.E. (1994). What price depression? The cost of depression and the cost-effectiveness of pharmacological treatment. *British Journal of Psychiatry*, **164**, 665–673.

Kavanagh, S. and Knapp, M.R.J. (1995a). Rationing, market rationales and rationality? The mixed economy of mental health care in England. *Health Affairs*, **14**, 260–268.

Kavanagh, S. and Knapp, M.R.J. (1995b). At the crossroads of health policy, health economics and family policy: whose interest to provide a family-oriented service? In M. Göpfert and J. Webster, eds, *Disturbed Mentally Ill Parents and Their Children.* Cambridge University Press.

Knapp, M.R.J. (1994). Mental health research in the PSSRU. *Journal of Mental Health*, **3**, 2, 273–281.

Knapp, M.R.J. (1995). The economic perspective: framework and principles. In M.R.J. Knapp, ed, *The Economic Evaluation of Mental Health Care.* Aldershot: Ashgate.

Knapp, M.R.J. (1996). The health economics of schizophrenia treatment. In M. Moscarelli, ed, *The Economics of Schizophrenia.* Chichester: John Wiley.

School of Public Health, University of Leeds, Centre for Health Economics, University of York, Research Unit, Royal College of Physicians (1993). The treatment of depression in primary care. *Effective Health Care No. 5*, University of Leeds, Leeds.

Secretaries of State for Health (1989a). *Working for Patients.* Cmd. 555. London: HMSO.

Secretaries of State for Health (1989b). *Caring for People: Community Care in the Next Decade and Beyond.* Cmd. 849. London: HMSO.

Stewart, A. (1994). Maintenance treatment for depression. *Mental Health Research Review*, **1**, 9–10.

World Bank (International Bank for Reconstruction and Development) (1993). *World Development Report 1993 Investing in Health.* Oxford University Press.

44

Description of the Mental Health Economics Research Program

AGNES RUPP
Services Research Branch, Division of Epidemiology and Services Research, US National Institute of Mental Health
Rockville, MD, USA

GOALS OF THE PROGRAM

The Mental Health Economics Research Program (MHERP) plans, stimulates, supports, and conducts policy-oriented scientific research on the role of economic factors in the delivery, accessibility, and use of mental health services. Objectives of the program are to promote the growth of scientific knowledge and assist in the development of improved mental health care financing. Research topics addressed by the MHERP include: cost of mental illness studies; cost–benefit evaluations of innovative treatment and financing programs; analyses of insurance benefits for mental health services; and studies of the financing of public and private mental health service delivery systems.

PROGRAM ACCOMPLISHMENTS

Since its establishment in 1979, when knowledge of mental health economics was limited largely to a scattering on studies on the cost of mental illness, the MHERP has supported a growing number of economists who have focused on an array of mental health topics. Branch-supported projects have: estimated elasticity of demand for mental health services; analyzed barriers to insurance coverage of treatment for mental illnesses; developed options for adequate mental health benefit plans based on the levels of service, aimed at improving financial access to mental health services; conducted cost–benefit evaluations of innovative treatment methods, systems of care, and financing mechanisms which have resulted in economic savings and contributed to economic competitiveness; and developed and evaluated several Medicare cost-containment mechanisms, including prospective payment for mental health care and the resource-based relative value scale for reimbursing providers.

The solid scientific knowledge base obtained through MHERP's extramural and intramural components ensures that the mental health field will continue to play an integral and compelling part in the national debate on the mental health component of the health care reform, at local, State, and Federal levels.

NEW RESEARCH DIRECTIONS AND INITIATIVES

Ongoing health care reform activities underscore the need to expand the field of mental health

Handbook of Mental Health Economics and Health Policy, Volume I, Schizophrenia. Edited by M. Moscarelli, A. Rupp and N. Sartorius.
© 1996 John Wiley & Sons Ltd.

economics research. Accordingly, the National Institute of Mental Health (NIMH) is actively seeking to expand its portfolio of research designed to find more efficient and equitable mechanisms of financing mental health care for people with mental disorders. Of particular interest given current trends in health care deliberations are studies related to capitated rate setting methodologies; reinsurance issues; development and evaluation of new supply- or demand-side cost-containment strategies; studies that refine understanding of the financing and provision of care in State and local public mental health systems and the relationship of these systems to the private service delivery sector; improved methods for estimating the negative economic consequences of mental illness and evaluating the cost-effectiveness of new treatment approaches.

PROGRAM ANNOUNCEMENTS

The foundation of MHERP's grant research activities, program announcements solicit investigator-initiated applications for research in all relevant areas of mental health economics. New announcements routinely are sent to health economists and other health services researchers working in academic and non-academic research settings in the USA and abroad; chairs of graduate programs in health economics; deans of schools of public health, and current grantees. Approximately 1000 people are on the mailing list of the MHERP.

CURRENT RESEARCH ACTIVITIES

The MHERP currently supports 40 research grants in mental health economics. Abstracts of currently funded grants are available from program staff. Funded grants focus on health insurance, managed mental health care, payment systems, cost-effectiveness evaluations, homelessness, and public sector financing. Principal investigators on these grants include health economists and mental health services researchers from disciplines including psychiatry, psychology, social work, political science, sociology, anthropology, and biostatistics. Approximately 10–15 new mental health economics research grants are awarded in a given fiscal year. The maximum amount awarded for a research project grant (RO-1) is approximately $250 000/year in direct costs. In addition to RO-1's, support mechanisms also include small grants, for preliminary or pilot studies; FIRST Awards, research demonstration grants, and Research Scientist Development Awards.

RESEARCH CENTERS

MHERP developed and supports four Centers for Research on the Organization and Financing of Care for the Severely Mentally Ill. These are located at the Johns Hopkins University; Rutgers University; University of California-Berkeley; and the University of Wisconsin-Madison. Centers comprise interdisciplinary research teams and are linked to a major public mental health system. The centers conduct research on the organization of publicly and privately financed mental health services; on the economics and financing of mental health care; considerations regarding financing mental health services for special populations; and methodology development. In addition to the four centers listed above, the Center for Rural Mental Health Care Research at the University of Arkansas also is developing a mental health economics research component.

RESEARCH TRAINING

The MHERP develops and administers research training grants in mental health economics, financing, and mental health policy. Predoctoral training currently is offered at the Department of Economics, University of Wisconsin-Madison; the Johns Hopkins University School of Hygiene and Public Health; and the JFK School of Government at Harvard University. Institutional training grants to the University of California-Berkeley, School of Public Health and Brandeis University provide both pre- and postdoctoral training. A collection of papers on "The Economics of Mental Health Administration," includes studies based on the doctoral dissertation of students in the research training program at Brandeis University, has been published in the journal *Administration and Policy in Mental Health* (guest editor, Thomas McGuire; September, 1990).

RESEARCH CONFERENCES

Integral to the MHERP's dissemination and research development program is a NIMH-sponsored biennial scientific conference convened exclusively for presentation and discussion of technical papers in mental health economics. The seventh biennial session, with the theme of Mental Health and Healthcare Reform was held in Washington, DC, September 1994.

A new addition to the program of the biennial mental health research conferences is the Carl Taube Lecture, a tribute to the legacy of the pioneering intellectual leadership of the late Dr. Taube in mental health economics research. This keynote lecture provides a forum for a senior mental health economist–researcher to discuss findings and new research directions relevant to mental health care financing policy.

PUBLICATIONS

Papers presented and discussed at the Biennial conferences have been published in refereed journals (e.g. *The Journal of Human Resources*, Vol. 21, No. 3, 1986; and *Inquiry*, Summer, 1989 issue) and books.

Papers presented at the Fifth Biennial Conference have been published in *Economics and Mental Health* (eds. R. Frank and W. Manning, The Johns Hopkins University Press, 1992).

Papers presented at the Sixth Biennial Conference on Research on the Economics of Mental Health (guest eds. T.-w. Hu and A. Rupp, in Vol. 14 in the series *Advances in Health Economics and Health Services Research* (eds. R. Scheffler and L. Rossiter, JAI Press Inc., December, 1994).

INTERNATIONAL COOPERATION

The MHERP has assisted the Association for Research into Costs and Assessment in Psychiatry (ARCAP), located in Milan, to organize with the Co-Sponsorship the World Health Organization and the World Psychiatric Association, a series of international meetings designed to respond to growing international interest in mental health economics. The ARCAP sessions provide a forum for both clinical and economic studies focused on evaluating the management of mental disorders. A selection of papers, including papers presented by MHERP grantees and intramural staff at the First Workshop on the Cost of Schizophrenia (Venice, Italy, October, 1990) has been published in the *Schizophrenia Bulletin* (Vol. 17, No. 3, 1991): a selection of papers presented at the Second Workshop on the Costs of Affective Disorders (Venice, Italy, October 1992) has been published in a supplement of the *British Journal of Psychiatry* (Vol. 166, Suppl. 27, April 1995) and on social psychiatry and psychiatric epidemiology (Vol. 30, No. 5, 1995).This handbook of mental health economics and health policy (Volume I, Schizophrenia) is part of the international cooperation.

NEWSLETTER

News, notes, announcements, research highlights related to MHERP are published twice a year in FOCUS, a newsletter of the Association for Health Services Research and the Foundation for Health Services Research.

REFERENCES

National Mental Health Advisory Council (1993). Health care reforms for americans with severe mental illness. *American Journal of Psychiatry*, **150**, 1447–1465.

Hohmann, A. A. (1995). Grant Funding in Mental Health Services Research: Methods and Mechanisms, pp. 1–9. September 1995. Unpublished manuscript.

McGuire, T. G. (1990). Growth of a field in policy research: the economics of mental health. *Administration and Policy in Mental Health*, **17**, 165–175.

National Insitute of Mental Health. (1995). *Annual Report*, pp. 1–94. September 1995.

U.S. Department of Health and Human Services. (1993). *Research on Mental Health Economics*. Program Announcement, PA94–018. December, 1993. pp. 1–10.

45

State Mental Health Systems: Their Evolution and Use of Economic Tools

MICHAEL F. HOGAN
Ohio Department of Mental Health, Columbus, Ohio, USA

INTRODUCTION

With the advent of employer-financed health insurance, there has been a remarkable growth in mental health care in the United States in the past generation. Atay *et al.* (1992) indicate that the volume of additions to outpatient care, for example, increased from 1.1 million in 1969 to 3.0 million in 1988. At the same time, government's role in providing or financing mental health care has remained proportionately larger than in the rest of health care. These public mental health responsibilities have involved the federal government, states, and local entities. Among the different levels of government, states have had the primary responsibility for funding and orchestrating the public health care system. The state role has evolved substantially, particularly in the last 30 years. During this period, the state mental health agencies (SMHAs) have moved from a focus on running asylums, to developing community alternatives, to orchestrating local or regional systems of care.

In response to these changes, states have developed varying levels of expertise in the portfolio of capabilities needed to orchestrate care systems, including planning, program development, financing, and therefore economic analysis. The range of capabilities of the states is quite variable, as is the size, structure, and auspices of the SMHAs. As mental health care has moved from state-operated hospitals to community care systems, the competencies required for state-level administration have increased dramatically. Despite this variability, analytic disciplines including economic studies are of increasing importance to the states, and there are signs that these tools are being used more frequently.

Impending changes in the larger American health care system will affect mental health care dramatically, although the dimensions of reform are not yet clear. It is safe to predict a movement toward closer relationships between mental health and other health care services, and between public and privately funded and managed services. As this takes place, the ability of states to use more sophisticated planning and management tools, including economic, organizational, and financing analyses, will increase. This chapter outlines the evolving role of the states in orchestrating mental health care, considers analytic needs and capacities of SMHAs, and reviews state experiences with economic analyses.

Handbook of Mental Health Economics and Health Policy, Volume I, Schizophrenia. Edited by M. Moscarelli, A. Rupp and N. Sartorius.
© 1996 John Wiley & Sons Ltd.

THE EVOLUTION OF AMERICAN MENTAL HEALTH POLICY, AND THE ROLE OF GOVERNMENTS

While a thorough treatment of these issues is beyond the scope of this chapter, some understanding of how mental health care and governmental roles have evolved is essential. First, the federal government has long resisted accepting basic responsibility for mental health care. In the mid-nineteenth century, during one of the periodic reform cycles that characterize American social policy, Congress was persuaded to enact a land grant program, providing funds to the states for the construction of asylums. The legislation was then promptly vetoed by President Pierce. Over a century later, during the administration of President Carter, comprehensive mental health reform legislation once again passed the Congress—this time to encourage creation of community mental health systems on a broad scale. But the 1980 elections intervened, and President Reagan signed the repeal of the Mental Health Systems Act. In each case, a limited view of the federal government's proper role coincided with general skepticism of the legitimacy of mental health care. These factors outweighed the social reform ideals that had temporarily promised a more significant place for mental health in the nation's agenda.

Marmor and Gill (1989) have observed that serious mental illness is precisely the kind of condition that the American government and approach to social policy are poorly suited to handle. The systems required to provide good care are comprehensive, and the population in need is poor and has little political power. In contrast, as Marmor and Gill point out, the dynamics of the American system favor incremental solutions to social problems. Additionally, the American public is chronically suspicious of publicly managed approaches to meet social needs.

A consequence of these national political dynamics, when coupled with the substantial incidence of mental illness, and the lack of private solutions, is that states were forced into the breach. Thus, when the federal government failed to build asylums during the Jacksonian era, reformers like Dorothea Dix visited state capital after state capital, convincing many to support asylums. And thus the seeds for state involvement were sown.

In most states, the early asylums were operated by Boards of Trustees, with the direct appropriation of some funds from the state legislature, and charges for care levied against the cities or towns who sent patients to the hospitals. In an early sign that economic dynamics were poorly understood, many states enacted "State Care Acts," to replace the cumbersome billing of local government with a more convenient approach of direct state appropriation of funds. This approach fundamentally undercut local responsibility, and ensured a brisk business for the asylums: providing "free" care to unfortunates who otherwise might have been cared for closer to home.

In most states, the creation of state agencies (to oversee the asylums) did not happen until well into the twentieth century. And the original mission of these agencies was clear—to coordinate the operation of hospitals. By the middle of this century, however, changes were in the air. And while the federal government would not accept responsibility for providing care—or substantially financing it—it would begin to play a substantial policy role. While reluctant to accept responsibility for mental health care, Congress and the federal government have not been loath to direct the states how to do the job.

This more activist federal role was catalyzed by several mental health factors emerging from the Second World War, including the very substantial numbers of draftees found unable to serve in the armed forces because of mental problems, and the development of treatment approaches to deal with combat-related stress disorders. The creation of the National Institute of Mental Health (NIMH) in 1946 was a prominent signal of this emerging federal role.

NIMH has played a prominent part in the evolution of mental health policy in America, and in developing a strong research portfolio, emphasizing basic research into the causes and treatment of mental illness. However, the lead responsibilities for services planning and administration stayed with the states. The Community Mental Health Centers (CMHC) Act in 1963 was a flawed variation on this theme. The implicit goal of the CMHC approach was to create a national network of community centers, which could provide alternative care for patients housed (or even "warehoused," in the rhetoric of the time) in state-run institutions. But the program was fatally flawed from the outset. First, the federal government, consistent with its long-standing ambivalence regarding support for the seriously mentally ill, never provided the funding needed to achieve this goal. Only about 700 centers were funded, while about 2600 would have been necessary to cover the country. And the funding approach for centers was to provide 7 years of "start-up" resources, with the requirement that CMHCs develop "fiscal independence" during this time. If the program had been carefully articulated with the phasedown of state hospitals during the same period, then state resources might have been transferred to fund the centers. But federal leadership was not trusting of states, and bypassed the SMHAs in the design of the program, with CMHC grants flowing directly to local organizations without state control. This design flaw combined with the startup funding strategy to virtually guarantee that CMHCs would tend to neglect poor persons with serious mental illness—those who had been cared for primarily in state institutions. The CMHCs needed to find paying customers to establish their financial viability, and poor, disabled clients were not likely to help. Thus, the CMHC initiative suffered from designed-in goal displacement—creating a new class of community agency with few incentives to serve the individuals who states had been responsible for—while also bypassing the thus eroding SMHA authority.

At the same time, the CMHC movement did build a community mental health infrastructure. The 1963 legislation initiated a substantial expansion of community mental health services. Although the logical target population of individuals from state hospitals was often poorly served, community capabilities were being created that states would return to and rely on heavily in the 1980s, when serving the seriously mentally ill in communities became a generally accepted goal. The community planning requirements of the CMHC Act also encouraged another significant development—the creation of substate entities to plan or orchestrate community services systems of care. In many states, these responsibilities were vested in county government, and in others local mental health authorities were created via state legislation. These local entities would become advocates for local/community resources, and create an infrastructure for administering the more robust community services to be developed in the 1980s. These local entities would also become a political counterforce to the SMHAs, increasing the complexity of state level coordination.

DATA AND EVALUATION CAPACITY

Another relative strength of the CMHC approach was an emphasis on evaluative approaches and data systems. The requirement to report annually to the federal government, and the competitive grant nature of the program, put a premium on program evaluation techniques such as community needs assessment and the formative evaluation of new services. The emphasis on planning and evaluation would help develop capacity that would be essential to manage the more complex community care systems that would evolve during the 1980s.

Another federal development during the 1960s would perhaps have an even more substantial impact on mental health services than the CMHC initiative. This was the enactment of the Medicaid program in 1965. Designed essentially as a health insurance program for the poor, Medicaid had an immediate, indirect impact on state mental health efforts. This was also somewhat paradoxical, as the program was specifically designed to avoid paying for care in mental hospitals, and thus to keep the federal government out of the arena of primary responsibility for mental health care. But Medicaid would pay for certain services that states could "substitute" for state-run and financed institutions. The first, and to this date the largest such "substitute" service was nursing home care. Medicaid has fueled enormous growth in nursing home care, and during the 1960s states transferred thousands of state hospital residents (most of them elderly) to nursing homes. In fact, the so-called "deinstitutionalization" of mental hospitals during the period 1965–80 could be more accurately—if equally inelegantly—referred to as "transinstitutionalization"; the transfer of typically elderly and disabled individuals from the former institution of choice (state-operated and funded psychiatric hospitals) to the new institution of choice—Medicaid reimbursed, but privately operated nursing homes.

The second Medicaid-funded mental health service that substituted for state psychiatric hospitals was hospitalization in general hospitals—whether in psychiatric units or in so-called "scatter beds" providing for psychiatric hospitalization in medical–surgical units. Kiesler and Sibulkin (1987) have documented the extraordinary and often underestimated effect of this substitution. Thus, there are today many more long-term mentally ill individuals in nursing homes than state psychiatric facilities, and many more episodes of short-term hospitalization in general hospitals than in state facilities.

Medicaid, through these trends, also increased the erosion of diffusion of SMHA authority. While the CMHC approach bypassed SMHA by providing funds directly to local providers, the SMHA was usually indirectly involved with CMHCs, at least by reviewing and commenting on CMHC funding applications. And the CMHCs were undeniably mental health organizations, with some general accountability to the SMHA. But the Medicaid approach undercut SMHAs more directly. First, the funding levels involved in Medicaid were much bigger. Second, the state-level responsibilities for Medicaid administration were generally not housed in the SMHA, but in another state agency. Third, the local Medicaid reimbursed providers were not primarily mental health entities, but acute or long-term care providers without ties to the SMHA. Thus, the ability of the states to coordinate mental health policy was substantially reduced by these federal initiatives. However, the advent of Medicaid would—like the CMHC approach—initiate trends that would in time require SMHAs to develop economic and other analytic tools to assess and influence policy.

INCREASING MANAGEMENT DEMANDS ON SMHAs

The advent of the federal CMHC and Medicaid programs set in motion second-order shifts in the management of state mental health responsibilities. Prior to the CMHC/Medicaid eras, mental health care consisted basically of state hospitals (providing both long-term care and acute treatment) with a small number of community alternatives for individuals with serious mental illness. For individuals with less disabling conditions, there was very limited private care, paid for out-of-pocket, or in rare cases reimbursed by health insurance. Medicaid and the CMHC approach changed this by building a third sector of not-for-profit agencies—some of them oriented to mental health, and others outside the mental health service sector. The CMHC approach increased the level of community care in the states but decreased SMHA control. Medicaid also increased mental health services mostly outside of the specialty mental health system, but had the same effect of decreasing state agency control. The complexity of public mental health funding (both to SMHAs and to local agencies) increased, while the degree of SMHA influence decreased. Economic perspectives and other analytic tools would become more relevant in this environment.

At the same time, the goals and focus of SMHAs were evolving. By the 1970s, the SMHAs had begun to move beyond simply running state psychiatric hospitals, to also supporting "alternative" community services, including group homes, case management, etc. Differential investments—in hospitals or community services; in the public or private sectors—were possible. The variety and complexity of funding sources increased. The boundaries between the public and private mental health systems grew more permeable.

AN ERODING SMHA MISSION

The 1970s produced a low point in the quality, relevance, and coherence of mental health systems in many states. The SMHA's traditional mission of running state institutions had been discredited. Criticism had come from sources ranging from academics like Goffman (1961) to the popular press. This criticism, particularly in the political environment of the 1960s, created a broad perception that institutions were themselves the problem. The moral high ground of community mental health had been appropriated by the federal CMHC program. Both this program and Medicaid weakened SMHA influence or control of mental health policy and resources at the state level. It was not yet recognized that deinstitutionalization would turn out to be as much of a policy disaster as institutionalization itself—in some measure due to the "dechaining" of community services funding and direction from the states. The failures of old SMHA policies were evident, and most states did not have credible alternatives to put forward. A coherent approach to community-oriented, longitudinal care of individuals with serious mental illness had not yet been advanced, and revitalization of state programs would depend on such a new direction.

MENTAL HEALTH POLICY IN THE 1980s

The decade of the 1980s saw both new federal policy direction for mental health services, and a continuation of the pattern of limited federal support for mental health care. This paradox was evident in the first days of the decade, as President Reagan's budget strategy led to repeal of the just-enacted Community Mental Health Systems Act. This legislation, a priority of the Carter administration, had proposed to modify the CMHC approach in several ways. First, it would put the program under state as well as federal control—ending the practice of bypassing states—and second, it would move the focus to community care systems for the serious mentally ill, and away from an emphasis on facilities. While advocates had seen mental health policy reach its highest prominence in decades with the work of the President's Commission on Mental Health, headed by first lady, Rosalyn Carter, the Reagan action should not have been too much of a surprise. In reality, it simply continued the pattern—now well over a century old—of occasional federal concern and rhetoric about mental health issues, without much commitment of resources to help address the problem.

The early 1980s would, however, see a small program in the NIMH exert enormous leverage on mental health policy. The work of the President's Commission—documenting the fragmentation of programs at the state and local levels, the need for a higher emphasis on practical supports such as income maintenance and housing, and the importance of a systems approach at the local level—found a home in the Community Support Program (CSP) within NIMH. A small but effective group of leaders within the CSP leveraged change in many states by recognizing that states were ready to change, and by using small system change grants, demonstration projects, and the convening power of the federal government. And, in many cases, the states were indeed ready to change. The policy failures of institutionalization and deinstitutionalization were evident. Additionally, the Reagan block grant/New Federalism approach had put the states back in charge of the limited federal mental health funds flowing to the states, and the leadership of the SMHAs had begun to change. One index of this change is in the professional identity of the SMHA directors. In 1977, three-quarters of the SMHAs were directed by physicians. By 1988, however, only one in 10 SMHA directors was a physician. The change signals the movement of SMHAs toward a broader managerial role, involving orchestration of systems of care. In the evolving SMHA environment, management and analytic capacities would be essential. During the 1980s, the SMHAs built on the basic directions of CSP (community care, systems approaches, egalitarian values, an emphasis on practical supports) in a wide variety of ways.

At one level, the work of SMHAs during the 1980s consisted of incrementally changing their services portfolio toward CSP services such as case management, housing programs, and rehabilitation. In order to move from hospital-dominated budgets (67% of SMHA budgets in 1981 were for inpatient care), states reallocated hospital funds to support community services, moved hospital staff to communities with patients, and used similar strategies. In general, this was done during a period of very limited SMHA budget growth. As a result, total SMHA expenditures for community services increased 262% from 1981 to 1990, while inpatient expenditures increased 72% and total expenditures increased only 100%. In constant dollars, SMHA expenditures over this period increased by only 2%. States actually reduced state hospital expenditures in constant dollars, and increased the constant dollar investment in community services by 34%. (Lutterman *et al.*, 1993).

The need to provide community support services outpaced state revenue growth during the 1980s for several reasons. Population growth, particularly in the early adult age cohort at greatest risk for onset of schizophrenia, fueled demand. Additionally, there was a need to "catch up" with unmet needs created to some extent by the deinstitutionalization of the 1970s, and more significantly by what might be termed "noninstitutionalization" (Kiesler, 1982)—the nonavailability of long-term hospitalization for the new generation of individuals with serious mental illness. While long-term institutionalization had proven to be a poor solution, at least it was a solution. Many persons with long-term conditions like schizophrenia required substantial and well-coordinated supports to function well, in addition to periodic brief hospitalization. In most locales, short-term hospitalization was available, but little else.

The combination of major unmet needs and limited state resources meant that states had to turn to sources other than state general funds, if they had any hope of financing the new, needed services. To some extent the CMHCs provided an infrastructure for this development, and increasingly CMHCs became the providers of community supports for needy persons that they had originally been designed to be. But additional funding was still required, and increasingly, especially in the late 1980s, states turned to "second generation" Medicaid financing to support the needed services. The initial uses of Medicaid for mental health care, as discussed earlier, had been for services in the general hospital and long-term care sectors—inpatient treatment, hospital-based outpatient care, and nursing homes. These services—which were not particularly responsive to the needs of seriously mentally ill persons, had expanded dramatically—creating a new supply and thus demand for mental health care while weakening the control of SMHAs and obscuring the boundaries of the public mental health system. However, several less well known Medicaid provisions were increasingly used by SMHAs in the 1980s to finance services which were more responsive to the needs of persons with long-term mental illness, particularly case management and rehabilitation. States adapted or rewrote their state Medicaid plans to finance these services. In the state of Ohio, for example, total Medicaid expenditures for community mental health services grew from $18 million in 1981 to $90 million in 1990, an increase of 500%.

THE EVOLVING SMHA AND ITS MANAGEMENT CHALLENGES

The developments of the past generation have created increasingly complex management environments in SMHAs, and increased the need for sophistication in planning and analysis. Public mental health systems prior to the CMHC era were dominated by state hospitals and a narrow range of alternatives under the control of states. The CMHC/Medicaid initiatives dramatically expanded publicly funded mental health services—some at the fringe of SMHA control, and others in sectors which were scarcely influenced by SMHAs. The CSP approach led to further development of community alternatives under partial SMHA control, financed both by state (and sometimes local) revenues, and by the new Medicaid approaches. The creation of local governing structures for mental health such as county boards had increased constituency and political support for community care, but had also weakened state control.

More sophisticated mental health data systems and program evaluation methods provided some tools to help manage this complexity. In the new mental health environment, economic and related analytic tools were increasingly relevant. The emerging mental health system was only partially operated by states, and was financed by a wide variety of sources. Understanding and utilizing economic levers and incentives became essential.

SMHA USE OF FINANCIAL INCENTIVES

The use of economic incentives by states to help reform their systems was reviewed by Dickey and Cohen (1993). They describe a range of state and local mental health authority strategies to influence patterns of care. One of the most widely used strategies involves the use of financial incentives to stimulate desired outcomes, such as payments to communities who brought residents home from state institutions. This approach was used in many states, with some of the best known programs being in Texas (where countries could "earn" $35.50 for each day that institutionalized residents were sustained in the community) and in Rhode Island, which used several similar methods to facilitate community placement of hospitalized clients.

One irony of this use of fiscal incentives is that it reverses an incentive put in place in many states in the nineteenth century state care acts, which made state funding of the asylums a permanent responsibility, and thus created a disincentive to serve mentally ill residents at home. The efforts by states to provide incentives for community placement during the 1980s were thus attempts to correct a century-old policy failure—and a belated recognition of the power of economic incentives.

Another goal which states pursued via economic incentives was to encourage community agencies and systems to serve needier, disabled individuals. These efforts linked state responsibility for needy individuals (formerly served in hospitals), to community agencies like CMHCs, which had frequently tended to serve less disabled persons. Ohio is perhaps the state in which these efforts were best documented. Ohio developed a definition and methodology to classify persons as "severely mentally disabled" and then used the numbers of "SMD" persons enrolled in local systems as a factor in allocating funds to these communities.

A third type of economic incentive used by states was "performance contracting," perhaps better defined as performance-based fund allocation. Pennsylvania's approach, described by Hadley *et al.* (1983) is perhaps the best known. Pennsylvania developed 10 indicators of "good" county system performance with quantitative measures of each indicator. Counties reported to the state on their performance on each variable annually, and comparative rankings of overall performance were then used as the basis for allocating funding increases for existing services. Counties that performed better would thus typically receive funding increases greater than the cost of inflation, and poorer performing counties would receive no funding increases. Additionally, other funds available to develop additional programs would only be available to counties with average or above performance. Hadley *et al.* reported several benefits of this approach, including that it decreased the annual bickering over funding allocation methods, and also focused localities on desirable service and administrative goals. Performance-based contracting or allocation methods have been used in a variety of other states, including California (California Department of Mental Health, 1983), Colorado (Berger *et al.*, 1989), and New Jersey (Kamis-Gould, 1987). In these states, performance criteria were used to shape directions for local systems of care (counties or comprehensive CMHCs).

Perhaps the most powerful financial incentives used by states were the simplest—making local systems accountable for state hospital use by giving them control of state hospital funds (and thus available for community services expenditures), but making the localities pay for state care actually used. Wisconsin's use of this mechanism was among the earliest (see Stein *et al.*, 1990). Ohio also implemented this approach as a key element in its 1988 reform legislation (see Robinson, 1991, and Hogan, 1992).

ANALYTIC TOOLS OF SMHAs

The evolution of SMHA functions—from coordinating institutions, the planning and implementing community alternatives, to orchestrating systems of care—has necessitated a corresponding evolution in the sophistication of planning and evaluation tools. The new tools required during the 1970s focused on community planning and program evaluation, as a response to the federal CMHC Act, with its formal–rational expectations regarding needs assessment and evaluation. The needs emerging during the 1980s were both broader and less clear. The CSP approach introduced fundamental shifts in problem definition and approach (for example, a shift from facility-centered acute treatment to community-centered social and clinical support).

At the same time, the complexity of public systems increased dramatically, as the scope of community care expanded, local systems developed their own status and constituencies, and increased use of Medicaid to finance mental health care expanded the size and diversity of the system, while introducing new funding sources outside the control of SMHAs.

States responded in highly variable ways to the management and analytic requirements, partly because there was no strong or consistent federal leadership in mental health during this period. After the CSP effort of the early 1980s, the priority of leaders at NIMH was unequivocally to emphasize basic and biological research studies into mental illness. The "New Federalism" policies of the Reagan era reinforced a diminished federal leadership role in mental health, by de-emphasizing federal activism in general. Thus, leadership in the mental health services arena took a back seat, just as states were entering a period of substantial change and innovation.

A small but significant exception to this lack of federal initiative was in the area of assisting states with development of management information systems and "services research"—studies more rigorous (e.g. using controlled trials and formal statistical methods) than the traditional mental health program evaluations. The information systems effort reflected an evolution of the NIMH Mental Health Statistics Improvement Program (MHSIP)—a long-standing collaborative effort between NIMH and states to cooperatively develop guidelines and criteria to improve mental health statistical and information systems. This effort had been limited to voluntary information sharing and planning. However, in 1988 Congress earmarked a portion of the Alcohol, Drug, and Mental Health block grant to be spent on program evaluation, technical assistance, and related functions. This created an opportunity for NIMH to provide funds to states for improvement of management information systems, following the guidelines developed by the MHSIP. By 1993, over $15 million had been spent in grants to virtually all of the states and territories, in three cycles of grants. The first cycle of grants was designed simply to stimulate information system improvement, and compliance with the standards developed by the MHSIP. The second round of funding allowed states to enhance particular information subsystems, and the third cycle focused on making information better suited for decision-making, and on supporting managers' decision needs. There has not at this time been a formal evaluation of the MHSIP grants. However, it is clear that the grants have significantly expanded the information and information capacity of most SMHAs, particularly in the smaller states—at a time when the growing complexity of state responsibilities made these capacities essential.

The block grant set aside also provided an opportunity for NIMH to provide funds to a small number of states to enhance their research capacity by engaging in research studies of their service innovations in partnership with academic researchers. Although only a half dozen of these grants were given, their impact was significant. States used the grants to evaluate timely and significant problems such as various methods of case management, changed reimbursement methods, and approaches to serve patients with dual mental illness and substance abuse problems. Additionally, in several states, such as New Hampshire and New York, the grants help expand research capacities.

This background makes it clear that the complexity of SMHA environments is increasing rapidly. The movement towards community support has greatly increased the number of mental health organizations that states must coordinate. Expanded insurance coverage—both through private insurance and public systems like Medicaid—has increased the complexity of payment and reimbursement systems. An increased local role in management of systems of care has further increased both complexity and political cross-currents.

At the same time, the analytic capacity of the states has advanced. Improved information systems and the ability of some states to conduct sophisticated research studies signal the availability of more data, and better use of the data. At the same time, the use of economic analyses by states, particularly the use of formal studies, has been modest at best. A review of some of these experiences indicates both the potential and the limited utilization of economic methods.

ECONOMIC STUDIES OF SMHA INITIATIVES

Despite the increasing use of economic "policy levers" by SMHAs, there are not many comprehensive analyses of these approaches using economic methods. The Dickey and Cohen (1993) article summarizes most of the known efforts to date.

However, there are several other examples of economic analyses of state systems. Frank and Gaynor (1991) analysed the economic effects of funding incentives built into Ohio mental health reforms. As described earlier, Ohio allowed local mental health boards to plan for and assume control over funds previously spent in state hospitals—thereby removing the long-standing, unintended "subsidy" of state hospital care. (In Ohio, and virtually every other state until the recent past, states bore the entire cost of state hospital care, but only partially funded the cost of community care. From an economic point of view, overuse of state hospitals should scarcely be a surprise. What is perhaps more surprising is how infrequently economic incentives were applied to address the problem.)

In their assessment of the effects of eliminating the subsidy for hospital care (under which care in the state hospital was no longer "free" to the board), Frank and Gaynor found that "eliminating the historical subsidy for use of state mental hospital services is a very effective approach to reducing use of these services. Given the difficulty with attempting to 'administer' reduced levels of hospital use or to impose new capacity constraints, altered subsidy arrangements appear to be a promising avenue for mental health policy (1991, p. 26)."

Frank and Gaynor also studied another economic incentive used by Ohio: including the number of SMD persons enrolled in care as a factor in funding allocations. They found that this incentive for enrollment of SMD individuals affected board actions in significant ways, even though these incentives were marginal in nature. They emphasize the potential utility of economic levers to achieve policy change, as opposed to the administrative or programmatic strategies typically employed.

There are few recorded efforts of states to employ economic analyses prior to changing policy, perhaps precisely because of the fact that economic tools for change have been underutilized. In one such approach, the state of New Hampshire adjusted its reimbursement methods for general hospital psychiatric inpatient care after consulting with economists (McGuire *et al.*, 1990). The approach used previously to reimburse for such care in New Hampshire had a number of unintended patterns. Reimbursement levels varied widely across facilities for patients with comparable diagnoses. There was also a "cross-subsidization effect" across three levels or types of inpatient care: "designated receiving facilities" intended to have the capability to treat all admissions, general purpose psychiatric units, and "scatter beds" (medical–surgical beds used for psychiatric care).

The New Hampshire economic consultation exposed the different forces affecting patterns of care, and thus helped shape a modified reimbursement system. The core of the revised system was based on reimbursement by episode of care, with different rates based on "diagnosis-related groups" (to link payments generally to severity). However, the new approach also created distinct rates for each of the three levels of care, to reduce cross-subsidization or patient transfers to "game" the reimbursement system. To remove a disincentive to serving needier patients, the new approach also added an "outlier payment," to compensate hospitals for most—but not all—of the cost of longer lengths of stay associated with needier patients. Although the new reimbursement approach described by McGuire *et al.* (1990) has not been thoroughly evaluated over time, the value of building economic analyses into policy decisions is well illustrated by this effort.

CONCLUSIONS

Despite the centrality of economics to many of the decisions made in mental health care, economic tools have not been broadly employed by the state mental health systems that are the foundation of mental health care in the United States. In large measure, this reflects the evolution of state systems and their leadership. The SMHAs have evolved from an emphasis on simply administering state hospitals to a contemporary focus on orchestrating systems of care. Economic tools are much more clearly central to this new mission, which explains the increased use of economic analysis by states.

The emerging challenges of health care reform will accelerate this trend, and place a premium on such analyses. Indeed, in a number of states that are planning statewide reforms of Medicaid, these studies are now commencing. For public mental health care to evolve successfully in this new environment, competence in this new arena will be essential.

REFERENCES

Atay, J.E., Mandersheid, R.W., Redick, R.W., and Withkin, M.J. (1992). *Specialty mental health system characteristics*, In R.W. Mandersheid and M.A. Sonnenschien, eds, *Mental Health, United States*. Washington, DC: US Department of Health and Human Services.

Berger, B.L., Glover, R.W., and Nelson, L.A. (1989). Performance contracting: The Colorado model. *Journal of Mental Health Administration*, **16**, 21–28.

California Department of Mental Health (1983). *Performance management system statewide overview fiscal year 1981–82*. Unpublished paper, Sacramento, CA.

Deutsch, A. (1949). *The Mentally Ill in America: A History of their Care and Treatment from Colonial Times*, 2nd ed. New York: Columbia University Press.

Dickey, B., and Cohen, M.D. (1993). Changing the financing of state mental health programs; using carrots, not sticks, to improve care. *Administration and Policy in Mental Health*, **20**.

Frank, R.G. and Gaynor, M. (1991). *Organizational failure and incentive contracts in the public sector: Evidence from an experiment in the financing of mental health care*. Unpublished paper. Baltimore, MD: Johns Hopkins University.

Goffman, E. (1961). *Asylums*. Garden City, NY.

Hadley, T.R., Nazar, K., Rossman, G.R., and Wilcox, J.T. (1993). Performance standards and allocation of funds in community mental health programs. *Administration in Mental Health*, **10**, 155–161.

Hogan, M.F. (1992). New futures for mental health care: the case of Ohio. *Health Affairs*, **11**, 69–83.

Kamis-Gould, E. (1987). The New Jersey performance management system: A state system and use of simple measures. *Evaluation and Program Planning*, **10**, 249–255.

Kiesler, C.A. (1982). Mental hospitals and alternative care: Noninstitutionalization as potential public policy for mental patients. *American Psychologist*, **37**, 349–360.

Kiesler, C.A. and Sibulkin, A.E. (1987). *Mental Hospitalization: Myths and Facts about a National Crisis*. Newbury Park, CA: Sage Publications.

Lutterman, T., Hogan, M.F., and Hollen, V. (1993). *Funding Sources and Expenditures of State Mental Health Agencies: Revenue/Expenditure Study Results Fiscal Year 1990*. Alexandria, VA: National Association of State Mental Health Program Directors Research Institute.

Marmor, T.R., and Gill, K.C. (1989). The political and economic context of mental health care in the United States. *Journal of Health Politics, Policy and Law*, **Fall**, 459–475.

McGuire, T.G., Mosakowski, W.S., and Radigan, L.S. (1990). Designing a state-level prospective payment system in Medicaid. *Administration and Policy in Mental Health*, **15**, 43–54.

Robinson, G. (1991). *Journey to Passage: The Ohio Mental Health Act*. Washington, DC: Mental Health Policy Resource Center.

Stein, L.I., Diamond, R.J., and Factor, R.M. (1990). A system approach to the care of persons with schizophrenia. In M.I. Herz, S.J. Keith, and J.P. Docherty, eds, *Handbook of Schizophrenia, Volume 4: Psychosocial Treatment of Schizophrenia*, pp. 213–246. New York: Elsevier.

46

The National Schizophrenia Fellowship: History, Structural Development, Service Provision and Campaigning

GARY HOGMAN
National Schizophrenia Fellowship, Kingston upon Thames, Surrey, UK

The National Schizophrenia Fellowship (NSF) has been in existence for 21 years. It is currently the largest voluntary organization in Europe providing support for, and campaigning on behalf of, people with a severe mental illness, their families and carers.

It began with a letter to *The Times* national newspaper regarding the situation faced by the families and carers of people with schizophrenia. At that time carers were experiencing a frustrating period at the hands of service professionals and receiving little support and help with their caring role.

The NSF was officially registered as a charity in 1972 after the establishment of four principal objectives: to help people who suffered from schizophrenia and their families; to seek to bring about improvements in public provision; to emphasize the need for a more intense research effort; and to promote greater knowledge and understanding of the condition. These four aims have remained central to the development of the NSF.

The national organization began forming local groups in England, Wales, Northern Ireland and Scotland (which later beame a separate charity due to differences in legislation). These groups consisted mainly of carers with some users in attendance. Regular meetings provided members with support and information about the illness and services. Groups were organized by co-ordinators who now provide a link between the national and regional offices (staffed by volunteers and paid professionals) and members.

The carers' main need, both in the past and at present, is for a comprehensive and up-to-date information service. This would include practical information such as how to deal with a crisis, phone numbers of emergency services, crisis hostels, etc. as well as information about the illness itself, medication and the future outlook. The general public still have little understanding of severe mental illness, its origins and prognosis. Many myths and much misunderstanding still remain and when relatives or friends are confronted with the symptoms their experience is often frightening and they feel helpless. The statutory services, who are primarily concerned with the needs of the sufferer, are less often able to appreciate fully the needs of carers. The role of carers as a very active part of the care team is similarly often overlooked.

Handbook of Mental Health Economics and Health Policy, Volume I, Schizophrenia. Edited by M. Moscarelli, A. Rupp and N. Sartorius.
© 1996 John Wiley & Sons Ltd.

PROFESSIONALS AND POLICY INFLUENCES

NSF have maintained strong links with the medical side of the professional services throughout its existence. In general terms, with the majority of members being carers, the role of the doctor in providing hospital treatment and medication has been the most important. The links with the Royal College of Psychiatrists (whose Research Director, Professor John Wing, is President of the NSF) are still strong. The Professional Advisory Committee, Medico-Legal Committee and Committee on Race and Culture all have psychiatrists and representatives from social work present. Psychiatrists, however, have a much greater presence overall at present and in the past.

Psychiatrists are also the main contributors to NSF advisory leaflets drafting six of the eight leaflets currently available.

Links with the social work profession have been weaker for a number of reasons. Early in the NSF's formation it was not uncommon for social workers, through their training, to view the family as being instrumental, if not responsible for, the development of schizophrenia in their children. This followed the literature written by Dr R. D. Laing in the 1960s and is still included in the training of social workers today. The role performed by social workers can be viewed as being opposed to the goals of the psychiatrist. Whereas the former is often advocating for the individuals' freedom from medication and hospital, the latter is often advocating for them.

This is only a general distinction but it does transmit the flavor of the development of the NSF's philosophy and policy regarding the various elements of mental health care. To continue with this point the voluntary organizations providing care and reprinting user and carer's views can also be differentiated along these lines. The National Association for Mental Health (MIND) have a much greater proportion of members who directly use mental health services. Their policies and campaigns over the years have sometimes had very different emphases from those of the NSF, calling for the accelerated closure of mental illness hospitals and more social and alternative care. NSF, on the other hand, has always been more cautious on these issues.

MEMBERSHIP AND STAFF STRUCTURE

The membership structure of the NSF now has at its base 6800 members based in England, Wales and Northern Ireland. All members are linked to a local group via the group co-ordinators and phone links and the group meetings themselves. There are about 200 groups and they meet once every month or 2 months, often with guest speakers attending. Many members are involved in health and social services planning teams for mental health and are well known in their localities. Professionals that they are in touch with are invited to address NSF meetings and sometimes are a semistructured part of the consultation process.

The groups in turn are linked to one of eight Regional Committees which consist of elected representatives from the region and who oversee the running of the regional office. They meet monthly or bi-monthly and in some cases have an Executive Regional Committee who oversee the financial and general business of the regions projects. At the same level are five committees which advise the Council of Management (CoM). The Medico-Legal, Parliamentary, Professional Advisory and Race and Culture, Committee on Race and Culture and Support and Service Committees, meet quarterly and advise NSF on specific subjects. The first four are mainly made up of professionals with "expertise" in certain areas. The fifth group consists of regional representatives and staff. Each advisory committee is chaired by a Member of the CoM.

The CoM meets six times a year, three policy and three business meetings. In between this schedule the Executive Committee meets to make decisions regarding the national operation of the organization. The Executive is comprised of the Chair, Vice Chair and Treasurer of the CoM plus each advisory committee chair and two other CoM representatives elected annually. Senior staff attend all the committees as advisers and to provide various services, e.g. taking minutes, drafting statements. They do not have voting rights.

The regional committees occupy the strata below the CoM. The CoM consists of nine regional representatives, five nationally elected representatives, the treasurer, the president and a member of VOICES. VOICES is a collection of people who have experienced the symptoms of severe mental illness and is part of the NSF. The CoM members are the trustees of the organization and responsible for the running of what is currently a £10.5 million business.

The staff structure of NSF is hierarchical. Staff based in projects, whether as volunteers or paid staff, are responsible to the line manager of the project who in turn is linked to an area manager and thus to the regional director. Each regional director is line managed by the director of development. The chief executive is responsible for the line management of the directors of development, finance, appeals (fund raising) and training, as well as the manager of the advice service and the officer in charge of the research/campaigning department. All these departments are based at the National Office in Kingston, Surrey (to the southwest of London).

The two parallel structures of staff and members interact on four main levels: project management committee; regional committee; advisory committees; and the Council of Management. NSF is a member-led organization and involves members in all aspects of operation from running projects via steering groups to being responsible for the financial management of the whole organization.

SERVICE PROVISION

The long-standing central government policy of hospital closure and care in the community lies behind NSF's decision to provide services for the severely mentally ill and not solely to be a campaigning organization. The closure of hospitals and the slow encroachment of community care have left many gaps between an acute admission and rehabilitation in the community. Other factors also inflenced this decision.

Private, "for-profit" independent sector organizations were entering the market. Their autonomy raised the question of who would be responsible for guaranteeing high levels of quality care. The worry was and still is that there will be an incentive to cut quality in order to achieve a profit. NSF members and staff perhaps felt that they would rather take over the running of a particular housing project rather than see it go to a private organization. Similarly, NSF members and staff wanted to make a change and an improvement to their local services. With carers and users on-board and being part of the decision-making (and management) process NSF could provide more appropriate care for their population.

As the NSF grew with an image and a growing voice in Parliament and the media, funds increased and groups and regions began to set up small projects. These usually took the form of either fund raisers (such as bookshops) or projects, which provided support and advice to sufferers and carers. Larger grants from Trusts and fund-giving bodies allowed NSF to become more firmly established in the southern England and Midlands regions, developing projects such as housing, day care and advice services.

The organization did not move into service provision without objection from the membership. Many people were concerned that NSF would become dependent on funders and develop in a direction not controlled by the membership and their needs but by the needs of health and local authorities providing services for their population.

Another stumbling block was the possible conflict between a campaigning department which is often critical of central and local government and a service provision section that seeks funds from the same people.

At present NSF has developed over 200 projects in England, Wales and Northern Ireland. The regional structure is divided into eight with England split into six areas: Midlands; Southern; Northern; South Western; Eastern; and London and the South East. Partly because of the intervention of funding bodies the development of these regions has not been consistent. Some, such as the Eastern and South Western regions have received much support from the National Office as the whole organization has tried to balance its development in relation to the needs of its members and non-members.

In 1991–92 the national turnover of NSF was about 3.5 million, by 1993–94 it had tripled to 10.4 million and is projected to increase by another £2–3 million in the following financial year (1994–95). Approximately 3000 people a week use NSF projects and about 300 of these are residents in NSF residential units.

A cynical view of this development might view the

government's policies of encouraging a wider marketplace filled with independent sector providers (for-profit and not-for-profit) saving them money, while at the same time releasing them from many of the responsibilities of providing care through the National Health Service.

The voluntary organizations who provide services are involved in competing with similar groups for local and health authority funds. Often more established organizations have an advantage over smaller newer groups and "win" the funds that are on offer. The use of volunteers, the ability to fund raise using the charities name and the tax-relief beneifts afforded to charities are three of the reasons for very competitive cost-effective services. Services for the mentally ill provided by health and local authorities are usually more expensive, in part due to various bureaucratic procedures, and therefore are very interested in using new providers.

About 90% of NSF's turnover is directly linked to contracts with health and local authorities to provide services that either they used to provide or that are new but replace or fulfill a similar function to old services.

CAMPAIGNING

NSF began life very much as a campaigning organization that provided support and information to families and friends of people with severe mental illness. Initial campaigning issues included the continuing call for a freeze of bed losses and hospital closures and changes/improvements to the Mental Health Act of 1959 (and subsequently the Mental Health Act 1983). NSF undertakes this role in three main ways:

1 Informing the "lobbying" Members of the House of Parliament (MPs) and the House of Lords.

2 Gaining coverage by the media of NSF's views and policies.

3 Producing research reports and other documents which are then made available to decision makers, journalists and the public.

Each of these methods can be pursued at both local and national levels. For example MPs are "lobbied" by their local constituents who are NSF members and informed about Government policy and practice. On April 1, 1993, NSF organized a national lobby of parliament to report on the first 2 years of Care in the Community for people with a mental illness. The Grand Committee Room at the House of Parliament was booked and over 300 NSF members from all over the country arrived to listen to a range of speakers including psychiatrists, social workers, members of other voluntary organizations and MPs. Following the speeches NSF members went through the lobbying process of obtaining passes to go and visit their local MP and speak to them about NSF's concerns. All people attending were given a copy of our campaigning document for the day. This included information about the Care Programme Approach, an initiative which began in April 1991, and some of the findings and recommendations which arose from NSF research into this area.

NSF maintains a list of about 300 MPs who are sympathetic to our concerns. They receive regular briefings that include statistics and information gathered from a variety of sources by NSF (including our own information) and includes NSF views of current policy. These are often used as the basis for questions which are asked (sometimes drafted by NSF).

NSF is in regular contact with key health and social services correspondents and specialist magazine journalists. Over the years NSF has built up a reputation for quality information (regarding such issues as hospital closure and reduction of beds, for example) journalists have been able to use. Recently, such independent sources of information have become more important as the Government devolves its responsibility for mental health care to localities. Much information that used to be held by central Government is no longer kept. Apart from information NSF responds to the media's requests to interview people suffering from severe mental illness and their carers. This is another way in which NSF is able to campaign through the media.

Members of staff at NSF's National Office are involved in research surveys which appear in national publications (e.g. *British Medical Journal*). An example of this is the report "Window Dressing", which was published by NSF in October 1993. The work has a dual focus looking at the Mental Illness Specific Grant (MISG) and the Care Programme Approach (CPA). Both initiatives were started on April 1, 1991 and the research concentrated on a representative sample of 14 areas in England. The findings along with NSF's recommendations comprised NSF's report which achieved wide publicity on its release.

NSF has also recently produced a leaflet in response to a 10-point plan put forward by the Secretary of State for Health, Virginia Bottomley, towards the end of the summer (1995). The leaflet has been sent to all MPs and was also distributed at the three main political party conferences by NSF staff. It sets out 10 items that NSF believes must be urgently addressed if care in the community is to have any chance of success. These include: a freeze on hospital closure, no more beds must be lost; £500 million a year extra for accommodation, day care, employment, respite and support for carers and training; a Community Care Ombudsman to oversee both health and social services and be fully able to investigate individual complaints regarding community care; a legal requirement to provide a personal care programme with a named key worker for everyone with a severe mental illness discharged from hospital.

It is hard to assess the effect of NSF's various campaigns over the years, but many commentators agree that overall NSF have been leading calls for policy and guidance chances which have taken place. The organization has regular meetings with the Department of Health and is invited to House of Commons cross-party select committees to give evidence on mental health matters. NSF is also called upon to give oral and written evidence from a national perspective to individual independent enquiries.

CONSUMER ORGANIZATIONS AND THEIR USE OF MENTAL HEALTH ECONOMICS DATA

The availability of any detailed information related to mental health is likely to increase an organization's effectiveness, especially with regard to campaigning activity. However, the way that information is processed and used can have a negative effect on an organization's ability to perform — it is not always a straightforward positivė.

Information is a weapon in the fight for higher quality services and the protection of people's rights. Consumer organizations, such as NSF in the UK, are also providers of services. As such economic information is useful for planning, budgeting and bidding for new services from statutory agencies, as well as for informed campaigning. Economics data are especially useful in picking out trends in service delivery. They will, over a period of time, aid organizations in their development as they will be able to see where the money is going and therefore what care and support services are in vogue. They will also enable service users and carers to ask more informed questions. For example, the hospital closure program in the UK and other parts of Europe caused uproar when money released from hospital sales was not spent on replacement facilities in the community. Carers' organizations and even the Audit Commission in the UK were not able to trace funds which in time became lost to mental health services.

However, some patterns can be misleading and if acted upon by managers and policy-makers too soon can have an adverse affect. An example might be the "un-holy alliance" between central Government and antipsychiatry user movement and researchers/academics keen to show that alternatives to hospital care were successful and cheaper. The hospital closure program was in part legitimized by research which indicated service users appreciation of life in the community and lower cost. The policy was further supported by the user movement and the "left" with words such as "institutionalized" and "Victorian buildings" becoming politicized. A Government trying to cut costs and shed accountability more or less received a mandate to speed-up the hospital closure program which has now left the UK in crisis with some acute wards in metropolitan areas running at 130% occupancy.

More information available to the consumer should mean more power. People on the receiving end of decisions are better placed to protect their rights and complain if they have good data behind them. In the current climate many people are suffering from "information overload". It is arriving all the time through fax machines and the internet, via the postal system and the plain old telephone. Consumer organizations can benefit from this facility but must be careful in using it. They must consider their own time and possess the skills to judge valid and usable data from the rest.

47

A Multinational Strategy on Mental Health Policy and Care. A WHO Collaborative Initiative and Consultative Program

WALTER GULBINAT
Division of Mental Health, World Health Organization, Geneva, Switzerland

RONALD W. MANDERSCHEID
Center for Mental Health Services, Substance Abuse and Mental Health Services Administration, Rockville, MD, USA

ALLAN BEIGEL
Harvard University, Cambridge, MA, USA

JORGE-ALBERTO COSTA E SILVA
Division of Mental Health, World Health Organization, Geneva, Switzerland

THE CURRENT SITUATION

Within the past several years, there have been several important developments that together are creating an international environment for significant initiatives for achieving improved mental health care throughout the world. Included among them are:

1 The realization that mental health problems are frequent, widely spread, and severe, which is demonstrated by: (a) the finding of a World Bank Study that mental illnesses are responsible for almost 10% of the total burden of diseases to mankind (World Bank, 1993); (b) the findings that every fourth patient seeking help in general health care suffers from a mental health problem usually unrecognized and hence inappropriately treated by general health care personnel (Bourdon *et al.*, 1994; Üstin & Sartorius, 1995); (c) the observation of health authorities in many countries that the number of people with mental health problems is increasing and that the lack of appropriate interventions causes a tremendous financial burden to societies (Rice *et al.*, 1990).

2 There are major international initiatives pointing to possible solutions of mental health problems; (a) the declaration of a Decade of the Brain and the significant scientific advances in understanding the origins and causes of different mental illnesses (Judd, 1990; Orsulak, 1994); (b) the increasing research data that document the effectiveness of specific treatments for many mental illnesses (Sartorius *et al.*, 1993; WHO, 1991); (c) the recent conclusions of a

Handbook of Mental Health Economics and Health Policy, Volume I, Schizophrenia. Edited by M. Moscarelli, A. Rupp and N. Sartorius.
© 1996 John Wiley & Sons Ltd.

Harvard study on World Mental Health regarding the problems of mental health care in developing countries and the need and potential for action to address them (Desjarlais *et al.*, 1995); (d) the repeated demonstration that mental health care can be effectively delivered by a wide variety of mental health and health care professions provided that they receive proper training (WHO, 1990; Busnello & Bertlote, 1983).

3 The political context for mental health action is changing both nationally and internationally in support of mental health action, which is evidenced by: (a) the adoption of the United Nations Resolution 46/119 (December 1991) on the Rights of People With Mental Illness and the Improvement of Mental Health Care (United Nations, 1994); (b) the increasing awareness of the escalating dollars being spent on health care and the resultant need for finding more cost-effective ways of delivering care (Udvarhelyi *et al.*, 1992); (c) the active search in many countries for system changes that will reduce the cost of care while maintaining its quality (Arons *et al.*, 1994; Ministry of Health, Republic of Chile, 1991); (d) the strengthening of non-governmental organizations (NGOs) and the expansion of their activities on behalf of improved mental health education, research, and service find broad support (WHO, 1992); (e) the recent initiative by the Secretary General of the United Nations to launch a multi-agency mental health programme and the recommendation to the United Nations to declare a Decade for Mental Health (1996–2006) (Boutros-Ghali, 1995).

MENTAL HEALTH POLICY—A PREREQUISITE FOR SUCCESSFUL MENTAL HEALTH CARE

Many mental health problems run a long-term course, and cure is currently an unattainable objective of clinical intervention. Important outcome measures of mental health intervention are reduction of the patient's disability, social integration, increase of social functioning, improvement of quality of life of both the patient and his/her family members or carers, and cost-effectiveness.

Without a sound mental health policy such objectives cannot be achieved.

National and regional plans and action for solving identified national mental health problems often have fallen significantly short of their intended objectives because of their failure to address structural and financial issues that are the principal barriers to success.

Examples include:

1 The deinstitutionalization movement that transferred many patients with severe conditions from the hospital to the community in countries, such as the United states and Italy, but failed to recognize how unprepared the structure and financing of the social and health care systems within the community were to receive them.

2 The significant increase in trained mental health professionals as a means of expanding access to care without sufficient attention to issues related to the qualty of care and a delination, through certification and other means, of specific roles based upon skills.

3 The expansion of care givers eligible to receive government and other forms of financial support for their work outside of any structure for evaluation and accountability that encouraged the most qualified professional to deliver the service that he or she is best trained to do.

4 The development of alternative systems of care, including family support, self-help groups and others, without any structural and financial linkages to more formal systems of care.

5 The utilization of primary care givers to deliver care to a signfiicant segment of the mentally ill population without any structural or financial linkages to the more formalized systems of mental health care.

There is no universally applicable blueprint for formulating a national mental health policy, as existing resources very tremendously between (and often even within) countries, resources that need to be tapped for developing cost/effective solutions. On the other hand, governments cannot afford to spend time and resources on long-term experiments to find—by trial and error—the mental health policy best suited to the needs of their populations commensurate with the financial resources available.

NATIONAL MENTAL HEALTH REFORMS—THE BENEFITS OF INTERNATIONAL COLLABORATION

At a time of economic scarcity, the more and more countries are reviewing and reorganizing the structure of their national health care services with the goal of containing costs without diminishing or even increasing effectiveness. This requires an understanding of strengths and weaknesses of the actual system in place, as well as knowledge of the alternatives which exist and may already be in operation in other countries, which may be used as a basis for clear health policy decisions.

The knowledge of how to plan and implement such mental health reforms is scarce. "To support and accelerate health policy reform, resources need to be redirected both domestically and externally to improve the evident mismatch between the need for health policy reform and the low levels of capacity for undertaking this effort in countries at different levels of development" (WHO & World Bank, 1993). This finding of the Conference on Future Partnership for the Acceleration of Health Development, organized jointly by WHO, the World Bank, and the Canadian International Development Research Center (IDRC) holds particularly true for the mental health sector. Health policy decision makers are looking for cost-effective options in the organization of mental health care at a time when international comparative studies of mental health services are extremely limited, indeed almost non-existent.

THE GOALS OF THE WHO STRATEGY

WHO has been developing an international initiative designed to provide access for decision and policy makers to data, information, and knowledge that are available from a larger body of experiences outside a specific national boundary.

The creation of this multinational strategy to expand shared data and knowledge is expected to lead to a more informed set of actions by those who are responsible for proceeding with mental health planning and action within their own specific country. These decision and policy makers will thus have a "new way" in which to approach both "old" and "new" problems as they proceed with their efforts to improve care within their countries at the same or reduced cost.

Three steps have been identified, each with their own set of tasks, for implementing this multinational strategy.

STEP 1: SURVEY EXISTING SOURCES

Task A

Develop a multinational consultative network on the structure, financing and costs of service that will be available to national decision and policy makers.

Task B

Build a comprehensive bibliography of existing information regarding structure, financing, and costs of mental health care and their impact on service quality, outcome, and cost effectiveness.

Task C

Complete a multinational problem analysis that identifies the significant structural and financial barriers to improved quality, outcome, and cost-effectiveness of care, and the range of policy options available to address them, as perceived by various constituencies within specific countries.

Task D

Conduct a multinational analysis to identify the key decisions that national policy makers need to make.

STEP 2: ESTABLISH A MULTINATIONAL INFORMATION RESOURCE BASED ON A COMMON FRAMEWORK

Task A

Establish a common framework for compiling information on structure, financing, and costs of services.

Task B

Use this framework for developing a preliminary

multinational knowledge base from existing information in different countries.

Task C

Identify gaps and areas of non-comparability in the preliminary multinational knowledge bases.

Task D

Expand the preliminary multinational knowledge base through requesting additional available information that can be integrated with the preliminary information into a permanent and continually updated information resource that can be used by national decision makers.

STEP 3: CONDUCT NEEDED STUDIES

Task A

Design needed comparative studies, based upon the problems and decision analyses conducted in step 1. Priority is given to:

1 A continuing comparative assessment of national mental health policies, services, and needs, financing, and costs in selected countries, with rapid feedback of results to participating countries.

2 A comparison of how different countries implement national mental health policies at various levels of the governmental structure, as well as the role of major costs considerations in these policies.

3 A comparative study of provider patterns of mental health care for specified mental illnesses within selected countries and related cost considerations.

4 A comparative study of how patients and their families seek care and utilize existing mental health services for specified mental illnesses within selected countries, and the role of costs in their decisions.

5 A comparative study of how different countries are defining cost-effectiveness and outcome measures as a means for setting and reviewing national goals and designing the structure and finances of programs to achieve these goals.

This work will lead to and provide essential input to an additional major initiative:

6 The development of a language for mental health. In a first step a mental health terminology will be developed (based on existing work in a certain number of countries). In a second step, internationally accepted classifications will be developed for mental health-related disability, for mental health interventions, for support systems for patients with mental illness, for financing and cost measures, for outcome measures of mental health interventions, and for mental health risk factors (stressors).

Task B

Build linkages to national decision makers, and to mental health professionals as a means for implementing the needed comparative studies, and for gathering information from different countries regarding the relationship of structure, financing, and costs to service quality, outcome, and cost-effectiveness.

ACKNOWLEDGMENTS

The following experts collaborated in the development of this WHO initiative: Dr G.P. Harnois, Director, Douglas Hospital Research Centre, Montreal (Quebec), Canada; Dr Rachel Jenkins, Principal Medical Officer, Mental Health, Elderly and Disability, Department of Health, London, United Kingdom; Dr Morton Kramer, Professor Emeritus, Johns Hopkins School of Hygiene and Public Health, Baltimore, USA; Dr Philip Leaf, Professor, Department of Mental Hygiene, Johns Hopkins School of Hygiene & Public Health, Baltimore, USA; Dr M. Linden, Professor of Psychiatry, Department of Psychiatry, Free University of Berlin, Germany, Free University of Berlin, Dr M. Tansella, Professor of Psychiatry, Institute of Psychiatry, Department of Medical Psychology, University of Verona, Italy; Dr H.A. Whiteford, Director of Mental Health, Queensland Health Central Office, Brisbane, Australia.

REFERENCES

Arons, B.S., Buck, J.A., Manderscheid R.W., and Sonnenschein, M.A. (eds) (1994) Mental health and substance abuse benefits under national care reform. *Mental Health, United States 1994*. pp. 1–7. Washington, DC: Center for Mental Health Services.

Bourdon, K.H., Rae, D.S., Narrow, W.E., *et al.* (1994) National prevalence and treatment of mental and addictive disorders. In R.W., Manderscheid, M.A., Sonnenschein, eds, *Mental Health, United States 1994*. pp. 22–34. Washington DC: Center for Mental Health Services.

Boutros-Ghali, B. (1995). Remarks at launch of *World Mental Health: Problems and Priorities in Low-income Countries, 15 May 1995*, New York.

Busnello, E. and Bertolote, J.M. (1983). *Training of Non-psychiatrist Physicians and Nursing-Aids in a Primary Health Care setting in Porto Alegre, Brazil*. New York: Plenum Press.

Desjarlais, R. Eisenberg, L. Good, B. *et al.* (1995) *World Mental Health: Problems and Priorities in Low-income Countries*. New York: Oxford University Press.

Judd, L.L. (1990). The decade of the brain: prospects and challenges for NIMH. *Neuropsychopharmacology*, **3**, 309–310.

Ministry of Health, Republic of Chile (1991). *Health Situation and Health Care in Chile*. Santiago: Ministry of Health.

Orsulak, P.J. (1994). The decade of the brain: recent developments in the neurochemistry of depression, mania, and other mood disorders. Proceedings of the 17th annual symposium, July 10, 1993, New York. *Clinical Chemistry*, **40**, 271–272.

Rice, D.P., Kelman, S., Miller, L.S., *et al.* (1990). *The Economic Costs of Alcohol and Drug Abuse and Mental Illness: 1985*. DHHS Pub. No. (ADM) 90-1694. Rockville, MD: National Institute of Mental Health.

Sartorius, N., de Girolamo, G., Andrews, G., *et al.* (eds) (1993) *Treatment of Mental Disorders: A Review of Effectiveness*. Washington, DC: American Psychiatric Press, Inc.

Udvarhelyi, S., Colditz, G.A., Rai, A., and Epstein, A.M. (1992). Cost-effectiveness and cost–benefit analyses in the medical literature. *Annals of Internal Medicine*, **116**, 238–244.

United Nations (1994). *Human Rights; A Compilation of International Instruments*. New York: United Nations.

Üstin, T.B., and Sartorius, N. (eds) (1995). *Mental Illness in General Health Care: An International Study*. Chichester: John Wiley & Sons.

World Health Organization (1990). *The Introduction of a Mental Health Component into Primary Health Care*. Geneva: World Health Organization.

World Health Organization (1991). *Evaluation of Methods for the Treatment of Mental Disorders*. 812. WHO Technical Report Series. Report of a WHO Scientific Group. Geneva: World Health Organization.

WHO Division of Mental Health (1992). *Non-governmental Organizations Collaborating with WHO's Mental Health Programme: Summary Descriptions*. WHO/MNH/92.6.

WHO and World Bank (1993). *Future Partnership for the Acceleration of Health Development: Report of a Conference 18–20 October 1993*, Ottawa, Canada. International Development Research Center, WHO.

World Bank (1993). *World Development Report 1993—Investing in Health. Executive Summary*. New York: Oxford University Press.

Index

Note: Page references in *italics* refer to Figures; those in **bold** refer to Tables

Index compiled by Annette J. Musker